THE PARAMEDIC
Companion

THE PARAMEDIC Companion
A Case-Based Worktext

Arthur Hsieh, MA, NREMT-P

San Francisco Paramedic Association
San Francisco, California

Kevin Boone, BSN, EMT-P

Paramedic Firefighter
Berkeley Fire Department
Berkeley, California

To accompany **The Paramedic** *textbook*

Will Chapleau, EMT-P, RN, TNS
Manager, ATLS Program
American College of Surgeons
Chicago, Illinois

Angel Clark Burba, MS, EMT-P, NCEE
Associate Professor
EMS Program Director
Howard Community College
Columbia, Maryland

Peter T. Pons, MD
Emergency Physician
Denver, Colorado

David Page, MS, NREMT-P
Faculty, Emergency Health Services Department
Inver Hills Community College
Inver Grove Heights, Minnesota

McGraw-Hill
McGraw-Hill
Higher Education

Boston   Burr Ridge, IL   Dubuque, IA   New York   San Francisco   St. Louis
Bangkok   Bogotá   Caracas   Kuala Lumpur   Lisbon   London   Madrid   Mexico City
Milan   Montreal   New Delhi   Santiago   Seoul   Singapore   Sydney   Taipei   Toronto

THE PARAMEDIC COMPANION, UPDATE: A CASE-BASED WORKTEXT

Published by McGraw-Hill, a business unit of The McGraw-Hill Companies, Inc., 1221 Avenue of the Americas, New York, NY, 10020. Copyright © 2012 by The McGraw-Hill Companies, Inc. All rights reserved. Previous edition © 2009. Printed in the United States of America. No part of this publication may be reproduced or distributed in any form or by any means, or stored in a database or retrieval system, without the prior written consent of The McGraw-Hill Companies, Inc., including, but not limited to, in any network or other electronic storage or transmission, or broadcast for distance learning.

Some ancillaries, including electronic and print components, may not be available to customers outside the United States.

This book is printed on acid-free paper.

1 2 3 4 5 6 7 8 9 0 QDB/QDB 1 0 9 8 7 6 5 4 3 2 1

ISBN   978-0-07-756389-9
MHID   0-07-756389-1

Vice President/Director of marketing: *Alice Harra*
Vice President/New product development: *John E. Biernat*
Director, digital products: *Crystal Szewczyk*
Developmental editor: *Kelly H. Lowery*
Digital development editor: *Kevin White*
Director, Editing/Design/Production: *Jess Ann Kosic*
Project manager: *Jean Starr*
Buyer II: *Sherry L. Kane*
Senior designer: *Srdjan Savanovic*
Senior photo research coordinator: *John C. Leland*
Photo researcher: *LouAnn Wilson*
Manager, digital production: *Janean A. Utley*
Cover and interior design: *Laurie B. Janssen*
Typeface: *10/12 Melior*
Compositor: *Laserwords Private Limited*
Printer: *Quad/Graphics*
Cover credit: *David Page, MS, NREMT-P*
Credits: The credits section for this book begins on page 719 and is considered an extension of the copyright page.

Library of Congress Cataloging-in-Publication Data

Hsieh, Arthur.
    The paramedic companion : a case-based worktext / Arthur Hsieh, Kevin Boone.
        p. cm.
    Includes bibliographical references and index.
    ISBN-13: 978-0-07-320265-5 (alk. paper)
    ISBN-10: 0-07-320265-7 (alk. paper)
    1. Emergency medical services--Case studies. 2. Emergency medical technicians.
I. Boone, Kevin, 1965- II. Title.
    [DNLM: 1. Emergency Medical Services--Problems and Exercises. 2. Emergency
Medical Technicians. WX 18.2 H873p 2008]
RA645.5.H75 2008
362.18--dc22

                                        2007019115

Dedication

EMS educators passionately care about how to improve the human condition. EMS educators teach people how to save lives and provide comfort when it is needed the most. EMS educators do not do it for the money or for the fame—they do it because it matters. We dedicate this book to them.

It's romantic to say that writing a book like this is a labor of love. It is also a product of sacrifice. I am forever grateful to my wife, Veronica, and my sons, Josh and Jacob, for the sacrifices that they have made to give me the time to bring this book to life. My parents taught me the value of hard work and sacrifice. Thank you.—AH

I want to thank Art for the opportunity to work together in sculpting this worktext. I dedicate this book my wife, Deanna, not only for her unyielding support during this project but also for her help in making this book a reality, and to our son Aiden for excusing me from some of our trips to the playground and the park so I could have time to work.—KB

About the Authors

Arthur Hsieh

Arthur Hsieh, MA, NREMT-P, is the Chief Executive Officer for the San Francisco Paramedic Association. He has been involved in EMS since 1982 and has worked as an EMT and Paramedic in both rural and urban environments. An educator since 1987 with a Master's degree in education, Art has been a chief training officer for a metropolitan fire department, a paramedic program director, and has trained both new providers and experienced medical professionals in the finer points of emergency medical care. He is a past president of the National Association of EMS Educators and has presented at conferences and workshops nationwide.

Kevin Boone

Kevin Boone, BSN, NREMT-P, is a Paramedic Firefighter with the Berkeley Fire Department and has been a practicing paramedic in San Francisco Bay Area for over twentyfive years. Kevin has been a paramedic program director and primary instructor and has also served as an instructor providing in-service training for the EMTs and paramedics of the SFFD. A majority of his nursing experience has been in intensive care and cardiopulmonary nursing.

Contents

Paramedicine is a highly technical profession. Not only must you have strength to lift and carry large amounts of weight, but you also need to perform fine motor tasks such as endotracheal intubation and intravenous therapy. The mastery of these skills depends upon clear instruction at the beginning and repetition training. *The Paramedic Companion* presents task training in two different ways: Step-by-Step (SBS) skill demonstrations (some in the worktext and others on the DVD and Online Learning Center) show how a skill is performed, using both pictures and text. Skill sheets outline skill progression in a "check off" format. SBSs and Skill sheets can be found in both printed and electronic format for ease of use and convenience. The table below provides a map for locating skills content.

Key:

DVD = Student DVD found in *The Paramedic Companion: A Case-Based Worktext*
N/A = Not applicable (i.e., no Step-by-Step exists)
OLC = Online Learning Center, found at www.mhhe.com/chapleau1e
SBS = Step-by-Step

No.	Title	Skill Sheet Location (PDF Format)	Electronic SBS Location (ShockWave and iPod Formats)	Print SBS location (Worktext chapter)
1	Airway Positioning and Maneuvers	DVD and OLC	DVD and OLC	N/A
2	Oropharyngeal Airways	DVD and OLC	DVD and OLC	N/A
3	Nasopharyngeal Airways	DVD and OLC	DVD and OLC	N/A
4	Bag-Mask Ventilation with 1 Rescuer	DVD and OLC	DVD and OLC	N/A
5	Bag-Mask Ventilation with 2 or More Rescuers	DVD and OLC	DVD and OLC	N/A
6	Foreign Body Airway Obstruction Removal—Advanced Techniques	Worktext Appendix A, DVD, and OLC	DVD and OLC	12
7	Endotracheal Intubation	Worktext Appendix A, DVD, and OLC	DVD and OLC	12
8	ALS Airway Adjuncts	DVD and OLC	N/A	N/A
9	Endotracheal Confirmation Techniques	DVD and OLC	DVD and OLC	N/A
10	End-Tidal Capnography	DVD and OLC	N/A	N/A
11	Endotracheal Suctioning	DVD and OLC	DVD and OLC	N/A
12	Pulse Oximetry	DVD and OLC	DVD and OLC	N/A
13	Rapid Sequence Intubation	Worktext Appendix A, DVD, and OLC	DVD and OLC	12
14	Nasal Intubation	DVD and OLC	DVD and OLC	N/A
15	Digital Intubation	DVD and OLC	N/A	N/A
16	Endotracheal Intubation in Face-to-Face Position	DVD and OLC	N/A	N/A
17	Extubation	DVD and OLC	N/A	N/A

No.	Title	Skill Sheet Location (PDF Format)	Electronic SBS Location (ShockWave and iPod Formats)	Print SBS location (Worktext chapter)
18	Continuous Positive Airway Pressure	Worktext Appendix A, DVD, and OLC	DVD and OLC	12
19	Needle Cricothyroidotomy	Worktext Appendix A, DVD, and OLC	DVD and OLC	12
20	Surgical Cricothyrotomy	Instructor Materials Only	N/A	N/A
21	Dual-Lumen Airway Device	Worktext Appendix A, DVD, and OLC	DVD and OLC	12
22	Meconium Suctioning	DVD and OLC	DVD and OLC	N/A
23	Suctioning of Stoma	DVD and OLC	DVD and OLC	N/A
24	Evacuation of Gastric Contents	DVD and OLC	DVD and OLC	N/A
25	Arterial Pulse Locations	DVD and OLC	N/A	N/A
26	Blood Glucose Assessment	DVD and OLC	DVD and OLC	N/A
27	Chest Auscultation	Worktext Appendix A, DVD, and OLC	DVD and OLC	11
28	Nystagmus Assessment	DVD and OLC	N/A	N/A
29	Orthostatic Vital Signs	DVD and OLC	DVD and OLC	N/A
30	Prehospital Stroke Evaluation	DVD and OLC	DVD and OLC	N/A
31	Trauma Scoring	DVD and OLC	N/A	N/A
32	Primary Survey	Worktext Appendix A, DVD, and OLC	DVD and OLC	14
33	Secondary Survey	Worktext Appendix A, DVD, and OLC	DVD and OLC	14
34	Chest Pain Assessment	DVD and OLC	N/A	N/A
35	Dyspnea Assessment	DVD and OLC	N/A	N/A
36	Abdominal Assessment	DVD and OLC	N/A	N/A
37	ECG Acquisition	Worktext Appendix A, DVD, and OLC	DVD and OLC	29, Section I
38	Synchronized Cardioversion and Defibrillation	Worktext Appendix A, DVD, and OLC	DVD and OLC	29, Section II
39	Transcutaneous Cardiac Pacing	Worktext Appendix A, DVD, and OLC	DVD and OLC	29, Section II
40	Vagal Maneuvers	DVD and OLC	N/A	N/A
41	Uncomplicated Childbirth	DVD and OLC	N/A	N/A
42	Intravenous Access	Worktext Appendix A, DVD, and OLC	DVD and OLC	16
43	Intravenous Access Using Saline Lock	DVD and OLC	DVD and OLC	N/A
44	Phlebotomy	DVD and OLC	N/A	N/A
45	Intraosseous Access and Drug Administration	Worktext Appendix A, DVD, and OLC	DVD and OLC	16
46	Umbilical Vein Cannulation	DVD and OLC	N/A	N/A
47	Central Line Access for Fluids and Drug Administration	DVD and OLC	N/A	N/A

No.	Title	Skill Sheet Location (PDF Format)	Electronic SBS Location (ShockWave and iPod Formats)	Print SBS location (Worktext chapter)
48	Intravenous Drug Bolus	Worktext Appendix A, DVD, and OLC	DVD and OLC	16
49	Intravenous Drug Infusion	Worktext Appendix A, DVD, and OLC	DVD and OLC	16
50	Intramuscular Drug Administration	Worktext Appendix A, DVD, and OLC	DVD and OLC	16
51	Intranasal Drug Administration	DVD and OLC	N/A	N/A
52	Nebulized Drug Administration	Worktext Appendix A, DVD, and OLC	DVD and OLC	16
53	Subcutaneous Drug Administration	Worktext Appendix A, DVD, and OLC	DVD and OLC	16
54	Sublingual Drug Administration	DVD and OLC	N/A	NA
55	Endotracheal Drug Administration	DVD and OLC	N/A	N/A
56	Eye Drop Drug Administration	DVD and OLC	N/A	N/A
57	Oral Drug Administration	DVD and OLC	N/A	N/A
58	Rectal Drug Administration	Worktext Appendix A, DVD, and OLC	DVD and OLC	16
59	Autoinjector Drug Administration Device	DVD and OLC	N/A	N/A
60	Putting On and Removing Gloves	DVD and OLC	N/A	N/A
61	Handwashing	DVD and OLC	DVD and OLC	N/A
62	Communication Challenges— Interpreter Services	DVD and OLC	N/A	N/A
63	Verbal Communications	DVD and OLC	N/A	N/A
64	Documentation	DVD and OLC	N/A	N/A
65	Physical Restraints	DVD and OLC	DVD and OLC	N/A
66	Bleeding Control and Shock	DVD and OLC	DVD and OLC	N/A
67	Bleeding Control with a Tourniquet	DVD and OLC	DVD and OLC	N/A
68	Seated Spinal Immobilization	DVD and OLC	DVD and OLC	N/A
69	Standing Spinal Immobilization	DVD and OLC	N/A	N/A
70	Supine Spinal Immobilization	DVD and OLC	DVD and OLC	N/A
71	Helmet Removal	DVD and OLC	DVD and OLC	N/A
72	Rapid Extrication	DVD and OLC	N/A	N/A
73	Appendicular Skeleton Splinting	DVD and OLC	N/A	N/A
74	Traction Splinting	DVD and OLC	DVD and OLC	N/A
75	Dislocation Reduction	Instructor Materials Only	N/A	N/A
76	Traumatic Brain Injury Assessment	DVD and OLC	N/A	N/A
77	Management of Chest Trauma	Worktext Appendix A, DVD, and OLC	DVD and OLC	21
78	Burn Percentage Estimation	DVD and OLC	N/A	N/A
79	Crush Injury Management	DVD and OLC	N/A	N/A

No.	Title	Skill Sheet Location (PDF Format)	Electronic SBS Location (ShockWave and iPod Formats)	Print SBS location (Worktext chapter)
80	Eye Irrigation	DVD and OLC	N/A	N/A
81	MAST/PASG Application	DVD and OLC	N/A	N/A
82	Pericardiocentesis	Instructor Materials Only	N/A	N/A
83	NREMT Patient Assessment Trauma	DVD and OLC	N/A	N/A
84	NREMT Ventilatory Management—Adult	DVD and OLC	N/A	N/A
85	NREMT Dual-Lumen Airway Device	DVD and OLC	N/A	N/A
86	NREMT Dynamic Cardiology	DVD and OLC	N/A	N/A
87	NREMT Static Cardiology	DVD and OLC	N/A	N/A
88	NREMT Oral Station	DVD and OLC	N/A	N/A
89	NREMT Intravenous Therapy	DVD and OLC	N/A	N/A
90	NREMT Pediatric Ventilatory Management	DVD and OLC	N/A	N/A
91	NREMT Pediatric Intraosseous Infusion	DVD and OLC	N/A	N/A
92	NREMT Spinal Immobilization (Seated Patient)	DVD and OLC	N/A	N/A
93	NREMT Spinal Immobilization (Supine Patient)	DVD and OLC	N/A	N/A
94	NREMT Bleeding Control/Shock Management	DVD and OLC	N/A	N/A

During my lifetime, I have developed a continuing interest in learning how we learn. The wide variety of thinking processes involved with each of the various intelligences, most specifically the complexities of the higher levels of thinking as they apply to patient care, and the interpersonal relationships that result, never cease to capture my interest. As a teacher of patient care providers, I pay particular attention to the textbooks and resources available, and find myself supplementing as I go, depending on the needs of the students in my care.

Therefore, I was particularly intrigued when asked to review *The Paramedic Companion: A Case-Based Worktext*, which I was told was no ordinary workbook. Much thought had gone into the need to supplement didactic information with exercises designed to stimulate long-term memory, promote "chunking" of like bits of information and enhance linking with other "chunks," and provide images to allow students to visualize conditions to facilitate understanding and thus store in long-term memory. Needless to say, I was interested and agreed to review the material.

What I found was an entirely new resource. It is a treasure trove of images, exercises, and games—all designed to stimulate thinking, promote "chunking," enhance relationships between bits of information, and ultimately make that bridge between textbook didactic learning and the field. The images and skills demonstra-tions are a gold mine that, with accompanying questions, open the students up to a wide variety of learning opportunities at all levels and in learning environments that include not only the novice student but also the experienced provider. What a wonderful resource for primary education, continuing education, and the biggest challenge of all, remediation.

The Problem-Based Learning Cases are additional resources that can be used independently with any other textbook. The games and other activities included provide easy, fun methods of promoting retention of facts and other material that students have traditionally found difficult to master.

Because of the wide variety of materials provided, I would heartily encourage use of this worktext as a companion for any primary education course, regardless of the textbook used. Instructors finally have a resource that will fill a number of needs and can be used for a variety of learners. My hope is that classroom teachers will realize the full potential of this resource and use it to the maximum. Congratulations to the authors of this wonderful product.

Alice "Twink" Dalton
Mountain View Fire Protection District
Longmont, Colorado

Preface

We began our paramedic training in the mid 1980s. At that time, the number of books we were required to purchase for class were few: a primary paramedic textbook and a basic ECG workbook. The American Heart Association ACLS reference text was available for us to use during class. Altogether, the number of pages to read and study was probably around a thousand.

The paramedic students of today are as motivated as we were back then. However, they are required by educators to buy textbooks that contain much more information than before. A paramedic textbook alone today may have nearly two thousand pages. The amount of information that today's paramedic student needs to digest, understand, and retain can be staggering. This volume of information runs the risk of overload. The effort to make sense of it all can overwhelm even the most well-intentioned student.

This concern forms the underlying theme of *The Paramedic Companion*. As you use this book, think of it as your companion during the journey to becoming a paramedic. Sometimes you will use it as a guide to your learning, as it directs you to resources needed in order to learn about specific concepts. Other times, it will support your exploration of the art and science of prehospital medicine by providing you with learning tools, still images, and exercises to better explain an idea or technique. The questions and exercises are challenging—they are not meant to prompt you to simply regurgitate ideas, but rather to explore them more fully. *The Paramedic Companion* is designed to help explain the concepts of paramedicine in a unique and fun way.

The Paramedic Companion is written in a simple and direct style, speaking clearly to paramedic students. The material in each chapter revolves around "Need To Know" content that the authors of both the textbook and worktext felt were necessary for the paramedic student to master. All features in the worktext were designed to ensure that learners can successfully master these key content areas.

Features

Special features in each chapter are designed to promote critical thinking based on real-life situations, an essential quality of the professional prehospital care provider. These include:

Are You Ready?

Each chapter begins with a vignette describing an incident that has direct relevance to the materials that will be presented next. Open-ended questions based on the vignettes help review basic concepts the student needs and prepare the learner for the chapter's lessons.

Active Learning

Self-directed, student-centered activities provide alternative methods for mastering the chapter's main concepts while promoting independent learning. Many are designed for use with partners or in small groups.

You Are There: Reality-Based Cases

The progressive case studies found in each chapter encourage students to build on and apply newly acquired information to real-world practice.

Test Yourself

This self-assessment section offers review of the textbook chapter contents in multiple-choice, short-answer, and fill-in question formats.

Need to Know

Need to Know content is summarized in Key Objectives and explanatory narrative to help the learner review what he or she has learned in the textbook chapter.

Need to Do

Paramedics must learn a wide range of skills and procedures in order to assess and manage ill and injured patients. This section outlines the relevant psychomotor skills and provides a map for finding skill sheets and Step-by-Step demonstrations in the worktext, at the Online Learning Center (www.mhhe.com/chapleau1e) and on the accompanying Student DVD. Skill sheets to support the in-text Step-by-Steps can be found in Appendix A and will help systematically guide the student through the repetitive process.

Connections

Links and cross-references to related textbook, work-text, and ancillary content, as well as other resources, help tie together information for the student.

Secrets

These hints and tips related to key chapter content share tried and true information from seasoned paramedics.

The Drug Box

Key content about drugs commonly used to treat the conditions covered in the text chapter is summarized here.

I Spy Photographs

These detailed photographs with hidden elements are a fun way for students to review key concepts of both proper and improper practices.

Answers

Not only are the answers provided for each question, but an in-depth explanation is provided as well. This way, students can determine immediately whether their answers and rationales are correct.

Problem-Based Learning Cases

Eight Problem-Based Learning Cases (PBLs) are included in the worktext to support each of the major parts of the textbook. Each problem is firmly grounded in the complexities of real-life situations—there is often more to the situation than meets the eye! Problem-based learning employs an open-ended, Socratic approach to student learning. By design, specific answers are NOT directly provided. Instead, an overview of the problem is presented to the reader to help exercise critical-thinking skills. Students are encouraged to answer the questions through research and analysis.

Companion DVD and Online Learning Center

Multimedia tools on the accompanying DVD and Online Learning Center will create an educational space that is rich with information. Content includes:

- Skills—Step-by-Steps in a ShockWave and iPod formats that show skills being correctly performed. Text "bubbles" and arrows point to key aspects of skill performance.
- 91 skill sheets
- Audio glossary with pronunciation of key terms
- New chapter review questions, including questions keyed to photographs and ECGs
- Anatomy and physiology animations
- Drug administration animation
- Games and exercises such as drug flashcards, ECG exercises, and puzzles
- I Spy Exercises—Detailed photographs with accompanying questions

As you use this worktext, we hope that you find it interesting, stimulating, challenging, and even fun. Use it to help master the critical concepts of prehospital emergency care. Make sure that you refer to the User's Guide to make full use of this book. We wish you well as you embark on this exciting voyage of discovery.

—AH and KB

Acknowledgments

Writing a worktext in a manner worthy of being read by our peers has proven to be a daunting task. For this work to come together, we have many people to thank, not only for their expertise, but also for their kindness and patience.

There have been countless patients, physicians, paramedics, EMTs, firefighters, and nurses who have helped to shape our clinical experiences and knowledge. Educators from all walks of life provided insights, tips, and pearls on how people learn. Students and their desire to learn drive us to provide relevant and timely knowledge in a readable, interesting format. We thank all of you for your contributions.

There are specific people in our industry who deserve special thanks. Twink Dalton is the EMS educator's educator. Her calm, quiet demeanor belies the passion and love she has for the profession and its professionals. Nick Klemenko helped us create the nearly 100 skill sheets. Tim Howey performed magic and created the electronic presentation of skill Step-by-Steps. The folks at FISDAP created the thought-provoking Test Yourself questions found in each chapter and the chapter quizzes found on the DVD and Online Learning Center. Rick Brady is our photographer, and we are grateful for his guidance, feedback and, most importantly, his eye for the photos that illustrate key points in this worktext. Greg Peterson supplied several effective photographs. Thanks to all of the volunteers who spent countless hours performing skills and acting out scenes depicted in this book.

The process of putting a book together is as challenging as the creative process itself. Sponsoring Editor Claire Merrick has steered this project to its completion over the past two years. Development Editor Kelly Trakalo was the one who listened to our pitch, years ago, about a case-based EMS workbook. Nancy Peterson is our Developmental Editor, angel, coach, taskmaster, spell checker, vent receiver, and ultimately, a good friend. Project Manager Jean Starr at McGraw-Hill helped us through the morass of copyedited manuscript and page proof known as production.

Finally, we wish to thank the textbook authors for envisioning an evidence-based paramedic textbook. Peter Pons, Will Chapleau, Angel Burba, and David Page have put together the definitive EMS education textbook. David has been instrumental in tying many of the project's pieces together and finding humor in the minutiae of this incredible project. When no humor could be found, he provided some of his own. It is an honor to have worked with such dedicated EMS professionals. Thanks!

Reviewers

The publisher and authors gratefully acknowledge the many professionals who shared their expertise and assisted in refining our plan and developing this worktext. These individuals include:

Linda M. Abrahamson, BA, RN, EMTP
*Silver Cross Hospital/Joliet Junior College
Joliet, Illinois*

David K. Anderson, BS, EMT-P
*NW Regional Training Center
Director of EMS Education
Vancouver, Washington*

Angel Clark Burba, MS, EMT-P, NCEE
*Associate Professor
EMS Program Director
Howard Community College
Columbia, Maryland*

Will Chapleau, EMT-P, RN, TNS
*Manager, ATLS Program
American College of Surgeons
Chicago, Illinois*

Gregory J. Chapman
*Hudson Valley Community College
Troy, New York*

Alice ("Twink") Dalton
*Mountain View Fire Protection District
Longmont, Colorado*

Dr. Daniel Finley
*Gulf Coast Community College
Panama City, Florida*

Lawrence Linder, MA, NREMTP
*Hillsborough Community College
Tampa, Florida*

Michael McGowan, NREMT-P
*Florida Medical Training Institute
Melbourne, Florida*

Louis N. Molino, Sr., CET
Fire and Safety Specialists, Inc
College Station, Texas

David Page, MS, NREMT-P
Faculty, Emergency Health Services Department
Inver Hills Community College
Inver Grove Heights, Minnesota

Peter T. Pons, MD
Emergency Physician
Denver, Colorado

Meghan Treitz, MD
Adjunct faculty at Arapahoe Community College
Littleton, Colorado

Guided Tour

This Guided Tour shows you how to put the features and ancillary components of *The Paramedic Companion* to work for you.

Worktext Features

Are You Ready?

The opening vignette is designed to get you thinking about the concepts that will be introduced in the chapter. A short, vivid case is followed by open-ended questions intended to help you apply the material to a real-world setting. Don't worry about answering each question right away—study the chapter and come back to any aspects of the case that you are unsure of when you feel more comfortable with the material.

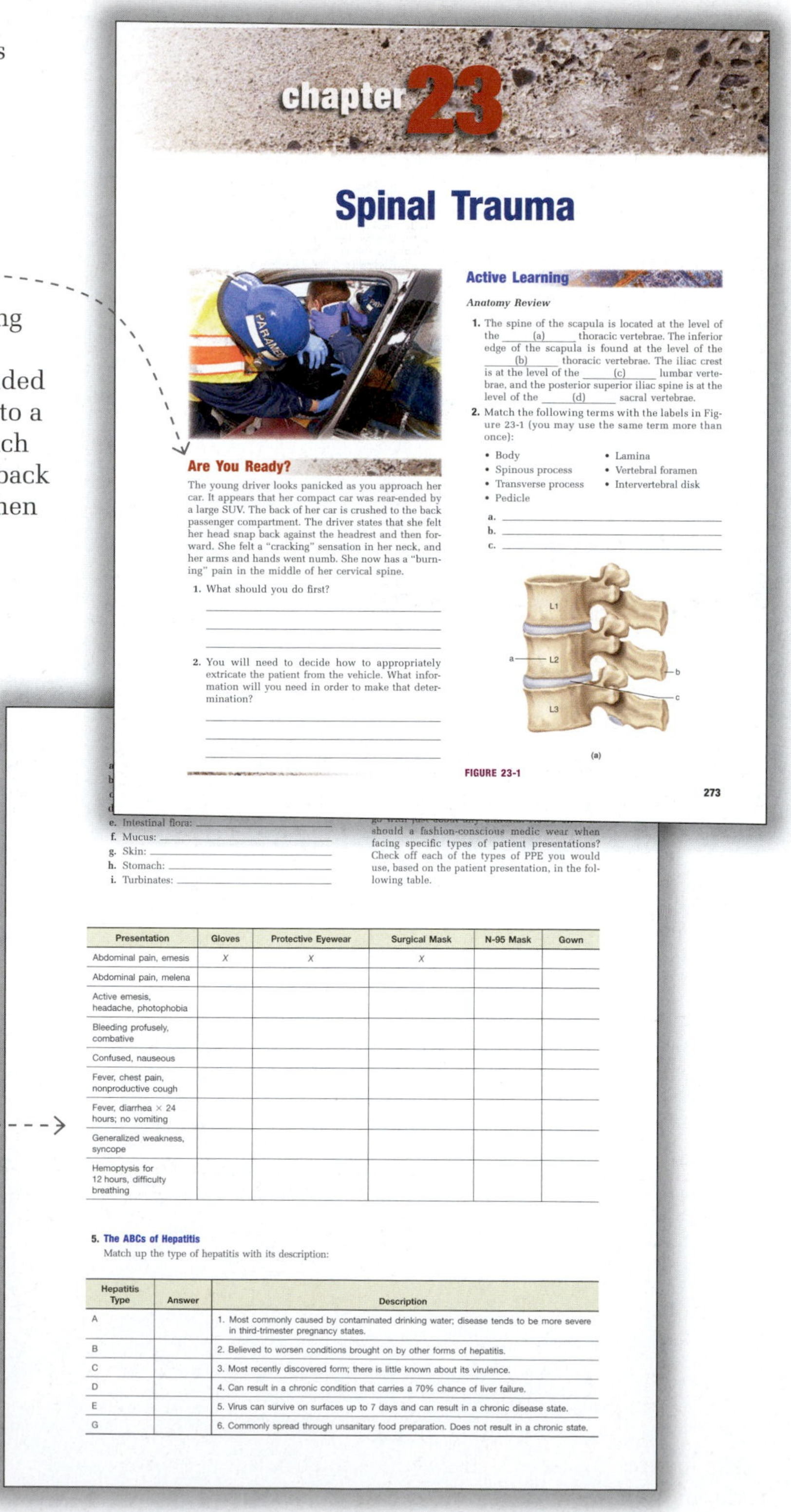

Active Learning

You will find a variety of exercises to help you increase your comprehension of the subject matter introduced in each chapter. Many of these exercises require active participation from you; the good news is, they're beneficial and fun to do! You will also find student-centered activities such as fill-in and matching exercises, as well as ideas to help you explore specific topics of interest. Use this section to promote your understanding of the chapter material.

chapter **23**

Spinal Trauma

Are You Ready?

The young driver looks panicked as you approach her car. It appears that her compact car was rear-ended by a large SUV. The back of her car is crushed to the back passenger compartment. The driver states that she felt her head snap back against the headrest and then forward. She felt a "cracking" sensation in her neck, and her arms and hands went numb. She now has a "burning" pain in the middle of her cervical spine.

1. What should you do first?

2. You will need to decide how to appropriately extricate the patient from the vehicle. What information will you need in order to make that determination?

Active Learning

Anatomy Review

1. The spine of the scapula is located at the level of the ____(a)____ thoracic vertebrae. The inferior edge of the scapula is found at the level of the ____(b)____ thoracic vertebrae. The iliac crest is at the level of the ____(c)____ lumbar vertebrae, and the posterior superior iliac spine is at the level of the ____(d)____ sacral vertebrae.

2. Match the following terms with the labels in Figure 23-1 (you may use the same term more than once):

- Body
- Spinous process
- Transverse process
- Pedicle
- Lamina
- Vertebral foramen
- Intervertebral disk

a. _____
b. _____
c. _____

FIGURE 23-1

273

e. Intestinal flora: _____
f. Mucus: _____
g. Skin: _____
h. Stomach: _____
i. Turbinates: _____

...should a fashion-conscious medic wear when facing specific types of patient presentations? Check off each of the types of PPE you would use, based on the patient presentation, in the following table.

Presentation	Gloves	Protective Eyewear	Surgical Mask	N-95 Mask	Gown
Abdominal pain, emesis	X	X	X		
Abdominal pain, melena					
Active emesis, headache, photophobia					
Bleeding profusely, combative					
Confused, nauseous					
Fever, chest pain, nonproductive cough					
Fever, diarrhea × 24 hours; no vomiting					
Generalized weakness, syncope					
Hemoptysis for 12 hours, difficulty breathing					

5. The ABCs of Hepatitis

Match up the type of hepatitis with its description:

Hepatitis Type	Answer	Description
A		1. Most commonly caused by contaminated drinking water; disease tends to be more severe in third-trimester pregnancy states.
B		2. Believed to worsen conditions brought on by other forms of hepatitis.
C		3. Most recently discovered form; there is little known about its virulence.
D		4. Can result in a chronic condition that carries a 70% chance of liver failure.
E		5. Virus can survive on surfaces up to 7 days and can result in a chronic disease state.
G		6. Commonly spread through unsanitary food preparation. Does not result in a chronic state.

You Are There: Reality-Based Cases

These real-life scenarios will help you push your fundamental understanding of the material to the next level. Although most of the questions center on the current chapter, additional concepts from other areas of the worktext and the textbook are integrated in a manner that will thoughtfully and realistically broaden the depth and breadth of your overall knowledge.

Need to Know

These key chapter objectives and narrative explanations will summarize critical information contained in each chapter. Make sure that you can meet these objectives before moving on to the next chapter. The "foundation" of paramedic knowledge is only as strong as each of the individual "blocks" of knowledge used to construct it.

Test Yourself

These questions will help you assess your strengths and weaknesses regarding the content of the chapter. Try to answer these questions without referring to the textbook first. You may want to wait until you have finished studying the chapter before completing this section—this way, you can rapidly identify the areas where you may still have some deficiencies and remediate them.

(Screenshot: page 552 — Part 5 Special Populations)

bring their bicycle helmets to school on the day that you will be there so that you can assist in helmet sizing and proper use. Attempt to find local businesses, public safety agencies, and bicycle helmet manufacturers that would be willing to donate helmets to children who cannot afford one. If you choose children of day care age, you might consider working with a representative of your local law enforcement agency to provide fingerprinting or identification cards for this age group.

There are a number of injury prevention topics that you can choose from, including motor vehicle safety, choking prevention, poisoning, bicycle and pedestrian safety, fire and burns, water safety, and firearms.

During the time spent with these children, you can experience firsthand how children of that age group function and behave. It is extremely helpful to have a teacher or a caregiver available to facilitate your interaction with the different age groups and assist you in learning about their normal behavior, growth, and development.

Once you have an idea of what is normal behavior, growth, and development, you will have a much better idea of what would be considered abnormal. After all, it is the abnormal presentations that you will be called to evaluate, treat, and transport.

When engaged with young children in these environments, you should always be accompanied by another adult to prevent any accusation of unethical behavior.

2. Assessment Practice

If you have the opportunity to spend time observing or volunteering in a pediatric clinic, a pediatrician's office, or the pediatric unit of a local hospital, you will be able to gain tremendous insight into the assessment and treatment of pediatric patients. Simply watching a practitioner who is well versed in the assessment of children is a wonderful way to develop your own assessment style, and if you have the opportunity to watch and then perform assessments with an experienced practitioner there to guide you, the experience will be even more valuable.

If you are unable to arrange such an experience, then practice assessing your children, children in your extended family, or of friends or neighbors if they are willing to let you practice assessing their children.

3. Just how Safe

Go to a store that sells infant-related furniture and devices. Find a changing table and measure the height of the changing surface to the floor. How does the height compare to the distance needed to meet trauma criteria? Repeat the measurement on

a high chair, and compare the heights. What did you find?

You Are There: Reality-Based Cases
Case 1

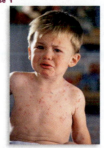

Ben is a 3-year-old who developed a rash over his entire body 3 days ago. He has stayed at home with his babysitter since the onset of the rash, and today he is complaining of abdominal pain and has a fever of 101°F.

The babysitter called 9-1-1 because she witnessed Ben having a full body seizure.

When you arrive on the scene, you find Ben in a fetal position in bed. He is hot to the touch, responds to painful stimuli appropriately, has a very pronounced deep respiratory pattern, and his radial pulse is rapid and weak.

The sitter reports that Ben had been very tired and had vomited several times this morning.

(Screenshot: page 256 — Part 3 Trauma)

Need to Know

The following represent the Key Objectives of Chapter 21:

1. *Explain why injuries to the thoracic cavity can become lethal very quickly.*

The chest houses many critical organs and structures that, when injured through blunt or penetrating trauma, can quickly bleed (Figure 21-3). In addition, air can also "spill" into the cavity in large amounts, either from an external opening, such as through the chest wall, or internally through the bronchial tree. If trapped, this air will compress organs such as the heart and lungs, as well as structures such as the great vessels.

2. *Detect and correct life-threatening injuries to the chest during the primary survey.*

The human body is very unforgiving when its primary systems are compromised. You must identify and treat these life-threatening conditions during the primary survey:

Condition	Intervention
Airway obstruction	Relieve obstruction or bypass (needle cricothyroidotomy).
Tension pneumothorax	Needle decompression (needle thoracotomy).
Open pneumothorax	Occlusive dressing.
Flail chest	Positive pressure ventilation; early intubation.
Massive hemothorax	Treat for shock; transport for surgical intervention.
Cardiac tamponade	Treat for shock; transport for surgical intervention; pericardiocentesis if authorized.

3. *Suspect both abdominal and chest involvement when an injury occurs between the umbilicus and nipple line.*

Unlike the photos and diagrams that show the diaphragm in a position that roughly cuts the thorax in half, in reality it rises a fair amount into the chest cavity during exhalation. Penetrating trauma during the respiratory cycle can cause injuries in the chest cavity, in the abdominal cavity, and/or to the diaphragm itself. It may be very difficult to ascertain exactly where the injury lies in the prehospital assessment. Assuming that an injury exists in all three areas will help keep your suspicion level high.

4. *Explain how to use your understanding of the mechanism of injury to "predict" patterns of injury, enabling you to react more quickly and manage life-threatening conditions of the chest.*

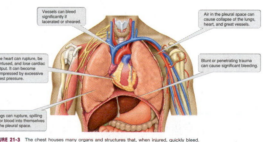

Vessels can bleed significantly if lacerated or sheared.

Air in the pleural space can cause collapse of the lungs, heart, and great vessels.

The heart can rupture, be contused, and lose cardiac output. It can become compressed by excessive chest pressure.

Blunt or penetrating trauma can cause significant bleeding.

Lungs can rupture, spilling air or blood into themselves or the pleural space.

FIGURE 21-3 The chest houses many organs and structures that, when injured, quickly bleed.

(Screenshot: page 349 — Chapter 29 Cardiology, Section I)

3. Which lead is most commonly used for general ECG monitoring, and where are the electrodes for this lead located?

4. The ability to initiate an electrical impulse without outside nervous system stimulation is called

5. The normal T wave represents repolarization of the ventricles. Why do you rarely see the repolarization of the atria on an ECG?

6. An ECG *cannot* tell you if the patient's heart is contracting.
   True
   False

7. The _____ leads get their name because of their placement around the heart on the chest.

8. Name the three layers of the heart and briefly discuss the function of each.

9. What is the Frank-Starling mechanism, and how does it apply to cardiac output?

10. Describe how the venous system serves as a reservoir for blood.

Test Yourself

1. List the five steps of systematic ECG interpretation.

2. You are interpreting an ECG that shows a slightly irregular rhythm. There are no marks visible at the top or bottom of the ECG paper. What method should you use to calculate the patient's heart rate?
   a. Use a heart rate meter
   b. The 300 counting method
   c. The triplicate method
   d. The 6-second strip method

Need to Do

Your technical skills must be as solid as your knowledge. Paramedic procedures can be invasive and pose risks as well as benefits to the patient. In this section, there are Step-by-Step demonstrations of specific chapter-relevant skills. There is also a summary of pertinent skills necessary to manage the patient presentations found in each chapter. Note that the skill summary table will refer to skill sheets, some of which can be found in Appendix A, and all of which are available on the Student DVD and the Online Learning Center (OLC) in PDF format. When applicable, the table also refers to Step-by-Steps, some of which are illustrated and printed in selected chapters, and all of which are found on the Student DVD and OLC in Shockwave and iPod formats. Use these skills resources to help you master the skills and assess your performance.

Connections

No single topic in paramedicine is learned or mastered in a void. This section will identify other chapters of the textbook and this worktext, as well as additional resources, to help you integrate the information into your practice.

The Drug Box

Paramedic students often find medication properties confusing and difficult to learn. This section provides the most relevant information about specific drugs as they relate to the subject matter found in individual chapters.

Secrets

Find "pearls" of information as well as tips of the trade that can help you work more efficiently as a paramedic. These tips are based on the combined knowledge and experience of many seasoned paramedics and health-care professionals.

Sample textbook pages

Need to Do

The following skills are explained and illustrated in a step-by-step manner, via skill sheets and/or Step-by-Steps in this text and on the accompanying DVD:

Skill Name	Skill Sheet Number and Location	Step-by-Step Number and Location
Bag-Mask Ventilation with 1 Rescuer	4 – DVD	4 – DVD
Bag-Mask Ventilation with 2 or More Rescuers	5 – DVD	5 – DVD
Endotracheal Intubation	7 – Appendix A and DVD	7 – Chapter 12 and DVD
Pulse Oximetry	12 – DVD	12 – DVD
Nasal Intubation	14 – DVD	14 – DVD
Digital Intubation	15 – DVD	N/A
Endotracheal Intubation in Face-to-Face Position	16 – DVD	N/A
Chest Auscultation	27 – Appendix A and DVD	27 – Chapter 11 and DVD
Primary Survey	32 – Appendix A and DVD	32 – Chapter 14 and DVD
Chest Pain Assessment	34 – DVD	N/A
Dyspnea Assessment	35 – DVD	N/A
Bleeding Control and Shock	66 – DVD	66 – DVD
Management of Chest Trauma	77 – Appendix A and DVD	77 – This chapter and DVD

Step-by-Step 77

Management of Chest Trauma

Conditions: The candidate should perform this procedure on a simulated patient under existing indoor, ambulance, or outdoor lighting, temperature, and weather conditions.

Indications: A patient who has experienced a medical or trauma mechanism to the chest that results in loss of normal lung expansion, either due to negative pressure loss (pneumothorax) or excessive positive pressure (tension pneumothorax)

Red Flags: Increased possibility of infection. Application of an occlusive dressing can result in a tension pneumothorax; needle decompression is unlikely to reduce hemothorax and will create an open pneumothorax.

—Continued

Steps:

1. Use appropriate standard precautions.
2. Evaluate mechanism of injury.
3. Expose and inspect the neck, chest, and (Figure SBS 77-1). Observe for symmetric rise and respiratory effort.

SBS 77-1

4. Immediately cover the open wound with hand.
5. Palpate for chest wall integrity, subcutaneous emphysema, and chest rise.
6. Auscultate all lung fields.
7. Percuss, listening for hyperresonance and hyporesonance.
8. Apply occlusive dressing and/or needle decompress the chest as necessary.

A. Occlusive Dressing

A1. Place an occlusive dressing over wound SBS 77-2).

SBS 77-2

B2. Locate landmarks (Figure SBS 77-3):
 • Second intercostal space, over the third rib
 • Or fourth intercostal space, over the fifth rib

Connections

- The Diver's Alert Network (DAN) is a nonprofit organization affiliated with the Duke University Medical Center in Durham, NC. Its mission is to help protect the safety and health of divers. The emergency number to contact DAN for the location of a hyperbaric facility is +1-919-684-8111. You can also call collect at +1-919-684-4DAN. When the phone is answered, advise the operator that you are managing a diving emergency and you will be connected directly to a DAN assistant or receive a return phone call. The DAN website is www.diversalertnetwork.org.
- The International Society for Mountain Medicine (ISMM) has a short tutorial on high-altitude illness at their website: www.ismmed.org/np_altitude_tutorial.htm. The ISMM's mission is to "encourage research on all aspects of mountains, mountain peoples and mountaineers and to spread scientific and practical information about mountain medicine around the world."[1]
- You may want to review other causes of noncardiac pulmonary edema in Chapter 29, Cardiology, and about intracranial pressure in Chapter 20, Head, Face, and Neck Trauma, in the textbook.
- Environmental conditions can often factor into complex cases. Problem Based Learning Case 6: Come Out Swinging will test your assessment and diagnostic abilities.
- Link to the companion DVD for a chapter-based quiz, audio glossary, animations, games and exercises, and, when appropriate, skill sheets and skill Step-by-Steps.

Street Secrets

- **Feel the Heat** On the patient, that is. Don't check for body surface temperature on the exposed areas of the skin—ambient temperature may cause you to feel inaccurately. Instead, check for temperatures close to the core, on the patient's chest or abdomen, or under the armpits. If these areas feel cool to the touch, you can be more confident that the patient may be in fact experiencing hypothermia. Don't forget to use the palmar side of your wrist to feel for skin temperature. Just be sure that your skin is intact in that region.
- **Be Safe** Many of the injuries and illnesses described in this chapter occur under risk-laden conditions—underwater, at high altitudes, and at the extremes of heat and cold. You must be

trained and prepared to handle yourself in these conditions, even as you help others. If you are working in an area where these types of events occur, take extra training to better protect yourself while working.

The Drug Box

Nifedipine: A calcium channel blocker that dilates the pulmonary vasculature; can help patients experiencing high-altitude pulmonary edema (HAPE).

Diazepam: A sedative that can help reduce the extreme shivering brought on by rapid cooling measures utilized during heat stroke emergencies.

Diuretics: Furosemide may be helpful in helping to shift interstitial fluid out of the pulmonary tissue during HAPE, but it also increases the risk of dehydration.

Reference

1. International Society for Mountain Medicine Website. "About 15mm." www.ismmed.org/ismm_info.htm (accessed November 18, 2006).

Answers

Are You Ready?

1. The irregular breathing pattern and level of unconsciousness is troubling. Because of the potential injury, you will need to manually stabilize the head and neck during the primary survey. It is possible that you will need to ventilate the patient, rather than simply providing supplemental oxygen. He will need to be exposed quickly and checked for any possible injuries that may be hidden by his clothing. The circumstances may be a clue to Ronald's medical condition. If Ronald is a creature of habit, perhaps something happened to him that took him out of his normal routine. He might have been drinking more than usual, causing him to not be able to get back to his normal place of sleep. Or, he may have been assaulted or fallen and struck his head, causing confusion and altered mental status. If it was fairly cool the night before, hypothermia may have caused him to become confused and disoriented.

2. Patients like the one described can be frustrating to manage, but still demand your respect and care. See Chapter 3, Professional Ethics for discussion on this topic.

I Spy Photographs

These photos are a snapshot of reality. Look for clues in each of the pictures that can help sharpen your power of observation and, in certain situations, maybe even save your life. Knowing what to look for in an emergency situation will give you an edge in your daily practice.

Answers

You will find comprehensive answers, including illustrations, to the questions from each section of the chapter in this section. Study the rationales that are provided to significantly increase your comprehension of the material.

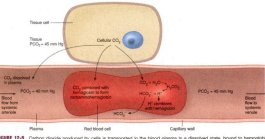

Problem-Based Learning Cases

Throughout this worktext, you will find a series of eight, in-depth and complex clinical cases to think about and solve. These activities use problem-based learning (PBL) to help you analyze information carefully and develop the critical-thinking skills needed by the successful paramedic. As you work your way through each case, consult not only the textbook but also other resources that can help you find the answer to each question posed by the problem. In some cases, you will be given information that may appear to be beyond what you are expected to know. However, if you research this information, you will find valuable clues as to the patient's condition and your management strategy.

When you review the problem in the "Debriefing" section, you will notice that often the "answers" are posed as an additional series of questions. Don't be frustrated; these questions will help guide you to the "real" answers, which are contained in the "Discussion" section.

Ancillary Components

Student DVD and Online Learning Center

Worktext ancillaries include the enclosed DVD and the Online Learning Center, found at www.mhhe.com/chapleau1e. Check them out to find:

- Step-by-Step Skills in ShockWave and iPod formats to show skills being correctly performed. Text "bubbles" and arrows point to key aspects of skill performance.
- 91 Skill Sheets
- Audio Glossary
- New Chapter Quizzes
- Anatomy and Physiology Animations
- Drug Administration Animation
- Drug Flashcards
- Anatomy and Physiology and ECG Exercises

Problem-Based Learning Case 3

An Awful Crash

Part I: The Case

Dispatch and Scene Size-Up

Your pager begins to go off in that familiar singsong: beep beep beep. There is static for a second, and then . . . beeeeEEEP. "Medic 17, Rescue 4, Battalion 2, Engine 42. Unconscious male after a fall. Willows Motocross Raceway, 27235 Highway 70. Medical personnel on scene reporting motocross rider down after collision."

You are at the track within 5 minutes. The rescue unit pulls into the lot as well. A track official waves you to the far gate, near the large mogul section where the riders can gain altitudes of 30 feet as they jump off the hills. You see the medical response truck parked off to the side, its amber lights flashing.

As you pull your gear off the ambulance, a track staff member comes running over. Quickly she tells you that the rider is at the bottom of a ravine that is adjacent to the course track. You follow the direction of her pointed finger and notice that the chain-link fence that separates the track from that area is heavily damaged, with the top of the fence bowed outward. It appears that the rider jumped his motorcycle in the wrong direction and sailed through the fence.

It is midafternoon. The ambient temperature is about 92°F, and the humidity is 90%.

282

1. *Describe your initial concerns about this situation.*

_____
_____

2. *List the equipment you will bring down with you to the patient's side.*

_____
_____

The Primary Survey (Initial Assessment) and Initial Differentials

The patient is lying prone on the ground about 20 feet below you. The terrain is not steep enough to require rope rescue techniques, but it is rocky and loose. There are three other people kneeling next to the patient. You see the demolished motorbike further down the hill, about 30 feet away from the rider. You make your way down the hillside with your EMT partner and one of the rescue firefighters. The other firefighter is staying at the top of the hill.

You reach the injured rider. One of the bystanders appears to be a first responder; he is using a pair of trauma shears to cut away the rider's clothing and protective pads and back shield.

The rider is still wearing his helmet. You can't determine how well he is breathing or his airway patency, but you hear strange sounds coming from underneath the helmet. His arms and legs are lying in odd positions. There are clear angulations of his right leg and both arms.

3. *What are the patient care priorities?*

_____
_____

4. *Is the first responder performing the correct procedure?*

_____
_____

THE PARAMEDIC Companion

Foundations of Paramedicine

part 1

chapter 1

The EMS Profession

Are You Ready?

It's a sultry summer evening in Middle America. At a bar in the center of town, a young man is enjoying the company of his date as they have several drinks. At approximately 10:30, they get up to leave. The man feels fine, although he laughs out loud as he fumbles with his keys and tries to start the motor. The Pontiac GTO fires up with a satisfying roar, the V-8 motor packing 360 impatient horses under the hood. Sliding the automatic three-speed transmission into drive, he puts his arm around the woman, and they roll out of the parking lot and into the warm night.

With the Supremes singing "Baby Love" on the AM radio, the GTO moves quickly onto State Route 34. A few miles away from the bar, the road begins a series of sharp, narrow turns. On the third turn, the man loses control of the car; it runs off the road and rolls over into a nearby ditch. The roof crushes under the weight of the car, and glass flies everywhere. In a few moments, the car comes to a stop on its side, and the night goes still. Inside, the man is dying, impaled by the steering column; the woman lies unconscious on the ground, halfway out of the passenger side window.

It is August 1966.

1. Imagine that you have just come across this crash in your own private vehicle. How will you contact the authorities? What type of emergency medical care will these victims receive on the scene? How and where will they be transported?

_____

_____

_____

Active Learning

1. The Passage of Time

Stand in a room, next to a wall. Use a tape measure to trace out the size of a rectangle that is 50 inches wide and 8 feet, 6 inches long. Step inside this "box" and now imagine you are inside a Civil War era Rucker's ambulance (Figure 1-1a). How does this compare with the back of a Type I ambulance

(a)

(b)

FIGURE 1-1   Vehicle Comparison.   (a) The Rucker ambulance, a Civil War era vehicle. **(b)** A Type I ambulance. Note the length of a modern ambulance is just under three times the length of the body of the Rucker ambulance.

of today (Figure 1-1b)? (As a guide, the federal government KKK-A-1822E standards specify a size of 96 inches wide and 22 feet long.)

2. A Vision of the Future, Circa 1996

Read the following vision, as laid out by the authors of *EMS Agenda for the Future*[1]:

The year is 2009 and it's a Thursday evening. Joe S. is a 60-year-old male who emigrated from Russia in 1995 to work for a software company. He does not speak English very well. He has several cardiac risk factors including hypertension, elevated cholesterol, a history of smoking (a pack a week), and he is 20% overweight. For the past two days he has had mild, intermittent chest discomfort unrelated to exercise.

However, at 11:00 p.m., the discomfort suddenly becomes more severe. Joe's wife, worried and anxious, instructs their computerized habitat monitor (CHM) to summon medical help. Through voice recognition technology, the CHM analyzes the command, interprets it as urgent, and establishes a linkage with the appropriate public safety answering center (PSAC). At the PSAC, a "smart map" identifies and displays the location of the call. Richard Petrillo, the emergency medical communicator (EMC) notes the type of linkage that has been established (not a telephone, personal communicator device, television, or personal computer).

He also knows what sort of query can be conducted through this linkage. Petrillo commands the PSAC computer to instruct the CHM to identify the potential patient, report his chief complaint, and provide his medical database identifiers. In the meantime, the "smart map" has identified the closest acute care response vehicle, and Petrillo instructs the computer to dispatch it.

Staffing the acute care response vehicle are Nancy Quam, Community Health Advanced Medical Practitioner (CHAMP), and Ed Perez, Community Health Intermediate Practitioner (CHIP). As Quam and Perez proceed toward Joe's home, a transponder in their vehicle changes all traffic signals in their favor. Also, digital displays in all area vehicles are alerted that there is an emergency vehicle in their vicinity. The PSAC computer informs Quam and Perez that neither a personal risk analysis (PRA) nor a domicile risk analysis (DRA) has been performed in the past five years.

As Quam and Perez arrive at the home, four minutes after the initial linkage with CHM, they notice substandard lighting on the home's outside walkways and front-porch steps in need of repair. They also note that a maintenance light is illuminated on the CHM annunciator panel. As they greet the patient, they realize that he does not speak English well. Perez puts the translator module into his PDA, and then he speaks to the PDA, which translates his voice to Russian.

The all-systems monitor is applied to the patient's arm and across his chest. Physiologic data is acquired by the monitor's computer chip, then it is analyzed on the scene and transmitted via burst technology to the medical command center 100 miles away. By communicating through their PDAs, Quam and Perez are able to acquire the patient's history. Through Quam's PDA video screen, she establishes a video connect with the MCC. The MCC EMS physician requests additional Level III monitoring, which reveals the patient's carbon monoxide level to be 14%.

Analysis of all the data by the MCC computer and EMS physician suggests a 96% probability of acute myocardial ischemia. Quam and the EMS physician confer, and the patient subsequently is administered short-acting thrombolytics and IV antioxidants. The nearest cardiac care center that is part of Joe's health network is identified and alerted by computer. Joe is transported there, even though other hospitals may be closer. He is examined very briefly in the emergency department and taken directly to the cardiac catheterization laboratory. There he undergoes complete laser debridement of his coronary arteries. Joe suffers no myocardial enzyme leak, there is no permanent cardiac damage, and he is discharged in two days.

This description of the EMS system in 2009 can be found in the beginning of *EMS Agenda for the Future.* Do you agree with this futuristic vision? Why or why not? Whether or not you agree, what do you think needs to occur in order for this vision to become reality?

3. A Preponderance of Evidence

Research will continue to drive the development of EMS systems. Although you may not want to perform actual research yourself, as a future paramedic practitioner, try to seek out new data and trends in medicine as they pertain to your practice. This includes knowing where to find research, how to read and interpret the data, and how to determine whether you agree or disagree with its conclusions.

Where do I find research?

Information about EMS practice can be presented in two general ways. Trade magazines such as *Emergency Medical Services Magazine* or *JEMS* (the *Journal of Emergency Medical Services*) provide monthly synopses of the latest information about the industry and profession. These publications are generally supported by a combination of subscriptions and advertising by industry manufacturers. Additionally national EMS organizations often publish newsletters to keep their members informed of issues specific to the members' interests.

Research findings are generally presented in scholarly journals. Researchers must submit their articles for review by the publication, which may or may not accept the findings based upon the recommendation of a reviewing panel of experts. This *peer review* of submissions is considered the most fair and unbiased approach in deciding whether an article is "fit" for publication. Examples of specific emergency medicine research publications include *Prehospital Emergency Care, Prehospital and Disaster Medicine, Academic Emergency Medicine,* and *Annals of Emergency Medicine.*

The Internet has made the ability to find research easier than ever before. All of the previously mentioned journals can be found on the Web. Additionally, there are medically focused search engines such as PubMed, a service of the National Library of Medicine and the National Institutes of Health (www.pubmed.gov). PubMed searches MEDLINE, an indexing service for research in medicine and related fields. General search engines such as Google or Yahoo! can also point to research articles. In many cases, much of the text of an article can be found directly on the Web.

There are also various websites that can provide valuable information about medicine, including www.emedicine.com and www.webmd.com. A cautionary note: There are sites on the Web that purport to be unbiased sources of information, but in fact are created by medical vendors. The information can be valuable, but you must be aware about the potential bias the site might contain.

How do I read a research article?

Research articles can be difficult and, quite frankly, boring to read. Knowing how a typical research article is constructed may help you understand the information more quickly. A research article typically begins with its *abstract,* a one- or two-paragraph-long summary statement of the article itself. A *hypothesis statement* describes why the research was conducted in the first place. A *literature review* provides background information related to the research question. The *methods* section provides a detailed description of how the data was collected, as well as the parameters of the study design. The data is reported in the *results* section, usually without any explanation. That is done in the *discussion* section, where the author(s) of the study interpret what was found and how it is related to the research question. The *conclusion* section summarizes the article and often provides additional questions related to the original hypothesis for future research.

It is tempting to scan through an article's abstract to find meaning in the article. Indeed the abstract can at least help you make an initial impression as to the relevancy of the information contained within. However, if the article is significant to you, read it in its entirety.

How do I interpret the research?

Read any research article critically. In other words, question the results of the study and the interpretation by the author(s). Does it make sense to you? Why or why not? Reading research with a critical eye and questioning what you read is not necessarily doubting what you read; it is simply allowing you to form your own opinions and draw your own conclusions about what you read.

Reading critically will also help you understand how the research can impact your own practice. For example, what were the parameters, or conditions, of the research? Did it take place in an urban environment, with short transport times? Your working environment may be more rural, with longer transport times. Maybe the research was conducted in a system in which paramedics work with EMT-Basics, whereas your system is "dual medic." You get the idea—the results and conclusions may be appropriate to apply to your practice, or they may be appropriate for other settings.

Frankly, you may not agree with the author's conclusions. Be prepared to explain to yourself why that's the case. If you are new to reading and interpreting research, ask a more experienced colleague to review your conclusion to help determine if it has merit compared to the conclusions of the author(s).

4. Explore Recertification in Your State

Investigate what your state's requirements are for maintaining your hard-earned paramedic status. You can try looking at your state office for EMS oversight; the National Council of State EMS Training Coordinators website has a map to locate most state offices (www.ncsemstc.org/members. htm). Answer the following questions:

a. Are paramedics required to attend a mandatory refresher training course? How long must the course be?

b. Can continuing education (CE) be used to fulfill renewal of license or certification requirements? How many units? Are there limitations to the type or topic of CE you can use for recertification purposes?

c. Are there any local requirements you need to fulfill before you can renew your license or certification?

You Are There: Reality-Based Cases

Case 1

It's a late fall evening, and the air outside the bar is crisp and cool. Inside the bar, a young man is enjoying the company of his date while they have several drinks. At approximately 10:30, they get up to leave. The man feels fine, although he laughs out loud as

he fumbles with his keys and tries to start the motor. The Pontiac GTO fires up with a low roar, the V-8 motor packing 400 impatient horses under the hood. After buckling his seat belt, he casually grasps the hand of the woman. They roll out of the parking lot and into the warm night.

With Christina Aguilera singing "Ain't No Other Man" on the CD player, the GTO moves quickly onto State Route 34. A few miles away from the bar, the road begins a series of sharp, narrow turns. On the third turn, the man loses control of the car; it strikes the guardrail, and sparks fly everywhere. The car is moving too quickly and with enough force to roll over the guardrail and land in a nearby ditch. The front and side air bags deploy while the safety glass breaks apart.

In a few moments, the car comes to a stop on its side, and the night goes still. Inside, the man tries to release his safety belt; he is bleeding from a laceration on his forehead. The woman is crying in pain and fear; it appears that her right lower leg may be broken. The vehicle's onboard computer, sensing the tremendous forces that the car just experienced, sends a wireless signal to a processing center several states away, notifying a communications operator of the crash.

It is October 2006.

1. Imagine that you have just come across this crash in your own private vehicle. How will you contact the authorities? What type of emergency medical care will these victims receive on the scene? How and where will they be transported?

_____

_____

_____

Test Yourself

1. What did the Highway Safety Act of 1966 achieve?

   _____

   _____

2. What is generally the difference between licensure and certification?

   a. Licensure is obtained with a 4-year college degree; certification is obtained with the completion of a specialized course.

   b. Certification is recognized only regionally; licensure is recognized both regionally and nationally.

   c. Licensure is granted by the state; certification is granted by a recognized organization at the local level.

   d. Certification indicates competency to do the job; licensure gives one permission to do the job while working for a provider.

3. In 1960, AT&T designated 9-1-1 as the national emergency phone number.

   True

   False

4. Why is it so difficult to implement evidence-based medicine into the prehospital setting?

   _____

   _____

5. In 1966, the White Paper officially recognized and classified _____ as a disease process for the first time.

6. You are caring for a critical trauma victim in the remote wilderness. The patient needs a lifesaving skill performed immediately, but you are unable to contact a medical control physician to obtain a verbal order. What should you do?

   _____

   _____

7. Online medical oversight occurs with real-time consultation from a physician (or approved designee) via telephone, two-way radio, satellite, or other device to permit two-way interaction.

   True

   False

8. What is the purpose of quality improvement?

   a. To find the best practices and implement them.

   b. To motivate employees to follow standards out of fear of losing their jobs.

   c. To determine which employees are best and reward them accordingly.

   d. To identify mistakes and initiate discipline.

9. In the 1950s, Dr. Peter Safar researched mouth-to-mouth resuscitation.

   True

   False

Need to Know

The following represent the Key Objectives of Chapter 1:

1. *Identify the attributes and behaviors required of an EMS professional.*

   The 1998 National Standard Paramedic Curriculum lists critical professional behaviors expected of paramedic practitioners, including:

   - Integrity
   - Empathy
   - Self-motivation
   - Appropriate appearance and personal hygiene
   - Self-confidence
   - Good written and verbal communication skills
   - Effective time management
   - Teamwork and diplomacy
   - Respect
   - Patient advocacy
   - Careful delivery of services

2. *Describe EMS as a single component of the entire health-care system, and explain why we must work as a team to better serve patients.*

   The EMS system is but one part of the continuum of health care. Our role is an important one—people call for our services when they believe they have a serious medical emergency. We respond to their request, assess the situation, and implement initial care. We transport the patient safely to a medical facility, where a team of nurses, health professionals, and physicians assume the responsibility of medical care that we began in the field. Often, the care that the emergency team provides is transferred to other health professionals, such as those who work in surgery, critical care, medical-surgical floors, rehabilitation, and primary care. It is important to remember that the care we provide to patients can impact the care and events further down the health-care chain.

3. *Describe the levels of providers that make up the EMS profession.*

   There are two broad categories of prehospital care practitioners. *Basic life support* (BLS) *level providers* include emergency medical responders and emergency medical technicians. They are trained to provide a basic level of patient care, including patient assessment, airway control and breathing management with basic airway adjuncts, bleeding control, trauma management, CPR, and automatic external defibrillators (AEDs). In many states, EMTs are trained to administer certain medications, including oxygen, glucose, and activated charcoal, and to assist patients in administering their own medications. *Advanced life support* (ALS) level providers perform all the skills of a basic-level provider. Additionally, advanced EMTs and paramedics are trained to perform more invasive procedures such as intravenous therapy, advanced airway control, and electrical therapy, and can administer many more medications than the BLS provider. A paramedic's training can require over 1,000 hours to complete, compared with the EMT-Basic at 120 hours.

4. *Describe the historical milestones that have shaped and defined the EMS profession.*

The history of EMS development in the United States is relatively brief compared with other medical professionals, such as physicians and nurses. However, much has been accomplished during its short existence. A summary of EMS history, as detailed in the 1996 *EMS Agenda for the Future,* is found in Table 1-1. Note that the pace of development increases as the time line approaches the current day.

5. *Describe the role you play in shaping the future of the EMS profession.*

The EMS profession continues to develop opportunities for career and growth. Where will you fit

TABLE 1-1   **Summary of EMS History**

Date	Event
1500 BC	The Good Samaritan aids an injured traveler alongside the road.
	Romans and Greeks use chariots to transport injured soldiers off the battlefield.
1797	Baron Dominique-Jean Larrey, chief physician in Napoleon's army, institutes the first prehospital system designed to triage and transport the injured from the field to aid stations.
1862	Ambulances developed by Dr. Jonathan Letterman are authorized by General McClellan during the Civil War to transport Union soldiers off the battlefield.
1865	Cincinnati General Hospital begins the first civilian ambulance service. New York City follows in 1869.
1928	The first Rescue Squad begins service in Roanoke, Virginia.
1958	Dr. Peter Safar demonstrates mouth-to-mouth resuscitation is superior to other methods of ventilation.
1960	CPR is shown to be effective.
1966	The National Academy of Sciences publishes "Accidental Death and Disability: The Neglected Disease of Modern Society."
1967	Dr. Frank Pantridge describes field resuscitation techniques in the British journal *Lancet.*
1967	Dr. Eugene Nagel trains firefighters as paramedics in Miami, Florida.
1968	9-1-1 is designated as the national emergency phone number.
1969	The NHTSA publishes the first national standard curriculum for training emergency medical technicians.
1970	The NREMT is organized.
1973	The EMS Systems Act is developed. It is funded in 1974 by President Ford.
1973	The Star of Life is developed by NHTSA.
1974	KKK-specifications for ambulances are developed by the GSA.
1984	EMS-C (EMS for children) funding is enacted.
1994	The NREMT begins the EMS Practice Blueprint.
1996	*EMS Agenda for the Future* is released.
1998	*EMS Education Agenda for the Future: A System's Approach* is published.
2005	The National EMS Workforce Initiative begins.

in—practitioner, supervisor, educator, researcher? Perhaps you will use your paramedic skills as a firefighter, or apply your training or experience to becoming a nurse, physician assistant, or other health-care professional. No matter what you do, remember to keep your eye on the ball: an EMS professional has the interests of the patient first.

Need to Do

There are no psychomotor skills that directly support this chapter content.

Connections

- Box 1-3, Major Milestones of National Impact, in Chapter 1 of the textbook summarizes EMS developments in the United States.
- Link to the companion DVD for a chapter-based quiz, audio glossary, animations, games and exercises, and, when appropriate, skill sheets and skill Step-by-Steps.

Street Secrets

- **Star of Life** Did you know that the six points of the Star of Life (Figure 1-2) represent the different phases of EMS response? They are
  a. Detection   d. Care on scene
  b. Reporting   e. Care en route
  c. Response   f. Transfer of care

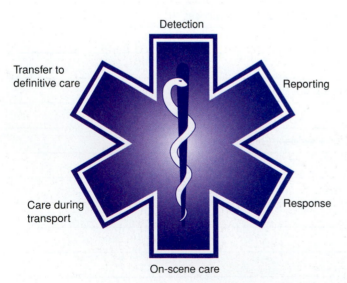

FIGURE 1-2 The Star of Life was designated as the symbol for EMS in 1977.

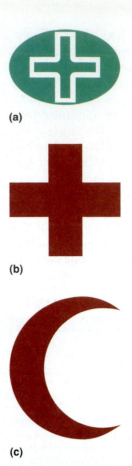

FIGURE 1-3   Other Emergency Symbols.   (a) The Green Cross. **(b)** The European Red Cross. **(c)** The Middle Eastern Red Crescent.

- **Other Emblems** Although the Star of Life is strongly associated with prehospital care today, other emblems have been used in the past to indicate that emergency care was available, such as the Green Cross (Figure 1-3a). In other parts of the world, other symbols of EMS include the Red Cross in Europe (Figure 1-3b) and the Red Crescent in the Middle East (Figure 1-3c).

The Drug Box

There are no specific drugs related to this chapter content.

Reference

1. National Highway Traffic Safety Administration. *EMS Agenda for the Future.* Washington, DC: US Department of Transportation, 1996. Publication DOT HS 808 441.

Answers

Are You Ready?

1. The year 1966 saw the release of "Accidental Death and Disability: The Neglected Disease of Modern Society," published by the National Academy of Sciences. In that year, 50,894 people died on American highways, translating to a rate of 5.497 deaths per million miles driven. If you had arrived on the scene of this vehicle crash, you would probably have had to wait until someone else drove by to tell that driver to go to the nearest pay phone and call for help using a local seven-digit telephone number. Although it may have been possible that some type of emergency ambulance was available, it is more likely that the police and fire department would work with the local funeral home to extricate and transport the victims. Little or no prehospital care would have been provided; it would be unlikely that a backboard or cervical collar would be used. The victims would be quickly driven to the closest hospital, which may or may not have had the appropriately trained personnel on-site to treat the victims.

You Are There: Reality-Based Cases

Case 1

1. Compared to 1966, the fatality rate fell to 1.48 deaths per million miles driven in 2003, for a total of 42,643 deaths. In addition to the prenotification by the onboard computer, it is likely that you would be contacting the authorities by using a cellular telephone to dial 9-1-1. Trained paramedics and/or EMTs would work with firefighters and police officers to extricate the victims, provide initial treatment to manage any life-threatening injuries, and transport them to the nearest trauma center, where a specially trained trauma team would quickly evaluate and further manage their injuries. It is likely that an air medical unit would be utilized for longer-distance transports and cases in which extrication is delayed.

   Compare this scenario to that in the chapter-opening case. In the 40 years between the two fictitious events, much has happened in the technology of automobiles, highway construction, and prehospital care that optimizes the long-term survival of crash victims.

Test Yourself

1. The formation of the Highway Safety Bureau

   With passage of the Highway Safety Act in 1966, the National Highway Traffic Safety Agency and the National Traffic Safety Agency were combined to form the Highway Safety Bureau within the Federal Highway Administration of the Department of Transportation.

2. d

   Generally, the certification process indicates that you are competent to do the job, but it does not give you permission to do the job. Licensure gives you permission to do the job while working for a provider. However, the actual definition of each term may vary from state to state. Each jurisdiction that grants permission to function as a paramedic will have specific terminology, and you bear the responsibility to understand what this means and how it impacts you as a professional.

3. False

   In 1968, AT&T designated 9-1-1 as the national emergency phone number.

4. There is a lack of research on EMS practices.

   There is surprisingly little actual research on EMS practices, so there is not a lot of information to draw upon to design treatment guidelines. While there will always be some who resist change, most EMS providers wish to move the field forward. There is federal support, and several national entities are lobbying for EMS research.

5. Trauma

   In 1966, the National Academy of Sciences–National Research Council (NAS-NRC) published a report entitled "Accidental Death and Disability: The Neglected Disease of Modern Society," known as the "White Paper." For the first time trauma was officially recognized and classified as a disease process. Once the majority of the medical scientists began thinking of accidents as a form of disease, proven clinical and public health models of management could be applied to help "cure" the disease. This represented a huge step forward in the progress of treating injuries as well as illness.

6. Perform the skill and document why you did so without a verbal order.

   You should perform the lifesaving skill without online medical direction and then document why you did so. Not performing the skill or waiting until you establish medical direction could result in the loss of life.

7. True

   Online medical direction is achieved when real-time consultation occurs between the prehospital provider and the doctor or their approved designee.

8. a

   The purpose of quality improvement is to find the best practices and implement them. It should never be used to target, scare, or discipline employees.

9. True

   Dr. Peter Safar researched mouth-to-mouth breathing in the 1950s. At this time, he did not research chest decompression, epinephrine administration, or spinal immobilization.

chapter 2

The Well-Being of the Paramedic

Are You Ready?

It's 8 a.m., and the firehouse is humming with activity. You have just finished stocking the medic unit when your stomach gives one of those growls that says, "Hey! Feed me!" You make your way to the kitchen, where you spy a big plate of donuts that were brought in by one of the firefighters. Simultaneously, another firefighter places a bowl of fresh fruit on the table next to the donuts.

1. Which food would you pick? Why? Provide an answer that relates to the food pyramid.

   _____

   _____

   _____

Active Learning

1. What Is Your Body Mass Index?

One method used to determine if an individual is overweight or obese is by calculating that individual's body mass index (BMI). The BMI is calculated mathematically by comparing the individual's height in inches to the individual's weight in pounds. The actual mathematical equation uses kilograms and meters to perform the calculation, but tables have been converted for use in the United States as well. Table 2-1 is the BMI chart used by the National Institutes of Health (NIH). An expert panel convened by the National Heart, Lung, and Blood Institute (NHLBI) in cooperation with the National Institute of Diabetes and Digestive and Kidney Diseases (NIDDK), both part of the NIH, identified *overweight* as a BMI of 25–29.9 and *obesity* as a BMI of 30 or greater. Remember, overweight and obesity are not mutually exclusive, since people who are obese are also overweight. Defining overweight as a BMI of 25 or greater is consistent with the recommendations of the World Health Organization and most other countries.

Calculating BMI is simple, quick, and inexpensive, but it does have limitations. One problem with using BMI as a measurement tool is that very muscular people may fall into the "overweight" category, even though they are actually healthy and fit. Another problem with using BMI is that people who have lost muscle mass, such as the elderly, may be in the "healthy weight" category according to their BMI, although they actually have reduced nutritional reserves. BMI, therefore, is useful as a general guideline to monitor trends, but by itself is not diagnostic of an individual's health status.[1]

TABLE 2-1 Body Mass Index (BMI) Table

To use the table, find the appropriate height in the left-hand column labeled "Height." Move across to a given weight. The number at the top of the column is the BMI at that height and weight. Pounds have been rounded off.

	BMI	Normal						Overweight					Obese										Extreme Obesity
		19	20	21	22	23	24	25	26	27	28	29	30	31	32	33	34	35	36	37	38	39	40
Height (Inches)	58	91	96	100	105	110	115	119	124	129	134	138	143	148	153	158	162	167	172	177	181	186	191
	59	94	99	104	109	114	119	124	128	133	138	143	148	153	158	163	168	173	178	183	188	193	198
	60	97	102	107	112	118	123	128	133	138	143	148	153	158	163	168	174	179	184	189	194	199	204
	61	100	106	111	116	122	127	132	137	143	148	153	158	164	169	174	180	185	190	195	201	206	211
	62	104	109	115	120	126	131	136	142	147	153	158	164	169	175	180	186	191	196	202	207	213	218
	63	107	113	118	124	130	135	141	146	152	158	163	169	175	180	186	191	197	203	208	214	220	225
	64	110	116	122	128	134	140	145	151	157	163	169	174	180	186	192	197	204	209	215	221	227	232
	65	114	120	126	132	138	144	150	156	162	168	174	180	186	192	198	204	210	216	222	228	234	240
	66	118	124	130	136	142	148	155	161	167	173	179	186	192	198	204	210	216	223	229	235	241	247
	67	121	127	134	140	146	153	159	166	172	178	185	191	198	204	211	217	223	230	236	242	249	255
	68	125	131	138	144	151	158	164	171	177	184	190	197	204	210	216	223	230	236	243	249	256	262
	69	128	135	142	149	155	162	169	176	182	189	196	203	210	216	223	230	236	243	250	257	263	270
	70	132	139	146	153	160	167	174	181	188	195	202	209	216	222	229	236	243	250	257	264	271	278
	71	136	143	150	157	165	172	179	186	193	200	208	215	222	229	236	243	250	257	265	272	279	286
	72	140	147	154	162	169	177	184	191	199	206	213	221	228	235	242	250	258	265	272	279	287	294
	73	144	151	159	166	174	182	189	197	204	212	219	227	235	242	250	257	265	272	280	288	295	302
	74	148	155	163	171	179	186	194	202	210	218	225	233	241	249	256	264	272	280	287	295	303	311
	75	152	160	168	176	184	192	200	208	216	224	232	240	248	256	264	272	279	287	295	303	311	319
	76	156	164	172	180	189	197	205	213	221	230	238	246	254	263	271	279	287	295	304	312	320	328

Weight (Pounds)

The National Heart, Lung, and Blood Institute, which is a part of the Department of Health and Human Services and the NIH, maintains an online resource for calculating BMI. Go to www.nhlbisupport.com/bmi/bmicalc.htm to see this and find other information from the Obesity Education Initiative section of their website at www.nhlbi.nih.gov/about/oei/index.htm.

2. Feel the Beat

You should try to achieve your *target heart rate* during exercise. The target heart rate is 60%–80% of the maximum rate the heart can tolerate during physical activity. These rates vary according to age and baseline activity level; there are several target rate calculators online, including one that can be found at the Mayo Clinic website www.mayoclinic.com/health/target-heart-rate/SM00083.

3. Eat Right

Managing your dietary intake does not have to be difficult or distasteful. As long as you keep in mind how to distribute your fat and caloric intake, eating healthy can be fun—and tasty! Learn more about the food pyramid at the government website www.mypyramid.gov (Figure 2-1). Enter the information requested under "My Pyramid Plan," and look at a recommended food pyramid customized for your age and exercise regimen. You can even track your own pyramid at www.mypyramidtracker.gov/.

4. Get Fit

The same site (www.mypyramidtracker.gov/) also has a physical activity tracker. Register first, and then use it to keep track of your progress.

Anatomy of MyPyramid

One size doesn't fit all
USDA's new MyPyramid symbolizes a personalized approach to healthy eating and physical activity. The symbol has been designed to be simple. It has been developed to remind consumers to make healthy food choices and to be active every day. The different parts of the symbol are described below.

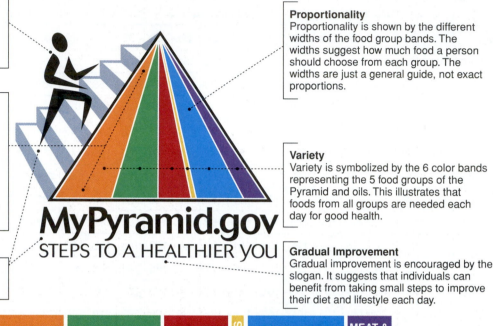

Activity
Activity is represented by the steps and the person climbing them, as a reminder of the importance of daily physical activity.

Moderation
Moderation is represented by the narrowing of each food group from bottom to top. The wider base stands for foods with little or no solid fats or added sugars. These should be selected more often. The narrower top area stands for foods containing more added sugars and solid fats. The more active you are, the more of these foods can fit into your diet.

Personalization
Personalization is shown by the person on the steps and the slogan.

Proportionality
Proportionality is shown by the different widths of the food group bands. The widths suggest how much food a person should choose from each group. The widths are just a general guide, not exact proportions.

Variety
Variety is symbolized by the 6 color bands representing the 5 food groups of the Pyramid and oils. This illustrates that foods from all groups are needed each day for good health.

Gradual Improvement
Gradual improvement is encouraged by the slogan. It suggests that individuals can benefit from taking small steps to improve their diet and lifestyle each day.

USDA U.S. Department of Agriculture
Center for Nutrition Policy and Promotion
April 2005 CNPP-16
USDA is an equal opportunity provider and employer.

| GRAINS | VEGETABLES | FRUITS | OILS | MILK | MEAT & BEANS |

FIGURE 2-1   The Food Guide Pyramid can help you make nutritious eating choices.

5. Physical Activity Levels

What exactly is moderate physical activity, and what constitutes vigorous physical activity? At this point, you've probably got the message: Exercise will go a long way in promoting long-term health and wellness. You may wonder, then, just what *exactly* constitutes "moderate" and "vigorous" physical activity? Well, the Centers for Disease Control and Prevention provides examples of exercise and other activities that will help you keep fit. Table 2-2 is a partial list of such activities. Do any of these examples interest you?

You can download the entire list at the following Web link: www.cdc.gov/nccdphp/dnpa/physical/pdf/PA_Intensity_table_2_1.pdf.

You Are There: Reality-Based Cases

Case 1

It has been a busy day—drills and a few EMS calls made the morning fly by. Lunch was served about an hour ago, and now your partner shows you that he has a copy of the latest hit movie on DVD. Meanwhile, it's time for your daily workout routine.

1. What will you do?

_____

_____

_____

_____

The shift continues, and it's 11 p.m. The dishes are put away, and the station is quiet. You're feeling a little tired, but you have a lot on your mind, and you're in the middle of a good book that is "calling" you.

2. Should you stay up?

_____

_____

_____

_____

TABLE 2-2   **Examples of Moderate and Vigorous Activities**

Moderate Activity 3.0–6.0 METs* (3.5–7 kcal/min)	Vigorous Activity Greater Than 6.0 METs (more than 7 kcal/min)
Walking at a moderate or brisk pace of 3–4.5 mph on a level surface inside or outside, such as • Walking to class, work, or the store • Walking for pleasure • Walking the dog • Walking as a break from work Walking downstairs or down a hill Hiking Roller skating or in-line skating at a leisurely pace	Race walking and aerobic walking—5 mph or faster Jogging or running Walking and climbing briskly up a hill Backpacking Mountain climbing, rock climbing Roller skating or in-line skating at a brisk pace
Bicycling 5–9 mph, level terrain, or with few hills Stationary bicycling—using moderate effort	Bicycling more than 10 mph or bicycling on steep uphill terrain Stationary bicycling—using vigorous effort
Aerobic dancing—high impact Water aerobics	Aerobic dancing—high impact Step aerobics Water jogging Teaching an aerobic dance class
Calisthenics—light Yoga Gymnastics General home exercises, light or moderate effort, getting up and down from the floor Jumping on a trampoline Using a stair climber machine at a light-to-moderate pace	Calisthenics—push-ups, pull-ups, vigorous effort Karate, judo, tae kwon do, jujitsu Jumping rope Performing jumping jacks Using a stair climber machine at a fast pace
Weight training and bodybuilding using free weights, Nautilus- or Universal-type weights	Circuit weight training
Boxing—punching bag	Boxing—in the ring, sparring Wrestling—competitive
Ballroom dancing Line dancing Square dancing Folk dancing Modern dancing, disco	Professional ballroom dancing—energetically Square dancing—energetically Folk dancing—energetically Clogging
Table tennis—competitive Tennis—doubles	Tennis—singles Wheelchair tennis
Golf, wheeling or carrying clubs	
Softball—fast pitch or slow pitch Basketball—shooting baskets Coaching children's or adults' sports	Most competitive sports Football Basketball Soccer Rugby Kickball Lacrosse

*METs = metabolic equivalents.

Test Yourself

1. You have achieved a high level of wellness if you
   a. have taken all necessary precautions to avoid becoming sick or injured, thus maintaining excellent physical health.
   b. have learned to balance all aspects of life, including the intellectual, emotional, and social areas.
   c. have learned to remain calm, focused, and capable of critical decision-making even under stressful situations.
   d. are capable of working long hours under physically demanding conditions any time of the day or night.

2. Any substance that is capable of causing a disease is called a(n)
   a. pathogen.
   b. virus.
   c. bacteria.
   d. infection.

3. Which of the following statements about tobacco use is correct?
   a. Chewing tobacco is a good alternative to smoking, since there is no inhalation of smoke involved.
   b. Secondhand smoke is almost as dangerous as inhaled smoke.
   c. Five years after quitting smoking, a person's risk of heart disease and stroke is similar to that for someone who has never smoked.
   d. Smokers have a higher risk for stomach, esophageal, pancreatic, bladder, and cervical cancer.

4. A 35-year-old patient has some concerns about the impact of nicotine on his health. His parents still smoke, and when he visits them it's hard to resist the temptation, and he's worried about the secondhand smoke. Name three things he can suggest to his parents to help them quit smoking.

   _____

   _____

   _____

5. Name the five risk factors that account for approximately 75% of all cancers.

   _____

   _____

6. The spiritual dimension of wellness involves having satisfying relationships and interacting well with others, and includes an appreciation for diversity.
   True
   False

Scenario: You are concerned about a fellow paramedic with whom you work on the night shift. She has been increasingly irritable and has put on some weight. Even more alarming, she has been clumsy lately and has had a number of minor accidents at work.

7. You should first suspect
   a. alcoholism.
   b. stress from fatigue.
   c. bipolar depression.
   d. drug use.

8. You should advise your coworker to
   a. act professionally or you'll report her.
   b. go for psychiatric therapy.
   c. change to a shorter day shift.
   d. drink more coffee or caffeinated soda.

9. A career in EMS is more stressful than many other careers, and paramedics are affected by a high level of stress.
   True
   False

10. It may be possible to lower your risk of heart disease and some forms of cancer by eating a diet that is high in
    a. lean protein like poultry and fish.
    b. low-fat milk, yogurt, and cheese.
    c. high-fiber grain products, fruits, and vegetables.
    d. organic produce and free-range meats.

11. The development of skill-related fitness is of prime importance for paramedics.
    True
    False

12. Which of the following is the most constructive way to fulfill your responsibility to encourage public wellness?
    a. Provide a positive example by improving and maintaining your own wellness.
    b. Lecture all your emergency patients on the importance of not smoking.
    c. Call attention to the weight of any obese patients and talk to them about dieting.
    d. Volunteer to give public health lectures whenever you are not working.

13. Name four of the six job conditions identified by the National Institute for Occupational Safety and Health (NIOSH) as the leading causes of stress in the workplace.

_____

_____

14. Briefly describe how you would handle a terminal patient who is nonviolent but verbally lashes out at you with anger and hostility.

_____

_____

Need to Know

The following represent the Key Objectives of Chapter 2:

1. *Identify the individual responsibilities of a paramedic in promoting, modeling, and maintaining wellness.*

   As a paramedic, you are responsible for being both physically and psychologically healthy, not only to yourself, but to your patients and coworkers. The EMS profession is demanding. You must be able to make choices in both your professional and personal lives that will promote a long-term state of health that will permit you to function at your best.

2. *Explain how behavior choices prevent wellness and how to avoid negative behaviors.*

   The EMS profession does not always lend itself well to promoting good behaviors that promote wellness. Long hours, little sleep, poor eating habits, little chance for exercise, and a stress-filled environment all contribute to less than optimal health. Understanding that these challenges exist can help you choose behaviors that promote a healthier lifestyle, such as eating sensibly, exercising, not smoking, and reducing intake of alcohol and caffeine.

3. *Describe behaviors that promote wellness, and explain how you can build them into your lifestyle.*

   Being keenly aware of your cardiovascular health will help shape your decisions about what you eat and drink, and whether you smoke and exercise. Reduce your chance of cancer through smoking cessation, exercise, and a healthy diet. Try to achieve a high level of wellness—integrate the physical, intellectual, and emotional aspects of a healthy lifestyle.

4. *Describe appropriate management strategies for dealing with the stress inherent in the EMS profession.*

   Working in the EMS profession can be stressful. It is what you do with excess stress that is important to understand. First, recognize the general signs of stress, such as headache, sleep disturbances, difficulty concentrating, short temper, and upset stomach. Second, learn to "calm" both the external and internal environments. Eat right, exercise, and sleep enough so that you can physically manage stress well. Limit stimulants like caffeine. Learn relaxation and time management techniques. Build time into your schedule to relax and exercise. Third, be positive. Being proactive about recognizing and managing excess stress allows you to have more control over the situation than just allowing it to happen. Finally, seek help if you need to. Talking to a trusted individual about an event or stressor can help you sort out your emotions, and the individual can be a sounding board for your thoughts.

Need to Do

There are no psychomotor skills that directly support this chapter content.

Connections

- The Centers for Disease Control and Prevention (CDC), located in Atlanta, Georgia, is an excellent resource. Many health-care personnel think of the CDC as the agency that assists in the management of contagious diseases such as measles or smallpox. However, the CDC is much more than that—it is the principal agency in the United States government for protecting the health and safety of all Americans and for providing essential human services. The CDC is involved in a wide range of population-based health issues, including overall health issues such as smoking and obesity. The main Web page is www.cdc.gov.
- The American Dietetic Association is the nation's largest organization of food and nutrition professionals. There is also a wealth of information on its website, www.eatright.org.
- The American Heart Association has resources to help support healthy living. Its Healthy Lifestyle Web page is www.americanheart.org/presenter.jhtml?identifier=1200009.

- The President's Council on Physical Fitness and Sports has a resource page, www.fitness.gov. The site contains links to publications and health fitness organizations. For tips on strengthening your back for lifting, try the American Academy of Orthopaedic Surgeons website for some valuable information: http://orthoinfo.aaos.org/fact/thr_report.cfm?Thread_ID=17. For knee strengthening, try www.chiroweb.com/archives/23/13/14.html. Of course, there are many resources on the Web—do a search!

- Link to the companion DVD for a chapter-based quiz, audio glossary, animations, games and exercises, and, when appropriate, skill sheets and skill Step-by-Steps.

Street Secrets

- **Exercise for Your Career** The adage of "An ounce of prevention is worth a pound of cure" most certainly applies to the job of the paramedic. Too often EMS providers are forced from their jobs because of injuries, especially to the back and knees. To help minimize your chances of getting hurt, try both a combination of isometric and isotonic exercises:

  a. *Isometric* exercises are ones that tighten your muscles but don't move them through a wide range of motion. Examples include abdominal muscle contractions ("crunches") during modified sit-ups, which help strengthen both the abdominal and back muscles; and arm and leg reaches that can strengthen back, buttock, and leg muscles.

  b. *Isotonic* exercises move the muscle group through a full range of motion, with strengthening occurring at the beginning and end of each motion. Lifting with simple weights is an isotonic exercise.

  c. *Aerobic* exercises help to increase endurance of not only your muscles, but also your cardiovascular system. Walking, jogging, running, and swimming are classic examples of aerobic exercise, but simply walking up one or two flights of stairs rather than taking the elevator will help build your aerobic fitness. Exercise in moderation and regularly—several times a week. Alternating between different types of exercises will keep it interesting and fun.

- **Exercise on the Run** Having a busy shift or not working at a fixed station does not necessarily mean that you can't exercise. Having a small set of weights or specially made rubber resistance bands in the ambulance will make it convenient to do a small workout. If the ambulance is parked at a standby location, getting out to stretch your muscles and walking briskly for a few minutes will contribute to a healthier heart.

The Drug Box

There are no specific drugs related to this chapter content.

Reference

1. "BMI-Body Mass Index." www.cdc.gov/nccdphp/dnpa/adult_bmi/about_adult_BMI.htm (August 26, 2006). accessed.

Answers

Are You Ready?

1. Although the donuts would certainly be tempting, the fruit is your better bet. The donuts have a high calorie and fat count, both of which can unbalance the food pyramid very quickly. Additionally the natural sweetness in fruit comes in the form of sugars that are much easier to digest.

You Are There: Reality-Based Cases

1. You know you *should* do your workout routine, but you may *want* to watch the movie with your crew. This dilemma is easily solved, though. Either ask your partner to delay the start of the movie until you're done exercising, or exercise after the movie. Avoid *not* exercising though!

2. If you have the opportunity to get some rest during your shift, you should do so. Fatigue can be a factor in making a mistake in clinical judgment, as well as compromising your overall physical health. Rest when you can!

Test Yourself

1. b

   Being healthy is much more than just not being sick or injured. A high level of wellness involves maintaining quality in your life. To achieve this requires balance in all aspects of life including the physical, intellectual, emotional, environmental, social, spiritual, and occupational areas.

2. a

   A pathogen is any substance (protein, bacteria, virus, etc.) that is capable of causing a disease.

3. d

   Smoking has been identified as a risk factor not only for lung cancer, but for stomach, esophageal, pancreatic, bladder, and cervical cancer as well. Smokeless tobacco users are also at risk for cancer. Secondhand smoke has twice the tar and nicotine, almost three times the carbon monoxide, and three times the ammonia of the inhaled smoke. A smoker's risk of heart disease and stroke is not similar to that of a person who has never smoked until 15 years after the smoker has quit.

4. Any three of the following: set a quit date; get rid of all cigarettes and ashtrays; do not let people smoke in their home, car, or place of work; avoid social situations where they might be tempted to smoke; try to distract them from urges to smoke; use substitute behaviors like exercising, reading, or socializing; calculate the dollar amount that would be spent on smoking in one year and instead use the money saved to plan a celebration or vacation on the 1-year anniversary of quitting; use the nicotine patch, nicotine gum, nicotine inhaler, or nicotine nasal spray.

5. Tobacco use, non-nutritious diet, infectious diseases, chemical exposure, and radiation exposure.

   Risk factors for cancer include tobacco use (smoking and chewing), non-nutritious diet, infectious diseases, chemical exposure, and radiation exposure. These five risk factors account for approximately 75% of all cancers. Approximately one-third of all cancer deaths are related to lack of physical activity and unhealthy diet.

6. False

   Having satisfying relationships and interacting well with others is what the social dimension of wellness involves. It includes an appreciation for diversity.

7. b

   Stress and fatigue have been associated with poorer perceived general health, increased injury rates, more illness or increased mortality, and unhealthy weight gain.

8. c

   Shift work has been shown to be associated with hypertension, cardiovascular disease, obesity, increased triglycerides, impaired glucose tolerance, increased sleep disorders, an increased risk of accidents, greater use of health-care services, interference of social life and social problems, and increased psychological problems.

9. True

   Even though a career in EMS is more stressful than many other careers, many paramedics do not believe they are affected by a high level of stress. This is called unrealistic optimism. Unrealistic optimism can lead to an inability to assess problems (because of a lack of awareness of them) and an inability to cope effectively with them.

10. c

    Fruits and vegetables provide essential vitamins and minerals and fiber associated with good health. Low-fat diets rich in fiber-containing grain products, fruits, and vegetables may reduce the risk of heart disease and some types of cancer. Milk products provide protein, vitamins, and minerals and are the best source of calcium.

11. False

    Of prime importance for the paramedic is the development of health-related fitness. Skill-related fitness includes many components involved with athletic performance.

12. a

    As a paramedic, you also have the responsibility of encouraging wellness in the public through education and by example. As individuals approach you for information about healthy living, you will be provided the opportunity to encourage wellness through education. It is important to maintain a list of wellness and community resources that, when the opportunity arises during patient interaction, you can pass on to the willing listener.

13. Any four of the following: design of the tasks, management style, interpersonal relationships, work roles, career concerns, environmental conditions.

14. When dealing with the patient, remain calm. Be honest about the seriousness of the patient's condition. Speak with hope, avoiding negative statements which may exacerbate the patient's emotional state.

    Do not make false reassurances or claims that "everything is going to be alright." Instead, reassure the patient that you are providing the best care you can and allow the patient to talk and vent his or her feelings. One of the most important things you can say in these situations is "I'm sorry." If the situation allows, you may give the patient some time alone with loved ones so the patient can say goodbye in private. Stay close by to provide support to the family.

chapter 3

Professional Ethics

Are You Ready?

You are helping your partner evaluate a homeless person who is passed out in a bus stop shelter. The patient is a woman in her late 40s or early 50s who reeks of alcohol. Your partner is unzipping the many layers of coats and clothing in order to perform a physical examination of the patient. Out of the corner of your eye, you notice that a small amount of money falls out of one of the patient's shirt pockets. Before you can say anything, your partner picks up the loose bills and stuffs them in his pant's pockets. He does not say anything and continues to evaluate the patient.

1. What did your partner just do? What will you do? Would it make a difference if your partner were also a close friend?

_____

_____

_____

Active Learning

1. **Things Aren't Always What They Seem**

Making an ethical decision is not as simple as it might seem. Consider the following scenario: You know a woman who is pregnant and who has had eight children already. Three of these children are deaf, two are blind, and one is mentally handicapped. Additionally, you know that this woman has syphilis. Would you recommend that she have an abortion?

After you have answered the question honestly, consider the following situation: You are given the decision to choose the next president. Here are the facts about the three leading candidates:

Candidate A associates with crooked politicians and consults with astrologers. He's had two mistresses. He also chain smokes and drinks up to five martinis a day.

Candidate B was ejected from office twice, sleeps until noon, used opium in college, and drinks a large amount of whiskey every evening.

Candidate C is a decorated war hero. He's a vegetarian, doesn't smoke, drinks an occasional beer, and hasn't had any extramarital affairs.

Who would you choose?

Returning to the first scenario, how did you come to a decision? Did you use the rules of thumb explained in Box 3-4 in Chapter 3 of the textbook in order to answer the question? Did you apply Iserson's three-step process for solving ethical dilemmas in an emergency setting (Figure 3-1)?

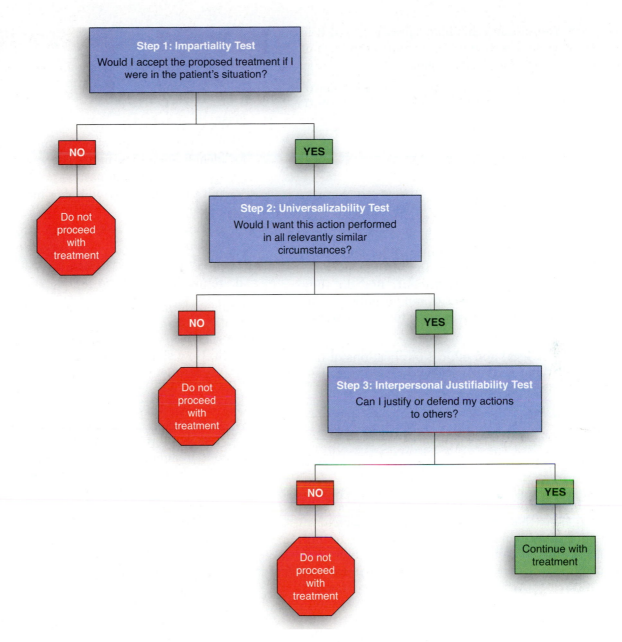

FIGURE 3-1 Three-step process for making an ethical decision developed by K. V. Iserson and associates.

You may be interested to know that, if you had recommended an abortion for the woman in the first scenario, Ludwig van Beethoven never would have been born.

Now, let's review the second situation about choosing the next president. Based on the information provided, it would appear that candidate C would be the most obvious choice. If you indeed chose this person, you would have decided that Adolf Hitler would be the next president. Franklin D. Roosevelt (candidate A) and Winston Churchill (candidate B) would seem less likely to be the best candidates, right? If you had known these names

beforehand, would your choice have been different? Why?

You Are There: Reality-Based Cases

Case 1

You arrive at the home of an elderly male patient who has been badly burned by a scalding hot bath. He has experienced first- and second-degree burns to the lower half of his body. He has a history of cancer. He is crying out in pain, and he begs you to give him some relief. You measure his blood pressure, and it is 86/64. Hypotension is a contraindication to the use of a narcotic such as morphine sulfate.

1. How could you approach the ethical dilemma of administering the morphine sulfate to this patient?

_____

_____

Case 2

An elderly female calls 9-1-1 at 4 a.m. She has had chest pain for 2 hours and admits to being "very scared." She is conscious, alert, and able to make an informed decision. After determining that the patient was "just panicky," the paramedics do not perform a complete or adequate assessment, nor do they explain to the patient the risks of not accepting treatment. They have her sign a refusal form and return to bed.

1. What are the legal and ethical implications of this incident? What should you have done if you had been on the call?

_____

_____

Case 3

You and your crew have been resuscitating a 25-year-old female who was found in her bedroom by her husband. It appears that she has overdosed on several of her medications. No suicide note has been found. After 35 minutes of resuscitation, which included advanced life support, she is apneic and pulseless, with asystole showing on the ECG. Your protocol allows you to terminate the resuscitation without transporting the patient. The husband is distraught and insists that you transport her to the hospital. The couple's two young children are crying while watching your interactions unfold from across the hallway. The husband pleads for you to not leave her here to "die in front of her children."

1. Will you follow protocol or the husband's wishes? Why?

_____

_____

2. What if the patient was a 75-year-old woman and no children were on the scene? Would it make a difference in your decision-making process?

_____

_____

Test Yourself

1. Ethically, an ambulance should be stationed where the majority of the population resides.
   True
   False

2. While searching the pocket of an unresponsive patient for identification, you find what you consider to be an unusually large sum of money. You should
   a. tell the police that you may have found "drug money."
   b. document and secure the money for the patient.
   c. apply the money toward the patient's bill.
   d. return the money to the pocket immediately.

3. While performing triage during a mass casualty incident, you find a small child who is breathing but has sustained catastrophic injuries certain to cause death. How should you deal with this patient?

_____

_____

4. While waiting to admit a patient who is experiencing a behavioral emergency, you are asked to respond to another call. An EMT-Basic who works at the hospital has offered to wait with the patient. What should you do?

_____

_____

5. The document that relates to the EMT's standards of professional behavior in practice is the EMS Code of Morals.
   True
   False

6. You are told in confidence by an elderly man that he is being abused by his family. It is not a breach of confidentiality to report the alleged abuse.
   True
   False

7. What is the term for the standards by which human beings should act as they live and function within a society?

_____

_____

8. A police officer has stopped you for speeding. You tell her that you are a paramedic and should only receive a warning. This behavior is illegal.
   True
   False

9. What is the best way for paramedics to develop their ethical problem-solving skills?

   _____

   _____

10. The set of principles and standards that paramedics use to determine what is right and wrong conduct within their profession is called _____.

Scenario: You respond to an apartment complex and find a very intoxicated 18-year-old patient who has attempted to harm himself by cutting his wrists.

11. Prior to treating this patient it is best to obtain
    a. family consent.
    b. informed consent.
    c. implied consent.
    d. a court order for treatment.

12. If the patient refuses your help you should
    a. treat the patient against his wishes in "good faith" because he is incompetent.
    b. allow the refusal since the patient is not a minor.
    c. wait until a court order is present to avoid the possibility of a lawsuit.
    d. have the patient sign a patient refusal form in order to document his wishes.

13. The patient tells you he'll give you $100 if you promise not to tell his parents about the intoxication or the suicide attempt. Ethically, you should
    a. accept his offer and promise to keep his information a secret.
    b. refuse the patient's offer and notify his parents because he is a minor.
    c. decline his offer and explain that his privacy will be respected.
    d. check with your shift supervisor prior to accepting the patient's offer.

Scenario: While at work, you overhear a fellow paramedic speaking with her husband on the phone about a recent motor vehicle crash involving a local city official. She is heard discussing a patient's name and his injuries with her husband who is a newspaper reporter covering the story.

14. The paramedic's actions are in violation of which of the following?
    a. The National EMS Accountability Act
    b. The Health Insurance Portability and Accountability Act
    c. The duty to act
    d. Local and state Good Samaritan laws

15. Considering all legal and ethical implications, this paramedic can divulge a patient's personal information if which of the following occurs?
    a. The information related to the patient came from a bystander, not directly from the patient.
    b. She was given verbal permission from law enforcement to discuss the patient's condition.
    c. She was not actually on the call in question and therefore is free to discuss the patient's condition.
    d. She is presented with a valid subpoena under a court order to provide information in a case.

Scenario: You are called to the home of an elderly patient who has been diagnosed with lung cancer. He is unresponsive and in a state of severe respiratory distress. You determine that the patient needs advanced airway management. However, his children cannot agree with each other. The man's daughter claims her father wanted to have "everything" done medically to save his life. The man's two sons claim their father didn't want a "breathing tube" or a respirator. Unfortunately, none of the children can produce any documentation stating the patient's wishes or desires.

16. In this situation, the best ethical choice for treatment would include which of the following?
    a. Proceeding with any medical treatment necessary under the doctrine of implied consent.
    b. Searching for an advance directive document that can clarify the patient's wishes.
    c. Any medical therapy would be considered futile and therefore should not be initiated.
    d. Medical treatment should not proceed until the patient's children can agree on what to do.

17. If a living will is found, the daughter's request to do "everything" for her father should be
    a. honored because the patient is unable to provide actual consent.
    b. considered, but it cannot supersede a legal document.
    c. formally made in writing with at least one witness.
    d. ignored because she is not in the majority opinion in the family.

Scenario: A patient has been given the incorrect dosage of a drug. It is unlikely that the patient will be harmed due to this medication error.

18. What is the best course of action for a paramedic to take in this scenario?

    a. Explain to the patient what has happened, document the medication error, and advise your supervisor and the nurse at the hospital.

    b. Medication errors are acceptable as long as the patient is not negatively affected.

    c. Medication errors are not uncommon and usually require no official documentation.

    d. If there is no adverse effect on the patient's well-being, there is no reason to report the error.

19. In this situation, an accidental incorrect drug dosage could be described as which of the following?

    a. An acceptable drug dosage error

    b. A felony assault with a deadly weapon

    c. A statistically acceptable deviation from protocol

    d. A deviation from a standard of care

Need to Know

The following represent the Key Objectives of Chapter 3:

1. *List the ethical characteristics appropriate for an EMS professional, and practice them in your personal and professional lives.*

    A study that surveyed a panel of EMS experts in the United Kingdom showed that the top 10 desirable attributes of EMS providers were[1]:

    • Honesty

    • Patient-centered

    • Caring, empathetic, and values life

    • Professionalism

    • Nonjudgmental, nondiscriminatory

    • Self-aware, recognizing personal responsibilities and limitations

    • Common sense

    • Skills and awareness of manual handling and health and safety

    • Awareness of and adherence to national and local guidelines and policies

    • Practical (pragmatic)

    Together, these behaviors can be taken to represent the ethical "code" of the profession. A paramedic whose personal moral standards closely mirror the professional ethics will find it easier to adhere to them.

2. *Explain the principles described in the EMT Code of Ethics.*

    The National Association of Emergency Medical Technicians Code of Ethics describes the conduct you should adhere to when practicing as a paramedic. The principles include

    • Save lives, alleviate suffering, and promote health.

    • Strive for quality EMS care for everyone.

    • Hold all private and personal information confidential unless required by law to divulge it.

    • Define and uphold standards of professional practice and education.

    • Uphold the laws that govern the practice of EMS care.

    • Advocate for legislation involving EMS care.

    • Ensure that EMS care is provided by competent professionals.

    • Work cooperatively with other members of the health-care continuum.

3. *Identify the laws, rules, regulations, policies, procedures, protocols, and standing orders of your organization so you can render care in an ethical manner.*

    A myriad of rules, policies, and guidelines define the scope of practice for the paramedic. Chapter 4, Legal Issues, in the textbook describes these issues in greater detail. For the moment, remember that as a professional, you are obligated to provide competent care to patients, regardless of who they are. Also, patients must consent to your care, or refuse it if they are competent to do so. Additionally, confidentiality of your care is not only ethical, but it is mandated by laws such as the Health Insurance Portability and Accountability Act (HIPAA).

4. *Rehearse ethical dilemma situations with coworkers so you can develop problem-solving abilities to use when such situations arise. Remember that there are a variety of patient care situations in which ethical dilemmas can arise.*

    • *Care in a futile situation.* In situations such as a cardiac arrest, there are many instances in which any further care would be considered futile. In these circumstances, systems have developed protocols and guidelines to assist the paramedic in making the decision to discontinue care.

    • *Obligation to provide care.* The care that you render should always be professional and appropriate, regardless of the patient's race, gender, socioeconomic status, and ability to pay. If the patient is combative or violent, you must continue to provide care after safety issues have been addressed.

- *Patient advocacy.* Ensure that your patient's health-care rights are protected. This includes the right to proper health care, the right to be transported to a preferred destination, and the right to refuse care if competent to do so.
- *Paramedic accountability.* You are accountable to your patient, the public, medical oversight, and the EMS system.
- *Role as physician extender.* You are accountable in your role as an extension of the physician in the out-of-hospital arena. This includes following both online and off-line (standing orders) medical protocols.

5. *Use problem-solving tools, such as Iserson's process, to help you work through ethical dilemmas. These tools will help you to develop a systematic and consistent approach to problem solving.*

Refer back to Box 3-4 in the textbook for rules of thumb to apply when answering an ethical question. Remember that your response should be free of emotion, made with reason and logic, and based in fact as much as possible, not only on what other people think or feel. Also review Iserson's three-step process to solving ethical dilemmas, which is summarized in Box 3-5 in the textbook and illustrated in Figure 3-1. When confronted with an ethical question, ask yourself the following three questions:

- Would I accept the proposed treatment if I were in the patient's situation? (Impartiality)
- Would I want this action performed in all relevantly similar circumstances? (Universality)
- Can I justify or defend my actions to others? (Interpersonal justifiability)

Answering no to any of these questions should stop you from performing that step.

Need To Do

There are no psychomotor skills that directly support this chapter content.

Connections

- The W. Maurice Young Centre for Applied Ethics, located at the University of British Columbia (Canada), maintains a website with resources regarding ethics and ethical behavior. A page that provides additional guidance in making ethical decisions is www.ethics.ubc.ca/people/mcdonald/decisions.htm.
- Link to the companion DVD for a chapter-based quiz, audio glossary, animations, games and exercises, and, when appropriate, skill sheets and skill Step-by-Steps.
- Ready to try your hand at solving a few ethical dilemmas? Look at Problem-Based Learning Case 1: The Partner Quandary.

Street Secrets

- **Personal Ethics** Look at every decision you make as an EMS professional with a personal ethical eye. When confronted with an ethical dilemma, ask yourself, "Can I justify my action to my parents? My spouse? My children?" If you cannot honestly answer the question in the affirmative, rethink your decision-making process before you act.

The Drug Box

There are no specific drugs related to this chapter content.

Reference

1. T. Kilner, "Desirable Attributes of the Ambulance Technician, Paramedic, and Clinical Supervisor: Findings from a Delphi Study." *Emergency Medicine Journal* 21, no. 3 (May 2004): 374–78.

Answers

Are You Ready?

1. The scenario, as written, does not have a solid "right" or "wrong" answer. It is designed to make you think carefully about the situation and your initial reactions. Based on your fleeting observation, what do you think happened? Was your partner stealing the patient's money? Was he trying to keep it safe in order to turn it in to the hospital staff? It is difficult right at this moment to fully understand what has happened, and your actions will depend on what happens next. If your partner did intend to keep the money, would you report his actions? What if your partner was in fact a close friend of yours? Should that make a difference? Would it?

You Are There: Reality-Based Cases

As with the scenario you encountered in the Are You Ready? section there are no clear-cut answers to each of these case studies. Use the questions in this section to formulate further responses to decide what *you* would do in these situations.

Case 1

1. Address this problem by using Iserson's approach to solving ethical dilemmas in the emergency setting:
   - *Step 1.* Would I accept the proposed treatment if I were the patient?
   - *Step 2.* Would I administer the medication to another patient under similar circumstances?
   - *Step 3.* Can I justify this action to my medical director?

Case 2

1. Did the paramedic team act in the best interests of the patient? Would you be able to apply Iserson's method of making an ethical decision in this situation? What is the possibility that a cardiovascular event may be happening? Answering these questions should allow you to make a better ethical decision than this paramedic crew. Do you think that this signed refusal form would stand up in a court of law?

Case 3

1. This is an extremely difficult situation. On one hand, you could simply follow your protocol and stop resuscitation, and then focus on taking care of the husband and children. Would the scene dynamics be conducive to this approach? You could decide to move the patient out to the ambulance, where you could either transport or terminate resuscitation efforts there. Would the family then incur additional grief in the hopes of a miracle that you know will not occur? If the resuscitation continues into the emergency department, will you now have saddled the family with additional medical bills?

2. Did you find yourself making a different decision with the change in age? What does that say about your perspective on age? Are you comfortable with your decision?

Test Yourself

1. True

   EMS planners base resource allocation upon need. It would not be ethical to place an ambulance in a jurisdiction where very few live at the expense of an area where the majority of the population resides.

2. b

   Paramedics must live as upstanding citizens with good and decent character, often putting their own interests behind those of their customers as they assume the role of patient advocates.

3. You should consider the child unsalvageable and move on to other salvageable patients.

   During a mass casualty incident, triage is used to save the greatest number of lives possible. Typically the critical (but salvageable) patients are transported first, followed by potentially unstable patients, and finally stable patients. Patients with catastrophic injuries may not be treated if their injuries are so resource intensive that treating them will result in delayed care of many other individuals. These patients are considered unsalvageable and are often moved to a secure, private, and if possible quiet, location where they die out of the view of media, salvageable patients, bystanders, and rescuers.

4. You should decline the EMT-Basic's offer and remain with your current patient.

   Legally, leaving a patient with an individual of lesser training after initiating care constitutes abandonment.

5. False

   The document that relates to the EMT's standards of professional behavior in practice is the EMS Code of Ethics. In order to establish a standard of professional behavior in practice, every profession needs an ethical code by which it can be measured. Dr. Charles Gillespe wrote the EMS Code of Ethics.

6. True

   As strict as the policies and laws are surrounding confidentiality, there may be occasional situations which arise that will require divulging information to fulfill other laws. An example is for a risk to public health, such as with the mandatory reporting of suspected child and elder abuse or neglect and domestic violence. In this situation, the patient may be at risk for further harm if the suspected abuse is not reported.

7. Morals

   Just as the definition of ethics relates to both personal and professional standards, morals relate to societal standards; specifically how humans should act, either good or bad, as they live and function within a society.

8. False

   There is no law against using your profession to talk your way out of a ticket. However, this type of behavior could be considered unethical. How a paramedic reacts in difficult situations, even in his or her personal life, is always a reflection on the profession.

9. Paramedics should rehearse ethical dilemma situations with coworkers so they can begin to develop problem-solving abilities for times when they occur.

   Many ethical situations are similar, and a paramedic can benefit from practice scenarios related to such issues as termination of resuscitation and determining patient competence.

10. Ethics

    The word *ethics* comes to us from the Greek word for "character" and relates directly to personal standards based on what is right and wrong. For paramedics, ethics is the set of principles and standards that determine what is right and wrong conduct within our profession.

11. b

EMS providers must always value the patient's autonomy. Before performing any treatment, explain the procedure, risks, benefits, and alternatives so the patient can make an informed decision whether or not to allow the procedure. Even though this patient is intoxicated, he should be allowed to make his wishes known and to participate in his own health-care decisions.

12. a

Incompetent means that the patient is not capable of making decisions that would represent his or her best interest. Testing this ability is not simple and can involve lengthy legal proceedings. Generally patients under the influence of mind-altering substances like drugs or alcohol should not be considered competent to make appropriate medical decisions.

13. c

It is unethical to receive money from a patient who is not competent or under duress. The patient is not a minor by definition, and any treatment the patient receives while in your care is private and can't be shared with family members without his consent.

14. b

Confidentiality is a fundamental legal right of every patient. Paramedics who violate this right may be sued or face legal charges or disciplinary action. In 1996 the United States Congress passed the Health Insurance Portability and Accountability Act (HIPAA). HIPAA details strict guidelines for patient privacy for both personal and medical information. Violators may be fined up to $250,000 and/or be imprisoned for up to 10 years for the malicious distribution of protected patient information.

15. d

As strict as the policies and laws are surrounding confidentiality, there may be occasional situations which arise that will require divulging information to fulfill other laws. An example is when subpoenaed under court order to provide information in a case. It is crucial to be aware of rules, laws, regulations, policies, and procedures and consult with an attorney when appropriate.

Remember what is written in the EMS Code: "The Emergency Medical Technician respects and holds in confidence all information of a confidential nature obtained in the course of professional work unless required by law to divulge such information."

16. a

When the patient is incapable of providing actual consent, the patient may be treated under the doctrine of implied consent. Implied consent states that a reasonable person in a similar situation would likely want treatment and would provide consent. In this scenario, the family cannot agree on what the man's wishes are; therefore, you must assume the man would want everything done to save his life. Taking extra time to search for a document that may not exist or obtaining a court order in a reasonable amount of time could be detrimental to the patient's health.

17. b

With the existence of advance directives like Do Not Attempt Resuscitation orders and living wills, paramedics must be guided by what the legal documents direct. Most difficulties arise when a patient has expressed his or her wishes to someone but has not written them down into a legal document. You must have a clear understanding ahead of time of the laws in your area that govern these situations. Lastly, family input may be utilized as a guide although it cannot supersede legal documents.

18. a

All paramedics are accountable to their protocols and standing orders. It is their responsibility to know the details of these documents so they can follow them at a second's notice in any situation. If a medication error occurs, even one without adverse consequences, it must be documented and the patient should be made aware of the error.

19. d

If something is not consistent with the standard of care, you have an obligation to discuss that with the person giving the order so the person understands it is out of the normal routine.

chapter 4

Legal Issues

Are You Ready?

"Mr. Konovich, can you confirm that this is your patient care record?" The plaintiff's attorney presents a photocopy of a chart to the paramedic.

Ron looks at it for a moment. Even though the City's attorney has prepared him for this moment on the stand, he feels his heart pounding. Ron has been named as one of the paramedics who the patient's family alleges failed to successfully secure the patient's airway during a cardiac arrest, which caused the resuscitation effort to be unsuccessful. The family seeks financial restitution for the loss of the patient, a 52-year-old man in the prime of his working life.

Ron feels terrible. Even though he is convinced that he did nothing wrong, being charged with negligence is difficult to handle.

1. What will the plaintiff's attorney need to prove in order to win a judgment against the paramedic?

_____

_____

_____

Active Learning

1. The Paramedic Said What?

Match each of the statements (on page 27) with the legal concept most closely related to it.

You Are There: Reality-Based Cases

Case 1

Ron reviews the chart he is holding. "Yes Ma'am, this is my patient care record." The attorney asks Ron to read out loud several lines of his narrative. The attorney then points out the section of the chart that contains information about airway management.

"Mr. Konovich, would you please summarize what is on the chart regarding the patient's airway?"

"I documented that I was unsuccessful at intubating the patient's airway after two attempts."

The attorney faces the jury box. "You do not deny that you failed at intubating the airway?"

"I do not deny that fact. The patient had features in his airway that made it very difficult to intubate."

"Do you believe that your failure to intubate the patient contributed to his death? After all, isn't securing the airway one of the most important tasks a paramedic must perform during a critical case such as cardiac arrest?"

1. Which element of the negligence charge is the attorney trying to prove with this discussion? If you were Ron, how would you prepare yourself for this type of encounter?

_____

_____

_____

Legal Term	Statement Letter	Statement
Abandonment		a. "It's 2 a.m. and Mrs. Smith is calling *again*? We shouldn't have to respond to *these* calls!"
Advance directive		b. "I should just write down on the report that the patient was drunk."
Assault		c. "Sam, I know your parents are not here, but you will still have to come with us to see the doctor for your injured arm."
Battery		d. "I don't care whether the patient wants to or not, he is going to the hospital with me."
Breach of duty		e. "No one is going to notice a few milligrams of morphine missing, right?"
Concurrent medical direction		f. "Hey, we've got another call. Let's leave the patient in the waiting room. The triage nurse will see her."
Criminal law		g. "10-4, I copy the order for a dopamine drip running at 8 micrograms per kilogram per minute."
Due process		h. "Mr. Jones, what should we do for your father?"
Duty to act		i. "I knew that the protocol said to do one thing, but I did the other anyway because I don't agree with the protocol."
EMTALA		j. "Medical Control, we are transporting from 123 Main Street to your facility with a 32-year-old female in labor."
Expressed consent		k. "Yes Doctor, I was trained to perform needle cricothyroidotomy, and I am permitted by state regulations to perform this procedure."
False imprisonment		l. "Your union representative should be at your disciplinary meeting scheduled for next week."
HIPAA		m. "Who says that the patient experienced a vertebral compression fracture just because I dropped her?"
Implied consent		n. "Based upon the last chart audit, it looks like you are having some difficulty with your intubation technique. Let's schedule some time in the OR."
In loco parentis		o. "I'm going to smack you if you don't stop crying right now."
Libel		p. "I don't care who hears me. I said that the patient's family is a pain in the neck."
Patient self-determination		q. "The patient was such a jerk. I put him in restraints just to shut him up."
Power of attorney		r. "The hospital wants us to divert to another emergency room? Can't they see we are pulling up to their doorway?"
Proximate causation		s. "How can you be so sure that he does not want resuscitation to be performed?"
Retrospective medical direction		t. "Yes, it is routine to immobilize a patient who complains of neck pain after a fall."
Scope of practice		u. "Hello, I am a paramedic. Can I help you?"
Slander		v. "I know that it's the end of shift, but there is no reason to transport the patient to the closest facility. He needs to go to his hospital."
Standard of care		w. "There is no pulse. Begin CPR."

Test Yourself

1. When is palliative care appropriate?

_____

_____

2. A Do Not Resuscitate/Do Not Intubate (DNR/DNI) order is the same as a Do Not Treat order.

   True

   False

3. Your unconscious patient requires immediate transportation. A neighbor overhears that you intend to take her to General Hospital and calls out, "You can't take her to General. That's where her husband died, and she swore she would never set foot in there again." You are required to

   a. ask the neighbor where he believes your patient would prefer to be transported.

   b. transport the patient to the facility best able to care for her needs.

   c. explain the alternatives to the neighbor.

   d. contact the next of kin to obtain consent before transporting the patient.

4. Your paramedic partner is getting ready to start an IV on a patient when the patient states, "I do not want an IV." Your partner tells the patient that he is following system protocol and proceeds to administer the IV. Your partner has just committed a(n)

   a. criminal act.

   b. civil act.

   c. negligent act.

   d. administrative act.

5. You and your partner transported a public official to the emergency room. The oncoming paramedic crew asks if you transported an official during your shift because they heard a rumor of suspicious activity. You should

   a. discuss the details of the call since your EMS crews work together.

   b. discuss the call because the activities of public officials are public record.

   c. remind the crew that patient confidentiality must be honored.

   d. report the oncoming crew to the supervisor due to HIPAA violation.

6. In order to be considered *informed,* patients must understand

   a. the need for cooperation, treatment alternatives, and the right to deny care.

   b. the diagnosis, the nature of the treatment, and the probable outcome.

   c. the benefit of care, risks of refusal, and health problem.

   d. the level of care needed, anticipated financial expense, and probable outcome.

7. List the four components of negligence with a short explanation of each.

_____

_____

8. You arrive at the scene of a single-car accident. The driver is an older male who is unconscious. His wife is in the passenger seat. She is conscious with multiple injuries. You request permission from her to treat both her and her husband. She says you can treat her, but she hopes he "rots in hell" and says you had "better not treat him" as long as she is there. She then spits on her husband and seems about to hit him. You should

   a. ignore her demands and have your partner treat her while you treat her husband under implied consent.

   b. not treat the man; as his wife and next of kin, she has the right to refuse treatment for her husband.

   c. treat her injuries and transport her, and then begin working on his injuries under implied consent.

   d. move her out of sight of her husband and treat her while your partner treats him under implied consent.

9. Four types of consent are

   a. implied, expressed, in loco parentis, and emancipated.

   b. implied, expressed, mitigated, and parents patria.

   c. implied, expressed, parents patria, and in loco parentis.

   d. implied, expressed, parents patria, and emancipated.

10. Do Not Resuscitate orders and advance directives are generally regulated by

    a. a federal agency.

    b. local government.

    c. state government.

    d. an advisory committee.

11. The federal laws concerning patient privacy are established by the Medicare Patients' Rights Association.

    True

    False

12. According to his friends, your 23-year-old patient is intoxicated. He is unconscious and withdraws

from tactile stimulus. You may treat him under which type of consent?

a. Immuned

b. Expressed

c. Informed

d. Implied

13. How have advance directives made treatment by a paramedic or emergency department staff less subjective?

_____

_____

14. Mikeal is an illegal immigrant to the United States and is very unfamiliar with the customs and laws of this country. His world is black and white. He believes that "you live until you die." He is critically injured in a farming accident, with the probability of being permanently paralyzed. How might his beliefs complicate the ability to obtain consent?

_____

_____

15. A man collapses while mowing his lawn. Before you arrived, he was unconscious, but he is now alert and oriented and understands the seriousness of his condition. His wife insists that he must go to the hospital. He does not want to go, saying that he will be just fine after he cools off. Who has the authority to consent to treatment or refuse medical care?

a. The man himself, as long as he is competent

b. His daughter, under whose medical insurance he is covered

c. His neighbor, a friend and confidante for over 40 years

d. The man's wife, his next of kin

16. Rolling up one's sleeve to accept an IV implies consent.

True

False

17. Which of the following is an example of prospective medical control?

a. Physician protocols and standing orders for EMS providers

b. Medical director operational control of paramedic clinical practice

c. Quality improvement run report review audit by medical director

d. Paramedic consulting with a medical control physician on the radio

18. Who has ultimate authority over patient care?

a. Medical director

b. Chief paramedic

c. EMS supervisor

d. EMS patient

19. Prospective medical control is

a. the hierarchical system of professional relationships in civil services that defines the roles of all emergency responders during a multiple casualty incident.

b. a way for paramedics and medical directors to evaluate the effectiveness of care rendered and discover opportunities for improvement.

c. when a paramedic contacts a physician or other advanced health-care professional by electronic means to collaboratively decide the best course of treatment.

d. a set of standards that establish the parameters for EMS clinical practice and set forth the expectations that EMS providers must satisfy in the delivery of patient care.

20. What is the difference between concurrent medical direction and retrospective medical direction?

_____

_____

21. What is the difference between assault and battery?

_____

_____

Scenario: You respond to a multiple casualty incident. Two women are lying next to each other. You check the condition of the first woman and request permission to treat her. As you begin the assessment, the second woman is repeating your conversation with the first patient to a third person via cell phone. She explains that the three of them are "like sisters."

22. What competing interests have to be considered while treating the first patient?

_____

_____

23. What should you do?

a. Take the woman's cell phone and return it to her after you have finished treating her friend.

b. Ask a police officer to remove the second woman from the area.

c. Explain that she is violating her friend's right to privacy, and ask her to hang up.

d. Stop speaking so that the second woman cannot repeat the information.

Need to Know

The following represent the Key Objectives of Chapter 4:

1. *Explain why consent is legally required prior to providing EMS care, including why every reasonable attempt should be made to attain it before you treat patients.*

The patient's right to self-determination requires you to seek and obtain permission to provide care, even when it is clearly needed. *Expressed consent* is explicitly provided by the patient or a legally responsible caregiver (one who has power of attorney). It does not need to be verbal; there must be some sign that there is an agreement for you to provide the care. *Implied consent* provides legal standing for the paramedic to provide care to patients who cannot provide explicit consent but present in such a way that under similar circumstances any person would reasonably expect to receive care. For example, a person who is unconscious due to a sudden blow to the head would want to be treated for the injury, even when he or she cannot say so.

2. *Explain the recommendation to "Always err on the side of treatment." That is, the job of an EMS provider is to perform patient care services; when there is some doubt whether the patient needs services, continue to provide care as you look for other information or obtain guidance from medical direction.*

In a sense, practicing conservative medicine implies that you want the patient to "prove" to you that he or she should *not* be treated. In other words, there must be a valid, legal reason why you should not treat a patient under your care. This might be in the form of an advance directive, a written document that clearly outlines the wishes of the patient experiencing a terminal disease such as cancer.

3. *Explain why professional appearance and actions, coupled with a high regard for customer service, are some of a paramedic's best legal defenses.*

Adhering to professional behaviors as a way to minimize potential litigation has been studied and written about by a wide variety of health-care professions.[1-3] Communicate with your patients and be honest in your interactions. If you act in the best interests of your patients, you will adhere to the highest ethical and legal standards.

4. *Identify circumstances that require additional reporting to social service, public service, or law enforcement agencies.*

Specific criteria may vary, but in general most states require health-care providers such as paramedics to report situations of pediatric or dependent elder abuse or neglect. Other situations that require reporting can include evidence of criminal activity, perceived threats to homeland security, animal attacks, discriminatory or harassing behaviors, and suspicion of communicable diseases.

5. *List the elements of malpractice/negligence, and explain how to avoid them.*

In order to prove negligence by the paramedic, the plaintiff must be able to prove the four elements of duty to act, breach of duty, injury, and proximate cause. These four elements provide the guidelines to follow when providing care:

- *Duty to act.* If you are on duty, or responding in an official capacity to a medical emergency, you are obligated to follow through and provide care.
- *Breach of duty.* Maintain professional behavior. Thoroughly understand your local protocols and scope of practice. Adhere to standards of care that will guide you through reasonable decisions regarding care.
- *Injury.* Document all observations about the patient's condition, even if the outcome is not what you expect or desire.
- *Proximate cause.* It can be very difficult to prove what your care may have contributed to the patient's outcome, good *or* bad. Again, the best defense you have is to document your interventions and your patient's responses to treatment accurately, completely, and in an objective manner.

Need To Do

The following skills are explained and illustrated in a step-by-step manner, via skill sheets and/or Step-by-Steps in this text and on the accompanying DVD:

Skill Name	Skill Sheet Number and Location	Step-by-Step Number and Location
Documentation	64 – DVD	N/A
Physical Restraints	65 – DVD	65 – DVD

Connections

- Legal rulings often begin as ethical issues. Review Chapter 3, Professional Ethics, in the textbook from time to time as you learn more about the clinical aspects of being a paramedic. You must pay attention to the legal and ethical aspects of every patient encounter, every time.
- Chapter 17, Documentation and Communication, in the textbook covers what you must and should document each time you contact a patient. Although it might not be exciting, documentation is a critical skill to master early.
- Link to the companion DVD for a chapter-based quiz, audio glossary, animations, games and exercises, and, when appropriate, skill sheets and skill Step-by-Steps.

Street Secrets

- **Documentation**   As you encounter more and more patients during your career, it will become difficult to remember the details of most of your cases. Develop a consistent method of charting to document ordinary or routine findings or treatments. If an unusual event occurs during a call, document it with some detail. Months or even years later, if you have to review the chart for possible litigation action, the detailed documentation of the unusual occurrence can trigger a memory of the event. Even if you cannot recall exactly what happened, your meticulous documentation will provide an accurate record of what occurred.
- **Be Nice!**   It pays to remember the Golden Rule during your patient encounters, no matter how the patient behaves. Malpractice suits often occur as a result of anger, not for injuries incurred.[4] Being

polite, empathetic, and professional with your patient will go a long way toward avoiding lawsuits.

The Drug Box

There are no specific drugs related to this chapter content.

References

1. A. Sukolsky, "Patients Who Try Our Patience." *American Journal of Kidney Diseases* 44, no. 5 (November 2004): 893–90.
2. M. Gentile, "Medicolegal Aspects of Respiratory Care and Leadership Responsibilities." *Respiratory Care Clinics of North America* 10 (2004): 281–93.
3. K. Worthington, "Customer Satisfaction in the Emergency Department." *Emergency Medicine Clinics of North America* 22 (2004): 87–102.
4. I. Press, *Patient Satisfaction: Defining, Measuring, and Improving the Experience of Care.* ACHE Management Series. Chicago, IL: Health Administration Press, 2002.

Answers

Are You Ready?

1. In order to prove the charge of negligence, the attorney must demonstrate four distinct elements:
   - *Duty to act.* The paramedic had a legal obligation to provide care.
   - *Breach of duty.* The paramedic did not perform his duty through either an omission or commission of an act inconsistent with a standard of care.
   - *Injury.* There was an injury or other form of harm that occurred to the plaintiff.
   - *Proximate cause.* The injury or harm to the plaintiff resulted from the breach of duty committed by the paramedic.

Active Learning

1. Abandonment (f); advance directive (s); assault (o); battery (q); breach of duty (i); concurrent medical direction (g); criminal law (e); due process (l); duty to act (a); EMTALA (r); expressed consent (u); false imprisonment (d); HIPAA (j); implied consent (w); in loco parentis (c); libel (b); patient self-determination (v); power of attorney (h); proximate causation (m); retrospective medical direction (n); scope of practice (k); slander (p); standard of care (t).

You Are There: Reality-Based Cases

Case 1

1. The attorney is trying to prove the proximate causation element of the negligence charge; the paramedic contributed to the death of the patient *because* he was unable to intubate the patient. In consultation with his attorney, Ron should be prepared to respond to the allegation by

   - Ensuring that his knowledge and skill of intubation meets at least the minimum standard of care as specified by local, state, or national guidelines.
   - Reviewing his actions and behavior during the event to see if they were consistent with a "reasonable" standard—that is, what any other reasonable paramedic would do under similar circumstances.
   - Understanding any studies that could link endotracheal intubation with resuscitation rates, as well as studies of the airway procedures that *were* used during the resuscitation.
   - Understanding any autopsy findings.
   - Reviewing all documentation that was completed after the incident.

Test Yourself

1. Palliative care is appropriate when lifesaving therapy is not indicated or allowed, such as when you are presented with a legal DNR order.

   Palliative care is the term applied to care measures meant to provide comfort to the patient. Often when lifesaving therapy is not allowed, palliative measures are appropriate. It allows for humane and compassionate treatment when lifesaving measures are not allowed.

2. False

   Do not resuscitate does not mean "do not treat" or "do not transport." There may be some treatments that can be administered that do not violate a person's wish and still be "giving care." Further, it could be that a patient, upon seeing the care given, chooses to change his or her mind.

3. b

   If your patient is not competent, you must act in the best interests of the patient without undue delay.

4. a

   If your partner starts the IV against the patient's wishes, it would most likely be considered assault and battery, which is a criminal act.

5. c

   It is important to protect patient privacy and honor patient protection. It is not appropriate to discuss or talk about any patient to anyone except for the purpose of patient care, continuation of treatment, health-care operations, and payment. It might be an overreaction to report the incident to the supervisor.

6. c

   Patients are informed if they understand their condition, the benefits of EMS care, and the risks if care is refused. Paramedics do not provide a diagnosis for patients and are not always aware of the likely outcome of care.

7. A duty to act: the EMS provider is obligated to assess and treat the patient. Breach of duty: this exists when the EMS provider fails to meet an objective standard of care. Damage: any harm or other loss suffered by the patient as a result of the negligence of the paramedic. Proximate causation: the damage or loss by the patient was most likely caused by the paramedic.

8. d

   The cornerstone of consent is that the patient or responsible decision maker is fully informed of the patient's condition, the risks of nontreatment, and the benefits of treatment. The patient or responsible decision maker must also be competent to grant consent for care (or to refuse it). Under these guidelines, this woman does not qualify as a fully informed, competent decision maker. You are therefore required to treat the man under his own implied consent. Since the woman is behaving aggressively toward her husband, it would be best if you moved her away from him before starting treatment for them both, if not contraindicated.

9. c

   Expressed consent is given by a patient or by his or her responsible decision maker either verbally or through some physical action indicating that the patient desires treatment. Implied consent means that an emergency health-care provider may presume that a patient who is ill or injured and for any reason unable to give consent would consent to treatment. Child welfare agencies may grant consent for emergency health care for a minor in their custody under the principle of parents patriae. The principle of in loco parentis empowers school officials to "stand in place of the parent."

10. c

    Each state has the responsibility of regulating DNR orders and advance directives. Federal and local government entities usually have no direct involvement in legislation. State agencies follow legislation, establish rules, and enforce the law.

11. False

    The federal laws concerning patient privacy are contained within the Health Insurance Portability and Accountability Act (HIPAA).

12. d

    When an adult is unable to give consent, the law states that it is implied. We must assume that the patient would want to be treated as would any awake, alert, and consenting person. Expressed and informed consent would be obtained only if the patient was awake. There is no such thing as immuned consent.

13. An advance directive is a document in which a competent person gives instructions to be followed with respect to his or her health care in the event the person later becomes incapacitated and unable to make or communicate those decisions to others. An advance directive typically does not become effective unless it is documented in writing, and until the patient becomes terminally ill and/or enters a permanent vegetative or nonresponsive state.

14. Implied consent assumes under U.S. law that any person, being fully aware of the options and the risks, would prefer treatment. Therefore, it is always permissible to begin treatment without the patient expressly giving you permission. With this patient, however, the assumption that he would prefer treatment may be incorrect. He may prefer to die from what he considers a "natural" accident than live in an "unnatural" state as a quadriplegic. This is why you should obtain expressed consent whenever possible.

15. a

A competent patient (or legally responsible decision maker) who is properly informed of the risks of non-treatment and the benefits of treatment is permitted to refuse medical care and/or transportation, even if that care would save the person's life. In any refusal situation, it is important to determine if the patient is both legally and mentally competent to make an informed refusal decision and that the patient understands the risks of refusal.

16. True

Nonverbal, physical expressions of express consent may include, for example, a nod of the head or rolling up a sleeve to allow the paramedic to initiate IV access.

17. a

The physician medical director is responsible for establishing standing orders and protocols for paramedics, including training and establishing expectations for EMS field practice. Radio consultation occurs during the EMS call, and run report reviews occur after the ambulance call. Medical direction typically has little to no control over the operations of EMS systems.

18. d

The patient is the primary decision maker during medical care on an EMS call. In most cases patients have the authority to determine their care. It is possible that the chief paramedic, supervisor, and medical director can override the patient's choice where the law allows, e.g., refusal and advance directives.

19. d

Prospective medical control is a set of standards that establish, in advance, the parameters for EMS clinical practice and set forth the expectations that EMS providers must satisfy in the delivery of patient care. In some EMS systems, physician medical directors are also required to prospectively approve paramedics for work in the field, typically upon the completion of a required course of training or preceptorship. In some states, a paramedic can be removed from clinical practice when a medical director believes the paramedic is not functioning according to prescribed standards.

20. Concurrent medical direction occurs when the paramedic consults (usually by telephone, radio, or other electronic means) with a physician or other medical professional while treating a patient. Retrospective medical direction results from paramedics and medical directors reviewing cases after the fact to learn about skill improvement, better protocols, or other aspects of patient care delivery.

Technological advancements have and will continue to impact the delivery of concurrent medical direction, with the ability to transmit real-time video and clinical information in digital form to improve the accuracy and timeliness of clinical decision-making directly at the patient's bedside. Retrospective medical direction or control is typically exercised through quality improvement mechanisms such as chart reviews, case reviews, and other methods after patient care has been completed.

21. Assault is speech or action that indicates to another that they are or will be in danger. Threatening to touch another (even to achieve a positive result) is considered assault. Battery is actual physical contact with another without their consent. For a patient, unauthorized treatment can be considered battery.

22. You must keep the first woman informed about her condition and treatment options and obtain permission to treat her. However, you also need to consider her right to privacy (HIPAA) and your possible exposure to legal liability.

The patient must be given sufficient information to make an informed decision on whether to accept a particular course of treatment. HIPAA requires that all individually identifiable health information be safeguarded and used only for purposes specifically permitted by the regulations.

23. c

You must continue to keep your patient informed, so you cannot stop speaking. You cannot remove the phone from the second woman's possession. You should try to briefly explain the need for patient privacy to the second woman, and ask her to hang up, before involving authorities.

Problem-Based Learning Case 1
The Partner Quandary

Part 1: The Case

Dispatch and Scene Size-Up

It's 0710 hours and your partner is late—again. This is the third time in the past five shifts that Bob has done this. In addition to being irritated that you have to check out the ambulance by yourself, you also wonder what is going on with your partner. Just then Bob appears at the back of the ambulance. With a bit of effort, he climbs into the patient compartment, mumbles a "good morning," and turns his attention to the equipment cabinets.

Bob looks tired. You notice that his eyes are bloodshot and he hasn't shaven.

"Hey, Bob, I already checked out the rig. Are you okay?"

Without looking at you, he responds, "Yeah, I'm fine. I didn't sleep so well last night. Do you mind driving first today? I'll feel better in a couple of hours."

1. *What would you say to your partner? Are you concerned about his appearance?*

_____

_____

The Primary Survey (Initial Assessment) and Initial Differentials

0712 hours: You step out of the rig and open the hood of the ambulance to check the fluids. There appear to be satisfactory levels of oil, brake fluid, transmission fluid, and coolant. The emergency and running lights appear to be in working order. As you start up the motor, you look up in the rearview mirror. You notice Bob working on the portable oxygen tank.

"Hey, Bob, I already checked that out. It's all set." He mumbles something back that you can't quite hear over the sound of the diesel engine.

The motor idles appropriately. You shut off the engine and climb out of the cab. Circling to the back of the ambulance you check in on what Bob's doing. Startled, Bob makes a quick motion to drop his hand down by his side. You realize that Bob has the nitrous oxide administration mask in his hand.

Bob laughs. "Hey, it's no big deal. I was making sure that the system worked. Guess it does!" He laughs again and puts away the mask.

Bob seems to move a bit slower than usual as he exits the ambulance. As he walks by, you catch an odd smell. Was that alcohol on Bob's breath? You stand there for a moment, thinking about what might be happening.

2. *Is Bob drunk? Is Bob impaired? Should Bob work today? What are you going to do? What other information would you like to know about Bob's behavior?*

_____

_____

History and Physical Exam (Secondary Survey and History)

0720 hours: In the crew sleeping quarters, you find Bob prone on his bed. He appears to be sleeping, in violation of the company's policy. As you lean forward to wake him, you smell the odor of alcohol on Bob's breath. Bob awakens easily when you shake him slightly. Although he swings his legs off the bed, he doesn't immediately rise. Instead, he holds his head in his hands, rubbing his eyes as if to wipe away the sleepy look. It doesn't help.

"Bob, are you sure that you're okay?" you ask. There is a brief silence.

"No, but . . . I'm fine. Really, I'm okay. Do I—we—have a call?" Bob appears to be tachypneic. His face is pale.

"Bob, you really don't look so good. Have you been drinking?"

Bob hesitates. "Um, ahh . . . guess I did last night. I had a couple of beers."

3. *Should Bob be working? What are your concerns about your partner? About yourself? Should you call your supervisor? What other information would you like to know in order to make these decisions?*

_____

_____

Field Impression(s) and Treatment Plan

0722 hours: Gently but persistently you ask Bob to talk about what is happening with him. It helps that Bob trusts you; after all, the two of you have been working together for the past 4 years. He tells you that his wife Lydia served him divorce papers two weeks ago and wants custody of their two children. He has been confused, angry, and frustrated about the situation. He insists that he is not drunk, but just tired; he was up until 3 a.m. trying to sleep. He had a couple of drinks to help him do that.

He can't afford to take time off from work. "The divorce is going to cost me a lot!" He asks if you could start an IV on him and administer a liter of normal saline to help with his headache.

4. *What are the ethical and legal ramifications of performing Bob's request? What options can you think of to handle this dilemma? What other information do you want to know to better decide on how to proceed?*

_____

_____

Transportation and Ongoing Care

0725 hours: The dispatch phone rings, interrupting your thoughts. Picking up the phone, you answer, "Medic 7."

"Good morning Medic 7. I need you to start heading toward the interstate. We are getting reports of a multivehicle collision on southbound 95. Medic 10 is already rolling. State troopers are on scene and should be giving an update shortly."

You look at Bob. The dispatcher says, "Did you copy, Medic 7?"

5. *How will you answer the question? What are the ramifications of your decision? What will you do now?*

_____

_____

Part 2: Debriefing

Responses to Part 1 questions:

1. At first glance, this situation doesn't seem unusual. Who hasn't had a late night before the beginning of a shift? Yet something doesn't seem quite right about this situation. What do you see about Bob's behavior that might raise some concerns?

2. How can you determine if Bob is drunk or impaired? A police officer may use a combination of manual sobriety tests and a Breathalyzer exam to determine whether an individual is impaired in the field. What tools do you have to make the same determination? Do you have the authority or right to prohibit Bob from working today?

3. Bob has just admitted to using alcohol recently, and he is also violating company policy regarding sleeping while on duty. Combined with a possible misuse of a controlled substance (nitrous oxide), do you have enough information to conclude that Bob is impaired and, if so, unable to work?

4. Can you ethically and/or legally start an IV on Bob and administer fluid? Could you consider Bob to be a patient? After all, he has a complaint ("headache") and has expressed consent to receive treatment. Do you put yourself out of service and request another ambulance to transport Bob? Or, do you help out your friend, provide the treatment, and hope he is able to work? Do you call a supervisor to document possible illegal activity?

5. This is a terrible dilemma. On the one hand, your friend and partner is exhibiting behavior that is understandable. His situation at home is very stressful. He is unable to sleep because of it. The financial pressure is high. Yet, on the other hand, his behavior may put him, you, and the public at risk. What you do next may determine Bob's future with the company, as well as any personal friendship you might have with him.

Part 3: Case Discussion

As in real life, this scenario is complex, and there is no one "right way" or "wrong way" to answer the related questions. Let's look at this problem through three lenses.

1. *Well-being.* While not explicitly stated, it seems that the changes in Bob's behavior are related to the pressures he faces at home. His tardiness seems to be tied to being served with the divorce papers. There is no mention of a substance abuse or dependency issue; in fact there is no clear information that Bob is even impaired or intoxicated.

However, the alcohol smell on his breath and some of his behaviors seem to suggest that at least he is struggling to maintain a sense of normalcy by remaining at work. Is Bob capable of making clinically sound decisions for the care of his (future) patients? Would you feel comfortable letting Bob drive the ambulance?

Is Bob's drinking and possible use of the nitrous oxide a one-time mistake or a sign of a larger problem? Abrupt changes in behavior are often indicative of deeper issues that need to be resolved.

2. *Ethics.* In the 1998 National Standard Curriculum, there is a list of attributes for the EMS profession. They are

- Integrity
- Empathy
- Self-motivation
- Appearance and personal hygiene
- Self-confidence
- Communications
- Time management
- Teamwork and diplomacy
- Respect
- Patient advocacy
- Careful delivery of service

As a close friend of Bob, you may feel obligated to help him out in what seems to be a moment of need. You could advise the dispatcher that your unit is unable to respond because your partner is ill. Simultaneously you could present Bob with your observations about his behavior and let him make the decision to leave work. However, if Bob insists that he can function normally, what will you do?

In addition, do you ask Bob about the possible misuse of the nitrous oxide? If he admits that he in fact did self-administer the medication, what would you do? What is your responsibility to yourself as a health-care provider? To the safety of the public?

3. *Legal.* The concept of "breach of duty" may apply in this situation. One could argue that a "reasonable" paramedic would not show up for work the way that Bob did. Conversely, is it true that, because Bob had not yet responded to a call for help, there was no duty to act in this situation, and therefore no breach of that duty had occurred?

Are there company policies that prohibit the type of behavior that Bob exhibits? If you do not report Bob's behavior, are you liable for events that might occur later?

If you do treat Bob, is he then a patient? If so, do you then document your actions on a patient care report?

In addition, the possible use of the nitrous oxide, while not covered by the federal Controlled Substances Act, may violate state and other federal laws (see www.usdoj.gov/dea/concern/inhalants. html, California penal code 381b; www.leginfo. ca.gov/cgi-bin/waisgate?WAISdocID=7530589929+ 1+0+0&WAISaction=retrieve).

The 1998 EMT-Paramedic National Standard Curriculum is a federally funded, public domain document held at the U.S. Department of Transportation. You can download a copy of this document from the National Highway Safety Transportation Administration (NHTSA) website at www.nhtsa.gov. Click on "Emergency Medical Services," and then look for the "National Standard Curricula" section. Also there are copies of the curricula for EMT-Basic, First Responder, and various refresher programs. As of this writing, work is under way to develop the new EMS Education Standards, which will eventually replace the National Standard Curriculum.

Part 4: Further Learning Paths

- Alcoholics Anonymous (AA) is a member-driven organization whose sole purpose is to help people suffering from alcoholism get help for their addiction. More information about AA can be found at www.alcoholics-anonymous.org.

- The National Association of EMTs is a membership organization representing, at the time of this writing, more than 20,000 EMS professionals across the country. With the world headquarters located in Clinton, Mississippi, their Web address is www.naemt.org.

- The American Medical Association has an online resource dedicated to medical ethics, which can be found at www.ama-assn.org/ama/pub/category/ 2416.html.

chapter 5

Clinical Decision-Making

Are You Ready?

You are assessing an 18-year-old female who appears to have fallen off her bicycle. She is alert as you approach her and appears to be in pain. She is holding her left arm with her right arm.

1. As you look at this scene, what clues can you find that will help you shape your assessment and management of this patient?

   _____

   _____

   _____

2. Based on the little information you have about this incident, are you able to make a quick decision regarding whether this patient needs to be transported?

   _____

   _____

   _____

Active Learning

1. Can't Make a Decision?

This text chapter may appear to cover some fairly complex-sounding concepts, but that's not necessarily true. Try the following exercise:

Think about a time when you had to make a simple decision. Perhaps it was deciding which brand of food product to buy at a market, or which type of gas to purchase for your car. Maybe it was what to have for lunch.

 a. How did you make your decision?

Now, think of a more complex decision that you have made. Maybe it was purchasing a large appliance, like a dishwasher or oven. Or maybe it was choosing a style of furniture or item of clothing like a suit or dress.

 b. How did you make your decision? What did you consider when making the decision? Did it take longer than the first example? At what point did you make the decision?

Finally, think of a time when you could *not* make a decision or you made a decision that you later regretted.

 c. Why was it so difficult to make the decision, or not make a decision at all? Did you wish you knew something that you didn't? If it was a poor decision, why did you regret it?

You Are There: Reality-Based Cases

Case 1

Your patient is a 56-year-old, top-level executive at a large business firm. She has been working long hours over the past several days trying to complete a significant project. This morning she awoke feeling a bit of anxiety about trying to finish the job. It worsened as she drove to work; by the time she arrived at the office, her

hands felt numb and her chest felt tight, like she couldn't catch her breath. She felt nauseous. Her assistant became concerned and called 9-1-1. You find her to be alert, tachypneic, and tachycardic. She appears frightened.

1. What do you think is causing the patient's condition? Write down as many potential causes of her signs and symptoms as you can. What other information do you need to know about her? What treatments will you provide?

_____

_____

_____

Case 2

Your patient is a 56-year-old, top-level executive at a large business firm. He has been working long hours over the past several days trying to complete a significant project. This morning he awoke feeling a bit of anxiety about trying to finish the job. It worsened as he drove to work; by the time he arrived at the office, his hands felt numb and his chest felt tight, like he couldn't catch his breath. He felt nauseous. His assistant became

concerned and called 9-1-1. You find him to be alert, tachypneic, and tachycardic. He appears frightened.

1. What do you think is causing the patient's condition? Write down as many potential causes of his signs and symptoms as you can. What other information do you need to know about him? What treatments will you provide?

_____

_____

_____

2. Compare what you wrote about the first patient with that of the second. Were there any differences, or did you answer them the same way? Did you think about them the same way? In other words, did you come to the same conclusion, but use different thought processes?

_____

_____

_____

Test Yourself

1. The EMS critical thinking process starts as soon as the paramedic arrives on the scene.
   True
   False

2. List some of the challenges unique to the prehospital environment.

   _____

   _____

3. One critical difference between the decision-making process for the physician and the decision-making process for the EMS provider is
   a. the EMS provider must synthesize both subjective and objective information.
   b. the EMS provider must use history taking to gather subjective information.
   c. the physician must come up with an actual diagnosis of the problem.
   d. the physician must make an evaluation based on the physical examination.

4. Why is making a diagnosis *less* important in the prehospital setting?

   _____

   _____

Scenario: You are called for a patient who has been found unconscious in a car at night. A neighbor states that she saw an unfamiliar car with "an old man slumped over the wheel." As you approach the vehicle, you notice the car is parked at an odd angle, but you do not notice any damage. The car's engine is not running. When you tap on the window, the man regains consciousness and explains he pulled over because he was "too tired to drive." His skin is warm and dry, there is no odor of alcohol on his breath, and his vital signs are within normal limits.

5. Given the preceding scenario, which of the following is an example of subjective information?
   a. It is nighttime.
   b. There is no damage to the car.
   c. The engine is not running.
   d. The car is not familiar to the neighbor.

6. At this point your patient is
   a. sick.
   b. not sick.
   c. not yet sick.
   d. becoming sick.

7. The patient assures you he "feels fine now." You should
   a. clear the scene; there is no medical problem.
   b. follow the patient as he drives home to make sure he gets there safely.
   c. perform a good assessment and anticipate the potential for a serious problem.
   d. ask the police to place the patient on a transport hold.

8. Appropriate interventional treatments must always be balanced with gathering information and performing an assessment.
   True
   False

9. One of the potential pitfalls of greater experience in the field of paramedicine is
   a. tunnel vision due to overconfidence when using the availability heuristic in problem solving.
   b. greater difficulty performing rapid evaluations and prompt treatments due to fatigue and burnout.
   c. using a "shotgun" approach to decision-making due to familiarity with a wide variety of tests and procedures.
   d. failing to value pertinent negatives as much as positive findings, due to rapid patient assessment.

10. Why is it important to combine the assessment elements before making a decision regarding treatment?

_____

_____

11. Which of the following scenarios is an example of using pattern recognition in problem solving?
   a. You suspect that a 1 a.m. call to a motor vehicle collision (MVC) may involve intoxication because you notice empty beer cans in the back seat.
   b. You suspect that a 1 a.m. call to an MVC may involve intoxication because you have found that is often the case.
   c. You suspect that a 1 a.m. call to an MVC may involve intoxication because the driver tells you she is drunk.
   d. You suspect that a 1 a.m. call to an MVC may involve intoxication because a passenger's blood alcohol content is 0.11%.

12. Name two technological devices used to assess for possible cardiovascular or respiratory problems in a prehospital setting.

_____

_____

13. Which of the following is a good way to improve your critical thinking abilities?
   a. Rule out negative evidence as superfluous to the assessment process.
   b. Fully explore each potential cause before committing to any particular treatment.
   c. Consider all the information available; do not rule anything out as distracting.
   d. Be alert for fresh evidence and keep your treatment strategies flexible.

14. In some cases pertinent negative findings are more important than other signs and symptoms.
   True
   False

Scenario: During the course of a week-long heat wave, you have treated a number of elderly patients for heat exhaustion. You are called to treat an 82-year-old woman in a stiflingly hot room presenting with dizziness, nausea, and headache.

15. You should
   a. immediately treat the patient for heat exhaustion by administering replacement fluids, via IV if necessary.

b. use the availability heuristic and assume the patient must be suffering from heat exhaustion.

c. suspect heat exhaustion as the most likely cause, but perform a targeted history and physical exam to verify.

d. administer oxygen and transport the patient emergently to the nearest stroke facility.

16. Using the evidence of the stifling room as a basis for a conclusion that this patient may be suffering heat exhaustion is an example of which problem-solving tool?

a. The representativeness heuristic

b. The availability heuristic

c. The anchoring heuristic

d. Confirmation bias

17. Using your critical thinking skills, you come to the conclusion that this patient is most likely suffering from heat exhaustion. In this situation, you should most be on guard for

a. fundamental attribution error.

b. confirmation bias.

c. self-serving bias.

d. hindsight bias.

18. Describe a method you should use to help control bias in the decision-making process.

_____

_____

19. List two pitfalls commonly encountered when applying critical thinking skills in real-life situations.

_____

_____

Need to Know

The following represent the Key Objectives of Chapter 5:

1. *Explain how paramedics provide emergency care to their patients by using an assessment-based approach.*

Both physicians and paramedics gather, evaluate, and synthesize information about a patient's condition. In this sense, both health-care practitioners use an assessment-based approach to determining patient care. However, the physician is compelled to *diagnose* the patient, that is, come to a conclusion about what exactly is causing the patient's current condition. The paramedic does not need to determine the exact underlying cause in order to begin emergency care and transport of the ill or injured patient. In fact it may be best to avoid coming to a "snap" judgment of the problem, in order to avoid tunnel vision.

2. *Describe the subtle differences in patient presentation among patients who are sick and those who are not yet sick.*

Chapter 14, Patient Assessment, in the textbook covers the critical concepts of the primary and secondary survey in detail. At this point, recognize that sometimes the line that divides sick patients from not yet sick patients can be very fine. The paramedic must remain vigilant about the patient's airway, breathing, and circulation status and carefully analyze both the environmental and patient findings. Ongoing assessment of the patient's vital signs and physical exam are critical to finding these subtle differences.

3. *Explain the differences between how problems might be solved by novice (new) and expert (appropriately experienced) paramedics.*

Imagine that the brain is an old-fashioned Rolodex, a rotating file device that is still commonly used to store business contact information on small cards. The brand-new paramedic has a brand-new Rolodex, full of blank cards. She experiences her first patient encounter and manages the event. In her Rolodex, she "writes down" the

information about this patient contact—let's say it was a 45-year-old male with chest pain. Mentally, she stores this information away. She contacts a second patient, then a third, and then more. For each contact, she mentally writes down information about that contact and stores it in her Rolodex.

One day she contacts a 49-year-old male with chest pain. She vaguely remembers that she managed a similar patient in the past. She "flips" her mental Rolodex to that first patient's card and recalls what she provided for management and treatment. This time, her treatment goes a little faster than the first time.

As she continues her practice, the paramedic adds more and more "cards" to her mental Rolodex. We call this experience, and this is how the paramedic becomes an expert in her craft. An experienced paramedic can have many thousands of "cards" in the Rolodex; she can flip through them very quickly, match patterns of what signs and symptoms she has seen in her past patients, and make what might appear to be "snap" decisions to an inexperienced paramedic. The novice who tries to make the same level of rapid decision-making may be less accurate simply because of the lack of sound experience.

If this analogy makes sense to you, then you will remember to be precise and diligent in assessing and managing your patients at the beginning of your career. Resist the urge to make a quick decision about a patient's condition. Over time you will get there!

4. *Determine when enough information is gathered to form an assessment of the problem, and balance that with the need to manage the patient, particularly when the problem is life-threatening.*

As a new paramedic, you may feel like you need to ask many questions and perform a detailed examination on every patient you contact—after all, who wants to miss a crucial piece of information that can make a difference in treatment and outcome? You must remember that the patient's airway, breathing, and circulatory status must be evaluated *first* and treated *first*. The paramedic will manage the most serious conditions first, followed by less threatening conditions. Indeed, minor conditions can be left alone if there is a life-threatening condition that needs immediate attention and care.

5. *Develop critical thinking skills that can be useful in EMS situations using heuristic tools commonly used by physicians.*

The term *heuristic* comes from the Greek word *heuriskein*, meaning "find." Medical practitioners can use a variety of methods to help solve problems presented by their patients. There are three basic approaches that are discussed in the text. They are:

a. *Representative heuristic.* You find out enough information about the patient's condition that causes you to believe that the pattern represents a specific disease or injury process.

b. *Availability heuristic.* You have experienced enough similar situations to the one you are facing now to make a judgment on it.

c. *Anchoring heuristic.* You make a few observations about the patient's condition, formulate an initial impression of what is occurring, and then try to fit your subsequent findings to that impression.

Each of these methods has both strengths and weaknesses associated with it. Regardless of which tool you might use, remember these basic tips to help you develop good critical thinking habits:

- *Avoid tunnel vision.* Although your textbooks might imply that your patients will always appear to be "black or white," many of them will in fact be found in the "grey" area. In other words, their presentation may be due to a variety of causes, not just one.

- *Sort and prioritize your information.* Focus on findings that lead to serious conditions first, followed by less critical ones.

- *Keep reassessing the patient.* Observing your patient is not like taking a photograph. It is more like filming a movie—things can change from one moment to the next.

- *The absence of findings can be just as important as the ones that you can observe.* These are called *pertinent negatives,* and you will want to keep them in mind as you sift through your clues.

- *When it's time to switch, switch!* The nature of patient care is a pattern of assessment, followed by management, followed by more assessment and more management. Be clear and confident when you decide when to evaluate and when to take care of your patient.

6. *Explain how biased thought processes can result in difficulties in problem solving and how being aware of possible biases and consciously filtering for them can minimize the impact they have on critical thinking.*

Being biased is not necessarily wrong; after all, we all are biased in one way or another in how we view others and ourselves in the world. What is more important to understand is how to recognize bias as it relates to critical thinking and decision-making skills in medicine.

Examples of bias in the thinking process include:

- *Hindsight.* Believing that past events will predict future events
- *Focalism.* Focusing on single points of detail of an event and not the big picture (tunnel vision)
- *Fundamental attribution error.* Thinking that the source of the patient's complaint is personality driven rather than clinically based
- *Confirmation bias.* Incorrectly judging a situation, and then trying to rationalize observations so that they support that judgment
- *Self-serving bias.* Taking credit for outcomes that are not necessarily related to your actions

If you can recognize these behaviors in yourself, then you can stop them and keep your mind open to the possibilities of what is really happening to the patient.

Need to Do

There are no psychomotor skills that directly support this chapter content.

Connections

- The accuracy and quality of emergency care that you provide to your patient rests squarely upon your ability to assess the patient. It is not too early to begin looking at the following chapters in the textbook: Chapter 9, Safety and Scene Size-Up; Chapter 10, Therapeutic Communications and History Taking; and Chapter 11, The Normal Physical Examination.
- The W. Maurice Young Centre for Applied Ethics, located at the University of British Columbia, Canada, has a website that outlines a sensible, ethical approach to clinical decision-making and advising. You can find that page at www.ethics.ubc.ca/people/mcdonald/decisions.htm.
- If you are interested in finding out more about the critical thinking process, try a Web search on the term *critical thinking.* One link is www.criticalthinking.org, which is the website for the Foundation for Critical Thinking (Dillon Beach, California). This site provides short readings on the thinking process, as well as links to other resources.

- Link to the companion DVD for a chapter-based quiz, audio glossary, animations, games and exercises, and, when appropriate, skill sheets and skill Step-by-Steps.

Street Secrets

- **Using Resources** You don't operate in a void. Remember to use your resources, including your partner, medical director, and protocols, to help guide you in making critical decisions. As you gain confidence in your abilities, you will rely on external resources less. However, having an extra "ear" or "second opinion" is helpful.
- **Closing the Loop** When possible, "close the loop." In other words, find out what happened to your patient after you transferred care. You may be surprised to find out that what you thought you were dealing with was in fact not the case! This "reflection-on-action" moment will help shape your experiences in a positive way.

The Drug Box

There are no specific drugs related to this chapter content.

Answers

Are You Ready?

1. This photo provides an opportunity for you to exercise an "open mind." Did you notice the following when you studied the scene?
   - The front rim of the bicycle wheel is bent, indicating some force. What could have created this force?
   - The patient appears awake and engaged with the paramedic.
   - Not all of the trees have leaves yet. Is it spring or fall?
   - The patient is on the sidewalk. Did she land there or walk to her current position?
   - An absence of a helmet. Was she wearing one?
2. Do you believe that she has an injury that warrants ambulance transport? Perhaps you used an *availability heuristic* approach to your decision-making, since you have seen many of these cases before. Or, maybe the mechanism of the incident, coupled with an apparent extremity injury, led you to use the *representative heuristic* to make the decision.

Active Learning

1. **a.** There was probably a wide range of options and prior information you considered before making a decision—information you knew about because of previous experience. The fact is, you may have made the decision without even thinking about it because the *pattern* was very similar to situations you were involved with in the past, like buying gas or a specific kind of cereal. How does this relate to *pattern matching* or the *availability heuristic* in clinical decision-making?

    b. Why might this decision have taken longer? Unlike the first situation, you may not have been familiar with the products that you had to choose from. Because of this, you may have needed to gather more information about the options, doing research and comparisons before deciding on which item to purchase. Consider the following: Did you have a sense of what you wanted before beginning the decision-making process? Did you then balance the different variables, such as cost and function, in order to identify the item that was most like your original mental image? How does this relate to the *representative heuristic* decision process?

    c. If you couldn't make a decision, perhaps it was because you felt that you did not have enough information, or that the outcome of your decision was too risk-laden or caused too significant of an impact to other parts of your life. These "high stakes" situations also occur in EMS situations, where the patient outcome is strongly influenced by what you decide to do. In these situations you must often make your decision even though you do not feel fully confident—and then live with the outcome afterward.

    If you have ever made a poor decision, you probably realized that perhaps there was some information that may have been available, but you missed or ignored it because you felt that it wasn't important at the time. Could this be an example of tunnel vision?

You Are There: Reality-Based Cases

Case 1

1. Did you write down more than one or two possible causes of her discomfort? What do you think is the most likely culprit? Is she "sick"? For more to this answer, go to patient 2.

Case 2

1. Compare the answers you provided for Case 1, the female businesswoman's condition, with those you gave for the businessman's complaints. Were there any differences between the two sets? Why do you think that is?

2. If there were no differences between your two answers, great! You have just demonstrated your ability to control bias as it relates to gender. The two cases are identical, with the exception of gender. Could the woman be experiencing psychogenic hyperventilation? Certainly.

Could she be experiencing a pulmonary embolus or cardiac ischemia? Absolutely!

Now, how likely were you to attribute the man's condition to psychogenic hyperventilation? If you initially thought the woman was more prone to that condition than the man, think about how you reached your conclusion. Can you think of which bias you might have inadvertently selected?

Test Yourself

1. False

    During a call, the EMS critical thinking process begins as soon as the EMS professional obtains information from the dispatcher.

2. The prehospital environment may include adverse weather conditions, poor lighting, uneven terrain, and even a possible shortage of equipment, supplies, or team members.

3. c

    The decision-making process for both the physician and the EMS provider involves gathering, evaluating, and synthesizing information. There are, however, substantial differences between the purposes of the two processes, the most notable of which is the need for the physician to come up with an actual diagnosis of the problem.

4. Many diseases have similar presentations of symptoms and signs. Ultimately, determining the cause of the symptoms and signs is less important than gathering pertinent information; recognizing the severity of the signs and symptoms; preventing or correcting abnormalities that impact the airway, breathing, and circulation; and providing safe, expeditious transportation to the most appropriate facility capable of caring for the patient.

5. d

    Objective findings are those that are measurable or observable by the paramedic. Subjective findings are those that the patient (or someone else) tells you.

6. c

    The patients who are between "sick" and "not sick" can be the most difficult ones for both experienced and novice paramedics to handle. These patients do not appear sick at the moment, or sick enough to warrant aggressive resuscitation measures, but if they are not watched carefully and handled correctly, they can become very sick and may even die. These are the ones referred to as "not yet sick."

7. c

    "Not yet sick" patients are difficult to assess and treat. You should always maintain a high index of suspicion. These are the patients who benefit most from a paramedic's experience and ability to perform a good assessment and anticipate the potential for the patient to have a serious problem.

8. True

    Sorting through the signs and symptoms may not be your first priority if the patient is unconscious and not breathing. Appropriate interventional treatments must always be balanced with gathering information and performing an assessment. What makes this difficult is in knowing where the balance between assessment and treatment lies. The old saying "experience is the best teacher" is true for the practice of paramedicine.

9. a

When tunnel vision occurs, a person's field of focus is too narrow, and possibilities that should be considered are frequently ignored. If signs or symptoms are not considered because they do not confirm the suspected diagnosis, the patient may be mismanaged.

10. It is important to consider all assessment findings before making a treatment decision, because there are certain conditions in which a "normal" vital sign, when combined with a specific chief complaint, is indicative of a life-threatening situation.

11. a

Pattern recognition involves the assessment of environmental clues (or lack of clues) based on known patterns to develop a hypothesis.

12. Responses include cardiac monitor, end-tidal CO_2 detector, and pulse oximeter. As the technology available in the prehospital environment is increasing, the use of tools such as the cardiac monitor, pulse oximeter, and end-tidal CO_2 detector are becoming more common. These devices are minimally invasive and are good tools to assess for possible cardiovascular or respiratory problems. They are becoming a standard of care for most cardiac and respiratory emergencies as well as serious trauma situations.

13. d

Be alert for fresh evidence, particularly evidence that demands a revision or deletion of the assessment conclusion: Until a person is dead, the person is in a dynamic state. The person's condition can improve or deteriorate rapidly. Your treatment strategies must be flexible as well.

14. True

In some cases, pertinent negative findings are more important than other signs and symptoms. With some diseases, like infectious diseases, they are critical to safety.

15. c

The anchoring heuristic is a problem-solving strategy that begins with the most likely cause as the anchor, and then the signs and symptoms needed to confirm that cause are assessed for first. This can be a powerful tool, but it can be used incorrectly if the paramedic does not perform a thorough assessment or gather history to justify his or her conclusions.

16. a

The representativeness heuristic means that the situation provides enough information for the paramedic to believe that the current signs and symptoms represent a particular disease.

17. b

Confirmation bias is the tendency to search for and interpret information in a way that confirms your preconceptions. In this case, although you suspect heat exhaustion, you should still consider contradicting signs and symptoms and be prepared to revise your treatment plan.

18. Remember that patient presentations are diverse and their problems evolve over time. Paramedics must be flexible to be effective. Ultimately, each and every call should be approached with the same question: "What is the most serious possible cause of this patient's presenting signs and symptoms?" Being aware of possible biases and consciously filtering for them can minimize the impact they have on your critical thinking abilities.

19. Failure to take the necessary equipment to the patient and failure to mobilize adequate personnel to support the management of the care of the patient are two common pitfalls.

Always take an ECG monitor-defibrillator, airway kit with oxygen, and IV kit with cardiac drugs to every patient that dispatch information indicates as "sick" or "not yet sick." A third common pitfall is performing assessments out of sequence so that a life-threatening problem, when it arises, is mismanaged.

chapter 6

Medical Terminology

Are You Ready?

Mr. Bond is a 76-year-old male who has a very extensive medical history, including insulin-dependent diabetes, cholecystitis, hyperlipidemia, hypertension, renal insufficiency, cardiomyopathy, inferior-lateral myocardial infarction, congestive heart failure, anemia, cerebrovascular accident with resulting right-sided hemiparesis, dysarthria, dysphasia, gout, and depression. Today Mr. Bond is complaining of a sore throat that he has had for the past 15 minutes.

1. Using the patient care report in Figure 6-1 and the table below, break down each of the components of Mr. Bond's past medical history (PMH) into prefix, root word, and suffix (where applicable) to assist you in defining each word:

Word	Prefix	Root	Suffix	Definition
Diabetes				
Cholecystitis				
Amyotrophic				
Sclerosis				
Hyperlipidemia				
Arteriosclerosis				
Cardiomyopathy				
Myocardial				
Anemia				
Cerebrovascular				
Hemiparesis				
Dysarthria				
Dysphasia				

Valley Fire Department Patient Care Report

Dispatch Date 01/02/07	*CASE NUMBER*	1	2	3	4	5	6	7	8	Pt Number 1 of 1	Page Number 1 of 1	Service Type	Scene Transfer

Incident Location 1234 49th Ave				Location Type	L	R	E	S	Estimated Incident Date & Time	01/02/07 @ 13:00 hrs

Patient Name (Last, First) Bond, James	Patient Address 1234 49th Ave	Telephone Number (415) 555-1234

Birthdate 12/28/30	SSN 123-45-6789	Insurance Information ☐ MediCare/Cal ☐ Kaiser ☐ Work Comp. ■ Pvt.	Policy Number 123456789

Age 76	Gender M F Unk.	Weight (kg) 70 kg	Medications ☐ Denies Insulin (Regular and NPH), Colchicine, DSS, Famotidine, Lipitor, HCTZ,

Past Medical History   ☐ Denies
■ MI ■ CHF ■ HTN ■ Other Cardiac ☐ Asthma ☐ COPD
☐ Pneumonia ☐ Other Respiratory ☐ Immunocompromised
■ Diabetes ■ Kidney Failure ☐ Cancer ☐ Psychiatric
☐ Seizures
■ CVA ☐ Neurological ☐ Pregnancy ☐ Recent Surgery
☐ Alcohol/Substance Abuse ☐ History of Current Complaint
■ Other_____

Plavix, Furosemide, Slow-K, Multivitamins, Digoxin, NTG, and

Zoloft.

Allergies   ☐ NKDA
PCN, Morphine, Codeine

Family History: *Cardiac disease, hypertension, diabetes mellitus, lupus, and amyotrophic lateral sclerosis (ALS).* **Past Medical History:** Insulin-dependent diabetes, cholecystitis, hyperlipidemia,

hypertension, renal insufficiency, cardiomyopathy, inferior-lateral myocardial infarction, congestive heart failure, anemia, cerebrovascular accident with resulting right-sided

hemiparesis, dysarthria, dysphasia, gout, and depression.

Primary MD.
Bracket, K.

FIGURE 6-1   Excerpt from the patient care report corresponding to the chapter-opening scenario.

Active Learning

1. Define each root word.

Root Word	Meaning
Append/o, appendic/o	*Appendix*
Arthr/o	
Derm/o	
Muc/o	
Hydr/o	
Neur/o	
Hemat/o	
Thromb/o	
Path/o	

2. For the following medical terms, place forward slashes between the individual word parts, and write the definition of the medical term.

Term	Meaning
Cardi/o/megaly	*Enlargement of the heart*
Acromegaly	

Term	Meaning
Macroglossia	
Histology	
Arthritis	
Pericarditis	
Splenomegaly	
Aleukocytosis	
Thoracocentesis	
Pericardiocentesis	
Pulmonary	
Gastrectomy	
Appendicitis	
Dermatology	
Neuritis	
Cardiac	
Supraclavicular	
Dysmenorrhea	
Hemolysis	
Osteomalacia	

Term	Meaning
Maxillary	
Encephalomyelitis	
Gastroenterology	
Laryngoscope	
Laryngectomy	
Hematoma	
Retrogastric	
Retroperitoneal	
Myeloid	
Gastritis	
Pneumothorax	
Dysphagia	
Mitral stenosis	
Hepatitis	
Adenectomy	
Dermatitis	
Laparotomy	
Intraosseous	
Aerotitis media	
Microscope	
Anoxia	

3. Choose the best medical term for the following descriptions. When writing the term, place forward slashes between each of its word parts.

Meaning	Term
Inflammation of the adenoids	*Adenoid/itis*
Immature cell from which a white blood cell develops	
Accumulation of blood in the pleural cavity	
Excessive carbon dioxide	
Inflammation of the liver	
Relating to the ribs	
Condition of having a split mind	
Inflammation around the heart	
Surgical removal of an embolus	

Meaning	Term
Bacteria that appear blue	
Condition of an overproductive thyroid gland	
Double vision	
Difficulty speaking	
A medication capable of relieving pain	
Relating to fat, or like fat	
To take water away from	
Slow heart rate	
Relating to something under the liver	
Inflammation of the brain	
Bones in the hand after the carpals	
Normal, or good, breathing	
Red blood cell	
Cancerous tumor	
Relating to mucus, or a mucous membrane	
Visual examination of the larynx	
A bluish discoloration of the skin	
Fast respiratory rate	
The process of recording carbon dioxide measurements	
Inflammation of the colon	
Under the sternum	
Surgical removal of the uterus	
Fever producing	
Loss of, or without speech	
Nasal discharge or flow	
The suturing of a severed nerve	
Agent that kills fungi	
Incision into the skull	
Surgical removal of the gall bladder	
Condition of being without feeling	
Capable of dissolving or digesting mucus	
Surgical repair of the larynx	

4. Read an article in your favorite EMS journal or medical journal and make a list of any medical terms that you do not understand. Break down each of these words into its prefix, root word, and/or suffix (where applicable) in an attempt to define these words. When you are done, look up each of these words in a medical dictionary to see if you are correct.

You Are There: Reality-Based Cases

Case 1

You are called to a prenatal clinic, where you find an unresponsive 35-year-old female on a gurney. The patient came into the clinic complaining of headache; blurred vision; nausea with vomiting; swelling of her face, hands, and ankles; sudden weight gain; confusion; anxiety; trouble catching her breath; right shoulder pain; and lower back pain.

The patient's physician tells you that she has been suffering from pregnancy-induced hypertension and preeclampsia, and that today she presented with proteinuria and hyperreflexia. The physician wrote an order for MS 4.0 g deep IM in each buttock and hydralazine 10 mg IV. The preceptor RN advised the student nurse to prepare the MS while she went to look for the hydralazine. The student nurse prepared the MS as she was instructed to do, but when the physician began to pressure the student nurse, she administered the MS without her preceptor present. As soon as the preceptor returned, she established an IV and administered the hydralazine. Approximately 10 minutes after the patient received the MS, she became unresponsive. The student nurse informs you that the patient's initial vital signs are: blood pressure, 240/110; pulse, 128; respirations, 22; and temperature, 98.9° F.

1. What is your general impression of this patient, and what additional information would you like to know about her?

_____

_____

The physician states that the patient did not exhibit any seizure activity during the time that the patient was under her care. The patient appears to have a patent airway, but has bradypnea and very shallow respirations. The patient has bounding pulses in her periphery. The patient was found in a left lateral position.

2. What are some other possible causes for the change in the patient's status?

_____

_____

After you test the patient's blood sugar (124 mg/dL), the patient stops breathing. You and your partner insert an NPA and ventilate the patient with a bag-mask attached to high-flow oxygen. You load the patient on the gurney, and, as you begin to wheel her to the ambulance, the head nurse frantically enters the room and asks the student nurse if she knows where the 80 mg of morphine from the drug cabinet is. The student nurse states that she administered the 80 mg of morphine to the patient as the physician had ordered, 40 mg IM in each buttock.

3. What action should you take upon discovery of the medication error?

_____

_____

This scenario depicts the downside of using medical abbreviations, especially when used to order and document the administration of medications. In this particular situation, the physician meant to order 4 grams of magnesium sulfate ($MgSO_4$ or MS) administered intramuscularly, 2 grams in each buttock. The student nurse interpreted the order as 40 milligrams of morphine sulfate (MSO_4 or MS) intramuscularly in each buttock and ended up giving the patient 80 milligrams of morphine. The abbreviation MS can mean magnesium sulfate or morphine sulfate; thus, it is imperative to write out the names of these medications. The student interpreted the order for the medication to be in milligrams, when in reality the physician had ordered grams.

If the medication order is unclear, or appears incorrect, confirm the order with the person who issued it, look up the medication if you are not familiar with its use or an appropriate dosage of the medication, and always follow the five rights of medication administration.

Another important point to make regarding this medication error is the use of a trailing zero. If you are giving 4 grams of something, *do not* write 4.0 grams. The decimal point between the 4 and the zero may not be seen by everyone, and the 4.0 can be interpreted as 40 (an error which would deliver 10 times the medication that was intended), which was the case in this example.

Test Yourself

1. Which of the following suffixes means "contraction, constriction"?
   a. -sclerosis
   b. -stenosis
   c. -stalsis
   d. -stasis

2. What does the term *adduction* mean?

   _____

   _____

3. The abbreviation *DT* means
   a. duodenal torsion.
   b. drop test.
   c. delirium tremens.
   d. deltoid tumor.

4. What does the medical term *leukocyte* mean, and what is its root word?

   _____

   _____

5. The suffix *-esthesia* means
   a. brain activity.
   b. ability to move.
   c. sensation.
   d. appearance.

6. What does the term *dysphagia* mean?

   _____

   _____

7. While treating an unconscious, elderly patient in her home, you notice a prescription bottle with the abbreviation *b.i.d.* on the label. What does this mean?

   _____

   _____

8. The term *periumbilical* describes the
   a. two glands of the throat.
   b. area surrounding the belly button.
   c. the "bag of waters" surrounding a fetus.
   d. area immediately behind the eye.

9. You have responded to a call for a 55-year-old woman complaining of chest tightness and difficulty breathing. In order to determine if the pain radiates anywhere, you ask, "Does the pain radiate down your left arm?" Explain why this question is poorly phrased.

   _____

   _____

10. The best way to learn medical terminology is to memorize medical terms.
    True
    False

11. You are treating a patient with suspected hemothorax. What common terms should you use to describe this condition to the patient?

    _____

    _____

12. *Arteriosclerosis* is a medical term meaning
    a. infection of the joints.
    b. widening of the arteries.
    c. inflammation of the joints.
    d. thickening and narrowing of the arteries.

13. What does the suffix *-centesis* mean?

    _____

    _____

14. The abbreviation *MVC* means
    a. motor and vasculature condition.
    b. motor vehicle collision.
    c. muscular veniform contraction.
    d. multiple ventricular contractions.

15. A nulligravida patient is a patient that has never been pregnant.
    True
    False

16. Medical terminology is best suited for conversations with
    a. the patient's family.
    b. other medical professionals.
    c. the patient.
    d. bystanders.

17. In your written report you could use which symbol to denote the patient's gender, if your patient is a female?
    a. ♀
    b. ♂
    c. μ
    d. ≠

18. The prefix *poly-* means
    a. porous.
    b. many.
    c. rare.
    d. red.

19. The term *meningitis* means
    a. inflammation of a peripheral nerve.
    b. inflammation of the heart.
    c. inflammation of the brain.
    d. inflammation of the meninges.

Scenario: You have responded to a call for a 76-year-old male complaining of chest pain immediately below his breastbone, difficulty breathing, and profuse sweating.

20. What term would you use to describe the location of his chest pain?

_____

_____

21. What medical terms would you use to describe his other symptoms?

_____

_____

Need to Know

The following represent the Key Objectives of Chapter 6:

1. *Outline the components of a medical term.*

   The need to understand medical terminology and abbreviated medical terms becomes glaringly evident as soon as the paramedic is exposed to a patient's medical record. For paramedics to become proficient in the use of medical terminology, they must have a basic grasp of the methods used in the construction of these terms. The paramedic's ability to identify, understand, and utilize *root words, prefixes,* and *suffixes* will allow for proficient written communication with other medical professionals.

2. *List common medical terms used in the EMS profession.*

   The use and misuse of abbreviated medical terms in the medical community can be problematic. Paramedics are no exception to this phenomenon. It is imperative that paramedics only use medical terms and abbreviations that they are familiar with and that are approved for use by their employer and the local or state EMS regulating agency. If there is any doubt as to the use of a medical term or abbreviation, the paramedic should spell out the word in its entirety. Keep in mind that spelling counts. If you are not a good speller, have a medical dictionary or an electronic spell-checker with you to check the words that you are unsure of.

3. *Avoid the use of abbreviations when documenting medication orders and the administration of medications on a prehospital care report.*

   Misuse of medical abbreviations, especially in the area of medication administration, have led to disastrous results. Table 6-1 shows the abbreviations that the Joint Commission on the Accreditation of Healthcare Organizations (JCAHO)[1] states should *not* be used due to the frequency with which they have been responsible for errors (medication and other). Table 6-2 lists additional abbreviations, acronyms, and symbols for possible future inclusion in the official "do not use" list.

TABLE 6-1 **Abbreviations That Should *Not* Be Used**

Do Not Use	Potential Problem	Use Instead
U (Unit)	Mistaken for 0, the number 4, or cc	Write "unit."
IU (International Unit)	Mistaken for IV (intravenous) or the number 10	Write "International Unit."
Q.D., QD, q.d., qd (daily) Q.O.D., QOD, q.o.d., qod (every other day)	Mistaken for each other Period after the Q mistaken for I, and the O mistaken for I	Write "daily." Write "every other day."
Trailing zero (X.0 mg) Lack of leading zero (.X mg)	Decimal point is missed.	Write "X mg." Write "0.X mg."
MS MSO$_4$ and MgSO$_4$	Can mean morphine sulfate or magnesium sulfate Confused for one another	Write "morphine sulfate." Write "magnesium sulfate."

TABLE 6-2 Abbreviations, Acronyms, and Symbols to Avoid

Do Not Use	Potential Problem	Use Instead
> (greater than) < (less than)	Misinterpreted as the number 7 or the letter L Confused for one another	Write "greater than." Write "less than."
Abbreviations for drug names	Misinterpreted due to similar abbreviations for multiple drugs	Write drug name in full.
Apothecary units	Unfamiliar to many practitioners Confused with metric units	Use metric units.
@	Mistaken for the number 2	Write "at."
cc	Mistaken for U (units) when poorly written	Write "mL" or "milliliters."
µg	Mistaken for mg (milligrams) resulting in one thousand-fold overdose	Write "mcg" or "micrograms."

Need to Do

The following skills are explained and illustrated in a step-by-step manner, via skill sheets and/or Step-by-Steps in this text and on the accompanying DVD:

Skill Name	Skill Sheet Number and Location	Step-by-Step Number and Location
Documentation	64 – DVD	64

Connections

- Chapter 17, Documentation and Communication, in the textbook further explains why it is critically important to understand the spoken and written language of medicine and the medical terminology that goes along with it.
- It's important to own or have access to a medical dictionary (print or electronic). Many electronic dictionaries can be downloaded onto a PDA or a laptop computer.
- Link to the companion DVD for a chapter-based quiz, audio glossary, animations, games and exercises, and, when appropriate, skill sheets and skill Step-by-Steps.

Street Secrets

- **Spelling Counts!** You could be the best paramedic in the universe, but if you are unable to prove that fact in writing, you may find yourself in considerable trouble. If you are required to testify in court concerning your care and documentation and there are spelling errors on your patient care report, you become a much less credible witness. It is a good practice to have a medical dictionary and, if you are a poor speller in general, a standard dictionary readily accessible while composing your prehospital reports. There are also "misspeller's dictionaries" available for download onto a PDA.

The Drug Box

There are no specific drugs related to this chapter content.

Reference

1. "Patient Safety 'Do Not Use' List." Joint Commission on the Accreditation of Healthcare Organizations. Available online at www.jcaho.org (accessed October 21, 2006).

Answers

Are You Ready?

Word	Prefix	Root	Suffix	Definition
Diabetes		Diabetes = "increased urine output"		Increased urine output
Cholecystitis	Chole = "bile"	cyst = "bladder"	-itis = "inflammation"	Inflammation of the gall bladder
Amyotrophic	A = "without"	myo = "muscle"	-trophic = concerned with nourishment	Pertaining to muscular atrophy
Sclerosis		Sclerosis = "hardening"		To harden
Hyperlipidemia	Hyper = "excessive"	lipid = "fat"	-emia = "blood"	Increased lipids in the blood
Arteriosclerosis		Arterio = "artery"	-sclerosis = "to harden"	Hardening of arteries
Cardiomyopathy	Cardio = "heart"	myo = "muscle"	-pathy = "disease"	Disease of the heart muscle
Myocardial	Myo = "muscle"	cardial = "heart"		Concerning the myocardium (heart muscle)
Anemia	An = "not"	emia = "blood"		A reduction in the number of red blood cells
Cerebrovascular	Cerebro = refers to the brain	vascular = "blood vessel"		Referring to the blood vessels of the brain
Hemiparesis	Hemi = "half"	paresis = "paralysis"		Paralysis affecting only one side of the body
Dysarthria	Dys = "difficult"	arthria = "to utter distinctly"		Difficult and defective speech
Dysphasia	Dys = "difficult"	phasia = "to eat"		Inability to or difficulty swallowing

Active Learning

1.

Root Word	Meaning
Append/o, appendic/o	Appendix
Arthr/o	Joint
Derm/o	Skin
Muc/o	Mucus
Hydr/o	Water
Neur/o	Nerve
Hemat/o	Blood
Thromb/o	Blood clot
Path/o	Disease

2.

Term	Meaning
Cardi/o/megaly	Enlargement of the heart
Acr/o/megaly	Enlargement of the extremities
Macro/glossia	Large tongue
Hist/o/logy	The study of tissue
Arthr/itis	Inflammation of the joints
Peri/card/itis	Inflammation around the heart
Splen/o/megaly	Enlargement of the spleen
A/leuk/o/cyto/sis	Absence of white blood cells
Thorac/o/centesis	Withdrawing fluid from the thorax or chest
Peri/cardi/o/centesis	Withdrawing fluid from around the heart
Pulmon/ary	Relating to the lungs
Gastr/ectomy	Removal of the stomach
Appendic/itis	Inflammation of the appendix
Dermat/o/logy	The study of the skin
Neur/itis	Inflammation of the nerves
Cardi/ac	Pertaining to the heart
Supra/clavicul/ar	Above the clavicles
Dys/men/orrhea	Painful menses

Hem/o/lysis	Destruction of the blood
Oste/o/malacia	Softening of the bones
Maxill/ary	Relating to the upper jaw
Encepha/lo/myel/itis	Inflammation of the brain and spinal cord
Gastr/o/enter/o/logy	The study of the stomach and small intestine
Laryng/o/scope	Instrument used to view the larynx
Laryng/ectomy	Removal of the larynx
Hemat/oma	A mass (or tumor) of blood that is usually partially clotted
Retro/gastric	Relating to something behind the stomach
Retro/periton/eal	Behind the peritoneum
Myel/oid	Like the marrow, or spinal cord
Gastr/itis	Inflammation of the stomach
Pneum/o/thorax	Accumulation of air in the pleural cavity
Dys/phag/ia	Difficulty swallowing
Mitral stenosis	Narrowing of the mitral valve
Hepat/itis	Inflammation of the liver
Aden/ectomy	Surgical removal of a gland
Dermat/itis	Inflammation of the skin
Lapar/o/tomy	Incision into the loin or abdomen
Intra/osse/o/us	Within the bone
Aerot/itis media	Inflammation of the middle ear by air pressure changes
Micro/scope	Instrument for viewing small objects
An/oxia	Without oxygen

3.

Meaning	Term
Inflammation of the adenoids	Adenoid/itis
Immature cell from which a white blood cell develops	Leuk/o/cyt/o/blast
Accumulation of blood in the pleural cavity	Hemo/thorax
Excessive carbon dioxide	Hyper/capn/ia
Inflammation of the liver	Hepa/titis
Relating to the ribs	Cost/al
Condition of having a split mind	Schiz/o/phrenia

Inflammation around the heart	Peri/card/itis
Surgical removal of an embolus	Embol/ectomy
Bacteria that appear blue	Cyan/o/bacteria
Condition of an overproductive thyroid gland	Hyper/thyroid/ism
Double vision	Dipl/opia
Difficulty speaking	Dys/phasia
A medication capable of relieving pain	An/alges/ic
Relating to fat, or like fat	Adip/ose
To take water away from	De/hydr/ate
Slow heart rate	Brady/cardia
Relating to something under the liver	Sub/hepatic
Inflammation of the brain	Encephal/itis
Bones in the hand after the carpals	Meta/carpals
Normal, or good, breathing	Eu/pnea
Red blood cell	Erythr/o/cyte
Cancerous tumor	Carcin/oma
Relating to mucus, or a mucous membrane	Mucous
Visual examination of the larynx	Laryng/o/scopy
A bluish discoloration of the skin	Cyan/o/sis
Fast respiratory rate	Tachy/pnea
The process of recording carbon dioxide measurements	Capn/o/graphy
Inflammation of the colon	Col/itis
Under the sternum	Sub/sternal
Surgical removal of the uterus	Hyster/ectomy
Fever producing	Pyro/genic
Loss of, or without speech	A/phasia
Nasal discharge, or flow	Rhino/rrhea
The suturing of a severed nerve	Neur/o/rrhaphy
Agent that kills fungi	Anti/fungal
Incision into the skull	Crani/o/tomy
Surgical removal of the gall bladder	Cholecyst/ectomy
Condition of being without feeling	An/esthes/ia
Capable of dissolving or digesting mucus	Muc/o/lytic
Surgical repair of the larynx	Laryng/o/plasty

You Are There: Reality-Based Cases

1. The patient is critically ill and needs rapid intervention and transport to a medical facility that is capable of appropriately treating a patient with preeclampsia. Additional information that would be beneficial at this point would be:
   - Did the patient experience a seizure?
   - Does the patient have a patent airway?
   - Is the patient breathing adequately?
   - Does the patient present with adequate perfusion?
   - Is the patient in a position that permits the protection of her airway and the optimum perfusion to the fetus?
   - What is the patient's past medical history, what medications does the patient take, and does the patient have any allergies to medications?
   - What is the patient's gynecological history (number of pregnancies, number of live births, last menstrual period, due date, prenatal care, anticipated complications, etc.)?

2. The best place to start when you are not sure why a patient has had a dramatic change in his or her level of consciousness is back at the beginning. Ensure that the patient has no threats to the airway, breathing, and circulation. If there is no problem with the ABCs, take a look at the medical history and the medications that the patient takes. If the patient has a history of a condition such as diabetes, you can test to see if the patient is hypoglycemic or hyperglycemic. If you are unable to gather a medical history on the patient but he or she has a list of medications that includes insulin or some sort of opiate, you then have more possibilities that you can rule out. Remember to consider the possibility of overdose of medications or noncompliance with prescribed medications.

   If the cause(s) of the patient's change in status cannot be determined after assessing the ABCs and reviewing the patient's medical and medication history, the use of mnemonics such as AEIOUTIPS (**a**lcohol, **e**pilepsy, **i**nsulin, **o**verdose, **u**nderdose, **t**rauma, **i**nfection, **p**sychoses, **s**epsis) are useful when faced with a patient experiencing an altered level of consciousness.

   When all else fails, continue to address the needs of the patient as far as the ABCs are concerned, treat the patient for any conditions within the bounds of your policies and protocols, and rethink the steps that were taken in treating the patient to determine if there is anything out of the ordinary.

3. Ventilatory support was maintained, and the patient was immediately given 2 mg of IV Narcan, which yielded minimal change in her status. Therefore, 2 additional milligrams of Narcan were administered, and in less than a minute the patient became responsive and shortly after was alert and oriented.

Test Yourself

1. c

   Stalsis = contraction, constriction. Peristalsis, for example, is the coordinated contraction of smooth muscle that moves food through the digestive system and urine through the ureters. Stasis = stopping, constant; stenosis = narrowing; sclerosis = hardening.

2. The term *adduction* means to move toward (usually the center of the body).

   This is the opposite of the term *abduction,* which means to move away from. These terms are commonly confused. A way to remember the difference is that if a person is abducted, he or she is taken away from somewhere.

3. c

   Delirium tremens is experienced by some chronically malnourished alcohol-addicted persons during alcohol withdrawal.

4. *Leukocyte* means "white blood cell." The term leukocyte consists of the root word *cyte* (meaning "cell") and the prefix *leuko-* (meaning "white").

5. c

   The suffix *-esthesia* means "sensation" and is often combined with the prefix *an-* meaning "without," which describes the medications and procedures used to prevent a patient from feeling pain.

6. Difficulty swallowing

   Phagia means swallowing. The prefix *dys-* means difficulty and is also used in the terms dyspnea (difficulty breathing), dysuria (difficult urination), and dysphasia (difficulty speaking).

7. The abbreviation *b.i.d.* means "twice a day."

   The abbreviation *b.i.d.* is an abbreviation of the Latin term *bis in die,* which means "twice a day." This abbreviation is found on medication containers and on medication orders that you might find in a patient's chart (skilled care facility patients, interfacility transfers). You may also see it written on discharge instructions from a patient's previous hospital visit or on an unfilled prescription found at the scene.

8. b

   The prefix *peri-* means "around or surrounding"; the umbilicus is commonly known as the belly button.

9. Most patients should be interviewed using common terms, rather than medical terms. The rare exception would be when you have another medical professional as your patient. This patient may not understand what you mean by "radiate" in this context. Also, by asking her about a specific location (left arm), the question is leading the patient. This may cause her to "feel" pain that is not really present.

   A better way to determine if the pain radiates anywhere would be to ask, "Do you feel the pain anywhere besides your chest?"

10. False

    Although memorization is an important tool in learning medical terminology, the best way to learn it is to use it often.

11. You should tell the patient he may have internal bleeding around his lungs.

    The term *hemothorax* is made of the word *hemo* meaning "blood" and *thorax* meaning "chest." The term specifically refers to blood in the pleural cavity, usually between the two pleura, and can be caused by chest trauma. Hemothorax is a life-threatening emergency.

12. d

    Arteriosclerosis is a medical term for the narrowing and hardening of the arteries; this is a common risk factor for myocardial infarction (MI).

13. *Centesis* means "puncture."

    The term is usually used when referring to withdrawing fluid, such as in pericardial centesis, where excess fluid is withdrawn from the pericardial sac.

14. b

    The term *motor vehicle collision* is starting to replace the term *motor vehicle accident.* The reason behind this change is that most collisions are preventable and not merely accidents.

15. True

    The prefix *nulli-* means "none or never," and the root word *gravida* means "pregnant."

16. b

    Medical terminology is best suited for conversations among medical professionals since it allows precision.

Becaue patients, bystanders and first responders may or may not know what these terms mean or may use them improperly, you should always ensure that you utilize terms understood by those you are speaking with.

17. a

    ♀ represents female; ♂ represents male; µ can represent micrograms, but it is *no longer used;* ≠ represents "not equal to."

18. b

    Poly- means "many or excess" and is often combined with terms describing bodily functions or structures.

19. d

    Meningitis is inflammation of the meninges (the lining of the brain and the spinal cord). Some forms of meningitis are contagious and therefore pose a risk to the paramedic.

20. Substernal

    Pain underneath the breastbone would be described as substernal (*sub* = "under," *sternum* = "breastbone"). *Episternal* means "upon the breastbone," *suprasternal* means "above the breastbone," and *circumferential* means "encircling."

21. Dyspneic and diaphoretic

    Dyspnea is the medical term for difficulty (dys-) breathing (-pnea); *diaphoretic* (from the Latin *diaphoreticus* meaning "promoting perspiration") is the medical term for "sweaty."

chapter 7

Anatomy Overview

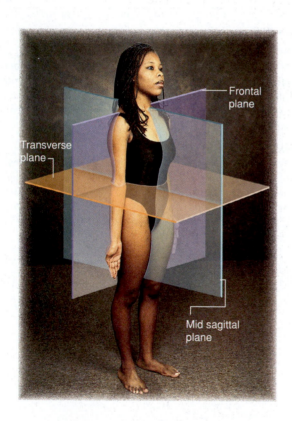

Frontal plane

Transverse plane

Mid sagittal plane

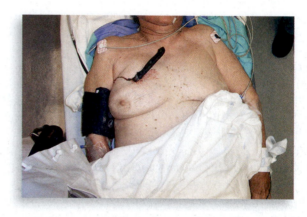

brother, saw what had happened and ran to her grandmother's aid. Colin, Marge's grandson, ran into the house and called 9-1-1.

1. Describe the location of the knife using anatomical terms.

   _____

   _____

   _____

2. What internal structures are likely to be involved based upon the photograph above?

   _____

   _____

   _____

3. After scene safety and body substance isolation (BSI), what are your priorities in caring for this patient?

   _____

   _____

   _____

Are You Ready?

Marge Robinson was cutting up a watermelon for her grandchildren on a warm summer day when she heard Carlie, her youngest granddaughter, scream at the top of her lungs from the backyard. Marge ran out the back door of the kitchen to see what was wrong, and as she scampered down the back steps, she lost her balance and fell forward. She reached out with her hands to break her fall, but landed on the knife that she had been carrying. She felt a sharp pain in her chest as she fell, and when she tried to get up from the ground, she noticed that the knife was stuck in her chest. Carlie, who had been sprayed with the hose by her

Active Learning

1. Describe anatomical position.

_____

_____

_____

2. In Figure 7-1, label A points to the (a) _____
surface of the body and label B points to the
(b) _____ surface of the body. Another
name for (a) is (c) _____, and another
name for (b) is (d) _____.

3. Label the planes of the body shown in Figure 7-2.

  a. _____

  b. _____

  c. _____

4. The spine is (a) _____ to the kidney, and
the skull is (b) _____ to the brain. The
nose is (c) _____ to the mouth, and
the xiphoid process is (d) _____ to the
sternum.

5. Identify the structures of the anterior chest and
abdominal wall, as shown in Figure 7-3.

  a. _____

  b. _____

  c. _____

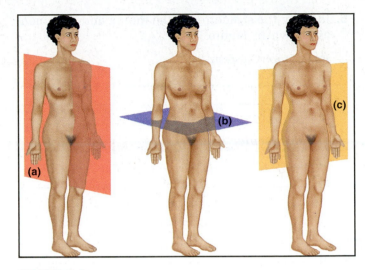

FIGURE 7-2

  d. _____

  e. _____

  f. _____

  g. _____

  h. _____

  i. _____

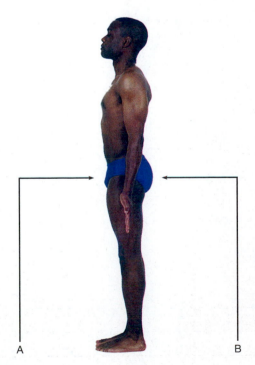

FIGURE 7-1

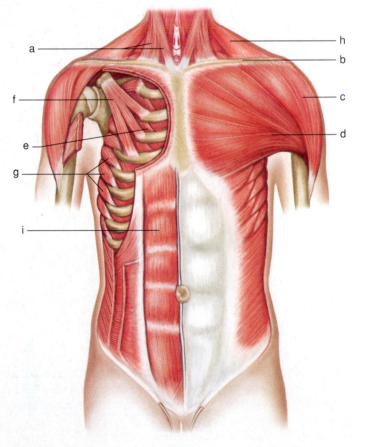

FIGURE 7-3

6. Identify the structures of the thorax and abdomen, as shown in Figure 7-4.

Pulmonary system

a. _____

b. _____

c. _____

Cardiovascular system

d. _____

e. _____

f. _____

g. _____

h. _____

i. _____

Genitourinary system

j. _____

k. _____

l. _____

m. _____

n. _____

o. _____

p. _____

q. _____

r. _____

s. _____

Male reproductive system

t. _____

u. _____

v. _____

w. _____

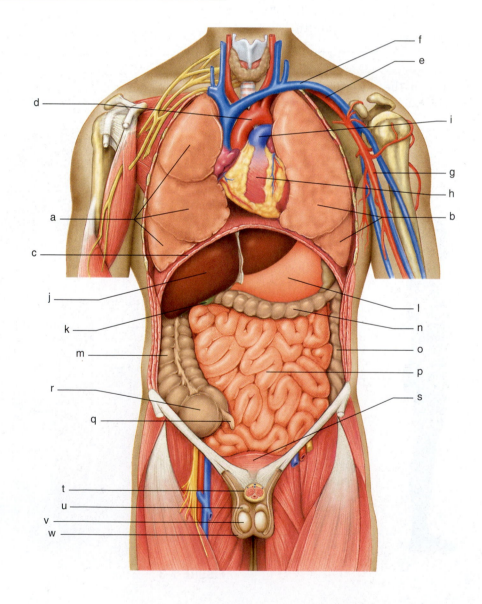

FIGURE 7-4

7. Identify the structures of the torso, as shown in Figure 7-5.

Cardiovascular system

a. _____

b. _____

c. _____

d. _____

e. _____

f. _____

g. _____

h. _____

i. _____

j. _____

Genitourinary system

k. _____

l. _____

m. _____

n. _____

o. _____

Female reproductive system

p. _____

q. _____

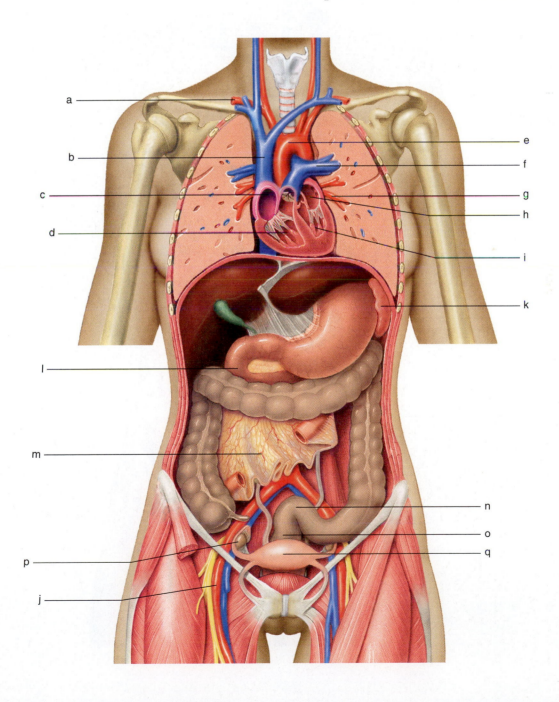

FIGURE 7-5

8. Identify the deeper structures of the torso, as shown in Figure 7-6.

Pulmonary system

a. _____

b. _____

c. _____

Cardiovascular system

d. _____

e. _____

Genitourinary system

f. _____

g. _____

h. _____

i. _____

j. _____

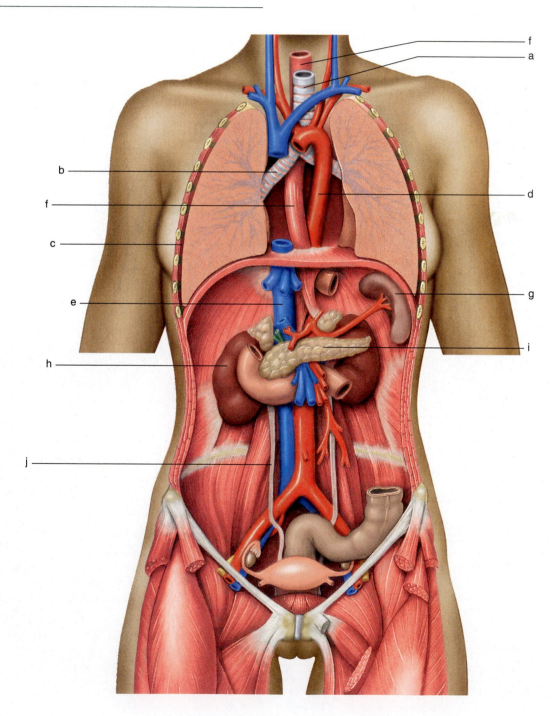

FIGURE 7-6

9. Identify the major bones of the skeleton, as shown in Figure 7-7.

a. _____

b. _____

c. _____

d. _____

e. _____

f. _____

g. _____

h. _____

i. _____

j. _____

k. _____

l. _____

m. _____

n. _____

o. _____

p. _____

q. _____

r. _____

s. _____

t. _____

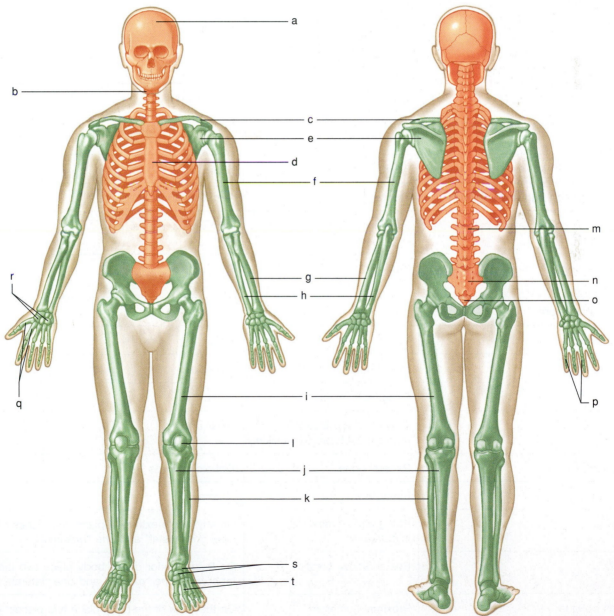

FIGURE 7-7

10. Referring again to Figure 7-7, the bones shown in orange make up the (a) _____ skeleton, and the bones shown in green make up the (b) _____ skeleton.

11. **The Anatomy Game**

    This game can be played in a group or with one partner. The player or team with all the correct answers in the shortest amount of time wins. The rules of the game are as follows:

    a. Decide who will be the "anatomical manikin" for this exercise. The manikin can also participate in locating structures.

    b. Take a roll of tape and write down the name of each of the body structures listed in the following table.

    c. Place the labeled tape segments on the manikin in the appropriate location. Record the time it takes to find and label all structures.

    d. When the other player or group is finished, you will check them for accuracy, and they will check you. Record any missed items. Add 3 seconds to the overall time for each mistake you find.

    e. Use your textbook and other resources to resolve any disputes.

    f. In the end, the player or team with the shortest time wins. If you are completing this exercise alone, when you have completed labeling the manikin, check yourself using a textbook or other resource.

Find the following structures:

1st lumbar vertebra	Femur	Proximal radius
2nd intercostal space, midclavicle line on right side	Fibula	Rectus abdominus
2nd metatarsal on left side of body	Frenulum	Spleen
3rd metacarpal on right side of body	Frontal bone	Temporal bone
5th intercostal space, lateral-axillary line on right side	Inferior scapula	Temporomandibular joint
5th intercostal space, midaxillary line on right side	Kidney	Thymus
7th cervical vertebra	Liver	Thyroid
Angle of Louis	Mandible	Tibia
Ascending colon	Manubrium	Trapezius
Bicep	Occiput	Tricep
Brachial artery	Ovaries (show location regardless of sex of manikin)	Ulnar artery
Carotid artery	Parietal bone	Xiphoid process
Distal clavicle	Pinnae	Zygoma
Distal ulna	PMI (point of maximal impulse)	On any single extremity place two pieces of tape: label one "distal" and one "proximal."
Ethmoid	Posterior iliac crest	On the posterior of the body place two pieces of tape: label one "*medial*" and one "lateral."
Externus oblique	Proximal humerus	On the trunk of the body place two pieces of tape: label one "dorsal" and one "ventral."

You Are There: Reality-Based Cases

Case 1

You and your partner just finished cleaning your ambulance after caring for a patient you picked up at the Senior Center with a case of uncontrollable diarrhea. It has taken the two of you the better part of 2 hours to clean and sterilize your equipment, the back of your ambulance, and yourselves. Even after all your efforts, you are still not sure if the odor remains in the ambulance, as it seems to have taken up permanent residence in your nose and in your brain.

Just as you toss out the last of the soiled cleaning supplies, your dispatcher calls your unit number and asks if you are ready to clear for another call. Hesitantly, and somewhat reluctantly, you advise dispatch that you are ready to go.

"Medic 72, respond code II for a painful rash at the Senior Center, 1203 W. 164th Ave. Cross street is Fairmont." You and your partner look at each other in horror because you are going back to the same spot where you picked up your last patient.

When you arrive at the Senior Center, one of the staff members meets you and asks you to follow her. As you walk down that familiar hallway, the staff member tells you that she called because one of the volunteers from the college has a painful rash on her buttocks.

You are led to a small locker room, where you are introduced to the patient. She is standing there with a towel wrapped around her waist. As you approach, she says that she is sorry to bother you, but she doesn't know what else to do. She says that the rash on her buttocks is getting worse, and the pain is becoming unbearable.

On examination, you find a rash that extends from the left lateral border of the spine at the superior border of the sacrum to the level of the third or fourth lumbar vertebra and then laterally and inferiorly, with the superior border of the rash passing along the superior border of the ischium and the area of the femoral head. The rash then appears to extend around to the anterior surface of the body.

The patient states that she has been really stressed out about finals at school and she has taken a second job to make ends meet. She begins to cry. You cover the patient with her towel and reassure her. She further explains that the rash has developed over the past 2–3 days and is isolated to one side of her body. The rash appears to be clusters of vesicles with an erythematous base that follow a path from the spine to the front of the body.

1. What is your general impression of this patient?

   _____

   _____

2. What is your greatest concern at this time?

   _____

   _____

3. What questions would you ask the patient in order to help you determine the cause of the rash?

   _____

   _____

4. What do you think is wrong with this patient?

   _____

   _____

Test Yourself

1. Health-care workers should describe body locations as if the patient were in the _____ position.
   a. Fowler's
   b. lateral recumbent
   c. supine
   d. anatomical

2. A head-injured patient reports that she is unable to smell. She may have damaged her _____ cranial nerve.

3. While listening to an intubated patient's lung sounds, you note that there is no air going into the left lung. This could indicate that
   a. the tube has moved past the esophagus and into the right main-stem bronchus.
   b. the tube has been misplaced into the secondary bronchi superior to the carina.
   c. the tube has been placed superior to the carina and is only inflating one lung.
   d. the tube has moved past the carina and into the right main-stem bronchus.

4. The substance that allows the alveoli to remain open is called _____.

5. The outermost portion of the eye is called the _____.

6. The midsagittal plane
   a. divides the upper torso from the lower extremities.
   b. runs parallel to the transverse plane on the body.
   c. divides the body midline into equal right and left halves.
   d. runs perpendicular to the midline of the body.

7. The property of _____ allows the heart to contract spontaneously without external stimulus.

8. What is the function of the parotid, submandibular, and sublingual glands?

   _____

   _____

9. The tunica intima controls the size of the opening in a blood vessel.

   True

   False

10. A patient lying face up on an ambulance gurney would be in the _____ position.

11. Partially digested food that empties into the small intestine is called

    a. peristalsis.

    b. bile.

    c. duodenum.

    d. chyme.

12. A sagittal plane is

    a. a dividing line running parallel to the midsagittal plane.

    b. a dividing line crossing the midsagittal plane at a 90-degree angle.

    c. a line that divides the body into equal right and left halves.

    d. a plane used to divide the body into top and bottom pieces.

13. What organs could be injured if a patient was struck in the right upper quadrant with a bat?

    _____

    _____

14. The layer of the meninges that lies closest to the brain and spinal cord is the _____.

15. A patient is lying supine with her arm adducted. She is unable to extend her arm. Which of the following describes the patient's position?

    a. She is lying face down, holding her arm close to her body, and is unable to bend her arm.

    b. She is lying face up, holding her arm close to her body, and is unable to straighten her arm.

    c. She is lying face down, holding her arm away from her body, and is unable to straighten her arm.

    d. She is lying face up, holding her arm away from her body, and is unable to bend her arm.

16. Movement of a patient's arm away from the patient's body is described as

    a. adduction.

    b. pronation.

    c. abduction.

    d. flexion.

17. On a male patient, the nipple usually corresponds to the fourth intercostal space.

    True

    False

18. Which of the following best describes a stab wound to a patient's right side, below his armpit, at the level of his nipples?

    a. The wound is lateral to the sternum and superior to the axilla.

    b. The wound is inferior to the right axilla and at the level of the fourth intercostal space.

    c. The wound is proximal to the right axilla and located in the right lower quadrant.

    d. The wound is superior to the sternum and located midaxillary.

Scenario: A patient fractured his right forearm when he fell from his bike. He has associated abrasions on his right palm and elbow.

19. Which best describes the location of the patient's elbow abrasions?

    a. The abrasions are distal to the shoulder.

    b. The abrasions are proximal to the shoulder.

    c. The abrasions are distal to the hand.

    d. The abrasions are superior to the shoulder.

20. The abrasions on the palm can be described as

    a. ventral.

    b. posterior.

    c. craniad.

    d. dorsal.

Need to Know

The following represent the Key Objectives of Chapter 7:

1. *Describe the location and function of anatomical structures on both the surface and inside of the body.*

   Successful paramedics have the ability to quickly and accurately assess and describe the pertinent positive and negative findings based on a solid foundation of normal and abnormal anatomy presentations. For example, paramedics with a solid understanding of the anatomical areas where they can auscultate the lung fields in a manner that will avoid large bony structures (e.g., the scapula and vertebral column) can quickly, accurately, and effectively assess and interpret a patient's lung sounds—and therefore provide appropriate patient care. In addition, paramedics with a solid grasp of anatomy will be able to deductively reason what internal structures are likely involved based on the mechanism of injury and injury patterns.

The study of anatomy constantly reminds us that the cells, tissues, and organs of the body are all part of one organism that depends upon other cells, tissues, and organs to survive. The cardiopulmonary system is an excellent example of this fact. Both of the main organs of the cardiopulmonary system (the heart and the lungs) share the purpose of providing nourishment to and removing waste products from the cells and tissues of the body. However, the heart and lungs (the cardiopulmonary system) would not be able to survive if it were not for the help of the vascular system.

Another example of how the different components of the body are dependent upon each other is the musculoskeletal system. One without the other would lead to a nonfunctioning system. The bones make up the frame of the body, whereas muscles, tendons, and ligaments hold the skeleton together and, with the help of the different types of joints, allow for movement and function. This holds true for all the body systems. If it were not for the ability of all the systems of the body to work together, the human organism would fail.

Need to Do

There are no psychomotor skills that directly support this chapter content.

Connections

- Mastery of the following chapters in the textbook is significantly dependent upon anatomical knowledge:

  Chapter 20, Head, Face, and Neck Trauma

  Chapter 21, Thoracic Trauma

  Chapter 22, Abdominal Trauma

  Chapter 23, Spinal Trauma

  Chapter 24, Skeletal Trauma

  Chapter 25, Soft Tissue and Muscle Trauma

  Chapter 26, Burn Trauma

- Link to the companion DVD for a chapter-based quiz, audio glossary, animations, games and exercises, and, when appropriate, skill sheets and skill Step-by-Steps.

Street Secrets

- **Pronunciations** During the process of learning or refreshing your knowledge of anatomical terms, make sure that you are pronouncing the terms correctly. Mispronunciation of anatomical terms is unprofessional and can lead to confusion and even mismanagement of patients. While mastering anatomy and anatomical terms, have a medical dictionary available and look up the phonetic pronunciation of any terms that you are not certain how to pronounce.

- **Anatomical Position** Remember that when you describe features of a patient using anatomical terminology, the description that you give needs to be related to the *patient's* anatomical position, not your perspective of anatomical position as you face the patient.

- **Precision** Be as precise with your anatomical description as possible. Attempt to give the location of something in anatomical position in both the vertical (sagittal or coronal/frontal) and the horizontal (transverse) planes. For example, instead of merely describing something using the sagittal plane ("Patient has a gunshot wound to his midclavicular line"), help to pinpoint the location by adding a transverse location ("Patient has a gunshot wound to his midclavicular line at the fourth intercostal space").

The Drug Box

There are no specific drugs related to this chapter content.

Reference

1. J. Tintinalli, G. Kelen, and J. Stapczynski, *Emergency Medicine: A Comprehensive Study Guide,* 6th ed. New York: McGraw-Hill, 2004, p. 1522

Answers

Are You Ready?

1. The knife is located in the midclavicular line at the level of the fifth intercostal space. The knife is impaled at a very shallow angle, with a pathway that extends from the midclavicular line laterally, with no exit wound noted.

2. Because of the very shallow angle that the knife takes and the lateral trajectory of the blade, the damage may be isolated to the subcutaneous tissue. However, it is best to err on the side of caution and assume that the right lung has been punctured.

3. Airway, breathing, circulation, disability, exposure. Treatments other than resolving any immediate life threats should be performed en route to a receiving facility that is capable of treating the patient's injury (a trauma center if possible).

Active Learning

1. The anatomical position is when the subject is standing erect (upright) with eyes facing forward, arms hanging down at the sides, and palms of the hands facing forward.

2. a. anterior or ventral; b. dorsal or posterior; c. ventral or anterior (whichever term was not used in answer b); d. posterior or dorsal (whichever term was not used in answer a)

3. a. sagittal or median plane; b. transverse or horizontal plane; c. frontal or coronal plane

4. a. medial; b. lateral; c. superior; d. inferior

5. a. sternocleidomastoid muscle; b. clavicle; c. deltoid; d. pectoralis major; e. external intercostal; f. pectoralis minor; g. serratus anterior; h. trapezius; i. rectus abdominus

6. **Pulmonary system:** a. right lung; b. left lung; c. diaphragm. **Cardiovascular system:** d. aortic arch; e. left subclavian artery; f. left subclavian vein; g. brachial artery; h. heart; i. pulmonary trunk. **Genitourinary system:** j. liver; k. gall bladder; l. stomach; m. ascending colon; n. transverse colon; o. descending colon; p. small intestine; q. appendix; r. cecum; s. urinary bladder. **Male reproductive system:** t. penis; u. epididymis; v. testis; w. scrotum.

7. **Cardiovascular system:** a. right subclavian artery; b. superior vena cava; c. right atrium; d. right ventricle; e. aortic arch; f. pulmonary artery; g. pulmonary vein; h. left atrium; i. left ventricle; j. femoral artery. **Genitourinary system:** k. spleen; l. duodenum; m. mesentery; n. sigmoid colon; o. rectum. **Female reproductive system:** p. ovary; q. uterus.

8. **Pulmonary system:** a. trachea; b. right bronchus; c. pleural cavity. **Cardiovascular system:** d. descending aorta; e. inferior vena cava. **Genitourinary system:** f. esophagus; g. spleen; h. right kidney; i. pancreas; j. ureter.

9. a. cranium; b. hyoid; c. clavicle; d. sternum; e. scapula; f. humerus; g. radius; h. ulna; i. femur; j. tibia; k. fibula; l. patella; m. vertebral column; n. sacrum; o. coccyx; p. phalanges; q. metacarpals; r. carpals; s. tarsals; t. metatarsals.

10. a. axial; b. appendicular

You Are There: Reality-Based Cases

Case 1

1. A stable patient with an erythematous vesicular rash

2. Since the patient's condition doesn't appear to be life-threatening, and she has a patent airway, unlabored breathing, and adequate perfusion, one of your greatest concerns should be isolating the patient and preventing the spread of her illness to others, including yourself.

3. • Has the patient ever had a rash similar to this in the past? If the patient has had a similar rash in the past, was she seen by a physician and what did the physician say that it was? Was it communicable, and how did he or she treat the rash?
   • Has the patient had chicken pox (varicella-zoster virus)?
   • Is the patient experiencing any pain associated with the rash?
   • Has the patient ever had an allergic skin reaction to anything (e.g., latex or laundry detergents)?
   • Does the patient have any sexually transmitted diseases?

4. There are many possibilities as to the source of the rash. However, if the patient states that she did have chicken pox as a child, she has no allergies to anything, and she has no sexually transmitted diseases, the fact that she has been under a considerable amount of stress, that the rash appears to follow a nerve pathway (dermatome) that is isolated to one part of her body, and that the rash is typical of herpes zoster, it is likely that she is suffering from a form of herpes zoster referred to as "shingles."[1]

Test Yourself

1. d

   To ensure consistency, health-care professionals should describe all body locations relative to their anatomical positions. This is true whether the patient is lying down or sitting.

2. Olfactory

   An injury to the olfactory nerve frequently affects the sense of smell.

3. d

   The trachea divides at the carina into the right and left main-stem bronchi, which then divide into secondary bronchi. Further subdivisions form respiratory bronchioles, alveolar ducts, and alveolar sacs. The tube has moved past the carina inferiorly into the right main-stem bronchus. As a result, the left lung is not being oxygenated and lung sounds will not be heard or will be diminished.

4. Surfactant

   The alveoli remain open because of a substance called surfactant that decreases the surface tension of the alveoli.

5. Cornea

   The outermost portion of the eye is the cornea. Behind the cornea is the fluid-filled anterior chamber. The colored part of the eye is the iris; its central opening is the pupil, which is the anterior limit of the posterior chamber. Moving posteriorly, the lens, which focuses images and light onto the retina, is next.

6. c

   The midsagittal plane passes through the midline of the body and divides it into equal left and right halves.

7. Automaticity

   The cardiac musculature is specially modified so that the heart is able to contract spontaneously without an external stimulus. This property, called automaticity, then permits the heart to generate its own electrical impulse.

8. They lubricate food and release digestive secretions.

   Three types of salivary glands (parotid, submandibular, and sublingual) lubricate the food and release digestive secretions into the oral cavity. The parotid glands are located at the base of each ear. The submandibular glands are located on each side of and beneath the lower jaw. The sublingual glands are located in the mucus membrane on the floor of the mouth beneath the tongue.

9. False

   Blood vessels are made up of three layers surrounding a lumen which is the opening of the vessels. They include the tunica intima (the innermost layer), the tunica media (the middle muscular level, which controls the size of the lumen), and the tunica adventitia (the outermost layer, which defines the maximum lumen size when the muscles relax).

10. Supine

    Supine indicates that the patient is lying horizontally with the face upward; prone describes a patient lying horizontally and with the face downward. Lateral recumbent indicates that the person is lying on his or her side, and the reverse Trendelenburg position places the patient supine with the head of the bed elevated 45 degrees.

11. d

    Partially digested food (called chyme once it is ejected from the stomach) next enters into the small intestine. Peristalsis is the rhythmic movement of the muscles of the digestive system that continues to propel the chyme through the body for processing. The duodenum is the most proximal part of the small intestine followed by the jejunum and then the ileum. The common bile duct is a conduit for digestive secretions from the liver and pancreas, and the duct empties into the duodenum. The liver is located in the right upper quadrant of the abdomen and secretes bile to digest fats. It also detoxifies many substances.

12. a

    The body can be described by using imaginary lines, called planes, to slice through it. The midsagittal plane passes through the midline of the body and divides it into equal left and right halves. A sagittal plane is any dividing line that runs parallel to the midsagittal plane.

13. The liver, gall bladder, pancreas, duodenum, colon, and right kidney

    The right upper quadrant (RUQ) contains the liver, gall bladder, head of the pancreas, part of the duodenum, right kidney, and part of the colon.

14. Pia mater

    Three layers of meninges surround the brain and spinal cord. The pia mater adheres closely to the brain and spinal cord. The arachnoid membrane is the second layer of the meninges and has a spiderweb-like appearance. The subarachnoid space lies between these two layers and contains the cerebrospinal fluid. The outer layer of the meninges is thick and fibrous and is called the dura mater.

15. b

    Supine means lying horizontal with the face upward, and adduction is a movement toward the body. Flexion is the act of bending, and extension is the act of straightening.

16. c

    Abduction is a movement away from the body, and adduction is a movement toward the body. Flexion is the act of bending, and pronation is the act of rotating the arm so that the palm of the hand is facing downward.

17. True

    On a male patient, the nipples are a good reference point for determining where a thoracic injury is located and what organs may have been affected by thoracic trauma.

18. b

    Inferior means toward the feet, and a stab wound at the nipple level on a male will usually lie at or near the fourth intercostal space. This wound is below the axilla; therefore it is not superior.

19. a

    An abrasion on the elbow is distal to the shoulder. In this instance, when comparing that same abrasion to the hand, it would be described as proximal.

20. a

    In the anatomical position, the palms face forward. Therefore, an abrasion on a patient's palm would be located ventrally.

chapter 8

Physiology Overview

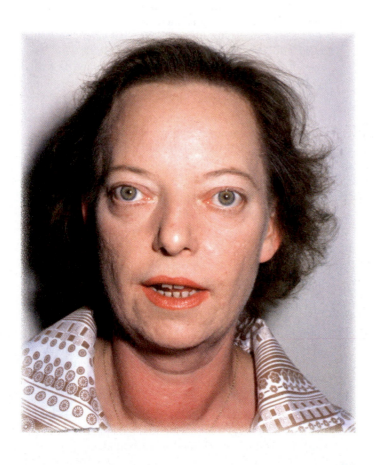

the patient, what is your general impression of the patient?

_____

_____

_____

2. Do you agree with the police officers' impression that the patient is under the influence of crack cocaine?

_____

_____

_____

3. What are other possible causes for the patient's presentation?

_____

_____

_____

4. What signs or behaviors did the patient display that led you to your general impression?

_____

_____

_____

Are You Ready?

You are called to the local police station, where you are asked to evaluate a 42-year-old female who the police believe is under the influence of crack cocaine. You find the patient pacing inside a holding cell, appearing agitated and tachypneic. The patient's skin is hot to the touch, and her radial pulse is rapid. You note that she has a goiter on her neck and her eyes appear to be bulging.

1. Based on the information that you have received from the police and the limited information that you have obtained in your brief encounter with

Active Learning

Regulation and Maintenance

1. Referring to Figure 8-1, summarize the process of energy adenosine triphosphate (ATP) production, including glycolysis, the Krebs (citric acid) cycle, and electron transport. Include the components involved in each step, where the

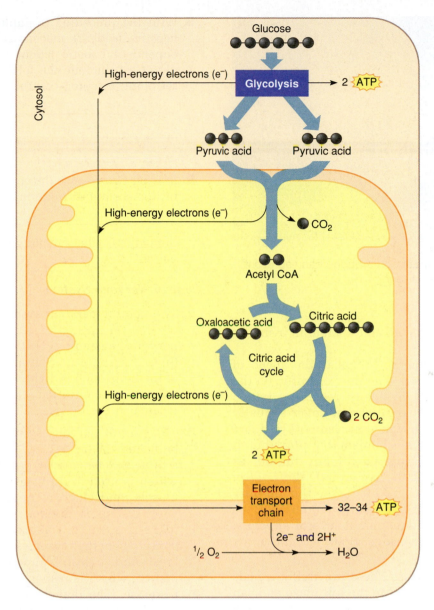

FIGURE 8-1   Cellular respiration occurs in three distinct, yet interconnected, series of reactions: glycolysis, the citric acid cycle (Krebs cycle), and the electron transport chain.

reactions take place, and the amount of energy yielded.

_____

_____

_____

2. Define _hypoxia_ and _hypoxemia_.

_____

_____

3. List three possible physiologic consequences of hypoxia and anaerobic metabolism.

_____

_____

_____

4. Feedback Mechanisms

The Oakland–San Francisco Bay Bridge is a major artery for motorists traveling into and out of San Francisco (Figure 8-2). The 4.5-mile-long bridge is used by over 270,000 vehicles per day. When traffic flows at a steady pace, the trip across the bridge takes a matter of minutes, but when there is an accident or heavy traffic, the travel time across the bridge can increase from minutes to hours.

The San Francisco Bay Bridge is, in a sense, a living being. The traffic on the bridge represents the blood that travels through the artery (the bridge). Like human arteries, the bridge needs feedback mechanisms to help maintain homeostasis (in this case, traffic flow). The feedback mechanisms for the bridge include all the components found in

FIGURE 8-2 Automobile traffic on a bridge can represent blood traveling through an artery.

a human feedback system and operate in a similar manner:

The *set point* for the bridge is the speed of vehicles traveling on it. The flow of traffic on the bridge is monitored by many *receptors* (video cameras and motion sensors) that cover virtually the entire span. If traffic flows smoothly, there are no homeostatic mechanisms at play, but if traffic flow is compromised for any reason (as identified by any of the receptors), the *control (integration) center* (in this case, the on-duty supervisor in the bridge control room) will be notified and will initiate one of several *effectors*. The effectors that the bridge supervisor has at his or her disposal are

- *The metering lights.* These are traffic signals that are located distal to the toll plaza and can be set at a variety of speeds depending on how slow traffic needs to be in order to resolve the problem in the artery. When there is no need to slow traffic, the metering lights can be turned off.

- *California Department of Transportation bridge crews.* The bridge has tow trucks immediately available to respond in order to clear disabled vehicles.

- *Emergency crews.* In the event of an emergency on the bridge, the bridge supervisor has direct access to the California Highway Patrol, Fire, and EMS agencies.

If the receptors measure changes in the flow of traffic from the set point, the control center activates effectors that return conditions toward normal. As the conditions on the bridge return to normal, the effectors are gradually shut down. This is an example of a *negative feedback mechanism*.

5. With the preceding example in mind, describe a negative feedback mechanism found in an insulin-dependent diabetic patient who took his insulin but didn't eat. Include the following in your example: set point, receptor, control center, and effectors.

_____

_____

_____

6. In what two ways is the endocrine system involved in homeostatic regulation?

_____

_____

_____

Central Nervous System

7. The central nervous system (CNS) is composed of the (a) _____, and the peripheral nervous system (PNS) is composed of the (b) _____. Sensations inside and outside of the body such as light, sound, temperature, and oxygen concentration are sensed by receptors located in the (c) _____.

8. The central nervous system is divided into two branches, the (a) _____, which is used to activate skeletal muscles, and the (b) _____, which is used to activate cardiac muscle, smooth muscle, and glands. The (c) _____ nervous system is divided into two branches, the (d) _____ branch, which helps the body conserve energy resources and maintain a state of "rest and digest," and the (e) _____ branch, which is responsible for the fight-or-flight response. The branch of the autonomic nervous system that is responsible for rest-and-digest functions is also responsible for (f) _____ heart rate, (g) _____ mean arterial pressure, and (h) _____ (an effect on the bronchioles). The branch of the autonomic nervous system that is responsible for fight-or-flight reactions is also responsible for (i) _____ heart rate, (j) _____ mean arterial pressure, and (k) _____ (an effect on the bronchioles).

Neurotransmitters and Receptor Sites

9. Use the following terms to fill in the blanks in the paragraphs below (terms may be used more than once):

- Beta
- Dopamine
- Epinephrine
- Norepinephrine
- Alpha
- Muscarinic
- Acetylcholine
- Nicotinic

The existence of many types of neurotransmitters, the varied receptors available for individual neurotransmitters, and different types of target cells bearing these receptors enables neurotransmitters to induce a range of physiologic responses.

The preganglionic fibers of the sympathetic and parasympathetic divisions of the autonomic nervous system (ANS) and a majority of the postganglionic fibers located in the parasympathetic nervous system secrete the neurotransmitter (a) _____. This neurotransmitter is involved in the control of skeletal muscle actions in the central nervous system (CNS) and the peripheral nervous system (PNS), stimulating skeletal muscle contraction at neuromuscular junctions. It can excite or inhibit ANS synapses.

Most of the postganglionic nerve fibers of the sympathetic division of the autonomic nervous system secrete the neurotransmitter (b) _____. In the CNS, this neurotransmitter creates a sense of feeling good, but in low doses it can cause feelings of depression. Depending on the receptor located in the PNS, this neurotransmitter can inhibit or excite ANS actions.

Acetylcholine can combine with two different types of cholinergic receptors. The first type is located in the membranes of effector cells at the ends of all postganglionic parasympathetic nerve fibers and at the ends of cholinergic sympathetic nerve fibers. These receptors are called (c) _____ receptors, and they produce an excitatory response that is relatively slow. (d) _____ receptors are located in the synapses between the preganglionic and postganglionic neurons of the parasympathetic and sympathetic pathways and produce an excitatory response that is rapid.

The two major chemical mediators (hormones) of the sympathetic nervous system, both of which are released by the adrenal glands, are (e) _____ and (f) _____. (g) _____ receptors are one of the two major receptors of the sympathetic nervous system and cause vasoconstriction in vascular smooth muscle when stimulated. (h) _____ receptors are the second of the two major receptors of the sympathetic nervous system and cause relaxation of uterine muscle, relaxation of bronchial smooth muscles, and increased inotropy and chronotropy in the heart when stimulated.

(i) _____ receptors are located in the brain. When stimulated, they create a sense of feeling good. A deficiency of the neurotransmitter that stimulates the previously mentioned receptors is associated with Parkinson's disease. Paramedics use a synthetic version of this neurotransmitter to treat patients who are suffering from cardiogenic shock.

Cardiovascular System

10. The inherent rate of the heart is between (a) _____ beats per minute in a normal adult. (b) _____ exists when the sinus rate is less than 60 beats per minute, and (c) _____ is greater than 100 beats per minute.

11. Define *cardiac cycle*.

_____

_____

_____

12. Define *stroke volume*.

_____

_____

_____

13. The average stroke volume per heartbeat is _____.

14. What are the three major influences on stroke volume?

_____

_____

_____

15. What is the formula for determining stroke volume?

_____

_____

_____

16. Mean arterial pressure is important because it reflects the average pressure driving blood flow into smaller vessels during the cardiac cycle. List two factors that influence blood flow and in turn influence mean arterial pressure.

_____

_____

_____

17. Use the following terms to fill in the blanks in the paragraphs below.

- Vasomotor center
- X (vagus)
- Rises
- Chemoreceptors
- Baroreceptors
- Sinoatrial (SA) node
- Baroreceptor reflex
- Falls
- Cardiac center
- Mean arterial pressure
- IX (glossopharyngeal)

Any factor that increases cardiac output and/or resistance increases mean arterial pressure (MAP); conversely, any factor that lowers cardiac output and/or resistance lowers MAP. Both neural and endocrine regulatory mechanisms exist for controlling MAP. The (a) _____ utilizes control centers in the medulla oblongata. The (b) _____ controls heart rate, and the vasomotor center controls vascular resistance. The (c) _____ normally activates a tonic state of vascular constriction, a state called vasomotor tone.

When mean arterial pressure falls, (d) _____ found in the aortic arch and in the carotid sinus are activated. Afferent nerves in cranial nerves (e) _____ and (f) _____ activate these control centers. The cardiac center sends a message through the sympathetic cardiac thoracic nerves to activate the (g) _____ to increase the heart rate and increase cardiac contractility (to increase stroke volume). Both of these processes elevate cardiac output and, as a result, (h) _____.

(i) _____ present in the aortic arch and the carotid sinus adjust MAP relative to plasma O_2 and pH. When plasma O_2 falls and/or pH falls, mean arterial pressure (j) _____; conversely, if plasma O_2 rises and/or pH rises, mean arterial pressure (k) _____.

18. Define the following terms:

   a. Shock _____
_____
_____

   b. Cardiogenic shock _____
_____
_____

   c. Neurogenic shock _____
_____
_____

   d. Hypovolemic shock _____
_____
_____

   e. Septic shock _____
_____
_____

   f. Anaphylactic shock _____
_____
_____

The Respiratory System

19. Determine whether the following statements are true or false:

   a. In order to inhale, atmospheric pressure must be higher than intra-alveolar pressure; in order to exhale, intra-alveolar pressure must be higher than atmospheric pressure.

   b. The diaphragm is stimulated to contract by the glossopharyngeal nerve, which causes it to move higher toward the heart.

   c. During inhalation, the size of the thorax increases and the intrathoracic pressure decreases.

   d. During exhalation, the thorax gets smaller, and intra-alveolar pressure falls.

Hypoxia

20. List three things that the body does to compensate for hypoxemia.

_____

_____

_____

21. What are the three ways in which CO_2 is carried in the blood?

_____

_____

_____

22. Ventilatory rate is normally controlled by the respiratory centers located in the (a) _____. The respiratory centers are most sensitive to changes in plasma (b) _____ and the (c) _____ of cerebrospinal fluid. When pCO_2 levels are too high, the respiratory center attempts to compensate by causing the body to (d) _____. When pCO_2 levels are too low, the respiratory center attempts to compensate by causing the body to (e) _____.

Urinary System

23. (a) _____ is released from the posterior pituitary gland when the blood plasma becomes too concentrated with solute or when blood pressure falls. It is a small peptide that enables the body to conserve H_2O. (b) _____ is released when atrial pressure increases, as it might if the blood volume was too high (it is released during hypervolumetric conditions or during congestive heart failure). This hormone appears to decrease aldosterone secretion by the adrenal cortex, increase the rate of renal filtrate formation, increase Na^+ retention, and decrease renin release.

Acid/Base Balance

24. The amount, or concentration, of (a) _____ in the body is the basis for the measurement of pH. The pH of blood plasma normally ranges from (b) _____. One of the primary sources of acid for body regulation is (c) _____. (d) _____ is a condition in which plasma pH falls below 7.35. Two conditions that a pH below 7.35 can cause are (e) _____ and (f) _____. (g) _____ is a condition in which the plasma pH rises above 7.45. Two conditions that a pH above 7.45 can cause include (h) _____ and (i) _____.

Respiratory and Metabolic Considerations

25. Hypoventilation increases (a) _____ and leads to (b) _____. When this occurs, healthy kidneys will compensate by eliminating (c) _____ in the urine and adding (d) _____ to the plasma. Hyperventilation blows off (e) _____ and leads to (f) _____. When the preceding conditions occur, healthy kidneys will compensate by eliminating (g) _____ in the urine and reabsorbing (h) _____. During metabolic acidosis, the kidneys will eliminate (i) _____ and (j) _____ to the blood, and (k) _____ will occur. During metabolic alkalosis, the kidneys will not eliminate and will attempt to reabsorb (l) _____, and (m) _____ will occur. (n) _____ and (o) _____ are causes of metabolic acidosis. (p) _____ and (q) _____ are causes of metabolic alkalosis. The normal range for pCO_2 is (r) _____. The normal range for bicarbonate (HCO_3^-) is (s) _____.

26. Action Potential Exercise

A toilet (the kind with a tank) is all you need for this exercise. The water in the toilet represents the ions in a cell, and the flushing mechanism represents a gate that will allow the ions to pass through. First, consider the toilet in its "resting" state. Would you agree that this would represent the resting potential of a cell? Now, pull the handle. What happens to the flushing mechanism? What happens to the water? What do these actions represent in a depolarizing cell?

At some point, the toilet begins to fill. How does it do that? (If you are not familiar with how a toilet works, lift the lid to the tank, and observe how it works.) What does this refilling represent in a repolarizing cell?

Wait only a few seconds before activating the flushing mechanism again. What happens? How does this relate to the concept of the refractory period?

The bowl will continue to refill. This time, wait a few more seconds and flush again. Observe what happens—is it the same as before? Repeat these steps a few more times, allowing a few more seconds between efforts until a change happens. What does this change in action represent in terms of refractory periods? How might this relate to the conduction of an electrical impulse in the heart or a muscle contraction?

What happens when the toilet is completely refilled? What state has this "cell" reached?

27. Frank Starling's Law of the Heart Exercise

This exercise can be done as a group or by yourself, but it is much more fun to do as a group (large or small). It is best performed outside on a lawn in warm weather wearing something that you don't mind getting wet. In fact, plan on getting wet!

Get 5 to 10 balloons that are of the same size. Imagine that each balloon represents a cardiac ventricle. The opening of the balloon represents the opening of the ventricle, where blood will exit the chamber when the ventricle contracts.

Give each person in the group a balloon. Have them line up in front of a sink or garden hose. The first person fills his/her balloon with just enough water to fill it without stretching it. Pinch the balloon opening so that it will not leak. The next person fills a balloon with roughly twice the amount of water as the first person. The third person fills his/her balloon with twice the amount of water as the second person, and so on until the last balloon is very nearly ready to burst. (Maybe it will burst—how does this relate to a heart chamber like the ventricle?)

Once the balloons are filled, have people line up shoulder to shoulder. The person with the least-filled balloon stands at one end, and the other participants line up in order of increasing amounts of water. With the tips of the balloons still pinched, carefully turn the balloons onto their sides so that the other hand supports each one.

Once everyone is in place, the person who has the least amount of water in their balloon releases his/her pinch hold on the balloon. What happens to the water? How far does it squirt from the balloon? If possible, measure the distance the water travels as it exits the balloon. Repeat the experiment with the next person, and then the next, until all have released the contents of their balloons. Measure the distance that the water traveled each time. What did you observe?

How do your observations relate to the concept of Starling's Law? Did you notice that there was a point of maximum distance that the water traveled? When did that occur? Was it with the last, highest-filled balloon? If not, why? Consider how this would relate to the filling of a ventricle with blood. Would you conclude that there is an "optimal" volume that produces the best flow, whether it is water from a balloon or blood from a ventricle?

You Are There: Reality-Based Cases

Case 1

The outside temperature has dropped dramatically over the past several days, and the forecast is for more of the same over the next week. The snowdrifts are growing, and power is out to almost half of the city. People are getting desperate to stay warm, and you are no exception to the rule. Just when you are beginning to thaw after your last run, the dispatch phone rings, and you are off to respond to an unconscious family in a home on the other side of town.

Several blocks away from the home, first responders advise you that there are two adults and two children who are unresponsive. They show contractures in their hands and feet, and their skin looks bright red. Upon your arrival, the battalion chief approaches you and states that the family lit a charcoal barbecue inside the house in an apparent attempt to stay warm. The two children were found upstairs in their bedroom, and the parents were found in the hallway

leading to the garage. The firefighters are moving the family into the garage to get them out of the contaminated environment. The garage door is open, and the firefighters are using fans to ventilate the house. You note that all of the victims are breathing rapidly.

1. On arrival, what is your greatest concern?

_____

_____

2. What is the likely cause of the family's unconsciousness, based on the reports that you have received from the first responders?

_____

_____

_____

3. What major physiologic processes are involved in this case?

_____

_____

4. What is the name of the condition that causes stiff, contracted muscles in the extremities, and what is it related to?

_____

_____

5. Explain physiologically how carbon monoxide can lead to the condition in which the patients were found.

_____

_____

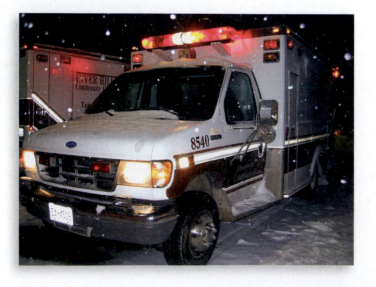

Test Yourself

1. Which of the following will result in increased cardiac output (CO)?
   a. Increased thoracic pressure
   b. Decreased afterload
   c. Decreased preload
   d. Increased end-systolic volume (ESV)

2. Hypoxia can result from
   a. oxygen delivery exceeding oxygen consumption.
   b. oxygen consumption exceeding oxygen delivery.
   c. increased blood oxygen carrying capacity.
   d. increased oxygen level in the environment.

3. Which of the following patients is most likely to be hypoxic, but *not* hypoxemic?
   a. A patient suffering from altitude illness
   b. A patient with a chronic lung disease
   c. A patient with a traumatic abdominal injury
   d. A patient with carbon monoxide poisoning

4. Your patient complains of excessive thirst and urination, but her blood glucose level is within normal range. She may be deficient in _____ hormone.

5. Narrowing pulse pressure is defined as
   a. the difference between the blood pressure reading and the rate of the brachial pulse.
   b. a decreasing difference between the systolic and diastolic blood pressure reading.
   c. a blood pressure reading with a substantial difference separating systole and diastole.
   d. a subtle change in the amount of pressure needed to inflate the blood pressure cuff.

6. Explain why aerobic metabolism is preferable to anaerobic metabolism.

   _____

   _____

7. _____ nervous system activity is associated with reduced heart rate, reduced mean arterial blood pressure, and bronchoconstriction.

8. Hyperventilation can lead to respiratory alkalosis.
   True
   False

9. The primary mechanism to ensure adequate renal pressure is the _____ mechanism.
   a. $NaHCO_3/H_2CO_3$ buffer
   b. antidiuretic hormone
   c. atrial natriuretic peptide
   d. renin-angiotensin

10. Given that each ventricle ejects the body's entire blood volume every minute under resting conditions, explain why the average healthy adult is able to hold his or her breath for longer than 1 minute.

    _____

    _____

11. Chemoreceptors in the carotid body trigger an increase in mean arterial pressure (MAP) if they detect
    a. an increase in plasma O_2 or pH.
    b. a decrease in plasma O_2 or pH.
    c. an increase in plasma O_2 or a decrease in plasma pH.
    d. a decrease in plasma O_2 or an increase in plasma pH.

12. Define the term *homeostasis,* and explain how it applies to physiology.

    _____

    _____

13. How does carbon dioxide leave the body?

    _____

    _____

14. A 24-year-old woman contracted food poisoning. She has had severe diarrhea for the past 3 days and has been taking aspirin for abdominal pain. She is lethargic, with rapid, shallow respirations. What pH imbalance is most likely?
    a. Respiratory alkalosis
    b. Respiratory acidosis
    c. Metabolic acidosis
    d. Metabolic alkalosis

15. Most of the body's control centers are located in the _____ system or in the _____ system.

16. Enzymes are complex molecules that
    a. catalyze (promote) a chemical reaction.
    b. stabilize the position of organelles within the cell.
    c. use nutrients to synthesize nucleic acids (DNA and RNA).
    d. are one of the components of all cell membranes.

17. Cell reactions that release the energy contained in the chemical bonds of complex molecules are known as
    a. anabolic reactions.
    b. anaerobic reactions.
    c. catabolic reactions.
    d. aerobic reactions.

18. Describe how receptors, control centers, and effectors work together to achieve homeostasis.

    _____

    _____

19. While treating a respiratory patient, your partner provides bag-mask ventilation at a rate of one small squeeze (about 500 mL) every 6 seconds. What is the approximate minute ventilation of this patient?
    a. 6 breaths per minute
    b. 5 L
    c. 10 breaths per minute
    d. 3 L

20. Normally, increased heart rate creates increased cardiac output (CO). Explain why very high heart rates (usually greater than 170 beats per minute) cause a *decrease* in cardiac output.

_____

_____

Need to Know

The following represent the Key Objectives of Chapter 8:

1. *Explain the terms* physiology *and* homeostasis.

Simply stated, physiology is the study of the function of living organisms. It is a basic understanding of how the human body functions that allows the paramedic to respond appropriately when there is something wrong with the human machine. Much of what we do as paramedics is in response to problems with homeostatic mechanisms. Without a basic understanding of how a healthy body maintains itself, we are powerless to intervene and correct deviations from normal physiologic parameters.

Homeostasis is a state of equilibrium of the internal environment of the body that is maintained by dynamic processes of feedback and regulation (a dynamic equilibrium). For homeostasis to work, many different components must be in place and functioning. The components of homeostasis include

a. *Set point.* The acceptable value for any variable (blood pressure, temperature, pH level, etc.). The set point is the value that homeostatic mechanisms strive to maintain.

b. *Control mechanism.* Reflex pathways that utilize structures outside of the affected organ to accomplish regulation. Each control mechanism has three essential elements: receptors, control center, and effectors.

- *Receptors* are specific sites on or inside a cell, a whole cell, or a group of cells together that receive (chemical, electrical, or electro-chemical) messages and are activated when a variable moves outside of its desired range.

- The *control (integration) center* assesses information registered by the receptor, compares it to its normal set point, and initiates a corrective change; control centers are typically located in the central nervous system or in endocrine glands.

- *Effectors* are the structures of the body that actually accomplish the desired effect.

c. A *negative feedback mechanism* is a homeostatic mechanism that prevents physiologic processes from deviating from their desired set point through the use of effectors and a control center.

d. An *afferent pathway* is the means by which electrical and chemical messages are passed from receptors to control (integration) centers.

e. An *efferent pathway* is the process that conveys electrical and chemical messages from control centers to effectors.

f. A *positive feedback mechanism* is a mechanism whereby one action creates additional actions of the same type (for example, clotting cascade).

It is because of these checks and balances that the human body is able to maintain

- An acceptable balance between oxygen and carbon dioxide
- pH levels within acceptable parameters
- Normal body temperature
- Fluid and electrolyte balances
- A heart rate and blood pressure capable of maintaining perfusion to the organs of the body

Need to Do

The following skills are explained and illustrated in a step-by-step manner, via skill sheets and/or Step-by-Steps in this text and on the accompanying DVD:

Skill Name	Skill Sheet Number and Location	Step-by-Step Number and Location
Pulse Oximetry	12 – DVD	12 – DVD
Blood Glucose Assessment	26 – DVD	26 – DVD

Connections

- See Chapter 7, Anatomy Overview, in the textbook for supportive information about anatomical form, function, and location with regard to physiologic processes.

- Chapter 13, Shock Overview, in the textbook discusses the different physiologic compensatory mechanisms that the body institutes in an attempt to maintain homeostasis.

- Chapter 15, Pharmacology, in the textbook has additional detail on the sympathetic and parasympathetic nervous systems and describes many of the receptors found in each branch.

- See Chapter 19, Hemorrhage and Hemorrhagic Shock, in the textbook for more information on the types of shock and the manner in which different types of shock impact the normal physiology of the body.

- Chapter 31, Endocrine, Electrolytes, and Acid/Base, in the textbook will enhance your understanding of conditions such as diabetes, as well as electrolyte and pH balance and their effects on homeostasis.

- Link to the companion DVD for a chapter-based quiz, audio glossary, animations, games and exercises, and, when appropriate, skill sheets and skill Step-by-Steps.

Street Secrets

- **Things Are Not Always What They Appear to Be**

   Hyperventilation should not be dismissed as an anxiety disorder; it may be a sign of a very serious medical condition such as a head injury or diabetic ketoacidosis (DKA).

   Hypoglycemia can mimic a cerebrovascular accident (CVA); as such, all patients with signs and symptoms of a CVA should have their blood sugar tested.

   Very aggressive and violent behavior is not always related to personality disorders, drugs, or alcohol ingestion—it could be caused by a head injury, hypoxia, hypoglycemia, and a number of other medical conditions.

   The alcoholic who you see on a regular basis deserves the same treatment as any other patient. The patient who falls and strikes his or her head on a regular basis is far more likely to sustain a serious head injury than most other patients. Assess and treat these patients as you would any other patient with a head injury. Failure to assess and treat patients because of preconceived notions about them could very well be a career-ending decision.

- **Think on Your Feet** You may not always be able to determine the exact cause of a patient's

condition, but you can always come back to maintaining the ABCs and treating problems as they arise. Continually reassess patients, and be ready to change your treatment plan with the patient's changing condition. Try to anticipate reactions that the patient may have to your interventions, and be prepared to react to those possibilities.

- **Putting It All Together** Be aware of all the subtleties that are brought to your attention. Don't dismiss any information that is provided to you, but do perform a thorough physical examination and obtain a detailed medical history. Pay attention to your surroundings, and do your best to put all the pieces of the puzzle together in a logical treatment plan. Do not forsake patient care or transport of a critical patient for a detailed and lengthy history and physical examination. If you do not have time to perform these tasks on the scene, bring medications and people who have information to the hospital or have someone (first re-sponders, etc.) gather information and convey it to you once it is obtained. This frees you up to provide prompt care and rapid transport for critical patients.

The Drug Box

There are no specific drugs related to this chapter content.

References

1. D. Shier, J. Butler, and R. Lewis, *Hole's Anatomy and Physiology*, 11th ed. New York: McGraw-Hill, 2007.
2. M. Edmond, "Fever and Hyperthermia," www.people.vcu.edu/~eric/adobe%20files/Fever.pdf.
3. J. E. Tintinalli, G. D. Kelen, and J. S. Stapczynski, *Emergency Medicine: A Comprehensive Study Guide*, 6th ed. New York: McGraw-Hill, 2004, pp. 1238–41.
4. D. Kasper, E. Braunwald, A. Fauci, S. Hauser, D. Longo, J. Jameson, *Harrison's Principles of Internal Medicine*, 16th ed. New York: McGraw Hill, 2005, p. 138.
5. Ibid, p. 1239.
6. E. Newton, "Hyperventilation Syndrome," p. 2, www.emedicine.com/EMERG/topic270.htm (accessed April 12, 2007).

Answers

Are You Ready?

1. The patient might have ingested crack cocaine, but there are several indicators that the patient may have another significant medical condition. The patient's

skin is hot to the touch and her radial pulse is rapid, both of which could be related to ingesting cocaine. The fact that she has a goiter and bulging eyes may also be significant.[1]

2. Whether you agree or not, it is good practice to assume that a patient has an intrinsic medical problem until proven otherwise by the patient's own admission or as the result of a complete medical workup.

3. Other possible causes of the patient's condition include heat-related illness, infection, malignant hyperthermia, neuroleptic malignant syndrome, endocrine hyperthermia (thyroid storm, pheochromocytoma crisis), and hyperglycemia (diabetic ketoacidosis).[2]

4. The pacing, agitation, tachypnea, tachycardia, and hot flushed skin are consistent with cocaine ingestion, but the goiter and the bulging out of the eyes (exophthalmus) should lead to a suspicion of thyrotoxicosis or thyroid storm.

Active Learning

1. **Glycolysis:** The 6-carbon sugar glucose is broken down into two 3-carbon pyruvic acid molecules with a net gain of 2 ATP and the release of high-energy electrons.

   Citric acid cycle: The 3-carbon pyruvic acids generated by glycolysis enter the mitochondria. Each loses a carbon (generating CO_2) and is combined with a coenzyme to form a 2-carbon acetyl coenzyme A (acetyl CoA). More high-energy electrons are released.

   Electron transport chain: The high-energy electrons still contain most of the chemical energy of the original glucose molecule. Special carrier molecules bring the high-energy electrons to a series of enzymes that convert much of the remaining energy to more ATP molecules. The other products are heat and water. The requirement of oxygen in the last step explains why the overall process is called aerobic respiration.

2. Hypoxia is a low-oxygen state. Hypoxemia is an abnormally low arterial oxygen tension within the blood.

3. Any three of the following: a state of energy deficiency, decrease in cellular pH (acidosis), increase in intracellular phosphate, decrease in enzyme functioning, decrease in DNA and RNA structure and replication, decrease in protein synthesis, and decrease in membrane transport.

5. An insulin-dependent diabetic took his insulin this morning, but because he was feeling nauseated, he didn't eat anything. As a result, the patient's circulating blood sugar has moved from the vascular space into the cells of his body to be used as energy. As the sugar is utilized, and no additional sugar is added to the body in the form of food, the cells of the body soon become starved for glucose. The sugar-poor cells send a message via the afferent pathway to the brain that they need sugar. The brain in turn sends a message to the endocrine system via the efferent pathway that the cells of the body need sugar. The message results in the release of the hormone glucagon, which converts glycogen, amino acids, and lactic acid to glucose and temporarily raises the blood sugar in an attempt to meet the demands of the cells. In this example the *set point* is a normal "random" blood glucose level, which is in the low to mid 100s range. The *receptors* are the cells of the body, the *control center* is the brain, and the *effectors* are the endocrine system (glucagon).

6. It serves as a control center and it produces hormones.

7. a. brain and spinal cord; b. cranial and spinal nerves; c. PNS

8. a. somatic branch; b. autonomic branch; c. autonomic; d. parasympathetic; e. sympathetic; f. reduced (or decreased); g. reduced (or decreased); h. bronchoconstriction (which increases airway resistance and reduces air flow during ventilation); i. increased; j. increased; k. bronchodilation (which reduces airway resistance and increases air flow during ventilation)

9. a. acetylcholine; b. norepinephrine; c. muscarinic; d. Nicotinic; e. epinephrine; f. norepinephrine; g. Alpha; h. Beta; i. Dopamine

10. a. 60–100; b. Bradycardia; c. tachycardia

11. The cardiac cycle is the time period extending from one heartbeat to the next heartbeat and includes both systole and diastole of the atria and the ventricles.

12. Stroke volume (in mL/min) is the amount of blood ejected by a ventricle each time it contracts.

13. 70 mL

14. Preload, contractility of the heart muscle, and afterload

15. Stroke volume (SV) (mL/beat) = End-diastolic volume (EDV) − End-systolic volume (ESV)

16. Any two of the following: vessel length, blood viscosity, and vessel radius.

17. a. baroreceptor reflex; b. cardiac center; c. vasomotor center; d. baroreceptors; e. IX (glossopharyngeal); f. X (vagus); g. sinoatrial (SA) node; h. mean arterial pressure; i. Chemoreceptors; j. rises; k. falls

18. **a.** A generalized failure to deliver oxygenated blood to tissues. For most all types of shock, low blood pressure and reduced urine formation characterize this disorder.

    b. Heart failure leading to reduced cardiac output.

    c. Failure of the vasomotor center to maintain vasomotor tone.

    d. Reduction in blood volume, leading to reduced stroke volume and cardiac output.

    e. Bacterial toxins induce vasodilation and reduce resistance.

    f. Massive immune reactions that lead to systemic vasodilation and increased capillary permeability.

19. **a.** True

    b. False. The diaphragm is stimulated to contract by the phrenic nerve, which causes it to pull lower toward the abdomen.

    c. True

    d. False. During exhalation, the thorax gets smaller, and intra-alveolar pressure rises.

20. An increased rate of ventilation (if plasma pO_2 falls below 60 mm Hg), an increased vasomotor tone (sensitivity of carotid and aortic chemoreceptors increases), and increased erythropoiesis (red blood cell production).

21. Approximately 7% dissolves in the plasma, approximately 23% binds to hemoglobin, and the remainder of the CO_2 reacts with water to form H_2CO_3 (carbonic acid).

22. a. medulla oblongata; b. pCO_2; c. pH; d. hyperventilate; e. hypoventilate

23. a. Antidiuretic hormone (ADH); b. Atrial natriuretic peptide (ANP)

24. a. hydrogen ions; b. 7.35–7.45; c. CO_2; d. Acidosis; e–f. any of the following: central nervous system depression, lethargy, coma, and death; g. Alkalosis; h–i. any of the following: hyperexcitability, numbness and tingling, muscle tetany, muscle paralysis, and death

25. a. CO_2 levels (and in turn H^+ ions); b. respiratory acidosis; c. H^+ ions; d. HCO_3; e. pCO_2; f. respiratory alkalosis; g. HCO_3; h. H^+ ions; i. H^+; j. HCO_3; k. hyperventilation; l. H^+ ions; m. hypoventilation; n–o. any of the following: renal compromise or failure, diabetic ketoacidosis, excessive emesis in which alkaline contents are lost, prolonged diarrhea in which alkaline contents are lost; p–q. any of the following: excessive antacid ingestion, prolonged emesis in which the acids of the stomach are lost, following gastric drainage or lavage, excessive use of diuretics; r. 33–44 mm Hg; s. 22–28 mEq/L.

You Are There: Reality-Based Cases

Case 1

1. Scene safety is the primary concern, that is, making sure that the public safety workers and the patients are out of the contaminated environment and that none of the emergency workers will be exposed to the substances that affected the family.

2. The combination of the initial radio report that the two adults and the two children were unresponsive, with contractures in their hands and feet, and had bright red skin, with the battalion chief's report that the family was using a barbecue inside their house to keep warm should lead you to a high index of suspicion that the family has been overcome by carbon monoxide.

3. Carbon monoxide (CO) is a colorless, odorless gas that enters the body by inhalation. Because the gas is inhaled, it involves the respiratory (pulmonary) system. The gas crosses the alveolar-capillary membrane and binds with hemoglobin (cardiovascular and hematology). In fact, CO has approximately 230–270 times the affinity for hemoglobin (Hb) that oxygen (O_2) has, and carboxyhemoglobin is cherry red in color, giving the skin of patients with high levels of carboxyhemoglobin a bright red appearance.[3] Because of hemoglobin's affinity for CO and the fact that the strong binding of CO makes it more difficult for the remaining O_2 to transfer to the tissues of the body, the processes of diffusion, pH balance, cellular respiration, and muscular contraction are impacted as well. The cascade of effects resulting from CO poisoning are even farther reaching than described here, but in relation to the prehospital management of CO poisoning, we will focus on those systems mentioned.

4. Carbon monoxide tetany, otherwise known as carpal-pedal spasm, is related to hyperventilation caused by CO-induced hypoxia.[4]

5. Carbon monoxide (CO) is the result of incomplete combustion, in this case, the incomplete combustion of charcoal in a barbecue that was placed inside a closed space in an attempt to heat a home in the wintertime when the power was out. CO is a colorless, odorless gas until it reaches extremely high concentrations, when it has a slight lavender odor. CO is inhaled and enters the bloodstream at the alveolar-capillary membrane. Once in the bloodstream, CO binds with hemoglobin at an affinity 230–270 times that of oxygen (O_2).[5] This being the case, CO has a tendency to replace O_2 on hemoglobin molecules and results in diminished O_2 delivery to the tissues of the body. Several reactions result from the decreased O_2 delivery to the tissues of the body: Hypoxia develops, and the cells of the body respond to the hypoxia that is developing by sending chemical and electrical messages to the brain to tell it to send more O_2 to the hypoxic tissues. The body's response is to increase the respiratory rate. The increased respiratory rate causes CO_2 to be blown off and, in turn, causes a shift in the pH balance in the body. The decrease in CO_2 creates an alkaline environment which impacts the normal functioning of skeletal muscle contraction. Acute metabolic changes result from intracellular shifts and increased protein binding of various electrolytes during respiratory alkalosis. Secondary acute hypocalcemia can result in CO tetany (carpal-pedal spasm).[6]

Test Yourself

1. b

   Cardiac output (CO) equals stroke volume multiplied by heart rate, so either stroke volume or heart rate or both must increase to increase CO. Decreased afterload (vascular resistance) will increase stroke volume because the ventricle will be fighting against less pressure. Increased thoracic pressure will decrease the amount of blood returning to the heart, thereby decreasing preload. Decreased preload will decrease stroke volume because it means there is less blood in the ventricle to be ejected. Increased ESV means that there is more blood left in the heart after ejection, again decreasing stroke volume.

2. b

   Hypoxia can result from a lack of O_2 in the environment, reduced O_2 carrying capacity of the blood, and any state in which O_2 consumption exceeds O_2 delivery.

3. c

   Hypoxia is defined as a lack of adequate O_2 in cells, resulting in an impairment of tissue function. Hypoxemia is an abnormally low amount of oxygen within the blood. The terms *hypoxia* and *hypoxemia* are often used interchangeably; however, one state can occur without the other. For example, a patient with severe hemorrhage (say from a traumatic abdominal injury) may have tissue hypoxia from inadequate blood volume, despite having a normal oxygen saturation level. Alternatively, a patient with chronic lung disease (like COPD) may have a low oxygen level within the blood (hypoxemia), but because the patient has polycythemia (a higher than normal amount of red blood cells) he or she may have no tissue hypoxia.

4. Antidiuretic

   Antidiuretic hormone (ADH), also called vasopressin, is a small peptide that stimulates the kidneys to conserve H_2O. ADH is manufactured by the hypothalamus and is stored and secreted by the posterior pituitary gland. A deficiency in secretion of ADH is called hypothalamic diabetes insipidus. Symptoms of diabetes insipidus are quite similar to those of untreated diabetes mellitus, with the distinction that the urine is not sweet and there is no hyperglycemia (elevated blood glucose). Causes of this disease include head trauma and infections or tumors involving the hypothalamus.

5. b

   Narrowing pulse pressure is a decreasing difference between the systolic and diastolic blood pressure reading. If normal blood pressure is around 120/80, an example of narrowing pulse pressure is 130/110, and widening pulse pressure is 140/50. Narrowing pulse pressure may go unnoticed if only one blood pressure reading is obtained. This example highlights the importance of continuous monitoring.

6. Without sufficient oxygen for aerobic metabolism, cells become hypoxic and are forced to use anaerobic methods. Anaerobic metabolism may cause a state of energy deficiency, a decrease in cellular pH (acidosis), and an increase in intracellular phosphate.

   Anaerobic metabolism is less efficient than aerobic metabolism. Anaerobic metabolism produces lactic acid, which can lead to a buildup of wastes in the blood that results in acidosis, organ impairment, organ failure, and eventually, if untreated, death.

7. Parasympathetic

   The goal of the parasympathetic nervous system (PNS) is to help the body conserve energy resources and maintain a state of rest and digest. As a result, parasympathetic nervous system activity is associated with reduced heart rate, reduced mean arterial blood pressure, and bronchoconstriction (which increases airway resistance and reduces airflow during ventilation).

8. True

   Carbonic acid (H_2CO_3) buffers excess bases, thereby preventing alkalosis. The amount of carbonic acid is inversely related to the ventilation rate, since it is formed from CO_2 and H_2O. Hyperventilation thus reduces the body's natural ability to buffer against alkalosis. Alkalosis is a condition in which the plasma pH rises above 7.45; it can lead to hyperexcitability, numbness and tingling, muscle tetany (spasms brought on by mineral imbalance), muscle paralysis, and death.

9. d

   The kidneys require pressure to filter the blood, and there are many mechanisms in place to ensure that renal pressure is maintained. Perhaps the most important of these mechanisms, systemically, is the renin-angiotensin mechanism. When renal pressure falls, or when the renal filtrate is dilute or slow moving, renin is released from kidney cells into the blood. Renin acts on angiotensinogen, forming angiotensin I. Angiotensin-converting enzymes (ACE) act on the angiotensin I, forming angiotensin II. Angiotensin II is a potent vasoconstrictor that elevates systemic pressure by elevating resistance with vasoconstriction.

10. Hemoglobin normally releases only 25% of the O_2 that it is carrying to tissues. The extra O_2 acts as a reserve.

    The extra reserve of O_2 becomes critically important under conditions of hypoventilation.

11. b

    Chemoreceptors are present to adjust MAP relative to plasma O_2 and pH. When plasma O_2 falls and/or pH falls, mean arterial pressure rises; conversely, if plasma O_2 rises and/or pH rises, mean arterial pressure falls. This allows mean arterial pressure to be adjusted relative to changes in metabolic rate.

12. Homeostasis is the healthy, well-balanced state where the internal environment is optimal for cellular function. The property of organisms that drives them to remain in this state is the central, unifying theme of physiology.

    Most of the processes that occur in the body function to maintain relative internal stability (hemostasis), even when external conditions are fluctuating. For example, when we get dehydrated, we become thirsty; when we are overheated, we sweat; and when we are oxygen deficient, we may hyperventilate. This is the basis of physiology.

13. Carbon dioxide is carried in venous blood to the lungs, where it is eliminated from the body during exhalation. It is also converted to carbonic acid; excess acid is eliminated through the urinary system.

    Carbon dioxide (CO_2) is a waste product produced by tissue cells. It is carried in three ways: a small amount (about 7%) dissolves in the plasma, approximately 23% binds to hemoglobin, and most of the CO_2 reacts with water to form H_2CO_3 (carbonic acid). When these various forms of CO_2 reach the lungs, the CO_2 will diffuse out of the capillaries into the alveoli and be eliminated from the body during exhalation. When not enough CO_2 is exhaled or too much carbonic acid remains in the system, acidosis occurs.

14. c

    Acidosis is a condition in which plasma pH falls below 7.35; it can lead to, among other things, central nervous system depression, lethargy, coma, and death. Metabolic acidosis can be caused by diabetic acidosis, lactic acidosis, $NaHCO_3$ loss (severe diarrhea), high fat intake, and ingested substances (aspirin, methanol, bleach). During metabolic acidosis, the kidneys will eliminate

H^+ and add $NaHCO_3$ to the blood, and hyperventilation will occur.

15. Central nervous, endocrine

    The central nervous system (CNS) contains many important control centers including those that regulate water balance, skeletal muscle tone, digestion, heart rate, blood pressure, and ventilation. The endocrine system is involved in homeostatic regulation by serving as a control center and by producing hormones. Endocrine glands themselves can serve as a control center for a variable, as in the case of the control of plasma glucose by the pancreatic hormones insulin and glucagon. Endocrine glands can also be activated by the CNS.

16. a

    Nutrients are used by cells to synthesize more complex molecules, such as enzymes, proteins, complex carbohydrates, lipids, and nucleic acids like DNA and RNA. Some of these molecules are structural; lipids, for example, are components of all cell membranes, and protein filaments stabilize the position of organelles within the cell. Other complex molecules act as enzymes (complex proteins made by cells that catalyze [promote] a chemical reaction), antibodies, signaling molecules, antigens, receptors, and ion channels; are involved in motility (movement) and contraction; or are involved in the regulation of DNA expression, cell division, and metabolism.

17. c

    Catabolic reactions release the energy contained in the chemical bonds of complex molecules. Anabolic reactions consume energy and are used to synthesize large biomolecules. Reactions that require an oxygenated environment are called aerobic, and reactions that occur without oxygen are called anaerobic.

18. A receptor is activated when a variable moves outside of its desirable range. A control (integration) center assesses information registered by the receptor, compares it to its normal set point, and initiates a corrective change. One or more effectors are then triggered. Effectors are the structures of the body that actually accomplish the desired action.

    For example, consider a patient with hypotension due to blood loss. Arterial receptors found in the arch of the aorta and in the carotid sinuses monitor both the force of blood coursing through the vessels and mean arterial pressure. When these receptors sense a change in blood pressure, they transmit a message along afferent pathways to the brain. The brain then interprets the data sent by the receptors and registers the low blood pressure. Signals from the brain then travel down the sympathetic nervous system (an efferent pathway) to the heart to increase both the rate and force of contractions in an attempt to preserve cardiac output and the blood pressure. In this case the arterial receptors are the receptors, the brain is the control center, and the heart is the effector.

19. b

    Minute ventilation is calculated as the tidal volume (amount of air moved in and out of the lungs during one breath) multiplied by the minute respiratory rate. In this case, one breath every 6 seconds equals a respiratory rate of 10 breaths per minute. This 10 breaths per minute multiplied by 500 mL per breath equals a minute ventilation of 5 L, which is the average minute ventilation of a healthy adult at rest.

20. The shorter duration of diastole limits the time available for ventricular filling. CO depends on both stroke volume and heart rate. With an extremely high heart rate, there is not time for the ventricles to fill completely, which drastically reduces stroke volume. In these circumstances, the stroke volume falls so much that the cardiac output decreases despite an increase in heart rate.

part

2

Foundations of Communication, Assessment, and Critical Care

chapter 9

Safety and Scene Size-Up

Are You Ready?

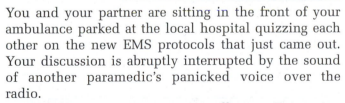

You and your partner are sitting in the front of your ambulance parked at the local hospital quizzing each other on the new EMS protocols that just came out. Your discussion is abruptly interrupted by the sound of another paramedic's panicked voice over the radio.

"Medic 13 . . . Emergency traffic . . . Emergency traffic! Shots fired . . . Repeating shots fired! Medic down! We need code 3 police and another ambulance!"

During the radio traffic, you hear shots in the background and then silence. The dispatcher repeatedly attempts to raise Medic 13 with no response. The dispatcher calls your unit identifier and tells you to respond code 3 to back up Medic 13 at 1234 56th St., cross streets of Maple and Elm. The protocol book that you and your partner were reading hits the ambulance floor as you fly out of the parking lot to respond to the call and go to your coworkers' aid.

1. What is your first priority?

_____

_____

_____

2. How should you proceed once you receive your dispatch information?

_____

_____

_____

3. What additional information do you need from the dispatcher to ensure the safety of everybody involved in this situation?

_____

_____

_____

_____

4. What do you need to do when you arrive on the scene?

_____

_____

_____

Active Learning

1. Comparison of Settings

Using the following scenario and chart, list several different factors that need to be taken into consideration when managing similar situations in different settings (the first row is completed as an example).

Scenario: A shooting at the local high school. There are reports of up to 15 students shot.

Settings			
Factors	Urban	Suburban	Rural
Response time	Because of the number and density of people located within a relatively small geographical area, there tend to be more ambulances that are located closer to incidents. However, due to the large population located in a small area, traffic can be a factor that slows the response time.	There tend to be less people per geographical area as compared with the urban setting, but there may not be as many EMS resources as seen in an urban setting. Traffic, on the other hand, may not be as difficult as in the urban setting, so response times may improve in this area.	The number of people per geographical area is significantly smaller than in an urban or suburban setting. Because of the relatively small number of people, the EMS resources tend to be relatively small. Some rural communities have EMS providers that cover hundreds of square miles, and their response times can be very long.
ALS ambulance availability			
BLS ambulance availability			
EMS aircraft availability			
Level of training			
Time to hospital			
Time to trauma center			
Law enforcement availability			

Driving and Scene Safety

2. A majority of serious collisions involving emergency vehicles occur at _____.

3. The size and shape of an ambulance creates several driving hazards. List three driving hazards that ambulances inherently possess.

_____

_____

4. List the five elements of scene size-up.

_____

_____

5. List three things that paramedics can do at the scene of a motor vehicle collision on the highway to protect themselves from other vehicles.

_____

_____

6. When responding to a potentially dangerous or violent scene, the paramedic should, as a very minimum, do what before entering the scene?

_____

_____

7. If you are approaching a potentially dangerous scene and you are not sure if the scene is safe, what should you do?

_____

_____

8. Define and give an example of the term *cover*.

_____

_____

9. Define and give an example of the term *concealment*.

_____

_____

10. List two things that paramedics can do when managing patients (especially potentially violent patients) to improve their own personal safety.

_____

_____

11. There are many nonverbal cues of aggressive behavior. Describe at least four of these nonverbal cues.

_____

_____

Safe Patient Interviews

12. There are many different methods that are used for interviewing patients. No matter which style you use in your everyday practice, there are several things that you can do during your interview that will increase your awareness of the scene and your overall safety. Describe each of the following:

a. Reactionary gap

b. Bladed stance

c. Contact and cover

13. Crew member safety can be improved by proper positioning of the members on the scene. What are the basic tenets of crew member positioning in relation to the patient and the physical scene setting?

You Are There: Reality-Based Cases

Case 1

You and your paramedic partner arrive on the scene of a multiple stabbing at a country bar approximately 50 minutes away from the small town in which you

work. En route to the scene, your dispatcher advises that the sheriff is on scene and the suspect has fled the scene. During the same radio transmission, you are told that there are eight patients with "serious stab wounds."

The town that you work in has a basic emergency department equipped with a helipad, and the closest trauma center is an hour and a half away from the scene by ground and a half hour away by helicopter. The neighboring town has already sent you its volunteer BLS ambulance and is trying to find a paramedic to jump on its volunteer ALS ambulance. The only other ALS ambulance from your town is still en route to the trauma center with a fall victim, and it will not be able to get to the scene for over 2 hours. There are two medical helicopters based near the trauma center.

1. Based on the information that you have received, what can you say about the scene safety and scene size-up?

_____

_____

2. What can you do with the scene size-up information that you have received over the radio to expedite patient care?

_____

_____

When you arrive on the scene, you and your partner begin the process of triaging the patients and organizing a treatment area. When you finish the process of triaging (utilizing the principles established by your local EMS agency—in this particular case, simple triage and rapid transport [START] triage), you determine that you have five immediate (red) patients, two delayed (yellow) patients, and one deceased (black) patient. As you complete your triage of the patients your dispatcher contacts you and states that the volunteer ALS ambulance will not be available. The trauma center states that it can take five patients, and the local emergency department can handle three patients.

3. How will you best utilize your resources in order to care for these patients?

_____

_____

The sheriff and the volunteer fire department have established a 100-foot by 100-foot landing zone across the street from the bar where the stabbing victims are located. The first helicopter is orbiting overhead and requesting a description of the landing zone and any possible hazards that exist.

4. What type of safety information can you convey regarding the scene and the landing zone?

_____

_____

5. What do you and the other emergency workers on the ground need to keep in mind when working around a helicopter (especially while the rotors are turning)?

_____

_____

Test Yourself

1. The scene size-up assessment begins when arriving at the scene.
True
False

2. Nonverbal cues of aggressive behavior include
   a. hands facing palm out.
   b. low-pitched, slow voices.
   c. hands clenched and raised.
   d. constantly looking at an exit.

3. When you activate an ambulance's lights and sirens, you are
   a. exercising operational interface.
   b. acting with due regard.
   c. driving in a defensive mode.
   d. operating in emergency mode.

4. Which is an example of personal protective equipment?
   a. Turnout coat and pants
   b. High-efficiency particulate air filter

   c. Reflective outer clothing
   d. Hearing and head protection

5. When soap and running water are not available, hands should be sanitized with which type of cleanser?
   a. Acidic
   b. Alcohol
   c. Alkali
   d. Enzyme

6. What is an iatrogenic disorder?

_____

_____

_____

7. With regard to emergency vehicle operations, what is the "zone of safety"?

_____

_____

_____

8. Why is it important for a paramedic to be aware of existing infectious disease outbreaks and to be vigilant for new outbreaks?

_____

_____

9. List some of the immunizations a paramedic should receive.

_____

_____

10. Which of the following statement regarding pushing or pulling is correct?
    a. Push or pull from the hips.
    b. Keep arms extended.
    c. Push or pull from the knees.
    d. Keep elbows straight.

11. The most important action taken by the paramedic at an emergency scene is to
    a. manage the airway of a trauma patient.
    b. utilize personal protective equipment.
    c. control bleeding of an open fracture.
    d. administer rescue breaths, eight per minute.

12. Describe the proper technique for lifting and moving patients.

_____

_____

13. When dealing with nerve agents, EMS personnel must be familiar with the administration of atropine.

    True

    False

14. The most common large-scale public health problem encountered by paramedics is _____.

15. The use of safety restraints in an ambulance is
    a. recommended for everyone in the vehicle.
    b. not possible for the attendant caring for the patient.
    c. mandatory if the passenger is younger than 16.
    d. optional for the driver when not on a call.

Need to Know

The following represent the Key Objectives of Chapter 9:

1. *Demonstrate how to apply and safely remove personal protective equipment.*

   Depending on the provider that you work for and the level of training that you possess, you will have varying types of personal protective equipment (PPE) available for your use. Make sure that you inspect your PPE on a regular basis, understand how to don and doff your PPE, and use them as indicated by the manufacturer, your provider's policies and procedures, and the policies and protocols of your state and local EMS regulatory agencies. You are ultimately responsible for your own safety and well-being. Personal protective equipment will not serve its function if it is not worn by emergency workers or if it is not used properly.

2. *Describe how to ensure the safety of a scene throughout the EMS call, including how to reduce the possibility of contamination while managing contaminated patients.*

   In the field, paramedics should demonstrate due diligence in ensuring the safety of all scenes. Scene safety should not only involve the time in which paramedics are physically caring for patients, but should be part of their consciousness at all times (before, during, and after the time that they are on a scene). Scene safety doesn't just involve protecting yourself and your patients from cars that are speeding by as you care for the victims of a traffic collision or the hazards at the scene of a violent crime. It also involves protecting paramedics and all others involved from objects that may not be obvious hazards. Paramedics must know how to assess and address problems associated with hazardous materials or other contaminants that may be present at a scene and/or on a patient. With proper training, paramedics should have a very clear idea of how to maintain safety in all aspects of their lives, both professional and personal.

3. *Identify the five elements of scene size-up.*

   When it comes to scene size-up, keep the following five elements in mind:
   1. Always take the time to ensure your own safety and the safety of your fellow emergency workers, the patient(s), and the public at large.
   2. Before you even get out of the ambulance, or out of your fire engine, look outside (when applicable) and see how many patients you are dealing with.
   3. Attempt to determine the cause of the illness or injury.
   4. Always use BSI and PPE when indicated.
   5. Know your limitations and ask for help early. When additional resources are needed, try to request them as early in the call as possible, hopefully while you are still in your apparatus or as soon as you recognize the need for assistance. Once you are involved in patient care it is difficult to remove yourself from the situation and ask for help.

Need to Do

The following skills are explained and illustrated in a step-by-step manner, via skill sheets and/or Step-by-Steps in this text and on the accompanying DVD:

Skill Name	Skill Sheet Number and Location	Step-by-Step Number and Location
Putting On and Removing Gloves	60 – DVD	N/A
Handwashing	61 – DVD	61 – DVD
Physical Restraints	65 – DVD	65 – DVD

Connections

- See Chapter 49, Ambulance Operations, in the textbook for more information on helicopter safety.

- Chapter 52, Teamwork and Operational Interface, includes a protocol in the form of an algorithm for handling special pathogen situations.

- See Chapter 53, Hazardous Materials Incidents, in the textbook for more detailed information on the various levels of PPE during hazmat situations and when each should be used.

- Link to the companion DVD for a chapter-based quiz, audio glossary, animations, games and exercises, and, when appropriate, skill sheets and skill Step-by-Steps.

Street Secrets

The following are safety secrets to keep in mind while working as a paramedic:

- Never allow a patient to move into a position that blocks your egress route.

- Never allow a patient to leave your sight. Accompany the patient, and alert your partner, if the patient needs to leave the room.

- When you first approach a patient, it is best to assume that the patient may pose some sort of threat until proven otherwise.

- Maintaining a safe distance between yourself and the person you are interacting with until you can determine whether or not the person is a threat, referred to as a *reactionary gap,* is a good practice to develop. If a person that you are interviewing has some sort of sharp object or potential weapon in his or her hand, you should have a reactionary gap of at least 21 feet from the person (preferably locked in your ambulance driving away from the scene while requesting the police). If the person

that you are interviewing has nothing in his or her hands and doesn't present any obvious threat, you should have a reactionary gap of at least 7 feet. The purpose of the reactionary gap is that it takes at least this amount of distance for you to react to some type of threatening act from this person and avoid personal injury.

- A *bladed stance* involves slightly widening your stance and standing at an angle of approximately 45 degrees to the interviewee. This position improves balance and center of gravity and allows for a quicker exit because you are already partially turned away from the person. Your "strong side" should be pointed away from the person.

- *Contact and cover* is a simple practice that allows for you to either be the contact member or the cover member of your EMS team; your partner will assume the duties of the other role. The role of the contact member is to make contact with the person at hand, whether that is a patient, a bystander, or a witness. The cover member's role is to provide a watchful eye over the contact member as well as the entire scene, monitoring potential threats that enter or exit the scene and maintaining responsibility for ensuring team safety. It is the cover member's responsibility to alert the contact member to any potential problems before they arise or to assist the cover member with any problems once they have occurred. The contact member is responsible for patient care. The cover member is responsible for continued scene safety. The cover member should never get so distracted as to lose sight of the big picture.

The Drug Box

There are no specific drugs related to this chapter content.

I SPY

Scenario:

You and your partner are pulling into the parking lot of your station when everything starts to shake, rattle, and roll.

"Earthquake!" exclaims your partner, as he grabs for the dashboard of the ambulance. The shaking eventually stops. For the next several minutes, the two of you just sit there, stunned by what just happened. Your dispatcher's voice comes over the radio:

"Medic 22, are you okay?" After you inform the dispatcher that you are okay, she immediately sends you to 32nd and Cypress Street for a freeway collapse to assist Engine 5 and Truck 1 already on scene.

I Spy Questions:

1. Identify at least five hazards at this scene.

_____

_____

_____

2. What should you do to minimize these hazards?

_____

_____

_____

_____

3. What is your first priority related to patient care?

_____

_____

_____

_____

Answers

Are You Ready?

1. The natural tendency when you hear radio traffic such as that described in this scenario is to get to the scene and save your friends and coworkers. Unfortunately, this can lead to devastating consequences unless you take a deep breath, slow down, and start to plan ahead. When a paramedic responds to a situation in an emotional, reactionary manner, it is referred to as "condition black." In this mode of operation, fear takes over, rational thought processes are difficult, and the paramedic will likely not be able to form a rational interpretation or response to the situation at hand. It is highly likely that someone (possibly the responder) will be injured or killed in this situation.

The *first priority* in every situation that you encounter as a paramedic is to think safety and continue to do so until the entire situation has been dealt with. (See the Awareness Color Coding System described by Colonel Jeff Cooper in Chapter 9 of the textbook for further information on awareness in potentially dangerous situations.)

2. The manner in which you proceed can have a dramatic impact on the outcome of the entire situation from a multitude of perspectives. First, you need to make sure that you get to the scene in a safe and efficient manner (wear your seat belts). When you are driving, before you put the ambulance in gear, take a deep breath or two and remind yourself to take your time and to drive safely.

Immediately begin thinking about safety. There are potentially two medics down, as the dispatcher has been unable to raise Medic 13. Call your dispatcher on the radio and request that at least one more ambulance be dispatched to the scene, in addition to your unit. If it turns out that you don't need the additional ambulance, you can cancel it once you arrive on the scene. However, if you do need the additional help, you will be glad that they are there. If definitive care (a trauma center) is a great distance away, consider requesting a helicopter earlier rather than later. Remember that it takes time for a helicopter to get into the air and get to the scene.

Plan ahead and remember that any additional resources that you request now can be cancelled if they are not needed. Have the dispatcher check with the trauma center to determine how many patients it can handle from this incident. Have a backup plan ready to implement if the trauma center is overloaded or if any of the resources that you have requested fail to materialize.

While you are driving to the call, pay special attention to the other drivers (both civilian drivers and other emergency vehicles that may be responding to the same or a different incident). Drive defensively, and have your partner keep his or her eyes open for you as well. (The passenger in front of the ambulance should call out any hazards as they approach, even if they seem obvious. The hazard that they thought you saw and didn't call out may be the one that keeps you from reaching the scene to help your coworkers.)

If the only thing that you can do is get to the scene safely and make sure that the scene is safe for you and your partner to enter (before you arrive), that is the first step to a successful outcome.

3. Ask the dispatcher to contact the police and have them advise you when the scene is secure. Stage your ambulance one to two blocks away from the scene until you have been advised that the scene has been secured. It goes without saying that you and your partner want to get to Medic 13's crew as soon as you can. However, if you enter a scene that has not been secured and you or your partner are injured or killed, the help that you intended to give will become a hindrance.

4. Ensure that you appropriately size up the scene, and report your findings to your dispatcher in a clear and concise manner. Use the following five steps to size up the scene:

a. Determine if the scene is safe and identify (and report) any hazards.

b. Determine the (approximate) number of patients. Try to do this before you get out of your ambulance, or as soon as possible afterward.

c. Establish the mechanism of injury or nature of the illness.

d. Ensure that every team member has the appropriate personal protective equipment and clothing, including body substance isolation (BSI).

e. If you have not already requested the additional information that you need, order it as early as you possibly can.

Active Learning

1. There are no "correct" answers, but the possible answers in the table on page 92 reflect general information about different settings. There are many different configurations and conditions throughout the country that may differ from the following table. No matter where you work, you will be faced with different challenges specific to your area, and it helps to understand the challenges that you could face ahead of time rather than during a critical situation.

2. Intersections

3. Because of their large size, ambulances tend to have a high center of gravity, and extreme caution needs to be exercised while driving ambulances to avoid rollovers; their squared-off design creates large "blind spots," so ambulance operators need to use all their mirrors and remain constantly aware of where vehicles are located around them; the large size negatively impacts high-speed maneuverability; ambulances are difficult to stop quickly once they are moving.

4. (1) Is the scene safe? (2) How many patients are there? (3) What is the mechanism of injury or nature of the illness? (4) Does every team member have the appropriate personal protective equipment and clothing, including BSI? (5) Do we need any additional resources for this situation?

5. Always consider your visibility to others; use all vehicle emergency lighting; wear high-visibility reflective outerwear over your uniform; provide a "zone of safety" in which to work (position the ambulance between the crash scene and oncoming traffic); use cones and flares to help identify the emergency scene; use law enforcement officers to provide assistance directing traffic around the scene.

6. Make sure that the police are on the scene and that the scene is secure (safe). No matter what terminology is used by local law enforcement to advise an EMS team that it is cleared to enter a dangerous scene, this clearance needs to be obtained before paramedics approach and subsequently enter a scene.

7. Stage a safe distance away until you can confirm that the scene is safe to enter.

8. Cover offers protection from view and provides a barrier to stop projectiles such as knives or bullets. For example,

Possible Answers to Active Learning Exercise 1.

	Settings		
Factors	**Urban**	**Suburban**	**Rural**
Response time	Because of the number and density of people located within a relatively small geographical area, there tend to be more ambulances that are located closer to incidents. However, due to the large population located in a small area, traffic can be a factor that slows the response time.	There tend to be fewer people per geographical area as compared with the urban setting, but there may not be as many EMS resources as seen in an urban setting. Traffic, on the other hand, may not be as difficult as in the urban setting, so response times may improve in this area.	The number of people per geographical area is significantly smaller than in an urban or suburban setting. Because of the relatively small number of people, the EMS resources tend to be relatively small. Some rural communities have EMS providers that cover hundreds of square miles, and their response times can be very long.
Advanced life support (ALS) ambulance availability	ALS ambulances tend to be the predominant type of response level used in this setting.	Tend to have a similar ALS ambulance availability to the urban setting with the possibility of a slightly larger BLS component.	The tendency for ALS ambulances in this area is less than the other settings primarily due to cost, size of population, and training factors.
Basic life support (BLS) ambulance availability	BLS ambulances may be used to supplement the ALS tier in this setting, but do not tend to be the predominant type of ambulance. BLS ambulances can be used in two-tier systems or as transfer units.	BLS ambulances can be used to supplement the ALS tier in this setting, but do not tend to be the predominant type of ambulance. BLS ambulances can be used in two-tier systems or as transfer units.	BLS ambulances, whether paid positions or volunteer, tend to be more prevalent in the rural setting than in urban or suburban systems.
EMS aircraft availability	This setting may have a large number of EMS aircraft available, but depending on the density of the city and the proximity to definitive care, their use may be minimal. EMS aircraft in this setting are more frequently used to transport patients between facilities, or from scenes in outlying (suburban or rural) areas to trauma centers and specialty care hospitals within the urban area.	This setting may have access to EMS aircraft, and probably more landing zone possibilities than an urban setting.	The rural areas may not have EMS aircraft available locally, but they tend to benefit from the use of EMS aircraft because of the long transport times to specialty care facilities (trauma centers, etc.).
Level of training	Personnel within an urban setting tend to have a high level of training and a high level of practical experience.	Depending on the size of the population and the availability of funds, the level of training can be very high.	Training facilities and funding for training can be a significant challenge for some rural settings.
Time to hospital	Usually is short as there tend to be more hospitals closer together than found in other settings.	Has the likelihood of being longer than in an urban setting, but may not have some of the traffic issues that an urban EMS system experiences.	Rural systems tend to have long transport times to hospitals, especially those specialty hospitals such as trauma centers.
Time to trauma center	Tends to be relatively short, mostly because there are usually more trauma centers in this setting than in any of the other settings.	Tends to be longer than in an urban setting.	Tends to be very long. Thus trauma patients in a rural setting may benefit from transport by EMS aircraft.
Law enforcement availability	More law enforcement officers with more specialized training.	Suburban settings tend to have smaller police/sheriff departments.	Many rural departments tend to be smaller and to cover greater areas than urban or suburban areas.

standing behind a concrete wall offers cover (and concealment).

9. Concealment provides visual protection, but it does not provide an appropriate barrier to stop projectiles. For example, standing behind a bushy shrub can provide concealment.

10. Never allow a patient to move into a position that blocks your egress route; keep an eye on your partner as well as on the position of the patient and bystanders; never allow a patient to leave your sight, even under the pretense of getting medication or information from another room. Accompany the patient and alert your partner when you leave the room.

11. Raised voices, agitated movements, quickly rising from a seated position, pacing back and forth like a caged animal, clenched or balled-up fists, hands raised in a threatening manner.

12. a.

When you first approach a patient, it is best to assume that the patient may pose some sort of threat until proven otherwise. If you begin to interview your patient using a tactical interview process, maintaining a safe distance between yourself and the person you are interacting with until you can determine whether or not the person represents a threat to you, you will have the upper hand if something goes wrong. The process of maintaining a safe distance from the person that you are interviewing is referred to as maintaining a *reactionary gap.* If a person that you are interviewing has some sort of sharp object or potential weapon in his or her hand, you should have a reactionary gap of at least 21 feet from the person (preferably locked in your ambulance driving away from the scene requesting the police). If the person that you are interviewing has nothing in his or her hands and doesn't present any obvious threat, you should have a reactionary gap of at least 7 feet. What this means is that it takes at least this amount of distance for you to react to some type of threatening act from this person to avoid personal injury.

b.

A *bladed stance* involves slightly widening your stance and standing at an angle of approximately 45 degrees to the interviewee. This position improves balance and center of gravity and allows for a quicker exit because you are already partially turned away from the person. Your "strong side" should be pointed away from the person (this would be your right-hand side if you are right-handed, and your left-hand side if you are left-handed).

c.

Contact and cover is a simple practice that allows for you to either be the contact member or the cover member of your EMS team. Your partner will assume the other role. The role of the contact member is to make contact with the person at hand, whether that is a patient, a bystander, or a witness. The cover member's role is to provide a watchful eye over the contact member as well as the entire scene, monitoring potential threats that enter or exit the scene and maintaining responsibility for ensuring team safety. It is the cover member's responsibility to alert the contact member to any potential problems before they arise or to assist the cover member with any problems once they have occurred. The contact member is responsible for patient care. The cover member is responsible for continued scene safety. The cover member should never get so distracted as to lose sight of the big picture that is occurring.

13. Position yourself between the patient and your egress route; do not let them cut you off from your exit. If you and your partner are interviewing two patients, you may wish to position yourselves so you and your partner can maintain eye contact and the patients or bystanders cannot readily see each other.

You Are There: Reality-Based Cases
Case 1

1. Scene safety and scene size-up begin long before you arrive on the scene. The process of ensuring safety as well as scene size-up for each individual call should begin when you are dispatched and continue throughout the entire call. With the information that you have received thus far, you have a decent start on scene size-up and scene safety. You can begin the process of scene size-up with a mental scene size-up checklist:

- Is the scene safe? The scene is safe according to the information that was relayed to you by dispatch about the sheriff being on the scene. Even though the scene has been declared safe, it is always good practice to be extremely cautious at the scene of a violent crime.

- How many patients are there? There are eight patients with "serious stab wounds" according to the sheriff.

- What is the mechanism of injury or nature of the illness? The mechanism of injury per the information that you have received is stabbing.

- Does every team member have the appropriate personal protective equipment and clothing, including BSI? You do not yet have this information, but you have a good idea based on past practice that all the people involved with the care of these patients will be utilizing appropriate BSI.

- Do we need any additional resources for this situation? Yes! With the report of eight patients with "serious stab wounds" you will definitely need additional resources.

2. With the information that you have received over the radio you know that you will not be able to handle the situation by yourselves. Now you are faced with the task of planning what you will do with eight potentially critical trauma patients with stab wounds.

First you will need to request additional resources. The volunteer BLS ambulance is 15 minutes behind you, and you are not sure if the volunteer ALS ambulance will be available or not. You contact your dispatcher and request that the two helicopters be dispatched and get an update on the availability of the volunteer ALS ambulance. Now that you have requested the helicopters, you need to make sure that there is a place to land them in relatively close proximity to the scene. You advise your dispatcher to contact the sheriff and the local volunteer fire department to identify and prepare one and preferably two landing zones (as the faster the patients receive definitive care, the better). The next thing you need to do is have your dispatcher contact the trauma center and the local hospital to see how many patients they can handle receiving (patients with non-life threatening wounds can be transported to the local hospital, and the patients with more critical wounds can be transported to the trauma center).

3. Based on the findings of your initial triage of the patients, the estimated times of arrival (ETA) of the resources that are responding to this incident, the proximity of the hospitals, and the number of patients that the hospitals can handle, you make the following decision: There are five critical patients, two delayed patients, and one deceased patient whom the sheriff will take care of. Of the two helicopters that are responding, one can transport one patient and the other has the capability of transporting two patients. You decide that the three most critical (immediate) patients will be transported by helicopter to the trauma center, and you and your partner will take the two remaining (immediate) critical patients in your ambulance (get one of the volunteers to drive) and head to the trauma center. The helicopter that is capable of transporting two patients will be loaded first because you figure that if they deliver the patients to the trauma center and then meet you at the local emergency department, they can transport the two remaining immediate patients to the trauma center much faster than you could drive them there. The two delayed patients will be transported to the hospital by the volunteer BLS ambulance.

4. The following information is important to convey when setting up or describing a landing zone (LZ). (The mnemonic HOTSAW can be used to assist in remembering the following LZ information):

   Hazards—wires, towers, debris
   Obstructions—trees, fences, signs
   Terrain—wet terrain, type of terrain
   Slope—5 degrees or less
   Animals—keep all animals at least 500 feet away
   Wind—speed, direction, gusts

5.
   - Remember the tail rotor is going in excess of 1600 revolutions per minute. It is nearly invisible and always fatal if someone walks into it.
   - Do not approach the LZ while the helicopter is landing or departing.
   - Do not approach the helicopter on your own. Make visual contact with the pilot first, and use hand signals to indicate that you want to approach the helicopter.
   - Approach the helicopter from the front or side. If the helicopter must land on a slope, always approach from the down-slope side.

   - When approaching the helicopter, walk in a crouched position. The blades of the helicopter are extremely flexible, and on some models they will dip down to about 4 feet as the helicopter turbines slow down.
   - If the helicopter lands on a hill, never approach from the uphill side.
   - Always take sheets off the stretcher before approaching the aircraft. Helicopters can generate hurricane-force winds.
   - Never leave a stretcher unattended near the landing zone.
   - Do not wear hats around a running aircraft. If wearing a rescue helmet, make sure your chin strap is buckled.
   - Never walk under the tail of the helicopter.
   - Never walk behind the helicopter.
   - Don't allow smoking within 100 feet of the aircraft.
   - Never shine bright lights or headlights at the aircraft during landing or liftoff.
   - Do not carry IVs above your head or use an IV pole.
   - No ambulances or other vehicles are permitted within 50 feet of the aircraft.
   - Keep bystanders back an additional 100 feet from the landing zone. If there is an undesirable event on the field, objects may be hurled from the site and cause serious injury or death.

Test Yourself

1. False
   The scene size-up assessment begins upon receipt of dispatch information.

2. c
   Nonverbal cues of aggressive behavior include hands clenched and raised. Low-pitched, slow voices and hands facing palm out typically do not represent aggressive behavior. Constantly looking at an exit may represent fear or anxiety.

3. d
   The use of lights and sirens is called "operating in an emergency mode."

4. b
   High-efficiency particulate air filter (HEPA) is personal protective equipment. Turnout coat and pants, hearing and head protection, and reflective outer clothing are safety equipment.

5. b
   When soap and running water are not available, hands should be sanitized with alcohol-based hand cleansers.

6. An iatrogenic disorder is any disorder that a patient develops that is caused by the treatment of a health-care provider. Iatrogenic conditions are thought to be conditions that would not have developed if proper care had been rendered.

7. The zone of safety pertains to safely positioning the ambulance between the crash scene and oncoming traffic to provide some protection.

8. Constant awareness of existing outbreaks and intervals is necessary to ensure the health of the paramedic.

   Many patients are contagious before symptoms develop. Patients transported by ambulance should receive nebulizer treatments or other infectious aerosol-producing treatments only if absolutely necessary to prevent disease transmission.

9. Paramedics should receive immunizations against infectious agents such as influenza, hepatitis, and tetanus. Check with your physician about your status in terms of screening for tuberculosis (PPD or chest X-ray), measles-mumps-rubella (MMR), hepatitis B, hepatitis A (if required by your agency), diphtheria-pertussis-tetanus (DPT), polio, chickenpox, influenza (annual immunizations), and rabies (if appropriate to your risk).

10. c

   When pushing or pulling, keep your elbows bent with your arms close to your body. If the weight is lower, push or pull from the knees.

11. b

   Perhaps the single most important action taken by a paramedic responding to any scene of a medical emergency is the utilization of appropriate personal protective equipment (PPE) to prevent accidental exposure to potentially contaminated body fluids.

12. When performing a lift, keep your body as close to what you're lifting as possible, keeping your arms tucked in close to your body. Grasp objects so that your hands are positioned with the palms facing up instead of down. Bend at the knees instead of the waist, and keep your back straight with your legs shoulder width apart.

13. True

   In the case of nerve agents, EMS personnel must be familiar with the administration of injectable antidotes like atropine and pralidoxime.

14. Influenza

   Influenza outbreaks occur every year. The flu is the most common large-scale health problem encountered by paramedics.

15. a

   Everyone in the vehicle should be in a safety restraint. The literature suggests that paramedics and patients in the back of the ambulance are at most risk for injury and have the lowest compliance for use.

I Spy

1. Hazards at this scene include:
   - The pillars from the upper deck of the freeway have fallen and are leaning against the pillars for the lower deck of the freeway.
   - The upper deck of the freeway has fallen onto the lower deck of the freeway.
   - The pillars for the lower deck appear to be damaged in places.
   - There is smoke pouring out of the area between the upper and lower deck.
   - There is rebar sticking out of the concrete and posing an impaling risk.
   - There are people wandering under and around the damaged structure.
   - It is getting dark (sunset), and visibility will become an issue.

2. The following are ways to minimize these hazards:
   - Coordinate efforts with other rescue workers through a unified command at a command post.
   - Make sure that all the civilians are clear of the structure in the event of further collapse.
   - Allow trained professionals with proper equipment to perform rescues of trapped people.
   - No "freelancing."
   - Maintain order by following tasks assigned by incident command; make sure that you work with a partner and that someone knows where you are at all times.
   - Wear appropriate PPE, and make sure that you have all the equipment that you need for your assigned task.
   - Make sure that you have adequate lighting to perform the tasks that you have been assigned.

3. Your first priority is rescuer safety. Then, the following can be undertaken:
   - If first on scene, take the role of medical group supervisor (MGS) and check in with the incident commander (it is difficult not to go to work helping people, but an organized effort will yield much better results than a disorganized "freelance" session).
   - Advise your dispatcher of the findings of your initial scene survey (type of incident, exact location, hazards, number of victims, access, egress, staging location, etc.).
   - Request additional resources as needed.
   - Locate and triage victims (if that is the task that you are assigned).
   - Establish a treatment area (if that is the task that you are assigned).
   - Establish a staging area (if that is the task that you are assigned, and it has not been done already).

chapter 10

Therapeutic Communications and History Taking

Are You Ready?

It's Sunday morning, and it promises to be another hot, muggy day. You groan as you get dressed in your heavy cotton uniform; at least the shirt is short-sleeved.

As you head out to the garage, you hear your unit being called for a "medical emergency at Saint Augustine's Church, 227 West 25th Street." Your partner starts up the diesel motor, and you head out of the bay and into the morning sunshine.

You can see people leaving the church as you arrive. As you make your way to the open door of the church, you are directed to an area of the pews where you find an elderly woman sitting down. Several people surround the woman fanning her with paper. The white-haired woman looks at you as you approach. In fact it seems that *everyone* is looking at you.

1. How do you begin your interactions with the patient and bystanders? What communication techniques would be helpful in this situation?

   _____

   _____

   _____

Active Learning

1. Know Thyself

You need to be aware of your bias and temperament before you can approach all your patients professionally and respectfully. Visit www.keirsey.com/ and take the free Keirsey Temperament Sorter. This might give you a better understanding of your personality type and temperament.

Another more widely used personality assessment tool is the Myers-Briggs Type Inventory (MBTI). An online version of this tool can be found at www.humanmetrics.com/cgi-win/JTypes2.asp.

Assessment tools such as these are sometimes criticized as being more "parlor trick" than science. Always take into account that any one test or tool is unlikely to reveal everything about a person's feelings, intuitions, and outlook on life. On the other hand, you might learn something about yourself if you answer the questions seriously and honestly.

2. Describe Thyself

a. Using the space provided, list adjectives that describe how you perceive yourself in various environments.

Public Self	Real Self	Future Self
How do others describe you?	What are your true feelings?	Who would you ideally like to become?

    b. List five positive qualities about yourself.

    _____

    _____

    c. List five negative qualities about yourself.

    _____

    _____

    d. How might these qualities affect your work as you encounter patients, bystanders, and other members of the health-care team in your work as a paramedic?

    _____

    _____

    e. How might you be able to actively change your own perceived negative qualities?

    _____

    _____

You Are There: Reality-Based Cases

Case 1 (continued from chapter opening)

You kneel down beside the woman and smile. "Hello my name is Bob, and I am a paramedic. What is your name?"

"My name is Marion McClure," the patient replies.

"Mrs. McClure, how can I help you?"

"I'm fine, young man. I'd just like to go home. Would you be able to take me home?" You gently rest your hand on the patient's arm. As you do, you quickly check for a radial pulse. It feels faint and slower than what you think is normal. She is also slightly diaphoretic. You consider how you will respond to her request. Meanwhile, you turn to your partner. "Sam could you . . . ."

1. What would you like Sam to do? Why?

    _____

    _____

2. In addition to positioning yourself on one knee, what other body movements can you perform that will help with your communications with the patient?

    _____

    _____

3. What might you say to Mrs. McClure at this point?

    _____

    _____

Case 2

You are beginning your evaluation of Eric Kaiser, a 54-year-old male who collapsed this morning while stepping out of his shower. His wife heard him call out and found him curled up on the floor near the bathroom door. He couldn't stand, and she called 9-1-1. He is alert and sitting on the floor in the hallway. He states that he has discomfort in his chest. Imagine yourself being part of the following dialogue.

1. Given the patient's response, fill in the blanks with the question you should have asked:

Patient's Statement	Your Question?
"I'm allergic to sulfa drugs."	*Are you allergic to any medications?*
"Medicine for my high blood pressure."	
"Like someone is stabbing me in the back, right between the shoulder blades."	
"I guess last night's dinner."	
"I can't find a comfortable position."	
"My doctor just told me that my blood pressure is too high."	
"I think I was taking a shower when the pain came on all of a sudden. I felt my legs go numb."	
"Yeah, it's a little hard to breathe."	
"It's pretty bad. Never felt anything like this before."	
"I haven't done any lifting recently."	
"No, the pain's right there."	

Test Yourself

1. While dealing with a difficult patient paramedics should
   a. conform to the patient's behavior.
   b. take offense at the patient's behavior.
   c. be aware of their own emotional bias.
   d. ignore their own emotional triggers.

2. Using the OPQRST acronym what does *onset* refer to
   a. The time of onset of the first symptoms
   b. The events that were occurring when symptoms started
   c. What occurred leading up to the request for assistance
   d. The time the symptoms significantly worsened

3. Which of the following is an open-ended question?
   a. Are you allergic to anything?
   b. Did you eat breakfast today?
   c. What medications are you taking?
   d. Have you seen the doctor lately?

4. Silence can be a useful technique during a patient interview because it
   a. encourages the patient to continue speaking.
   b. can let the patient focus on his or her breathing.
   c. gives the paramedic time to think of questions.
   d. allows the paramedic to write patient notes.

5. When using the SAMPLE and OPQRST acronyms,
   a. transport should be delayed until all information is collected.
   b. collect SAMPLE information before OPQRST information.
   c. information can be collected throughout the patient transport.
   d. information should be collected in the order of each acronym.

6. The essence of _____ has been described as the ability to see other people as they see themselves.

7. A patient states he has chest pain, cannot catch his breath, feels sick to his stomach, and is dizzy. These are an example of _____ findings.

8. A patient's statement, "I was mowing the lawn when the pain started," would address the _____ element of the OPQRST acronym.

9. During the primary assessment, the paramedic
   a. confirms scene safety.
   b. forms the general impression.
   c. checks for life threats.
   d. obtains past medical history.

10. Avoiding silence is a component of effective communication.

    True

    False

11. The chief complaint the patient tells the paramedic
    a. is documented as a patient quote.
    b. is the same as the dispatch information.
    c. provides the patient's medical history.
    d. remains the same throughout the call.

12. For the patient to discuss personal information with the paramedic, the patient will need to have a
    a. degree of disclosure with the paramedic.
    b. reliability of information with the hospital.
    c. degree of comfort with the paramedic.
    d. level of disclosure with the ambulance service.

13. When communicating with the patient or family members, the paramedic should avoid using what kinds of communication?

    _____

    _____

14. After the patient concludes his or her comments, the paramedic should summarize the information given. This is known as paraphrasing.

    True

    False

15. Using the OPQRST acronym, what does *time* refer to?
    a. What occurred leading up to the request for assistance
    b. The events that were occurring when symptoms started
    c. The time of onset of the first symptoms
    d. The symptom starting suddenly or gradually

16. A general impression of the patient is formed before the primary assessment.

    True

    False

17. The reason that a patient seeks care from EMS is known as the _____.

18. You park on the patient's lawn, enter the patient's home without knocking, and track mud onto their carpet. This type of communication is _____ and _____.

19. The term for the noticeable absence of a symptom typically expected for a certain disease process is a _____.

20. During the secondary assessment, the paramedic
    a. obtains the past medical history.
    b. forms the general impression.
    c. checks for life threats.
    d. makes the scene safe.

Need to Know

The following represent the Key Objectives of Chapter 10:

1. *Establish a professional rapport with the patient.*

   How you begin your interaction with your patient is key to building a successful relationship quickly.

   • Look professional. (See Box 10-1 in the textbook for a list of behaviors that a professional provider will demonstrate during a call.)

   • Be aware of your body language. Remember that what is considered personal space can vary from one culture to the next. Speaking to the patient in a clear and measured voice, while at the patient's eye level, will convey that you care.

   • Although looking directly at a patient while speaking is considered to be a cultural norm in our society, other cultures may see that as a sign of disrespect or as a threat. Be conscious of how the patient responds to your body cues during the first moments of contact, and adjust accordingly.

   • Address the patient in a formal manner first. If the patient asks you to use an informal tone, by all means do so.

2. *Communicate with the patient to effectively elicit an appropriate history.*

   Allow the patient to provide you with the initial details of his or her illness or injury as much as possible. Interrupting the patient early or often can in fact increase the amount of time it takes to elicit a history.

   Maintain objectivity and avoid premature interpretation of the patient's statements by using active listening techniques or appropriate moments of silence to ensure that you clearly understand the information that the patient is trying to provide.

   Most importantly, be as empathetic as you can. As you gain experience you may believe that the patient's complaint may not be of an emergent nature. However, your patient may have been compelled to call you because he or she felt that it was. Don't belittle or insult your patient—it won't help you gain the patient's confidence, which you will need to accurately assess the patient's condition.

3. *Use basic mnemonics to organize your line of questioning.*

The information that the patient provides is part of the subjective assessment that you help guide through thoughtful, concise questioning techniques. Using a combination of closed- and open-ended questions to guide this part of history taking is both a skill and an art. Using the SAMPLE and OPQRST mnemonics is a useful jump-off point for further questions.

4. *Integrate patient autonomy concepts with patient care plans (e.g., consent issues, destination decisions, and refusal of care).*

You must determine your patient's ability to consent to care early. Simply asking the question, "Can I help you?" can provide you the answer quickly. Explain what you are doing for the patient clearly, using vocabulary that is appropriate to his or her comprehension level. Be sure to review Chapter 4, Legal Issues, in the textbook for situations in which implied consent exists, or when consent is needed from the guardian of a child or dependent adult.

5. *Communicate with health-care providers to effectively relay patient information and findings during the transfer of care.*

As part of the care continuum you will need to transmit the information you find about a patient's condition to the next link of the health-care system. Basic assessment findings that need to be summarized effectively include:

- Appropriate scene information, including nature of injury (NOI) and mechanism of injury (MOI)
- Primary assessment findings
- Appropriate history-taking findings, including pertinent negatives
- Appropriate physical findings, including pertinent negatives

6. *Communicate with family, friends, and bystanders to effectively elicit additional history and provide reassurance.*

Bystanders can provide valuable observations and other information about the patient's current condition. It is your responsibility to elicit those findings in the same way you would with the patient. Often the family or friends of the patient will feel stressed or frightened by what they see happening to their loved one. Your ability to reassure them and gain their trust will be critical to the success of the call.

Need to Do

The following skills are explained and illustrated in a step-by-step manner, via skill sheets and/or Step-by-Steps in this text and on the accompanying DVD:

Skill Name	Skill Sheet Number and Location	Step-by-Step Number and Location
Communication Challenges—Interpreter Services	62–DVD	N/A
Verbal Communications	63 – DVD	N/A
Documentation	64 – DVD	N/A

Connections

- Your ability to gain the trust of your patient is essential to conducting a thorough and accurate assessment. Integrate what you learn here with the information presented in Chapter 14, Patient Assessment, in the textbook.
- Remember that age-specific populations, such as pediatrics and geriatrics, may require different communication techniques. Chapters 43 and 44 in the textbook cover these differences in more detail.
- Chapter 48, Patients from Diverse Cultures, in the textbook discusses issues and concerns relative to diverse population subsets. Although there are many differing cultural norms, respect, honesty, and professionalism cross all borders.
- Link to the companion DVD for a chapter-based quiz, audio glossary, animations, games and exercises, and, when appropriate, skill sheets and skill Step-by-Steps.

Street Secrets

- **Patients with Hearing Loss**   Speaking very loudly at someone who is hearing-impaired will likely not help. Age-related hearing loss occurs generally over a long period of time. People learn to read the lips of the persons speaking at them, as well as their body language. Rather than speaking in a loud voice, make sure people can see your face clearly and speak to them in a normal, clear voice. This way they can read your lips and try to interpret what you are saying. In some cases, the hearing loss is in specific frequencies in the sound range, often the higher ones. You can try to accommodate this by speaking in a lower tone; however, you will need to keep the volume of your voice at a normal level.

■ **Communication Tools**   There are a variety of tools to help with communication issues (Figure 10-1). One example is written medical questions and answers that are organized for quick location and retrieval. These written instructions can be helpful for deaf patients and can be written in several lan-

guages to assist with non-English-speaking patients.

The Drug Box

There are no specific drugs related to this chapter content.

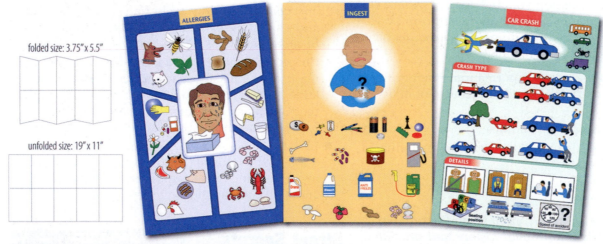
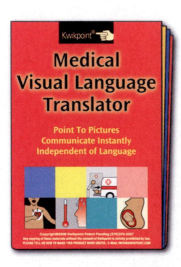

Pocket-sized picture guide that breaks down language barriers.

Enables communication of critical information items for triage.

Facilitates communication when an interpreter is not available.

Ensures better understanding even when an interpreter is used.

www.kwikpoint.com

FIGURE 10-1   Examples of pictures and written questions on boards used to help communicate with deaf and non-English-speaking patients.

I SPY

Scenario:

Compare and contrast the paramedic's interaction in these two photographs.

I Spy Questions:

1. What observations can you make about the paramedic's interaction with the patient in the photo on the left?

2. Identify at least three behaviors that the paramedic in the photo on the right has done to improve her communication with the patient.

Answers

Are You Ready?

1. Based on your observations, you can see that people are concerned about the welfare of their fellow parishioner. Treat these bystanders with respect, and politely ask them to step aside so that you can approach the patient. Although this is likely a safe scene, you should still maintain an awareness of your surroundings. An easy way to do this is to be in continual contact with the group. Asking questions and having bystanders help with minor scene control will allow people to feel helpful during a time of crisis.

   A person who is older than you deserves your full attention and respect. Your patient is sitting down; you will need to get on her level to initiate eye contact. An older person may have eyesight and hearing issues, which you can overcome with clear speech and good lighting so she can see you form your words. Using formal language such as "Ms. Smith" or "Ma'am" to address your patient is another way to convey your respect.

You Are There: Reality-Based Cases

Case 1

1. From your EMT-Basic training, you should recognize that your patient's primary assessment findings are not normal. You will need to begin your interventions immediately, while you continue to assess the patient. Your partner can help by placing your patient on oxygen, attaching the electrocardiogram (ECG) electrodes, and asking bystanders for more information about the patient's history of present illness (HPI) and any past medical history (PMH).

2. Place yourself in full view of the patient's line of sight. Avoid having the patient twist her head or body uncomfortably. When speaking, do so clearly. You may not need to speak loudly; patients with gradual hearing loss can even unconsciously learn to lip-read and understand

what you are saying if they are able to see your facial movements.

3. Your response might be, "Mrs. McClure, I might be able to answer your question more accurately if we can evaluate your condition first. Will that be okay?" Responding this way will allow you to gain further cooperation with the patient without immediately turning down her request.

Case 2

1.

Patient's Statement	Your Question
"I'm allergic to sulfa drugs."	Are you allergic to any medicine?
"Medicine for my high blood pressure."	Are you taking any medications?
"Like someone is stabbing me in the back, right between the shoulder blades."	What does it feel like?
"I guess last night's dinner."	When did you last eat?
"I can't find a comfortable position."	Does anything make it feel better?
"My doctor just told me that my blood pressure is too high."	What medical history do you have?
"I think I was taking a shower when the pain came on all of a sudden. I felt my legs go numb."	Do you remember what you were doing when this happened?
"Yeah, it's a little hard to breathe."	Does anything else bother you?
"It's pretty bad. Never felt anything like this before."	How severe is the pain? Have you ever had this pain before?
"I haven't done any lifting recently."	Have you done anything differently lately, like lifting something heavy?
"No, the pain's right there."	Does the pain go anywhere else?

Test Yourself

1. c

   Some general tips for dealing with difficult patients include trying not to take personal offense at their behavior and being aware of your own biases and emotional triggers. This is important so that you do not get frustrated and drawn into a confrontation with a patient.

2. b

   Onset refers to the events that were occurring when symptoms started. The time of onset of the first symptoms, and the time the symptoms significantly worsened refers to *time*. What occurred leading up to the request for assistance refers to *events* in the SAMPLE acronym.

3. c

   An open-ended question cannot be answered with a simple yes or no.

4. a

   Silence can be a useful technique during an interview. It may seem uncomfortable to sit there in silence, but remaining quiet and letting the patient talk will encourage the patient to continue speaking.

5. c

   The order in which the information in the SAMPLE history is collected does not need to match the acronym. The complete interview often does not have to occur just on the scene. Information should be collected throughout the transport of the patient, and transport should not be delayed if information can be gathered while en route to a hospital. Whenever possible, every one of the elements in SAMPLE and OPQRST should be collected and reported to the receiving care provider at the hospital.

6. Empathy

   To a large extent your ability to perform an accurate assessment, effectively communicate with a patient, and simply help a patient feel better depends on your empathy skills. Empathy is a form of understanding, both intellectually and emotionally. It is different from compassion or sympathy. Sympathy is more like feeling sad or sorry for someone. Compassion implies a desire to alleviate someone's distress. Demonstrating empathy shows patients that you have a concern for their well-being beyond their physical injury (see Figure 10-3 in the textbook).

7. Subjective

What the patient says is considered the subjective portion of your assessment and involves the patient's report of symptoms. This implies that it cannot be seen, felt, heard, or even verified by the paramedic. Take the information at face value as there is a limited ability to substantiate the information.

8. Onset

The acronym OPQRST is a mnemonic used to remember the classic questions that help clarify the attributes of a symptom. *Onset* refers to the events that were occurring when symptoms started. *Provocation* or *palliation* refers to anything that makes the symptoms worsen or improve, including any interventions performed by the patient. *Quality* refers to the nature or character of the symptom or pain. *Region* or *radiation* refers to the location of the symptom and where it is referred or radiates to. *Severity* is the patient's self-assessment of a pain level on a scale from 0–10. And *time* refers to the time of onset of the first symptoms.

9. c

During the primary assessment the paramedic quickly determines if the patient requires life-saving interventions. Further questioning during the primary assessment is accompanied by an assessment and status of the airway, breathing, and circulation. Questions during this time should be linked directly to the ABC assessment. The general impression is made prior to the primary assessment. Making the scene safe is part of the scene size-up. Past medical history is part of the secondary assessment.

10. False

Silence can be a useful technique during an interview. It may seem uncomfortable to sit there in silence, but remaining quiet and letting the patient talk will encourage the patient to continue speaking. The classic components of effective communication in western culture are active listening, eye contact, allowing choices, and appropriate touch and nonverbal communication.

11. a

The chief complaint is traditionally documented in the patient's own words, in quotes, exactly as the patient states it. It may not be what was called in to the 9-1-1 dispatcher and may change if the patient's condition changes. It may provide medical history, but it may be a new complaint.

12. c

Since human interaction is complex, it should be noted that patients will have different degrees of comfort openly admitting personal information to health-care professionals.

13. When communicating with patients, avoid using euphemisms and avoidance language, professional jargon and medical terminology, and leading or biased questions.

Don't use euphemisms or avoidance language like "passed away" for someone who has died. Instead, use direct language in a respectful and gentle way. This will help the patient and family confront bad information in a more real and therapeutic way. Use of medical terminology can be confusing to patients or make it seem like you are "talking down" to them. You will get more information if you ask straightforward, open-ended, nonbiased questions that the patient and family members can understand clearly.

14. True

As the patient concludes his or her comments, restate or paraphrase what you have heard using a summary or fewer words. Paraphrasing is important to test your understanding of what the patient has said, and it helps clarify what you think you heard.

15. c

The time of onset of the first symptoms refers to *time*. The events that were occurring when symptoms started and the symptom starting suddenly or gradually refers to *onset*. What occurred leading up to the request for assistance refers to *events* in the SAMPLE acronym.

16. True

A general impression, conducted immediately prior to initiating the primary assessment, helps identify life-threatening problems quickly. If the patient is able to speak clearly and distinctly, the patient's airway is open and probably not obstructed. The patient's speech pattern can give you an immediate idea of level of consciousness and if there is any difficulty in breathing. If the patient speaks only in one- or two-word sentences or seems out of breath, dyspnea is likely present. Nonverbal communication (the position and actions of the patient) is also an important clue to determine how sick the patient may be.

17. Chief complaint

The reason care is being sought is traditionally called the chief complaint. The chief complaint is traditionally documented in the patient's own words, in quotes, exactly as the patient states it. Studies show that patients usually have more than one primary complaint. To conduct a more patient-centered interview it is best to let the patient describe what is wrong.

18. Nonverbal; disrespectful

Initial communication with the patient is nonverbal. The manner of approach and entrance to the scene sends a message. Parking on the patient's lawn, entering the patient's home without knocking, and tracking mud onto a clean carpet can communicate disrespect before the first word is ever exchanged.

19. Pertinent negative

Just as important as discovering what symptoms are present is the noticeable absence of symptoms typically expected for a certain disease process. This noticeable absence is known as a pertinent negative, and it can help you differentiate between possible causes and sometimes rule out causes.

20. a

Past medical history is part of the secondary assessment. Checking for life threats is part of the primary assessment. The general impression is made prior to the primary assessment. Making the scene safe is part of the scene size-up.

I Spy

1. The paramedic is towering over the patient, which can be very intimidating. The look on the paramedic's face is stern. Her body position is also an assertive one, with her hand placed on her hip.

2. The paramedic has positioned herself to be at the patient's level. The paramedic is also looking directly at the patient, which allows the patient to see the paramedic's face clearly. The body position and facial expression of the paramedic convey a feeling of being attentive to the patient's needs.

chapter 11

The Normal Physical Examination

Are You Ready?

You are called to the home of a middle-aged female who is having difficulty breathing. When you arrive on scene, there is no doubt in your mind that your patient is desperately trying to breathe. Her mouth is open, and her eyes are glazed over as she struggles to move air in and out of her lungs.

1. During your time with this ill patient, you will be continually evaluating and treating her condition.

What physical exam techniques will you use to get a full picture of her condition?

_____

_____

_____

Active Learning

1. Just What Is Baseline?

This chapter is about understanding what *normal* findings are on real patients, so that you can recognize *abnormal* ones more easily. In order to build your baseline knowledge on vital signs, write down a list of people you know—family, friends, and coworkers—who would be willing to have their vital signs taken as part of this project. The trick is to have as wide a variety of age groups, gender, and body shape as possible. Measure each person's vital signs, making sure that his or her body position is the same as everyone else that you measure (i.e., they are all sitting or standing at the time of measurement). Use Table 11-1 to track your findings.

Try to measure as many sets of vital signs as you can. When you are done, compare your subjects. Do you notice any trends in the vital signs related to age, gender, or weight? What if the subjects were overweight or in excellent physical health? What was the span of "normal findings" overall?

2. Listen Up!

Or "listen down" may be more accurate. Ask your instructor if he or she has access to a CD or audiotape of lung sounds that you may borrow. Cue up a recorded sound on the playback machine, but

TABLE 11-1   **Baseline Vital Signs**

Name	Age	Gender	Height	Weight	Pulse Rate	Respiratory Rate	Blood Pressure
Example: John S.	45	Male	5'10"	220	72	12	114/92

don't play it yet. Cover the speaker with a piece of clothing, like a T-shirt. Turn the volume *down* to the point at which you can barely hear it with your ear from 6–12 inches away. Now, put on your stethoscope and place the bell over the speaker, on the cloth. Play the sound and listen to what it sounds like. Try this a few times, and then take the cloth off the speaker. Play the sound again with normal volume. Were there any differences in the sound of the recording? Try to listen to examples of the basic sounds—clear, crackles, wheezes, and rhonchi.

If your instructor has a recording of heart tones, borrow that as well and try to listen to the basic elements—S_1, S_2, split sounds, S_3. If you do not have access to these recordings, try the resources listed in the Connections section of this chapter.

3. Feel the Beat

Using Skill Sheet 25, Arterial Pulse Locations (found on the accompanying DVD), find a partner and work your way through the body to assess as many pressure points as possible. Become familiar with the amount of pressure it takes for palpating the various pulses. Place an "X" with a pen to mark the site of each pulse. If you are doing this as a classroom activity, try to check another classmate's pulses and compare how much finger pressure it takes to check pulses in similar sites on different bodies.

4. Try a Beat

Try your hand, actually your *fingers,* at some percussion techniques. Locate a classmate or friend's liver in the right upper quadrant of the abdomen, just below the costal margin. Place your index and middle fingers together, side by side on the skin, with just enough force to dimple it. Raise the two fingers of your other hand about 4–6 inches above the fingers resting on the skin. With a swift motion,

strike the last set of knuckles of the resting fingers with the fingertips of the raised ones several times. The force should be enough to generate a drumlike sound. Vary the intensity of the strike until the sound is as "clear" or unmuffled as it can be. Then, move to your thigh and repeat the same finger position and strike force. Can you tell the difference in the sound? Puff one cheek of your mouth out with air and hold it. Repeat the striking motion. What do you hear now?

You Are There: Reality-Based Cases

Case 1

You are dispatched for a "bicycle accident." Upon arrival you find a 10-year-old girl on the ground holding her elbow. She is crying and cringes as you approach.

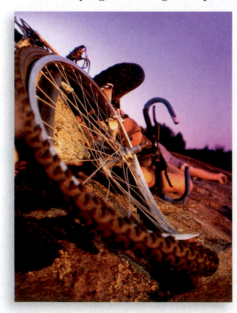

1. List the physical examination techniques that you would use to assess this pediatric patient.

   _____

   _____

   _____

2. How might your questioning and examination of this young patient be different from interviewing an adult?

   _____

   _____

   _____

Case 2

Mr. Ed Kendricks is a 61-year-old African American male who has been ill for several days. He is complaining of feeling chilled and nauseous and has vomited several times. He has not been able to eat much and has had little fluid intake. He has had intermittent sharp chest pain since yesterday that increases when he coughs.

1. List the physical examination techniques that you would use to assess Mr. Kendricks.

   _____

   _____

   _____

2. What questions would you like to ask your patient about his condition?

   _____

   _____

   _____

Test Yourself

1. You would use auscultation to help determine a patient's
   a. glucose level.
   b. blood pressure.
   c. pulse rate.
   d. eye reactivity.

2. What term describes the technique of applying mild to moderate pressure to the body?
   a. Percussion
   b. Palpation
   c. Auscultation
   d. Inspection

3. What are the minimum blood pressures for both systolic and diastolic hypertension in an adult?
   a. 140 mm Hg systolic and 90 mm Hg diastolic
   b. 130 mm Hg systolic and 90 mm Hg diastolic
   c. 140 mm Hg systolic and 80 mm Hg diastolic
   d. 130 mm Hg systolic and 80 mm Hg diastolic

4. Which of these rates falls within the range of normal resting adult respiration?
   a. 38 cycles per minute
   b. 28 cycles per minute
   c. 8 cycles per minute
   d. 18 cycles per minute

5. Which of the following rates are within the range of normal adult pulse rate?
   a. 45 beats per minute
   b. 55 beats per minute
   c. 65 beats per minute
   d. 35 beats per minute

6. Where is a pulse oximeter typically attached?
   a. The neck
   b. The chest
   c. The finger
   d. The wrist

7. What is the most common method for determining a patient's pulse rate when the patient's pulse is regular?
   a. Count for 1 minute
   b. Count for 2 minutes and divide by 2
   c. Count for 30 seconds and multiply by 2
   d. Count for 15 seconds and multiply by 4

8. To quickly and accurately assess a patient's temperature, you should touch the patient's
   a. underarm or wrist.
   b. forehead or wrist.
   c. underarm or chest.
   d. forehead or chest.

9. Percussion of the chest can be useful to determine
   a. sternum tenderness.
   b. heart tone.
   c. respiration depth.
   d. lung tissue density.

10. Your patient has a minor abrasion on his knee. Should you perform a physical examination? Why?
    a. No, because it is an unnecessary invasion of the patient's privacy.
    b. Yes, because you are likely to discover other medical concerns.

c. No, because you can use your time more effectively elsewhere.

d. Yes, because it helps strengthen your understanding of normal conditions.

11. Which of the following tasks is *not* important when assessing a patient's lower extremities?

a. Grasping the toe to determine whether the patient can feel your touch

b. Finding the popliteal, dorsalis pedis, and/or medial malleolus pulses

c. Examining the patient's reflexes by gently striking a flexed tendon

d. Checking the leg for deformities or tenderness

12. When examining the patient's lungs, what is a normal finding?

a. Lung sounds resemble a quiet wheeze

b. Lungs produce a faint crackling sound

c. Lung sounds are difficult to hear

d. Lungs produce a slight moan

13. Blood pressure readings are affected by the position of the patient's arm or the size of the blood pressure cuff.
True
False

14. A pulse that is too strong can be a sign of abnormalities.
True
False

15. Under normal conditions, after you squeeze a patient's fingertip to blanch it, color should return within 4–6 seconds after releasing the finger.
True
False

16. Paramedics are considered physician extenders because they perform many critical procedures under physician oversight.
True
False

17. You are attempting to test a patient's blood pressure, but because of background noise you cannot hear the pulse with your stethoscope. How should you proceed?

_____

_____

18. What is trending and why is it important?

_____

_____

19. What are point-of-care tests, and what are their advantages and disadvantages?

_____

_____

20. You notice that a patient seems to slow his breathing when he sees you are timing it. What is one way you can capture a true respiration rate?

_____

_____

Need to Know

The following represent the Key Objectives of Chapter 11:

1. *Explain normal findings associated with a physical examination.*

Recognizing what *normal* looks, feels, sounds, and smells like is crucial. It will help you to rapidly and accurately identify when something is not right with a patient. In order to develop your baseline knowledge, begin utilizing physical examination procedures in a consistent and commonsense way. Chapter 14, Patient Assessment, in the textbook will help you develop a consistent approach.

2. *Relate normal findings of the physical examination to normal physiological processes.*

It will be easier for you to remember what normal findings should be if you understand the basic physiological principles for how the body functions. For example, a patient is suddenly losing a large amount of blood due to some form of trauma. The body, recognizing a sudden drop in blood pressure, triggers the sympathetic nervous system to initiate a fight-or-flight response. Part of that response is to release epinephrine and norepinephrine into the bloodstream. These two hormones have many stimulating properties, including the shunting of blood from the outer skin into the deeper tissues of the body; this results in the patient's skin quickly becoming cool, pale in color, and perspiring, which are some of the first indications you will detect in this hypoperfusing patient.

3. *Identify which tests and evaluations are appropriate for emergency situations and which can help expand your understanding of the human body but do not add any value to managing a patient in an emergency situation.*

There are a wide variety of techniques that a paramedic must learn. Just as important is the understanding of which techniques should be performed all the time, which ones are crucial to be done quickly with a sick or injured patient, and which techniques will help provide additional information but can be done later in the process.

Chapter 14, Patient Assessment, in the textbook outlines the following techniques as "nice to know"—in other words, helpful but not definitively needed in an emergent situation:

- 1-minute cranial nerve exam
- Accommodation test
- Corneal reflex
- Visual acuity—confrontation
- Excursion of the chest
- Tactile fremitus
- Bronchophony
- Whispered pectoriloquy
- Egophony
- Point of maximal impulse
- Heart sounds
- Abdominal reflexes
- Extremity reflex assessment
- Babinski plantar response

Critical exam techniques that should be performed *every time* you have contact with a patient include:

- Establishing level of consciousness (AVPU)
- Looking and feeling for skin signs
- Listening for upper airway sounds
- Looking for potential airway obstructions
- Observing respiratory rate, depth, and effort
- Palpating for location, rate, and quality of a pulse

You will notice that these techniques all relate to the *primary assessment* of a patient. For more details see Chapter 14, Patient Assessment, in the textbook. The *secondary assessment* is where you will perform many of the techniques described in this chapter. The frequency of using specific techniques may vary. For example, you will need to establish a full set of vital signs on virtually every patient. Or, you may only perform a 12-lead electrocardiogram on patients who you suspect are experiencing cardiac ischemia. As you read through the different chapters of the textbook and this manual, pay attention to the examination procedures specific to each complaint. Take a look at the Need to Do section to find examples of specific assessments, such as chest pain or shortness of breath.

Need to Do

The following assessment skills are explained and illustrated in a step-by-step manner, via skill sheets and/or Step-by-Steps in this text and on the accompanying DVD:

Skill Name	Skill Sheet Number and Location	Step-by-Step Number and Location
Pulse Oximetry	12 – DVD	12 – DVD
Arterial Pulse Locations	25 – DVD	N/A
Blood Glucose Assessment	26 – DVD	26 – DVD
Chest Auscultation	27 – Appendix A and DVD	27 – This Chapter and DVD
Orthostatic Vital Signs	29 – DVD	29 – DVD
Trauma Scoring	31 – DVD	N/A
Primary Assessment	32 – Appendix A and DVD	32 – Chapter 14 and DVD
Secondary Assessment	33 – Appendix A and DVD	33 – Chapter 14 and DVD
Chest Pain Assessment	34 – DVD	N/A
Dyspnea Assessment	35 – DVD	N/A
Abdominal Assessment	36 – DVD	N/A
ECG Acquisition	37 – Appendix A and DVD	37 – Chapter 29, Section I, and DVD
Traumatic Brain Injury Assessment	76 – DVD	N/A

Chest Auscultation

Conditions: The candidate should perform this skill on a simulated patient under existing indoor, ambulance, or outdoor lighting, temperature, and weather conditions.

Indications: Any patient who is being evaluated by EMS personnel.

Red Flags: Must be conducted over bare skin.

Steps:

1. Use appropriate personal protective equipment.

2. Clean diaphragm of stethoscope with alcohol prep pad or other disinfectant.

3. Adjust auricles (earpieces) of stethoscope to fit properly.

4. Expose and inspect chest prior to listening to breath sounds.

5. Position patient so you can easily auscultate all lung fields (Figure SBS 27-1).

SBS 27-1

6. Using light to moderate finger pressure, place bell on bare chest beginning at the fourth intercostal space, midclavicular line, on the side closest to you (Figure SBS 27-2).

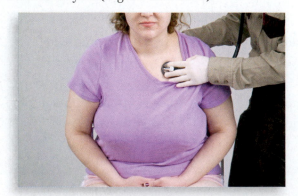

SBS 27-2

7. Direct patient to inhale deeply, and then exhale.

8. Listen, and then immediately listen to the same lung field on the opposite side (Figure SBS 27-3).

SBS 27-3

9. Repeat previous steps, performing auscultation bilaterally at the following additional sites:
   - Midclavicular, second intercostal space
   - Midclavicular, above clavicles
   - Midaxillary, fifth intercostal space
   - Midaxillary, fourth intercostal space

   Posterior chest (each side)
   - Area between top of scapula and spine
   - Area between bottom of scapula and spine

Critical Criteria:
- Use appropriate standard precautions.
- Listen bilaterally across lung fields.
- Place bell over bare skin.

Connections

- This chapter is closely tied to Chapter 14, Patient Assessment, in the textbook. Refer to that chapter as needed to determine how examination skills are integrated into the patient assessment.

- Each of the subsequent clinical chapters in the textbook will also contain references to when examination procedures should be conducted.

- There are several Web sites that have recordings of both lung and heart sounds. A few examples include The R.A.L.E. Repository (www.rale.ca/), Blaufuss Medical Multimedia Laboratories (www.blaufuss.org/), and the McGill University Virtual Stethoscope (http://sprojects.mmi.mcgill. ca/mvs/mvsteth.htm).

- Link to the companion DVD for a chapter-based quiz, audio glossary, animations, games and exercises, and, when appropriate, skill sheets and skill Step-by-Steps.

- The patient assessment is the foundation of excellent prehospital care. Problem-Based Learning Case 2, found right after Chapter 14, will test your physical exam skills.

Street Secrets

- Stethoscopes do get cold! Try to warm up the bell of your "scope" by briskly rubbing it prior to placing it on the patient's chest.

- Similarly, the gel found in patient ECG monitoring electrodes can be cold to the touch. While you may not be able to warm them, warn the patient to be ready for their application, so that there are no surprises.

- Repetition bears repeating—the more physical examination techniques you perform, the more comfortable you will be in performing them. Further, the more times you determine what a "normal" finding looks, feels, or sounds like, the more likely you'll be able to recognize an "abnormal" finding.

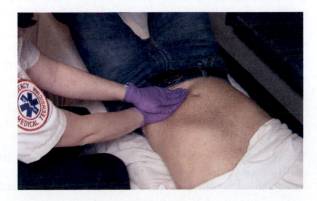

- In order for you to perform a true abdominal assessment, your patient must lay supine with his or her legs bent at the knees. This allows the organs to be in their anatomical position and the abdominal muscles to be in a relaxed position. When palpating, don't be shy! You will want to press deeply enough to get past the abdominal musculature and fascia.

The Drug Box

There are no specific drugs related to this chapter content.

Answers

Are You Ready?

1. Physical exam techniques include:

   Inspect. Respiratory rate and rhythm, evidence of accessory muscle use, skin signs, pedal edema, jugular venous distention, medical alert bracelet.

   Auscultate. Audible sounds, lung sounds, heart tones

   Palpate. Pedal edema, sacral edema.

   Vital signs. Blood pressure, pulse rate, respiratory rate.

   Others. Pulse oximetry, capnography, electrocardiograph (ECG).

   You may have identified additional techniques, which is terrific at this point. By listing the techniques, you get the idea that examining patients is a complex act, especially for a sick patient like the one in this scenario.

You Are There: Reality-Based Cases

Case 1

1. Reassure and calm the patient. Begin your assessment visually, and proceed to the physical exam slowly while continually explaining your actions to the patient. (You will also want to try to contact a parent or guardian if possible.) You will need to palpate not only the injured extremity, but also the rest of the patient's body to make sure there are no more serious, underlying injuries. Evaluating the distal circulatory, sensory, and motor function of the extremity is necessary. Obtain a full set of vital signs.

2. A child may be more fearful of your approach than an adult might be. If your visual overview of the patient indicates a "stable" presentation, you may want to take a little more time in creating the trusting relationship with the child. Sometimes a toe-to-head approach to the physical exam may be appropriate for a child at even this age. Be supportive and clear with your directions and explanations. Never lie about what you will do—if some procedure may cause additional pain, let the child know that before proceeding.

Case 2

1. Physical exam techniques include:

   Inspect. Respiratory rate and rhythm, evidence of accessory muscle use, skin signs, chest wall for redness, abdominal region for contour.

   Auscultate. Lung sounds, heart tones, presence of abdominal sounds.

   Palpate. Chest wall for tenderness, abdomen for tenderness, masses, rigidity. Consider percussion of the chest wall for areas of dullness.

   Vital signs. Blood pressure, pulse rate, respiratory rate, and orthostatic vital signs.

   Others. Pulse oximetry, capnography, ECG.

2. Your responses should include questions involving the OPQRST and SAMPLE mnemonics. Review Chapter 10, Therapeutic Communications and History Taking, in the textbook to confirm your line of questioning.

Test Yourself

1. b

   Auscultation refers to listening with a stethoscope. The pulse rate is found through palpation. Eye reactivity is found by observing the eyes when exposed to light. The glucose level is determined using a glucometer. A complete blood pressure is auscultated.

2. b

   Palpation is applying pressure to the body, such as when finding a pulse rate or checking for tenderness. Auscultation is listening with a stethoscope. Inspection is a visual examination. Percussion involves tapping an area and listening to the resulting sounds.

3. a

   Blood pressures of 140 mm Hg systolic over 90 mm Hg diastolic are considered hypertensive. Normal systolic pressure is defined as less than 120 mm Hg, and a normal diastolic pressure is less than 80 mm Hg.

4. d

   The average resting respiratory rate of an adult ranges from 12 to 20 times per minute.

5. c

   The normal resting heart rate of an adult is between 60 and 100 beats per minute.

6. c

   Typically a sensor probe is placed on a finger, but probes are also available for earlobes, an infant's foot, or even the nose.

7. d

   For regular pulses, the rate is measured by counting the number of pulsations felt over a 15-second period and multiplying by 4 to calculate the number of beats per minute. If the pulse is irregular, count the rate for 30 seconds (and multiply by 2) or for a full 60 seconds.

8. c

   Cool or cold ambient temperatures will cause the skin to naturally blanch as the peripheral capillary beds constrict. Because of this response, feeling the forehead or arms for skin temperature may be inaccurate. Placing the back of your hand against the chest or under the axilla (underarm) may provide a more accurate assessment of the body's temperature.

9. d

   Percussion involves tapping an area and listening to the resulting sound. Dense lung tissue produces a lower-pitched sound. Sternum tenderness is best determined through palpation. Heart tone and respiration depth are best determined through auscultation.

10. d

   Performing physical examinations often, even for minor injuries or illnesses, helps sharpen your appreciation of "normal" and will improve your ability to quickly detect "abnormal" situations. While you may discover other medical concerns, this is not likely. Naturally, if the patient objects, you should not perform the examination, but this is not typical.

11. c

   While it is nice to know them, checking the patient's reflexes is often not performed in a prehospital setting, while finding the pulse, inspecting and palpating the legs, and ensuring the patient can feel you typically are.

12. c

   Normal lung sounds should be difficult to hear initially, since there should be no restriction to airflow. They should be clear of any unusual noises, such as wheezes, crackles, rubbing, or moaning-type sounds.

13. True

   There are a surprising number of factors that can affect the accuracy of blood pressure measurement. Incorrect bladder size (as opposed to cuff size), improper patient or arm positioning, as well as poor cuff and stethoscope placement can all contribute to an inaccurate blood pressure measurement.

14. True

   A pulse should be neither weak nor excessively strong. A strong or bounding pulse indicates excessive force being generated by the left ventricle.

15. False

   The blanched area should become pink again within 2–3 seconds. Environmental conditions such as cold weather may increase capillary refilling time dramatically.

16. True

   As physician extenders, paramedics on the scene are the eyes, ears, and hands of the physician. The point is that you will use your senses to detect both normal and abnormal findings and will need to communicate these findings to the physician continuing to care for the patient.

17. You may test blood pressure by palpation. With the BP cuff properly positioned and deflated, begin the process by first locating the patient's radial pulse. The BP cuff

is inflated until the radial pulse can no longer be felt. Add 30 mm Hg more pressure to the BP cuff before starting to deflate. The pressure in the cuff is then slowly released until the radial pulse can be felt again. The reading at the point the pulse is first felt correlates with the systolic pressure.

Only the systolic pressure is measured with this technique. Blood pressure by palpation has been shown to be relatively accurate compared to an auscultated blood pressure. Palpated blood pressures are within 8–10 mm Hg of auscultated blood pressures.

18. Trending is the practice of using vital signs to detect changes in a patient's condition. Subtle changes in the patient's condition can go unnoticed unless frequent vital sign monitoring is occurring. Vital sign readings may change in one direction or another; for example, a steady increase in pulse and respiration can signal that shock is worsening.

19. Point-of-care tests are medical tests that can be performed in the field, such as using a glucometer to test a patient's glucose level. Compared to laboratory tests, point-of-care tests may not be as accurate, but they can be performed much more quickly. In urgent or emergent conditions such as those found in an EMS system or emergency department, the advantage of significant time savings using point-of-care testing may outweigh the more accurate findings of laboratory testing.

20. In order to capture a true respiratory rate, begin by counting the pulse rate. After an appropriate amount of time for the pulse (typically 15 or 30 seconds with a regular rhythm or a full 60 seconds with irregularity), keep your hand on the pulse and switch your attention to counting respirations. Patients will be unaware you are counting their respiratory rate, and you are more likely to obtain a true reading.

chapter 12

Airway Management, Ventilation, and Oxygenation

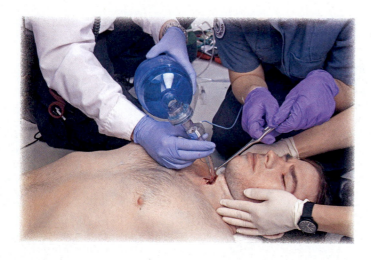

Are You Ready?

You and your classmates are attending the paramedic class graduation banquet at a Chinese restaurant following your graduation ceremony. Mike Johnson is the class clown and also the class valedictorian. He gave a speech at the graduation ceremony that brought the audience from hysteria to tears.

Mike tried to convince the class not to eat at a Chinese restaurant because he has a severe allergy to peanuts. The class outvoted him, and here you all are. The class called ahead and ordered the food, making a point to order a special dish for Mike, one that did not contain any peanut products.

The banquet is a huge success. The students, families, and staff from the school are all having a wonderful time when Mike starts to complain of itching and shortness of breath. He gets up from the table and walks outside. Most of the students are used to this type of behavior from Mike, as he was constantly walking in and out of the classroom. When Mike comes back into the restaurant, he says that he really can't breathe. He looks very anxious.

Mike is looking flushed and, as he gets closer to the table, an audible wheeze can be heard. Another student, Emily Brown, walks over to Mike, holding up her hands as she approaches him as if to tell the students to be quiet. The room becomes silent, and the wheezing can be heard very clearly. Emily sees that Mike is visibly anxious and appears to be having considerable difficulty breathing. She turns to the class and says, "Somebody call 9-1-1."

1. What is your general impression of Mike at this point in time? What is his level of distress?

   _____

   _____

   _____

2. Knowing some of Mike's medical history, what is the likely cause of Mike's shortness of breath?

   _____

   _____

   _____

3. What part of the airway is typically responsible for wheezing?

   _____

   _____

   _____

4. What is likely causing Mike's wheezing?

   _____

   _____

   _____

You assess Mike's airway, breathing, and circulation, and provide high-flow oxygen by non-rebreather mask.

Your partner obtains a baseline set of vital signs (a blood pressure [BP] of 132/66, heart rate [HR] of 124, and respiratory rate [RR] of 28) and establishes an IV of normal saline at a keep vein open (KVO) rate.

5. Based on Mike's presentation and his medical history, what type of medication would be most beneficial to treat Mike's wheezing? How does this medication work?

_____

_____

_____

Active Learning

1. Draw and Describe

Draw and describe the path that air takes from the point it enters the body to the point at which it exits. Describe the major structures of the upper and lower airways and their significance with regard to the movement and processing of the inhaled air. Be sure to include the:

- Nose
- Nasal hair
- Nasal conchae
- Nasal cavity
- Nasopharynx
- Oropharynx
- Laryngopharynx
- Epiglottis
- Larynx
- Glottic opening
- Vocal cords
- Trachea
- Carina
- Bronchi (secondary and tertiary)
- Bronchioles (interlobular and tertiary)

_____

_____

_____

2. Restricted Airways

As a paramedic you will see people suffering from a multitude of physical ailments firsthand. If you have never experienced an asthma attack, try the following exercise to help you empathize with asthma patients.

First, consider the basic pathophysiology surrounding an asthma attack:

- When an individual with asthma experiences an episode of bronchospasm, the smooth muscles of the lower airways contract and cause a narrowing of the internal lumen.
- Individuals with asthma tend to have less difficulty getting air in (during inspiration) than they do trying to get air out (during exhalation). This phenomenon is referred to as "air trapping."

Second, try the following method of mimicking what it feels like to try to breathe through constricted airways. (Remember, stop at any time if you begin to feel uncomfortable!)

- Sit and breathe in a relaxed manner.
- Take a drinking straw in one hand, and pinch your nose closed with the other hand.
- Place the drinking straw in your mouth, and wrap your lips firmly around the straw (so that air doesn't escape from the outside edge of the straw). With your nose remaining plugged, breathe normally through the straw.
- Keep breathing through the straw. You should notice that it takes a much greater effort to breathe in a relaxed manner.
- Now walk around the room or up and down a flight of stairs with the straw in your mouth and your nose plugged.
- You should notice that it is even more difficult to breathe with a diminished airway size when you exert yourself.

The final step of this exercise is to attempt to replicate air trapping:

- Continue to pinch your nose closed and breathe through the straw. Now, partially pinch off the straw during exhalation after you have exhaled approximately one-quarter of your tidal volume.
- As soon as you have exhaled one-quarter of your tidal volume, inhale.
- To restrict your airway even more, use a hollow stirring straw and repeat the experiment. What did you experience?
- Repeat this process for several cycles, and you will get an idea of how difficult it is for an individual with asthma to breathe during an episode of bronchospasm.

You Are There: Reality-Based Cases

Case 1

It is five o'clock in the morning when you and your partner clear the hospital from your last call. With only 1 hour left in your shift, in your mind, you are already in bed. The last hour of the shift is always the hardest. Trying to stay awake, coupled with an underlying fear that you will get a late call leaves you with an uneasy feeling. Just as you get into the ambulance and sink into the front seat, your text pager goes off. Your hopes of getting off on time are dashed by a call to a convalescent hospital on the other side of town. You are responding for a patient with severe shortness of breath.

When you arrive on scene, you find the fire department tracking the patient's ventilations with a bag-mask. The patient is an 87-year-old male whom the firefighter states has a history of CHF, HTN, CAD, MI, diabetes, and renal insufficiency. As you approach the patient, you note considerable supraclavicular retractions, accessory muscle use with ventilations, and audible crackles. The patient appears fatigued and frightened.

Your partner goes off to gather a history from the staff as you begin your assessment. The patient's airway appears to be patent, and the firefighter who is tracking the patient's ventilations states that the oxygen is going in with minimal resistance. The patient's oxygen saturation is 92% on supplemental oxygen, and his initial vital signs are BP of 92/54; HR of 104; irregular, labored respiratory rate of 24; and temperature of 98.5°F.

1. What is your general impression of this patient?

   _____

   _____

   _____

2. What do you suspect is wrong with the patient based on the information that you have obtained thus far?

   _____

   _____

   _____

3. What is your primary concern at this point?

   _____

   _____

   _____

4. Considering the patient's medical history, what is a likely cause for the patient's low blood pressure?

   _____

   _____

   _____

As you continue to assess the patient, you notice that he is becoming more lethargic and appears to have no more "fight" left in him. The patient has an O_2 saturation of 99%, and the electronic capnography device that you applied to the bag-mask reads: CO_2: 20 mm Hg and RR: 36. Because the patient appears to be more fatigued, you reassess his vital signs and obtain the following: BP of 74/40; HR of 110; and an irregular ventilatory rate of 36.

5. What is your general impression of the patient now?

   _____

   _____

   _____

6. Are the capnography and oxygen saturation readings appropriate for this patient?

   _____

   _____

   _____

7. What are some probable causes for the change in vital signs and patient status?

   _____

   _____

   _____

8. Is there anything that you can do to improve the patient's condition?

   _____

   _____

   _____

Test Yourself

1. You have just finished intubating a patient in cardiac arrest. Your partner asks another rescuer to take over ventilating the patient and prepares to start an IV while you are applying the ECG. You notice a reduction in the $ETCO_2$ level. The oxygen saturation appears unchanged, however. After checking the patency of the airway, you should consider

   a. decreasing the volume and rate of ventilations.
   b. fluid challenge.
   c. increasing the volume and rate of ventilations.
   d. replacing the endotracheal (ET) tube.

2. During inspiration, the pressure inside the lungs can be described as relatively _____ compared to the atmosphere.

   a. equal
   b. hyperbaric

c. positive

d. negative

3. The majority of rescuers provide ventilation at the appropriate rate and volume.

True

False

4. What are the five primary techniques you should use to confirm proper intubation?

_____

_____

5. You have responded to a 16-year-old male who is unconscious after being struck in the face with a baseball. There is a laceration across the bridge of his nose, epistaxis from both nares, and general deformity to the nose. You can hear audible gurgling of blood, and the patient shows signs of hypoxia. You should

a. perform nasotracheal intubation with manual stabilization.

b. insert a nasopharyngeal airway.

c. perform orotracheal intubation with manual stabilization.

d. perform immediate cricothyroidotomy.

6. In premature infants, lack of _____ can result in alveolar collapse.

7. A class of medications that frequently cause angioedema is called

a. angiotensin-converting enzyme inhibitors.

b. corticosteroids.

c. benzodiazepines.

d. Beta-blockers (β-blockers).

8. What are some of the common causes of airway obstruction?

_____

_____

9. You must have the ability to perform advanced invasive airway management skills in order to manage most airway problems.

True

False

10. You have responded to a 78-year-old female patient with a history of COPD. You find her sitting in a chair, leaning forward, and resting her elbows on her knees. She is pale and diaphoretic; her pulse is 128; respirations are 26 and very labored; she complains of being "hungry for air"; and her BP is 124/84. She is on 2 L/min O_2 via nasal cannula as prescribed by her physician. You obtain a pulse oximetry reading of 82%. As the EMT from the fire department reaches for a non-rebreather mask, the patient's son states that his mother cannot have a higher concentration of oxygen because it "may knock out her respiratory drive." You should

a. follow the son's instructions.

b. have the EMT continue applying high-concentration oxygen.

c. transport immediately without any supplemental oxygen.

d. begin bag-mask ventilations without oxygen.

11. Define aspiration, and list two complications associated with it.

_____

_____

12. When the head of an unconscious patient is flexed at the neck, it

a. can obstruct the airway.

b. provides clearer visualization of the airway.

c. opens up the airway.

d. has no effect on the airway.

13. When providing assisted ventilations through a bag-mask device, you should ventilate at a rate of approximately one breath every _____ seconds for most patients.

14. Discuss the negative effects of tachypnea.

_____

_____

15. Receptors in the carotid artery and in the medulla oblongata stimulate an increased respiratory rate in response to

a. increased O_2.

b. decreased pH.

c. decreased CO_2.

d. increased pH.

16. Define the term *atelectasis*.

_____

_____

17. What three factors should guide your decision to intubate (or use any other aggressive airway technique)?

_____

_____

18. The most important method of ensuring airway patency is
    a. colorimetric exhaled CO_2 detectors.
    b. pulse oximetry.
    c. end-tidal CO_2 monitoring (capnography).
    d. systematic and redundant reassessment.

19. What is the difference between hypoxia and hypoxemia?

    _____

    _____

20. You have responded to the scene of a house fire. The occupants were able to self-evacuate the building a short time after the fire started, and the fire chief would like you to "check them over." They all appear anxious but unhurt. You have some concerns regarding possible carbon monoxide poisoning. Your best course of action for these patients would be to
    a. apply a pulse oximeter to look for abnormal readings.
    b. transport them to the emergency department for further evaluation.
    c. remain on scene and observe the patients for signs of carbon monoxide poisoning.
    d. look for the classic "cherry red" face color.

21. What is the normal range for end-tidal CO_2?

22. In assessing a 45-year-old unresponsive diabetic patient, you notice that she is exhibiting classic Kussmaul's respiration. This type of respiration is probably an attempt by the body to
    a. increase the amount of inspired O_2.
    b. eliminate excess CO_2.
    c. increase glucose absorption.
    d. eliminate excess water in the lungs.

23. Prolonged suctioning can cause increased hypoxia.
    True
    False

24. External respiration occurs at the
    a. alveolar-capillary membrane.
    b. pharynx.
    c. lips and nose.
    d. trachea.

25. The lower airway begins at the
    a. pharynx.
    b. alveolar-capillary membrane.
    c. vocal cords.
    d. cricothyroid membrane.

26. Vocal cord spasm (laryngospasm) is a complication most frequently associated with
    a. tricyclic antidepressants.
    b. hypertension.
    c. use of airway adjuncts in BLS airway management.
    d. paralytic agents used in rapid sequence intubation.

27. You have responded to the airport for an international flight that made an emergency landing due to a medical emergency. As you board, you find that the flight crew has applied oxygen to a patient in obvious respiratory distress. You are unable to speak with her due to a language barrier, and no interpreter is available. You complete your assessment and find that she has a patent airway and her lung sounds appear clear, but aircraft noise has limited your ability to auscultate fully. Her vital signs are HR of 128 and BP of 134/P, and the ECG shows sinus tachycardia. You apply a pulse oximeter, which reads 92%, and capnography, which shows slightly reduced CO_2 and a right-sided curve shift. Your partner has established an IV. You contact medical control. The physician would be most likely to order
    a. transportation to a hyperbaric chamber.
    b. administration of albuterol.
    c. immediate transport of the patient on her left side.
    d. immediate intubation.

28. In the average-sized adult, the tip of the endotracheal tube should be placed about _____ cm from the teeth.

29. What are the two primary mechanisms that cause cyanosis?

    _____

    _____

30. What is the Sellick maneuver, and how is it performed?

    _____

    _____

31. Assisted ventilation techniques create a positive pressure inside the chest, which can lead to changes that worsen perfusion and cardiac output.
    True
    False

32. The high-pitched, raspy sound made on exhalation as a result of airway obstruction is called snoring.

   True

   False

33. Oxygen and carbon dioxide are moved across the alveolar-capillary membrane by

   a. diffusion.

   b. the Krebs cycle.

   c. osmosis.

   d. the sodium-potassium pump.

34. You have responded to a patient in cardiac arrest. Bystanders have performed CPR for 3 minutes prior to EMTs arriving about 5 minutes ago. The EMTs have been providing CPR with bag-mask ventilation since their arrival. During the resuscitation you notice that the patient has jugular venous distention. This is probably a result of

   a. diminished venous return.

   b. occluded pulmonary vessels.

   c. abdominal aortic aneurysm.

   d. carotid aneurysm.

35. You have responded to a 14-year-old male who has ingested a toxin. He presents with a pulse rate of 72, respirations of 14, and a progressively diminishing level of consciousness. Medical control orders intubation, followed by administration of activated charcoal. Which of the following routes would most likely be ordered by medical control (assuming all are permitted under your protocols)?

   a. Intravenous (IV)

   b. Rectal (PR)

   c. Nasogastric tube (NGT)

   d. Oral (PO)

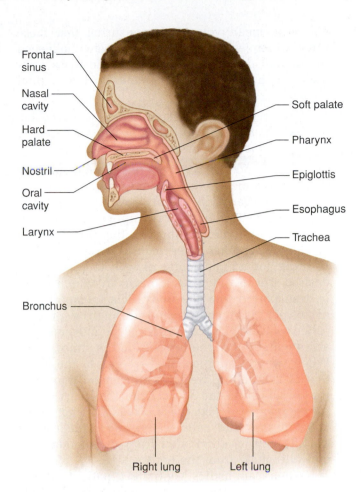

FIGURE 12-1 Organs of the respiratory system.

Need to Know

The following represent the Key Objectives of Chapter 12:

1. *Describe the anatomy, physiology, and pathophysiology of the airways, including the importance of airway patency.*

   There are many conditions that can affect the different components of the upper and lower airways. A basic understanding of the anatomy, physiology, and pathophysiology of the airway affords the paramedic a distinct advantage when it comes to assessing and treating airway problems.

Figure 12-1 shows the organs of the respiratory system. Anatomically, the airways are divided into upper and lower airways; the upper airway extends from the nose and mouth to the extrathoracic trachea, and the lower airway continues to the point at which the alveoli come into contact with the pulmonary capillaries (where gas exchange in the lungs takes place).

Patency of the airway is essential for life to exist. The airway is at the pinnacle of emergency care yet is overlooked easily. The simple act of positioning a patient in such a manner that his or her airway is open can make the difference between life and death.

In order for the respiratory system to function efficiently, the orchestration of many different components (gases, muscles of the upper and lower airways, nerves, the respiratory control center in the brain stem, blood cells, chemoreceptors, etc.) of the respiratory system needs to take place. Airway, breathing, and circulation are vital to life. They allow for oxygen to get to the tissues and cells of the body, and for carbon dioxide and waste products to be removed from the body. As a paramedic, you will spend your career ensuring that these three principles are met. When you are challenged by difficult cases, you will depend on these principles to help get your patients to the hospital alive.

2. *Explain oxygenation and ventilation, including factors paramedics should consider when ventilating a patient who is hypoventilating or not breathing.*

Two very important concepts regarding the airway that deserve mentioning are oxygenation and ventilation. *Oxygenation,* simply stated, is to supply with oxygen. This in no way implies that the supplied oxygen is moved through the airway or exchanged with other gases such as carbon dioxide. In order for supplemental oxygen to provide its desired effect, it requires a means by which it can be transported into the body. The transportation of oxygen is accomplished through a process called ventilation. *Ventilation* is the movement of air into and out of the lungs from the atmosphere. When we add supplemental oxygen to the equation of ventilation, we have a means of transporting oxygen from the source into the lungs where gas exchange can take place, oxygen can get to the target tissues and cells of the body, and carbon dioxide can be eliminated from the bloodstream and ultimately from the body.

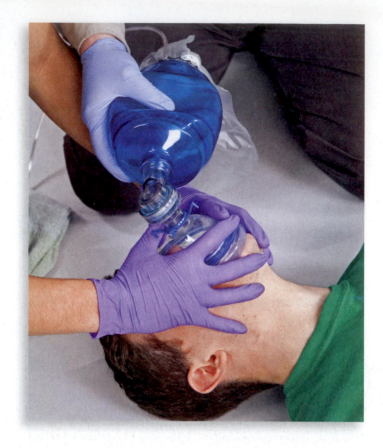

When paramedics ventilate a patient who is either hypoventilating or is apneic, several points need to be kept in mind:

- When mechanical ventilation (ventilation via a bag-mask or a ventilator) is used to aid in the movement of gases into and out of the lungs, the pressure inside the thoracic cavity changes from a negative pressure system to a positive pressure system.
- When the pressure inside the thoracic cavity is changed from negative pressure to positive pressure, there are some noteworthy physiologic changes that take place:
  a. The positive pressure inside the thoracic cavity can impair the venous return to the

right side of the heart (blood is pulled into the atria by negative pressure).
  b. Subsequently, the delivery of blood from the left side of the heart to the organs and cells of the body (cardiac output) is also decreased (what comes in goes out).
  c. Slowing down ventilations during your care of patients to a rate of 8–12 per minute makes great strides toward improving cardiac output and overall patient care.
  d. Positive pressure ventilation, especially in patients suffering from chronic lung disease (particularly patients with COPD), can increase the risk of barotrauma developing.

Need to Do

The following airway skills are explained and illustrated in a step-by-step manner, via skill sheets and/or Step-by-Steps in this text and on the accompanying DVD:

Skill Name	Skill Sheet Number and Location	Step-by-Step Number and Location
Airway Positioning and Maneuvers	1 – DVD	1 – DVD
Oropharyngeal Airways	2 – DVD	2 – DVD
Nasopharyngeal Airways	3 – DVD	3 – DVD
Bag-Mask Ventilation with 1 Rescuer	4 – DVD	4 – DVD
Bag-Mask Ventilation with 2 or More Rescuers	5 – DVD	5 – DVD
Foreign Body Airway Obstruction Removal—Advanced Techniques	6 – Appendix A and DVD	6 – This chapter and DVD
Endotracheal Intubation	7 – Appendix A and DVD	7 – This chapter and DVD
ALS Airway Adjuncts	8 – DVD	N/A
Endotracheal Confirmation Techniques	9 – DVD	9 – DVD
End-Tidal Capnography	10 – DVD	N/A
Endotracheal Suctioning	11 – DVD	11 – DVD
Pulse Oximetry	12 – DVD	12 – DVD
Rapid Sequence Intubation	13 – Appendix A and DVD	13 – This chapter and DVD
Nasal Intubation	14 – Appendix A and DVD	14 – DVD
Digital Intubation	15 – DVD	N/A
Endotracheal Intubation in Face-to-Face Position	16 – DVD	N/A
Extubation	17 – DVD	N/A
Continuous Positive Airway Pressure (CPAP)	18 – Appendix A and DVD	18 – This chapter and DVD
Needle Cricothyroidotomy	19 – Appendix A and DVD	19 – This chapter and DVD
Dual Lumen Airway Device	21 – Appendix A and DVD	21 – This chapter and DVD
Meconium Suctioning	22 – DVD	22 – DVD
Suctioning of Stoma	23 – DVD	23 – DVD
Evacuation of Gastric Contents	24 – DVD	24 – DVD

Foreign Body Airway Obstruction Removal—Advanced Techniques

Conditions: The candidate should perform this skill on a simulated patient in the supine position under existing indoor, ambulance, or outdoor lighting, temperature, and weather conditions.

Indications: Any patient with a complete foreign body airway obstruction that is not relieved with BLS interventions.

Red Flags: Do not force object further down trachea. Incomplete airway obstructions usually do not require ALS intervention.

Steps:

1. Don appropriate personal protective equipment.
2. Position unconscious patient in the supine position and open the airway.
3. Verify complete obstruction by attempting ventilation. If unable to ventilate, reposition airway and reattempt ventilation. If still unable to ventilate, look inside mouth for visible obstructions.
4. Perform abdominal thrusts and finger sweeps as indicated.
5. Keep suction readily available.
6. Check laryngoscope; ensure the light is tight, white, and bright (Figure SBS 6-1).

SBS 6-1

7. Hold Magill forceps in right hand (Figure SBS 6-2).

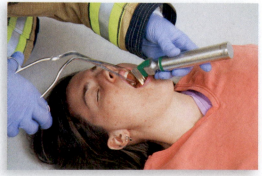

SBS 6-2

8. Slowly insert laryngoscope blade into mouth and anterior pharynx, advancing into pharynx and glottic opening. *Do not rapidly advance blade deep into pharynx or push object further down airway.*

9. If the obstruction is visualized:
   a. Remove with Magill forceps.
   b. Remove remaining small particles with suction.

10. If unable to remove object, your partner should continue abdominal thrusts, or you should do the following:
    a. Attach meconium aspirator to suction tubing.
    b. Cut cuff off of ET tube and attach to meconium aspirator. (Figure SBS 6-3).
    c. Create an airtight seal between obstruction and ET tube. Remove object carefully past glottic opening.

SBS 6-3

11. Ensure adequate ventilation following object removal.

12. If the object cannot be removed, consider cricothyroidotomy.

- Verify complete obstruction.
- Perform BLS maneuvers.
- Do not advance blade deep into pharynx (do not force object further into airway).

Critical Criteria:

- Use appropriate personal protective equipment.

Step-by-Step 7

Endotracheal Intubation

Conditions: The candidate should perform this skill on a simulated patient in the supine position under existing indoor, ambulance, or outdoor lighting, temperature, and weather conditions.

Indications: Patients in respiratory failure or respiratory arrest, patients with an altered level of consciousness and an inability to protect their own airway, and patients in cardiopulmonary arrest.

Red Flags: Consider intubation as a tool for airway management, not as a goal. Esophageal placement can be fatal if unrecognized. *The total time of ventilation interruption should not exceed 30 seconds.*

Steps:

1. Don appropriate personal protective equipment.

2. Evaluate for possible difficult intubation (e.g., due to anatomical considerations).

3. Consider use of an alternative technique or ET tube introducer.

4. Select appropriately sized ET tube:
   a. Adult: 8.0–8.5 for average males; 7.0–7.5 for average females.
   b. Pediatric: If available, use length-based tape to determine size. Otherwise, use formulas: (age/3) + 4 for uncuffed tubes and (age/4) + 4 for cuffed tubes.

5. Open the proximal end of the sterile package.

6. Inflate the cuff with 10–12 mL of air.

7. Squeeze distal obturator cuff to check for leaks.

8. Deflate the cuff and leave the syringe in place (Figure SBS 7-1).

SBS 7-1

—Continued

9. Select proper laryngoscope blade:
   a. Adult: Usually size 3 or 4.
   b. Pediatric: Use length-based tape to determine size.

10. Attach blade and ensure laryngoscope bulb is tight, white, and bright.

11. Prepare suction.

12. Stop ventilations, remove the airway adjunct (if present), and position patient's head (Figure SBS 7-2).

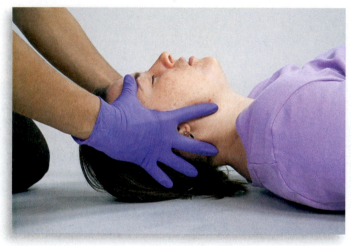

SBS 7-2

13. Apply or direct an assistant to apply cricoid pressure, as needed.

14. Insert the laryngoscope blade into the right side of the mouth and advance toward the base of the tongue (Figure SBS 7-3).

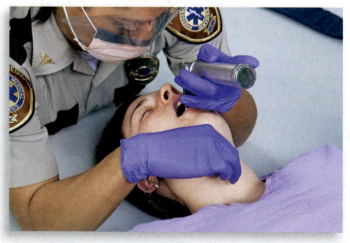

SBS 7-3

15. Sweep the tongue to the left, and visualize the epiglottis.

16. Straight blade: lift epiglottis directly. Curved blade: place in vallecula and lift epiglottis.

17. Verbalize visualization of the vocal cords and arytenoid cartilage.

18. Insert the ET tube into the right side of the mouth and advance through the vocal cords (Figure SBS 7-4).

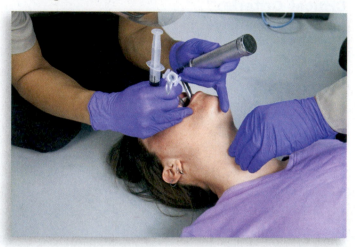

SBS 7-4

19. Verbalize passing of the tube through the vocal cords.

20. Withdraw the laryngoscope and close blade against handle. Set aside.

21. Secure the tube against the upper teeth, noting the depth of the tube.

22. Inflate the tube cuff until firm with a syringe.

23. Remove stylet, and attach bag (Figure SBS 7-5). (If using an esophageal detector device, utilize before attaching bag.)

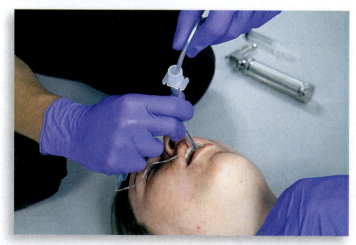

SBS 7-5

24. Attempt ventilations (Figure SBS 7-6). *Total time of ventilation interruption should not exceed 30 seconds.*

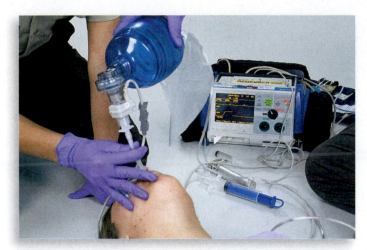

SBS 7-6

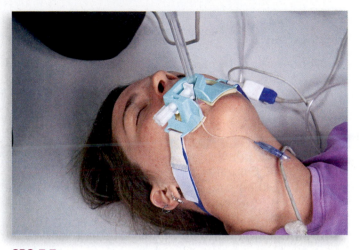

SBS 7-7

25. Auscultate.
   a. Over epigastrium; gurgling on ventilation indicates esophageal placement.
   b. All lung fields; no lung sounds indicates esophageal placement.

26. Use other secondary methods of tube confirmation as appropriate.

27. Secure tube with tape or commercial device (Figure SBS 7-7).

28. Place a cervical collar to help maintain tube position.

Critical Criteria:

- Use appropriate personal protective equipment.
- Use sterile technique.
- Total time of ventilation interruption should not exceed 30 seconds.
- Frequently reassess ET tube placement during patient encounter.

Step-by-Step 13

Rapid Sequence Intubation

Conditions: The candidate should perform this skill on a simulated patient under existing indoor, ambulance, or outdoor lighting, temperature, and weather conditions.

Indications: Patients in respiratory failure or respiratory arrest, patients with an altered level of consciousness and inability to protect their own airway, and patients whose airways cannot be managed by conventional means (due to gag reflex, trismus, etc.)

Red Flags: Consider intubation as a tool for airway management, not as a goal. Esophageal placement can be fatal if unrecognized.

—Continued

Steps:

Preparation

1. Don appropriate personal protective equipment.

2. Apply LEMON law to evaluate patient's anatomy:
   - **L**—Look externally for masses, goiter, receding mandible, obesity.
   - **E**—Evaluate 3-3-2 rule: adequate mouth opening (Figure SBS 13-1), hyoid–chin distance, mouth–thyroid cartilage distance.
   - **M**—Mallampati scale: classes I through IV (I and II, uncomplicated; II and IV, difficult)
   - **O**—Obstruction: abscesses, soft tissue swelling in upper airway.
   - **N**—Neck mobility: limited range of motion of the neck.

SBS 13-2

Preoxygenate

9. Oxygenate patient with 100% oxygen.

10. Assist ventilations as needed with bag-mask (Figure SBS 13-3).

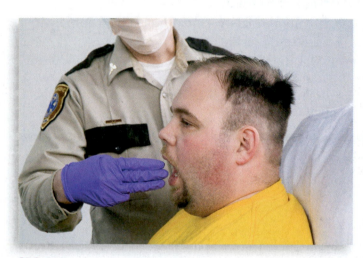

SBS 13-1

3. Inquire about allergies and previous medication reactions.

4. Assign specific duties to personnel on scene (e.g., ventilation, drawing up meds).

5. Monitor patient's vital signs, SpO$_2$, and ECG.

6. Prepare intubation equipment (have backup airways available in case intubation is not successful).

7. Prepare suction.

8. Establish at least one IV for medication administration (Figure SBS 13-2).

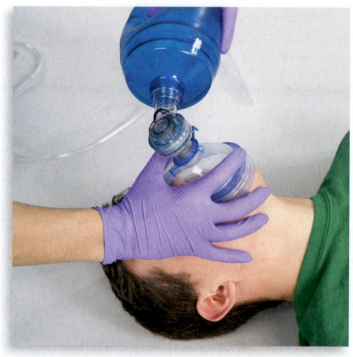

SBS 13-3

Pretreatment

11. *Atropine* for all pediatric patients and adult patients who exhibit or are at risk for bradycardia.

12. *Lidocaine* for patients with head injury to prevent or reduce an increase in intracranial pressure caused by intubation.

Paralysis and Anesthesia

13. Choose and administer a sedative medication. *Do not administer paralytics without sedation* (Figure SBS 13-4).

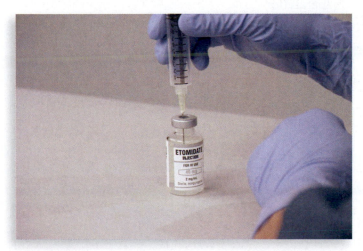

SBS 13-4

14. Choose and administer a paralytic agent.

Intubate and Confirm Proper Placement

15. Perform endotracheal intubation (Figure SBS 13-5).

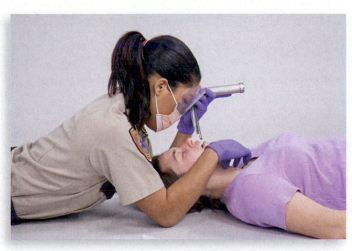

SBS 13-5

16. If intubation is not successful, insert alternative airway, such as dual lumen airway, laryngeal mask airway, oropharyngeal airway, or nasopharyngeal airway. Cricothyroidotomy is a last resort.

17. Confirm ETT placement using at least two methods (Figure SBS 13-6).

SBS 13-6

18. Continually monitor end-tidal CO_2 using device with waveform if available (Figure SBS 13-7).

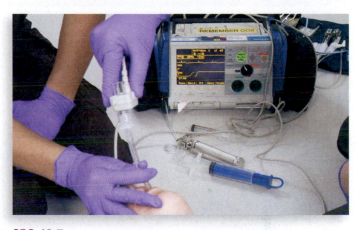

SBS 13-7

Post-Intubation Management

19. Secure ETT with tape or a commercially available tube-securing device.

20. Place cervical collar to help maintain ETT position (Figure SBS 13-8).

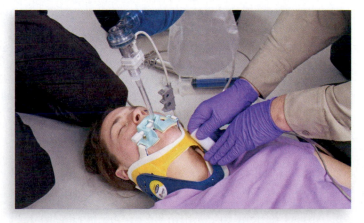

SBS 13-8

—Continued

21. Oxygenate and ventilate the patient. *Do not hyperventilate the patient.* This can have a detrimental effect, especially on patients suffering from head injuries, patients in shock, and patients with cardiac failure.

22. Reassess the patient (ABCs, vital signs, SpO_2, $ETCO_2$).

23. If patient needs to remain sedated, administer a sedative such as a benzodiazepine (Versed or Valium).

Critical Criteria:

- Use standard precautions.
- Check for patient allergies and sensitivities to medications.

- Check expiration date of medication.
- Ensure that the five rights of medication administration have been followed.
- Evaluate anatomy for intubation approach.
- Administer sedative prior to administration of paralytic.
- Ensure alternative airways are available if intubation is not successful.
- Confirm tube placement (and reconfirm frequently).

Step-by-Step 18

Continuous Positive Airway Pressure (CPAP)

Conditions: The candidate should perform this skill on a simulated patient in the sitting position under existing indoor, ambulance, or outdoor lighting, temperature, and weather conditions.

Indications: A patient experiencing respiratory insufficiency or failure, including pulmonary edema or bronchoconstrictive disease, is able to follow commands and has oxygen saturations less than 90%.

Red Flags: Contraindicated in patients with pneumothorax, apnea, unconsciousness, and full cardiopulmonary arrest. Relative contraindications include trauma with suspicion of elevated intracranial pressure, abdominal distention with risk for vomiting, and hypotension. Patients who have emphysema should be monitored closely when CPAP is applied, as they are at increased risk for barotrauma and pneumothorax.

Steps:

1. Don appropriate personal protective equipment.

2. Assess patient to confirm he or she is candidate for CPAP. Assess lung sounds, pulse oximetry, ECG, peak flow, and $ETCO_2$, if available.

3. Initiate BLS care.

4. Explain procedure to patient.

5. Assemble equipment according to manufacturer's recommendations (Figure SBS 18-1). Connect CPAP generator to a 50-psi oxygen source.

SBS 18-1

6. Assemble mask and tubing.

7. Set device parameters (rate and frequency, oxygen concentration, tidal volume, positive end expiratory pressure [PEEP], etc.) and test pressure relief valve (Figure SBS 18-2).

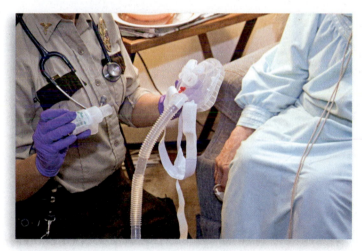

SBS 18-2

8. Occlude tubing to test for peak pressure required to activate pressure relief valve, and adjust as necessary.

9. Place mask on patient; have patient hold it to his or her face if possible (Figure SBS 18-3).

SBS 18-3

10. When patient is comfortable with the mask on his or her face, attach straps around head and ensure proper mask seal. Insert CPAP valve into the mask, and check for air leaks (Figure SBS 18-4).

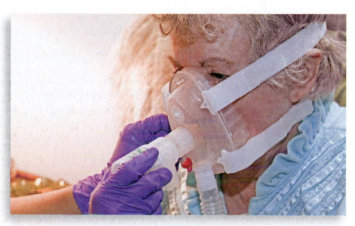

SBS 18-4

11. Coach the patient to breathe normally and adjust to air pressure.

12. Monitor the patient for desired and adverse effects. Continue other treatments.

Critical Criteria:
- Use standard precautions.
- Assess patient prior to and frequently after the application of the CPAP device.
- Ensure patient understands procedure.
- Ensure proper parameters (pressure relief, tidal volume, oxygen concentration, rate, etc.).
- Test pressure relief valve prior to application.

Needle Cricothyroidotomy

Conditions: The candidate should perform this skill on a simulated patient under existing indoor, ambulance, or outdoor lighting, temperature, and weather conditions.

Indications: A patient whose airway cannot be managed by BLS or other ALS airway procedures.

Red Flags: This procedure cannot be used if the trachea is transected or if there is significant trauma to the cricoid cartilage or larynx. This technique is designed for short-term use only. Requires a high-pressure source of oxygen, which poses a great risk for spraying blood and body fluids on rescuers and can cause barotrauma in patients (pneumothorax, subcutaneous air, etc.). Does not isolate the airway; thus, aspiration of blood, emesis, etc., is a continued risk.

Steps:

1. Don appropriate personal protective equipment.

2. Properly assemble ventilation delivery device, including needle jet insufflator.

3. Attach a large-bore needle to a 10-mL syringe.

4. Place patient supine and hyperextend the head if not contraindicated.

5. Locate the cricothyroid membrane below the thyroid cartilage and above the cricoid ring (Figure SBS 19-1).

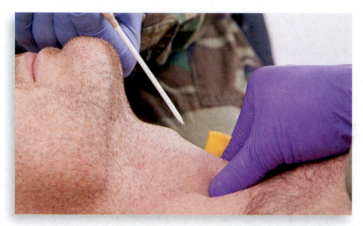

SBS 19-2

9. Advance needle while aspirating for air (Figure SBS 19-3).

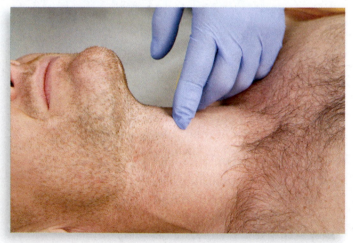

SBS 19-1

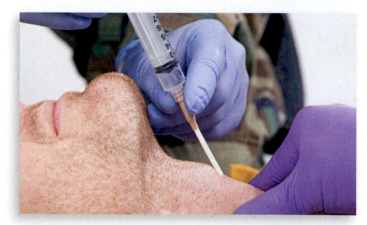

SBS 19-3

6. Cleanse the area with alcohol and/or iodine.

7. Direct partner to stabilize the trachea.

8. Insert the needle through the membrane at a 45-degree angle with the bevel up (Figure SBS 19-2).

10. Stop when air is aspirated.

11. Advance the catheter and withdraw the needle (Figure SBS 19-4).

12. Attach oxygen delivery device to catheter.

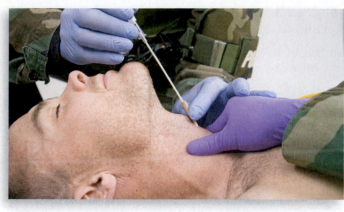

SBS 19-4

13. Attempt ventilation, allowing adequate time for exhalation (inspiratory/expiratory ratio of 1:3). Observe for chest rise and fall.

14. Secure the catheter (Figure SBS 19-5).

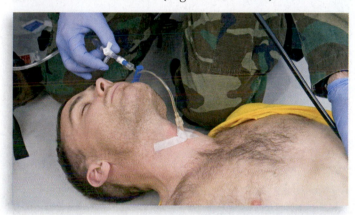

SBS 19-5

15. Auscultate over the epigastrium and all lung fields.

16. Discontinue if esophageal perforation or placement outside to the trachea is suspected.

17. Control any bleeding and monitor for pneumothorax.

18. Transport rapidly and monitor the patient closely for adverse effects.

Critical Criteria:
- Don standard precautions (gloves, mask, and eye protection recommended).
- Insert needle/catheter at a 45-degree angle toward feet.
- Aspirate syringe while needle is advanced.
- Recognize incorrect placement.
- Dispose of needle immediately into appropriate sharps container.
- Monitor patient continuously for desired effects and complications associated with procedure.

Step-by-Step 21

Dual Lumen Airway Device

Conditions: The candidate should perform this skill on a simulated patient in the supine position (stretcher, bed, or floor) under existing indoor, ambulance, or outdoor lighting, temperature, and weather conditions.

Indications: Patients in respiratory failure or arrest, without a gag reflex. Basic airway maneuvers do not maintain a patent airway.

—Continued

Red Flags: Consider the dual lumen airway as a tool for airway management use, not as a goal. Not designed for patients under 5 feet or over 7 feet tall. Other contraindications are recent ingestion of caustic substances, latex allergy, esophageal varices, trauma to trachea, and bleeding below the pharynx. *The total time of ventilation interruption should not exceed 30 seconds.*

Steps:

1. Don appropriate personal protective equipment.

2. Position patient in the "sniffing" position, unless contraindicated.

3. Inspect airway for secretions or obstructions, and check for stoma.

4. Test cuffs prior to placement (Figure SBS 21-1) by filling 100 mL of air in blue port and 20 mL of air in white port using syringes.

SBS 21-1

5. Remove syringes to check for leaks in valve.

6. Deflate and ready device for insertion.

7. Lubricate distal tip with water-soluble jelly.

8. Suction airway prior to attempt.

SBS 21-2

9. Control jaw and tongue with left hand (Figure SBS 21-2).

10. Insert in right side of mouth, advancing midline. Advance until teeth are between black lines (Figure SBS 21-3).

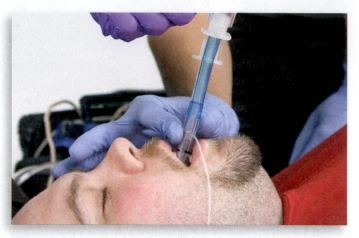

SBS 21-3

11. Inflate pharyngeal balloon (up to 100 mL) and distal balloon (up to 15 mL).

12. Ventilate through blue tube (Figure SBS 21-4). *Do not interrupt ventilations for more than 30 seconds.*

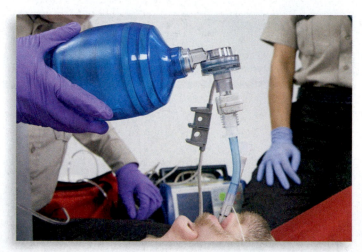

SBS 21-4

13. Check epigastric sounds; gurgling on ventilation indicates tracheal placement.

14. Check lung sounds. Present and equal sounds indicate esophageal placement; otherwise, suspect tracheal placement.

15. Ventilate through second tube if tracheal placement is suspected (Figure SBS 21-5).

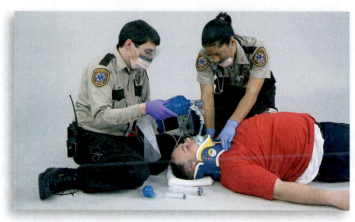

SBS 21-5

16. Reassess tube placement.

17. Secure tube.

18. Place cervical collar.

19. Continually reassess during transport.

Critical Criteria:

- Use appropriate standard precautions.
- Ventilation interruption does not exceed 30 seconds at any one time.
- Continually confirm tube placement during patient encounter.

Connections

- For a detailed discussion on allergies and anaphylaxis, see Chapter 32, Allergies and Anaphylaxis, in the text. Other related text chapters include Chapter 13, Shock Overview, and Chapter 29, Cardiology.
- See the 2005 American Heart Association Guidelines (*Handbook of Emergency Cardiovascular Care*) for more information on current standards for cardiopulmonary resuscitation and research findings related to airway and ventilatory management.[1]
- Link to the companion DVD for a chapter-based quiz, audio glossary, animations, games and exercises, and, when appropriate, skill sheets and skill Step-by-Steps.
- Get ready for Problem-Based Learning Case 2, where your airway thinking skills will be tested!

Street Secrets

- **AHA Guidelines** The American Heart Association 2005 evidence-based standards show that, in addition to slowing down respiratory rate and decreasing overall respiratory volume during positive pressure ventilation, the process of allowing for full recoil of the chest during cardiac compressions (CPR) may briefly return the inside of the chest to a negative pressure state. Fewer interruptions in compressions, coupled with full recoil of the chest during CPR, results in improved filling of the heart and perfusion to the heart itself. Patients who receive CPR with these changes stand a chance for a much better outcome.

The Drug Box

Rapid Sequence Intubation (RSI)

Pretreatment

Lidocaine (Xylocaine): Used as a pretreatment for RSI because of its reported ability to prevent or blunt any increase in intracranial pressure that may occur during this procedure.

Atropine sulfate (parasympathetic blocker): An antimuscarinic agent that blocks acetylcholine at parasympathetic sites; useful when administered prior to orotracheal intubation to blunt the effects of vagus nerve stimulation.

Sedatives (Induction Agents)

Fentanyl (Sublimaze, narcotic agonist): A short-acting narcotic analgesic used in conscious sedation and as an induction agent for general anesthesia. Also used to treat postoperative pain and restlessness. The onset of action for fentanyl is 1–2 minutes, and the duration of action is approximately 30 minutes.

Midazolam (Versed, benzodiazepine): A short-acting benzodiazepine used as an inducing agent for general anesthesia and as an adjunct to sedate mechanically ventilated patients. The use of midazolam for IV induction purposes requires high doses that have corresponding dramatic cardiovascular effects. The onset of action for midazolam is 2–5 minutes, and the duration of action is approximately 30–60 minutes.

Etomidate (Amidate, nonbarbiturate hypnotic): A short-acting hypnotic used to assist with endotracheal intubation. It is frequently the induction agent of choice due to its noteworthy cardiovascular profile in patients who are not suffering from hypovolemia. Care must be taken in the hypovolemic patient because etomidate can decrease cardiac output by up to 30%. The onset of action for etomidate is less than 1 minute, and the duration of action is 3–7 minutes.

Propofol (Diprivan, alkylphenol nonbarbiturate hypnotic): A sedative-hypnotic used in the induction and maintenance of anesthesia. Its onset of action is less than 30 seconds, and the duration of action is dependent on the means of administration. Propofol can be administered as a bolus or as an infusion. The duration of action for a propofol bolus is 1–5 minutes, and the duration of action for a propofol infusion (once discontinued) is less than 30 seconds.

Paralytics (Muscle Relaxants)

Succinylcholine (Anectine, Quelicin, Sucostrin): A depolarizing, noncompetitive muscle relaxant used in general anesthesia to facilitate endotracheal intubation and to induce skeletal muscle relaxation during mechanical ventilation. It has a rapid onset of action (30–45 seconds) and a short duration of action (approximately 5–10 minutes). *Cautions and side effects*: About 10–15 seconds after the administration of succinylcholine, fasciculations occur together with a brief increase in intracranial pressure, intraocular pressure, and intragastric pressure; transient hyperkalemia; malignant hyperthermia; trismus; and cardiac arrhythmias (such as sinus bradycardia, junctional rhythms, ventricular arrhythmias, and even asystole). (Bradycardia and asystole can be prevented as well as treated with atropine.) Despite the potential for these possible complications and side effects, succinylcholine remains one of the most frequently used muscle relaxants due to its rapid onset and short duration of action.

Rocuronium (Zemuron, aminosteroid): A nondepolarizing muscle relaxant used to induce paralysis with intubation and mechanical ventilation. It does not have the cautions or side effects associated with succinylcholine. It has a rapid onset of action (approximately 60–90 seconds), but a relatively long duration of action (30 minutes).

Vecuronium (Norcuron, aminosteroid): A nondepolarizing neuromuscular blocker used to induce paralysis with intubation and mechanical ventilation. It does not have the cautions or side effects associated with succinylcholine. It has a rapid onset of action (approximately 1–3 minutes) and a longer duration of action (45–60 minutes) than succinylcholine and rocuronium.

Nasal Intubation

Phenylephrine (Neo-Synephrine): An alpha-adrenergic agonist used to constrict nasal vasculature prior to insertion of nasal airway adjuncts to help reduce the risk of inducing epistaxis.

Lidocaine jelly (Xylocaine jelly): A topical anesthetic and lubricant that is typically applied to the nasotracheal tube (NTT) and the nasopharyngeal airway (NPA) if an NPA is used prior to insertion of an NTT. If lidocaine jelly is not part of your local EMS protocol for nasotracheal intubation, any water-based lubricant can and should be used to facilitate insertion of the NPA and/or NTT. (Note: Prior to the insertion of an airway adjunct, lidocaine jelly, or any water- based lubricant, first administer the Neo-Synephrine. If any lubricant is inserted prior to administration of the Neo-Synephrine, the lubricant will prevent the efficient absorption of the Neo-Synephrine.)

20% benzocaine: A topical anesthetic agent used to numb the oropharynx and hypopharynx in an attempt to blunt the gag reflex prior to insertion of a nasotracheal tube in a conscious patient with an intact gag reflex.

Reference

1. 2005 AHA Guidelines, *Handbook of Emergency Cardiovascular Care*, Dallas, TX: American Heart Association, 2006.

Answers

Are You Ready?

1. Mike should be classified as critically ill. Anybody with a history of severe allergic reactions who is short of breath and is complaining of itching and shortness of breath needs to be taken very seriously.

2. An allergic reaction.

3. The lower airways (typically the bronchioles).

4. Wheezing is typically caused by constriction of the smooth muscle of the bronchioles. It can also be caused by fluid as a result of conditions such as congestive heart failure and by mucus or phlegm as a result of an infection.

5. Beta$_2$-specific bronchodilators are typically administered to patients who are experiencing bronchospasm because administration of these bronchodilators results in the relaxation of the smooth muscles of the bronchioles.

   In some EMS systems, protocol dictates that paramedics immediately administer 1:1,000 epinephrine subcutaneously for patients with allergic reactions. However, keep in mind that, despite the fact that epinephrine has several beneficial (alpha and beta) effects, it can also produce several undesirable side effects. For a patient who is currently relatively hemodynamically stable (i.e., has a blood pressure that affords adequate perfusion to the vital organs), a conservative treatment

FIGURE 12-2 Use of a bronchodilator nebulizer.

of oxygen, IV fluid as needed, and a beta$_2$-specific bronchodilator nebulizer is an appropriate start (Figure 12-2).

For paramedics who work in an EMS system that differentiates between the severity of allergic reactions (mild, moderate, or severe, for example) and specifies different treatment regimens to treat the different severities of allergic reactions, it is good to know why different treatments are used for different severities of allergic reactions. If the beta$_2$-specific bronchodilator nebulizer doesn't appear to be improving the patient's respiratory status, and/or if the patient becomes hemodynamically unstable (altered mental status, hypotension, evidence of significant fluid shifts—third spacing, etc.), the administration of subcutaneous 1:1,000 epinephrine is very appropriate (with considerations for age and preexisting cardiac conditions). In this setting epinephrine will likely not only have the desired effect on the bronchiole smooth muscle, but it will likely exert its alpha effects on the vasculature and decrease vessel size and permeability, thus helping reduce fluid shift and increase blood pressure.

Active Learning

1. Oxygen enters the body during the process of inhalation. Air enters the nose and passes through nasal hair, where any large foreign particles are trapped and prevented from entering the lower airways. Just beyond the nasal opening lie the nasal conchae (turbinate bones), which are covered with pseudostratified ciliated epithelium and a rich supply of blood vessels. The air becomes turbulent as it passes through the nasal conchae and, as a result, bounces off the walls of the nasal cavity. As the air strikes the walls of the nasal cavity it is further filtered by the cilia, moistened by the mucus, and warmed by the heat from the rich blood supply that lines the nasal cavity. The mucus of the nasal cavity also traps small foreign particles such as dust, further filtering the air entering the body.

Once warmed, moistened, and filtered, air continues through the nasopharynx, the oropharynx, and the laryngopharynx. It passes the epiglottis (a small flaplike structure attached to the upper border of the thyroid cartilage), which allows air to enter the larynx but prevents food and liquid from entering the lungs during their consumption. The glottic opening is the point at which there is a "fork in the road." For a person in the supine position, there is a low road and a high road. The low road leads to the esophagus, and the high road leads to the larynx. Air tends to take the high road, and food hopefully takes the low road.

As air enters the larynx and passes the vocal cords it makes its way into the cartilaginous ringed tube known as the trachea. From the vocal cords to the carina (a bifurcation in the trachea), the trachea measures approximately 10–12 cm in adults. The trachea is lined with a ciliated epithelium that helps bring any foreign material that got past the filtering structures of the upper airway as well as mucus and phlegm to the glottic opening, where it can be swallowed and removed from the body or coughed up. The cartilage rings of the trachea are C shaped, with the opening of the C pointing toward the spine. The opening of the tracheal cartilage is closed by smooth muscle and connective tissue. The smooth muscle of the trachea allows the esophagus to expand as food passes through it. The cartilage of the trachea prevents the tube from collapsing and allows for the efficient movement of air. The carina is the point at which the trachea divides into right and left main-stem (primary) bronchi. From this point, the bronchi continue to branch into secondary (lobar) bronchi and tertiary (segmental) bronchi.

Here, air enters bronchioles that divide even more. The interlobular bronchioles follow the tertiary (segmental) bronchi and are followed in turn by the terminal bronchioles, and finally the respiratory bronchioles. The bronchi and bronchioles are surrounded by smooth muscle and blood vessels. As the air passages move from the trachea to the alveoli, the amount of cartilage decreases and the smooth muscle becomes more and more plentiful. Along with the decreasing amount of cartilage comes a decrease in the number of mucus-producing goblet cells and a decrease in the number of ciliated epithelial cells. With the increase in the smooth muscle of the smaller air passages comes a dense capillary network that will ultimately play a key role in the exchange of gases at the alveolar-capillary membrane (Figure 12-3).

The smooth muscle that surrounds the lower airways is responsible for controlling the diameter of the air passages. Pressure gradients at the alveolar-capillary membrane and at the tissue-capillary membrane allow for the exchange of oxygen and carbon dioxide, respectively, from areas of greater pressure to areas of lesser pressure (Figure 12-4). This allows for oxygen (O_2) to enter the bloodstream at the alveolar-capillary membrane and off-load at the tissue-capillary membrane.

Likewise, carbon dioxide (CO_2), following the same principles of moving from a greater pressure area to a lesser pressure area enters the bloodstream at the tissue-capillary membrane (Figure 12-5) and exits the bloodstream at the alveolar-capillary membrane (Figure 12-6).

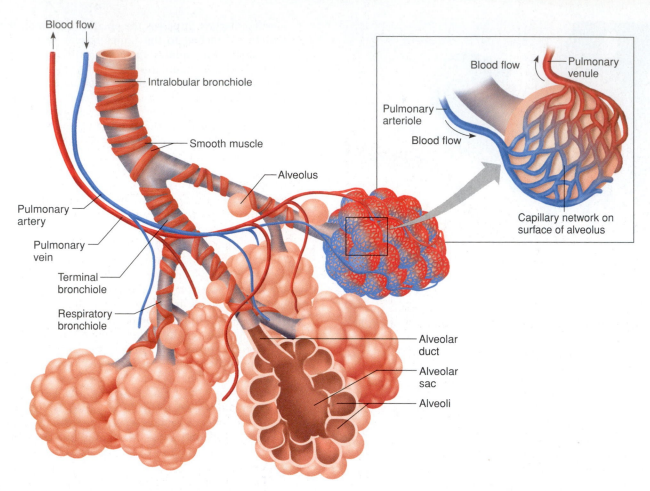

FIGURE 12-3 The respiratory tubes end in tiny alveoli, each of which is surrounded by a capillary network.

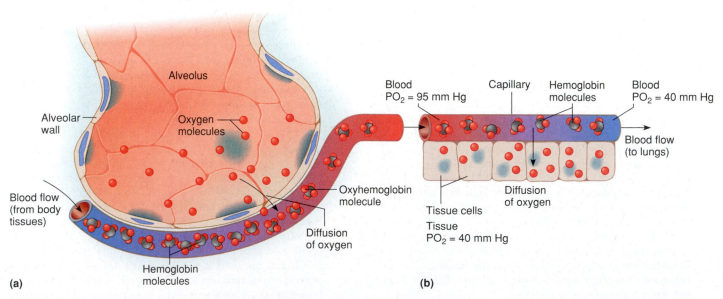

FIGURE 12-4 Blood transports oxygen. **(a)** Oxygen molecules, entering the blood from the alveolus, bond to hemoglobin, forming oxyhemoglobin. **(b)** In the regions of the body cells, oxyhemoglobin releases oxygen.

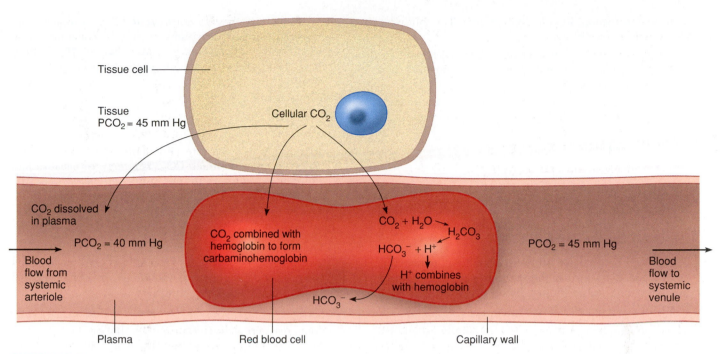

FIGURE 12-5 Carbon dioxide produced by cells is transported in the blood plasma in a dissolved state, bound to hemoglobin, or in the form of bicarbonate ions (HCO_3^-).

The transport of these respective gases in the bloodstream is accomplished for the most part through plasma and bicarbonate ions (CO_2), the hemoglobin component of red blood cells.

You Are There: Reality-Based Cases

Case 1

1. The patient appears to be in severe distress, is fatigued, and has hemodynamically unstable vital signs (especially for a patient with a history of HTN).

2. With the patient's medical history and his presentation, one would expect that the patient is suffering from pulmonary edema as a result of CHF. The blood pressure might be expected to be high, but the fact that it is low suggests that there is another underlying issue that needs to be addressed.

3. The primary concern at this point is managing the patient's ABCs. The airway can be managed in a number of ways; one of the most significant factors affecting your decision will be what capabilities you have for

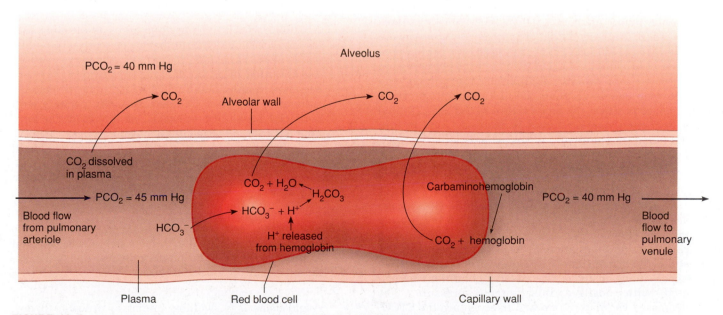

FIGURE 12-6 In the lungs, carbon dioxide diffuses from the blood into the alveoli.

airway management in your EMS system. The following are several possibilities:

  a. Place the patient in a position that will maintain his blood pressure and allow for the most efficient mechanics of ventilation.

  b. Continue to track the patient's ventilations with a bag-mask and high-flow oxygen (consider adding a BLS airway [OPA, NPA, etc.]).

  c. Consider CPAP.

  d. Consider RSI and oral intubation.

  e. Consider nasotracheal intubation.

4. With a history of CHF and MI and no signs of infection or fever, it is likely that the hypotension has a cardiac origin (cardiogenic shock).

5. The patient is critically ill. He appears to be worsening, as evidenced by further fatigue and a decompensating hemodynamic status (falling blood pressure and rising heart rate).

6. The capnography readings are CO_2 of 20 mm Hg and RR of 36 with an oxygen saturation reading of 99% being delivered by a bag-mask with high-flow oxygen. A normal CO_2 reading is 40 mm Hg (range = 35–45 mm $Hg^{+/-}$); thus the CO_2 reading is low and the oxygen saturation reading is in the desired range.

7. There are a number of reasons why the vital signs decompensate. One of the more likely reasons for the precipitous drop in blood pressure is the change from the normal physiologic negative intrathoracic pressure to the positive intrathoracic pressure that may have occurred as the patient's ventilations were supplemented with a bag-mask. Because the heart refills with blood under a negative pressure, when the pressure within the thorax changes from a negative to a positive pressure, the heart has a much more difficult time filling. This is especially true with patients in shock or cardiac arrest. When the heart can't fill efficiently, it cannot pump efficiently. (Remember Starling's law: The more in, the more out. The inverse is true as well: The less in, the less out.) This means that, when you have a patient with an already compromised perfusion status, if you provide ventilations too quickly and with too much volume, the intrathoracic pressure becomes positive, the blood return to the heart (filling) is decreased, cardiac output is decreased, and in turn the blood pressure falls. When patients with poor perfusion status experience these conditions, the chances for survival decrease.

8. The most simple and probably the most effective means of managing this patient would be slowing the ventilatory rate down to approximately 8 breaths per minute. This is a rate that will provide adequate oxygenation and ventilation to meet the patient's needs, and at the same time it will prevent the patient from experiencing many of the adverse conditions associated with positive intrathoracic pressure. The decreased ventilatory rate will likely return the $ETCO_2$ reading closer to normal (40 mm $Hg^{+/-}$).

If these changes do not have the desired effect, then further treatment algorithms need to be considered (see Chapter 13, Shock Overview, and Chapter 29, Cardiology). The point is that ventilation is not a benign procedure.

Test Yourself

1. a

   It is likely that the rate and depth of respirations are "blowing off" too much CO_2. This may be because less volume is required in the intubated patient, or the rescuer who assumed the "bagging" duties used a higher rate or volume than your partner.

2. d

   During inspiration, the diaphragm and intercostal muscles retract, expanding the size of the chest cavity; this also expands the size of the lungs, creating negative pressure and "sucking" in air.

3. False

   Most rescuers deliver ventilations that are both too fast and with too much volume, especially to critically ill patients. This can lead to excessive intrathoracic pressure, inhibiting effective circulation.

4. (1) Observe the ET tube pass through the vocal cords, (2) see equal chest rise with positive pressure ventilation, (3) during auscultation hear no sounds over the epigastrium and hear equal bilateral breath sounds, (4) observe a positive reading on an esophageal detector device, and (5) note the presence of CO_2 in the exhaled air.

   Once the ET tube is passed, tracheal placement must be confirmed. A single mistake in the placement or confirmation of placement of an advanced airway may result in the preventable death of your patient. Your approach therefore should be calm, calculated, systematic, and provide continual reassessment of redundant checks to ensure proper placement and patency of the patient's airway.

5. c

   A patient who is unconscious and has bleeding into the airway should be intubated as soon as possible. Until intubation can be performed, aggressive suctioning, insertion of an oropharyngeal airway (OPA), and bag-mask ventilation should be incorporated. Patients suffering from facial trauma (especially patients with midfacial instability, epistaxis, etc.) should not have their airways managed with nasopharyngeal airways or nasotracheal intubation. Cricothyroidotomy should be used only if other methods of advanced airway management fail and the patient cannot be managed with a BLS airway.

6. Surfactant

   Surfactant is first produced toward the end of uterine life for the fetus. Premature infants can thus be deficient in surfactant, causing respiratory distress due to the collapse of their alveoli (atelectasis).

7. a

   Angioedema is a swelling similar to urticaria (hives), but the swelling is beneath the skin rather than on the surface. The welts associated with angioedema usually occur around the eyes and lips. They may also be found on the hands and feet. If the welts occur in the throat, they can cause difficulties in airway management, including difficulty visualizing vocal cords during intubation. Angioedema can result from certain allergies. Corticosteroids often cause swelling to the face with prolonged use.

8. An airway can become obstructed from a wide variety of causes including blood, broken teeth, food, vomitus, saliva, foreign bodies, and the tongue.

   Because of its mobility and its tendency to fall backward when a patient with altered mentation is placed in a supine position, the tongue is the most common cause of airway obstruction. Airway obstruction by the tongue can be managed by repositioning the patient's head and jaw or by inserting one of several devices used for lifting or bypassing the tongue. Suctioning can clear the airway of blood, saliva, and vomitus. Total obstruction of the airway by a piece of food or foreign body can be managed with finger sweeps, abdominal thrusts, or use of the Magill forceps to remove the object. If an obstruction is located at the glottis, and it cannot be removed with abdominal thrusts or Magill forceps, a surgical airway may be the next appropriate step.

9. False

   Basic emergency medical technicians (EMT-Bs) entering paramedic education programs should have a working knowledge of simple, noninvasive airway maneuvers, adjuncts, and ventilatory techniques. It is important to note that these basic skills alone have been shown to be effective in managing most airway problems. This is a very important point that is easily overlooked as you learn new and more advanced invasive skills. Performing basic airway skills flawlessly is the first and possibly the most important step to becoming a skilled advanced care provider.

10. b

    Even though there is a possibility that a COPD patient's drive to breathe may be "knocked out," this is a rare occurrence in the prehospital setting. If the patient is hypoxic (as in this scenario), the patient *must* receive oxygen. You must carefully observe the patient's respirations. If the patient's respiratory drive should decline, you can assist ventilations with a bag-mask device. *Never deprive a hypoxic patient of oxygen.*

11. Aspiration is the inhalation of foreign substances into the lungs. Aspiration can cause both airway obstruction and lung infections.

    Patients who have an altered level of consciousness or suffer from a medical condition that impairs their ability to maintain their own airway (e.g., CVA) are at risk for aspiration. This is a very serious problem both because of the potential for airway obstruction (with larger substances) and because of the possibility that aspirated contents will later cause an infection in the lungs (pneumonia).

12. a

    If the head is flexed at the neck (chin to chest), the tongue can come into contact with the soft palate, obstructing the airway. This is especially dangerous for unconscious patients.

13. 8

    Assisted ventilation should approximate the rate and volume (minute volume) of a person at rest; this can be achieved through a one-hand squeeze of about 700 mL every 8 seconds.

14. A tachypneic respiratory system cannot completely exchange air, resulting in hypoxia and hypoxemia.

    It is important to understand that the breath you just took into your lungs does not go directly to the alveoli. The molecules first mix with air that is being exhaled as they begin to move into the bronchi and distal airways. The next respiratory cycle moves it deeper into the bronchioles, and eventually it reaches the alveoli. In a tachypneic system, "dirty air" can be trapped in the distal airways while "fresh air" is moved quickly in and out of the tracheo-bronchial tree but does not reach the alveoli. The result is a patient with inadequate ventilation. This patient may require some level of ventilatory support to control rate and depth of ventilation in addition to oxygen administration to prevent further deterioration.

15. b

    Receptors in the medulla oblongata and in the carotid artery are stimulated by decreased pH (which indicates increased acidity), usually as a result of increased CO_2 in the blood. This is the primary stimulus to breathe. The secondary "drive" is reduced O_2, usually found in patients with COPD.

16. Atelectasis is the collapse of the alveolar sac, resulting in total or partial collapse of the lung.

    When the alveolar sac collapses, that area then becomes unavailable for gas exchange, thereby reducing respiration.

17. (1) Failure of airway maintenance or protection, (2) failure of ventilation or oxygenation, and (3) anticipated clinical course for further treatment.

    Airway management should be supportive and minimally invasive whenever possible. If the anticipated clinical course leads you to suspect further deterioration, such as in the case of status epilepticus or seizures of suspected intracranial hemorrhage from a stroke or trauma, intubation should be strongly considered. If an obstruction is located at the glottis, and it cannot be removed with abdominal thrusts or Magill forceps, a surgical airway may be the next appropriate step. Protocols can help guide some of these clinical decisions, but so should experience and maturity.

18. d

    Tools such as end-tidal CO_2 monitoring (capnography), colorimetric exhaled CO_2 detectors, pulse oximetry, and physical assessment are only parts of ensuring airway patency. The most important method is utilization of systematic and redundant checks. You must frequently reassess all the indicators of airway adequacy. These include physical examination (chest rise and fall, lung sounds, skin color, accessory muscle use, and mental status) and use of secondary devices or tools such as capnography, pulse oximetry, and colorimetric detectors. When using secondary devices keep in mind that they are only tools to help you assess your patient.

19. Hypoxia is a term that means that the patient is not carrying enough oxygen in the blood to the cells in the body. Hypoxemia is a low level of oxygen in the blood.

   It is possible for a patient to be hypoxic but not hypoxemic; for instance, the red blood cells (RBCs) may be carrying enough oxygen, but the cells may not be getting enough oxygen due to low blood volume from a traumatic injury. The terms do not mean the same thing, although they are often used interchangeably.

20. b

   Patients who have been exposed to carbon monoxide, even in low levels, should be evaluated in the emergency department, especially if they exhibit signs and symptoms of altered mental status (e.g., anxiety as in this scenario). Cherry red skin color is a late sign in CO poisoning. Pulse oximeters measure the amount of gas attached to RBCs, and CO and O_2 are measured identically. Therefore patients can have a 100% saturation on the pulse oximeter and still have a significant amount of CO bound to their RBCs. CO displaces oxygen; in other words, it prevents oxygen from being transported by the RBCs.

21. 35–45 mm Hg

   The normal range for end-tidal CO_2 is 35–45 mm Hg.

22. b

   Kussmaul's respiration in patients with diabetic ketoacidosis (DKA) usually represents an effort by the body to "blow off" excess CO_2, thereby reducing the acidity of the body.

23. True

   The biggest complication that can occur with suctioning comes with prolonged suctioning of the patient. Patients who need suctioning are often hypoxic to begin with, and prolonged suctioning can cause increased hypoxia. Therefore suctioning should be limited to 15 seconds or less. Every second the suction unit is operating is a second the patient is being deprived of air. When the patient's pulse oximetry is being monitored, it can help provide you with information valuable to performing suction. If you note the pulse oximeter is dropping, stop suctioning and ventilate the patient for 30–60 seconds before suctioning again.

24. a

   Respiration is the exchange of gases between a living organism and its environment, and it occurs in two places, the alveolar-capillary membrane of the lungs (external) and the level of the cells (internal).

25. c

   The lower airway begins at the vocal cords and ends at the alveolar-capillary membrane.

26. d

   As strange as it sounds, the paralytic medications used in rapid sequence intubations (RSI) can cause airway obstruction by way of laryngospasm. This is an important risk to be aware of before making the decision to use RSI versus other means of airway control.

27. b

   A right-sided shift during capnography is usually indicative of asthma or lower airway trapping.

28. 20–22

   In the *average*-sized adult, if the ET tube is placed correctly, the tip will be approximately 20–22 cm from the teeth. There is great variation in anatomy between different patients, so you should not rely on this measurement to ensure accurate placement; it is just another part of your overall assessment. Use primary confirmations such as chest rise and fall, lung sounds, and visualizing the tube going through the cords combined with secondary confirmations to ensure proper placement.

29. Cyanosis occurs either because the air is not exchanging well in the airway or because the blood is not moving well through the lungs.

   Cyanosis is a condition that occurs when the amount of oxygen passing between the lungs and the RBCs decreases. As the amount of oxygen in the blood drops, a bluish tint develops, first in the nail beds, the conjunctivas of the eyes, the lips, and the tongue. As cyanosis worsens, the skin will appear bluish gray. The primary cause of cyanosis is poor exchange of air in the airway. Many different respiratory problems can result in a poor exchange of air in the airway, such as airway obstruction, asthma, emphysema, severe pneumonia, and tachypnea. Cyanosis can also occur due to conditions that decrease blood flow through the lungs. Tension pneumothorax, cardiac tamponade, massive pulmonary embolism, and severe congestive heart failure diminish blood flow into the thorax and result in less oxygen getting into the blood, producing cyanosis. Both are important causes of cyanosis, and both must be considered by the rescuer.

30. The Sellick maneuver is a technique that closes the esophagus (decreasing the chances of regurgitation) and may assist in the visualization of the vocal cords during orotracheal intubation. It should be performed by placing the thumb and finger on the cricoid cartilage, not the thyroid cartilage, and applying gentle pressure to occlude the esophagus.

   The Sellick maneuver should be utilized on patients with altered levels of consciousness who require assisted ventilation to decrease the amount of air that may be blown into the esophagus and stomach, as well as to decrease the risk of vomiting and aspiration. If the Sellick maneuver is used, it should not be stopped until an invasive airway device such as a dual lumen airway, laryngeal mask airway (LMA), or ET tube is placed. This technique is not necessary once an ET tube, LMA, or Combitube is placed. The maneuver has also been the traditional technique to assist in visualization of the vocal cords. Recently, however, this procedure has been questioned, and some research studies seem to indicate the procedure may not be as helpful as once thought.

31. True

The heart pumps out the blood that it receives, and it receives that blood by sucking it back via a slight negative pressure. When air is blown into a patient's lungs during assisted ventilation, this action creates a positive pressure inside the thorax and impairs the venous return of blood to the heart. In patients with normal circulation, such as in patients undergoing routine surgical procedures under anesthesia, assisted ventilation usually has very little negative effect on blood return to the heart and thus on cardiac output. However, in patients with circulatory problems, such as shock, dehydration, or cardiac arrest, raising pressure inside the thorax through assisted ventilation can dramatically decrease venous return and thus greatly decrease cardiac output, worsening shock.

32. False

Snoring is associated with a raspy sound on inhalation. Stridor is a high-pitched sound heard on exhalation. When stridor is heard both on inhalation and exhalation, this suggests a very high grade of obstruction.

33. a

Oxygen, carbon dioxide, nitrogen, and other gases diffuse across the alveolar membrane.

34. a

During resuscitation, gastric distention, positive pressure ventilations, and chest compression all increase the pressure in the chest cavity. This can inhibit venous return and therefore circulation.

35. c

Since activated charcoal is designed to absorb certain toxins in the gastrointestinal (GI) tract, it must therefore reach the GI tract. IV administration would not be ordered, and PR administration would have limited effect since the majority of absorption would have occurred by the time the substance reaches the rectal area. Oral, nasogastric, and orogastric tube administrations are the most common routes. The patient in this scenario had a progressively diminishing level of consciousness and would therefore be at risk for aspirating the thick charcoal slurry. Nasogastric tube administration, if allowed, would be the most appropriate in this situation and would likely be accompanied by an order for intubation (in order to secure the airway).

chapter 13

Shock Overview

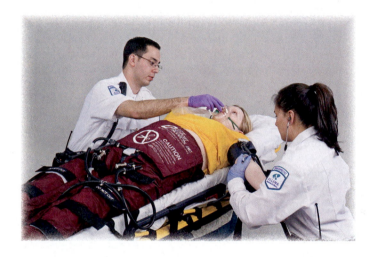

2. Is the patient in shock?

_____

_____

_____

3. If the patient is in shock, what type of shock is she likely experiencing?

_____

_____

_____

4. If the patient is in shock, what is the probable cause of her shock?

_____

_____

_____

Are You Ready?

Myra Acevito and her husband Julio are 15 minutes away from landing at Los Angeles International Airport (LAX) and have been sitting in first class for the past 12 hours. Myra and her husband are getting back from a trip where they celebrated their 15th wedding anniversary. Julio starts to notice that Myra, age 42, is becoming agitated, but he doesn't worry too much about it. She has acted this way before when she has not been able to smoke for an extended period of time.

All of a sudden, Myra grabs Julio's arm and says that she has chest pain and she can't breathe. She becomes acutely pale, begins to sweat profusely, and appears profoundly short of breath. Julio stands up and looks for the flight attendant. Myra has no history of cardiac or respiratory problems.

1. What is your general impression of the patient?

_____

_____

_____

Active Learning

1. Causes of Shock

List at least two causes for each of the following types of shock:

Type of Shock	Causes
Hypovolemic shock (hemorrhagic)	
Hypovolemic shock (nonhemorrhagic)	
Distributive shock	
Cardiogenic shock	
Obstructive shock	
Metabolic shock	

2. How Shocking!

Shock is a syndrome, that is, a group of symptoms that occur together. Shock can result from a variety of mechanisms, which can be confusing. Let's try the following series of exercises to help differentiate the causes of shock.

Hypovolemic shock: You will need the following items:

- Three 1-quart resealable plastic storage bags (such as Ziploc® bags)
- A 1-gallon resealable plastic storage bag
- A sharp needle able to make a small hole in the bags
- Red food dye or Kool-Aid
- Water source
- A measuring cup
- A quarter cup of cereal, like corn flakes

First, fill one of the 1-quart plastic bags about four-fifths full. Add red dye to the mixture until the fluid becomes a noticeable red color, without making it so dark that you cannot see through it. After you have injected the dye, seal the bag. Hold the entire apparatus over a sink or garbage bag. Imagine now that this bag represents the vasculature, and the fluid represents blood. If you filled the bag correctly, it should be nearly full. Resist the temptation to use it as a water balloon!

Now, poke a small hole in the bottom of the bag. What happens? What does this represent? Poke another small hole, and another, until you have 5 or 6 holes. What is happening, both to the fluid as well as the bag? As the experiment continues, you can imagine that the "vasculature" is changing. In fact, "shock" is setting in. What kind of shock does this represent?

Let the experiment continue for 10 minutes. During this time, fill the measuring cup with water. Carefully open the seal about 1 inch and begin to pour the clear water into the bag. What does this represent? As you add the fluid, note the color of the water. What is happening to it? What does this change represent and how might it affect the patient?

If you let the experiment continue for another 10 minutes and refill the bag with another cup of water, what would be the color of the fluid then?

Take another 1-quart bag and fill it halfway with the corn flakes. Add water until it is nearly full. Do not add red dye. Seal the bag. This mixture represents blood in the vasculature, with the water representing plasma and the corn flakes representing red blood cells (RBCs). Like the previous experiment, poke several small holes at the bottom of the bag. As the fluid drains, imagine how this relates to the body's vasculature again. What condition does this represent now? What is happening to the relative concentration of corn flakes?

Let the experiment continue for 10 minutes. In the meantime, fill the measuring cup with water. Carefully open the seal about 1 inch and begin to pour the clear water into the bag. What does this represent? What is happening to the concentration of corn flakes? Compare your findings to the first experiment. In which situation does refilling the bag with water bring it back to its original condition?

Finally, fill the third 1-quart bag with water. This time, though, pour that amount of water into the 1-gallon bag. Seal the 1-gallon bag and observe your results. If the bags represent the vasculature, what just happened? What kind of "shock" did you just create?

For a discussion of this exercise, see the answer section of this chapter.

Distributive shock: There are two key physiologic responses associated with distributive shock that we can demonstrate: increased blood vessel permeability and the effects of vasodilation.

To demonstrate increased blood vessel permeability, take a long, slender balloon and stretch it out several times. Once the balloon is stretched out, take the tip of a permanent marker that has a relatively fine point and make multiple fine marks approximately one-quarter to one-half inch apart. By the time you are finished you should have multiple dots located along the length of the balloon. Turn the balloon slightly and repeat the process along the length of the balloon until there are dots spaced along the surface of the balloon. Attach the balloon to a faucet and fill it just enough to give shape to the balloon. This is a simulated blood vessel, and the dots on the balloon signify closed pores on the vessel surface. When the pores are closed, the amount of fluid that can cross the vessel wall is negligible.

Now, imagine that the patient is suffering from some form of distributive shock (e.g., anaphylactic or septic). The body's natural response to this type of shock is increased blood vessel size (dilation) and increased permeability. Add enough water to the balloon to at least double the diameter of the balloon and then pinch off the opening of the balloon. You will notice that the size of the dots (pores) increases. With the increase in the size of the dots (pores) comes an increase in their permeability. The diameter of the blood vessels increases as well.

Now, instead of adding more water, blow air into the balloon. As you add more air to the balloon, you will notice that the water is no longer occupying the entire area of the blood vessels. The combination of increased permeability (fluid shifting out of the blood vessel) and increased vessel diameter results in a container that holds a smaller and smaller relative fluid volume.

You Are There: Reality-Based Cases

Case 1 (continuation of chapter opener)

You awaken to the sound of the flight attendant announcing that the captain has turned on the fasten seat belt sign and you are beginning your descent into Los Angeles International Airport. You rub your eyes and stretch as you slowly awaken. Before you finish your stretch, the flight attendant comes back on the intercom and requests that any medical personnel identify themselves by pressing the flight attendant button in the overhead panel.

You press the button and almost immediately the flight attendant appears in the aisle next to your seat and asks what type of medical training you have. You tell her that you are a paramedic, and she asks if you will take a look at the woman in 2B, who appears to be having difficulty breathing.

As you approach Mrs. Acevito, you note that she appears profoundly short of breath and extremely anxious. A flight attendant has placed her on high-flow oxygen via face mask. Her husband states that she has never had any breathing problems before, nor has she had any cardiac conditions. A flight attendant produces a surprisingly extensive medical kit and places it by your side.

Myra is a 42-year-old woman who appears slightly overweight. Her husband tells you that she has high blood pressure and smokes a pack and a half of cigarettes per day. She takes medications for high blood pressure, type 2 diabetes, and high cholesterol, and she takes birth control pills.

You listen to the patient's lungs, which are clear, but note that she is very tachypneic and appears to have very shallow respirations. Her radial pulses are barely palpable, and her auscultated blood pressure is 80/70 with a heart rate of 130. You attach her to an automated external defibrillator (AED) and note that she is in sinus tachycardia. She has jugular venous distention without peripheral edema. There is a pulse oximeter that you apply and discover that she has an O_2 saturation of 87%. You ask the patient to nod if she is having sharp chest pain. She nods in an affirmative manner.

1. With further information and a set of vital signs, what is your general impression?

   _____

   _____

   _____

2. What is your first priority in caring for Myra?

   _____

   _____

   _____

3. How will you address the hypotension, tachycardia, and hypoxia?

   _____

   _____

   _____

4. What is the definitive treatment for this patient, and how can you best ensure that the patient receives this treatment?

   _____

   _____

   _____

Test Yourself

1. When treating a pediatric patient who is in shock, what is the *most* important thing to remember in order to prevent serious complications?
   a. Pulse, respiration, and blood pressure vary with age.
   b. Dehydration can quickly lead to hypovolemic shock.
   c. Children may not be able to communicate their complaints effectively.
   d. Children appear normal until they are in profound shock.

2. In the expanded acronym for treating shock, ABCDE, D and E stand for _____ and _____.

3. What three components are necessary to maintain homeostasis?

   _____

   _____

4. A 74-year-old male fell from an extension ladder while cleaning the gutters. He complains about pain in his left hip. When you ask about his medical history, he tells you that he is taking propranolol to control his hypertension. While examining him, you notice his respiration rate is steadily increasing, his pelvis is sensitive to palpation, and his heart rate is 68. You should be most concerned about
   a. hypovolemic shock.
   b. cardiogenic shock.
   c. pain control.
   d. metabolic shock.

5. The vital sign that most distinguishes compensated from decompensated shock is
   a. heart rate.
   b. respiration rate.
   c. skin temperature.
   d. blood pressure.

6. Cardiac output is equal to
   a. stroke volume times heart rate.
   b. blood pressure times systemic vascular resistance.
   c. heart rate times blood pressure.
   d. systemic vascular resistance times stroke volume.

7. A patient with _____ is least likely to need IV fluid boluses.
   a. emesis
   b. gastrointestinal bleeding
   c. an *E. coli* infection
   d. acute myocardial infarction

8. Why is oxygen support a crucial element of shock treatment?

   _____

   _____

9. What are the primary differences between compensated and decompensated shock?

   _____

   _____

10. Which of these is *not* a primary controller of the heart and blood vessels?
   a. Sympathetic nervous system
   b. Parasympathetic nervous system
   c. Immune system
   d. Endocrine system

11. A 40-year-old female is unconscious. Her vital signs are HR of 148, RR of 32, and BP of 90/48. Her skin is cold and cyanotic. She is most likely in which stage of shock?
   a. Irreversible shock
   b. Compensated shock
   c. Reversible shock
   d. Decompensated shock

12. Shock progresses from the decompensated stage to the compensated stage, and finally to the irreversible stage.
   True
   False

13. Shock is best defined as
   a. inadequate perfusion of oxygen and glucose to body tissue.
   b. a systemic failure of internal organs.
   c. severe blood loss.
   d. overcompensation of the body's self-preservation techniques.

14. The difference between systolic and diastolic blood pressure is the
   a. pressure index.
   b. point pressure.
   c. pulse pressure.
   d. pressure window.

15. In addition to vital signs, what are some indications of hypovolemic shock?

   _____

   _____

16. Patients experiencing nontraumatic hypotension have a greater mortality rate than those who are not.
   True
   False

17. Anaerobic metabolism can lead to
   a. hypoglycemia.
   b. acidosis.
   c. anemia.
   d. alkalosis.

18. Treatment of shock in the prehospital setting centers on airway management, oxygen administration, hemodynamic support, and rapid transport to an emergency care facility.
   True
   False

19. The stages of shock are
    a. compensated, irreversible, and decompensated.
    b. irreversible, compensated, and reversible.
    c. decompensated, reversible, and irreversible.
    d. reversible, decompensated, and compensated.

20. Overall, patients who suffer from shock have a mortality rate of roughly
    a. 5%
    b. 1%
    c. 45%
    d. 20%

21. What are the problems caused by anaerobic metabolism?

    _____

    _____

22. Why might you *not* want to administer fluids to a patient in shock?

    _____

    _____

23. Which of the following could lead to hypovolemic shock?
    a. Vomiting
    b. Pulmonary embolism
    c. Acute myocardial infarction
    d. Cerebrovascular accident

24. When might you treat a patient for shock, even if the patient does not display classic shock symptoms?

    _____

    _____

25. Name three factors that could impact a patient's response to shock.

    _____

    _____

Need to Know

The following represent the Key Objectives of Chapter 13:

1. *Explain the state of homeostasis and what happens when the body's homeostatic mechanisms fail.*

   The never-ending attempt to maintain homeostasis is a main theme found in any discussion surround-

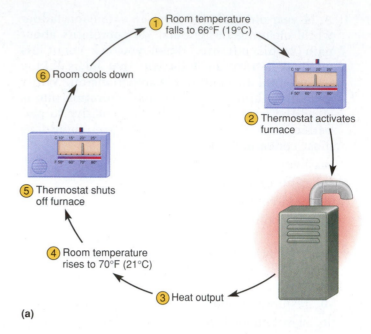

(a)

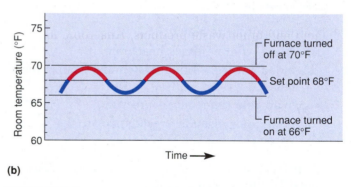

(b)

FIGURE 13-1   Negative Feedback in a Home Heating System. **(a)** The negative-feedback loop that maintains room temperature. **(b)** Fluctuation of room temperature around the thermostatic set point.

ing the topic of shock. The principles of homeostasis and negative feedback can be understood by the analogy of a home heating system (Figure 13-1). When you set your thermostat at a specific temperature, you are establishing the set point. When the room becomes too cold or too warm, a temperature-sensitive switch in the thermostat turns the furnace on or off accordingly. In the latter situation, the temperature rises until it is above the set point; then, the switch breaks the circuit and turns off the furnace. This process represents a negative-feedback mechanism that restores the temperature to the set point.

The homeostatic mechanisms needed to prevent shock include an intact and functioning heart and circulatory system and an adequate blood volume that contains the vital nutrients necessary for cellular life (e.g., oxygen and glucose). When all the mechanisms are functioning properly and the cells and tissues of the body are well perfused and functioning optimally, they are said to be functioning under aerobic metabolism (metabolism with adequate oxygen and fuel). The sympathetic and parasympathetic nervous systems, along with the endocrine system, provide control over the heart and blood vessels in maintaining homeostatic balance. It is when these homeostatic mechanisms fail and the tissues and the cells of the body are not perfused adequately (i.e., they do not receive the oxygen and glucose that they need) that a state of shock exists.

When the tissues and cells do not get the fuel they need for cellular metabolism (energy production), they begin to function in an anaerobic state. Anaerobic metabolism is a cell's attempt to keep alive when it no longer receives the fuel needed to stay alive. It is during this type of metabolism that the cells of the body begin to produce lactic acid and other waste products. Anaerobic metabolism has a very detrimental effect on the cells of the body and the human organism as a whole.

Shock is a state that the body cannot maintain for an indefinite period of time. If shock is left untreated, it can lead to irreversible organ failure and ultimately death. It is crucial that the paramedic be able to quickly recognize and treat the signs and symptoms of shock.

2. *Describe the presentation of shock, including its three stages.*

The manner in which patients present with shock (otherwise known as hypoperfusion) has some common threads, but not all patients present with the classic signs and symptoms. Because the body can do such a good job of trying to compensate for shock, the paramedic must not only treat obvious signs and symptoms, but also treat patients based on history and mechanisms when appropriate. A normal set of vital signs does not rule out the presence of shock.

Shock tends to progress through three distinct stages:

1. *Compensated shock.* Compensatory mechanisms attempt to protect the body by trying to normalize blood, oxygen, and glucose delivery to the tissues and cells of the body.

2. *Decompensated shock.* The point at which the compensatory mechanisms begin to fail. Delivery of blood, oxygen, and glucose to the cells of the body is interrupted.

3. *Irreversible shock.* The point at which resuscitative efforts are likely to fail due to the progression of damage to the body.

3. *Describe how to provide care to patients experiencing shock.*

The treatment of the shock patient begins with the recognition of shock or a history or mechanism that strongly suggests that shock may be present. The second most important fact to recognize is that the treatment of shock is best accomplished in the hospital setting and that rapid transport to an appropriate facility is essential. This is not to say that there is nothing that the paramedic can do to help treat shock.

The prehospital treatment of shock brings us back to the ABCs:

- Airway management with basic or advanced adjuncts.
- Breathing support with ventilatory assistance if needed and administration of supplemental oxygen.
- Circulatory (hemodynamic) support through prevention of fluid loss and cautious fluid replacement (when indicated).

Specific treatment for shock varies based on the type of shock and the presenting signs and symptoms.

- Hypovolemic shock: typically treated with crystalloid fluid and/or blood transfusions (usually administered in the hospital setting).
- Distributive shock (related to atypical vascular tone:
  - Anaphylactic—epinephrine, crystalloid IV fluids, antihistamines, bronchodilators, and possibly steroids.
  - Neurogenic—crystalloid IV solution and, if necessary, dopamine or another vasopressor.
  - Septic—similar to neurogenic shock.

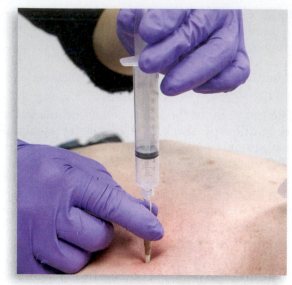

FIGURE 13-2   Pleural decompression.

- Cardiogenic shock:
  - Small fluid boluses in the absence of pulmonary edema.
  - Control of rate-related conditions
    - Bradycardia—transcutaneous pacemaker or pharmacologic interventions such as atropine sulfate.
    - Tachycardia—vagal maneuvers, synchronized cardioversion, or pharmacologic interventions such as adenosine, beta-blockers, and antiarrhythmics.
  - Administration of vasopressors and inotropic agents (e.g., dopamine and dobutamine).
- Obstructive shock:
  - Tension pneumothorax—pleural decompression (Figure 13-2).
  - Pericardial tamponade—pericardiocentesis (Figure 13-3).

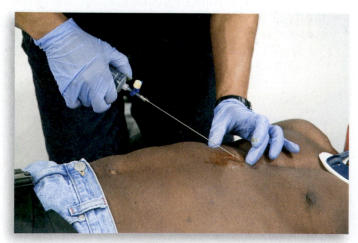

FIGURE 13-3   Pericardiocentesis.

Need to Do

The following skills are explained and illustrated in a step-by-step manner, via skill sheets and/or Step-by-Steps in this text and on the accompanying DVD:

Skill Name	Skill Sheet Number and Location	Step-by-Step Number and Location
Orthostatic Vital Signs	29 – DVD	29 – DVD
Intravenous Access	42 – Appendix A and DVD	42 – Chapter 16 and DVD
Bleeding Control and Shock	66 – DVD	66 – DVD
MAST/PASG Application	81 – DVD	N/A
NREMT Bleeding Control/Shock Management	94 – DVD	N/A

Connections

- Hemorrhagic shock is discussed in more detail in the following textbook chapters: Chapter 19, Hemorrhage and Hemorrhagic Shock; Chapter 29, Cardiology; Chapter 31, Endocrine, Electrolytes, and Acid/Base; Chapter 34, Gastroenterology; and Chapter 41, Obstetrics and Gynecology.
- Distributive shock is covered in more detail in the following textbook chapters: Chapter 23, Spinal Trauma; Chapter 30, Neurology; Chapter 32, Allergies and Anaphylaxis; Chapter 33, Infectious and Communicable Diseases; and Chapter 35, Toxicology.
- Cardiogenic shock is further discussed in Chapter 29, Cardiology, in the textbook.
- Obstructive shock is covered in more detail in the following textbook chapters: Chapter 21, Thoracic Trauma; Chapter 28, Pulmonary; and Chapter 29, Cardiology.
- Metabolic shock is discussed in more detail in Chapter 35, Toxicology, in the textbook.
- Link to the companion DVD for a chapter-based quiz, audio glossary, animations, games and exercises, and, when appropriate, skill sheets and skill Step-by-Steps.

Street Secrets

- **Rapid Transport** Despite our abilities as paramedics to address some of the basic needs of patients with shock, shock is best treated in the hospital setting. An overall goal to rapidly package and transport patients in shock should be at the top of the paramedic's priority list. Other than securing the cervical spine and establishing a patent airway in patients who are unable to maintain their own airway, the paramedic should perform all treatments for shock patients en route to the hospital.

The Drug Box

0.9% sodium chloride: A crystalloid isotonic IV solution that is used for volume replacement for patients in various types of shock.

Lactated Ringer's solution: A crystalloid isotonic IV solution that is used for volume replacement for patients in various types of shock.

Epinephrine: A vasopressor with alpha and beta properties that is the drug of choice in the management of anaphylactic shock.

Dopamine (Intropin): A vasopressor that is useful in treating various types of shock, including cardiogenic and distributive shock.

Dobutamine (Dobutrex): A vasopressor that is useful in treating cardiogenic shock, particularly when it is accompanied by congestive heart failure (CHF) and pulmonary edema, due to its positive inotropic effects.

Answers

Are You Ready?

1. The patient is critically ill. She has profound shortness of breath and complains of chest pain. She has cutaneous signs of shock.

2. Yes. The patient's presentation strongly suggests that she is experiencing compromised oxygenation. She is anxious, severely dyspneic, pale, and diaphoretic. Myra is a 42-year-old woman who smokes cigarettes and has been sedentary during her 12-hour flight.

3. A reasonable general impression would be obstructive shock.

4. Pulmonary embolism

Active Learning

1.

Type of Shock	Causes
Hypovolemic shock (hemorrhagic)	• Trauma • Gastrointestinal bleeding • Vaginal bleeding • Ruptured abdominal aortic aneurysm
Hypovolemic shock (nonhemorrhagic)	• Gastrointestinal losses (e.g., vomiting and diarrhea) • Insensible losses (e.g., burns) • Sequestration (e.g., ascites)
Distributive shock	• Sepsis • Anaphylaxis • Spinal cord injury
Cardiogenic shock	• Acute myocardial infarction • Dysrhythmias (e.g., ventricular tachycardia and atrial fibrillation) • Overdose (e.g., beta-blocker or calcium channel blocker)
Obstructive shock	• Pulmonary embolism • Cardiac tamponade
Metabolic shock	• Carbon monoxide poisoning • Hydrogen cyanide poisoning • Hydrogen sulfide poisoning

2.

The first part of this experiment demonstrates what happens when the vasculature is injured and blood begins to leak out of the system. As the fluid leaves the bag, the bag begins to collapse, much like the body's blood vessels. We can attempt to the "refill" the bag with a volume expander such as water, and in fact it does refill. But, did you notice that the red color of the water slowly became lighter, more pink? That is because you are diluting the "blood," as would happen inside the body when we use volume expanders such as lactated Ringer's or normal saline.

The second experiment should have taught you the difference between shock caused by hemorrhagia (the first experiment) and dehydration. In the second experiment, did you recognize that providing replacement fluid in this case would be helpful? You may have also considered this to be a form of anaphylactic or septic shock, where the vessel walls become more permeable to fluid. In either condition, plasma shifts from inside the blood vessels into the interstitial space while the red blood cells remain inside, just as in a state of dehydration. This is why fluid resuscitation would be very helpful in either of these cases.

The third experiment should have clued you into a form of distributive shock. The container suddenly became much larger when you poured the fluid from the 1-quart bag to the 1-gallon bag. This represents a dilation of the vasculature, a condition associated with anaphylaxis, sepsis, or neurogenic shock.

You Are There: Reality-Based Cases

Case 1

1. The primary assessment and vital signs, combined with the initial information conveyed by the patient's husband, confirm that the patient is critically ill.

2. The first priority in caring for this patient is similar to the priorities for any patient: protecting and supplementing (where needed) the patient's airway, breathing, and circulation.

3. Because there is no guarantee that the cause of the patient's condition is a pulmonary embolism or that the patient is in obstructive shock (as opposed to any other form of shock), you should treat the patient's hypotension in the same manner in which you would treat any patient who is in shock of an unknown etiology. First, place the patient on high-flow oxygen, because breathing comes before circulation (Myra has already been placed on O_2 via face mask). Since the patient has an O_2 saturation of 87% on this concentration of O_2 and her respirations are fast and shallow, you should consider tracking the patient's ventilations (respirations) with a bag-mask device and, if needed, a BLS airway adjunct if the patient can tolerate one. Whatever the means, you need to be sure that the patient has a patent airway and is receiving adequate oxygenation and ventilation. The tachycardia is likely a result of the hypoxia or hypotension, but keep your mind open to the fact that the tachycardia, although highly unlikely at a rate of 130, may be the cause of the hypotension and respiratory distress.

   The next step in the process of caring for this patient should address her hypotension; as with most of the treatment that we provide patients, the care should progress from the least invasive treatments to the most invasive treatments. First determine if the patient is in a position that optimizes perfusion. If not, should you place the patient in such a position, or would that have a negative effect on the patient's airway or breathing? If it would negatively impact the patient's airway or breathing, is there some position that the patient could be placed in that would partially address and have no negative impact on the airway, breathing, or circulation? It is likely that if you change the position of the patient and that makes the patient uncomfortable or exacerbates the dyspnea, the patient will let you know.

   An IV containing an isotonic crystalloid solution would also be appropriate for this situation. Once you establish an IV, you can consider small fluid boluses to see if that has any impact on the blood pressure or the heart rate. If repeated fluid boluses have no effect on the blood pressure, consider the administration of a vasopressor such as a dopamine drip, which you should titrate to effect (a systolic blood pressure of 100 or more).

4. If in fact a pulmonary embolism is causing obstructive shock, the patient needs hospitalization, heparinization and/or thrombolysis. In your setting, the best thing that you can do is to ensure that transportation is standing by when you get off of the plane. Have the flight attendant notify the captain to have transportation standing by for the patient when you arrive at LAX. In the meantime, continue your supportive care and if possible mentally perform a thrombolytic checklist so that you have the information ready when you turn over care to the transporting care provider.

Test Yourself

1. d

   Children appear to compensate for a long time, and then they quickly decompensate. If the mechanism or history leads you to suspect shock, trust your instincts and treat for shock. While the other statements are at least partially true (dehydration-induced shock occurs primarily in infants), forgetting them is less likely to lead to a life-threatening situation than assuming a child is not at risk for shock until the child presents with severe symptoms.

2. Delivery, endpoint

   Delivery means ensuring adequate oxygen delivery, and *endpoint* means achieving the endpoints of a successful resuscitation. Although a patient in shock may be able to draw oxygen into the lungs, the oxygen may not be reaching the cells (inadequate delivery). The normal endpoints in resuscitation from shock, as measured in the field setting, are normal blood pressure and heart rate. Urine output can also serve as an endpoint, but it is rarely monitored in the field.

3. Adequate cardiac function (pump), appropriate vascular tone (container), and adequate blood volume.

   If any of these components fail, shock may result. Knowing which component failed may affect your treatment of the patient. For example, you are more likely to administer inotropic drugs to a patient with inadequate cardiac function than you are to a patient with insufficient blood volume.

4. a

   You must be highly suspicious when evaluating geriatric patients for signs of shock, as they often fail to mount an appropriate physiological response. This, combined with the fact that he is taking propranolol (a beta-blocker, which may prevent tachycardia), means that the patient is less likely to display symptoms. As there is no other cause evident, the increase in respirations should be assumed to be shock. The most likely cause of shock in this scenario is internal hemorrhage caused by the fall (a form of hypovolemic shock).

5. d

   During the compensated stage of shock, the body is often able to respond to shock in a manner that maintains or elevates blood pressure. However, these responses fail when entering decompensated shock, and blood pressure will fall dramatically.

6. a

   Cardiac output is the total amount of blood pumped by the heart in a minute, and it equals the heart rate times the stroke volume. Stroke volume is also one of the factors that determines blood pressure (along with systemic vascular resistance). If a patient goes into shock, his or her body may attempt to raise cardiac output to maintain blood pressure.

7. d

Acute myocardial infarction and other forms of cardiogenic shock result in a failure of the heart to adequately circulate blood (a broken "pump"), not in an absolute loss of fluid or a relative loss (increased "container" size). As such, adding more fluid to a system is not as useful, and indeed may cause more harm than good.

8. A patient who is in shock has an insufficient perfusion of oxygen to meet the metabolic demands of the body. The objective of initial therapy is to maximize the oxygen concentration in the blood in order to maximize oxygen delivery to tissues.

All patients in shock should, at a minimum, be placed on 15 liters of oxygen using a non-rebreather face mask. If respiratory failure has occurred or is perceived to be imminent, oxygenation and ventilation should be provided using a bag-mask and a basic airway or a more invasive airway such as an endotracheal tube.

9. During compensated shock, the patient's body attempts to correct physiological imbalances. For example, the heart rate may rise to increase cardiac output, blood may divert from the extremities to feed the heart and brain, and the respiration rate will increase to intake more oxygen and expel carbon dioxide. When the body is no longer able to mount an effective resistance, the patient enters the decompensated stage. Blood pressure drops, the mental state degenerates, and the blood's pH falls (acidosis occurs).

10. c

The sympathetic, parasympathetic, and endocrine systems work together to control the heart and blood vessels. In a shock situation, they will cause an increased heart rate and vasoconstriction because the sympathetic system overrides much of the parasympathetic system.

11. d

The patient's hypotension and altered mental status suggest that she is in the decompensated phase of shock. However, the elevated pulse and respiration rates indicate that she probably has not yet reached the irreversible stage.

12. False

The proper order of stages is compensated, decompensated, and irreversible.

13. a

Shock (or hypoperfusion) is a state of inadequate tissue perfusion with reduced amounts of oxygen and glucose being delivered to the body cells and tissues. Shock is a common clinical problem encountered by paramedics, and it requires rapid recognition and appropriate treatment.

14. c

The difference between the systolic and diastolic blood pressure is the pulse pressure. It is this change in pressure that you feel when palpating a patient's pulse. A decreasing pulse pressure is a potential sign of shock.

15. Other signs of hypovolemic shock include pale cool skin, sweating, altered mental status, weak peripheral pulse, and poor capillary refill rate. Many of these signs are common to all forms of shock, though patients in distributive shock usually have warm skin rather than cool.

16. True

In a large clinical study of out-of-hospital hypotension, investigators found that nontraumatic hypotension was associated with a significantly higher rate of in-hospital mortality. In this study, a single episode of hypotension prior to hospital arrival conferred a 26%–32% in-hospital mortality rate, whereas those patients who were never hypotensive had in-hospital mortality rates ranging from 8% to 11%. Do not wait until you observe vital signs deteriorating to begin aggressive intervention if the patient seems at risk of hypotension.

17. b

Anaerobic metabolism overproduces the waste product lactic acid. As lactic acid concentrations rise in the cells, the lactate diffuses across cell walls and into the blood, resulting in increased systemic acidosis. Acidosis contributes to organ impairment, and if left untreated, organ failure and death.

18. True

Prehospital airway management includes providing oxygen and ventilatory support in an effort to maximize the concentration of oxygen in blood in order to improve the oxygen supply to tissues. Hemodynamic support is primarily provided by infusion of crystalloid solutions, namely, isotonic saline. Transport follows the standard procedures.

19. a

The three stages of shock are compensated, where the body compensates and maintains near-normal blood flow; decompensated, where the body is unable to compensate; and irreversible, where the organs are too damaged to recover.

20. d

Overall, shock has an estimated mortality rate of roughly 20%, but some specific forms of shock have a much higher mortality rate. For example, approximately 60%–90% of patients who have cardiogenic shock and 30%–40% of those with septic shock die within 1 month of the onset of shock.

21. Anaerobic metabolism produces less energy than aerobic metabolism, and it also produces more lactic acid. Anaerobic metabolism only produces 5%–10% as much ATP (adenosine triphosphate). The overproduction of lactic acid can lead to acidosis, which in turn leads to further organ impairment.

During shock, if the body's mitochondria do not receive enough oxygen, they will shift to produce ATP through anaerobic (without oxygen) metabolism. The alterations associated with anaerobic metabolism and lactic acidosis result in organ impairment if left untreated. Organ impairment is followed by organ failure and death.

22. Fluids may not always benefit a patient in shock. When the cause of shock is unrelated to blood volume (during cardiogenic shock, for example), additional fluid may lead to serious complications such as pulmonary edema. In a patient suffering from hemorrhagic shock, excess fluid can lead to the dislodging of blood clots and additional bleeding or hemodilution.

    Work closely with your medical director to keep abreast of any updates regarding fluid resuscitation.

23. a

    Hypovolemic shock is caused by a decreased vascular fluid volume and is divided into hemorrhagic and non-hemorrhagic shock. Vomiting is a potential cause of nonhemorrhagic shock. Other forms of nonhemorrhagic hypovolemic shock include insensible losses (such as fever in an infant, or the result of burn trauma) and sequestration (or third spacing) of fluids.

24. You should assume a patient is in shock if the situation suggests it. The most obvious example is if a patient has lost blood through hemorrhage. This is especially true if there are factors that might suppress symptoms, such as the patient's age or certain medications.

    For example, a geriatric patient who is taking beta-blockers is less likely to develop tachycardia. Also, children are capable of maintaining a normal appearance for a long time during compensated shock.

25. Factors include age, medications, comorbid factors, ambient and body temperature, and recreational drug use.

    Pediatric patients may appear normal for a while and then have a precipitous drop in their condition, while signs of shock may be subtle in geriatric patients. Some medications (such as beta-blockers or calcium channel blockers) can mask symptoms of shock, while others (such as diuretics) may decrease fluid levels. Many illnesses also deplete fluids through vomiting or diarrhea.

chapter 14

Patient Assessment

Are You Ready?

"Lisa, be careful! You're really close to the stairs," John warned. They were hanging posters in the hallway of the biology building for next week's concert, and Lisa wanted to hang the last one just above the stairway. "No worries," Lisa replied as she started to ascend the ladder they were using. "Can you get the tape gun? I left it by the last poster we put up." She pointed down the hallway. John turned and went down the hallway to retrieve it; just as he reached the end of the hallway, he heard a sickening crashing sound. He ran back to the stairway and saw Lisa lying at the bottom of the stairwell. She was not moving. "Somebody call 9-1-1!" John shouted as he made his way down the stairs.

As the EMS crew approached the patient they could see that the patient was "sick." She was lying at the bottom of a long stairwell; a pool of blood had formed on the floor behind her head. Her eyes were closed, and snoring respirations could be heard on approach. John was kneeling beside her and turned to the crew to give a quick description of what happened.

1. If you were the paramedic, what would you do first to assess this situation?

_____

_____

_____

2. What details do you observe that are of real concern to you at this point?

_____

_____

_____

_____

Active Learning

1. **The Right "Mime-Set" for Physical Assessment**

   Because it is tempting to "voice-assess" simulated patients during practice sessions, try this exercise. Work in a group of three. The first student is the paramedic, the second is the victim, and the third is the evaluator.

   - The victim decides what complaint he or she will present to the paramedic, such as shortness of breath, abdominal pain, or cervical spine pain. Try using one of the skill sheets that describes a specific assessment method (located in Appendix A at the back of this book and on the student DVD.)
   - The victim begins to play the part. The paramedic begins to assess the victim, *but* here is the trick: the paramedic cannot speak! The paramedic must demonstrate the appropriate assessment using only his or her actions.
   - Using the skill sheet, if available, the evaluator checks off the assessment steps as they are completed.

2. A Man (or Woman) of Few Words

Work with two or more classmates. One person in the group chooses a specific complaint or disease process, for example, diabetic ketoacidosis. (That person may have to do some research on the condition in order to become familiar with it.) One at a time, each of you gets to ask one question of the patient, who may only respond with simple yes or no answers. If you believe that you have the diagnosis, raise your hand and state the answer. The patient will then either agree with your response, and you win, or disagree, and you lose. If you guessed wrong, you must drop out of the game. The game continues until someone gives the right answer or all guess wrong. Repeat the game with another student playing the patient.

You Are There: Reality-Based Cases
Case 1

A 60-year-old man fell off a ladder while trying to clean the gutters of his home. As you arrive, you notice the scene depicted in the photo to the right.

1. What should you do first?

   _____

   _____

   _____

You and your crew bring your equipment as you make your way toward the side of the house.

2. Identify two facts about the scene that could play a part in the patient's presentation?

   _____

   _____

   _____

One of your crew members secures any hazards that are present, allowing you to approach the patient. Another crew member kneels down to manually stabilize the cervical spine.

3. What should you do now? How would you do this?

   _____

   _____

   _____

   The patient looks at you as he states, "I'm so embarrassed. It was stupid for me to try to hold the

leaf blower with one hand. Seemed to make sense at the moment! I think I broke my ankle."

4. Now that you have established responsiveness, what should you do next? Describe your step(s) very clearly and completely.

   _____

   _____

   _____

You note the following: There are no unusual sounds coming from the patient's airway. His breathing is regular, not too fast, and not too slow. His chest rises and falls with each breath. There is no bleeding that you can see, and his pulse rate feels fast and strong.

5. How critical is your patient? What would you do next in your assessment?

   _____

   _____

   _____

Case 2

A 56-year-old male began experiencing chest discomfort that felt like "burning" while playing the 16th hole at a golf course. Nevertheless he finished the full 18 holes, trying to relieve the sensation with some chewable antacids his playing partner had with him. He called his wife to pick him up from the club. His wife suspected a serious problem and called 9-1-1 to have an ambulance take him to the hospital instead.

You arrive on scene and begin your evaluation.

1. What would you do first? Describe your assessment and any initial treatment you might perform.

_____

_____

The patient's name is Henry Wilcox. He tells you that he is not having trouble breathing, but the pain in his chest is "incredibly" uncomfortable. He has a regular radial pulse.

2. What part of your assessment should happen next?

_____

_____

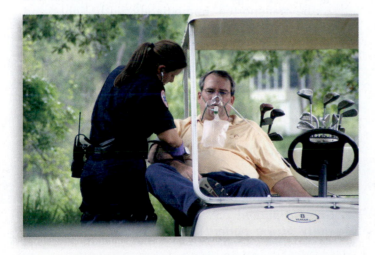

3. What physical examination techniques would be helpful to you in obtaining additional relevant information?

_____

_____

Test Yourself

1. What regions of the body are inspected during the secondary assessment?

_____

_____

2. The basic approach to patient care can be divided into four distinct categories. What are they?

_____

_____

3. The standard use of the AVPU scale during the primary assessment can rapidly identify any patient's level of consciousness.
   True
   False

4. List one example of each of the following types of standard protective gear available to the paramedic.
   - BSI (body substance isolation) equipment
   - Respiratory equipment
   - Outerwear

5. Which of the following should be determined during the scene size-up?
   a. Nature of illness, working diagnosis, and need for additional resources
   b. Need for additional resources, patient history, and need for additional caution
   c. Nature of illness, patient history, and working diagnosis
   d. Mechanism of injury, nature of illness, and need for additional caution

6. A patient would *not* immediately be considered "sick" if he presented with
   a. abdominal pain.
   b. acute scrotal pain.
   c. unconsciousness.
   d. a broken ankle.

7. List some of the equipment that may be used to gather information during a secondary assessment.

_____

_____

8. What do you need to consider before transporting a patient?

_____

_____

9. Your patient is an unconscious woman lying on her back. Her respirations are shallow with some stridor. You should
   a. assume there is an upper airway obstruction.
   b. continue primary assessment looking for signs of trauma.
   c. assume there is a lower airway obstruction.
   d. obtain an ECG reading and check other vital signs.

10. An elderly woman is found in a parked car, slumped over in her seat unconscious. After a primary assessment, you should look for all the following *except*
    a. needle marks on the abdomen.
    b. trauma to the tongue.
    c. medical alert jewelry.
    d. the condition of her hearing aid.

11. Your elderly patient is found lying on her kitchen floor. She is unconscious and has a contusion on her forehead. You should assume that her altered mental status is the result of head trauma.
    True
    False

12. Which of the following patients would not be classified as "sick"?
    a. A 4-year-old boy with full-thickness burns
    b. A 29-year-old man with a fractured clavicle
    c. A 19-year-old woman having an allergic reaction to a bee sting
    d. A 40-year-old woman with a fractured femur and tibia

13. What are the elements of scene size-up?

_____

_____

14. Conscious and unconscious patients are assessed in the same manner.
    True
    False

15. Which of the following may indicate that your patient has poor perfusion?
    a. Hot skin
    b. Pale skin
    c. Jaundiced skin
    d. Dry skin

16. Which of the following conditions would *not* require transportation to a trauma facility?
    a. Crushing injury to the hand
    b. Extremity trauma with partial-thickness burns
    c. Penetrating injury to the neck
    d. A depressed skull fracture

17. In the case where a patient has a faint radial pulse and is pale, what is the advantage of raising the feet several inches above heart level?
    a. It helps to reestablish cardiac rhythm.
    b. It increases the flow of blood to the head.
    c. It increases oxygen delivery to organs.
    d. It reduces the workload on the heart.

18. Tachypnea is
    a. an irregular constriction of the diaphragm.
    b. an increased respiratory rate.
    c. a slow rate of respiration.
    d. a cessation of breathing.

19. The patient position that takes weight off the patient's diaphragm is called
    a. lateral recumbent.
    b. sitting with head back.
    c. tripod.
    d. prone.

20. Why is it important to check the patient's airway early in the assessment process?
    a. Airway status can usually be determined quickly and easily.
    b. If the patient is apneic, he or she will need to be transported immediately with lights and siren.
    c. If the body cannot ventilate, oxygenate, and perfuse, it will cease to properly function.
    d. It is possible to diagnose many conditions based on respiratory symptoms alone.

Need to Know

The following represent the Key Objectives of Chapter 14:

1. *Given a patient presentation, determine the criticality of the patient's condition based upon the*

primary assessment, and describe how to intervene immediately in any life-threatening conditions.

This crucial step determines what you will ultimately do with your patient. Your *primary assessment* identifies the initial condition of the patient's airway, breathing, and circulatory status. *Any* abnormal findings *must* be corrected as soon as they are found. Let's integrate the examination techniques you learned in Chapter 11 in the textbook with the primary assessment:

Primary assessment Section	Assessment Techniques
General impression	Establish level of consciousness (AVPU) Look and feel for skin signs
Airway patency	Listen for upper airway sounds Look for potential airway obstructions
Breathing status	Observe respiratory rate, depth, and effort Observe patient body position
Circulation status	Palpate for location, rate, and quality of a pulse Observe for capillary refill

It is critically important to intervene when problems are detected during the primary assessment. Fortunately most initial interventions are straightforward to do.

Primary assessment Section	Management Techniques
General impression	Establish scene safety.
Airway patency	Manually open the airway (e.g., head tilt, chin lift). Clear foreign body obstruction with back blows and abdominal thrusts, suction, or Magill forceps. Needle or surgical cricothyroidotomy. Needle thoracotomy.
Breathing status	Apply supplemental oxygen. Assist ventilations with basic devices such as a bag-mask. Assist ventilations with advanced devices such as oral endotracheal intubation.
Circulation status	Control severe bleeding. Body positioning. Temperature control. Chest compressions.

Remember that assessment and treatment are not necessarily sequential. The competent, experienced paramedic has already initiated therapies at appropriate times during the primary assessment. For example, he or she may have placed the patient on supplemental oxygen when the patient first described shortness of breath, and aspirin and nitroglycerin might have been administered as soon as the OPQRST suggested a cardiac origin.

2. *Explain the approach to the secondary assessment based upon the primary assessment, scene findings, and the mechanism of injury (MOI) or nature of the illness (NOI).*

Your scene size-up and general impression will uncover whether the source of the patient's condition has a trauma component, a medical one, or, on occasion, both. Further questioning will reveal the forces associated with the trauma mechanism or the patient's level of consciousness. Based on these findings, you may need to modify your secondary assessment approach.

The flowchart in Figure 14-1 illustrates how you might organize your secondary assessment.

3. *Describe the assessment of a trauma patient with a significant mechanism of injury.*

Recovery from significant injuries sustained as a result of a major trauma mechanism is time dependent. The sooner this patient reaches the definitive care provided by a surgical team, the better the chance for survival. To achieve this in the prehospital phase, the paramedic must keep one mental "eye" on the time spent on scene. Efforts by the paramedic and the entire crew are coordinated to continuously move the patient to the trauma center. From the patient assessment perspective, the primary assessment is what is usually done on the scene, while the secondary assessment is done during transport.

Body regions are covered in a systematic manner during the secondary assessment. Table 14-2 in Chapter 14 in the textbook describes the findings you should be seeking. A detailed physical examination of the entire body may be conducted if time and the condition of the patient permit.

4. *Describe the assessment of a trauma patient with a minor mechanism of injury.*

If you are certain that the forces involved with the trauma mechanism are minor and isolated to the injured area, you may focus your attention on the site itself.

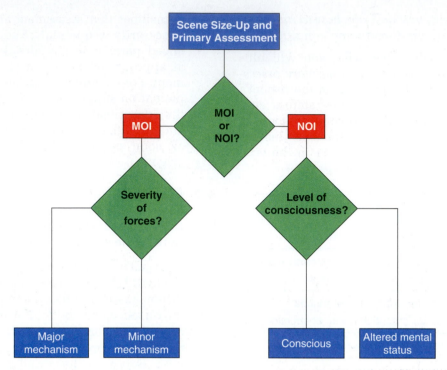

FIGURE 14-1   A simplified approach to patient assessment.

5. *Describe the assessment of a conscious medical patient.*

Patients with medical complaints are somewhat different from trauma patients. Whereas the paramedic can determine the types of injury and level of severity based upon a clear mechanism and physical findings, it is often more of a challenge to decide what *is* happening with an ill patient. The paramedic ends up spending more time being a medical "detective"—that is, the paramedic will gather clues about the patient's medical background and physical findings in a logical way and then consider a variety of working impressions or a "differential diagnosis" that could explain what is happening with the patient.

A conscious patient is generally your best source of information about the circumstances surrounding the medical condition and the past medical history. Physical findings, though helpful, can be more of an adjunct. It is not unusual for an ill patient to have very few positive signs of the illness itself, yet he or she can provide a very detailed and complete description of the events. For this reason, history taking comes generally first after the primary assessment is completed and any life-threatening issues have been managed. In reality, most patient-care providers begin questioning the patient while simultaneously placing the patient on a monitor, assessing vital signs, performing a physical exam, and so forth.

One of the greatest challenges for the new paramedic student is determining which questions to actually ask. While it seems daunting right now, as you learn about various medical conditions you will also learn which questions to ask, and when. Meanwhile, the AMPLE history and OPQRST complaint mnemonic will at least initially provide elemental information about the patient's condition. Over time you will be able to focus these questions into a logical, organized format.

Similar to history taking, the physical exam of the conscious medical patient appears daunting initially. Again, over time you will learn to focus your assessment based upon the patient's chief complaint. For example, most of your examination of the patient in respiratory distress will involve the chest (auscultation of the lungs, palpation of the chest wall for pain or abnormalities, and inspection for accessory muscle use). However, you may end up inspecting and palpating the patient's ankles or sacral area for pitting edema to find signs of congestive heart failure (CHF), as well as the neck for jugular venous distention (JVD). You can begin refining your physical exam technique by practicing the procedures previously described in Chapter 11.

6. Describe the assessment of a patient with altered mental status.

Unlike the conscious medical patient, the altered or unresponsive medical patient can only provide limited, if any, verbal information about the circumstances of the event or about his or her past medical history. In these situations the physical exam findings become more important in determining the underlying conditions that are causing the signs and symptoms. This is why a more comprehensive exam is conducted early, coming right after the primary assessment. Vital signs are obtained shortly after the examination, or during the exam itself.

Because the altered patient may not be able to interact with you, bystanders may be the primary source of historical information. Additional information may be obtained from on-scene clues.

7. Explain why it is important to keep an open mind as you assess your patient.

Remember that in some cases there may be *both* a medical event and a trauma mechanism that exist in the same situation. For example, a driver of a car may experience a sudden syncopal episode while driving, lose control of the vehicle, and crash. Conversely, a trauma patient experiencing hypovolemia or hypoxia may experience cardiac ischemia.

8. Explain the importance of continually reassessing the patient as conditions warrant.

A conscientious paramedic will be constantly conducting a primary assessment on the patient. Being vigilant for subtle changes in the patient's condition will allow you to anticipate what to do next as a call progresses.

Need to Do

The following assessment skills are explained and illustrated in a step-by-step manner, via skill sheets and/or Step-by-Steps in this text and on the accompanying DVD:

Skill Name	Skill Sheet Number and Location	Step-by-Step Number and Location
End-Tidal Capnography	10 – DVD	N/A
Pulse Oximetry	12 – DVD	12 – DVD
Arterial Pulse Locations	25 – DVD	N/A
Blood Glucose Assessment	26 – DVD	26 – DVD
Chest Auscultation	27 – Appendix A and DVD	27 – Chapter 11 and DVD
Nystagmus Assessment	28 – DVD	N/A
Orthostatic Vital Signs	29 – DVD	29 – DVD
Prehospital Stroke Evaluation	30 – DVD	30 – DVD
Trauma Scoring	31 – DVD	N/A
Primary Assessment	32 – Appendix A and DVD	32 – This chapter and DVD
Secondary Assessment	33 – Appendix A and DVD	33 – This chapter and DVD
Chest Pain Assessment	34 – DVD	N/A
Dyspnea Assessment	35 – DVD	N/A
Abdominal Examination	36 – DVD	N/A
ECG Acquisition	37 – Appendix A and DVD	37 – Chapter 29, Section I, and DVD
Traumatic Brain Injury Assessment	76 – DVD	N/A

Primary Assessment

Conditions: The candidate should perform this skill on a simulated patient under existing indoor, ambulance, or outdoor lighting, temperature, and weather conditions.

Indications: Every patient every time.

Red Flags: Life-threatening conditions must be identified and managed during the primary survey.

Steps:

1. Don appropriate standard precautions and ensure scene safety.

2. Survey scene for mechanism of injury (Figure SBS 32-1).

SBS 32-1

3. Determine number of patients.

4. Evaluate need for additional resources and call for more help if necessary.

5. Manually stabilize head and neck if indicated (Figure SBS 32-2).

SBS 32-2

6. Assess level of consciousness using AVPU.

7. Assess and manage airway.
   - Basic airway methods.
   - ALS interventions if BLS-level techniques fail to establish airway patency.

8. Assess and manage breathing.
   - Basic techniques such as supplemental oxygen and/or assisted ventilations.
   - Close any open neck or chest wound with manual pressure.

   - If indicated, advanced techniques such as needle chest decompression (needle thoracotomy).

9. Assess and manage circulation.
   - Control major bleeding.
   - Check skin color, temperature, and condition.
   - If indicated, treat for shock.
   - If indicated, begin chest compressions.

10. Assess and manage disability (Figure SBS 32-3).
    - Evaluate for neck or spine injury.
    - If indicated, prepare to apply cervical collar.
    - If indicated, prepare to immobilize the spine.
    - Stabilize major deformities.

SBS 32-3

11. Expose patient as needed to conduct physical exam.

12. Inspect torso for major bleeding and life-threatening injury.

13. Inspect pelvis and lower extremities for major bleeding or hip fracture.

14. Decide if patient is critical and whether rapid transport is indicated.

Critical Criteria:
- Use standard precautions.
- Consider scene safety issues.
- Establish need for cervical spine stabilization.
- Manage airway threats immediately.
- Manage breathing threats immediately.
- Manage circulation threats immediately.

Secondary Assessment

Conditions: The candidate should perform this skill on a simulated patient under existing indoor, ambulance, or outdoor lighting, temperature, and weather conditions.

Indications: Any patient who is being evaluated by EMS personnel. The secondary assessment focuses on the areas of the patient's past medical history and the body system(s) related to the presenting condition(s) or chief complaint(s).

Red Flags: The patient's condition can prevent the paramedic from obtaining a complete medical history. Life threats found during the primary assessment must be addressed before conducting a secondary assessment. This checklist is not designed to be followed in the order presented, nor is it implied that all steps must be done each time.

Steps:

1. Don appropriate standard precautions.

2. Gather statistical information (age, sex, weight).

3. Assess chief complaint.
   - O—Onset
   - P—Provocation
   - Q—Quality
   - R—Radiation
   - S—Severity
   - T—Time

4. Gather history.
   - A—Allergies
   - M—Medications
   - P—Past medical history
   - L—Last oral intake
   - E—Events leading up to incident

5. Note current health status and prior health history.

6. Evaluate patient's general appearance.

HEENT

7. Inspect skull for trauma (Figure SBS 33-1).

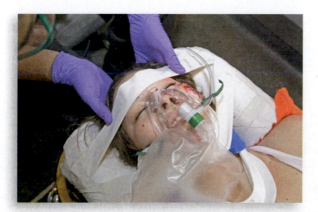

SBS 33-1

8. Inspect eyes for bleeding, swelling, and injury.

9. Check pupils for size, equality, and response to light.

10. In the alert patient, inquire about visual impairment.

11. Check ears for blood, fluids, trauma, and hearing loss.

12. Inspect nose for bleeding, discharge, and trauma (Figure SBS 33-2).

SBS 33-2

13. Inspect mouth for bleeding, trauma, loose teeth, etc.

14. Palpate thyroid and assess trachea for midline positioning.

15. Observe neck for jugular venous distention (JVD).

Chest

16. Palpate, auscultate (breath sounds and heart tones), and percuss chest (Figure SBS 33-3).

—Continued

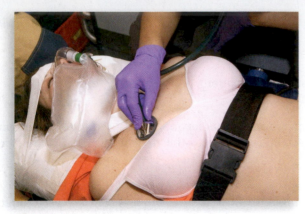

SBS 33-3

Abdomen and Pelvis

17. Palpate all four abdominal quadrants, observing for pain, rigidity, masses, and rebound tenderness (Figure SBS 33-4).

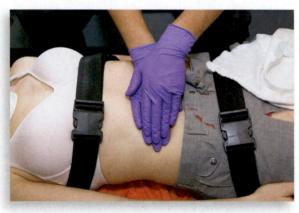

SBS 33-4

18. Check stability of pelvis.

19. In men, check for priapism.

Extremities

20. Check both legs and feet for trauma and dependent edema.

21. Check circulatory, motor, and sensory status (Figure SBS 33-5).

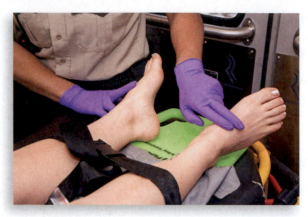

SBS 33-5

22. Check arms and hands for trauma.

23. Check circulatory, motor, and sensory status.

Critical Criteria:

- Use appropriate standard precautions.
- Speak to the patient professionally and with respect.
- Use appropriate body language to convey empathy and respect.
- Adjust interview technique for age or diversity factors.
- Use a consistent, logical format to frame questions.
- Use a combination of open- and closed-ended questioning techniques.

Connections

- *Textbook.* Nearly every textbook chapter is linked in some manner to this worktext chapter, reinforcing the concept that it is difficult to accomplish anything without an accurate patient assessment. Key chapters that will help you tie the components of assessment together include: Chapter 5, Clinical Decision-Making; Chapter 9, Safety and Scene Size-Up; Chapter 10, Therapeutic Communications and History Taking; Chapter 11, The Normal Physical Examination; and Chapter 12, Airway Management, Ventilation, and Oxygenation. To get a better grasp on forces that differentiate major from minor mechanisms of injury, consult Chapter 18, Mechanism of Injury.

- *Lung Sounds on the Web.* The RALE Repository (www.rale.ca/) is an online resource of lung sounds that can be played using your Web browser. The site is fairly extensive. The Emory University School of Medicine hosts a site where multiple resources containing online lung sounds are listed in one easy-to-navigate page. The address is www.emory.edu/WHSCL/grady/inetgrp/hplung.html.

- *Problem-Based Learning Case.* Try your hand at Problem-Based Learning Case 2, The Interfacility Transfer, following this chapter. Remember, not all answers will be available to you right away as you work through the case. Just like in real life, you may have to research some information and really think about the case.

- Link to the companion DVD for a chapter-based quiz, audio glossary, animations, games and exercises, and, when appropriate, skill sheets and skill Step-by-Steps.

Street Secrets

- **Don't Ignore the Smallest Details!** For example, you may want to extend your hand when you introduce yourself to your patient. Observe the interaction. Does the patient shake your hand with the speed and firmness you would consider to be normal? Is it slower or weaker, perhaps indicating a neurological or degenerative dysfunction, such as arthritis? Or does he or she not grasp your hand at all, perhaps a sign of altered mental status?

- **Stethoscope Etiquette** The bell of your stethoscope may be uncomfortable on your patient's bare skin, especially when it's cold. Tuck the scope inside your jacket or uniform shirt during wintry days,

taking it out just before use. Speaking of stethoscopes, sometimes they can be useful for your hard-of-hearing patients. Just have *them* wear the scope while you pick up the bell and speak normally. (You may want to have an inexpensive, disposable stethoscope handy just for this purpose.)

- **Double Gloving** For really messy calls, consider "double gloving," that is, wearing two sets of gloves during the call. If you get your hands full of blood or other bodily discharge during your assessment, you'll be able to quickly take those off using the technique described in Chapter 9, Safety and Scene Size-Up, in the textbook and still have standard hand protection. Keep in mind that the two sets of gloves may blunt your sense of touch.

The Drug Box

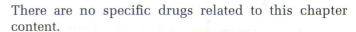

There are no specific drugs related to this chapter content.

Answers

Are You Ready?

1. We can assume that the scene is safe, but making one visual sweep of the scene to make sure nothing will fall on you or the crew would be prudent. It appears that there is a single patient, with a bystander who is able to give an accurate description of what happened.

2. Judging from the photo, assuming that Lisa was near the top of the ladder, the combined height of the fall might have been nearly 20 feet. She appears to be unconscious; you will need to establish where she is on the AVPU scale. The active bleeding is also of concern, but even more pressing is the unstable airway. You can begin controlling both the airway and potential cervical spine injury by utilizing a jaw thrust. Based upon what you find next on your primary survey, you may need to further control her airway, support her breathing with oxygenation and/or ventilation, and control the active bleeding. Further, you will need to examine her as soon as possible to help find any other injuries to her chest that may compromise her ABCs.

You Are There: Reality-Based Cases

Case 1

1. Perform a scene size-up, establish scene safety, don standard precautions, estimate the number of patients, and consider the need for additional resources.

2. The length of the ladder; a leaf blower nearby with a torn electrical line, implying a potential live wire; hardness of surface.

3. Establish responsiveness by introducing yourself and asking if you can help. If the patient speaks to you, you can assume for the moment that the patient has adequate perfusion to his brain. Of course, this assumption might change as you elicit more information about the patient's condition.

4. Your answer should describe a primary assessment clearly. Did you specifically state that you checked for airway patency, breathing, and cardiovascular status?

5. This patient fits into the "not yet sick" category. Although the fall suggests a major mechanism of injury, his primary assessment findings appear to be fairly normal. Nevertheless, you should continue to immobilize the patient's cervical spine and survey the patient to find any injuries.

Case 2

1. Although this appears to be a very safe scene, you still want to size up the situation. What is the weather like? Is he in an area where a flying golf ball might appear at any moment? Where are the last two holes on the course—and did he ride in the cart or did he walk?

   After taking basic precautions, begin your primary assessment. Is there any compromise to his airway, breathing, or circulation? He appears to be awake and alert. What are his skin signs? He has a significant complaint of discomfort in his chest—that warrants the immediate use of supplemental oxygen.

2. Ideally, you should perform several actions simultaneously: take a full set of vital signs, obtain an electrocardiogram and pulse oximetry reading, and take an OPQRST and AMPLE history of the chief complaint. As you gain proficiency as a paramedic you will be able to perform these steps simultaneously. Otherwise your partner or another member of the crew can obtain the vital signs and other objective findings while you question the patient on the complaint.

3. A physical exam for Mr. Wilcox should include the following techniques:

   • Inspection of general body position and overall health
   • Inspection and palpation of the anterior chest wall
   • Auscultation of breath sounds
   • Application of a 12-lead ECG
   • Inspection for the presence of jugular venous distention
   • Palpation for bilateral pulses
   • Inspection for pedal edema
   • Auscultation of heart sounds (nice to know)

Test Yourself

1. During the secondary assessment, you should inspect the head, neck, anterior chest, abdomen and pelvis, lower extremities, upper extremities, and back, buttocks, and flanks.

2. Scene size-up, primary assessment, secondary assessment, ongoing assessment.

3. False

   Pediatric patients, especially toddlers and infants, present specific communication challenges when evaluating level of consciousness. Use of the AVPU scale may need to be adjusted for these differences. Similarly, geriatric patients may have different cognitive issues that may require you to deviate in your examination and analysis.

4. BSI equipment includes gloves, gown, goggles, and mask. Respiratory equipment includes N95 class face masks and respirators. Outerwear includes steel-toed boots, cut- and tear-resistant clothing, and helmets. It is better to enter the scene wearing the appropriate PPE and BSI equipment than to become involved in patient care and realize that protective equipment is not readily available.

5. d

   The scene size-up gives valuable insight as to the nature of illness, mechanism of injury, and possible need for additional caution and resources.

6. d

   Some specific injuries, findings, and complaints that must be treated as "sick" as soon as they are discovered are unconsciousness; unstable airway; severe difficulty breathing or apnea; tension pneumothorax; open pneumothorax; massive bleeding; severe head trauma with altered mental status; multiple long-bone fractures; obvious signs of shock; pain, tenderness, distention, or guarding of the abdomen; acute nonmusculoskeletal back pain in patients > 60 years old; acute chest pain in patients > 35 years old; profuse hematuria (blood in the urine); major hemoptysis or hematemesis; wheezing or crackles in the lungs upon auscultation; unexplained diaphoresis; acute severe headache; acute onset of motor weakness, including dysphasia and paralysis; pulseless extremity; acute edema to the lower extremities; seizures; syncope; acute neck stiffness with signs of fever; immersion event (drowning or near-drowning); lightning strike; caustic ingestion or poisoning; complicated pregnancy; profuse vaginal bleeding; imminent birth; and acute scrotal pain.

7. Common devices include electrocardiogram (ECG), limb-lead based (3- or 4-lead ECG); pulse oximetry to check percent oxygen saturation (SpO_2); glucometers to check blood glucose levels (BGL); and capnography to check carbon dioxide levels.

8. Does the patient consent to transport (or do you persuade them)? How will the patient be extricated from the scene? How quickly should the patient be extricated? How quickly should the patient be transported? To which facility should the patient be transported?

9. a

   Upper airway obstruction may cause stridor, a harsh raspy sound that can be heard without a stethoscope during inspiration. Other obstruction sounds include grunting, snoring, or gurgling. If such an obstruction exists, the primary assessment is interrupted, and action is taken immediately.

10. d

A patient who has a severely altered level of consciousness or is unconscious will be unable to provide reliable information about complaints or medical history. Assessing the unconscious medical patient requires a different approach than does the conscious medical patient. After the primary assessment, a rapid head-to-toe physical examination is performed in the secondary survey. During this exam, the paramedic should assess for the findings listed in the chapter, including trauma to the tongue, needle marks on the abdomen, and medical alert jewelry.

11. False

Medical incidents and trauma incidents are not always easily differentiated. For example, an older female falls down a flight of stairs, breaking her arm and injuring her hip. It may appear to be purely trauma at first glance, but subsequent questioning of family reveals that the patient complained of feeling faint and then she lost her balance and fell.

12. b

A person with an allergic reaction to a bee sting, a critically burned patient, or one with several long-bone fractures are all examples of "sick" patients. The patient with the fractured clavicle should be classified as "not yet sick."

13. The elements of the size-up include safety assessment, determining the number of patients, assessment of the mechanism of injury or the nature of the illness, BSI and protective equipment assessment, and additional resource assessment.

You must carefully take note of the various findings of the scene, both for your own information as well as for other health-care providers in the continuum of care. The scene size-up gives valuable insight as to the nature of the illness, mechanism of injury, and possible need for additional caution and resources. With the exception of the safety assessment, which starts every call and is an ongoing issue, the remaining elements of the scene size-up can be performed in any order.

14. False

Conscious patients should be questioned regarding their past medical history and nature of their complaint. It is also important to keep the conscious patient informed and to obtain express consent. A patient who has a severely altered level of consciousness or is unconscious will be unable to provide reliable information about complaints and medical history. You may have to obtain pertinent information from family, friends, or bystanders.

15. b

Normal skin will be "pink," warm, and dry. (Remember, in patients with dark complexions, you may need to look at the mucosa, nail beds, and palms to check for adequate color.) Patients with skin that is pale, cool or cold, clammy (cold and damp), diaphoretic, mottled, or cyanotic may have poor perfusion, indicating potential inadequate blood volume, impaired circulatory blood flow, or capillary wall pathology.

16. a

The American College of Surgeons (ACS) recommends that the following injury patterns should direct a transport decision to a trauma facility: penetrating injuries to head, neck, torso, and extremities proximal to elbows and knees; flail chest; a combination of trauma with burns; two or more proximal long-bone fractures; pelvic fractures; open or depressed skull fractures; paralysis; amputation proximal to wrist and ankle; and major burns.

17. d

If during the assessment the patient has faint, rapid radial pulses and/or poor skin signs like pallor or cyanosis, lay the patient supine or lateral recumbent, and try to raise the legs 12 inches or more above the level of the heart. Placing the patient in this "shock position" helps reduce workload on the heart and increase preload pressure back to the right atrium. However, you should at all times ensure patient comfort to the extent possible.

18. b

Tachypnea may be the first indication of a potentially serious condition.

19. c

A patient who needs to lean over and support her weight on her hands and arms is in a "tripod" position; this position allows the weight of the chest to be distributed off the diaphragm.

20. c

The purpose of the primary assessment is to detect and treat any problems threatening the airway, breathing, and perfusion status. The body must maintain a steady flow of oxygen to its tissues as well as eliminate waste products from them in order to continue functioning effectively.

Problem-Based Learning Case 2
The Interfacility Transfer

Part I: The Case

Dispatch and Scene Size-Up

You stop at the coffee shop and order your first cup of coffee of the day. It's been a busy morning, and the communications center is now sending you to the Evergreen Convalescent Home, a large skilled nursing facility (SNF) on the south side of town. A patient is waiting for an interfacility transfer. You and your partner are to transport the patient to the community hospital for admission. It is the perfect opportunity for you and your partner to grab a cup of coffee and go.

Just 15 minutes later you are wheeling your gurney into the facility's ambulance entrance. The walk to the SNF unit is short. You are directed to room 27, bed B, where you find Mrs. Ella Freeman lying in the semi-Fowler's position in bed. She is dressed in a hospital gown, and you note that she has a tracheostomy tube. You also recognize that she is pale and appears unresponsive.

The nurse assistant is moving about the room, gathering some of the patient's belongings into a plastic bag. The patient's chart is sitting on the bedside table, next to a portable suction unit. The aide tells you that the patient just experienced an explosive bowel movement; she describes the stool as dark in color and watery in consistency.

1. *Based upon the scene presentation, what is your initial impression of Mrs. Freeman?*

_____

_____

2. *What other information should you gather in the next several minutes?*

_____

_____

3. *What actions might be indicated next?*

_____

_____

The Primary Assessment and Initial Differentials

While your partner reviews the patient's record and receives a report from the nurse who has just entered the room, you approach the patient. You attempt to awaken Mrs. Freeman by gently shaking her shoulder and calling her name. She coughs weakly, but she gives no other response. Her chest rises and falls minimally with each breath, and you hear a faint rattle from the tracheostomy tube when she inhales. As you palpate a radial pulse, you note that her skin is warm and moist. She has a weak radial pulse that feels slow.

4. *Is this patient sick? If so, how sick is she? Is her condition stable or unstable? What actions should you immediately perform? What physical findings and medical history would you like to obtain in order to help you understand this patient's condition more completely?*

_____

_____

History and Physical Exam (Secondary Assessment)

Your partner provides you with the following information: Mrs. Freeman has a history of myasthenia gravis (MG), hypertension, and type 2 diabetes mellitus. Although her record indicates that the tracheostomy tube was placed about 30 days ago, there is no information as to why it was inserted. She has been prescribed and, according to the staff, compliant with the following medications: azathioprine, pyridostigmine, Avandamet, hydrochlorothiazide (HCTZ), and Docusate (DSS). She has no allergies to medications.

Mrs. Freeman has had MG for the past 10 years. According to the nurse, she entered the facility about 1 year ago after her family was no longer able to help her at home. She has been admitted to the hospital twice since then for acute exacerbation of her condition. During the past 12 hours, the patient appears to have lapsed back into another episode, but at a much faster rate. There is no recorded recent history of infection, fever, or diarrhea.

You record the following observations during the secondary survey:

Head: Pupils are equal, dilated, and react minimally to light. Face appears symmetrical. Lips and oral mucosa appear hydrated. Secretions are noted from the nose and mouth.

Neck: Flat neck veins. Trachea midline. No medical alert tag. Tracheostomy site appears well healed, without redness or drainage. No stridor auscultated.

Chest: No accessory muscle use noted. Coarse crackles, wheezing, and rhonchi auscultated in both lung fields.

Abdomen: Nondistended, soft, nontender. No masses visualized or palpated.

Pelvis: Unremarkable. Record indicates previous urinary catheterization, but none noted now.

Extremities: Equal pulses bilaterally. Unable to examine for range of motion (ROM) and strength. Weak Babinski responses.

Back: Unremarkable. Evidence of well-healed decubitus.

You measure the following vital signs:

Pulse: 54 and regular

BP: 94/68

RR: 28 and shallow

SpO$_2$: 84% room air

ETCO$_2$: 65 mm Hg

ECG: Sinus bradycardia

Blood glucose level: 156 mg/dL

5. *Does this information confirm your first impression of the patient's condition? What are possible explanations for Mrs. Freeman's presentation? How does myasthenia gravis affect the body?*

_____

_____

Field Impression(s) and Treatment Plan

As you treat Mrs. Freeman you note that flecks of white, frothy sputum are coating the inside of the tracheostomy tube. The SpO$_2$ monitor indicates a saturation of 81%, and the ETCO$_2$ is now 68 mm Hg. The patient's respiratory rate remains at 28.

6. *What will you do now to correct Mrs. Freeman's condition? What indicators will you focus on to determine whether your interventions are helping or worsening her condition?*

_____

_____

Transportation and Ongoing Care

As you are treating the patient, your partner brings in the gurney and lowers it to the height of Mrs. Freeman's bed. You mentally review your hospital destinations. Community Hospital is a 25-minute drive to the south. University Hospital, a Level I trauma center, is 15 minutes to the north; and Oak Valley Medical Center is 15 minutes away, close to Community.

7. *Should you transport Mrs. Freeman to Community Hospital or another facility? Why or why not? Is this an urgent or routine transport?*

_____

_____

Transfer of Care, Follow-Up, and Outcome

When you arrive at the hospital, the attending physician and two of the nurses are waiting to receive your patient in the "code" room. You begin to provide information to the doctor, who starts her examination of the patient by auscultating her breath sounds. You hear your pager being activated; dispatch is asking you to clear the hospital for a priority 1 call. You and your partner quickly go back in service.

Later in the shift you return to the ED with another patient. After transfer, you go to the nursing station to check on Mrs. Freeman's status. When you had originally arrived at the hospital, the physician had ordered a blood sample for analysis of the patient's arterial blood gases (ABGs). You see these results:

$$pH = 7.46 \qquad PaCO_2 = 32$$
$$HCO_3 = 29.3 \qquad PaO_2 = 95$$

The physician also ordered a complete blood count (CBC). The test results include:

$$Hb = 13 \text{ g/dL} \qquad HCT = 40\%$$
$$PLT = 216,000/mL \qquad WBC = 5,640$$

8. *What do these tests measure? From the ABG results, what can you determine about any intervention(s) that you provided in the field? Do the CBC results support your original impression of the patient's underlying condition and subsequent treatment?*

_____

_____

Long-Term Outlook

One month later you are back at Evergreen Convalescent Home for a routine transfer of a patient to the hospital. You recognize room 27 as being Mrs. Freeman's, but this time you are transporting her roommate. Mrs. Freeman is not in the room, but the nurse assistant who was helping last time is helping you now. When you ask about Mrs. Freeman, the nurse assistant smiles and reports that she is doing much better now that her medications have been adjusted. She has not had another occurrence since the last episode.

Part II: Debriefing

Responses to Part I questions:
1. Mrs. Freeman certainly looks "sick." Her skin color is poor, and she does not appear to be engaged with her environment. In the primary survey, did you ask yourself the following questions?
   - Is the patient really unresponsive?
   - Does the patient have a patent airway?
   - Is the patient breathing adequately?
   - Does the patient have a pulse?
2. You will want to obtain a full set of vital signs; ECG, pulse oximetry and capnography readings; and a blood glucose level. You should also determine from interviewing the staff and reviewing the patient's medical record the reason for the transfer, as well as any pertinent information related to her mental status and airway condition. An OPQRST history can help get you started, and the AMPLE method will gather at least basic information about her past medical history.
3. The primary assessment is where you will need to find *and* correct life-threatening conditions. Can you list the possible procedures you might consider performing based upon your survey results?
4. Is the rattle from the tracheostomy tube an indication of airway compromise? How can you further evaluate airway patency, oxygenation, and ventilatory needs? What might be causing her altered

level of consciousness? Are there any tests you can perform to support your suspicions?
5. How many possible underlying conditions could you identify? Did you think of it from a system perspective, i.e., cardiovascular, respiratory, gastrointestinal (GI), and endocrine? Did you organize your findings so that they made logical sense?
   Myasthenia gravis is an autoimmune disease that worsens over time. What structure(s) are involved in this devastating disease? How do the patient's medications affect this condition?
6. Is caring for a patient with a tracheostomy tube the same as caring for a patient with an endotracheal tube? Are there differences?
   When considering indicators for patient improvement or deterioration, did you think about physical exam findings as well as monitored values such as SpO_2 or $ETCO_2$?
7. This patient appears to be an emergent transport. The question is, where should she be transported? Does a trauma center provide additional services for her condition that a community hospital might not?
8. ABGs and CBCs are lab tests that are routinely ordered for seriously ill patients. They measure basic components of the blood and its characteristics. By following up on the results of these tests, a paramedic can refine the possible underlying conditions of the patient. For example, was the CBC normal in this case? How did that relate to the finding of dark, loose stools that were reported by the aide when you first entered the room?
   Was the ABG analysis normal? If not, which values were abnormal? Were you able to relate these results back to your treatment?

Part III: Case Discussion

Dispatch and Scene Size-Up

Dispatch information can be misleading. Depending upon how a call for service is received, the dispatcher may not be able to triage or prioritize the incident accurately. This call reminds us that a paramedic should always anticipate unusual or unexpected presentations.

Your "across the room" assessment of the patient should have noted the poor skin color and initial level of consciousness. Although a more detailed assessment may later show that these are "normal" signs for the patient, at least for now you must assume that a serious condition exists.

Did you note the presence of the tracheostomy tube and suction unit? These observations should alert you to the potential for a primary airway issue that needs to be assessed as soon as possible. The primary assessment seeks to find and reverse major problems with the patient's airway, breathing, and circulation status. It is crucial that you perform this task with speed and accuracy.

Actions that should be performed in the next several minutes include: airway positioning; suctioning; ventilatory assistance and/or oxygenation, using either basic or advanced airway management techniques; patient positioning; and providing a painful stimulus to confirm the patient's level of consciousness.

How might the description of the patient's bowel movement relate to the patient's initial presentation? The presence of dark, watery stool can indicate a gastrointestinal (GI) bleed; it can also indicate significant volume loss (dehydration). Either of these conditions can result in hypoperfusion, which can cause pale skin and a change in mental status.

The Primary Assessment and Initial Differentials

Yes, the patient is sick. She not only has some form of airway compromise that is presenting itself as a rattling noise from the tracheostomy tube and a minimal rise and fall of her chest with each breath, but she also has moist skin, a weak and slow radial pulse, and an altered level of consciousness.

Any patient who requires an intervention during the primary assessment is considered unstable. Because Mrs. Freeman requires an intervention during the primary assessment, she is considered unstable.

Because an airway issue (the rattling heard from the tracheostomy tube) was discovered during the primary survey, it needs to be addressed until it is resolved. If you are unable to adequately address this issue, you must maintain vigilance and continue your attempts to establish a patent airway and provide adequate ventilation and oxygenation until you do resolve the issue or you are able to turn over care to a higher medical authority.

Rattling from the tracheostomy tube is likely due to the presence of some form of secretion, bodily fluid, or foreign substance. The most appropriate first step in trying to clear the tracheostomy tube and resolve the rattling is to provide sterile tracheal suctioning (see Chapter 47, Patients with Chronic Illnesses, in the textbook for information on tracheal suctioning and troubleshooting tracheostomy tubes).

During the process of suctioning the tracheostomy tube, make sure that the patient maintains adequate oxygenation. Application of suction should not exceed 15 seconds, and the patient should be well oxygenated before and after the suctioning takes place. Heart monitoring and continuous oxygen saturation readings should accompany tracheal suctioning. At the first

sign of hypoxia, the suctioning should be discontinued, and the patient should be oxygenated.

Because the patient presents with minimal chest rise and fall, an altered level of consciousness, and what appear to be cutaneous signs of shock (pale, moist skin with a weak radial pulse), the paramedic should attempt to assist the patient's ventilations with a bag-mask device via the tracheostomy tube and place the patient into a shock position (lower the head of the bed and raise the patient's feet).

To further understand the patient's condition, the paramedic would benefit from obtaining a list of the patient's medications. (Are there any medications that could lead to the patient's presentation? Is the patient compliant with her medications? Who administers the medications? Is there a possibility of overdosing or underdosing of the patient's medications? Are there any new medications that the patient could be allergic to or are incompatible with any of her other medications? What are the actions and side effects of the medications?) A complete past medical history is also necessary—especially the reason why the patient received the tracheostomy tube—and the history that led up to the patient's current condition. (Has the patient complained of any symptoms of illness or injury? Has the patient had a fever, vomiting, diarrhea, infections, etc.? Are there any preexisting conditions such as hypertension, diabetes, or cardiac problems that could be contributing to the patient's current condition?)

History and Physical Exam (Secondary Assessment)

The secondary assessment reveals a wealth of information—in fact, maybe too much! How do you "filter" through all the information so that you can focus on the points that give you the *most relevant and important* information about the patient's immediate condition? You can begin by mentally sorting the findings from the secondary assessment by the order of the primary survey. For example:

Primary Assessment	Associated Secondary Findings
Airway	Secretions around nares and mouth; absence of stridor
Breathing	Crackles, rhonchi, and wheezing auscultated in lung fields; no accessory muscle use; tachypnea; low SpO_2 reading; high $ETCO_2$ reading; midline trachea
Circulation	Tachycardia; hypotension; good hydration of lips and mucosa; no obvious signs of infection

These findings surrounding the patient's airway and breathing status point to a serious issue with ventilation and oxygenation. Your initial interventions to suction the airway and assist ventilations with a bag-mask device were appropriate. Her circulatory status may be a result of her inability to breathe well.

How does the patient's reported medical history relate to her current condition? It is possible that the patient's diabetes is causing a change in mental status. Hypertension can result in an acute stroke, and it can also cause an acute myocardial infarction of the left ventricle, causing cardiogenic shock. By now you should have determined that myasthenia gravis affects the body by reducing the number of acetylcholine (ACh) receptors at the neuromuscular junction, resulting in reduced muscle strength and increasing weakness. A rare autoimmune disorder, MG once had a high mortality rate, but with close monitoring and medications, patients with MG can expect to live a near-normal life span. The records indicate that Mrs. Freeman has had MG for quite some time, and her condition is being managed using several medications: pyridostigmine and azathioprine. These medications must be administered in precise doses in order to avoid accidental overdosing or underdosing.

Did you learn that an overdose of pyridostigmine can cause symptoms very similar to organophosphate poisoning? Does your patient present with signs related to an excessive parasympathetic response?

Did you also learn that azathioprine use has a side effect of darkening stool? How does that relate to the patient's condition?

Field Impression(s) and Treatment Plan

At this stage of treatment, your focus is on working systematically to clear the airway, increase oxygen levels, and remove excess carbon dioxide from the body. After suctioning, assisting the patient's breathing with a bag-mask device and high-flow oxygen may help with her ventilatory status. In addition to monitoring the pulse oximeter and capnograph, observing changes in the patient's skin condition, mental status, and pulse rate can tell you whether your actions are helpful or not.

Transportation and Ongoing Care

Transportation destination decisions can be difficult. How well the patient responds to your therapies may guide your decision; if the patient improves, transporting to the patient's hospital of choice may be most appropriate. However, if you cannot reliably manage the patient's airway, breathing, and circulatory status, you may be required to transport to the closest facility. In this case, if your actions did not improve Mrs. Freeman's airway, then either University or Community Hospital would have been the appropriate destination. If her condition improved, then the hospital of her physician's choice would be appropriate.

The presence of the trauma center may imply a greater level of care at that facility; on the other hand, those resources may not be necessary for managing this particular patient's condition. There was very little in the patient's presentation that would have warranted the services of a trauma center.

Transfer of Care, Follow-Up, and Outcome

An arterial blood gas (ABG) test measures how much carbon dioxide is being carried in arterial blood ($PaCO_2$), its acidity/alkalinity level based on the presence or absence of carbon dioxide (pH), and how well the body buffers that acidity level (bicarbonate or HCO_3). Although it also measures oxygen levels, an ABG is not generally used for this purpose. The normal values for an ABG are:

pH: 7.35–7.45

$PaCO_2$: 35–45 mm

HCO_3: 22–26 mL/L

What can we tell from the patient's original ABG? Her carbon dioxide levels are near normal; in fact, they may be just a little low. This would have resulted from effective ventilations. As a result, her pH level is a little high, indicating a slight alkalosis from the lower than expected CO_2 level. Finally, her HCO_3 level is high; this is expected, because she was hypercarbic to begin with and the bicarbonate buffering system is slower to respond to changes in carbon dioxide levels. In summary, you can infer that your interventions in the field were helpful.

A complete blood chemistry (CBC) checks for the amount of specific blood components—hemoglobin (Hb), hematocrit (HCT), platelets (PLT), and red and white blood cells (RBC and WBC). Normal values for a CBC test are:

Hematocrit (varies with altitude):

Male: 40.7%–50.3%

Female: 36.1%–44.3%

Hemoglobin (varies with altitude):

Male: 13.8–17.2 g/dL

Female: 12.1–15.1 g/dL

RBC (varies with altitude):

Male: 4.7–6.1 million cells/mcL

Female: 4.2–5.4 million cells/mcL

WBC: 4,500–10,000 cells/mcL

Based on this information, you can surmise that this patient's CBC is normal, which may reduce the possibility of blood loss in the patient. That explosive, dark, and loose stool that was reported early in the case may have led you to suspect a GI bleed, but the CBC results rule that out. Subsequent tests revealed that a nurse had accidentally overdosed Mrs. Freeman on pyridostigmine, causing a cholinergic crisis.

Part IV: Further Learning Paths

- In November 1999 the Institute of Medicine (IOM) released *To Err Is Human: Building a Safer Health System,* a report that researched the extent of human error in medical care across the United States. Mistakes in medication administration were found to be a significant problem. The Agency for Heathcare Research and Quality has posted a synopsis of the scope of the problem at www.ahrq.gov/qual/errback.htm. You can view the entire report at http://fermat.nap.edu/books/0309068371/html/index.html.

- Myasthenia gravis is a debilitating disease. You can find out more about the condition at the Myasthenia Gravis Foundation Web site at www.myasthenia.org.

chapter 15

Pharmacology

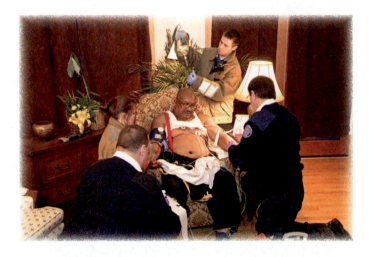

Are You Ready?

This 57-year-old man began complaining of squeezing pressure in his chest about an hour ago. As you evaluate him, you notice he looks pale and is diaphoretic. He has no medical history to relate and takes no medications. You begin an intravenous line of 0.9% sodium chloride and record a 12-lead electrocardiogram of his heart. Your interpretation of the patient's condition is that he is having a heart attack. You consider administering nitroglycerin sublingually and having him chew four baby aspirin.

1. How will the nitroglycerin help his condition? What type of route is sublingual administration? Why should the patient chew the aspirin rather than swallow it?

   _____

   _____

   _____

Active Learning

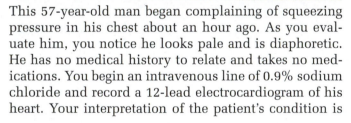

1. **Routes of Administration**

   Using the table below, place the following 10 drugs in the appropriate route of administration. (Hint: Some drugs may have more than one route of administration.)

   • Aspirin
   • Glucagon

Enteral		Parenteral	
Ingestion	Absorption	Injection/Infusion	Inhalation

- Diphenhydramine
- Albuterol
- Epinephrine
- Valium
- Glucose paste
- Amiodarone
- Naloxone
- Nitroglycerin

2. Achieving Balance

Refer to Table 15-8 in the textbook, and write down one or more medications that will balance each of the scales that is "weighed down" by a problem.

Homeostasis		Homeostasis
Heart too slow; blood pressure falls		
Bronchioles are constricted; breathing is difficult		
Blood glucose levels low; level of consciousness falls		
		Heart too fast; blood pressure falls
		Severe pain from fractured hip; anxiety rises
Low cardiac output; low blood pressure occurs		

You Are There: Reality-Based Cases

Case 1

Stan Horowitz nearly passed out while shopping for some hobby supplies. Store employees were able to help him sit down before contacting 9-1-1. He is awake, but cool and diaphoretic. You evaluate his heart rate and find out it is dangerously slow—about

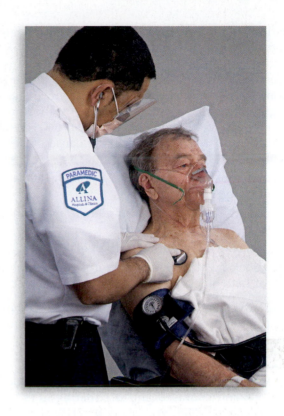

30 beats per minute. His blood pressure is low at 78/60.

1. Based upon this information, what should you do to help correct Mr. Horowitz's condition?

_____

_____

_____

You consider the drugs that you have available to correct your patient's condition. You know that epinephrine and atropine have the same desired effect.

2. Which drug would you choose, and why?

_____

_____

_____

Test Yourself

1. _____ are the class of medications that prevent thrombi by interrupting the clotting cascade.

2. You respond to a call for a patient complaining of a "headache." Your patient's vital signs are BP of 220/160, HR of 150, and RR of 20. Her history includes hypertension, diabetes, and asthma. Your

patient's medications include atenolol, glyburide, and albuterol. She tells you that she took a few "extra" atenolol because she thought her blood pressure might be high. Shortly after administration of the drug, she complains of dizziness and begins to wheeze and complain of shortness of breath. Her vital signs are BP of 90/64, HR of 48, and RR of 24. What is the likely cause of her new symptoms?

   a. A sympathetic response triggered by the patient's anxiety

   b. A drug interaction precipitated by administration of the beta-blocker

   c. An allergic reaction to the beta-blocker

   d. Blockage of beta receptors due to the high dose of beta-blocker administered

3. The primary neurotransmitter for the sympathetic nervous system postganglionic neurons is _____.

4. You respond to a call for a "person down." Upon arrival, you find your patient sitting on the floor. He is weak and confused and is suffering from altered mental status. His vital signs are HR of 36, BP of 80/56, and RR of 20. You should administer medication from the _____ class of drugs.

5. You determine the need to administer an Atrovent updraft treatment for your wheezing COPD patient. You learn that the patient has no allergies, including those to peanuts. This would be an example of the right _____.

   a. circumstance

   b. time

   c. patient

   d. drug

6. Headache is a contraindication for antihypertensive agents.

True

False

7. The _____ route of medication administration has the fastest rate of absorption.

8. Why is a person with hepatitis more likely to suffer from drug toxicity?

_____

_____

_____

9. Your patient complains of a syncopal episode. She is exhibiting signs and symptoms of weakness and dizziness. Her vital signs are BP of 82/58, HR of 160, and RR of 20. She has a history of hypertension

and takes ACE inhibitors. Based on your knowledge of ACE inhibitors, what is the most likely cause of the patient's symptoms?

   a. Stimulation of the sympathetic nervous system

   b. Inhibition of vasoconstriction by blood vessels

   c. Inhibition of calcium transportation across membranes

   d. Beta adrenergic receptor blockade

10. Which type of drug should be used to treat an oral overdose of any given medication?

_____

_____

_____

11. After you administer nifedipine (a calcium channel blocker), your patient develops hypotension and flushing. These signs and symptoms are examples of side effects.

True

False

12. After administering a medication for sedation, it is important to reassess _____.

13. Which of the following would be included in a treatment regimen for an asthma patient?

   a. Beta agonists

   b. Beta-blockers

   c. Antiemetics

   d. Antipsychotics

14. Organophosphate poisoning causes the inhibition of acetylcholinesterase (AChE), an accumulation of acetylcholine (ACh), and profound parasympathetic effects. The _____ class of drugs would be used to reverse these effects.

15. A patient taking an ACE inhibitor and a beta-blocker likely has the chronic condition of _____.

16. Impulses travel across the _____ before reaching a receptor site on a dendrite.

   a. dendrite

   b. axon

   c. synapse

   d. neurotransmitter

17. Your 48-year-old patient is complaining of dyspnea and chest pain. Your patient is unsure of his history, but currently takes Lasix (a loop diuretic), nitroglycerin, baby aspirin, and potassium chloride. Your physical exam reveals pitting edema to the extremities and crackles and wheezing in the lungs. Vital signs are BP of 160/90, HR of 140,

and RR of 24, and the ECG reveals atrial fibrillation. What treatment plan would be most effective in managing this patient?

   a. Treat for CHF: nitroglycerin, loop diuretic, morphine, and oxygen

   b. Treat the arrhythmia: oxygen and calcium channel blocker or beta-blocker

   c. Treat for respiratory complications: albuterol and oxygen

   d. Treat for an MI: nitroglycerin, oxygen, morphine, and aspirin

18. Pharmacodynamics describes how drugs are absorbed by the body, distributed to the target organs, and eliminated from the body.

True

False

19. An antagonist is a drug that binds to a receptor

   a. but does not cause it to initiate a response by an agonist.

   b. and causes it to initiate a response by an agonist.

   c. and stimulates some of its effects, but blocks others.

   d. and causes a deformity to the binding site.

20. After administering nitroglycerin to a patient with chest pain, you should be most concerned about what possible development?

_____

_____

_____

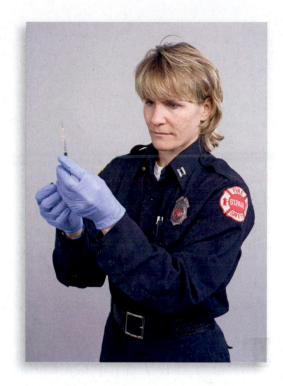

3. Right dose

4. Right route

5. Right time

An expansion of the classic five rights includes four more "rights," resulting in the nine rights of medication administration:

6. Right documentation

7. Right technique

8. Right circumstances

9. Right indication

You are accountable for the management and storage of the medications while they are in your care:

• Ensure that the medications are neither expired nor tampered with prior to use.

• Maintain the correct ambient temperature to keep drugs at their maximum efficacy.

• Keep track of and secure federally controlled drugs like narcotics, benzodiazepines, and other habit-forming medications.

2. *Explain how drugs interact with the body in both therapeutic and harmful ways, as well as how drugs can interact with each other to produce unexpected effects.*

As a paramedic, you should be familiar with the following terms that relate to this area of understanding:

   a. *Pharmacokinetics* is the study of how a drug enters the body and how the body removes

Need to Know

The following represent the Key Objectives of Chapter 15:

1. *Identify the paramedic's responsibilities and scope of practice related to medication administration.*

Paramedics are permitted to administer medications under the orders of a physician. Many of these drugs can be harmful or even lethal when administered inappropriately too much or too quickly. You can minimize your risk of hurting a patient by remembering the "five rights" of medication administration.

1. Right patient

2. Right drug

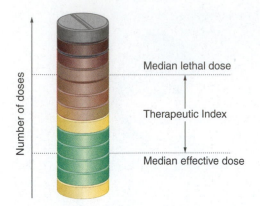

FIGURE 15-1 The relationship between median effective dose, median lethal dose, and the therapeutic index.

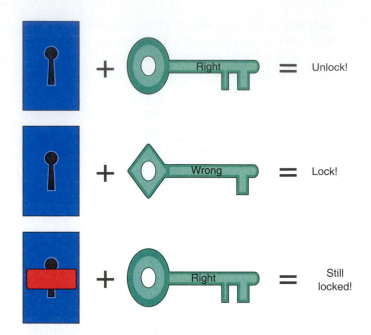

FIGURE 15-2 Pharmacodynamics and the lock and key mechanism.

the drug or its by-products once it has been used.

b. Drugs can be ingested, injected, absorbed, infused, or inhaled. Many of the drugs that paramedics deliver in the field are injected, which makes sense since the patients are often experiencing serious illnesses that require quick intervention. However, it also means that it is relatively easy to injure the patient if the wrong drug or dose is given through injection.

c. Many of the drugs that paramedics deliver are eventually removed by the liver. As such, patients with impaired or decreased liver function can achieve toxic levels of drugs more quickly than normal. Drugs also are excreted through the kidneys and GI tract.

d. How drugs enter and exit the body is related to the *bioavailability* of the medication in the body, its *median effective dose* (the amount of drug that when given to an experimental population, half will have the desired effect), and the *median lethal dose* (a desired amount that when given will kill half a population of experimental animals). The difference between the amount of a drug needed to achieve the median effective dose and the amount needed to achieve the median lethal dose is known as the *therapeutic index* (Figure 15-1).

e. Pharmacodynamics studies how a drug interacts with the body itself.

f. Many of our medications engage the body through the concept of receptors. How a drug interacts with a receptor site is similar to the concept of a key and door lock (Figure 15-2). If you insert the right key into a lock, the lock will turn and you will be able to then open the door. Conversely, if you insert the wrong

key into the same lock, or cover the keyhole with a piece of electrical tape, you will not be able to turn it and therefore not be able to open the door. In fact, even having the right key in your hand will not allow you to open the door since the keyhole is blocked.

Let's review the analogy, this time in pharmacodynamic terms. The right key is called an *agonist*. The wrong key that fits and blocks the opening of the lock to the right key, or the piece of electrical tape blocking the opening, is called an *antagonist*. The lock is the *receptor*. Opening the door after it has been unlocked is the *effect* you wanted.

g. Unlike the lock and key you find at the hardware store, our receptors are much more variable. It's as if you could somehow open a lock more quickly with one type of key than with one that was "less right." In some cases, the wrong key will fit *better* than the right one. The carbon monoxide and oxygen example given in the textbook is a great example of this concept. Finally, the effects are much more diverse than simply opening a door.

h. Having a fundamental understanding of how drugs interact with the body at the receptor level will help you to grasp what exactly is happening to the patient as you administer medications. Remember that ultimately the selection of the right medication, dose, route, and timing is based upon your desire to produce homeostasis. You might want to speed up a heart rate that is too slow. Your patient may have fluid overload due to congestive heart failure, and you want to speed up the production of urine to help remove the excess fluid. The patient's blood glucose level is too low so you want to reverse that. In each of these cases you will provide a medication that in some way engages with a receptor to produce that effect.

i. Now you know how drugs can interact with the body; drugs can interact with each other as well, sometimes for the better. For example, a patient may be prescribed two types of antihypertensive medications to control high blood pressure. These two medications, administered at lower doses, may be as effective as just one of the medications that is delivered at a higher dose. However, it may be safer to receive the lower dose combination rather than the single, higher dose. This is an example of *duplication*.

j. Two drugs can also be *antagonistic* with each other. You may be treating a patient who is experiencing respiratory distress. You assess her and decide to administer albuterol, a beta agonist that is very effective in opening constricted bronchioles in the lungs. However you find out that she is on a beta-blocker to control high blood pressure. It is possible that your preferred treatment may not work, as the beta-blocker antagonizes, or opposes, the desired effect of the albuterol.

k. Finally drugs can be *synergistic*; that is, when taken in combination, the cumulative effects are greater than just the sum of them. HIV "cocktails," which consist of several drugs taken together, are an example of a beneficial synergistic effect. Related to this concept is *potentiation,* in which one drug can enhance the effects of the other. Alcohol can significantly potentiate the effects of sedative drugs like diazepam by worsening the side effects of drowsiness and respiratory depression.

3. *Classify drugs by their specific drug actions.*

You read in the textbook that there are several ways of classifying medications, including

- American Heart Association classes of recommendations
- Controlled Substances Act
- Through body systems
- Chemical groups

Table 15-8 in the textbook contains a comprehensive listing of medications classified by their intended actions. As you review this list, there are several observations to be made:

a. Some drugs are included in more than one category. For example, epinephrine is classified as a catecholamine/sympathomimetic, an inotrope, and a vasopressor. They are all related; epinephrine is a *catecholamine* that stimulates both alpha and beta receptor sites throughout the body (Figure 15-3). Alpha sites, when stimulated, cause the peripheral vascular beds to constrict (*vasopressor*). Stimulating beta receptors will cause the heart to contract faster (*chronotrope*) and with more force (*inotrope*), as well as cause smooth muscle to relax and bronchioles to dilate, a desired effect for someone experiencing severe bronchoconstriction during status asthmaticus or anaphylaxis (*respiratory agent*).

b. Epinephrine is a good example of why it's important to relate a medication's properties to its actual physiological actions. Can you imagine trying to memorize just those actions listed in the example? It's much easier to remember that a *sympathomimetic* is a substance that stimulates the sympathetic side of the nervous system. (The "mime" reminds you that it mimics a sympathetic response.) Stimulating the sympathetic nervous system causes the heart to increase in rate and contractility, shunts blood away from the skin and other unimportant body areas back to its central core and deep skeletal muscles, and increases oxygen uptake through bronchodilation and increased respiratory rate.

If this makes sense, knowing that epinephrine, norepinephrine, vasopressin, dopamine, dobutamine, and Isuprel all have sympathetic properties can help you more quickly remember which drugs to consider using when you desire this type of response from the patient. Consider a patient in cardiac arrest. Because the heart is not contracting, no blood pressure is created, and target organs such as the heart, lungs, and brain are not perfused, causing death. Of the choices of sympathomimetics to use, epinephrine is often used first because it directly stimulates the peripheral vasculature to constrict and promote better blood flow to the critical organs during CPR. If the heart begins to beat again and blood pressure rises, yet remains too low, you may elect to use dopamine to help increase heart contractility without necessarily increasing its rate, helping it to keep its oxygen demand in check.

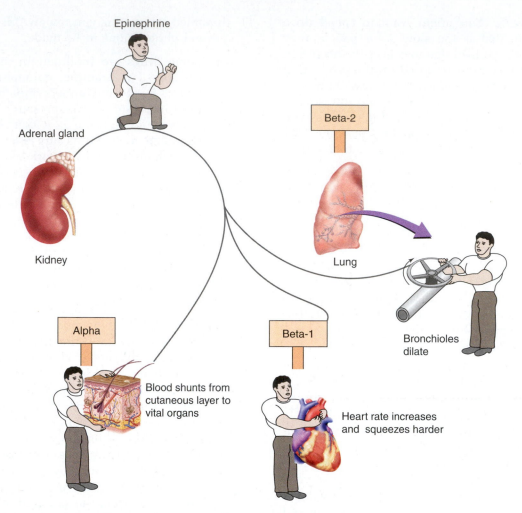

FIGURE 15-3 How epinephrine affects various organs through receptor sites.

c. Not all these drugs are typically used in pre-hospital care. That might make you believe that those particular medications are unimportant. In fact, knowing why a patient may be taking a specific medication may clue you into an unsuspected part of his or her medical history; it may also help you avoid an untoward or undesired effect. For example, a patient who is taking beta-blockers to help control hypertension may not be able to compensate well for sudden blood loss associated with trauma, because the medication is preventing his heart from responding appropriately to such an insult. Another example would be a patient who is taking a type of antidepressant medication called monoamine oxidase (MAO) inhibitors. Giving this patient the pain medication meperidine could precipitate a serious reaction that can cause death.

Need to Do

There are no psychomotor skills that directly support this chapter content. Please see Chapter 16, Medication Administration and IV, in this worktext for step-by-step medication administration skills.

Connections

■ The *Clinician's Pocket Drug Reference* (also called the *Scut Monkey Drug Manual*) is packaged with the textbook. Become familiar with this handy guide and its features and layout. Look especially at the section that begins on page 1. This section lists many medications by their category of action, which you have some understanding of by now. The generic forms of these drugs are described in more detail beginning on page 25.

- Link to the companion DVD for a chapter-based quiz, audio glossary, animations, games and exercises, and, when appropriate, skill sheets and skill Step-by-Steps.

The Drug Box

There are no specific drugs related to this chapter content.

Street Secrets

- **Mini References** Many paramedics keep either a homemade or commercially made reference guide that contains a list of both prescription and over-the-counter medications that they commonly encounter. Rather than contain every piece of information about the drug, these guides basically contain the generic and trade names and classifications. These mini-references can be very handy when you are trying to understand the patient's medical history through his or her prescription medications.

- **Electronic Drug References** There are also electronic programs available for personal digital assistants (PDAs) that are updated regularly.

- **Sound Alikes** Similar-sounding drugs can in fact to be related to one another. For example, prochlorperazine, hydroxyzine, and promethazine are all antiemetics. Esmolol, labetalol, metoprolol, and propranolol are examples of beta-blockers.

- **Poison Control** The U.S. Poison Control System is an excellent resource in helping to identify medications and treatment for overdoses. They have a universal telephone number: 800-222-1222. Often your local public safety answering point (PSAP) can link you directly to them.

Answers

Are You Ready?

1. Nitroglycerin is classified as an antianginal agent. It relaxes the smooth muscle surrounding the vasculature, allowing the arteries throughout the body to dilate. In the heart, the now larger-diameter coronary arteries promote greater blood flow and oxygenation to ischemic areas. Sublingual means "under the tongue." This is an *absorption* route. Aspirin, or acetylsalicylic acid (ASA), is an antiplatelet agent. If the ischemia in the cardiac muscle is due to a partially blocked coronary artery, coating it with ASA will prevent the blockage from becoming larger. Having the patient chew the ASA promotes a faster absorption through the oral mucosa, rather than waiting for it to be processed in the gastrointestinal tract.

You Are There: Reality-Based Cases

Case 1

1. In order to preserve homeostasis, speeding up the slow heart may help elevate the patient's blood pressure and therefore resolve his condition.

2. Both medications will increase the heart rate, which is the desired effect. As a sympathomimetic, epinephrine works like an accelerator in a car: you step on the pedal, and the engine works harder in response to the increased amount of gas being delivered. On the other hand, atropine, a parasympathetic blocker, is like stepping off the brake of the same car. As you release the brake, the car begins to move, slowly at first, but gently increasing

Active Learning

1.

Enteral		Parenteral	
Ingestion	Absorption	Injection/Infusion	Inhalation
Aspirin	Nitroglycerin (paste, spray, or tablet)	Glucagon	Albuterol
Glucose paste	Valium	Diphenhydramine	Epinephrine
	Aspirin	Epinephrine	
	Glucose paste	Valium	
		Naloxone	
		Amiodarone	

2.

Homeostasis		Homeostasis
Heart too slow; blood pressure falls		Epinephrine, atropine, Isuprel
Bronchioles are constricted; breathing is difficult		Albuterol, aminophylline, epinephrine, terbutaline, Atrovent
Blood glucose levels low; level of consciousness falls		Glucagon, dextrose 50%, glucose paste
Adenosine, beta-blocker, calcium channel blocker, lidocaine, amiodarone		Heart too fast; blood pressure falls
Narcotic analgesic, NSAID		Severe pain from fractured hip; anxiety rises
Low cardiac output; low blood pressure occurs		Vasopressors—epinephrine, dopamine, dobutamine, norepinephrine

speed, without the workload of being given gas. In the end, the car gains speed.

Turning back to the patient, you might be able to increase the heart rate by simply removing the "brake," or parasympathetic stimulus to the heart, by administering the blocker atropine. This may be safer than giving epinephrine, which can possibly "over-rev" both heart rate and contractility and cause irritability of an already sick heart.

Test Yourself

1. Anticoagulants

   Anticoagulants interfere with the clotting mechanism at various points in the cascade (see Box 15-15 in the textbook).

2. d

   The action of a beta-blocker is to block beta receptor sites, which results in a decrease in the rate and force of cardiac contraction, vasodilation, and tracheal and bronchial constriction or spasms. This is especially a concern for a patient with asthma as a block of the beta$_2$ receptors may result in an asthma attack that may not respond to beta agonists (see Boxes 15-10 and 15-15 in the textbook).

3. Norepinephrine

   Norepinephrine is the neurotransmitter for the sympathetic nervous system postganglionic neurons (see Box 15-9 in the textbook).

4. Parasympatholytic

   This patient is bradycardic (slow heart rate) and hypotensive (low blood pressure). Parasympatholytics mimic the sympathetic nervous system, which would cause an increase in pulse and blood pressure in the patient (see Box 15-15 in the textbook).

5. a

   The right circumstance is knowing when to give and when to withhold the administration of medications and confirming that no contraindications exist for using the drug, such as an allergy (see Box 15-13 in the textbook).

6. False

   A contraindication identifies when a drug should not be used. You could administer an antihypertensive agent to a patient with a headache; the headache could be an indication or a side effect associated with antihypertensive agents. Hypotension is a contraindication of antihypertensive agents, because administering an antihypertensive agent to a patient who is already hypotensive will cause an additional, unsafe drop in blood pressure.

7. Intravenous (IV)

   In general, the parenteral route has the fastest rate of absorption. Subcutaneous (SQ) and intramuscular (IM) routes take time for absorption to occur and allow the medication into the bloodstream, whereas an intravenous (IV) route injects the medication directly into the bloodstream, where it passes through the liver and lungs on its way to the target organ (see Box 15-3 in the textbook).

8. Hepatitis reduces liver function, and detoxification of drugs occurs in the liver.

   Hepatitis is a term used to describe any inflammation of the liver. The most common causes of hepatitis are the hepatitis viruses (hepatitis A, hepatitis B, hepatitis C, etc.), but hepatitis also may be caused by medications or alcohol abuse. Although filtration via the kidneys is a common means of elimination of drugs from the blood, the liver also detoxifies drugs (see Box 15-15 in the textbook).

9. b

   ACE inhibitors interfere with the conversion of angiotensin I to angiotensin II, which causes an inhibition of blood vessel vasoconstriction in order to decrease the blood pressure (see Box 15-15 in the textbook). A beta adrenergic blockade would likely result in the same symptoms if the patient were taking beta-blockers. Calcium channel blockers inhibit the transport of calcium across membranes, resulting in decreased peripheral vascular resistance and hypotension. Beta agonists cause a stimulation of the sympathetic nervous system, directly affecting cardiovascular and respiratory systems.

10. A gastric decontaminant

    Gastric decontaminants, such as activated charcoal, bind to and eliminate toxic ingested substances (see Box 15-15 in the textbook). Activated charcoal has become the treatment of choice for most oral overdoses. Syrup of ipecac is an emetic that is used less frequently in the out of hospital setting.

11. True

    Calcium channel blockers slow conduction (see Box 15-15 in the textbook), resulting in a decreased heart rate and vascular smooth muscle relaxation. A drop in blood pressure along with initial facial flushing may occur as side effects.

12. Level of consciousness, airway, breathing, pulse, and blood pressure

    When administering a medication for sedation, it is important to reevaluate the level of consciousness, airway, breathing, pulse, and blood pressure, because sedative medications depress the central nervous system. Careful monitoring ensures that the right amount of sedation has been given. If overmedication should occur, the patient will need airway and breathing management and a reversal agent should be considered.

13. a

    Selective beta agonists will cause tracheal and bronchial relaxation (dilation) without causing excessive stimulation of cardiac effects. Beta-blockers should be used with caution in asthmatics. Antipsychotic and antiemetic drugs would do nothing for a patient's asthma symptoms (see Box 15-15 in the textbook).

14. Anticholinergics

    Organophosphate poisoning is characterized by overstimulation of the parasympathetic nervous system. Treatment is aimed at inhibiting the parasympathetic response by stimulating the sympathetic nervous system. Anticholinergics stimulate the sympathetic nervous system (see Box 15-15 in the textbook).

15. Hypertension

    ACE inhibitors and beta-blockers are generally used as antihypertensive agents (see Box 15-15 in the textbook). Another possible answer is cardiac disease, since the majority of patients with cardiac disease suffer from hypertension.

16. c

    After the nerve cell receives an impulse stimulus (message) from the axon of another nerve cell, it travels across the synapse to a receptor site on a dendrite (see Figure 15-2 in the textbook).

17. a

    Treatment for congestive heart failure should be aimed at removing fluid from the patient in order to decrease obstructive shock and increase the number of alveoli available for oxygen exchange to reduce the patient's hypoxia. Nitroglycerin and morphine will reduce the myocardial oxygen demand while decreasing the workload on the heart, which should, in turn, relieve the chest pain (see Box 15-15 in the textbook).

18. False

    Pharmacokinetics is the study of how drugs are delivered to and removed from affected organs, including how drugs are processed in the body through absorption, distribution, metabolism, and excretion. Pharmacodynamics is the study of the action or effects of drugs on living organisms.

19. a

    Drugs that bind to receptors and then inhibit (or prevent) the binding of the endogenous agonist are antagonists. These compounds may produce a desired effect by simply inhibiting the action of the agonist.

20. Hypotension from vasodilation

    Nitroglycerin is an antianginal agent that improves oxygenation by causing the coronaries to vasodilate and the vascular smooth muscle to relax. It reduces the workload on the heart and reduces myocardial oxygen demand. The vasodilation may cause hypotension, headache, and nausea, but hypotension is the most significant finding. It requires immediate intervention by the paramedic to prevent further life-threatening complications.

chapter 16

Medication Administration and IV

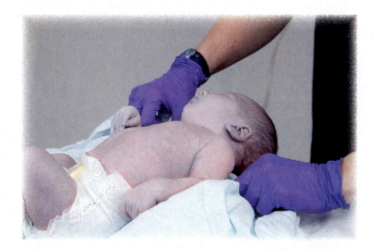

Are You Ready?

As you arrive on the scene of an "unknown medical emergency," a hysterical woman runs out of her house carrying an infant who appears blue and is actively seizing. You yell to your partner, "Seizing kid," as you open the side door of the ambulance and grab the pediatric kit and O_2 bag. Your partner takes the baby from the mother and steps up into the ambulance as you open the O_2 bag.

1. What is your general impression of this patient?

_____

_____

_____

2. What is your first priority?

_____

_____

_____

3. List four possible causes of this child's seizure.

_____

_____

_____

4. What test should you perform on this infant before any medications are administered, and why?

_____

_____

_____

5. What are the possible routes of medication administration for this patient (list in order of your preference and explain).

_____

_____

_____

Active Learning

Some people are great at math, and then there are the rest of us. There is a certain amount of common sense that goes into calculating drug dosages, but for the most part it is based on simple formulas and calculations.

1. Equivalents

Before you begin calculating drug dosages, there are several things that you will need to commit to memory:

a. _____ pound(s) (lb) make up 1 kilogram (kg).

b. 1 kg is equal to _____ gram(s) (g).

c. 1 g is equal to _____ milligram(s) (mg).

d. 1 mg is equal to _____ microgram(s) (mcg).

e. 1 liter (L) is equal to _____ milliliter(s) (mL).

f. 1 cubic centimeter (cc) is equal to _____ mL.

g. 1 teaspoon (tsp) is equal to _____ mL.

h. 1 tablespoon (T) is equal to _____ mL.

i. 1 fluid ounce (fl oz) is equal to _____ mL.

j. 1 grain (gr) is equal to _____ mg.

k. 1 deciliter (dL) is equal to _____ L.

l. 1 centimeter (cm) is equal to _____ meter(s) (m).

m. 1 milligram (mg) is equal to _____ g.

n. 1 mcg is equal to _____ g.

2. Calculation Methods

There are several ways to determine how much of a medication you are supposed to administer to a patient. No matter what method you choose to use, if performed properly, they should all come up with the same answer. Following are three methods for determining the appropriate dose based on information that you have available to you.

Method 1

The first method is based on the following *formula*:

$$\text{Volume to be administered } (X) = \frac{\text{Volume on hand} \times \text{Ordered (or calculated) dose}}{\text{Concentration (in units of mg, mcg, g, etc.)}}$$

Example: Medical control orders you to administer 5 mg of morphine sulfate IV to your 84-year-old female patient who has signs and symptoms of a hip fracture. The morphine in your formulary contains 10 mg in 1 mL. How many milliliters of morphine sulfate do you need to administer to this patient in order to deliver 5 mg?

You have the following information:

Order: 5 mg morphine sulfate IV

On hand: 10 mg/1 mL

Fill in the formula:

$$X = \frac{1\ \text{mL} \times 5\ \text{mg}}{10\ \text{mg}}$$

Cancel any common values (volumes or concentrations) that exist on the top and on the bottom, and multiply across the top.

$$X = \frac{1\text{mL} \times 5\ \cancel{\text{mg}}}{10\ \cancel{\text{mg}}}$$

$$= \frac{1 \times 5\ \text{mL}}{10}$$

$$= \frac{5\ \text{mL}}{10}$$

$$= 0.5\ \text{mL}$$

You need to administer 0.5 mL of morphine sulfate to your patient.

Method 2

This second method involves *ratio and proportion*. The symbol for proportion is ::, and the symbol for ratio is : .

Using the same problem as in method 1, start with the known ratio on the left side of the proportion:

$$10\ \text{mg} : 1\ \text{mL} ::$$

Place the unknown ratio on the right side of the proportion in the same sequence as the ratio on the left side of the proportion. This ratio is usually the physician order or the dosage that you are permitted to administer based on standing orders:

$$10\ \text{mg} : 1\ \text{mL} :: 5\ \text{mg} : X\ \text{mL}$$

First, multiply the extremes (*the far outside values:* 10 mg and X mL) and place the result on the left side of the equation. Second, multiply the means (*the numbers on either side of the proportion symbol:* 1 mL and 5 mg) and place this value on the right side of the expression:

$$10X = 1 \times 5$$

Multiply:

$$10X = 5$$

Divide both sides by the number in front of the X:

$$\frac{10X}{10} = \frac{5}{10}$$

$$X = 0.5\ \text{mL}$$

You need to administer 0.5 mL of morphine sulfate to your patient.

Method 3

The third method is referred to as the **cross multiplication method.** This method sets the problem up using fractions. The first fraction is the concentration, and the second fraction is the physician's order over the volume of medication being administered.

$$\frac{10 \text{ mg}}{1 \text{ mL}} = \frac{5 \text{ mg}}{X \text{ mL}}$$

Cross multiply the fractions by multiplying numerators by the denominator on the opposite side. Express the results as an algebraic equation the same as used in the proportion method.

$$10X = 5 \times 1$$
$$= 5$$
$$X = 0.5 \text{ mL}$$

You need to administer 0.5 mL of morphine sulfate to your patient.

3. Fluid Volume over Time

To calculate a volume to be infused over a specific time frame, you need the following information:

- The volume to be administered
- The delivery of volume of the administration set (drops [gtt]/mL)
- The total time to infuse the fluid (always expressed in minutes)

Example: The physician orders the administration of 400 mL of 0.9% sodium chloride solution over 1½ hours using a 10 gtt/mL (macro-drip) administration set. At what drip rate will you set the infusion?

Volume to be infused: 400 mL

Administration set size: 10 gtt/mL

Total time of infusion: 90 minutes

The following formula should be used when calculating this type of problem:

$$\frac{\text{Drip rate}}{(\text{gtt/min})} = \frac{\text{Volume to be infused} \times \text{Drip chamber size}}{\text{Total time of infusion (minutes)}}$$

$$= \frac{400 \text{ mL} \times 10 \text{ gtt/mL}}{90 \text{ min}}$$

Simplify:

$$\text{Drip rate} = \frac{400 \text{ mL} \times 10 \text{ gtt/mL}}{90 \text{ min}}$$
$$= \frac{400 \text{ gtt}}{9 \text{ min}}$$
$$= 44.4 \text{ gtt/min}$$

This same formula can be used to find out how long it would take to administer the entire contents of an IV bag using a specific drip rate.

- Place the drip rate on the left side of the equation.
- The total volume of the IV bag multiplied by the drip chamber size is the numerator on the right side of the equation.
- The total time of infusion is the denominator on the right side of the equation.
- Solve the equation for X (the time needed to administer the entire contents of an IV bag).

Example: You have a 250-mL bag of 5% dextrose in water (D_5W) and have been ordered to infuse it at 90 gtt/min using a 60-gtt/mL administration set. How long will it take to infuse this amount of fluid?

Volume to be infused: 250 mL

Administration set size: 60 gtt/mL

Total time of infusion: X minutes

Ordered gtt/min: 90 gtt/min

Set up the formula with the information that you have on hand:

$$90 \text{ gtt/min} = \frac{250 \text{ mL} \times 60 \text{ gtt/mL}}{X \text{ Time}}$$

Multiply each side of the equation by X. Milliliters cancel one another.

$$X(90 \text{ gtt/min})(X \text{ Time}) = 15{,}000 \text{ gtt}$$

Divide each side by 90 gtt/min:

$$X \text{ Time} = 167 \text{ min}$$

It will take 167 minutes, or 2 hours and 47 minutes, to infuse the 250-mL bag of D_5W.

4. IV Infusions

There are also several methods for determining IV drip rates for patients receiving IV infusions. The following methods are examples of how this can be done.

Formula Method

This method finds the ordered dosage over time based on the patient's weight.

Example: You have a resuscitation patient who has a return of spontaneous circulation (ROSC) after you defibrillate her out of ventricular fibrillation. You reassess the patient and discover that she is in a normal sinus rhythm, but she is hypotensive. Fluid boluses do not affect the patient's blood pressure, so you decide to start the patient on a dopamine infusion at 10 mcg/kg/min per your protocols. The patient weighs 132 pounds.

You have premixed dopamine IV bags that contain 200 mg of dopamine in 250 mL of D_5W. Your policy for administration of dopamine mandates the use of a 60-gtt/mL IV tubing. How many drops per minute will need to be delivered in order to achieve the 10 mcg/kg/min dosage?

First convert the patient's weight in pounds into kilograms:

$$132 \text{ lb} \div 2.2 \text{ lb/kg} = 60 \text{ kg}$$

Next insert the information that you have on hand into the formula below, and you will get

$$\mathcal{X} = \frac{\text{IV bag volume (mL)}}{\text{Amount of drug in IV bag}} \times \frac{\text{Concentration ordered (mg, mcg, g)}}{1 \text{ min}} \times \frac{\text{Administration set (gtt)}}{1 \text{ mL}}$$

$$= \frac{250 \text{ mL}}{200 \text{ mg}} \times \frac{10 \text{ mcg/kg}}{1 \text{ min}} \times \frac{60 \text{ gtt}}{1 \text{ mL}}$$

Because the concentration ordered is weight based, the 10 mcg needs to be multiplied by the patient's weight in kilograms (60 kg):

$$10 \times 60 = 600 \text{ mcg}$$

$$X = \frac{250 \text{ mL}}{200 \text{ mg}} \times \frac{600 \text{ mcg}}{1 \text{ min}} \times \frac{60 \text{ gtt}}{1 \text{ mL}}$$

Next convert the amount of drug in the bag from milligrams to micrograms because the order is in micrograms:

$$200 \text{ mg} = 200,000 \text{ mcg}$$

$$X = \frac{250 \text{ mL}}{200,000 \text{ mcg}} \times \frac{600 \text{ mcg}}{1 \text{ min}} \times \frac{60 \text{ gtt}}{1 \text{ mL}}$$

Simplify the problem (cancel out zeros and units):

$$X = \frac{250 \text{ mL}}{200,000 \text{ mcg}} \times \frac{600 \text{ mcg}}{1 \text{ min}} \times \frac{60 \text{ gtt}}{1 \text{ mL}}$$

$$= \frac{25}{20} \times \frac{6}{1 \text{ min}} \times \frac{6 \text{ gtt}}{1}$$

Now multiply:

$$X = \frac{25}{20} \times \frac{6}{1 \text{ min}} \times \frac{6 \text{ gtt}}{1}$$

$$X = \frac{900 \text{ gtt}}{20 \text{ min}}$$

Simplify the problem:

$$X = \frac{90 \text{ gtt}}{2 \text{ min}}$$

Reduce the fraction:

$$\frac{45 \text{ gtt}}{1 \text{ min}} = 45 \text{ gtt/min}$$

Clock Method—Dopamine Clock

The clock method is a way in which paramedics can simplify calculating how many drops per minute they need to infuse once they have determined the dosage of the medication that they need to administer. It helps determine drops per minute based on the concentration of medication per a specific volume of fluid and the number of drops per volume of the administration set.

Example: Dopamine comes in premixed bags with various concentrations of medication. For the sake of this example, we will say that the premixed bag contains 800 mcg/mL of fluid. If you are using a 60-gtt/mL administration set (which is typical for the administration of dopamine), the clock tells us that for every 60 gtt or 1 mL of fluid, the patient will receive 800 mcg of the solution. The 800 mcg and the 60 gtt/min go at the top of the clock (at 12:00). To complete the clock, you need to use basic division and addition. We need to fill in the clock at the 3:00, 6:00, and 9:00 positions. In order to do this, we need to divide both the 800 mcg and the 60 gtt by 4: 800 divided by 4 is 200, and 60 divided by 4 is 15. The 3:00 position is filled in by 200 mcg/mL and 15 gtt/mL. Add another 200 mcg/mL and 15 gtt/mL, respectively, to these numbers to get the correct volume and drip rate for the 6:00 position (400 mcg/mL and 30 gtt/mL). To complete the clock and fill in the 9:00 position, add another 200 mcg/mL and 15 gtt/mL, respectively, to the 6:00 calculation (obtaining 600 mcg/mL and 45 gtt/mL).

Dosage: 10 mcg/kg/min → 10 mcg/60 kg/min → 600 mcg/min

Premix IV bag: 200 mg/250 mL → 200,000 mcg/ 250 mL

Concentration: 800 mcg/mL

IV administration set: 60 gtt/mL

You are looking for the drip rate for dopamine in drops per minute. To accomplish this, you need to make sure that you are dealing with like values in your clock. For example, the volume that you are using in your administration set needs to match that of your concentration (if the volume of the administration set is measured in milliliters, then the concentration of the medication needs to be measured in a like volume [mL]). Once this has been confirmed, you are ready to set up your clock:

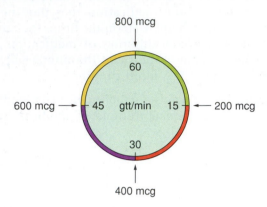

Since you are going to deliver 600 mcg/min, look at the clock to determine how many drops per minute you will need to deliver that amount of dopamine: 45 gtt/min will give you the desired 600 mcg/min.

Find the ordered dosage over time: The information that is needed from the problem is

- The ordered dose
- The size of the drip chamber
- The amount of drug on hand
- The total volume on hand (the volume of the IV bag being used)

The physician orders a 2-mg/min maintenance infusion of lidocaine for a patient who was experiencing ventricular tachycardia. You have a premixed solution of lidocaine that has 1 g of lidocaine in 250 mL of normal saline. You have a 60-gtt/mL administration set. At what drip rate will you set this infusion?

Physician's order: 2 mg/min
Administration set size: 60 gtt/mL
Amount of drug on hand: 1 g
Volume on hand: 250 mL

The following formula should be used when calculating these types of problems:

$$\text{Drops per minute} = \frac{\text{Volume on hand} \times \text{Drip chamber} \times \text{Ordered dose}}{\text{Amount of drug on hand}}$$

First, convert grams to milligrams to allow for consistency between the requested dosage and the concentration of medication on hand:

$$1g = 1{,}000 \text{ mg}$$

Apply the information that you have to the equation:

$$\text{Drops per minute} = \frac{250 \text{ mL} \times 60 \text{ gtt/ mL} \times 2 \text{ mg/ min}}{1{,}000 \text{ mg}}$$

Simplify: Milliliters cancel one another and milligrams cancel one another, leaving gtt/min.

$$\text{Drops per minute} = 30 \text{ gtt/ min}$$

Run the infusion at 30 drops per minute to infuse 2 mg of lidocaine per minute (check your work on the following lidocaine clock).

Clock Method—Lidocaine Clock

Lidocaine drips are typically 1 g of lidocaine in 250 mL or 2 g of lidocaine in 500 mL of D_5W. These drips are not weight based, but instead are based on milligrams per minute (mg/min).

The first thing that needs to be done is to convert the grams of lidocaine to milligrams so that the drip rate will reflect the established mg/min infusion rate.

- 1 g = 1,000 mg

Next divide the volume found in the IV bag by the concentration of the lidocaine to obtain the ratio of mg:mL.

- 1,000 ÷ 250 = 4 mg/mL
- 2000 mg ÷ 500 = 4 mg/mL

Now simply apply this ratio to a clock:

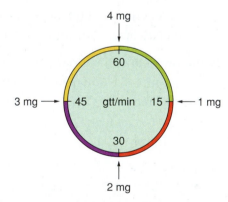

5. Calculation Problems

Using any of the preceding methods, solve the following dosage calculation problems.

a. You have been instructed by medical control to administer an initial dosage of 0.1 mg/kg of IV adenosine to your 33-lb pediatric patient followed by a rapid fluid bolus. Based on the available packaging of adenosine (depicted in the photo at the top of page 187), you will need to administer _____ mL.

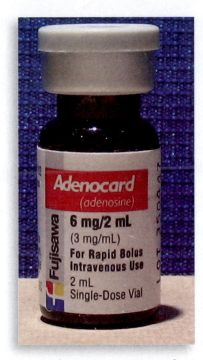

b. You are working up a patient who is in ventricular fibrillation. The patient has been defibrillated following the administration of 1 mg of epinephrine 1:10,000, CPR is in progress, and the patient is now ready for her first round of lidocaine at 1.5 mg/kg. The patient weighs 132 lb. Based on the order and the lidocaine that you carry in your formulary (depicted below), you will need to administer _____ mL of lidocaine.

c. You are treating an infant who is suffering from a symptomatic bradycardia at a heart rate of 40 beats per minute. The patient has not responded to oxygen therapy, ventilation, or epinephrine administration. Your base hospital physician has ordered you to administer 0.02 mg/kg to this 22-lb child. You should administer _____ mL of atropine (depicted below) to the patient.

d. You have a 27-year-old (80 kg) male patient who has suffered second- and third-degree burns over 56% of his body. You are transporting the patient to the burn center, which is just under 1 hour away. The patient has received a considerable amount of morphine, which barely seems to be taking the edge off of the pain. You calculate your fluid infusion for the patient based on the Parkland formula and realize that you will need to infuse 1,120 mL per hour for the first 8 hours. You will need to deliver _____ drops per minute in order to administer 1,120 mL/hour.

e. You are monitoring a 500-mL bag of normal saline that is dripping at a rate of 120 gtt/min through a 10-gtt/mL administration set. It will take _____ min for the bag to finish.

f. You have been given an order to infuse a 300-mL fluid bolus to your patient over 45 minutes with a 10-gtt/mL administration set. You will need to set the drip rate at _____ gtt/min in order to accomplish this goal.

g. The physician orders 3 mcg/kg/min of dopamine to be administered to your patient in cardiogenic shock. You place 200 mg of dopamine into a 250-mL bag of D_5W to mix the infusion. You have a 60-gtt/mL administration set, and your patient weighs 165 lb. You will run the infusion at the rate of _____ gtt/min.

h. You have been given an order for dobutamine for your hypotensive CHF patient. The order is 15 mcg/kg/min. Your protocol states that you are to use a dobutamine infusion consisting of 250 mg in 500 mL of normal saline. The patient weighs 165 lb. You will need to administer _____ gtt/min if you are using a 60-gtt/mL administration set.

i. Your preceptor is quizzing you about dosage calculations, and he states that he wants you to administer dopamine in the alpha range to a hypothetical 65-year-old, 88-lb patient. You remember that alpha effects are seen at 20 mcg/kg/min, and you have been drilled and drilled that you are supposed to always use a microdrip (60 gtt/min) administration set when administering IV piggyback medications and that your local protocols require 200 mg of dopamine to be mixed into a 250-mL bag of D_5W. Your preceptor wants to know how many drops per minute you will need to administer to this patient in order to see the desired effects. The answer you give is _____ gtt/min.

j. You have achieved a return of spontaneous circulation on a ventricular fibrillation cardiac arrest patient following your second defibrillation. Your partner boluses the patient with lidocaine and asks that you prepare a lidocaine drip. Your protocols require that you begin a lidocaine infusion at 2 mg/min. You carry premixed lidocaine (2 g in 500 mL). Using a 60-gtt/mL administration set, you will set the lidocaine infusion at a drip rate of _____ gtt/min to deliver 2 mg/min.

You Are There: Reality-Based Cases

Case 1

As you are inspecting your ambulance at the beginning of your shift, an elderly man shuffles up to the back of the ambulance and says, "Excuse me young man, may I have some help? I am having chest pain and I really don't feel well." You pull out the gurney from the back of the ambulance and ask the gentleman to sit down so that you can check him out. The patient complies, and as you are about to begin your assessment, your partner walks up to the ambulance. The two of you immediately go to work.

You assess the patient as your partner hooks him up to the ECG monitor and the pulse oximeter (his oxygen saturation is 92% on room air) and then places the patient on O_2 at 10 L by non-rebreather mask. The patient's vital signs are BP of 188/96, HR of 112, and irregular and slightly labored respirations of 28. The ECG shows the rhythm in Figure 16-1. The patient presents with cool, pale, moist skin and speaks in five- to six-word sentences. He is alert and oriented and follows basic commands. He states that he is having a heavy sensation in his chest, very similar to the pressure that he felt when he had an MI 2 months ago. The pressure (6 on a scale of 10) is nonradiating and is associated with

nausea. The onset of this episode was 30 minutes ago while walking.

The patient states that he had a stent placed, but he doesn't know which artery it was placed in. He takes digoxin, atenolol, Coumadin, Glucophage, and Lipitor. He has no allergies to medications.

You discover that the patient has jugular venous distention (JVD), slight supraclavicular retractions with his ventilations, trace pedal edema, and faint crackles in the bilateral bases of his lungs. He has had no recent illnesses and has had no sputum production. He states that he has had trouble breathing when he sleeps at night, so he has been sleeping in a recliner in his living room. He also states that he has trouble breathing when he walks.

As you establish an IV, your partner administers one metered dose of sublingual nitroglycerin and 325 mg of aspirin. Your partner states that he would like to complete the MONA algorithm and asks if you would like to contact medical control to get an order for morphine sulfate or if you would like him to make the call.

1. What is your general impression of the patient?

   _____

   _____

   _____

2. What is your first priority in the treatment of this patient?

   _____

   _____

   _____

3. Describe your basic treatment of the patient prior to administration of medications.

   _____

   _____

   _____

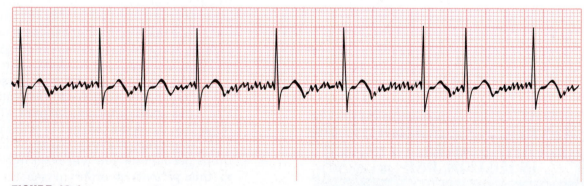

FIGURE 16-1

4. What do you need to know about the patient before you can administer medications?

_____

_____

_____

5. What do you need to know about a medication prior to administering that medication?

_____

_____

_____

6. What are the five "rights" of medication administration?

_____

_____

_____

7. What is likely the single most important thing that a paramedic can do following medication administration to prevent unnecessary exposure to contaminated items?

_____

_____

_____

8. Explain why your partner was able to administer nitroglycerin and aspirin but needed to contact medical control in order to administer morphine sulfate.

_____

_____

_____

9. During the process of obtaining a history, what is an important question to ask the patient regarding medications—other than the names of the medications and any known allergies that the patient may have to medications—that can have a dramatic impact on the patient's current condition?

_____

_____

_____

Test Yourself

1. You are called to an apartment building by law enforcement officials who have discovered a man whom they believe to be delusional. The patient tells you that he has been hearing people talking all day long, like "a radio playing in my head." In the kitchen you find several bottles of Abilify, an antipsychotic medication; all the bottles are full, and the prescriptions were filled several months ago. You should suspect
   a. a medication overdose.
   b. a manic depressive disorder.
   c. a traumatic head injury.
   d. a medication underdose.

2. In regard to medication administration, what is a contraindication?

_____

_____

3. When administering a medication, you should check the patient's vital signs
   a. after administering the medication.
   b. before and after administering the medication.
   c. every 10 minutes after administering the medication.
   d. before administering the medication.

4. Next to a patient's bathroom sink, you find a prescription sleep aid, an over-the-counter (OTC) pain reliever, an herbal remedy, and a toothpaste that contains fluoride. Which of the following must be documented in your report?
   a. The prescription and OTC medications
   b. The prescription medication only
   c. The prescription, OTC medication, and herbal remedy
   d. The prescription, OTC medication, herbal remedy, and toothpaste

5. Like medications, IV catheters and tubing have expiration dates.
   True
   False

6. Your patient is in hypovolemic shock and requires immediate fluid replacement therapy. While preparing to administer the IV, you drop the needle and it falls to the ground. What should you do?
   a. Retrieve a new needle.
   b. Wipe off the needle with a clean, dry piece of gauze.
   c. Wipe the needle with an antiseptic.
   d. Use your breath to steam the surface of the needle.

7. Sharps should be disposed of in
   a. a plastic bag clearly marked "Caution."
   b. any public trash receptacle.
   c. a jar containing alcohol.
   d. a biohazard receptacle.

8. _____ drugs need to be accounted for at the beginning and end of your shift, should be kept secure throughout your shift, and require detailed custody logs.

9. In accordance with your local protocols, you should frequently inspect your ambulance's medication supply. List three specific factors you should note when performing this task.

   _____

   _____

10. Although needle-less systems do not require needles, they are compatible with traditional needles.
    True
    False

11. Your partner has been experiencing chronic bumps and raised, red areas on her hands. When she went on vacation for 2 weeks, the symptoms gradually disappeared, but a week after returning to work, the symptoms have returned. She is always very careful to wear gloves when handling medications and during any patient contact. You should suspect
    a. a reaction to handling a medication.
    b. contact dermatitis contracted from a patient.
    c. a fungal infection.
    d. a latex allergy.

12. Which of the following statements regarding injectable medications is true?
    a. Most injectable medications should not be frozen.
    b. Most injectable medications have a very short shelf life.
    c. Most injectable medications can only be stored in glass bottles.
    d. Most injectable medications cannot be exposed to light.

13. List the three acceptable methods for sterilization of medical equipment.

    _____

    _____

14. EMS providers can emulate pharmacies by using a three-step system to confirm that the correct medication is being administered. Briefly describe these three steps.

    _____

    _____

15. You have responded to a remote location for a patient in hemorrhagic shock. En route to the hospital you are attempting to obtain IV access to begin fluid resuscitation, but the road that you are traveling on is bumpy, and you are unable to safely perform the procedure. To minimize the possibility of an accidental needle stick, you would likely
    a. wait until you reach the main highway before reattempting to obtain IV access.
    b. have the driver pull over, and obtain IV access while the ambulance is stopped.
    c. concentrate on alternative forms of treatment until you reach the hospital.
    d. continue to carefully attempt to obtain IV access until you are successful.

16. A drug in your supply expires December 2012. What is the last date that you can administer the drug?
    a. December 1, 2012
    b. November 1, 2012
    c. December 31, 2012
    d. November 31, 2012

17. How are the majority of health-care workers accidentally exposed to blood during their occupational training?
    a. Eye splashes
    b. Non-intact skin exposure
    c. Mucous membrane exposure
    d. Needle sticks

18. Most patients who regularly take prescription medication are compliant with their prescribed dosing regimen.
    True
    False

19. Who can authorize the administration of medication?
    a. The team leader
    b. The patient
    c. The online physician
    d. The most senior paramedic

20. You are called to a "man down" in a supermarket. When you arrive, the adult male patient is unresponsive and apneic. The ECG monitor reveals that the patient is in cardiac arrest. You need to administer epinephrine, but you cannot confirm the patient's

medical history or allergies because none of the immediate bystanders know the man. You should

   a. administer the epinephrine immediately.

   b. provide care without administering any medications.

   c. use the man's cell phone to contact a family member.

   d. use the store's public address system to ask any friends or family to come forward.

Need to Know

The following represent the Key Objectives of Chapter 16:

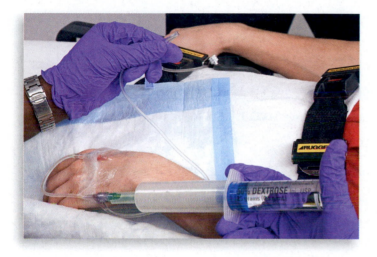

1. *Describe the safe and appropriate administration of medications based upon the selected route.*

With administration of medications comes a great deal of responsibility. The process of administering medications needs to be methodical, well thought out, and based on sound judgment. There is no room for complacency in medication administration, for when the paramedic becomes complacent, mistakes are made, and when it comes to medication administration, mistakes can be lethal.

All medication administration decisions need to be based on the results of assessments that include past medical history, any known allergies to medications (specific medications [e.g., morphine] or general classifications of medications [sulfa-based medications]), physical examination, and vital signs (e.g., heart rate, blood pressure, respiratory rate, temperature, ECG tracing, pulse oximetry). Paramedics must have a basic knowledge of any medications that they may administer, including indications, contraindications (absolute or relative), potential side

effects or complications, precautions, any possible interactions with other medications, and the expected therapeutic effects, based on their scope of practice and the formulary of their provider. Is the paramedic able to administer the medication based on standing orders, or does the medication administration require consultation with medical control?

Because most medication dosages are based on a patient's weight, the paramedic must be able to perform drug calculations so that the patient does not receive an overdose or an underdose of a medication. Since some medications do not come packaged as ready to administer, paramedics need to know how to prepare medications for administration. For example, glucagon comes in two vials. One of the vials contains a powder, and the other vial contains a liquid. The powder needs to be combined with the liquid and thoroughly dissolved before it can be administered. Similarly, some medications need to be mixed with an IV solution in an IV bag before they can be administered as an IV drip (infusion). If given such a medication undiluted as an IV bolus, the patient could experience undesired effects.

Standard medication administration must follow safe administration techniques via the appropriate administration route while maintaining asepsis. Contaminated disposable medication administration equipment needs to be disposed of in the appropriate disposal container, and reusable medication administration equipment needs to be cleaned and maintained per the manufacturer's instructions.

Any preexisting medication administration device that is used by paramedics must be approved by the EMS agency and the EMS provider that the paramedic works for. Any medication administration device that the paramedic is not familiar with or specifically trained how to use should not be used by the paramedic.

Other than ensuring that the five rights of medication administration are followed and the patient is not allergic to the medication that you are administering, perhaps the most important step in medication administration is to reassess the patient following the administration of a medication to see if it had the desired or any undesired effects. Make sure that the medication administration is clearly and accurately documented on your patient care report. This report is a part of the patient's medical record and may be referred to by medical personnel to direct them in further treatment of the patient.

Need to Do

The following medication administration skills are explained and illustrated in a step-by-step manner, via skill sheets and/or Step-by-Steps in this text and on the accompanying DVD:

Skill Name	Skill Sheet Number and Location	Step-by-Step Number and Location
Intravenous Access	42 – Appendix A and DVD	42 – This chapter and DVD
Intravenous Access Using Saline Lock	43 – DVD	43 – DVD
Phlebotomy	44 – DVD	N/A
Intraosseous Access and Drug Administration	45 – Appendix A and DVD	45 – This chapter and DVD
Umbilical Vein Cannulation	46 – DVD	N/A
Central Line Access for Fluids and Drug Administration	47 – DVD	N/A
Intravenous Drug Bolus	48 – Appendix A and DVD	48 – This chapter and DVD
Intravenous Drug Infusion	49 – Appendix A and DVD	49 – This chapter and DVD
Intramuscular Drug Administration	50 – Appendix A and DVD	50 – This chapter and DVD
Intranasal Drug Administration	51 – DVD	N/A
Nebulized Drug Administration	52 – Appendix A and DVD	52 – This chapter and DVD
Subcutaneous Drug Administration	53 – Appendix A and DVD	53 – This chapter and DVD
Sublingual Drug Administration	54 – DVD	N/A
Endotracheal Drug Administration	55 – DVD	N/A
Eye Drop Drug Administration	56 – DVD	N/A
Oral Drug Administration	57 – DVD	N/A
Rectal Drug Administration	58 – Appendix A and DVD	58 – This chapter and DVD
Autoinjector Drug Administration Device	59 – DVD	N/A
NREMT Intravenous Therapy	89 – DVD	N/A
NREMT Pediatric Intraosseous Infusion	91 – DVD	N/A

Intravenous Access

Conditions: The candidate should perform this skill on a simulated patient under existing indoor, ambulance, or outdoor lighting, temperature, and weather conditions. *Establish a patent IV line within 6 minutes.*

Indications: Patients who require or may potentially require administration of fluids or intravenous medications.

Red Flags: Prep the site with aseptic or medically clean technique as field conditions permit. Avoid starting an IV on the same arm as a dialysis shunt. IV infiltration, especially when medications are being administered, can cause serious and irreversible tissue damage. Avoid using areas of burned skin or heavy vein scarring.

Steps:

1. Use appropriate standard precautions.

2. Select proper fluid and check its expiration date and clarity.

3. Select proper IV tubing.

4. Close roller clamp.

5. Remove tab from IV bag and cap from spike end of IV tubing. Insert spike into IV bag administration port (Figure SBS 42-1).

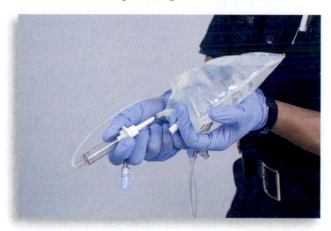

SBS 42-1

6. Squeeze the drip chamber until IV solution reaches fluid line or the drip chamber is half full.

7. Run fluid through the tubing until fluid fills tubing and air bubbles are removed.

8. Gather equipment (IV needle, tourniquet, tape, gauze, alcohol prep, etc.).

9. Apply tourniquet proximal to desired site.

10. Select site (Figure SBS 42-2). (Possible sites include between knuckles, dorsal thumb, back of hands, forearms, or antecubital fossa.)

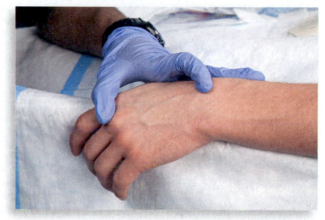

SBS 42-2

11. Cleanse area with alcohol prep.

12. Control site by pulling skin firmly, taking care to keep your fingers out of the needle path.

13. Insert needle at less than a 45-degree angle with the bevel up (Figure SBS 42-3).

SBS 42-3

14. Advance needle in a smooth motion.

—Continued

15. Monitor for flashback, and verbalize when flashback is visualized.

16. Advance catheter into vein while retracting needle until it locks.

17. Avoid catheter shear by not reinserting needle into catheter.

18. Remove tourniquet if blood sample is not required.

19. Hold hub, and tamponade vein to prevent bleeding (Figure SBS 42-4).

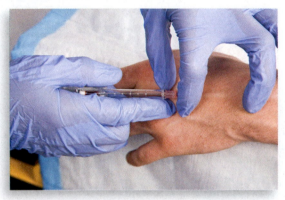

SBS 42-4

20. Remove needle from hub and place in a sharps container.

21. Connect administration set to catheter hub.

22. Open roller clamp and observe for free flow through drip chamber (Figure SBS 42-5).

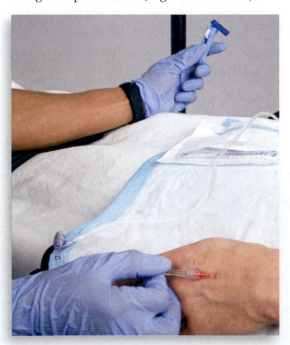

SBS 42-5

23. Inspect and palpate for infiltration at IV site.

24. Secure site and tubing with tape or a commercial device (Figure SBS 42-6).

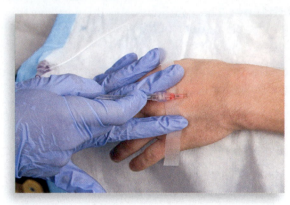

SBS 42-6

Critical Criteria:

- Use appropriate standard precautions.
- Maintain aseptic or medically clean technique throughout procedure.
- Avoid catheter shear by not reinserting needle into catheter.
- Observe for infiltration.
- Establish a patent IV line within 6 minutes.
- Dispose of sharps in an appropriate container.

Intraosseous Access and Drug Administration

Conditions: The candidate should perform this skill on a simulated patient under existing indoor, ambulance, or outdoor lighting, temperature, and weather conditions.

Indications: A patient who requires intravascular access for medication administration and/or volume resuscitation and for whom IV access is not readily available.

Red Flags: Long-bone deformity distal to access site on same bone; unable to locate landmarks.

Steps:

1. Use appropriate standard precautions.

2. Select appropriate device and prepare equipment. A manual IO needle is shown here.

3. Locate intraosseous (IO) site (Figure SBS 45-1). (Possible sites include tibia, distal femur, humerus, sternum, or iliac crest.)

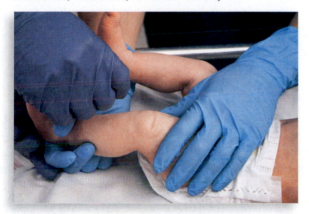

SBS 45-1

4. Cleanse site with alcohol and/or iodine.

5. Place IO device against bone.

6. Insert needle straight into bone at a 90-degree angle (Figure SBS 45-2).

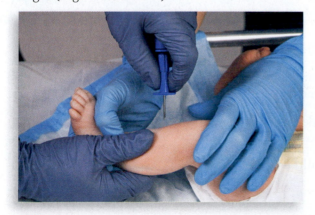

SBS 45-2

7. Stop at proper depth or when resistance is no longer felt ("popping" sensation).

8. Stabilize IO catheter and remove needle.

9. Dispose of sharps in appropriate sharps container.

10. Attach syringe to IO needle.

11. Aspirate bone marrow and administer saline flush (Figure SBS 45-3).

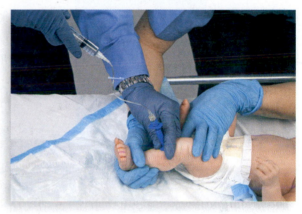

SBS 45-3

12. Inspect site for infiltration. If swollen, remove needle and apply pressure.

13. Attach administration set, and run fluid wide open.

14. Ensure free flow and no swelling, and adjust to desired rate.

15. Secure device (Figure SBS 45-4).

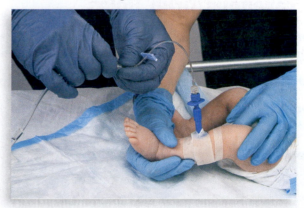

SBS 45-4

—Continued

Drug Administration

16. Ensure that five patient rights of drug administration are met.

17. Draw medication using aseptic technique.

18. Dispose of needle in a sharps container.

19. Cleanse port with alcohol prep.

20. Attach syringe to port.

21. Occlude line between fluid and port by pinching line or adjusting three-way stopcock (Figure SBS 45-5).

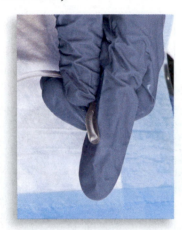

SBS 45-5

22. Push medication at proper rate, and flush tubing after administration.

23. Monitor patient for desired and adverse effects.

Critical Criteria:

- Use appropriate standard precautions.
- Use intraosseous needle in a safe manner.
- Immediately dispose of sharps in appropriate container.
- Observe for infiltration at site.
- Ensure that five rights of medication administration are followed.

Step-by-Step 48

Intravenous Drug Bolus

Conditions: The candidate should perform this skill on a simulated patient under existing indoor, ambulance, or outdoor lighting, temperature, and weather conditions.

Indications: A patient who requires a medication bolus delivered intravenously.

Red Flags: Medications given through the IV route are rapid acting. Deliver medications at appropriate rate and at appropriate time intervals. Always observe for infiltration.

Steps:

1. Use appropriate standard precautions.

2. Explain procedure to a conscious patient.

3. Ensure patient is not allergic to the medication.

4. Ensure IV flows without infiltration.

5. Ensure that five patient rights of drug administration are met.

6. Assemble pre-filled syringe, or draw medication into syringe (Figure SBS 48-1).

SBS 48-1

7. Expel air from syringe.

8. Cleanse IV port with alcohol prep.

9. Attach syringe to IV port (Figure SBS 48-2).

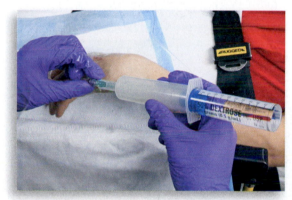

SBS 48-2

10. Occlude IV line between port and IV bag, or close roller clamp.

11. Push medication at the proper rate (Figure SBS 48-3) while observing for infiltration.

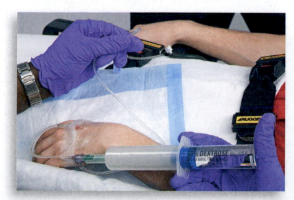

SBS 48-3

12. Withdraw needle from IV tubing and dispose in sharps container.

13. Flush IV tubing, and set flow to desired rate (Figure SBS 48-4).

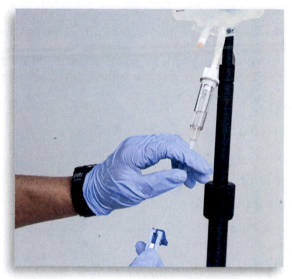

SBS 48-4

14. Thoroughly document medication administration.

15. Monitor patient for desired and adverse effects.

Critical Criteria:

- Use standard precautions.
- Check for patient allergies and medication reactions.
- Ensure that five rights of medication administration have been met.
- Cleanse the IV port prior to injection.
- Immediately dispose of sharps in an appropriate container.
- Monitor patient for changes in condition.

Intravenous Drug Infusion

Conditions: The candidate should perform this skill on a simulated patient under existing indoor, ambulance, or outdoor lighting, temperature, and weather conditions.

Indications: A patient who requires medications continuously delivered intravenously.

Red Flags: Medications given through the IV route are rapid acting. Pay close attention to the rate of administration. Always observe for infiltration of primary IV.

Steps:

1. Use appropriate standard precautions.

2. Explain procedure to a conscious patient.

3. Ensure patient is not allergic to the medication.

4. Ensure IV flows without infiltration.

5. Ensure that five patient rights of drug administration are met.

6. Calculate drug dosage in drips per minute (gtt/min).

7. Prepare IV solution or spike premixed bag (Figure SBS 49-1).

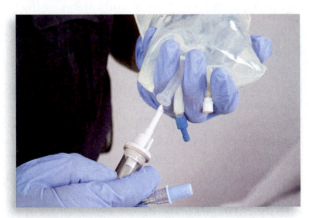

SBS 49-1

8. Fill drip chamber, and flush tubing (Figure SBS 49-2).

SBS 49-2

9. Mark bag with drug name and concentration, date and time of administration, and initials of person preparing and administering infusion.

10. Dispose of any sharps in appropriate container.

11. Cleanse IV port with alcohol prep.

12. Connect infusion IV set to main IV and stop flow of main IV (Figure SBS 49-3).

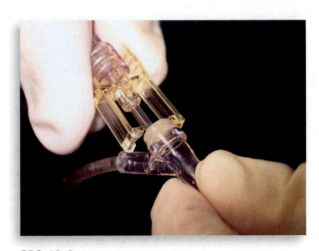

SBS 49-3

13. Secure line with tape (Figure SBS 49-4).

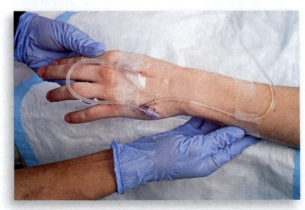

SBS 49-4

14. Adjust to proper drip rate.

15. Thoroughly document medication administration.

16. Monitor patient for desired and adverse effects.

Critical Criteria:
- Use standard precautions.
- Check for patient allergies and medication reactions.

- Ensure that five rights of medication administration have been met.
- Cleanse medication port prior to insertion.
- Dispose of sharps immediately after use.
- Ensure that infusion is set at proper rate.
- Monitor patient for desired and adverse effects.

Step-by-Step 50

Intramuscular Drug Administration

Conditions: The candidate should perform this skill on a simulated patient under existing indoor, ambulance, or outdoor lighting, temperature, and weather conditions.

Indications: A patient whose condition requires the administration of a medication through the intramuscular route. A patient who does not have vascular access, and the required medication can be administered intramuscularly.

Red Flags: May not be effective in poorly perfused tissue.

Steps:

1. Use appropriate standard precautions.

2. Explain procedure to a conscious patient.

3. Ensure patient is not allergic to the medication.

4. Ensure that five patient rights of drug administration are met.

5. Using a 20-gauge or smaller needle, draw medication into syringe (Figure SBS 50-1).

6. Expel air from syringe.

7. Locate administration site (deltoid, thigh, or buttocks).

8. Cleanse site with alcohol prep.

9. Stabilize skin with fingers, or pinch to raise skin slightly (Figure SBS 50-2).

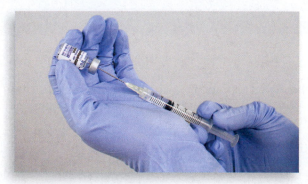

SBS 50-1

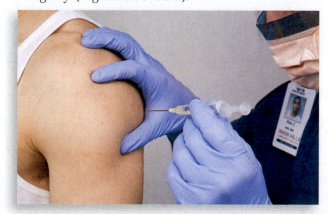

SBS 50-2

—Continued

10. Insert needle at 90-degree angle, and quickly advance into muscle.

11. Attempt to aspirate for blood (Figure SBS 50-3). If blood returns, withdraw needle and try a different site.

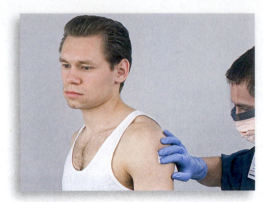

SBS 50-4

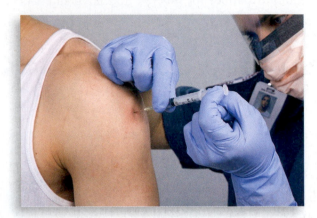

SBS 50-3

15. Thoroughly document medication administration.

16. Monitor for redness and swelling.

17. Monitor patient for desired and adverse effects.

12. Slowly inject medication.

13. Withdraw needle from patient, and dispose of needle and syringe in appropriate sharps container.

14. Apply sterile gauze and direct pressure to site (Figure SBS 50-4).

Critical Criteria:

- Use standard precautions.
- Check for patient allergies.
- Ensure that five rights of medication administration have been met.
- Insert needle at 90-degree angle.
- Aspirate for blood prior to medication administration.
- Immediately dispose of sharps in appropriate container.

Step-by-Step 52

Nebulized Drug Administration

Conditions: The candidate should perform this skill on a simulated patient in a sitting or supine position (stretcher, chair, or bed) under existing indoor, ambulance, or outdoor lighting, temperature, and weather conditions.

Indications: A patient whose condition requires the administration of a medication through the nebulized route.

Red Flags: Equipment used to nebulize medications can vary significantly. Practice with your local system's equipment until you are comfortable with assembly and use.

Steps:

1. Use appropriate standard precautions.

2. Explain procedure to a conscious patient.

3. Ensure the patient is not allergic to the medication.

4. Ensure that five patient rights of drug administration are met.

5. Place medication in nebulizing chamber (Figure SBS 52-1).

SBS 52-1

6. Screw on chamber cover.

7. Attach oxygen tubing to nebulizer chamber, and attach tubing to oxygen source (Figure SBS 52-2).

SBS 52-2

8. Assemble administration set according to manufacturer's instructions, ensuring nebulizer chamber remains upright.

9. Attach T-piece to nebulizing chamber (Figure SBS 52-3).

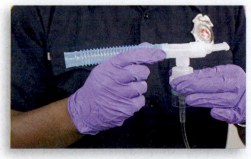

SBS 52-3

10. Adjust flow of oxygen to nebulizer to create a steady mist of medication (6–8 L/min).

11. Instruct patient to seal lips around mouthpiece, and direct him or her to breathe slowly and deeply (Figure SBS 52-4).

SBS 52-4

12. *Alternately*, attach set to an in-line adapter, and ventilate with a bag-mask at 12–20 breaths/min timed with patient's inspiratory effort (Figure SBS 52-5).

SBS 52-5

13. *Alternately*, attach nebulizer to simple mask (Figure SBS 52-6) and adjust the flow of oxygen to create a steady mist of medication (6–8 L/min).

SBS 52-6

14. Refill chamber per local protocol.

—Continued

15. Thoroughly document medication administration.

16. Monitor patient for desired and adverse effects.

Critical Criteria:
- Use standard precautions.
- Ensure that five rights of medication administration are met.

- Assist ventilations as necessary.
- Keep in-line nebulizer chamber upright.

Step-by-Step 53

Subcutaneous Drug Administration

Conditions: The candidate should perform this skill on a simulated patient under existing indoor, ambulance, or outdoor lighting, temperature, and weather conditions.

Indications: A patient whose condition requires the administration of a medication through the subcutaneous route.

Red Flags: May not be effective in poorly perfused tissue.

Steps:

1. Use appropriate standard precautions.

2. Explain procedure to a conscious patient.

3. Ensure patient is not allergic to the medication.

4. Ensure five patient rights of drug administration are met.

5. Using a 22-gauge or smaller needle, draw medication into syringe (Figure SBS 53-1). May give maximum of 1 mL of fluid.

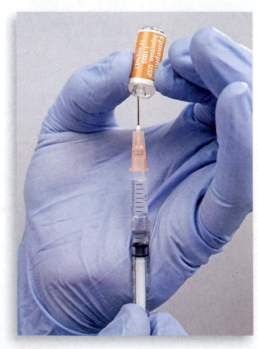

SBS 53-1

6. Expel air from syringe.

7. Locate administration site (upper arm, abdomen, or thigh).

8. Cleanse site with alcohol prep.

9. Pinch skin to lift it slightly (Figure SBS 53-2).

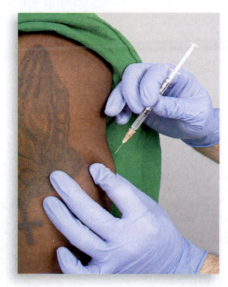

SBS 53-2

10. Insert needle at a 45-degree angle.

11. Smoothly advance needle into subcutaneous tissue (Figure SBS 53-3).

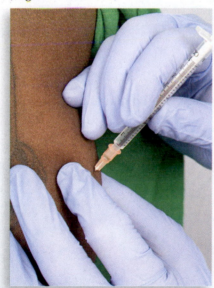

SBS 53-3

12. Attempt to aspirate for blood with syringe (should be difficult). If blood returns, withdraw and try a different site.

13. Inject the medication (Figure SBS 53-4).

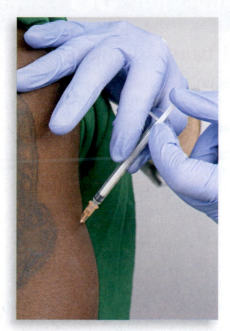

SBS 53-4

14. Withdraw needle, and dispose of needle and syringe in appropriate sharps container.

15. Place gauze over injection site, and apply direct pressure.

16. Thoroughly document medication administration.

17. Monitor administration site for redness and swelling.

18. Monitor the patient for desired and adverse effects.

Critical Criteria:

- Use standard precautions.
- Check for patient allergies.
- Check expiration date of medication.
- Ensure that five rights of medication administration have been met.
- Insert needle at 45-degree angle.
- Immediately dispose of sharps in appropriate container.
- Aspirate for blood prior to medication administration.
- Monitor for desired and adverse effects.

Rectal Drug Administration

Conditions: The candidate should perform this skill on a simulated pediatric patient under existing indoor, ambulance, or outdoor lighting, temperature, and weather conditions.

Indications: A pediatric patient whose condition requires the administration of a medication via the rectal route.

Red Flags: Feeding tube or syringe must be inserted deep enough into rectal space in order to deliver medication. Forceful insertion can perforate the bowel wall. Remove needle prior to insertion of syringe into rectum.

Steps:

1. Use appropriate standard precautions.

2. Explain procedure to a conscious patient or parents.

3. Ensure patient is not allergic to the medication.

4. Ensure that five patient rights of drug administration are met.

5. Draw up medication using aseptic technique (Figure SBS 58-1).

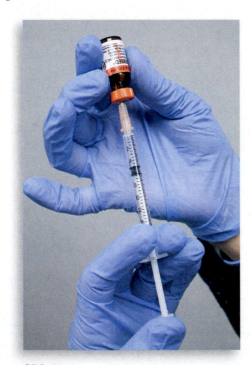

SBS 58-1

6. Remove and dispose of needle in appropriate sharps container.

7. Choose administration option:
   a. Attach an extension: large-bore IV catheter without needle or cut 3.0 ET tube.
   b. Use a tuberculin (TB) syringe without needle.
   c. Insert a suppository with gloved finger.

8. Lubricate administration device or suppository and finger with water-soluble jelly only.

9. Gently insert into anus (Figure SBS 58-2). If using a suppository, insert with gloved finger.

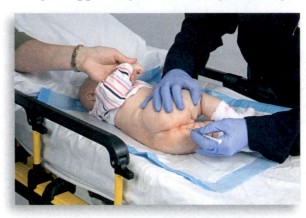

SBS 58-2

10. Advance past both sphincter muscles.

11. Slowly deliver medication.

12. Remove syringe and hold buttocks together (Figure SBS 58-3).

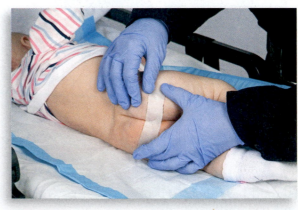

SBS 58-3

13. Dispose of syringe in appropriate container.

14. Thoroughly document medication administration.

15. Monitor patient for desired and adverse effects (Figure SBS 58-4).

SBS 58-4

Critical Criteria:

- Use standard precautions.
- Check for patient allergies and medication reactions.
- Ensure that five rights of medication administration have been met.
- Lubricate administration device or suppository and finger before administration.
- Pinch buttocks closed after administration.
- Immediately dispose of sharps in appropriate container.
- Monitor patient for desired and adverse effects.

Connections

- Chapter 15, Pharmacology, in the textbook contains additional information on medication indications, contraindications, precautions, and special considerations. See Box 15-6 in the textbook for a description of the patient "rights" that are identified in the DOT curricula.
- Chapter 10, Therapeutic Communications and History Taking, in the textbook describes techniques that can be helpful in obtaining information from patients.
- Chapter 9, Safety and Scene Size-Up, in the textbook includes additional information on BSI precautions.
- Chapter 17, Documentation and Communication, in the textbook details information on performing a radio consultation and what elements of medication administration documentation are important to capture on the patient care report.
- Link to the companion DVD for a chapter-based quiz, audio glossary, animations, games and exercises, and, when appropriate, skill sheets and skill Step-by-Steps.

Street Secrets

- **Shortcuts** Drug dosage calculations can be a nightmare for many paramedics. The need to perform them in any situation—let alone a situation in which one is caring for a critical patient who has a very low blood pressure—can send the most confident paramedic into a meltdown. The following simple formulas are shortcuts that will give you a close estimate of the number of drops per minute that you need to administer to a patient receiving a dopamine infusion. *These shortcuts are based on the use of a 60-gtt/mL IV administration set. This method should not be used in a testing environment because it is not 100% accurate.* Shortcut 1 is for use with a dopamine IV bag that has a concentration of 1,600 mcg/mL and is used to obtain a 5-mcg/min dose.

> (Weight in kg ÷ 10) (2) − 1 = drip rate in gtt/min for patient receiving 5-mcg/min dose.

Example: The patient weighs 80 kg.

$$80 \div 10 = 8$$
$$8 \times 2 = 16$$
$$16 - 1 = 15 \text{ gtt/min}$$

Shortcut 2 is for use with a dopamine IV bag that has a concentration of 800 mcg/mL and is used to obtain a 5-mcg/min dose.

> (Weight in kg ÷ 5) (2) − 2 = drip rate in gtt/min for patient receiving 5-mcg/min dose.

Example: The patient weighs 60 kg.

$$60 \div 5 = 12$$
$$12 \times 2 = 24$$
$$24 - 2 = 22 \text{ gtt/min}$$

Note: The paramedic should always ensure the patency of the IV by aspirating prior to injecting any medication. This is crucial because drugs injected into the tissues instead of the bloodstream could have a detrimental effect on the patient.

The Drug Box

There are no specific drugs related to this chapter content.

Answers

Are You Ready?

1. The patient is critically ill. The infant is seizing and blue (cyanotic). This alone is evidence of a life-threatening emergency.

2. Airway, airway, airway! Followed by breathing and circulation.

3. Any four of the following: fever, hypoglycemia, head injury, ingestion (poisoning), hypoxia, arrhythmia, epilepsy, hypovolemia, and electrolyte imbalance.

4. You should perform a blood sugar test. If the patient is hypoglycemic and you stop the seizure with an anticonvulsant, you may not remember to check the patient's blood sugar, and a blood sugar level low enough to cause seizures can cause significant damage if left untreated.

5. Administration of medications needs to be in compliance with local EMS policies and protocols, but for the sake of this exercise general guidelines are as follows:

   a. The first choice would be IV administration of medications because of the relative ease of establishing an IV, the relatively minimal invasiveness of the procedure, and the rapid onset of action of medications administered intravenously. You also have a route to administer IV fluids in the setting of hypovolemia.

   b. The second choice would be based on the type of medication being administered. If you are delivering an anticonvulsant such as a benzodiazepine, the rectal route should be considered next. This route does not allow for correction of hypovolemia or hypoglycemia.

   c. If the patient is hypoglycemic and/or hypovolemic, another more invasive, yet very effective, means of delivering medications to a critical patient is via the intraosseous route (Figure 16-2).

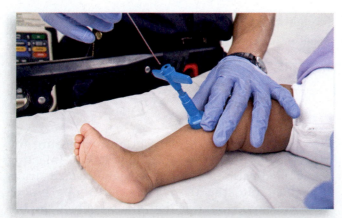

FIGURE 16-2 The intraosseous route is an effective alternative to the intravenous route of medication and fluid administration.

d. Another possibility for the administration of some medications is the intranasal route, but the absorption rate is not as rapid, and there is no possibility for addressing fluid deficits or hypoglycemia.

Active Learning

1. a. 2.2 lb; b. 1,000 g; c. 1,000 mg; d. 1,000 mcg; e. 1,000 mL; f. 1 mL; g. 5 mL; h. 15 mL; i. 30 mL; j. 65 mg; k. 1/10 or 0.1 L; l. 1/100 or 0.01 m; m. 1/1,000 or 0.001 g; n. 1/1,000,000 or 0.000001 g

5.

   a. In order for you to administer 0.1 mg/kg of adenosine to this 33-lb (15 kg) patient, you will need to administer 0.5 mL.

   b. In order to administer 1.5 mg/kg of lidocaine to this 132-lb cardiac arrest patient, you will need to deliver 4.5 mL.

   c. To administer a 0.02-mg/kg dose of atropine to this 22-lb (10 kg) child, you must administer 2 mL of atropine.

   d. In order to deliver 1,120 mL/hour, you will need to deliver 187 gtt/min.

   e. The 500-mL bag of normal saline dripping at a rate of 120 gtt/min through a 10-gtt/mL administration set will be completed in 41.66 or about 42 minutes.

   f. In order to administer 300 mL of fluid over 45 minutes via a 10-gtt/min administration set, you will need to set your drip rate at 67 gtt/min.

   g. Drops per minute = 16.8 gtt/min. Run the infusion at 17 drops per minute to infuse 3 mcg/kg/min of dopamine to your patient.

   h. For your 165-lb patient to receive 15 mcg/kg/min of dobutamine from an IV bag that contains 250 mg of dobutamine in 500 mL of normal saline, using a 60-gtt/min administration set, the patient needs to get a 135-gtt/min infusion.

   i. In order for your 88-lb patient to receive 20 mcg/kg/min of dopamine (200 mg/250 mL D_5W) via a micro-drip administration set, you will need to administer 60 gtt/min.

   j. In order to deliver 2 mg/min, you will need to set the IV drip rate of the 60-gtt/mL administration set at 30 gtt/min.

You Are There: Reality-Based Cases

Case 1

1. The patient is sick: he has chest pain and shortness of breath, and he is hypertensive, tachycardic, and tachypneic. He has an oxygen saturation of 92% on room air, and he speaks in five- to six-word sentences. He has JVD, pedal edema, supraclavicular retractions, and crackles in the bilateral bases of his lung fields.

2. The first priority in this patient, or any patient for that matter, is airway, breathing, and circulation.

3. Perform complete primary and secondary examinations including vital signs, ECG, and pulse oximetry; take a medical history, including medications and allergies to medications.

4.
- Does the patient have any allergies to medications?
- Will the patient's current hemodynamic status allow for the administration of the chosen medication?
- Will the administration of the chosen medication negatively impact the patient's medical condition(s)? (For example, if the patient has a history of ulcers, will the administration of aspirin have a negative impact on the patient?)
- Will the administration of the chosen medication interact negatively with any of the medications that the patient takes on a regular basis?

5. Prior to administering any medication, a paramedic should be aware of its indications, contraindications, precautions, side effects, interactions, and therapeutic effects. The paramedic should also be familiar with the appropriate route of administration for that particular medication, as well as the appropriate rate of administration.

6.
- The right patient
- The right medication
- The right dosage
- The right route
- The right time

7. Immediately dispose of sharps in an approved container. Never re-cap sharps!

8. There could be several reasons why a paramedic may administer some medications and not others. It is likely that the nitroglycerin and aspirin were administered according to standing orders. (Standing orders are pre-established medication orders that paramedics may administer based on specific parameters. A complete assessment, history, and physical examination must be performed prior to medication administration by standing orders.) For some medications and procedures, a paramedic must consult with a physician prior to administering the medications or performing the procedures.

9. Determine whether the patient has been compliant with his or her prescribed medications. (Is there any chance the patient is taking either too much or too little of the prescribed medication? An overdose or an underdose of medication can have a dramatic impact on the patient's condition.)

Test Yourself

1. d

The unopened pill bottles in the patient's kitchen are a good indication that he has not been taking his prescribed medication. Medications such as antipsychotics (which help control delusions) must be taken continually to maintain their effectiveness.

2. A contraindication is a reason that a medication should not be considered. Common contraindications include sensitivity, pregnancy, and certain diseases.

3. b

Prior to administering any medication you should collect enough information through history taking and from the physical examination to ensure a correct diagnosis is made so the proper therapy is selected. Postadministration follow-up procedures include reassessing and monitoring the patient for effects.

4. c

When looking for medications in a patient's home you should be alert for prescription medication, OTC medications, herbal preparations, drug paraphernalia, and any signs of medication abuse or misuse.

5. True

Check all expiration dates on a regular basis. To make it easier to check for expiration, mark the box clearly with the expiration date or circle the date on the container.

6. a

The fallen needle must be replaced with a new, sterile needle. Before performing an administration, it is a good idea to collect extra supplies in case something becomes contaminated or is not appropriate for use.

7. d

Used needles and syringes should be disposed of in an appropriate biohazard receptacle. These storage devices may be red or yellow and often carry warning labels.

8. Narcotic

9. Answers may include: ensure that all necessary medications have not expired. Confirm that all medications have been stored and handled in accordance with their manufacturers' recommendations. Make sure the appropriate supplies are available to prepare and administer every medication in the formulary (an adequate number and selection of syringes, needles, IV solutions, IV administration sets, etc.).

Every agency will have its own guidelines regarding the management of medications. Some services require a thorough count and expiration date check with the change of every shift, while other services may require weekly, monthly, or random spot checks. Make sure you are informed of, and abide by, your agency's guidelines.

10. False

Attempting to use a needle in a needle-less system will contaminate or damage it.

11. d

Given the location of your partner's rash, and knowing that her symptoms cleared when she was away from her job and then returned, you should suspect an allergic reaction to her latex gloves. Between 5% and 17% of all health-care workers are estimated to be allergic to latex.

12. a

When familiarizing yourself with your service's formulary, you should read the accompanying literature from the medication package box (called the package insert) to determine if there are any special storage or handling requirements.

13. Extreme heat from steam under pressure (autoclaving), dry heat, and ethylene oxide gas.

Sterilization kills all biotic material, including bacterial spores. Human tissue and some equipment cannot be sterilized.

14. To confirm that the correct medication has been selected for administration, you can first repeat the drug name and dosage when received during consultation; then carefully read the medication name before taking it out of the box; and finally ask another member of the patient care team to verify the name on the medication container.

This three-step approach is a good, systematic way to make sure you are administering the correct medication. Although it may not always be practical to follow all three steps in the field, you should *always* check to confirm that the right medication has been selected for administration.

15. b

Minimize the possibility of an accidental needle stick by performing all injections or IVs while the ambulance is stationary. If patient transport has begun, gather and prepare the equipment while the ambulance is moving. When ready, ask the driver to pull over and stop for a minute while you perform the venipuncture. Once the flash of blood is seen in the needle chamber, if the road surface is relatively smooth, the driver can go while you finish securing the line.

16. c

For expiration dates that only list the month and year, the last day of the month is considered the expiration date.

17. d

A 1998 survey of 3,162 emergency medicine residents found that over 50% reported having at least one occupational exposure to blood during their training, and over 70% of the exposures were from a needle stick or sharp object.

18. False

A study observed that over three-fourths of all people taking a prescription medication were not taking it according to the directions.

19. c

Administration of medication requires authorization from medical direction. This permission may take the form of off-line written protocol and standing orders, or it may require real-time, online physician direction via telephone, radio, or satellite consultation.

20. a

Although it is important to know whether a patient is taking medication or has any known allergies, this information should not delay treatment during life-threatening events.

chapter 17

Documentation and Communication

Are You Ready?

Traffic is at a standstill on the freeway as your engine company slowly makes its way along the shoulder to a motor vehicle crash. As you arrive on scene you note that one vehicle, a Buick Regal, has rear-ended a Chevrolet. There is not a lot of damage; the Chevy's bumper is pushed in, but there appears to be little damage to the Buick. The driver of the Buick, who is still inside the vehicle, appears dazed. The Highway Patrol officer is standing near the driver's door.

You ask the officer for any details of the event. "According to the driver of the Chevy, everyone was moving slowly when he was rear-ended. He said that the guy who hit him"—he motions to the Buick's driver—"didn't say anything when he approached him to exchange paperwork."

You ask what happened next. "He hasn't gotten out of the car. I think he might be under the influence, I can smell booze in the car. But, he's not cooperative. I was about ready to order him out of his car when you showed up."

1. Is the officer's report to you important? How will you document the officer's statements in your report?

_____

_____

_____

Active Learning

1. The Power of Observation

Try this exercise with a classmate: Have a sheet of paper and a pen in front of you. When you are ready, look at Figure 17-1 on page 215 for no more than 5 seconds. Your partner should *not* look at the photograph. Now, close the book and proceed to write down every detail of that photograph that you can remember. When you are done, let your partner read what you wrote, and then ask him or her to draw what was written using colored crayons or markers. Compare the drawing to the original photograph. How similar are they to each other? What did you learn from this exercise in regard to observation and documentation?

2. Failure to Communicate

Do this exercise with a partner. Have available some 8 × 11½ sheets of paper and some pencils, pens, and colored pencils or crayons. Sit with your backs to each other. One of you will have the writing implements, and the other will have access to Figure 17-2 on page 215. The person who has the figure will take 2 minutes to describe what he or she sees to the other person. The other person tries to draw the figure using the materials provided. The person who is drawing may not give any feedback to the person describing the image during this time. When the 2 minutes are up, compare what was drawn with the actual figure. How close are they? If the two images are really close, discuss what was effective in the communication that was provided. If they did not resemble each other, discuss what was said—or wasn't said—that made it difficult to be accurate.

Now reverse roles and repeat the exercise using Figure 17-3 on page 215. This time, the person drawing the image can provide feedback to the person describing the new image. Take 2 minutes to complete the exercise, and again compare the two images. Were they closer this time? If so, why? Did the feedback help to clarify details? How can this apply to communication techniques between patient and caregiver?

3. Listen In

Make arrangements to visit a local EMS communications center. When at the center, carefully observe the methods that telecommunicators use to draw information out of callers. In addition, try to get a sense of the overall functioning of the EMS system. For example, how many calls for service are there in an hour? How many units are out on runs? What types of runs are currently in progress? If it's possible, try to listen to a radio report being provided by a paramedic to medical direction. How is the information being provided? Is there any discussion between the paramedic and medical direction?

You Are There: Reality-Based Cases

Case 1 (continuation of chapter opener)

The Buick's driver continues to stare straight ahead as you approach him. His seat belt is still fastened, and no air bag was deployed. His hands are still holding the steering wheel. After you call to him several times, he looks at you but does not say a word. He appears pale and is sweating profusely. You can smell alcohol; there is a spilled bottle of beer in the passenger side wheel well.

The driver appears to be in his 40s. He does not seem to be hurt—you do not see any bruises, lacerations, or other signs of injury. His breathing is unlabored. Through the open window, you are able to palpate a fast, faint radial pulse. With your commands, the driver

is able to open the door of the car. He is sweating, even though it's not warm out. He follows your commands, but he appears confused.

You provide him oxygen via a non-rebreather mask and attach the ECG monitor. His vital signs are HR of 110, BP of 96/60, and RR of 20. There is a bracelet on his left wrist that says "IDDM." His lung sounds are clear, and there is no complaint of pain when you palpate his head, neck, chest, or abdomen. He denies chest pain, but tells you that he feels weak and dizzy.

Ten minutes later the ambulance arrives on scene. In the meantime you have provided treatment and the patient is now alert and responding to your questions. He cannot remember how he got here; the last event he remembers is that he stopped at a store to get a can of soda because he "needed it." He knows that he is allergic to sulfa drugs, but he cannot recall if he takes any medications or whether he has any medical conditions.

1. Using a separate piece of paper, document this incident using one of the formats described in Chapter 17 in the text.

Test Yourself

1. You respond to a residence for a patient with difficulty breathing. Upon arrival, you are met at the front door by a family member who directs you to the patient. The patient is refusing evaluation and wants to be left alone. What action would be most appropriate?

   a. Respect the patient's wishes and leave.

   b. Obtain a legal refusal from the patient.

   c. Ask the family member to sign a refusal for the patient.

   d. Contact the police.

2. List five nonclinical professionals who may have a legal right to access a patient care report.

   _____

   _____

   _____

3. Grammatical correctness is not a necessary component of the patient care report.

   True

   False

4. Which of the following items should be omitted from the patient care report?

    a. Abbreviations

    b. Subjective comments by patients

    c. Short sentences and phrases

    d. Jargon

5. Which piece of information should be left out of the patient care report?

    a. The patient denies any abdominal pain.

    b. The patient was arrested 2 weeks ago for robbery.

    c. The patient denies shortness of breath with a complaint of chest pain.

    d. The patient denied drinking alcohol but smells of ETOH.

6. You should document the time the call was received by the dispatch center in the patient care report.

    True

    False

7. You respond as additional assistance for a multivehicle accident on the interstate. Once you arrive, you report to command and are released from the scene. How should your patient care report reflect this response?

    a. Document a complete scene size-up and the number of patients transported by the other units.

    b. Document the person who released your unit in your report.

    c. Document "no patient found" in your report.

    d. Obtain a refusal of care from the patients refusing transport.

8. When writing patient care report narratives, how should you report patient or bystander comments?

    _____

    _____

    _____

9. Which of the following is *not* a necessary "where" statement in the patient care report?

    a. Medic one was dispatched for chest pain.

    b. The patient was found in the bedroom unconscious.

    c. The patient was sitting on the curb clutching his chest.

    d. The vehicle was found 50 feet off the roadway, resting on its roof.

10. What is the legal purpose of a patient care report?

    _____

    _____

    _____

11. You are called to the home of a terminally ill patient. You are met at the door by the patient's daughter who informs you that she is the patient's power of attorney. She requests that you evaluate her unconscious mother. You perform an assessment and determine the need for patient transport to the hospital, but the patient's daughter is refusing. Who has the legal right to refuse transport for the patient in this situation?

    _____

    _____

    _____

12. List three things that must be documented in order to obtain a legal refusal of care.

    _____

    _____

    _____

13. You should report your opinion of the patient's condition in the patient care report.

    True

    False

14. You and your partner are involved in a minor vehicle accident in the parking lot where you are refueling. You notice one of the occupants is unable to get out of her vehicle, but she refuses care. What actions should you take in this situation?

    a. Ask everyone if they are okay and then return to quarters.

    b. Do nothing; there is no duty to act or document anything.

    c. Obtain informed legal refusals on each patient involved not requesting transport.

    d. Call for an additional unit to obtain informed legal refusals on each patient.

Need to Know

The following represent the Key Objectives of Chapter 17:

1. *Explain why written reports and recorded online consultations should be concise, precise, and professional.*

   As suggested in the textbook, your patient care report should be your "legal shield" and not your "legal handicap." Potential litigation cases often begin with a review of any and all documentation of patient assessment and care. Your ability to document your actions clearly, plainly, and objectively will provide a clear picture to the reviewer that you were thoughtful and professional in the manner in which you provided care to the patient.

   There are several methods of ensuring consistent documentation. Examples include the CHART method, as well as several variants of the SOAP method. In many EMS systems you will be provided guidance as to which method to use. Regardless of which approach to documentation you utilize, remember that two key attributes should always be evident:

   - *Accuracy.* Be truthful in your reporting. Do not guess or assume anything about what you observed or did. If you committed a medical error, do not omit any findings or actions. Your patient care report is a legally binding document, and efforts to conceal or otherwise alter the circumstances are not only unethical but criminal.

   - *Objective.* Eliminate your personal emotions and opinions from your documentation. Bias has no place in your report. Stick to the facts as you see them. If it is crucial to report other statements as part of the record, use quotation marks to clearly identify those statements and attribute them appropriately. For example, part of your narrative might contain: "On scene with a 42-y/o M presenting with AMS. Police officer on scene reports patient was 'weaving all over the road' while operating a motor vehicle at slow speed."

   In addition to these general principles, there are a couple of special circumstances described in the textbook that bear repeating. When documenting on a patient who is refusing your services, take care to ensure that:

   - The patient has the legal capacity to refuse your care.
   - The patient has the mental capacity to refuse your care.
   - The patient has received adequate information and understands it well enough to make an informed decision.

   If you are cancelled prior to initiating patient contact, you should document the circumstances of the cancellation and the authority of the person who cancelled the response. If you begin any type of patient contact, you should document the circumstances that prevented you from completing an informed refusal.

2. *Explain how the quality of your written documentation and verbal communication conveys your level of professionalism to other members of the health-care team.*

   a. For professional written documentation, there are several attributes that should be evident:

      - Your report should be to the point (concise) and accurate (precise).
      - Standard English must be used. That means using full sentences with correct grammar and punctuation.
      - Words are correctly spelled and appropriately used.
      - Jargon and slang terms are avoided.
      - Approved abbreviations and symbols are used. The JCAHO list of approved abbreviations is a good foundation to use when documenting; your local EMS system may have additional terms.

   b. For verbal communications, there is a minimum set of key information to be provided.

      For the transfer of patient care:

      - Pertinent patient demographic information
      - Chief complaint

- Current medical and mental condition
- Description of medical history
- List of current medications and allergy history
- List of assessments performed
- List of treatments rendered
- Any information deemed critical for the receiving provider

For radio communication:

- Your radio identifier
- Confirmation of an authorized person to provide medical direction
- Estimated time of arrival (ETA) to the receiving facility and patient priority
- Your initial impression of the scene
- Age, sex, and weight of the patient
- Chief complaint
- Level of consciousness of the patient
- Level of distress of the patient
- Vital signs, assessment findings, and history information
- Treatments provided so far and the patient's response to the treatments
- Your request for treatments or medications that require medical direction
- Any orders or requests repeated back

Need to Do

The following skills are explained and illustrated in a step-by-step manner, via skill sheets and/or Step-by-Steps in this text and on the accompanying DVD:

Skill Name	Skill Sheet Number and Location	Step-by-Step Number and Location
Communication Challenges—Interpreter Services	62 – DVD	N/A
Verbal Communications	63 – DVD	N/A
Documentation	64 – DVD	N/A

Connections

- Review Chapter 4, Legal Issues, for additional information regarding documentation
- Link to the companion DVD for a chapter-based quiz, audio glossary, animations, games and exercises, and, when appropriate, skill sheets and skill Step-by-Steps.

Street Secrets

- **Consistency** Develop a consistent style to your documentation skills. When something unusual occurs during an EMS call, take care to document it well. Years later, if you have to recall what you did on that call, you can review your chart, and any documentation you provided that stands out from your "routine" statements may help trigger a memory of the event.
- **Look It Up!** Knowing that spelling is a weakness does not excuse you from spelling words correctly on your patient care record (PCR). If you have any questions on how to spell a word, look it up in a pocket or electronic dictionary. Proofread your writing when you are done as well.

The Drug Box

There are no specific drugs related to this chapter content.

Answers

Are You Ready?

1. Since you have not yet begun your assessment of the patient, it is important to document the police officer's statements as either quotes or using qualifying terms, such as "Police officer on scene states that . . ." This choice of words indicates that you did not make these observations or conclusions.

You Are There: Reality-Based Cases

Case 1

1. Using the CHART method, your report might look like this:

   C = Chief complaint: Altered mental status.

   H = History:

S = Symptoms:
  O = Unknown. PO states patient appeared to be "under the influence" when he first made contact.
  P = Provocation or palliation: Unknown. Patient was observed to be "weaving" in and out of the traffic lane prior to low-speed collision into a second vehicle.
  Q = Quality: Not applicable. Patient appears confused.
  R = Region or radiation: Patient denies any pain or related injuries.
  S = Severity: N/A.
  T = Time: Unknown.
A = Allergies: Sulfa drugs.
M = Medications: Unknown. Patient unable to recall.
P = Past and pertinent medical history: Medical alert bracelet indicates IDDM.
L = Last oral intake: Unknown.
E = Event leading up to the injury or illness: Unknown.

A = (Physical) Assessment: Pale, cool skin, no signs of obvious illness or injury. Denies neck and back pain. Denies chest pain or shortness of breath. Moves all extremities; responds to simple commands. Originally diaphoretic, but skin signs improve after treatment. Blood glucose level tested; glucometer reading of 18 mg/dL obtained.

R = Rx = Treatment: Oxygen 15 L/min non-rebreather; initiated IV NS TKO with 18-gauge needle, left antecubital. 50 g $D_{50}W$ administered IV. Patient LOC increased after administration; is alert and able to answer questions.

T = Transport and transfer (utilizing the TTFN acronym): Patient transported to Suburban Hospital without incident. Additional 50 g $D_{50}W$ administered. Patient A & O × 3 on arrival at Suburban.

Test Yourself

1. b

You may be charged with abandonment and negligence if you leave the scene or have the family member sign the refusal on behalf of the patient. You should explain the need for medical assessment and make sure that the patient is a mentally competent adult capable of making an informed decision. The risks and benefits of refusal should be explained to, and understood by, the patient. Documentation should reflect the same. At this point, if the patient still wishes to refuse care, he or she may sign the refusal and you may return to service.

2. Possible answers include: billing agents; insurance auditors; local, state, or federal investigators; risk managers; EMS administrators; forensic specialists; attorneys; expert witnesses; or jurors.

Other medical professionals such as physicians, nurses, respiratory therapists, physical therapists, social workers, and other allied health professionals have a legal right to access a patient care report with the purpose of gathering facts from the prehospital component of care. However, there are other professionals, who may be nonclinical in nature, who may have a prospective interest in the facts revealed in your documentation. Their interest may stem from a financial drive, a legal drive, or a combination of both.

3. False

You are judged by the mechanical aspects of your report. The mechanics of transferring the facts of a call into the run sheet are important. Spelling, sentence structure, proper capitalization, punctuation, and the use of proper English are required. Because your run sheet is an extension of your care, if your run sheet is mechanically substandard, it leaves a poor perception of the care provided to the patient or may be construed as a general lack of intellect. The use of simple basic writing skills, proper mechanics, punctuation, and correct spelling in the prehospital report reflects a professional and knowledgeable provider.

4. d

Jargon has no place in the patient care report. Jargon can be defined as a hybrid language of technical terminology, characteristic of a special activity or group. Like colloquialisms, the meaning of jargon is generally appreciated by those belonging to the group, such as prehospital providers, but not to the medical community at large.

5. b

Pertinent negatives are critical findings (or more accurately nonfindings) from the assessment or history provided by the patient. They are items that are generally present for a given disease process but are not present in the current patient's presentation. The recording of pertinent negatives provides evidence that a thorough history was performed, as well as providing valuable information to the receiving healthcare professionals. When pertinent negatives are not recorded, it may convey the impression that an incomplete assessment or history was performed. In this case, the absence of abdominal pain and the lack of shortness of breath proves that the patient was assessed and questioned. The fact that the patient smells of ETOH does not prove intoxication; there are other conditions that may cause the fruity odor produced by the body after alcohol consumption. In the absence of a blood glucose meter, this finding, coupled with the patient's statement, may indicate the presence of diabetic ketoacidosis (DKA). The fact that the patient was arrested 2 weeks ago and that it was for a robbery are null points that do not pertain to the current medical complaint.

6. True

It is necessary to document the time the call was received, the time of dispatch, the time the unit went responding and on the scene, the time patient contact was made, when the unit left or was dismissed from the scene, the time of arrival at the destination, the time returning in service, and the time when returning to quarters. It is also important to document the time medications or other interventions were performed, including vital signs.

7. b

When responding to a scene or arriving on a scene prior to making patient contact, it is necessary to document who dismissed your unit's response. It may also be necessary to document that no patient contact was made.

8. Use quotation marks around patient or bystander comments.

This separates comments made by the patient or bystander from those of the paramedic or EMT providing objective information.

9. a

"Where" provides descriptors for the word picture of the on-scene setting and environment the patient was found in. It contributes to an appreciation for the overall landscape of the call. It can also provide information directly connected to the on-scene time.

FIGURE 17-1 Use for Active Learning exercise 1: The Power of Observation.

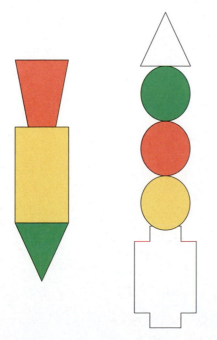

FIGURE 17-2 Use for the first part of Active Learning exercise 2: Failure to Communicate.

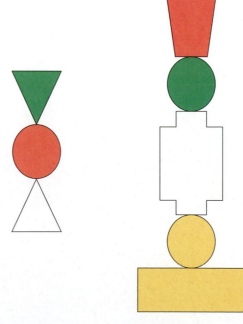

FIGURE 17-3 Use for the second part of Active Learning exercise 2: Failure to Communicate.

10. The legal purpose of a patient care report is to provide a concise and accurate account of events regarding patient care.

    The patient care report, as a legal document, provides proof of medical care and patient assessment findings. Although it may serve as evidence in a court case, it will not have any bearing on whether a crime was committed by anyone other than the prehospital provider.

11. The daughter, as power of attorney

    Because the patient is unable to make an informed decision and the daughter is the power of attorney, the daughter may legally refuse care for her mother.

12. In order to obtain a legal refusal of care, one must document the patient's legal date (date of birth), current mental capacity and function, and ability to make a well-informed decision as any rational adult would in this situation. In addition, the patient must indicate an understanding of the risks and benefits involved in refusing care. An individual on the scene (other than you or your partner) must also witness the refusal.

13. False

    A well-written report should be factual and include only those facts that pertain to the patient's history and condition. It should also include subjective information, in quotation marks, about things the patient and/or bystanders said relating to the incident. Objective findings, such as vital signs and a physical exam, are also necessary components. Your opinion should never be placed in the patient care report.

14. d

    Because you were involved in the incident, you must request an additional unit (and a supervisor and police) because you are on duty. There is a duty to act and determine the well-being of all those involved in the accident, but this must be performed by a unit not involved in the accident. It is necessary to write a patient care report and obtain refusals on all parties involved in the accident.

part 3

Trauma

Mechanism of Injury

Are You Ready?

Barbara Jones is running late to pick up her children from preschool. If she doesn't hurry, she'll be late to pick them up for the third time this month. Barbara is driving as fast as she can and, unfortunately, she is not wearing. her seat belt. When she is three blocks away from the school, a child comes flying out of a driveway on his scooter. Barbara slams on her brakes and swerves to miss the child. Her car runs up onto the curb and strikes a lamppost.

1. Based on the information in the scenario and the photograph of Barbara's wrecked car, what are the possible pathways that Barbara's body took when she impacted the lamppost?

   _____

   _____

   _____

2. What types of injuries might Barbara have sustained based on the pathway(s) that she may have taken upon impact?

   _____

   _____

   _____

Active Learning

1. Bullet Ballistics

This exercise can be performed in several different settings. If you have access to a swimming pool and you know how to swim, you may opt to perform this exercise at the pool, using either the diving board or edge of the pool to conduct your experiment. If you do not have access to a swimming pool, you can substitute a bucket filled with water for the swimming pool.

Note: The experiment in the pool should only be performed by individuals who know how to swim, and preferably when there is a qualified lifeguard present.

If you dive into the pool in as streamlined a position as possible, you will likely create minimal splash and go fairly deep, as compared to when you jump off of the diving board or the edge of the pool and perform a cannonball or a belly flop. When you perform a cannonball or a belly flop, there is a great deal of splash, and you do not go nearly as deep into the pool.

If you use a bucket of water, you will also need a streamlined object such as a pencil or a pen, as well as an object with considerably more mass (size) such as a baseball. With the pencil tip pointing toward the bucket of water (at a given height above the bucket), let the pencil fall and watch how it enters the water and how fast and far it travels in the water.

Now hold the baseball (or whatever object you have chosen) the same distance above the bucket and drop that object into the water. Change the height of the object above the bucket and repeat the process. What do you notice in relation to changes in the different variables? As you change the height of the object that you are dropping, and in turn change the velocity at which the object is traveling when it strikes the water, what do you see?

This demonstration should yield the same type of results that can be seen with different caliber bullets and how they react when they strike the human body.

Most bullets are made of lead and encased in a hardened metal shell, called a jacket, which is typically made of copper. The copper jacket prevents the softer lead from deforming when fired. Some bullets have a "full metal jacket" (typically used by the military) that prevents the lead from deforming when striking tissue (Figure 18-1). This prevents the bullet from slowing too fast and allows it to penetrate more deeply, often passing completely through the victim (much like the streamlined diver or the pencil in this experiment). These bullets generally cause less damage than bullets that do not have a full metal jacket.

Soft-point or hollow-point bullets leave a proportion of the lead exposed, allowing the bullet to deform on contact with tissue (Figure 18-2). The bullet fragments and deforms into a blunt, mushroom-shaped projectile that can leave a permanent cavity 2.5 times larger than the original bullet and a much larger temporary cavitation cavity (similar to the cannonball, belly flop, or the blunt object that you used in this experiment).

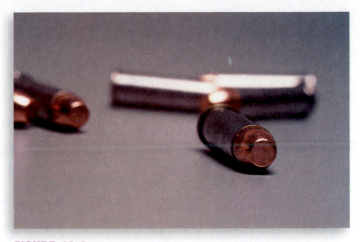

FIGURE 18-2 Soft-point and hollow-point bullets fragment and deform into blunt, mushroom-shaped projectiles when they strike their target. These bullets often do not penetrate very deep, but they can cause considerable damage.

These bullets often do not penetrate as deep but can cause far more damage. Hollow-point bullets are illegal in many areas and are also referred to as "cop killers" because of their destructive design.

You Are There: Reality-Based Cases

Case 1

You and your partner are on your way back from a 3-hour interfacility transfer. Your partner and the patient are in the back of the ambulance discussing politics and baseball. You decide to take the scenic route, because traffic on the freeway is at a complete standstill. The route that you have chosen has practically no traffic at all, but just as you start to think that you have made a terrific decision, you see an accident that is just about to happen.

Approaching a signal intersection, you notice that the light is about to turn red, but the traffic traveling in the opposite direction does not appear to be slowing down. There is a delivery truck, followed by a small sedan, behind which is a large 18-wheeler. The light has already turned red, and the driver of the delivery truck slams on the brakes. The sedan begins to slow, but the 18-wheeler seems completely unaware that the signal has changed. The next few seconds seem to take place in slow motion. The 18-wheeler, without any evidence of braking whatsoever, crashes into the back of the

FIGURE 18-1 Full metal jacket rounds are considered to be for military use because of their stopping ability with less associated trauma. These bullets tend not to deform when they strike their intended target.

sedan and thrusts it forward into the back of the stopped delivery truck. The impact is so great that the delivery truck is propelled halfway into the intersection. Dust and glass are flying, and the sedan is crumpled between the two large trucks like an accordion.

1. Which of Newton's laws were involved in this accident?

_____

_____

_____

2. Based on your answer to question 1, describe how you believe Newton's laws were involved in this crash.

_____

_____

_____

3. What type of collision(s) was the sedan driver's body involved in?

_____

_____

_____

4. Based on the mechanism of injury of this crash, what potential injuries might the driver of the sedan have suffered based on the kinematics of the crash?

_____

_____

_____

Test Yourself

1. The more severe the force that is applied to the body
   a. the more signs of penetrating trauma you will see.
   b. the more damage that is present whether it is visible or not.
   c. the less important preexisting medical illnesses become.
   d. the more signs of blunt force trauma you will see.

2. You are called to an unconscious patient lying in his front yard. Upon physical examination, you find that he has a small laceration across his forehead, severe bruising and abrasions along his left arm, and both ankles are swollen and deformed. The most likely mechanism of injury is
   a. your patient fell from his roof and landed feet-first.
   b. your patient tripped over his front step and hit his head.
   c. your patient was assaulted and left in front of his house.
   d. your patient fell from his roof and landed head-first.

Scenario: You are treating a 26-year-old man who was involved in a bar fight. He has a stab wound from a broken bottle to his left lower arm.

3. You should be most concerned about
   a. vascular compromise.
   b. tension pneumothorax.
   c. septic shock.
   d. cardiac tamponade.

4. You should
   a. check with law enforcement before transporting to make sure your patient is not charged with a crime.
   b. apply direct pressure to the stab wound and reassess frequently throughout transport.
   c. apply a tourniquet to the upper left arm and transport your patient emergently.
   d. test your patient's blood alcohol level and report it to the police immediately if it is over 0.10.

5. After controlling the bleeding, the best way to assess the patient for arterial compromise is to
   a. wait until you've splinted the arm to assess pulse, sensation, and motor function.

    b. assess both arms with a blood pressure cuff and compare the readings.

    c. use palpation to continually reassess the blood pressure of the injured arm.

    d. perform a capillary refill test to monitor tissue perfusion in the injured arm.

6. Anytime a victim has a penetrating wound, you must consider it was a violent act by an assailant until proven otherwise.

    True

    False

7. What three issues should you consider if you are called to evaluate a patient who has been incapacitated by a Taser?

    _____

    _____

    _____

8. Describe some of the common symptoms of crush syndrome.

    _____

    _____

    _____

Scenario: Your 39-year-old patient was severely injured in an explosion at the factory where she works. She has a large piece of glass protruding from her right lower abdomen. She also has blood coming from her ears and a fractured arm. She is alert and oriented.

9. This patient's injuries were most likely sustained by which of the four blast injury mechanisms?

    a. Primary, tertiary, and quaternary

    b. Secondary, tertiary, and quaternary

    c. Primary, secondary, and tertiary

    d. Primary, secondary, and quaternary

10. Which organ is most likely to be affected by the penetrating injury?

    a. Spleen

    b. Heart

    c. Liver

    d. Lungs

11. You notice a bluish discoloration across the surface of her abdomen. You should be most concerned about

    a. cardiac tamponade.

    b. tension pneumothorax.

    c. blood in the pleural cavity.

    d. blood in the peritoneum.

12. You should

    a. stabilize the glass with bulky dressings and tape, and transport in a position of comfort.

    b. carefully remove the glass and control the bleeding with direct pressure.

    c. carefully remove the glass and control the bleeding by clamping the vessel.

    d. stabilize the glass with bulky dressings and tape, take spinal precautions, and transport.

13. Describe the three-collision model that a person experiences during a motor vehicle crash.

    _____

    _____

    _____

14. According to Newton's first law, what is the relationship between the mass of an object, its velocity, and its kinetic energy?

    a. Both the mass of an object and its velocity have a linear effect on the object's kinetic energy.

    b. The mass of an object has an exponential effect on its kinetic energy, while its velocity has a linear effect.

    c. Both the mass of an object and its velocity have an exponential effect on the object's kinetic energy.

    d. The mass of an object has a linear effect on its kinetic energy, while its velocity has an exponential effect.

15. During a motor vehicle collision (MVC), the driver of the vehicle flew forward, hitting his head on the windshield. When his head hit, the windshield pushed back with equal force. This is an example of

    a. Newton's first law.

    b. Newton's third law.

    c. Newton's fourth law.

    d. Newton's second law.

Scenario: You are called to the scene of a multiple-vehicle collision. The driver of a sedan ran a red light and drove into the passenger side of a minivan in which a restrained 8-year-old boy was seated. There is minimal damage to the front of the sedan, but the passenger side of the minivan has collapsed inward.

16. Your patient is the driver of the minivan. Given the mechanism of injury, which of the following injuries should you suspect?

    a. Neck hyperextension

    b. A spinal fracture

    c. Dislocated knees

    d. A ruptured liver

17. Which patient is most likely to need immediate treatment?

    a. The 34-year-old driver of the minivan

    b. The 75-year-old driver of the sedan

    c. The 49-year-old passenger in the sedan

    d. The 8-year-old passenger in the minivan

18. A 7-year-old boy has been in a bicycle accident. He has a closed arm fracture and a severe laceration to his right leg. He is awake and breathing regularly, and his systolic blood pressure is 64. You estimate his weight at about 50 pounds. Calculate your patient's Pediatric Trauma Score (PTS), and summarize your course of treatment.

    _____

    _____

    _____

19. List four risks common in elderly patients who have fallen and are unable to get up.

    _____

    _____

    _____

Need to Know

The following represent the Key Objectives of Chapter 18:

1. *Evaluate the mechanism of injury of patients who have experienced traumatic injuries.*

   During your career as a paramedic you will see many injuries ranging in severity from scratches to decapitations, and all the different types of injuries in between. The traumatic injuries that are associated with external findings such as abrasions, lacerations, and bruises are much easier to identify and treat than internal injuries that exist without obvious external findings.

   The paramedic must also consider the possibility of internal injuries in the absence of obvious external trauma. Paramedics must develop a thought process that makes them acutely aware of how people are injured. The process of determining how somebody is injured, also known as the mechanism of injury, should be evaluated with every patient who has sustained a traumatic injury.

2. *Predict injury patterns based on the mechanism of injury.*

   The study of mechanism of injury has yielded predictable patterns of injury based on particular mechanisms of injury. The paramedic should evaluate the mechanism of injury of every trauma patient and apply these predictable patterns of injury. Even patients with no obvious external trauma can have internal injuries that paramedics can discover by applying their knowledge of kinematics and predictable patterns of injury. Paramedics must be particularly aware of very young and very old trauma patients and of patients suffering from preexisting medical conditions. These populations have the worst outcomes following a traumatic injury.

3. *Apply basic physics principles to evaluate the mechanism of injury.*

   Paramedics must be familiar with basic physics while evaluating the mechanism of injury of trauma patients. The following are several important factors to consider while evaluating the mechanism of injury:

   - There doesn't need to be any external evidence of injury for there to be a life-threatening internal injury. Always look at the big picture.
   - Kinematics: The study of trauma and what the forces of energy do to the body.
   - Newton's first law (law of inertia—also known as the law of motion): A body at rest will remain at rest and a body in motion will remain in motion until acted upon by an outside force.
   - Kinetic energy (the energy possessed by an object in motion) = ½ Mass × Velocity². Kinetic energy is described in units known as joules. The speed of an object is critically important in this equation.
   - Potential energy = Mass (weight) × Force of gravity × Height.
   - Newton's second law (law of acceleration): Force = Mass × Acceleration.
   - Newton's third law (law of reciprocal actions): For every action there is an equal and opposite reaction.
   - Motor vehicle crashes, falls, and a number of other traumatic mechanisms that involve energy changing form tend to create injuries as the result of more than one force. Motor vehicle

Lung
Heart
Spleen
Liver
Stomach
Intestine

FIGURE 18-3 The three separate impacts that occur as kinetic energy is transferred.

crashes, for example, are frequently described in terms of three collisions (Figure 18-3):

1. The first collision takes place when the vehicle crashes into an object.
2. The second collision takes place when the patient's body strikes the vehicle or another object.
3. The third collision occurs when the organs within the cavities of the patient's body strike the interior surface of the body.

- Impaled objects are not to be removed unless they interfere with CPR or other life-saving interventions (e.g., airway management).
- Paramedics' ability to provide quality patient care and to advocate for trauma patients depends in part on their ability to recognize

potential injuries based on the mechanism of injury in the absence of obvious signs and symptoms.

Connections

- Chapter 9, Safety and Scene Size-Up, in the text presents additional information on rescuer and patient safety.
- Link to the companion DVD for a chapter-based quiz, audio glossary, animations, games and exercises, and, when appropriate, skill sheets and skill Step-by-Steps.
- The mechanism of injury can help you predict patterns of injury, even before contacting the patient. Problem-Based Learning Case 3, An Awful Crash, will illustrate this concept vividly.

Street Secrets

- **Examine the Entire Patient** Approach every trauma patient with an open mind and open eyes. Make sure that you don't have tunnel vision about the obvious injuries; instead, examine the entire patient for the not-so-obvious injuries. Examination of the back of every trauma patient is necessary, yet it is frequently overlooked. Quality patient care involves the entire patient.
- **Wound Size** When it comes to penetrating trauma of the gunshot or stabbing variety, do not let the small size of the wound or the lack of external bleeding allow you to believe that all is well. Take off the blinders, and take a look at the big picture. Think about the underlying internal structures (e.g., organs and blood vessels), and remember that there is plenty of room within the body cavities to empty the entire circulating blood volume. A wound doesn't need to be big to be bad.

Need to Do

The following skills are explained and illustrated in a step-by-step manner, via skill sheets and/or Step-by-Steps in this text and on the accompanying DVD:

Skill Name	Skill Sheet Number and Location	Step-by-Step Number and Location
Trauma Scoring	31 – DVD	N/A
Primary Assessment	32 – Appendix A and DVD	32 – Chapter 14 and DVD
Rapid Extrication	72 – DVD	N/A
NREMT Patient Assessment Trauma	83 – DVD	N/A

- **Penetrating Wounds**   Never dismiss a puncture wound (especially to the torso, head, face, or neck) as being "superficial" and not worthy of transport to the hospital for evaluation. Paramedics do not have an accurate or appropriate means of determining the depth of penetrating wounds. Transport patients with penetrating wounds to a hospital where they can be evaluated by a physician.

- **Gunshot Wounds**   When describing the size and location of gunshot wounds, do not state that the patient has an "entrance wound" at a specific location and an "exit wound" at another location if you did not witness the person getting shot and you do not know for a fact that a specific wound is an entrance or an exit wound. Instead, simply state what you see. For example, "Patient has a 1-cm wound to the inferior lateral border of his left scapula and a 4-cm wound in the mid-sternal line superior to the xiphoid process." Remember that external wounds are not always a reflection of the injuries that may have occurred inside the body. Gunshot wounds are a glaring example. What appears to be a very small hole with very little bleeding on the surface of the body can in fact be a completely different story on the inside of the body. Bullets have a tendency to deform or fragment when they strike a person, especially when they hit bones as they enter the body. The size of the bullet and the velocity at which the bullet was traveling, in addition to the physical characteristics of the person who was shot, all influence the cavity that is produced and the damage that is created internally.

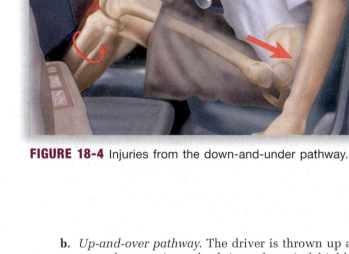

FIGURE 18-4 Injuries from the down-and-under pathway.

The Drug Box

There are no specific drugs related to this chapter content.

Answers

Are You Ready?

1. Drivers of cars involved in head-on, or frontal impact, collisions frequently react to the impact in one of two ways:
    a. *Down-and-under pathway.* The driver continues to travel downward into the seat and forward into the dashboard or steering column; the knees strike the dashboard; the upper legs absorb most of the impact (Figure 18-4).
    b. *Up-and-over pathway.* The driver is thrown up and over the steering wheel into the windshield or inside roof of the car; the head is usually the leading point in this type of collision, crashing into the windshield (Figure 18-5).

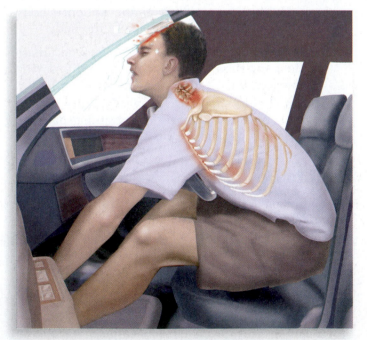

FIGURE 18-5 Injuries from the up-and-over pathway.

2. The resulting injuries from the two previously discussed pathways are as follows:

   a. Down-and-under pathway

- Dislocated knees, fractured femurs, and a fractured pelvis or dislocated hips; thoracic spine fractures.
- If the upper body strikes the steering wheel or the dashboard, the patient can suffer broken ribs or sternum, flail chest, pulmonary contusion, myocardial contusion, or ruptured liver or spleen.
- Vertebral fractures, crushed larynx, fractured facial bones.

   b. Up-and-over pathway (Figure 18-6)

- Scalp lacerations, skull fractures, or cerebral contusions and/or hemorrhage.
- Compression fractures of the cervical spine, fracture or dislocation of the vertebrae, spinal cord compression.
- The larynx or the facial bones can be crushed if they strike the steering wheel.
- If the chest or abdomen strikes the steering wheel, the patient can suffer broken ribs or sternum, flail chest, pulmonary contusion, myocardial contusion, or ruptured liver or spleen.

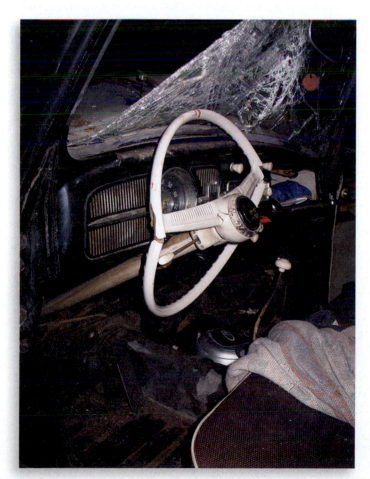

FIGURE 18-6 Actual example of up-and-over pathway.

You Are There: Reality-Based Cases

Case 1

1. Newton's first law (law of inertia), Newton's second law (law of acceleration), and Newton's third law (law of reciprocal actions).

2. All three vehicles involved in this accident were traveling in the same direction at approximately the same speed. The drivers of the delivery truck and the sedan applied their brakes and were able to come to a complete stop (Newton's first law, the law of inertia: a body at rest will remain at rest, and a body in motion will remain in motion until acted upon by an outside force). Newton's first law, second law (law of acceleration), and third law (law of reciprocal actions) all played a role in the collision that took place between the 18-wheeler, the sedan, and the delivery truck.

The 18-wheeler (a body in motion [first law]) strikes the sedan (a body at rest [first law]), propelling the sedan forward and slowing down the 18-wheeler (the rate of change of momentum of a body is equal to the resultant force acting on the body, and that force needs to be in the same direction that the original body was traveling [second law]). The energy was transferred from the forward-moving 18-wheeler to the stationary sedan; in turn, the sedan now has a forward momentum. The energy will once again transfer when the sedan crashes into the delivery truck, causing the stationary delivery truck to propel forward. The brakes of the delivery truck will eventually bring it, the sedan, and the 18-wheeler to a stop. The entire transfer of energy that occurred in this collision transferred directly through the driver of the sedan (Newton's first, second, and third laws).

3. The driver of the sedan was barely moving in a forward direction (Newton's second law [law of acceleration]: the rate of change of momentum of a body is equal to the resultant force acting on the body, and that force needs to be in the same direction that the original body was traveling) when his vehicle was struck from behind. When his car was struck and propelled forward, his body pushed back (Newton's third law [law of reciprocal actions]: for every action there is an equal and opposite reaction) against the force that was applied by the velocity and the mass of the 18-wheeler. The sedan and the driver continued forward until the sedan struck the delivery truck [Newton's first law [law of inertia]: a body at rest will remain at rest, and a body in motion will remain in motion until acted upon by some outside force]. When the front end of the sedan struck the back of the delivery truck, the body of the sedan driver flew forward into the windshield and steering wheel of his car, at which point the surface of his body stopped its forward momentum [Newton's third law [law of reciprocal actions]: for every action there is an equal and opposite reaction]. When the surface of his body stopped, his internal organs, great vessels, etc., continued moving in a forward direction until they were stopped by the internal surface of the body cavities (Newton's first law).

4. Rear impact: Head and neck hyperextension (whiplash), torn neck muscles, spinal cord damage.

Frontal impact (up and over or down and under):

- Impact of head with windshield or steering wheel: scalp lacerations, skull fractures or cerebral contusions and/or hemorrhage (coup-contrecoup injury), compression fractures of the cervical spine, fracture or dislocation of the vertebrae, spinal cord compression
- Impact with the face or neck: crushed larynx and the facial bones if they strike the steering wheel, transected trachea
- Impact with the chest: broken ribs or sternum, flail chest, pulmonary contusion, myocardial contusion, transected aorta
- Impact with the abdomen: ruptured liver, ruptured spleen

Test Yourself

1. b

Many times injuries cannot be seen externally or the patient is unable to tell you where the pain is coming from. In these cases, you have to look for clues but also remain suspicious based on your knowledge of predictable patterns of injury gained from understanding kinematics. The more severe the force applied to the body, the more severe the damage, whether it is obviously visible or not. These forces can cause life-threatening problems such as a liver laceration, torn aorta, cavitation injury from gunshot wounds, and hemorrhage.

2. a

Those patients who land feet-first also usually sustain a series of collisions resulting in a predictable pattern of injuries. When the feet strike the ground, fractures of the calcaneus or ankles generally result. As the momentum of the body continues downward, forces act to fracture the femurs, hips, or pelvis. Then the trunk will usually bend at the waist, often causing spinal fractures and possibly intra-abdominal injury. Patients will subsequently attempt to brace their fall with their outstretched arms, causing fracture to one or both of the upper extremities. Finally, the head will strike the ground, causing possible head and cervical spine injury.

3. a

Penetrating trauma to the extremities is associated with vascular compromise. Septic shock, tension pneumothorax, and cardiac tamponade are associated with penetrating wounds to the chest and/or abdomen.

4. b

If the patient has significant bleeding, it should be controlled with direct pressure. Tourniquets should be avoided in all but the most extreme cases. Accommodate the law enforcement officers as much as you can, but do not compromise patient care in the process.

5. b

If time permits, the injured extremity should also be assessed with a blood pressure cuff and the reading compared to the unaffected extremity. The palpation method of blood pressure assessment is adequate for gross changes but will become less useful as the injury worsens and the pulses are no longer palpable. Capillary refill testing is not always a reliable tool. It is always vital to assess pulse, sensation, and motor function both before and after splinting an injured extremity.

6. True

The first important thing to do is to assess scene safety. It does the patient little good if you become a patient yourself. Always make sure there are no more uncontrollable threats to the victim or yourself before entering the scene. Anytime a victim has a penetrating wound, you must consider it was a violent act by an assailant until proven otherwise.

7. The barbs will be impaled into the patient's body; the patient may be in cardiac arrest; the patient may have sustained traumatic injuries when he or she fell down.

First, the barbs will be impaled into the subject's body. They are only 4 mm long and can usually be removed easily. However, it is important to know one's local protocols as to who can remove them and under what circumstances. Second, there have been rare instances of cardiac arrest in patients who have been incapacitated by a Taser. If a paramedic discovers on primary survey that a patient is in cardiac arrest, then appropriate ACLS measures should be taken as discussed in Chapter 29 in the text. Third, if you are called to evaluate a patient on whom a Taser has been used, you should take into account that the patient likely fell and do an appropriate trauma evaluation including cervical spine immobilization if indicated.

8. Systemic manifestations of crush syndrome include rhabdomyolysis (the muscle cells that break down release their protein, which damages the kidneys), electrolyte abnormalities, acid-base abnormalities, hypovolemia, acute renal failure, and perhaps compartment syndrome.

Crush syndrome is a systemic disorder of severe metabolic disturbances resulting from the crushing of skeletal muscle. For crush syndrome to occur, the skeletal muscle must be exposed to the high-pressure crushing forces for an extended period of time. The shortest time documented for crush syndrome to occur is 4 hours. The continual pressure results in minimal or no circulation of blood into the compressed areas, and the tissue undergoes ischemia followed by necrosis (tissue death). When the pressure is released, the toxins that are released from the necrotic tissue contain myoglobin, phosphate, potassium, lactic acid, and uric acid. These toxins can overwhelm the heart (disrupting the electrical system and causing life-threatening dysrhythmias), and the liver and kidneys cannot remove them fast enough to prevent damage. Death can occur rapidly in these patients.

9. c

This patient most likely sustained the ear injury from the blast itself (the primary mechanism). She sustained the penetrating injury when glass thrown by the blast became shrapnel (the secondary mechanism). She sustained the fracture when she landed after being thrown by the blast (the tertiary mechanism).

10. c

The liver is a right-sided organ.

11. d

The presence of blood in the peritoneum can also cause hemorrhagic shock, abdominal pain and tenderness, rigidity, or a sensation of dread and doom. When enough blood is present in the peritoneum, it may be visible on the surface of the abdomen as a bluish discoloration. This finding is known as Cullen's sign.

12. d

In this case (an explosion), spinal precautions would be indicated. If the patient has an impaled object protruding from her body, leave it in place. Never remove an impaled object unless it poses an immediate life threat and medical direction has ordered it to be removed. Removing the object may cause further damage, leading to destabilization of the patient. The object may be tamponading (compressing) a bleeding vessel, and removing it may result in an uncontrolled bleed. The object should be secured in place with bulky dressings and tape.

13. During crash one, the vehicle strikes an object. During crash two, the patient strikes the vehicle or other object. During crash three, the organs within the patient strike the inner surfaces of the patient.

   The first collision occurs when the vehicle comes into contact with an object that alters its direction of movement. The alteration of direction results in a transfer of energy between the two objects. This transfer causes the second collision. This occurs as the vehicle occupant continues to travel in the original direction, striking the interior of the vehicle or another object. The third collision occurs as the organs within the patient strike the inside of the compartment they reside within.

14. d

Kinetic energy = ½ Mass × Velocity². The critical component of this equation to remember is that velocity (speed) is squared. When speed is doubled, the mathe-matical result is a quadrupling, or a multiplying of the force by four times! The speed of the projectile is critically important.

15. b

Newton's third law states, "For every action, there is an equal and opposite reaction." In other words, as the person pushes on the steering wheel and windshield of the car, those objects push back with equal force against the person.

16. b

Fractures of the spine are more common with lateral collisions than with rear collisions. Dislocated knees are associated with frontal collisions, neck hyperextension is associated with rear-impact collisions, and a ruptured liver is most likely to affect persons on the passenger side during a lateral collision.

17. d

Given the damage to the vehicles, the passenger side of the minivan seems to have absorbed the majority of the energy from the collision. Also, children are more vulnerable to traumatic injury because they do not respond to trauma in the same manner that adults do. Their heads are proportionately larger (making them top-heavy), and their nervous systems are less well developed. Their ability to compensate for shock is less driven by catecholamines, and they have less cardiac reserve than adults. The internal organs of children are not as well protected by bony structures as adults, and children's immune systems are less mature and not as efficient as those of adults.

18. To calculate this patient's PTS, you would count 2 points each for weight (> 20 kg), mental status (awake), and airway (normal); 1 point each for BP (50–90) and skeletal (closed fracture); and −1 point for the wound (major open). This patient's PTS is 7, so he should be taken to a pediatric trauma center.

   A child with a revised trauma score of less than 12 (see Table 18-7 in the textbook) or a PTS less than 8 (see Table 18-6 in the textbook) should be taken to a pediatric trauma center.

19. Patients who are unable to get up from a fall are at risk for dehydration, hypothermia, electrolyte imbalance, and rhabdomyolysis.

   Fifty percent of elderly individuals who fall are unable to get up without assistance.

chapter 19

Hemorrhage and Hemorrhagic Shock

1. What is your general impression of this patient?

_____

_____

_____

2. What is your first priority?

_____

_____

_____

3. What is the process for achieving hemostasis in a patient with severe external bleeding?

_____

_____

_____

Are You Ready?

You are taking a much deserved week off of work and getting as far away from anything to do with medicine as you possibly can. You flew home to spend time with family and friends and to volunteer for the organization "Christmas in April." You and the rest of your group are putting a new roof on the home of an elderly woman in a low-income part of town. You are thoroughly enjoying the physical work and the camaraderie of your fellow workers when the sound of laughter is interrupted by a commotion on the other side of the building.

You fear that your dream of a medicine-free vacation is about to come to an abrupt end. You scramble up to the peak of the roof and look over to the other side. One of the volunteers has sustained a significant laceration to the medial part of his left thigh. Bright red blood is squirting into the air through the fingers of the worker as he tries to control the bleeding.

Active Learning

1. Hemodilution Exercise

What effects IV fluid administration has on trauma patients suffering from hemorrhagic shock in the prehospital setting is a debate that continues to this day. Studies show that the administration of large amounts of crystalloid IV solutions to critical trauma patients who are suffering from hypovolemic shock can be harmful.

This exercise demonstrates the effects of fluid challenges to trauma patients suffering from hemorrhagic shock.

Materials needed:

- Liter bag of IV solution
- 500-mL bag of IV solution

- 10-gtt/min administration sets
- 18-gauge or larger needle
- Bucket or basin
- 10-mL syringe with needle (may use the same 18-gauge or larger needle for both applications)
- Red food coloring
- IV pole or means of elevating one of the IV bags
- Table

Spike both of the IV bags and flood the IV tubing. Use the 10-mL syringe to draw up the food coloring and inject it into the 500-mL bag of IV solution (use a minimum of 5 mL and up to 10 mL as needed to create the appearance of blood or a dark solution in this IV bag). Mix the food coloring by shaking the IV bag. Once the solution is mixed, aspirate 10 mL of the fluid from the 500-mL IV bag and place the syringe off to the side for use later in the experiment. Attach the needle from the syringe to the end of the IV tubing from the 1,000-mL IV bag and insert it into the medication port of the 500-mL IV bag.

Place the 500-mL IV bag on a table, and place the tubing from this IV into the basin or bucket on the floor (make sure that the cap is off the end of the IV tubing). Hang the 1,000-mL bag of IV fluid on the IV pole or on a hook above the level of the 500-mL bag that you have placed on the table.

Open the roller clamps for both of the IV bags and watch what happens. The end of the IV tubing from the 500-mL IV bag represents a break in the blood vessels of a trauma patient and the subsequent bleeding. The 500-mL IV bag represents the patient's circulating blood volume, and the 1,000-mL IV bag represents the IV fluid that is being administered to the trauma patient who is suffering from hemorrhagic shock.

Let the experiment continue until all the fluid has emptied out of the 1,000-mL IV bag. Note the color of the fluid in the 500-mL IV bag as the experiment progresses, and also look at the color of the fluid that ends up in the bucket.

When you are done with this experiment, compare the color of the fluid in the syringe that you took out of the 500-mL IV bag with the color of the fluid in the bucket or basin. This experiment is designed to show the effects of hemodilution.

You Are There: Reality-Based Cases
Case 1

Today is your first day as a flight medic for the local air medical service. You arrived at work early, checked all of the equipment at least three times, and now you are going over the mechanical check of the helicopter with the pilot. When the mechanical check of the helicopter is complete, the flight nurse explains that she will provide a majority of the care for critical care transfers while you learn and become more comfortable with the different biomedical equipment, medications, and procedures needed to care for these patients. As she begins to explain the process of hemodynamic monitoring utilizing a Swan-Ganz catheter, your pagers begin to sound.

You have been requested to respond to the Coast Highway for a car over a cliff. The fire department is on scene and in the process of extricating a patient trapped in his car. In a matter of minutes you are orbiting over the scene, assessing the landing zone established by the fire department for any potential hazards. You spot the firefighters hauling the patient up the cliff in a Stokes basket.

As soon as you land, the flight nurse motions for you to follow her. You comply with her gestures, exit the aircraft, and head directly for the patient. When you reach the patient, a paramedic from the engine crew begins to give you a report. She explains that the 62-year-old male patient was the restrained driver of a vehicle that plunged over 80 feet off of a cliff onto the rocks below. When they reached the patient, he was unconscious, yet he responded to deep painful stimuli by withdrawing. Both of the patient's legs were trapped under the dashboard of the car, the steering wheel was deformed, and the windshield was spiderwebbed. The patient sustained multiple

glass lacerations to his forehead and has bruising to the anterior chest wall in the shape of the steering wheel, with instability to the right anterior axillary line from the area of the third intercostal space to the subcostal margin. The patient also presents with instability to the pelvis and multiple open fractures to the bilateral lower extremities. The patient's vital signs are: blood pressure 84/56; pulse 124; respirations 26 and shallow on 15 L of oxygen via non-rebreather mask. The patient is in full c-spine precautions and has two large-bore IVs established.

You thank the paramedic for the report and perform your own assessment of the patient. The patient is awake but confused and able to follow simple commands. His skin is cool and moist. The brachial pulses are palpable yet rapid and weak. The carotid pulses are more readily palpable than the brachial pulses. The bleeding from the glass lacerations to the patient's forehead appears to be controlled by the application of 4 × 4 dressings and the tape from securing the c-spine. The patient's airway appears to be patent, but his breathing is shallow, with slightly diminished breath sounds on the right-hand side. The oxygen saturation is 92% on 15 L of oxygen via non-rebreather mask. Examination of the chest wall reveals a large steering wheel–shaped bruise, slight paradoxical movement of the chest wall with ventilations, and crepitus upon palpation of the right anterior axillary line. The abdomen appears soft and non-distended. When you apply pressure to the pelvis, you feel crepitus and a definite instability.

The legs have been wrapped with rolling bandages, and there does not appear to be any uncontrolled external bleeding. The patient is able to feel when you squeeze his toes, and he is able to wiggle his toes as well. The upper extremities appear to be intact, and the patient is able to squeeze your fingers with equal strength bilaterally. The patient's vital signs are: blood pressure 80/50; pulse 130; respirations 26 and shallow; oxygen saturation 92% on 15 L of oxygen via non-rebreather mask. The firefighter paramedic hands you a card that states that the patient has a history of hypertension and takes benazepril. He has no allergies to medications.

1. What is your general impression of this patient?

_____

_____

_____

2. What are your priorities in treating the patient?

_____

_____

_____

3. If the patient is in shock, what type of shock do you suspect he is suffering from? Explain your reasoning.

_____

_____

_____

4. Describe the physiological process of maintaining perfusion to the tissues of the body that occurs when hemorrhage begins (mild fluid deficit).

_____

_____

_____

5. Describe (pathophysiologically) how the body initiates hemostasis.

_____

_____

_____

6. What class of medication is benazepril?

_____

_____

_____

7. Does the patient's medication have any impact on the body's compensatory mechanisms in terms of preventing shock?

_____

_____

_____

Test Yourself

1. _____ shock is the result of a decrease in the heart's ability to supply needed oxygen and nutrients to the tissues and cells of the body.
   a. Neurogenic
   b. Distributive
   c. Cardiogenic
   d. Hemorrhagic

2. At the venous end of the capillary (the distal end), _____ are returned to the vascular system where they are excreted by the lungs, liver, and kidneys.
   a. fluids, oxygen, and waste products
   b. fluids, water, and waste products

c. fluids, carbon dioxide, and waste products

d. fluids, CO, and waste products

3. _____, or SIR, is the pathway in the worsening state of shock where there is a release of inflammatory mediators like cytokines, arachidonic acid metabolites, and free radicals.

a. Subcellular inhibitory response

b. Systemic inhibitory response

c. Severe inflammatory response

d. Systemic inflammatory response

4. What is the first phase of multiple organ failure due to shock?

a. Ischemic phase

b. Cellular phase

c. Washout phase

d. Capillary stagnation phase

5. How does care of a patient with penetrating injuries differ from care of a patient with blunt force injuries?

a. You are less likely to administer volume resuscitation for patients with penetrating injuries.

b. Patients with blunt force injuries have little to no risk of major blood volume loss.

c. You should not delay treatment in patients with blunt force injuries by taking the time to fully expose them.

d. Patients with penetrating injuries are more likely to require rapid transport to a trauma center.

6. Your patient is exhibiting signs of shock. While assessing the ABCDEs, you palpate the carotid pulse and note that the heart rate, rhythm, and quality seem to be within the normal range. You should

a. check the radial pulse and compare the two.

b. note that the patient's circulation is fine and rule out hemorrhagic shock.

c. move on and assess the patient for disability.

d. recheck the carotid pulse to obtain an actual heart rate.

7. List some findings and injuries that may indicate life-threatening internal bleeding.

_____

_____

8. Describe each of the classes of hemorrhage in terms of the amount of blood loss.

_____

_____

9. Explain why the compression of pressure points to stop bleeding is controversial.

_____

_____

10. How does zeolite powder (sold as QuikClot) work to stop bleeding?

a. It elevates the temperature around the wound site to 42°C–44°C.

b. It absorbs water and concentrates clotting factors at the wound.

c. It attracts cells necessary to the clotting process toward the wound.

d. It causes vasoconstriction in the affected vessels near the wound.

11. Pneumatic anti-shock garments (PASGs) have been shown to increase survivability in patients who suffered from thoracic trauma.

True

False

12. Your 61-year-old patient has a suspected head injury following a car collision. Vital signs are BP of 88/50, HR of 116, and RR of 28, and the patient has a history of heart disease. You estimate the patient's weight at about 120 pounds. Should this patient receive fluid resuscitation?

a. No. Trauma patients in compensated shock should not receive fluid resuscitation to avoid causing pulmonary edema, which can increase the patient's mortality.

b. Yes. Two large-bore intravenous lines in the upper extremities should be used to infuse fluid at an initial bolus dose of 2,400 mL; then the patient should be reassessed.

c. Yes. One large-bore intravenous line in the upper extremity should be used to infuse fluid at an initial bolus dose of 1,100 mL; then the patient should be reassessed.

d. Yes. Administer the 1,100-mL bolus of fluid in several divided doses with continuous evaluation of the vital signs and clinical response during the treatment.

13. What three questions help a health-care provider determine whether fluid resuscitation is indicated?

_____

14. Hemorrhage and shock from traumatic injuries can be treated definitively in the field and may not require surgical intervention.

True

False

15. List the clinical cause of shock and some of its consequences.

_____

_____

Need to Know

The following represent the Key Objectives of Chapter 19:

1. *Describe the pathophysiology of shock.*

    Many EMS scenarios involve a discussion of homeostasis. Hemorrhagic shock is a perfect example of how badly things can go when the ability to maintain homeostasis is compromised. The cells of the body function very well when they receive all the oxygen and nutrients they need and they are able to rid themselves of waste products. When a traumatic injury results in hemorrhagic shock, the cells of the body lose the ability to function using aerobic metabolism. When an individual who has suffered a traumatic injury is no longer capable of delivering oxygen and vital nutrients to the cells of the body, anaerobic metabolism begins.

    Decreased perfusion first affects the skeletal muscles and visceral organs. The cellular effects of anaerobic metabolism are decreased adenosine triphosphate (ATP) production and increased lactic acid production. When levels of lactic acid begin to increase, the body begins to convert lactic acid to lactate. Lactate is transported to the liver, where it is neutralized and converted to bicarbonate and water. As tissue perfusion continues to decrease, lactic acid production increases. At some point, the body will no longer be able to keep up with the conversion of lactic acid to lactate and the conversion of lactate to bicarbonate. It is at this point that metabolic acidosis develops, causing myocardial irritability, decreased cardiac output, and depressed cardiac contractility. The effect of metabolic acidosis on the heart further decreases peripheral blood flow and exacerbates the state of shock.

    Continually decreasing production of ATP and continually increasing metabolic acidosis have a profound effect at the cellular level. The sodium and potassium ATP pumps begin to fail and are no longer capable of preventing intracellular contents from leaving the cell and interstitial contents from entering the cell. The sodium potassium ATP pump failure will eventually lead to cellular ischemia and ultimately cellular death.

2. *Describe the effects of hemorrhagic shock on blood pressure.*

    Blood pressure is the by-product of cardiac output (CO) and peripheral vascular resistance (PVR). With this in mind it becomes easy to see how blood loss can dramatically lower blood pressure. Because hemorrhage causes a decrease in stroke volume, and the hormones that are released in response to bleeding result in an increase in heart rate and/or an increase in vasoconstriction (Cardiac output = Stroke volume [SV] × Heart rate [HR]), it becomes clear that cardiac output is profoundly affected by hemorrhage.

3. *Describe the three stages of hemorrhagic shock.*

    * *Compensated shock.* Occurs as the body adjusts to the fluid loss and organ perfusion is maintained.

    * *Decompensated shock.* If compensated shock is not treated and the compensatory mechanisms begin to fail, the patient enters a state of decompensated shock.

    * *Irreversible shock.* If the decompensated shock is not treated, the patient enters a state of shock that will ultimately lead to death.

4. *Discuss hemostasis in the prehospital setting.*

    The process of hemostasis in the prehospital setting depends on several factors:

    * Is the hemorrhage internal or external?
    * Is the bleeding controlled or uncontrolled?
    * What is the location of the bleeding (e.g., abdomen or extremity)?

    Internal hemorrhage is, in virtually all cases, a problem that needs to be treated in the hospital and is a condition that requires surgery until proven otherwise. Thus, patients suspected of having an internal hemorrhage (whether it be medical or due to trauma) need to be transported as soon as possible to an appropriate receiving facility, with any prehospital interventions performed en route to the hospital.

External hemorrhage is much easier to identify and control. Some areas of the body, such as the neck, offer special challenges when it comes to controlling bleeding, due to the other associated anatomical structures. The paramedic needs to take special care in applying direct pressure to the neck, because excessive pressure can cut off blood supply to the brain. Other associated structures that the paramedic needs to keep in mind when managing external hemorrhage of the neck include the airway, spine, nerves, and great vessels.

External trauma to the extremities resulting in hemorrhage can be managed using the basic principles of bleeding control in a progression from least invasive to most invasive:

- Apply direct pressure.
- Elevate the extremity above the level of the heart.
- Apply pressure dressings.
- Apply pressure to pressure points (major artery proximal to point of bleeding).
- Application of a tourniquet.

For suspected uncontrolled internal bleeding, the paramedic must rely on the patient's physiological presentation, which is typically consistent with signs and symptoms of hemorrhagic shock. Patients with suspected internal hemorrhage should be treated for shock even if they do not yet present with the signs and symptoms of shock.

5. *Describe the treatment for patients suffering from hemorrhagic shock.*

First and foremost, as previously discussed, patients with hemorrhagic shock need to be transported as early as possible after the suspicion or determination of hemorrhagic shock is made. Control of the patient's airway and breathing needs to take place en route to the hospital, if not necessitated earlier. Control of external hemorrhage needs to take place as soon as it is discovered. If c-spine precautions are required due to trauma, this procedure needs to take place prior to moving, packaging, and loading the patient into the ambulance for transport. If at all possible, interventions should be performed en route to the hospital, not on scene, and prehospital interventions should not delay transport.

The textbook (Chapter 19, Hemorrhage and Hemorrhagic Shock) describes the following method to determine how to approach fluid resuscitation in patients suspected of suffering from hemorrhagic shock.

Paramedics need to answer three questions:

1. Is the hemorrhage controllable or uncontrolled?
2. What is the mechanism of injury (blunt or penetrating)?
3. Is the patient in shock or showing signs of hypotension?

Once the paramedic controls the bleeding, volume resuscitation is recommended if there is evidence of shock (altered mental status, hypotension, or poor peripheral perfusion).[1] The volume of fluid should be administered in small boluses to a total volume that reverses the signs of shock.

For patients in whom the paramedic suspects continued uncontrollable bleeding, the current recommendation is to obtain intravenous access and administer fluids at a low maintenance rate or KVO. In the event that the patient becomes unstable, approaching circulatory arrest, volume resuscitation can be attempted but is unlikely to provide much benefit.[2]

Patients with hypotension as a result of blunt injury pose a particular problem. There is no compelling evidence to support aggressive fluid resuscitation. However, the recommendation for volume resuscitation to reverse the signs of trauma still stands.[3] Clinicians must resist over-resuscitation in these patients to avoid causing pulmonary edema, which can increase the patient's mortality. Conversely, in patients with suspected head trauma, it is especially important to support their blood pressure with fluids as necessary to provide adequate cerebral perfusion. This pressure is equivalent to 90 mm Hg systolic.

Connections

- Chapter 30, Neurology, in the text includes a discussion on the role of the nervous system in hemostasis.
- Chapter 20, Head, Face, and Neck Trauma, in the text outlines techniques specific to providing bleeding control for head, face, and neck wounds.
- Chapter 25, Soft Tissue and Muscle Trauma, in the text includes an in-depth explanation of hemostasis.
- Link to the companion DVD for a chapter-based quiz, audio glossary, animations, games and exercises, and, when appropriate, skill sheets and skill Step-by-Steps.

Need to Do

The following skills are explained and illustrated in a step-by-step manner, via skill sheets and/or Step-by-Steps in this text and on the accompanying DVD:

Skill Name	Skill Sheet Number and Location	Step-by-Step Number and Location
Bleeding Control and Shock	66 – DVD	66 – DVD
Bleeding Control with a Tourniquet	67 – DVD	67 – DVD
Rapid Extrication	72 – DVD	N/A
MAST/PASG Application	81 – DVD	N/A
NREMT Patient Assessment Trauma	83 – DVD	N/A
NREMT Bleeding Control/Shock Management	94 – DVD	N/A

Street Secrets

- **QuikClot** The military has had good results with a product called QuikClot, which has been used in combat situations since 2003. QuikClot is a powder that is applied to small and medium-sized wounds to provide hemostasis. When the powder is poured into the wound, it absorbs water and active substances in the blood, causing a concentration of clotting factors and ultimately hemostasis. QuikClot is similar to another product on the market called microporous polysaccharide hemosphere (MPH), also known as TraumaDEX, but it is inert and nonallergenic. One point of concern regarding the use of QuikClot is that, when the powder is applied, the temperature of the tissue exposed to the powder rises to somewhere between 42°C and 44°C. Newer compositions reduce the temperature closer to 38°–39°C.

- **Tourniquet Use** The use of a tourniquet is seldom necessary. However, when all other attempts at controlling bleeding have failed, it can truly be a lifesaving procedure. Keep in mind that, when a tourniquet is applied, the blood supply to the distal extremity is cut off. Because of this fact, once a tourniquet has been applied, the patient is transported to a hospital, preferably a trauma center, as quickly as possible. Prolonged tourniquet use can cause cell death distal to the tourniquet and result in conditions similar to crush syndrome. Make sure that the time of tourniquet application is clearly displayed on the patient.

- **IVs and Hemorrhagic Shock** Patients presenting with signs and symptoms of hemorrhagic shock should have IVs started en route to an appropriate receiving facility as soon as possible. As peripheral blood vessels constrict (shunt blood to the

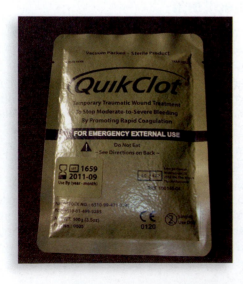

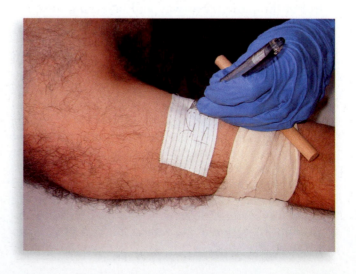

central circulation) and blood pressure drops, IV access becomes more difficult.

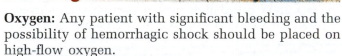

The Drug Box

Oxygen: Any patient with significant bleeding and the possibility of hemorrhagic shock should be placed on high-flow oxygen.

0.9% sodium chloride solution: An isotonic crystalloid solution used for volume replacement as the result of blood loss.

Lactated Ringer's solution: An isotonic crystalloid solution used for volume replacement as the result of blood loss.

References

1. P. E. Pepe, V. N. Mosesso, and J. L. Falk, "Prehospital Fluid Resuscitation of the Patient with Major Trauma." *Prehospital Emergency Care* 6 (2002): 81–91.
2. Ibid.
3. Ibid.
4. American College of Surgeons Committee on Trauma, *Advance Trauma Life Support for Doctors–Student Manual*, 6th ed. Chicago, IL: American College of Surgeons, 1997, p. 98.
5. G. Regel et al., "Prehospital Care, Importance of Early Intervention on Outcome." *Acta Anaesthesiologica Scandinavica* 110 (1997): 71–76.

Answers

Are You Ready?

1. The patient is sick. Any arterial bleeding, *characterized by pulsatile spurting,* is considered life-threatening until proven otherwise.

2. The first priority is scene safety. A panicked patient on a roof is a dangerous patient on a roof. Securing the patient on the roof or getting the patient safely to the ground should be a top priority. Then your priorities are bleeding control and the assurance that the patient has been assessed for airway, breathing, circulation, disability, and exposure (ABCDE).

3. The first step in achieving hemostasis in a patient with a severe external bleed is the application of direct pressure over the wound with sterile dressings. Elevate the affected extremity above the level of the heart if possible. If bleeding continues after direct pressure and elevation have been provided, pressure dressings and/or proximal pressure points **can** be utilized. If bleeding continues after the previous steps have been taken, the use of a tourniquet may be considered as a last-ditch effort to provide hemostasis. If a tourniquet is applied, the time of application needs to be clearly labeled on the patient's forehead, and the patient needs to be transported to an appropriate medical facility immediately. Note: When a tourniquet is applied, it cuts off all circulation distal to the point of application. Therefore, it is considered a technique of last resort.

You Are There: Reality-Based Cases

Case 1

1. The patient is seriously injured. The patient was involved in a motor vehicle collision that involved a tremendous mechanism of injury. The patient was initially unconscious upon the arrival of first responders, and he now presents with confusion. The patient presents with cutaneous signs of shock (cool, pale, moist skin) and vital signs indicative of hemodynamic instability. The patient's breathing is shallow and rapid with decreased breath sounds on the right side and an oxygen saturation of 92% on 15 L of oxygen via non-rebreather mask. There is an obvious chest injury with bruising and instability of the chest wall. The pelvis is unstable, and the lower extremities are severely injured.

2. The priority treatment for this patient will involve rapid transport to a trauma center following rapid sequence intubation. The patient's airway appears to be patent, but due to the fact that the ventilatory effort is inadequate (unstable chest wall, shallow and rapid respirations, oxygen saturation of 92% on oxygen at 15 L via non-rebreather mask), you should secure the airway and provide positive pressure ventilation for the patient.

3. Hemorrhagic shock. The patient was involved in a significant automobile crash. He has obvious bleeding from his lower extremities with multiple fractures, an unstable pelvis, and an unstable chest wall. He has the potential for critical bleeding from multiple sites. The patient doesn't appear to have any signs of sepsis, he has no history of cardiac problems, there doesn't appear to be any evidence of allergic reaction, and the patient appears to be neurologically intact.

4. When there is a decrease in blood flow to the kidneys as a result of hemorrhage, receptors in the kidneys increase the production of rennin (Figure 19-1). Renin decomposes a blood protein molecule called angiotensinogen, which releases a peptide called angiotensin I. An enzyme called angiotensin-converting enzyme (ACE), located in the lungs, converts angiotensin I to angiotensin II. Angiotensin II is carried in the bloodstream; when it reaches the adrenal cortex, it stimulates the release of aldosterone with the assistance of acetylcholine (ACh). Aldosterone functions to retain sodium (Na^+) ions and secrete potassium (K^+) ions. The retention of Na^+ ions results in the retention of water by osmosis in the tubules of the kidneys. The brain assists in this process by releasing antidiuretic hormone (ADH), which stimulates water reabsorption in the distal tubule of the kidney as well as increases the sensation of

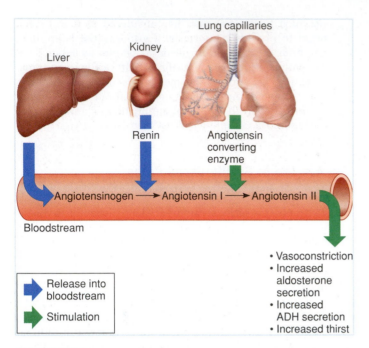

FIGURE 19-1   The formation of angiotensin II in the bloodstream involves several organs and multiple actions that conserve sodium and water.

thirst, which will hopefully make the person replace fluid that is being lost.

Another critical component to help with fluid loss from hemorrhage is the fluid found in the interstitial space. When hemorrhage occurs, the fluid from the interstitial space shifts into the intravascular space. This acts as a short-term stopgap to compensate for the fluid that is being lost through hemorrhage.

5. Hemostasis involves four components: vasoconstriction, platelet aggregation, fibrin formation, and fibrinolysis. Vasoconstriction begins almost immediately as arteries, arterioles, and some veins constrict in response to injury. This response helps to reduce bleeding and may even completely stop bleeding—at least temporarily. In addition, the cut ends of larger vessels can retract (through vasospasm), which also reduces bleeding. This physical reaction to vascular injury occurs rapidly and provides time for the coagulation phase of bleeding control to begin.

Platelets (thrombocytes) are free-floating structures in the bloodstream. When the platelets come into contact with damaged or injured blood vessels, they swell and change from a smooth slippery shape to a spiked shape. The platelets become sticky and secrete chemicals that activate other platelets to come and join together to form a plug. This process is referred to as aggregation. These activated platelets actually stick to one another and form a "platelet plug" at the site of the damage to the blood vessel. This event is referred to as agglutination or clumping. If the injury is minor, this may be the only control necessary to stop bleeding. If the injury is major, coagulation will begin.

The coagulation cascade is a complex chemical and biological process used to control bleeding. From initiation of the first signal indicating the injury to the vessel until the formation of a blood clot, usually less than 30 minutes is required.[4,5] When a blood vessel is injured, a complex process is set into motion to create a blood clot (Figure 19-2), Basically, a network of protein fibers, called fibrin, weave themselves together and trap red blood cells in order to form a blockage in the blood vessel and stop hemorrhage. The blood clot forms in three stages:

1. Stage I: Injury activates clotting factors that produce prothrombin activator (PTA).

2. Stage II: Platelets, calcium, and PTA activate prothrombin to create thrombin.

3. Stage III: Thrombin activates fibrinogen and forms the fibrin fibers (the net), which trap other blood cells to form the clot (thrombus). Once hemostasis has been achieved, the vessel can be repaired and the fibrin clot is destroyed (fibrinolysis) so that blood flow can resume.

6. Benazepril is an angiotensin-converting enzyme inhibitor, otherwise known as an ACE inhibitor.

7. Benazepril inhibits the conversion of angiotensin I to angiotensin II (a potent vasoconstrictor), resulting in decreased peripheral arterial resistance, decreased aldosterone production, and in turn decreased reabsorption of water. The net effect is lower blood pressure. When the body attempts to maintain blood pressure through the use of the renin-angiotensin-aldosterone system, the

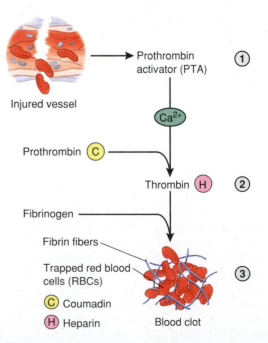

FIGURE 19-2   Following an injury, a complex sequence of events is set into motion that involves fibrin fibers weaving themselves together to form the framework of a blood clot and promote hemostasis.

presence of benazepril in the system will prevent these mechanisms from compensating for the hemorrhage.

Test Yourself

1. c

Cardiogenic shock is the result of a decrease in the heart's ability to supply the needed oxygen and nutrients to the tissues and cells, usually the result of a heart attack.

2. c

Carbon dioxide is the gaseous waste product of cellular respiration that is returned to the lungs for excretion.

3. d

The systemic inflammatory response (SIR) is the initiation of irreversible shock.

4. a

When compensatory mechanisms for shock cause peripheral vasoconstriction, blood flow to organ tissue decreases, and the cells are said to be in an ischemic phase.

5. a

The differences between blunt and penetrating trauma will directly affect the care that is required for the patient. For example, the recommendations for volume resuscitation of uncontrolled hemorrhage depend on the mechanism of injury. One study found that increased blood pressure from volume resuscitation resulted in more brisk bleeding, dislodgment of newly formed blood clots, and dilution of clotting factors in patients with penetrating injuries. Therefore, the current recommendation for patients with penetrating injuries is to obtain intravenous access and administer fluids at a low maintenance rate or KVO, which stands for "keep the vein open." However, both penetrating injuries and blunt force injuries are likely to require exposure and rapid transport, and both can cause major blood volume loss.

6. a

Evaluation of circulation is especially important in patients who are potentially suffering from hemorrhagic shock. The carotid and radial pulses are easily accessible and can be checked simultaneously and compared for rate, rhythm, and quality. Differences in quality or intensity between the carotid and radial pulses may signal that peripheral vasoconstriction exists and that the compensatory mechanisms for shock have begun.

7. Pneumothorax, chest deformity, evidence of rib fractures, significant chest deformities, small flail segment, rapidly distending abdomen, ecchymosis over the inferior abdominal wall, or evidence of a pelvic fracture.

Internal hemorrhage can be elusive, especially with the limitations of the out-of-hospital evaluation process. Many tools used to identify internal hemorrhage, like nuclear imaging and CT scans, are not available in the prehospital setting, so a high index of suspicion is required.

8. Class I is up to 15% blood volume loss (up to 750 mL). Class II is 15%–30% blood volume loss (750–1,500 mL). Class III is 30%–40% blood volume loss (1,500–2,000 mL). Class IV is greater than 40% blood volume loss (> 2,000 mL).

Because patients with Class I hemorrhage are virtually asymptomatic, these classes are most useful to emphasize the fact that significant blood loss can occur before the patient shows signs of shock or changes in hemodynamic status.

9. The compression of pressure points to achieve hemostasis is controversial because it can have some negative consequences. For instance, improper compression could occlude venous return but not the arterial supply to the limb, which could worsen bleeding. Finding the pulse to compress in a hypotensive patient can be quite difficult, and searching for the pressure point could divert attention away from the proven treatment of direct compression. Finally, there is no data in the medical literature to support its use.

Pressure points are areas of the body where an artery is either lying close to the surface of the skin or found directly over a bone. These are the places where a pulse can be felt when fingertip pressure is applied. When this area is compressed, the artery is pushed against the bone, limiting blood flow to the distal region of that portion of the body. Because use of pressure points for hemostasis is controversial, direct pressure over the bleeding site should always be attempted first.

10. b

Mineral zeolite powder (sold as QuikClot) absorbs water and concentrates clotting factors at the wound to stop bleeding. QuikClot is inert and nonallergenic, but the absorption of water can elevate the local temperature to 42°C–44°C, which is several degrees above the normal body temperature of 37°C. QuikClot is a powder that is poured directly on the wound from a single-use envelope.

11. False

At least two studies have shown that use of a PASG can increase mortality, especially for patients with thoracic trauma. These findings are also supported by animal studies, which found that if a PASG was inflated directly over the site of bleeding in the pelvic and abdominal areas, there was improved survival. However, if the source of hemorrhage was in the chest, survival was decreased.

12. d

In patients with suspected head trauma it is especially important to support their blood pressure with fluids as necessary to provide adequate cerebral perfusion. For a patient with existing cardiac and respiratory disease, or a patient who has any disease process that requires fluid restriction (for example, a dialysis patient), the patient should receive the 20-mL/kg bolus of fluid in several divided doses with continuous evaluation of the vital signs and clinical response during the treatment.

13. Is the hemorrhage controllable or uncontrolled? What is the mechanism of injury (blunt or penetrating trauma)? Is the patient in shock or showing signs of hypotension?

    Controllable or uncontrolled hemorrhage: in patients with uncontrolled bleeding, the only measure to take is rapid transport while continued efforts are made to control the bleeding. Mechanism of injury: studies show that patients with penetrating injuries may have a higher mortality and complication rate with prehospital fluid resuscitation. Shock: prudent volume resuscitation to reverse the signs of shock is recommended.

14. False

    Hemorrhage and shock from traumatic injuries have only one definitive treatment, and that is surgical intervention.

15. Shock is caused by inadequate oxygen and nutrient delivery to tissues. Shock causes anxiety, restlessness, altered mental status, tachycardia, tachypnea, pallor, cool and clammy skin, cyanosis, and hypotension. Untreated shock leads to organ failure and ultimately results in death.

    Although definitive treatment for hemorrhagic shock often requires surgical intervention, several interventions are effective and can be delivered in the out-of-hospital setting. Treatments may include: bleeding control, oxygen, ventilatory support, fluid resuscitation, cardiovascular support with catecholamines (depending on the type of shock and local protocols), calming and reassuring the patient, conserving the patient's body heat, and rapid transport.

chapter 20

Head, Face, and Neck Trauma

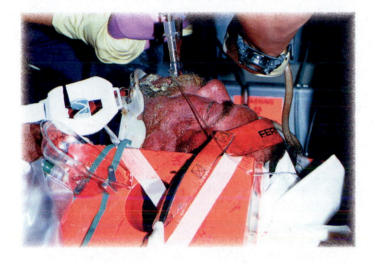

Are You Ready?

John Cruz is a 23-year-old male day laborer who was cleaning the gutters of the Smith family home when he slipped off of the ladder and fell into the bushes. When Mr. Smith returned home and noticed that John was nowhere to be found, he walked around the outside of the house to look for him. When he got to the back of the house, Mr. Smith saw the ladder on the ground and heard moaning coming from the bushes next to the storage shed. When Mr. Smith parted the leaves of the bush, he found John lying on his right side in a pool of blood, impaled by a gardening stake. The stake entered John's neck on the right anterior-lateral aspect just superior to his right clavicle. It exited the left side of his neck just inferior to the mastoid process. Mr. Smith ran to call 9-1-1.

1. What is your general impression of this patient?

_____

_____

_____

2. What zone of the neck did the stake enter, and what zone did the stake exit?

_____

_____

_____

3. Name three structures found in each of the zones described in question 2.

_____

_____

_____

4. What is your first priority after scene safety?

_____

_____

_____

5. Should the stake be removed in order to manage the airway?

_____

_____

_____

6. How will you manage the patient's cervical spine?

_____

_____

_____

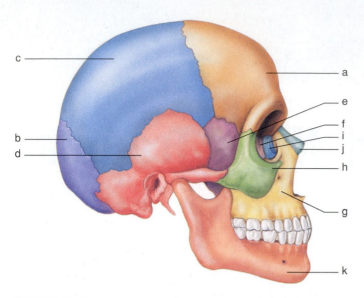

FIGURE 20-1

Active Learning

1. Anatomy Review

Label the bones of the skull in Figure 20-1:

a. _____

b. _____

c. _____

d. _____

e. _____

f. _____

g. _____

h. _____

i. _____

j. _____

k. _____

2. The opening at the base of the skull through which the spinal cord passes is called the _____.

3. Glasgow Coma Scale

Using the table on the next page, calculate a Glasgow Coma Scale score for patients a–h.

You Are There: Reality-Based Cases

Case 1

Max and Zach are known throughout town as two of the biggest bullies at the local high school. Today, as they were driving home from school, they spotted Jim Jones, a quiet kid riding his scooter in front of them.

Zach told Max to pull alongside Jim. As Max did so, Zach reached out the window and tried to poke at Jim with a golf club that he had in the car. Suddenly, Jim noticed that the road was making a sharp turn to the left and quickly stopped his scooter. Max failed to notice the turn and crashed the car head-on into a telephone pole.

When Max's car struck the telephone pole, Max flew face-first into the steering wheel, and Zach was ejected from the vehicle, flying head-first into a parked car.

Jim yelled at a woman in front of her house to call 9-1-1, and then ran over to check on Max and Zach.

Max was sitting in the driver's seat awake and alert with blood pouring out of his nose and a look of horror on his face. As Jim was checking on Max, a car pulled up and a man who saw the crash got out to help. Jim asked the man to hold Max's head still while he went to check on Zach.

Jim found Zach unconscious in the street in a prone position. He had snoring respirations and was bleeding from a large laceration to his forehead along his hairline. Jim could see a large dent in the door of the car that Zach had struck with his head after being ejected from the car. He had abrasions on the right side of his face, and his right forearm was deformed. Jim stayed with Zach, holding his head still, making sure that he could breathe, until help arrived.

A fire engine was the first to arrive. Jim gave the firefighters the abridged version of what had happened. The firefighter asked Jim to continue to hold the patient's head still while he performed an assessment.

Minutes later, you and your partner arrive on scene. When you arrive, you see that there are two patients being assessed by the fire crew.

1. Based on the preceding description of the patients, what is your general impression of Max and Zach's conditions?

_____

_____

_____

Active Learning Exercise 3				
Patient Information	Eyes	Verbal	Motor	Total GCS Score
a. 18-y/o male. Fell out of a cherry tree onto his head. He does not awaken to a sternal rub, but he mutters inappropriate words and groans. There is no response when you ask him to open his eyes. His pupils are dilated and slow to react.				
b. 6-y/o female struck by a car. Patient has obvious deformity to right side of head. Pupils are reactive to light. Patient is awake and confused. Patient does not know the month or year, but she tries to answer by saying, "Next week is my birthday, and I will be 3 years old." When you ask her to show you two fingers, she gives you a blank stare and does not respond. She swats your hand away when you pinch her arm.				
c. 87-y/o female. She was found on the floor of her bedroom this morning by her husband. She has vomited three times. Her husband says she hit her head hard last week but refused to go to the doctor. She opens her eyes to a sternal rub. She mutters when you ask her the date and is unable to show you two fingers when asked. She flexes her arms and balls up her fists when you pinch her shoulder, but she does not move out of the way or attempt to brush away your hand.				
d. 18-y/o male in an MVC. Patient is awake. He tells you it is April 4, 1993, when you ask the day/date (the actual date is the current date). When you ask him to show you two fingers, he giggles and flips you off with both hands. You note a strong odor of alcohol on his breath and track marks on his arms.				
e. 12-y/o female fall victim. Patient was thrown down 12 wooden steps by her older brother during a fight. She landed on a concrete basement floor. She opens her eyes to a shoulder pinch and mumbles nonsensical words when you ask her the day/date. When you pinch her hand, she pulls it into her body. Her pupils are sluggish but do react to light.				
f. 24-y/o male assault patient. He was struck on the side of his head with a baseball bat during a bar fight. No fractures are noted upon exam. The patient is unconscious, yet his eyes open to pain. He grunts and says "1963" when you ask him the date (the actual date is the current date). He lifts his arm and does not show two fingers when you ask him to. He withdraws his hand upon painful stimulus to the back of his hand.				
g. 28-y/o female struck in the head by a surfboard. The patient was pulled from the water unconscious with ABCs intact. Patient awakens when you say "Hey, are you okay?" She shows you two fingers when asked and is confused on the date. She keeps asking you "What happened?" over and over again.				
h. 65-y/o interfacility transport patient. Your patient is on a ventilator and suffered a stroke 7 days ago. His eyes are closed, but they react slowly to light. The patient cannot speak due to the ET tube. He is unconscious. The patient extends his hand and fans out his fingers with a strong pinch to his dorsum.				

2. What is your first priority?

_____

_____

_____

3. What are the priorities of treatment for Max and Zach?

_____

_____

_____

As you approach Max, you see that there is a firefighter in the back seat of the car holding manual cervical alignment, and there is another firefighter who is sizing up and about to apply a cervical collar. The patient continues to have blood pouring out of his nose, and you notice that he is retching (dry heaving). The first thing that you do when you approach is introduce yourself and feel the patient's wrist to check for a radial pulse. The patient's skin appears slightly pale and moist, but he has a strong, regular radial pulse at a rate of approximately 80 beats per minute. You introduce yourself to the patient, and ask the patient his name. In a shaky voice, he responds by saying that his name is Max. The patient is able to follow simple commands and appears to be maintaining his airway adequately. In addition to bilateral epistaxis, your assessment reveals instability to Max's midface with associated crepitus and ecchymosis. Max complains of neck pain and pain to his bilateral knees.

4. How will you secure Max's cervical spine?

_____

_____

_____

5. What types of fractures are associated with midface instability?

_____

_____

_____

6. How can you help control the epistaxis?

_____

_____

_____

As the firefighters place Max in c-spine precautions, you go over to assist your partner with Zach. He remains unconscious and, as you approach, your partner is completing his assessment of the posterior aspect of Zach's body after cutting off his clothes. Your partner is concerned about Zach's level of consciousness and his snoring respirations. He has placed a long spine board beside Zach. Zach does not open his eyes to painful stimuli and he has no verbal response, but he responds to pain by withdrawing. Zach has periods of apnea lasting up to 30 seconds, followed by gradually increasing depth and frequency of respirations.

7. What is Zach's Glasgow Coma Scale score?

_____

_____

_____

8. How will you manage Zach's airway?

_____

_____

_____

9. How would you describe Zach's respirations?

_____

_____

_____

A firefighter takes over manual cervical spine alignment from Jim, and your partner applies an appropriately sized c-collar. The firefighter positions himself for the log-roll and states, "We will roll on my count, on three. One . . . two . . . three." As the firefighter says "three," you, your partner, and the firefighter log-roll the patient while the other firefighter positions the long board. When the roll is complete, the firefighter at the head continues to maintain manual c-spine alignment, your partner assesses the patient's airway, and you complete the removal of the patient's clothing so that the anterior surface of the patient can be assessed. Your visual assessment of the patient's anterior surface reveals no new obvious findings, other than the fact that the patient's right pupil is dilated and fixed, and the left pupil is 4 mm and reactive to light. Your partner states that the patient has trismus and he can't open the patient's mouth.

10. What is the significance of unequal pupils (the patient's right pupil is dilated and fixed, and the left pupil is 4 mm and reactive to light)?

_____

_____

_____

11. If you decide to perform rapid sequence intubation (RSI) on this patient with a possible head injury and trismus, what are some possible negative consequences of oral intubation in a patient with this presentation?

_____

_____

_____

12. Are there any steps that you can take to reduce or prevent the negative consequences you listed for question 11?

_____

_____

_____

13. List several positive and negative consequences of ventilating a potentially head-injured patient with a bag-mask via an endotracheal tube.

_____

_____

_____

Test Yourself

1. Explain how facial injuries can cause significant airway compromise.

_____

_____

2. Your intoxicated patient was involved in a fight. His vital signs are BP of 80/52, HR of 120, and RR of 8. Further assessment reveals cerebrospinal fluid leaking from the nose and ears, as well as Battle's sign presentation and preservation. You are unable to make a conclusion about your patient's condition based on your neurological exam. What is likely complicating the assessment process?

_____

_____

3. Your patient opens his eyes, withdraws to pain, and attempts to speak in incomprehensible sounds. What is this patient's Glasgow Coma Score?

_____

_____

4. Your patient has suddenly collapsed. A detailed history reveals that your patient fell off a second-story roof yesterday. You learn that your patient had a brief lapse of consciousness and was diagnosed with a concussion. Prior to collapsing, your patient was complaining of a headache and visual disturbances. A check of the vital signs reveals a BP of 200/110, HR of 50, and erratic respirations. What is likely the cause of your patient's signs and symptoms?
  a. Diffuse axonal injury
  b. Subarachnoid hematoma
  c. Cerebral contusion
  d. Epidural hematoma

5. What is the goal of prehospital treatment of traumatic brain injury?

_____

_____

6. List some of the structures in the neck that can be easily damaged with neck trauma.

_____

_____

7. Your patient jumped from the second-story balcony while trying to escape a fire. He struck his head on the concrete below. You note obvious trauma to the posterior region of his skull; however, your patient is exhibiting bizarre and uncharacteristic behavior. What is likely the cause of his condition?
  a. A coup-contrecoup injury affecting the cerebellum
  b. A coup-contrecoup injury affecting the frontal lobe
  c. A coup-contrecoup injury affecting the temporal lobe
  d. A coup-contrecoup injury affecting the parietal lobe

8. Your patient has sustained a closed head injury as a result of an MVC. You note a large hematoma along the frontal-parietal margin on the right side. Vital signs are BP of 110/80, HR of 120, RR of 16, and GCS of 10 (E-2, V-3, M-5). En route to the hospital the patient's mental status begins to deteriorate. Reassessment of the patient reveals that the right pupil is dilated and is nonreactive to light. The left pupil is normal. Updated vital signs are BP of 180/110, HR of 48, RR of 6, and GCS of 4 (E-1, V-1, M-2). You should suspect
  a. transection of the brain stem.
  b. herniation of the brain.
  c. compression of the vagus nerve (X).
  d. lesion in the brain.

9. Your patient was a restrained driver involved in an MVC. Your patient has a hoarse voice, stridor, and subcutaneous emphysema. You should suspect
  a. dissection of the carotid artery.
  b. transection of nerves in the neck.
  c. laryngeal fracture.
  d. pulmonary effusion.

10. Damage to the reticular activating system (RAS) may result in changes in _____.

11. You respond to a single-car MVC—car versus parked car. Your patient's vehicle has minor front-end damage on the passenger's side. The windshield is intact. The patient was a restrained driver with no air bag deployment. Assessment reveals that he is unconscious with snoring respirations and a GCS of 9 (E-2, V-3, M-4), BP of 106/72, HR of 120, and RR of 8. He appears uninjured. You note a prescription for insulin on the passenger seat with the patient's name on it. What is the most likely cause of the patient's altered mental status, and the easiest cause to determine and treat?

   a. LeFort's II fracture

   b. Epidural hematoma

   c. Basilar skull fracture

   d. Hypoglycemia

12. Your patient is a small child who was attempting to imitate a magic trick by placing peas up his nose. In an attempt to show off his trick, he ran into the next room where he tripped and fell. The peas broke free from his nasal cavity and were released into his airway. The child is conscious, unable to speak or cough, and is not moving any air. How should you manage this patient?

   a. Leave the remaining peas in his nose and perform the Heimlich maneuver.

   b. Remove the remaining peas from his nose and perform the Heimlich maneuver.

   c. Leave the remaining peas in his nose and suction his airway.

   d. Remove the remaining peas from his nose and suction his airway.

13. The total displacement of a tooth from its socket is called _____ .

14. Septal fractures and epistaxis are often associated with nasal trauma.
True
False

15. Hemotympanum can be caused by penetrating or blunt trauma that fractures the _____ .

16. Which of the following are most likely to cause secondary brain injury?

   a. Hypoxia and hypotension

   b. Hypoxia and hypertension

   c. Hyperventilation and hypertension

   d. Hyperventilation and hypocarbia

17. Your patient with facial trauma is complaining of nausea, vomiting, and a headache. Your assessment reveals pain with eye movement and decreased vision. The right globe and pupil appear to be misshapen. What is the most appropriate treatment to prevent an increase in intracranial and/or intraocular pressure?

   a. Treat nausea and vomiting.

   b. Treat your patient's headache.

   c. Bandage the injured eye with a sterile dressing.

   d. Provide the patient with a 20-mL/kg bolus of isotonic IV fluid.

18. You suspect your patient has a closed head injury. Your assessment reveals damage to the right orbit causing a protruding globe. Vital signs are BP of 160/100, HR of 68, RR of 6, and GCS of 8 (E-2, V-3, M-3). Your patient begins to vomit. You should be most concerned about which of the following possibilities?

   a. Decreased intraocular pressure

   b. Blood loss from the eye injury

   c. Decreased intracranial pressure

   d. Increased intracranial pressure

19. In which of the following situations would you most likely suspect a spinal injury?

   a. A witnessed trip and fall in which the patient is complaining of arm pain only.

   b. A witnessed fall from a standing position with a hip injury, no loss of consciousness, and no additional injuries or complaints.

   c. A fall from a chair with an isolated leg injury and no additional complaints, no loss of consciousness, and no neck or back pain.

   d. A fall from a third-story roof with a head injury and loss of consciousness.

20. The major vessels of the neck, the esophagus, and the larynx lie in zone III.
True
False

Need to Know

The following represent the Key Objectives of Chapter 20:

1. *Assess, formulate a field impression, and implement a treatment plan for patients with:*

- *Traumatic brain injuries and skull fractures*
- *Facial fractures*
- *Fractured larynx and penetrating trauma to the neck*
- *Injuries to the eyes and ears*

Injuries to the head, face, and neck are some of the most serious injuries that an individual can sustain. In fact, traumatic brain injury (TBI) is one of the leading causes of death and disability in the United States. Head injuries can range from very minor to life threatening. Objective assessment findings that are indicative of severe head injuries include, but are not limited to, altered mental status, unequal pupils, irregular respirations, severe hypertension or hypotension, and posturing.

Head injuries are often associated with neck and spinal injuries; the use of cervical spine immobilization on these patients is very important. If you have a patient with trauma above the clavicle, that individual is automatically a strong candidate for c-spine precautions.

Head injuries are also often accompanied by facial injuries. These injuries offer some challenges as far as airway management and bleeding control. Neck injuries, like facial injuries, are also serious and present many challenges for the paramedic. The most life threatening are injuries directly to or affecting the airway. Additionally, the neck has a number of very large and important blood vessels and nerves. An injury to the neck can lead to life-threatening bleeding.

2. *Describe the management of a patient with traumatic brain injury (TBI).*

Assessment of the initial level of consciousness (LOC) and frequent reassessment of the LOC when treating a patient with a suspected head injury or TBI is crucial. The Glasgow Coma Score (GCS) is a widely used and accepted means of assessing a patient's LOC. Rapid recognition of a patient with a potential TBI is critical; once a TBI is suspected, rapid transport to a facility capable of appropriately treating a TBI patient is crucial. The paramedic must be aware of the appropriate treatments that should be performed for the TBI patient en route to the trauma center. These treatments include protecting the airway and providing adequate oxygenation, supporting ventilation as necessary, and preventing hypotension.

Connections

- Chapter 30, Neurology, in the textbook describes and illustrates the 12 cranial nerves.
- Chapter 12, Airway Management, Ventilation, and Oxygenation, in the textbook describes end-tidal CO_2, capnography, and advanced airway maneuvers.
- Chapter 35, Toxicology, in the textbook reviews the effects of alcohol intoxication.
- Chapter 11, The Normal Physical Examination, in the textbook reviews assessment of the pupils.
- Link to the companion DVD for a chapter-based quiz, audio glossary, animations, games and exercises, and, when appropriate, skill sheets and skill Step-by-Steps.

Street Secrets

- **Head Injury and Intoxication** Patients with head injuries can display behavior very similar to an intoxicated individual. The difference between patients with head injuries and intoxicated individuals is that, if you disregard head-injured patients as "just drunks" and do not treat them, they can die or suffer permanent disability. If, on the other hand, you treat intoxicated patients as if they have head injuries, there will be no negative consequences. Even the intoxicated individual whom you are called to treat on a regular basis can fall and suffer a head injury. In fact, the intoxicated individual you see frequently stands a far greater chance of suffering a head injury than most people who do not partake of alcohol to excess on a daily basis.
- **Need for Suction** Because patients with head injuries can present with an altered level of consciousness, nausea, and vomiting as a result of increased intracranial pressure, it is always a good idea to have a suction device readily available in the event that clearing the airway becomes necessary.

The Drug Box

There are no specific drugs related to this chapter content.

Need to Do

The following skills are explained and illustrated in a step-by-step manner, via skill sheets and/or Step-by-Steps in this text and on the accompanying DVD:

Skill Name	Skill Sheet Number and Location	Step-by-Step Number and Location
Airway Positioning and Maneuvers	1 – DVD	1 – DVD
ALS Airway Adjuncts	8 – DVD	N/A
Needle Cricothyroidotomy	19 – Appendix A and DVD	19 – Chapter 12 and DVD
Blood Glucose Assessment	26 – DVD	26 – DVD
Trauma Scoring (includes GCS)	31 – DVD	N/A
Bleeding Control and Shock	66 – DVD	66 – DVD
Seated Spinal Immobilization	68 – DVD	68 – DVD
Standing Spinal Immobilization	69 – DVD	N/A
Supine Spinal Immobilization	70 – DVD	70 – DVD
Helmet Removal	71 – DVD	71 – DVD
Traumatic Brain Injury Assessment	76 – DVD	N/A
NREMT Patient Assessment Trauma	83 – DVD	N/A
NREMT Spinal Immobilization (Seated Patient)	92 – DVD	N/A
NREMT Spinal Immobilization (Supine Patient)	93 – DVD	N/A
NREMT Bleeding Control/Shock Management	94 – DVD	N/A

Answers

Are You Ready?

1. John is sick. Any penetrating trauma to the neck is life threatening until proven otherwise.

2. The stake entered zone I and exited from zone III (Figure 20-2).

3. Zone I: Any three of the following: vertebral arteries, carotid arteries, thoracic vessels, lung apex, esophagus, trachea, thoracic duct, and spinal cord.

   Zone III: Any three of the following: vertebral arteries, carotid arteries, pharynx, and spinal cord.

4. The greatest priority is airway. Because there is so much potential for critical bleeding from this area, be aware of any uncontrolled hemorrhage. There is also a strong possibility of cervical spine involvement, so c-spine precautions need to be taken.

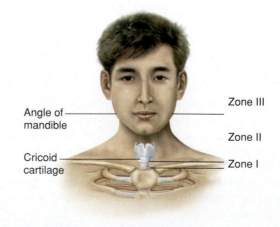

FIGURE 20-2 Zones of the neck.

5. No. Only as an absolute last resort should an impaled object be removed. It should only be removed if there is absolutely no other way to manage the airway. If the object is causing a considerable airway obstruction, consider the use of an advanced airway such as a surgical or needle cricothyroidotomy, for example.

6. After the stake has been cut at the base so that the patient can be transported to the hospital, the patient should be placed on a spinal immobilization board utilizing manual cervical spine immobilization. The use of a cervical collar can result in further injury or airway compromise, so creative c-spine immobilization may need to take place. This could include the use of pillows, foam blocks, a rolled-up sheet or blanket wrapped around the top of the head, or other means that allow you to prevent movement of the head or neck—without interfering with the impaled object or the airway. Please consider local policies and protocols when making this decision, and, if necessary, consult medical direction or your clinical supervisor.

Active Learning

1. a. frontal; b. occipital; c. parietal; d. temporal; e. sphenoid; f. ethmoid; g. maxilla; h. zygomatic; i. lacrimal; j. nasal; k. mandible

2. Foramen magnum

3. GCS Exercise

Patient	Eyes	Verbal	Motor	Total
a	1	2	1	4
b	4	3	5	12
c	2	2	3	7
d	4	4	6	14
e	2	2	3	7
f	2	4	4	10
g	3	4	6	13
h	1	1	2	4

You Are There: Reality-Based Cases

Case 1

1. Max is sick. He has a significant mechanism of injury and, due to the epistaxis, he has a potentially serious airway compromise issue. Zach is very sick. He not only has a significant mechanism of injury (ejection from a vehicle), but he has a significant head injury and is unconscious with snoring respirations.

2. The first priority is scene safety. It is also a good idea, very early on, to make sure that you have sufficient resources. If you don't, request them before you become committed to patient care.

3. The priorities for Max are maintaining a patent airway while immobilizing his cervical spine and completing a

primary (ABCDE) assessment. Priorities for Zach are the same.

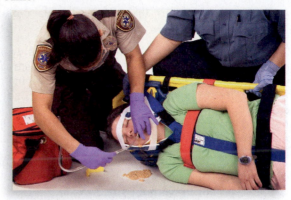

4. There are a couple of possibilities for securing the c-spine in patients suffering from severe epistaxis, and the method that you choose should be based on local policies and protocols, or the standards set forth by your provider. Placing the patient in an appropriately sized c-collar and then applying a Kendrick Extrication Device (KED) or short spine board, while keeping the patient in a seated position, is one possibility. This method does not offer true immobilization of the spine and, unless the patient is leaning forward, blood can still be swallowed and cause nausea, emesis, and airway compromise. Another possibility is to thoroughly immobilize the patient on a long spinal board (torso first, followed by the head) and then turn the entire spine board, keeping the patient on his or her side to allow for drainage of blood and to prevent or reduce the risk of emesis and aspiration of blood.

5. LeFort fractures. Typically midface instability is indicative of a LeFort fracture, of which there are three types (Figure 20-3):

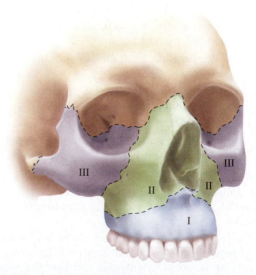

FIGURE 20-3 LeFort fractures.

a. LeFort I—a fracture through the floor of the maxillary sinuses

b. LeFort II—a fracture through the maxillary sinuses

c. LeFort III—a fracture through the orbits

6. Treatment for a patient with epistaxis is generally aimed at protecting the airway, but controlling bleeding by applying digital pressure to the nose and applying cold packs or ice to decrease or limit swelling may be attempted. The practices of packing the nose or inserting nasal tampons or balloons are typically reserved for the hospital setting.

7. Zach has a GCS of 6 (he does not open his eyes to painful stimuli [1], he has no verbal response [1], but he responds to pain by withdrawing [4]).

8. There are several factors to consider regarding the management of Zach's airway:

   • Zach has a closed head injury. You do not want to increase intracranial pressure during the process of establishing an airway.

   • If you do not isolate Zach's airway, he will have an increased risk of aspiration.

   • Zach may have a c-spine injury and, because of the need to maintain Zach's spine in an in-line position, the insertion of an advanced airway becomes more challenging.

   • With Zach in a prone position, you have been unable to adequately evaluate his airway, and as such, you don't know what to expect.

   Because of your concerns and several unanswered questions regarding Zach's airway, you must be prepared with a number of airway adjuncts that could be used in the management of his airway.

9. A respiratory pattern marked by periods of apnea lasting up to 30 seconds, followed by gradually increasing depth and frequency of respirations, is referred to as *Cheyne-Stokes respirations*.

10. One large fixed pupil in an unconscious patient indicates herniation until proven otherwise.

11. Some of the negative consequences of oral intubation in a head-injured patient include:

    • Risk of aspiration from emesis produced by laryngoscope manipulation.

    • Risk of increased intracranial pressure.

    • Risk of bradycardia stimulation by stimulating the vagus nerve during intubation.

    • An inability to successfully intubate the patient once the RSI medications have been delivered will leave the airway unprotected.

12. The following are measures that can be taken in order to avoid some of the complications identified in question 11:

    • Until the airway is isolated, there is always the risk of aspiration of stomach contents. Ensuring that the airway is properly opened and that the ventilations being delivered are not too rapid or too forceful will decrease the chances of gastric insufflation and potential emesis.

    • Although there is currently no evidence to support the use of intravenous lidocaine as a pretreatment for RSI in patients with head injury, lidocaine administration 3 or more minutes prior to intubation is said to decrease the incidence of increased intracranial pressure and is part of the RSI protocol in many EMS systems.

    • A failure to intubate and thus isolate the trachea with an endotracheal tube (ETT) following the administration of RSI medications is not a hopeless scenario. The airway can be maintained and oxygenation and ventilation performed without an ETT, as there are other means of providing for an open airway (e.g., oropharyngeal airway [OPA], nasopharyngeal airway [NPA], laryngeal mask airway [LMA], or dual-lumen airway), although they do not isolate the trachea.

13. The advantages of ventilating a head-injured patient with an ETT are providing oxygenation; providing or supplementing ventilation; and controlling CO_2 levels, influencing intracranial pressure (ICP) and cerebral perfusion pressure (CPP). The disadvantage of ventilating a head-injured patient via an ETT is inadvertently hyperventilating the patient, which can lead to hypocarbia and vasoconstriction.

Test Yourself

1. Injuries to the lips, teeth, and tongue may result in aspiration or obstruction from fractured teeth or dentures. Significant facial trauma can also cause bleeding into the airway.

   It is particularly important to evaluate patients with facial injuries for obstruction of the airway or aspiration from a fractured tooth, dentures, or blood.

2. Alcohol can lead to respiratory depression and hypotension.

   Alcohol intoxication and head injury is a common combination. Acute and chronic alcohol abuse can lead to hemodynamic and respiratory depression. Alcohol also acts as a CNS depressant and can mask clinical symptoms. Because these patients have an unreliable neurological exam that prevents clinical clearance of injury, they should be assumed to have spinal and intracranial injury until proven otherwise.

3. (Eye opening to pain = 2) + (Incomprehensible sounds = 2) + (Withdrawing from pain = 4) = GCS of 8.

   The GCS gives an objective measurement of the level of consciousness. It is a simple test for the initial assessment of the level of consciousness and is repeated to determine improvement or deterioration from the initial assessment. The three components are based on eye, motor, and verbal responses (see Box 20-3 in the textbook).

4. d

   The classic presentation of a patient with an epidural hematoma is a brief loss of consciousness, followed by a period of lucidity that lasts from a few minutes to hours, and then rapid and severe decompensation with a headache, vomiting, and loss of consciousness. Many times these patients are erroneously diagnosed with a concussion.

5. The goal in traumatic brain injury (TBI) is to prevent further damage by preventing and treating secondary causes of TBI, which include hypoxia and hypotension.

    TBI is somewhat unique in that it involves two components of injury, one which the paramedic can do nothing about (the primary injury), and the other which it is critical that the paramedic do something to prevent (secondary injury). Oxygenation, ventilation, and prevention and treatment of low blood pressure and low pulse oximetry readings are critical to prevent secondary brain injuries.

6. Carotid and vertebral arteries, jugular veins, esophagus, trachea, lower cranial nerves, thyroid gland, and brachial plexus.

    The neck has little to protect it from traumatic injuries, including injuries to the carotid and vertebral arteries, jugular veins, esophagus, trachea, lower cranial nerves, thyroid gland, brachial plexus, and spinal cord. Although the spinal cord can be injured with significant neck trauma, it is well protected by the bony vertebral column.

7. b

    Coup-contrecoup often occurs during deceleration injuries in which the head strikes an object, damaging that region of the brain, and then the brain is driven into the skull on the opposing side of the brain (contrecoup, see Box 20-1 in the textbook). In this case the posterior region, most likely the occipital region, was struck initially and likely damaged the frontal lobe, which affects personality and accounts for the patient's bizarre and uncharacteristic behavior.

8. b

    During uncal herniation of the brain, the oculomotor nerve (III) is compressed, creating dilation of the pupil on the affected side. The pupil on the affected side becomes nonreactive to light, while the unaffected pupil functions normally. The presence of Cushing's triad also indicates a herniating brain.

9. c

    A hoarse voice, stridor, and subcutaneous emphysema are signs and symptoms associated with tracheal laceration, laryngeal fracture, and expanding hematomas that lead to airway compromise.

10. Level of consciousness

    The reticular activating system is a part of the reticular formation that extends from the brain stem to the midbrain and thalamus with connections distributed throughout the cerebral cortex. It controls the degree of activity of the central nervous system and is thus responsible for level of consciousness (see Box 20-1 in the textbook).

11. d

    It is important to check blood glucose in all patients with altered mental status. It is possible that the patient's hypoglycemia was the cause of the MVC; however, don't discount the possibility of internal injuries to the head, chest, and abdomen.

12. a

    Because the peas were released into the airway, the child has begun to choke and possibly aspirate the peas. The Heimlich maneuver is beneficial in the conscious patient. Suctioning the airway may not release the peas, and the remaining peas should not be removed from the nose because further airway compromise may result.

13. An avulsion

    Avulsion accounts for up to 16 percent of all injuries to teeth. It is necessary to reimplant avulsed permanent teeth as soon as possible. Reimplantation is possible if performed within 2 to 3 hours. To minimize this time, ideally the patient or health-care provider at the scene should reimplant the tooth.

14. True

    Traumatic fracture of the nose is common with head and neck fractures and is associated with septal fractures and epistaxis.

15. Base of the skull

    Penetrating or blunt trauma that fractures the base of the skull can cause bleeding within the middle ear (hemotympanum) that likewise compromises hearing and may disrupt the normal sense of balance by damaging the vestibular labyrinth.

16. a

    Secondary brain injuries occur after the primary injury when the patient is allowed to become hypotensive and hypoxic.

17. a

    A globe rupture may produce symptoms of an irregular-shaped pupil and globe. It is important not to apply pressure to the globe. Both eyes should be covered to prevent sympathetic eye movement. The headache in this case is of little consequence. The nausea and vomiting should be treated quickly as vomiting increases intraocular pressure that may worsen the injury.

18. d

    Vomiting can cause airway concerns, especially aspiration in the unconscious patient. Additionally, vomiting can increase intraocular and intracranial pressure, thus worsening the head injury.

19. d

    Suspect a spinal injury any time a patient presents with a head injury or the mechanism of injury is unknown or unwitnessed (e.g., "person down") and take appropriate spinal precautions.

20. False

Zone I contains the vertebral and carotid arteries, thoracic vessels, lung apex, esophagus, trachea, thoracic duct, and spinal cord. Zone II contains the vertebral and carotid arteries, jugular vein, esophagus, larynx, and spinal cord. Zone III contains the vertebral and carotid arteries, pharynx, and spinal cord (see Box 20-4 in the textbook).

chapter 21

Thoracic Trauma

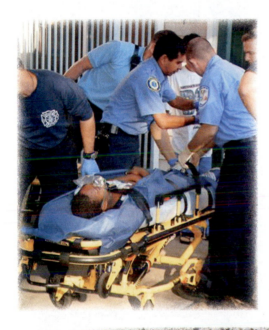

Are You Ready?

A 15-year-old male has just been stabbed in the right lower anterior chest, just to the left of the sternal border. He presents sitting on the street curb, his shirt and pants bloody and torn. He is alert and denies having difficulty breathing. Exposing the chest revealed a half-inch incision that is steadily oozing blood.

1. What are your initial treatment steps? Which step will you perform *first*?

_____

_____

_____

Active Learning

Anatomy Review

1. Name the landmarks identified in Figure 21-1.

a. _____

b. _____

c. _____

d. _____

e. _____

2. What five structures do the ribs protect?

_____

_____

_____

3. In a male patient, the _____ intercostal space is typically located at the level of the nipple.

4. The _____ nerve innervates the diaphragm and assists with respiration.

5. Identify the structures in Figure 21-2.

a. _____   e. _____

b. _____   f. _____

c. _____   g. _____

d. _____   h. _____

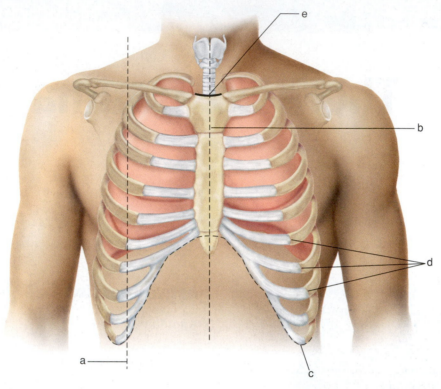

FIGURE 21-1

6. Barbecue Anyone?

The next time you are at the supermarket, stop by the meat section. You should be able to find beef or pork ribs in the refrigerated section; make sure they are not frozen! Once you locate a side of ribs in its packaging, close your eyes for a minute and "palpate" the ribs with the fingers of one hand. Imagine that you have a 12-gauge needle in your other hand. Keeping your eyes closed, imagine guiding the tip of the needle into an appropriate site, just over the rib. It may help to imagine placing the tip of the needle directly on top of the rib and then dragging it up and into the intercostal space. (Another option is to purchase the ribs, bring them home, and try the exercise. Afterward, you can then "eat what you learned"!)

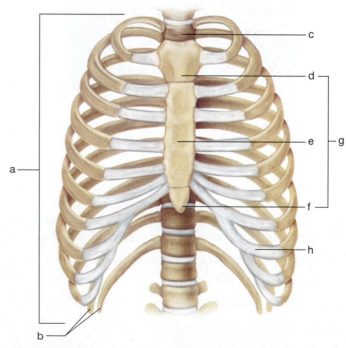

FIGURE 21-2

7. Tap Dance

Percussing the chest wall for the presence of free air or blood in the cavity is an old technique, dating back to 1754 when Leopold Auenbrugger noted that percussed sounds could indicate an abnormality under the skin.[1] As you read in Chapter 11, The Normal Physical Examination, in the textbook, the technique of percussion is limited in the out-of-hospital arena due to ambient noise issues. However, with practice you might be able to use this technique to help differentiate different resonant sounds.

You can try this technique using common fruit found in the supermarket. Find a large cantaloupe. First, using the technique described in Chapter 11, tap the side of the melon. You should be able to hear a specific sound. Tap a bit harder until the sound becomes clear to you, even in a noisy environment. Now, try placing your index and middle fingers side by side and tap with *two* fingers of the other hand over the first two fingers. Is it louder?

Move to a different type of melon, such as a watermelon. Better yet, place two types of melons side by side and tap each one. Go back and forth and see if you can hear the difference. Now here is the *pièce de résistance:* Buy both melons and bring them home. Cut open each melon widthwise. Is there a difference in the internal structure? One may be hollow in the center, the other full of flesh all the way through. Can you correlate the sound you heard with the hollowness of the fruit? How might that relate to the hollowness of an air-filled chest cavity or the fullness of a blood-filled one?

Bonus: Do this exercise at a moment when you are hungry. Just before eating, percuss over areas of the body that are dense, such as the liver in the right upper quadrant. Then, percuss over the stomach, which should be mostly empty. Do you hear a difference? Is it similar to the melons you've been working with?

You Are There: Reality-Based Cases

Case 1 *(continuation of chapter opener)*

You have finished your primary assessment of the patient from the opening scenario and have begun transport. While trying to palpate a blood pressure, you observe that the patient is becoming restless. He is supine on the gurney but is trying to sit up. You try to coax him to stay lying flat. You realize that his breathing rate

has increased significantly. His radial pulse has become weak and faster than before.

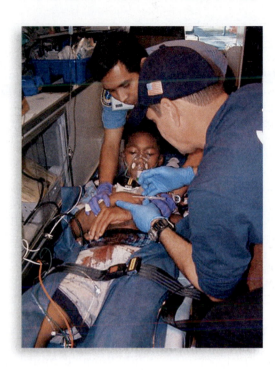

1. What might be causing the patient's change in presentation (identify at least three possible reasons)? How can you try to differentiate between them?

_____

_____

_____

2. Of the possible causes you listed in question 1, which one will be most life threatening? What can you do to correct the situation?

_____

_____

_____

Lifting the occlusive dressing off the wound does not relieve the patient's respiratory distress. He is quite pale now and diaphoretic. You auscultate the lung fields; the right side is much fainter now than compared with when you listened on scene. The blood pressure monitor now reads 84/68. The ECG indicates a sinus tachycardia at a rate of 138.

3. What other physical findings should you recheck now? Based on your findings, what would you do next?

_____

_____

_____

At the trauma center the surgical team performs a thoracotomy. A liter of blood is evacuated from the right chest cavity. Later you learn that the team also repaired a perforated diaphragm during surgery. The patient remains in surgical intensive care for another 2 weeks.

4. Do these findings confirm your suspicions?

_____

_____

_____

Test Yourself

1. The most common major thoracic injury in the pediatric population is _____.

2. During an assault, a patient was struck in the chest several times with a metal pole. He is presenting with hemoptysis and mild dyspnea. You should suspect a pulmonary laceration.
   True
   False

3. What is the potential advantage of administering a narcotic analgesic to a patient with rib fractures?

   _____

   _____

4. How should you treat a patient with a flail chest segment?

   _____

   _____

5. A patient was struck in the chest by flying debris during a tornado. He complains of weakness, shortness of breath, and left-sided chest pain. He appears pale and is cool to the touch. His pulse is rapid and thready. When listening to his lung sounds, you note decreased breath sounds in his

right hemithorax. His vital signs are BP of 80/60, HR of 130, and RR of 36. What is the most likely cause of these findings?

_____

_____

6. Breathing carefully with less than normal volume in an effort to avoid pain is called _____.

7. A 22-year-old male patient has been extricated from a motor vehicle that was involved in a high-speed frontal collision with a large tree. Upon examination, you find the patient unresponsive with irregular, shallow breathing and significant subcutaneous emphysema throughout the upper chest, neck, and face. The patient was not wearing a seat belt, and the vehicle did not have an air bag. You have determined that the patient has a partial transection of his trachea. What is the best option for managing this patient's airway?

   _____

   _____

8. A small child began experiencing dyspnea, tachypnea, tachycardia, and cyanosis a few hours after being kicked in the chest by a horse. Upon examination, you notice a paradoxical chest movement and decreased breath sounds. What is the most likely cause of these findings?

   _____

   _____

9. The _____ tethers the aortic arch to the pulmonary artery outflow tract.

10. Explain the importance of negative pressure in the chest cavity.

    _____

    _____

Scenario: While rock climbing, a patient is struck in the chest by a large falling rock. The patient is complaining of pain, general weakness, and difficulty breathing. His lung sounds are diminished on the side of the injury, and you notice paradoxical movement of the chest wall during respirations.

11. Which best describes the patient's trauma?
    a. Blunt force compression injury to the thorax
    b. A combination of compression and shearing force trauma

   c. Blunt force trauma caused by a shearing force
   d. Penetrating force trauma to the thorax

12. What is the likely cause of this patient's presentation?
   a. Flail chest injury
   b. Cardiac tamponade
   c. Lung laceration
   d. Lung contusion

Scenario: Your patient was thrown to the ground during an explosion in a garage. She complains of shortness of breath. Your physical exam reveals several lacerations and puncture wounds on her anterior body.

13. The paramedic should suspect barotrauma to the patient's
   a. face and neck.
   b. brain and spinal cord.
   c. alveoli and lungs.
   d. arms and legs.

14. While transporting the patient, you observe that her trachea is deviated to the left and her lung sounds are absent on the right. You should suspect
   a. right-side tension pneumothorax.
   b. right-side simple pneumothorax.
   c. left-side hemothorax.
   d. left-side tension pneumothorax.

Scenario: You have responded to a call at an auto repair shop where you find a 25-year-old male with noticeable purple discoloration of the face, head, and neck. Bystanders tell you that a car slipped off of a jack and onto the patient's chest.

15. What is the most likely cause of the patient's discoloration of the face, head, and neck?
   a. Pulmonary laceration
   b. Traumatic asphyxia
   c. Hemothorax
   d. Tension pneumothorax

16. The patient is alert and orientated and complains of chest, head, and back pain. Treatment should include
   a. supplemental oxygen, cervical spine protection, and transport.

   b. spinal immobilization and immediate needle decompression.
   c. airway, breathing, and circulation assessment and an infusion of heparin.
   d. oxygen, endotracheal intubation, and needle decompression.

Scenario: A patient has a knife lodged in his sternum. He complains of chest pain and a feeling of impending doom. His vital signs are BP of 88/68, HR of 130, and RR of 30. Breath sounds are clear and equal bilaterally, and heart tones are muffled.

17. The paramedic should suspect
   a. pericardial tamponade.
   b. tension pneumothorax.
   c. pulsus paradoxus.
   d. massive hemothorax.

18. Initial treatment of this patient should include
   a. stabilization of the impaled object and oxygen and morphine for pain management.
   b. oxygen, intravenous fluid replacement, and emergent transport.
   c. endotracheal intubation, emergent transport, and cardiac monitoring.
   d. fluid challenge, oxygen, and cardioversion for the rapid heart rate.

Scenario: An elderly patient fell down six stairs approximately 1 hour ago. She is alert and oriented and is complaining of point tenderness at the level of the fifth rib on her right side. Her vitals are as follows: BP of 150/90, HR of 98, and shallow RR of 24.

19. The paramedic should
   a. perform a needle thoracotomy on the right side to improve the respiratory rate.
   b. immobilize the patient and provide ventilatory support with a bag-mask and oxygen.
   c. administer oxygen, establish two large-bore IVs, and initiate rapid transport.
   d. maintain oxygenation, evaluate for underlying serious injury, and manage pain.

20. Which of the following injuries is most likely associated with this patient's rib injury?
   a. Lung injury   b. Diaphragm injury
   c. Cardiac injury   d. Esophageal injury

Need to Know

The following represent the Key Objectives of Chapter 21:

1. *Explain why injuries to the thoracic cavity can become lethal very quickly.*

   The chest houses many critical organs and structures that, when injured through blunt or penetrating trauma, can quickly bleed (Figure 21-3). In addition, air can also "spill" into the cavity in large amounts, either from an external opening, such as through the chest wall, or internally through the bronchial tree. If trapped, this air will compress organs such as the heart and lungs, as well as structures such as the great vessels.

2. *Detect and correct life-threatening injuries to the chest during the primary assessment.*

   The human body is very unforgiving when its primary systems are compromised. You must identify and treat the following life-threatening conditions during the primary assessment:

Condition	Intervention
Airway obstruction	Relieve obstruction or bypass (needle cricothyroidotomy).
Tension pneumothorax	Needle decompression (needle thoracotomy).
Open pneumothorax	Occlusive dressing.
Flail chest	Positive pressure ventilation; early intubation.
Massive hemothorax	Treat for shock; transport for surgical intervention.
Cardiac tamponade	Treat for shock; transport for surgical intervention; pericardiocentesis if authorized.

3. *Suspect both abdominal and chest involvement when an injury occurs between the umbilicus and nipple line.*

   Unlike the photos and diagrams that show the diaphragm in a position that roughly cuts the thorax in half, in reality it rises a fair amount into the chest cavity during exhalation. Penetrating trauma during the respiratory cycle can cause injuries in the chest cavity, in the abdominal cavity, and/or to the diaphragm itself. It may be very difficult to ascertain exactly where the injury lies in the pre-hospital assessment. Assuming that an injury exists in all three areas will help keep your suspicion level high.

4. *Explain how to use your understanding of the mechanism of injury to "predict" patterns of injury, enabling you to react more quickly and manage life-threatening conditions of the chest.*

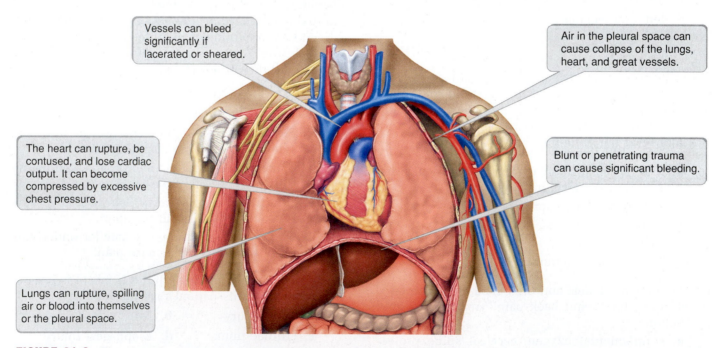

Vessels can bleed significantly if lacerated or sheared.

Air in the pleural space can cause collapse of the lungs, heart, and great vessels.

The heart can rupture, be contused, and lose cardiac output. It can become compressed by excessive chest pressure.

Blunt or penetrating trauma can cause significant bleeding.

Lungs can rupture, spilling air or blood into themselves or the pleural space.

FIGURE 21-3 The chest houses many organs and structures that, when injured, quickly bleed.

Blunt force is transmitted through the chest cavity wall and distributed into the organs and structures. The closer the structure is to the point of impact, the more force it will experience.

There are three major types of blunt force trauma.

- *Shearing forces* can tear at points of attachment during deceleration of internal organs. The aortic arch, which is held in place by the ligamentum arteriosum, is an example of a structure susceptible to this type of force. Think of a balloon filled with water and tied off at the end with a string. If the string was long enough and you were careful enough, you could probably swing the balloon around by the string and nothing would happen, as long as the swings were gentle and smooth. But, allow the balloon to fall toward the ground and jerk up on the string very quickly, and most likely the balloon will tear and spill all the water. This phenomenon is similar to how the ligamentum arteriosum can cause the aorta to tear when very high deceleration forces are applied.

- *Compression forces* can damage the entire chest wall as well as the lungs and heart. Take the water-filled balloon again. You could toss the balloon to a partner carefully, and it would probably not burst. But throw it a far distance, or with some force, and your partner will get wet, no matter what your partner does to slow the balloon down while catching it.

- *Blast forces* are a combination of both compression and shearing. In addition, if the victim is close enough to the explosion that causes the blast, he or she may also experience penetrating trauma as a result of the shrapnel embedded in the blast wave.

Penetrating forces create actual cavities inside the chest cavity. There are two types:

- *Low-velocity* or impaling forces tend to inflict damage right at the source. Examples of this type of force include knives and other sharp objects. Remember that if an object becomes impaled in the chest, do not try to remove it.

- *High-velocity* or projectile forces are more significant in their impact. (Remember from Chapter 18, Mechanism of Injury, in the textbook that the amount of force increases dramatically with the speed or velocity of an object, not its weight.)

Depending upon its actual speed of entry, a projectile like a bullet can pass straight through the body or, worse, ricochet off bony structures and strike a variety of structures. Either way, injuries can take the form of significant bleeding, such as a hemothorax, or introduce a large volume of air into the cavity, such as a pneumothorax. Sometimes injuries can cause both! The space within the chest cavity is quite large—up to 2 liters of blood can be held by one side alone.

Need to Do

The following skills are explained and illustrated in a step-by-step manner, via skill sheets and/or Step-by-Steps in this text and on the accompanying DVD:

Skill Name	Skill Sheet Number and Location	Step-by-Step Number and Location
Bag-Mask Ventilation with 1 Rescuer	4 – DVD	4 – DVD
Bag-Mask Ventilation with 2 or More Rescuers	5 – DVD	5 – DVD
Endotracheal Intubation	7 – Appendix A and DVD	7 – Chapter 12 and DVD
Pulse Oximetry	12 – DVD	12 – DVD
Nasal Intubation	14 – DVD	14 – DVD
Digital Intubation	15 – DVD	N/A
Endotracheal Intubation in Face-to-Face Position	16 – DVD	N/A
Chest Auscultation	27 – Appendix A and DVD	27 – Chapter 11 and DVD
Primary Assessment	32 – Appendix A and DVD	32 – Chapter 14 and DVD
Chest Pain Assessment	34 – DVD	N/A
Dyspnea Assessment	35 – DVD	N/A
Bleeding Control and Shock	66 – DVD	66 – DVD
Management of Chest Trauma	77 – Appendix A and DVD	77 – This chapter and DVD

Step-by-Step 77

Management of Chest Trauma

Conditions: The candidate should perform this procedure on a simulated patient under existing indoor, ambulance, or outdoor lighting, temperature, and weather conditions.

Indications: A patient who has experienced a medical or trauma mechanism to the chest that results in loss of normal lung expansion, either due to negative pressure loss (pneumothorax) or excessive positive pressure (tension pneumothorax)

Red Flags: Increased possibility of infection. Application of an occlusive dressing can result in a tension pneumothorax; needle decompression is unlikely to reduce hemothorax and will create an open pneumothorax.

—Continued

Steps:

1. Use appropriate standard precautions.

2. Evaluate mechanism of injury.

3. Expose and inspect the neck, chest, and back (Figure SBS 77-1). Observe for symmetrical chest rise and respiratory effort.

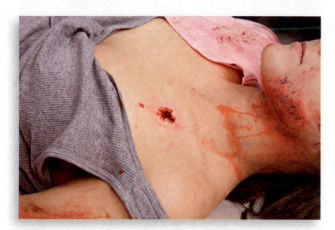

SBS 77-1

4. Immediately cover the open wound with gloved hand.

5. Palpate for chest wall integrity, subcutaneous emphysema, and chest rise.

6. Auscultate all lung fields.

7. Percuss, listening for hyperresonance and hyporesonance.

8. Apply occlusive dressing and/or needle decompress the chest as necessary.

A. Occlusive Dressing

A1. Place an occlusive dressing over wound (Figure SBS 77-2).

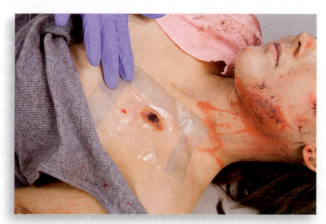

SBS 77-2

A2. Tape three sides.

A3. If a tension pneumothorax develops, tape the fourth side and needle decompress the affected side.

A4. Monitor the patient for changes and transport rapidly.

B. Chest Needle Decompression

B1. Confirm need for decompression.

B2. Locate landmarks (Figure SBS 77-3):
  - Second intercostal space, over the third rib
  - Or fourth intercostal space, over the fifth rib

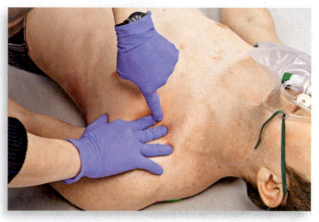

SBS 77-3

B3. Cleanse with alcohol and/or iodine.

B4. Insert a large-bore straight needle over rib (Figure SBS 77-4).

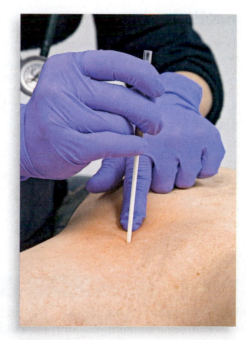

SBS 77-4

B5. Continue until air escape is heard or resistance decreases.

B6. Advance catheter, and remove needle. If using a syringe on needle, aspirate while removing needle (Figure SBS 77-5).

B7. Dispose of needle in appropriate sharps container.

B8. Tape hub securely in place, and connect the flutter valve (Figure SBS 77-6).

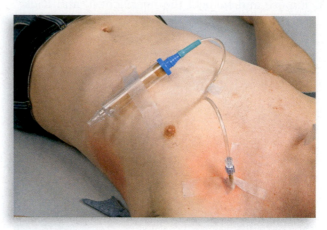

SBS 77-6

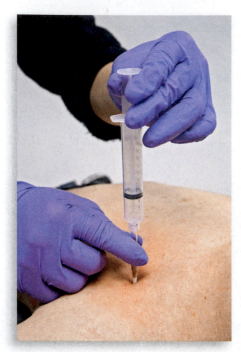

SBS 77-5

Critical Criteria:

- Use appropriate standard precautions.
- Identify tension pneumothorax quickly.
- Insert needle over the top of the inferior rib.
- Recognize developing tension pneumothorax after occlusive dressing application.

Connections

- The following textbook chapters are closely related to the content in this chapter: Chapter 7, Anatomy Overview; Chapter 11, The Normal Physical Examination; Chapter 12, Airway Management, Ventilation, and Oxygenation; Chapter 13, Shock Overview; Chapter 14, Patient Assessment; Chapter 18, Mechanism of Injury; and Chapter 19, Hemorrhage and Hemorrhagic Shock.
- Link to the companion DVD for a chapter-based quiz, audio glossary, animations, games and exercises, and, when appropriate, skill sheets and skill Step-by-Steps.

Street Secrets

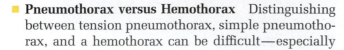

- **Pneumothorax versus Hemothorax** Distinguishing between tension pneumothorax, simple pneumothorax, and a hemothorax can be difficult—especially given a noisy environment, poorly lit conditions, and a moving platform. In these cases you consider the *entire* picture of your patient, not just one or two signs or symptoms. Moreover, consider your patient's overall condition before deciding to treat—do you believe that he or she will succumb to the injuries before you reach the trauma center? Or, is the patient relatively stable, maintaining perfusion and ventilation status during transit? Asking these questions will help guide you in making your decision accurately and quickly.

- **Automatically Sick?** Just because a patient has a pneumothorax, this doesn't mean he or she is automatically sick. In fact, a patient can have equal lung sounds, yet have a small (less than 15%) pneumothorax in one lung. Therefore, the absence or presence of lung sounds does not automatically determine the absence or presence of a pneumothorax. Consider it to be a possible cause for respiratory distress, even in the presence of equal lung sounds.

- **Decompression** Not all tension pneumothoraces need to be decompressed in the field. As with all other situations, size up your patient *overall*. Is he or she decompensating because of the condition? If not, monitor the patient's condition closely and transport. However, if you suspect that the patient has a tension pneumothorax, *and* has decreasing mental status, *and/or* transitions from respiratory distress into respiratory failure, you will need to decompress in order to restore breathing and circulatory effectiveness.

- **The Abdomen** Remember that the abdomen extends further up into the chest cavity than it seems. If the trauma mechanism involves the area of the chest below the fourth rib, consider which abdominal organs may be involved as well.

- **Need for Speed** For patients with significant chest trauma, it pays to remember that they need to be "healed with cold steel"—in other words, they must have access to a trauma surgeon as quickly as possible. Carefully weigh the modes of transportation available to you; what will be the fastest way to transport your patient, by air or by ground?

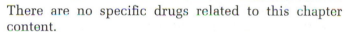

The Drug Box

There are no specific drugs related to this chapter content.

Reference

1. "Josef Leopold Auenbrugger." www.whonamedit.com/doctor.cfm/309.html (accessed November 27, 2006).

Answers

Are You Ready?

1. The primary assessment is your first concern. Despite his initial appearance, the patient has a wound in a critical part of his anatomy, his chest. Quickly but carefully evaluate his perfusion status by ensuring that his airway is patent, breathing is indeed unlabored, and he has a radial pulse. The wound is in an area that can hide a significant amount of blood or air. You will need to cover this wound with an occlusive dressing as soon as possible. Once your primary assessment is complete, you will need to rapidly assess the rest of the body to make sure there are no other injuries.

Active Learning

1. a. midclavicular line; b. midsternal line; c. costal margin; d. costochondral junction; e. suprasternal notch

2. Heart, lungs, liver, spleen, and kidneys

3. Fourth

4. Phrenic

5. a. ribs (12); b. floating ribs (vertebral ribs); c. thoracic vertebra; d. manubrium; e. body; f. xiphoid process; g. sternum; h. costal cartilage

You Are There: Reality-Based Cases

Case 1

1. The patient may have become agitated due to a hypoperfusing state; for some reason there is a decreasing flow of blood and oxygen to his brain. This may be due to a pump, volume, and/or vasculature problem, or an increase of free air in the space. The mechanism of injury and location of the wound point to a combination of all these:

   - *Pump.* The pericardial sac might be lacerated; the knife may have penetrated deep enough to cause the myocardium to bleed into the sac, causing cardiac tamponade.

   - *Volume.* The lungs may have been involved and are now bleeding into the chest cavity.

   - *Vasculature.* An artery or vein might have been lacerated and is bleeding (hemothorax).

   - *Free air.* Loss of chest wall integrity creates a path of air movement into the chest cavity, or from a punctured lung (simple pneumothorax). In addition, the air may become trapped and build pressure inside the chest, crowding and crushing the lungs, heart, and great vessels (tension pneumothorax).

   - *Lacerated diaphragm.* The diaphragm may also be lacerated, causing a loss of ventilatory capacity and subsequent hypoxia.

   A rapid, thorough examination of the chest is paramount. Auscultate breath sounds for their presence or absence. Check for the presence of jugular venous distention, subcutaneous air (emphysema), a hyperinflated chest wall, and an asymmetrical chest rise. Percuss the chest loudly for resonance.

2. A tension pneumothorax is perhaps the most serious possibility, along with cardiac tamponade. In most EMS systems, the tension pneumothorax is the condition that can be corrected by a paramedic. It is possible that the occlusive dressing is contributing to the increasing intrathoracic pressure; lifting the bandage off the wound may relieve some pressure. A needle decompression may be necessary.

3. Have you checked for JVD? Asymmetrical chest rise? A hyperresonant or hyporesonant chest wall? Did you palpate the upper abdominal quadrants for pain, tenderness, or rigidity? Did you reconsider the mechanism of injury to see if your suspicions match the forces involved? The patient's vital signs point to a significant shock condition. If you still suspect a developing tension pneumothorax as the primary problem, a needle thoracotomy is warranted. If you suspect a massive hemothorax, ensuring that the patient remains in a supine position and is kept warm, transported emergently, and that large-bore intravenous

access is obtained while en route are critical actions. Don't forget about the patient's ventilatory capacity—you may need to assist his respiratory effort with a bag-mask and early intubation, especially if the diaphragm is involved.

4. If your answer did not match the final events in this case, reconsider the mechanism of injury and findings that were provided. See if the clues make more sense to you now that you know about the patient's outcome.

Test Yourself

1. Pulmonary contusions

   Pulmonary contusions have been reported to occur in 30%–50% of patients with major blunt trauma. Additionally they coexist with extrathoracic trauma in 87% of patients. They are also the most common major thoracic injury in the pediatric population as the pediatric chest wall is more deformable, affording the lungs less protection.

2. True

   A blunt injury that causes the sharp end of a broken rib to project inward can lacerate the lung. Pulmonary laceration causes hemo- or pneumothorax. In addition to the symptoms and signs of hemo- or pneumothorax, the patient may also present with hemoptysis, which is bloody sputum coming from the lungs.

3. Administering an analgesic should minimize pain upon inspiration.

   If you can minimize the pain on inspiration, it's possible the patient can breathe more effectively and will require fewer aggressive measures.

4. Treatment could include supplemental oxygen, bag-mask, endotracheal intubation, and continuous positive airway pressure (CPAP) ventilation.

   Because a flail segment may seriously compromise the mechanics of breathing, early detection and intervention are very important. Positive pressure ventilation with the bag-mask unit is recommended as well as early endotracheal intubation. Ventilation not only assists with oxygenation and lung inflation, but it may also effectively serve as an internal splint. CPAP ventilation can also be utilized if available in your EMS system.

5. Hemothorax

   The patient is most likely suffering from a hemothorax. Signs and symptoms of a massive hemothorax may include: hypotension and obvious shock, pain, tachypnea, shortness of breath, low pulse oximeter reading, tachycardia, and decreased breath sounds. Tracheal deviation and JVD may be present in the late stages of hemothorax.

6. Autosplinting

   All the structures that make up the chest wall are very well innervated and will cause significant pain if injured. Signs and symptoms of thoracic injury include rapid breathing (tachypnea) and an effort on the patient's part to breathe carefully and with less volume (autosplinting).

7. Bag-mask with high-flow oxygen

   With tracheobronchial injuries, blind nasotracheal intubation and even orotracheal intubation with direct laryngoscopy can be risky. A disruption of the trachea could be made worse with the endotracheal tube. The tube may even transect the trachea and enter into the adjoining soft tissues. If possible, the patient should be supported with high-concentration oxygen and a bag-mask until intubation can be performed in the emergency department. Ideally the patient would be intubated with a fiber-optic bronchoscope, which would allow direct visualization of the trachea.

8. Pulmonary contusion

   Patients with pulmonary contusions can present with dyspnea, tachypnea, tachycardia, and possibly cyanosis. Hemoptysis may occur in up to 50% of cases. On exam, decreased breath sounds or rales may be noted. Evidence of concomitant rib fractures and, especially, a flail chest segment should actively be looked for.

9. Ligamentum arteriosum

   A piece of fibrous tissue called the ligamentum arteriosum, which is a remnant of the embryological circulatory system, tethers the aortic arch to the pulmonary artery outflow tract.

10. Negative pressure draws air into the lungs and draws venous blood flow back into the heart.

    The negative pressure in the chest created when a person expands the chest wall and contracts (drops) the diaphragm is not only necessary to draw air into the lungs, it may have other important cardiovascular effects as well. Recent research shows that negative pressure in the chest also helps draw venous blood flow back into the heart.

11. a

    The two types of forces that cause chest injuries are blunt and penetrating. Rapid deceleration forces cause shearing forces. Compression injuries occur when the thorax gets crushed. If the ability of the ribs to withstand force applied to them is exceeded, it causes injury to the chest wall and internal organs. Blast injuries are a combination of compression and shearing, as well as penetrating trauma from flying debris and shrapnel.

12. a

    A flail chest injury occurs when three or more adjacent ribs are fractured in two or more places, resulting in a free-floating segment of the chest wall called a flail chest. On exam there may be a palpable deformity of the flail segment. Additionally, by watching the patient's respirations, you may notice paradoxical chest wall motion with respirations. This is when the flail chest wall segment moves inward during inspiration and outward during expiration.

13. c

    Blast injuries are a combination of compression and shearing, as well as penetrating trauma from flying debris and shrapnel. Air-filled spaces, like the alveoli of the lungs, are in danger of barotrauma from the over-pressurized blast wave.

14. a

If air is actively entering the pleural space and is not able to escape, the trapped air may begin to put pressure on the heart, great vessels, and opposite lung. This is known as a tension pneumothorax. Clinical signs suggesting a tension pneumothorax include tachycardia, hypotension, asymmetrical breath sounds, and a deviated trachea.

15. b

Traumatic asphyxia is a rare entity caused when the thorax undergoes a significant compression forcing blood backward into the pulmonary system and into the veins of the neck and head. Because the large veins of the head and neck do not have valves, the full force of the blood being pushed in reverse is transmitted to the capillaries of the head, face, and neck, causing blood to leak out into the subcutaneous tissues. Clinically a patient may present with a flushed face; purple discoloration of the head, face, and neck; and bilateral subconjunctival hemorrhages.

16. a

From the prehospital standpoint, treating traumatic asphyxia includes providing supplemental oxygen, protection of the cervical spine if indicated, and transport to the emergency department.

17. a

Prehospital recognition of pericardial tamponade may be very difficult. You should maintain a high index of suspicion with any trauma to the chest. This patient has many of the signs and symptoms of pericardial tamponade, including hypotension, tachycardia, and muffled heart tones. Other signs and symptoms include pulsus paradoxus, JVD, and narrowing pulse pressure.

18. b

Pericardial tamponade is a very serious condition that can be rapidly fatal. If it is suspected, the patient must be supported with oxygen, a trial of fluid replacement, and emergent transport to the hospital.

19. d

A patient with rib fractures will complain of significant point tenderness at the site. Increased breathing depth may cause extreme pain, so patients will purposely take shallow breaths (splinted respirations) in order to minimize the pain. Management of these patients is directed at evaluation for underlying serious injury, maintenance of oxygenation, and pain relief.

20. a

Rib fractures signify that force was transmitted to the thorax and that significant injury may have occurred to the underlying organs of the thorax and the upper abdomen. Fractures to the first and second ribs are uncommon because they are protected by the shoulder and other bones. If the impact is strong enough to cause injury to these ribs, other injuries are likely, and mortality is increased by 50%. The fourth through tenth ribs are more likely to be injured and are also more likely to cause injury to the lungs.

chapter 22

Abdominal Trauma

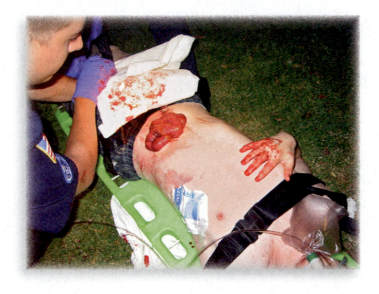

Are You Ready?

Peter Davis and his friends were hanging out in front of his house drinking some beers when one of Peter's neighbors walked by. Stephanie Wu is a shy 19-year-old who lives down the block from Peter. Peter's friend Glen saw her coming and immediately approached her and began to try and strike up a conversation. Stephanie kept trying to walk around Glen, but each time she attempted to pass him, Glen would step in front of her and stop her from doing so. Finally, Peter walked over to Glen and tried to hold him so that Stephanie could pass. Glen grabbed Stephanie by the arm, stumbled, and fell to the ground, pulling her down with him.

Just then, Stephanie's older brother pulled up in his car, jumped out and ran over to help his sister.

Stephanie was crying now, and her brother went straight for Glen. He ran up, jumped on top of Glen, and began to beat him about the face. Peter tried to pull him off of Glen; when he did, Stephanie's brother pulled out a knife and stabbed Peter once in the left inferior chest and sliced him across his abdomen.

By the time your unit arrives, Peter has been placed on a long board, and the first responders have covered the stab wound to Peter's chest with an airtight dressing taped on three sides. They have covered the abdominal laceration with a trauma dressing. Your partner walks over to Glen to assess him, and you begin to assess Peter.

1. Based on the photograph, what type of abdominal wound did Peter receive?

   _____

   _____

   _____

2. How will you treat this wound?

   _____

   _____

   _____

3. What are your priorities in treating this patient?

   _____

   _____

   _____

Active Learning

Anatomy Review

1. Describe how the abdomen is divided into four quadrants using anatomical terms and names of structures.

   _____

   _____

   _____

2. The lateral aspect of the abdomen is often called the (a) _____. The point at which the twelfth rib attaches to its corresponding vertebra can be found on the back and is called the (b) _____.

3. Identify the arteries shown in Figure 22-1 and the abdominal organs that they supply.

   a. _____

   b. _____

   c. _____

   d. _____

   e. _____

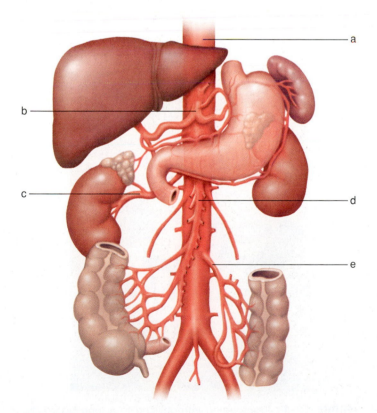

FIGURE 22-1

4. Abdominal Examination Exercise

This exercise is performed with a partner.

Abdominal injuries, especially blunt abdominal injuries, can be very difficult to detect. Because of the difficulty of identifying abdominal injuries, it is important that paramedics understand what a healthy, atraumatic abdomen looks, feels, and sounds like.

In a professional manner, have your partner lie in a supine position and expose the abdomen. There is a definite sequence that needs to be followed when examining the abdomen:

a. Inspection of the abdomen. Look for bruising, distention, abrasions, penetrating injuries, lacerations, pulsatile masses, etc.

b. Auscultation of the abdomen. In the prehospital setting auscultation of the abdomen has not been proven to be effective. If this is part of your local EMS standard of care, it should take place following inspection of the abdomen. In the prehospital setting auscultation is simply used to ascertain if there are active sounds present.

c. Palpation of the abdomen. This should take place after auscultation, because if palpation takes place prior to auscultation, the process of palpating can decrease the activity (motility) of the intestines and give a false negative finding when bowel sounds are not present. During palpation of the abdominal quadrants, look for point tenderness, rigidity, distention, pulsating masses, etc.

Examine the abdomens of as many people as you can, because it is a keen familiarity with the healthy abdomen that allows the paramedic to identify the subtle changes that can occur in a traumatized abdomen.

You Are There: Reality-Based Cases

Case 1

It is a hot summer day in the Midwest. You and your EMT partner are standing in a long line at the Fosters Freeze waiting to get an ice cream cone when your dispatcher calls your unit number. You respond to State Route 48 for a head-on collision involving a tow truck and a compact sedan.

When you arrive on the scene, you find a 45-year-old male driver and an 18-year-old female front seat passenger in the sedan.

FIGURE 22-2   Bent steering wheel of Mark's car.

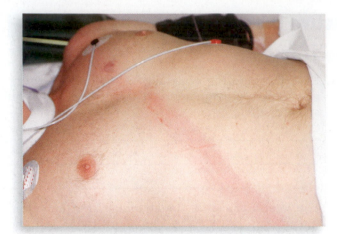

FIGURE 22-3   Seat belt sign.

The driver, Mark Jenkins, and his daughter, Tracy, had been arguing about what time Tracy would come home that night from a party. Mark became distracted and crossed over the center line into oncoming traffic, colliding with the tow truck. Both Mark and his daughter were restrained, but the vehicle that they were driving was not equipped with air bags. During your size-up and initial assessment of Mark, you notice that there is moderate damage to the front end of his vehicle, but considerable damage to the steering wheel (Figure 22-2).

Mark has minor complaints of chest discomfort with a positive seat belt sign (Figure 22-3) but no instability of the rib cage. Tracy has a complaint of left leg pain where she feels she struck the dashboard, but otherwise she has no complaints of pain or obvious injury (Figure 22-4).

1. What is your general impression of these two patients?

   _____

   _____

   _____

2. Based on the condition of the steering wheel, what type of injuries is Mark likely to have? What injuries should you monitor Tracy for, other than her complaint of left leg pain?

   _____

   _____

   _____

3. Do you have sufficient resources on the scene to deal with your patient load?

   _____

   _____

   _____

Mark and Tracy are in the process of being placed in c-spine precautions. The trauma center is 30 minutes away by ground, which you and your partner have decided is an appropriate means of transportation.

FIGURE 22-4   Tracy being immobilized to a long board by rescuers.

You and your partner get in the back of your ambulance, and one of the firefighters begins to drive you to the trauma center.

Approximately 10 minutes into the 30-minute drive, during your reassessment of Tracy's ABCDEs and her vital signs, you note that Tracy is guarding the left upper quadrant of her abdomen. Her heart rate has increased, and her skin is pale and moist. Your updated blood pressure is within a couple of points of the initial blood pressure. When Tracy is questioned about her abdomen, she states that it hurts when you push on her left upper quadrant.

4. What is your impression of the new findings discovered during Tracy's reassessment?

_____

_____

_____

5. How will you respond to the changes that you have discovered in Tracy's condition?

_____

_____

_____

Test Yourself

1. Name the solid organs of the abdomen.

_____

_____

2. The epigastric region is located inferior to the xiphoid process and superior to the periumbilical region.

True

False

3. You respond to the scene of a motor vehicle collision. A 37-year-old patient was ejected from her car during a rollover crash. The patient is alert and denying significant pain. You find only minor external injuries during your assessment. Her vitals are BP of 80/62, HR of 120, and RR of 28. What condition should you most suspect when accounting for these vital signs?

_____

_____

4. The abdominal and thoracic cavities are separated by the _____.

5. Falls from twice the height of the patient are associated with an increased risk of intra-abdominal bleeding.

True

False

6. Your 20-year-old patient fell from the roof of a house and has only minor external injuries. Vital signs are BP of 88/60, HR of 114, and RR of 24. What type of abdominal injury most likely accounts for these vital signs?

_____

_____

7. The most commonly injured hollow organ in cases of blunt trauma is the _____.

Scenario: A seat-belted passenger of a car involved in a head-on collision is complaining of pain in the upper quadrants of his abdomen and right shoulder pain. His vital signs are BP of 92/68, HR of 100, and RR of 22.

8. The most likely cause of this patient's pain is an injury to his
   a. liver and spleen.
   b. small bowel and bladder.
   c. diaphragm and colon.
   d. stomach and kidneys.

9. The pain in the patient's shoulder is most likely caused by
   a. bleeding that is irritating the diaphragm.
   b. a whiplash injury caused by the crash.
   c. a probable acute myocardial infarction.
   d. his state of decompensated shock.

10. Prehospital management of this patient should include
   a. complete stabilization on scene prior to transporting.
   b. applying a sling and swath to the right arm and shoulder.
   c. transportation to a trauma center with surgical capabilities.
   d. maintaining the patient's blood pressure at 80 mm Hg systolic.

Scenario: A 24-year-old male patient has suffered a large knife wound to his abdomen. You note small bowel protruding through the wound.

11. Management of this injury should include
    a. flushing the evisceration with any source of clean potable water.
    b. covering the bowel with moist, sterile, or occlusive dressings.
    c. covering the bowel with dry, sterile dressings taped on all sides.
    d. making one attempt to replace the bowel back into the abdomen.

12. Management of this patient should include
    a. transporting the patient in a prone position.
    b. leaving the wound uncovered to avoid injury.
    c. applying a pneumatic anti-shock garment.
    d. initiating fluid replacement with large-bore IVs.

Scenario: A 72-year-old man was struck and pinned for a short time by a falling tree. He is complaining of abdominal tenderness and seems somewhat confused. He takes a beta-blocker medication daily. His vitals are BP of 86/56, HR of 70, and RR of 20.

13. What is the significance of the patient's prescribed beta-blocker medication?
    a. Beta-blockers may be blunting signs of shock.
    b. Beta-blockers are increasing the heart rate.
    c. Beta-blockers have no relevance in this situation.
    d. Beta-blockers are prohibiting the clotting process.

14. Management of this patient should include
    a. slowly transporting this noncritical patient.
    b. administration of beta-blocker medication.
    c. application of a sandbag to the injury site.
    d. assessment of the mechanism of injury.

Need to Know

The following represent the Key Objectives of Chapter 22:

1. *Identify the structures located within the four abdominal quadrants so that potential injuries can be considered.*

   Some organs are located in more than one quadrant; thus they may be listed more than one time. The great vessels (the aorta and the inferior vena cava) run through the abdominal quadrants along the spine.

Right Upper Quadrant (RUQ)	Left Upper Quadrant (LUQ)
Liver	Spleen
Gall bladder	Pancreas
Pancreas	Stomach
Right kidney	Part of the liver
Ascending colon	Transverse colon
Transverse colon	Descending colon
Duodenum (small intestine)	Small intestine
Right Lower Quadrant (RLQ)	**Left Lower Quadrant (LLQ)**
Appendix	Descending colon
Cecum	Sigmoid colon
Ascending colon	Small intestine
Small intestine	Part of the kidney
Part of the kidney	Ureter
Ureter	Ovary (female)
Ovary (female)	Fallopian tube (female)
Fallopian tube (female)	Uterus +/−
Uterus +/−	Bladder +/−
Bladder +/−	Common iliac artery
Common iliac artery	

2. *Assess, formulate, and implement a treatment plan for a patient with abdominal trauma.*

   Abdominal trauma is one of the more difficult types of trauma to manage. This is especially true in the case of blunt abdominal trauma because there are not always external clues to lead the paramedic to the conclusion that a traumatic injury has occurred and that an underlying injury exists.

   The abdomen is a large structure that houses a number of solid and hollow organs, and it has the space to hold a person's entire circulating blood volume, and then some. The abdomen is relatively unprotected compared with the thoracic cavity and the cranium (which are protected by the rib cage and the skull, respectively). As such, the abdomen is subject to blunt and penetrating traumatic injuries.

   The solid organs of the abdomen (liver, spleen, kidneys, and pancreas) are very vascular and subject to severe bleeding when injured. The hollow organs of the abdomen (small intestine, colon, stomach) are not nearly as vascular as the solid organs found in the abdominal cavity and do not pose a significant threat of severe bleeding. The hollow organs of the abdomen do, on the other hand, pose a threat of severe infection if their contents spill into the abdominal cavity. In the event that gastric and intestinal contents spill into the abdominal cavity, especially if the incident is initially undetected, the chance for developing severe septic shock is great.

Because the abdomen and the thoracic cavity border one another, and the diaphragm (the structure that divides these two cavities) has such a wide range of movement, penetrating injuries between the nipple line and the umbilicus must be considered to be both abdominal and thoracic injuries until proven otherwise by a qualified physician, such as a trauma surgeon.

In the absence of penetrating injuries, blunt injuries with obvious external findings, and specific pain to the abdomen, abdominal injuries are often very difficult to identify. In fact, one of the best indicators of abdominal injury, especially in the prehospital setting, is the presence of early signs of shock. Because this is the case, paramedics must be vigilant in assessing the mechanism of injury as a means of determining the potential for abdominal trauma; when such a mechanism exists, the patient should be transported to an appropriate facility capable of assessing the potential injuries, and appropriate treatment (oxygen administration and IV access) should be provided en route to the hospital.

Rapid detection, transport, and treatment of patients suffering from abdominal injuries is crucial, because unrecognized abdominal injuries can have an associated mortality rate of greater than 50%.[1]

Connections

- Chapter 7, Anatomy Overview, in the textbook provides more information on the location and function of the organs located in the four abdominal quadrants.
- Chapter 19, Hemorrhage and Hemorrhagic Shock, in the textbook outlines information on the treatment of bleeding and shock.
- Chapter 34, Gastroenterology, in the textbook discusses preexisting medical conditions of the abdomen that may affect your assessment and treatment of the patient with abdominal trauma.
- Chapter 41, Obstetrics and Gynecology, in the textbook gives an overview of the gravid uterus and a discussion on trauma during pregnancy.
- Link to the companion DVD for a chapter-based quiz, audio glossary, animations, games and exercises, and, when appropriate, skill sheets and skill Step-by-Steps.

Street Secrets

- **Intra-abdominal Bleeding** The detection of bleeding in the abdomen as the result of blunt or penetrating trauma is difficult at best. The mech-

Need to Do

The following skills are explained and illustrated in a step-by-step manner, via skill sheets and/or Step-by-Steps in this text and on the accompanying DVD:

Skill Name	Skill Sheet Number and Location	Step-by-Step Number and Location
Abdominal Examination	36 – DVD	N/A
Bleeding Control and Shock	66 – DVD	66 – DVD
MAST/PASG Application	81 – DVD	N/A
NREMT Patient Assessment Trauma	83 – DVD	N/A

anism of injury, with or without signs or symptoms of shock, is one of the leading indicators of how paramedics treat patients with abdominal trauma. The use of abdominal ultrasound in the prehospital setting to detect free fluid in the abdomen is one up-and-coming method of helping paramedics confirm their suspicions about bleeding into the abdominal cavity, and in turn support their decision to transport such a patient to an appropriate receiving facility (a trauma center if possible).

Even with the use of ultrasound as a tool to help identify free fluid in the abdominal cavity, the mechanism of injury, presenting signs and symptoms, and a concerted effort to err on the side of the patient are effective indicators for deciding where to transport patients who have suffered abdominal trauma.

The Drug Box

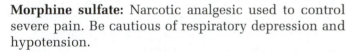

Morphine sulfate: Narcotic analgesic used to control severe pain. Be cautious of respiratory depression and hypotension.

References

1. P. C. Ferrera et al., "Injuries Distracting from Intraabdominal Injuries after Blunt Trauma." *American Journal of Emergency Medicine* 16, no. 2 (1998): 145–49.
2. C. D. Newgard, "Steering Wheel Deformity and Serious Thoracic or Abdominal Injury Among Drivers and Passengers Involved in Motor Vehicle Crashes." *Annals of Emergency Medicine* 45, no. 1 (January 1, 2005): 43–50.

Answers

Are You Ready?

1. Peter received an abdominal evisceration.

2. Dress the wound with saline-soaked sterile dressings or an occlusive dressing, and do not attempt to push the intestines back into the abdominal cavity.

3. The priorities are to assess and maintain ABCDEs. The stab wound to the chest is likely the more serious of the two wounds (although the stab wound is not as visually dramatic, the chance of sustaining a life-threatening stab wound to the chest is more likely than sustaining a life-threatening evisceration). The

patient needs to be monitored closely for signs of shock or respiratory compromise. Treatment should take place on the way to a trauma center (if possible). The treatment includes supplemental oxygen and two large-bore IVs with frequent reassessment of the ABCDEs en route to the hospital.

Active Learning

1. A midsagittal line spanning from the xiphoid process to the symphysis pubis separates the right from the left abdomen. This line is intersected by a horizontal line through the umbilicus, which separates the upper from the lower quadrants.

2. a. flank; b. costovertebral angle (CVA)

3. a. abdominal aorta (branches of the aorta supply blood to the abdominal organs); b. celiac trunk (supplies arterial blood to the stomach, part of the duodenum, liver, gall bladder, pancreas, and spleen); c. renal arteries (supply the kidneys); d. superior mesenteric artery (supplies the remaining portions of the duodenum and the proximal colon up to two-thirds of the way along the transverse colon); e. inferior mesenteric artery (supplies the remainder of the colon).

You Are There: Reality-Based Cases

Case 1

1. Based on the mechanism of injury, the bent steering wheel, and a positive seat belt sign on the driver's chest, Mark will be assessed and treated as a critical trauma patient until proven otherwise. Tracy experienced the same mechanism of injury as her father, but she didn't strike the steering wheel and she doesn't have any outward signs of trauma other than her subjective complaint of left leg pain. Nonetheless, Tracy falls into the same category as her father based on mechanism and the potential for internal injuries. Tracy will be treated as a critical trauma patient.

2. A recent study on the usefulness of bent steering wheels as a predictor for abdominal injuries points to the need for a careful assessment of the steering wheel after a motor vehicle crash.[2] This retrospective study examined crash data from 1995 to 2002 and found a direct correlation between the degree of steering wheel damage and injuries to the thorax and abdomen. Severity of steering wheel damage was directly correlated with severity of thoracic injuries in drivers and with abdominal injuries in passengers. The authors of this study theorize that when the driver's chest strikes the steering column, this may protect the abdomen from further injury. This study helps emphasize the importance of carefully inspecting the steering wheel at the scene of a crash. It also points to increasing your suspicion of abdominal injuries in passengers of a vehicle that sustained steering wheel damage. Thus Mark's assessments and treatments need to continue to focus on his thoracic injuries. Tracy, on the other hand, needs to be assessed

for the pain in her leg and for potential abdominal injuries.

3. If you have a total of two patients, you have sufficient resources to transport these patients. If you have more than two patients, then you will need to request additional resources.

4. The new findings support the need to continually reassess patients in the front passenger seat of a car where the steering wheel has been bent. They also suggest that Tracy is in the beginning stages of shock and that she has likely suffered an internal abdominal injury.

5. You can consider establishing a second IV line on Tracy, and you can always reassess the means of transportation that you have chosen. If another means of transportation would deliver Tracy to a trauma center more efficiently, then that means should be considered. Because you were 20 minutes out from the trauma center when you made this discovery, it would not make any difference to attempt another means of transportation. You should continue with your transport, notify the trauma center of the new findings, and continue to closely monitor Tracy's status.

If the pneumatic anti-shock garment (PASG) is in your protocols, you can consider its application. If Tracy becomes hemodynamically unstable, you may choose to inflate its various compartments.

Test Yourself

1. The solid organs of the abdomen include the liver, spleen, kidneys, and pancreas.

It is important to differentiate between solid and hollow organs as injury to these two types of organs may produce different signs and symptoms, and the severity of these injuries is usually quite different. Solid organs are highly vascularized, meaning they have a rich blood supply. The primary concern with injuries to these (mainly the liver and spleen) is the potential for there to be substantial or even fatal blood loss.

2. True

The center section is over the belly button and is called the periumbilical region. Immediately above this and just inferior to the xiphoid is the epigastric region. The suprapubic region (sometimes called hypogastric) is just below the periumbilical region and is just superior to the symphysis pubis.

3. Abdominal hemorrhage

Maintain a high index of suspicion for bleeding in the abdomen when a patient has unexplained shock, or shock seemingly out of proportion to injuries, even with a "normal" abdominal exam.

4. Diaphragm

The muscular diaphragm, which separates the abdominal and thoracic cavities, moves from the fifth intercos-

tal space to as low as the bottom of the costal margin at the lateral ribs.

5. False

The height of a fall is important, as falls from greater than 20 feet (or 3 times the height of the patient) in an adult are associated with an increased likelihood of intra-abdominal bleeding.

6. A fractured solid visceral organ

Injuries to the solid visceral organs, such as the liver, spleen, kidneys, and pancreas, can cause substantial blood loss, with the potential to cause rapid development of tachycardia and hypotension.

7. Small bowel

In the case of blunt abdominal trauma, the small bowel is the most commonly injured hollow organ, followed by the colon/rectum, duodenum, and stomach.

8. a

Liver and splenic injuries often cause pain directly over the injured organs, in the right upper quadrant and left upper quadrant, respectively.

9. a

If injuries result in bleeding that irritates the diaphragm, pain is often referred to the shoulder on the same side as the irritation. This referred pain to the shoulder is known as Kehr's sign.

10. c

Prehospital management of severe abdominal injuries, regardless of the actual source of the injury and bleeding, is as follows: rapid assessment, identification as a high-priority patient, package for transport, transport to a trauma center with immediate surgical capabilities, control obvious bleeding, dress open wounds, secure any impaled objects, treat shock aggressively with fluids to a systolic BP of 90–100 mm Hg, and administer high-concentration oxygen to maintain the SpO_2 at greater than 95%.

11. b

In the case of evisceration of abdominal organs, handling exposed structures more than necessary should be avoided. Do not attempt to replace them into the abdominal cavity. Cover the evisceration with moist, sterile dressings or an occlusive dressing. Cover that dressing with additional soft, light padding to help maintain body heat. Avoid using dry dressings as these may adhere to the wound, causing problems for the surgical team. Sterile saline should be used to keep the dressing moist, which decreases evaporation and, therefore, drying of the organs. If the organs dry, they likely will die and will require surgical removal.

12. d

Open trauma with hypotension or tachycardia should be managed with fluid resuscitation. In cases of evisceration, establish two large-bore IVs and initiate fluid replacement in addition to applying a moist, sterile or occlusive dressing over the eviscerated bowel.

13. a

Injuries to the solid visceral organs, such as the liver, spleen, kidneys, and pancreas, can cause substantial blood loss, with the potential to cause rapid development of tachycardia and hypotension. Along with these findings, rapid blood loss can cause skin and mental status changes consistent with shock. In older patients, these findings may develop rapidly or may actually be blunted due to chronic use of certain medications (e.g., beta-blockers). In younger patients, on the other hand, substantial blood loss may result in only minimal signs or symptoms, so the care provider must remain ever-vigilant.

14. d

Mechanism of injury is an important part of every trauma assessment conducted by the paramedic. Due to the patient's hypotension and decreased mental status, this patient should be considered a high priority for transport to an appropriate trauma facility.

chapter 23

Spinal Trauma

Are You Ready?

The young driver looks panicked as you approach her car. It appears that her compact car was rear-ended by a large SUV. The back of her car is crushed to the back passenger compartment. The driver states that she felt her head snap back against the headrest and then forward. She felt a "cracking" sensation in her neck, and her arms and hands went numb. She now has a "burning" pain in the middle of her cervical spine.

1. What should you do first?

_____

_____

_____

2. You will need to decide how to appropriately extricate the patient from the vehicle. What information will you need in order to make that determination?

_____

_____

_____

_____

Active Learning

Anatomy Review

1. The spine of the scapula is located at the level of the _____(a)_____ thoracic vertebrae. The inferior edge of the scapula is found at the level of the _____(b)_____ thoracic vertebrae. The iliac crest is at the level of the _____(c)_____ lumbar vertebrae, and the posterior superior iliac spine is at the level of the _____(d)_____ sacral vertebrae.

2. Match the following terms with the labels in Figure 23-1 (you may use the same term more than once):

- Body
- Spinous process
- Transverse process
- Pedicle
- Lamina
- Vertebral foramen
- Intervertebral disk

a. _____

b. _____

c. _____

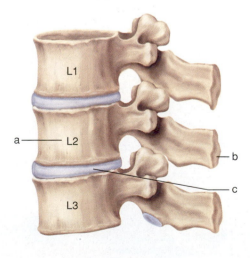

(a)

FIGURE 23-1

Posterior

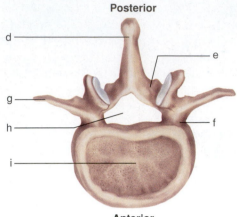

Anterior

(b)

FIGURE 23-1 *(Continued)*

d. _____

e. _____

f. _____

g. _____

h. _____

i. _____

3. Name the three horns of the spinal cord.

  a. _____

  b. _____

  c. _____

4. Identify which horn of the spinal cord contains the pain, temperature, and vibration signals from the body.

5. The _____ horn includes the fibers that transmit information to and from the body's arms and legs.

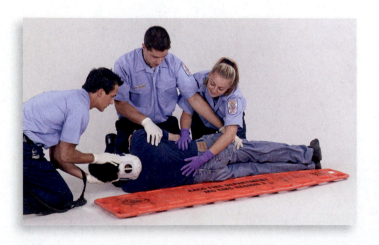

6. Why Is That?

There are several studies that look at the act of immobilization causing pain and discomfort in otherwise healthy volunteers.[1-3] Make an effort to review these articles if possible. In general, what all three studies found was that proper spinal immobilization on healthy volunteers with no previous history of back injuries would result in pain or discomfort within 60 minutes of application. What could be an explanation for this phenomenon?

You Are There: Reality-Based Cases
Case 1

During the busy commute, a subway train is just beginning to leave the station when it comes to an abrupt stop. Most of the passengers are fine, but several are thrown to the floor of the train. The initial dispatch sends a first-alarm response and three ambulances from the fire department, including yourself.

After making your way down the stairway, you begin triaging the victims. Most of the noninjured and "walking wounded" have already moved onto the station platform; you see several patients remaining in the subway car.

Your first patient (patient 1) is a 64-year-old woman sitting on one of the benches. She states that she was thrown from her seat and landed on her outstretched hand. She was assisted back to a seat and now complains of pain, tenderness, and swelling of her left wrist. She has no other complaints or injuries.

Patient 2 is a 6-month-old infant who was being held in her father's arms when the train stopped. The father lost his grip on the infant, and she fell to the train floor from a standing position. The baby, held by her father, is crying quietly.

Patient 3 is a 27-year-old male who does not speak English. He appears to be holding a bloody shirt against a very deep laceration located on his right lower leg. He has a hematoma to the right lateral side of his head and a bruise and abrasion to his right cheek. He is crying out in pain.

Patient 4 is a female who appears to be in her 50s and is lying on her side, unconscious, on the floor. She has a scalp laceration to the occiput of her head.

1. Which of these patients require cervical immobilization? Why?

_____

_____

_____

Test Yourself

1. A force applied to the top or bottom of the spine that is directed along the length of the spine is
   a. extension compression.
   b. vertical compression.
   c. flexion compression.
   d. anterior compression.

2. A complete spinal cord injury above C4 results in all the following *except*
   a. hypoventilation.
   b. paraplegia.
   c. loss of diaphragmatic function.
   d. hemorrhagic shock.

3. The major divisions of the spinal column are
   a. lumbar, anterior, sacrum/coccyx, and cervical.
   b. cervical, sacrum/coccyx, thoracic, and lumbar.
   c. thoracic, anterior, lumbar, and flexion.
   d. flexion, cervical, lumbar, and sacrum/coccyx.

4. List two types of spinal injury that are usually unstable.

_____

_____

5. List the most common kinds of external force that lead to spinal trauma, and indicate the complications that result from each.

_____

_____

6. Your patient was found lying unconscious in a prone position partially under an all-terrain vehicle (ATV). Friends pulled the ATV off of the injured man but otherwise left him as is. You should
   a. perform a thorough primary assessment and then decide whether or not to prepare for a log-roll maneuver.

   b. perform a rapid ABC assessment and then have your partner help you perform a log-roll maneuver if not contraindicated.
   c. rapidly assess ABCs, apply an appropriately sized cervical collar, and treat the patient in the prone position.
   d. rapidly assess ABCs and the patient's back while the other care providers prepare for a log-roll maneuver.

7. All spinal fractures result in spinal cord injury, and all spinal cord injuries are associated with spinal fractures.
   True
   False

8. Which of the following is the *least* likely cause of hypotension?
   a. Cardiac tamponade
   b. Neurogenic shock
   c. Tension pneumothorax
   d. Ongoing blood loss

9. Methylprednisolone (Solu-Medrol) is useful in the hospital setting for the management of spinal injuries. Therefore it should be used for patients with spinal injuries in the prehospital arena.
   True
   False

10. Common symptoms that present in complete spinal cord transection include all the following *except*
   a. loss of ligament connectivity.
   b. loss of position sensation.
   c. absence of motor function.
   d. loss of temperature sensation.

11. The majority of acute spinal cord injuries are caused by
   a. penetrating trauma.
   b. gunshots.
   c. hanging.
   d. blunt trauma.

12. Describe your course of treatment for a patient with suspected neurogenic shock.

_____

_____

13. In addition to the standard elements for every patient care report, the spinal-injured patient's report should contain what information?

_____

_____

14. A compression fracture resulting in the crushing of the C1 ring is called a
    a. Jefferson fracture.
    b. Brady fracture.
    c. burst fracture.
    d. Hangman's fracture.

15. A patient with a spinal cord injury is most likely to become paraplegic if the injury is at or below
    a. T3.
    b. C6.
    c. T1.
    d. C2.

16. Identify the name, location, and number of vertebrae of each section of the spinal column.

    _____

    _____

17. Why is it important to document and report the evolution of a spinal injury?

    _____

    _____

18. The vertebral canal
    a. houses the vertebral arch.
    b. houses the fibrocartilaginous ligament.
    c. forms a protective barrier for the transverse process.
    d. houses and forms a protective barrier for the spinal cord.

19. When should you *not* perform manual stabilization and repositioning of a patient with a suspected spine injury?

    _____

    _____

Scenario: On Sunday, a man went hiking in the mountains and did not return. You are among a team of rescuers sent to search for him on Tuesday morning. He is found sitting at the bottom of a crevasse, propped against a boulder. He says that he struck his head when he fell. When you grasp his toe, he is not sure whether he can feel it, saying that he has been "cramped between the rocks" for too long. You suspect a spinal injury.

20. After performing your preliminary examination, you should *first*
    a. ask him if he feels any tingling, numbness, or burning.
    b. administer oxygen.

    c. administer an IV of normal saline.
    d. provide manual immobilization of the cervical spine.

21. Would you in this case suspect a secondary spinal injury? Why or why not?

    _____

    _____

22. You should take spinal precautions using
    a. a short board.
    b. a long board.
    c. towel rolls.
    d. a soft collar and rolled-up blanket.

Need to Know

The following represent the Key Objectives of Chapter 23:

1. *Describe the anatomy of the spinal column and spinal cord as it relates to forces that can cause injury.*

   The relationship between the spinal column and the spinal cord is similar to that of the skull and the brain: the spinal column does a very good job of protecting the delicate cord from injury. Compared with the rigid skull, the spine is very flexible, allowing us to rotate and bend with ease—most of the time! However, this similarity is a two-edged sword: if the spinal cord is injured, the swelling from the injury will become trapped within the vertebral canal, causing pressure to build and cause further damage to the cord itself.

   Review Chapter 7, Anatomy Overview, in the textbook. Remember that the spine consists of 33 vertebrae stacked on top of one another in such a way as to form a double-S shape. This curved shape, along with the vertebral disks, allows for the mobility of the spine as well as its ability to absorb forces associated with functions like walking or sitting.

   • *Compression forces* can overcome the natural resiliency of the spine, causing disks to misalign, bulge, or rupture. Significant compression can even cause burst fractures of the vertebrae. On the other hand, *distraction forces,* such as with hanging, can cause two vertebrae and the spinal cord to pull apart.

   • Forces associated with *flexion* or *extension* can cause the spine to move excessively forward or backward, respectively. This is particularly noticeable in the cervical spine region, where the weight of the skull can accelerate these forces. Flexion can cause anterior *wedge* fractures or *subluxation* of one or more vertebral bodies. Extension can cause fractures to the posterior portion of the spine, where the pedicles and lamina are located.

- *Blunt* trauma can cause hematoma within or around the spinal cord, transection of the cord, or cord impingement by fractured bone. *Penetrating* trauma can completely transect a cord or cause injury through fragments or swelling.

- *Rotational* forces can force the vertebral bodies beyond the normal range of motion, causing injury to the ligaments, tendons, and vertebral disks.

2. *Identify the signs and symptoms of the major types of spinal injuries.*

   Damage to the spinal column and spinal cord can produce very frightening signs and symptoms, ranging from severe pain at the injury site to paralysis of the entire body and loss of respiratory effort.

   - *Primary* spinal injuries are a direct result of the force involved—compression, stretching, or transection (laceration). *Secondary* injuries result from spinal cord ischemia, resulting from diminished blood flow or tissue edema at the site. The paramedic must remain vigilant for evolving spinal injuries as the swelling of the cord may not occur for some time after the initial event.

   - Sprains of the bone ligaments and strains of the tendons of the muscles surrounding and supporting the spinal column occur frequently and often cause significant, immediate pain.

   - Fractures of the spine range from being stable, such as a spinous process fracture, to an unstable and potentially fatal C1 fracture resulting from compression forces. The pain from fractures can be indistinguishable from ligament or tendon injuries, so X-rays or CT scans must be performed to definitively show their presence or absence.

   - Dislocations are caused by forces that push the flexibility of the spine too far, causing one vertebra to improperly align with the next one, resulting in point tenderness and a reduction in range of motion (ROM).

   - Actual injuries to the spinal cord range from transection, in which the cord is completely severed, to partial injuries that affect only a certain part of the cord. Several examples of partial spinal cord injuries include anterior, central, and Brown-Séquard. An *anterior*

injury to the cord will result in the classic pattern of decreased sensation and strength below the level of the injury. A *central cord injury* tends to affect the upper extremities rather than the legs because of the more centrally located motor neuron fibers for the arms. A *Brown-Séquard injury* results from an injury sustained on the side of the spinal cord, which results in an unusual presentation of sensory loss on the side of the body opposite the injury and motor loss on the same side. This is due to the location of the motor and sensory tracts in the cord itself, with the sensory fibers crossing over to the opposite side of the cord prior to exiting the column.

- Spinal shock, also known as *areflexia,* is a temporary loss of spinal reflex activity. These reflexes help govern autonomic functions such as blood pressure and body temperature regulation. Box 23-3 in the textbook discusses more specific details of spinal shock.

- Neurogenic shock—Because the sympathetic nervous system fibers are contained within the spinal cord, any injury to the cord could possibly damage this part of the nervous system. Without the sympathetic side functioning, the parasympathetic side becomes dominant, resulting in bradycardia, hypotension, and warm, dry skin distal to the injury site.

3. *Explain when spinal immobilization precautions must be taken to protect the patient from possible further injury of the spine.*

   Box 23-4 in the textbook provides a list of signs and symptoms of a spinal cord injury. They include:
   - Pain, deformity, edema, or tenderness at the site of the injury
   - Altered nervous system responses, such as numbness, tingling, weakness, or paralysis of the extremities
   - Dyspnea or apnea
   - Priapism and/or loss of rectal sphincter tone

   Immobilization will reduce the chances of further injury during the extrication and transport of the patient. Immobilization should begin the moment a spinal cord injury is suspected; do not walk a patient complaining of neck pain into the ambulance and *then* attempt immobilization. Remember that alcohol ingestion, altered mental status, and painful distracting injuries can mask the signs of a spinal injury. If you are in doubt, reconsider the forces involved in the mechanism of injury, and immobilize the patient as necessary.

4. *Describe the general principles of appropriate and effective spinal immobilization.*

There are several key principles to remember when immobilizing a patient for a possible spinal injury:

- Complete the primary assessment first. Manually stabilizing the head only during the primary assessment is appropriate.
- It takes more than two people to immobilize a patient. Coordinate the team's efforts to minimize confusion and misdirection.
- Establish the patient's baseline neurological status before performing the procedure.
- The cervical collar must fit correctly!
- The body of the patient should be secured first, followed by the head.
- Pad voids under and around the patient to provide a degree of comfort and support.
- Strapping techniques may vary; however, whatever method you use must secure the shoulders and pelvic girdle to the backboard.
- Strapping should not be tight enough to cause the patient to have difficulty breathing.
- Reevaluate the patient's neurological status after the procedure is complete. Document your findings.
- The speed and precision you apply to the technique depends upon the overall presentation of the patient. It is not wise to spend a significant amount of time immobilizing a victim of a car crash with a short extrication board if she is in shock. Conversely, rapidly extricating this victim would not be appropriate if her vital signs are stable and she is complaining of numbness or weakness in her legs.

Connections

- Review Chapter 7, Anatomy Overview, in the textbook for the structure and relationship of the spinal *column* and the spinal *cord*. For example, does the spinal cord extend all the way down the column? If not, where does it exit?
- Chapter 18, Mechanism of Injury, in the textbook speaks to the forces that you want to uncover when assessing a patient for cervical spine immobilization.
- Jim Lubin is a C2 quadriplegic who is completely paralyzed from the neck down and depends upon a ventilator to breathe. He has compiled an extensive resource page of links to various spinal cord injury websites. You can find it at www.makoa.org/sci.htm.
- The National Spinal Cord Injury Association (NSCIA) advocates for people with SCI in regards to public policy. Their website has a significant number of resources and is located at www.spinalcord.org.
- Get ready to "race" against time as you work your way through Problem-Based Learning Case 3, An Awful Crash.
- Link to the companion DVD for a chapter-based quiz, audio glossary, animations, games and exercises, and, when appropriate, skill sheets and skill Step-by-Steps.

Need to Do

The following skills are explained and illustrated in a step-by-step manner, via skill sheets and/or Step-by-Steps in this text and on the accompanying DVD:

Skill Name	Skill Sheet Number and Location	Step-by-Step Number and Location
Seated Spinal Immobilization	68 – DVD	68 – DVD
Standing Spinal Immobilization	69 – DVD	N/A
Supine Spinal Immobilization	70 – DVD	70 – DVD
Rapid Extrication	72 – DVD	N/A
NREMT Spinal Immobilization (Seated Patient)	92 – DVD	N/A
NREMT Spinal Immobilization (Supine Patient)	93 – DVD	N/A

Street Secrets

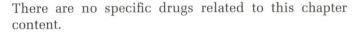

- **Push-Me Pull-You** Remember the two-headed animal in the story of Doctor Dolittle? It was called a Push-Me Pull-You. As amusing as it sounds, remember this animal when you are strapping a patient to a board. Here's why: Most straps tighten by pulling on them. Fine, but the act of pulling can in fact place unnecessary force upon the patient, causing the body to possibly twist. You can minimize this force by pushing the end of the strap feeding *to* the buckle while pulling the other end of the strap that is *leaving* the buckle.

- **"Clearing" C-Spine** Based upon the recent studies of the frequency of true cord injuries and the not-so-benign effects of nonselective spinal immobilization, EMS systems are beginning to build in treatment protocols that permit certain patients to *not* be immobilized simply on mechanism alone. Most protocols will have at least the following requirements:

    Does *not* have cervical spine tenderness

    Does *not* have an unusual sensory-motor presentation

    Does *not* have mentation changes or altering substances "on board"

    Does *not* have a "distracting" injury

  Regardless of the specifics of your system's spine clearance protocol, make sure that you understand them well!

The Drug Box

There are no specific drugs related to this chapter content.

References

1. J. A. March, S. C. Ausband, and L. H. Brown, "Changes in Physical Examination Caused by Use of Spine Immobilization." *Prehospital Emergency Care* 6 (2002): 421–24.
2. R. N. Barney, W. H. Cordell, and E. Miller, "Pain Associated with Immobilization on Rigid Spine Boards" (abstract). *Annals of Emergency Medicine* 18 (1989): 918.
3. D. Chan, R. Goldberg, and A. Tascone, "The Effect of Spine Immobilization on Healthy Volunteers." *Annals of Emergency Medicine* 23 (1994): 48–51.

Answers

Are You Ready?

1. A rescuer must gain control of the head and neck immediately to help prevent any further injury to the patient's cervical spine. Based on the mechanism of injury and the patient's symptoms, there is a significant potential for spinal injury.

2. You will need to identify and treat any problems found during the primary assessment first. If there is a problem with her airway, breathing, or circulatory status that requires immediate intervention, you may need to rapidly extricate her from the vehicle to a backboard. On the other hand, if she is stable, you may end up spending a significant amount of time immobilizing her to a short board first, and then removing her carefully from the vehicle in order to minimize any further compromise to the spine.

Active Learning

1. a. third; b. seventh; c. fourth; d. second
2. a. body; b. spinous process; c. intervertebral disk; d. spinous process; e. lamina; f. pedicle; g. transverse process; h. vertebral foramen; i. body
3. a. anterior; b. posterior; c. lateral
4. Posterior
5. Anterior

You Are There: Reality-Based Cases

Case 1

1. Patient 1 may have a so-called distracting injury to her wrist that may keep any cervical spine discomfort "hidden." However, the mechanism—a fall from a seated position—seems relatively minimal. There are no other injuries or complaints. Your index of suspicion may rise if the patient has a history of osteoporosis, but you will need to determine that information. For now, it would seem unnecessary to immobilize her.

   Patient 2 may have been thrown to the ground at a distance greater than 3 times her height, which constitutes a significant mechanism. Immobilization is indicated.

   Patient 3 is unable to communicate with you and has injuries consistent with a fall. In addition, there may be a distracting injury. Immobilization is indicated.

   Patient 4 is unable to communicate with you and has an injury consistent with a fall. Immobilization is indicated.

Test Yourself

1. b

   Vertical compression is a force applied to either the top or bottom of the spine that is directed along the length of the spine.

2. d

   The muscles of the diaphragm are controlled by the nerves originating at the fourth cervical vertebra. If the spinal cord injury occurs at or above this level, there will be little or absent diaphragm motor function leading to hypoventilation or apnea. Secondly, a complete spinal cord lesion (injury) leads to loss of sympathetic tone below the level of the lesion, which results in neurogenic shock.

3. b

The normal spinal column consists of 33 vertebrae aligned one on top of another. The upper seven vertebrae comprise the cervical spine. The next twelve vertebrae constitute the thoracic spine, and the five vertebrae below this are the lumbar spine. The remaining nine vertebrae are fused into two separate segments called the sacrum and the coccyx, which form the posterior, or back, of the pelvis.

4. Any two of the following: Jefferson fractures, Hangman's fractures, wedge-shaped compression fractures with accompanying ligament injury, trauma to the spine resulting in improper alignment or dislocation of one vertebra on another.

The most common type of spinal fracture is a wedge-shaped compression fracture. In isolation, this is a stable fracture, but if accompanied by ligament injury from a severe flexion mechanism of injury, it can be very unstable. Jefferson fractures are an injury in which the ring of C1 is pushed down on the dens of C2, resulting in a break in the ring of C1. It is usually a very unstable injury with high mortality. Bilateral fractures of the pedicles of the second cervical vertebra are also unstable. Although this pattern of injury is called a Hangman's fracture, there are a number of mechanisms that can cause it.

5. The most common types of externally applied forces include: vertical compression, flexion, extension, rotation, and distraction. Vertical compression can result in several fracture patterns (burst fracture and Jefferson fracture). Flexion is when part of the spine moves forward relative to the rest of the spine. This may result in an extreme injury called a wedge fracture, or it can result in the complete disruption of the spinal cord's supporting ligaments. Extension injuries happen when the head and spine are pushed backward relative to the torso (as happens in a rear-end accident). Rotation injuries occur when forces cause one side of the vertebral column to act as a fulcrum against which the opposite side turns. Distraction injuries happen when part of the spine remains in a fixed position while the adjacent area of the spine is pulled in the opposite direction.

6. d

Evaluating and treating a patient who is in the prone position is exceedingly difficult. Consequently, if a trauma patient is found facedown and unresponsive, there should be no delay in preparing for a log-roll maneuver. Time and steps can be saved if a long board can be placed next to the patient, with the back quickly assessed prior to rolling the patient. In most instances, this procedure requires four care providers.

7. False

One of the most important points to remember is that not all spinal fractures result in spinal cord injury and,

similarly, not all spinal cord injuries are associated with a fracture.

8. b

Hypotension in the prehospital setting should rarely, if ever, be attributed to neurogenic shock. Other causes of shock such as ongoing blood loss, cardiac tamponade, or a tension pneumothorax should be the focus of therapy.

9. False

Methylprednisolone may be beneficial in reducing inflammation in spinal cord injuries, but due to its controversial nature in the early phases of treatment, it should not be considered unless directed by local protocol or in systems where there is a long transport time.

10. a

Complete spinal cord injuries occur when there has been transection of the cord at a specific vertebral level. As a result, the patient will lose motor and sensory function below the level of the injury.

11. d

The mechanism of injury resulting in injuries to the spine has been fairly consistent over the past 3 decades. Acute spinal cord injury is caused by blunt trauma 85%–90% of the time.

12. Assess the scene, and complete a primary (ABCDE) assessment. During the primary assessment, neutralize the cervical spine and head. Immobilize as the assessment warrants. Look for potential neurological compromise. Give fluid resuscitation (with isotonic crystals) and maintain arterial pressure as needed. Search for and treat causes of hypotension and blood loss. Determine the transport priority.

13. A scene description including the patient's position; incident details (including a photo); the where, when, and how of the environment; results of the physical exam, especially the condition of the patient before and after stabilization including any changes; a time line of events, including any change in sensory or motor response or a change in the location of any deficits; a report of any deviations from the normal standard of care with justification.

14. a

In the lumbar spine, the vertical compression forces are directed toward the middle aspect of the vertebral bodies. When these forces exceed the ability of the vertebrae to resist them, the vertebral body shatters outward from within. This is called a burst fracture. A similar mechanism occurs in the upper spine, but it is directed toward the C1 and C2 vertebrae. In this case, the ring of C1 is pushed down on the dens of C2, resulting in a break in the ring of C1. This pattern is called a Jefferson fracture, and it is usually a very unstable injury with high mortality.

15. a

Injuries at or below the thoracic spine (T3) are more likely to cause the patient to become paraplegic, while injuries above this level will affect all the limbs and cause the patient to become quadriplegic.

16. The normal spinal column consists of 33 vertebrae aligned one on top of another. The upper seven vertebrae comprise the cervical spine. The next twelve vertebrae constitute the thoracic spine (and there is one vertebra for each pair of ribs in the thoracic cage), and the five vertebra below this are the lumbar spine. The remaining nine vertebrae are fused into two separate segments called the sacrum and the coccyx, which form the posterior, or back, of the pelvis.

17. Documenting the evolution, especially through markings on the body, helps medical staff at the hospital identify at what levels the patient had sensation and how that changed through time as you treated them. This enables the hospital staff to better determine where the potential injury is actually located.

    Let's use the patient from the textbook as an example: You report that your patient had sensation at the belly button upon your arrival on scene, but you note that upon repeat assessment 10 minutes later the patient had lost sensation in that area. Upon arrival at the hospital you report that the patient now has lost sensation below the nipple line. This information, along with an approximate time line, can be valuable to the neurosurgery team treating the patient as it helps them determine the progression of the injury.

18. d

    The importance of the vertebral canal is that it houses and forms a protective barrier for the spinal cord. This is critical because the spinal cord links the brain and motor capabilities of the rest of the body. This component of the body must remain flexible (allowing us to move and walk) and yet stiff enough to protect the delicate operations contained therein.

19. Patients who experience severe pain, have resistance to movement, or who develop or have an increase in neurological symptoms.

While manual stabilization with neutral repositioning is appropriate for the initial care of most patients with the potential for spine injury, there are certain cases where it is contraindicated. In particular, patients who experience severe pain, have resistance to movement, or who develop or have an increase in neurological symptoms should not undergo manual stabilization and repositioning. As well, if there is severe misalignment of the head or if airway compromise develops, repositioning should be deferred.

20. d

    Although it is virtually impossible to determine if an actual spinal injury exists in the out-of-hospital setting, it is best to treat the potential spinal injury with stabilization and immobilization.

21. Yes. You should suspect that he has a secondary spinal injury. He may have diminished mental capacity and be unable to tell you the extent of his injuries. Often secondary injuries occur hours or days later as the primary injury evolves.

    Primary injuries occur as the traumatic event causes compression, stretching, or laceration of the spinal cord. Secondary cord injuries occur minutes, hours, days, or weeks later as the primary injury evolves. Spinal cord ischemia has been suggested as the principal cause of secondary injury, although other mechanisms like edema may also exist. A patient can be considered to be unreliable for a number of reasons. Significant injury, particularly long-bone fractures, may be sufficiently distracting as to render a physical exam unreliable. Altered mental status, particularly secondary to head injury, may also prevent a reliable history or exam.

22. a

    Short spine boards are primarily used to immobilize the neck and back of patients who are sitting upright or are in a confined space. A simple short board can be used in combination with a cervical collar and tape to provide intermediate immobilization, although there are many commercial devices that include all the necessary equipment.

Problem-Based Learning Case 3
An Awful Crash

Part I: The Case

Dispatch and Scene Size-Up

Your pager begins to go off in that familiar singsong: beep beep beep. There is static for a second, and then . . . beeeeEEEP. "Medic 17, Rescue 4, Battalion 2, Engine 42. Unconscious male after a fall. Willows Motocross Raceway, 27235 Highway 70. Medical personnel on scene reporting motocross rider down after collision."

You are at the track within 5 minutes. The rescue unit pulls into the lot as well. A track official waves you to the far gate, near the large mogul section where the riders can gain altitudes of 30 feet as they jump off the hills. You see the medical response truck parked off to the side, its amber lights flashing.

As you pull your gear off the ambulance, a track staff member comes running over. Quickly she tells you that the rider is at the bottom of a ravine that is adjacent to the course track. You follow the direction of her pointed finger and notice that the chain-link fence that separates the track from that area is heavily damaged, with the top of the fence bowed outward. It appears that the rider jumped his motorcycle in the wrong direction and sailed through the fence.

It is midafternoon. The ambient temperature is about 92°F, and the humidity is 90%.

1. *Describe your initial concerns about this situation.*

   _____

   _____

2. *List the equipment you will bring down with you to the patient's side.*

   _____

   _____

The Primary Assessment and Initial Differentials

The patient is lying prone on the ground about 20 feet below you. The terrain is not steep enough to require rope rescue techniques, but it is rocky and loose. There are three other people kneeling next to the patient. You see the demolished motorbike further down the hill, about 30 feet away from the rider. You make your way down the hillside with your EMT partner and one of the rescue firefighters. The other firefighter is staying at the top of the hill.

You reach the injured rider. One of the bystanders appears to be a first responder; he is using a pair of trauma shears to cut away the rider's clothing and protective pads. It looks like he is about to remove the shoulder pads and back shield.

The rider is still wearing his helmet. You can't determine how well he is breathing or his airway patency, but you hear strange sounds coming from underneath the helmet. His arms and legs are lying in odd positions. There are clear angulations of his right leg and both arms.

3. *What are the patient care priorities?*

   _____

   _____

4. *Is the first responder performing the correct procedure?*

   _____

   _____

5. *What are your immediate management steps?*

_____

_____

There is frank blood coming from the patient's mouth through clenched teeth. It is bubbling and spraying into the airway with each breath. The inside of the helmet is coated with blood. The patient's breathing pattern is fast and shallow, and you hear stridor with each breath. He does not respond to your voice or a trapezius pinch.

The chest plate of his protective gear is fractured in several places. As you release the shoulder pads, you see multiple abrasions and contusions stretching across his chest. A laceration is bleeding freely in the left upper side of the chest, just inferior to the clavicle.

6. *What are your immediate next steps?*

_____

_____

7. *Name the possible injuries sustained by the patient based on your initial findings.*

_____

_____

Field Impression(s) and Formulation of Treatment Plan

With all the riding gear removed, you see the amount of damage the rider sustained when he crashed through the fence.

- *HEENT.* Bleeding from the mouth has stopped. Trismus noted. Blood noted in left ear canal. No accessory muscle use noted. Medical pendant around neck. Neck veins are flat.
- *Chest.* Laceration to left upper chest as noted. Bruising, abrasions throughout chest wall. Crackling under skin noted on palpation to left upper third of anterior-lateral chest wall. Diminished or absent breath sounds on left, poor on right. Symmetrical chest rise.
- *Abdomen.* Bruising, hematoma, abrasions to left upper and lower quadrants. Rigidity on palpation.
- *Pelvis.* Contusion, left lateral hip. Open wound, minimal bleeding, distal to contusion.
- *Legs.* Deformity, hematoma, left femur. Deformity, distal right tibia and fibula.
- *Arms.* Deformity, both wrists. Lacerations and abrasions to both arms.
- *Back.* Abrasions, contusion left flank.

- *Vitals.* Heart rate: 126 and regular, at the carotid. Respiratory rate: 28. Skin condition: pale, warm, and diaphoretic.

You package the patient onto a backboard and strap him securely for the extrication process back up the hillside. There is a brief debate among you as to which interventions to perform on scene and which to delay until the team reaches the ambulance. Agreement on a treatment plan is made and, after another minute of on-scene time, the patient is moved up the hill and to the ambulance.

8. *List the possible injury patterns that the patient may have sustained based on your findings.*

_____

_____

9. *What prehospital interventions could be performed on the patient?*

_____

_____

10. *Which interventions were performed prior to extrication? Why?*

_____

_____

11. *How can you manage the challenges presented in the airway?*

_____

_____

Transportation and Ongoing Care

Twenty-five minutes have passed since your initial contact with the patient. You brace yourself against the back of the bench seat as the ambulance jostles around due to the bumpy trail surface. Once back out on the highway you continue your survey of the patient. His SpO_2 is 90% with supplemental oxygen; PCO_2 is 21; blood pressure is palpated to be approximately 70 mm Hg systolic. His ECG is shown in Figure PBL 3-1. Pupils are dilated and slow to react. Breath sounds remain the same. Your patient is now moaning.

You have two EMTs assisting with the care of your patient. You have a transport time of 20 minutes. The air medical service is not available.

12. *What interventions should you perform now?*

_____

_____

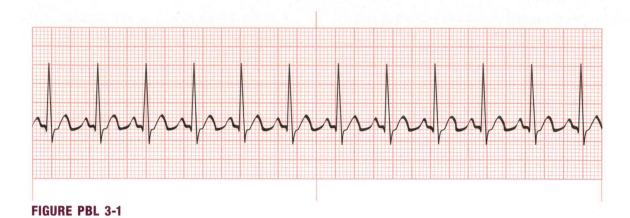

FIGURE PBL 3-1

13. *Did the additional vital sign measurements match what you expected based upon your earlier survey results?*

_____

_____

History and Physical Exam (Secondary Assessment and History)

One of the EMTs reports that the patient's right foot is considerably cooler than his left. No distal pulse can be palpated on that extremity.

The medical pendant reads "Seizure Hx."

Your estimated time of arrival is 7 minutes. The driver is notifying the receiving facility of your impending arrival and the patient's condition.

14. *How does the EMT's finding affect your care? Will you act upon this finding?*

_____

_____

15. *How might the identification of a medical history affect your assessment and management of this patient?*

_____

_____

16. *Verbalize a radio report to the receiving facility.*

_____

_____

Transfer of Care, Follow-up, and Outcome

The attending physician looks to you expectantly. As the crew and hospital staff prepare to transfer the patient to the hospital gurney, you begin your report.

The room ECG and gas monitors are attached to the patient. A swarm of surgeons, residents, nurses, and technicians goes to work. Bloods are drawn, and the patient's body is reexamined. A chest tube is inserted at the fifth intercostal space of the left chest at the midaxillary line. Blood pours into the Pleur-Evac. Radiographic films of the chest, abdomen, and head are taken and sent to the lab for processing. A Foley catheter is inserted.

After cleaning yourself up, you begin your documentation of the incident.

17. *What does the blood in the Pleur-Evac indicate?*

_____

_____

18. *Assume that a chest X-ray was taken before the placement of the chest tube. What would you expect to see on the film? Why?*

_____

_____

19. *Write a narrative of your findings and treatment of the patient.*

_____

_____

Long-Term Outlook

You later learn that the rider may have experienced a generalized seizure prior to the crash. Crash reconstruction indicated that he may have been moving as fast as 40 miles per hour as he launched himself off the last hill. Witnesses reported that the bike nearly cleared the height of the fence, which was 12 feet high at that point. However, the front wheel collided with the top of the fence, and the patient became partially entangled with his bike as it flipped over the fence.

Both the bike and rider struck the ground nearly simultaneously, which caused them to separate. The force of the impact caused the rider to tumble another 15 feet before coming to a stop.

The patient has multiple surgeries to repair his long bones and remains in the surgical intensive care unit for 3 weeks before being transferred to a surgical floor. He spends the next year in physical therapy to regain the strength in his legs and arms. He never remembers the crash or any specific details of that day.

20. *Were the injury patterns in line with the described mechanism?*

_____

_____

21. *What may have caused the open laceration of the patient's left upper chest?*

_____

_____

Part II: Debriefing

Responses to Part 1 questions:

1. It appears that an extended extrication of the patient will be necessary, depending upon how far down the ravine he is. How might this impact your transportation decision? Did you consider the terrain and weather conditions as possible safety hazards?

2. Your list of equipment should take into account the distance from the patient to the ambulance. The further the distance, the less likely you can run back to the unit to retrieve equipment. From the initial reports, it sounds like you will need equipment for spinal immobilization, airway control, breathing management, and circulatory support. Does your list match this answer?

3. How well can you conduct your primary assessment while your patient is in the prone position?

4. It would appear that the patient does need to be exposed to find any injuries hidden by the clothing and hidden gear. But is now the appropriate time?

5. In this case, should the helmet remain on or should it be removed? What about any other protective gear that the patient might be wearing—should that also be removed?

6. If you were thinking of additional assessment steps, reconsider your findings so far. What interventions can you perform right now to correct any life-threatening conditions?

7. Did your suspicions relate to life-threatening conditions? If so, that's great. If you were considering others, remember that you are still in the primary assessment, trying to figure out what might kill the patient *now*.

8. There are several possible injury patterns to be identified, many of them serious in nature. How can you organize them? Were any of them not originally identified in the primary assessment that could still be life threatening?

9. Did you include all the BLS procedures in addition to ALS?

10. Does it make sense that most of the care you provided on the scene was BLS? Why or why not?

11. If you were considering the use of succinylcholine to paralyze the patient and control the trismus, what might be a significant complication with the medication itself?

12. Go back to your original list of treatment options. Which ones were appropriate to perform while en route to the hospital? Which ones can you delegate to the EMTs to perform?

13. Which condition(s) might be causing the vital signs to present the way they do?

14. Have you dealt with all the life-threatening conditions? Perhaps now is the time to manage the limb-threatening concerns. Did you describe what you or the EMT would do?

15. What is your suspicion now that there may be a medical component to this event?

16. Radio reports are usually very short, 30 seconds in length. For a trauma patient, the report should include the MOI, injuries sustained, vital signs, and treatment rendered. Did yours fit within that time frame?

17. Did you expect to see blood in the evacuation chambers of the Pleur-Evac? Where did it originate?

18. Radiography will reveal the presence of fluid such as edema or blood, as well as free air. Did you find out how?

19. Did you use SOAP or CHART as a template? Compare your verbal radio report with your written one. Which details did you stress on the radio report?

20. Given the velocity associated with the fall, there were multiple types of impacts involved, both blunt and possibly penetrating. It's not surprising that the patient sustained a significant number of injuries.

21. Could it have been a fractured clavicle that broke the skin, or part of the bike, or something on the ground? You might not think about the blunt end of the handlebar, but with that much force behind it, that may well have been the culprit.

Part III: Case Discussion

The management of prehospital trauma is an exercise in organization. It begins with determining what resources you will need to bring to the patient's side, as well as what you will need to prepare so that transport is not delayed. It continues with your assessment approach. Is your primary assessment conducted so that there is not one wasted moment in the process? Do you identify the most serious injuries, those that could kill the patient without your immediate intervention? Are your team members provided with enough direction to work on managing different aspects of the incident, yet in coordination with each other? These are the fundamental actions that, as the lead paramedic, you must strive to perform each and every time you deal with a critically injured patient.

The forces involved in this case were significant. The rate of speed as estimated by witnesses, coupled with the distance and height traveled by the rider, combined to inflict a large amount of energy that needed to be dissipated upon impact. The rider was wearing protective clothing and a helmet, which may have prevented him from being killed outright. However, the ongoing crashes that occurred after the initial impact continued to inflict serious damage, as evidenced by your assessment.

The distance from your unit to the patient is significant and plays a factor in determining how much equipment you will need to bring down to the patient's side (and bring back up to the ambulance). Equipment needed to control the airway would be a combination of BLS adjuncts, suction, and possibly ALS airway equipment. Oxygen and ventilation equipment will be needed to support any respiratory deficiency. Given the amount of research data regarding fluid replacement in the trauma patient, that skill may be less of a priority in this case. Extrication and carrying equipment will be important, though.

Can you adequately assess a prone patient? As well-meaning as it may be, the first responder was spending precious minutes exposing the patient when the greater priority was to establish the patient's airway patency. With the blood coming from under the helmet, there's an immediate need to gain control of the head and neck and roll the patient to a position in which adequate airway control can be provided. You might consider rolling the patient to a lateral position first, a more difficult position to maintain if you need to remove the helmet. However, with the blood coming from the airway, it may be helpful to allow continued drainage while preparing to suction the patient (you *did* bring your suction, didn't you?). There are five of you, so it might be possible to perform the "half roll."

You know that you will need to remove the helmet. What about the protective pads and other gear? The general rule of thumb is to remove everything if the helmet is coming off, or leave everything on if the patient is stable. In this particular case, you will need to remove as many pieces of the gear as possible. Your bystanders can assist here, especially if they are more familiar with how a rider would put the gear on.

Trismus (involuntary clenching of the jaw) and a bloody airway both indicate a serious problem with the management of this airway. It will be hard to suction or find the source of bleeding in the oropharynx if you are not able to get past the teeth. Assisted ventilations may also be ineffective, especially if the nasopharyngeal passage is also blocked. You could consider a paralytic to relax the contracted muscles, but you definitely will need to control the patient's airway.

With a brain injury as a possible cause of the loss of consciousness, the associated mechanism of injury may have also injured the spinal cord. This will also complicate the management of the airway, because a jaw thrust will need to be done. If the jaw thrust does not adequately maintain the airway, perform a chin lift as minimally as possible.

Suction aggressively. Try to determine where the bleeding source is located; if it is in the soft tissues of the oropharynx, you might be able to control the bleeding. Assist ventilations between suctioning attempts using a bag-mask; if suctioning does not maintain airway patency, you may need to intubate or use a supraglottic airway such as a dual-lumen airway.

The possible head injury is also worrisome. Coupled with a dangerously low blood pressure, this is a recipe for disaster. The brain is not receiving enough blood, oxygen, and nutrients when it needs them the most. The mean arterial pressure is in all likelihood not high enough to maintain cerebral perfusion pressure. However, the other sources of bleeding that may not be controllable in the prehospital arena diminish the benefit of fluid therapy.

Did you seal the open chest wound immediately? Signs of bubbling or sounds of sucking are *not* needed to confirm the presence of an open chest wound. The same would also go for the presence of a flail segment; paradoxical chest wall movement may not occur for some time, especially if the victim is young and can "self-splint" the broken ribs.

Did you determine whether the patient had a pneumothorax, a tension pneumothorax, a hemothorax, or a pneumohemothorax? It's not as easy as it might seem. Remember to look at the *entire picture*, not just one or two signs or symptoms. In this case, there was a clear absence of lung sounds over the affected side, no jugular venous distention, the presence of subcutaneous air, and symmetrical chest rise. You could have percussed the chest wall for hypertympany or hypotympany, but the patient is also not exhibiting accessory muscle use, which implies that the passage of air is not restricted. It seems less likely to be a tension pneumothorax. The later vital signs would appear to support that exclusion.

There appears to be significant hypotension, which might imply a source of internal bleeding, perhaps into the chest cavity. The draining of blood through the inserted chest tube appears to bear out that possibility. However, the presence of subcutaneous air may point to an open pneumothorax, along with the open chest wound. Certainly, a combination pneumohemothorax is quite possible here.

The abdomen may also be a source of internal bleeding. The external injury pattern may indicate more serious conditions beneath. The rigidity of the abdomen may not necessarily be from a large volume of blood; more likely it is from the irritation of the peritoneum by blood or free air. In either case, it is a worrisome area. Pneumatic anti-shock garments may be of value here if an abdominal bleed is suspected.

Typically, complete splinting of extremities is withheld in critical cases such as this, at least until other, more pressing problems are addressed. Placing the limbs into near-anatomical positions on the back-board is usually sufficient. However, the loss of a pulse and/or sensation of the distal part of the affected extremity is of concern. You may need to direct the EMT to realign the broken extremity in hopes of reperfusing the limb.

Despite all these injuries, the patient survives neurologically intact. This may be due to the patient's relatively good health, age, and protective gear that may have reduced the forces just enough for him to escape death.

Part IV: Further Learning Paths

- This case study reviews multiple chapters in the trauma section of the textbook. You will want to review the chapters relevant to the injuries described in this PBL.

- The Prehospital Trauma Life Support (PHTLS) Program and the International Trauma Life Support (ITLS) Program are 2-day courses that help to bring together various trauma concepts similar to this case. More information may be found at the PHTLS home page on the National Association of EMTs website, www.naemt.org/PHTLS/default. htm and at the ITLS website, www.itrauma.org/.

- The American College of Surgeons Committee on Trauma (ACS-COT) maintains a website of resources at www.facs.org/trauma/index.html.

chapter 24

Skeletal Trauma

Are You Ready?

Sixteen-year-old Rex and his friends were enjoying a summer afternoon at the skate park when Rex came off of his skateboard at the top of the half-pipe and fell approximately 15 feet over the back side, landing on his outstretched right arm. Rex's friends found him sitting on the ground, cradling his badly deformed right forearm. Rex had a blank look on his face as he stared at the new angle that had been created in the middle of his forearm. He muttered, "Dude, I don't feel so hot," and then passed out. Rex's friends quickly ran to a phone and called 9-1-1.

When you arrive on scene, you find Rex sitting on the ground, awake and alert, complaining of severe pain to his right forearm and numbness in the fingers on his right hand. You note that the right forearm is obviously deformed, and there is considerable swelling to the extremity.

1. What are your initial priorities when you arrive on scene?

_____

_____

_____

2. How do you assess the right forearm, and what are you looking for during the assessment?

_____

_____

_____

3. Should you straighten this injury? Why or why not? If yes, how?

_____

_____

_____

4. Should you manage the patient's pain? If so, when and how will you take care of it?

_____

_____

_____

_____

Active Learning

Anatomy Review

1. Identify the structures of the upper limbs shown in Figure 24-1.

a. _____

b. _____

c. _____

d. _____

e. _____

f. _____

g. _____

h. _____

i. _____

j. _____

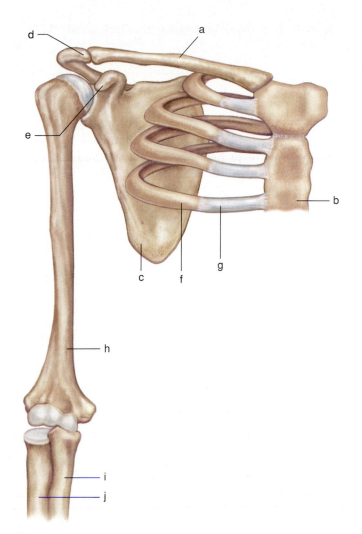

FIGURE 24-1

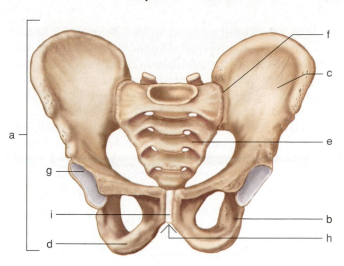

FIGURE 24-2

gently manipulate the bone ends a little. You will feel the grating, cracking sensation of the two bone ends rubbing against each other.

Bonus: Try to create a "greenstick" fracture with another turkey bone. How much force did you need to apply?

4. Can You Feel the Beat?

Distal pedal pulses can be very difficult to find, even under normal conditions. Take the time to evaluate as many pedal pulses as possible. First try to find them on classmates, friends, and relatives. Have the person stand, as well as lay supine, and try to find at least the dorsalis pedis and posterior tibial pulses. With time and practice, these pulse sites will become easier to find.

5. See the Big Picture

Or at least look at a few radiographs, or X-rays. The next time you are in the emergency department, see if you might be permitted to review a few X-ray films of patients who have sustained extremity fractures. As you view the injury, imagine how that might feel on palpation. Sketch how the limb might look upon visualization.

You Are There: Reality-Based Cases

Case 1

You and your partner have responded to a "fall off a bicycle" in one of the more remote areas of the national park located in your response district. Park rangers have escorted the fallen rider out of the woods and meet you at the trailhead. You can see the rider's mountain bike in the back of the park rangers' truck; it appears to be in good shape, with the only obvious damage being the handlebar twisted to one side.

2. Identify the structures of the pelvic girdle shown in Figure 24-2.

a. _____

b. _____

c. _____

d. _____

e. _____

f. _____

g. _____

h. _____

i. _____

3. Snap! Crackle! Pop!

Many EMS providers will state that the feeling of crepitus upon palpation is unforgettable. In order to simulate the sound and sensation of broken bones rubbing against each other, don a pair of gloves and pick up the drumstick of a turkey *before* it's been cooked. Hold both ends firmly, and bend the shaft of the bone until it breaks (this might require significant force). Once it is broken,

Mrs. Strickland appears to be a woman in her 50s who is in good physical shape. She is sitting on a bench located at the trailhead. Sheepishly, she tells you that she had lost her concentration for a moment while coming to a stop and forgot to unclip her shoes from the bicycle's pedals. As she toppled over, she instinctively extended her left arm out and fell onto her hand. Almost immediately she felt her wrist snap. She was wearing a helmet that was secured to her head, but she doesn't recall striking her head on the ground. The fall happened about 30 minutes ago.

1. Based on this information, what is your general impression of the patient?

   _____

   _____

   _____

2. What are your first steps in approaching this patient?

   _____

   _____

   _____

3. Based on the mechanism of injury, what injuries might this patient have sustained?

   _____

   _____

   _____

Your general impression of the patient reveals a 57-year-old female in excellent physical condition. In your primary assessment, you determine that her airway is patent, she is breathing without excessive effort, and her skin signs are warm, pink, and slightly diaphoretic. Her chief complaints include pain in the left wrist and left shoulder and clavicle. No damage to the helmet is noted, and she does not complain of any head or cervical spine pain. An examination of the affected extremity shows deformity in the left wrist. The patient is able to squeeze your finger with her left hand with reasonable strength and does not complain of any neurological deficits distal to the wrist. You are able to find a weak radial pulse on the left wrist as compared to the right.

The patient is also complaining of pain to the left anterior shoulder. You can palpate deformity in the area, and the patient is unable to rotate the arm without significant discomfort.

4. Based upon your findings, describe your management approach to the patient's injuries.

   _____

   _____

   _____

5. Will you need to reduce the left wrist? Why or why not?

   _____

   _____

   _____

As you treat her injuries, you notice that she is leaning a little to her left. You ask if she feels okay. She smiles and nods her head, but there seems to be a little anxiety showing on her face. "I think I might have hit my left side on something when I fell. It's beginning to hurt now." She motions to the left upper quadrant of her abdomen. She winces when you lightly palpate the area.

6. What do you want to know now? What should you do next?

   _____

   _____

   _____

Test Yourself

1. While sliding down a fire pole, a firefighter loses his grip and falls to the apparatus floor. The height of the fall was about 10 feet. He is complaining of significant left thigh pain. Upon assessment you note deformity to the femur midway between the knee and hip. Your patient appears to have no other injuries. He is awake, alert, and is otherwise not in any other distress. How should you care for this patient?

   a. Long backboard, analgesia, O_2, transport
   b. Reeves stretcher, IV, transport
   c. Traction splint, IV, analgesia, transport
   d. Long board splint, IV, O_2, transport

2. You are caring for a patient with a suspected hip injury who is presenting with a flexed hip that appears to be externally rotated. This patient has most likely sustained a(n) _____ dislocation.

3. In addition to assessing for DCAP-BTLS, what other signs should you assess for when treating a patient with a suspected extremity fracture or dislocation?

   a. Decreased pulse, decreased range of motion, increased strength
   b. False movement, increased circulation to the area, paresthesia
   c. Crepitus, false movement, increased range of motion
   d. Crepitus, pain, decreased range of motion

4. Injuries to bones, muscles, cartilage, tendons, and ligaments are rarely life threatening.
   True
   False

5. You have been called to the local baseball field for an injured player. Upon examination you note angulation to the distal, lateral aspect (thumb side) of the forearm with noted pain and swelling to the extremity, leading you to suspect a radial fracture. You should also suspect a possible _____ fracture.

6. Which of the following is a common fracture site in geriatric patients?
   a. Calcaneus
   b. Humerus
   c. Clavicle
   d. Femur

7. How should dislocations be immobilized?
   a. Splint in found position and apply hot packs to increase vascular supply to the area.
   b. Immobilize the dislocation in the position found to reduce pain.
   c. Attempt to reposition as many times as necessary until adequate vascular supply is achieved.
   d. Reposition the dislocation so you may splint the injury in a position of comfort.

8. Differentiate between a sprain and a strain.

   _____

   _____

9. The radius is one of the bones of the _____ skeleton.

10. You have responded to the local ice rink for an injured hockey player. Upon examination you discover that your patient has a painful right upper extremity that appears pale and pulseless. A neurological exam of this extremity reveals weakness and painful movement throughout the range of motion. What immediate injury complication might affect this patient?
    a. Infection
    b. Fat embolism
    c. Compartment syndrome
    d. Hemorrhage

11. The most frequently fractured foot bone is the _____.

12. What is the function of an osteoclast?

    _____

    _____

13. Which of the following are signs of compartment syndrome?
    a. Pulselessness, paresthesia, paralysis, paradoxus
    b. Pulselessness, pallor, paresthesia, priapism
    c. Pain, pallor, pressure, paresthesia
    d. Pain, petechiae, pressure, paralysis

14. A subluxation is a type of partial dislocation.
    True
    False

15. Which of the following is a contraindication for use of a traction splint with a femur fracture?
    a. Closed femur fracture
    b. Pulseless lower extremity
    c. Hip fracture
    d. Unconscious patient

Need to Know

1. *Assess, formulate a field impression, and treat a patient with a fracture, sprain, or strain of an extremity.*

Injuries to the skeletal muscles and extremities can be deceptively simple to manage. Moreover, the pain and discomfort produced by these injuries can mask more serious injury patterns to the head, chest, and abdomen. Therefore, regardless of how "minor" the patient's complaint may be, it is wise to remember the basics and ensure that the patient's airway, breathing, and circulatory status are intact and functioning well before focusing on the isolated skeletal injury.

Specific management of isolated skeletal injuries involves several basic principles. The paramedic must assess the circulatory and neurological condition of the extremity involved in the injury before and after immobilization efforts. Additionally, the use of splints, application of cold to reduce swelling, and pain control will provide a great deal of comfort to the patient.

A specific circumstance deserves special mention. When the neurovascular status of an extremity is impaired due to angulation, realignment of the dislocation or fracture will be necessary. This situation requires immediate, careful attention in order to minimize long-term disabling effects.

There are many bones to injure and seemingly the same number of ways of splinting them. Immobilization devices range from pillows to vacuum splints. However, all methods of splinting an isolated injury have common points to remember. Table 24-1 summarizes these points:

TABLE 24-1   General Splinting Principles

Procedural Step	Discussion Points
Use standard precautions.	Open wounds may be bloody, so at a minimum gloves and eye protection must be used.
Assess the affected extremity for distal sensation, motor response, and perfusion.	If the distal hand or foot has good sensation, motor function, and perfusion, splint the limb in the position found. If neurological function and/or perfusion are compromised, attempt to straighten the extremity once by providing gentle traction while moving the extremity ends into a more natural position. Follow similar principles if the injury is associated with an open wound caused by broken bone piercing the skin or by a penetrating mechanism.
Place the extremity into a position of function.	By having the patient passively grasp a small roll of roller gauze, the tendons, ligaments, and muscles of the arm are in their most neutral or relaxed position. This *functional position* provides both maximal comfort as well as minimal damage to the injury site. If an Achilles tendon injury is suspected, splint the leg with the foot slightly extended (plantar flexion) to reduce pain.
Apply an appropriate splinting device.	There are many commercial and noncommercial splinting devices, ranging from pillows and sheets to vacuum and traction splints. Train with the splinting equipment used in your local EMS system to be fully prepared to use those devices.
Pad any voids with soft, supportive material.	Any large gaps between the extremity and splint may allow for excessive movement within the device with resulting pain and the potential for further injury.
Secure the splint to the extremity, making sure that the limb is immobilized above and below the affected area and at the joints above and below the injury site.	The splint should be secured enough to immobilize the extremity bones and muscles, but not so tight it reduces blood flow and impairs neurological function. Splinting the joints above and below the injury site also reduces further swelling and potential injury.
Reassess the distal extremity for sensation, motor response, and perfusion.	The splint may need to be loosened slightly if pulses and neurological function that were present prior to the splint application are now diminished or absent. Once pulses return, secure the splint with enough force to immobilize the injury without reducing circulation.
Apply cold if possible.	Cold will help reduce the amount of inflammation and swelling at the site of injury, promote faster healing times, and reduce pain.
Consider additional pain management measures.	Your local EMS system may have protocols that allow for the judicious use of pain control medication in the case of isolated extremity injuries and for reducing dislocations if transport times are lengthy. Consider the use of analgesics prior to splinting or dislocation reduction.

Need to Do

The following skills are explained and illustrated in a step-by-step manner, via skill sheets and/or Step-by-Steps in this text and on the accompanying DVD:

Skill Name	Skill Sheet Number and Location	Step-by-Step Number and Location
Appendicular Skeleton Splinting	73 – DVD	N/A
Traction Splinting	74 – DVD	74 – DVD

Connections

- Remember to carefully understand the mechanism of injury and accurately assess the patient before focusing your attention on the isolated injury. Is there any potential for less obvious but more significant injuries? Is the isolated injury so painful that it distracts the patient from noticing cervical spine pain? Review Chapter 18, Mechanism of Injury, and Chapter 27, Trauma Patients and Trauma Systems, in the textbook for further information.

- Link to the companion DVD for a chapter-based quiz, audio glossary, animations, games and exercises, and, when appropriate, skill sheets and skill Step-by-Steps.

Street Secrets

- **RICE** Although management of isolated musculoskeletal injuries is generally considered a basic skill, it is easy to overlook simple but essential points. *Elevation* of an injury is very helpful in promoting venous return from the injury site to the body. Application of *cold* will reduce excessive swelling to the site that might otherwise impair needed blood flow to the injury site. In addition, it can reduce pain and discomfort to the injury, a very important aspect in the management of the patient. For injuries such as sprains and strains, compression of the site using an elastic bandage may also help slow excessive swelling. A simple mnemonic to remember these steps is RICE—*R*est, *I*ce, *C*ompression, and *E*levation.

- **Age and Skeletal Injuries** The extremes of age influence the rate and type of skeletal injuries. Geriatric patients are prone to more fractures due to bone density loss. This means that you will want to reconsider even minor mechanisms of force as potential causes of fractures. For the pediatric patient, the bones are more pliable. On the one hand, this means that the bones can flex a bit more, allowing them to deflect some of the force involved.

However, that force is transferred elsewhere into the body, such as to the organs. Therefore, look carefully for additional underlying injuries beyond the simple fracture.

The Drug Box

Morphine sulfate: An analgesic such as morphine sulfate will provide a good deal of comfort to a patient with a painful isolated musculoskeletal injury. Local protocols vary, but it is not unusual to administer greater amounts IV or IM to provide pain relief.[1]

Nitrous oxide: An anesthetic can help to reduce pain by depressing the central nervous system. Nitrous oxide is a gas that is self-administered by the patient.

Benzodiazepines (e.g., diazepam, Ativan, midazolam): Although these drugs do not manage pain directly, anxiolytics are very helpful in the management of the anxiety and emotional stress a patient can experience with these very painful injuries. Ativan and midazolam are rapid-onset, short-duration sedatives; diazepam (Valium) is a commonly found prehospital drug that has a rapid onset of action but also has a greater potential for respiratory depression and a longer duration of action than Ativan or midazolam.

References

1. M. Steele, "Fractures, Tibia and Fibula." www.emedicine.com/emerg/topic207.htm (accessed 14 Aug. 2005).
2. P. Rosen and R. Barkin, *Emergency Medicine: Concepts and Clinical Practice,* 5th ed., St. Louis: Mosby, 2003.

Answers

Are You Ready?

1. Establish scene safety. Regardless of the patient's complaint, begin with a primary assessment to determine any potential threats to the patient's airway, breathing, and circulatory status.

2. Your primary assessment of an angulated extremity fracture should take place in the position in which the extremity is found. Assessment should address color, movement, sensation, temperature, and perfusion to the distal extremity. Look for the "P"s: pain, pallor, paresthesia, paralysis, and pressure.

3. Although the numbness of the distal arm is of real concern, check to see if a pulse is present at the wrist. If the pulse is absent or very diminished compared with the unaffected arm, you may need to straighten the angulated fracture to preserve the limb. Apply gentle traction, and place the extremity in an anatomical position, with the hand in a position of function. Apply a splint that immobilizes the joint above and below the fracture and supports the area beneath the suspected fracture.

4. Initial pain management can take place by immobilizing, elevating, and icing the extremity. Pain management via the administration of IV or IM analgesics should be considered prior to manipulation or splinting of the injured extremity if the assessment of the patient's pain dictates.[2]

Active Learning

1. a. clavicle; b. sternum; c. scapula; d. acromion process; e. coracoid process; f. rib; g. costal cartilage; h. humerus; i. ulna; j. radius

2. a. pelvis; b. ischium; c. ilium; d. pubic bone; e. sacrum; f. sacroiliac joint; g. acetabulum; h. pubic arch; i. symphysis pubis

You Are There: Reality-Based Cases

Case 1

1. The initial scene size-up and patient presentation indicate a stable, isolated trauma patient. However, a primary assessment still must be conducted to confirm the original impression.

2. Consider cervical spine precautions, and confirm the patient's level of consciousness and airway, breathing, and circulatory status.

3. Dislocation and/or fracture of the left shoulder; fracture of the left wrist.

4. Splint the isolated wrist injury, and apply cold to help reduce swelling. Immobilization of the shoulder can be done through the use of a sling and swath. Consider pain management if permitted by local protocol.

5. Although the pulse strength is *reduced,* it is not *absent.* Reduction of any angulated injury carries a degree of risk of further harm. Joints such as the wrist, knee, and especially elbow are very complex structures that are difficult to manipulate even in the presence of radiographic confirmation. Therefore, in this situation, it is best to splint it in the position found. Transport and frequently reassess the perfusion status while en route to the hospital.

6. This new complaint is alarming. The spleen is located in the left upper quadrant and is highly vascular. It can

bleed profusely if it is injured. The delay in symptoms may be due to the spleen's capsule controlling the bleeding to a certain extent. This late finding reminds us that ongoing assessment and a reconsideration of the mechanism of injury is warranted even for minor-appearing injuries. Examine the area carefully to see if there is any apparent bruising to the area. Assume that bleeding may be present and try to have the patient lay supine. Keep the patient warm and administer oxygen. You may need to initiate intravenous access in case signs of shock appear.

Test Yourself

1. c

The basis for identification of skeletal injuries is history, mechanism of injury, and assessment findings. From this information, a field impression can be generated and a plan developed for specific management. Depending on the patient's vital signs, the paramedic may decide that IV fluid administration and splinting with sufficient analgesia is indicated, followed by transport to an emergency department for definitive care.

2. Anterior hip

An anterior dislocation usually occurs when the hip is extended and externally rotated at the time of impact. The classic presentation of this injury is a flexed, abducted, and externally rotated hip.

3. d

In addition to the DCAP-BTLS signs, look for crepitus, pain on palpation or movement, decreased range of motion, false movement (unnatural movement of an extremity), and decreased or absent sensory perception or circulation distal to the injury.

4. True

Injuries to bones, muscles, cartilage, tendons, and ligaments are rarely life threatening because major organs and blood vessels are generally not involved.

5. Ulnar

Because the radius and ulna bones work together as a unit, a fracture to one is usually associated with a fracture or dislocation to the other. Fractures of both forearm bones or one bone with a concomitant joint injury are more common occurrences than a fracture of either bone by itself. Because the injury described involves the radius, it can be assumed that the ulna is also involved.

6. d

Common sites of fractures are the vertebrae, the femoral neck, shoulder, and distal radius or wrist.

7. b

Immobilize dislocations in the position found or the position of comfort to ensure good vascular supply and pain reduction. To alleviate swelling, elevate and apply cold packs to the extremity if possible. The application of cold packs helps to decrease inflammation in the area of injury, thereby decreasing swelling and subsequent pain. You should attempt to realign a pulseless extremity only once in the prehospital setting according to local protocol, as you may cause more damage and deficit through realignment.

8. A sprain is the result of stretching or tearing a ligament (bone to bone), and a strain is the stretching or tearing of a tendon (muscle to bone).

9. Appendicular

The appendicular skeleton includes the paired long bones of the body, such as the humerus, radius, and ulna. These attach to the axial skeleton by the clavicle and scapula (commonly referred to as the pectoral girdle). Also part of the appendicular skeleton are the bones of the lower extremities, specifically the femur, tibia, and fibula, that attach to the axial skeleton by the pelvic girdle which consists of three bones: two innominate bones and the sacrum. The innominate bones are further subdivided into the ilium, ischium, and pubis.

10. c

The lower leg and forearm are the most common locations for compartment syndrome to develop. Pain with passive range of motion of the fingers or toes is thought to be the most sensitive early sign. Late signs of arterial insufficiency caused by compartment syndrome include: pain, pallor, paresthesia, paralysis, and pulselessness. If nerve or muscle ischemia has been present long enough, paralysis, paresthesia, and tissue damage are likely. Pulselessness is not reliable, as it does not always occur in the late stages of compartment syndrome.

11. Calcaneus (heel)

The calcaneus (heel) is the most frequently fractured tarsal (foot) bone. The calcaneus is frequently fractured during a fall from a height.

12. Osteoclasts serve to reabsorb bone for the purpose of repairing and growing new bone tissue.

The other two types of bone cells are osteoblasts and osteocytes. Osteoblasts are the bone-forming cells. Once they lay down new bone tissue the osteoblasts become osteocytes. Osteocytes are imprisoned within the mineralized matrix of the bone, becoming a component of the bone.

13. c

Compartment syndrome is characterized by pain, pallor, pressure, paresthesia, and paralysis.

14. True

A subluxation is a partial displacement of a joint. A dislocation may be either a partial or complete dislocation of a joint; therefore, a subluxation is a type of partial dislocation.

15. c

Contraindications of the traction splint include injuries to the pelvis, hip, knee, tibia-fibula, ankle, and foot on the affected side when using a bipolar device and on both sides when applying the unipolar Sager splint.

chapter 25

Soft Tissue and Muscle Trauma

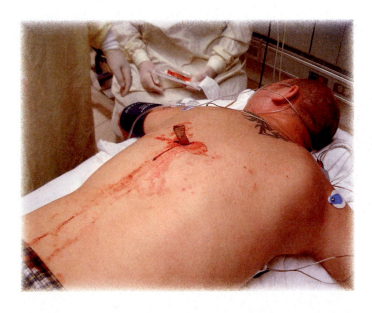

Are You Ready?

Six months ago Michael started to date a woman by the name of Sarah. All was going well until one afternoon when Sarah got off work early and decided to surprise Michael. She rented a movie and went over to his apartment to see it with him.

As Sarah walked through Michael's kitchen, she found Michael and her best friend kissing on Michael's couch. Sarah became enraged and, before Michael even knew that she was there, grabbed a knife off of the kitchen counter, ran over to Michael, and stabbed

him in the back. Sarah stabbed Michael with such force that the handle of the knife broke off, leaving the blade sticking out of his back.

1. Based on the photograph, and having no other patient information, what is your general impression of Michael's condition?

_____

_____

_____

2. Based on the location of the impaled knife, what internal structures might be involved?

_____

_____

_____

3. What is your priority in treating this patient?

_____

_____

_____

4. How will you manage this injury?

_____

_____

Active Learning

Anatomy Review

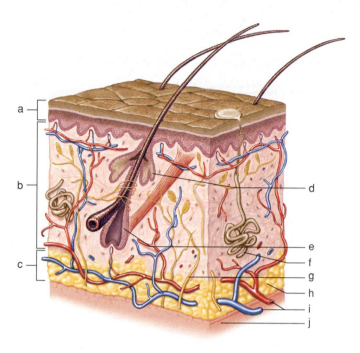

FIGURE 25-1

1. Identify the structures in Figure 25-1.

a. _____

b. _____

c. _____

d. _____

e. _____

f. _____

g. _____

h. _____

i. _____

j. _____

2. Volunteer Opportunity: Wound Care

Abrasions, contusions (bruises), hematomas, lacerations, avulsions, incisions, and punctures are soft tissue injuries that paramedics see and care for on a regular basis. The care that we perform is basic and is by no means the definitive care that the patient will receive for a particular injury.

Become more familiar with the care of wounds by observing how they are managed along the continuum of care. You can see how this care is provided in several venues:

Emergency department: If there is a trauma center in your area, you may have the opportunity to see more serious wounds.

Surgical or trauma ICU: Specialty care units like these treat patients with many different types of wounds and incisions. You may encounter patients whose wounds are not healing properly and the problems that result from impaired healing.

Wound care clinics: Some hospitals handle wound care so frequently that they have special clinics that patients visit for dressing changes and checkups.

Home health: Home health nurses perform wound care on a regular basis, and an observation in this setting would not only benefit your knowledge of wound care, but would offer the home health nurse an extra set of hands, which can be quite welcome.

You Are There: Reality-Based Cases

Case 1

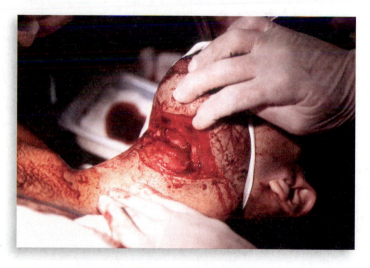

Tim is a 20-year-old male who loved the security and fringe benefits that associating with a gang afforded him. Tim partied and gambled with his new friends almost every day for several months, and during that time he incurred a very large gambling debt. When his "friends" came to collect their money, and Tim had none, they took him to a garage and began to torture him. They tied him up and cut off all the fingers on his left hand with a pair of pruning shears.

Then, just as they began to cut Tim's throat, they were interrupted by the police crashing through the door. Tim was pushed over backward and fell to the floor. The last thing he remembers hearing was one of the police officers requesting medical assistance right away.

When you and your partner approach Tim, he is unconscious, laying supine on the floor in a pool of what you assume is his own blood. The digits from his left hand are neatly placed in a cup on a table next to where he is lying. His left hand, minus the fingers that are in the cup, has very little bleeding, and a large incision is visible on his anterior neck, stretching from one side to the other.

With each of Tim's slow, shallow respirations, bubbles are created by the blood from the laceration on his neck, and there is still blood oozing out of the wound. A firefighter who arrived just before you did tells you that the patient has no radial pulses and that his brachial pulses are extremely weak and rapid. The patient has no verbal response, and he doesn't open his eyes to pain, but he does withdraw to the stimulus.

1. What is your first priority following scene safety and BSI?

_____

_____

_____

2. How will you execute the steps needed to accomplish the priority that you established in the answer to question 1?

_____

_____

_____

3. Describe the different classifications of blood loss and how patients with these types of blood loss present.

_____

_____

_____

4. Based on Tim's presentation, what class of hemorrhage has he experienced?

_____

_____

_____

5. What critical structures in the neck are likely involved with this injury?

_____

_____

_____

6. How will you manage the bleeding of the neck wound? Are there any special considerations you need to be aware of when managing bleeding from wounds to the neck?

_____

_____

_____

7. How will you manage Tim's left hand injuries?

_____

_____

_____

8. What is the appropriate management for the amputated fingers?

_____

_____

_____

9. Describe two factors associated with poor healing of soft tissue injuries, and identify patients who are most susceptible to these complications.

_____

_____

_____

10. What simple prophylactic measure can people take to help avoid some of the complications associated with soft tissue injuries?

_____

_____

_____

Case 2

Daniel Washington is a 76-year-old male who had just gone to a lumberyard to pick up fencing materials. Returning to his farm, Mr. Washington drove his truck up onto the hill where most of the fence work was located. He got out of his truck and tried to pull some of the posts out of the uphill side of the truck, but the load was too tight. Daniel walked around to the downhill side of the truck where he had secured the load, and he began to loosen the load. Just as he finished loosening the first strap, the entire load shifted and came crashing down onto him. Daniel tried to turn and run, but the entire load of fence posts came down on his legs and knocked him to the ground.

When the dust settled, Daniel realized that he was stuck under the posts. Despite a great deal of pain in both of his legs, he tried to free himself from the pile. No matter what he tried, the load wouldn't budge, and he decided to just lie there and wait for help.

Daniel looked at his watch and noticed that it was 1:00 p.m. Over the next 6 hours he went from experiencing severe pain in his legs to barely being able to feel his legs. It wasn't until 6:30 p.m. that his neighbor and longtime friend Myron Peterson found him.

Myron ran to Daniel's house and called 9-1-1, and at 6:50 p.m. the first volunteers arrived on the fire engine. Minutes later, as the volunteers were attempting to determine how to remove the load without causing any further damage to Daniel, you and your partner arrive in your ambulance. You find Daniel awake and alert with a palpable irregular radial pulse and slightly pale and moist skin. You stop the volunteers from lifting the entire load and pulling Daniel out from underneath.

1. What is your impression of the patient at this point in time?

   _____

   _____

   _____

2. Why should you stop the volunteers from removing the load from Daniel's legs?

   _____

   _____

   _____

3. Describe pathophysiologically what may happen if the load is rapidly removed from Daniel's legs.

   _____

   _____

   _____

4. What should your treatment consist of prior to releasing the load from Daniel's legs?

   _____

   _____

   _____

As your partner coordinates the release of the patient, you begin the prerelease treatment of the patient. During the process of assessing and treating Daniel, you discover that he has a history of an MI and hypertension. He takes Plavix, digoxin, and atenolol. Once you have readied all your equipment and delivered your preextrication medications, the volunteers carefully lift the load. Daniel screams in pain and then has a look of relief on his face as he is quickly placed on a long board. Like clockwork, the first responders cut away Daniel's blood-soaked pants and reveal his lower extremities.

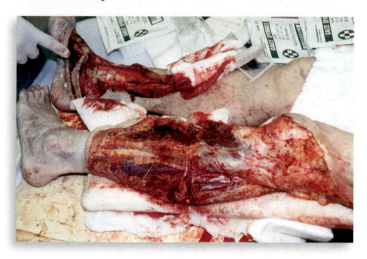

5. Do any of the medications that Daniel is taking concern you in relation to his current injuries? If so, what are your concerns?

   _____

   _____

   _____

6. Describe Daniel's injuries to his lower extremities based on the photograph.

   _____

   _____

   _____

7. How will you package the injured extremities?

   _____

   _____

   _____

8. Where should patient care take place?

   _____

   _____

Test Yourself

1. Identify and explain three barriers to normal wound healing.

_____

_____

Scenario: A heavy bookcase fell on your patient's legs and was immediately removed by two of his friends. There is no sign of external bleeding, but you note redness and swelling in the patient's thighs and lower legs. His hands and feet are cold and clammy. The patient is unable to wiggle his toes and cries out in pain when you stretch the toes of his left foot.

2. You should classify this injury as
   a. dual femoral fracture.
   b. crush syndrome.
   c. rhabdomyolysis.
   d. a crush injury.

3. You should most suspect
   a. muscle necrosis.
   b. neurogenic shock.
   c. a dangerous hematoma.
   d. compartment syndrome.

4. The most appropriate patient care should include
   a. transporting emergently to the nearest trauma center.
   b. applying cold packs directly to the skin of both legs.
   c. performing a fasciotomy to avoid permanent injury.
   d. palpating both legs to feel for possible fractures.

5. An occlusive dressing
   a. will cling to a wound and close the wound.
   b. prevents air from entering the wound.
   c. is capable of soaking up blood, pus, or other secretions.
   d. is called a "sponge" in surgical medicine.

6. List three functions of the skin.

_____

_____

7. Describe a method you could use to prevent re-bleeding.

_____

_____

Scenario: You are called to a 37-year-old patient who has cut off his hand at the wrist in an industrial accident. The wound is dirty, ragged, and bleeding profusely, and your patient presents with tachycardia, decreased pulse pressure, restlessness, and anxiety.

8. Given these clinical findings, the patient has most likely sustained
   a. greater than 40% blood volume loss.
   b. 30%–40% blood volume loss.
   c. up to 15% blood volume loss.
   d. 15%–30% blood volume loss.

9. You cannot immediately find the hand. You should
   a. transport the patient, applying direct pressure and administering an analgesic or sedative en route.
   b. apply direct pressure and transport the patient emergently, treating for shock en route to the nearest trauma center.
   c. cleanse the wound with sterile saline or lactated Ringer's solution, control bleeding, and treat for shock while your partner looks for the hand.
   d. transport the patient, using a hemolytic material and treating for shock with crystalloid solutions en route.

10. In order to control the bleeding, you apply direct pressure. The bleeding slows somewhat but does not stop. You should next
    a. elevate the wound above the heart to reduce arterial pressure.
    b. apply pressure at the pulse site immediately proximal to the injury.
    c. use a hemolytic (blood stopper) material such as ActCel or QuikClot.
    d. apply a wide tourniquet approximately 1–2 inches proximal to the injury.

11. What should be done with the hand once it is found?
    a. It should be rinsed with sterile water and then kept cool during transport.
    b. It should be wrapped in sterile dressing, placed in a plastic bag, and put on ice.

c. It should not be considered for reimplantation because the wrist was so damaged.

d. It should be kept dry and cool in a plastic bag in a cooler with dry ice.

12. What special considerations should be made when treating a patient with a laceration to the neck?

   _____

   _____

13. Internal tissue continuity is reestablished during the _____ phase of normal wound healing.

14. Sweat glands are found in the subcutaneous layer.

   True

   False

15. When treating a minor abrasion, you should be most concerned about infection.

   True

   False

Need to Know

The following represent the Key Objectives of Chapter 25:

1. *Describe the pathophysiology of soft tissue injury.*

   The sound of the term "soft tissue injury" may not bring visions of profound life-threatening injuries to your mind. By themselves, they frequently do not pose a threat to life. But when we dig a little bit deeper, we become aware that soft tissue injuries such as uncontrolled bleeding, amputations, impaled objects, crush injuries, and compartment syndrome all pose a certain threat to life. Of course, bumps, bruises, abrasions, avulsions, and lacerations are also included in this category of injuries.

   The skin is a large part of any discussion of soft tissue injuries, not only because it is typically involved in the physical trauma of a soft tissue injury, but because it plays an important role in the daily maintenance of the human organism, offering (for instance) protection from external pathogens, prevention of water loss, temperature regulation, and self-repair.

   Hemostasis, likely the most important aspect of managing soft tissue injuries, is a very important and complex process that can potentially be compromised by a number of factors. The basic components of hemostasis include:

- Vasoconstriction
- Platelet aggregation
- Fibrin formation
- Fibrinolysis

Neuromuscular damage can result from soft tissue injuries (see Chapter 25, Soft Tissue and Muscle Trauma, in the textbook).

2. *Describe how to manage a soft tissue injury.*

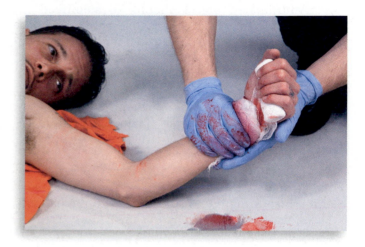

When soft tissue injuries occur, treatment of these wounds involves application of direct pressure in an attempt to control the bleeding. When bleeding is difficult to control, a basic sequence of steps should be followed in an attempt to get the bleeding under control. These steps include:

- Elevation
- Pressure points
- Pressure dressings
- Application of a tourniquet

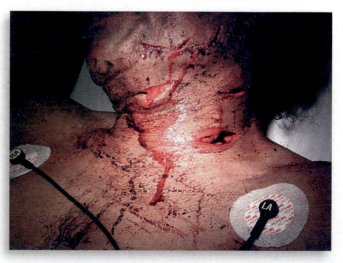

Some soft tissue injuries, simply by their location in proximity to vital structures and organs, warrant a high index of suspicion that there may indeed be a life-threatening injury present. Lacerations to the neck, for instance, may not appear serious on the surface, but under the skin they may involve the airway or vital arteries and could pose a great threat to life. Patients with soft tissue injuries to the neck deserve to be treated as critical trauma patients and transported to a trauma center where they can be appropriately evaluated and treated.

An impaled object should be stabilized in place and transported with the patient to a trauma center. The only time an impaled object should be removed is when it poses an immediate threat to the patient's life. Amputations are very dramatic injuries but do not tend to cause life-threatening bleeding by themselves. If a patient with an amputation shows obvious signs of shock, it is prudent to search for other injuries that may be causing those signs and symptoms. The care of an amputated part involves placing it in a plastic bag, keeping it cool without causing freezing of the part, and transporting it to the hospital with the patient. Label the bag so that it is not mistakenly thrown away as trash.

Serious forms of soft tissue trauma that can pose an increased life threat are crush syndrome and compartment syndrome. The injuries seen with these conditions are by themselves frequently not deadly. It is the pathophysiologic consequences of these injuries that make them so dangerous.

Need to Do

The following skills are explained and illustrated in a step-by-step manner, via skill sheets and/or Step-by-Steps in this text and on the accompanying DVD:

Skill Name	Skill Sheet Number and Location	Step-by-Step Number and Location
Bleeding Control and Shock	66 – DVD	66 – DVD
Crush Injury Management	79 – DVD	N/A
NREMT Bleeding Control/Shock Management	94 – DVD	N/A

Connections

- Chapter 19, Hemorrhage and Hemorrhagic Shock, in the textbook includes a discussion on hemostasis.
- Chapter 21, Thoracic Trauma, in the textbook discusses penetrating and soft tissue injuries to the thorax.
- Chapter 24, Skeletal Trauma, in the textbook provides further discussion on compartment syndrome.
- Chapter 32, Allergies and Anaphylaxis, in the textbook discusses the immune system defense and how the body fights off infection caused by breaks in the skin.
- Chapter 45, The Abused and Neglected, in the textbook discusses signs and symptoms of abuse and neglect as they relate to soft tissue injuries.
- Link to the companion DVD for a chapter-based quiz, audio glossary, animations, games and exercises, and, when appropriate, skill sheets and skill Step-by-Steps.

Street Secrets

- **Medication Clues** Be aware of patient medications when treating patients with soft tissue injuries. Medications will tell you quite a bit about some of the complications that you may face in dealing with issues such as control of hemorrhage, as well as some of the longer-term problems associated with risk of infection and poor healing tendencies. Medications such as Coumadin or Plavix may interfere with your efforts to control bleeding. Plavix is of particular concern because it takes up to 5 days once the medication has been discontinued for the drug's effects to stop. This is particularly problematic when it comes to patients who require surgery. When you have a trauma patient who has a significant mechanism of injury and signs of shock except for a rapid heart rate, check his or her medications. Drugs like beta-blockers and calcium channel blockers will not allow the heart rate to increase due to their mechanism of action. Do not take a slow heart rate as a sign that the patient is not in shock.

The Drug Box

Morphine sulfate: A narcotic analgesic used in the management of pain associated with soft tissue and muscle trauma.

References

1. S. A. Santer, "Transfusion Therapy." Chapter 223 in *Tintinalli's Emergency Medicine*. McGraw-Hill Online (accessed June 11, 2006).
2. C. K. Stone and R. L. Humphries, "Orthopedic Emergencies." Chapter 28 in *Current Emergency Diagnosis and Treatment*. McGraw-Hill Online (accessed June 10, 2006).
3. Ibid.
4. H. P. Ehrlich and T. K. Hunt, "Effects of Cortisone and Vitamin A on Wound Healing." *Annals of Surgery* 167 (1968): 324.
5. P. J. E. Cruse and R. A. Foord, "A Prospective Study of 23,649 Surgical Wounds." *Archives of Surgery* 107 (1973): 206.
6. M. Michaelson et al., "Crush Syndrome: Experience from the Lebanon War, 1982." *Israel Journal of Medical Sciences* 20 (1984): 305.
7. O. Better, "Rescue and Salvage of Casualities Suffering from the Crush Syndrome after Mass Disasters." *Military Medicine* 164, no. 5 (1999): 366–69.

Answers

Are You Ready?

1. Any patient with an impaled object embedded in the back is a critical trauma patient (sick) until proven otherwise by a qualified physician (at a trauma center in your area, if available).

2. The knife is impaled just to the left lateral side of the thoracic spine approximately at the level of T6–T8. The possibilities for injuries resulting from this impaled knife (depending on the length of the blade and the angle that the knife took when it entered the body) include the left lung, the aorta, the superior aspect of the left kidney, the diaphragm, thoracic vertebrae, the spinal cord, spinal nerves, ribs, intercostal nerves and blood vessels, the spleen, and the esophagus.

   A concept referred to as the "cone of injury" can be useful in determining the extent of internal injury when a person is stabbed (Figure 25-2). There are several factors

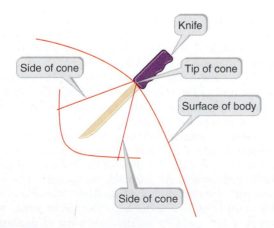

FIGURE 25-2   The cone of injury.

that one needs to keep in mind when assessing such an injury, including the length of the blade, the angle at which the blade entered the body, whether the blade was manipulated while it was in the body, and if it was pulled straight out. The cone is used to describe the possible areas involved once the blade enters the body. It starts at the point of insertion and flares out from that point (the point of insertion is the tip of the cone, and potential pathways of the blade are the flared-out sides of the cone).

3. Priorities are scene safety, BSI, maintaining the patient's ABCs, and transporting the patient to a trauma center with supportive care provided en route to the hospital.

4. Secure the knife in place with bulky dressings (use occlusive dressings surrounding the knife if there is any potential for air to enter the wound). Consider immobilization of the spine. Because of the impaled object, spinal immobilization would be difficult to accomplish without compromising the position of the knife. Assess and continue to monitor for any changes in the patient's condition, including vital signs, mental status, skin signs, lung sounds, ECG, oxygen saturation, and establishing at least one, if not two, large-bore IVs en route to the trauma center.

Active Learning

1. a. epidermis; b. dermis; c. subcutaneous layer; d. sebaceous gland; e. hair follicle; f. sweat gland; g. nerve cell process; h. adipose tissue; i. blood vessels; j. muscle layer

You Are There: Reality-Based Cases

Case 1

1. There are multiple factors that suggest that Tim is a critical trauma patient who has a significant airway compromise issue. The first priority is to secure his airway.

2. Managing Tim's airway requires more than inserting an airway adjunct. Because of the bleeding from his neck, Tim is at a significant risk for aspiration, particularly because there is a direct route for the blood to enter the airway (through the hole in his neck). Stop the bleeding and apply an occlusive dressing over the hole in the airway. This prevents the possible entrance of air into the vasculature of the neck; it may also prevent the development of an air embolus. Once an occlusive dressing has been applied, the patient can be suctioned and an airway can be placed.

   Tim's condition has multiple factors that point toward the placement of an advanced airway: unconsciousness, bleeding into the airway, risk of aspiration, hypoventilation, low GCS score, probable hypoxia, and a definite need to go to the operating room (OR) for treatment of his wounds. If he is already intubated, the time in the emergency department before he can be taken to the OR will be reduced significantly.

   The means by which the intubation is performed will be based primarily on patient presentation. For example, does he have a gag reflex? Is he responsive at all? Is RSI an option for airway management in your particular EMS system? If you are unable to intubate the patient due to distorted anatomy as a result of the trauma, or because of swelling of tissues of the airway, consider the use of a needle cricothyroidotomy or a surgical tracheostomy.

If you are confident that Tim has an airway that is secure enough to manage with BLS maneuvers until you start your transport, then do so. Tim needs care that can only be provided in a hospital (i.e., blood infusion and an operating room). The quicker you get Tim to the hospital (trauma center), the better his chance of surviving this injury.

3. The American College of Surgeons classifies hemorrhage according to estimated blood volume loss correlated with clinical findings.

   - *Class I hemorrhage* is any amount up to 15%. Typically patients do not begin to exhibit any signs of shock until a 10%–15% blood loss occurs, and even then the signs may be subtle and include mild tachycardia, anxiousness, and mild tachypnea.

   - *Class II hemorrhage* corresponds to an estimated 15%–30% (up to 1,500 mL) blood volume loss with clinical manifestations of sustained tachycardia, decreased pulse pressure, restlessness, and anxiety. It can be tolerated by young, healthy patients when treated with crystalloid solutions, but it is not tolerated well by older patients and patients with chronic illness.

   - *Class III hemorrhage* is an estimated 30%–40% blood volume loss with clinical manifestations of tachycardia, tachypnea, systolic hypotension, and mental status changes.[1]

4. Tim was found in a large pool of blood. He has a rapid pulse that can barely be felt at the brachial artery (an indicator that he is hypotensive), and he is unconscious (a significant mental status change). It is safe to assume, based on the above information, that Tim has experienced a *class III hemorrhage.*

5. The more critical structures in the neck that may be involved in this injury are the airway (larynx and trachea), the carotid arteries, the jugular veins, several nerves in the neck (most notably, the vagus nerve), and the thyroid gland (depending on the position of the patient's head when the incision was made).

6. In general, a paramedic manages bleeding in a similar fashion regardless of bleeding site, but there are some structures of the body that require special consideration, such as the neck. Following the standard methods of controlling hemorrhage to a bleeding neck injury can in fact lead to disastrous results. If excessive pressure is applied to the neck, several negative consequences may result, including interference with the airway, slowing of the heart rate and resulting drop in blood pressure, and reduction of cerebral blood flow. You must be vigilant for these effects as you attempt to control bleeding. In most situations, it may be necessary to hold direct pressure over the wound rather than wrapping a circumferential dressing around the neck and compromising the trachea

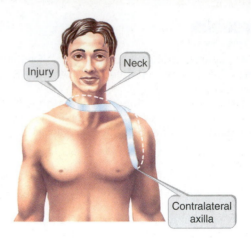

FIGURE 25-3   Figure-eight method of controlling neck bleeding.

and airway. Occlusive dressings are appropriate if damage to blood vessels of the neck is suspected.

If bleeding has been controlled with direct pressure and sterile dressings, applying a cervical collar can help maintain cervical alignment in a patient with a suspected c-spine injury. It can also maintain pressure to the wound and free up the hands of the person who was tasked with applying the pressure. This method can be used even if there is no suspicion of c-spine injury as a means of maintaining continuous pressure on a neck wound. However you must continue to monitor for bleeding and possible signs and symptoms of a compromised airway.

Another option for controlling bleeding to the neck, especially the lateral neck, is the use of sterile dressings followed by the application of roller bandages starting at the lateral aspect of the neck on the affected side and continuing with a figure eight around the neck and contralateral axilla (Figure 25-3).

7. Bleeding control can usually be accomplished with bulky trauma dressings and direct pressure. Since Tim's left hand has minimal bleeding, direct pressure will likely control the bleeding. Assume that there is an open fracture associated with the injury. Manage the patient's pain with analgesics.

8. In many cases, amputated limbs and other body parts can be recovered and transported to the trauma center with the patient. However, do not delay transporting the patient if access to the limb is delayed. In such a case, have a second crew transport the amputated limb in another unit to the trauma center. Sharp, guillotine-type amputations without crush or avulsion damage are the best candidates for reimplantation.[2]

Keep the amputated part clean, wrap it in a sterile dressing moistened with sterile saline, place it in a plastic bag labeled with the time of the injury, and put the plastic bag on ice. An ice pack works best. The amputated part should not come into direct contact with ice. The main objective is to keep the tissue cool, which increases the viability of the tissue for reimplantation from 6 to 24 hours from the time of the amputation.[3]

9. Any of the following factors contribute to impaired wound healing:

   - *Infection.* Infection delays healing.
   - *Aging.* Most surgeons believe that aging produces intrinsic physiological changes that result in delayed or impaired wound healing.
   - *Hypoxia.* Low oxygen tension (saturation in the blood) has a profoundly negative effect on all aspects of wound healing.
   - *Steroids.* Large doses or chronic usage of glucocorticoid steroids reduce collagen synthesis and wound strength.[4]
   - *Diabetes.* Diabetes mellitus is the best known of the metabolic disorders contributing to increased rates of wound infection and failure to heal.[5]
   - *Poor nutrition.* Poor nutritional intake or lack of individual nutrients significantly alter many aspects of wound healing.

   The two populations that tend to have complications with wound healing are the elderly and individuals with diabetes.

10. All patients treated for any type of open wound should be seen by a physician and preventively treated for the disease tetanus, commonly called lockjaw. Tetanus is an acute, often fatal, infectious disease caused by the anaerobic, spore-forming bacillus *Clostridium tetani,* an agent that most often enters the body through a contaminated wound. Tetanus shots are typically effective for a 10-year period.

Case 2

1. Daniel is an elderly man who is awake and alert with a palpable radial pulse but cutaneous signs of shock. He has a potentially serious injury to his lower legs, and he has been trapped under a heavy load for approximately 6 hours. Daniel deserves to be treated as a critical trauma (sick) patient.

2. Daniel has a crush injury. Because of the length of time that his legs have been trapped under a heavy load, he has the potential to be suffering from crush syndrome. If the volunteers lift the load before you and your partner are prepared to care for Daniel, he could bleed to death (the weight removed from his legs can release the tamponade that the load is offering), and if Daniel is not pretreated appropriately, he could also suffer the effects of crush syndrome.

3. Crush syndrome tends to occur when skeletal muscle is exposed to extreme pressure for an extended period of time. The shortest time documented for crush syndrome to occur is 4 hours.[6] The constant pressure that the skeletal muscle is exposed to results in minimal if any perfusion into the crushed tissues. As a result, the tissue becomes ischemic and eventually necrotic. This leads to a condition called rhabdomyolysis, which can lead to complications such as disseminated intravascular coagulopathy (DIC) and acute renal failure (ARF).

   When the crushing load is released, blood reperfuses the damaged or dead tissue, and a number of harmful substances (by-products of cell death) are released into the bloodstream. The harmful substances include myoglobin, potassium, phosphate, lactic acid, and uric acid. These substances can have a profound effect on the heart, liver, and kidneys. They can result in life-threatening dysrhythmias (from excessive potassium levels), hypovolemic shock, metabolic acidosis (from the release of lactic and uric acid from necrotic tissue), acute myoglobinuric renal failure (due to the kidney's inability to clear the buildup of myoglobin that exists as a result of muscle tissue death), and perhaps compartment syndrome (due to swelling or bleeding into the inelastic fascia found with skeletal muscle).[7] Death can occur rapidly in these patients.

4. All treatments prior to the release of a patient suspected of experiencing crush syndrome should be based on local policies and protocols. The following treatments are possibilities for treating crush syndrome:

   - High-flow oxygen (to keep oxygen saturation high)
   - ECG monitoring (to be aware of any arrhythmias that may develop)
   - Two large-bore IVs established (fluid administration tends to help decrease the development of myoglobinuric renal failure) using an approved IV solution, typically isotonic or hypertonic solutions
   - Sodium bicarbonate (keeps myoglobin in the circulation and helps prevent hyperkalemia)
   - Calcium chloride administration (to correct hypocalcemia and to help manage hyperkalemia, which shifts potassium into cells)
   - Nebulized albuterol (to help manage hyperkalemia, which shifts potassium back into cells)
   - D_{50} and insulin (as insulin transports dextrose into the cell, it pulls potassium with it)
   - Analgesics (for the management of pain: follow local protocols and beware of hypotension)
   - Lasix (offers some renal vasodilation, decreases oxygen demand by the kidneys, and increases renal intratubular flow)

5. Daniel is taking Plavix, digoxin, and atenolol.

   - *Plavix* (clopidogrel) hinders platelet aggregation by inhibiting the binding of adenosine diphosphate (ADP) to its platelet receptor, impeding ADP-mediated activation and subsequent platelet aggregation. Plavix irreversibly modifies the platelet ADP receptor. The main concern is bleeding control. With this specific medication, platelet aggregation will not return to normal for 5 days after the medication has been discontinued.
   - *Digoxin* inhibits sodium potassium–activated ATP, causing an increased movement of calcium from the extracellular to the intracellular environment. The net result is an increase in cardiac contractile force. Digoxin also acts on the CNS to enhance vagal tone, resulting in a slowing of conduction of electrical impulses through the sinoatrial (SA) and atrioventricular (AV) nodes (slowing the heart rate) and providing an antiarrhythmic effect. The main concern with this medication is that, despite the increased

contractile force of the heart, the slowing of the conduction through the SA and AV nodes will make it difficult for the heart to compensate for shock if hemorrhage is severe or cannot be controlled due to the fact that Daniel is taking a medication that will interfere with his ability to form clots.

- *Atenolol* is a beta-blocker that selectively blocks beta adrenergic receptors; decreases cardiac output, peripheral resistance, and cardiac oxygen consumption; and depresses renin secretion. The main concern with this medication in relation to Daniel's situation is that it lowers blood pressure (by decreasing cardiac output), which can prove to be a detriment if hemorrhagic shock becomes a factor. The other concern regarding this medication is that it has a propensity to slow the heart rate, which can be problematic when it comes to the body's physiological attempts to compensate for shock (the heart rate will not be able to increase).

6. Daniel has severe degloving injuries to both of his lower extremities. There is exposure of bone, muscle, fascia, etc. The left lower extremity is degloved from above the knee (on the dorsal aspect of the leg) to several inches above the left ankle. The right lower extremity is degloved from the medial aspect of the lower leg, halfway between the ankle and the knee, to the dorsal aspect of the foot just above the point where the toes meet the foot. The injury extends medially to the area of the Achilles tendon.

7. The degloved tissue may have accumulated in one area, or it may have been placed back over the bone and muscle. In any case, bleeding control is the top priority at this point. Because the degloving injury is to the legs, it is easier to dress the wounds and elevate them. Large, saline-moistened trauma dressings can be placed around the exposed bone, muscle, and tissue so that the dressings do not stick and create further bleeding when they are removed, and so the muscle, bone, and tissue do not dry out. Roller bandages or elastic bandages can then be applied from distal to proximal. The legs can be splinted with whatever leg splinting device is available (if the patient has significant bleeding from the injuries to the legs, air splints may not only prevent movement and decrease bleeding in that manner, but they may also act to help tamponade the bleeding). No matter what type of splint you use, make sure that you assess motion, sensation, and perfusion prior to and upon completion of placing splints and frequently during your transport. Another device that can be considered to help splint and stop bleeding, if approved for use in your EMS system, is the use of the pneumatic anti-shock garment (PASG). Do not hesitate to contact medical control for consultation if you have any questions about applying the PASG or if you need guidance for the treatment of a patient with crush syndrome. Elevation of the extremities above the level of the heart will also help control the bleeding. Because of Daniel's age, and the fact that he has already been placed on a backboard, it would be adventitious to place him in c-spine precautions (the pain to the lower extremities is a significant distracting injury).

8. All care, other than that for life-threatening conditions (e.g., airway management for an unstable airway), should take place in the ambulance on the way to the trauma center.

Test Yourself

1. Hypoxia is a barrier to wound healing because oxygen is needed for effective blood clotting and collagen synthesis. Use of steroids also inhibits healing because steroids inhibit the inflammatory phase. Diabetes is a barrier to healing, because uncontrolled diabetes results in reduced inflammation, angiogenesis, and collagen synthesis. Other barriers to healing include infection, aging, and poor nutrition.

2. d

   A crush injury is defined as a mechanism of injury in which skeletal muscle, as well as the overlying skin, subcutaneous tissue, and associated structures such as bones, nerves, and blood vessels are locally compressed by high-pressure forces. For crush syndrome to occur, the skeletal muscle must be exposed to high-pressure crushing forces for an extended period of time. The shortest time documented for crush syndrome to occur is 4 hours. Rhabdomyolysis is a potential complication from crush syndrome. An avulsion is an open wound, and external bleeding would be evident.

3. d

   The lower leg and forearm are the most common locations for compartment syndrome to develop. Pain with passive range of motion of the fingers or toes is thought to be the most sensitive early sign.

4. a

   An immediate surgical procedure, called a fasciotomy is indicated to avoid permanent injury from compartment syndrome. This procedure is not performed by paramedics, so recognition of the problem and rapid transport are appropriate treatments.

5. b

   An occlusive dressing is a nonporous dressing (often plastic) placed directly over a wound to prevent air from entering the wound. It may or may not be clear in color. Using a sterile surface for the dressing is optimal. The inner portion of the package from a sterile trauma pad or large sterile dressing is a good source for this type of material.

6. Protection from the outside environment and infection, prevention of water loss, temperature regulation, and self-repair are the most important functions of the skin.

   The skin is the largest, thinnest, and one of the most important organs of the body. Along with nails, sweat glands, and sebaceous glands, the skin makes up the integumentary system. The skin also synthesizes vitamin D. Emotional well-being, including one's response to the daily stresses of life, is also reflected in the skin.

7. When treating lacerations of the arms or legs, splinting the limb will reduce movement and prevent re-bleeding. Make sure you maintain direct pressure for a long enough period

of time to prevent re-bleeding. Remove dressings carefully, particularly adherent, absorbent, or dry dressings.

Re-bleeding is when bleeding starts again following initial control attempts. This can happen when the patient moves and the clot controlling the hemorrhage is disrupted, when direct pressure is not applied for a long enough period of time, or when bandages are removed.

8. d

Class II hemorrhage corresponds to an estimated 15%–30% blood volume loss with clinical manifestations of sustained tachycardia, decreased pulse pressure, restlessness, and anxiety. While young, healthy patients can tolerate blood loss of up to 25%–30%, or 1,500 mL, when treated with crystalloid solutions, older patients and patients with chronic illness such as cardiac diseases may not tolerate similar blood loss without cardiac or neurological decompensation.

9. b

With high-priority patients, transportation should never be delayed for dressing and bandaging wounds; however, initial attempts to control bleeding must be started prior to moving the patient from the scene. Do not delay transporting the patient if access to the limb is delayed. Have a second crew transport the amputated limb in another unit to the trauma center.

10. a

If direct pressure alone is not sufficient to control the hemorrhage, simple elevation of the wound above the level of the heart in addition to direct pressure will help slow bleeding.

11. b

Keep the amputated part clean. The amputated limb should be wrapped in a sterile dressing moistened with sterile saline, placed in a plastic bag, and put on ice. An ice pack works best. If real ice must be used, the limb should not come into direct contact with the ice or water. Never use dry ice as this can lead to freezing.

12. Maintaining an open airway is your primary responsibility. Lacerations to the neck should be considered life threatening. Bleeding control of a neck laceration needs to be handled carefully because too much pressure applied to the neck can lead to interruption of blood flow to the brain or stimulation of the vagus nerve. An occlusive dressing should be placed over the laceration to prevent an air embolism.

Facial and neck trauma may distort physical features and landmarks for intubation. Cervical in-line stabilization or immobilization must be maintained throughout the prehospital phase of care for trauma patients with suspected spinal injury. Neck lacerations often require exploration in the operating room, and patients with this type of injury should be transported to an appropriate trauma center.

13. Proliferation

The proliferation phase spans 4 to 12 days, depending upon the severity, size, and depth of the wound. During this phase, tissue continuity is reestablished. Fibroblasts and endothelial cells infiltrate the healing wound.

14. False

Hair and hair follicles, sweat glands, sebaceous (oil) glands, sensory nerves, muscles, and pressure receptors are located in the dermis. Subcutaneous tissue, also called the hypodermis, lies directly under the dermis. Its extensive network of blood vessels makes it an ideal route for medication administration.

15. True

Abrasions are the rubbing away of the skin through a mechanical process. This wound is the result of friction against exposed skin (i.e., sliding along concrete after falling from a bicycle). If there is any bleeding associated with this wound, it will be capillary bleeding (small droplets of blood are formed). There is usually considerable pain with this type of injury and a high risk for infection. The pain results from the nerve endings being exposed to the air, and the infection risk is from the protective surface of the skin having been scraped away, exposing open blood vessels, and from debris being ground into the wound.

chapter 26

Burn Trauma

Active Learning

1. How Much BSA?

Using Figure 26-1 and the rule of nines (Figure 26-4 in the textbook), calculate the percentage of body surface area (BSA) that is shaded in red—both for an adult and a pediatric patient.

Are You Ready?

You and your crew arrive at a shed that is engulfed in flames. As you step down from your engine, a police officer runs from across the street and directs you to a smoldering mass on the ground near the building. What looks like a pile of smoking clothing is, in fact, a young man. He is moaning as you approach.

1. What are your first priorities for this incident?

_____

_____

_____

2. What are your first actions in the management of this patient?

_____

_____

_____

	Adult	Child
A	% BSA _____	% BSA _____
B	% BSA _____	% BSA _____

FIGURE 26-1

(Continued)

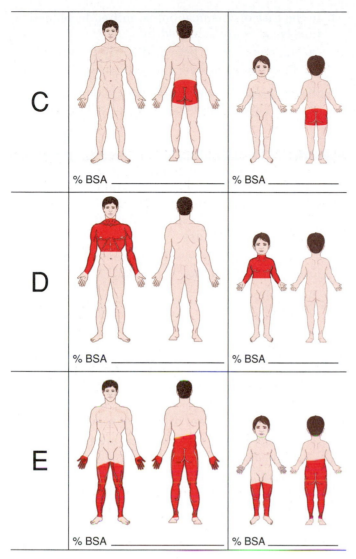

FIGURE 26-1

C   % BSA _____   % BSA _____

D   % BSA _____   % BSA _____

E   % BSA _____   % BSA _____

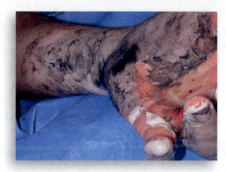

b. **FIGURE 26-3** _____

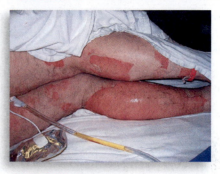

c. **FIGURE 26-4** _____

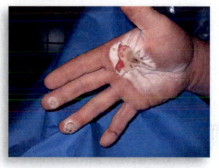

d. **FIGURE 26-5** _____

2. To What Degree?

For each of the photos in Figures 26-2 through 26-5, describe the degree of the burn (i.e., first, second, third, or deep third).

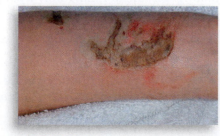

a. **FIGURE 26-2** _____

3. Volunteer Opportunity: Burn Care

If possible, arrange to visit a burn center. Take the opportunity to observe various processes involved with the postresuscitation care of the burn patient. Ask the burn center staff for any tips or tricks they may have in dealing with the emotional impact of severely burned victims and the steps you should perform in the prehospital arena to help with the long-term care of the patient. You can check the Web resources in the Connections section of this chapter to find the nearest burn center.

You Are There: Reality-Based Cases

Case 1 *(continuation of chapter opener)*

You douse the patient with water and then remove as much of the wet clothing as possible. Simultaneously you perform a primary assessment that reveals the following:

- *Airway.* You note audible stridor. There are soot and burns around the mouth, and the patient's hair is burned.
- *Breathing.* The respiratory rate is fast, about 30 times per minute. Lung sounds are diminished bilaterally and nearly drowned out by the stridor.
- *Circulation.* You can palpate peripheral pulses that are rapid.
- *Disability.* The patient is moaning and does not react to your voice. He is not moving any of his extremities.
- *Exposure.* You note second- and third-degree (partial- and full-thickness) burns on his hands, arms, and the front of his thorax.

1. What interventions will you perform, based upon your primary assessment findings? What other concerns do you have, in addition to the burn injury?

_____

_____

_____

As you prepare the patient for transport to the trauma center, a police officer comes over, asking if the patient is "going to make it." He goes on to tell you that the shed was an illegal drug lab that law enforcement was monitoring when it exploded. The patient came staggering out almost immediately and then collapsed on the ground where you found him.

2. How does this information impact your actions and management approach to the patient? How might it impact his outcome?

_____

_____

_____

Test Yourself

1. When treating a burn victim, which step should be performed *first*?
   a. Ensure that the burning process has stopped.
   b. Treat any immediate threats to life.
   c. Perform a primary assessment of the patient.
   d. Undress the patient and cover with a dry, sterile sheet.

2. Most deaths at the scene of a fire are a result of
   a. smoke inhalation.
   b. direct effects of burns.
   c. increased risk of infection.
   d. carbon monoxide poisoning.

3. In the case of chemical burns, initial decontamination is generally achieved by
   a. submersing the patient directly in water.
   b. flushing water over the patient.
   c. covering the patient in dry blankets.
   d. applying a counteragent to neutralize the chemical.

Scenario: A 31-year-old male is injured in a meth lab explosion. He has second- and third-degree burns covering his back, the back of his head and neck, and both arms. His vital signs are BP of 70/40, HR of 139, and RR of 28. You cannot locate the dorsalis pedis pulse or medial malleolus pulse.

4. Using the rule of nines, what percent of the patient's total body surface area is burned?
   a. 40.5%
   b. 36%
   c. 27%
   d. 31.5%

5. Which of the following would you suspect?
   a. Hypovolemia caused by another source of trauma
   b. Pulmonary edema caused by smoke inhalation
   c. Pulmonary edema caused by another source of trauma
   d. Hypovolemia caused by plasma shifting from the vascular system to body tissues

6. When you transport that patient, he should be taken to
   a. a burn center only.
   b. a trauma center only.
   c. a trauma center, and later transferred to a burn center.
   d. a burn center, and later transferred to a trauma center.

7. Describe the likely appearance of a superficial partial-thickness burn.

_____

_____

8. When evaluating for smoke inhalation, what signs should you look for?

_____

_____

9. Provide at least five examples of burn injuries that would require transportation to a burn center.

_____

_____

10. How does the treatment of chemical burns differ from the treatment of thermal burns? How is it similar?

_____

_____

11. What are signs that a child's burns may be the result of abuse?

_____

_____

12. You should never apply ice to cool a burn.
    True
    False

13. Decontamination of patients exposed to radiation is generally performed at specially equipped facilities.
    True
    False

14. It is appropriate to enter a burning building to rescue a patient when
    a. you have appropriate protective gear and are trained to do so.
    b. you can reach the patient without directly contacting the fire.
    c. the fire department has not yet arrived on the scene.
    d. the patient's life is in immediate danger.

15. According to the Baux formula for burned patients, the likelihood of mortality is equal to
    a. the patient's age plus half the total body surface area critically burned.
    b. half the patient's age plus half the total body surface area critically burned.
    c. the patient's age plus the total body surface area critically burned.
    d. half the patient's age plus the total body surface area critically burned.

Need to Know

The following represent the Key Objectives of Chapter 26:

1. _Describe the relationships between the pathophysiology and mechanism of burn trauma with the typical presenting signs and symptoms of patients with burn trauma._

   Our skin helps give us our shape, protects us from infection, and regulates our body temperature. Multiple layers of tissue combine to perform these functions, while being flexible and sensitive to our environment. It is no wonder why disrupting the skin with a burn can be devastating, crippling, and painful.

   a. A burn is classified by the depth of the injury, or how many layers of the skin are involved.
      • First-degree burns involve the superficial layer of the skin, the epidermis.
      • Second-degree burns involve the dermal layer, causing blisters to form at the site of injury. They are also called partial-thickness burns.
      • Third-degree burns involve the epidermis, the dermis, and the layers beneath, causing a full-thickness injury.
      • Review Table 26-1 in the textbook for more information about burn classification.

   b. The mechanics of a burn can vary. Sources that cause burns include thermal, chemical, electrical, and radiation.
      • Thermal burns include scalds from hot water or other liquids, contact with high-heat sources, and direct flame. The severity of the burn is dependent upon the temperature of the heat and the length of contact time.
      • Chemical burns result from the absorption, inhalation, ingestion, or injection of a chemical substance. The severity of the burn depends upon the concentration and amount of the chemical, the duration of contact, the depth of exposure, and the route of entry. The eye is particularly sensitive to chemical injuries.
      • Electrical burns pose an especially hazardous situation. Ensure that trained personnel shut down the power to any wires or cables lying around the scene prior to your entry. Electricity, like water, will always flow through routes of least resistance. In the body that means the nervous system tissue, blood vessels, and muscles are especially vulnerable to electrical burns. This implies that while surface burns due to contact with electricity may appear small and isolated, you must suspect that greater injuries may exist under the skin.
      • Exposure to large doses of ionizing radiation (gamma or beta) can cause burns similar to the other mechanisms. Like electricity, scene safety is paramount, and appropriate protective equipment and training are required to remove patients from hazardous environments and, if necessary, decontaminate them prior to transport.

- Systemic inflammatory response syndrome (SIRS) can occur if the burn is severe enough to cause blood plasma to leak out of the capillary beds. The shift of fluid disturbs the homeostatic balance of the blood and tissues, increasing the workload of many organ systems, especially the metabolic, cardiovascular, and coagulation systems. In later stages blood pressure falls as the volume in the vasculature is reduced by the third spacing effect.

2. *Identify the key signs of immediate life-threatening burn trauma.*

You may have realized that, after reading the chapter in the textbook, burns generally do not kill a patient immediately. It may take some time for the body to succumb to even the worst burns. However, any involvement to the airway by the burn mechanism will pose an immediate threat to life. In addition, compromise of the respiratory system through smoke and other toxic gas inhalation will pose an immediate threat as well.

Keep these conditions in mind as you perform the primary assessment. Look for signs of soot and burns around and in the mouth and nose. Be especially alert for signs of any swelling to the upper airway; stridor, hoarseness, and drooling are all signs of possible impending closure of the airway. Inhalation signs and symptoms include dyspnea, coughing, restlessness, sputum production, and wheezing.

3. *Evaluate and appropriately manage different types of burn injuries.*

There are a few general principles to adhere to in managing burns:

a. The mechanisms that cause burns can also cause severe injury or death to the rescuer. *Be safe!* Be properly trained and protected before attempting to rescue or resuscitate a burn patient.

b. Stop the burning process before initiating treatment. That includes putting out any active fire on the patient, washing away chemicals with copious amounts of water, turning off electrical power, or removing the patient from a radioactive environment.

c. Because of the nature of burn mechanisms, assume that multisystem trauma is involved until proven otherwise. If your burn patient presents with signs and symptoms of shock, search aggressively for possible causes in addition to the burn itself.

d. Always ensure the patency of the airway, the ability of the patient to breathe, and the circulatory status before managing the burn.

e. The very old, very young, and those individuals with significant cardiac or pulmonary histories are very susceptible to the effects of burns.

Intravenous fluid therapy is indicated for adults with burns greater than 18%–20% of total body surface area (TBSA) and children with burns involving more than 12%–15% of TBSA. Fluid administration of Ringer's lactate will range from 120 cc/h in young children to 500 cc/h in an adult.

Pain management should be considered, especially in the absence of major system trauma. Narcotics should be given in small amounts often, to help avoid respiratory depression.

Transportation to a burn center is preferred in cases in which there are no other mechanisms that suggest multisystem trauma. Box 26-6 in the textbook lists the referral criteria for burn center transport.

Need to Do

The following skills are explained and illustrated in a step-by-step manner, via skill sheets and/or Step-by-Steps in this text and on the accompanying DVD:

Skill Name	Skill Sheet Number and Location	Step-by-Step Number and Location
Endotracheal Intubation	7 – Appendix A and DVD	7 – Chapter 12 and DVD
Rapid Sequence Intubation	13 – Appendix A and DVD	13 – Chapter 12 and DVD
Needle Cricothyroidotomy	19 – Appendix A and DVD	19 – Chapter 12 and DVD
Burn Percentage Estimation	78 – DVD	N/A

Connections

- Refer to the textbook for additional background information related to this chapter. Suggested chapters include Chapter 7, Anatomy Overview; Chapter 9, Safety and Scene Size-Up; Chapter 12, Airway Management, Ventilation, and Oxygenation; Chapter 13, Shock Overview; Chapter 14, Patient Assessment; and Chapter 18, Mechanism of Injury.

- The American Burn Association (ABA) is dedicated to improving the lives of individuals affected by burn injury through patient care, education, research, and advocacy.1 The ABA sponsors an educational program named Advanced Burn Life Support (ABLS). There are two classes, one of which is geared toward prehospital providers. You can find more information on the ABA and ABLS at the ABA website at www.ameriburn.org.

- Shriners Hospitals for Children are world renowned for treating pediatric patients. A listing of their facilities can be found at www.shrinershq.org/ Hospitals/_Hospitals_for_Children/Shriners_ Hospitals/burns.aspx.

- Trauma.org is an online organization that promotes and disseminates the knowledge and practice of injury prevention and trauma care throughout the world.2 It has a comprehensive reposi-tory of trauma photographs that can be found at www.trauma.org/imagebank/imagebank.html.

- Get ready to respond to your next trauma patient presented in Problem-Based Learning Case 4, A Tragic Fall.

- Link to the companion DVD for a chapter-based quiz, audio glossary, animations, games and exercises, and, when appropriate, skill sheets and skill Step-by-Steps.

Street Secrets

- **Need for Compassion** Burns are perhaps some of the most horrific injuries that a paramedic must manage. They are visually dramatic, and the odor of burnt skin and hair is unforgettable. In addition, the pain involved with these injuries can be unimaginable. Be prepared to be as professional and compassionate as possible—your patients will appreciate these behaviors in their time of need.

The Drug Box

Morphine sulfate: Burns can be extremely painful, which can drive up metabolism in the critically injured patient. Local protocols may allow the use of a narcotic such as morphine sulfate if the burn is uncomplicated by a trauma mechanism. Carefully observe the patient's respiratory effort as the medication is being administered, often in large amounts.

Succinylcholine: A common paralytic used in medication-assisted intubation procedures. However, its use is contraindicated in the severely burned patient, due to the risk of hyperkalemia. It appears that the peak risk period is 7–10 days after the injury. The large areas of tissue destruction may predispose the patient to release dangerously high amounts of potassium into the bloodstream upon succinylcholine administration, which may cause sudden cardiac arrest.

References

1. American Burn Association, "Mission statement." www. ameriburn.org/about.php?PHPSESSID=7e96978dbb82d d34530d11d142622d6f (accessed December 5, 2006).
2. Trauma.org. www.trauma.org/traumaorg.html (accessed October 25, 2006).

Answers

Are You Ready?

1. Your own safety is paramount. The mechanisms that cause a burn have great potential to harm the rescuer as well. Be sure to take appropriate precautions and be properly trained for these types of incidents.

2. The burning process needs to be abated immediately. Cooling the smoldering clothes with water for up to 1 minute is appropriate. Afterward, or simultaneously, conduct a primary assessment to determine if there are any threats to the airway patency, breathing ability, or circulatory status and treat them. Try to determine if the mechanism that caused the fire, such as an explosion, may have also caused additional injuries. You will also need to begin the process of conserving body temperature, since the air exposure, coupled with any wet clothing, will lower the patient's body temperature.

Active Learning

1.

	Adult	Child
A	front leg + back leg = 4.5 + 4.5 = 9%	front leg + back leg = 4 + 4 = 8%
B	Front arm = 4%–5%	Front arm = 9%

(Continued)

	Adult	Child
C	Area equivalent to about half of posterior thorax = 9%	Area equivalent to about half of posterior thorax = 9%
D	Front of both arms + anterior thorax = 10 + 9 = 19%	Front of both arms + anterior thorax = 18 + 9 = 27%
E	Front of both legs + back of both legs + posterior thorax + both hands = 18 + 18 + 9 + 2 = 47%	Front of both legs + back of both legs + posterior thorax + both hands = 16.5 + 16.5 + 9 + 6 = 48%

2.
   a. Second-degree burn (from oven cleaner chemical)
   b. Second-degree and deep third-degree burns (patient's hand was held down on a campfire)
   c. Second-degree burns (from sodium hydroxide exposure following an industrial explosion)
   d. Second- and third-degree burns (from contact with a 7,200-volt line)

You Are There: Reality-Based Cases

Case 1

1. This patient clearly has suffered an insult to his airway and breathing ability. It requires an aggressive approach to circumvent the signs of impending airway closure secondary to soft tissue swelling. This may include intubation, perhaps with the assistance of a paralytic agent such as succinylcholine or a non-defasciculating agent such as vecuronium after induction. If oral entry is not possible, a needle cricothyroidotomy may be required to preserve the airway. With the amount of burn damage to the body (36%), chances are high that there may be additional injuries underneath. Your primary assessment should check for the presence of tension pneumothorax, hemothorax, and other possible sources of bleeding.

2. The suspected presence of an illegal drug manufacturing site adds significant worry. First, there may be chemical containers still burning in the building that could explode and cause further damage. You may need to relocate your patient to a safer location. Second, the patient may have experienced significant forces when the explosion occurred. Third, there may have been toxic gases that the patient inhaled or chemicals he may have absorbed through the skin to complicate his thermal burns. You will need to assess the patient carefully for signs of these possibilities and document accordingly. As you read in the text, victims of clandestine drug lab fires are at greater risk for death because of exposure to atypical flammables such as white phosphorus, inhaling toxic by-products such as ammonia, and preexisting use of the drug, which increases metabolic demands of the body.

Test Yourself

1. a

   Once the patient is presented to your team for treatment, first stop the burning process by putting water on smoldering clothing. Work quickly so you do not chill the patient. All the other steps are performed after the burning has stopped.

2. a

   The majority of deaths from fire are due to smoke inhalation. Of fire deaths on the scene, 50%–60% are secondary to inhalation injury.

3. b

   A large amount of water flushed over the patient is still the mainstay of initial decontamination. White phosphorus is the only chemical for which direct immersion (soaking) in water is recommended as the initial treatment. Blankets are used after the decontamination process to preserve body heat.

4. a

   According to the rule of nines, the back is 18% total BSA, the back of the head and neck is 4.5%, and the arms are 18% (9% each).

5. a

   Because vital signs should be near normal at this stage of the injury, patients with signs of hypovolemic shock immediately after being burned are that way because of blood volume loss. Depending upon the cause of the burn, other traumatic injuries should be suspected and searched for during the trauma patient assessment. Symptoms of pulmonary edema include difficulty breathing, coughing up blood, excessive sweating, anxiety, and pale skin. They do not generally include tachycardia, absent peripheral pulses in non-burned extremities, or lower blood pressure.

6. c

   The hypervolemia indicates another source of trauma, and the TBSA justifies bringing the patient to a burn center. Patients with both burns and major trauma should go to the trauma center first and then be transferred to a burn center once the trauma is stabilized.

7. Superficial partial-thickness burns are pink or red, blistered, and painful. They are edematous and elastic, and they will blanch (turn white) when pressure is applied to the skin. Hair does not pull out easily.

8. When evaluating for smoke inhalation, think about the following: stridor, increasing hoarseness, drooling, burns occurring in a closed structure or vehicle (smoke), inhalation injuries caused by steam (thermal airway trauma), and inhalation injuries involving chemicals. Signs and symptoms of possible inhalation injury include: complaints of dyspnea; facial burns; singed hair, eyebrows, and nasal hair; soot present in the airway and sputum; coughing; wheezing; episode of unconsciousness related to the event; burns in the mouth; and unexplained anxiety and restlessness (assume hypoxia).

9. Any five of the following:
   - Partial-thickness and full-thickness burns totaling greater than 10% TBSA in patients under 10 or over 50 years of age.
   - Partial-thickness and full-thickness burns totaling greater than 20% TBSA in other age groups (those between ages 10 and 50).
   - Partial-thickness and full-thickness burns involving the face, hands, feet, genitalia, perineum, or major joints.
   - Full-thickness burns greater than 5% TBSA in any age group.
   - Electrical burns, including lightning injury.
   - Chemical burns.
   - Inhalation injury.
   - Burn injury in patients with preexisting medical disorders that could complicate management, prolong the recovery period, or affect mortality.
   - Any burn with concomitant trauma (e.g., fractures) in which the burn injury poses the greatest risk of morbidity or mortality. If the trauma poses the greater immediate risk, the patient may be treated initially in a trauma center until stable before being transferred to a burn center.
   - Burn injury in children admitted to a hospital without qualified personnel or equipment for pediatric care.
   - Burn injury in patients requiring special social, emotional, and/or long-term rehabilitative support, including cases involving suspected child abuse.

10. Decontamination is an important part of treating chemical burns. Clothing should always be assumed to be contaminated and a threat to prehospital providers and receiving medical facility staff, so it must be immediately removed. A large amount of water flushed over the patient is still the mainstay of initial decontamination. After decontamination, the burn should be treated as any other burn would be, by first monitoring and treating any threats to airway, breathing, and circulation and then treating the burn with the application of dry sterile dressings.

11. Child abuse should be suspected in children with multiple burns or bizarre descriptions of events. Reports of falling into a hot bathtub are suspicious, especially if there are no burns to the chest or head (children are top heavy) or the child is too young and unable to walk.

12. True

   Never apply ice to cool a burn. Frostbite can occur too easily to injured tissue.

13. False

   Most radiation control measures, such as decontamination, covering wounds, and removing clothing, will be performed on the scene. The decontaminated patient will then be transferred to the ambulance and transported.

14. a

   Even if the patient is seriously injured, it is not appropriate to endanger yourself or members of your crew trying to rescue a patient from a burning environment unless you have the appropriate protective clothing and gear and are trained to do so.

15. c

   The Baux score is a rule of thumb that calculates mortality by adding the patient's age to the percentage of body surface area burned. Certainly this score should never be used as a tool to determine whether or not to withhold treatment, but it may help paramedics better understand the severity of what they are dealing with.

Problem-Based Learning Case 4
A Tragic Fall

Part I: The Case

Dispatch and Scene Size-Up

As you and your partner are sitting down to eat lunch with the engine crew at your station, the alarm that has so frequently interrupted your meals goes off. You silently hope that the run is going to be for the engine, but the call is for you and the engine company closest to Broadmoor University. The loudspeaker screeches, "Medic 4, Engine 56 . . . Respond for a fall at the university's Drama Department, 1234 56th Ave; cross streets are Blakemore Street and University Drive. The time is 12:14 hours."

You arrive on scene simultaneously with the fire department EMTs. You load a backboard and all your equipment onto the gurney and make your way toward the front door. As you enter the building and head up the stairs, you see a young female lying on the stairway landing. A tall ladder is lying on its side in the stairwell, partially blocking access to the patient. Posters and other papers are strewn about. The patient appears unconscious and has agonal respirations.

1. *What is your general impression of the scene and of the patient? Do you have any safety concerns about the scene?*

_____

_____

The Primary Assessment and Initial Differentials

You hear the patient gasp as you kneel down to begin your primary assessment. You can hear gurgling in the throat. Her breathing is slow and irregular. You find a slow radial pulse. A sternal rub produces no response from the patient. There is a laceration at the left temporal side of the patient's head. It is bleeding, but not profusely.

2. *What condition(s) could explain the primary assessment findings? How will you manage these findings, and when will you begin your treatment? Do you treat the bleeding from the laceration now? What is the patient's GCS score?*

_____

_____

History and Physical Exam (Secondary Assessment and History)

A man runs up to the scene. He says that the patient's name is Nicole. They were hanging posters announcing an upcoming concert, using the ladder to get higher on the walls. He was helping to stabilize the ladder as she climbed up. As he was positioning the ladder near the stairway, someone down the hall called to him, and he went over to talk to that person. He heard Nicole cry out and turned around to see her fall with the ladder into the stairway. He estimates that she fell nearly 20 feet.

After exposing the patient, you note that she has a contusion near the center of her chest. You also observe that her jugular veins are distended. She has clear lung sounds. As you palpate the back of Nicole's head, you can feel that it is soft. Your gloved hand is now bloody.

3. *Based upon the description of the incident, what injuries did Nicole suffer? What other information will you need to better differentiate your suspicions? Of the injuries you identified, which one should you focus on first?*

_____

_____

Field Impression(s) and Formulation of Treatment Plan

As you continue to assess the patient you discover:

Blood pressure: 70/60

Heart rate: 42

Respiratory rate: 6

Oxygen saturation: 86% on room air

Pupils: right: 3 mm and reactive; left: 9 mm and non-reactive

4. *At this point, has your impression of the patient changed? What is the most appropriate treatment for the patient at this time? How did you come to your conclusion regarding the prioritization of treatment for the patient? Are there any considerations regarding the initial treatment that could negatively affect the patient? If so, how will you address these issues? What is the patient's mean arterial pressure (MAP)? What is cerebral perfusion pressure (CPP), and why would it be important to know the CPP of this patient?*

_____

_____

Transportation and Ongoing Care

Your patient is now in the back of the ambulance. Your transport time to the regional trauma center is 30 minutes by ground once you are en route. The center's medical helicopter is already in the air and heading to your destination. The fire lieutenant reports that it will arrive within the next 7–10 minutes.

You note that the patient's body begins to stiffen. A few seconds later, the patient begins to spasm rhythmically. Vomit and blood begin to flow out of her mouth.

5. *Should you utilize the helicopter or the ground ambulance to transport Nicole? What is the status of the patient's airway? Describe how you would control and manage this situation.*

_____

_____

Transfer of Care, Follow-up, and Outcome

At the medical center you transfer the care of the patient to the trauma team. A baseline assessment is performed, yielding the following results:

GCS: 4

BP: 92/78

HR: 96 and regular

RR: Controlled manually at 10 breaths per minute

ECG: Sinus rhythm

Partial lab results include:

CBC
  Hemoglobin: 14 g/dL
  Hematocrit: 38%
  PCO$_2$: 26 mm Hg

Glucose: 106 mg/dL

BUN: 27 mg/dL

Creatinine: 0.5 mg/dL

6. *How do these lab values coincide with Nicole's condition and your management? How does her MAP compare to the field measurement? How does that relate to your patient's condition?*

_____

_____

Long-Term Outlook

On the morning of your next workday you transport a trauma patient to the trauma center. While you are there, you go to the ICU to check on the patient from the university. As you approach the patient's room you notice that there is a technician in the room performing an electroencephalogram (EEG). The charge nurse sees that you are approaching the room and greets you. She informs you that the patient had a severe epidural bleed, and the CT scan showed herniation of her brain stem. The patient had a pericardiocentesis in the ED and underwent a craniotomy. The patient experienced decerebrate posturing after she was admitted to the ICU. The patient has no respiratory effort and continues to be hypotensive, despite the use of high-dose vasopressors. Her family has been at the hospital since the incident, and the trauma surgeons have explained to them that her prognosis is extremely poor. The doctors and the family are discussing the possibility of organ harvesting.

7. *Is the patient a good candidate for organ donation? Why or why not? What are the criteria for organ donation? How does organ donation pertain to your practice?*

_____

_____

Part II: Debriefing

Responses to Part I questions:

1. Did you consider the following questions as they relate to the primary assessment:
   - Is the patient really unresponsive?
   - Does the patient have a patent airway?
   - Is the patient breathing adequately?
   - Does the patient have a pulse?

   The stairway landing looks narrow, which can present an extrication challenge. In addition to scene safety issues (Did she fall? Why did she fall?), did you consider ergonomic issues for yourself and other members of the team?

2. Nicole's condition is very serious. The primary assessment reveals instability to her airway and breathing status. It is essential that these conditions are reversed as quickly as possible. Given the situation, will bandaging the head injury be helpful at this point?

3. Based on the described mechanism of injury, there is a strong possibility that your patient has both chest and head injuries. A closer survey of these areas will provide you with additional information to confirm your suspicions. (Do not neglect other major areas, though—you have learned that occult bleeding can easily happen in the abdominal cavity.) Assuming that Nicole has both of these injury patterns, which one is most life threatening? What other specific information do you need to help you develop a treatment plan?

4. At this point, you are faced with the task of determining the extent of the patient's injuries and how you are going to address them. Because the patient has more than one life-threatening condition, it is imperative that you prioritize your treatments in a manner that will not negatively affect the patient's overall condition. Treatment of some conditions may not be in your scope of practice; thus some treatment decisions may be made for you.

5. Many EMS systems have local policies and protocols to help guide EMS providers in making decisions about the utilization of air medical transport. There is controversy about the risk versus benefit of air ambulances, and it will be important for you as a health-care professional to make a rational decision about the transport method of your patient.

6. Did you research the lab values? They can provide you with some valuable feedback as to the patient's baseline physiological status. Look carefully at the amount of carbon dioxide (how were your ventilations?), the blood urea nitrogen (BUN) and creatinine levels (what do they suggest about the

kidneys' perfusion status?), and the glucose level (why would you want to know about this in a patient with altered mental status?).

7. It is upsetting when a young adult experiences such a devastating injury. However, in death might come life: because of Nicole's overall health, her organs are probably in excellent shape to be harvested by a donor team. Her low perfusion status may be a challenge that needs close monitoring.

Part III: Case Discussion

Trauma management is the ultimate race against time. Recovering from a critical injury after the insult is strongly related to the amount of time it takes for the patient to reach definitive surgical treatment. Balancing this urgency are the needs to accurately identify and reverse life-threatening conditions and the ability to protect the patient from further harm. Meeting all these requirements takes a well-practiced, consistent approach to assessment and treatment.

Begin with an accurate scene size-up. It appears that there has been a fall. Based on the ladder type, it would seem likely that it was set up at the top of the stairs above the landing. If true, assuming the worst-case scenario in which the patient was standing at the top of the ladder, the combined height of the fall is significant.

Ensure that the scene is safe for you and the team. Look above you as well as around you. However remote, check to see if there is a violent mechanism associated with this fall—did someone push the ladder over? Size up your working area. It appears to be narrow and tight where the patient landed—you will want to be very conscious of your own body ergonomics when lifting and moving this patient out of the area.

The primary assessment identifies critical problems. The patient appears to have a very low GCS score and is unresponsive even to pain, which signals the loss of a spontaneous gag reflex. The airway is not patent and requires immediate intervention of suctioning and the placement of an oral airway. Simultaneous manual stabilization of the head and neck is needed to protect the cervical spine from any further harm. The respiratory effort is too slow to be considered adequate, even for a young patient. Supplemental oxygen will not be enough—assisting her respiratory effort with a bag-mask will be needed. Her slow radial pulse is another source of concern. It may be an ominous sign of impending failure and cardiac arrest. Based on these findings of the primary assessment, it is imperative that you safely begin moving her to the hospital as quickly as possible. Dressing the scalp laceration will not be helpful at this point—putting down some 4 × 4s or a trauma dressing to absorb some of the blood may be helpful in minimizing contamination, but speed is now of the essence. The recorded hypotension may be indicative of blood loss, but it doesn't appear to be from the scalp.

There is a contusion to the patient's chest, which might indicate injury beneath. However, her lung sounds are clear. Her jugular veins are distended, but she is lying supine, and observable neck veins are expected. The head injury is clearly of greatest concern, meaning that careful control of ventilation is a must. The unequal pupils and subsequent seizure are indicative of a herniating brain. The hypotension may be a terminal sign of total respiratory failure. There needs to be a two-front war to keep her alive: improving blood flow to the brain by controlled ventilation and raising her blood pressure to overcome a higher than normal ICP.

The usefulness of the aircraft is probably minimal. The time it will take to rendezvous with the helicopter, perform the landing procedure, transfer the patient from the ambulance to the helicopter, and perform the takeoff procedure will likely negate any time savings of the faster transit time.

This case has no happy ending for the patient and her family. However, her desire to be an organ donor will permit others to live better, more fulfilling lives. She is an excellent candidate for donation, as a young and healthy individual. The biggest concern is the hypoperfusion state of the body and how long various tissues and organs can withstand that state and not be injured. It is yet another reason to make sure that blood pressure remains adequate to keep organs viable for harvesting.

Part IV: Further Learning Paths

- The Brain Trauma Foundation website contains resources that can be researched for this case. Go to www.braintrauma.org/to find out more.
- Review Chapter 19, Hemorrhage and Hemorrhagic Shock, and Chapter 20, Head, Face, and Neck Trauma, in the textbook, for more detailed information related to this case.

chapter 27

Trauma Patients and Trauma Systems

fatality from the wreck and a critical victim trapped and requiring extrication. There are at least two other seriously injured patients, along with four or five "green," or low-priority, victims.

The Level I trauma center is 30 minutes away by ground transport from the crash scene. A Level II facility is 20 minutes away, in the opposite direction. Two other community hospitals are within 20 minutes by ground as well. AirCare, the air medical services provider, has been alerted to the situation by the dispatch center. Two other ambulances have begun traveling to the scene, with estimated times of arrival of 20 and 25 minutes, respectively.

1. Which hospitals should receive which patients? Should the victims be transported by ground or by air?

   _____

   _____

   _____

Are You Ready?

Your service area covers an area of the county that has seen a rapid, significant increase in population over the past 4 years. Unfortunately the road system has not kept up with the surge in growth, often producing slow traffic patterns during rush hour. Impatient with the traffic, commuters often find alternative routes to reach their jobs. One such road is a narrow stretch of country highway that winds through the hills, separating your bedroom community from the main urban area. Your coworkers have nicknamed this road "Blood Alley" for all the crashes that have occurred there over the years.

At 5 a.m. the tones of your pager sound for the report of a multivehicle crash on that highway. Your response time is 15 minutes traveling at Code 3. First responders arriving on the scene report at least one

Active Learning

1. A Look at Trauma Systems

Most of the public—and even more than a few EMS providers—believes that their community's trauma system is comprised of the ambulance service and the hospital "trauma center." In fact, you now know that a trauma system is made up of many components. List as many of these components as you can.

_____

_____

_____

2. Volunteer Opportunity: Trauma Center

Is there an American College of Surgeons' (ACS) designated trauma facility in your area? If so, make arrangements to visit with the director or other staff of that center. Review the criteria for the different levels of trauma care (I, II, and III), and see if you can find evidence of each point during your visit. If you are visiting a surgical intensive care unit (SICU), ask the staff what actions you could take as the prehospital provider

that could help the patient later in the care continuum.

3. Developing a Trauma System

If you live in an area where there is no designated trauma center, check out some of the resources listed in the Connections section of this chapter. There are several documents produced by the federal government and national organizations that speak to the trauma care system. As you read these documents, assume that you are now the person who is responsible for analyzing your local EMS system and assessing the option of developing a trauma system. What barriers and challenges would have to be overcome to create such a system?

_____

_____

_____

4. A Closer Look at Trauma Decision-Making

By now you have learned the trauma triage criteria explained in the textbook. Let's apply this knowledge to a few practical situations. For each of the presentations listed in the table below, decide whether the patient requires transport to a trauma center.

Patient	Patient Presentation	Transport to Trauma Center? (Yes/No)
A	A 45-year-old male is an unrestrained driver in a motor vehicle crash. His vehicle was struck on the driver's side by another car. Damage to the patient's car is moderate, with 3 inches of intrusion into the rear passenger space. The patient denies any loss of consciousness and is alert. He complains of neck pain, left shoulder pain, and left hip pain. His vital signs are HR of 92, BP of 136/84, and RR of 22.	
B	Same presentation as patient A, but the patient is a 71-year-old female.	
C	A 17-year-old female presents with possible bilateral ankle injuries after jumping from a balcony. The distance from the balcony to the ground is 15 feet. She is awake and alert and has significant swelling, deformity, and pain to both ankles. She denies any neck or back pain. Her vital signs are HR of 86, BP of 124/84, and RR of 20.	
D	Same presentation as patient C, but the distance between the balcony and ground is 18 feet.	
E	Same presentation as patient C, but the patient's blood pressure is 94/76.	
F	A 27-year-old male has been shot. He is awake and oriented. He has a wound located in the left midthigh region. The mild bleeding is controlled with direct pressure. His vital signs are HR of 100, BP of 122/82, and RR of 24.	
G	Same presentation as patient F, but the wound is located in the left midtibial region.	
H	Same presentation as patient F, but the wounds are in the left midtibial and right midulnar regions.	

You Are There: Reality-Based Cases
Case 1 (continuation of chapter opener)

You arrive at the scene, where the rescue lieutenant advises you that the extrication of the patient may take another 7–10 minutes. Behind him, you can see that the roof of the car has been cut off by the rescue crew, who are using hydraulic cutting tools to open the passenger door.

You continue to sort out the patients and prepare them for transport. The other ambulances are arriving. AirCare-1 has lifted off from its hangar and has a 7-minute estimated time of arrival to your location. Once in the area, it will take another 2–3 minutes to orbit and land the aircraft, and then another 10 minutes before the helicopter can lift off the scene and begin its 10-minute flight to the Level I trauma center.

1. Does this information help to confirm your transport decision-making process?

_____

_____

_____

Test Yourself

1. You have arrived on the scene of a single-vehicle, multiple-rollover accident. The patient is standing outside his vehicle with a contusion and laceration to the forehead and complaining of a "sore neck." The patient states that he was belted and was not ejected from the vehicle. The patient is alert and oriented × 3. You should
   a. request that the patient sign a refusal form before you release him, since he is not seriously injured.
   b. perform a quick physical exam and tell the patient to call 9-1-1 if he feels worse after he arrives home.
   c. encourage the patient to make an immediate appointment the following day with his family physician.
   d. encourage the patient to let you take c-spine precautions, perform a complete trauma examination, and transport.

2. Who is responsible for making recommendations to revise practices, changing EMS protocols, and identifying areas for improvement?
   a. The chief of operations
   b. The quality improvement/quality management (QI/QM) committee
   c. The company administrator
   d. The medical director

3. In communities where resources are limited and distances to the trauma center are great, deployment of _____ can save valuable time.
   a. air medical evacuation resources
   b. rapid transport teams
   c. medical "Go Teams"
   d. paramedic chase vehicles

4. Protocols, standards of care, and _____ help providers determine which patients would be better served at a trauma center versus a local hospital.
   a. standing orders
   b. administrative standards
   c. triage criteria
   d. online consults

5. Patients meeting the trauma decision criteria should be rapidly transported to a trauma center with treatment
   a. postponed until arrival at the trauma center.
   b. performed on the scene.
   c. continued during transport.
   d. delayed until a trauma consult is obtained.

6. You have arrived at a single-vehicle MVC. As you approach, the vehicle's single occupant appears unresponsive. You announce loudly, "Sir, don't move your head. My partner is going to hold your head and neck still." The patient begins mumbling. You notice a contusion over the patient's left eye. He does not want to cooperate and is becoming more and more combative; you smell alcohol. You should suspect
   a. a head injury with an altered level of consciousness (LOC). The altered LOC and combativeness could be the result of the head injury. This is a high-priority patient who needs immediate transport.
   b. a head injury and/or hypoglycemia. The patient will be immobilized in a KED-like extrication device and then transferred to a full backboard. While this is in progress, you can initiate an IV, test the patient's blood glucose level, and apply oxygen. The patient can then be transported to the hospital.
   c. intoxication. However, because he may have a neck injury, you will apply a cervical collar, immobilize the patient, and transport.
   d. an unsafe scene. Because the patient is becoming combative, you will need to notify law enforcement for the safety of you and your

crew. Move everyone away from the patient until law enforcement arrives to avoid bystander and crew injury.

7. Why is it important to handle the patient assessment of both medical and trauma patients the same way each time?

_____

_____

8. A recent Canadian study showed that trauma patients treated by EMTs with only BLS skills had a(n) _____ mortality rate when compared to patients treated by paramedics or physicians.

   a. equal
   b. lower
   c. higher
   d. similar

9. An 18-year-old male was ejected during a two-vehicle MVC. He is pulseless and apneic, and you observe no apparent signs of life. The cardiac monitor reveals no signs of organized electrical activity. You should begin resuscitation.

   True
   False

10. Your patient was ejected during an MVC. He is unconscious, has a flail section to his right chest with decreased breath sounds, a distended and rigid abdomen, and a fractured right femur. Following your primary assessment to correct all life-threatening conditions, vital signs are BP of 100/70, HR of 90, and shallow respirations of 20. To what type of center should you transport this patient?

_____

_____

11. A specialty medical facility located in a large urban area with capabilities to treat all types of injury and illness 24 hours a day, 7 days a week is known as a _____.

12. Paramedics should educate the public in injury prevention to reduce morbidity and mortality.

    True
    False

13. Driving under the influence of alcohol accounts for 40% of all traffic fatalities.

    True
    False

14. While trauma is the fifth leading cause of death across all age groups and has a significant economic impact on society, it is the leading cause of death for people under the age of 45.

    True
    False

15. You are dispatched to a reported drive-by shooting. After law enforcement has secured the scene, you find a single patient with a "through and through" gunshot wound to the left side, midclavicular, approximately 3 inches above the nipple. The patient is conscious, cyanotic around the lips, and experiencing severe difficulty breathing. Formulate a treatment plan for this patient.

_____

_____

Need to Know

The following represent the Key Objectives of Chapter 27:

1. *Describe the attributes of a comprehensive trauma system, including the different levels of care.*

A comprehensive trauma system contains the following elements:

- A concerted effort to prevent injuries from occurring
- Easy access to emergency medical care
- Rapid response by the EMS system
- Appropriate destination to receive trauma patients
- Appropriate resources to manage trauma patients

- Comprehensive rehabilitation services
- Data collection and research to improve trauma resuscitation processes

Table 27-1 in the textbook describes the various levels of trauma center designations. The Level I trauma center is capable of managing critically injured patients around the clock; Level II and III facilities have less availability and fewer resources. Services required by a medical facility to receive Level I trauma include:

- A specially trained surgical team
- In-house or on-call surgical staff
- Surgical critical care
- Support services, including a blood bank, radiology, and pharmacy

These services are expensive to provide and must receive a minimum number of patients annually. For these reasons, Level I trauma centers are regionally based, covering large populations.

2. *Explain how and when air medical transport should be utilized to maximize its effectiveness.*

The transportation of a critically injured patient by helicopter can save valuable time in delivering the patient into the hands of a surgeon. However, it is not without risk and cost. The decision to "fly" a patient must be made deliberately. Factors such as weather, time of day, and road congestion are as important to consider as the distance to the trauma center, the time it takes for a helicopter to arrive and land, the load time it takes to move the patient into the aircraft, and the time it takes for the helicopter to lift off the scene and arrive at the facility. System protocols and common-sense judgment are needed to make a sound medical decision.

Need to Do

The following skills are explained and illustrated in a step-by-step manner, via skill sheets and/or Step-by-Steps in this text and on the accompanying DVD:

Skill Name	Skill Sheet Number and Location	Step-by-Step Number and Location
Trauma Scoring	31 – DVD	N/A
Verbal Communications	63 – DVD	N/A

Connections

- Review Chapter 18, Mechanism of Injury, and Chapter 14, Patient Assessment, in the textbook for assessment information critical to the trauma transport decision-making process.
- Additional information about trauma systems, including planning information, can be found at the following NHTSA website: www.nhtsa.dot. gov/people/injury/ems/emstraumasystem03/ traumasystem.htm. You might want to refer to this document as you work on the first activity in the Active Learning section of this chapter.
- The trauma registry is an important piece of the data collection puzzle. Without the ability to collect and analyze information about trauma patients, it is difficult to understand whether the trauma system is functioning effectively. The federal Health Resources and Services Administration (HRSA) has additional information about trauma registries at its website at www.hrsa.gov/trauma/registries. htm
- The American College of Surgeons' Committee on Trauma (ACS-COT) has updated its resource guide for trauma patient management. Titled Resources for the Optimal Care of the Injured Patient: 2006, this document can be purchased over the Web at web2.facs.org/timssnet464/acs-pub/frontpage.cfm?product_class5trauma.
- The International Association of Flight Paramedics (IAFP) (www.flightparamedic.org) represents the professional interests of EMS flight personnel.

- Link to the companion DVD for a chapter-based quiz, audio glossary, animations, games and exercises, and, when appropriate, skill sheets and skill Step-by-Steps.

Street Secrets

- **Be Alert** Many EMS systems have routine announcements made by the communication center regarding the receiving status of the area's hospitals, including trauma centers. Keep a mental note of any closures that might impact your decision-making process for trauma destination.

The Drug Box

There are no specific drugs related to this chapter content.

Answers

Are You Ready?

1. This is a complex decision-making situation. You have many patients, an extended extrication process, and transport resources that will take some time to arrive. Preparing patients for immediate transport will be key to successfully getting patients to interventional care within the Golden Period. It is very possible that the Level II trauma center can receive the two seriously injured patients, allowing you to reserve the Level I trauma center resources for the critically injured patient. If extrication is prolonged, the air ambulance may be able to arrive in time to immediately transport the critical victim to the Level I center. The later-arriving ground units can take several of the "walking wounded" to the community hospitals.

Active Learning

1. Injury prevention; immediate access to care (9-1-1 system); an efficient EMS response system; an appropriate transport destination for immediate trauma care; a comprehensive way to rehabilitate a trauma patient and return him or her to as normal a life as possible; the collection of data from trauma registries and EMS system performance to determine if the system is effective in reducing morbidity and mortality from trauma; and ongoing research to refine the approach and care of the trauma patient.

3. The answer to this question will vary from one area of the country to another. However, factors that can limit the development of a trauma center include lack of funding, political and legislative issues, and lack of facilities for both the provision of care as well as data collection and research.

4. Patient A: no; patient B: yes (age); patient C: no; patient D: yes (distance of fall is 3 times the height of the patient); patient E: yes (hypotension, although it might be normal for her); patient F: yes (site of injury is proximal to knee); patient G: no; patient H: no.

You Are There: Reality-Based Cases

Case 1

1. It appears that the helicopter arrival time will work well with the extrication time of the critical patient. The ground units can package the remaining patients and transport them to the Level II trauma center and community hospitals. You will want to retriage the patients, in case there has been a change in their conditions. If you are in any doubt, develop a plan to transport the patients to a higher level of care. Overtriage is better than undertriage.

Test Yourself

1. d

   Even if the patient shows only minor trauma, because of the mechanism of injury in addition to cervical tenderness he should be encouraged to accept a backboard and transportation to the ED.

2. b

   The QI/QM committee can make recommendations to revise practice, change EMS protocols, identify areas for improvement, and suggest education programs to ensure the standards are met.

3. a

   In some communities resources may be limited and distances to trauma centers may be great. In such communities, the deployment of air medical evacuation resources can save valuable time.

4. c

   Prehospital guidelines, protocols, standards of care, and triage criteria help providers determine which patients would be better served at a trauma center versus the local hospital.

5. c

   As a rule, patients meeting the trauma decision criteria should be rapidly transported to a trauma center with treatment continuing during transport.

6. a

   There are many reasons why the patient could have an altered LOC. The head injury, however, is the most serious and requires immediate attention. All patients experiencing an altered LOC require immediate transport.

7. Performing patient assessments the same way each time will ensure you do not miss an important step in the process.

   For both medical and trauma patients, immediately correct any and all life-threatening conditions (airway, breathing, circulation, and bleeding). Next, perform a primary survey and then continue to repeatedly assess your patient. Assessments and reassessments are necessary to evaluate the patient's condition and any interventions that you may have performed. If the patient's condition is worsening, then a reassessment of the patient is required. You may observe something missed during the initial assessment. You should also reevaluate your intervention and stop or modify it if necessary.

8. b

   Similarly, a much more recent study investigating prehospital systems in Canada showed that patients cared for by EMTs with only BLS skills had a lower mortality rate than those cared for by paramedics or physicians. This suggests that there may be no direct increase in survival of trauma patients when ALS procedures are performed. Delay at the scene to perform procedures does not appear to improve survival. Therefore make every effort to minimize scene time. A direct correlation has been shown between shorter prehospital times and decreased mortality of trauma patients.

9. False

   A recent position paper by the National Association of EMS Physicians proposed the following guidelines to use when deciding to initiate resuscitative efforts with trauma patients: (1) Do not attempt to resuscitate blunt trauma patients who are pulseless, apneic, and have no organized cardiac electrical activity. (2) Patients with penetrating trauma have a slightly higher chance of survival, even if they are pulseless, apneic, and without organized electrical cardiac activity; therefore, attempt resuscitation.

10. A regional Level I trauma center

    The patient is suffering from multisystem trauma and should be transported to a Level I trauma center where his injuries can be addressed immediately. Going to a facility other than a Level I trauma center may require the patient to wait for physicians to respond from their homes or offices.

11. Level I trauma center

    Level I trauma centers are frequently located in areas with large populations at major university medical centers. They are uniquely equipped with a large number of specialty services and mechanisms to care for patients with complex injuries and illnesses.

12. True

    Injury prevention organizations have created programs to promote safety in daily living as well as at play. Paramedics can make a significant impact by supporting these programs as well as by setting a safe example for the public to follow.

13. True

    Driving while under the influence of alcohol is the most frequent cause of fatal motor vehicle crashes.

14. True

    Trauma is the leading cause of death in children and adults under the age of 45.

15. You should first treat the open chest wound. Then perform a primary assessment, place the patient on a backboard, put him on the cot, and transport him to a trauma center.

    Life-threatening conditions need to be treated immediately. All other interventions can wait until you are en route to a trauma center.

Medical Issues

chapter 28

Pulmonary

Five days after Mrs. Jones' choking episode, you are called to Shady Acres to evaluate her because she appears to be experiencing a decreased level of consciousness and respiratory distress with perioral and peripheral cyanosis. When you arrive, you note that Mrs. Jones is in moderate to severe respiratory distress and responds to pain by withdrawing.

1. Based on the preceding information, what is your general impression of Mrs. Jones' condition?

   _____

   _____

   _____

2. What is a likely cause of Mrs. Jones' condition?

   _____

   _____

   _____

3. List several signs and symptoms that you would expect to see that would support your impression of what is causing Mrs. Jones' altered level of consciousness and respiratory distress.

   _____

   _____

   _____

Are You Ready?

Muriel Jones is a 72-year-old female who has been residing at the Shady Acres Convalescent Home for the past month to undergo rehabilitation after suffering a right hemisphere cerebrovascular accident. Mrs. Jones has left-sided hemiparesis, dysarthria, and dysphagia.

Two weeks after her admission to the long-term care (LTC) facility, Mrs. Jones had a choking episode during a meal, despite the fact that she was on a special diet of nectar-thickened liquids and pureed foods. She was taken to a nearby hospital for evaluation and discharged with instructions to have another swallowing evaluation by an occupational therapist at the LTC facility.

4. What are your priorities for treating Mrs. Jones?

   _____

   _____

   _____

   _____

Active Learning

Anatomy Review

1. Identify the structures of the upper airway in Figure 28-1 and describe the functions of those structures marked with an asterisk (*).

   a. _____

   b. _____

   c. _____

   d. _____

   e. _____

   f. _____

   g. _____

   h. _____

   i. _____

   j. _____

   k. _____

   l. _____

   m. _____

   n. _____

2. Identify the respiratory structures in Figure 28-2.

   a. _____

   b. _____

   c. _____

   d. _____

   e. _____

   f. _____

   g. _____

   h. _____

   i. _____

   j. _____

   k. _____

   l. _____

3. The name of the substance that lubricates the alveolar surfaces and keeps them from sticking together is _____.

4. The serous membrane that adheres to the surface of the lungs and is insensate is called the (a) _____ pleura. The serous membrane that lines the thoracic cavity, contains nerve fibers, and forms part of the mediastinum is know as the (b) _____ pleura. The potential space between the two opposing pleural layers is referred to as the (c) _____. This potential space contains a thin film known as (d) _____, which helps prevent friction between the two surfaces during respiration.

5. Blood is supplied to the lungs by two separate systems. The first involves the transport of oxygen and cellular waste products (carbon dioxide, etc.). In this system deoxygenated blood is transported from the heart to the lungs by the (a) _____, where carbon dioxide can be eliminated and oxygen can be brought into the blood. Once oxygen has been diffused into the blood, it leaves the lungs via the (b) _____ and is distributed to the rest of the body by way of the (c) _____. The lungs themselves receive blood from the (d) _____, which are branches of the aorta. Blood is returned by veins called the (e) _____ and the (f) _____, which empty into the (g) _____ and back to the heart.

6. Restricted Airways

Repeat the Active Learning exercise in Chapter 12, entitled "Restricted Airways," for a refresher on the effects of bronchospasm and other causes of restricted airways.

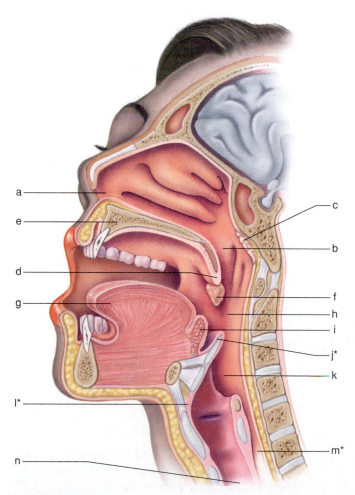

a
e
d
g
l*
n

c
b
f
h
i
j*
k
m*

FIGURE 28-1

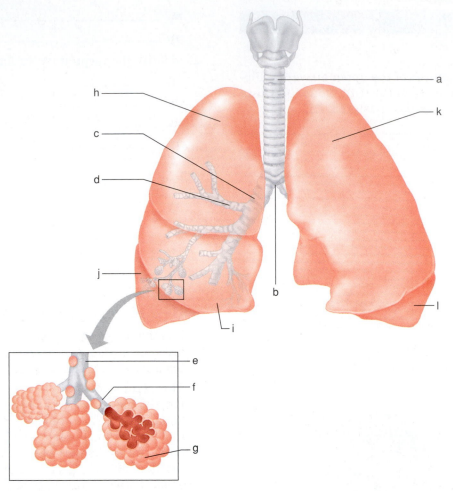

FIGURE 28-2

7. Capnography versus Pulse Oximetry

This is an exercise that can be done individually or in a group, although it tends to be more interesting in a group setting.

You will need the following equipment:

- Oxygen saturation monitor to measure SpO_2
- Electronic capnography—in-line (bag-mask or endotracheal tube [ETT]) or standard monitoring (cannula)—to measure $ETCO_2$
- Stopwatch or a watch or clock with a second hand

This experiment requires an individual to be hooked up to SpO_2 and $ETCO_2$ monitors. The individual should be healthy and free of significant preexisting medical conditions (especially cardiac and respiratory conditions), as this exercise can have a slight impact on the cardiopulmonary system.

a. Once the individual is attached to the SpO_2 and $ETCO_2$ monitors, obtain and record baseline readings for SpO_2 and $ETCO_2$.

b. Have the individual hold his or her breath as long as possible. Make sure that the individual begins to breathe as soon as he or she experiences any atypical signs or symptoms, lightheadedness, or discomfort, and continually monitor the SpO_2 and the $ETCO_2$ monitors, documenting any changes in readings over time. When the individual needs to take a breath, instruct him or her to take one and then resume holding his or her breath. The goal is for the individual to experience marked hypoventilation.

- Which do you expect to change first, SpO_2 or $ETCO_2$?
- Which do you think will change more significantly, SpO_2 or $ETCO_2$?
- What are your findings?

c. With the same individual or another person hooked up to the SpO_2 and $ETCO_2$ monitors, again obtain and record baseline SpO_2 and $ETCO_2$ readings.

d. Next, have the individual begin to hyperventilate (again, make sure that the individual begins to breathe normally as soon as he or she experiences any atypical signs or symptoms, lightheadedness, or discomfort) as you observe and record any changes in the SpO_2 and $ETCO_2$ readings.

- Which do you expect to see change first (SpO_2 or $ETCO_2$)?
- Which do you think will change most significantly (SpO_2 or $ETCO_2$)?
- What are your findings?
- Based on your findings, which of the two monitoring devices do you think would be more beneficial to apply to a patient in ventilatory distress?

8. Oxygen and Carbon Dioxide Pathways

Describe the path that oxygen (O_2) must take to get from the atmosphere into a cell and the path that carbon dioxide (CO_2) must take to get from cells to the atmosphere.

_____

_____

_____

You Are There: Reality-Based Cases

Case 1

As fate would have it, as soon as you clear the hospital, your dispatcher sends you back to Shady Acres Convalescent Hospital for a patient with shortness of breath. As you drive up into the parking lot, a nurse sees the ambulance through a window and comes running out to greet you. She says, "I'm so glad that you came back. . . . Mr. White is having severe respiratory distress, and we need your help."

You grab all your equipment and follow the nurse into the facility. When you arrive at Mr. White's bed, you find him sitting up on the edge of the bed in a tripod position, using multiple accessory muscles to breathe, and unable to speak in more than two-word sentences. You grasp his wrist to check for his pulse and note that he is cool, pale, diaphoretic, and tachycardic. He appears very anxious.

1. What is your general impression of Mr. White's condition based on the information that you have gathered thus far?

_____

_____

2. What is your initial priority for Mr. White?

_____

_____

_____

You obtain the following information:

Mr. White is a 72-year-old male who was admitted to Shady Acres for rehabilitation from hip replacement surgery two weeks ago. He had a follow-up appointment with his orthopedic surgeon yesterday at which time he appeared to be healing well.

Symptoms:

Onset: Mr. White began to complain of mild shortness of breath earlier this morning (06:00 hrs.) with gradual worsening throughout the morning (it is now noon).

Provocation/palliation: Mr. White has an extremely poor exertion tolerance. He became very short of breath when he tried to walk to the bathroom, and he became incontinent to urine.

Quality: While he denies pain, he feels that he can't "catch his breath."

Radiation/related symptoms: He denies chest pain, chest pressure, or chest discomfort of any type.

Severity: He rates his level of distress at 8 or 9 on a 1–10 scale.

Time: This episode is about 6 hours long.

Allergies: No known allergies.

Medications: Albuterol, Atrovent, Intal, Azmacort, prednisone, HCTZ, Lipitor, metoprolol, and NTG as needed. The patient has been compliant with his medications and the staff denies any possibility of under- or overdosing of his medication.

Past Medical History: Asthma, COPD, and angina. diet-controlled diabetic and has a history of hyperlipidemia, hypertension, and the beginning signs of renal insufficiency.

Last Oral Intake: Several sips of juice at breakfast.

Events Prior to Incident: He has no history of recent illness or injury. He has been using his inhalers throughout the morning with no appreciable improvement.

Physical Findings: Mr. White appears fatigued, but he continues to be able to follow simple commands. He has a patent airway with diminished breath sounds bilaterally. Scattered expiratory wheezing with crackles in the bases of his lung fields can also be heard. Supraclavicular retractions and abdominal muscle use with breathing are evident. His oxygen saturation is 86% on 4 liters of O_2 by nasal cannula, and $ETCO_2$ is 47 mm Hg. His vital signs are BP of 180/100, pulse of 112, and a respiratory rate of 32. His ECG shows a sinus tachycardia. The nurse informs you that Mr. White's peak expiratory flow measurement (PEFR) is less than half of his best measurement today.

3. What are the classifications of Mr. White's medications, and what are the desired effects?

_____

_____

_____

4. Describe the basic differences between asthma and emphysema.

_____

_____

_____

5. Has your impression of Mr. White's condition changed based on the information that you have gathered?

_____

_____

_____

6. Based on Mr. White's presentation and his past medical history, what do you think is the etiology of his current ventilatory distress?

_____

_____

_____

7. How will you prioritize your treatment for this patient?

_____

_____

_____

Mr. White is placed in a sitting position and started on CPAP. He receives in-line albuterol and Atrovent nebulizer treatments. When he is reassessed, you discover that his air movement has dramatically improved and his wheezing is gone, but now he has crackles up to the nipple line and his respiratory distress has worsened. He can no longer hold his head up and he is no longer able to follow your basic commands. His SpO_2 saturation has dropped to 78% on 15 liters per minute via CPAP.

8. What is your priority treatment now?

_____

_____

_____

9. List several possible causes for Mr. White's difficulty breathing, along with your rationale for these possibilities.

_____

_____

_____

_____

Test Yourself

1. Rattling noises in the chest caused by mucus in the bronchial tree are called _____.

2. List the indications for application of continuous positive airway pressure (CPAP).

_____

_____

3. Your COPD patient has an SpO_2 of 80% and an $ETCO_2$ of 60 mm Hg. These findings indicate significant respiratory compromise in this patient.
   True
   False

4. _____ is an effective and noninvasive tool to help you indirectly evaluate carbon dioxide levels in the blood.

5. Which of the following best describes the physiology of wheezing?
   a. Inflammation of the bronchioles causes excess fluid accumulation in the bronchioles.
   b. Air trapping in alveoli creates a whistling sound.
   c. Leaky pulmonary capillaries cause fluid to accumulate in the alveoli.
   d. Constriction of the bronchioles causes narrowed airways.

6. The structure that covers the trachea during swallowing is the _____.

7. How is end-tidal carbon dioxide useful in the pre-hospital setting?
   a. It determines how efficiently the patient is using oxygen.
   b. It determines the amount of exhaled carbon dioxide.
   c. It determines the amount of oxygen to administer.
   d. It measures the pH of the blood.

8. List three structures of the lower airway.

   _____

   _____

9. Which of the following findings assessed during the primary assessment would most likely require rapid intervention?
   a. Flushed skin
   b. Respiratory insufficiency
   c. Increased heart rate
   d. Normal appearance

10. Your dyspnea patient is wheezing. First, you need to determine the cause of the wheezing.
    True
    False

11. In COPD patients, the stimulus to breathe is a response to changes in _____ levels.

12. The process by which gases move from high concentration to low concentration is called _____.

13. Why are patients with emphysema sometimes called "pink puffers"?

    _____

    _____

14. What is the nature of the pulmonary edema associated with acute respiratory distress syndrome (ARDS)?

    _____

    _____

15. In a healthy person, the principal stimulus to breathe is based upon a decrease in oxygen in the blood.
    True
    False

16. One modifiable factor that can increase the chance of developing COPD is
    a. lung cancer.
    b. environmental pollutants.
    c. obesity.
    d. smoking.

17. What is the pathophysiology of COPD?
    a. Increased fluid in the interstitial space
    b. Obstruction of the bronchioles
    c. Blood clots in the pulmonary arteries
    d. Chronic inflammation of the upper airway

18. COPD patients commonly demonstrate features of which two diseases?

    _____

    _____

19. List five diseases or respiratory problems that can produce wheezing.

    _____

    _____

20. The most common breath sound associated with a patient suffering from an acute asthma attack is _____.

21. What structures of the upper airway may be affected by an upper respiratory infection?

    _____

    _____

22. You respond to a call for shortness of breath. You find a 63-year-old female on home oxygen and note several full ashtrays. Your patient has audible wheezing and rapid respirations. What treatment would immediately benefit this patient?
    a. Corticosteroids
    b. Positive pressure ventilation
    c. Intubation
    d. Albuterol nebulizer treatment

23. Respiration is the process of the exchange of air between the lungs and the environment.
    True
    False

24. Your emphysema patient is complaining of dyspnea and has normal oxygen saturation but increased end-tidal carbon dioxide levels. Your patient's respirations are 30 and labored with pursed lips. How should this patient's condition be managed?
    a. Nebulized steroids
    b. Nebulized albuterol with CPAP
    c. High-flow oxygen
    d. Administration of sodium bicarbonate

25. Why do asthmatic patients have a higher risk of developing a pneumothorax during assisted ventilation than other patients?

    _____

    _____

26. Calculate the minute volume for a patient with a tidal volume of 250 mL, breathing 30 breaths per minute.

_____

_____

27. How does the cause of bronchospasm in asthma patients differ from that of patients with COPD?

_____

_____

Scenario: A 19-year-old female with a history of asthma attends a bonfire. She suddenly feels short of breath and realizes that she forgot her inhaler. About 20 minutes later another partygoer finds her severely short of breath and lethargic. You arrive to find your patient pale, sweaty, and speaking only in two- and three-word sentences. You note paradoxical motion of the chest, nasal flaring, and bilaterally decreased lung sounds with faint wheezes. You are informed by another partygoer that the last time this happened the patient was intubated and spent two weeks in the ICU.

28. What physical exam findings indicate the severity of acute asthma exacerbation?
    a. The onset of signs and symptoms
    b. Her signs and symptoms
    c. Her vital signs
    d. The delay in seeking or receiving treatment

29. Which medications are indicated?
    a. Albuterol and ipratropium bromide
    b. Epinephrine and methylprednisolone
    c. Methylprednisolone and ipratropium bromide
    d. Albuterol and methylprednisolone

30. What other options are available to this patient if she does not respond to the initial treatment?
    a. CPAP
    b. BiPAP
    c. Continuous albuterol nebulizer treatments
    d. Intubation

Need to Know

The following represent the Key Objectives of Chapter 28:

1. *Describe pulmonary pathophysiology as it relates to upper and lower airway illnesses.*

The airways are divided into the upper and lower airways, with the upper airway beginning at the nose and mouth and the lower airway extending from the end of the upper airway at the inferior aspect of the laryngopharynx to the point at which the alveoli come into contact with the pulmonary capillaries.

An important point to make when discussing pulmonary function is the difference between respiration and ventilation. *Ventilation* is defined as the process of exchange of air between the lungs and the environment, including inspiration and expiration. *Respiration* is a term that is frequently misused. Many people use it to describe the rate at which people breathe or the effort required to breathe (the level of "respiratory distress"). In reality, that process is better described as "ventilatory rate" or "ventilatory distress." Respiration is actually more accurately used to describe the diffusion of gases (oxygen and carbon dioxide) between the tissues of the body and the bloodstream and the diffusion of gases between the lungs and the bloodstream. Diffusion is the process by which molecules move from an area of high concentration gradient to an area of lesser concentration. In the case of the alveolar-capillary membrane (in the lungs), there is a large amount of oxygen inside the alveoli and a lesser oxygen concentration in the capillary blood; conversely there is a large amount of carbon dioxide in the capillary blood and a smaller concentration of carbon dioxide inside the alveoli. As a result, the oxygen that we breathe into our lungs moves into the bloodstream to be delivered to the tissues of the body, and the carbon dioxide that is created in the process of cellular respiration moves out of the bloodstream and into the lungs. A similar process takes place between the tissues of the body and the capillaries that feed them, but in this setting oxygen diffuses into the tissues and carbon dioxide diffuses into the capillaries. The following are the pathophysiological reasons for the more common conditions associated with upper and lower airway diseases:

Upper Airway

a. *Upper respiratory infections.* Upper respiratory infections (URIs) are caused predominantly by airborne viruses. Viral URIs typically present with runny nose (rhinorrhea), coughing, and/or hoarseness. The patient may report a fever as well as discomfort or pain. Bacterial upper respiratory infections occur less frequently and tend to cause specific infections in the upper airway, such as pharyngitis and tonsillitis. These infections lack the general symptoms seen in viral infections, such as runny nose, cough, hoarseness, fever, and discomfort or pain.

b. *Stridor*. Stridor, or narrowing of the upper airway, can result from:

- Burns (see Chapter 12, Airway Management, Ventilation, and Oxygenation, and Chapter 26, Burn Trauma, in the textbook)
- Allergic reactions and anaphylaxis (see Chapter 32, Allergies and Anaphylaxis, in the textbook)
- Trauma (see Chapter 20, Head, Face, and Neck Trauma, in the textbook)

c. *Upper airway obstruction*. Upper airway obstructions due to tissue swelling and edema can be caused by:

- Epiglottitis
- Peritonsillar abscess
- Posterior pharyngeal abscess
- Angioedema
- Croup

Review Chapter 12, Airway Management, Ventilation, and Oxygenation, in the textbook.

Lower Airway

a. *Asthma*. Asthma is an inflammatory disease of the lower airways that has both acute and chronic components. In acute asthma, an antigen binds with cells, releasing inflammatory mediators. Inflammation causes airway hyperresponsiveness (an exaggerated acute bronchoconstrictive response). Early phase changes include airflow limitation and wheezing (bronchospasm) in the first few minutes to hours. The treatment of choice for bronchospasm is administration of nebulized beta$_2$ agonists.

Late phase changes that occur after a few hours to days or weeks include: inflammation progresses; the pulmonary vasculature begins to leak, resulting in lower airway swelling; mucus is secreted and plugs form, causing bronchial obstruction and air trapping (difficulty exhaling air). Late phase changes are less reversible than bronchospasm.

b. *Chronic obstructive pulmonary disease (COPD)*. COPD is defined as conditions *other than asthma* that are characterized by dyspnea, cough, sputum production, airflow limitation, and impaired gas exchange.[1]

Prolonged or severe COPD can result in pulmonary hypertension and cor pulmonale.[2] Because the COPD patient has a constantly elevated carbon dioxide level, the primary drive for respiration comes from oxygen rather than carbon dioxide levels. This change in respiratory drive is referred to as the *hypoxic drive*. Despite the fact that high concentrations of oxygen can negatively affect a COPD patient's respiratory drive, oxygen should never be withheld from COPD patients who present with respiratory distress or failure.

c. *Chronic bronchitis*. Chronic bronchitis is defined as a productive cough that is present for at least 3 months per year for at least 2 years. It is characterized by a chronic productive cough due to excessive bronchial mucus production and airway inflammation. Patients with chronic bronchitis are chronically short of breath and have a decreased capacity to exchange oxygen and carbon dioxide secondary to a ventilation/perfusion mismatch.

Chronic bronchitis affects both small and large bronchi. Obstruction of the airways is caused by inflammation of the lining of the bronchi with associated smooth muscle constriction and mucus production. The obstruction leads to difficulty breathing, which typically presents as dyspnea on exertion (DOE) and causes hypoxia and hypercarbia. The body responds to hypoxia by producing more red blood cells (polycythemia). The combination of hypoxia and polycythemia results in chronic cyanosis.

d. *Emphysema*. Emphysema is defined as a disease process involving dilation of air spaces that results in the destruction of lung tissue, starting in the smallest airways and involving the alveoli (Figure 28-3). Eventually this destruction causes a loss of elastic recoil, which leads to the collapse of bronchi and significant obstruction to airflow.[3]

e. *Pulmonary embolism*. The following are the three predominant mechanisms for developing a pulmonary embolism (PE), along with their risk factors:

1. Pooling (stasis) of blood—increased risk with prolonged immobility.
2. An increased likelihood of clotting (hypercoagulability)—inflammatory conditions.
3. An injury to the inner lining of a blood vessel (intimal injury)—frequently caused by trauma or surgery.

Patients with a history of a deep vein thrombosis (DVT) are highly susceptible to developing a PE. The risk of developing a PE increases with age from around 50 and up.[4]

f. *Pneumonia*. Pneumonia is an infection of the lung(s) caused by viruses, bacteria, fungi, and parasites. Patients in the following categories are at increased risk for developing pneumonia: extremes of age (very young and very old),

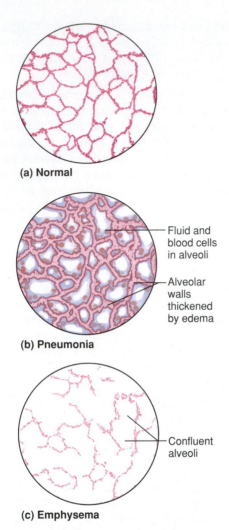

(a) Normal

Fluid and blood cells in alveoli

Alveolar walls thickened by edema

(b) Pneumonia

Confluent alveoli

(c) Emphysema

FIGURE 28-3 Pulmonary Alveoli in Health and Disease
(a) In a healthy lung, the alveoli are small and have thin respiratory membranes. **(b)** In pneumonia, the respiratory membranes (alveolar walls) are thick with edema, and the alveoli contain fluid and blood cells. **(c)** In emphysema, alveolar membranes break down and neighboring alveoli join to form larger, fewer alveoli with less total surface area.

patients with chronic illnesses, alcoholics, cancer patients, and patients with compromised immune systems.

Once the pathogen establishes itself in the lung(s), the patient's immune system mounts a response to fight the infection. The response progresses as follows:

- The first response is inflammation and fever.
- Then the body's defense system attacks and surrounds the infection (consolidation); fluid is produced and enters the alveoli.
- If the infection does not remain isolated in the lung(s), it can spread to the bloodstream (bacteremia).
- Bacteremia can lead to septic shock and hypotension.

g. *Spontaneous pneumothorax.* Spontaneous pneumothoraces are typically caused by blebs (air-filled sacs), which are associated with weak connective tissue in the lung. Blebs can spontaneously burst without any discernible provoking factor, causing a leak of air between the lung and the inside of the chest cavity. Blebs are separated into primary (without any lung disease) and secondary (caused by an underlying lung disease such as COPD, pneumocystis carinii pneumonia in AIDS patients, tuberculosis, and lung cancer). The leak of air causes the lung to collapse, resulting in increasing pressure and space between the lung and the pleura lining the thoracic cavity.

h. *Acute (adult) respiratory distress syndrome (ARDS).* ARDS is a type of noncardiogenic pulmonary edema. It is caused by damage to the lung from a number of illnesses and injuries. In ARDS, direct injury to the lung or circulating inflammatory mediators causes inflammation of the alveolar membrane. The damaged alveolar membrane becomes leaky, and fluid and protein enter the alveoli. Causes of ARDS include:

- Burns
- Direct injury
- Near drowning
- Toxic gas or smoke inhalation
- Opiate overdose
- Pancreatitis
- Pulmonary aspiration
- Sepsis
- Shock
- Trauma
- Viral infections (pneumonia or other infections)

i. *Hyperventilation.* Not all individuals who breathe fast are hyperventilating. The term for rapid respiration is "hyperpnea," and this condition alone may be a normal condition. Hyperventilation syndrome, a condition that is often dismissed as an emotional condition, may in fact be an indication that something very serious is taking place. Patients who experience hyperventilation syndrome exhibit an excessive loss of CO_2. Causes for hyperventilation syndrome include:

- Acidosis (diabetic ketoacidosis)
- Asthma
- CHF

- COPD
- Emphysema
- Fever
- Pain
- Pregnancy
- Pulmonary embolism

j. *Neoplasms of the lung.* Lung cancer is the leading cause of cancer deaths in many developed countries. Figure 28-4 shows the effects of smoking on the lung tissue. Patients with neoplasms of the lung can develop many complications. Space-occupying tumors can obstruct bronchioles, causing difficulty breathing. Other cancers can cause damage to blood vessels, resulting in bleeding (evidenced by hemoptysis). Treatments for lung neoplasms, such as chemotherapy, frequently carry side effects that can weaken patients' immune systems and make them vulnerable to opportunistic infections, such as pneumonia and URIs, further complicating their condition.

2. *Recognize a patient in respiratory failure during the primary assessment.*

When a patient is unable to keep up with the body's oxygenation and ventilation demands, or the work of breathing exceeds a patient's energy expenditures, the patient experiences respiratory failure. Many resources list parameters for oxygen saturation and end-tidal carbon dioxide ($ETCO_2$) levels to determine when a patient is in respiratory failure. These parameters vary from resource to resource, and there are a number of factors that can interfere with accurate measurement of these values. If, however, a patient presents with signs of severe ventilatory distress, has an oxygen saturation of less than 90%, and $ETCO_2$ levels greater than 45 mm Hg, the patient is likely experiencing respiratory failure.

A paramedic should be able to determine if a patient is in respiratory failure during the primary assessment. Because there does not need to be a specific cause or exact differential diagnosis identified in order to address these conditions and parameters, the paramedic can intervene immediately upondiscovery of respiratory failure.

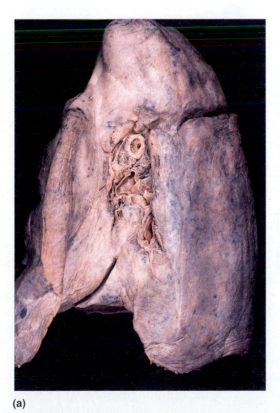

(a)

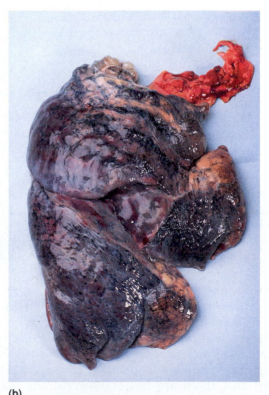

(b)

FIGURE 28-4   **Effects of Smoking (a)** Healthy lung, mediastinal surface. **(b)** Smoker's lung with carcinoma.

The paramedic can assist ventilations with a bag-mask whether the patient is suffering from an acute asthma attack or pulmonary edema from congestive heart failure.

When it comes to patients in respiratory distress without signs of failure, providing supplemental oxygen may be adequate to manage the distress. For example, if the paramedic is treating a patient in ventilatory distress with signs and symptoms of pulmonary edema and a history of CHF, the paramedic may provide supplementary interventions, such as high-flow oxygen by non-rebreather mask and supplementary treatments such as the administration of nitrates and diuretics. On the other hand, if the patient presents with signs and symptoms of pulmonary edema but has in addition cutaneous signs of shock, cyanosis, altered level of consciousness, and agonal respirations, the patient would need to be treated more aggressively, and the patient's ventilations would need to be assisted with the use of a bag-mask and a basic or an advanced airway.

3. *Recognize and manage the signs and symptoms of respiratory illnesses encountered in the prehospital field.*

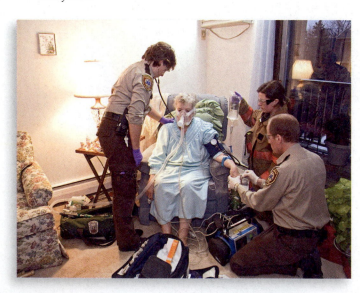

Ventilatory and respiratory problems are frequently obvious. Almost all will be identified during the primary assessment. This is not to say that all patients with ventilatory distress are easily managed, as respiratory and ventilatory conditions can be very complex and difficult to treat. Keep in mind that there are basic interventions that paramedics should follow when treating a patient in ventilatory distress. Place the patient in a position that allows for comfort and optimizes the patient's ease of ventilation. Provide supplemental oxygen and, if necessary, assist ventilations. When possible, determine the patient's prior medical history, medications, and allergies to medications, as this can be extremely beneficial in developing a treatment plan. Use mnemonics such as SAMPLE and PASTE to organize your history and physical examination. Mnemonics help to prevent omission of pertinent information. The SAMPLE mnemonic is:

S—signs and symptoms
A—allergies
M—medications
P—past medical history
L—last oral intake (food or fluid)
E—events leading to current patient condition

The PASTE mnemonic is:

P—progression
A—associated symptoms (chest pain, etc.)
S—sputum production
T—talking (number of words in sentences)
E—exertion tolerance

Connections

- *Expert Panel Report 2: Guidelines for the Diagnosis and Management of Asthma,* published in 1997 by the National Institutes of Health as a Clinical Practice Guideline (EPR 2).[5] This was updated in 2002, and a new panel is expected to convene in 2007.

- Chapter 12, Airway Management, Ventilation, and Oxygenation, in the textbook describes ventilation/perfu sion (V/Q) mismatch.

- Chapter 29, Cardiology, in the textbook presents a discussion on the relationship between cardiac and respiratory function and disease.

- Chapter 32, Allergies and Anaphylaxis, in the textbook describes the impact that allergies have on the respiratory system.

- The Asthma and Allergy Foundation of America provides information on education, advocacy, research, publications, and support groups for people with asthma and allergies at www.aafa.org/.

- Link to the companion DVD for a chapter-based quiz, audio glossary, animations, games and exercises, and, when appropriate, skill sheets and skill Step-by-Steps.

Need to Do

The following skills are explained and illustrated in a step-by-step manner, via skill sheets and/or "Step-by-Steps" in this text and on the accompanying DVD:

Skill Name	Skill Sheet Number and Location	Step-by-Step Number and Location
End-Tidal Capnography	10 – DVD	N/A
Pulse Oximetry	12 – DVD	12 – DVD
Continuous Positive Airway Pressure	18 – Appendix A and DVD	18 – Chapter 12 and DVD
Chest Auscultation	27 – Appendix A and DVD	27 – Chapter 11 and DVD
Dyspnea Assessment	35 – DVD	N/A
Nebulized Drug Administration	52 – Appendix A and DVD	52 – Chapter 16 and DVD
Endotracheal Drug Administration	55 – DVD	N/A

Street Secrets

- **Nebulized Saline for Comfort** Patients who are placed on oxygen for an extended period of time will attest to the fact that oxygen can be very drying and can become quite uncomfortable. Humidification of oxygen is one method of offering relief from the drying effects of long-term oxygen use, but this option adds the increased risk of infection, especially if the setup is not changed and the equipment is not sterilized on a regular basis. Relief from the drying effects of oxygen with less risk of infection can be achieved by providing nebulized sterile saline, if the equipment used to nebulize and deliver the saline is itself sterile.

- **Nebulized Saline for Mucous Plugs** Patients with asthma or COPD, or any respiratory condition that produces mucus, are at increased risk for the production of mucous plugs. Mucous plugs can obstruct airways and result in difficulty breathing. If the mucus that is formed by these conditions is kept thin, mucous plug formation is dramatically decreased, and obstruction of the airways is prevented or significantly diminished. One way to prevent the thickening of mucus and the formation of mucous plugs is to provide intermittent doses of nebulized sterile saline. For patients who have difficulty breathing and signs of bronchospasm, a bronchodilator along with sterile saline may be administered.

- **Shortness of Breath versus Ventilatory Distress** Like pain, shortness of breath is something that patients experience personally. As such, shortness of breath is a *subjective* complaint. Ventilatory distress, on the other hand, is anx *objective* sign that can be observed.

The Drug Box

Albuterol (Proventil, Ventolin): A beta adrenergic sympathomimetic bronchodilator. This selective beta agonist relaxes the smooth muscle of the bronchioles and is thus used to treat bronchospasm.

Ipratropium (Atrovent): A synthetic anticholinergic similar to atropine that is more likely to be used to treat chronic COPD than to treat acute exacerbations of asthma due to its relatively slow onset of action (compared to beta agonists). It antagonizes acetylcholine at the muscarinic receptors on bronchial smooth muscle, causing relaxation and dilation.

Cromolyn sodium (Intal, Nasalcrom, Opticrom): An antihistaminic mast cell stabilizer that helps prevent or reduce inflammation in patients with asthma and COPD.

Triamcinolone (Azmacort): A topical steroid used for the long-term management of the inflammation associated with asthma and other inflammatory pulmonary disorders.

Prednisone (Deltasone): A steroid anti-inflammatory used to manage acute exacerbations or for chronic maintenance of asthma. Steroids do not offer rapid relief of bronchospasm and should be used in conjunction with rapid-acting bronchodilators.

Hydrochlorothiazide (HCTZ) (HydroDIURIL, Esidrix): A thiazide diuretic that inhibits the reabsorption of sodium and chloride in the distal segment of the nephron, thus lowering blood pressure by means of diuresis.

Nitroglycerin (NTG) (Nitrostat, Nitrolingual, Nitro-Bid ointment, Nitro-Bid IV, Nitrodisc, Transderm-Nitro): A vasodilator that relaxes vascular smooth muscle, dilates coronary arteries, and decreases myocardial oxygen demand by decreasing preload to the heart. It is used as a treatment for congestive heart failure.

Furosemide (Lasix): A loop diuretic that decreases sodium and chloride reabsorption in the ascending loop of Henle and the distal tubule. It is used as a treatment for congestive heart failure.

Diphenhydramine (Benadryl): An antihistamine used in the treatment and prevention of allergic reactions.

References

1. "Chronic Obstructive Pulmonary Disease," in A. Harwood-Nuss, ed., *The Clinical Practice of Emergency Medicine*, 3rd ed. Baltimore, MD: Lippincott, Williams & Wilkins, 2001, p. 746.
2. "Chronic Obstructive Pulmonary Disease," in J. Marx, *Emergency Medicine: Concepts and Clinical Practice*, 5th ed. St. Louis, MO: Mosby, 2002, pp. 957, 962.
3. Ibid., 957, 961.
4. S. D. Chunilal et al., "Does This Patient Have Pulmonary Embolism?" *JAMA* 290, no. 21 (December 3, 2003): 2849–2858.
5. National Institutes of Health, National Heart, Lung and Blood Institute. Clinical Practice Guideline. *Expert Panel 2 Report: Guidelines for the Diagnosis and Management of Asthma.* July 1997. NIH Publication Number 97-4051. Available online at http://nhlbli.nih.gov/nhlbi/nhlbi.htm (accessed December 12, 2006).
6. F. Sciurba, "Physiologic Similarities and Differences Between COPD and Asthma." *Chest* 126 (2004): 117S–124S. Available online at http://www.chestjournal.org/cgi/content/abstract/126/2_suppl_1/117S (accessed December 12, 2006).
7. J. Brochard, "Noninvasive Ventilation for Acute Respiratory Failure." *JAMA* 288 (2002): 932–35.

Answers

Are You Ready?

1. Mrs. Jones is sick. She presents with respiratory distress and has a significant alteration in her level of consciousness (withdrawing to pain only), as well as perioral and peripheral cyanosis, which is suggestive of profound hypoxia.
2. The sequence of events and the time line suggest that Mrs. Jones is suffering from aspiration pneumonia.
3. Signs and symptoms consistent with a patient suffering from aspiration pneumonia include: respiratory distress, tachypnea, tachycardia, elevated temperature (not always seen in the geriatric population—see Chapter 44, Geriatric Patients, in the textbook for details) with associated chills, low oxygen saturation (< 90% SPO$_2$), cough with sputum production, a variety of possible lung sounds including crackles, areas of consolidation, rhonchi, wheezing, and diminished breath sounds. If the infection has spread to the bloodstream, the patient can present with hypotension as the result of septic shock. If the patient has associated vomiting and/or diarrhea, the patient may present with signs of hypovolemic shock.
4. The first and most important priority is to assess and provide a patent airway for Mrs. Jones. Assess and support breathing by providing high-flow oxygen in an attempt to improve saturation to 94% or better. If the patient presents with wheezing in the absence of pulmonary edema, administer an approved bronchodilator nebulizer. Continually monitor oxygen saturation and ETCO$_2$ (if available) along with the overall patient presentation to determine the effectiveness of your interventions. If the patient has a presentation consistent with shock (septic or hypovolemic), establish an IV and provide fluid replacement. Transport the patient to an appropriate receiving facility.

Active Learning

1. a. nose; b. nasopharynx; c. pharyngeal tonsil; d. uvula; e. hard palate; f. palatine tonsil; g. tongue; h. oropharynx; i. lingual tonsil; j. Epiglottis—serves to protect the airway from food during swallowing; k. laryngopharynx; l. larynx—the passageway for air into and out of the trachea, which serves as a protective structure to keep foreign objects out of the trachea; m. esophagus—serves as a passageway for food from the pharynx into the stomach; n. trachea
2. a. trachea; b. carina; c. right main-stem (primary) bronchi; d. secondary (lobar) bronchi; e. respiratory bronchioles; f. alveolar ducts; g. alveolar sacs (alveolus); h. right upper (superior) lobe; i. right middle lobe; j. right lower (inferior) lobe; k. left upper (superior) lobe; l. left lower (inferior) lobe
3. Surfactant
4. a. visceral; b. parietal; c. pleural space; d. pleural fluid
5. a. pulmonary artery; b. pulmonary veins; c. aorta; d. bronchial arteries; e. azygos; f. hemiazygos; g. superior vena cava
8. Oxygen enters the body during the inhalation phase of the ventilatory process through the nares, where the air is filtered, warmed, and humidified as it makes its way through the nasopharynx, oropharynx, and laryngopharynx. It passes the glottis, enters the larynx, and makes its way into the trachea, where it branches into the right and left main-stem bronchi at the carina. The oxygen continues down progressively narrowing bronchioles until it ends up in the alveoli. Pressure gradients at the alveolar-capillary membrane and at the tissue-cell-capillary membrane allow for the exchange of oxygen and carbon dioxide, respectively.

You Are There: Reality-Based Cases

1. Mr. White appears to be very sick. He has multiple signs of severe respiratory distress (tripod position, using multiple accessory muscles to breathe, and unable to speak in more than two-word sentences) and cutaneous signs of shock (cool, pale, diaphoretic skin, tachycardic, and appears very anxious), which are likely the result of hypoxemia stemming from his respiratory distress.

2. The initial priority for Mr. White is assessment and management of his ABCs. If any life threats are discovered during the primary assessment, they need to be addressed immediately. The administration of high-flow oxygen via non-rebreather mask is a minimum at this stage of assessment.

3. You can find information on many of the patient's medications in the Drug Box section of this chapter.
   - Atorvastatin calcium (Lipitor) is a HMG-CoA reductase inhibitor that interferes with the biosynthesis of cholesterol (lowers cholesterol). It is used in treatment of hypercholesterolemia.
   - Benazepril (Lotensin) is an ACE inhibitor that lowers blood pressure by reducing peripheral arterial resistance, decreasing aldosterone secretion, and in turn reducing sodium and water retention.

4. In its classic presentation, asthma is a condition that tends to begin early in life in nonsmokers. It is associated with periods of exacerbation (asthma attacks), and it is a reversible airway disorder marked by airway hyperresponsiveness. Classic emphysema, on the other hand, is characterized by a history of tobacco smoking, a progressive onset, fixed airflow obstruction that is associated with a loss of lung elastic recoil, resting and dynamic lung hyperinflation, and abnormalities in gas diffusion.[6]

5. No, the history and physical examination only support the general impression that was expressed earlier. Mr. White is in severe ventilatory distress and showing signs of progressing toward respiratory failure (poor oxygen saturation and high $ETCO_2$ readings accompanied by fatigue).

6. Mr. White appears to be experiencing bronchospasm (wheezing) that could be the result of asthma, COPD, or early pulmonary edema (cardiac asthma). He has crackles in his bases, which could be the result of a number of conditions such as CHF, infection, or acute respiratory distress syndrome (ARDS). His high blood pressure, tachycardia, and hyperpnea could support some theories as to what is causing his ventilatory distress, or they could be part of a compensatory mechanism to the hypoxia that is resulting from his distress. He has a low oxygen saturation on 4 liters of oxygen by nasal cannula, and he has a relatively high $ETCO_2$, despite a rather rapid respiratory rate. This may be indicative of a patient with COPD or a patient with a number of other conditions transitioning from respiratory distress to respiratory failure. Mr. White has a poor peak expiratory flow rate, and he has not been responding to inhaled bronchodilators. The key point to take away from this example is that *diagnosing the root cause of the breathing problem is not as important as properly assessing and making wise treatment decisions.*

7. Because Mr. White is in severe ventilatory distress with low O_2 saturation, high $ETCO_2$, and fatigue, you must intervene before he goes into respiratory failure, ventilatory arrest, and cardiopulmonary arrest. He is already on O_2 at 4 liters by nasal cannula, and that is not providing sufficient oxygenation. He needs a greater concentration of oxygen and ventilatory assistance as well. The patient may be able to be managed with a nasopharyngeal airway and tracking of his ventilations with a bag-mask and positive end expiratory pressure (PEEP), if available, and high-flow O_2. Another possibility for ventilatory assistance is the use of continuous positive airway pressure (CPAP). This is an effective alternative to intubation that reduces the complications associated with intubation and reduces overall time of hospital admission.[7] In-line medications (bronchodilators, steroids, etc.) can be delivered while the patient is being assisted with a bag-mask, CPAP, or ETT. If the patient doesn't respond, he may need to be intubated (e.g., rapid sequence intubation [RSI], nasal intubation). Make a good-faith effort at a BLS approach to ventilatory assistance before attempting advanced airway interventions.

8. Mr. White is no longer a candidate for CPAP because he is no longer able to follow simple commands. Because of the decreased level of consciousness, increased level of ventilatory distress, increase in pulmonary edema (crackles), and decreasing SpO_2, the patient would likely benefit from intubation. The administration of nitrates and diuretics may be helpful. The patient will definitely benefit from positive pressure ventilation via bag-ETT and, if possible, the patient would benefit from the effects of gravity by being placed in a semi-Fowler's position once he is intubated and the tube is secured. *Note*: Beware of position changes with the intubated patient, and frequently reassess ETT placement along with constant monitoring of SpO_2 and $ETCO_2$. As soon as the patient is stable enough to transport, or if there is any indication that the airway will be difficult to manage, transport should be initiated.

9.
   - *Pulmonary embolism (PE)*. Any time that a patient presents with shortness of breath during or following a period of prolonged immobility, PE should be considered. This condition is typically acute and is frequently associated with chest pain.
   - *Asthma*. This condition is part of the patient's history, and he presents with scattered wheezing and diminished breath sounds bilaterally possibly due to severe bronchospasm.
   - *COPD*. This condition is also part of the patient's history, and he presents with low SpO_2 readings and a high $ETCO_2$ reading, which is typical of patients with COPD.
   - *CHF (pulmonary edema)*. The patient has a history of angina, HTN, and hyperlipidemia, which places him at increased risk for myocardial infarction and, in turn, CHF. He presents with respiratory distress and crackles in the bases of his lungs.

Test Yourself

1. Rhonchi

   Rhonchi are the rattling noises that mucus makes in the bronchial trees during breathing.

2. Indications for CPAP include: rising levels of $ETCO_2$ above 45 mm Hg despite treatment; dropping oxygen saturations; and exhaustion and inability to keep up with the work of breathing; all combined with the clinical findings of an awake, alert patient, able to follow commands, with continued respiratory effort.

   In order for CPAP to be applied, the patient *must* be awake and alert enough to follow commands, have adequate respiratory effort, and have the ability to protect his or her own airway. In addition, CPAP is better utilized for conditions that are reversible in a time frame of minutes to hours (such as pulmonary edema and acute respiratory failure) rather than for chronic respiratory failure. Contraindications include apnea, unconsciousness, and full cardiopulmonary arrest. Relative contraindications include trauma with suspicion of elevated intracranial pressure and abdominal distention with risk of vomiting or hypotension.

3. True

   COPD patients commonly present with lower-than-normal SpO_2 levels (90%–95%) and elevated $ETCO_2$ readings (45–50 mm Hg). However, a COPD patient with an SpO_2 of 80% and an $ETCO_2$ of 60 mm Hg can be determined to be in severe respiratory distress, not only because of the profound hypoxia, but because of the hypercarbia as well.

4. $ETCO_2$ monitoring

   Ventilation is driven by carbon dioxide levels in the blood. Exhaled carbon dioxide (CO_2) is reflective of carbon dioxide levels in the blood and can be measured (in a noninvasive manner) by using end-tidal carbon dioxide detectors. Exhaled CO_2 levels are closely related to arterial CO_2 levels in the bloodstream most of the time.

5. d

   Wheezing is characterized by lower airway obstruction (by mucus) or by narrowed airways, not by fluid accumulation.

6. Epiglottis

   The epiglottis covers the trachea during swallowing. Inflammation of the epiglottis due to infection (epiglottitis) may result in a life-threatening condition because air may not be allowed to enter the trachea.

7. b

   End-tidal carbon dioxide detectors measure the amount of CO_2 a patient exhales. This may be one useful factor in determining if a patient requires CPAP or intubation for respiratory distress.

8. Possible answers include: trachea, bronchi, bronchioles, alveolar ducts, and alveoli.

   The larynx is the dividing point between the upper and lower airway and is sometimes included with the lower airway. The trachea, bronchi, bronchioles, alveolar ducts, and alveoli are distal to the larynx and are therefore part of the lower airway.

9. b

   A patient with respiratory insufficiency should be managed quickly, as the patient may progress into respiratory arrest. The other findings listed are general and do not necessarily require immediate intervention on your part.

10. False

    Correcting hypoxia, regardless of the cause, should be the most important goal in any dyspneic patient. After treating hypoxia, you should focus on treating the wheezing. Obtaining a thorough history can help determine the best treatment. For instance, if the patient has a history of chronic heart failure, nitrates and a diuretic may be the most beneficial treatment and a beta agonist may exacerbate the condition. If the patient has a history of asthma, a beta agonist would be beneficial to correct the wheezing. However, determining the exact cause of the wheezing should not be a primary concern.

11. Arterial oxygen

    The dominant stimulus for breathing in a healthy person comes from an increase in carbon dioxide. This is also called the hypercarbic respiratory drive. In COPD patients with chronically high CO_2 levels, over time the brain adjusts the control mechanism because it detects something is wrong with the "sensors," which continuously send impulses to increase respirations to compensate for the high acid level. Little by little, the COPD patient's brain adjusts the sensors to pay more attention to the concentration of oxygen in the arterial blood. After this change occurs, when the oxygen levels drop (hypoxia), the patient's brain receives a signal to take another breath. The patient is now operating with a hypoxic drive instead of the hypercarbic drive. This mechanism will continue to operate for the remainder of the person's life. It is important to note that not all COPD patients develop hypoxic drive.

12. Diffusion

    Diffusion occurs as molecules or gases move from a high concentration or pressure to that of a low concentration or pressure.

13. Increased red blood cell production gives the skin a pink appearance.

    As the body of an emphysema patient becomes chronically hypoxic, it responds by producing more red blood cells in order to increase the body's overall oxygen-carrying capacity.

14. Acute respiratory distress syndrome (ARDS) is a form of noncardiogenic pulmonary edema caused by damage to the lungs from a variety of illnesses and injuries.

    ARDS is caused by fluid occurring in the interstitial spaces around the pulmonary capillary beds, but it is not cardiac in nature. Normally, pulmonary edema is associated with increased vascular pressure. But with ARDS, pulmonary pressures are not high. Instead, direct injury to the lungs or circulating inflammatory mediators causes inflammation of the alveolar membrane.

Once damaged the alveolar membrane becomes leaky and fluid and protein enter the alveoli. Some common causes of ARDS include: direct injury, pulmonary aspiration, severe viral infections, near drowning, and toxic gas or smoke inhalation.

15. False

    A "normal" stimulus to breathe is based upon high levels of carbon dioxide in the cerebral spinal fluid (CSF). This is called the hypercarbic drive. In patients with COPD, however, the stimulus to breathe is usually based upon low oxygen levels in the blood. This is called the hypoxic drive.

16. d

    COPD is usually caused by smoking or long-term exposure to environmental pollutants. Smoking is a habit that can be changed, but it is nearly impossible to escape environmental pollutants. Obesity is modifiable, but it is not a risk factor for COPD.

17. b

    COPD is by definition a result of chronic obstruction or inflammation of the bronchioles.

18. Emphysema and chronic bronchitis

    Chronic obstructive pulmonary disease (COPD) is usually defined as conditions other than asthma characterized by dyspnea, cough, sputum production, airflow limitation, and impaired gas exchange. COPD is characterized by chronic sputum production that leads to inflammation of the bronchioles (in patients with chronic bronchitis) and air trapping due to collapsed alveoli (in patients with emphysema). Despite emphysema and chronic bronchitis being two separate diseases, COPD patients rarely have just one but commonly demonstrate features of both diseases.

19. Possible answers include: asthma, COPD (chronic bronchitis and emphysema), pneumonia, exacerbations of congestive heart failure (pulmonary edema), foreign body ingestion or aspiration, smoke or toxic gas inhalation, and laryngeal fracture.

    Wheezing can be caused by many diseases other than asthma and by problems other than respiratory diseases such as foreign body obstruction and toxic gas inhalation. A common medical saying, "all that wheezes is not asthma," is especially helpful when evaluating the cause of a patient's wheezing. Patients with foreign body ingestion or aspiration can manifest wheezing. In these cases the wheezing will be more focal rather than generalized. Patients with exacerbations of congestive heart failure may have fluid buildup in their lungs. Air movement will be restricted enough that the patients will wheeze or edema will cause bronchospasm. In this case the "wheezing" may be more prominent in the bases bilaterally.

20. Wheezing

    Wheezing is generally associated with asthma, since wheezing is a result of narrowed or obstructed lower airways.

21. Pharynx, larynx, epiglottis

    The pharynx, larynx, and epiglottis are upper airway structures, and all are susceptible to upper respiratory infections.

22. d

    This patient likely has a history of COPD and would benefit from an albuterol treatment more than any of the other treatment methods listed.

23. False

    Respiration is defined as the exchange of gases at the alveolar-capillary membrane. It involves the diffusion of oxygen from the alveoli across the capillary membrane and the exchange of gases between the blood and the cells of the body.

24. b

    The fact that the oxygen levels are normal and the carbon dioxide levels are elevated indicates that this patient is retaining CO_2. This indicates a problem with ventilation (air going into and leaving the lungs), and the patient may require the administration of albuterol to dilate the bronchioles and potentially reduce excess CO_2 trapped by narrowed airways. The use of CPAP to remove excess CO_2 will help maintain open airways. Use CPAP with caution in a patient with emphysema because the increased pressure may cause barotrauma.

25. By definition, patients with asthma have constricted airways, which puts them at risk for air trapping. If too much air is trapped in the lungs (for instance, as a result of rapid assisted ventilations), a pneumothorax may develop.

    In an asthmatic patient who is intubated or receiving positive pressure ventilation, it is important to use slow ventilations, also called "controlled hypoventilation" or "permissive hypercapnia." This slow ventilation is necessary to allow time for the patient to exhale. Ventilation forces air into the lungs, but exhalation still depends on passive relaxation of the chest. If air is being trapped by constricted airways, a longer expiratory phase is critical to allow as much emptying as possible.

26. 7,500 mL/min

    Minute volume is calculated as Tidal volume × Respirations per minute. In this example, 250 mL/breath × 30 breaths/min = 7,500 mL/min.

27. Bronchospasm in asthma patients is due to hyperresponsiveness of the airway.

    Asthma and COPD are both characterized by airflow obstruction as a result of chronic bronchoconstriction. However, asthma is characterized by hyperresponsiveness of the airway, while with COPD bronchoconstriction is caused by either inflammation of the bronchioles (chronic bronchitis) or destruction of the alveolar walls and enlargement of the alveolar air spaces (emphysema). Ultimately, asthma is considered the most reversible disease, while COPD is more a chronic progressive disease that is less reversible.

28. b

The patient's symptoms indicate that she is in severe distress (nasal flaring and the absent lung sounds with faint wheezing). The onset of symptoms and the delay in treatment do not indicate severe asthma exacerbation. The patient's vital signs do not indicate the severity of the attack, only that the patient is in distress.

29. a

Albuterol (a beta agonist) and ipratropium bromide (an anticholinergic) are well-suited together to combat the initial bronchospasms brought on by the smoke. Epinephrine is not indicated in this situation with methylprednisolone (a corticosteroid with a long onset of action). The same holds true for albuterol and methylprednisolone.

30. d

Because the patient's work of breathing is dramatically increased and the patient is suffering from two- to three-word dyspnea with mental status changes, she is a likely candidate for intubation. CPAP and bilevel positive airway pressure (BiPAP) would not be effective for a patient with mental status changes because of her hypoxic state. Remember: Patients with normal SpO_2 and elevated $ETCO_2$ are candidates for CPAP and BiPAP. Continuous nebulizer treatments would not fully correct the patient's condition. In addition, because the patient has a history of intubation with hospitalization, she is a candidate for intubation.

chapter **29**

Cardiology

Section I: Physiology and ECG Interpretation

Are You Ready?

Mrs. Willits looks up at you as you check for her pulse. You are in the back of the church on a warm Sunday. Services were just beginning when your older patient felt "faint" and weak. Friends helped her to lie

down on the pew, where you find her. She appears a bit apprehensive and embarrassed. You reassure her while your partner obtains a set of vital signs. You place the ECG monitor leads on the patient as you evaluate her. You see the rhythm in Figure 29-1.

1. What is this rhythm? What information do you need to elicit from Mrs. Willits?

_____

_____

_____

Active Learning

Anatomy Review

1. Describe the location of the heart in relation to the different structures of the thoracic cavity.

_____

_____

_____

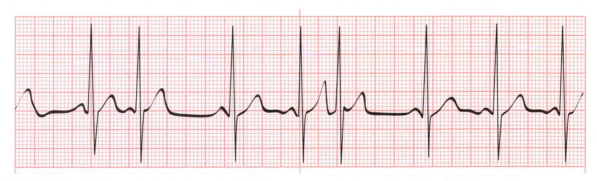

FIGURE 29-1

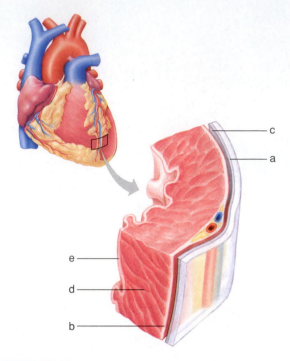

FIGURE 29-2

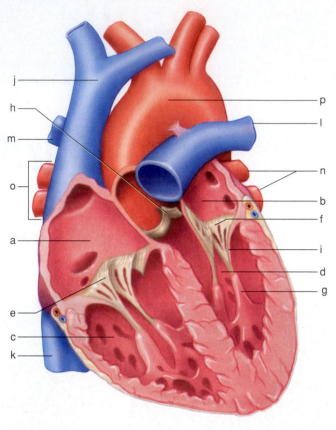

FIGURE 29-3

2. Identify the structures of the heart wall in Figure 29-2.

  a. _____

  b. _____

  c. _____

  d. _____

  e. _____

3. Identify the structures of the heart in Figure 29-3.

  a. _____

  b. _____

  c. _____

  d. _____

  e. _____

  f. _____

  g. _____

  h. _____

  i. _____

  j. _____

  k. _____

  l. _____

  m. _____

  n. _____

  o. _____

  p. _____

4. Which layer of the heart muscle provides the most bulk?

  _____

  _____

  _____

5. Name the three layers of a blood vessel (from the lumen to the exterior).

  _____

  _____

  _____

6. Identify the coronary vessels in Figure 29-4.

  a. _____

  b. _____

  c. _____

  d. _____

  e. _____

  f. _____

  g. _____

  h. _____

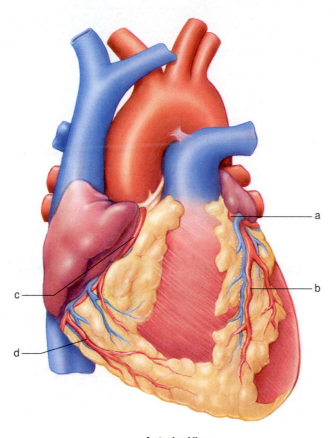

Anterior View   **Posterior View**

FIGURE 29-4

7. At what phase of the cardiac cycle do the coronary arteries fill with blood, and why does this happen during this particular phase?

_____

_____

_____

8. Practice Makes Better

There are many books and electronic products available to you to practice your ECG interpretation skills. In fact, you may already have one assigned to you by your instructor. Included on the DVD that came with this book are approximately 75 ECG exercises. Practice! The more you look at strips, the sooner you will begin to recognize patterns and shapes. When practicing, make sure that you don't cheat yourself and look at the answer before you have provided one first.

There are also websites that give you instant feedback when you provide an answer. Try searching for "ECG interpretation" or "EKG interpreta-

tion." One primer site available through Gateway Community College (AZ) is www.gwc.maricopa. edu/class/bio202/cyberheart/ekgqzr.htm. Another site that provides a review of basic ECG interpretation is available through the University of Wisconsin–Madison at www.fammed.wisc.edu/ pcc/ecg/ecg.html. There are many others out there—try a few!

9. ECG Basics

Identify the basic elements of the ECG strip shown in Figure 29-5.

a. _____

b. _____

c. _____

d. _____

e. _____

f. _____

g. _____

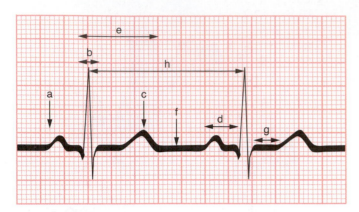

FIGURE 29-5

c. II, III, aVF: _____

d. V_2, V_3, V_4: _____

e. I, aVF: _____

f. I, aVL: _____

g. III, aVL: _____

h. V_3, V_4: _____

i. I, V_1, MCL_1: _____

j. V_3, V_4, V_5, V_6: _____

10. You Do the Math

Your patient is in a ventricular fibrillation cardiac arrest. Effective CPR is being performed. Your partner has defibrillated the patient, IV access has been obtained, and epinephrine has already been administered. You are preparing to administer amiodarone. Your protocol is to deliver 300 mg of amiodarone intravenously over 3–5 seconds, diluted with D_5W to 20 mL total. You carry amiodarone in 3-mL vials, each with a concentration of 50 mg/mL. You are using a microdrop administration set.

a. How many milliliters will you need to draw into a syringe? How many vials will you use? How many milliliters of D_5W will you need to deliver the appropriate dose?

_____

_____

You have been treating a patient who is experiencing profound hypotension secondary to a complete heart block. Your next intervention is to infuse epinephrine at a rate of 6 micrograms per minute (mcg/min). You have a multidose vial of epinephrine (1:1000), a 250-mL IV bag of normal saline, and a microdrip set. It is typical to inject 1 mg of epinephrine into the 250 mL of normal saline.

b. How many milliliters of epinephrine will you draw out of the vial and into the saline IV bag? What is the drip rate in drops per minute?

_____

_____

11. Continuous or Contiguous?

Which of the following sets of leads are contiguous? For each contiguous set you identify, name the area of the heart that the leads are indicating.

a. I, II, III: _____

b. II, III, aVR: _____

You Are There: Reality-Based Cases

Case 1 *(continuation of chapter opener)*

Your partner reports that the 72-year-old patient's blood pressure is 106/78. Her heart rate is 82, and she is breathing at a rate of 22. She appears pale, but her skin is warm and dry. A focused history reveals relatively little information. She had been experiencing the sensation of her heart "skipping a beat" occasionally during the past 5 days. She takes no medications and recently saw her physician for a checkup. She is feeling much better now, she says, and would like to sit up. She wonders aloud what the fuss is all about.

1. Should you let the patient sit up? What are your concerns?

_____

_____

_____

2. What other information would be helpful to you at this point?

_____

_____

_____

You are packing away some of your gear when the patient puts her hand to her chest and says, "There it goes again. I feel my heart skipping." You see the ECG tracing in Figure 29-6.

Mrs. Willits continues, "I'm feeling dizzy again."

3. What should you assess at this moment?

_____

_____

_____

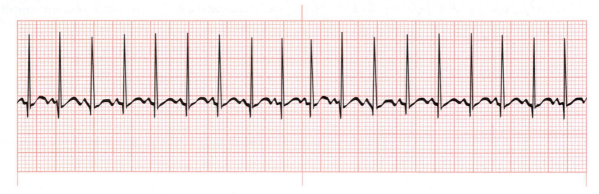

FIGURE 29-6

4. What dysrhythmia do you see in Figure 29-6?

_____

_____

_____

You ask the patient to take a breath and bear down as hard as she can, as if to have a bowel movement. She is able to do so. The ECG reverts back to the original rhythm you saw. Her dizziness resolves; however, she agrees to go to the emergency department with you to investigate her condition.

5. Can you explain what happened when the patient followed your directions? (Hint: Look to Section II of Chapter 29 for help on this question, as well as Chapter 8, Physiology Overview, both in the text-book). What should you evaluate while preparing this patient for transport?

_____

_____

_____

Test Yourself

1. List the five steps of systematic ECG interpretation.

_____

_____

2. You are interpreting an ECG that shows a slightly irregular rhythm. There are no marks visible at the top or bottom of the ECG paper. What method should you use to calculate the patient's heart rate?
   a. Use a heart rate meter
   b. The 300 counting method
   c. The triplicate method
   d. The 6-second strip method

3. Which lead is most commonly used for general ECG monitoring, and where are the electrodes for this lead located?

_____

_____

4. The ability to initiate an electrical impulse without outside nervous system stimulation is called

_____ .

5. The normal T wave represents repolarization of the ventricles. Why do you rarely see the repolarization of the atria on an ECG?

_____

_____

6. An ECG *cannot* tell you if the patient's heart is contracting.
   True
   False

7. The _____ leads get their name because of their placement around the heart on the chest.

8. Name the three layers of the heart and briefly discuss the function of each.

_____

_____

9. What is the Frank-Starling mechanism, and how does it apply to cardiac output?

_____

_____

10. Describe how the venous system serves as a reservoir for blood.

_____

_____

11. An infarction involving the inferior aspect of the heart will most likely be "seen" by leads _____, _____, and _____.

12. An absent or very small Q wave is a cause for concern.
    True
    False

13. List three potential sources of electrical interference (artifact) during ECG monitoring.

    _____

    _____

14. Which of the following is the primary pacemaker site?
    a. The atrioventricular node
    b. The protein gates
    c. The sinus node
    d. The Purkinje fibers

15. The absolute refractory period is unstable and occurs when the cardiac cycle is not finished.
    True
    False

16. The shorter the length of the diastolic period, the less the amount of time available for coronary blood flow.
    True
    False

17. What are the three primary functions of the atrioventricular (AV) node?

    _____

    _____

18. P waves that are over 2.5 mm in amplitude are called _____.

19. Which location is the optimal position to listen with a stethoscope to the closure of the heart valves?
    a. Just right of the sternum at the third rib
    b. Just left of the sternum at the fourth rib
    c. Directly over the sternum at the fourth rib
    d. Just left of the sternum at the fifth rib

Scenario: You are called to a 79-year-old female who is "feeling sick." She is alert and oriented, and denies chest pain and shortness of breath. Her vital signs are BP of 110/60 and RR of 25. Her ECG reading is shown in Figure 29-7:

20. Calculate this patient's approximate heart rate.
    a. 60 bpm
    b. 40 bpm
    c. 50 bpm
    d. 70 bpm

21. What type of rhythm is this?
    a. Sinus tachycardia
    b. Normal sinus rhythm
    c. Sinus arrhythmia
    d. Sinus bradycardia

22. How should you treat this patient?
    a. Start an IV, provide low-flow O_2, and perform a 12-lead ECG.
    b. Consider external cardiac pacing en route to the hospital.
    c. Administer atropine by IV drip and begin bag-mask ventilations.
    d. Begin assisted ventilation and consider administering isoproterenol.

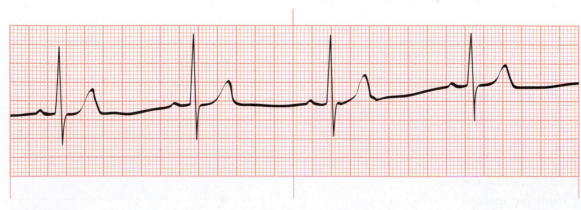

FIGURE 29-7

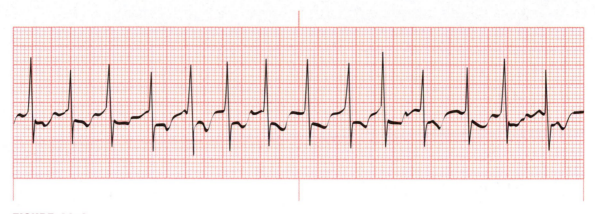

FIGURE 29-8

Scenario: You are called to the home of a patient who has fallen. Upon arrival, you find an 85-year-old woman lying on her kitchen floor. She is alert and oriented but complaining of severe (9 out of 10) pain in her left hip. She tells you she fell only about 20 minutes ago, and she has a history of hypertension. Her vital signs are BP of 110/80 and RR of 28. Her ECG is shown in Figure 29-8.

23. What is this rhythm?
  a. Junctional tachycardia
  b. Sinus tachycardia
  c. Atrial fibrillation
  d. Atrial flutter

24. What two risks are frequently associated with this rhythm?
  a. Myocardial infarction and stroke
  b. Digitalis toxicity and hemodynamic compromise
  c. Digitalis toxicity and embolism
  d. Hemodynamic instability and embolism

25. After performing your patient assessment, what should be your next step?
  a. Administer an analgesic and observe the patient for changes in the rhythm.
  b. Perform defibrillation while transporting emergently to the nearest hospital.
  c. Immobilize the hip and treat the patient's symptoms during transport.
  d. Attempt to determine the underlying cause of the arrhythmia, and then treat the cause.

Scenario: You are called to the home of an elderly patient who is experiencing chest pain. Initial assessment reveals a 75-year-old man who is alert and oriented. His vital signs are BP of 70/40 and RR of 28. His ECG shows the rhythm in Figure 29-9.

26. Calculate the patient's approximate heart rate.
  a. 80 bpm
  b. 40 bpm
  c. 100 bpm
  d. 60 bpm

27. This rhythm should be classified as
  a. essentially regular.
  b. regular.
  c. irregularly irregular.
  d. regularly irregular.

28. What type of rhythm is this?
  a. Junctional escape rhythm
  b. Idioventricular rhythm

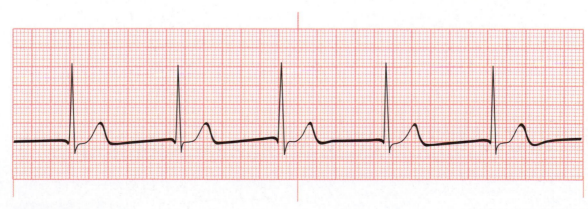

FIGURE 29-9

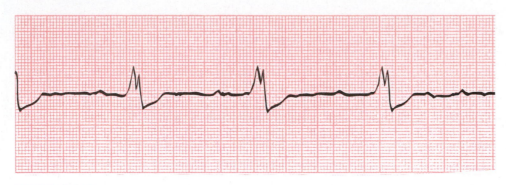

FIGURE 29-10

c. Premature junction contraction

d. Sinus bradycardia

Scenario: Your patient is a 64-year-old man with a history of acute myocardial infarction and hypertension. He presents with dizziness, fatigue, and shortness of breath. His ECG is shown in Figure 29-10.

29. Calculate the PR interval (PRI).

a. 0.42 s

b. 0.12 s

c. 0.24 s

d. 0.18 s

30. What type of rhythm is indicated by the length of the PR interval?

a. Third-degree AV block

b. Left bundle branch block

c. Right bundle branch block

d. First-degree AV block

31. What type of rhythm is indicated by the shape of the QRS complex?

a. Left bundle branch block

b. Right bundle branch block

c. Third-degree AV block

d. First-degree AV block

32. What is the most likely cause of this patient's presenting symptoms?

a. Embolism

b. Right bundle branch block

c. Hypertension

d. Bradycardia

Scenario: Your patient is a 54-year-old woman presenting with chest pain and shortness of breath. You cannot find a pulse, and your patient's mental status is rapidly deteriorating. Her ECG is shown in Figure 29-11.

33. Identify the rhythm.

_____

_____

34. Explain why you cannot find a pulse.

_____

_____

35. How should you treat this patient?

a. Perform chest compressions and defibrillate.

b. Attempt synchronized cardioversion and transport.

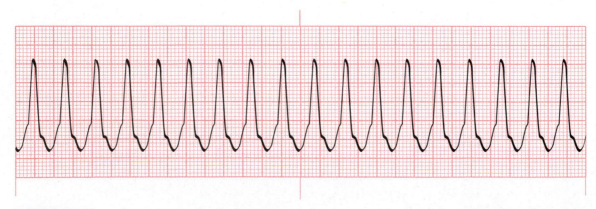

FIGURE 29-11

c. Attempt to determine the underlying cause of the rhythm.

d. Treat the patient's symptoms of shock.

Need to Know

The following represent the Key Objectives of Chapter 29, Section I:

1. *Describe the anatomy and physiology of the cardiovascular system as it relates to normal blood flow.*

   After studying Chapter 29, Cardiology, in the textbook you might feel a bit more in awe of your cardiovascular system. From the moment it is developed inside the fetus to the day it stops functioning, it works at nearly any cost to provide the function of *perfusion*—to bring oxygen- and nutrient-rich blood to all cells in the body. It also removes toxins and waste from the cells and carries away dead cells to be excreted by the lungs, kidneys, and gastrointestinal tract, respectively. It is wise to take a moment to ensure that you have a solid understanding of the cardiovascular system's centerpiece, the heart.

   The heart's four chambers can be functionally divided in two ways:

   a. The right and left atria squeeze downward to force blood into the right and left ventricles, respectively. This *top-to-bottom* movement results in the ventricles filling to their capacity (the "atrial kick"), which allows them to contract more forcefully (the Frank-Starling mechanism). Blood flows only in one direction because the AV valves (tricuspid on the right, bicuspid on the left) prevent backflow from the ventricles to the atria during ventricular contraction.

   b. The right side of the heart moves blood to the left side of the heart through the pulmonary circulation, where oxygen and carbon dioxide are exchanged at the level of the alveoli and pulmonary capillaries. The left side of the heart moves blood to the right side of the heart through the systemic circulation, where blood is distributed to nearly every cell in the body. This *side-to-side* movement of blood creates a circulatory system that is efficient and fully connects both sides of the heart. Blood flows only in one direction because the semilunar valves (pulmonic on the right, aortic on the left) prevent backflow from the great vessels to the ventricles during ventricular refilling.

   The two sets of valves open and close *opposite* each other, creating the "lub dub" sound that you can auscultate with your stethoscope. Again, this causes blood to flow in one direction, taking the following path: from the right atrium, to the right ventricle, through the pulmonary circulation, to the left atrium, to the left ventricle, out through the aorta into systemic circulation, and back into the right atrium through the vena cava.

   When the ventricles contract, blood is squeezed out of the chambers under pressure. This pressure adds to the pressure in the circulatory system, causing blood to flow. This is the *systolic* phase of the cardiac cycle. When the ventricles relax and refill with blood, the pressure falls back to its resting or baseline level, known as the *diastolic* phase (Figure 29-12).

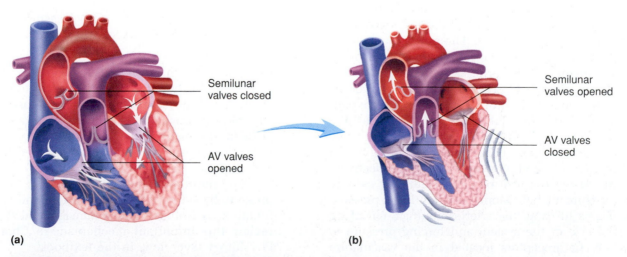

(a)

Semilunar valves closed

AV valves opened

(b)

Semilunar valves opened

AV valves closed

FIGURE 29-12 The Two Phases of the Cardiac Cycle (a) Diastole: the relaxation and filling of both the atria and ventricles. **(b)** Systole: contraction of the atria and ventricles.

The heart muscle comprises three layers: the top layer known as the epicardium, the thick middle layer called the myocardium, and the smooth inner layer, namely, the endocardium. The heart's own circulation, the coronary arteries and veins, are located on the epicardium.

The heart only perfuses itself through the coronary arteries during diastole, or when the ventricles are relaxing.

Review Figure 29-11 in the textbook for the locations of the major coronary arteries:

- Left and right main coronary arteries (LCA and RCA, respectively)
- Circumflex and left anterior descending (LAD) arteries, branching off the left main coronary artery
- The posterior descending artery, which is what the RCA is called when it reaches the back of the heart

The heart is the pump that drives the cardiovascular system, similar to your automobile's water pump, which causes coolant to circulate through pipes to keep the engine at a normal operating temperature. Unlike your car's pipes, your vasculature is able to respond to changing conditions quickly and effectively. The vasculature includes the arteries, capillaries, and veins.

- The capillaries are literally one cell thin, allowing for easy diffusion of gases, nutrients, and waste across cell membranes.
- The veins are relatively fixed, allowing blood to return to the heart. One-way valves exist in veins to allow one-way flow to occur.
- The arteries have the marvelous property of being able to expand and contract. This flexibility allows blood to flow smoothly from the heart out to the most distal tissues without too much loss of pressure. The bolus of blood as it leaves the left ventricle causes temporary expansion of the arterial walls, which then "snap" like an elastic band to push the bolus to the next section of artery, where the expansion of the arterial walls again pushes the bolus onward, and so forth.

    Additionally, the arteries can respond to increasing blood pressure by dilating, effectively increasing the size of the system and causing pressure to fall. More importantly, if pressure begins to drop, the arteries contract, shrinking the size of the system and forcing pressure to rise. Baroreceptors located in the vasculature sense falling blood pressure and signal the adrenal glands through the autonomic nervous system to secrete norepinephrine, which activates the alpha receptors located in the arterial walls that cause the arterial muscle to contract.

The system's vasculature has to have a certain amount of existing pressure for two reasons:

a. Blood must flow into the atria in order for the ventricles to fill adequately. There has to be a certain amount of pressure in the ventricle at the end of its diastolic phase, when it is passively filled with blood from the atria. Called *preload*, this pressure controls the ventricle's cardiac output. If preload is too high, the heart has to work harder to pump. If preload is too low, cardiac output falls.

b. There has to be a certain amount of pressure in the systemic circulation in order for the squeeze of the left ventricle to be effective in pushing blood to the body's tissues (known as *afterload*). If the afterload is too high (hypertension), there will be significantly more workload on the myocardium. Conversely, if it is too low (hypotension), blood will not circulate effectively.

The fluid in the automobile coolant analogy has a certain viscosity or thickness to it, contributing to its effectiveness in carrying heat better than simply water would do. Our blood has a certain viscosity as well, which contributes to blood pressure maintenance (the heavier density of blood causes "drag" during flow, creating additional resistance inside the vasculature).

Components of the blood related to this chapter include the red blood cells, which carry oxygen, and platelet cells, which trigger the clotting process.

2. *Explain how blood flow and pressure are controlled by the cardiovascular system to maintain homeostasis.*

Remember that the body's ultimate goal is to maintain a state of homeostasis. At the cardiovascular level, the three components—heart, vasculature, and blood—work in concert to maintain blood pressure (perfusion) throughout the body, particularly the critical organs, the brain, kidneys, lungs, and the heart itself.

The renin-angiotensin mechanism regulates pressure by acting upon both cardiac and vascular function, as well as volume management. You can review this important mechanism in Chapter 8, Physiology Overview, in the textbook.

When stimulated, the sympathetic nervous system will release epinephrine from the adrenal glands into the bloodstream. Epinephrine will activate *beta receptors* in the heart and produce chronotropic effects (faster heart rate) as well as inotropic effects (more forceful contractions).

Conversely, the parasympathetic system uses acetylcholine to counter the effects of the sympathetic side of the autonomic nervous system, causing the heart to slow, reducing contractility, and dilating blood vessels.

These mechanisms will interact with each other to increase cardiac output into a smaller vasculature as pressure falls, or much less effectively, try to decrease cardiac output into a larger vasculature when pressure is high.

3. *Describe the cardiac cycle in terms of mechanical and electrical function.*

How the heart controls the direction of sequence of the atrioventricular contraction is yet another marvel.

Cardiac cells possess the properties of automaticity (spontaneous generation of an electrical impulse) and excitability (easily stimulated by an electrical impulse). In addition, they are connected to each other in such a way as to promote rapid conduction of action potentials from one to the next. Even more specialized conduction fibers allow for even faster propagation of electrical signals. These properties allow for the fast, coordinated spread of an electrical signal throughout the heart.

An electrical impulse is generated typically at the sinoatrial pacemaker site, or SA node, located on the posterior side of the heart next to where the superior vena cava enters the right atrium. This impulse travels throughout the right atrial cells, across Bachmann's bundle to the left atrium, and down the internodal pathways to depolarize both atria nearly simultaneously.

The electrical wave reaches the cardiac skeleton that physically and electrically separates the atria from the ventricles. However, at the bottom of the left atrium are the AV node and AV junction, which allow electrical transmission through the skeleton and into the ventricular structures. From the AV junction, the impulse travels down the bundle of His, which is electrically isolated from the myocardium. The bundle of His divides into the left and right bundle branches.

The left bundle branch has to cover a great deal of ventricular muscle mass. It does so by dividing again into the anterior and posterior fascicles which spread out across the walls of the left ventricle.

Near the apex (bottom) of the heart, each bundle branch terminates in a network of conduction fibers called the Purkinje network. From here the impulse rapidly propagates throughout the remainder of the ventricular wall.

The electrical conduction system of the heart contains three naturally occurring pacemakers—the SA node, AV node, and Purkinje fibers (Figure 29-13). The AV and Purkinje pacemaker sites function as backups for the SA node in case it fails. Both generate impulses at a slower rate than the SA node as well.

With your knowledge of both the mechanical and electrical aspects of the heart, let us now relate the two:

- Based upon the signals it receives from the autonomic nervous system, the SA node generates electrical impulses (depolarizes) at a specific rate necessary to maintain perfusion. Each beat travels out of the SA node through the internodal pathways and Bachmann's bundle. Upon receipt of the signal, the cardiac cells begin to contract. Since the impulse travels as a wave, the atria contract with a wavelike motion. This effectively causes the atria to squeeze from top to bottom, maximizing the amount of blood leaving the chambers.

- As the atria are squeezing, the electrical wave enters the AV junction. There is a slowing of the impulse as it travels through this section. This allows the atria to fully contract their contents through the AV valves into the ventricles.

- The electrical impulse then travels into the bundle of His, down the bundle branches, and back up the Purkinje fibers. The cells at the apex begin to contract first, followed by the remainder of the ventricular cells from the bottom of the heart up.

- As the ventricles contract, the AV valves slam shut and pressure inside the chambers increases. The semilunar valves snap open once the pressure reaches a certain level, causing the blood to eject forcefully into the vasculature.

- The energy from the original electrical impulse dissipates, and the contraction phase stops. The semilunar valves close, just before the next electrical impulse causes the atria to contract and push more blood into the ventricular chambers.

- The cells must electrically return to their resting state before they can depolarize again. This is called repolarization. During this phase, cells cannot respond easily or at all to any electrical signal sent to them; they are either relatively refractory (can only partially respond) or absolutely refractory (cannot respond at all).

1. Electrical impulses originate in the SA node and travel across the wall of the atrium (*arrows*) from the SA node to the AV node.

2. Electrical impulses pass through the AV node and along the bundle of His, which extends from the AV node, through the fibrous skeleton, into the interventricular septum.

3. The bundle of His divides into right and left bundle branches, and electrical impulses descend to the apex of each ventricle along the bundle branches.

4. Electrical impulses are carried by the Purkinje fibers from the bundle branches to the ventricular walls.

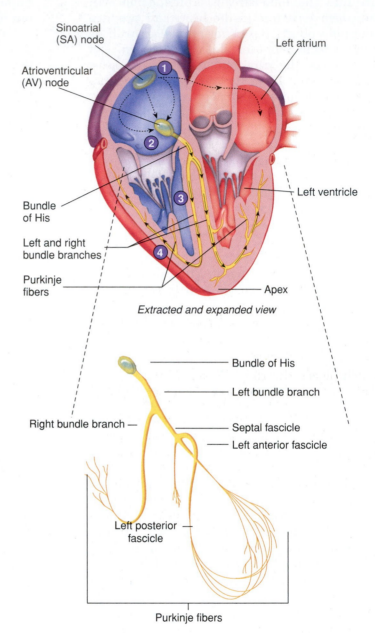

Extracted and expanded view

FIGURE 29-13   The heart's conduction system generates and carries electrical impulses throughout the heart. The enlarged section shows the His-Purkinje system.

4. *Analyze and identify an electrocardiogram (ECG).*

As a paramedic, you will be observing the electrical properties of the cardiac system through the use of a cardiac monitor (the science is called electrocardiography). By viewing an electrocardiogram (ECG), you may be able to identify a variety of problems associated either with the electrical rhythm itself, the health of the cardiac muscle, or both.

An electrical signal can be imagined as a flow of particles moving from an area of high concentration to an area of low concentration. In the case of the ECG, the point of high concentration of these particles (electrons) is a *negative pole,* and the low point is a *positive pole.* The ECG records the flow of electricity from the negative to the positive poles, using electrodes to record the flow. Each pair of negative and positive electrodes is called a lead.

To identify how electricity flows through the heart, a paramedic typically uses *limb leads.* Leads I, II, and III are examples of limb leads. Lead II is generally used to record the tracing both on paper and the oscilloscope (screen) of the

ECG monitor. Limb leads are affixed to the patient's skin with gel-coated electrodes. In lead II, the negative electrode is located on the right arm, with the positive at the left leg. In order to reduce artifact, the limb leads are often attached close to or directly on the patient's trunk closest to the limbs.

Electricity is "seen" by the ECG monitor as it flows from the negative to the positive electrode. The monitor views it from the point of the positive electrode, so like a camera, the wave of electricity is coming toward it. The monitor translates this movement into a *positive deflection,* which is seen as an upright tracing from the isoelectric line on the screen or tracing paper.

Each part of the heart produces a wave that is seen by the ECG monitor.

- The first deflection seen is the one caused by the depolarization of the SA node into the atria. This is the *P wave.*

- The second deflection is caused by the wave traveling through and depolarizing the much bigger ventricles. Therefore the tracing is also much bigger, dwarfing the size of the P wave. This is the *QRS complex.* There are several shapes associated with the QRS complex, and not all parts of the wave need be there. However, the common trait among all the complexes is that they should be shorter than 0.12 second long in duration, the time it takes for the ventricles to depolarize.

- The third deflection is called the *T wave,* and it is a recording of the repolarization of the ventricles.

- There are intervals between the different waveforms that you should know about. One is the *PR interval* (PRI), measured from the beginning of the P wave to the beginning of the QRS complex (the Q part of the QRS complex may not be seen all the time, and the R wave is usually noticeable). This represents the time it takes for depolarization to run from the SA node to the bundle of His, usually 0.12–0.20 second.

- The second interval is the *ST segment* located between the end of the QRS complex, as measured by the J point, to the beginning of the T wave. Under most circumstances, the ST segment should be equal in height to the isoelectric line. More on this in a moment.

- The third interval is called the QT interval, the distance between the beginning of the QRS complex and the end of the T wave. It should be less than half the length of the cardiac cycle, as measured from one R wave to the next (the RR or "R to R" interval).

I	aVR	V_1	V_4
II	aVL	V_2	V_5
III	aVF	V_3	V_6

FIGURE 29-14 Leads I, aVL, V_5, and V_6 (shown in green) look at the lateral wall; leads II, III, and aVF (red) look at the inferior wall; leads V_1 and V_2 (blue) look at the septal wall; and leads V_3 and V_4 (yellow) look at the anterior wall.

The limb lead ECG is usually sufficient to identify gross disturbances with the rhythm. Use the five-step method outlined in Table 29-1 to identify dysrhythmias, and recall that all dysrhythmias are evaluated against the standard normal sinus rhythm (NSR). Refer to Chapter 29, Cardiology, in the textbook in order to identify and describe the different rhythms encountered by the paramedic.

The limb leads will provide an image of the electrical heart in one plane. To "see" the heart in three dimensions, a 12-lead ECG is taken. The 12 leads are the 3 limb leads (I, II, III), the 3 augmented leads (aVL, aVR, aVF), and the 6 ventral leads (V_1 through V_6). Figure 29-36 in the textbook shows you where to accurately place the V leads.

The 12-lead ECG can help you identify areas of ischemia in the heart muscle. Most notably, the ST segment may either elevate above or depress below the isoelectric line in two or more contiguous (areas of the heart adjoining each other) leads. Boxes 29-8 through 29-14 in the textbook show the different leads that are affected by specific parts of the heart. Figure 29-14 shows the leads shaded in different colors. Leads shaded in a specific color "look" at that part of the heart.

Need to Do

The following skills are explained and illustrated in a step-by-step manner, via skill sheets and/or Step-by-Steps in this text and on the accompanying DVD:

Skill Name	Skill Sheet Number and Location	Step-by-Step Number and Location
ECG Acquisition	37 – Appendix A and DVD	37 – This chapter and DVD

TABLE 29-1   **Five-Step Method for Identifying Dysrhythmias**

Step	Should Be (Normal Sinus Rhythm)	Unusual	Rhythm Characteristic
1. Rate	60–100 bpm	Slow (< 60)	• Sinus bradycardia • Junctional rhythm • Idioventricular rhythm (IVR) • Heart blocks, especially second and third degree
		Fast (> 100)	• Sinus tachycardia • Supraventricular tachycardia (SVT), including PSVT, MAT • Ventricular tachycardia (VT) • Rapid atrial fibrillation/flutter
2. Rhythm regularity	Regular	Regularly irregular	• Second- and third-degree heart blocks • Sinus arrhythmia
		Irregularly irregular	• Atrial fibrillation (AF)
		Occasional additional beat.	• premature atrial contraction (PAC), premature ventricular contraction (PVC), premature junctional contraction (PJC)
3. P:QRS relationship	P is present; 1:1 relationship (P = QRS)	P > QRS	• Second- and third-degree heart blocks
		QRS > P	• Slow VT • PVCs
		No relationship between P and QRS	• Third-degree heart block
		P not present	• AF (atrial waves) • A flutter (flutter waves) • SVT • VT • Ventricular fibrillation (VF)
4. PR interval duration	0.12–0.20 s duration	> 0.20 s	• First-degree heart block • Second-degree heart block
		< 0.20 s	• Junctional rhythm • PACs
5. QRS complex width	< 0.12 s wide	> 0.12 s wide	• VT • Wide complex tachycardia • Aberrantly conducted SVT

ECG Acquisition

Conditions: The candidate should perform this skill on a simulated patient under existing indoor, ambulance, or outdoor lighting, temperature, and weather conditions.

Indications: Any patient exhibiting chest pain of probable cardiac origin, or other symptoms of a possible myocardial infarction.

Red Flags: Avoid attaching electrodes to skin that is burned, injured, or otherwise not intact. Do not delay the management of life threats for acquisition of an ECG.

Steps:

1. Don appropriate standard precautions.

2. Explain procedure to patient.

3-Lead ECG Acquisition

3. Place limb leads:
   - White on right arm
   - Black on left arm
   - Green on right leg
   - Red on left leg (Figure SBS 37-1)
   - MCL_1, if utilized, should be placed in the fourth intercostal space, right of the sternum

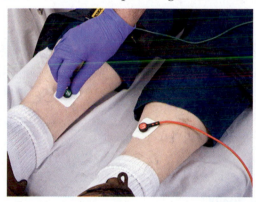

SBS 37-1

4. Turn monitor on and assess the baseline rhythm (Figure SBS 37-2).

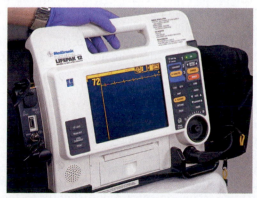

SBS 37-2

5. Print ECG strip as necessary.

12-Lead ECG Acquisition

6. Treat life-threatening rhythms prior to 12-lead.

7. Expose the chest.

8. Ensure skin is intact, and shave hair as necessary.

9. Cleanse area with alcohol if necessary. Alcohol must dry prior to placing electrodes.

10. Attach cables to self-adhesive leads.

11. Attach precordial leads (Figure SBS 37-3):
    - V_1—fourth intercostal space, right of sternum
    - V_2—fourth intercostal space, left of sternum
    - V_4—fifth intercostal space, midclavicular line
    - V_3—on a line midway between V_2 and V_4
    - V_5—anterior axillary line on same horizontal level as V_4, between V_4 and V_6
    - V_6—midaxillary line at same level as V_4 and V_5

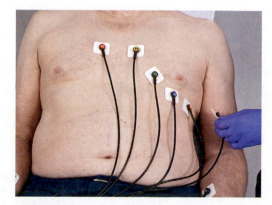

SBS 37-3

12. Connect precordial leads to monitor.

13. Direct patient to remain still and breathe normally (Figure SBS 37-4).

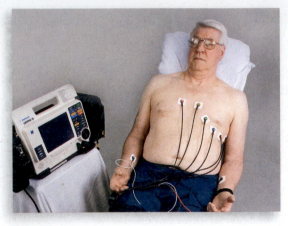

SBS 37-4

14. Acquire 12-lead ECG.

15. If data is "noisy," adjust appropriate lead and retake 12-lead ECG.

Critical Criteria:

- Use appropriate standard precautions.
- Accurately place leads on patient.
- Ensure skin is clean and clear prior to lead placement.

Connections

- Several of the textbook chapters warrant review to help strengthen your knowledge of cardiology: Chapter 7, Anatomy Overview; Chapter 8, Physiology Overview; Chapter 28, Pulmonary, and Chapter 31, Endocrine, Electrolytes, and Acid/Base.

- Several websites have examples of heart tones. The University of Michigan has an image showing where to place the stethoscope and the corresponding sound: www.med.umich.edu/lrc/coursepages/M1/anatomy/html/surface/thorax/hsounds.html. The Auscultation Assistant at the University of California at Los Angeles has both heart sounds and lung sounds at its site: www.med.ucla.edu/wilkes/inex.htm.

- A wonderful animation site showing the cardiac cycle, ECG interpretation, and other aspects of cardiology can be found at www.blaufuss.org/. Created by Blaufuss Medical Multimedia Laboratories, there is an excellent animation and tutorial on the various forms of supraventricular tachycardia (SVT), including Wolff-Parkinson-White syndrome.

- Link to the companion DVD for a chapter-based quiz, audio glossary, animations, games and exercises, and, when appropriate, skill sheets and skill Step-by-Steps.

Street Secrets

- **A Sticky Situation** It can be a challenge to get the ECG electrodes to stick to the patient's skin when the patient is very diaphoretic. Wiping the area with an alcohol pad or iodine swabs can help reduce the amount of moisture and increase the stickiness factor.

- **Things Might Get a Little Rough** Another way to make electrode pads adhere better to the skin and increase electrical pickup is to "rough up" the skin a little. By rubbing an alcohol pad briskly over the skin you will remove the upper layers of the epidermis, which may create a better electrical contact between the electrode and the skin.

The Drug Box

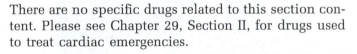

There are no specific drugs related to this section content. Please see Chapter 29, Section II, for drugs used to treat cardiac emergencies.

Answers

Are You Ready?

1. This rhythm is a sinus tachycardia with premature atrial contractions. Is this enough information to begin any treatment? No, you still need to find out more about what happened just prior to your arrival; the patient's past medical history, prescription medications, and allergies; and any physical findings, such as her vital signs and a description of any pain she may be experiencing. In other words, you need to treat the patient, not *just* the monitor.

Active Learning

1. The heart is bordered on both sides by the right and left lungs, respectively; anteriorly by the sternum; and posteriorly by the vertebral column. Its base (the wide portion of the heart that holds the great vessels) lies beneath the second rib, and its apex (the pointed portion of the heart) lies facing downward and slightly to the left at the level of the fifth intercostal space.

2. a. parietal pericardium; b. epicardium (visceral pericardium); c. pericardial cavity (containing fluid); d. myocardium; e. endocardium

3. a. right atrium; b. left atrium; c. right ventricle; d. left ventricle; e. right atrioventricular (tricuspid) valve; f. left atrioventricular (bicuspid or mitral) valve; g. papillary muscles; h. aortic valve; i. chordae tendineae; j. superior vena cava; k. inferior vena cava; l. left pulmonary artery; m. right pulmonary artery; n. left pulmonary veins; o. right pulmonary veins; p. aorta

4. The myocardium

5. Tunica intima (interna), tunica media, and tunica adventitia (externa)

6. a. left coronary artery; b. left anterior descending artery; c. right coronary artery; d. marginal artery; e. circumflex artery; f. posterior descending artery; g. coronary vein; h. coronary sinus

7. The coronary arteries fill with blood during diastole. The reason the coronary arteries fill with blood during diastole rather than systole is because the opening to the coronary arteries lies just distal to the aortic valves. When the heart contracts (systole), the valves open and the cusps from the valves cover the opening to the coronary arteries. When the heart relaxes (diastole), the aortic valve cusps return to their resting phase, and the openings to the coronary arteries are exposed. Thus, it is during diastole that the coronary arteries are perfused.

9. a. P wave; b. QRS complex; c. T wave; d. PR interval; e. QT interval; f. isoelectric line; g. ST segment; h. RR interval

10. a. Each vial contains 150 mg of amiodarone (3 mL × 50 mg/mL = 150 mg). You will need two vials to make a 300-mg bolus. Since you are drawing up a total of 6 mL of fluid, you will need 14 mL of D_5W to create the 20-mL bolus indicated by your protocol.

    b. An epinephrine vial of 1:1000 concentration has a concentration of 1 mg/mL. You will need to draw 1 mL of epinephrine to give you 1 mg of epinephrine; 1 mg of epinephrine in 250 mL of normal saline will produce a concentration of 4 mcg/mL. Therefore, you will need to infuse 1.5 mL of this solution per minute to provide the patient the appropriate dose of 6 mcg/min. The drip rate would be 90 drops per minute (1.5 mL × 60 gtt/mL = 90 gtt). However, because 90 drops per minute is too fast to count, you could increase the amount of epinephrine in the IV bag in order to create a drip rate below 60 per minute. For example, adding 2 mg would double the dose, thereby cutting the drip rate in half, or to 45 gtt/min. It's still fast but is easier to count than 90.

11. a. not contiguous; b. not contiguous; c. contiguous: inferior aspect; d. contiguous: anteroseptal; e. not contiguous; f. contiguous: lateral wall; g. not contiguous; h. contiguous: septal wall; i. not contiguous; j. contiguous: septal – lateral wall

You Are There: Reality-Based Cases

1. With the events being described, there is a distinct possibility that your patient may have suffered a near—or full—syncopal episode. Although her blood pressure is not technically hypotensive, given her age you might expect it to be higher than what is reported. Her blood pressure may fall if she sits or stands; in addition to another syncopal episode, the preload pressure back to the heart may become inadequate. This can lead to cardiac ischemia or injury.

2. There are several reasons why she may be syncopal. Hypovolemia may be one cause. Cardiac dysrhythmia and/or ischemia that lead to sudden decreased output are other possible causes. You will need to elicit more information about the patient's past medical history. For example, does she have a recent flu or fever history with vomiting and diarrhea episodes? She may have become dehydrated. Is there any chest discomfort or sudden, unexplained shortness of breath associated with the episode, indicative of a possible coronary event? Other information will include a physical exam. You will need to look for signs that back up your suspicions. For example, you may look for ST segment elevation on two or more contiguous leads on the ECG if she is complaining of cardiac-type discomfort. An absence of neck vein distention, skin tenting, and a sunken eye appearance may help to reinforce the suspicion of hypovolemia secondary to dehydration.

3. This is an abrupt change in the patient's cardiac rhythm. You must assess whether any or all of these beats are creating a pulse that you can palpate peripherally. A patient who complains of feeling dizzy or faint *while supine* must be quickly evaluated to determine if hypotension is the cause. If this sounds familiar, it should—you are back to performing a primary survey of the patient's airway, breathing, and circulatory status.

4. Use the five-step method to compare this ECG tracing against normal sinus rhythm.

    Step 1. *Calculate the heart rate.* This is a tachycardia, at approximately 180 beats per minute.

    Step 2. *Classify the rhythm.* It appears fairly regular.

    Step 3. *Inspect the P wave and its relationship to the QRS complex.* There appear to be P waves that look alike, but they are not shaped in the round manner that you would expect. There is a P wave for every QRS complex, and a QRS complex for every P wave. This implies that there is a focus in the atria, and not the sinoatrial node, that is able to depolarize the ventricles each time it reaches the AV node.

    Step 4. *Calculate the PR interval.* It appears shorter than expected, just less than 0.08 second long. This reinforces the possibility that this is an atrial-based rhythm, not a sinus-based rhythm.

    Step 5. *Inspect the QRS complex.* The ventricular response appears normal, with a narrow, upright shape. This implies that the beat is originating within the electrical conduction fibers of the bundle of His.

In summary, this rhythm appears to originate in the atria, is conducting very quickly, and follows the remaining electrical pathway normally. This would all point to a supraventricular tachycardia, most likely an atrial tachycardia.

5. You have just asked your patient to perform a Valsalva maneuver. Pressure against the glottic opening transiently increases parasympathetic tone and stimulates the vagus nerve, which in turn slows down electrical conduction through the AV node. If the SVT is due to a reentry mechanism, the slowing can "break" the cycle and terminate the tachycardia. Keep your fingers on the patient's pulse when she performs the vagal maneuver to check for slowing. (You may also want to have this patient remain supine, in case she lowers her blood pressure along with her heart rate.)

Test Yourself

1. Calculate heart rate; classify rhythm (including the presence of ectopic beats); check for the presence and shape of the P wave and the P wave's relationship to the QRS complex; calculate the PR interval; inspect the QRS complex.

   For every ECG, you should train yourself to identify the rhythms by following the five-step process. Following these five steps will ensure that you do not miss anything and make an incorrect reading. The learning process can be frustrating, but after you have had some experience applying the systematic approach to rhythm interpretation, you will learn to identify a few ECG patterns by sight, such as the life-threatening dysrhythmias.

2. b

   For regular or slightly irregular rhythms, and when the markings may not be visible, you can estimate the heart rate by identifying the R waves of two consecutive complexes, counting the number of large (5 mm) boxes between them, and dividing that number into 300. For even more accuracy, count the number of small (1 mm) boxes between the R waves and divide that number into 1,500. Neither of these counting methods works very well with irregular rhythms. The 6-second strip method only works when you can see the 3- or 6-second markings at the top or bottom of the ECG paper. Both the triplicate method and heart rate meters can only be used with regular rhythms.

3. Lead II is the most commonly used; in lead II, the negative electrode is on the right shoulder, the positive electrode is on the left leg, and the ground is on the left shoulder.

   Lead II is the most commonly used lead for general monitoring, because it usually gives the tallest ECG complex and also because it observes the impulse traveling "down" through the conduction pathway.

4. Automaticity

   The heart is made up of specialized muscle tissue found nowhere else in the body. It has the normal properties of muscle tissue in that it will contract and relax when stimulated by electrolytes such as calcium and magnesium. These specialized cells express the additional unique properties of automaticity, the ability to initiate an electrical impulse without outside nervous system stimulation, and excitability, the ability to readily receive and respond to an electrical impulse.

5. Repolarization of the atria occurs during depolarization of the ventricles (the QRS complex).

   The QRS complex primarily represents the depolarization of the ventricles. The repolarization of the atria occurs at the same time and is therefore factored into the QRS complex. Because of the strength of ventricular depolarization and the relative weakness of atrial repolarization, atrial repolarization is rarely "seen" on an ECG.

6. True

   The ECG monitors the electrical impulses in the heart but cannot tell you if the heart is responding to these impulses by actually contracting.

7. Precordial

   The precordial leads get their name because of their placement around the heart on the chest. The precordial leads are also known as unipolar leads because, just as in the augmented leads, the negative component is calculated using three limb leads. These, in conjunction with the six limb leads, create the standard 12-lead ECG.

8. The epicardium is the outermost layer, which protects the heart. The myocardium is the muscular middle layer, which performs the work of the heart. The endocardium is the inner layer, which lines the chambers of the heart and contains the Purkinje fibers.

   The epicardium serves as the "skin" of the heart and is a protective layer that contains most of the heart's blood vessels, lymph vessels, and nerve fibers. The myocardium makes up the bulk of cardiac muscle tissue and also contains a rich blood supply from capillaries. The endocardium is comprised of mostly connective tissue, a few blood vessels, and the system of nerve fibers known as the Purkinje fibers.

9. The Frank-Starling mechanism (also sometimes described as a "law") states that the force of blood ejected by the heart is determined primarily by the length of the fibers of its muscular wall. Simply stated, the more a cardiac muscle is stretched, the harder it will contract. Therefore, the more blood that is pushed into the ventricles (thus stretching them more), the harder they will contract, increasing cardiac output.

10. The venous system serves as a reservoir for blood by increasing or decreasing its size through venous constriction or dilation (sometimes also called "pooling"). By increasing or decreasing its capacity, it can control how much blood is being returned to the heart. This mechanism allows the body to adjust to blood loss, dehydration, and overhydration by altering the container size to accommodate the fluid volume.

    This system is influenced by blood pressure, psychogenic (emotion-controlled) factors, and medication. Simple fainting, which is also called vasovagal syncope, may be the result of increased capacitance (or size changes) of the vascular system, which decreases blood flow to the heart and ultimately to the brain. Like all compensatory mechanisms, vascular system constriction or dilation has its limitations.

11. II, III, and aVF

    Think of each electrode as an "eye" looking toward the heart. Each eye looks at a very specific portion of the heart. Since the electrical conduction travels many different directions in different areas of the heart, the ECG pattern from each lead will appear slightly different. Keep in mind that the measurements of waves and intervals shouldn't change. This also means that a change involving only one portion of the heart will only be seen in the leads that look to that area. Leads II, III, and aVF look at the heart's inferior aspect; they are referred to as the inferior leads. Leads V_1 and V_2 look at the septal region. Leads V_3 and V_4 look at the anterior aspect, while leads V_5, V_6, I, and aVL look at the lateral wall.

12. False

    The Q wave is the first negative deflection from the isoelectric line. After the impulse pauses at the AV node, it travels through the AV node, reaching the bundle of His and the bundle branches. As the impulse hits the left bundle branch, the septum begins to depolarize, and once again some electrical movement is detected by the monitor. Since the left bundle branch depolarizes the ventricular septum, the impulses travel across the septum to the right bundle branch. The result is a very tiny deflection away from the positive electrode called a Q wave. This wave is usually so small it often isn't seen at all.

13. Muscle movement, loose leads, and 60-cycle interference

    The ECG measures all electrical activity in the body, although this is minimized by a series of filters. The three common types of artifact include muscle movement, loose leads, and 60-cycle interference (the latter is caused by proximity to other electrical devices).

14. c

    The primary pacemaker, or sinus node, is able to initiate depolarization at a rate of 60–100 times per minute. Should the sinus node fail to initiate an impulse, the AV node will then fire. Should both fail, the Purkinje fibers take over at an intrinsic rate of 20–40 bpm. When lower-positioned pacemaker sites fire because a higher site has failed, the term "escape" is used to describe the rhythm that results.

15. False

    The absolute refractory period occurs once the cardiac cell is in the depolarized state and the electrical gradient is such that no matter how strong an incoming electrical impulse is, the cell is not capable of responding to it. Therefore, the absolute refractory period is stable. The relative refractory period occurs when the cardiac cycle is not finished and it is unstable. A strong enough electrical impulse hitting at this time may be sufficient to interfere with the coordinated activity of the conduction system, effectively destabilizing the entire heart. This destabilization could result in chaotic electrical activity known as ventricular fibrillation or ventricular tachycardia and could be life threatening.

16. True

    As the heart begins to relax and refill during diastole, some of the blood that was pushed out into the aorta during systole is "sucked" back toward the heart, into the coronary system. At this time the coronary arteries are opened and blood quickly flows into them, perfusing the heart. Thus, the shorter the length of the diastolic period, the less the amount of time available for coronary blood flow.

17. The AV node connects the atria to the ventricles electrically. It slows down the conduction by an average of 0.08 ms. And it acts as the secondary pacemaker.

    The AV node allows impulses to cross from the atria to the ventricles. A 0.08-ms delay in conduction provided by the AV node allows the atria a little extra time to fill the ventricles with blood before the ventricles themselves begin to contract. In the event that the sinus node or the conduction system of the atria fails, the AV node would begin to fire at a rate of 40–60 bpm.

18. P-pulmonale

    The first deflection noted with the start of the cardiac cycle is called the P wave. It identifies atrial depolarization and shows the impulse originating in the sinus node. The P wave is usually upright and rounded in lead II, and the duration is 0.10 second or less and is rarely over 2 mm high. P-pulmonale waves are over 2.5 mm in amplitude and may be associated with respiratory problems. This P wave is usually peaked instead of rounded.

19. d

    The pointed portion of the heart is called the apex. It is the closest part of the heart to the chest wall, located just left of the sternum at the fifth rib. This location is the optimal position to listen with a stethoscope to the closure of the valves found between both the left and right atria and ventricle. This auscultatory site is called the point of maximal impulse (PMI).

20. b

    You can approximate the patient's heart rate by counting the number of large boxes between the R wave of one QRS complex and the R wave of the next. Then divide 300 by that number: 300/7 large boxes ≈ 43 beats per minute.

21. d

    The diagnostic criteria for sinus bradycardia are: heart rate < 60; rhythm regular to essentially regular without any ectopy; P waves present and preceding each QRS complex with a 1:1 relationship; PRI of 0.12–0.20 second; QRS complex < 0.12 second and uniform in shape.

22. a

    Treatment for sinus bradycardia should be based on the clinical presentation of symptoms and not on the actual heart rate. A patient mentating properly (who is awake; alert; and oriented to person, place, time, and situation), with no serious symptoms like hypotension, chest pain, or difficulty breathing, may simply be observed until a cause is determined. However, it would be a good idea to have an IV and oxygen support in place in case the patient's condition starts to deteriorate.

23. c

    Similar to atrial flutter, atrial fibrillation is the result of rapid atrial depolarization, except that it is the result of multiple ectopic sites within the atria, resulting in an atrial depolarization rate of 350–600. The hallmark of this rhythm is the gross irregularity of the ventricular response. Because of the sheer volume of atrial impulses, it is impossible to predict which impulse will be conducted to the ventricles and when.

24. d

The first concern with this rhythm is the rate of ventricular response. The faster the ventricles depolarize, the less time they have to fill, thus reducing cardiac output and leading to hemodynamic instability. The second main concern with this rhythm is the risk that the chaotic arrhythmic action will release blood clots into the general circulation, resulting in embolisms. If this occurs, it is very likely that one of them might lodge in the brain and cause a stroke.

25. c

Atrial fibrillation may be paroxysmal or chronic in nature with no apparent cause. Disorders associated with atrial fibrillation include congestive heart failure, arterial hypertension, coronary artery disease (CAD), valvular heart disease, cardiac surgery, electrolyte disturbances, ethanol intoxication, pulmonary disease, and sepsis. Whatever the cause, atrial fibrillation is a very malignant, difficult to control arrhythmia. In the prehospital environment, treatment should be based upon the degree of hemodynamic instability demonstrated by the patient.

26. d

You can approximate the patient's heart rate by counting the number of large boxes between the R wave of one QRS complex and the R wave of the next. Then divide 300 by that number: 300/5 large boxes = 60 bpm.

27. b

A rhythm may be classified one of many ways. The choices are regular, essentially regular, regularly irregular, and irregularly irregular. To be considered regular, the timing intervals (measured as the distance between each RR interval) should march across the ECG strip from R wave to R wave without major changes. The faster the rhythm, the more exact it should be. Slower rhythms may be up to two small boxes off either way and may still be considered essentially regular. If the distance between the shortest RR and the longest RR interval is greater than 0.16 second (four small boxes), the rhythm is considered irregular.

28. a

The diagnostic criteria for junctional escape rhythm include: heart rate of 40–60 bpm; regular rhythm; P waves prior, during, or after QRS complex; PRI < 0.12 second; QRS complex < 0.12 second and uniform in shape. The junctional escape rhythm is the AV junction doing its job as the secondary pacemaker in the event of failure of the SA node to function properly. This rhythm would be treated as a bradycardic rhythm.

29. a

The PRI is calculated by adding the time from the beginning of the P wave to the end of the PR segment. This

interval normally measures between 0.12 and 0.2 second in duration. This interval is very important and will serve as one of the measurements used to name rhythms captured by the ECG tracing. Usually, any PRI of less than 0.2 second (one large box) with an upright P wave is considered normal.

30. d

The first-degree AV block can be identified by the prolonged PRI (> 0.12 s) in conjunction with the fact that every P wave results in the formation of a QRS.

31. b

During right bundle branch block, the impulse traveling down the bundle of His is not allowed to propagate normally down that branch. The ventricle must then be depolarized from impulses traveling across the ventricular septum from the left bundle branch. Electrically, you will see a small R wave signifying septal depolarization; a deep S wave will appear as the left ventricle depolarizes normally. Finally, a wide, slurred R wave will appear as the left ventricle finishes depolarization and the right ventricle is depolarized. This gives a classic triphasic, "M," or "rabbit ear" appearance to the right bundle branch pattern.

32. d

First-degree AV block is typically considered to be a nonmalignant rhythm because it doesn't produce any real symptoms unless the rhythm is accompanied by bradycardia significant enough to cause symptoms. In this case, the patient's heart rate (50 bpm) has indeed been slowed sufficiently to be classified as bradycardia. Common signs and symptoms of bradycardia include fatigue, light-headedness or dizziness, fainting, and shortness of breath.

33. Monomorphic ventricular tachycardia

This rhythm can be identified as a ventricular dysrhythmia because the QRS complexes are wide and bizarre in appearance, and because the T wave has an opposite polarity from the QRS complex. This rhythm can be identified as a monomorphic ventricular tachycardia because the rhythm is sustained and regular and the heart rate is > 100 bpm.

34. At rates exceeding 150, ventricular filling time decreases to the point where hemodynamic compromise starts becoming a problem. Ventricular tachycardia without a pulse indicates that the heart is perfusing so poorly that no pulse can be perceived.

35. b

When treating patients with pulseless ventricular tachycardia, there should be no delay in treatment to try to determine the cause; if synchronized cardioversion is unsuccessful, ventricular tachycardia should be treated just as ventricular fibrillation (VF), using defibrillation. The acute lack of perfusion will cause this rhythm to progress to VF or asystole very quickly if immediate steps are not taken to correct the problem.

Cardiology

Section II: Cardiovascular Diseases

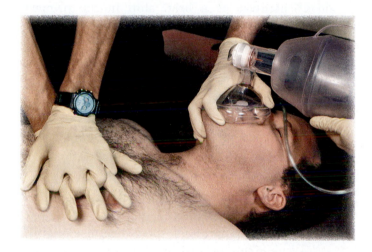

Are You Ready?

It is Christmas Eve, and you and your partner are sitting in an ambulance on a street corner watching the last-minute shoppers scurry about. Holiday cheer is definitely in the air, and you are enjoying watching the people as they pass by when the screen on your mobile data terminal lights up and call information is displayed. You notice that the address is only three blocks away and right next to the local fire station.

The dispatcher tells you that you are responding for a collapse of a 32-year-old male. CPR instructions are being given over the phone. Before the dispatcher has the chance to finish what she is saying, you are on your way. You arrive on the scene in less than 3 minutes, and the firefighters from the station across the street from the patient's address are already in the house. You and your partner grab all your equipment and hurry into the house.

The engine crew is performing CPR on a young adult male. His wife and two young children, along with many other relatives, are weeping nearby.

The fire crew reports that the patient collapsed without warning, and the family was performing CPR upon their arrival. They inform you that ventilations are being performed without resistance, and there is no gastric distention. They have not yet attached their automated external defibrillator (AED) to the patient.

You attach the patient to the ECG and see the rhythm in Figure 29-15.

1. What ECG rhythm is the patient in?

_____

_____

_____

2. Following the recognition of the ECG rhythm, what should your next step be?

_____

_____

_____

3. What is the 2005 American Heart Association (AHA) ratio for compressions to ventilations in an adult patient?

_____

_____

_____

4. What is the slogan that the AHA emphasizes for rescuers performing CPR on adult patients (regarding how CPR is supposed to be performed) to emphasize the science-based changes made in 2005?

_____

_____

_____

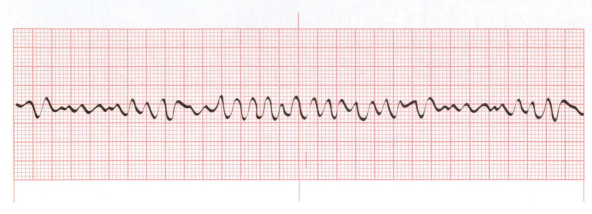

FIGURE 29-15

5. When using a monophasic defibrillator, according to the 2005 AHA standards, what energy setting is used for the initial defibrillation?

_____

_____

_____

Active Learning

1. Get Real

The Get Real ACLS Algorithm (Figure 29-16) is a simplified method of approaching patients who have signs and symptoms that are consistent with the AHA emergency cardiac care algorithms. The initial focus of the Get Real Algorithm is not the patient's presenting ECG rhythm. Rather, it is one basic question: "Is the patient dead or alive?"

The "dead" patient has no pulse and is not breathing; the "almost dead" patient is not breathing but has a pulse; and the "alive" patient has a pulse and is breathing. Treatment for the dead patient who doesn't meet any criteria that would prevent you from initiating resuscitation (e.g., rigor mortis, dependent lividity, and decomposition of the body—any criteria for death in the field that has been established by your local EMS regulatory entity) would focus on quality basic life support with an emphasis on CPR no matter what ECG rhythm the patient presents with. According to the AHA, "Push hard and fast (100/min) with full recoil and minimal interruptions in compressions, while avoiding hyperventilation," is the strategy that will yield the greatest chance of surviving a cardiac arrest.

The algorithm for the dead patient addresses two basic pathways that center around CPR: the shockable rhythms (ventricular fibrillation and pulseless ventricular tachycardia) and pulseless electrical activity (PEA)/asystole. The "almost dead" pathway is a brief stop in the primary assessment that leads the paramedic to identify and treat respiratory arrest on the path to further assessment in the "alive" pathway.

Finally, after addressing any immediate threats to airway, breathing, and circulation, the alive pathway leads to one important factor: heart rate. The alive pathway asks four important questions regarding heart rate:

- Is it slow (less than 60/min)?
- Is it fast (greater than 180/min)?
- Is it stable (normal blood pressure)?
- Is it unstable (altered mental status, hypotension, chest pain of a suspected cardiac origin)?

A separate treatment pathway exists for each of the possible options presented by these questions.

2. Starling's Law of the Heart and the Effects of Preload and Afterload

(This exercise is an abbreviated form of the exercise presented in Chapter 8 of this worktext.)

Preload is how tightly stretched the ventricular myocardium is just prior to contraction and is measured by the ventricular pressure just before each heart contraction. It is assessed by left ventricular end-diastolic pressure (LVEDP) and measured in the hospital using a direct LV catheter, or by using a Swan-Ganz balloon catheter wedged in the smaller pulmonary arteries (a wedge pressure).

This demonstration of how preload affects cardiac function uses a balloon and can be done anywhere. Simply blow up a balloon with two breaths and then release it. The air exits the balloon with low pressure, making minimal noise.

Get Real ACLS Algorithm

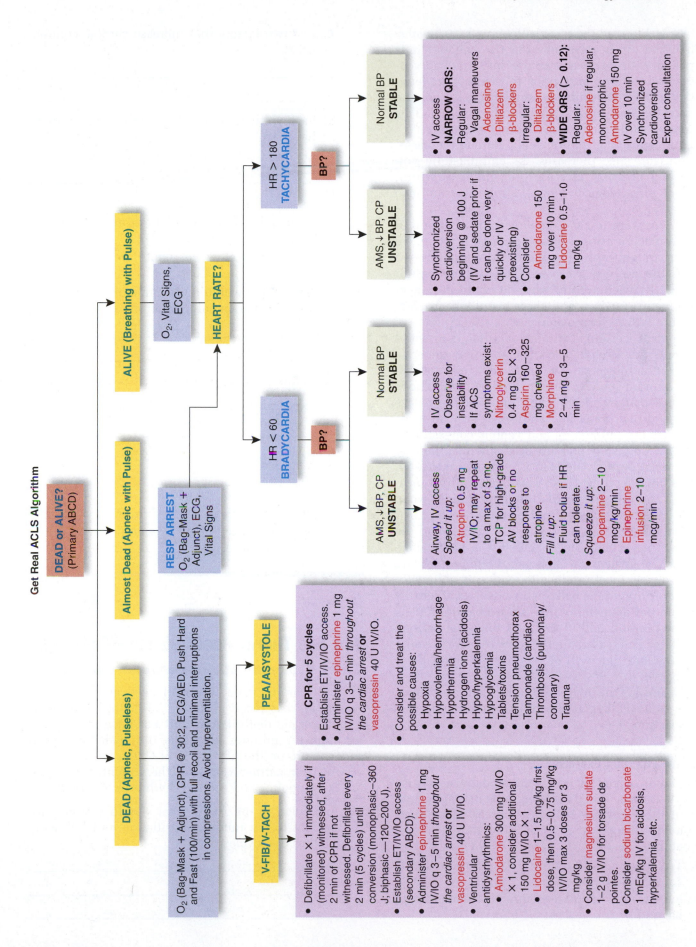

FIGURE 29-16   Get Real ACLS Algorithm.   (Copyright 2007 Arthur Hsieh.)

Now, blow up the same balloon with 10 breaths. When the air is released from the balloon, it is expelled with much greater pressure. Cardiac ventricular distention just prior to contraction (end-diastolic volume) is directly correlated to the volume of blood ejected with systole (stroke volume). This is known as the *Frank-Starling relationship.*

As ventricular end-diastolic volume increases, its pressure also increases. As end-diastolic volume and pressure increase (i.e., preload) within normal physiological ranges, stroke volume also increases.

If you were to keep blowing up the balloon, it would reach a critical point at which it would no longer stretch to produce more and more pressure when the air was released. The balloon would eventually reach a point where it could no longer stretch any further, and there would be a catastrophic failure (explosion).

After a certain limit, myocardial contractile elements are stretched too far, and they generate less contractile force. The once beneficial mechanism of more stretch yielding stronger contractions becomes compromised. The Frank-Starling curve flattens at this point, and additional preload leads to worsening pulmonary and venous congestion.

Afterload is the pressure against which the ventricle must pump. Afterload is clinically measured as systolic blood pressure. This is an indirect measure of the pressure inside the left ventricle when the aortic valve is open and blood is ejected, barring any obstruction between the ventricle and the artery from which blood pressure is being measured. The greater the afterload, the more pressure the ventricle must produce to empty its volume.

Returning to the balloon exercise, if we narrow the internal diameter of the inflated balloon's neck by pinching off half of the neck once the balloon is inflated (increased afterload or resistance), more pressure and time will be required for the balloon to empty.

Examples of increased afterload are aortic valve stenosis, hypertension, and peripheral vasoconstriction.

3. Cardiac Function Exercise

The force of contraction generated by a cardiac muscle fiber is directly related to its resting length. When the ventricles fill with increasing volumes of blood, the force of contraction increases proportionately.

a. The name of the preceding relationship is _____.

b. Factors that increase contractility are said to have a(n) _____ effect.

c. List two factors that increase cardiac contractility.

_____

_____

d. Factors that reduce contractility are said to have a(n) _____ effect.

e. List two factors that reduce cardiac contractility.

_____

_____

f. Factors that increase heart rate are said to have _____ effects.

g. Factors that slow heart rate are said to have _____ effects.

h. What effect would a heart rate of 180 beats per minute have on cardiac output (CO) and why?

_____

_____

i. Define pulse pressure.

_____

_____

j. How is pulse pressure calculated?

_____

_____

k. Mr. Smith has a blood pressure of 188/56. His pulse pressure is _____.

You Are There: Reality-Based Cases

Case 1 (continuation of chapter opener)

The 32-year-old male who collapsed at the holiday celebration has received his initial defibrillation with a monophasic defibrillator. CPR has been in progress for almost 2 minutes since the initial defibrillation, and you are on the fifth cycle of CPR.

As your partner ventilates the patient, you check the ECG monitor and see the rhythm in Figure 29-17.

1. According to the AHA, what should you do subsequent to the initial defibrillation and following another five cycles of CPR?

_____

_____

_____

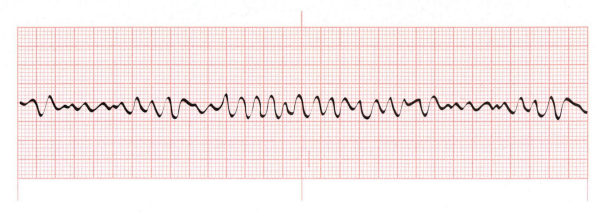

FIGURE 29-17

2. At what point should intubation and intravenous (IV) or intraosseous (IO) access be attempted?

_____

_____

_____

3. Once the airway has been secured and IV/IO access has been established, what is the first medication that should be administered to the patient (include dosage, route, and frequency)?

_____

_____

_____

4. After the administration of the first cardiac medication, another five cycles of CPR, and a third defibrillation (if the patient remains in a shockable rhythm), what type of medication should be delivered (include dosage, route of administration, and frequency)?

_____

_____

_____

As team leader, you assign tasks to the different personnel on the scene. You establish an external jugular IV, and your partner intubates the patient. You instruct one of the firefighters to continue chest compressions and the other firefighter to ventilate the patient once the tube placement is confirmed and the tube is secured. The third firefighter takes over compressions as the first firefighter completes five cycles of 30:2. You document the interventions performed and the patient's response to those interventions, and your partner administers the medications and any other interventions that need to be performed.

After you have administered an antiarrhythmic medication and delivered a fifth defibrillation, the patient converts into the rhythm shown in Figure 29-18.

5. Identify the ECG rhythm on the ECG strip shown in Figure 29-18.

_____

_____

_____

6. Describe the algorithm to treat this rhythm.

_____

_____

_____

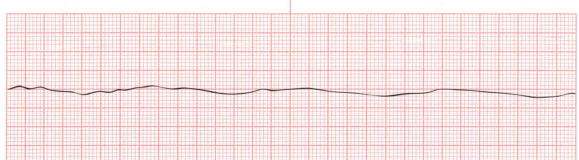

FIGURE 29-18

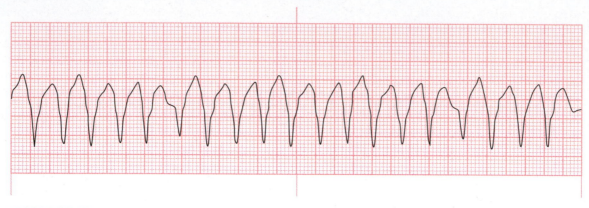

FIGURE 29-19

CPR is continued, and the treatment regimen for the preceding rhythm has been initiated. At the end of the fifth cycle of CPR, the patient presents with the rhythm shown in Figure 29-19.

7. Identify the rhythm on the ECG strip in Figure 29-19.

_____

_____

_____

8. What should your first priority be at this point?

_____

_____

_____

The patient has a palpable carotid pulse with the rhythm change but very weak brachial pulses and no apparent respiratory effort. You obtain a blood pressure of 72/44, and the carotid pulse is slower than the rate on the ECG.

9. What is the most appropriate treatment of the patient's ECG rhythm based on your reassessment of the patient?

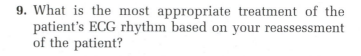

_____

_____

_____

Following your intervention, the patient presents with the ECG rhythm found in Figure 29-20.

10. Identify the rhythm on the ECG strip in Figure 29-20.

_____

_____

_____

11. What should your first treatment priority be at this point?

_____

_____

_____

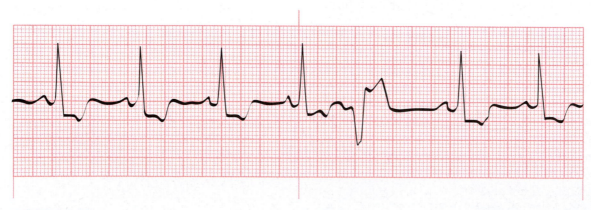

FIGURE 29-20

The patient has readily palpable pulses that correspond to the rate seen on the ECG, a blood pressure of 102/66, and a respiratory rate of 8 breaths per minute.

12. What, if any, treatment considerations should you have at this point?

_____

_____

_____

13. How should you proceed with patient care?

_____

_____

_____

Case 2

Sixty-year-old Jay Sideman has been promising his wife Sandy that he would get into shape for over 10 years. Jay is, by all accounts, a type-A workaholic, well over his target weight, and his only exercise for the past 10 years has been his weekly golf game with his friends (and they use a golf cart).

Yesterday when Jay went to work, the elevators in his office building were out of service, and he was forced to walk up five flights of stairs. After the second flight, Jay began to feel winded, and by the fourth floor he felt like he was going to pass out and needed to sit down on the stairs to catch his breath.

That night, Jay went home and told Sandy about his experience with the stairs and the fact that he was determined never to have that happen again. That weekend Jay and Sandy went to the local gym and signed up for a deluxe membership, which included one month of free assistance from a personal trainer

who would help Jay and Sandy develop personalized workouts.

After meeting, the trainer started by warning Jim that, due to his lack of physical activity for a number of years, Jim needed to take it slow and ease himself into a workout that would allow him to increase his exercise efforts over a period of time. The trainer wanted to start with an assessment of Jay's cardiovascular ability, so he led Jay over to the treadmill. The trainer explained to Jay that he wanted him to start out walking, and every 2 minutes he would increase the speed. Jay stepped onto the machine, and the trainer slowly started the machine and gradually increased the speed to level 3.

Sandy sat on a bench next to the machine and smiled as Jay jogged along on the treadmill. The trainer told Jay that he needed to let him know if he experienced shortness of breath, chest pain or discomfort, or became light-headed. Jim nodded his head in agreement and continued to jog. At 2 minutes Jay was panting and sweating, and when the trainer asked how he was doing, he gave the trainer a thumbs-up and said, "Speed it up."

The trainer did as Jay asked, and at 4 minutes Jay was panting heavily and drenched in sweat. The trainer asked him if he wanted to stop, to which Jay struggled to say, "Speed it up!" He then collapsed onto the treadmill, and rolled off of the back. Sandy screamed and quickly got up. As Jay landed on the floor, he rolled onto his back and grabbed his chest. He gasped for air and tried to sit up. Sandy and the trainer tried to help him, and as soon as they got Jay into a sitting position, the trainer ran and called 9-1-1. When the trainer returned, Jay was still gasping for air and complaining of chest pain and dizziness. Within 4 minutes three firefighters came into the gym carrying their medical equipment. Jay was propped up against a wall, still gasping for breath and complaining of chest pain.

1. Describe the similarities and differences in the presentations of patients experiencing an acute coronary syndrome (angina, unstable angina, and myocardial infarction).

_____

_____

_____

2. What are the risk factors associated with cardiovascular disease that predispose people to experience a cardiac event?

_____

_____

_____

As you arrive on the scene, you approach Jay to introduce yourself and begin your assessment while your partner approaches Sandy to obtain Jay's medical history.

You notice that Jay is short of breath. He is very pale, and he is rubbing his chest and left shoulder. You ask him how he feels as you reach for his radial pulse. Jay struggles in very short sentences to explain that he doesn't feel good. You are having trouble palpating a radial pulse. Jay tells you that he feels very dizzy, he can't breathe, he has chest pain, and he thinks he is going to vomit. Another firefighter places Jay on oxygen at 6 liters via nasal cannula.

3. Based on the information that you have obtained about Jay thus far, how would you describe his overall condition?

_____

_____

_____

4. Have you obtained enough information to complete the primary assessment on Jay (if you have, please describe your findings)?

_____

_____

_____

5. What are your primary concerns, and how will you address them?

_____

_____

_____

6. What additional information do you need in order to develop a general assessment and a treatment plan?

_____

_____

_____

As you complete your secondary examination and your partner finishes gathering Jay's medical history from Sandy, you obtain the following information: Jay is a 50-year-old male with a history of hypertension, high cholesterol, and "borderline diabetes," which he has been attempting to control through diet and "exercise." He has not taken his hypertension medication in 2 months because it interfered with his sex life (erectile dysfunction), and he is a "social smoker." His father died at a young age of a "heart attack," and his mother suffers from cardiac disease and an "enlarged heart."

Onset. Jay admits that he has had a heavy sensation in his chest since he had to climb up the stairs to his office several days ago.

Provocation. Nothing seems to make the pain better, and exertion definitely makes the pain worse.

Quality. The chest discomfort is described as "heaviness."

Region/radiation. The chest heaviness is located in the substernal area, and it radiates to his neck and left shoulder.

Severity. The chest heaviness is rated as 8 on a 0–10 scale (0 is no pain at all, and 10 is the worst pain that you have ever experienced).

Time. Jay has had the heaviness for several days, but it became unbearable while he was running on the treadmill.

Signs and symptoms. Chest pain, shortness of breath, diaphoresis, pallor, tachypnea, hypotension, and tachycardia.

Allergies. Jay denies any allergies to medications, latex, tape, etc.

Medications. HCTZ (noncompliant for 2 months) and Lipitor.

Past medical history. HTN, "borderline diabetes," smoker, overweight, high cholesterol.

Last oral intake. Jay ate a sausage omelet and bacon and drank a large coffee with cream for breakfast approximately 3 hours ago.

Events leading up to the emergency. The events that led up to the condition that Jay is experiencing started some time ago with lifestyle decisions and genetics, but the real beginning of this event started when he had to walk up five flights of stairs several days ago and was exacerbated by his session on the treadmill.

Jay presents with a patent airway and moderate to severe shortness of breath with supraclavicular retractions and abdominal muscle use with respiration. He speaks in two- to three-word sentences and has a labored regular respiratory rate of 34 breaths per minute. He displays crackles in the lower half of his bilateral lung fields, and his initial oxygen saturation (on 6 liters of oxygen by nasal cannula) is 90%. Jay has slight pedal edema and JVD with no history of recent illness or injury. There is no increase or change in the chest heaviness with palpation, inspiration, or movement. Jay has a blood pressure of 76/54, a heart rate of 120, and equal brachial pulses bilaterally that are weaker than his carotid pulses (unable to palpate radial pulses). Jay's initial 12-lead ECG is shown in Figure 29-21.

7. What are Jay's cardiovascular risk factors?

_____

_____

_____

8. How do you interpret Jay's 12-lead ECG?

_____

_____

_____

9. What are the three components necessary to make a diagnosis of myocardial infarction?

_____

_____

10. List two cardiac-related causes of JVD.

_____

_____

_____

11. With all the information that you and your partner have gathered, what is your general impression of Jay's condition?

_____

_____

_____

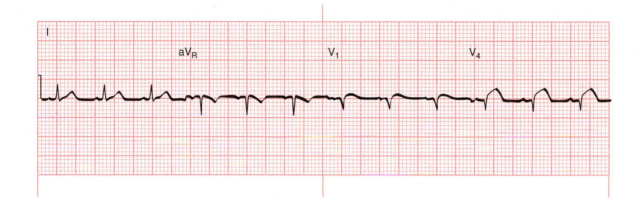

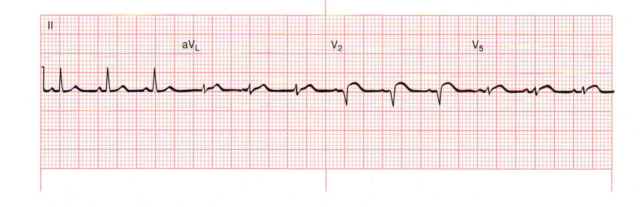

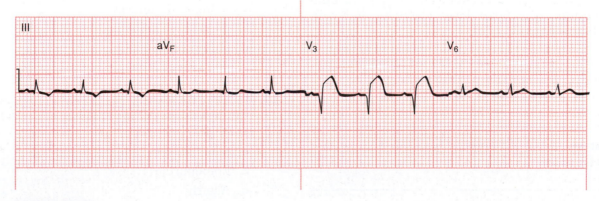

FIGURE 29-21

12. How will you begin to treat the conditions that you have discovered?

_____

_____

_____

Test Yourself

1. Which of the following types of disorders is *least* likely to present with chest pain?
   a. Musculoskeletal
   b. Reproductive
   c. Psychological
   d. Gastrointestinal

2. What is the difference between cardioversion and defibrillation?

3. Which of the following conditions is most likely to lead to other cardiovascular diseases?
   a. Acute myocardial infarction
   b. Pulmonary edema
   c. Cardiac tamponade
   d. Chronic dysrhythmia

4. Compare the use of nitroprusside to nitroglycerin for treating a patient with a hypertensive emergency.

5. A(n) _____ occurs when the pericardium surrounding the heart loses elasticity and constricts the heart.

6. In order to maximize tissue oxygenation, you should hyperventilate patients during CPR.
   True
   False

7. What are some differences between venous and arterial ulcers?

8. When treating a patient with chest pain, you must first try to rule out which three conditions?

9. All the following patients are in cardiopulmonary arrest and are not responding to resuscitation efforts. According to the National Association of EMS Physicians, you should consider stopping resuscitation efforts for which patient?
   a. A 36-year-old man with multiple stab wounds to the abdomen and chest whose pupils react to light
   b. A 54-year-old man who was in a head-on collision and who is 20 minutes away from the nearest hospital
   c. A 14-year-old girl who was rescued 25 minutes after friends saw her fall into a cold lake
   d. A 23-year-old woman who fell from a third-story window and whose ECG readings show electrical activity

10. What are some indications that a patient has a ruptured abdominal aortic aneurysm?

11. How does the administration of diuretics benefit a patient with congestive heart failure?

12. While you are treating a patient for left ventricle heart failure, she develops shortness of breath and a "frothy" cough. You auscultate the lungs and hear a crackling sound. This patient has most likely developed
   a. pulmonary fibrosis.
   b. pulmonary embolism.
   c. pulmonary edema.
   d. pulmonary arrest.

13. Which of these drugs is often used to treat a patient who has no pulse but still has electrical readings on an ECG?
   a. Beta-blockers
   b. Epinephrine
   c. Aspirin
   d. Morphine

14. A patient has suffered a myocardial infarction and has gone into cardiogenic shock. Which of the following are you *least* likely to administer?

   a. Epinephrine

   b. Oxygen

   c. Heparin

   d. Aspirin

15. If a patient has no signs or symptoms of shock 4 hours after an AMI, the patient is unlikely to develop cardiogenic shock.

   True

   False

16. What are some general risk factors for cardiovascular disease?

   _____

   _____

17. Which of the following steps should you *not* perform when managing a patient with acute arterial occlusion?

   a. Administer morphine.

   b. Administer dopamine.

   c. Remove compressive stockings.

   d. Keep the affected limb below heart level.

Scenario: You enter the home of a patient complaining of "feeling ill." The 65-year-old man is sitting upright in a chair with pale skin and closed eyes. As you approach, he opens his eyes and says that "breathing is getting harder and harder." His pulse is rapid and irregular; his skin is clammy and cool. He has a BP of 154/92, irregular HR of 120, and shallow RR of 24. The monitor reveals atrial fibrillation with a rapid ventricular response at a rate of 120. Your patient has no allergies, does not take his prescribed medications, but did take his daily aspirin approximately 15 minutes ago. His ankles have pitting edema, and his lung sounds reveal faint crackles throughout.

18. This patient is suffering from

   a. congestive heart failure.

   b. chronic obstructive pulmonary disease.

   c. pulmonary embolism.

   d. mitral valve prolapse.

19. In addition to 12-lead ECG and continuous cardiac and vital sign monitoring, your actions should include:

   a. administration of oxygen 15 L/min via nonrebreather face mask, establishment of central IV,

administration of nitroprusside 5 mcg/kg/min, synchronized cardioversion at 100 J, and transportation in Fowler's or semi-Fowler's position.

   b. administration of oxygen at 2 L/min via nasal cannula, administration of nitroglycerin 1 tablet sublingual, administration of albuterol 2.5 mg via nebulizer, ventilation assistance as necessary with bag-mask to improve rate, and transportation while supine.

   c. asking the patient to walk to the ambulance, administration of oxygen at 2 L/min via nasal cannula, transportation in Trendelenburg position, nitroglycerin spray 0.4 mcg up to 5 times administered 3 minutes apart, and preparation for thrombolytic therapy.

   d. administration of oxygen at 15 L/min via nonrebreather face mask, establishment of a peripheral IV line, administration of nitroglycerin 1 tablet sublingual, administration of furosemide 40 mg IV, administration of morphine 4 mg IV, and transport in a position of comfort with head elevated and legs dependent.

20. His wife tells you he has not been sleeping well lately. He frequently awakens gasping for air, sweating profusely, and wheezing. This is a condition known as _____.

Scenario: Your crew has just finished lunch at a local diner when the waitress asks you to help one of the cooks. He is in his mid-fifties, obese, and very pale. He is standing at the counter with one hand on his chest. He tells you that the pressure in his chest has "come and gone" over the past 2 or 3 days and worsens when the restaurant is full. He has no prior history and has not seen a physician for several years. You help him sit and assess his vital signs: BP of 158/90, HR of 100, RR of 20, and oxygen saturation of 94%. You administer oxygen, attach the monitor and obtain a 12-lead ECG that appears normal, and establish an IV. He tells you that his chest pain seems to be easing. He asks to go back to work, as the diner is too busy to be without a second cook.

21. At this point, the best course of action is to

   a. reassess his vital signs, ask about the onset of this episode and previous occurrences of this pain, and obtain a full SAMPLE history and OPQRST assessment of this event.

   b. ask the patient to sign a refusal of treatment form, and advise him to make an appointment with his regular physician as soon as possible.

   c. contact medical control, advise them of the patient's situation, and ask the physician for clearance to not transport.

   d. wait for the chest pain to abate, and then reassess vital signs. If he appears stable, remove the IV and advise him to seek medical attention within the next day or so.

22. The patient's pain returns as he attempts to stand up. You repeat the ECG and note ST segment depression and a rare PVC as he becomes diaphoretic. He agrees to go to the hospital. Your treatment of this patient should include

   a. repeat vital signs every 15 minutes en route; administer oxygen at 15 L by non-rebreather mask, aspirin, nitroprusside, and morphine while transporting without lights and sirens to the closest appropriate facility.

   b. repeat vital signs every 15 minutes en route; administer oxygen at 15 L by non-rebreather mask, aspirin, nitroprusside, and morphine while transporting with lights and sirens to the closest appropriate facility.

   c. reassess vital signs every 5 minutes en route; repeat ECG as patient's condition changes; administer aspirin, nitroglycerin, and morphine; and transport quickly and safely to the closest appropriate facility.

   d. repeat vital signs every 5 minutes en route; repeat ECG as patients condition changes; administer albuterol, nitroglycerin, and morphine; and transport without lights and siren to the closest appropriate facility.

23. As you are completing the history and pain assessment, which of these statements should concern you the most?

   a. "I had a heart murmur when I was a baby."

   b. "My dad had a heart attack when he was my age."

   c. "The pain feels like someone is squeezing my chest."

   d. "I sometimes have heartburn, but it goes away if I take an antacid."

Scenario: A 62-year-old woman was camping in a wilderness area when she began experiencing chest pain. Upon arrival, your patient is alert and oriented.

She tells you the pain began an hour ago and has been moderate but persistent. Her vital signs are BP of 140/90, HR of 96, and RR of 24. The ECG shows a regular rhythm with ST elevation. The patient has a history of hypertension. There is a small hospital 20 minutes away by ambulance, but it does not have a catheterization lab. A large regional medical center is 2 hours away by ambulance.

24. Where should you transport this patient?

   _____

   _____

25. What type of treatment(s) should you consider administering during transport?

   _____

   _____

Need to Know

The following represent the Key Objectives of Chapter 29, Section II:

   1. *Understand basic pathophysiological processes associated with cardiovascular disease.*

   a. *Myocardial ischemia.* Also called acute coronary syndrome (ACS), ischemia comes in several different forms, based on varying degrees of coronary artery occlusion. The cause of myocardial ischemia is typically a ruptured or eroded atherosclerotic plaque in one or more of the coronary arteries.

   Some of the different forms of myocardial ischemia include:

   • *Stable angina.* Tends to be brought on by exertion (activity) and can be caused by a partial blockage of a coronary vessel or by spasm of a coronary vessel. Symptoms are typically relieved by rest and/or the administration of nitroglycerin.

   • *Unstable angina.* Tends to be caused by a partially occluding thrombus that produces signs and symptoms that are new, occur at rest, are prolonged, or are different from previous presentations (i.e., are more severe than previous episodes, take less exertion to provoke, are experienced in a different location, etc.).

   • *Myocardial infarction.* There are two forms of MI: a non-ST-segment elevation MI (NSTEMI), and an ST-segment elevation MI (STEMI). Myocardial infarction is associated with chest pain lasting longer than several minutes and unrelieved by rest, oxygen, or nitroglycerin. If a thrombus occludes a coronary blood vessel, a STEMI is likely to result. Figure 29-22 shows key ECG changes associated with ischemia, injury, and infarction.

Acute coronary syndrome is the most common cause of sudden cardiac death.

b. *Aneurysm.* An aneurysm is a focal dilation or expansion of an artery (1.5 times) compared with an adjacent arterial segment (Figure 29-23). Aortic aneurysms can occur at any location along the aorta, but they are generally classified as thoracic or abdominal aneurysms. Risk factors for aortic aneurysms include: age, gender, cigarette smoking, atherosclerosis, hypertension, and family history.

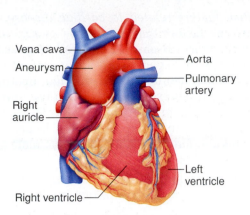

FIGURE 29-23   Heart in Marfan syndrome, showing aortic aneurysm.

c. *Hypertension.* See Chapter 8, Physiology Overview, in the textbook for a complete discussion of hypertension.

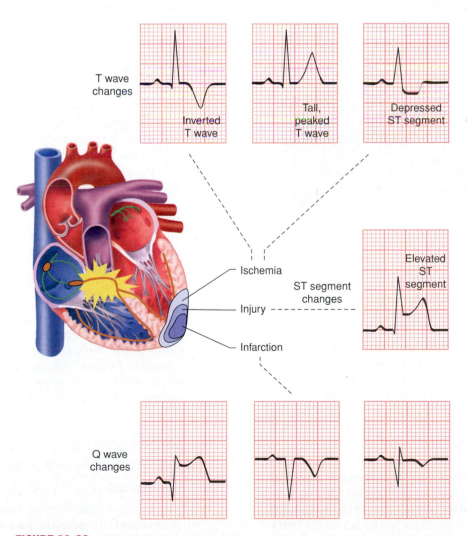

FIGURE 29-22   Key ECG changes associated with ischemia, injury, and infarction.

d. *Risk factors related to cardiac disease.* These are the factors that predispose people to coronary artery disease (CAD) and increase their chances of experiencing some sort of cardiac event (ischemia, injury, sudden death). Box 29-15 in the textbook provides a list of risk factors known to contribute to CAD, including: abnormal cholesterol levels, hypertension, smoking, family history, diabetes, male gender, renal disease, and obesity.

2. *Describe a general assessment approach to a patient experiencing a cardiovascular emergency.*

It is beneficial for paramedics to develop a standard approach to efficiently and effectively assess and treat patients experiencing cardiovascular emergencies. The following is an approach to a *standard cardiac assessment* that can be adopted to manage these patients:

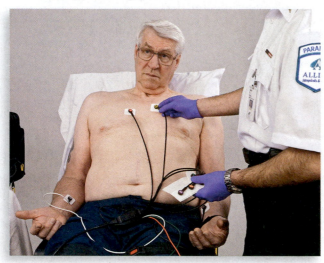

a. Primary Assessment (ABCDE)
   - General impression of patient's condition.
   - Airway—Is the airway open and patent?
   - Breathing—Is the patient breathing? Assess not only the presence or absence of breathing, but in the breathing patient assess rate, depth, and quality of breathing.
   - Circulation—Assess the perfusion status of the patient. This is not limited to checking for the presence of a pulse; also assess its rate and quality and any skin signs.
   - Disability—Assess the patient's mental status (i.e., GCS, AVPU, and the ability to respond or follow simple commands).
   - Exposure—Expose the patient in such a manner that a complete and accurate physical examination can be performed. When the exam is complete, make sure that the patient is covered back up in order to maintain body temperature and dignity.

b. Secondary Assessment

History. To obtain a complete history on your patient, ask every cardiac patient the same questions. The use of mnemonics such as OPQRST and/or SAMPLE help organize history taking and allow for a more complete, well-structured history.

Features of chest pain. Table 29-1 in the textbook outlines the causes and typical features of chest pain, including:
   - Cardiac—angina, unstable angina, myocardial infarction, and pericarditis
   - Vascular—aortic dissection and pulmonary embolus
   - Pulmonary—pneumonia and pneumothorax
   - Gastrointestinal—esophageal reflux, esophageal spasm, peptic ulcer disease (PUD), gall bladder disease, and pancreatitis
   - Musculoskeletal—costochondritis
   - Psychological—panic disorder or anxiety
   - Infectious—herpes zoster (shingles)

General health status. Inquire about any recent illness and/or injury and any preexisting medical conditions. Has the patient been healthy until the onset of this condition, or is he or she frequently ill? Family history? Tobacco use? Exercise regimen?

Current event related to past events. Has the patient ever experienced a similar episode? If so, has the patient ever been seen for the condition by a physician? If so, what was the problem and how was the patient treated for the problem? A correlation between events experienced in the past and present events can be a valuable tool in helping to determine the course of treatment for a patient.

3- or 4-lead ECG. This is the standard of care for monitoring a patient for rhythm, rate, and regularity. A 12-lead ECG is but one tool in a series of tests that help determine the underlying cause of cardiac-related conditions. Other useful tools include a pulse oximeter to measure oxygen saturation, end-tidal CO_2 monitoring, bilateral peripheral pulse check, comparison between central and peripheral pulses, accurate and regular monitoring of vital signs (BP, pulse, respiration rate, temperature, ECG), and serial cardiac enzymes.

Physical Examination Findings
   - Auscultation

      Lung sounds—equal bilaterally, any adventitious sounds (crackles, wheezing, rhonchi, etc.)

Heart sounds—Prehospital auscultation of heart sounds is not a common practice, but if you do auscultate heart sounds in the field, make sure that you listen to all your patients' heart sounds so that you have a very good idea of what a healthy heart sounds like ($S_1:S_2$) and can differentiate them from abnormal heart sounds (S_3, clicks and murmurs).

- Pedal edema—could also be edema of any dependent body part (e.g., sacral edema on a person confined to bed); can be an indication of right-sided heart failure (Figure 29-24).

- Jugular venous distention—can be an indication of right-sided heart failure (Figure 29-25).

- Equal peripheral pulses—Compare equality of radial, brachial, posterior tibial, and dorsalis pedis pulses (especially in a patient suspected of having an aortic aneurysm).

- Compare pulses—Compare central to peripheral pulses (e.g., carotid pulses to radial or brachial pulses) to get an idea if peripheral vasoconstriction is taking place.

  Pulsus paradoxus refers to a 10 mm Hg or greater drop in the systolic blood pressure that occurs during inspiration. It is classically noted in cardiac tamponade, constrictive pericarditis, and restrictive cardiomyopathy.

  Pulsus alternans describes a pulse intensity that alternates between weak

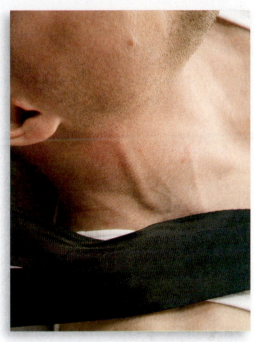

FIGURE 29-25   Jugular venous distention.

and strong. The changing intensity of the pulse indicates that the ventricle is alternating between stronger and weaker contraction forces. These pulses generally differ by at least 20 mm Hg and signify severely depressed cardiac function.

- Palpation—Does pain or discomfort increase or decrease with palpation (inspiration or movement may reproduce or alleviate pain as well)?

- Pallor—can be a result of the peripheral blood supply being shunted to the central circulation (lack of blood flow to the capillary beds results in pallor) or poor oxygen status.

- Diaphoresis—In the presence of cardiac ischemia, the sympathetic nervous system can produce diaphoresis.

- Nausea and vomiting—can be due to reflex stimulation of vomiting centers by pain fibers or vagus nerve reflexes from the area of the ischemic myocardium; can impact the GI tract.

- ST segment elevation in contiguous leads—The absence of findings such as ST elevation, ST depression, and reciprocal changes does not rule out a possible cardiac event, but the presence of these findings is strongly suggestive of one.

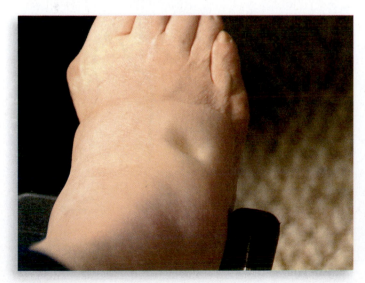

FIGURE 29-24   Example of pedal edema.

3. *Describe the management of acute coronary syndrome (ACS).*

The initial treatment for a patient experiencing signs and symptoms of ACS includes oxygen, aspirin, nitroglycerin, and morphine sulfate. The common way to remember these medications is MONA:

- Morphine Sulfate—2–4 mg IV slow every 5–30 minutes (treatment per local protocol)
- Oxygen—supplemental amounts if the patient is dyspneic, hypoxic, or in heart failure
- Nitroglycerin—0.3–0.4 mg sublingual repeated for a total of 3 doses at 5-minute intervals (treatment per local protocol)
- Aspirin—160–325 mg by mouth (PO)

Additional prehospital treatment for patients experiencing ischemic chest pain includes beta-blockers, heparin or other anticoagulants, ACE inhibitors, and tissue plasminogen activator (tPA).

Percutaneous coronary intervention (PCI) is the preferred method for treating patients with coronary vessel occlusion if performed in a timely manner. An important advantage of primary PCI is that it restores normal cardiac blood flow in more than 90% of cases[1,2] compared with only 50%–60% with fibrinolysis.[3–5]

Determine if the patient is a fibrinolytic candidate. Fibrinolytic medications improve outcomes in MI compared to no intervention at all, but they have associated complications and therefore multiple contraindications. A generally accepted way to approach the MI patient who may be a candidate for fibrinolysis is the following:

- Has the patient experienced chest pain for greater than 15 minutes and less than 12 hours?
- If the answer to the preceding question is "yes," and if any of the questions listed in Box 29-21 in the textbook are answered "yes," thrombolytics are probably contraindicated.
- Does the patient have cardiogenic shock or severe heart failure, making PCI preferable? These are typically clinically evident based on evaluation, including absence of hypotension, cold and clammy extremities, and lung crackles or pulmonary edema.[6, 7]
- Boxes 29-20 and 29-21 in the textbook comprise a typical fibrinolytic checklist that includes inclusion and exclusion criteria.

Classic presentations are typically sudden onset with retrosternal pain (pressure, tightness, constriction, burning, or a squeezing, bandlike sensation of compression around the chest) and radiation to the left shoulder or arm or the neck, dyspnea, diaphoresis, nausea and vomiting, and a sense of impending doom. Atypical presentations are more common in the elderly, women, and diabetic individuals.

ST segment changes may indicate the location of the event.

- Changes in one or more of the precordial leads (V_1 to V_6) and in leads I and aVL are consistent with acute transmural anterior wall ischemia, often with lateral extension (Figure 29-26).
- Changes in leads V_1 to V_3 are consistent with anteroseptal ischemia (Figure 29-27).
- Changes in leads I, aVL, V_5, and V_6 are consistent with lateral ischemia (Figure 29-28).
- Changes in leads II, III, and aVF are consistent with inferior wall ischemia (Figure 29-29).

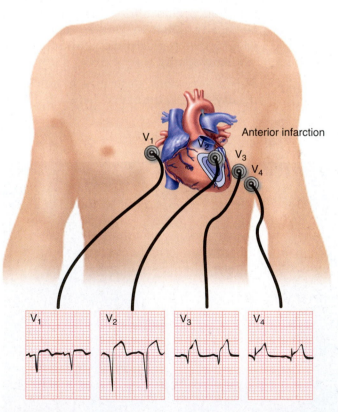

FIGURE 29-26 Leads V_1 to V_4 are used to identify anterior myocardial infarction.

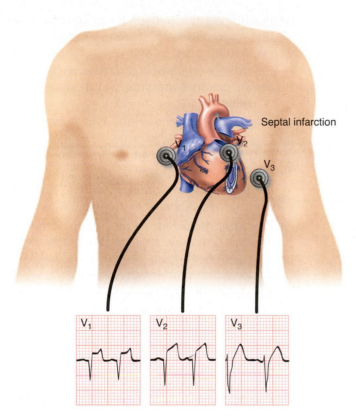

FIGURE 29-27 Leads V₁ to V₃ are used to identify septal myocardial infarction.

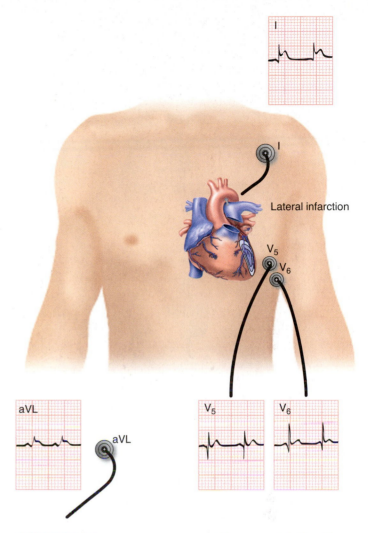

FIGURE 29-28 Leads I, aV_L, V₅, and V₆ are used to identify lateral myocardial infarction.

Figure 29-30 shows the leads and corresponding areas of the heart that are viewed by each of the different leads.

It is important to identify STEMI patients for destination criteria. Patients presenting with ST segment changes in the prehospital setting are better served if they are transported to a cardiac center (a hospital equipped to manage ACS patients with state-of-the-art care) for treatment with PCI. Diagnosis of myocardial infarction is based on:

- History
- ECG (ST segment changes in contiguous leads)
- Cardiac enzyme (troponin, CK, CK-MB, etc.)

Patients suspected of an AMI in the prehospital setting should be treated based upon the history and physical exam regardless of the findings of the ECG or the availability of enzyme tests.

4. *Describe the managment of acute heart failure.*

Acute heart failure results when cardiac output is insufficient to meet the body's metabolic demands.

Right-sided heart failure: The most common cause of right-sided heart failure is left-sided heart failure. The result of right-sided heart failure is the backup of blood into the systemic circulation, which frequently results in peripheral edema and jugular vein distention (JVD).

Left-sided heart failure: Left-sided heart failure is caused by an ineffective left ventricle and/or increased peripheral vascular resistance. It causes a backup of blood into the lungs, which leads to pulmonary edema and respiratory complications associated with poor alveolar-capillary gas exchange. It is frequently associated with paroxysmal nocturnal dyspnea, which causes the patient to wake up in the middle of the night with difficulty breathing and the need to sit up (caused by fluid building up in the lungs). If the patient has had the condition for some time,

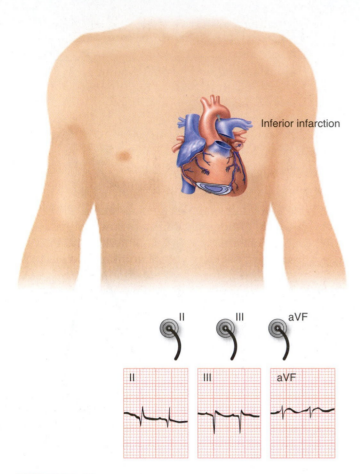

Inferior infarction

II   III   aVF

II   III   aVF

FIGURE 29-29   Leads II, III, and aVF are used to identify inferior myocardial infarction.

he or she may opt to sleep propped up on several pillows in order to avoid having shortness of breath at night (orthopnea).

The most significant finding in acute heart failure is pulmonary edema. The treatment of acute pulmonary edema in the prehospital setting involves:

Lead I Lateral Wall	Lead aVR Quality Control	Lead V$_1$ Septal Wall	Lead V$_4$ Anterior Wall
Lead II Inferior Wall	Lead aVL Lateral Wall	Lead V$_2$ Septal Wall	Lead V$_5$ High Lateral Wall
Lead III Inferior Wall	Lead aVF Inferior Wall	Lead V$_3$ Anterior Wall	Lead V$_6$ High Lateral Wall

FIGURE 29-30   Leads and the corresponding areas of the heart that are viewed by each of the different leads. Leads I, aVL, V$_5$, and V$_6$ (shown in green) look at the lateral wall; leads II, III and aVF (red) look at the inferior wall; leads V$_1$ and V$_2$ (blue) look at the septal wall; and leads V$_3$ and V$_4$ (yellow) look at the anterior wall.

- Positioning the patient in an upright position to decrease venous return to the already overloaded heart
- Providing supplemental oxygen with noninvasive positive pressure ventilation (CPAP) if needed
- Providing intravenous diuretics if available
- Providing nitrates to reduce venous return to the heart by way of vasodilation
- Occasionally giving inotropic agents (such as dopamine or dobutamine) in cases of cardiogenic shock with hypotension
- Providing intravenous morphine sulfate to decrease venous return, dilate the coronary blood supply, decrease anxiety, and decrease the work of breathing

Ultimately, the underlying cause of the acute increase in intracardiac pressures that lead to acute pulmonary edema will need to be addressed.[8,9]

5. *Describe the management of cardiogenic shock.*

Cardiogenic shock is inadequate tissue perfusion as a result of cardiac dysfunction. It typically occurs within the first 24 hours following an AMI. Cardiogenic shock is accompanied by pulmonary edema more than 67% of the time.

- *Do not* treat pulmonary edema in the cardiogenic shock patient without addressing the cardiogenic shock condition first.
- Treatment for cardiogenic shock includes fluid resuscitation, vasopressor support, and airway management.

6. *Describe the management of pericardial tamponade.*

Pericardial tamponade occurs when the heart is restricted by accumulation of fluid in the pericardial sac. Medical causes of tamponade include infections and inflammation, HIV, cancer, and bleeding. Classic assessment findings for pericardial tamponade are called Beck's triad and include:

- JVD—caused by increased venous pressure from the right side of the heart
- Hypotension—caused by decreased cardiac output
- Muffled heart sounds—a result of the excess fluid in the pericardial sac

Pulsus paradoxus (a cyclic decrease in systolic blood pressure during inspiration) and pulsus alternans (an alternating peripheral pulse amplitude) can also be seen in a patient with cardiac tamponade.

The only treatment for pericardial tamponade is drainage of the excess fluid in the pericardial sac. The emergent procedure for removal of fluid from the pericardial sac is pericardiocentesis.

7. *Describe the management of a hypertensive emergency.*

A hypertensive emergency is an acute, marked elevation in blood pressure that results in damage to vital organs. A hypertensive emergency can occur in people with long-standing or uncontrolled hypertension, patients who have abruptly stopped taking their antihypertensive medications, patients suffering from renal artery stenosis, and pregnant patients with preeclampsia. Uncontrolled hypertension can cause endothelial damage to blood vessels with eventual occlusion, cerebral edema, and clinical signs of hypertensive encephalopathy.

- The goal of treatment is to reduce the diastolic blood pressure to approximately 100 mm Hg over the first 2–6 hours. Do not drop the patient's pressure quickly!
- Nitroprusside is a very effective medication for treating hypertensive emergencies. It dilates both arterioles and veins with a rapid onset and a short half-life (2–5 minutes). The significant drawback to nitroprusside is that it metabolizes to cyanide.
- Nitroglycerin (NTG) tends to dilate veins more than arteries and causes headache and reflex tachycardia, but it doesn't metabolize to cyanide. NTG is particularly useful when treating a hypertensive emergency in a patient presenting with cardiac ischemia. The onset of action is within 2–5 minutes and lasts for 5–10 minutes.
- Labetalol is an alpha- and beta-blocker that has an onset within 5 minutes. It reduces peripheral vascular resistance.

8. *Describe the management of arterial emergencies.*

Arterial emergencies include embolism, thrombosis, and aneurysm.

Aneurysm. An aneurysm is a focal dilation or expansion of an artery (1.5 times) compared with an adjacent arterial segment. Aortic aneurysms can occur at any location along the aorta, but they are generally classified as thoracic or abdominal aneurysms. Risk factors for aortic aneurysms include: age, gender, cigarette smoking, atherosclerosis, hypertension, and family history.

Dissection. The initial event for an aortic dissection is a tear in the intimal layer. This tear allows pulsatile blood to contact the media,

separating the intima from the media and/or adventitia. This causes a false lumen within the wall of the aorta, which can spread both proximally and distally, causing a variety of symptoms (sharp or tearing pain—chest pain is more common with a dissection of the ascending aorta, and back pain is more common with dissection of the descending aorta). Other signs and symptoms of dissection include:

- Pulse and blood pressure deficits
- Tearing back or chest pain
- Syncope
- Numbness and tingling in distal extremities
- Dyspnea
- Hypertension or hypotension
- Tachycardia
- Shock
- Dizziness

Treatment of an aortic dissection in the field includes:

- Rapid transport to a hospital capable of treating a patient with an aortic dissection.
- Lowering the blood pressure
- Supportive care
- Treating sequelae of the dissection (MI, CHF, CVA, etc.). *Avoid the use of heparin.*

Peripheral arterial disease (PAD). The cause of PAD is atherosclerosis obstructing the blood flow to the extremities. The major complications of this process are thrombosis and limb ischemia.

The signs and symptoms of limb ischemia include the following "P"s:

pain, pallor, paresthesias, and paralysis.

The management for acute arterial occlusion as the result of PAD includes:

- Administer analgesics.
- Position the affected extremity below the level of the heart.
- Remove restrictive clothing, socks, etc.
- Ensure rapid transport to a hospital capable of managing such an emergency.

Deep vein thrombosis. With this condition there is a risk of the thrombus breaking loose and having the clot produce a pulmonary embolism. Risk factors for pulmonary embolism include:

- Prolonged immobility (lengthy periods of being bedridden, long airline flights, etc.)
- Recent surgery

- Obesity
- History of venous thromboembolism
- Lower extremity trauma
- Malignancy
- Use of oral contraceptives or hormone replacement therapy, particularly in smokers
- Pregnancy or postpartum status
- CVA

Classic DVT symptoms include swelling, redness, and pain in the affected limb. The initial DVT management includes:

- Immobilizing the affected limb
- Administering oxygen
- Establishing IV access
- Rapid transport to a hospital capable of managing such a condition

Definitive treatment of DVT includes prompt anticoagulation to prevent extension of the clot and embolization to the lungs.[10]

9. *Describe the management of a cardiac arrest.*

Approach all cardiac arrests in a similar manner. The assessment should start with scene safety and BSI, and then a quick assessment of the patient's level of responsiveness, airway, breathing, and circulation should be performed. A team approach tends to yield the best results as long as there is one team leader who is responsible for coordinating resuscitation efforts. Management of all cardiac arrests emphasizes solid basic life support with effective and efficient CPR. The CPR should follow the current AHA guidelines, including 2 minutes of CPR prior to defibrillation for unwitnessed cardiac arrests. Compressions are performed at a ratio of 30:2 with full recoil of the chest wall and infrequent interruptions for pulse and rhythm checks. IV or IO access should be established with minimal interruption to CPR. Be mindful of advanced directives such as Do Not Resuscitate orders, and follow your local policies and protocols for discontinuation of resuscitation efforts if such an endpoint is reached.

Need to Do

The following skills are explained and illustrated in a step-by-step manner, via skill sheets and/or Step-by-Steps in this text and on the accompanying DVD:

Skill Name	Skill Sheet Number and Location	Step-by-Step Number and Location
Chest Auscultation	27 – Appendix A and DVD	27 – Chapter 11 and DVD
Chest Pain Assessment	34 – DVD	N/A
ECG Acquisition	37 – Appendix A and DVD	37 – Section I of this chapter and DVD
Synchronized Cardioversion and Defibrillation	38 – Appendix A and DVD	38 – This chapter and DVD
Transcutaneous Cardiac Pacing	39 – Appendix A and DVD	39 – This chapter and DVD
Vagal Maneuvers	40 – DVD	N/A
Sublingual Drug Administration	54 – DVD	N/A
NREMT Dynamic Cardiology	86 – DVD	N/A
NREMT Static Cardiology	87 – DVD	N/A

Synchronized Cardioversion and Defibrillation

Conditions: The candidate should perform this skill on a simulated patient under existing indoor, ambulance, or outdoor lighting, temperature, and weather conditions.

Indications: Defibrillation: ventricular fibrillation, pulseless ventricular tachycardia; when synchronization circuit is not working. Synchronized cardioversion: unstable supraventricular tachycardia (SVT), unstable ventricular tachycardia (VT), stable SVT or VT refractory to pharmacologic interventions.

Red Flags: Do not delay CPR for any interval of time when defibrillating. Sedate alert patients if possible prior to cardioversion. *Electrical therapy is dangerous and can harm rescuers if they are in contact with the patient during delivery of electrical charge.*

Steps:

1. Don appropriate standard precautions.

2. Place patient in safe environment, avoiding water and other conductive materials.

3. If possible, explain procedure to patient.

4. If using pads, choose appropriate size and check expiration date.

5. Attach pads to monitor. *Or*, apply gel to paddles and attach to monitor.

6. Ensure skin is intact, and shave hair if necessary.

7. Cleanse area with alcohol if necessary. Alcohol must dry prior to placing electrodes.

8. Place pads/paddles in either the sternum-apex (Figure SBS 38-1) or anterior-posterior (Figure SBS 38-2) position. Apply firmly and completely.

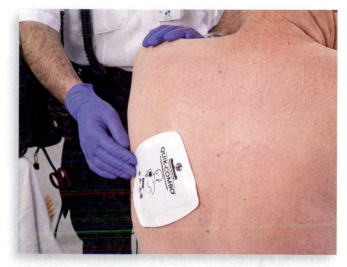

SBS 38-2

9. If appropriate, sedate patient prior to electrical therapy.

10. Check rhythm, and confirm need for electrical therapy.

11. Set to desired energy level (Figure SBS 38-3).

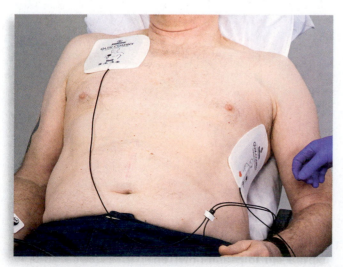

SBS 38-1

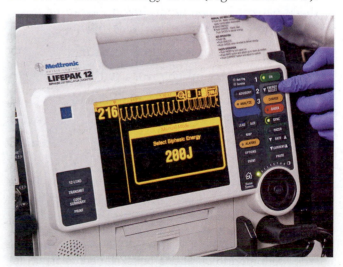

SBS 38-3

12. For synchronized cardioversion, ensure "sync" is on between each shock.

13. Charge defibrillator.

14. Ensure no one is touching patient prior to shock. Say, "One, I'm clear. Two, you're clear. Three, shocking."

15. Deliver shock.

16. Reassess patient and rhythm.

17. Continue treatment according to current cardiac guidelines.

Critical Criteria:
- Use appropriate standard precautions.
- Apply gel to paddles.
- Ensure good contact between pads/paddles and patient.
- Clear patient contact before delivering electrical charge.
- Assess patient and ECG rhythm before and after therapy.

Step-by-Step 39

Transcutaneous Cardiac Pacing

Conditions: The candidate should perform this skill on a simulated patient under existing indoor, ambulance, or outdoor lighting, temperature, and weather conditions.

Indications: Patient experiencing symptomatic bradycardia secondary to high-grade block; symptomatic bradycardia refractory to atropine.

Red Flags: Significant patient discomfort; consider sedation if IV access available. Ensure good contact between pads and patient to minimize energy levels needed for capture.

Steps:

1. Don appropriate standard precautions.

2. Place patient in safe environment, avoiding water and other conductive materials.

3. If possible, explain procedure to patient.

4. Place limb leads and confirm need for pacing.

5. Select appropriate size pads and check expiration date.

6. Attach pad leads to monitor.

7. Ensure skin is intact, and shave hair as necessary.

8. Cleanse area with alcohol if necessary. Alcohol must dry prior to placing pads.

9. Place pads in either the sternum-apex or anterior-posterior position. Apply firmly and completely (Figure SBS 39-1).

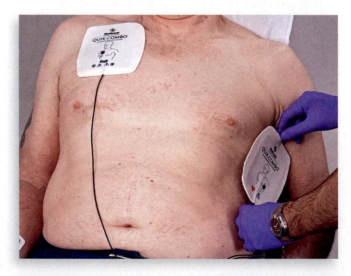

SBS 39-1

10. If appropriate, sedate patient prior to pacing.

11. Reconfirm rhythm and patient symptomatology.

12. Set desired rate (typically around 80 pulses per minute) (Figure SBS 39-2).

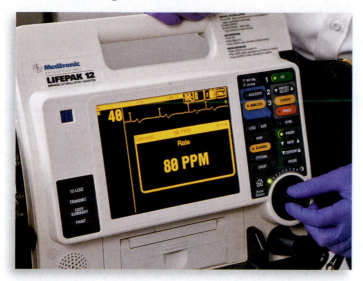

SBS 39-2

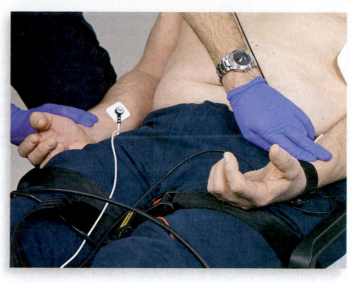

SBS 39-3

13. Increase current until you see electrical capture.

14. Look for QRS and T waves following every pacer spike.

15. Set current 10% above point of capture.

16. Confirm mechanical capture (pulse matches rhythm) (Figure SBS 39-3).

17. If mechanical capture is not obtained, consider alternate therapies.

18. Continuously monitor patient.

Critical Criteria:

- Use appropriate standard precautions.
- Place pads correctly.
- Ensure good contact between pads and patient.
- Always check for mechanical capture.

Connections

- The American Heart Association's *Handbook of Emergency Cardiovascular Care* (2010 CPR and ECC Guidelines) presents national standards regarding cardiovascular care.[11]
- Chapter 7, Anatomy Overview, in the textbook discusses the structure and function of the heart.
- Chapter 8, Physiology Overview, in the textbook explains how the heart works (from its most basic cells to its electrical system).
- Chapter 13, Shock Overview, in the textbook describes cardiogenic shock.
- Chapter 28, Pulmonary, in the textbook explains the relationship between the respiratory and the cardiovascular systems.
- Chapter 34, Gastroenterology, in the textbook identifies abdominal complaints that may have a cardiac origin.
- Chapter 44, Geriatric Patients, in the textbook describes the effects that aging has on the cardiovascular system.

- Link to the companion DVD for a chapter-based quiz, audio glossary, animations, games and exercises, and, when appropriate, skill sheets and skill Step-by-Steps.

Street Secrets

- **Inferior Wall Ischemia** ST segment ECG changes in leads II, III, and aVF are indicative of ischemia in the inferior wall of the heart. When there is ischemia in this area, there is a possibility of ischemia in the right ventricle, so whenever ST segment elevation is noted in leads II, III, or aVF, it is important to evaluate the right ventricle for ischemia. To evaluate the right ventricle, move V_4 from the fifth intercostal space at the left midclavicular line to the same position on the right side of the chest (V_{4R}) to check for right ventricular infarct. Lead V_{4R} is approximately 90% specific and 90% sensitive for determining the presence of right ventricle ischemia. Therefore, as a minimum, V_{4R} needs to be evaluated, and if possible, V_{3R} to V_{6R} should be evaluated (V_{3R} to V_{6R} are evaluated by moving the precordial leads V_3 to V_6 to the same location on the right side of the chest). Right ventricular infarction can be associated with hypotension, supranodal and atrioventricular blocks, atrial fibrillation, atrial flutter, and premature atrial contractions (PACs). It is extremely important to evaluate for right ventricular infarction because standard treatment for ischemic chest pain (e.g., MONA) can cause a worsening of the patient's condition (e.g., severe hypotension).

The Drug Box

Adenosine: A Vaughn-Williams Class IV antidysrhythmic that slows AV node conduction speed. Used to terminate SVT and monomorphic, regular wide-complex tachycardia in the stable patient.

Amiodarone: A Vaughn-Williams Class III antidysrhythmic used to terminate a wide variety of rhythm disturbances, including ventricular fibrillation (VF), ventricular tachycardia (VT), supraventricular tachycardia (SVT), and atrial fibrillation (A-Fib).

Aspirin: A prostaglandin inhibitor administered to patients at high risk for myocardial infarction (MI)

Atropine: Parasympathetic blocker used to increase vagal-mediated, symptomatic bradycardia. May be less effective in second-degree type II, or third-degree heart blocks.

Beta adrenergic blockers: Used in the MI and angina patient to control heart rate and blood pressure so that myocardial oxygen demands will not increase.

Beta blockers: Class of drugs used to control SVT and other narrow-complex tachycardias by blocking the effects of epinephrine on both beta-1 and -2 receptor sites.

Diltiazem: A calcium channel blocker used to control atrial fibrillation or atrial flutter in the stable patient.

Dopamine: Dosage-dependent positive inotropic agent used to support blood pressure in patients with perfusing rhythms. A mid-range dose of 2–10 mcg/kg/min will produce a predominantly beta effect; a high-range dose of 10-20 mcg/kg/min will cause predominantly alpha effects.

Epinephrine: An adrenergic agonist with both beta and alpha properties. Used as a repeating bolus during cardiac arrest to constrict peripheral vasculature and coarsen fibrillatory waves. May be used as a drip infusion to help support blood pressure in severely bradycardic patients.

Lidocaine: A Vaughn-Williams Class IB antidysrhythmic used to terminate ventricular-based rhythm distur-

bances such as VF or VT. Unclear efficacy in cardiac resuscitation; currently assigned a class IIB recommendation for use by the American Heart Association (AHA). Dosage is reduced for patients with hepatic disorders or those who are elderly.

Magnesium sulfate: Electrolyte used to terminate torsades de points or multiform VT by increasing QRS duration and prolonging the QT interval.

Morphine: A narcotic analgesic used for pain control and sedation (anxiety reduction) in patients suffering from myocardial ischemia and chest pain.

Nitroglycerin: Used for relaxation of vascular smooth muscle and dilation of coronary arteries to increase blood flow to myocardium.

Oxygen: Administered to patients with cardiovascular compromise to compensate for diminished cardiovascular function and shock by increasing the overall concentration of oxygen being delivered to the tissues and cells of the body.

Sodium bicarbonate: Alkalinizing agent used to help reverse metabolic acidosis, hyperkalemia, and the effects of a tricyclic acid (TCA) overdose. Not used to reverse respiratory acidosis.

Vasopressin: Posterior pituitary hormone with potent peripheral vasoconstriction effects. Used as a bolus during cardiac arrest to maintain pressure within the vasculature.

References

1. R. H. Mehta et al., "Clinical and Angiographic Correlates and Outcomes of Suboptimal Coronary Flow in Patients with Acute Myocardial Infarction Undergoing Primary Percutaneous Coronary Intervention." *Journal of the American College of Cardiology* 42, no. 10 (2003): 1739–46.

2. G. W. Stone et al., "Comparison of Angioplasty with Stenting, with or without Abciximab, in Acute Myocardial Infarction." *New England Journal of Medicine* 346, no. 13 (2002): 957–66 (see comment).

3. J. L. Anderson, L. A. Karagounis, and R. M. Califf, "Metaanalysis of Five Reported Studies on the Relation of Early Coronary Patency Grades with Mortality and Outcomes after Acute Myocardial Infarction." *American Journal of Cardiology* 78, no. 1 (1996): 1–8.

4. Anonymous, "An International Randomized Trial Comparing Four Thrombolytic Strategies for Acute Myocardial Infarction. The GUSTO Investigators." *New England Journal of Medicine* 329, no. 10 (1993): 673–82 (see comment).

5. Anonymous, "The Effects of Tissue Plasminogen Activator, Streptokinase, or Both on Coronary-Artery Patency, Ventricular Function, and Survival after Acute Myocardial Infarction. The GUSTO Angiographic Investiga-

tors." *New England Journal of Medicine* 329, no. 22 (1993): 1615–22 (see comment). [Erratum appears in *New England Journal of Medicine* 330, no. 7 (February 1994): 516.]

6. D. P. Zipes et al. (eds.), *Braunwald's Heart Disease*, 7th ed. Elsevier Science, 2005.

7. E. M. Antman et al., "ACC/AHA Guidelines for the Management of Patients with ST-Elevation Myocardial Infarction—Executive Summary. A Report of the American College of Cardiology/American Heart Association Task Force on Practice Guidelines (Writing Committee to Revise the 1999 Guidelines for the Management of Patients with Acute Myocardial Infarction)." *Journal of the American College of Cardiology* 44, no. 3 (2004): 671–719 (see comment). [Erratum appears in *Journal of the American College of Cardiology* 45, no. 8 (April 2005): 1376.]

8. G. Gardner, D. S. Pinto, and S. Lewis, "Flash Pulmonary Edema," UpToDate, October 22, 2004 (cited May 12, 2005). Available from www.utdol.com/application/topic.asp?file=hrt_fail/2458&type=A&selectedTitle=1~7.

9. S. K. Frankel and M. A. Fifer, "Heart Failure." In L. S. Lilly, ed., *Pathophysiology of Heart Failure*, 2nd ed. New York: Lippincott, Williams & Wilkins, 1998, pp. 193–216.

10. S. Landaw, "Approach to the Diagnosis and Therapy of Suspected Deep Vein Thrombosis," UpToDate, 2004 (cited April 15, 2005), version 13.1. Available from: www.uptodate.com.

11. American Heart Association, *Handbook of Emergency Cardiovascular Care* (2010 ECC Guidelines), 2006.

Answers

Are You Ready?

1. Ventricular fibrillation
2. Perform CPR for five cycles or 2 minutes and then defibrillate the patient, with immediate resumption of CPR following the defibrillation.
3. 30:2
4. "Push hard and fast (100/min) and release completely (full recoil) and minimize interruptions in compressions."
5. 360 joules

Active Learning

3. a. Starling's law of the heart; b. positive inotropic effect; c. the sympathetic nervous system and drugs (such as digitalis); d. negative inotropic; e. beta adrenergic blockers and calcium channel blockers; f. positive chronotropic; g. negative chronotropic; h. A heart rate of 180 would decrease CO. The shorter duration of diastole limits the time available for ventricular filling. In these circumstances, the stroke volume falls (due to decreased length of diastole) so much that the cardiac output decreases, despite an increase in heart rate; i. Pulse pressure is the difference between the systolic arterial pressure and the diastolic arterial pressure; j. Pulse pressure = Systolic BP − Diastolic BP; k. Pulse pressure = 188 − 56 = 132

You Are There: Reality-Based Cases
Case 1

1. Check the rhythm, and perform a second defibrillation at 360 joules (performing CPR while the defibrillator charges). Resume CPR immediately following defibrillation.

2. Optimally, the patient is intubated and an IV/IO is established while CPR is in progress. If intubation and IV/IO access cannot be accomplished with CPR in progress, then CPR should be interrupted at the end of the fifth cycle of 30 compressions to 2 ventilations in order to attempt these skills. The main point is that *CPR should be interrupted as little as possible.*

3. A vasopressor is the first medication that should be administered, and it should be administered while CPR is in progress (no interruption for medication administration unless the administration of endotracheal (ET) medications is necessary, and even then, the interruption should be as short as possible). The two vasopressors that are typically administered are epinephrine (1:10,000 1 mg IV/IO, repeated every 3–5 minutes) or one dose of vasopressin (40 units [U] IV/IO to replace the first or second dose of epinephrine).

4. With CPR in progress, administer the first round of an antiarrhythmic medication. Typically one of these antiarrhythmic drugs is utilized in this setting:
   a. Amiodarone (300 mg IV/IO × 1; consider an additional 150 mg IV/IO × 1)
   b. Lidocaine (1–1.5 mg/kg first dose; then 0.5–0.75 mg/kg IV/IO with a maximum of three doses, or 3 mg/kg)
   Less likely:
   c. Magnesium sulfate (2 g IV/IO for torsades de pointes or hypomagnesemia)
   d. Consider $NaHCO_3$ (1 mEq/kg IV for acidosis, hyperkalemia, etc.)

5. Asystole

6. Assuming that CPR is in progress, remember that CPR should be performed in the following manner:
   - Push hard and fast (at least 100/min)
   - Full recoil with compressions
   - Minimal interruptions in compressions
   - Avoid hyperventilation
   Administer:
   - Epinephrine—1 mg IV/IO every (q) 3–5 minutes *throughout the cardiac arrest*
     or
   - Vasopressin—40 U IV/IO

Consider and treat the possible causes (H's and T's):

- Hypoxia, hypovolemia or hemorrhage, hypothermia, hydrogen ions (acidosis), hypokalemia or hyperkalemia, hypoglycemia

- Tablets or toxins, tension pneumothorax, tamponade (cardiac), thrombosis (pulmonary or coronary), trauma

7. Ventricular tachycardia

8. Reassess your patient at this point (at the end of five cycles of CPR). Reassess ABCs and, if the patient has a pulse, attempt to obtain a blood pressure. If the patient is breathing, track the patient's ventilations; if he or she is not breathing, provide ventilations with the bag-mask device (or whatever device is approved for your EMS system).

9. Synchronized cardioversion starting at 100 joules and increasing in prescribed increments if the patient does not convert with the first attempt.

10. The ECG shows a sinus rhythm with one PVC.

11. Reassess ABCs and, if the patient has a pulse, attempt to obtain a blood pressure. If the patient is breathing, track the patient's ventilations; if the patient is not breathing, provide ventilations for the patient with a bag-mask device (or whatever device is approved for your EMS system).

12. The patient's ABCs should continue to be assessed on a frequent basis, and the patient's oxygen saturation, ETCO$_2$, and ECG need to be monitored. Any alterations in these assessment findings need to be addressed immediately. Because the patient initially converted his rhythm after the administration of an antiarrhythmic medication, you should consider giving another bolus of the medication and initiating an infusion (depending on the antiarrhythmic administered). The patient's blood pressure is within an acceptable range, but you need to be prepared to support it should the pressure drop.

13. The patient needs to be packaged and prepared for transport to an appropriately skilled receiving hospital.

Case 2

1. *Angina* can present with retrosternal chest pain, pressure, burning, and heaviness; can radiate to the jaw, neck, epigastrium, shoulders, or arms; becomes worse with exertion, distress, and cold; often lasts 2–10 minutes; and is relieved by rest and/or nitroglycerin.

   Unstable angina can present with retrosternal chest pain, pressure, burning, and heaviness; can radiate to the jaw, neck, epigastrium, shoulders, or arms; includes any change to the typical angina pattern, such as new angina, angina at rest, angina that occurs with much less exertion than in the past, and angina that requires a longer period of time or more nitroglycerin to resolve.

   Myocardial infarction can present with retrosternal chest pain, pressure, burning, and heaviness; can radiate to the jaw, neck, epigastrium, shoulders, or arms; can be more severe or longer lasting than angina. It is more likely to have a sudden onset; last more than 30 minutes; and be associated with shortness of breath, nausea, and vomiting.

The cause of myocardial ischemia is typically ruptured or eroded atherosclerotic plaque in one or more of the coronary arteries. Exceptions include conditions such as *variant* or *angiospastic angina,* where the pain is a result of a spasm of the coronary artery.

2. Cardiovascular risk factors include: abnormal cholesterol levels, hypertension, smoking, family history, diabetes, male gender, renal disease, and obesity.

3. Jay is sick. He has chest pain, shortness of breath, dizziness, nausea, and diaphoresis (although at this point it is difficult to determine if the sweating is from the exercise or a result of a cardiac event). You are having difficulty palpating a radial pulse.

4. There is enough information to complete a primary assessment:

   a. Jay's airway is clear, and he is able to speak with no apparent obstructions.

   b. His breathing is labored several minutes after he stopped exercising (no lung sounds at this point).

   c. Jay's perfusion is impaired (as evidenced by the fact that you cannot palpate a radial pulse).

   d. Jay appears alert and answers your questions appropriately, although he speaks in very short sentences due to difficulty breathing.

   e. At this point you have not exposed the patient, but even without exposing the patient you can see that he is experiencing severe shortness of breath.

5. The primary concerns are maintaining Jay's airway (ensuring that he doesn't aspirate if he vomits), addressing his chest pain and shortness of breath, and improving his hemodynamic status. The means by which these concerns are addressed will depend on the information that you obtain in your secondary assessment, the information that your partner obtains from Jay's wife, and the presentation of the patient. At this point it is safe to say that you will address your concerns by continuing the patient on oxygen and increasing the oxygen if Jay is able to tolerate a nonrebreather mask (with his nausea); establishing an IV; obtaining a set of vital signs (including oxygen saturation, blood pressure, pulse, respiratory rate, temperature, and 3-lead ECG); a 12-lead ECG; and a complete secondary assessment.

6. Since Jay's airway appears to be patent, and he is alert enough to maintain it by himself, the following information is needed before treatment can begin:

   - *Vital signs.* Since radial pulses are not readily palpable, it is good practice to assume that Jay is hypotensive. It would be a good idea to place him in a supine or shock position, but we should also be concerned about his breathing. If he turns out to have pulmonary edema, lying him flat or placing him in a shock position could worsen his respiratory distress.

   - *Lung sounds.* Since Jay's respiratory distress has not diminished with rest, we need to be concerned that there is some underlying respiratory component to this event.

- *Oxygen saturation.* Obtain a baseline reading to help evaluate improvement or worsening of Jay's respiratory status.

- *3-lead and 12-lead ECG.* The 3-lead ECG will monitor rate, regularity, presence of P waves, width of QRS complexes, and ST segment height, whereas the 12-lead ECG will better evaluate the cause of Jay's chest pain and shortness of breath, looking for the presence of ST segment elevation or depression in contiguous leads and to help determine an appropriate facility to transport Jay to. *Remember:* The presence of ST segment changes in contiguous leads is suggestive of myocardial injury or infarction, but the absence of ST segment changes alone does not rule out myocardial injury or infarction.

- *Presence of peripheral (dependent) edema or JVD.* This is suggestive of possible preexisting heart failure.

- *Medical history.* Questions should be asked about Jay's general health status, current and past medical history, whether he has ever experienced a similar episode, and, if so, whether he was ever evaluated for the problem. If he was evaluated, what was the result of the evaluation (was there a diagnosis, and what was the treatment)?

- *Equality of peripheral pulses.* Differences in pulses on one side of the body compared with the other may be suggestive of conditions such as aortic aneurysm.

- *Comparing central pulses to peripheral pulses.* Differences between central and peripheral pulses may be suggestive of peripheral vasoconstriction, which can be an indicator of shock.

7. HTN, diabetes, male gender, obesity, abnormal cholesterol, smoker

8. There is ST elevation in leads V_2 through V_5, which suggests an anteroseptal MI with some lateral extension.

9. History, serial 12-lead ECGs, and serial cardiac enzymes

10. Any of the following are acceptable answers: congestive heart failure (right heart failure), pericardial tamponade, tension pneumothorax, and pulmonary embolism.

11. He appears to be suffering from a myocardial infarction, CHF with pulmonary edema, and cardiogenic shock.

12. Major problems that must be managed are the MI, pulmonary edema, and cardiogenic shock. In an attempt to prioritize a treatment plan, you must consider the ramifications of every action and treatment on the coexisting medical conditions. For example, something as simple as patient positioning can have a dramatic effect on the patient's status. Placed in a shock position, the patient could experience an exacerbation of his shortness of breath. If he is seated upright, his blood pressure could fall, decreasing his ability to perfuse his vital organs.

The MI is likely the root cause and is high on the treatment priority list. There are consequences of the standard treatment for an MI that may affect this patient. There is a small concern that Jay may vomit into his oxygen mask. However the benefits appear to outweigh the risks in this situation, especially since Jay is awake, alert, and able to reach up and take off his mask if he vomits. Aspirin is appropriate and will have no major negative effects on his hemodynamic status. Therefore 325 mg of aspirin is a good choice. Nitroglycerin is a very effective vasodilator and would be very helpful in the treatment of Jay's MI and pulmonary edema, but his already low blood pressure of 76/54 precludes its use. Morphine sulfate and its venous pooling, analgesic, and calming effects would be a desirable medication to deliver if it were not for its propensity to cause hypotension and respiratory depression.

In order for Jay to be able to receive these beneficial medications, his blood pressure must be high enough to support them. This can have a profound impact on his heart. The options for raising the blood pressure include fluid boluses, which could exacerbate his pulmonary edema, and the use of a vasopressor such as dopamine or dobutamine, which can increase the workload of the heart, increase myocardial oxygen demand, and exacerbate his existing condition. If fluid boluses are to be administered, ensure that they are small, and reassess the patient frequently (hemodynamic status, lung sounds, oxygen saturation, ECG, etc.). Keep in mind that if the patient is not hypovolemic, the added fluid may worsen the pulmonary edema. If dopamine or another vasopressor is used, make sure that you start at the lower end of the dosage range and titrate to the desired effect (normal blood pressure). Once blood pressure has risen to an acceptable level, administer nitrates very cautiously. If the patient has a right-sided MI, the administration of nitroglycerin may drop the patient's blood pressure quickly.

Beta-blockers are indicated for a patient experiencing myocardial infarction with ST segment elevation, but due to Jay's hypotension and pulmonary edema, beta-blocker administration is contraindicated.

Some EMS systems utilize fibrinolytics in the prehospital setting. In order for a patient to be eligible for fibrinolytic administration, the patient must be evaluated for eligibility through the use of a fibrinolytic checklist (see Boxes 29-20 and 29-21 in the textbook for an example of a fibrinolytic checklist).

Diuretic medications, such as furosemide, can cause hypotension as a result of increased urine production and output. Transport this patient as soon as possible. Time is muscle. Transportation of this patient should be to a facility that is capable of performing a percutaneous coronary intervention (PCI) or to the local hospital for fibrinolytic therapy. In any case, time should not be wasted on scene trying to perform ongoing treatments.

Test Yourself

1. b

It is often easiest to think of the possible causes of chest pain in a system-based manner, with the most common systems affected being cardiac, pulmonary, vascular, gastrointestinal, musculoskeletal, and psychological. Other systems almost never lead to chest pain.

2. Cardioversion delivers energy synchronized with the cardiac cycle. Defibrillation is an unsynchronized delivery of energy, meaning the shock is delivered randomly during the cardiac cycle without any regard for the refractory period.

Because it synchronizes with the existing ECG complex, cardioversion is less likely to accidentally cause ventricular fibrillation in patients experiencing some cardiac dysrhythmias. However, if the patient is already experiencing ventricular fibrillation or ventricular tachycardia, cardioversion is less effective and defibrillation should be used.

3. a

Myocardial infarctions vary in degree, but all cause some level of damage to the heart muscle, which puts the patient at risk for a host of problems (including heart failure, chronic dysrhythmias, or vascular disease). If a patient reports a history of acute myocardial infarction, you should maintain a heightened level of suspicion when responding to complaints.

4. Both drugs are vasodilators. Nitroprusside is slightly more effective, as it dilates both arterioles and veins, whereas nitroglycerin only dilates veins. However, nitroprusside is difficult to prepare and can lead to cyanide toxicity. Nitroglycerin is relatively easy to prepare, and the possible side effects are headache and tachycardia.

Because it is easier to prepare and carries less risk of toxicity, you are most likely to use nitroglycerin in the field.

5. Cardiac tamponade

The most common causes of cardiac tamponade are malignant (cancer-induced) effusions, bacteria (including tuberculosis and mycobacteria), fungus, infections associated with human immunodeficiency virus, and bleeding into the pericardial sac, known as hemopericardium.

6. False

Hyperventilation increases pressure in the thorax, which in turn decreases the amount of venous blood that can return to the heart. If less blood returns to the heart, less blood can be pumped out, defeating the purpose of CPR.

7. Venous ulcers are usually painless, irregular at the margins, superficial, exudative, and located along the inner ankle bone or along veins. Arterial ulcers tend to be painful, sharply demarcated, deep, dry, and located along the outer ankle bone and other pressure points.

Determining the type of ulceration can help you establish whether a patient has chronic venous insufficiency or arterial disease.

8. Acute myocardial infarction, aortic dissection, and pulmonary embolism

In the real world, patients may have more than one cause for their chest pain, and symptoms are seldom "classic" in appearance. Therefore paramedics must have all possible disorders in mind when evaluating a patient with chest pain. A thorough understanding of the life-threatening potential is extremely important. The most life-threatening causes of chest pain are acute myocardial infarction (AMI), aortic dissection, and pulmonary embolism (PE). The paramedic must therefore be adept at distinguishing the characteristics of these three disorders. This is done by using clinical judgment and evaluating the patient for the risk factors as well as current signs and symptoms.

9. b

The National Association of EMS Physicians has published two position papers to help guide local policies regarding cessation of resuscitative efforts in the prehospital setting. One recommendation is that traumatic cardiopulmonary arrest patients with a transport time to an ED or trauma center of more than 15 minutes after the arrest is identified may be considered nonsalvageable, and termination of resuscitation should be considered.

Trauma patients who show signs of life, such as pupil reactivity or organized electrical activity, should have resuscitation performed. In situations of hypothermia complicating trauma, patients should be aggressively resuscitated and transported to a center capable of actively rewarming the victim.

10. A patient with a ruptured abdominal aortic aneurysm typically describes an acute onset of abdominal or back pain, often described as "gnawing" and constant. A pulsatile mass can sometimes be felt in the abdomen, and the abdomen is tender to palpation.

Because the pain is not specific to this problem, it is not surprising that up to 30 percent of all aneurysms are initially misdiagnosed. Prompt identification and treatment are crucial, as the mortality of a ruptured abdominal aortic aneurysm is over 50 percent.

11. Many of the body's efforts to compensate for congestive heart failure, such as the renin-angiotensin system and antidiuretic hormone, work to retain water and sodium. However, there will be a point where the heart cannot handle the increase in intravascular volume and preload. Thus diuretics are administered to help relieve the increased pressure.

Diuretics act by inhibiting sodium and water reabsorption at the kidneys, thus decreasing the volume overload and intracardiac pressures. Loop diuretics such as furosemide and bumetanide are the primary drugs of choice for patients with congestive heart failure. However, a major concern with loop diuretics is the risk for hypokalemia; therefore, patients are typically on potassium replacement in combination with their diuretic.

12. c

In the failing left ventricle, the left atrium and subsequently the pulmonary vasculature receive increased pressures, resulting in acute pulmonary edema. Acute pulmonary edema is a rapid fluid increase within the pulmonary interstitium and alveoli, resulting in a rapid onset of shortness of breath, hypoxia, pulmonary rales, a "frothy" cough, and usually tachycardia with hypertension. Treatment of acute pulmonary edema in the field is aimed at the underlying cause of the increase in intracardiac pressures that led to the edema.

13. b

Other drugs used include vasopressin. Every patient in PEA needs CPR and regular pulse checks. If a pulse returns or a recognizable rhythm comes on the monitor, change algorithms accordingly.

14. a

Oxygen, aspirin, and heparin are all traditionally administered to patients in cardiogenic shock caused by myocardial infarction (assuming there are no contraindications). While epinephrine is a potent catecholamine drug that increases myocardial contractility, it has systemic side effects that may be undesirable.

15. False

Two large clinical trials (the GUSTO-I and SHOCK trials) showed cardiogenic shock occurs within the first 24 hours after an AMI, and often develops after hospital admission (5.3% of patients). In the SHOCK trial, the median time from AMI to onset of cardiogenic shock was 5.5 hours, and 75% of the patients who developed cardiogenic shock did so within 24 hours.

16. Risk factors include: abnormal cholesterol levels, high blood pressure, diabetes mellitus, tobacco abuse, male gender, family history, obesity or metabolic syndromes, and kidney disease.

You should examine patients with these risk factors with heightened suspicion, but the absence of these factors should never rule out the possibility of heart disease.

17. b

Acute arterial occlusion is when the blood flow is completely blocked to a limb. As a vasopressor, dopamine would only make the problem of acute arterial occlusion worse. You should administer morphine to control pain, lower the limb to use gravity to your advantage, and remove stockings as they may constrict blood flow.

18. a

Your patient's peripheral edema is evidence of right-sided heart failure; the crackles in the lungs are evidence of left-sided failure and indicate pulmonary edema.

19. d

The proper treatment for acute pulmonary edema includes transportation in an upright position, oxygen (preferably high-flow), CPAP, possible diuretics, nitrates, morphine, and inotropic agents. Your patient is experiencing atrial fibrillation, which does not need to be cardioverted at this time.

20. Paroxysmal nocturnal dyspnea

An abnormal condition of the respiratory system, paroxysmal nocturnal dyspnea is often associated with left ventricular failure and pulmonary edema.

21. a

This patient is experiencing an acute coronary event, despite the ECG findings. It is appropriate to reassess him when his pain changes and to determine the likelihood of an ischemic event. Even if he is stable, undiagnosed angina needs to be evaluated. The patient is under stress due to the workload of his job, which is causing an increased myocardial oxygen demand, thus leading to the chest pain. You cannot force him to go to the hospital, but by calmly completing your assessment and reassuring him, you are more likely to have a compliant patient.

22. c

Treatment for this patient includes MONA—morphine, oxygen, nitroglycerin, and aspirin. It also includes transporting the patient without undue stress or risk of injury. At times, it is appropriate to use lights and sirens, but that increases your risk of collision. It also can increase the patient's stress level and cause further ischemia or injury. Nitroprusside is not indicated in this patient, and helicopter transport is not needed based on the condition of your patient. Helicopter transport may also not be an option due to the obesity of your patient.

23. b

A family history of heart disease is a strong risk factor for myocardial infarction. Pain reliably relieved by antacids is likely gastroesophageal in origin, although occasionally patients with ACS have reported improvement of their cardiac symptoms with antacids. Squeezing pain is frequently described by patients with both angina and infarction and should be regularly suspected. Infant murmurs are not related to heart disease and may be very functional. They usually resolve and need no further care.

24. To the smaller, nearer hospital

Although percutaneous coronary intervention (PCI) is the preferred method for managing acute myocardial infarction (AMI), in this situation PCI cannot be performed in a timely manner. This patient has no contraindications for thrombolytic agents; therefore she should be transported to the nearest hospital where thrombolytics can be administered.

25. En route treatment should focus on managing pain, maintaining cardiac output, performing serial 12-lead ECGs to monitor for hemodynamic compromise or other worsening conditions, and treating any other symptoms as they arise. If you have time, you should initiate additional IVs to help the receiving facility provide thrombolytic medication sooner upon arrival. Medications you should consider administering to an AMI patient include: MONA (morphine, oxygen, nitroglycerin, and aspirin), beta-blockers, and anticoagulants.

Paramedics can prevent complications and initiate treatment for acute myocardial infarction before hospital arrival, resulting in a reduction of time between the AMI event and reperfusion therapy. Patients treated for AMI require medication delivered early, including: aspirin, beta-blockers, heparin or other anticoagulants, morphine or other IV pain medication, oxygen, and more recently indicated medications such as clopidogrel (Plavix). The use of lipid-lowering agents (called statins) and ACE inhibitors is beneficial in ACS/AMI patients but not a priority for paramedics.

chapter 30

Neurology

study while his wife was preparing dinner in the kitchen. He heard a crash and something falling on the floor, so he ran into the kitchen. Kathy had apparently dropped the knife she was using and was leaning over the counter holding her head and mumbling about a headache. She barely recognizes that you are there.

1. What are your next steps in identifying the possible causes of Kathy's presentation? What are your initial interventions?

_____

_____

_____

Active Learning

Anatomy Review

1. Identify each of the lobes of the cerebral hemispheres (Figure 30-1) and describe their functions.

   a. _____

   b. _____

Are You Ready?

You have been called to a residential address to evaluate a 43-year-old female with "altered mental status." You find Kathy Ross in her kitchen, sitting on a chair and being supported by her husband, Jon. Your general impression is that the patient is awake but appears tired and confused. You note a clear droop on the right side of her face, and it appears that she is having difficulty sitting upright. Jon reports that he was in the

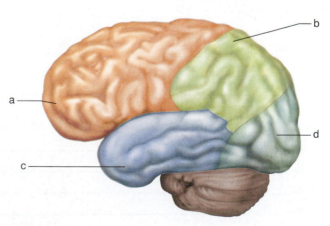

FIGURE 30-1

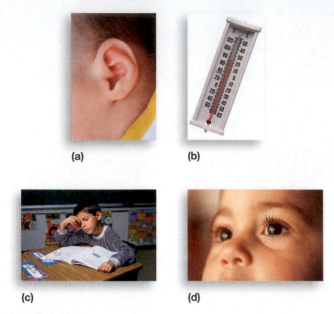

(a)   (b)

(c)   (d)

FIGURE 30-2

c. _____

d. _____

2. Match the function shown in each photo in Figure 30-2 with the correct area of the brain.

a. _____

b. _____

c. _____

d. _____

3. Using the diagram in Figure 30-3 and the photos in Figure 30-4, select which of the images best matches the function of each of the brain structures:

Structure	Location	Function
Medulla oblongata	b	5
Midbrain		
Cerebrum		
Pons		
Cerebellum		

4. Identify each of the structures in Figure 30-5.

a. _____

b. _____

c. _____

d. _____

e. _____

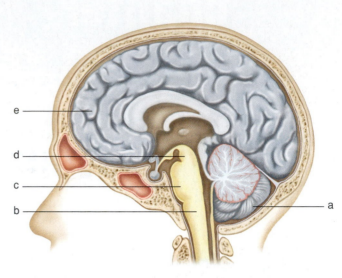

FIGURE 30-3

5. The space between the dura mater and the arachnoid mater is called the (a) _____. The space between the dura mater and the skull is called the (b) _____.

1   2

3   4

5

FIGURE 30-4

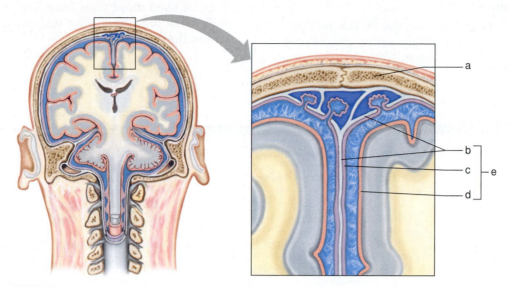

FIGURE 30-5

6. (a) _____ nerves conduct nerve impulses from a receptor along a sensory neuron to the central nervous system as part of a reflex arc. (b) _____ nerves conduct impulses from the central nervous system along a motor neuron to an effector muscle or gland as part of a reflex arc.

7. The following table lists the cranial nerves and their functions. Fill in the blanks with the missing information.

Cranial Nerve Numbers, Names, and Functions		
Number	**Name**	**Function**
I		Sense of smell
	Oculomotor	Controls four of the six eye muscles; controls eyelid (upper); constricts pupil
XII	Hypoglossal	
IX		Taste and sensation to back of tongue
		Controls muscles of facial expression, taste sensation, and tear and salivary glands
IV		Controls one of the six eye muscles
VI	Abducens	
		Hearing and balance
	Vagus	
XI	Accessory	
	Optic	
V		Sensation of face; controls muscles of chewing

8. Using Your Head

Match each of the cranial nerves in the left column of the table to one of the testing procedures described in the right column. Note that answers may be used more than once, and a cranial nerve may have more than one test associated with its evaluation.

Cranial Nerve	Answer	One Minute Cranial Nerve Exam
I Olfactory		a. "Close your eyes. Can you smell this? What is it?"
II Optic		b. Lean in close. Whisper, "Can you hear me?"
III Oculomotor		c. "Open your eyes. Hold your head still and follow my penlight." Move light in front of eyes in an "H" pattern. Check for pupil response to light.
IV Trochlear		d. "Please clench your teeth." Palpate the masseter and temporal muscles for tone.
V Trigeminal		e. "Keep your teeth clenched and smile. Show me your teeth."
VI Abducens		f. "Say 'Ahhhh.'" Watch the uvula move.
VII Facial		g. "Stick out your tongue."
VIII Vestibulocochlear		h. Test sensation at forehead, chin, and each cheek.
IX Glossopharyngeal		i. "Please stand straight with your feet together. Now close your eyes and stand still." Observe if patient sways.
X Vagus		j. Ask patient to shrug shoulders upward while you push downward and to rotate head to the left and right while you put gentle counterpressure on each side of the face.
XI Accessory		k. Test gag reflex with tongue blade.
XII Hypoglossal		

9. Neuromuscular Match

Match the disease process with the appropriate description in the table.

Disease	Answer	Signs and Symptoms
Amyotrophic lateral sclerosis		a. Begins with fever, neck stiffness; may progress rapidly to full body paralysis
Bell's palsy		b. Spasmodic contraction and relaxation of muscles; may be seen in generalized seizures
Dystonia		c. Sudden one-sided facial numbness and facial droop
Multiple sclerosis		d. Progressive muscle weakness that begins in the extremities
Parkinson's disease		e. Abnormal muscle flexion that may be reversed with diphenhydramine
Myoclonus		f. Begins with numbness and paresthesia, and progresses as myelin sheaths degenerate
Poliomyelitis		g. Tremors of the hands that worsen at rest; facial muscles may freeze and cause a masklike appearance

You Are There: Reality-Based Cases

Case 1 (*continuation of chapter opener*)

Kathy's airway is patent, but she is tachypneic. Her radial pulse is thready and fast. Her skin is cool to the touch, diaphoretic, and pale. She looks at you when you speak with her. When you ask her questions, she mumbles a response, but you are unable to clearly make out what she is trying to say. Your team begins basic care and rapidly assesses the patient's physical condition. Your findings include:

Vital signs: HR of 86; BP of 96/72; RR of 22

ECG: Sinus tachycardia, no ectopy

SpO_2: 97% with supplemental oxygen

$ETCO_2$: 42 mm Hg

Pupils: Midrange, slow to react, equal

Lung sounds: Clear, equal bilaterally

Neuro exam: Decreased grip, strength, and plantar flexion on the right side

Past medical history: Hypertension, diabetes (Type 2) and hypercholesterolemia

Medications: Tenormin

Allergies: No known allergies (NKA)

1. Based on your findings, what is Kathy's Glasgow Coma Scale score?

   _____

   _____

   _____

2. Based upon your findings thus far, what are possible causes for this patient's presentation? What further information should you elicit now?

   _____

   _____

   _____

Kathy is now supine on a gurney. She continues to respond to your questions, but her responses are shorter and even more difficult to discern. She is flaccid on the right side. SpO_2 continues to be in the high 90s, and $ETCO_2$ is in the 30s. Her heart rate is 90. A team member has initiated an IV of normal saline at KVO rate. An Accu-Chek reading of the blood sample reveals a blood glucose level of 15 mg/dL. There is no JVD or pedal edema on visual examination.

3. What do these findings tell you? Are there other possible reasons you have not yet considered that could be causing the presentation findings?

   _____

   _____

   _____

Case 2

You arrive at the high school for a "man down" call. Firefighters report that a student found someone in one of the men's bathrooms "passed out." The engine company EMTs found a male patient who appeared to be seizing on the floor of a toilet stall. With manual cervical spine precautions in place, they quickly extricate him from the stall, and you find him supine. Another teacher recognizes the victim as the principal of the school, 58-year-old John Lee. As you size up the scene, you notice that the patient is pale, incontinent of urine, and has a contusion to his right forehead. He has snoring respirations.

1. What will you do first? What will you try to find out about the patient as quickly as possible?

   _____

   _____

   _____

A jaw thrust reduces the snoring respirations, and an EMT inserts a nasopharyngeal airway in the right nares. The patient is breathing quickly and deeply. His pulse rate is 100 and bounding at the radial. One of the office assistants runs down the hall. She reports that John has recently been diagnosed with hypertension. She shakes her head when you ask whether he has any medications for the condition. She then pulls you to one side and quietly reports that John had just returned from a drug rehabilitation center, where he was treated for narcotic addiction secondary to pain medications for an old knee injury. Other than a little blood in his oropharynx, there are no other signs of bleeding. His pupils are constricted, equal, and nonreactive to light.

2. Based on the information provided, what are possible causes for the patient's presentation? What are your treatment priorities?

_____

_____

En route to the hospital, John's breathing effort becomes more erratic and shallow. His blood pressure is now 260/156, and his pulse rate is 64. Pupils are pinpoint and fixed. His blood glucose level is 106 mg/dL. You observe that both wrists are abnormally flexed.

3. Is hyperventilation warranted for this patient? What other clinical parameters should you monitor closely?

_____

_____

_____

Test Yourself

1. If a patient exhibits neurological signs and symptoms of stroke that last less than 24 hours and resolve without any intervention, it is referred to as a cerebrovascular accident.
   True
   False

2. Describe the facial appearance of a patient with a "facial droop."

   _____

   _____

3. _____ is a temporary disruption in normal neuronal activity resulting in abnormal repetitive and synchronous firing (action potentials) of neurons in the brain.
   a. Seizure
   b. Stroke
   c. Syncope
   d. TIA

4. The brain receives its blood supply through anterior and posterior circulations. The internal carotid arteries branch into the left and right middle _____ .

5. The neuron generates an electrical impulse called _____ that travels along the axon to the synaptic terminals.

6. An anterior cerebral artery (ACA) stroke produces neurological deficits. How might a patient with an ACA stroke describe his or her symptoms?

   _____

   _____

7. High levels of arterial carbon dioxide result in
   a. cerebral vasodilation.
   b. cerebral vasoconstriction.
   c. cerebral occlusion.
   d. cerebral vasospasm.

8. Which of the following is most likely to cause a hemorrhagic stroke in a young patient?
   a. Atrial fibrillation
   b. Hangings
   c. Drug use
   d. Breath holding

9. The primary respiratory control center of the brain is located in the _____ .

10. On the Cincinnati Prehospital Stroke Scale, an abnormal exam finding in the arm drift includes which of the following:
    a. both arms move in opposite directions.
    b. one arm stays stationary and one drifts down.
    c. neither arm moves.
    d. both arms move in the same direction.

11. Patients with a head or brain injury may be unable to manage their own airway. As a result, they may be at risk for
    a. coughing.
    b. pneumonia.
    c. wheezing.
    d. aspiration.

12. Cerebral perfusion pressure (CPP) is equal to the mean arterial pressure (MAP) minus the
    a. venous resistance.
    b. diastolic blood pressure.
    c. systolic blood pressure.
    d. intracranial pressure.

13. The vestibulocochlear nerve supplies the superior oblique muscle of the eye.
    True
    False

14. The midbrain, pons, medulla, and reticular formation are located in the _____.

15. While assessing a patient you notice that the patient experiences difficulty speaking with halting speech. This is referred to as
    a. induced aphasia.
    b. expressive aphasia.
    c. receptive aphasia.
    d. perceptive aphasia.

16. If a patient is alert and oriented, then the _____, a part of the nervous system, is most likely intact and functioning.

17. Which condition results in a temporary loss of consciousness and postural tone usually caused by a brief, sudden drop in cerebral perfusion?
    a. Aura
    b. Petit mal seizure
    c. Orthostasis
    d. Syncope

18. _____ neurons detect changes and stimuli in the environment and carry electrical signals into the CNS.

    _____

    _____

19. A patient appears to have normal vital signs and body temperature and is adequately hydrated. Which part of the brain influences these functions?
    a. Hypothalamus
    b. Medulla oblongata
    c. Limbic system
    d. Auditory cortex

20. A stroke is a disruption in the blood supply to the brain and is most likely caused by either a
    a. tear or plaque.
    b. hemorrhage or clot.
    c. aneurysm or rupture.
    d. pressure or clot.

21. Which of the following relays messages between the cerebrum and medulla and between the cerebrum and cerebellum?
    a. Pons
    b. Basal ganglia
    c. Cerebral hemispheres
    d. Hypothalamus

22. Increased blood pressure, tachycardia, and fluctuating respirations are associated with
    a. Cushing's triad.
    b. Waddell's triad.
    c. Beck's triad.
    d. the perfusion triad.

23. Your patient is able to move her arms and feel rain against her skin. The _____, a part of her brain, must still be intact.

Scenario: You are treating a patient with a traumatic brain injury who presents with persistent unconsciousness, flaccid paralysis, and pupils unresponsive to light.

24. What dangerous condition is imminent?

    _____

    _____

25. Should you hyperventilate this patient? Why or why not?

    _____

    _____

Need to Know

The following represent the Key Objectives of Chapter 30:

1. *Describe the pathophysiology associated with altered mental status.*

   The cerebrum and reticular formation act in concert to create consciousness. Alterations to either structure can cause changes in the level of consciousness. These changes range from structural issues such as stroke, head injury, and tumor to metabolic concerns in the form of hypoxia or hypoglycemia. The brain is a well-defined organ, with specific areas and structures associated with specific functions. The cerebrum is thought to be the center of higher thought processes and is the essential decision-making center as well as the attenuator for motor control. The cerebellum controls and regulates basic motor functions of the body, including balance. The pons is more closely related to the spinal cord than it is to the brain and is responsible for basic control of autonomic systems such as respirations and heart rate.

   In addition to function, the brain can also be divided into left and right halves, or hemispheres.

Injuries specific to an organ or hemisphere will also produce specific patterns of signs and symptoms. For example, an area of brain ischemia located on the left side of the brain can produce right-sided weakness and loss of sensation. A blow to the occipital region of the brain can produce bright flashing lights as the ocular nerves are injured.

The brain is not one solid mass; open areas within the brain mass called ventricles help to circulate cerebral spinal fluid in and around the brain tissue, providing cushioning for it. These ventricles can also contain excess blood or build pressure, causing intracranial pressure (ICP) to rise to dangerous levels.

Covering the brain are the meningeal layers, or membranes that provide protection and much of the blood supply. The meninges can become infected (meningitis) or bleed (epidural or subdural hematoma, or arachnoid bleed). Review Chapter 30, Neurology, in the textbook for more specific information about these conditions.

2. *Describe an effective, logical assessment approach to a patient experiencing altered mental status.*

Your assessment begins with a scene size-up and general impression of the patient. When you begin the primary assessment, there may be several clues that can key you in to a patient who is experiencing an altered level of mentation.

- It may be simple—a patient who responds to a verbal or physical stimulus, for example. It may be more subtle—for example, generalized absence seizures in a child can go unnoticed by the parents and teachers for some time. (In such cases, a careful solicitation of past medical history and the events leading up to the condition will be needed.)
- Patients with altered mental status can have difficulty controlling their airway, even while conscious.
- Changes in breathing patterns can be associated with conditions involving mental status changes. For example, Kussmaul's respirations can be indicative of diabetic ketoacidosis. Central neurogenic hyperventilation, such as Biot's respirations, can reflect a brain stem injury.
- A slow pulse rate can indicate increased intracranial pressure.

Secondary assessment findings can help you refine your suspicions about the cause of the altered mental status. A simple mnemonic is AEIOU-TIPS:

- **A**lcohol involvement—the odor of ethanol on the breath; signs of liver dysfunction (ascites, jaundice)

- **E**pilepsy—wounds from generalized, tonic-clonic seizure activity; incontinence; lingual trauma
- **I**nsulin—high or low blood glucose levels; respiration patterns associated with diabetic ketoacidosis (DKA); evidence of injection sites on abdomen; fruity, acetone odor from mouth
- **O**verdose—unexplained loss of medications, whether prescribed, over-the-counter, or herbal-based; pill or tablet fragments in emesis
- **U**remia—signs of renal failure; dialysis shunt; peritoneal shunt
- **T**rauma—head injury; blood loss resulting in hypotension
- **I**nfection—fever, nausea, vomiting history; dehydration; signs of sepsis
- **P**sychiatric—bizarre behavior, presence of (or missing) psychotropic medications; dystonia
- **S**troke—hemiparalysis, hemiparesis

Elicit as accurate a history as is possible. You may need to ask friends, family, neighbors, or even strangers about any observations they made and any medical history information. Confirm this type of "third-party" information with a second source, such as medication bottles in the patient's name or official medical record transcripts.

3. *List the steps of conducting a prehospital neurological exam.*

Review Tables 30-2 and 30-3 in the textbook, which outline how to utilize the Los Angeles Prehospital Stroke Screen and the Cincinnati Prehospital Stroke Scale, respectively. Also see Skill Sheet and Step-by-Step 30, Prehospital Stroke Evaluation, on the Student DVD.

4. *Describe the prehospital findings and management of key neurological presentations.*

As with all patients, the focus of your initial care is to manage any problems found during the primary assessment. Don't delay treatment while trying to determine the underlying cause. Airway control, appropriate ventilation and oxygenation, and basic circulatory measures are particularly important in the patient with altered mental status, because the patient may not be able to provide you with an accurate chief complaint. Note any trauma mechanism that might make cervical spine immobilization necessary. Observe and record any environmental clues that might suggest a cause for the patient's change in mental status—prescription medications, recreation-al drugs, and alcohol use are but a few examples. See Table 30-1 for additional findings associated with each of these key neurological presentations.

TABLE 30-1 **Key Findings and Treatment Guidelines for Neurological Disorders**

Disorder	Key Findings	Related Treatment	Additional Comments
Alcohol abuse	Smell of alcohol on breath; open and/or empty containers	Supportive; continually assess patency of airway	Alcohol is often a factor in other illness or injury patterns. It can mask more serious underlying problems. Alcohol poisoning is a true medical emergency.
Acidosis	High glucose count (DKA or HHNS); acetone or fruity odor on breath (ketones); Kussmaul's respirations; history of the "3 polys"—polyuria, polyphagia, polydipsia; dehydration	Supportive; large volume infusion if blood glucose levels are high	The ketone breath of diabetics can be mistaken for alcohol.
Epilepsy	Tonic-clonic movements (generalized); sudden loss of attention (absence); focal movements; incontinence of urine; lingual trauma (bit tongue); postictal state	Control active seizures with benzodiazepine; clear area around patient to minimize trauma during seizure activity	Seizures can be confused with muscle twitching, which is sometimes seen after a syncope event. Seizures can occur just prior to cardiac arrest, secondary to hypoxia, or at the onset of acute hypoglycemia. Status epilepticus should be considered an emergency and be treated immediately.
Infection	Severe headache; associated neck stiffness; fever; nausea, vomiting, diarrhea; petechiae or purpura in later stages of sepsis	IV fluid replacement if hypotensive or in shock; passive cooling measures if high fever present	Meningitis is highly communicable; use mask and eyewear to reduce potential for cross infection.
Overdose	Presence of medication containers; insulin syringes, drug paraphernalia; combination of different drugs and/or alcohol	Naloxone for reversal of narcotic overdoses; $D_{50}W$ or glucagon for Insulin overdoses; glucagon for beta-blocker overdoses	See Chapter 35, Toxicology, in the textbook for more information.
Uremia	Presence of dialysis shunt; evidence of peritoneal dialysis; gradual onset of headache, nausea, vomiting, fatigue; increased thirst; cramps; dehydration signs; extremity edema, uremic "frost"	Supportive treatment; acute treatment for associated hyperkalemia may be indicated.	See Chapter 36, Urology, in the textbook for more information. Hyperkalemia can be present.
Trauma	Trauma mechanism to the head; Cushing's triad; posturing; abnormal pupil reaction to light	Protect cervical spine; control ventilations for adequate O_2 and CO_2 levels; hyperventilate if signs of herniation develop; restrict fluid unless hypotensive	Refer to Chapter 20, Head, Face, and Neck Trauma, in the textbook for more information about brain trauma.
Tumor	Gradual onset of headache, visual disturbances, personality changes. May be prescribed anti-inflammatory medication.	Supportive; control active seizure activity	Witnesses may report a period of days to weeks of behavioral changes prior to any acute onset of symptoms.
Toxins	See *Overdose;* in addition, hazardous material containers, industrial cleaners, and agricultural materials	Decontamination in cases of hazardous materials contact	See Chapter 53, Hazardous Materials Incidents, in the textbook for more information.
Insulin	Excessively high or low blood glucose levels; history of insulin injection with decrease in dietary intake; history of increased metabolism rate; medical alert jewelry; symptoms and signs similar to *Acidosis*	$D_{50}W$ IV or glucagon IM for hypoglycemia; fluid therapy for hyperglycemia	See Chapter 31, Endocrine, Electrolytes, and Acid/Base, in the textbook for additional information.

Disorder	Key Findings	Related Treatment	Additional Comments
Psychosis	Blank stare; combative, violent behavior; visual and auditory disturbances (seeing and hearing)	Supportive treatment; chemical or physical restraints if necessary for safety of patient and EMS providers	Many causes of behavioral change mandate a thorough assessment for possible medical causes in addition to psychiatric ones.
Poisoning	See *Toxins.*		
Stroke	Risk factors of diabetes and stroke; sudden onset of severe headache, nausea, and vomiting (hemorrhagic); loss of sensation, paralysis, balance, or sight, especially on one side; slurred speech; loss of sensory input	Use of CPSS or LAPSS to identify likelihood of stroke; supportive treatment; rapid transport to appropriate receiving center	Other conditions can mimic stroke. Some are reversible, such as acute hypoglycemia, hypoxia, and hypotension. The use of a validated screening test such as the CPSS or LAPSS can help identify stroke accurately.
Seizure	See *Epilepsy.*		
Sepsis	See *Infection.*		
Syncope	May have presyncope complaints (dizziness, light-headedness, sudden sweating or feeling hot)	Keep supine; may try modified Trendelenburg position. IV fluids may be needed. Determine underlying cause.	Can be associated with a cardiac dysrhythmia (see Chapter 30, Neurology, in the textbook). Witnesses may describe seizure-like movements. Protect cervical spine if a fall is suspected.

You should have a general awareness of several neuromuscular diseases, including multiple sclerosis, muscular dystrophies such as Parkinson's disease, amyotrophic lateral sclerosis (ALS), and peripheral neuropathy. Paramedic-level care for the majority of these cases is supportive, with attention focused on airway control and respiratory management.

Need to Do

The following skills are explained and illustrated in a step-by-step manner, via skill sheets and/or Step-by-Steps in this text and on the accompanying DVD:

Skill Name	Skill Sheet Number and Location	Step-by-Step Number and Location
Blood Glucose Assessment	26 – DVD	26 – DVD
Prehospital Stroke Evaluation	30 – DVD	30 – DVD

Connections

- Review each of the following chapters in the textbook for specific information as it relates to the assessment of the patient with altered mental status:
  - Chapter 5, Clinical Decision-Making
  - Chapter 7, Anatomy Overview
  - Chapter 10, Therapeutic Communications and History Taking
  - Chapter 11, The Normal Physical Examination
  - Chapter 14, Patient Assessment
  - Chapter 20, Head, Face, and Neck Trauma
  - Chapter 35, Toxicology
  - Chapter 36, Urology
  - Chapter 38, Environmental Conditions
  - Chapter 40, Behavioral and Psychiatric Disorders

  It should be readily apparent that the potential underlying causes of a patient's confusion or altered level of consciousness can be numerous. Avoid making a snap judgment about the cause of the patient's presentation.

- A PDF file of the National Institutes of Health (NIH) Stroke Scale can be found at www.ninds.nih.gov/doctors/stroke_scale_training.htm.

Training for the use of the instrument can also be found at the same website.

- The Internet Stroke Center, located at Washington University in St. Louis, has a collection of resources for families, health-care professionals, and students about the ongoing research of stroke management. Their Web link is www.strokecenter.org/.

- The Epilepsy Therapy Development Project's mission is to advance new treatments for people living with epilepsy. They host a Web information site, www.epilepsy.com/, containing resources and links about this condition.

- Link to the companion DVD for a chapter-based quiz, audio glossary, animations, games and exercises, and, when appropriate, skill sheets and skill Step-by-Steps.

Street Secrets

- **Stroke Scales** Both the Cincinnati Prehospital Stroke Scale and the Los Angeles Prehospital Stroke Screen test for pronator drift with the patient's arms extended. For patients who already may be too weak or have preexisting diseases or injuries that prevent full arm extension, ask them to bend their arms at their elbows slightly and keep their forearms straight out, palms up.

- **Double Checking** Patients with subtle forms of altered mental status can at first glance appear to be fully alert and oriented. If there is any reason for you to be concerned about your patient's level of mentation, try to re-ask questions occasionally. For example, you might want to recheck a patient's past medical history by saying, "Now, Mr. Smith, I just wanted to confirm your past medical history. What did you tell me before?" If the answer is missing part of the previous answer, or adding more, follow up with, "That's interesting Mr. Smith. Earlier you did (did not) mention X [*the extra or missing history*]. Can you think for a moment to be sure?"

- **Mnemonics** Try using a mnemonic as a way to remember the cranial nerves in order:

On **O**ld **O**lympus **T**owering **T**op **A** **F**amous **V**ocal **G**erman **V**iewed **S**ome **H**ops.

The **bold letters** stand for:

olfactory, optic, oculomotor, trochlear, trigeminal, abducens, facial, vestibulocochlear, glossopharyngeal, vagus, spinal accessory, hypoglossal.

There are other memory devices that can be found with an Internet search.

- **Countdown** It can be difficult to remember the numbers for the Glasgow Coma Scale. Try this mnemonic: for motor, think about a *V6* engine in a car—the motor response is on a 6-point scale. For verbal, think of the *Jackson 5* singers—the verbal response is on a 5-point scale. And for the last category, think "*4-eyes,*" (the elementary school taunt for the kid with glasses)—the eye opening is a 4-point scale.

The Drug Box

Dextrose: Administered when blood glucose levels are too low (hypoglycemia).

Naloxone: A narcotic agonist that reverses the effect of a narcotic upon the nervous system.

Glucagon: A hormone that promotes the release of glycogen stores in the body's skeletal muscles and liver. Used in hypoglycemic patients when IV access cannot be obtained for dextrose administration. May not be effective in pediatric patients or patients with malnutrition or hepatic disease due to inadequate glycogen stores in the body.

Answers

Are You Ready?

1. Based upon the husband's description, it appears that your patient has experienced the very rapid onset of a serious condition. As you begin your assessment, ensure that Kathy's airway is patent, her breathing is adequate, and that she has a radial pulse. Supplemental oxygen is indicated, and you may need to assist her ventilations. She may be hypotensive; checking radial pulses immediately is critical. You may need to place her supine if her pulse is weak or absent. Once any potentially life-threatening conditions are addressed, quickly but methodically obtain a history from the patient and conduct a physical examination. Consider using the AEIOU-TIPS mnemonic to help guide your questions and exam. Obtain a set of vital signs, including the use of pulse oximetry, an ECG, and capnography. Kathy may have a significant past medical history that has caused or contributed to her current condition; perform a SAMPLE history. If Kathy is experiencing altered mental status, conducting a history will become challenging. You will have to depend upon the husband's recall of Kathy's medical history to fill in any gaps of information. Pay special attention to any medications that may be on scene. Your physical findings may become the primary source of information—be thorough and pay attention to any findings.

Active Learning

1. a. frontal lobe—controls movements of voluntary skeletal muscles; carries out higher intellectual processes, such as concentrating, planning, complex problem solving, and judging the consequences of behavior. b. parietal lobe—provides sensations of temperature, touch, pressure, and pain involving the skin; functions in understanding speech and in using words to express thoughts and feelings. c. temporal lobe—responsible for hearing; interprets sensory experiences and remembers visual senses, music, and other complex sensory patterns. d. occipital lobe—responsible for vision; combines visual images with other sensory experiences.

2. a. hearing—Hearing is done in the auditory cortex, located in the temporal lobe; b. regulation of body temperature—The hypothalamus controls body temperature; c. thought—The frontal lobe is responsible for higher thought and emotional behavior; d. vision—Vision is processed in the occipital cortex.

3.

Structure	Location	Function
Medulla oblongata	b	5
Midbrain	d	2
Cerebrum	e	4
Pons	c	1
Cerebellum	a	3

4. a. skull; b. dura mater; c. arachnoid mater; d. pia mater; e. meninges

5. a. subdural space or cavity; b. epidural space

6. a. Afferent; b. Efferent

7. Answers are listed in the table below.

8. I—a; II—c; III—c; IV—c; V—d, h; VI—c; VII—e; VIII—b, i; IX—f, k; X—k; XI—j; XII—f, g

9. Amyotrophic lateral sclerosis—d; Bell's palsy—c; dystonia—e; multiple sclerosis—f; Parkinson's disease—g; myoclonus—b; poliomyelitis—a

You Are There: Reality-Based Cases

Case 1

1. 11 (E = 4, V = 2, M = 5)

2. An immediate suspicion is a stroke; she has two risk factors in her medical history (high blood pressure and high cholesterol levels) and shows signs of right-sided weakness. Another possible cause would be her diabetic condition. A blood glucose level should be checked as soon as possible. She is hypotensive, although not tachycardic, as one might expect with a shock condition. Why might that be?

3. Kathy's low blood glucose level is cause for alarm. Acute insulin shock can mimic the signs of a stroke. Her other signs and symptoms validate this as the primary suspect of her condition. Dextrose should be administered intravenously. Alternatively, glucagon

Active Learning Exercise 7

Cranial Nerve Numbers, Names, and Functions

Number	Name	Function
I	Olfactory	Sense of smell
III	Oculomotor	Controls four of the six eye muscles; controls eyelid (upper); constricts pupil
XII	Hypoglossal	Motor function of tongue muscles
IX	Glossopharyngeal	Taste and sensation to back of tongue
VII	Facial	Controls muscles of facial expression, taste sensation, and tear and salivary glands
IV	Trochlear	Controls one of the six eye muscles
VI	Abducens	Controls one of the six eye muscles
VIII	Vestibulocochlear (auditory)	Hearing and balance
X	Vagus	Sensory and motor function of palate, pharynx, and larynx
XI	Accessory	Motor function of neck and back muscles (trapezius and sternocleidomastoid)
II	Optic	Sight
V	Trigeminal	Sensation of face; controls muscles of chewing

may be administered intramuscularly if an IV cannot be inserted successfully. Her oxygen and carbon dioxide levels appear to be normal, reducing the likelihood of a respiratory or metabolic cause of her altered mental status. She is on Tenormin, a potent beta-blocker that may be artificially depressing her heart rate and causing her blood pressure to be lower than expected.

Case 2

1. Maintain cervical spine precautions. Establish a patent airway with a manual airway maneuver; a jaw thrust is appropriate, but be prepared to lift the chin if it does not displace the tongue. Assess breathing, and provide ventilations if necessary. Check for the presence of a radial pulse and any major bleeding. A rapid survey of the body will be necessary. You will need to find any potential traumatic injuries as well as signs of a medical condition. Perhaps the teacher can find additional information in the patient's office, such as medication bottles.

2. At this point in your assessment, there are several possibilities, including a seizure, drug overdose, stroke, undiagnosed hypoglycemia, hypoxia, and even cardiac disease. Additional examination is needed, including a blood glucose check, ECG, a full set of vital signs, and SpO_2 and PCO_2 monitoring. Stay focused on the primary life threats. Given the patient's level of unconsciousness, he is at high risk of aspiration.

3. John is exhibiting signs of brain herniation. His heart rate is slowed, his blood pressure is dangerously high, and he is in respiratory failure. These are classic signs of Cushing's triad. Hyperventilation is warranted in this case as a last-ditch attempt to lower the intracranial pressure (ICP). Ventilations should be conducted at a rate that drives carbon dioxide levels to normal or slightly low values (see Chapter 20, Head, Face, and Neck Trauma, in the textbook for more information on traumatic brain injury management).

Test Yourself

1. False

   If a patient exhibits neurological signs and symptoms of stroke that last less than 24 hours and resolve without any intervention, it is referred to as a transient ischemic attack (TIA).

2. A facial droop will appear as a flattening of the nasolabial fold and the inability to raise the corner of the mouth in a smile.

   If there is asymmetry, determine if this is a new event, an ongoing situation, or perhaps the person's normal, baseline appearance.

3. a

   A seizure, or ictus, is a temporary disruption in normal neuronal activity resulting in abnormal repetitive and synchronous firing (action potentials) of neurons in the brain.

4. Cerebral arteries

   The internal carotid arteries branch into the left and right middle cerebral arteries (MCAs) and the anterior cerebral arteries (ACAs). The MCAs provide most of the cerebral blood flow to the hemispheres. Interruption of blood flow within these arteries causes dramatic neurological deficits.

5. An action potential

   The neuron generates electrical impulses called action potentials that travel along the axon to the synaptic terminals. Dendrites are the projections that contain receptors for specific substances and carry electrical signals toward the cell body of the neuron. The electrical signal is carried away from the cell body via the axon, which then branches into axon terminals.

6. When an anterior cerebral artery stroke occurs, the patient usually describes it as a feeling of heaviness, numbness, or weakness of the legs.

   Anterior cerebral artery (ACA) strokes produce deficits of one of the legs, which the patient usually describes as a feeling of heaviness, numbness, or weakness. Posterior cerebral artery (PCA) strokes result in a visual field deficit on the opposite side of the stroke (a right PCA stroke will result in a left visual field deficit).

7. a

   High levels of arterial carbon dioxide cause cerebral vasodilation and increase intracranial pressure.

8. c

   Hemorrhagic stroke in young patients is commonly due to drug use (typically cocaine) or a ruptured vascular malformation such as an aneurysm or arteriovenous malformation (AVM).

9. Medulla

   The primary respiratory control center is located in the medulla. It regulates rate, rhythm, and depth of breathing. In the event of damage to this center, others can take over.

10. b

    In the Cincinnati Prehospital Stroke Scale, an abnormal exam finding in the arm drift is present when one of the patient's arms stays stationary and one drifts down.

11. d

    Patients who are obtunded may suffer from a partially obstructed airway when in the supine position as the tongue blocks the pharynx. Patients who have suffered a brain injury may not be able to cough or gag, thereby placing them at risk for aspiration of gastric contents.

12. d

    Blood flow to the brain is constant despite changes in blood pressure and metabolic activity. The cerebral perfusion pressure (CPP) is equal to the mean arterial pressure (MAP) minus the intracranial pressure (ICP).

13. False

    The trochlear nerve supplies the superior oblique muscle of the eye (which is not innervated by cranial nerve III).

14. Brain stem

    The brain consists of distinct regions: the cerebrum (basal ganglia and cortex), the diencephalon (thalamus and hypothalamus), the limbic system, the brain stem (midbrain, pons, medulla, and reticular formation), and the cerebellum.

15. b

    As you speak to the patient, note any difficulties in language such as halting speech (expressive aphasia).

16. Reticular formation

    The reticular formation (or the reticular activating system [RAS]) is responsible for arousal and alertness. The RAS is a complex network of nerve fibers scattered throughout the medulla, pons, and midbrain.

17. d

    Syncope is a temporary loss of consciousness and postural tone usually due to a brief, sudden drop in cerebral perfusion. It may be caused by a cardiac dysrhythmia or by an alteration in blood volume or distribution. Absence or petit mal seizures are commonly seen in childhood epilepsy and are characterized by a loss of interaction, with patients staring off into space and returning to normal with no memory of the event. Patients may smack their lips, blink their eyes, or perform another repetitive action. An aura is a smell or visual disturbance or other sensation signaling a seizure is coming.

18. Sensory (or afferent)

    Sensory (or afferent) neurons detect stimuli and changes in the environment and carry electrical signals into the CNS.

19. a

    The hypothalamus regulates autonomic functions and homeostasis by linking the nervous and endocrine systems. Specifically the hypothalamus regulates heart rate and arterial blood pressure, body temperature, water, and electrolyte balance.

20. b

    A stroke is a disruption in the blood supply to the brain and can be caused by either a hemorrhage or a clot (from an embolus or thrombus) in one or more of the cerebral arteries.

21. a

    The pons separates the midbrain from the medulla oblongata. It relays messages between the cerebrum and medulla and between the cerebrum and cerebellum.

22. a

    As the body tries to compensate for increasing intracranial pressure, tachycardia develops and blood pressure must also rise or the brain will not be perfused. As pressure continues to rise the heart rate will begin to decline. Respiratory patterns change as pressure is applied to the brain stem (respiratory center).

23. Cerebral cortex

    The cortex covers the convolutions of the brain and dips into the sulci and fissures. It contains nearly 75% of all neuron cell bodies in the nervous system. The cortex is responsible for motor and sensory functions.

24. Herniation of the brain

    Signs of herniation resulting from increased intracranial pressure include altered mental status (persistent unconsciousness), decerebrate posturing or flaccid paralysis, and one or both pupils become dilated and unresponsive to light.

25. You should moderately hyperventilate the patient using 100% oxygen at a rate of approximately 20 breaths per minute for adults. Hyperventilation will reduce the arterial CO_2 levels and cause cerebral vasoconstriction, which reduces intracranial pressure, but the trade-off is that it also reduces cerebral perfusion pressure. Only hyperventilate a patient who has the three distinct signs that herniation is imminent.

    Prophylactic hyperventilation for suspected brain injury is not recommended in the absence of signs of herniation, as the reduction in cerebral perfusion may further compromise an already damaged brain.

chapter 31

Endocrine, Electrolytes, and Acid/Base

Are You Ready?

Colin Harkin and his girlfriend Holly were deep in the backcountry practicing for the Desert Off-Road Classic when the four-wheel-drive truck that Colin was driving got stuck in a muddy bog. Holly looked over at Colin and smiled. "We need work on these crossings."

Colin gave the steering wheel a good smack and then jumped out of the truck right into the mud. He grabbed some boards out of the bed of the truck and placed them under the wheels. Holly slid into the driver's seat and gave the truck some gas. The truck started to slide toward Colin. The front end of the truck caught a rock on the right side of the vehicle, went up into the air, and tipped over onto the driver's side. It landed on Colin, crushing him between the driver's side door and the rock that he was sitting on.

Holly yelled for Colin as she climbed up toward the passenger side door. When she got out, she could see that the truck was wedged between several large

rocks and Colin's legs were trapped. He was awake but in excruciating pain. They were 3 miles from the nearest road and in a valley where there was no cell phone reception. Colin told Holly to walk out to the main road and get help. She covered him with her jacket, gave him a bottle of water, and began to jog down the road toward help.

1. With a patient who is trapped under a heavy object for an extended period of time, what condition are you concerned about?

   _____

   _____

   _____

2. What is typically the least amount of time required for this type of injury to occur?

   _____

   _____

   _____

3. What happens to the part of the body that is trapped under the heavy object?

   _____

   _____

   _____

4. What are the consequences of freeing the trapped body parts in relation to other organs in the body?

   _____

   _____

   _____

5. Describe the treatment for this patient and what physiological effect your treatment will have on the patient.

_____

_____

_____

Active Learning

Anatomy Review

1. Identify the major organs of the endocrine system in Figure 31-1.

a. _____

b. _____

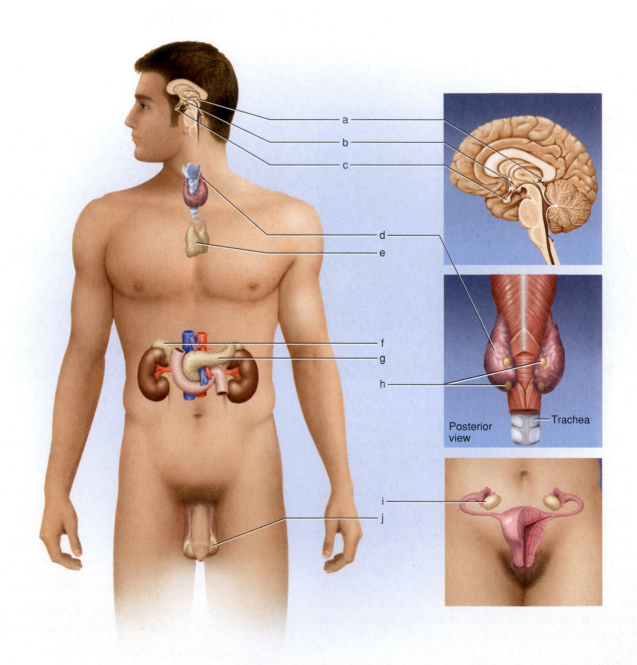

FIGURE 31-1

c. _____

d. _____

e. _____

f. _____

g. _____

h. _____

i. _____

j. _____

2. List the hormones that each portion of the pituitary gland secretes.

a. Posterior pituitary

_____

_____

_____

b. Anterior pituitary

_____

_____

_____

3. Use the textbook and other resources to complete the table below.

You Are There: Reality-Based Cases

Case 1

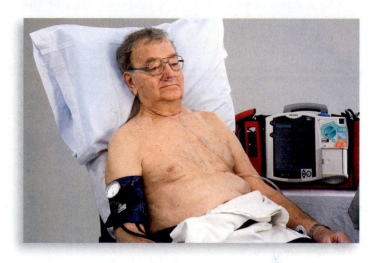

Every paramedic experiences a patient who falls into the "frequent flyer" category at some point in his or her career. Some frequent flyers are reasonable, and some have the ability to push every one of your buttons, but Mr. Schneider is one of the kindest men on the face of the planet. He is the kind of patient you don't mind seeing again and again.

Overview of Endocrine Glands			
Gland	**Location**	**Substance Secreted**	**Function**
Pituitary gland	*Located at the base of the brain.*		
Hypothalamus		*Secretes hormones that stimulate or suppress the release of hormones in the pituitary gland.*	
Pancreas			*Plays a role in hormone production (affecting the body's absorption of glucose) and in digestion of fats, carbohydrates, proteins, and nucleic acids (through its exocrine functions).*
Adrenal cortex			
Adrenal gland			
Thyroid gland			
Parathyroid glands			
Gonads			
Thymus			
Pineal body			

Mr. Schneider is a very brittle diabetic, whom you are called to evaluate on a regular basis by his wife Penny.

As a basic review of type 1 diabetes, answer the following questions:

1. Describe the role of insulin in the uptake of glucose into cells.

   _____

   _____

   _____

2. Explain the renal plasma threshold of blood sugar and what happens when that threshold is passed.

   _____

   _____

   _____

3. Describe the effects of hyperglycemia on fluid and electrolyte balances.

   _____

   _____

   _____

4. Explain how and why ketones are developed, and list the principles of diabetic ketoacidosis.

   _____

   _____

   _____

5. Describe the physiological concerns to keep in mind when correcting hyperglycemia or diabetic ketoacidosis (DKA).

   _____

   _____

   _____

Mr. Schneider and his wife give a good-faith effort to control his insulin-dependent diabetes mellitus. Despite their best intentions, you have seen him with a blood sugar of 8 mg/dL and a blood sugar greater than 1,000 mg/dL—and just about everything in between. Today you are called by Mrs. Schneider because Mr. Schneider has been lethargic and confused. As you approach Mr. Schneider, you note that his skin is cool, pale, and moist; his speech is slightly slurred; and he appears to have slight tremors in his upper extremities.

6. Based on the information you have obtained thus far, what is your general impression of Mr. Schneider's condition?

   _____

   _____

   _____

7. In relation to his diabetes, what would you say is Mr. Schneider's condition based on his presentation?

   _____

   _____

   _____

8. How will you approach this situation?

   _____

   _____

   _____

You begin to assess Mr. Schneider while your partner places him on 4 liters of oxygen via nasal cannula. Your assessment yields the following information: His GCS is 11 (eye opening—2; motor—5; verbal—4); his skin is cool, pale, and diaphoretic; his airway is clear; and he has no signs of respiratory distress with a room air oxygen saturation of 97% and a saturation of 100% on 4 liters of oxygen via nasal cannula. He has strong, regular radial pulses at a rate of 76 (corresponding with a sinus rhythm on the ECG), a blood pressure of 142/84, a temperature of 37°C, and a capillary blood sugar of 42 mg/dL.

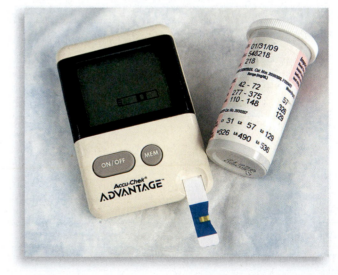

9. Based on your assessment findings, how will you proceed with your treatment of Mr. Schneider?

   _____

   _____

   _____

10. If Mr. Schneider has no vascular access, what are your other options for treatment?

_____

_____

_____

Following the treatment that you rendered, Mr. Schneider gradually increased his level of consciousness to his baseline (GCS of 15) and was grateful for the care that you provided for him.

Case 2

Your dispatch pager goes off as you stand in line for your morning coffee at a local coffee shop. The text screen reads:

Call Type: CODE-3 response possible cardiac arrest

Address: 1234 Broadway # 601

Cross Streets: E. 17th Ave. and E. 18th Ave.

Time Out: 08:35 hours

Run #: 0123456

When you arrive on scene, you find firefighters performing CPR on a 56-year-old female lying on the living room floor. As you approach the patient, you see the item in the following photograph lying on the floor next to the patient.

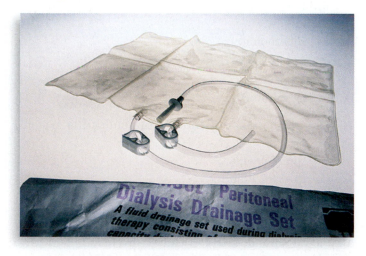

Apparently, the patient had collapsed onto the couch as she was sitting down. There is no trauma, and the AED screen that the first responders applied to the patient shows asystole. The patient was moved to the floor by friends, and CPR was performed as soon as the patient was removed from the couch.

1. What is your general impression of the patient's condition?

_____

_____

_____

2. What is the significance of the bag by the patient's head?

_____

_____

_____

3. What questions should you ask the family or friends in relation to this bag?

_____

_____

_____

4. What is your initial priority in treating this patient?

_____

_____

_____

Your partner intubates the patient, and you establish an external jugular IV while CPR is being performed on the patient. You administer epinephrine and atropine according to the American Heart Association pulseless arrest algorithm. The patient remains in asystole, and CPR is continuing with a fresh compressor. When you attempt to obtain a history from the patient's friends, they tell you that she is a peritoneal dialysis patient and that she had been complaining of difficulty breathing since yesterday. She has not received her dialysis for 2 days because she has an infection at her dialysis catheter. Her friend tells you that the patient has been staying with her for the past 3 days due to a domestic violence situation. She had to leave in a hurry, and her medications didn't make it into the box with all her dialysis supplies.

5. What physiological changes might you expect to see in a dialysis patient who has not received dialysis in the past 2 days? In what ways will the patient's medical condition and recent medical history alter your treatment approach?

_____

_____

_____

Test Yourself

1. The element that is essential for cell function, neural transmission, membrane stability, bone structure, and blood coagulation is _____.

2. Type 1 diabetes, also referred to as insulin-dependent diabetes mellitus (IDDM) or juvenile onset diabetes (JODM), develops due to a lack of

a. thiamine.

b. insulin.

c. sodium.

d. glucose.

3. Individuals with adult onset diabetes (AODM), or type 2 diabetes, have enough insulin to avoid the development of

   a. insulin shock.

   b. alkalosis.

   c. lactic acidosis.

   d. diabetic ketoacidosis.

4. _____ coma is primarily seen in individuals with long-standing untreated hypothyroidism.

5. What is the function of insulin?

   _____

   _____

6. Respiratory alkalosis occurs when there are decreased respirations and decreased removal of CO_2.

   True

   False

7. Patients with hypoglycemia have too little

   a. thiamine.

   b. glucose.

   c. insulin.

   d. dextrose.

8. Graves' disease is a severe form of hyperthyroidism.

   True

   False

9. The ideal pH for the body is between _____ and _____.

10. The best way to determine whether patients are intoxicated is to observe their behavior.

    True

    False

11. Metabolic acidosis occurs when there is

    a. a fluid shift.

    b. an increase in acid.

    c. an increase in base.

    d. a decrease in acid.

12. Describe the function and therapeutic uses of magnesium.

    _____

    _____

13. A 45-year-old patient has a complaint of nausea, vomiting, and diarrhea for 3 days. Physical assessment reveals hypotension, tachycardia, and the presence of orthostatic vital signs. In this scenario, the recommended fluid to use for fluid replacement is _____.

14. In diabetic ketoacidosis, the presence of ketone bodies results in

    a. hyperglycemia.

    b. hypercalcemia.

    c. hypernatremia.

    d. hyperketonemia.

15. An elderly diabetic patient is unconscious and responsive to noxious stimuli. His wife reports that the patient had been complaining of abdominal pain and vomiting the night before. The patient has warm, flushed skin and is tachycardic, hypotensive, and experiencing Kussmaul's respirations. You should suspect

    a. respiratory acidosis.

    b. metabolic acidosis.

    c. respiratory alkalosis.

    d. metabolic alkalosis.

16. Which system is responsible for regulating pH by influencing the concentration of bicarbonate in the blood?

    a. Bicarbonate

    b. Renal

    c. Cardiac

    d. Respiratory

17. One of the major glands of the endocrine system is

    a. the stomach.

    b. the gall bladder.

    c. the pancreas.

    d. the liver.

18. Acute adrenal crisis is caused by insufficient levels of

    a. sodium.

    b. cortisol.

    c. norepinephrine.

    d. epinephrine.

19. Which of the following is considered to be an electrolyte?

    a. Red blood cells

    b. Calcium

    c. Glucose

    d. Membrane

20. An adult patient is experiencing excessive perspiration, palmar erythema, hyperkinesis, and double vision. Extension tremor is present when the patient fully extends his arms. Vital signs are HR of 124, BP of 162/80, and RR of 22. The most likely cause of these findings is _____.

21. Which gland is responsible for producing norepinephrine and epinephrine in the fight-or-flight syndrome?
    a. Pituitary
    b. Pineal body
    c. Adrenal
    d. Thyroid

22. Glucagon is produced by the alpha cells of the _____ gland.

23. The _____ gland controls the functions of many other endocrine glands.

24. What three symptoms are referred to as the three P's?

    _____

    _____

Need to Know

The following represent the Key Objectives of Chapter 31:

1. *Explain how positive and negative feedback in the endocrine system helps maintain homeostasis.*

   The endocrine system is regulated by a complex feedback system that is similar to a thermostat. When an individual sets a particular temperature on a thermostat, the device then measures the actual temperature. If the temperature exceeds the set point, the thermostat turns off the heating system, and when the temperature falls below the set point, it turns the system back on. The endocrine system works in much the same fashion.

   A *positive-feedback mechanism* is a mechanism whereby one action creates additional actions of the same type. For example, in the extrinsic clotting mechanism, when an injury occurs, blood contacts the blood vessel wall or the tissue outside of the blood vessel, causing the release of a complex of substances called tissue thromboplastin (factor III). Factor III, along with calcium ions, activates factor VII, which along with calcium ions activates factor X. These are the initial steps in the clotting cascade, which is a classic example of a positive-feedback mechanism.

A *negative-feedback mechanism* is a check-and-balance system that helps to maintain homeostasis. It utilizes receptors to detect deviations from a set point and effectors that help compensate for the abnormal condition. Once the condition returns to normal, the set point is once again achieved, and the effectors shut down (see the Active Learning Exercise on negative feedback in Chapter 8, Physiology Overview, in the textbook). Figure 31-2 illustrates negative-feedback inhibition in the pituitary-thyroid axis.

2. *Describe the systemic effects of alterations in pH balance.*

   The pH that is being referred to in this section is the pH of blood. It is a direct reflection of the number of hydrogen ions in the blood. The normal range of pH in the blood (7.35–7.45) is inversely

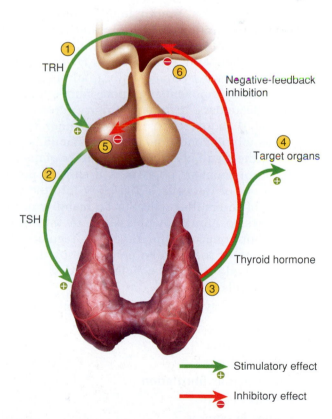

FIGURE 31-2   Negative-Feedback Inhibition in the Pituitary-Thyroid Axis (1) The hypothalamus secretes thyrotropin-releasing hormone (TRH). **(2)** TRH stimulates the anterior pituitary to secrete thyroid-stimulating hormone (TSH). **(3)** TSH stimulates the thyroid gland to secrete the two thyroid hormones, T_3 and T_4. **(4)** T_3 and T_4 stimulate the metabolism of most cells throughout the body. **(5)** T_3 and T_4 also *inhibit* the release of TSH by the pituitary. **(6)** To a lesser extent, T_3 and T_4 also *inhibit* the release of TRH by the hypothalamus.

related to the concentration of hydrogen ions in the blood. In other words, as the concentration of hydrogen ions increases, the pH begins to fall; as the level of hydrogen ions begins to drop, the pH begins to increase.

Acidosis is the condition that exists when the pH of the blood drops below 7.35. *Alkalosis* is the condition that exists when the pH of the blood rises above 7.45.

To maintain a homeostatic balance of pH, the body utilizes three primary buffer systems: the chemical buffer system; the respiratory system; and the renal system. Increases or decreases in HCO_3- are referred to as metabolic alkalosis or acidosis, respectively. Increases or decreases in PCO_2 are referred to as respiratory acidosis or alkalosis. (Table 31-4 in the textbook discusses the primary types of acid/base disorders.)

3. *Discuss the systemic effects of electrolyte imbalances.*

   a. *Potassium* is a predominantly intracellular electrolyte (95% of K+ is located intracellularly) that affects muscle tissues, digestion and metabolism, and homeostasis. *Hyperkalemia* can be caused by renal failure, adrenal insufficiency, and movement of potassium out of the cells secondary to trauma (injury [crush syndrome, rhabdomyolysis], surgery, tumor, burns, or hemolytic conditions). Hyperkalemia is typically the result of an increased intake of dietary or supplementary potassium, a shift of potassium out of the cells of the body into the vascular or interstitial space, or an inability of the kidneys to eliminate potassium in the urine. The hormone aldosterone helps regulate the excretion of sodium and potassium by the kidneys; if aldosterone deficiency exists, potassium levels will rise.

   Signs and symptoms of hyperkalemia include:
   - Nausea
   - Bradycardia
   - Heart blocks
   - Ventricular fibrillation
   - Weakness
   - Muscle cramps
   - Diarrhea
   - Gastrointestinal distress
   - ECG: peaked T waves, depressed ST segment, depressed P waves, widened QRS complex

   Hypokalemia can be caused by renal or GI losses, inadequate potassium intake, transcellular shift, and certain medications. Potassium can be lost through vomiting and diarrhea caused by GI conditions, and through excessive urination, as seen in diabetics who have hyperglycemia and in patients taking certain medications such as some diuretics (thiazides). Diabetic patients who are being treated for hyperglycemia have likely experienced a shift of potassium out of the cell and into the bloodstream as a result of the high concentration of intravascular blood sugar. Once insulin is administered, glucose will enter the cells of the body, and potassium will follow, creating hypokalemia.

   Signs and symptoms of hypokalemia include:
   - Palpitations
   - Skeletal muscle weakness
   - Paralysis
   - Constipation
   - Nausea, vomiting, and/or diarrhea
   - Abdominal cramping
   - Polyuria, nocturia, and/or polydipsia
   - Psychosis, delirium, and/or hallucinations
   - Depression, lethargy
   - Hypotension
   - Cardiac arrhythmias, bradycardia, or tachycardia
   - Hypoventilation and respiratory distress or failure
   - Cardiac arrest

   b. *Sodium* plays a significant role in the regulation of water. Where sodium goes, water will follow. *Hypernatremia* can be caused by problems with the renal concentrating mechanism (renal or hormonal) and by water losses. Severe hypernatremia can have a significant impact on the cerebral vasculature and, in severe cases, can lead to subarachnoid hemorrhage.

   Hyponatremia tends not to be clinically significant until it results in a reduction in serum osmolality (excess of total body water compared to electrolytes) due to electrolyte depletion, dilution of the electrolytes, or both. Hyponatremia influences cellular edema and central nervous system function. Hyponatremia is associated with neurological symptoms; the severity of these symptoms is influenced by the acuteness of the onset. The slower the onset, the less likely the symptoms will be severe.

   The neurological symptoms of hyponatremia include headache, seizures, and coma and are typically associated with a significant and rapid drop in serum sodium. Hyponatremia is also associated with nausea, malaise, and flulike symptoms. (See Table 31-3 in the textbook for a summary of hyponatremia and hypernatremia.)

c. *Magnesium* is associated with the regulation of the absorption of calcium and myocardial function and assists in relaxing the smooth muscle of the bronchioles and arterioles. *Hypermagnesia* is somewhat unusual, but it can be caused by chronic renal disease and rhabdomyolysis.

Signs and symptoms of hypermagnesia include:

- Nervousness, confusion
- Decreased blood pressure
- Widened QRS complex
- T wave segment elevation
- Respiratory distress
- Flushing
- Nausea and/or vomiting

Hypomagnesia tends to be caused by conditions that create shifts in electrolyte balances, which include renal disease; diuretic therapy; some antihypertensive medications; hyperthyroidism; diabetes; pancreatitis; parathyroid disorders; and diarrhea.

Signs and symptoms of hypomagnesia include:

- Fatigue, irritability, anxiety
- Weakness
- Muscle tightness or spasms
- Dysmenorrhea
- High blood pressure
- Cardiomyopathy
- Nerve conduction problems
- Anorexia
- Insomnia
- Sugar cravings
- Poor nail growth

Specific cardiac findings can include widening of the QRS complex and peaking of the T wave, as well as prolongation of the PR interval and flattening of the T wave.

d. *Calcium* is needed for normal cell function, neural transmission, membrane stability, bone structure, and blood coagulation. *Hypercalcemia* can develop as a result of several conditions including hyperparathyroidism, malignancy, and certain medications. Parathyroid-hormone-mediated hypercalcemia is caused by an increase in calcium absorption from the intes-

tine, and non-parathyroid-hormone-mediated hypercalcemia is typically caused by malignancy that increases resorption within the bone.

The symptoms associated with hypercalcemia are not unique to this condition; thus prehospital identification of hypercalcemia is unlikely. Signs and symptoms include:

- Nausea, vomiting
- Abdominal or flank pain
- Constipation
- Depression, ALOC, lethargy
- Weakness
- Polyuria
- Hypertension
- Bradycardia
- ECG: shortened QT interval, various degree of heart blocks

Hypocalcemia can be caused by a number of factors. The more common causes include hypoalbuminemia (the most common cause), a decreased ability to utilize calcium stored in bone; an increased loss of calcium from the kidneys into the urine; a decreased absorption of calcium in the intestine; and abnormal binding of calcium. (See Chapter 31 in the textbook for a complete list of the causes of hypocalcemia.) There are varying degrees of hypocalcemia with both acute and chronic presentations. The chronic hypocalcemic patient tends to have more generalized complaints, whereas the patient with acute hypocalcemia may present with cardiac dysrhythmias and cardiovascular collapse.

Signs and symptoms of hypocalcemia include:

- Muscle cramps or spasms
- Seizures or syncope
- Tingling sensations, focal numbness
- Angina
- Dry skin or brittle nails
- Hypotension
- Rales, bronchoconstriction, wheezing
- Laryngeal stridor
- Dysphagia
- Altered mental status
- Bradycardia

4. *Describe the different types of diabetes and their effects on the body.*

a. *Hyperosmolar hyperglycemic nonketotic syndrome (HHNS).* HHNS is severe hyperglycemia (frequently > 600 mg/dL) with associated fluid and electrolyte imbalances and the possibility of ketones in the blood and metabolic acidosis. Seen in type 2 diabetics; the scant amount of insulin circulating in the bloodstream paradoxically increases the blood glucose level by allowing just enough sugar intake by the cells to continue metabolism. However, the body continues to demand more glucose intake, causing the dramatic rise in blood sugar levels. HHNS is seen frequently in the elderly and presents with ALOC and fluctuations in hemodynamic status, poor skin turgor, dry mucous membranes, sunken eyeballs, and hypotension.

b. *Diabetic ketoacidosis (DKA).* DKA is most frequently seen in type 1 diabetics and is characterized by hyperglycemia (blood sugar > 300 mg/dL) that causes osmotic diuresis (and in turn electrolyte imbalances and dehydration), hyperketonemia, and metabolic acidosis. The classic symptoms for DKA include polyuria, polydipsia, and polyphagia, as well as general malaise. Other classic signs include Kussmaul's respirations and acetone odor on the breath. Again, the metabolism of lipids that occurs in DKA is considered by some to be the differentiating factor between HHNS and DKA.

c. *Hypoglycemia.* The normal range of blood sugar is 60–120 mg/dL, but the normal range varies between different sources. In general if you are dealing with a known diabetic who has a relatively low blood sugar and any of the following signs and symptoms, it is prudent to administer some form of glucose to this patient. A slightly high blood sugar is more desirable for the patient's well-being than a very low blood sugar:

- Tremors
- Dizziness, headache, impaired vision
- Confusion, altered mental status, or abnormal behavior
- Seizures
- Loss of consciousness
- Slurred speech
- Pale skin, diaphoresis
- Sympathetic nervous system response:
  - Anxiety
  - Sweating
  - Vasoconstriction (pale, cool skin)
  - Tachycardia
- Parasympathetic nervous system response:

- Hypotension
- Bradycardia
- Nausea
- Hunger

d. *Insulin-dependent diabetes (type 1).* Type 1 diabetes is characterized by the inability of the pancreas to secrete insulin. This is most often due to autoimmune destruction of the pancreatic beta cells. Because glucose requires insulin to cross the cell membranes and provide the fuel for cellular metabolism, patients with type 1 diabetes are required to take exogenous insulin in order for this process to take place. Type 1 diabetics are responsible for regulating their own homeostasis when it comes to their blood sugar level.

e. *Non-insulin-dependent diabetes (type 2).* Type 2 diabetics have the ability to secrete endogenous insulin. They produce levels of insulin that may be insufficient to allow for optimal glucose metabolism. However, in contrast to type 1 diabetics, insulin levels in type 2 diabetics may be sufficient enough to prevent diabetic ketoacidosis from occurring.

f. *Gestational diabetes.* Gestational diabetes mellitus (GDM) can be defined as any degree of glucose intolerance with an onset or first recognition during pregnancy. Untreated GDM can lead to fetal macrosomia (overly large fetus), hypoglycemia, hypocalcemia, and hyperbilirubinemia. In addition, mothers with GDM have higher rates of cesarean delivery and chronic hypertension.

g. *Diabetes insipidus.* Diabetes insipidus is caused by the inadequate secretion of antidiuretic hormone (vasopressin) by the pituitary gland, resulting in polyuria and polyphagia.

5. *Describe the effects of corticoadrenal insufficiency, hypopituitarism, hyperthyroidism, and thyrotoxicosis.*

a. *Corticoadrenal insufficiency.* Acute adrenal crisis is a life-threatening condition caused by insufficient levels of cortisol, a hormone that is produced in the adrenal gland. Adrenal crisis can develop if the adrenal gland deteriorates, such as in the case of *Addison's disease*, or primary adrenal insufficiency; if the pituitary gland is injured; or if preexisting adrenal insufficiency is not treated appropriately. Symptoms associated with adrenal crisis include:

- Dizziness
- Weakness

- Sweating
- Abdominal pain
- Nausea, vomiting
- Altered level of consciousness
- Weight loss
- Fever
- Tachycardia

b. *Hypopituitarism.* Occurs when the pituitary gland fails to produce adequate amounts of one or more of its hormones. This can be a particularly serious condition because the pituitary gland produces hormones that control many other endocrine glands.

c. *Hyperthyroidism (thyroid storm) and thyrotoxicosis.* Hyperthyroidism occurs because of an overactive thyroid gland. It is a subset of thyrotoxicosis, which is caused by excess synthesis and secretion of thyroid hormone by the thyroid. Although they are distinct disease processes, the terms hyperthyroidism and thyrotoxicosis are sometimes used interchangeably. Graves' disease (an autoimmune disorder) is the cause of greater than 50% of the cases of hyperthyroidism.

An excess of thyroid hormone results in:

1. Increased metabolic rate
   a. Increased body heat
   b. Increased cardiac contractility
   c. Vasodilation
2. Increased sympathetic nervous system symptoms

Symptoms associated with hyperthyroidism include:
- Periorbital edema
- Chemosis or conjunctival edema
- Proptosis weakness, muscle weakness
- Weight loss
- Nervousness, anxiety, tremors, hyperactive state
- Heat intolerance, warm skin, diaphoresis

- Oligomenorrhea (abnormally light menses)
- Tachycardia, palpitations
- Hypertension
- Smooth skin
- Atrial fibrillation or high output failure (in elderly individuals)

Younger patients tend to exhibit more sympathetic activation, such as anxiety, hyperactivity, and tremor. *Older patients* have more cardiovascular symptoms, such as dyspnea and atrial fibrillation with unexplained weight loss.

Connections

- The U.S. Food and Drug Administration (www.fda.gov/diabetes/insulin.html) provides additional information on insulin.
- See Chapter 25, Soft Tissue and Muscle Trauma, in the textbook for more detailed information on crush syndrome.
- Link to the companion DVD for a chapter-based quiz, audio glossary, animations, games and exercises, and, when appropriate, skill sheets and skill Step-by-Steps.

Street Secrets

- **When in ROME** Use the following mnemonic to help remember what happens with pH and carbon dioxide (PCO_2) in respiratory acidosis and alkalosis, and what happens with pH and bicarbonate (HCO_3) in metabolic acidosis and alkalosis (remember that PCO_2 is associated with respiratory conditions and HCO_3 is associated with metabolic conditions):

ROME

Respiratory = **O**pposite
- pH is high, PCO_2 is down (alkalosis)
- pH is low, PCO_2 is up (acidosis)

(*continued*)

Need to Do

The following skills are explained and illustrated in a step-by-step manner, via skill sheets and/or Step-by-Steps in this text and on the accompanying DVD:

Skill Name	Skill Sheet Number and Location	Step-by-Step Number and Location
End-Tidal Capnography	10 – DVD	N/A
Blood Glucose Assessment	26 – DVD	26 – DVD

Metabolic = Equal

- pH is high, HCO_3 is high (alkalosis)

- pH is low, HCO_3 is low (acidosis)

■ **Treat the Patient, Not the Monitor** If you have an insulin-dependent diabetic patient with an altered level of consciousness and signs and symptoms of hypoglycemia, but a glucometer reading that does *not* suggest hypoglycemia, treat the patient rather than the glucometer. The patient with a normal or high blood sugar will be far better off receiving dextrose than would a hypoglycemic patient who did not receive dextrose. Many EMS regulatory agencies go as far as to include this advice in their protocols so that glucometer malfunctions do not result in harm to the patient.

The Drug Box

Dextrose 50%: Used to correct hypoglycemia and, in some cases, along with insulin, help move potassium back into the cells (crush syndrome, etc.).

Normal saline (0.9%): A crystalloid solution used for fluid replacement in patients suffering from hypovolemia as a result of crush syndrome or hyperglycemia (DKA, etc.).

Lactated Ringer's solution: A crystalloid solution used for fluid replacement in patients suffering from hypovolemia as a result of crush syndrome or hyperglycemia (DKA, etc.).

Sodium bicarbonate: A synthetic buffer used to treat metabolic acidosis and to help prevent the deposition of myoglobin in the kidneys leading to renal failure in crush syndrome.

Calcium chloride: Acts as a cell wall stabilizer and helps shift potassium back into the cells.

Albuterol: Offers some assistance in moving potassium back into the intracellular space.

References

1. O. Better, "Rescue and Salvage of Casualities Suffering from the Crush Syndrome after Mass Disasters," *Military Medicine* 164, no. 5 (1999): 366–69.
2. D. Shier, J. Butler, and R. Lewis, *Hole's Human Anatomy and Physiology,* 11th ed., New York: McGraw-Hill, 2007, p. 519.
3. Ibid., p. 809.
4. "The Healing Handbook for People with Diabetes," www.umassmed.edu/diabeteshandbook/chap01.htm (accessed May 24, 2006).
5. D. L. Kasper et al., *Harrison's Principles of Internal Medicine,* 16th ed., New York: McGraw-Hill, 2005, pp. 2159–61.
6. J. E. Tintinalli, G. D. Kelen, and J. S. Stapczynski, "Emergencies in Renal Failure and Dialysis Patients," in *Emergency Medicine—A Comprehensive Study Guide,* 6th ed. New York: McGraw-Hill, 2004.

Answers

Are You Ready?

1. Crush syndrome

2. Four hours

3. The continual pressure results in minimal or no circulation of blood into the compressed area, and the tissue undergoes ischemia followed by necrosis (tissue death).

4. The toxins that are released into the bloodstream when trapped body parts are released can overwhelm the heart, kidneys, and liver. Patients suffering from crush syndrome typically present with hyperkalemia, hypocalcemia, metabolic acidosis, acute myoglobinuric renal failure, hypovolemic shock, and possibly compartment syndrome.[1] Even if treated aggressively, patients suffering from crush syndrome can fall victim to "smiling death" (i.e., the patient has a moment of relief, hence the smile, followed by rapid death due to the massive release of toxins into the bloodstream, causing disruption in the electrical system and/or life-threatening dysrhythmias).

5. It is important to anticipate the development of crush syndrome and try to establish IV therapy prior to releasing the patient from the crushing object. It will permit the administration of fluids, analgesia, and drugs for resuscitation or stabilization. Isotonic solutions (normal saline and lactated Ringer's solution) have been shown to be effective in the treatment of hypovolemic shock associated with crush syndrome. Sodium bicarbonate has been used to help prevent the deposition of myoglobin in the kidneys that leads to renal failure as well as treatment for metabolic shock. Calcium chloride and albuterol help shift potassium back into the cells.

Active Learning

1. a. pineal gland; b. hypothalamus; c. pituitary gland; d. thyroid gland; e. thymus; f. adrenal gland; g. pancreas; h. parathyrozid glands; i. ovary (female); j. testis (male)

2. a. posterior pituitary—secretes oxytocin and antidiuretic hormone (ADH); b. anterior pituitary—secretes thyroid-stimulating hormone (TSH), adrenocorticotropic hormone (ACTH), follicle-stimulating hormone (FSH), luteinizing hormone (LH), and prolactin (PRL)

3. See Table 31-1.

TABLE 31-1   **Overview of Endocrine Glands**

Gland	Location	Substance Secreted	Function
Pituitary Gland	Located at the base of the brain.	Secretes hormones to stimulate the adrenals, thyroid, pigment-producing skin cells, gonads, growth hormone, antidiuretic hormone, prolactin, and oxytocin	Controls many functions of the other endocrine glands.
Hypothalamus	Located in the brain.	Secretes hormones that stimulate or suppress the release of hormones in the pituitary gland.	Influences water balance, sleep, temperature, appetite, and blood pressure.
Pancreas	Located across the back of the abdomen, behind the stomach.	Secretes insulin, glucagon, and pancreatic juices— exocrine products (pancreatic amylase and pancreatic lipase).	Plays a role in hormone production (affecting the body's absorption of glucose) and in digestion of fats, carbohydrates, proteins, and nucleic acids (through its exocrine functions).
Adrenal cortex	The outer portion of the adrenal gland is located on top of each kidney.	Secretes hydrocortisone, androgen hormone, and aldosterone.	Affects metabolism, blood pressure, and saline balance.
Adrenal glands	Located on top of each kidney.	Secrete hydrocortisone, androgen hormone, and aldosterone.	Work in conjunction with the hypothalamus and pituitary gland.
Thyroid gland	Located in the lower portion of the anterior neck.	Secretes thyroxin, triiodothyronine, and calcitonin.	Plays an important role in the body's metabolism, body heat, bone growth, and regulation of calcium balance.
Parathyroid glands	Located on the surface of the thyroid gland.	Secrete parathyroid hormone.	Affect calcium levels in the blood.
Gonads	Male—testes	Secrete androgens: testosterone and dihydrotestosterone.	Development of secondary sex characteristics
	Female—ovaries	Secrete estrogen and progesterone.	Development of secondary sex characteristics and changes that occur in the uterus during the female reproductive cycle, respectively.
Thymus	Located in the upper part of the chest.	Produces T-lymphocytes, which are white blood cells.	Fights infections and destroys abnormal cells.
Pineal body	Located in the middle of the brain.	Produces melatonin.	Regulates the wake-sleep cycle of the body.

You Are There: Reality-Based Cases

Case 1

1. Insulin promotes the facilitated diffusion of glucose through the cell membrane when it binds with insulin receptors on the cell surface. Individuals with insulin-dependent diabetes lackz functioning pancreatic beta cells that are capable of producing insulin; thus, insulin-dependent diabetics depend on synthetic insulin to allow glucose to cross the cell membrane and maintain reasonable blood glucose levels.[2]

2. Because insulin-dependent diabetics lack pancreatic beta cells that produce insulin, they rapidly become hyperglycemic without the use of exogenous insulin. Once blood glucose levels reach the *renal plasma threshold*[3] (approximately 180 mg/dL), the kidneys begin to spill glucose into the urine.[4]

3. The relatively high concentration of glucose in the vascular space draws potassium out of the cells, creating a relatively hyperkalemic environment. Because glucose is such a large molecule, water and some important electrolytes such as potassium and sodium tend to follow the glucose into the urine and are eliminated from the body. As potassium is eliminated in the urine, the potassium level begins to decrease. This process of glucose drawing water and electrolytes into the urine is known as *osmotic diuresis* and results in one of the classic presenting symptoms of a person with diabetes mellitus: polyuria, the excessive excretion of urine, resulting in profuse and frequent urination. Along with polyuria and the relative hypovolemia caused by the hyperglycemic osmotic diuresis comes an increased and prolonged sense of thirst (*polydipsia*). When the hyperglycemic condition is addressed by the administration of insulin, potassium is shifted back into the cells of the body along with glucose. If the potassium that was eliminated in urine is not replaced, the patient can experience life-threatening arrhythmias caused by hypokalemia.

4. With no ability of cells to utilize glucose, blood sugar level continues to rise. The cells of the body send chemical and electrical messages to the brain to *further* increase glucose levels. This results in another classic symptom of diabetes mellitus known as *polyphagia*. Polyphagia is an increase in hunger that results in an increase in food consumption. At the same time the brain increases the sense of hunger, it begins to convert stored sugar (glycogen) into glucose by releasing the hormone glucagon, which further increases blood glucose levels. After the stores of glycogen are exhausted, the body begins to break down fat, protein, and muscle for energy use. In the process, ketones in the form of ketoacids are formed, resulting in a metabolic acidosis.

5. Fluid replacement is particularly important in the prehospital setting because administration of insulin and potassium is frequently not in the paramedic's scope of practice. In-hospital care for the DKA patient may involve arterial blood gas analysis, electrolyte (especially potassium and sodium) analysis, and frequent blood glucose analysis. The treatment is based on replacing fluid loss, returning blood glucose to an acceptable level through the use of insulin administration, correction of the metabolic acidosis, correction of the hypokalemia through the administration of potassium, and the monitoring of the patient's status in response to treatments. Because electrolyte analysis is not readily available in the prehospital setting, monitor the patient for signs and symptoms of hypokalemia.[5]

6. Mr. Schneider has cool, pale, moist skin; his speech is slightly slurred; and he appears to have slight tremors to his upper extremities. Because these are signs and symptoms that could be caused by a number of serious conditions, he is sick until proven otherwise.

7. Mr. Schneider is presenting with classic signs of hypoglycemia.

8. The priority for Mr. Schneider is to assess and manage his ABCs. If no life threats are discovered in the primary assessment, Mr. Schneider would benefit from supplemental oxygen administration, an assessment of his vital signs (blood pressure, heart rate, respiratory rate and quality, temperature, ECG, pulse oximetry, and blood sugar analysis), and a focused physical exam and medical history should be completed rapidly.

9. Mr. Schneider appears to be relatively stable except for the fact that he has a capillary blood sugar of 42 mg/dL. This can be addressed by administering glucose. With a GCS of 11, it is not advisable to administer oral glucose due to the increased risk of aspiration. If IV access is possible, an IV should be established and, after any allergies to medications are clarified, Mr. Schneider should receive IV dextrose 50%. Monitor the patient for the desired response and any possible adverse reactions to the medication that you administered, document the time and dosage of medication administered, update vital signs, update blood sugar level, and transport Mr. Schneider to an appropriate receiving facility.

10. Alternative treatments for hypoglycemia depend largely on the patient's level of consciousness. If the patient is awake, able to follow commands and has an intact gag reflex, glucose can be administered by mouth with glucose paste or juice. If the patient is not able to self-administer the oral glucose, an alternative route needs to be considered. If the patient is too altered for oral administration of glucose, and there is no vascular access to administer IV dextrose, then IM administration of glucagon should be considered.

Case 2

1. This patient is very sick.

2. The bag is a peritoneal dialysis bag. If it belongs to the patient, it could have a significant impact on the way in which you treat her.

3. Is the patient on peritoneal dialysis? If so, when was she last dialyzed? Does she produce any urine? What medications does the patient take, and is the patient compliant with her medications? Was she complaining of anything prior to her collapse?

4. Continue CPR and assess the effectiveness of the compressions, ensuring that the compressor is compressing

at an appropriate depth and rate (1½ –2 inches deep at ± 100 compressions per minute) with complete recoil of the chest. Compressors should be switched out after five cycles of CPR (approximately 2 minutes) to avoid compressor fatigue and ineffective CPR. If IV cannulation and endotracheal intubation cannot be accomplished during CPR, these tasks should be attempted after five cycles of 30 compressions to 2 ventilations, or at approximately 2 minutes. IV epinephrine (1:10,000 concentration) should be administered every 3–5 minutes throughout the resuscitation, and atropine sulfate should be administered per the American Heart Association ACLS standards (pulseless arrest algorithm). All dialysis patients should have their blood glucose levels evaluated.

5. Noncompliance with dialysis for the past 2 days can result in the retention of metabolic waste and the inability to eliminate excess fluid. Patients in acute or chronic renal failure can develop uremia (contamination of the blood with urine) and azotemia (the buildup of blood nitrogen). Tintinalli et al.[6] state that excretory failure can lead to the buildup of over 70 different chemicals in the blood, including BUN, serum potassium, serum sodium, serum chloride, serum phosphate, and metabolic acids. The fact that the patient was complaining of difficulty breathing since yesterday likely indicates that she is suffering from fluid overload; IV fluid administration during treatment should be monitored carefully and limited to necessary fluid administration only. Because of the buildup of a number of substances in the blood, there are additional medications that can be considered to treat her asystolic cardiac arrest:

- Sodium bicarbonate, calcium chloride or calcium gluconate, albuterol, dextrose 50%, and insulin can all be used to help shift potassium to the intracellular compartment. It is also useful in the management of metabolic acidosis.
- Dextrose 50% can be beneficial if the patient is hypoglycemic.
- Magnesium sulfate can be useful to treat ventricular fibrillation (especially in the presence of hypomagnesemic VF) that is refractory to other antiarrhythmics and polymorphic ventricular tachycardia.

It is difficult to correct the chemistry abnormalities in a noncompliant dialysis patient without performing dialysis on the patient; since the patient is in cardiopulmonary arrest, dialysis is not an option at this time.

Test Yourself

1. Calcium

Calcium is needed for cell function, neural transmission, membrane stability, bone structure, and blood coagulation. Calcium balance is maintained through a variety of mechanisms, including parathyroid hormone (PTH), vitamin D, calcitonin, and magnesium.

2. b

IDDM develops due to a lack of insulin. Because of this, the individual administers exogenous insulin.

3. d

In type 2 diabetes there is usually enough insulin to avoid the development of diabetic ketoacidosis.

4. Myxedema

Myxedema coma is a severe and potentially life-threatening condition that can occur during the progression of hypothyroidism. It is usually precipitated in patients with chronic hypothyroidism by a secondary insult such as hypothermia, infection, other systemic diseases, or drug therapies.

5. The key function of insulin is to allow glucose into a cell. Insulin also stimulates liver and muscle cells to store glucose in glycogen and create proteins.

Insulin is produced by the beta cells of the pancreas. It is required by almost all the body's cells. Its major targets include the liver, fat cells, and muscle cells. When glucose is released into the circulation, it interacts with insulin to allow glucose to enter the cell. Without insulin, the amount of glucose that enters the cell is insufficient to meet the body's demands.

6. False

Respiratory alkalosis results from increased respirations and excessive removal of CO_2. It can result from a variety of causes, including hyperventilation, anxiety, overventilation of patients on assisted ventilation, CNS disorders, liver failure, coma, and fever. Increased respiratory rate and depth lead to hyperventilation, leading to excessive loss of CO_2 in expired air. As the PCO_2 and cerebral tissue PCO_2 fall, plasma and brain pH rise. Cerebral vasoconstriction results and may produce cerebral hypoxia.

7. b

Hypoglycemia involves low blood sugar. Hyperglycemia is an excess of blood sugar.

8. True

Graves' disease, an organ-specific autoimmune disorder, is a severe form of hyperthyroidism that involves a swollen thyroid. It accounts for more than 50% of the cases of hyperthyroidism.

9. 7.35, 7.45

High pH (> 7.45) is alkalosis, whereas low pH (< 7.35) is considered to be acidotic. Disturbances of acid-base metabolism can influence carbon dioxide (CO_2) and bicarbonate (HCO_3^-) concentrations. Increases or decreases in HCO_3^- are referred to as metabolic alkalosis or acidosis, respectively. Increases or decreases in PCO_2 are referred to as respiratory acidosis or alkalosis (see Table 31-4 in the textbook).

10. False

Intoxicated behavior does not always mean the patient is intoxicated. For instance, hypoglycemic patients may appear to be intoxicated due to their low blood sugar. It is essential to thoroughly assess all patients, especially when altered mental status is present.

11. b

Metabolic acidosis occurs when there is an excess of acid and the body is unable to compensate.

12. Magnesium helps regulate myocardial function and the absorption of calcium, relaxes smooth muscles, and may be used in the treatment of asthma and hypertension.

13. Normal saline

Aggressive fluid replacement will help restore intravascular volume, reduce blood sugar levels, and assist with the replacement of electrolyte loss.

14. d

Ketones are produced by the metabolism of fatty acids. Ketones can lead to metabolic acidosis.

15. b

Symptoms of metabolic acidosis include vomiting, abdominal pain, weakness, cardiac arrhythmias, tachycardia, and warm and flushed skin.

16. b

The respiratory system assists with the removal of CO_2, the bicarbonate system responds to changes in hydrogen concentration, and the renal system regulates pH by influencing the concentration of bicarbonate in the blood.

17. c

The glands of the endocrine system include: the hypothalamus, pituitary, thyroid, parathyroid, adrenals, pineal body, pancreas, and reproductive organs.

18. b

Cortisol assists in glucose regulation and influences the body's response to stress.

19. b

Calcium is one of the key electrolytes of the human body.

20. Graves' disease

Graves' disease is an autoimmune disorder affecting the thyroid gland. It is characterized by an increase in the production of thyroid hormones, potentially leading to thyrotoxicosis. The thyroid gland is typically enlarged, and the eyes protrude from the sockets. Signs of thyrotoxicosis include: sinus tachycardia; atrial fibrillation; systolic hypertension; soft, smooth skin; excessive perspiration; palmar erythema (red palms) and sweating; lid lag; extension tremor (when a limb is fully extended, it trembles); hyperkinesis (abnormal and sometimes uncontrolled muscle movements); and large-muscle weakness. Graves' disease should be suspected if any evidence of thyroid eye disease exists, including periorbital edema, diplopia (double vision), or proptosis (eyes protrude outward).

21. c

The adrenal medulla produces hormones called catecholamines, including epinephrine and norepinephrine.

22. Pancreas

Glucagon is a protein hormone that is produced and secreted by the alpha cells of the pancreas. Glucagon acts on the same cells as insulin, but it has opposite effects. It stimulates the liver and muscles to break down stored glycogen (glycogenolysis) and release glucose. It also stimulates the liver and muscles to stimulate gluconeogenesis (the formation of glucose) in the liver and kidneys.

23. Pituitary

Located in the brain beneath the hypothalamus, the pituitary gland controls the functions of many other endocrine glands and is therefore considered to be the master gland.

24. Polyuria, polydipsia, and polyphagia

The three P's include: polyuria (increased urine), polydipsia (increased thirst), and polyphagia (increased appetite). The three P's are a common set of findings in diabetic patients and can be an indicator of hyperglycemia or ketoacidosis.

chapter 32

Allergies and Anaphylaxis

Are You Ready?

It's early December, and the holiday season is well under way. A call for a "sick female" sends your unit into the chilly night air. Flashes of red and white light reflect off the storefront windows as you cautiously make your way through the traffic. As you arrive outside of the community hall, you see that a large party is being held at the facility.

Two young women, dressed in black evening dresses, are standing near the front entrance. One has her arms around the second. Both appear to be shivering, but the second woman has a look of distress on her face. They make their way toward your ambulance, with the first woman helping the second maintain her balance.

In the ambulance, you take a look at the patient. Fiona appears to be in her early twenties and in good physical health. She is breathing faster than normal, although her tidal volume seems normal. Her skin appears pale, and she feels cool to the touch. A strong odor of alcohol is on her breath, and her speech is slurred.

The other woman, Alyssa, is the patient's "best friend." She too appears to have been drinking, although she appears more alert and speaks more clearly. Alyssa reports that they had gone to a company holiday party. Because of the open bar they started to drink early and often. The buffet tables were filled with all kinds of food. She relates that the patient had gone to the bathroom earlier and was in there for awhile—more than just a few minutes. She went in to check on Fiona and found her kneeling on the floor, vomiting into the toilet. After assisting Fiona to her feet, Alyssa then helped her clean up a bit and get her coat. They originally tried to hail a cab to go home, but Fiona felt progressively sicker and finally asked Alyssa to "take me to the doctor's." Alyssa was concerned and had the doorman call 9-1-1.

1. Is Fiona sick or not yet sick? Why?

   _____

   _____

   _____

2. What are your first steps to manage Fiona's condition?

   _____

   _____

   _____

3. What are the possible reasons for Fiona's condition?

   _____

   _____

   _____

Active Learning

1. Get Your Peanuts Here!

In your readings, you learned that nuts are one of the most common allergens. Go to a supermarket near you and take some time walking through the aisles where the processed food is stocked. Look at the ingredient labels of many of the products available. How many products contain peanut oil or nut by-products? Which products do not have it clearly labeled in the ingredient label that they contain these additives?

2. The Pen Is Mightier Than . . .

. . . the stinger, one might say. Is a friend, family member, or coworker known to be prone to anaphylaxis? Does he or she carry an epinephrine autoinjector? If you have never seen one, ask if you can see it, and become familiar with the device and how it is used. If the individual does not carry one, encourage him or her to seek advice from a qualified physician about obtaining one.

3. Put IT in Order

Place the steps of an immediate-reaction allergy (shown in Figure 32-1) in order, leading to an allergic reaction:

Step 1: _____

Step 2: _____

Step 3: _____

Step 4: _____

Step 5: _____

You Are There: Reality-Based Cases

Case 1 (continued from chapter opener)

You can see that it's beginning to snow outside the back windows as you continue to assess Fiona's condition. She is still awake, although her speech remains slurred. She appears to tire and become short of breath as she speaks. Her breathing is rapid and shallow. You

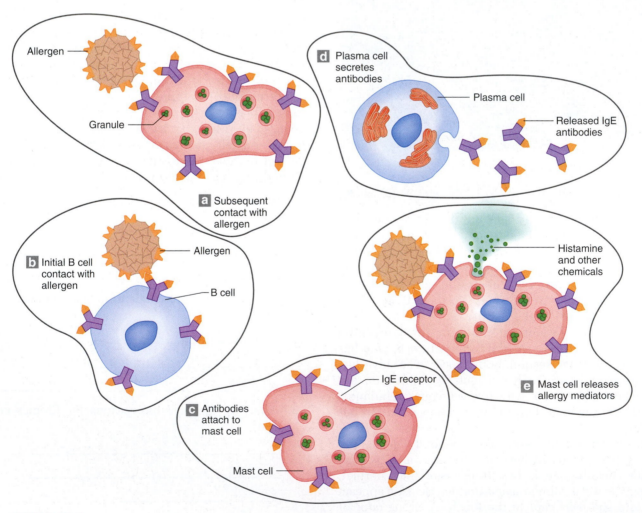

FIGURE 32-1

believe that you can palpate a radial pulse, although it is very faint and rapid.

Exposing her chest, you see no signs of hives, weals, or a rash. It's difficult to auscultate lung sounds, and you encourage her to breathe deeply. The sound of the idling ambulance drowns out most of what you're trying to hear. You conclude that her lung sounds seemed diminished bilaterally, especially at the bases.

Meanwhile your partner has evaluated Fiona's vital signs. She reports that the patient's heart rate is 130, blood pressure is 86/60, and respiratory rate is 26. The pulse oximeter reads 88%. Your partner has already placed an oxygen non-rebreather mask over Fiona's face and is applying the ECG electrodes.

1. Based on these findings, is Fiona still sick or not yet sick? Why?

_____

_____

_____

2. What other information should you elicit now?

_____

_____

_____

3. What might be causing Fiona's blood pressure to be low?

_____

_____

_____

The rest of the physical examination is unremarkable. Fiona's neck veins are flat. No accessory muscle use is evident. Her chest wall is nontender, as is her abdomen, which is soft upon palpation. With patient in the supine position, radial pulses are stronger and equal. No dependent edema is noted. There are no signs of needle marks or medical alert jewelry. Fiona admits to drinking alcohol but denies drug use. She has no medical history or prescribed medications. She is not allergic to any medications, although she is allergic to shellfish. She did have something to eat during the party, along with the alcohol.

4. What is your course of action now? Describe how you would treat this patient.

_____

_____

_____

Later that evening you return to the hospital to find Fiona still in the emergency department with her friend Alyssa. She looks significantly better and is a bit sheepish sitting on the gurney with a hospital gown on. It appears that during the excitement of the party Fiona had forgotten about her allergy to shellfish and had eaten some of the crab dip that was available. It is possible that her rapid intake of alcoholic beverages prevented her from sensing the ensuing anaphylactic reaction until it was almost too late.

Test Yourself

1. Autoimmunity is when the body relabels "friendly" substances inside the organs as foreign, "nonself" cells and attacks them.
   True
   False

2. What upper respiratory signs and symptoms are associated with an allergic reaction or anaphylaxis?

_____

_____

3. Which antibody is primarily responsible for promoting inflammation and allergic reactions?
   a. IgE
   b. IgA
   c. IgG
   d. IgD

4. Diphenhydramine inhibits muscarinic receptors.
   True
   False

5. What is the general difference between the way the first and second lines of immunity defense respond to invasion?

_____

_____

6. At what point does a person have an allergic or anaphylactic reaction to a substance?
   a. After immunotolerance is developed
   b. During the second exposure
   c. After autoimmunity is developed
   d. During the initial exposure

7. What symptoms and signs would you expect to find in a patient suffering from atopic rhinitis?

_____

_____

8. When managing the airway of a patient experiencing respiratory collapse as a result of an allergic reaction, what techniques should be *avoided*?

_____

_____

9. _____ is the process by which the body destroys the invading antigen along with the normal cell.

10. What role do natural killer (NK) cells play during the immune response?

_____

_____

11. In dealing with a patient experiencing an anaphylactic reaction, what is the first medication (after oxygen) that you will administer in order to reverse bronchoconstriction and wheezing?

   a. DuoNeb

   b. Diphenhydramine

   c. Epinephrine

   d. Albuterol

Scenario: You are called to a residence for a woman with dyspnea. Upon arrival, you find the 40-year-old patient sitting in a chair, struggling to breathe. You note swelling of her face and airway and stridor. There is no evidence of hives or itching. Your patient states that she is allergic to peanuts, but she denies ingesting any. During your scene survey you note a loaf of freshly baked banana bread that your patient appears to have eaten. She tells you she made it with some flour her mother brought her from Europe.

12. What is most likely the source of this patient's reaction?

   a. Bananas

   b. Soy products

   c. Peanuts

   d. Lupin flour

13. What medication would be contraindicated in this patient?

   a. Epinephrine

   b. Albuterol

   c. Ipratropium bromide

   d. Diphenhydramine

Scenario: You respond to the local nursing home for a patient experiencing localized facial swelling, along with swelling of the tongue, lips, and upper airway. The patient appears to be in some distress. You learn from your SAMPLE history that your patient takes lisinopril (an ACE inhibitor) for high blood pressure.

14. What should you suspect your patient is experiencing?

   a. Angioedema

   b. Anaphylaxis

   c. Severe allergic reaction

   d. Mild allergic reaction

15. What treatment would *not* be effective in treating this patient?

   a. DuoNeb

   b. Corticosteroids

   c. Epinephrine

   d. Albuterol

Need to Know

The following represent the Key Objectives of Chapter 32:

1. *Assess and provide care for a patient with an allergic reaction.*

   It is critical to determine whether your patient is experiencing a simple allergic reaction or a possible life-threatening anaphylactic reaction. Your primary assessment of a simple allergic reaction should reveal a patient who is alert, has a patent airway, has adequate tidal volume and rate of respirations, and exhibits no signs of poor perfusion. During your secondary assessment you may find signs and symptoms of an allergic reaction that might include a rash, urticaria, petechiae, purpura, and itching.

   Care for a simple allergic reaction is mostly supportive. Diphenhydramine delivered intramuscularly or by mouth can be used to diminish the uncomfortable itching associated with the allergic reaction. Epinephrine is *not* indicated for this presentation; the risk/benefit analysis of epinephrine use is weighted toward risk of cardiac irritability, dysrhythmia, and possible cardiac arrest.

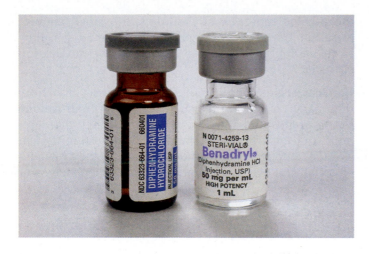

2. *Assess and provide care for a patient experiencing anaphylaxis.*

Anaphylaxis is differentiated from a simple allergic reaction by the presence of hypotension and difficulty breathing, or potential compromise of the upper airway due to swelling. These rare situations can be life threatening, so speed and accuracy of assessment and treatment are paramount. Remember that, in general, the faster the onset of symptoms, the higher the morbidity and mortality of the patient.

Initially support airway, breathing, and circulatory status through BLS procedures. Assist ventilations with a bag-mask and high-flow oxygen if the patient is unable to breathe adequately. Be prepared to manage the airway using advanced techniques if it becomes nearly or completely obstructed. As soon as anaphylaxis is suspected, administer epinephrine intramuscularly or subcu-

taneously immediately to reverse the signs of anaphylaxis. If perfusion to the skin and muscles is extremely poor, administer epinephrine intravenously. Diphenhydramine should be delivered IV to stop the histamine-mediated overresponse of the immune system. The patient may also require large volumes of fluid to overcome the loss of plasma from the intravascular space.

💿 Connections

- Did you have difficulty identifying Fiona's underlying condition? You may want to review the textbook for information on hypoperfusion and shock (Chapter 13, Shock Overview), respiratory emergencies (Chapter 28, Pulmonary), and of course allergies and anaphylaxis (Chapter 32).
- See Chapter 16, Medication Administration, in the textbook to review the proper administration of epinephrine subcutaneously or intramuscularly and diphenhydramine intravenously.
- See Chapter 12, Airway Management, Ventilation, and Oxygenation, in the textbook to review the procedures of bag-mask ventilation, endotracheal and nasotracheal intubation, and needle and surgical cricothyroidotomy.
- Link to the companion DVD for a chapter-based quiz, audio glossary, animations, games and exercises, and, when appropriate, skill sheets and skill Step-by-Steps.

Need to Do

The following skills are explained and illustrated in a step-by-step manner, via skill sheets and/or Step-by-Steps in this text and on the accompanying DVD:

Skill Name	Skill Sheet Number and Location	Step-by-Step Number and Location
Endotracheal Intubation	7 – Appendix A and DVD	7 – Chapter 12 and DVD
Nasal Intubation	14 – DVD	14 – DVD
Needle Cricothyroidotomy	19 – Appendix A and DVD	19 – Chapter 12 and DVD
Intramuscular Drug Administration	50 – Appendix A and DVD	50 – Chapter 16 and DVD
Nebulized Drug Administration	52 – Appendix A and DVD	52 – Chapter 16 and DVD
Subcutaneous Drug Administration	53 – Appendix A and DVD	53 – Chapter 16 and DVD
Autoinjector Drug Administration Device	59 – DVD	N/A

Street Secrets

- **Hives** Look thoroughly for the presence of hives. They may not always be readily apparent (e.g., on exposed arms). Expose the chest, back, and abdomen in order to visualize these areas if you suspect anaphylaxis or allergic reaction.

- **Don't Jump to Conclusions** Not all anaphylaxis will *always* have one symptom or another. If the patient provides an accurate history of contacting a known allergen, quickly check for signs of poor perfusion, decreasing blood pressure, or constricting airway. If your patient is not exhibiting any of these signs, do *not* administer epinephrine! In these situations, the risk of cardiac injury is greater than any benefit that epinephrine might provide.

- **Anaphylaxis versus Simple Reaction** Be *very* cautious in differentiating anaphylaxis from a simple allergic reaction. The administration of epinephrine in an allergic reaction will not provide any benefit in management and can cause significant cardiovascular compromise. Ensure that the patient has signs of hypoperfusion and/or hypoxia before considering such a risky intervention.

The Drug Box

Epinephrine: As a catecholamine, epinephrine temporarily reverses the effects of the anaphylactic reaction by increasing heart rate, dilating the small bronchioles, and constricting the peripheral vascular system in order to increase core perfusion. Because of its cardiotonic effects, epinephrine is generally administered through a subcutaneous or intramuscular route. It may be delivered intravenously if the reaction is severe enough to minimize peripheral circulation. Patients may feel very anxious after administration, and their cardiovascular system must be monitored very closely.

Diphenhydramine: The antihistamine effect of diphenhydramine blocks the receptor sites of the cells prone to IgE overstimulation. By blocking the sites, the body cannot shift fluids and the anaphylactic reaction slows or stops. Diphenhydramine may be administered intramuscularly for mild reactions or intravenously for severe ones. It may cause sleepiness for certain patients, so monitor the patient for any mental status changes after administration.

Albuterol: A beta agonist, albuterol is used to reverse the effect of bronchoconstriction, which can occur during an anaphylactic reaction. Albuterol is fairly well tolerated by most patients, having fewer side effects than Alupent. Albuterol is administered through the inhaled route, usually diluted in a small amount of saline. Care is taken to ensure that the oxygen flow is at the appropriate rate to aerosolize the medication correctly.

Corticosteroids: Because of a delayed onset of action, the use of corticosteroids such as methylprednisolone in the prehospital arena has a lower priority than epinephrine and diphenhydramine. While steroids can reverse the effect of bronchoconstriction, they have no effect on the cardiovascular problems associated with anaphylaxis.

Answers

Are You Ready?

1. Fiona appears ill. Although her condition may be due to excessive alcohol in her system, there are enough signs and symptoms to begin a full assessment on the patient—she is breathing rapidly, has slurred speech, and is unable to walk without assistance.

2. Perform a primary assessment and begin providing supplemental oxygen.

3. There are a number of possible causes for the patient's presentation. You will need to find out more about the history of the event and about Fiona's condition before moving forward on differential diagnosis.

Active Learnzing

3. Step 1: b; Step 2: d; Step 3: c; Step 4: a; Step 5: e

You Are There: Reality-Based Cases

1. The primary assessment confirms that the patient is seriously ill. Although her airway is open, she is breathing rapidly and has a faint, fast pulse. She is hypotensive, even for a person of her size and age. Her lung sounds are diminished, and her blood oxygen saturation is low enough for concern.

2. Fiona's past medical history is important to elicit. It may be difficult to obtain this from the patient herself, as she struggles to breathe. Her friend Alyssa may be able to provide more information about the patient's past medical history, any medications she might be taking, and any allergies she has to medications.

3. There could be several reasons why the patient is hypotensive. Physiologically, it could be her heart rate (pump), a loss of vascular resistance (pipe), and/or a loss of fluid in the vasculature (volume). There are no obvious signs that point to an underlying condition. However, it is unlikely that the alcohol consumption is causing her blood pressure to be low. She has not vomited significantly, nor is her heart rate high enough to cause significantly decreased cardiac output. Is it possible that she is third spacing secondary to some type of allergic reaction? It will be important to find out exactly what the patient ate.

4. There are two primary problems that need immediate intervention: her respiratory distress and low blood pressure. It appears that Fiona is having some type of anaphylactic reaction, possibly as a result of eating some shellfish during the party. After the administration of high-flow oxygen, she should receive an adrenergic agent such as epinephrine administered subcutaneously or intramuscularly, followed by diphenhydramine intravenously. She should also receive hydration therapy—IV boluses of normal saline or lactated Ringer's solution to help place volume into her vasculature quickly. The patient's condition requires extremely close monitoring and reassessment. The rapidity of the onset is of concern; as a rule, the faster the onset, the worse the situation.

Test Yourself

1. True

   When the immune system malfunctions, it can turn against the body's own cells. It relabels "friendly" substances inside the organs as foreign, "nonself" cells and attacks them. This process is called autoimmunity. When this occurs, the patient may develop chronic diseases that have episodic flare-ups during times when the immune system is actively damaging body cells and tissues. Some examples of autoimmune disorders that are encountered in the prehospital setting include: lupus, type 1 diabetes mellitus, Graves' disease, hemolytic anemia, and multiple sclerosis.

2. Signs and symptoms of an allergic reaction or anaphylaxis that are evident in the zupper respiratory system include: nasal congestion, nasal itching, sneezing, hoarseness, laryngeal edema, hypersalivation, and supraglottic edema.

   Of these, you should be most concerned about laryngeal edema and its related signs (hoarseness, laryngeal stridor, hypersalivation, supraglottic edema), as laryngeal edema is potentially life threatening.

3. a

   IgE antibodies are responsible for promoting the inflammatory process and initiating the allergic reaction.

4. True

   Diphenhydramine is an H1 blocker and is used for several other conditions. Since they are effective in inhibiting muscarinic receptors, these medications have an anticholinergic effect. They are especially useful for reversing capillary permeability (responsible for swelling), itching, and some smooth muscle contraction. They are also central nervous system (CNS) depressants and cause sedation.

5. The first line of defense functions by helping prevent or limit penetration and exposure or helping the body shed the allergenic substance. The second line of defense is an internal response that occurs once an allergen penetrates the body. The body recognizes these foreign hostile cells and begins attacking back.

   Examples of the first line of defense include simple reflexes (like coughing), mechanical barriers (like the skin), and chemical barriers (like tears or stomach acids).

The second line of defense includes natural killer cells, neutrophils, and monocytes.

6. b

   During the initial exposure the patient is sensitized to the antigen and the body produces antibodies; on second and subsequent exposures the antibodies recognize the invader and produce an exaggerated response.

7. In an atopic rhinitis type reaction the nasal passages are irritated, causing sneezing, itching, runny nose, and itchy, watery eyes.

   Atopic rhinitis is generally associated with outdoor allergies. By itself it is not life threatening.

8. Placement of oropharyngeal and nasopharyngeal airways should be avoided as they may generate laryngospasm.

   If the patient is apneic, or the rate and quality of respirations are insufficient, initiate ventilatory support using a bag-mask with supplemental oxygen.

9. Allergic reaction

   During an allergic reaction the body labels an antigen as an enemy, but for some unknown reason the reaction is overblown and excessive. Instead of simply destroying the allergen and returning the body to homeostatic balance, the body sets into motion a process that destroys normal cells as well.

10. The natural killer cells destroy any infected body cells in an attempt to limit further spread of the antigen. Natural killer cells also secrete chemicals that enhance the development of inflammation.

    Natural killer cells are special lymphocytes that provide protection by secreting cytolytic (cell-cutting) substances called perforans that lyse (cut) cell membranes.

11. c

    The mainstay of prehospital care for severe anaphylaxis is epinephrine. Administer 0.3 mg epinephrine intramuscularly or subcutaneously as soon as possible, followed by the administration of diphenhydramine or another approved antihistamine.

12. d

    Lupin flour is used in Europe and other countries as a replacement for soy flour. Persons with known allergies to peanuts need to avoid foods containing lupin flour.

13. c

    Administration of ipratropium bromide (Atrovent) is contraindicated in persons who are allergic to peanuts.

14. a

    Angioedema usually involves swelling of the lips, tongue, oral cavity, and upper airway. The swelling is non-pitting and has a tendency to manifest itself in areas where the skin is not taut (like the face). There are two main causes for the reaction. Typically it is an allergic reaction to angiotensin-converting enzyme (ACE) inhibitor medications.

15. c

    Angioedema from this type of allergic reaction is not mediated by IgE and will usually not respond to standard treatments such as epinephrine and antihistamines.

Problem-Based Learning Case 5
Happy New Year

Part I: The Case

Dispatch and Scene Size-Up

You respond for a dispatch of "shortness of breath" at an address in the heart of Chinatown. As you approach the scene, you realize that it is the beginning of the Lunar New Year, and the streets are very crowded with people trying to see the parade winding its way through the narrow streets. After trying to navigate through the crowd, you decide to park the ambulance and walk the remaining block to the address.

1. *How does this situation impact your ingress to and egress from the patient? What strategies can you employ to help mitigate the situation? What pieces of equipment should you bring to the patient?*

_____

_____

After making your way through the crowd, you arrive at the apartment building address where the patient is located. You climb up two flights of narrow stairs and work your way down a narrow, dimly lit hallway. Other apartment residents are also in the hallway. Everyone appears to be Asian, and they stare at you as you make your way around them. The door to the apartment is ajar. As you knock, you can smell a strong, sharp odor of camphor mixed with menthol, as well as a more subtle incense smell.

2. *Based on your observations, what are some of your concerns about the situation? What strategies can you employ to help mitigate your concerns?*

_____

_____

The Primary Assessment (Initial Assessment) and Initial Differentials

A young Asian female greets you at the door and motions for you to follow as she rushes down a long hallway that leads to a small bedroom. You see an approximately 60-year-old woman sitting on the edge of a bed. The patient appears to be in moderate to severe respiratory distress and looks fatigued. You introduce yourself to the patient, and she responds in Chinese, struggling to speak in four- to six-word sentences. She appears to be working hard to breathe with supraclavicular retractions and abdominal muscle use. As you palpate the woman's radial pulse, you note that she has warm, moist skin and a rapid, irregular radial pulse. The odor that you had detected at the doorway is now very strong as you lean close to the patient.

The woman who greeted you at the door responds to the patient's comments in Chinese. When you ask them if they speak English, they both shake their heads indicating that they do not.

3. *What is your initial impression of the patient, and what is your priority in caring for this patient?*

_____

_____

History and Physical Exam (Secondary Assessment and History)

Next to the patient on a bedside table you see several prescription pill bottles, two types of metered dose inhalers, and several bottles of what you think are Chinese medications. The pill bottles, which were dated from yesterday, are penicillin, dextromethorphan, and prednisone. The metered dose inhalers are albuterol and Advair. One of the Chinese medication bottles is a jar with "Tiger Balm" printed on the label.

4. *What do the medications on the patient's bedside table suggest as far as her past medical history? Do the medications give you any clues as to her current presentation?*

_____

_____

As you and your partner begin to perform a physical examination on the patient, a middle-aged Asian male enters the room and says something to the patient that you do not understand. The patient does not answer. He then turns to you and in very broken English asks, "What is wrong with my wife?" You explain that you are in the process of trying to determine what is going on. He offers that his wife has a history of asthma and for the past 4–5 days she has been complaining of fever, nausea, vomiting, diarrhea, and a cough. She called her private doctor yesterday and was prescribed several of the medications that you found on her table.

The patient's vital signs are:

HR: 116, irregular
BP: 94/72

RR: 24

You note the following monitor readings:

SpO$_2$: 84%
ETCO$_2$: 50 mmHg
ECG: See Figure PBL 5-1
Physical exam findings include:
General appearance: Height and weight proportionate; middle-aged Asian female; appears in significant distress; palms on knees; torso leaning forward
HEENT: Jugular venous distention
Chest: Wheezing scattered throughout both lung fields; S$_3$ heart tone
Abdomen: Mildly distended, soft, nontender
Pelvis: No remarkable findings
Extremities: Edema in lower extremities; full range of motion (ROM); pulses noted × 4; rashes on medial aspects of both arms

5. *What is your primary suspicion as to the patient's underlying condition? Explain why you believe this to be the case. Can you provide another explanation as to what is causing the patient's respiratory distress? What will be your next steps in the management of this patient's presentation?*

_____

_____

Field Impression(s) and Formulation of Treatment Plan

The patient's name is Han Roon Lin, according to one of the medication labels. Her level of distress does not decrease with oxygen administration. Her husband also appears anxious, although he does not say anything to her.

There is a knock on the apartment door. A middle-aged woman looks surprised as the husband opens the door. She is holding a pot of what smells like soup, but the pot lid is covering it. She enters the room, while the husband talks quickly to her, pointing at the

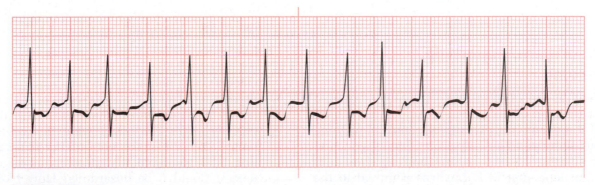

FIGURE PBL 5-1

pot. He becomes quite animated, as the woman holding the pot appears defensive.

The husband looks at you and says that his wife is allergic to peanut oil. You can see that what is in the pot is similar to what is in the rice bowl sitting near the patient.

6. *Does this information change your impression of the patient's presentation? What other information do you seek now? How will you treat this patient?*

_____

_____

Transportation and Ongoing Care

You have moved the patient to the ambulance, which took nearly 20 minutes because of the crowd situation. The police arrived, however, and helped you clear a path through the masses. The noise is deafening, making it difficult to auscultate lung sounds.

Mrs. Lin's condition has not worsened, nor has it improved. She became more diaphoretic during the extrication process, but her vital signs remain nearly the same as originally measured. The pulse oximeter now reads 95%, and her $ETCO_2$ reading is 46%.

During your treatment, a translator was located and brought to your location. In the course of your questioning, the patient reports that she has had nausea and vomiting for the past 2 days. She has had very little food or drink during that time. She complains of "burning" in her chest and abdomen, while rubbing both areas with her hand. In addition, the soup that was provided by the neighbor contained no peanut-based product.

A 12-lead ECG indicates ST segment elevation in leads V_4 through V_6. The QRS complexes appear wider than normal.

7. *Does this additional information reinforce or weaken your suspicions? Does it introduce any new theories as to the cause of her condition?*

_____

_____

Transfer of Care, Follow-Up, and Outcome

Upon arrival at the hospital, the attending physician takes over the care of the patient. You provide a brief history of the event, your treatment, and the ongoing assessment findings. The physician thanks you and turns her attention to the patient and her husband. You find out later that Mrs. Lin was admitted to the critical care unit. The emergency department staff was able to support the patient's blood pressure with an inotropic medication, although with difficulty. Additional lab values include:

Creatinine phosphokinase (CPK): 30–200 units/L
CPK, MB fraction: 0.0–8.8 ng/mL
CPK, MB fraction percent of total CPK: 0%–4%
CPK, MB2 fraction: < 1 unit/L
Troponin I: 0.0–0.4 ng/mL
Troponin T: 0.0–0.1 ng/mL

8. *What is your final set of differential impressions? Do you have one very likely suspicion? Which pieces of information provided the clues you needed to strengthen your theory? Which inotrope did the ED staff most likely use to support the patient's blood pressure?*

_____

_____

Long-Term Outlook

Mrs. Lin is discharged 10 days after admission. During the next year, she visits a cardiologist for follow-up and to adjust her new medication regimen.

Part II: Debriefing

Responses to Part I questions:

1. Emergency responders try to get as close to the scene as safety concerns permit. The key factor here is safety. The crowd is large and very dense, preventing you from reaching your destination with the ambulance. Can you clear a path through the crowd without injuring a bystander? If not, can someone else do that for you while you are engaged with patient care? Since egress from the patient appears to be a challenge, you will need to carry equipment a distance to the patient's side. Did you anticipate specific pieces of equipment you might need based on the original dispatch? Did the weight of the equipment factor into your decision? Did you consider how you might need to transport the patient out of the address and back to the ambulance?

2. Entering a culturally foreign environment can present several challenges. Did you consider language, customs, and beliefs about emergency health care? If you did, what actions did you consider taking to try to overcome those challenges? Are there specific resources you might want to look for at the scene? Did you make note of the hallway conditions? Do you have any ideas about the odor you detect? Could it be hazardous? How likely could that be, based on your current observations?

3. What did you find on your primary assessment? How was her level of consciousness? Is her airway patent? What is her breathing status? Are you satisfied with the circulatory status? Regardless of the language barrier, your patient does appear to be in respiratory distress. Does she require ventilatory assistance, or will supplemental oxygen be sufficient? Justify your response.

4. Not only does the patient have Western-style medications, but she also uses "alternative" medication forms, in this case Chinese medicine. To what degree does this impact your care of the patient? Did you make the link that the Tiger Balm is the source of the odor? Is the date of the medications meaningful? What does it mean to you? Did you look up the medications?

5. Throughout any EMS incident, you will shift your "view" of the patient constantly. At times you will be very focused on the task at hand; for example, an intubation attempt will require your complete attention, if only for a few seconds. At other times you will mentally step back and review all your findings thus far. This is one of those situations. Visualize the patient; she certainly appears to be experiencing significant distress. Now, review the information the husband provided. What acute or chronic conditions could cause the history as described? Then, consider your physical findings. Based on your original set of possible causes, do any of them rise to the top of your suspicion index?

   Even if you are not exactly certain what the underlying cause is, you must still provide effective treatment to improve the patient's respiratory status. Did you consider any therapies? What risks do you take in order to provide the greatest benefit?

6. There are several connections to make. First, does the husband imply that the soup contains peanut oil? Second, is the food in the pot the same as what is in the bowl? Third, did the patient eat what was in the bowl? Fourth, when did she eat? Finally, could an allergic or anaphylactic reaction be a root cause of the patient's presentation?

7. You may have guessed by now that your patient's condition is a complex one to differentiate. In reality, many cases that seem to be straightforward are more complicated than they appear. It is not the goal of the paramedic to declare a diagnosis; instead, keeping your options open in terms of what might be happening to your patient can help prevent tunnel vision. Did you find out if the atrial fibrillation is related to the ST segment changes on the 12-lead ECG?

8. How many possible causes did you consider? Based on the provided information, did you consider asthma, COPD, congestive heart failure, anaphylaxis, myocardial infarction, dehydration, or infection? For maintenance of blood pressure, the hospital probably used a combination of vasopressors such as dopamine and dobutamine.

Part III: Case Discussion

Mrs. Lin is a complicated patient. As a paramedic you will need to put on your detective's cap and sleuth your way through the myriad of findings. This can be a challenge to the paramedic student. Take a deep breath, and think your way through this case.

First consider the environment. Although it may not be intentionally hazardous, the large crowd in the street, the distance from the ambulance to the apartment building, and the need to climb flights of stairs and maneuver down a narrow, dark hallway present challenges to ingress to and egress from the scene. Did you consider performing any of the following actions to minimize the risk of injury to yourself and your crew?

- Increase lighting using flashlights or portable lamps.
- Decrease body profile.
- Anticipate scene needs and pack appropriate equipment.
- Distribute the weight of carried gear evenly to keep your balance.
- Stay with your partner or crew to maintain group awareness of the situation.

In a predominantly ethnic environment, be acutely aware of how you engage with the patient, family, and bystanders. You may want to review Chapter 48, Patients from Diverse Cultures, in the textbook for more information on this subject. If language differences present a challenge, finding an interpreter who can accurately and calmly translate information between you and the patient would be very helpful. Learning simple medical phrases in the more common languages is relatively easy and can help not only with language translation but also winning your patient's trust.

Your assessment began of course with a primary assessment of the patient. Although her airway is patent, she is in moderate to severe respiratory distress. She has a radial pulse; however, it is rapid and irregular. Her skin signs are abnormal. These signs tell you that you will need to intervene immediately and quickly determine important pertinent findings to help develop an effective treatment plan.

You establish the patient's mental status by introducing yourself. She responds to you. This implies that she is perfusing her brain well enough to engage appropriately with her environment. You have not yet objectively measured her oxygen and carbon dioxide levels in the blood, but at least clinically it would be a safe approach to provide her with supplemental high-flow oxygen as opposed to assisting her ventilations with a bag-mask.

The patient's medications provide a wealth of clues. She is taking a recently prescribed antibiotic and a cough suppressant, which implies some type of respiratory infection. The local and systemic corticosteroids, coupled with albuterol, point to a possible history of asthma or COPD. The Chinese medicines pose another challenge. Alternative medications can have synergistic or antagonistic properties, similar to "Western" medications. There may be drug interactions that could complicate, or even be the cause of, the patient's current presentation. (Tiger Balm, by the way, is a common salve used by many Asian cultures to soothe general discomfort.)

At the end of the secondary assessment, did you have a cause of the patient's underlying condition in your mind? Or was the overall picture of the patient still too fuzzy? Did you pick up on the fact that the patient *spoke with the physician* and may not necessarily have seen the physician? Again, clues to the problem can be subtle.

Review your findings. The pertinent findings include JVD, even though the patient is borderline hypotensive. How can this happen? Is the wheezing related somehow to this finding, or is it caused by her chronic asthma? Bronchoconstriction can occur as a result of several mechanisms, not just asthma.

How might you treat Mrs. Lin at this point? A beta agonist such as albuterol is typically used to reverse bronchoconstriction. This may help to improve the oxygenation status of the patient. However, even though albuterol is a very specific *beta$_2$ agonist,* it may still have cardiac effects. This means that if your patient is experiencing a myocardial infarction, you may be placing additional workload on the heart muscle. This is a typical *risk versus benefit analysis* that you must be comfortable making each time you consider an intervention such as a medication administration—will it help or hurt the patient? In this case, the potential for benefit probably outweighs the potential for harm, so the delivery of the albuterol may be appropriate for this patient.

As you begin treatment, you will also be continuing to assess the patient and gather more information. If you recall from Chapter 5, Clinical Decision-Making, in the textbook, collecting more information about the patient's condition is vital to refining your field impression. In this case, a 12-lead ECG and an ETCO$_2$ reading may provide you with more clues to help you differentiate your suspicions.

As the case continues, the possibility of anaphylaxis is presented. How likely is this possibility? It would seem that a severe allergic reaction would be less likely to cause the patient's condition, especially if it were determined that a significant amount of time had passed between ingestion and symptom onset. However, the language barrier can cloud your ability to be precise on chronology, so you will need to work diligently to determine if there were any peanut-based products in the meal. It is later reported that there weren't any, so anaphylaxis is unlikely. You cannot discount the theory entirely, though, since many of the signs and symptoms can be attributed to a severe allergic reaction.

The 12-lead ECG findings are a cause for concern. In your research you may come across the fact that the atrial fibrillation, coupled with the change in ST segment elevation and emergence of a Q wave, are indications for a lateral wall myocardial infarction. This may be causing a drop in the blood pressure secondary to loss of myocardial contractility. There may be a corresponding fluid shift out of the pulmonary capillary beds and into the interstitial space, which may be causing the bronchioles to constrict, causing the wheezing.

Did you determine that the hospital lab values seem to confirm this chain of events? The CPK values are elevated, as are the troponin markers, which is highly indicative of an AMI. An echocardiogram and other tests may be conducted to help even further solidify this diagnosis.

Part IV: Further Learning Paths

- Review the following chapters for additional resources for this case:
  - Chapter 9, Safety and Scene Size-Up
  - Chapter 10, Therapeutic Communications and History Taking
  - Chapter 28, Pulmonary
  - Chapter 29, Cardiology
  - Chapter 48, Patients from Diverse Cultures
- The American Medical Student Association has a section on how to increase cultural awareness in medicine. Their website is www.amsa.org.
- Speaking of Web searches, did you try key words such as cultural awareness, cultural competency, medicine, Asian, Chinese?
- The Henry J. Kaiser Family Foundation has compiled a list of resources surrounding cultural competence in health care. A PDF file of this report can be located at the foundation's website at www.kff.org. At the main page, type in "Compendium of Cultural Competence Initiatives in Health Care" in the search field to bring up the link.

chapter 33

Infectious and Communicable Diseases

Your scene assessment reveals a typical college student's dorm room: clothes are strewn across the floor, and books and papers are scattered everywhere. On the nightstand are bottles of cough suppressant and over-the-counter acetaminophen. Some empty beer cans are lying on the floor. There is a garbage can next to the bed that is covered with emesis. Shari is curled up in her bed, partially covered by a bedsheet. She is wearing a nightshirt that is also stained with emesis. She does not respond to your voice when you call her name, and her eyes do not open. She is diaphoretic. As you pull back the bedsheet, you see that she is incontinent of urine.

The roommate doesn't believe that Shari had been drinking. She doesn't know exactly; she was away for the weekend and just got back into town.

1. What are your initial steps?

_____

_____

_____

2. Identify some of the possible causes of Shari's condition based on the scene findings.

_____

_____

_____

Are You Ready?

In a college dorm room, you evaluate Shari Lewiston, an up-and-coming basketball player who is very popular among her teammates. Her roommate called campus police after she found Shari in her bed throwing up. The police contacted EMS after they were unable to get Shari to stand up.

Active Learning

1. Matching the Bugs

Match each of the following examples of pathogens or their diseases with the appropriate classification.

Examples	Answer	Classifications
AIDS		a. Bacteria
Botulism		b. Fungi
Chickenpox		c. Parasites
Chlamydia		d. Viruses
Giardia		
Gonorrhea		
H. influenzae		
H5N1		
Head lice		
Hepatitis B		
Meningococcus		
Pertussis		
Rabies		
Rocky Mountain Spotted Fever		
Rubeola		
Scabies		
Smallpox		
Staphylococcus		
Tetanus		
Thrush		
Tuberculosis		

Start Here
Healthy patient

_____ period:
agent present,
reproducing, no
symptoms

Virulence + Dose +
Route of entry −
Resistance = Infection

_____ phase:
period between initial
infection and onset of
symptoms

_____ phase:
agent can spread from
one host to the next

_____ period:
symptoms appear

2. Drive the Stagecoach

A pathogen will create a pathway that has distinct phases or stages. It's like a stagecoach that moves from one stop to the next along the route. See if you can name each "stage" of an illness created by a pathogen, and then link them in order of progression by drawing arrows from one stage to the next in the following figure.

3. All's Fair in Love and War

Think about this: Your body is in a constant state of war—battling the pathogens out in the environment that are intent on getting in to grow and reproduce. Fortunately your body has a variety of mechanisms to fight off infection. For each of the following terms, describe how it is involved with "germ warfare."

a. Cilia: _____

b. Diarrhea: *Forces pathogen out of the body*

c. GI tract: _____

d. Inflammatory response: _____

e. Intestinal flora: _____

f. Mucus: _____

g. Skin: _____

h. Stomach: _____

i. Turbinates: _____

4. Does This Make Me Look Protected?

Personal protective equipment (PPE) is a must-have for the stylin' paramedic. You just can't go wrong with a pair of latex or nitrile gloves—they go with just about any uniform. However, what should a fashion-conscious medic wear when facing specific types of patient presentations? Check off each of the types of PPE you would use, based on the patient presentation, in the following table.

Presentation	Gloves	Protective Eyewear	Surgical Mask	N-95 Mask	Gown
Abdominal pain, emesis	X	X	X		
Abdominal pain, melena					
Active emesis, headache, photophobia					
Bleeding profusely, combative					
Confused, nauseous					
Fever, chest pain, nonproductive cough					
Fever, diarrhea × 24 hours; no vomiting					
Generalized weakness, syncope					
Hemoptysis for 12 hours, difficulty breathing					

5. The ABCs of Hepatitis

Match up the type of hepatitis with its description:

Hepatitis Type	Answer	Description
A		1. Most commonly caused by contaminated drinking water; disease tends to be more severe in third-trimester pregnancy states.
B		2. Believed to worsen conditions brought on by other forms of hepatitis.
C		3. Most recently discovered form; there is little known about its virulence.
D		4. Can result in a chronic condition that carries a 70% chance of liver failure.
E		5. Virus can survive on surfaces up to 7 days and can result in a chronic disease state.
G		6. Commonly spread through unsanitary food preparation. Does not result in a chronic state.

You Are There: Reality-Based Cases

Case 1 (continued from chapter opener)

Shari's breathing rate is fast. While diaphoretic and pale, her skin is very warm to the touch. You can feel a weak, rapid radial pulse. There is no smell of alcohol on her breath. You find nothing else of significance during your primary assessment. The only response you elicit is a moan when you log-roll her on her side to inspect her back.

The physical examination also reveals little information. You note a faint rash across the patient's upper chest and arms. Her lung sounds are clear bilaterally. You do not elicit pain upon palpation of the chest and abdomen, and no bruising or other signs of trauma are evident. Her legs feel tense as you palpate them, and the patient moans again when you do. None of the medicine bottles on the table are empty. In fact they appear mostly full. Upon inspection, you note that the vomitus is mostly yellow in color and liquid in nature.

You obtain her vital signs: HR of 130, BP of 84/50, and RR of 26. ECG is a sinus tachycardia. SpO_2 = 85% on high-flow oxygen, and $ETCO_2$ = 54 mm Hg. A glucometer reading shows a blood glucose level of 90 mg/dL.

1. What diseases or illnesses do you suspect are causing Shari's condition?

   _____

   _____

   _____

2. Are any of your original possibilities less likely with this information?

   _____

   _____

   _____

3. How would you manage Shari's condition?

   _____

   _____

   _____

You prepare to insert a 16-gauge catheter into the patient's left cubital fossa. As the needle penetrates the vein, she jerks her arm back. Blood sprays out of the catheter, splashing your right eye. You blink and close your eye instinctively.

4. What should you do next?

   _____

   _____

   _____

Test Yourself

1. You accidentally stuck yourself with a bloody needle. After washing the site, you should
   a. immediately seek the assistance of a physician.
   b. ask about the infection status of the patient and report exposure if the patient has an infectious disease.
   c. report exposure to your supervisor and request the infection status of the source patient.
   d. make sure you are up-to-date on your immunizations and remain alert for symptoms.

2. What agents cause communicable diseases?

   _____

   _____

3. You are treating a patient with a skin rash. She mentions that she recently had a staph infection. You should be aware that she may be taking
   a. immunoglobulin.
   b. antiviral medication.
   c. antifungal medication.
   d. antibiotic medication.

4. Why is the respiratory tract more prone to pathogen invasion than the skin?

   _____

   _____

5. Health-care providers must use universal precautions
   a. only during patient contact when the risk of exposure to bodily fluids is high.
   b. only with patients who show signs of having an infectious disease.
   c. only with patients known to have an identified infectious disease.
   d. with every patient, even those without symptoms of infectious disease.

6. Describe the correct method for removing gloves.

   _____

   _____

7. List three instances in which a paramedic should practice social isolation.

_____

_____

8. Your HIV-positive patient slit his wrists. Upon arrival, you find the patient coughing and spitting. What type of face masks should be used?
   a. N-95 class face mask for the paramedic and a surgical mask for the patient
   b. Surgical masks for both the paramedic and the patient
   c. N-95 class face masks for both the paramedic and the patient
   d. N-95 class face mask for the paramedic and an oxygen mask for the patient

9. Which phases of infection are most likely to overlap?
   a. The incubation phase and the communicable phase
   b. The incubation phase and the disease period
   c. The latent period and the disease period
   d. The latent period and the communicable phase

10. You are called to a 19-year-old college student who presents with sudden onset of a fever, headache, and stiff neck. How should you proceed?

_____

_____

11. How is the avian flu (H5N1) transmitted?

_____

_____

12. Your 63-year-old patient presents with a cluster of painless ulcerations on his chest and a "deep, gnawing pain" in his lower right leg. This is an example of
   a. secondary syphilis.
   b. tertiary syphilis.
   c. primary syphilis.
   d. peripheral syphilis.

13. The childhood viruses chickenpox, mumps, measles, and rubella are all primarily spread
   a. by the oral route.
   b. through indirect fecal contact.
   c. through respiratory droplets.
   d. parenterally.

14. List five conditions that increase the risk of developing active tuberculosis.

_____

_____

15. As a paramedic, it is your responsibility to ensure that you stay up-to-date on such immunizations as
   a. diphtheria-pertussis-tetanus, hantavirus, and mononucleosis.
   b. measles-mumps-rubella, Lyme disease, and influenza (annual immunizations).
   c. measles-mumps-rubella, diphtheria-pertussis-tetanus, and polio.
   d. diphtheria-pertussis-tetanus, hepatitis C, and screening for tuberculosis.

16. List three national agencies involved in public health.

_____

_____

Scenario: You are called to a 4-year-old boy who presents with low-grade fever, swollen lymph nodes, and a generalized rash.

17. You should suspect
   a. rubeola.
   b. rubella.
   c. pertussis.
   d. mumps.

18. This case may present what additional public health risk?
   a. This virus may reactivate later in the patient's life, causing painful pustules that are contagious until scabbed over.
   b. This patient has been contagious for 2–4 weeks and will continue to be contagious for another 2 weeks.
   c. If the boy's mother is pregnant, the fetus could be at risk for deafness, blindness, and mental retardation.
   d. If this patient infects the paramedic, she could be at risk for meningitis, pancreatitis, and deafness.

19. What are some of the differences between hepatitis A (HAV) and hepatitis C (HCV)?

_____

_____

20. In patients with liver disease, or who have had their spleen removed, which aspect of the immune system is impaired?

_____

_____

Need to Know

The following represent the Key Objectives of Chapter 33:

1. *Explain how paramedics can protect themselves, their patients, and their families from exposure to infectious disease.*

Universal precautions means exactly that: If you assume that *any* patient has the potential to harbor and transmit a communicable disease, you will be more likely to use a minimum set of personal protective equipment such as latex or nitrile gloves and eyewear. Additional barrier devices such as gowns and masks should be used as the situation dictates. For example, you may be assessing a patient for a routine complaint, but as you begin to expose her you realize that she has head lice. You may need to stop your assessment and don a gown before continuing care.

Precautions go in both directions. *You* may be not feeling well! It will be important for you to reduce the chance of passing a communicable disease to your patients. You may need to wear a surgical mask, or better yet, use a sick day. And make sure you wash your hands after each patient contact!

Clean and disinfect your equipment and ambulance routinely. Use cleaning solutions appropriately and according to the manufacturer's directions. Remember to gross decontaminate the unit—sweep and mop the floor of any blood, dirt, and discarded medical items before disinfecting it. Cleaning the unit has the secondary effect of looking professional

to your next patient, which helps to instill confidence in you.

2. *Explain the importance of personal health history and immunization.*

You should be clear about your own immunization history. As you know by now, there are several childhood diseases such as measles or mumps that, while uncomfortable, pose little risk to the pediatric patient. However, contracting those diseases as an adult can cause great harm. If possible, minimize your exposure to these patients if you are not sure of your immunization status.

Consider the health and immunization status of your patient when a communicable disease process is a possible underlying cause of his or her presentation. Because many of the diseases discussed in this chapter can have signs that are subtle or that mimic more obvious conditions, we might assume that the patient is adequately immunized and not think about these diseases as possible culprits. Furthermore, understanding that your patient may be immunocompromised due to other disease states (such as cancer) may make you more acutely aware of potential pathogenic causes.

3. *Identify the infectious agents that have the potential for use as weapons of mass destruction (WMDs).*

Pathogens that may be used for human-made events have high virulence ability and can survive outside the host body for some time. Smallpox, anthrax, and even botulism have been implicated as high-risk bioweapons. Although it is beyond the scope of this chapter to delve into these agents, you should become familiar with the signs and symptoms of their infectious states. Regardless of the actual disease, remember that your first line of defense is awareness and universal precautions!

4. *Explain the value of establishing relationships with public health offices in prevention, surveillance, and response to virulent outbreaks.*

Having a fundamental understanding of public health principles can help you understand the implications of managing a sick and potentially contagious patient. Notifying the rest of the health-care continuum and isolating the patient from the general population is as important as protecting yourself and the rest of the rescuers from becoming infected. The local public health agency can be a great resource for information related to the diseases described in this chapter. In fact, EMS systems and public health agencies can work hand in hand in protecting the community's health by enhancing each other's strengths. For example, EMS providers may realize that, in the course of 24 hours, a certain part of the city is recording an increased number of service calls for people having a rapid development of debilitating flu-type symptoms. Receiving hospitals may not realize the increase of patients because patients are being distributed by the EMS system. However, EMS system managers, following a predetermined protocol, could contact the local public health agency to initiate an investigation sooner than waiting for hospital notification.

Need to Do

The following skills are explained and illustrated in a step-by-step manner, via skill sheets and/or Step-by-Steps in this text and on the accompanying DVD:

Skill Name	Skill Sheet Number and Location	Step-by-Step Number and Location
Putting On and Removing Gloves	60 – DVD	N/A
Handwashing	61 – DVD	61 – DVD

Connections

- The federal Centers for Disease Control and Prevention (CDC) is "at the forefront of public health efforts to prevent and control infectious and chronic diseases, injuries, workplace hazards, disabilities, and environmental health threats."[1] Major releases of information about communicable diseases often come through this agency. There is also a large amount of consumer-level information about diseases available through its website at www.cdc.gov/.
- Chapter 2, The Well-Being of the Paramedic, in the textbook has many ties to this chapter. Review the information about hygiene practices and universal precautions to help keep you safe.
- The American Public Health Association (APHA), located in Washington, DC, "is the oldest and largest organization of public health professionals in the world, representing more than 50,000 members from over 50 occupations of public health."[2] Its mission is to improve the overall health of the public at large. Various position papers and research findings involving community-based medicine can be accessed at its website (www.apha.org).

- The Agency for Toxic Substances and Disease Registry (ATSDR) is a federal public health agency whose aim is to "prevent harmful exposures and diseases related to toxic substances."[3] Located within the CDC, the ATSDR website (www.atsdr.cdc.gov) contains information about hazardous materials and their toxic effects.
- Link to the companion DVD for a chapter-based quiz, audio glossary, animations, games and exercises, and, when appropriate, skill sheets and skill Step-by-Steps.

Street Secrets

- Whose Face Is Behind the Mask? A face mask or, worse, a non-rebreather oxygen mask on a patient will provide a poor barrier to airborne pathogens. If you are concerned about the potential for contamination, mask yourself with the appropriate level of mask protection.
- Stop That Vehicle! The "vehicle" that can carry disease, that is. Regularly clean common tools and items such as BP cuffs, stethoscope heads, ECG patient cables, commonly used grab handles in the ambulance, and so forth.

The Drug Box

There are no specific drugs related to this chapter content.

References

1. CDC, www.cdc.gov/about/default.htm (accessed November 3, 2006).
2. APHA, www.apha.org/about/ (accessed November 3, 2006).
3. ATSDR, http://atsdr.cdc.gov (accessed November 3, 2006).

Answers

Are You Ready?

1. With bodily fluids on the scene, exposure concerns exist. Consider wearing a higher level of personal protective equipment, if you haven't already put on masks and eyewear. Apply a painful stimulus to see if the patient responds. Then assess and manage her airway, breathing, and circulatory status. Are there any signs of trauma? Consider whether you might have to immobilize the patient's cervical spine. Meanwhile, someone should check to see if the acetaminophen bottle still contains any tablets or if it is empty. The same should be done for the cough suppressant.

2. The beer, acetaminophen, and cough suppressant bottles may point to a possible ingestion or overdose. However, the medications may also indicate an infection issue. The emesis can point to either cause; regardless, there may be a dehydration state to manage. Incontinence of urine indicates a deep level of unconsciousness, possibly caused by a generalized seizure.

Active Learning

1.

Examples	Answer
AIDS	d
Botulism	a
Chickenpox	d
Chlamydia	a
Giardia	c
Gonorrhea	a
H. influenzae	a
H5N1	d
Head lice	c
Hepatitis B	d
Meningococcus	a
Pertussis	a
Rabies	d
Rocky Mountain Spotted Fever	a
Rubeola	d
Scabies	b
Smallpox	d
Staphylococcus	a
Tetanus	a
Thrush	b
Tuberculosis	a

2.

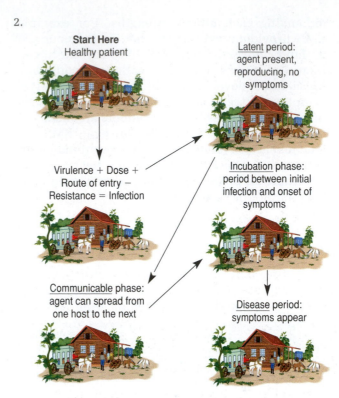

Start Here
Healthy patient

Latent period: agent present, reproducing, no symptoms

Virulence + Dose + Route of entry − Resistance = Infection

Incubation phase: period between initial infection and onset of symptoms

Communicable phase: agent can spread from one host to the next

Disease period: symptoms appear

3. a. Cilia: Hairlike projections in upper respiratory tract move mucus up and out.

b. Diarrhea: Forces pathogen out of the body.

c. GI tract: Acids secreted here help to destroy the pathogens.

d. Inflammatory response: Swelling due to fluid buildup reduces blood flow out of the area, slowing the spread of the pathogen. Also brings in white blood cells.

e. Intestinal flora: Compete with pathogens for resources.

f. Mucus: Lines the respiratory tract and traps pathogens.

g. Skin: Physical barrier to pathogens

h. Stomach: Acids destroy many pathogens here.

i. Turbinates: Disrupt laminar airflow, causing pathogens to crash into mucus-lined walls of airway.

4.

Presentation	Gloves	Protective Eyewear	Surgical Mask	N-95 Mask	Gown
Abdominal pain, emesis	X	X	X		
Abdominal pain, melena	X				
Active emesis, headache, photophobia	X	X		X	X
Bleeding profusely, combative	X	X	X		X
Confused, nauseous	X	X			
Fever, chest pain, nonproductive cough	X			X	
Fever, diarrhea × 24 hours, no vomiting	X				
Generalized weakness, syncope	X				
Hemoptysis for 12 hours, difficulty breathing	X	X		X	

5. A: 6; B: 5; C: 4; D: 2; E: 1; G: 3

You Are There: Reality-Based Cases

Case 1

1. There are several possibilities to consider regarding the cause of Shari's presentation. Alcohol or drug overdose should be considered. An infectious state is a real possibility due to the rash, vomiting, and possible fever. Could a seizure have caused the incontinence? Are there undiscovered signs of trauma?

2. A few of the findings seem to reduce the likelihood of alcohol or drug overdose or hypoglycemia as causes of her altered mental status. She is retaining carbon dioxide and also not able to increase her oxygen saturation levels, which are signs of possible respiratory or, more precisely, ventilatory failure.

3. Shari's condition is very serious. Even though she is athletic, the altered mental status, tachypnea, and sustained tachycardia are all signs of stress on her body systems. Her blood pressure is low, as is her oxygen saturation. With evidence of profuse emesis, fluid therapy is indicated. Breath sounds will need to be evaluated before volume is infused. Ventilations will need to be assisted with a bag-mask in the hopes of improving gas exchange. The "rash" needs to be investigated, as several conditions could be causing it, such as sepsis or anaphylaxis.

4. After wishing that you had worn your protective eyeglasses, have someone gain control of the bleeding IV site with gauze pads while you find a way to rinse your eye as soon as possible. Using a bottle of saline in the ambulance may be effective if no source of running water is immediately available. Report this exposure to your supervisor as soon as possible. You may need follow-up at a clinic or hospital for evaluation and prophylactic treatment.

Test Yourself

1. c

   Significant contact is defined as any blood or other bodily fluid coming into contact with the eyes, mouth, or mucus membrane, or through puncture wounds in the skin. Any paramedic who experiences a significant contact should report it to the appropriate authorities. The United States Government passed the Ryan White Comprehensive AIDS Resources Emergency Act of 1990, which gives health-care workers the right to request the infection status of the source patient.

2. Communicable diseases are those diseases that are caused by living organisms, such as bacteria, viruses, fungi, and parasites. Those organisms that cause human disease are referred to as agents or pathogens.

3. d

   Staph infections are caused by the staphylococcus bacteria and would be treated with an antibiotic. Several types of antibiotic have been shown to cause sensitivity to sunlight and skin rashes.

4. The membranes that line the respiratory tract are more permeable than the skin. Furthermore, the environment within the respiratory tract is warm and moist, making it an ideal incubator.

5. d

   Universal precautions must be used in all these scenarios, but it is important to realize that universal precautions must be used for every patient contact. You must get in the habit of treating every patient as if they have an infectious disease so that you never put yourself at risk.

6. Gloves should be removed after the contact with the patient has been concluded or after the procedure if the gloves have become contaminated. The proper method of removing gloves involves using one gloved hand to grab the palm of the other glove, pulling it off the hand, and turning it inside out at the same time. Then, the fingers of the bare hand are slid under the cuff of the glove still being worn, lifting it off the hand, and turning it inside out. This method prevents contact with the external, contaminated surface of the gloves. Both gloves are immediately thrown into an appropriate container.

7. The practice of staying home from work when ill to prevent the spread to others is called social isolation. You should avoid work when you have diarrhea, a draining wound or wet lesions (you may return to work when the lesions are crusted over), jaundice, infectious mononucleosis, scabies or lice, strep throat (you may return to work when you have been treated with antibiotics for 24 hours), or if you have a cold. If you must go to work when you have a cold, wear a mask.

8. d

   Face masks should be worn to prevent exposure to an airborne infection. As a rule, the paramedic should wear a mask whenever the patient is coughing. It is also sensible to place a mask on the patient to protect others. Masks are classified by the amount of protection they confer. Particulate filters such as the N-95 class of face masks should be worn to protect against respiratory pathogens such as tuberculosis. Because of the high prevalence of tuberculosis in patients with AIDS, all patients with a cough should have a mask placed. Since this patient has probably sustained serious blood loss from his self-inflicted wounds, an oxygen mask would provide treatment for possible hemorrhagic shock and protect the health-care providers from infectious disease.

9. a

   A latent period occurs when the infectious agent is present and reproducing but causes no signs or symptoms. During the latent period, the agent generally cannot be transmitted to another host. The communicable phase is that period during which the infectious agent can be spread to another host. Note that not all diseases are communicable, and symptoms may or may not occur during this phase. The incubation phase is the time period between initial infection and the onset of symptoms. The disease period begins with the onset of symptoms.

10. This is a classic presentation of meningococcal meningitis. You should wear a face mask and shield, and special

care should be paid to body substance isolation. Pay particular attention to the patient's fluid status, and notify the receiving facility of "a suspected case of meningitis" before arrival.

11. H5N1 is a virus that is transmitted to humans through close contact with birds, probably through their saliva, nasal secretions, feces, and blood.

    The greatest fear regarding H5N1 is that the virus will mutate and allow efficient person-to-person transmission. To date, no person-to-person infection has been definitively proven, but some possible cases have been documented. Thus, the use of respiratory protection by the EMS crew is paramount when treating a possible case of H5N1.

12. b

    Tertiary syphilis is characterized by skin lesions, cardiovascular complications, and neurological disorders. The signs and symptoms of tertiary syphilis may present several decades after secondary syphilis. The classic skin lesion of tertiary syphilis is called the gumma. These are large, painless ulcerations that occur on the skin. Gummas can also occur on bone, causing deep, gnawing pain.

13. c

    All these viruses are spread through respiratory droplets, and suspected cases indicate the use of face masks.

14. Factors that contribute to an increased risk of tuberculosis (TB) include HIV infection, immigration from countries where TB is endemic, living in cramped quarters with infected individuals (including homeless shelters), substance abuse, diabetes, low body weight, and immunodeficiency from prolonged corticosteroid use, cancer, or end-stage renal disease.

15. c

    Check with your physician about your status in terms of screening for tuberculosis (PPD or chest X-ray), measles-mumps-rubella (MMR), hepatitis B, hepatitis A (if required by your agency), diphtheria-pertussis-tetanus (DPT), polio, chickenpox, influenza (annual immunizations), and rabies (if appropriate to your risk). There is no vaccine for Lyme disease, hantavirus, HCV, or mononucleosis (EBV).

16. National agencies involved in public health include the Department of Defense, Federal Emergency Management Agency (FEMA), National Fire Protection Association (NFPA), U.S. Fire Protection Administration, International Association of Firefighters (IAFF), Occupational Health and Safety Administration (OSHA), Centers for Disease Control and Prevention (CDC), and National Institute for Occupational Safety and Health (NIOSH).

17. b

    Rubella is caused by the rubella virus and is also called German measles because it was first reported in Germany. The virus is spread through respiratory droplets and has an incubation period of 2 weeks. Symptoms include low-grade fever, swollen lymph nodes, and a generalized rash.

18. c

    Symptoms of rubella include low-grade fever, swollen lymph nodes, and a generalized rash. Patients are contagious from one week before the onset of rash to one week after the rash has resolved. Symptoms usually last 3 days, and the disease is without complications. If a pregnant woman is infected with rubella, however, it can be passed through the placenta, causing congenital rubella syndrome in the fetus. This syndrome can be devastating, causing deafness, blindness, mental retardation, and occasionally death. Infants with congenital rubella syndrome may be contagious for up to 1 year after birth. Mumps, not rubella, can create complications in adults like meningitis, inflammation of the testicles with subsequent sterility, pancreatitis, and deafness. Chickenpox, not rubella, may be reactivated later in life as zoster (also called shingles), which causes painful pustules that are contagious until scabbed over.

19. Hepatitis A accounts for nearly half of all hepatitis cases each year, as opposed to HCV, which accounts for only 15%. HAV is transmitted via the oral-fecal route, while HCV transmission occurs through the parenteral route. There is a vaccine for HAV, but no vaccine exists for HCV. There is no chronic hepatitis associated with HAV, whereas chronic hepatitis occurs in 55%–85% of persons infected with HCV, regardless of the presence of acute hepatitis.

    Of those patients with chronic hepatitis from HCV, 70% will develop chronic liver failure, and 1%–5% will die as a result of their disease. Because of the lack of vaccine and the risk of development of chronic disease, healthcare workers should be especially wary of contracting HCV, despite the fact that HAV is more common.

20. The reticuloendothelial system

    The reticuloendothelial system (RES) is the collection of white blood cells found outside the bloodstream, namely, in the liver, spleen, lungs, lymph nodes, bone marrow, and intestines. These white blood cells help to clear the blood of any debris that results from fighting an infection. This system also stores T cells and B cells when they are not active in an immune response. Patients with liver disease or who have had their spleen removed are less capable of clearing an infection and are therefore more prone to prolonged infection.

chapter 34

Gastroenterology

Are You Ready?

At 0800 hrs you and your partner are called to the local gym. Once inside, you are led to the aerobics room, where a young woman is sitting on a bench in front of the window. She appears to be uncomfortable. The woman tells you that she has not been feeling well since last night, but she thought that she would come and take an aerobics class to see if that would make her feel better. She states that she had to leave the class early because she started to experience abdominal pain.

1. Based on the information that you have obtained thus far, what is your general impression of the patient, and what might be causing her pain?

_____

_____

_____

Your partner obtains a baseline set of vital signs as you gather a history from the patient and begin your physical examination. The patient, Sarah Pierce, is a 26-year-old female who has no prior medical history. She denies any history of pelvic inflammatory disease (PID), ectopic pregnancy, endometriosis, ovarian cysts, or therapeutic abortion. She takes oral contraceptives and has been compliant with her medications. She has no known allergies to medications. Sarah states that her symptoms started while she was reading before she went to sleep. The only thing that she can do to make the pain feel better is to sit perfectly still. Sarah states that the pain is intermittent. She has difficulty describing the pain, but she states that it is in the area surrounding her navel. There is no apparent radiation of the pain. Sarah also has difficulty rating the severity of the pain because she states that it has varied in intensity over the past 8–10 hours.

Sarah doesn't think that she has eaten anything that may have given her food poisoning. Her last menstrual period was almost 6 weeks ago, but she states that she has very irregular menses. She believes that it is unlikely that she is pregnant. She is sexually active and denies vaginal bleeding or vaginal discharge. She doesn't smoke or drink alcohol and denies the use of recreational drugs.

Sarah states that, in addition to the discomfort in her abdomen, she is feeling nauseated, and that she has chills. She denies diarrhea or vomiting. No pain, burning, or urgency is associated with urination, and she has no changes when you test orthostatic vital signs. When you examine her abdomen, you notice no distention, pulsating masses, or trauma. She has active bowel sounds upon auscultation, and general discomfort and guarding to her periumbilical region. The pain increases on palpation and movement. During your examination of her abdomen she states that there is rebound tenderness to the right lower quadrant of her abdomen and that there is sharp pain to that region.

2. Based on the information that you have obtained in the history and physical examination, what is the most likely cause of Sarah's abdominal pain?

_____

_____

_____

3. Based on your answer to question 3, will your treatment for this condition differ from the treatment for a patient suffering from an ectopic pregnancy?

_____

_____

_____

4. Using the description of different types of pain described in the Need to Know section of this chapter, what type of pain is Sarah experiencing?

_____

_____

_____

Active Learning

Anatomy Review

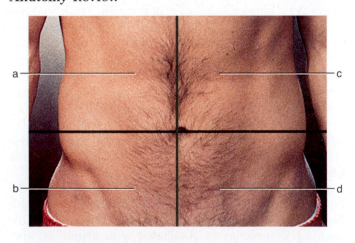

1. Name the four abdominal quadrants, and list at least two structures located in each one.

   a. _____

   b. _____

   c. _____

   d. _____

2. Abdominal Examination Exercise

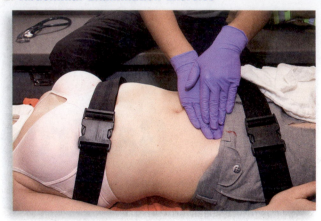

Practice makes perfect. This is especially true for the practice of physical examination and, in this case, abdominal examination. Find a partner and place him or her in the appropriate position for an abdominal examination. In the appropriate order (see the Need to Know section later in this chapter), inspect, palpate, and percuss your partner's abdomen. Follow the sequence and look, listen, and feel for the items listed in the Need to Know section.

Try this examination on several different people and compare the differences that you find in people with different body types, genders, and so forth. Keep in mind that, even though this is practice, professionalism needs to be observed at all times. Take into consideration the individual's modesty and accommodate any request to maintain privacy.

If you have the opportunity to practice the abdominal examination in the presence of an experienced practitioner, ask for any tricks of the trade based on the practitioner's experiences.

3. Digestive Tract

Trace a bite of food through the GI tract. Using the following terms, identify the structures in Figure 34-1 and describe their basic function, when applicable.

- Anus
- Appendix
- Ascending colon
- Cecum
- Descending colon
- Duodenum
- Esophagus
- Gall bladder
- Ileum
- Jejunum
- Large intestine
- Liver

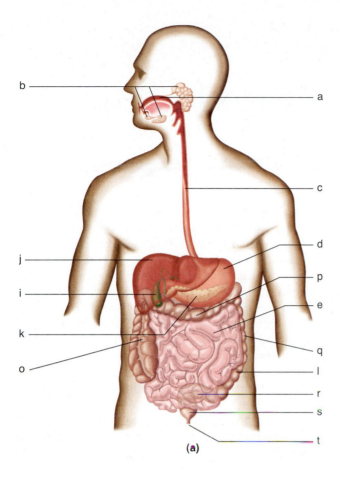

(a)

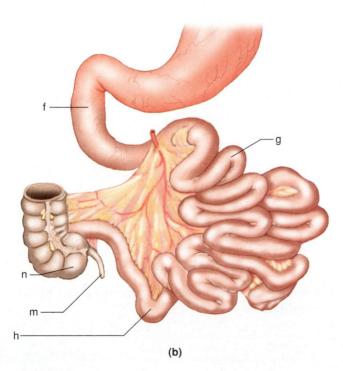

(b)

FIGURE 34-1

- Mouth
- Pancreas
- Rectum
- Salivary glands
- Sigmoid colon
- Small intestine
- Stomach
- Transverse colon

a. _____

b. _____

c. _____

d. _____

e. _____

f. _____

g. _____

h. _____

i. _____

j. _____

k. _____

l. _____

m. _____

n. _____

o. _____

p. _____

q. _____

r. _____

s. _____

t. _____

You Are There: Reality-Based Cases

Case 1

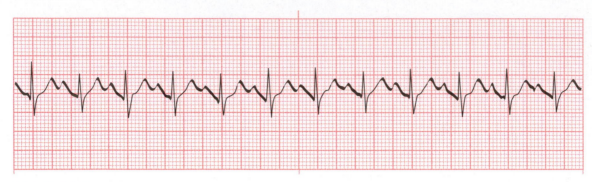

FIGURE 34-2

Molly woke up feeling awful. She and Fred had partied hard the night before, and Molly was paying the price. She had a throbbing headache and felt dizzy and nauseated. Molly stumbled out of bed and into her bathroom, where she searched for some Alka-Seltzer. Fred came into the bathroom and turned on the shower. "I'm going to be late again if I don't hurry up," he said to Molly as he stepped into the shower. Molly didn't reply—she just walked out of the bathroom and headed into the living room. Fred emerged from the bedroom less than 10 minutes later, fully dressed and frantically heading toward the door. When he entered the hallway, he found Molly sprawled out on the floor. He ran to her and tried to wake her, but she wouldn't respond.

Fred called 9-1-1 for help. He explained to the operator that he had tried to wake Molly, but she would not respond. She appeared to be breathing. The dispatcher instructed Fred to turn her onto her side so that her airway would be protected in case she vomited. This is the position that you find Molly in when you and the local fire crew arrive on the scene. You have the engine officer take Fred into the living room, and you and your partner begin to assess Molly.

1. Based on the information that has been presented thus far, what is your general impression of Molly's condition?

   _____

   _____

   _____

2. What is your initial priority in caring for Molly?

   _____

   _____

   _____

3. What additional information do you need to obtain to help determine an appropriate treatment plan?

   _____

   _____

   _____

During the primary and secondary assessments, you obtain the following information: Molly is a 38-year-old female whom Fred describes as a "functional alcoholic." She is unconscious and responds to deep painful stimuli by moaning. She and Fred drank heavily last night. Molly appears to have a patent airway, breathing 10 times a minute with adequate tidal volume, and clear, equal breath sounds bilaterally. She has faint, rapid (124 beats per minute) radial pulses and cool, pale, and slightly moist skin. Her blood pressure is 90/68, and her ECG is as shown in Figure 34-2.

Molly has a room air oxygen saturation of 90% and a blood glucose level of 70 mg/dL. Her pupils are equal at 4 mm and react sluggishly to light, and there is no apparent external trauma noted on the secondary assessment. Her abdomen is slightly distended. Fred tells you that Molly had been informed by her physician that she had something wrong with her liver. In a series of some routine blood tests, her liver panel appeared abnormal. Molly never followed up with the doctor in regards to the test. Fred states that Molly has no other medical problems, takes no medications, and doesn't believe that she has any allergies to any medications. She has had no recent illnesses (e.g., fever, emesis, diarrhea, cough, or congestion).

4. Based on the information that you have at this point in time, what are your priorities for treatment?

   _____

   _____

   _____

5. Do you currently have any concerns about Molly's condition?

   _____

   _____

   _____

Your partner places Molly on a non-rebreather mask at 15 liters per minute as you establish an IV attached to a crystalloid (isotonic) IV solution. You administer a 250-mL fluid bolus, and your partner administers a 50% dextrose IV push. When you reassess Molly following these interventions, you note that there is no change to her airway and breathing, although her oxygen saturation has improved to 98%. Her heart rate has slowed to 110 beats per minute, and her blood pressure is 92/70. A repeat blood glucose measurement approximately 5 minutes after the administration of the 50% dextrose is 120 mg/dL, and Molly starts to move around and speak. You assess her level of consciousness. Molly opens her eyes wide with a look of horror on her face, attempts to sit up, and suddenly vomits a copious amount of bright red blood into her oxygen mask. You and your partner both reach for Molly in an attempt to remove the blood-filled mask and protect Molly's airway. Just as quickly as she tried to sit up, Molly falls back, landing on the carpeted floor. Working in synchrony, your partner pulls off the oxygen mask, and you quickly turn Molly on her side as blood continues to flow out of her mouth. Molly appears to be unconscious.

6. What is your top priority now?

7. How will you proceed?

8. What is the most likely cause of the bleeding?

9. What is the definitive care for Molly?

10. What is a likely cause of hypoglycemia in this situation?

Test Yourself

1. Any bleeding that occurs above the _____ is considered upper gastrointestinal bleeding.

2. Elderly patients have an increased risk of
   a. diverticulitis.
   b. pancreatitis.
   c. appendicitis.
   d. peritonitis.

3. What are the four primary life-threatening conditions that frequently cause a patient to present with abdominal pain?

4. Patients with peritonitis will often rock back and forth or move about, searching for a comfortable position.
   True
   False

5. Pain in the shoulder or neck may indicate injury or illness in the upper abdomen.
   True
   False

6. List all six parts of the large intestine.

7. Although local protocols vary, the administration of narcotic analgesics to patients with abdominal pain is advisable.
   True
   False

8. Why is the swallowing of a button battery a life-threatening situation?

9. Chest pain resulting from an esophageal condition may worsen if the patient is given medications such as nitroglycerin, oxygen, or other medications frequently used to treat cardiac chest pain.
   True
   False

10. Your 72-year-old female patient is complaining of sudden-onset, upper abdominal pain. She is alert and oriented, and her vital signs are BP of 115/75, HR of 70, and RR of 22. Your primary assessment

reveals no other abnormal findings. Which of the following conditions should you consider first?

a. Cholecystitis

b. Peptic ulcer

c. Hiatal hernia

d. Abdominal aortic aneurysm

11. The stretching of pain fibers located in the walls of the hollow organs and capsules of the solid organs of the abdomen causes

a. visceral abdominal pain.

b. somatic abdominal pain.

c. referred abdominal pain.

d. parietal pain.

12. Which of the following cases is of greatest concern?

a. A 25-year-old man complaining of dull, periumbilical pain that was followed by vomiting

b. A 34-year-old woman complaining of intermittent lower abdominal pain

c. A 74-year-old woman complaining of abdominal discomfort and hard stools during the past 2 days

d. A 43-year-old man with a history of ulcers complaining of recurring pain

13. Which of the following patients is *most* at risk for esophageal varices?

a. A 65-year-old man with hypertension

b. A 39-year-old woman with gastroesophageal reflux

c. A 41-year-old woman with a history of chronic alcohol use

d. A 22-year-old man with a duodenal ulcer

14. Patients with mesenteric ischemia usually present with mild pain, hypotension, and bradycardia.

True

False

15. A man called 9-1-1 when his girlfriend experienced a brief episode of syncope. The 25-year-old woman is now alert and oriented. She is complaining of lower abdominal pain and appears pale. What condition should you immediately suspect as the cause of this woman's symptoms?

_____

_____

16. Concerned parents called 9-1-1 because their 2-year-old daughter will "not stop crying." Her father thinks that she might have a "stomachache" after eating a bowl of ice cream. The child does not

answer your questions. How might you determine whether she is suffering from abdominal pain?

_____

_____

17. When a patient's cystic duct is obstructed by a gallstone, it is likely to result in

a. hepatitis.

b. cholecystitis.

c. ascites.

d. gastroenteritis.

18. You are called to the home of a 76-year-old woman who has been having diarrhea all morning. She describes the feces as dark, almost black, with an appearance like coffee grounds. She is alert and oriented. Her vital signs are BP of 130/85, HR of 72, and RR of 18; her skin is pink, warm, and dry. How should you treat this patient?

a. Ensure that the patient is adequately hydrated and recommend that she make an appointment with her doctor.

b. Maintain the patient's ABCs, obtain IV access, and transport emergently.

c. Administer an antidiarrheal medication.

d. Obtain a detailed history and perform a thorough physical exam before making any further treatment decisions.

19. When performing a physical exam on a patient with abdominal pain, how should the patient be positioned?

_____

_____

20. When a patient has peritonitis, she has an inflamed

a. gall bladder.

b. pancreas.

c. peritoneum.

d. liver.

21. A 75-year-old man calls you because he has had diarrhea. He describes the feces as normal in color, but "loose and watery." Other than mild abdominal discomfort, the man has no other complaints. Your assessment reveals no abnormal findings, and you see no evidence of dehydration. The patient wants to be transported to the emergency room. You should

a. manage the patient's ABCs, administer fluid therapy, and transport the patient emergently.

b. explain that his condition is not serious and advise him to seek medical attention if his symptoms worsen or continue for more than 24 hours.

c. administer an antidiarrheal medication and tell the patient to drink plenty of fluids.

d. transport the patient nonemergently.

22. Explain why pediatric patients with foreign body esophageal obstructions are more likely to experience airway complications than adult patients.

_____

_____

23. Jaundice is an indication of possible illness affecting the _____.

24. A patient complaining of localized abdominal pain experiences no increased discomfort when you palpate the area, but as you are pulling your hand away, the patient visibly winces. This is an example of

a. referred pain.

b. abdominal tenderness.

c. rebound tenderness.

d. guarding.

25. If your patient is experiencing nausea and vomiting, you should suspect gastroenteritis.

True

False

26. Your 18-year-old female patient was a belted passenger in a car that was rear-ended at low speed. The driver and the other two passengers are uninjured. Your patient is pale, tachypneic, and complains of abdominal pain. During your assessment, you learn that the patient had just eaten a cheeseburger and fries, takes amitriptyline (a tricyclic antidepressant), and is recovering from mononucleosis. What should you suspect?

a. Appendicitis

b. Cholecystitis

c. Ruptured spleen

d. Toxic drug reaction

Scenario: A 16-year-old boy began experiencing abdominal pain a few hours ago. Originally, he was experiencing intermittent periumbilical pain, but now (a few hours after his symptoms began) the pain is constant, sharp, and located in the lower right quadrant. You note guarding when you palpate the lower right quadrant.

27. His pain was originally _____, and now it has become _____.

a. referred/somatic

b. visceral/referred

c. visceral/somatic

d. somatic/referred

28. You should suspect

a. kidney stones.

b. pancreatitis.

c. appendicitis.

d. bowel obstruction.

Scenario: Your 28-year-old patient is recovering from an appendectomy. He has been suffering from cramping periumbilical pain that began approximately 6 hours ago and has grown progressively worse. He called 9-1-1 because he has been vomiting for the past 2 hours. He says that he has been unable to eat or drink anything since his symptoms began and describes his emesis as watery and colorless. His vital signs appear normal. You note abdominal distention during the physical exam.

29. What is the most likely cause of the patient's symptoms?

a. Upper gastrointestinal bleeding

b. Lower gastrointestinal bleeding

c. Bowel obstruction

d. Peritonitis

30. How should you treat this patient?

a. Maintain the patient's ABCs, administer fluid therapy, and transport.

b. Administer an antiemetic and ask the patient to call 9-1-1 again if his symptoms do not abate.

c. Maintain the patient's ABCs, obtain IV access, administer vasopressin, and transport emergently.

d. Maintain the patient's ABCs, administer oxygen, and transport emergently.

Need to Know

Gastroenterology literally means "the study of the gastrointestinal (GI) tract." This means that it covers all the structures and associated problems from the mouth to the anus. There is a spectrum of possible problems and complaints associated with the GI tract, from gas pain to life-threatening bleeding, and many problems in between. There are a number of problems that present with GI complaints that are not specific to the GI tract at all (perhaps the most serious being myocardial infarction) and, in turn, there are GI-specific problems that may not present with abdominal complaints (e.g., cholecystitis, can present with shoulder pain). It is imperative that paramedics keep an open mind and a high index of suspicion while treating patients with GI complaints.

The following represent the Key Objectives of Chapter 34:

1. *Explain the relationship between abdominal pain and myocardial infarction.*

   The causes of abdominal complaints are not always related to pathology in the gastrointestinal tract. Myocardial infarction is likely the most serious of these possible causes and should be considered whenever a patient has vague complaints of nausea, vomiting, pain, or discomfort in the upper abdominal region—especially when the patient has a cardiac history and no GI problems, or when the patient fits into a category of individuals who are prone to atypical presentations of cardiac ischemia (e.g., women, the elderly, diabetics, and smokers). Keeping these possibilities in mind when assessing and treating patients with these types of complaints will prevent time wasted treating GI symptoms in a patient suffering from a cardiac problem.

2. *Identify four key life-threatening conditions that the paramedic should detect during the primary assessment of a patient with GI complaints.*

   Gastrointestinal problems may or may not be associated with abdominal pain. When abdominal pain is present, it can be difficult to assess and treat. Part of the reason for the complexity in assessing and treating abdominal pain is that there are a number of different types of organs located within the abdominal cavity. There are gastrointestinal organs, circulatory vessels, genitourinary organs, and reproductive organs located within the abdominal cavity. Abdominal pain can be a potential symptom for the following four key life-threatening conditions:

   a. *Abdominal aortic aneurysm (AAA).* A dilation of the abdominal aorta that is associated with leaking or rupture. Patients with an AAA can present with hypotension, abdominal and/or back pain, and a pulsatile abdominal mass. However, these classic signs and symptoms will not always be present; patients can be normotensive and without obvious pulsatile masses, and some patients can present without pain. Unequal femoral pulses are sometimes associated with AAA, but this finding cannot be relied upon as a diagnostic feature as it is not a condition found in all AAA patients.

   b. *Ruptured spleen.* A condition that is typically associated with abdominal trauma but can also be seen in patients who have recently suffered from mononucleosis. They can develop splenomegaly that can result in splenic rupture.

   c. *Ruptured ectopic pregnancy.* A condition that results in the implantation of a fertilized egg outside of the uterine cavity (typically in a fallopian tube). The potentially life-threatening condition of a ruptured ectopic pregnancy occurs as the developing fertilized egg grows and stretches the walls of the fallopian tube to the point that it ruptures, resulting in severe bleeding. A paramedic evaluating any woman of childbearing age with a complaint of abdominal pain should consider the possibility of an ectopic pregnancy.

   d. *Gastrointestinal bleeding.* Because blood is an irritant to the different organs located within the abdominal cavity, bleeding into the abdominal cavity often causes a generalized pain that is referred to as *hemorrhagic abdominal pain.*

3. *List possible sources of GI bleeds.*

   Potential sources of gastrointestinal bleeding include:
   - Boerhaave's syndrome
   - Mallory-Weiss syndrome
   - Tracheoesophageal fistula
   - Esophageal varices
   - Pancreatitis
   - Peritonitis
   - Peptic ulcer perforation

   GI bleeding can manifest itself as:
   - Hematemesis—blood in vomit
   - Hematochezia—free blood in stool
   - Melena—tarry processed blood in stool
   - Rectal bleeding—bright red blood from rectum
   - Hemoptysis—coughing up blood

4. *Describe the characteristics of the three types of abdominal pain that are most commonly encountered.*

   a. *Visceral pain.* Caused by stretching of the visceral pain fibers located in the walls of hollow organs (e.g., gall bladder) and in the capsules of solid organs (e.g., liver, spleen, and kidney). The pain is often felt in the midline of the abdomen and tends to be diffuse (difficult to pinpoint), intermittent, dull, or cramping and increases in severity over time. Patients experiencing visceral pain tend to find it difficult to sit still and frequently complain of nausea and vomiting.

b. *Somatic (parietal) pain.* Caused by irritation of the fibers that innervate the parietal peritoneum or abdominal wall and tend to produce more localized pain. Somatic pain is frequently described as constant, sharp, and aggravated by any movement.

c. *Referred pain.* Felt at a location away from the source of the pain and typically referred to as intense. Nerve segments that overlap and provide sensation to two or more areas can lead to pain originating in the abdomen but sensed at an extra-abdominal site (e.g., pain resulting from pathology in the upper abdominal regions, near the diaphragm, can stimulate nerve fibers that indicate pain in the shoulder or neck).

5. *Describe the different aspects of, and the sequence of, an abdominal examination (also see Skill Sheet 36, Abdominal Assessment).*

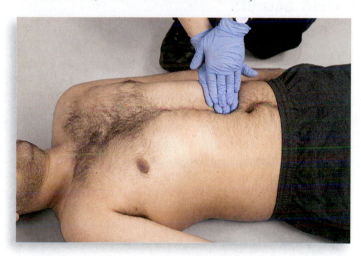

Optimally, the examination of the abdomen should take place with the patient in a supine position with the knees slightly bent. The examination of the abdomen can include inspection, palpation, auscultation, and percussion. Inspection and palpation are the minimum standard for the paramedic's examination of the abdomen, and auscultation and percussion practices vary considerably depending on local philosophy and training.

- *Inspection* involves visualizing the abdomen for any distention, masses, scars, discoloration, bruising, or trauma. Because inspection does not require manipulation of the abdomen, it is frequently the first step in the examination process.

- If *auscultation* of the abdomen is included in your scope of practice, then it should take place early in the examination process and before palpation or percussion, as these two procedures can decrease bowel activity and therefore bowel sounds. There is little information gained from the auscultation of bowel sounds. Absent bowel sounds can indicate injury or disease, but this is not always a reliable indicator. Auscultation of the abdomen requires a quiet environment and can take several minutes to properly perform.

- *Palpation* is performed using the fingertips in a location furthest from any complaints of pain or discomfort. Palpation should be performed over each of the four abdominal quadrants in a smooth and coordinated manner. During the palpation portion of the abdominal examination, look for abdominal tenderness, guarding, rebound tenderness, abdominal masses, an enlarged liver, and an enlarged spleen.

- *Percussion* can be performed in all the abdominal quadrants and can be helpful in detecting the presence of blood or other fluid in the abdominal cavity by producing a dull sound rather than the tympanic sound that is typically heard over gas-filled intestines. The presence of dullness upon percussion of the abdomen is not conclusive for blood or even fluid in the abdomen. Percussion of the abdomen is not typically utilized in the prehospital setting due to a noisy environment.

The assessment of vital signs is also important, as the results give us an idea of the patient's hemodynamic status and a baseline from which to compare. Orthostatic vital signs can be an indicator of blood or fluid loss (see Skill Sheet 29, Orthostatic Vital Signs).

6. *List the appropriate elements of a history for a patient with abdominal pain.*

Beyond the standard OPQRST of the complaint and SAMPLE history, additional pertinent questions may include:

- Are there any associated symptoms (nausea, vomiting, diarrhea, difficulty breathing, or chest pain)?

- Has the patient ever had a similar pain? If so, was he or she seen by a physician for the pain? If so, what was the diagnosis and what was the treatment (medication, hospitalization, surgery, etc.)?

- Is the pain constant or intermittent?

- Is the patient taking steroids or antibiotics? Both have the ability to mask infections and could be a clue to the cause of the abdominal pain.

- Women of childbearing age need to be asked about sexual activity or simply the chance of being pregnant but should not be asked in front of family or friends of the patient. A less direct way to determine the possibility of pregnancy is to ask the date of the patient's last menstrual period.

- The astute paramedic will ask questions regarding cardiac risk factors and symptoms.

7. *Discuss the determination of differential diagnosis and treatment of patients with abdominal pain.*

The determination of the cause of abdominal pain is difficult, if not impossible, to make in the prehospital setting. Abdominal pain and the severity of the pain that a patient experiences is not directly correlated to the criticality of the patient's condition. It is important for the paramedic to assume that the cause of the pain is potentially life threatening until proven otherwise. A treatment plan based on this approach will include a hospital destination capable of caring for this type of patient, IV access, fluid resuscitation (if the patient presents with signs and symptoms of hypoperfusion or shock), and pain control (based on local protocols). The definitive treatment for patients presenting with abdominal pain may include surgery or transfusion of blood products; as such, patients should be transported to a facility capable of providing these services as soon as possible.

Connections

- Chapter 13, Shock Overview, in the textbook includes more information on hypovolemic shock.
- Chapter 29, Cardiology, in the textbook includes more information regarding abdominal complaints associated with myocardial infarction.
- See Chapter 41, Obstetrics and Gynecology, in the textbook for more information on ectopic pregnancies.
- Link to the companion DVD for a chapter-based quiz, audio glossary, animations, games and exercises, and, when appropriate, skill sheets and skill Step-by-Steps.

Street Secrets

- **Differential Diagnosis** Keep in mind that it is very difficult to determine an accurate differential diagnosis for a patient with abdominal pain in the prehospital setting. Determination of the exact cause of abdominal pain is not nearly as important as being able to recognize the signs and symptoms of a patient who has a life-threatening condition. Abdominal complaints do not always have an abdominal origin, and patients experiencing conditions such as myocardial infarction can have vague abdominal complaints without any classic cardiac complaints. Rather than stay on scene and attempt to diagnose what physicians with sophisticated diagnostic equipment can have difficulty diagnosing, time is far better spent

Need to Do

The following skills are explained and illustrated in a step-by-step manner, via skill sheets and/or Step-by-Steps in this text and on the accompanying DVD:

Skill Name	Skill Sheet Number and Location	Step-by-Step Number and Location
Evacuation of Gastric Contents	24 – DVD	24 – DVD
Orthostatic Vital Signs	29 – DVD	29 – DVD
Abdominal Assessment	36 – DVD	N/A
Oral Drug Administration	57 – DVD	N/A
MAST/PASG Application	81 – DVD	N/A

attempting to, for example, stabilize a hypotensive patient with a GI bleed en route to a facility capable of providing appropriate care.

■ **Gettin' Buggy with It**   When questioning a patient about a GI-based complaint, ask about any recent out-of-country travel. It would be reasonable to suspect a parasitic infection as a possible cause of the complaint.

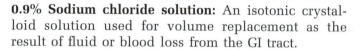

The Drug Box

0.9% Sodium chloride solution: An isotonic crystalloid solution used for volume replacement as the result of fluid or blood loss from the GI tract.

Lactated Ringer's solution: An isotonic crystalloid solution used for volume replacement as the result of fluid or blood loss from the GI tract.

Promethazine: A phenothiazine that reduces the sensation of nausea and emesis (antiemetic).

Answers

Are You Ready?

1. Based on the minimal information that you have obtained thus far, the patient should be considered critical until proven otherwise. There could be a number of different causes for her abdominal pain, but because she is a woman of childbearing age, you should consider the possibility of ectopic pregnancy because of the potential for life-threatening hemorrhage.

2. Based on the signs, symptoms, and history that were obtained during the primary and secondary assessment, another possible, if not likely, cause of Sarah's abdominal pain is appendicitis.

3. The treatment for a ruptured ectopic pregnancy and a ruptured appendix are virtually the same. They both involve the rapid recognition of the emergent condition, maintenance of a patent airway, supply of supplemental oxygen, and support of hemodynamic status by placing the patient in the shock position and keeping him or her warm, establishing IV access, giving and fluid bolus(es) as needed en route to a facility capable of treating a surgical patient in a timely manner.

4. Initially Sarah appeared to be experiencing a visceral type of pain (vague pain in the periumbilical region that was difficult to describe or rate in severity), but during the abdominal examination, her pain appeared to be more somatic (sharp pain in the right lower quadrant).

Active Learning

1. a. right upper quadrant (RUQ): the liver, gall bladder, head of the pancreas, part of the duodenum, right kidney, and part of the colon. b. right lower quadrant (RLQ): the appendix, ascending colon, small intestine, and in the female the right ovary and the right fallopian tube. c. left upper quadrant (LUQ): the spleen, tail of the pancreas, stomach, left kidney, and part of the colon. d. left lower quadrant (LLQ): the small intestine, descending colon, and in the female the left ovary and left fallopian tube.

2. a. mouth—chewing (mechanical breakdown of food); point at which the chemical breakdown of carbohydrates begins (saliva). b. salivary glands—secrete saliva, which contains salivary amylase (breakdown of carbohydrate) and mucus (provides lubrication and binds small food particles). c. esophagus—transports food from the mouth to the stomach by way of voluntary and involuntary muscles during the process of swallowing. d. stomach—secretes acids and enzymes, which initiate the enzymatic digestion of proteins (breaks proteins down into amino acids) and further breakdown of other foods. e. small intestine—the point at which food comes into contact with bile and pancreatic juices; digestive enzymes continue to break down food, and most nutrient absorption takes place here. f. duodenum—common bile duct empties into the duodenum. g. jejunum. h. ileum. i. gall bladder—stores the bile that is produced in the liver and secretes it into the duodenum via the common bile duct when needed for the breakdown of fat. j. liver—produces bile (breakdown of fat) and has considerable detoxification properties. k. pancreas—has both endocrine and exocrine functions. Its *exocrine* function is to secrete pancreatic juices and digestive enzymes into the small intestine (duodenum) via the pancreatic duct to aid in the digestion of food. Its *endocrine* function is to release hormones from the islets of Langerhans. The hormones are secreted by the following cells: *alpha cells*—secrete glucagons (stimulate the liver to break down glycogen into glucose); *beta cells*—secrete insulin (facilitates the uptake of glucose into the cells of the body and stimulates the liver to convert glucose into glycogen); and *delta cells*—secrete somatostatin (helps regulate glucose metabolism by inhibiting the secretion of insulin and glucagon). l. large intestine—absorbs water and electrolytes and forms feces. m. appendix—has no digestive function; contains lymphatic tissue. n. cecum—proximal section of the colon; point at which the ileum joins the large intestine (iliocecal valve). o. ascending colon—absorbs water and electrolytes and forms feces. p. transverse colon—absorbs water and electrolytes and forms feces. q. descending colon—absorbs water and electrolytes and forms feces. r. sigmoid colon—final portion of the colon before it turns into the rectum. s. rectum—regulates the elimination of feces. t. anus—point at which elimination of feces takes place; houses the internal and external anal sphincters.

You Are There: Reality-Based Cases

1. Molly is sick. She has not responded to any of Fred's attempts to arouse her.

2. The initial priority in caring for Molly is assessing her airway, breathing, and circulation and addressing any life-threatening conditions discovered during that assessment.

3. Determine if the patient has a patent airway. If she is breathing, is that breathing adequate to support vital functions? Determine if the patient has a pulse, as well as the rate and quality of the pulse. Additionally, it would be beneficial to gather a complete set of vital signs including pulse, blood pressure, respiratory rate (depth and quality), temperature, ECG, SpO_2 (baseline reading), and blood glucose analysis. A complete secondary assessment is needed and, when combined with the preceding information, can be very beneficial in determining an appropriate treatment plan. For example, if the assessment of the patient's breathing reveals that she has shallow, agonal respirations, and the secondary assessment reveals that the patient has pinpoint pupils and track marks in her antecubital fossa, you may elect to administer naloxone (Narcan) to rule out a narcotic overdose.

4. Although Molly's airway is patent, her ventilations are slow and shallow (adequate tidal volume) and her room air oxygen saturation is 90%. Molly should initially be placed on a non-rebreather mask at 15 liters per minute. If that doesn't appear to improve her SpO_2, her ventilations can be tracked with a bag-mask attached to a high-flow oxygen source. Because of the ALOC, relatively low blood pressure, rapid pulse, shocky skin signs, and low blood sugar, an IV should be established, and fluid boluses, as well as 50% dextrose administration, should be provided.

5. Since Fred states that the two of them drank rather heavily last night, there is a concern that Molly could vomit and, with her altered level of consciousness, she could easily aspirate. Therefore, a significant airway concern exists. Additionally, Molly has signs of shock: cool, pale, and moist skin, ALOC, a blood pressure of 90/68, and a heart rate of 124 beats per minute. Although the cause of shock is not clear, the fact that it exists is worrisome. Furthermore, Molly has a blood glucose level of 70 mg/dL; although this is not immediately life threatening by itself, it, too, needs to be addressed.

6. The top priority is airway management. The copious amount of blood needs to be cleared from the airway so that the airway remains patent and the patient doesn't aspirate any of the blood. Since Molly is already on her side, the next step is to suction the blood out of her airway (likely with a mechanical suction device and a rigid suction catheter).

7. As soon as the airway is cleared, Molly's level of consciousness needs to be reassessed, and she needs to have a primary and secondary assessment repeated. Preparation for transport needs to be initiated and, in light of the recent hematemesis and Molly's ALOC, isolation of the airway is desirable. Rapid sequence intubation would be appropriate if this is a skill that you are permitted to perform; if not, nasotracheal intubation would be appropriate if Molly is breathing and she has an intact gag reflex. As soon as the airway is secure, the patient needs to be transported emergently to a receiving facility that has surgical capabilities. All other interventions can take place en route to the hospital (if Molly is hypotensive, fluid resuscitation can begin as the airway is being secured since an IV has already been established).

8. The combination of signs and symptoms is indicative of esophageal varices. There are other causes of copious bright red hematemesis, such as a Mallory-Weiss tear, but this condition is typically preceded by violent coughing that tears the esophagus.

9. The definitive care for Molly is found at the hospital. Possibilities for treatment include:

   - Blood transfusions.
   - Endoscopic therapy—injection of clotting medications into the bleeding veins and placing rubber bands around the bleeding veins (band ligation) to stop the bleeding.
   - Balloon tamponade—typically a temporary means of controlling bleeding.
   - TIPS procedure—insertion of a transjugular intrahepatic portosystemic shunt decreases pressure on the portal system.
   - Octreotide and vasopressin administration (medication approach).
   - Surgery (insertion of portocaval shunt, removal of esophagus, etc.)—typically performed as a last resort due to a high mortality associated with it.

10. Molly's hypoglycemia is likely the result of the regular and frequently excessive use of alcohol. Because the liver is trying to break down and metabolize a large quantity of alcohol in the bloodstream, it is not able to appropriately maintain blood sugar levels, and hypoglycemia may occur.

Test Yourself

1. Ligament of Treitz

   The ligament of Treitz is the suspensory ligament of the duodenum.

2. a

   Causes of abdominal pain for which the elderly are at increased risk include: abdominal aortic aneurysm, mesenteric ischemia and infarction, carcinoma leading to bowel obstruction, diverticulitis, volvulus from immobility, myocardial infarction, and acute cholecystitis (which represents the most common surgical emergency in the elderly). See Box 34-2 in the textbook.

3. Ruptured aortic aneurysm, ruptured ectopic pregnancy, ruptured spleen, gastrointestinal bleeding

   Immediately life-threatening conditions in patients with GI-related complaints need to be identified quickly and treated aggressively. Generally, the greatest threats to life are conditions that cause significant bleeding.

4. False

   Patients with peritonitis tend to remain very still.

5. True

   Referred pain occurs when injury or illness within the abdomen stimulates nerve fibers that indicate pain outside of the abdominal region. Illness of the spleen, liver, or gall bladder, for example, may manifest as pain in the right shoulder or neck.

6. The large intestine is made up of the cecum, transverse colon, descending colon, sigmoid colon, rectum, and anus.

7. True

   At one time, it was believed that administering an analgesic would make eventual diagnosis more difficult, but this assumption is outdated.

8. The alkaline substances inside the battery may leak into the gastrointestinal tract, causing chemical burns and bleeding.

   Most objects that get to the stomach will ultimately pass through the rectum without intervention, but exceptions may include irregularly shaped, sharp, or elongated objects and button batteries. Field care is primarily supportive.

9. False

   Some esophageal conditions, particularly gastroesophageal reflux disease (GERD), may respond to treatments such as oxygen therapy or nitroglycerin, just as cardiac disease may respond to antacids or H2 receptor blockers typically used to treat some esophageal or gastric disorders. Since most pain caused by esophageal disorders is not immediately life threatening, while pain caused by cardiac ischemia obviously can be, it is prudent for the prehospital provider to assume a cardiac cause of a patient's complaints.

10. d

    The symptoms of an abdominal aortic aneurysm are often difficult to detect, and it should be immediately considered in all patients over the age of 65 who present with abdominal pain. More than 75% of patients with an abdominal aortic aneurysm are normotensive, and the characteristic pulsating mass is notoriously difficult to detect.

11. a

    Visceral abdominal pain is caused by the stretching of visceral pain fibers, which are located in the walls of hollow organs (such as the intestines or gall bladder) and the capsules of solid organs (such as the liver, spleen, and kidneys).

12. a

    Abdominal pain that occurs before the onset of vomiting is a cause for concern. Other warning signs that may be discovered during the patient interview include: pain that has lasted less than 48 hours, pain that is constant, and patients who have had no previous episodes of similar pain.

13. c

    Esophageal varices are dilated veins in the esophagus resulting from venous pressure from a backup from the liver. They are often a complication of alcoholic liver disease (portal hypertension). Patients with esophageal varices may develop massive bleeding and should be treated aggressively with oxygen and fluids as necessary.

14. False

    Patients with mesenteric ischemia, where the vascular supply to the bowel provided by the mesenteric artery or vein is compromised, frequently present with severe pain that is disproportionate to the physical findings. It is a life-threatening condition that should be suspected when the physical exam does not explain the patient's degree of pain, especially in the elderly.

15. Ectopic pregnancy

    Ectopic pregnancy is a life-threatening condition that should be immediately considered in all women of childbearing age who are complaining of abdominal pain.

16. It can be difficult to assess children for abdominal pain, especially when they cannot communicate well. You may consider asking the child to jump up and down. If the child is hesitant or jumps once and then stops immediately, it can be an indication of abdominal pain. You should also look closely for corresponding symptoms such as irritability, anxiety, lethargy, altered level of consciousness, affected gait, and posture. Also, carefully note how the child responds during the physical exam when you gently palpate the abdomen.

    In 2- to 6-year-old patients, tonsillitis has been a well-described source of abdominal pain. Lower lobe pneumonias can also result in a primary complaint of abdominal pain. When treating a pediatric patient who may be in pain, you may be able to determine the child's level of pain by utilizing a pediatric pain scale. This scale is comprised of expressions on pictured faces, with the first face representing a happy expression and the last face describing a grimacing face suffering from intolerable pain. The child is shown the scale and asked to point to the picture that best describes how he or she is feeling.

17. b

    Cholecystitis is the acute inflammation of the gall bladder, which usually occurs when the neck of the gall bladder or cystic duct is obstructed, often by a gallstone.

18. b

    Given the patient's description of her feces, you should suspect gastrointestinal bleeding. Mortality from GI bleeding may be as high as 10%, and most of those deaths occur in persons older than 60. Although the patient appears stable, patients with GI bleeds can become unstable quickly and without warning.

19. Ideally, the patient should be supine, with the head down and the knees slightly flexed. You must also consider the patient's position of comfort, however.

    The supine position will allow you to perform a thorough inspection, palpation, and auscultation of the abdomen. Inspection should be performed before palpation or auscultation, since the appearance of the abdomen may give you clues where to begin palpation. Inspect the abdomen for obvious distention or masses, as well as any surgical scars, discoloration, or bruises that might be present. Then palpate the abdomen gently, using fingertip pressure, beginning at the place furthest from the point of maximal pain. Auscultation in the prehospital setting is of questionable value and should not be performed if the patient is potentially unstable.

20. c

Inflammation or infection of organs within the peritoneal cavity can result in inflammation of the peritoneum, otherwise known as peritonitis.

21. d

Although most people do not seek emergency medical attention for diarrhea, there are potential complications, particularly in the elderly and patients with HIV. The patient should be transported nonemergently. Fluid therapy is unnecessary as there is no evidence of dehydration.

22. Ingested foreign bodies in pediatric patients may become caught in the proximal esophagus, where they can cause an accompanying airway obstruction. In contrast, foreign body esophageal obstructions in the adult population are often related to underlying esophageal disease and lodge in the distal esophagus.

Foreign body esophageal obstructions are more likely to occur at the three anatomical constrictions within the esophagus: one at the top, at the level of the cricopharyngeus muscle (most common in pediatric patients); another at the level of the aortic notch; and a third at the gastroesophageal junction as the esophagus enters the stomach.

23. Liver

Jaundiced patients will present with a yellowing of the skin, sclera, or other tissues. Jaundice can develop when there is excessive heme breakdown, failure of the liver to take up bilirubin, failure of the liver to conjugate and excrete bilirubin, or an obstruction of biliary excretion into the intestines.

24. c

Rebound tenderness is characterized as an increase of pain when the palpating hand is released. It should not be used in the prehospital setting as it increases patient discomfort, does not affect the prehospital treatment, and may lead to decreased patient cooperation. If it is noted, however, it should be documented.

25. False

Gastroenteritis has been referred to as a "wastebasket" diagnosis, used when other diagnoses are unclear. Serious conditions such as appendicitis, bowel obstruction, and even meningitis have been misdiagnosed as gastroenteritis. It is better to maintain a high index of suspicion than fail to identify a potentially life-threatening condition.

26. c

Given the patient's recent history of trauma and mononucleosis, you should immediately suspect a ruptured spleen.

27. c

Visceral pain is often dull, cramping, and not easily located. Patients will generally describe it as midgut. Somatic pain, however, is usually sharp, constant, and located in the region of the affected tissue.

28. c

Appendicitis will cause visceral pain initially, but as the disease progresses, somatic pain will develop.

29. c

Given the patient's recent history of abdominal surgery and his symptoms (cramping pain occurring before the onset of vomiting and abdominal distention), you should suspect a bowel obstruction.

30. a

The patient is suffering from an obstructed bowel, and definitive care will most likely require surgery. Prehospital care should include the administration of fluids (to treat dehydration caused by vomiting) and transportation.

chapter 35

Toxicology

Are You Ready?

You and your partner have tried to get a meal four times in as many hours, and each time you request a meal break, your dispatcher gives you another call. Finally, it looks as though you will get a break. You and your partner walk across the parking lot of the emergency department where you dropped off your last patient to buy a meal at the diner.

Right after you place your order, a patron comes out of the bathroom and tells you that a man is passed out on the floor.

When you enter the bathroom, you discover an unkempt male lying in a fetal position on the floor next to the toilet. He appears to be in his mid-twenties. He is unconscious with pale skin, perioral cyanosis, agonal respirations, and a strong radial pulse. On the floor next to the patient, you see the scene depicted in the photo to the right.

1. Based on the information that you have obtained thus far and using your knowledge of toxidromes, what is the likely cause of this patient's condition?

_____

_____

_____

2. Based on the answer to question 1, and completing the toxidrome, what size pupils will the patient likely have?

_____

_____

_____

3. What is an appropriate treatment for this patient?

_____

_____

_____

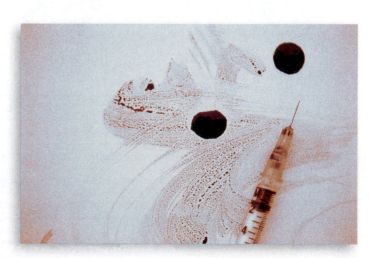

Active Learning

1. Volunteer Opportunity: Poisoning Management

There are several ways in which to expand your knowledge of medications and poisons. Perhaps one of the best ways is to observe a poison control center in action. Because of decreased funding for poison centers in recent years, it may be a challenge to find one nearby. However, even if you have a distance to travel, try to arrange an observational visit to the local poison center. Understanding the types and number of resources available to the specialists working at these centers will give you a greater perspective on this valuable resource.

Another beneficial resource for information about medications and their toxic effects is your local hospital pharmacy. Pharmacists and pharmacy technicians are well versed in the effects of medications, their actions, interactions, side effects, therapeutic ranges, and toxic effects. When they are not familiar with a specific medication and its effects, they have access to very sophisticated pharmacology databases that contain vast medication information.

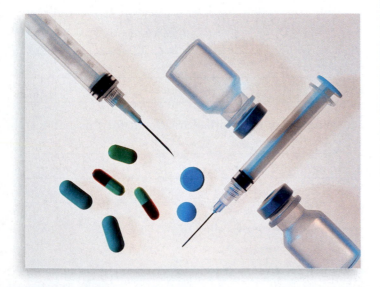

2. Which of These Is Not Like the Others?

Many recreational drugs will manifest similar signs and symptoms when a person has overdosed on them. For each of the conditions listed in the table below, choose the drug that does *not* cause that effect.

You Are There: Reality-Based Cases
Case 1

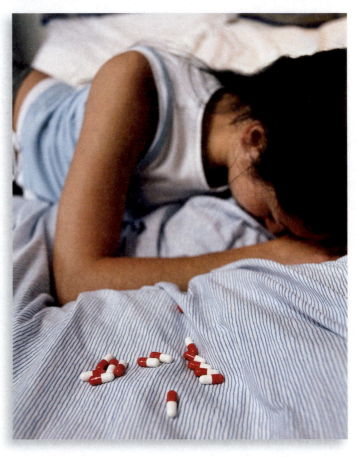

Maggie is a 15-year-old female who lives with her aunt. Maggie's aunt went into Maggie's room to tell her that dinner was ready. When she opened the door, she

Active Learning Exercise 2

Action	Drug Menu	Which One Is Not Like the Others?
a. Pupil constriction	Opiate, alpha$_2$ receptor agonist, tricyclic antidepressant	
b. Respiratory depression	Barbiturate, opiate, ethanol, cannabis	
c. Somnolence	Gamma-hydroxybutyrate, hallucinogen, lithium	
d. Agitation	Amphetamine, cocaine, barbiturate	

saw Maggie lying on her bed with some pills strewn on the bed next to her. Her aunt ran over to Maggie and shook her. Maggie moaned and tried to raise herself off the bed, but she only got to her elbows before she collapsed back onto the bed.

Her aunt noticed that Maggie had a black eye on the left side and bruising in the shape of a handprint on her left arm. There were two pill bottles on Maggie's nightstand. One was a brand-new bottle of Extra Strength Tylenol (acetaminophen 500 mg, 100 count) that appeared to be about half full. The other bottle belonged to Maggie's aunt—a new bottle that contained Restoril (15-mg pills, 2 of the 25 pills remained).

Maggie's aunt called 9-1-1, and within 5 minutes you and your partner arrive on the scene. The police have already arrived, and they inform you that the scene is safe to enter.

1. Based on the information that you have obtained so far, what is your general impression of Maggie's condition?

   _____

   _____

   _____

2. Are you concerned about either of the medications that Maggie has ingested?

   _____

   _____

   _____

3. Describe your treatment of Maggie.

   _____

   _____

   _____

4. Are there antidotes for acetaminophen or Restoril?

   _____

   _____

5. Were the amounts of medications ingested enough to cause health problems for Maggie?

   _____

   _____

   _____

6. What type of mandatory reporting, if any, is required as a result of the possible signs of abuse that were discovered (the black eye and the bruising in the

shape of a hand on Maggie's left arm) during your physical examination?

   _____

   _____

   _____

Case 2

Al has been sick with the flu for the past 3 days. He has a fever, nausea, vomiting, and diarrhea. He has been unable to hold down anything for the past 36 hours. He called his doctor and told him what he was feeling, and his doctor called in an order for an antiemetic, antidiarrheal, and antibiotic. Al's roommate Paul picked up the prescriptions for him, and as soon as Paul walked in the door, Al took the pills. He laid down on his bed, hoping more than anything that the nausea would end.

Approximately 15 minutes later, Paul went to check on Al. What he saw really frightened him: Al was lying on the bed drooling with strange contortions to his face, neck, and arms. Al was trying to speak to Paul, but only garbled words came out.

1. What is a likely cause for the contortions that Al is experiencing?

   _____

   _____

   _____

2. After you arrive on scene and assess Al's ABCDEs and vital signs, what information do you need to elicit from Al or his roommate?

   _____

   _____

   _____

Paul tells you that Al is usually quite a healthy guy. He eats very healthy food, and he doesn't drink alcohol, smoke, or take recreational drugs. He exercises religiously, but the past 3 days he has spent most of the time in the bathroom vomiting or having diarrhea. He also informs you that Al took the medications that his doctor prescribed, Compazine, Imodium, and Cipro, just prior to the onset of the contortions.

3. What is the medical term for the type of condition that Al is likely experiencing?

   _____

   _____

   _____

4. Which of the new medications is likely responsible for the contortions?

_____

_____

_____

5. Describe the pathophysiology for this type of reaction.

_____

_____

_____

6. What is the appropriate treatment for this type of reaction?

_____

_____

_____

Approximately 10 minutes after the administration of your treatment plan, Al begins to show signs of relaxation of his face, neck, and upper extremities, and his speech becomes more understandable.

Test Yourself

1. List the four most common ways that the body may absorb poison.

_____

_____

2. What advantages and disadvantages does activated charcoal have over other forms of gastric decontamination?

_____

_____

3. A 46-year-old female accidentally took her husband's medication instead of her own. She regularly takes zafirlukast (a leukotriene receptor antagonist) to manage her asthma. Instead she took her husband's propranolol (a beta-blocker), which he uses to manage hypertension. You examine her, and she appears normal. What should you do?

  a. Administer intravenous fluids and vasopressors.

  b. Tell the patient that you do not expect an adverse drug interaction and release her.

  c. Administer glucagon and calcium.

  d. Transport the patient and monitor her closely.

4. Most toxicological causes of seizures do _not_ respond well to standard doses of

  a. benzodiazepines.

  b. propofol.

  c. phenytoin.

  d. barbiturates.

5. In which of the following patients is activated charcoal contraindicated?

  a. An unresponsive 5-year-old who began vomiting after ingesting a bottle of vitamin D capsules.

  b. A 19-year-old who admits attempting suicide by taking painkillers containing codeine.

  c. An awake and alert 3-year-old who ingested half of a bottle of her grandmother's digoxin pills.

  d. An elderly patient who ingested several antihistamine tablets.

6. Which of the following is _most_ likely an intentional poisoning?

  a. A 42-year-old male unconscious in the driver's seat of his car, in his garage, with the garage door closed and all the windows in his car rolled down. The car is in park and still idling.

  b. A 28-year-old male complaining that the government is leaking nerve gas into his apartment. His skin, mouth, and eyes are dry, and his pupils are dilated.

  c. A 4-year-old female complains of a "real bad tummy ache." While examining the scene you find an open and mostly empty bottle of fruit-flavored iron supplements.

  d. A 31-year-old female has severe respiratory depression. When you take her medical history, you find she was recently prescribed morphine for pain management.

7. How does the size of a drug's therapeutic window affect a patient's likelihood of suffering toxic effects?

_____

_____

8. The extent of poison absorption depends _directly_ on all the following _except_

  a. duration of contact.

  b. the property of the poison.

  c. the route of exposure.

  d. the reason for exposure.

9. Generally speaking, which type of poisoning presents the greatest risk to the patient?

  a. Malicious poisoning

  b. Drug abuse

c. Intentional self-harm

d. Adverse drug reactions

10. What is the most common method of gastric decontamination?

  a. Activated charcoal

  b. Gastric lavage

  c. Whole bowel irrigation

  d. Induced vomiting

11. What generalization could you draw regarding the differences between the cholinergic and anticholinergic toxidrome symptoms?

_____

_____

12. When providing supportive care to an intoxicated patient, endotracheal intubation is rarely performed unless the patient is unconscious or apneic.

True

False

13. Which of the following toxins has an antidote that can be administered in the prehospital setting?

  a. Antipsychotics

  b. Acetaminophen

  c. Cyanide

  d. Food poisoning

14. You suspect that your unresponsive patient has been poisoned when you find an open, unlabeled pill bottle lying next to him. What resources are available to help you identify the toxin?

_____

_____

15. Children are generally at the greatest risk of

  a. iron poisoning.

  b. magnesium poisoning.

  c. lead poisoning.

  d. mercury poisoning.

16. The most accurate data regarding a specific toxic product can generally be found

  a. by contacting a poison center.

  b. on the manufacturer's material safety data sheet.

  c. by contacting a supervising physician.

  d. on the product's packaging.

17. The most commonly abused drug and leading cause of drug death is _____.

18. Your patient presents with vomiting, wheezing, pulmonary edema, diarrhea, and muscle weakness. What type of substance should you most suspect?

  a. A sympathomimetic

  b. A cholinergic

  c. An opioid

  d. An anticholinergic

19. Which of the following organs is more likely to be affected by an ingested poison *first*?

  a. Skin

  b. Skeletal muscles

  c. Eyes

  d. Heart

20. Most toxin-related instances of pulmonary edema are cardiogenic.

True

False

Need to Know

According to the Society of Toxicology and the National Library of Medicine, toxicology is defined as, "The study of the adverse effects of chemical, physical or biological agents on living organisms and the ecosystem, including the prevention and amelioration (improvement) of such adverse effects."[1]

The following represent the Key Objectives of Chapter 35:

1. *Describe poisonings commonly encountered by paramedics in the prehospital setting.*

  Poisoning can result from exposure to medications, recreational drugs, environmental hazards, and natural toxins. Over-the-counter medications taken in large quantities can have effects just as lethal as those of controlled prescription medications. Prescription medications, such as cardiac medications, sedatives, hypnotics, antidepressants, and antipsychotics are common in poisonings and can result in death from both accidental and purposeful exposures.

  Alcohol (ethyl alcohol, ethanol, ETOH) is one of the most frequently abused legal substances, and it plays a role in many of the patients that paramedics encounter.

  In the world of terrorism and weapons of mass destruction, paramedics and other emergency workers must learn about the effects of many poisons that are designed to have lethal effects on large groups of people. Nerve agents such as VX or sarin, blister agents, and organophosphates are deadly poisons that are used by terrorists to wreak havoc on a large scale.

2. *List common modes of exposure to poisons.*

Exposure to drugs and other chemicals occurs through various routes, including dermal (through the skin), ingestion (by mouth), injection, and inhalation. Of these, injection and inhalation represent the fastest routes of absorption.

3. *Identify factors that affect poisoning victims and produce toxicity.*

Factors that impact how quickly and seriously a toxic substance affects a patient include its concentration, duration of exposure, route of exposure, and the actual substance itself.

4. *Describe specific toxidromes and their treatments.*

A *toxidrome* is a combination of symptoms that is characteristic of a specific classification of poison. Toxidromes are important to paramedics because they lead the paramedic to a probable cause and likely treatment based on presenting signs and symptoms.

Following are commonly encountered poison classifications and their toxidromes:

a. *Organophosphates.* Organophosphates function as cholinesterase inhibitors, thereby affecting neuromuscular transmission. Organophosphates are commonly found in pesticides. Sarin is an example of an organophosphate nerve gas used in terrorism. Exposure is typically by inhalation or dermal exposure, but ingestion is another possible route.

The toxidrome for organophosphate (cholinergic) exposure can be remembered by the acronym SLUDGE:

- **S**alivation
- **L**acrimation
- **U**rination
- **D**efecation
- **G**astric distress
- **E**mesis

The treatment for organophosphate poisoning following removal of the patient from the area of exposure, decontamination, and support of ABCs is administration of atropine and pralidoxime.

b. *Narcotic overdose.* Narcotics are used as analgesics and also as recreational drugs. Accidental and purposeful overdoses are seen in both analgesic and recreational use. Morphine sulfate is a common narcotic analgesic, and heroin is a commonly abused recreational narcotic drug. Narcotic exposure is typically by ingestion or injection, but it can be also by the dermal route or inhalation.

The toxidrome for narcotic overdoses is:
- Respiratory depression
- Constricted pupils
- Altered level of consciousness (unconscious)

Treatment for narcotic overdose is support of ventilations, administration of high-flow oxygen, and the administration of naloxone.

c. *Anticholinergic poisoning.* Anticholinergic medications are used to relieve cramps, reduce uncontrollable movements, prevent bladder spasms, relax the smooth muscles in the airways, and dry the nose and chest. Thus anticholinergics are helpful in the treatment of stomach cramps, Parkinson's disease, colds, chronic obstructive pulmonary disease (COPD), urinary incontinence, and muscle spasms from cerebral palsy. Substances with anticholinergic properties competitively antagonize acetylcholine muscarinic receptors; this predominantly occurs at peripheral postganglionic parasympathetic muscarinic receptors.

The toxidrome for anticholinergic medication poisoning includes:
- Dry skin, mouth, and eyes
- Dilated pupils and blurred vision
- Tachycardia
- Confusion
- Diminished bowel sounds
- Constipation

d. *Sympathomimetic poisoning.* Sympathomimetic medications are used to treat a variety of conditions, such as asthma, cardiogenic shock, and allergic rhinitis. Pseudoephedrine, epinephrine, albuterol (beta$_2$ specific), MAO inhibitors, and phencyclidine are sympathomimetic medications. Some recreational drugs, such as cocaine and amphetamines, also fall into this category. Sympathomimetics have an effect on alpha and beta receptors and can cause vasoconstriction, tachycardia, increased cardiac output, and bronchodilation. Exposure to sympathomimetic drugs typically occurs through injection, ingestion, and inhalation.

The toxidrome for sympathomimetic poisoning is:
- Tachycardia (palpitations)
- Hypertension
- Agitation (irritability)
- Dilated pupils

- Headache
- Nausea
- Tremors
- Dilated pupils
- Diaphoresis

Note: Antidotes for common poisonings are listed in Table 35-3 in the textbook.

5. *Given a patient scenario, identify the poison and outline appropriate treatment.*

Identification of poisons can be difficult because many times medications and poisons are in atypical forms and/or are not in their original packaging. Simply finding small white pills next to an unconscious patient does not necessarily help the paramedic identify the medication.

There are several very good resources that paramedics can use to help identify poisons and appropriately manage the effects of exposure to that poison. One of the most easily accessible resources are poison control centers. A regional poison control center can be reached anywhere in the United States by calling 1-800-222-1222. Poison centers can help identify poisons based on a description of symptoms, and professionals can also provide information on the appropriate treatment for poisonings.

Another useful resource for managing a poisoning patient is the manufacturer's material safety data sheets (MSDS), which are typically found in all medication packages and products that contain poisons. These sheets will contain the specific concentrations of the substances in the container, and some even contain treatment information in case the substance is ingested, inhaled, or absorbed.

If possible, bring the substance to the hospital with you for identification, but do so only if bringing it to the hospital will not expose you or the people in the hospital to the same poisonous substance.

6. *Given that the amount of poison absorbed is directly proportional to the duration of the exposure, describe ways in which exposure time can be minimized.*

Decontamination is the principle of limiting absorption by shortening the duration of exposure.

a. *Inhalation.* Patients who are exposed to poisons due to inhalation should be removed from the toxic environment and placed in an environment free of the poisonous substance (e.g., a patient in a storage shed where there is a chlorine leak). The patient should be evaluated for patent airway, breathing status, and circulatory status and placed on high concentrations of oxygen.

b. *Ingestion.* Trapping a substance in the intestinal lumen (activated charcoal) or moving a poison through the GI tract so rapidly that it doesn't have time to absorb (whole bowel irrigation) are ways in which absorption can be decreased.

c. *Dermal and ocular exposures.* Dermal and ocular exposures are reduced by the rapid removal of the substance from the skin or the eyes. Solid particles on the surface of the skin can be brushed off or irrigated if the substance will not react with water. Irrigation of the eyes is the primary method of decontamination.

d. *Injection.* Because absorption of most poisons by injection is immediate, decontamination is not easily performed or beneficial.

Need to Do

The following skills are explained and illustrated in a step-by-step manner, via skill sheets and/or Step-by-Steps in this text and on the accompanying DVD:

Skill Name	Skill Sheet Number and Location	Step-by-Step Number and Location
Rapid Sequence Intubation	13 – Appendix A and DVD	13 – Chapter 12 and DVD
Evacuation of Gastric Contents	24 – DVD	24 – DVD
Eye Irrigation	80 – DVD	N/A

💿 Connections

- Epocrates (www.epocrates.com), a provider of handheld and Web-based clinical reference tools for health-care professionals, offers a very beneficial drug reference that can be used with your personal digital assistant (PDA). It is an efficient way to look up drugs that you are not familiar with while working in any medical setting—whether it be as a paramedic student, a novice paramedic, or an expert paramedic.

- Chapter 45, The Abused and Neglected, in the textbook includes additional information on how to interact with and manage a patient who may have been abused.

- Chapter 53, Hazardous Materials Incidents, in the textbook discusses the decontamination and treatment of patients exposed to hazardous poisons.

- Chapter 55, Responding to WMD Events, in the textbook outlines information on rescuer protection, decontamination, treatment, and transport of patients who are victims of a WMD incident.

- The *2004 Emergency Response Guidebook* published by the U.S. Department of Transportation (DOT) provides information on identifying hazardous materials. An online PDF file can be downloaded from the DOT website at http://hazmat.dot.gov/pubs/erg/gydebook.htm.

- Link to the companion DVD for a chapter-based quiz, audio glossary, animations, games and exercises, and, when appropriate, skill sheets and skill Step-by-Steps.

Street Secrets

- **Safety First** Whenever you are faced with a toxicology-related emergency, such as a poisoning or overdose, ensure that you and your fellow emergency workers are safe and utilizing all appropriate BSI and PPE applicable to the particular situation.

- **Resources** If you have any doubt about what is causing the patient's presenting signs and symptoms, or you are not sure how to manage a patient who has been exposed to a particular medication or poison, utilize all the resources that you have at your disposal for help. Resources such as poison control centers will prove extremely helpful in the identification and development of a treatment plan for almost any poisoning or overdose.

The Drug Box

Activated charcoal: An adsorbent that binds to many drugs and chemicals, preventing their absorption by the stomach and intestines into the bloodstream.

Albuterol (Proventil, Ventolin, Volmax): A beta2 specific agonist that causes relaxation of bronchiole smooth muscles; when taken in large quantities, it can result in sympathomimetic toxicity.

Amyl nitrite: Part of a cyanide antidote kit in an ampule form. When the ampule is crushed, the released gas is inhaled by the patient. This causes the formation of methemoglobin in the bloodstream, which in turn combines with cyanide to form cyanomethemoglobin. Cyanomethemoglobin converts to thiocyanate in the presence of sodium thiosulfate, another part of a cyanide kit. Thiocyanate is readily excreted by the kidneys. Amyl nitrite should be used as a temporizing measure only if IV access is not immediately available.

Atropine: An antimuscarinic agent that blocks acetylcholine at parasympathetic sites and is useful in high doses for the treatment of organophosphate poisonings.

Diphenhydramine (Benadryl): An antihistamine used in the treatment of dystonic (extrapyramidal) reactions caused by phenothiazine medications.

Epinephrine (Adrenalin): A synthetic catecholamine that has both alpha and beta adrenergic effects. An overdose of epinephrine can result in sympathomimetic toxicity.

Flumazenil (Romazicon): A benzodiazepine receptor antagonist that is used to reverse the side effects of benzodiazepines.

Glucagon: Hormone used to circumvent beta receptor sites blocked by an overdose, thereby increasing cardiac rate and contractility.

Naloxone (Narcan): A competitive narcotic antagonist used to treat patients suspected of suffering from a narcotic (opiate) overdose.

Pralidoxime (2-PAM chloride): Reactivates cholinesterase that is inactivated by organophosphate pesticides and related compounds, allowing for degradation of excess acetylcholine and the return of normal functioning to neuromuscular junctions.

Sodium bicarbonate: Alkalinizing agent used to reverse cardiac conduction effects of tricyclic acid overdoses.

References

1. The Society of Toxicology, www.toxicology.org/AI/PUB/SI05/SI05_Define.asp (accessed December 1, 2006).
2. E-medicine, "Toxicity, Medication-Induced Dystonic Reactions," www.emedicine.com/emerg/topic157.htm (accessed December 2, 2006).

Answers

Are You Ready?

1. Based on the presentation of the patient (unconscious, agonal respirations, strong radial pulses, and a 1-mL syringe lying on the floor next to the patient), the likely toxidrome to follow would be that of a narcotic overdose.
2. Constricted pupils, possibly pinpoint.
3. An appropriate treatment for a patient suffering from a narcotic overdose should include ventilatory assistance and supplementary oxygen. Naloxone can be administered intranasally, intramuscularly, or intravenously to block further effects of the narcotic.

Active Learning

2. a. tricyclic antidepressant; b. cannabis; c. lithium; d. barbiturate.

You Are There: Reality-Based Cases

Case 1

1. Maggie appears unresponsive after possibly taking an overdose of acetaminophen and Restoril. Any unresponsive patient is at risk for aspiration and should be classified as critical.
2. Acetaminophen (analgesic and antipyretic) overdoses are thought by many people to be benign because the product is sold over the counter. Initially acetaminophen overdoses present without signs or symptoms, but over the 24–72 hours after ingestion, liver damage and ultimately death can occur as a result of liver failure. Restoril (a benzodiazepine) can cause ALOC, hypotension, and respiratory depression. Airway protection with ALOC, hemodynamic compromise secondary to hypotension, and hypoxia resulting from respiratory depression are concerns when dealing with a Restoril overdose.
3. Initial management of Maggie's condition centers on airway, breathing, and circulation. Also, because she has a black eye that the aunt has not seen before and an altered level of consciousness, Maggie needs to be treated as a trauma patient and placed in c-spine precautions.

   Because Restoril can cause respiratory depression, ventilatory support and monitoring of SpO_2 and $ETCO_2$ would be beneficial. Assessment and frequent monitoring of Maggie's hemodynamic status (ECG, vital signs, etc.) are important because of the potential for hypotension as a result of the Restoril ingestion. It will be important to obtain IV access and give fluid boluses PRN to manage any hypotension that may occur. If the hypotension does not resolve with fluid boluses, consider the use of vasopressors to raise Maggie's blood pressure. Prevention of further absorption of the medications through the GI tract is important and can be accomplished via activated charcoal. The concern with such a medication in a patient who is unconscious is aspiration. Even if the patient is intubated, there is still the issue of how the activated charcoal will be administered. If your EMS system allows for the administration of activated charcoal via a nasogastric or orogastric tube, then this is an appropriate step to take.

4. N-acetylcysteine is an antidote for acetaminophen overdose, and flumazenil (Romazicon) is an antidote for benzodiazepine overdose. Neither is commonly administered in the prehospital setting. Paramedics should address any immediate life threats, prevent further absorption of the medications (if within your local EMS protocols), and transport the patient to the hospital.

5. For acetaminophen overdoses in adults, < 5 g is not toxic; with 5–7.5 g, hepatotoxicity is unlikely; and > 7.5 g is potentially hepatotoxic. In children, ≥ 150–200 mg/kg is potentially hepatotoxic.[1] Maggie appears to be a slender teenager (approximately 50 kg) who ingested half of a bottle of one hundred 500-mg tablets of acetaminophen.

   The amount of acetaminophen Maggie ingested is

   $$50 \text{ pills} \times 500 \text{ mg/pill} = 25,000 \text{ mg} = 25 \text{ g}$$

   which is over 3.5 times the potentially hepatotoxic adult dosage.

   The potentially hepatotoxic pediatric dosage for Maggie is

   $$50 \text{ kg} \times 150 \text{ mg/kg} = 7,500 \text{ mg}$$
   $$= 7.5 \text{ g}$$

   to

   $$50 \text{ kg} \times 200 \text{ mg/kg} = 10,000 \text{ mg}$$
   $$= 10 \text{ g}$$

   Thus the 25 g Maggie ingested is 2.5–3.5 times the potentially hepatotoxic pediatric dosage.

   For Restoril overdoses, the 50% lethal dose (LD50) for rabbits was 1,963 mg/kg (the amount of drug it took to kill 50% of the subject group, usually animals). Since Maggie possibly ingested twenty-three 15-mg pills, she may have ingested 345 mg, which is not close to the LD50 for rabbits, let alone humans. This is not to say that the effects of the Restoril are harmless or they cannot be fatal; you still need to be concerned about the effects of the ALOC, respiratory depression, and hypotension that can be caused by the Restoril.

6. Mandatory reporting for child abuse, elder abuse, and domestic violence differs from state to state. If you have any suspicion of abuse or domestic violence and you are not sure what your responsibilities are, contact your immediate supervisor, medical direction, or local law enforcement for assistance.

Case 2

1. Because Al's contortions started shortly (15 minutes) after the ingestion of his new medications, it would be logical to assume that the medications that he just took were responsible.

2. The information that would be beneficial to obtain would include the results of the primary and secondary assessment as well as Al's past medical history and history of present illness, including medications and allergies to medications.

3. The signs and symptoms that Al is displaying are consistent with a dystonic (extrapyramidal) reaction.

4. Compazine is a phenothiazine and therefore is likely responsible for the reaction.

5. Dystonic reactions are frequently idiosyncratic and therefore not accurately predictable. They are thought to be the result of a drug-induced alteration of dopaminergic-cholinergic balance in the basal ganglia. High-potency dopamine receptor antagonists are most likely to produce an acute dystonic reaction.[2]

6. Prehospital treatment of dystonic reactions begins with assessment and management of the ABCs as needed. The pharmacological treatment is typically diphenhydramine, but benztropine (Cogentin) and benzodiazepines such as diazepam (Valium) have proven effective in treating dystonic reactions as well.

Test Yourself

1. Injection, inhalation, ingestion, transdermal

   Absorption can also occur through the ocular, vaginal, urethral, or rectal mucosa.

2. Activated charcoal is easier to administer and is more pleasant for the patient than most other methods of decontamination (such as stomach pumping or induced vomiting). However, charcoal can be life threatening if aspirated, so you should not administer it if there is risk of aspiration. Also, there are several common poisons that are not bound by activated charcoal, including ethanol, methanol, ethylene glycol, iron, and lithium.

   Activated charcoal is the most common method of gastric decontamination. It absorbs many poisons and remains in the intestines, effectively trapping the poison and preventing systemic absorption.

3. d

   This is a case of accidental exposure. Most accidental ingestions are clinically insignificant, and many interventions are more likely to cause harm than to help. However, you should not dismiss the woman. Transport her to a care center, and monitor her to ensure her vital signs remain normal.

4. c

   While phenytoin may be an effective anticonvulsant in other circumstances, it is not considered useful for toxicological causes of seizure. Benzodiazepines are the most common treatment for toxicological seizures. Barbiturates and propofol are also considered useful.

5. a

   Charcoal aspiration can be life threatening, so charcoal should not be used if the patient is at risk for aspiration.

6. a

   The man in his garage has most likely attempted suicide. The woman prescribed morphine may have intentionally overdosed (an intentional poisoning), but there is also a good chance that her condition results from a therapeutic error or an adverse drug reaction. If the nerve gas victim's allegations are true, this would be an example of intentional poisoning, but he does not display symptoms of nerve gas poisoning. The 4-year-old probably mistook the iron supplements for candy and did not realize they could be harmful.

7. The narrower the therapeutic window, the more likely a patient will suffer toxic effects.

   The therapeutic window is the difference between the dose of a medication that causes the desired effects and the dose that causes toxic effects. Only a small overdose of a drug with a narrow window would cause toxic effects, while a much larger overdose of one with a wide window would be required.

8. d

   The reason for exposure can affect the extent of poison absorbed, but it does so indirectly. For example, a patient who desires to do self-harm is more likely to increase the duration of contact. The increased duration directly affects the amount of poison absorbed.

9. c

   Patients who intentionally expose themselves to toxins are often at the greatest risk of developing serious effects. They typically take as much poison as they can obtain, frequently ingesting multiple products. Furthermore, these patients may deny taking poison and may hide initial symptoms. It is important that these patients be carefully monitored.

10. a

    Activated charcoal is the most common method of gastric decontamination due to its effectiveness and ease of use. However, care should be taken to ensure the patient does not aspirate the charcoal. Whole body irrigation is used to decontaminate sustained-release medications, toxins not bound by charcoal (such as iron and lithium), and instances of body packing.

11. Many cholinergic symptoms are the opposite of anticholinergic symptoms. For example: sweating versus dry skin, salivation versus dry mouth, lacrimation versus dry eyes, constricted pupils versus dilated pupils. Another way to think of it is that cholinergic symptoms tend to be "wet," while anticholinergic symptoms tend to be "dry."

    Cholinergic symptoms include: salivation, lacrimation, vomiting, wheezing, pulmonary edema, diarrhea, urination, small pupils, seizures, fasciculations, and muscle weakness. Anticholinergic symptoms include: dry skin, mouth, and eyes; delirium; dilated pupils; tachycardia; and decreased bowel sounds.

12. **False**

Because vomiting is common in many poisonings, there should be a low threshold to intubate poisoned patients with a decreased level of consciousness. Patients with airway swelling or secretion should be intubated as soon as possible, as they will likely deteriorate with time.

13. c

Cyanide poisoning requires a three-step antidote of amyl nitrite, sodium nitrite, and sodium thiosulfate. The other toxins listed have no specific prehospital interventions.

14. Resources include: poison control centers, manufacturer's safety data sheet, product packaging, and witness accounts.

Poisons often cause nonspecific symptoms. Therefore diagnosis often depends on information gathered from witnesses or at the scene.

15. a

While advances in treatment and new packaging restrictions have dramatically decreased the risk of death from iron poisoning, vitamins containing iron are still a concern. Ingestion of large amounts of these vitamins will cause gastrointestinal symptoms and can progress to coma and shock. Lead, on the other hand, is only dangerous with chronic exposure. Acute mercury poisoning only occurs if mercury is heated to a gas or if mercury salts are ingested.

16. a

Poison centers are the most readily accessible and up-to-date source of poison information. Packaging and manufacturer's material safety data sheets also contain useful information, but this may be out of date. You can reach a regional poison center by calling 1-800-222-1222 anywhere in the United States.

17. Ethanol (alcohol)

Ethanol is undoubtedly the most common drug of abuse and is the leading cause of drug abuse death. Although ethanol is sold as a beverage, it is also in a variety of medicinal and cosmetic preparations, including cough suppressants, mouthwash, perfumes, colognes, and industrial solvents.

18. b

Several of the symptoms for cholinergic toxins can be remembered using the acronym SLUDGE (Salivation, Lacrimation, Urination, Defecation, Gastrointestinal distress, Emesis). Other symptoms include miosis, bronchospasm and pulmonary edema, fasciculations (twitching muscles), and muscle weakness.

19. d

Organs with high blood flow, such the heart, become saturated with the poison more quickly than those with lower blood flow. Other high-blood-flow organs include the liver, brain, and kidneys.

20. **False**

Most toxin-related instances of pulmonary edema are non-cardiogenic. Therefore diuretics, nitrates, and morphine are of little value.

chapter 36

Urology

rudimentary care to the patients. Tonight one of the caretakers points out Mrs. Sarah Sidner, a 72-year-old female who recently entered the home. The caretaker reports that Mrs. Sidner did not wake up from her afternoon nap. She could not arouse her for dinner.

Your patient presents supine in her bed. Speaking her name loudly does not cause her to stir. A mild trapezius pinch causes her to wince, but she remains silent. Her airway appears patent, and her ventilatory rate is fast. You can feel a faint, rapid radial pulse; her skin is warm and mottled.

The caretaker indicates that your patient has a history of diabetes and high blood pressure. She has prescriptions for Humulin NPH, HCTZ, and Colace.

1. Is your patient sick or not yet sick?

   _____
   _____
   _____

2. What are your initial steps in caring for this patient?

   _____
   _____
   _____

3. What information do you need to know about your patient at this point in time?

   _____
   _____
   _____

Are You Ready?

"Medic 7, A Delta response to 675 Liemert Street, cross of Park Boulevard. Unconscious elderly female." You make your way to the ambulance, where your partner has already started the motor. "It's the Board and Care home again," she says, tapping the mobile data terminal (MDT). You head through the evening traffic and shortly arrive at a nondescript, single-family home in a middle-class neighborhood.

The scene appears safe as you make your way into the home. From past experience, you know that there are eight older clients who live here. A husband and wife team manages the home and provides

Active Learning

Anatomy Review

1. Identify the structures of the urinary system in Figure 36-1.

a. _____

b. _____

c. _____

d. _____

e. _____

f. _____

g. _____

2. Note how the kidney is connected to the circulatory system. How might this connection be impacted during a rapid deceleration force?

_____

_____

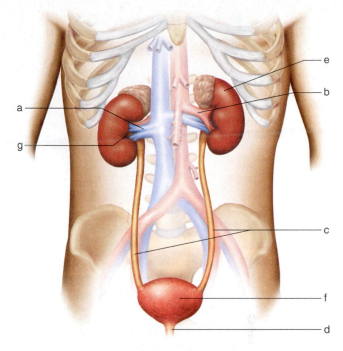

FIGURE 36-1

3. Identify the structures of the urinary system in Figure 36-2.

a. _____

b. _____

c. _____

d. _____

e. _____

f. _____

g. _____

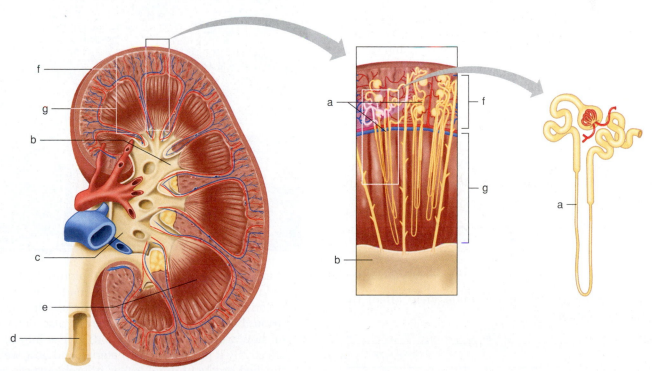

FIGURE 36-2

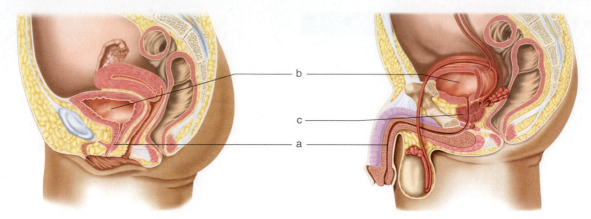

FIGURE 36-3

4. Trace the formation of urine through the structures shown in Figure 36-2.

5. Identify the structures of the male and female urinary systems shown in Figure 36-3.

    a. _____

    b. _____

    c. _____

Refer to Figure 36-3 to answer questions 6 through 8.

6. Note and compare structure "a" in the female and male views. Based on your observation, what are a female's chances of contracting a urinary tract infection (UTI) compared with a male's?

    _____

    _____

    _____

7. Note the position of organ "b" in the female view. How is it impacted by the organ immediately superior to it?

    _____

    _____

    _____

8. How can organ "c" in the male view affect the urinary system?

    _____

    _____

    _____

9. In and Out

Similar to the industrial plant pictured here, the kidney is a complex structure made up of pipes (arteries and veins) and filters (glomeruli) that "create" urine. Like this plant, the kidney is also dependent on how well raw product (blood) comes into it, how effectively it processes that material, and how well the finished product (urine) leaves it. Problems can occur with the kidney if any of these routes are affected.

Using the table below, organize the conditions listed here into the areas of prerenal, intrinsic, and postrenal "flow control" for the kidney?

- Aortic aneurysm
- Atherosclerosis
- Benign prostatic hypertrophy
- Bladder cancer
- Burns
- Diabetes
- HIV
- Hypovolemic shock
- Kidney stones
- Lupus erythematosus
- Myocardial infarction
- Renal artery thrombus
- Retroperitoneal tumors
- Streptococcal infection
- Vasculitis

Prerenal	Intrinsic	Postrenal
Atherosclerosis		
	HIV	

You Are There: Reality-Based Cases

Case 1 (continued from chapter opener)

You ascertain that Mrs. Sidner had chills, nausea, and a low-grade fever for the past 48 hours. She seemed to respond to oral doses of acetaminophen. She had eaten this morning, and her insulin was adjusted appropriately for her cold. She began complaining of lower abdominal pain last night.

Her vital signs are HR of 104, BP of 108/78, and RR of 20. A finger stick for blood glucose reveals a level of 165 mcg/dL. Her ECG tracing in lead II is shown in Figure 36-4.

Mrs. Sidner's physical examination is unremarkable. Her breath sounds are clear, and you cannot auscultate unusual heart tones. Her abdomen is soft; she does not moan when you palpate the four quadrants. You can palpate both femoral and radial pulses, and they feel faint but equal bilaterally. Her SpO_2 reading is 98%.

Upon further questioning, the caretaker believes that the patient's last bowel movement was "normal," and it occurred yesterday evening. Mrs. Sidner's last urine output was this morning. She reported some worsening of her abdominal pain when she urinated.

1. Based on the information thus far, what are the possible causes of your patient's condition?

   _____

   _____

   _____

2. List the interventions you would perform in this case.

   _____

   _____

   _____

Case 2

"Okay, the IV is in," reports your partner. Thank goodness, you think to yourself; your patient definitely needs it right now! Mavis Thomas, a 69-year-old female, is sitting upright on the edge of her bed, struggling to breathe. Family members had not heard from her and went to her apartment to find out if she had fallen. They found her having trouble breathing and called 9-1-1. You arrived to find a heavyset woman supine in bed in respiratory distress, speaking in only three- to four-word sentences. A quick blood pressure check

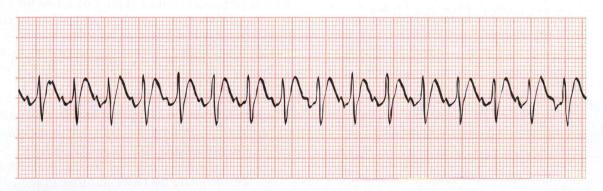

FIGURE 36-4

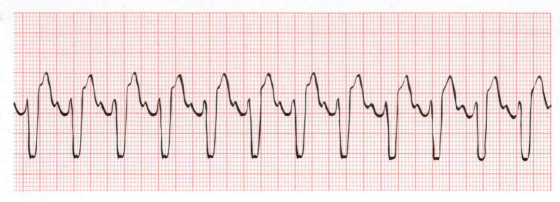

FIGURE 36-5

confirmed that she was not hypotensive, and you moved her to a sitting position. You have already placed her on a non-rebreather mask and have completed your primary assessment, which shows the following:

- The airway appears to be patent.
- She is tachypneic, and crackles are auscultated in both lung fields.
- She is tachycardic, with pulses felt at both radials. The ECG is shown in Figure 36-5.

Your secondary exam findings include:

- JVD and pedal edema are evident.
- There is an AV shunt in the left forearm.
- Her past medical history includes hypertension, chronic renal failure, and diabetes.
- Her medications include Lotensin and Glucophage.

In addition, she has missed her dialysis treatment that should have occurred 2 days earlier. She complains of chest discomfort as well as tingling around her face and hands.

When you ask her, Mrs. Thomas states that she was too weak to get to the taxicab that was to take her to the dialysis center. She also felt a little guilty about the whole situation; she had eaten a plate of fried bananas the day before her dialysis, something her doctor had told her not to do, but she missed them a lot and wanted to have "just a bite."

1. What are possible causes of her condition?

_____

_____

_____

2. How should you treat this situation?

_____

_____

_____

_____

Test Yourself

1. You are called to an office building for a patient experiencing lower abdominal and back pain. During the interview, you learn that it "burns" when she urinates. Your patient is an otherwise healthy 36-year-old female. You should suspect
   a. an upper UTI.
   b. an ovarian cyst.
   c. a kidney infection.
   d. a lower UTI.

2. List five organs associated with the genitourinary system.

_____

_____

3. Which of the following are signs and symptoms associated with kidney stones?
   a. Abdominal tenderness with hyperactive bowel sounds
   b. Constipation, weight gain, and radiating abdominal pain
   c. Dysuria, urinary urgency, and flank tenderness
   d. Severe flank pain, relieved by assuming the fetal position

4. You respond to the local nursing home for a patient who is lethargic. The nursing staff tells you that the patient has been decreasing in mental status since last night. The patient has a history of end-stage renal disease (ESRD) and was unable to attend her last dialysis treatment due to a fever. What treatments should you consider in order to address expected complications in this patient?
   a. The use of albuterol and calcium chloride for the potentially hyperkalemic patient
   b. The administration of an IV bolus followed immediately by Lasix in order to increase perfusion to the kidneys

   c. The use of succinylcholine to facilitate endotracheal intubation should the patient be unable to protect her airway

   d. The use of BiPAP or CPAP to manage any respiratory issues

5. Acute renal failure (ARF) can result in the deterioration of renal function over a period of hours.

True

False

6. What ECG waveform changes are associated with hyperkalemia?

_____

_____

7. Which of the following statements about renal failure is true?

   a. Diseases and disorders of blood vessels are causes of postrenal failure.

   b. Postrenal failure is the most common cause of acute renal failure.

   c. Rhabdomyolysis and nephrotic syndrome are causes of prerenal failure.

   d. Renal artery thrombi and renal artery stenosis are causes of intrinsic renal failure.

8. You are treating a 22-year-old male patient complaining of urinary frequency, burning, and discharge with scrotal swelling. Which of the following is the most likely cause of these symptoms?

   a. Chlamydia

   b. *Ureaplasma urealyticum*

   c. Syphilis

   d. Fecal coliform bacteria

9. You respond to a residence for a 29-year-old male complaining of extremely painful urination with a foul discharge. He tells you that he first noticed the symptoms about 2 days ago and that he had a one-night stand about a week ago. The most likely cause of his symptoms is _____.

10. Differentiate between peritoneal dialysis and hemodialysis.

_____

_____

Need to Know

The following represent the Key Objectives of Chapter 36:

1. *Assess and care for a patient complaining of pelvic or flank pain.*

Begin by addressing any conditions identified in the primary assessment. Is the airway patent? Is work of breathing adequate? Does the patient have enough circulation to create end-organ perfusion? As always, address problems found with airway, breathing, and circulation *first*.

Attempt to localize the point of discomfort during your secondary exam. Is the pain more anterior or posterior? Is it more of a visceral complaint (i.e., achy, dull, crampy) or is the discomfort more somatic (i.e., sharp and well-defined)? An OPQRST assessment of the pain can reveal a lot of information; for example, a pain that is slow to develop and difficult to localize is more indicative of an infection, whereas a relatively rapid onset of sharp pain in the flank region that moves downward with time can be indicative of kidney stones.

Establish a baseline set of vital signs and obtain a SAMPLE history. A previous history of dialysis or urinary tract infections can provide clues about the current complaint.

Unfortunately, there is little a paramedic can do to help alleviate the pain or discomfort associated with urinary conditions. Judicious fluid therapy can help a volume-depleted patient, and aggressive pain control may be needed to help the patient achieve a level of comfort that allows examination. While evaluating patients experiencing altered mental status that is possibly secondary to metabolic disorders brought on by a urological emergency, remember to check blood sugar, oxygen, and carbon dioxide levels as part of your workup.

2. *Identify and manage a patient experiencing complications secondary to renal failure.*

Renal failure can be described using three general categories. *Prerenal failure* refers to conditions that decrease perfusion to the kidneys. Shock, renal artery stenosis, and rhabdomyolysis are examples of prerenal causes. *Intrinsic failure* includes conditions within the kidney itself. For example, infection, vasculitis, and diabetes mellitus can impair kidney function. *Postrenal failure* refers to conditions that result in blockage of the urinary tract. Kidney stones, clots, and prostatic enlargement are examples of postrenal conditions.

Renal failure can be acute or chronic. Acute renal failure (ARF) results most commonly in electrolyte and acid/base imbalances and volume issues. The most serious condition is hyperkalemia. The ECG may provide valuable clues to this condition—look for peaked T waves and a shortened QT interval. As serum potassium levels rise, a bundle branch block may appear, along with a lengthened PR interval and flattened P waves. If the patient becomes hypotensive and/or the QRS interval begins to widen, 10% calcium carbonate or calcium chloride may be administered to help offset the increased potassium levels. Other treatment considerations include sodium bicarbonate, albuterol nebulizer, and a combination of insulin and 50% dextrose.

Also associated with ARF is excessive fluid loss or retention. In hypovolemic patients, carefully administer IV fluid, perhaps 200–500 mL at a time. Check for lung sounds and vital signs to avoid overhydrating the patient. For ARF patients who are hypervolemic, typical methods of clearing fluid from extravascular spaces such as the lungs may not be effective. CPAP or BiPAP may be helpful for hypervolemic patients with crackles or rales in the lung fields.

Other complications of ARF include urinary outlet obstruction that is relieved with bladder catheterization. These patients will complain of abdominal pain and the inability to urinate even though they have the urge to void. Recognizing these patients and transporting them as soon as possible will be of great help to relieve the pressure.

Chronic renal failure (CRF) refers to the gradual, permanent loss of kidney function. CRF eventually leads to end-stage renal disease (ESRD), which is fatal unless dialysis is begun or a kidney transplant occurs. The most common causes of ESRD are diabetes, hypertension, and glomerular disease.

Uremia is the clinical syndrome associated with ESRD. Toxins such as urea build up in the bloodstream, causing a variety of conditions to develop. They include anemia, acidemia, hyperkalemia, hyperparathyroidism, malnutrition, and hypertension. Patients can present in respiratory distress secondary to pulmonary edema. A patient may become lethargic, confused, and ultimately unresponsive as toxin levels rise in the blood.

Prehospital treatment is limited. Like ARF, think of other possible causes of the condition that are not related to renal failure. Check blood glucose, oxygen, and, if available, carbon dioxide levels. Obtain an ECG tracing to look for signs of hyperkalemia.

Patients with ESRD will most likely be on dialysis. It may be hemodialysis, in which external filtering of the blood takes place with the use of filters, or it may be peritoneal dialysis, in which the patient administers the dialysate fluid into the peritoneal cavity and allows for wastes and fluids to filter through the peritoneum. Common complications include infection of the access sites (AV shunt in hemodialysis or peritoneal catheter) and occlusion of the shunt or catheter.

During hemodialysis a patient can become hypotensive secondary to an excessive or a too-rapid removal of fluid from the body. Carefully administer small boluses of fluid and monitor heart rate, blood pressure, and lung sounds. A patient can also experience cerebral edema during or just after dialysis, causing disequilibrium syndrome.

3. *Identify and provide care to a patient experiencing symptoms related to infection of the urological system.*

Infection can occur in many of the structures associated with the urinary system. A urinary tract infection (UTI) can occur in the *lower* structures, such as the bladder (cystitis), resulting in frequent urination, burning upon urination, lower abdominal or back pain, fever, nausea, and weakness associated with the infection. An upper UTI involves the kidney and ureters, which results in flank pain, fatigue, chills, and fever. There may be pain upon palpation or percussion of the patient's flank region.

Care for patients with a UTI is mostly supportive. In circumstances in which infection becomes widespread, sepsis or septic shock may require prehospital fluid volume support.

Need to Do

There are no psychomotor skills that directly support this chapter content.

Connections

- The American Urological Association sponsors a patient-centered website at www.urologyhealth.org. Information about many urological conditions can be found here.
- Link to the companion DVD for a chapter-based quiz, audio glossary, animations, games and exercises, and, when appropriate, skill sheets and skill Step-by-Steps.

Street Secrets

- **Classic Kidney Stones** Kidney stones that lodge or drag their way through the ureter (ureterolithiasis) can be exquisitely and extremely painful. A classic presentation is the patient, usually male, who is unable to find a position of comfort.

An analgesic such as morphine sulfate may be needed to help dull the pain and assist in transport.

- ■ **UTI in the Elderly** Is your elderly patient experiencing an altered mental status (AMS)? Carefully evaluate for the presence of infection using the AEIOU-TIPS mnemonic. A UTI that has become systemic may not necessarily present with a fever in older patients. A focused history that checks for urinary frequency and pain, as well as urine quantity, color, and clarity can reveal an underlying infection that is causing the AMS.

The Drug Box

Albuterol: A beta$_2$ agonist that increases the secretion of insulin into the bloodstream. The insulin in turn drives the available glucose into the cell, taking potassium along with it. In hyperkalemia, the potassium level in the bloodstream can be reduced with an albuterol treatment.

Calcium chloride: In hyperkalemia, the cell's resting potential is unusually elevated, making it closer to its threshold potential. Calcium increases the threshold potential of the cell, so the normal difference between the two potentials is reestablished.

Sodium bicarbonate: Combines with hydrogen ions, causing an alkaline environment. In hyperkalemia, this results in a shift of potassium out of the extracellular environment back into the cell.

Dextrose and insulin: For the same reason given for the use of albuterol, administration of insulin and glucose can help facilitate potassium back into the cell.

Furosemide: This diuretic promotes the excretion of water from the loop of Henle and, along with it, potassium. However, its onset is slow and unpredictable. Moreover, depending upon the exact mechanism, it may not be effective in patients with renal failure.

Answers

Are You Ready?

1. Mrs. Sidner is sick. Your primary assessment indicates that she is compensating for a serious condition (tachypnea and tachycardia), which may include a poor perfusion status (weak quality of the pulse).

2. Your patient responds poorly to a painful stimulus. At this diminished level of consciousness, you will want

to pay attention to the patency of her airway. Is she ventilating adequately? Assess her ventilatory rate and depth, and evaluate her oxygen level. For the moment, providing supplemental oxygen with a non-rebreather mask is necessary. Is her perfusion adequate to raise her head to help control her airway? You will need to evaluate her blood pressure quickly in order to answer that question.

3. A full set of vital signs is needed right away, as well as ECG, glucometer, and SpO$_2$ readings. Ask the caretaker what had transpired with the patient within the past 24 hours, and review the patient's medical record for any clues to the current presentation. Perform a rapid medical examination, taking special note of lung sounds, areas of dependent edema, and abdominal findings.

Active Learning

1. a. renal vein; b. renal artery; c. ureters; d. urethra; e. kidney; f. urinary bladder; g. hilum

2. Bleeding at the site of the hilum is a potentially serious problem during a deceleration injury, as the forces can shear the organ off the renal vein.

3. a. nephrons; b. calyx; c. renal pelvis; d. ureter; e. renal pyramid; f. renal cortex; g. renal medulla

5. a. urethra; b. urinary bladder; c. prostate gland

6. The urethra is shorter in women as compared to men, giving bacteria a shorter distance to travel from the environment to the bladder. Because of this anatomical difference, females are more likely to experience a UTI than males.

7. In the pregnant female, the uterus will push down on the bladder as the fetus grows, causing the woman to need to urinate more frequently.

8. The prostate gland can enlarge due to age or disease, causing pressure on the ureter that passes through it. This in turn can be a postrenal source of problems for the kidney.

9.

Prerenal	Intrinsic	Postrenal
Atherosclerosis	Diabetes	Kidney stones
Myocardial infarction	Lupus erythematosus	Retroperitoneal tumors
Hypovolemic shock	Streptococcal infection	Bladder cancer
Burns	HIV	Aortic aneurysm
Renal artery thrombus	Vasculitis	Benign prostatic hypertrophy

You Are There: Reality-Based Cases

Case 1

1. Mrs. Sidner is a complex patient. Using the AEIOU-TIPS mnemonic, several of your findings fit a few of the possible reasons for her altered mental status:

A—There do not appear to be any findings related to alcohol use.

E—She has no history of seizures, nor any signs of generalized seizure activity.

I—She is an insulin-dependent diabetic. However, there appears to be an accurate description of her recent insulin use, and the glucometer reported a near-normal blood glucose level.

O—There appears to be no misuse or abuse of the patient's prescribed medications.

U—While there is no apparent history or sign of a urological problem, there is a decreased level of urine output.

T—There appear to be no signs or report of a trauma mechanism.

I—There are several signs pointing toward an infection, including the chills and fever history that was reported by the caretaker. Abdominal pain in an elderly patient can be a warning sign of a serious condition, as pain perception is altered or reduced (see Chapter 44, Geriatric Patients, in the textbook for more information). Her skin color and condition may also be indicative of a state of low perfusion related to sepsis.

P—There does not appear to be any known history of psychiatric disorders, although it is not yet known what the patient's baseline level of consciousness is.

S—There is the possibility that the patient is experiencing a cerebral event such as a stroke. Given the other presenting signs, it would be less likely than an infection. On the other hand, her vital signs are reflective of compensatory shock that may be caused by a condition such as urinary tract infection.

2. Her airway and breathing status appears to be managed. Her circulatory status may be compromised; no urine output may indicate a dehydrated state. It will be important to determine whether she has been able to drink any fluids during the past 24 hours. To help support her circulation, initiating an intravenous line of volume expander such as normal saline or lactated Ringer's solution will be helpful; 200–500 mL boluses of fluid may help reduce her heart rate and help to maintain perfusion to the kidneys. Be cautious, because fluid overload is not well tolerated by geriatric patients.

Case 2

1. Several possible causes exist, including myocardial infarction (right-sided and/or left-sided) and congestive heart failure. The history of chronic renal failure makes her prone to electrolyte disturbances. The recent history of eating fried bananas, combined with the missed dialysis appointment, may have created a hyperkalemic condition. The abnormal shape of the QRS complex and the peaked T wave may be key findings. If she is hyperkalemic, the condition can reduce her cardiac output and increase the possibility of electrical dysrhythmias.

2. A key piece of missing information is the patient's blood pressure. If she is hypotensive, treatment modalities for the fluid in the lungs, such as nitrates or continuous positive airway pressure (CPAP), may be contraindicated. However, a combination of albuterol, sodium bicarbonate, and calcium chloride can help to drive down the elevated potassium levels. This in turn can permit the heart to increase its pumping effectiveness and improve perfusion. In-hospital treatment may include the administration of insulin and dextrose (D50) to help push potassium back into the cell. On the other hand, if the patient is hypertensive, CPAP can be very beneficial in reducing excessive preload and afterload to the heart, improving cardiac output, and forcing fluid out of the lungs, improving oxygenation.

Test Yourself

1. d

A lower UTI, also known as a bladder infection or cystitis, is often associated with burning on urination, frequency, urgency, and lower abdominal pain in the suprapubic area. Patients may also experience low back pain, nausea, and malaise. Referred pain to the flank may be present. Physical examination often reveals suprapubic tenderness and occasionally low back tenderness.

2. The genitourinary tract consists of several organs including the kidneys, ureters, bladder, urethra, prostate, and testicles.

The genitourinary system organs occupy several different parts of the human body, including the abdomen, pelvis, and external genitalia.

3. c

The symptoms of ureterolithiasis (the presence of a kidney stone in the ureter) vary depending on where the stone is on its trip from the kidney to the bladder. The pain is caused by both ureteral spasm and obstruction. Patients passing kidney stones are frequently found writhing in pain, unable to remain still, and unable to find a comfortable position. The patients may complain of pain that waxes and wanes in the flank, abdomen, or groin, and they may complain of radiation to the vulva or testicles. Other symptoms include nausea, diaphoresis, dysuria, urinary urgency or frequency, and the urge to defecate.

4. a

The paramedic should consider hyperkalemia in every CRF or ESRD patient encountered. Just as in hyperkalemia due to acute renal failure (ARF), decompensation of the ECG due to elevated serum levels of potassium should be treated with calcium. Administration of inhaled albuterol by either metered-dose inhaler or nebulizer promotes the movement of potassium across the cell membranes, thus temporarily reducing the serum levels in CRF patients. This treatment may be used in patients with ECG evidence of hyperkalemia. The administration of succinylcholine, sometimes used in rapid sequence intubation procedures, can exacerbate life-threatening hyperkalemia and should be avoided. Lasix should be administered in the presence of pulmonary edema, while fluids should be reserved for those hypovolemic patients with some remaining renal function.

5. True

   Acute renal failure is the deterioration of renal function over a period of hours or days that results in the accumulation of metabolic waste products, primarily nitrogenous compounds, in the blood. The etiologies of acute renal failure can be classified into prerenal, intrinsic renal, and postrenal causes.

6. Peaked T waves with shortened QT intervals

   Hyperkalemia is the most common metabolic cause of death in ARF patients. The accumulation of potassium in the body with the resulting elevated serum potassium levels can result in skeletal muscle weakness and cardiac arrest. The ECG in hyperkalemia changes as the serum concentration rises and initially may show peaking of the T wave, as well as shortening of the QT interval and ST depression. As the serum level rises, these changes may be followed by bundle branch block, flattening of the P wave, and increases in the PR interval.

7. c

   Prerenal failure is the most common cause of ARF, accounting for 40%–80% of all cases. As its name suggests, prerenal describes any condition that decreases perfusion before blood reaches the kidneys, such as poor systemic perfusion (e.g., shock) or narrowing and blockage of vessels.

8. a

   The most common cause of intrascrotal inflammation and infection is epididymitis. From puberty to age 35, chlamydia is responsible for nearly 50%–60% of cases of epididymitis. Epididymitis is the inflammation or infection of the epididymis, a convoluted, wormlike structure that lies against the posterior surface of the testicle.

9. Urethritis

   Urethritis is inflammation of the urethra due either to trauma or infection. Traumatic causes of urethritis include frequent bladder catheterization and surgical instrumentation. Infections of the urethra occur primarily in adult males and are usually caused by sexually transmitted bacteria such as *Neisseria gonorrhea*, *Chlamydia trachomatis*, *Ureaplasma urealyticum*, *Mycoplasma hominis*, or *Trichomonas vaginalis*. The signs and symptoms of urethritis primarily include dysuria and urethral discharge. Prehospital care includes the use of appropriate infection control methods. Long-term complications of urethritis include urethral stenosis or abscess formation.

10. In hemodialysis, an external filter replaces the diseased or absent kidney nephrons. In peritoneal dialysis, the peritoneum acts as the dialysis filter.

    To begin hemodialysis, access to the vascular system must be obtained by creating a surgical fistula in which an artery and a vein are directly connected to each other in the patient's arm via an AV shunt. Blood is drawn from the AV shunt and circulated through the dialysis machine at a rate of 300–500 mL per minute. Wastes from the patient diffuse across the external filter, and then the filtered blood is returned to the body through the shunt, minus urea, excess fluid, certain dialyzable drugs, and other waste products. In peritoneal dialysis, dialysate fluid is circulated into the peritoneal cavity through a catheter inserted through a hole made in the abdominal wall. Wastes and fluids diffuse across the peritoneum, which acts as the dialysis filter, and into the dialysate. The dialysate fluid containing the waste materials and fluids is then drained from the abdomen by gravity after a prescribed time interval.

chapter 37

Hematology

Are You Ready?

Ashanti Washington is a 20-year-old female who immigrated to the United States from Tanzania (Africa) 2 years ago. Ashanti's cousin called 9-1-1 for her because she has been experiencing vomiting and diarrhea with an associated fever for the past day and a half. When you and your partner arrive on the scene, you find Ashanti bundled up on the couch in her living room complaining of nausea, vomiting, diarrhea, and dizziness, but her main complaint is severe pain in her joints that came on after the flu-type symptoms and the dizziness.

1. What condition is Ashanti's pain likely related to?

_____

_____

_____

2. What is likely causing the pain to occur now?

_____

_____

_____

3. Describe the basic pathophysiology of the disease process that causes this type of pain.

_____

_____

_____

4. Describe the basic treatment for the patient's condition.

_____

_____

_____

Active Learning

1. Volunteer Opportunity: Hematology

There is no better way to learn about different hematological conditions than to see patients who have these conditions and discuss the conditions with the patients and the medical professionals who treat them. Arrange for an observational session in any of the following specialty areas: hematology, oncology, histology, pathology, blood bank, or laboratory.

Go to these observational sessions with questions and an open mind. Discuss management strategies and assessment techniques that can help you improve your performance in the prehospital setting. However, if you are feeling sick, please reschedule your visit to oncology or any other area in which patients' immune systems are potentially compromised.

2. Blood Typing

If you are not sure what your blood type is, there is an easy way to find out at home or in the classroom. Simply search the Web for "home blood type testing kit," and you will see that there are many inexpensive home blood type testing kits available (if you do this exercise with a partner or two, the price per kit can drop significantly). These kits can test for ABO and Rh blood types. Compare your results with your classmates. What is the most common blood type? Does the breakdown of different blood types mirror the national average?

You Are There: Reality-Based Cases
Case 1

"Medic 9, Medic 12, Engine 12, Heavy Rescue 1, Battalion 2: Respond to State Route 13 at Ranch Road for a head-on collision with people trapped." You and your partner turn on your lights and siren and head toward the location of the collision. While you are en route to the scene, Medic 12 arrives on the scene and states that they have two critical patients. One is trapped and is being extricated by the heavy rescue squad, and the other is being packaged for transport and will be awaiting your arrival.

When you arrive on the scene, you are given a report for the driver of a car that crashed head-on with another vehicle. Per witnesses, both vehicles were traveling at greater than 60 miles per hour. Your patient's vehicle sustained major front-end damage. The patient is an 18-year-old female who was restrained. Although the air bags deployed, she still sustained major head, neck, chest, and abdominal injuries. She presents unconscious with stridor on inspiration and exhalation. One of the medics from Medic 12 attempted intubation but was unable to pass the endotracheal tube due to distortion of the airway.

The patient is being ventilated with a bag-mask and an oropharyngeal airway. She continues to have stridor with ventilation. She has been placed in c-spine precautions, and two large-bore IVs have been established. She has had two episodes of emesis, which were managed by rolling the patient on her side and suctioning the airway. The trauma center is over an hour away, but there is a community hospital less than 5 minutes away.

1. Based on the information that you have been given, how would you describe the patient's condition?

   _____

   _____

   _____

2. Where will you transport the patient?

   _____

   _____

   _____

You and your partner decide to take your patient to the community hospital. Immediately upon your arrival the patient receives a tracheostomy and is typed and crossed for a blood transfusion. After being informed that it would take 2 hours for a helicopter to arrive at the hospital to transfer the patient to the trauma center, the attending physician calls the trauma center and arranges for you and your partner, along with a nurse from the emergency department, to transfer the patient there. Two nurses check the blood that the physician has ordered to make sure that it is the right type. The check is completed, and the infusion is started. You load the patient into the ambulance and begin your transport to the trauma center.

Ten minutes into the transport you begin to reassess the patient and notice that the patient appears to be tachypneic. You look over at the ECG monitor and notice that the patient's heart rate has increased from 92 to 124 beats per minute; her face is red; and you note hives on her face, neck, and upper extremities. She appears to be shivering, and when you touch her skin she seems hot to the touch. You put on your stethoscope to auscultate her lungs and discover that she is wheezing.

3. What do you suspect is happening with the patient?

_____

_____

_____

4. What should your initial action be?

_____

_____

_____

5. How will you manage the patient's current problem?

_____

_____

_____

6. When determining a person's blood type, there are actually two blood types that need to be determined. What are these two different blood types?

_____

_____

_____

7. For each blood type that needs to be determined prior to initiating a blood transfusion, there are different blood subtypes. List the different blood subtypes for each of the two blood types discussed, and describe how they differ from one another.

_____

_____

_____

Test Yourself

1. A child fell on the playground and sustained a minor laceration that continues to bleed despite your efforts to control the bleeding. You notice multiple bruises on the child's body. The disease this child likely suffers from is _____.

2. Your patient is presenting with dyspnea on exertion, tachycardia, and hypotension due to anemia. Your treatment should include
   a. administration of blood.
   b. administration of corticosteroids.
   c. administration of anticoagulants.
   d. maintaining the ABCs.

3. Your transfusion patient is exhibiting signs and symptoms of a hemolytic reaction. The most important treatment would include giving glucocorticoids.
   True
   False

4. Why is transport to the hospital critical for patients who are having a sickle cell crisis?

   _____

   _____

5. You respond to a residence for a child with leukemia. The family states that the patient has been febrile and experiencing nausea and vomiting for 2 days. Which of the following treatments is most appropriate for the patient?
   a. Antiemetics
   b. Heparin
   c. Albumin
   d. Corticosteroids

6. The hematological condition prolonged hypoxia may lead to is _____.

7. The spleen
   a. detoxifies and filters the blood.
   b. houses Kupffer cells that phagocytize worn-out RBCs.
   c. manufactures RBCs and platelets.
   d. houses macrophages that phagocytize worn-out RBCs.

8. Sickle cell anemia results from
   a. the destruction of bone marrow.
   b. premature rupture of the RBC membrane.
   c. excessive loss of RBCs through bleeding.
   d. misshapen red blood cells.

9. Prehospital management of a patient with a sickle cell crisis includes pain management.

   True

   False

10. A patient with a history of lymphoma is complaining of nausea, vomiting, and dizziness. How should this patient be managed?

   a. Maintain the ABCs and administer corticosteroids.

   b. Maintain the ABCs.

   c. No prehospital treatment is necessary for this patient.

   d. Maintain the ABCs and treat the nausea, vomiting, and dizziness.

Need to Know

Hematology is defined as the study of blood and blood-forming tissue and the disorders associated with them.

The following represent the Key Objectives of Chapter 37:

1. *Identify and care for a patient who presents with complications associated with the bleeding disorders disseminated intravascular coagulation and hemophilia.*

   a. *Disseminated intravascular coagulation (DIC).* DIC results in widespread thrombus formation within the microvasculature. It uses large numbers of platelets and other clotting factors that are not quickly replaceable. During the DIC process, bleeding and thrombosis occur simultaneously. The most common presentation of DIC in the prehospital setting is unexplained bleeding from multiple sites. Because DIC can present in a similar manner to a number of conditions, the prehospital treatment is based on the presenting problems and includes supporting ABCs and providing high-flow oxygen and fluid resuscitation in an attempt to maintain hemodynamic status while transporting the patient to the hospital.

   b. *Hemophilia.* Hemophilia is a sex-linked, inherited bleeding disorder that is caused by a deficiency or absence of certain clotting factors. The severity of the disease is proportionate to the amount of clotting factor that is available. Signs and symptoms of hemophilia are typically hemarthrosis (bleeding in a joint), bleeding from the gums, nosebleeds, and intracranial bleeding. The prehospital treatment of hemophilia includes supporting the ABCs and providing high-flow oxygen and fluid resuscitation in an attempt to maintain hemodynamic status while transporting the patient to the hospital.

2. *Describe the different types of anemias, including their causes and appropriate prehospital management.*

   a. *Aplastic anemia.* Aplastic anemia develops when bone marrow is not capable of producing sufficient numbers of red blood cells secondary to declining numbers of pluripotent stem cells. Prehospital care focuses on presenting signs and symptoms and typically involves bleeding control (if bleeding is evident), supplemental oxygen administration, and IV access to correct any hemodynamic issues that may be present.

   b. *Megaloblastic anemia.* Megaloblastic anemia is mostly an inherited condition that results from vitamin B_{12} and/or folate deficiency secondary to an inability of the GI tract to absorb these substances. It can also be related to intestinal or stomach surgery or Crohn's disease. The definitive treatment is correction of the underlying problem, and prehospital care is primarily supportive.

   c. *Hemolytic anemia.* Hemolytic anemia is characterized by destruction of RBCs. It can be caused by conditions such as abnormal microvasculature, thrombotic thrombocytopenic purpura, and DIC. Definitive care is based on treating the underlying cause, and the prehospital treatment is based on the presenting signs and symptoms and includes supporting the ABCs and providing high-flow oxygen and fluid resuscitation in an attempt to maintain hemodynamic status as needed.

3. *Describe the effects and treatments of the white blood cell disorders leukemia, lymphoma, and multiple myeloma.*

   a. *Leukemia.* Leukemia is a cancer of the blood-forming stem cells of the bone marrow. The two major types of leukemia are *myelogenous* and *lymphocytic,* and there is a chronic and an acute form of each type. Signs and symptoms of leukemia include frequent infections; poor healing of minor wounds; anemia; bleeding or easy bruising; fatigue; fevers; night sweats; weight loss; headache; confusion; balance problems; blurry vision; abdominal pain and/or swelling; pain in other areas including the neck, underarms, groin, bones, joints, and testicles; loss of muscle control; and seizures.[1]

Prehospital treatment of leukemia patients consists of addressing presenting signs and symptoms, practicing impeccable aseptic technique if IV access or access of a preexisting vascular access device is required, and attempting to protect patients from any other microorganisms that they could be exposed to during their care and transport. Be aware of dehydration due to infection and emesis as a result of chemotherapy.

b. *Lymphoma.* Lymphoma is cancer of the lymphocytes. Hodgkin's lymphoma affects a specific type of B-lymphocyte, and non-Hodgkin's lymphoma affects other types of B-lymphocytes and/or T-lymphocytes. Signs and symptoms of lymphoma include swollen and painful lymph nodes, enlarged spleen, fever, chills, unexplained weight loss, night sweats, lack of energy, and itching.[2] Prehospital treatment of lymphoma is the same as for patients with leukemia.

c. *Multiple myeloma.* Multiple myeloma is a disorder that affects plasma cells and is characterized by replacement of healthy bone marrow with cancerous cells, bone destruction, and the formation of abnormal serum globulins that do not function normally. The cancerous plasma cells cause a decrease in the production of RBCs, WBCs, and platelets. Patients with multiple myeloma frequently contact 9-1-1 because they are experiencing problems associated with renal failure, hematuria, pain, or pathological fractures due to destruction of bone. The most common presenting complaints are those related to anemia, bone pain, and infection. Bone pain is by far the most common complaint for these patients. It is generally localized to the back or ribs. Lumbar pain is the primary symptom in over 70% of all patients with myeloma.[3,4] Prehospital treatment includes support of the ABCs; administration of oxygen as tolerated; IV fluid for patients experiencing dehydration from the nausea, vomiting, or fever; and analgesics for patients experiencing pain. Special attention should be paid to using aseptic techniques to protect the patient from infection.

4. *Describe SaO$_2$ and PaO$_2$, including their relevancy to prehospital treatment.*

a. SaO$_2$ is a *ratio* of the amount of oxygen bound to hemoglobin. It measures the total amount of oxygen currently bound and compares it to the amount that could be bound if all the available hemoglobin was used.

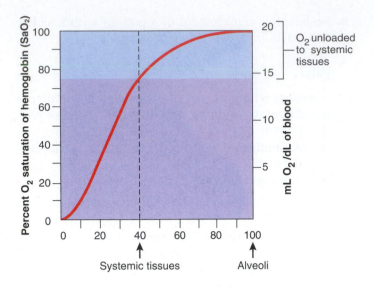

FIGURE 37-1   The oxyhemoglobin dissociation curve.

b. PaO$_2$ is the amount of oxygen actually bound to hemoglobin (the *partial pressure of oxygen*) expressed as a percentage that only considers the amount of oxygen that is currently bound to hemoglobin.

The oxyhemoglobin dissociation curve expresses how readily hemoglobin releases oxygen (Figure 37-1). The curve is typically divided into two parts. The first represents what happens at the alveolar-capillary membrane; oxygen binds with hemoglobin because the partial pressure of oxygen in the lungs is relatively high—a left shift of the standard curve, which means that a lesser partial pressure of oxygen is necessary for oxygen to bind to hemoglobin. The second represents what happens at the tissue-capillary juncture; oxygen is released (unbound) from hemoglobin for use by tissues because the partial pressure of oxygen in the tissues is relatively low—a right shift of the standard curve, which means that a greater partial pressure of oxygen is necessary for oxygen to bind to hemoglobin.

The curve of the graph shifts to the left or the right in response to the ability of oxygen to bind or unbind, depending upon the direction of shift, because of various factors. The most common factors that affect the standard curve are pH of the blood, temperature, and 2,3-diphosphoglycerate levels. Exercise and PCO$_2$ levels also affect the curve.[5]

Need to Do

The following skills are explained and illustrated in a step-by-step manner, via skill sheets and/or Step-by-Steps in this text and on the accompanying DVD:

Skill Name	Skill Sheet Number and Location	Step-by-Step Number and Location
Intravenous Access	42 – Appendix A and DVD	42 – Chapter 16 and DVD
Central Line Access for Fluids and Drug Administration	47 – DVD	N/A
Intravenous Drug Bolus	48 – Appendix A and DVD	48 – Chapter 16 and DVD
Intravenous Drug Infusion	49 – Appendix A and DVD	49 – Chapter 16 and DVD
Handwashing	61 – DVD	61 – DVD

Connections

- Chapter 13, Shock Overview, in the textbook discusses shock related to fluid loss, bleeding, and sepsis.
- Chapter 32, Allergies and Anaphylaxis, in the textbook provides further information on the signs, symptoms, pathophysiology, and treatment of allergic reactions.
- Chapter 33, Infectious and Communicable Diseases, in the textbook explains the factors that lead to infection and sepsis.
- Chapter 47, Patients with Chronic Illnesses, in the textbook provides information on devices that paramedics will see in the home care setting, including how to manage these devices.
- Link to the companion DVD for a chapter-based quiz, audio glossary, animations, games and exercises, and, when appropriate, skill sheets and skill Step-by-Steps.

Street Secrets

- **Opportunistic Infections** Patients suffering from white blood cell (WBC) disorders are at extremely high risk of acquiring any opportunistic infection that they come into contact with. Take the time to ensure that you do not contribute to their development of an infection. Do this by practicing precise aseptic or sterile technique when performing procedures such as starting an IV or accessing a preexisting vascular access device. If you are feeling sick, place a surgical mask on yourself and the patient so that the patient is not subjected to any of your germs.

Make sure that you practice adequate handwashing technique, including cleaning under your fingernails and washing the patient compartment of the ambulance and the gurney with a disinfectant on a regular basis.

The Drug Box

Diphenhydramine (Benadryl): An antihistamine used to treat allergic reactions seen in transfusion reactions.

Epinephrine (Adrenalin): An alpha and beta adrenergic medication that can be used to treat anaphylaxis (severe allergic reactions seen in transfusion reactions) by exerting its vasoconstrictive and bronchodilatory effects.

Systemic steroids (glucocorticoids): Examples are hydrocortisone, methylprednisolone, dexamethasone, prednisone, and prednisolone. They may be used for their anti-inflammatory properties in patients experiencing allergic reactions resulting from transfusion reactions.

Furosemide (Lasix): A loop diuretic used in transfusion reactions to help increase the functioning of the kidneys.

References

1. L. M. Tierney et al. (online eds.), *Current Medical Diagnosis and Treatment 2006,* McGraw-Hill Online, 2006.
2. eMedicine Heath.com, "Lymphoma Overview," www.emedicinehealth.com/Articles/25799-1.asp (accessed May 5, 2005).

3. Tierney, *Current Medical Diagnosis and Treatment 2006*.

4. R. L. Humphries and K. Stone, *Current Emergency Diagnosis and Treatment*, McGraw-Hill Online, 2004.

5. J. E. Tintinalli et al., *Tintinalli's Emergency Medicine: A Comprehensive Study Guide*, 6th ed., American College of Emergency Physicians, McGraw-Hill Online, 2004.

6. E. Mayfield, "New Hope for People with Sickle Cell Anemia," *FDA Consumer* (May 1996), www.fda.gov/fdac/features/496_sick.html (accessed May 9, 2005).

7. A. Taher, "Sickle Cell Anemia," (January 2005), www.emedicine.com/emerg/topic26.htm (accessed May 13, 2005).

8. G. E. Morgan, M. S. Mikhail, and M. J. Murrar, *Clinical Anesthesiology*, 4th ed., McGraw-Hill Online, 2006.

Answers

Are You Ready?

1. Sickle cell disease. Sickle cell crisis can be triggered by dehydration, low oxygen states, low pH, infection, trauma, extremes in temperature, and strenuous physical activity. Since Ashanti has had nausea, vomiting, diarrhea, and a fever for the past day and a half, it is likely that she is dehydrated. Dehydration is one of the conditions that can cause sickle cell crisis.

2. Hemoglobin in sickle cell anemia is called hemoglobin S and has a characteristic sickle shape. Hemoglobin S crystallizes when it is exposed to low oxygen states, causing the red blood cells to sickle in shape (Figure 37-2). The odd shapes tend to clump together, making it difficult for the cells to pass through the capillary beds. This results in localized ischemia and pain.

3. Sickle cell anemia is an autosomal recessive disease, which means that the gene must be obtained from each parent in order to actually develop the disease. Sickle cell trait results when only one recessive gene is inherited. Patients with sickle cell trait rarely experience any symptoms of the disease, except in low-oxygen environments such as at high altitudes.[6,7] Sickle cell crisis occurs when the sickle-shaped cells become lodged in the microvasculature of the body, interrupting blood flow. Patients suffer severe pain as a result of the interruption in blood flow and subsequent lack of oxygen being supplied to areas distal to the blockage.

4. Treatment of sickle cell disease begins in the same manner as any condition that a paramedic treats in the prehospital setting, by assessing and managing any problems with the ABCs. Because sickle cell crisis pain is associated with insufficient oxygen delivery distal to the blockage in blood flow, and sickling of the red blood cells occurs in a low-oxygen environment, the patient should be placed on high-flow supplemental oxygen. If the primary and secondary assessments for Ashanti support a dehydration treatment approach, IV access should be obtained and fluid resuscitation should be initiated. Pain control should proceed based on local pain management protocols and frequently requires medications such as Demerol or morphine sulfate to manage the pain.

You Are There: Reality-Based Cases

Case 1

1. The patient is a critical trauma patient with an unstable airway. She is unconscious with head, neck, chest, and abdominal injuries. She has stridor, she has had two episodes of emesis, and RSI was unsuccessful due to distortion of the anatomical structures of the airway.

2. The patient would benefit from the care that she would receive at a trauma center, but due to the fact that she has an unstable airway, she may benefit from going to the community hospital to have her airway secured before she is transported to the trauma center.

3. Based on the onset of signs and symptoms shortly after the initiation of a blood transfusion, the patient is likely experiencing a transfusion reaction (Figure 37-3).

4. Your initial action should be to discontinue the blood infusion.

5. After the transfusion has been discontinued, and ABCs reassessed, ensure that the patient is on high-flow oxygen and then replace all IV tubing. Start two large-bore IVs and begin to infuse normal saline or lactated Ringer's solution to maintain an adequate hemodynamic status (hypotension is common during a transfusion reaction). Consult medical direction if you do not have standing orders for the treatment of a transfusion reaction. Be sure to frequently assess lung sounds for signs of fluid overload as you infuse the fluid. If evidence

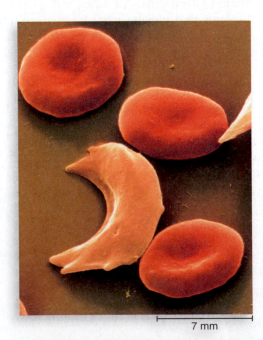

FIGURE 37-2 Blood cells of an individual with sickle cell disease showing one deformed, pointed erythrocyte and three normal erythrocytes.

7 mm

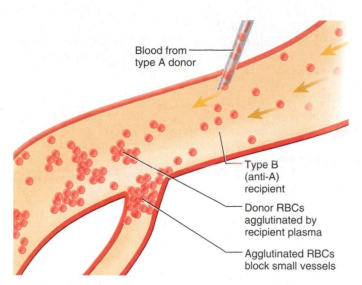

Blood from type A donor

Type B (anti-A) recipient

Donor RBCs agglutinated by recipient plasma

Agglutinated RBCs block small vessels

FIGURE 37-3   Effects of a mismatched transfusion. Donor RBCs become agglutinated in the recipient's blood plasma. The agglutinated RBCs lodge in smaller blood vessels downstream from this point and cut off the blood flow to vital tissues.

of fluid overload is detected, slow the IVs to a KVO rate.[8] Medications such as diphenhydramine (Benadryl), epinephrine, and steroids may be indicated if signs and symptoms of an allergic reaction appear. Furosemide (Lasix) and other diuretics can be administered to promote excretion of toxins (resulting from hypotension) from the body. Rapid transport is critical for these patients. Continue to monitor the patient throughout transport.

6. ABO blood types and Rh blood types

7. There are four ABO blood types and two Rh blood types. The ABO blood types are A, B, AB, and O. The blood type is based on the surface antigen (or lack of surface antigen) on the RBC and the antibody (or lack of antibody) that is produced. Table 37-1 shows the antigen and antibody associated with each blood type.

   Because blood type AB doesn't have anti-A or anti-B antibodies, blood type AB is called the universal

recipient. A person with this blood type can receive blood from any other blood type without a transfusion reaction. Because blood type O doesn't have an A antigen or a B antigen, but has both anti-A and anti-B antibodies, blood type O is called the universal donor. It can be given to any of the other blood types without any transfusion reaction.

Rh blood types are differentiated by the presence or absence of the Rh surface antigen. Individuals with Rh+ blood have the Rh surface antigen, and those with Rh- blood do not have the Rh surface antigen.

Both the ABO and Rh types need to be determined prior to administration of blood to avoid a hemolytic reaction.

Test Yourself

1. Hemophilia

   The child likely has a bleeding disorder that is responsible for the multiple bruises and the cut that will not stop bleeding. This set of signs and symptoms is characteristic of hemophilia.

2. d

   Initial treatment for all patients with hematological disorders should target airway, breathing, and circulation followed by treatment of other presenting symptoms.

3. False

   The most important treatment for a patient with a hemolytic reaction is to stop the transfusion, maintain the ABCs, and give a fluid bolus. Beta-blockers are not indicated for these patients.

4. The patient may require a blood transfusion.

   Patients experiencing a sickle cell crisis often require blood transfusions, in addition to oxygen, fluid therapy, and pain management.

5. a

   Treatment for a patient with a hematological disorder should be aimed at maintaining the ABCs and treating the underlying symptoms (e.g., nausea and vomiting).

6. Polycythemia

   Polycythemia is the production of excess RBCs, to increase the oxygen-carrying capacity of the blood, as a

TABLE 37-1   Antigens and Antibodies of the ABO Blood Groups

Blood Type	Antigen	Antibody
A	A	Anti-B
B	B	Anti-A
AB (universal recipient)	A and B	Neither anti-A nor anti-B
O (universal donor)	Neither A nor B	Both anti-A and anti-B

result of prolonged hypoxia (such as in the case of emphysema).

7. d

Macrophages phagocytize worn-out RBCs in the spleen. Kupffer cells phagocytize RBCs in the liver, which is also where the blood is filtered. RBCs are produced by stem cells in bone marrow in the adult patient.

8. d

Sickle cell anemia is the result of sickle-shaped red blood cells with diminished oxygen-carrying capacity.

9. True

Patients experiencing a sickle cell crisis often require the use of analgesics for pain, including Demerol and morphine.

10. d

Treatment for a patient with a hematological disorder should include maintenance of the ABCs and any additional complicating symptoms, such as the use of an antiemetic to control nausea and vomiting. Corticosteroids are not indicated for this situation.

chapter 38

Environmental Conditions

1. What are your initial priorities? Why are the circumstances of his presentation worth noting?

_____

_____

_____

2. How do you maintain a professional attitude and provide an equal level of care to all of your patients, desirable or not?

_____

_____

_____

Are You Ready?

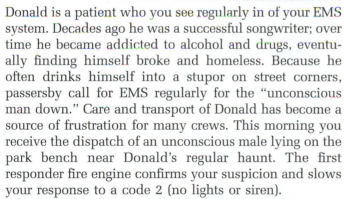

Donald is a patient who you see regularly in of your EMS system. Decades ago he was a successful songwriter; over time he became addicted to alcohol and drugs, eventually finding himself broke and homeless. Because he often drinks himself into a stupor on street corners, passersby call for EMS regularly for the "unconscious man down." Care and transport of Donald has become a source of frustration for many crews. This morning you receive the dispatch of an unconscious male lying on the park bench near Donald's regular haunt. The first responder fire engine confirms your suspicion and slows your response to a code 2 (no lights or siren).

The firefighters are standing off to one side as you approach. Donald is hidden underneath a pile of smelly clothes, his legs sticking out. The clothes are damp, which is unusual—not that they are wet from the cool morning dew, but that Donald stayed outside overnight. You remember that it was fairly cool the night before. Once you remove the clothing, you try to awaken Donald with a trapezius pinch. He does not respond. You observe that his breathing is slow and erratic and that he appears cyanotic. His face is cold to the touch; the alcohol smell on his breath is quite strong. There are a variety of older bruises and hematomas around his face and head, but one appears to be fresh.

Active Learning

1. Sweat It Out

How well does your body cope with changes in temperature? Try the following experiment. Choose a partner. Then bundle yourself into many layers of clothing. Make sure to cover every part of the skin, including the head and hands. Next, start exercising, walking briskly or otherwise to increase the body's metabolic rate. You should quickly become warm. Continue physical activities until you are sweating. **If at any time you feel exhausted, stop the activity.** Rapidly remove as many layers of clothing as possible.

During the exercise, have your partner record the following observations:

- Using a digital thermometer if possible, take an oral temperature before the exercise begins. Take a temperature again when sweating begins and every 5 minutes thereafter.

- Measure your heart rate and respiratory rate. Feel the skin on your chest and record the relative temperature.

- About 5 minutes after sweating begins, remove the coverings to your head and hands. After 1 minute, determine whether you feel some relief.

- Make sure to drink plenty of fluid after the activity and rest. Continue to record your heart rate, respiratory rate, and oral temperatures every 5 minutes during cooldown.

Review the recordings. Did the oral temperature rise during the activity? If so, how much? What about the heart rate? Did taking off the head and hand covers make you feel better? Why? *Bonus:* Did you begin to shiver during the cooldown period? Why would that happen?

2. Up and Down . . . and Way Down

Identify each of the following dysbaric conditions in the table from the description of the patient's complaint. Then, identify its associated phase of diving.

Complaint	Condition	Diving Phase
a. "I can't move, my joints hurt so bad!"		*Ascent*
b. "My ears were ringing. I felt so anxious. I felt like I was going to throw up. Toward the end I thought I wasn't going to make it; it was so hard to move."	*Oxygen toxicity*	
c. "She was really having trouble breathing when we took off her mask. She said her chest hurt, and she was coughing up blood."		
d. "My ears were hurting. Then I heard a pop, and I got dizzy right after that."		
e. "I don't know what happened. Suddenly my friend started to take off his face mask, trying to offer it to the fish."		

3. Bites and Stings

Mark the statements in the table as true or false:

Statement	True	False
a. If you get stung by a jellyfish, urinate on the area that was stung to neutralize the venom.		
b. A severe case of snake envenomation is marked by signs that include blood in the urine.		
c. You can reduce the effects of a sting ray's toxin by soaking the affected body part in hot water for 90 minutes.		
d. Use tweezers to pluck out a bee's stinger, because grabbing the stinger with fingers is difficult.		
e. If bitten by a snake, make "X" marks with a small knife over the puncture wounds and suck out the venom to minimize its effects.		

You Are There: Reality-Based Cases

Case 1 (*continued from chapter opener*)

Donald's breathing rate continues to be slow and irregular. You palpate slow femoral and carotid pulses. As you expose the patient, you find that he feels cold to the touch in his axillae and abdomen. Other than various scars on his upper extremities and legs, you do not find any other signs of trauma. Both his hands and feet are edematous. His breath sounds are faint but equal bilaterally. His pupils are dilated, equal, and very slow to respond. His gaze is unusually disconjugate.

His vital signs are HR of 60, RR of 6, and BP of 86/40. SpO_2 was 91% originally, and now it is about 94%.

In addition to his well-known history of alcohol and drug use, you also know that Donald has a history of traumatic brain injury, pneumonia, and chronic malnutrition. He had been taking several medications for a psychiatric condition, but none can be found today.

1. List several possible underlying conditions for Donald's presentation.

   _____

   _____

   _____

2. Describe your management of this patient.

   _____

   _____

   _____

Case 2

You are ascending Mount McKinley (Denali) with an experienced group of climbers. At 14,000 feet, your party comes across another two climbers moving toward you. One is waving at you for help. He asks you for assistance in carrying his partner back down the mountain. He tells you that his partner is "sick."

The other climber, Chris, is a 32-year-old male. He appears unsteady on his feet and doesn't respond when you call his name. He looks quite pale, and his lips are blue. You can find a carotid pulse, which is weak, thready, and fast. He is tachypneic.

The first climber provides you with more information. Chris began complaining of feeling ill about

2 days ago. He had a cough and felt like he had a fever. Chris wanted to continue on, so they resumed the ascent. Chris began vomiting this morning and complained of feeling very nauseous, as well as having a severe headache. He became disoriented and confused later in the day, which forced the climbers to turn back.

Wishing you had some medical equipment, you assess Chris. Pressing your ear close to Chris's mouth, you can hear crackles as he exhales. His neck veins are flat, and his lips are cracked and dry. There is no obvious bruising on what little exposed skin you can see.

1. What might Chris be experiencing?

   _____

   _____

   _____

2. What is the most effective way to treat his condition?

   _____

   _____

   _____

   _____

Test Yourself

1. Which group is at greatest risk for heat illness?
   a. Professional drivers
   b. Landscapers
   c. Construction workers
   d. Athletes

Scenario: Your patient has been camping and hiking in the Sonoran Desert. Although she was careful to drink water continuously, her husband believes that she has become dehydrated. She is complaining of fatigue, headache, and nausea. She is diaphoretic and her body temperature is 99.1°F.

2. You should suspect
   a. heat syncope.
   b. heatstroke.
   c. hyponatremia.
   d. heat edema.

3. How should you treat this patient?

   _____

   _____

4. How is prickly heat, also known as heat rash, caused and how can it be prevented?

_____

_____

5. Young, active people are particularly susceptible to classic heatstroke.
   True
   False

6. A soccer coach pulled one of his players out of the game when he noticed that the player seemed clumsy and disoriented. When you arrive 20 minutes later, the patient is sitting in the shade with his head between his knees. He is confused, feels "light-headed," and is sweating profusely. His body temperature is 39.8°C (103.6°F). How should you treat this patient?
   a. Remove the patient's clothing and apply ice or cold packs to the neck, groin, and armpits; administer a pressor and transport.
   b. Remove the patient to an air-conditioned building and encourage him to drink a salt-containing sport drink.
   c. Cool the patient with water or by fanning, administer a bolus set to deliver 250 mL of normal saline over an hour, and transport.
   d. Immerse the patient in ice water, administer a bolus set to deliver 1,000 mL of normal saline over 30 minutes, and transport.

7. A patient is hypothermic when her body temperature drops below _____°C (_____°F).

8. Which of the following patients is at greatest risk for hypothermia?
   a. A febrile 12-year-old
   b. A 23-year-old intoxicated male
   c. A 64-year-old with hyperthyroidism
   d. A 45-year-old obese woman

Scenario: Your elderly patient wandered away from his home and became confused. He is found lying in a snow-covered field a mile away. He responds to voice and is bradycardic and hypoxic. His body temperature is 29.6°C.

9. How would you classify this patient?
   a. Moderately hypothermic
   b. Severely hypothermic
   c. Local cold injury
   d. Mildly hypothermic

10. How would you treat this patient?

_____

_____

11. You are part of a team sent to rescue a hiker who has been lost for 3 days in damp and cool conditions. When you find the patient, he is pale and unresponsive. You are unable to obtain vital signs, and the ECG indicates that the patient is in cardiac arrest. His core temperature is 22.6°C (72.7°F). You should
   a. begin active rewarming techniques and administer CPR.
   b. begin active internal rewarming and administer atropine.
   c. remove cold or wet clothing and defibrillate.
   d. do nothing; the patient is deceased.

12. Frostbite is classified based on
   a. the minimum temperature of the affected tissue.
   b. the amount of surface area affected by the injury.
   c. the depth of the injury.
   d. the color of the injury.

13. Your patient was shoveling snow when he realized that he could no longer feel his fingertips. The tissue on his fingers felt hard, and now, 30 minutes after rewarming began, his fingers remain cool and pale. You should suspect
   a. chilblains.
   b. frostnip.
   c. superficial frostbite.
   d. deep frostbite.

14. _____ are a superficial injury caused by skin inflammation and tissue hypoxia when the skin is exposed to above-freezing, often windy, conditions.

15. You are called to a remote location for a woman who was cross-country skiing in the forest. When she noticed that her socks had become wet, she stopped to change them and discovered that the tissue on her feet was cold, blue, and hard. Because of the location, you had to park the ambulance a mile away. The patient feels that she can ski out. You should
   a. massage the damaged tissue and then treat it as you would a burn.
   b. wait until you return to the ambulance before beginning rewarming.

c. administer an analgesic before beginning rewarming.

d. begin active rewarming of the damaged tissue immediately.

16. Summarize Boyle's law.

_____

_____

17. Your patient has returned from an extended deep dive. She is confused and agitated and complains of nausea and blurry vision. As you perform a physical examination, you note that her eyelid is twitching. What is the likely cause of her symptoms?

_____

_____

18. Divers most commonly experience barotrauma during ascent.
True
False

19. What are the symptoms of nitrogen narcosis?

_____

_____

20. Which of the following diving disorders requires recompression therapy in a hyperbaric chamber?

a. Gastrointestinal barotrauma

b. Subcutaneous emphysema

c. Oxygen toxicity

d. Decompression illness (type 1)

21. Thermosensors are temperature-sensitive neurons located in the skin, spinal cord, limb muscles, and the anterior hypothalamus.
True
False

22. Vigorous shivering is characteristic of the _____ stage of hypothermia.

_____

_____

23. Divers who experience arterial gas embolism (AGE) should be transported

a. by ground in the Trendelenburg position.

b. by ground in the supine position.

c. by air in the Trendelenburg position.

d. by air in the supine position.

24. Which group of nonhuman animals causes the greatest number of human deaths?

a. Nonhuman mammals (including bears and large cats)

b. Fish (including sharks and stingrays)

c. Arthropods (including insects and spiders)

d. Reptiles (including snakes and lizards)

25. Which of the following statements is true regarding the removal of a bee stinger?

a. Use the side of a credit card to scrape the stinger away.

b. Do not remove the stinger in the prehospital setting.

c. Apply a compress of sodium bicarbonate before removing the stinger.

d. Gently pluck the stinger with your fingers.

26. The black widow spider has a dark hourglass-shaped spot on its dorsal side.
True
False

27. Your patient was involved in a fight. She has slight edema around her left cheekbone and a series of small gashes across the knuckles of her right hand. She thinks the hand injury occurred when she "finally hit him in the face." What should you suspect regarding the injury to her hand, and what actions should you take?

_____

_____

28. A boy was trying to feed a raccoon in his backyard when he was bitten. You should immediately be suspicious of

a. hemorrhage.

b. acute allergic reaction.

c. rabies.

d. bacterial infection.

29. Your patient was stung by a bee while picking apples in an orchard. He is now complaining of dyspnea, tightness in his chest and throat, and watery eyes. His fiancée tells you that he is asthmatic and has a hay allergy. You should be most suspicious of

a. an anxiety attack.

b. an allergic reaction to the hay that is being baled in a nearby field.

c. an asthma attack.

d. an anaphylactic reaction to the bee sting.

Scenario: You were picnicking on the beach with a group of friends when one of them accidentally stepped on a jellyfish. She is in extreme pain. You do not have any medical supplies immediately available to you.

30. You should
    a. ask her if she will let someone urinate on the affected area.
    b. have your friend rinse and vigorously scrub her leg in the ocean water.
    c. douse the affected area in orange juice.
    d. scrape the surface of her skin with the side of a credit card.

31. After decontaminating the wound, you should
    a. apply shaving cream or baking soda and shave the area.
    b. immerse the leg in cold water.
    c. immobilize the leg.
    d. bandage the wound using the cleanest materials on hand.

32. Your patient has traveled to the Colorado Rockies to ski during his spring break. He awakens in the middle of the second night with severe dyspnea. His friends tell you that he was complaining of a cough, fatigue, and a headache before he went to bed. How should you treat this patient?

_____

_____

33. _____ injuries occur when an object (such as a house or a tree) is struck by lightning and the dissipating current jumps to a nearby person.

34. You are part of a crew rescuing a swimmer who became tangled in lake weeds and has been submerged below the surface of a lake for nearly 10 minutes. The ambient temperature is 68°F. The patient's head and shoulders are now above the surface, and divers are working to disentangle her legs. You are able to safely access the patient in an inflatable raft. She is apneic and has a pulse rate of 41 beats per minute, weak and regular. You note a minor laceration on her right shoulder that is bleeding sluggishly. While the divers finish extricating the patient you should first
    a. apply a heat pack to the back of her neck.
    b. administer rescue breaths.
    c. continue to monitor her ABCs.
    d. control the bleeding of her shoulder.

Need to Know

The following represent the Key Objectives of Chapter 38:

1. *List the signs and symptoms associated with exposure to extremes of temperature, and describe the management of those conditions.*

Our bodies do fairly well when exposed to high or low temperatures. When it gets warm, we dilate our peripheral vasculature, allowing blood to pool near the surface of the body and heat to escape. We also sweat, which allows for evaporation to enhance internal heat loss. Conversely, being exposed to cooler temperatures reverses those effects; blood is shunted away from the skin, causing us to become pale. We begin to shiver, which uses mechanical friction to generate heat. Our heart rate also changes, increasing blood flow when it's hot and decreasing it when it's cold.

The human body runs into trouble when these mechanisms can no longer compensate for the ambient temperature. The severity of the condition is correlated with the level of heat gained or lost from the body. Heat- or cold-related emergencies are also affected by the patient's preexisting medical conditions, medications that can reduce the body's cooling or heating powers, clothing, and age.

Heat-related illnesses include heat cramps, heat exhaustion, and heatstroke. Heatstroke is a true medical emergency and requires rapid intervention of airway control, ventilatory and circulatory support, and rapid cooling of the body. Benzodiazepines such as diazepam may be used to control shivering brought on by rapid cooling. Fluid resuscitation may be necessary, especially if the patient was dehydrated when the illness began.

Patients who are experiencing heat exhaustion can be thought of as being in a "compensatory state" despite the elevated temperature—they continue to perspire and have a fully functional thermoregulatory mechanism. However, the core body temperature will still be elevated, and the patient may be hypovolemic. Passive cooling measures will be helpful, along with fluid replacement therapy.

Heat cramps are an example of a local tissue injury produced by the effects of heat. Loss of water and body salts through sweating and other dehydrating mechanisms can cause skeletal muscles to cramp uncontrollably. Drinking an excessive amount of water during high exertional periods without replacing the salts can also result in muscle cramping. Cramps will usually self-resolve with rest or with rehydration using salt-containing fluids.

Cold-related illnesses include local tissue injuries, such as frostbite, and systemic conditions, such as hypothermia. Hypothermia can be classified as mild, moderate, or severe. Be alert for signs of significant cooling, including altered mental status, stiffening limbs, loss of reflexes, the *absence* of shivering, and the emergence of Osborn waves on the ECG. The primary focus of prehospital care is to prevent further cooling and begin warming measures. Passive warming is appropriate for cases of mild hypothermia, but active external warming methods will be needed in moderate or severe cases.

Patients with moderate to severe forms of hypothermia must be handled gently and carefully. There is a possibility of inducing ventricular fibrillation in "cold" hearts. Advanced life support procedures such as defibrillation and medication administration may have little or no effect when the body is very cold. If the patient is in cardiac arrest and is hypothermic, begin CPR and continue resuscitation until the body has been warmed to near-normal temperatures.

Frostbite is an example of a local tissue injury in which the cells actually freeze. The frozen fluid expands and causes cells to rupture and die. The length of time of exposure and the amount of tissue involved will determine the extent of the injury. The skin of the affected area will become white, without any signs of blanching. In most cases, a loss of sensation occurs. Emergency care will involve rapid transport to an area or facility where rewarming can occur without the chance of refreezing. Analgesics may be needed for the significant pain that is felt as the tissue thaws.

2. *Describe the effects of submersion, immersion syndrome, and diving-related injuries and illnesses, including the prehospital treatment of those conditions.*

Submersion events occur when the patient is under water long enough to cause an adverse effect. They are graded by the level of effect on the body, from 1 (very mild) to 6 (cardiac arrest). In practical terms, there are no differences between drowning in fresh versus salt water conditions. Treatment for immersion incidents is focused on protecting the patient's cervical spine if a diving injury is suspected, establishing and maintaining the airway, and supporting breathing and circulatory systems. Care must be taken by the paramedic to exercise extreme caution when rescue from water is needed.

Immersion events are submersion events that occur in very cold water. General theory holds that the coldness of the water induces the mammalian diving reflex, in which the oxygen need of the body is suddenly reduced significantly. In these situations, it is possible to resuscitate victims successfully, even after prolonged periods of apparent cardiac arrest. Current treatment guidelines include basic life support (CPR) while the body is rewarmed, and withholding advanced life support treatment until the body temperature rises closer to normal. In a small percentage of immersion victims, *post-immersion* syndrome can occur, in which respiratory distress begins a few hours to days after the submersion event.

Dysbarisms are conditions that arise from excessive atmospheric pressure experienced during diving or from a too-rapid loss of pressure when ascending too quickly from significant depths of water. Most of the conditions involve oxygen and nitrogen gases that are dissolved within the body. Examples of conditions associated with descent include barotraumas, nitrogen narcosis, oxygen toxicity, and hypothermia. Ascent problems include vertigo, arterial gas embolism, pneumothorax, pneumomediastinum, and decompression sickness. Treatment of dysbaric conditions involves the identification of patients requiring recompression therapy and rapid transport to facilities equipped to perform such treatment. The Diver's Alert Network (DAN) can provide assistance in identifying the nearest appropriate facility for your patient.

3. *Describe the signs and symptoms of exposure to high altitudes and the management of patients experiencing high-altitude illnesses.*

In contrast to dysbarisms, high-altitude emergencies result from an underpressured environment, most notably at elevations high above sea level. At higher altitudes, atmospheric oxygen levels are thin compared to those at sea level. The body can make gradual adjustments over time, but rapid changes in altitude can cause heart rate, blood pressure, and peripheral resistance to increase. Cerebral blood flow also increases, resulting in possibly higher intracranial pressure (ICP).

Acute mountain sickness (AMS) develops within a few hours of achieving an altitude of 8,000 feet or higher. Lasting generally 3–4 days, signs and symptoms include headache, nausea, fatigue, dizziness, anoxia, or difficulty sleeping. It usually self-resolves or resolves by descending to lower altitudes.

High-altitude pulmonary edema (HAPE) is a much more serious condition than AMS, occurring at higher altitudes (typically greater than 14,500 feet). In addition to the signs seen in AMS, the patient with HAPE also is in respiratory distress, coughing up clear to bloody sputum as fluids build within the lung tissue. In fact, HAPE is an example of non-cardiogenic pulmonary edema. Treatment includes descent to lower levels, administration of supplemental oxygen, and artificial pressurization through hyperbaric chambers and portable Gamow bags. IV diuretics may be helpful, and nifedipine may help to lower vascular resistance.

High-altitude cerebral edema (HACE) occurs generally 1–3 days after the onset of AMS. The signs and symptoms of severe headache, nausea and vomiting, altered mental status, seizures, and coma point to a significant increase of pressure inside the brain. Rapid descent to a lower altitude is critical. Oxygen and dexamethasone may be helpful in addition to respiratory support. Diuretics may help, but they can worsen a hypovolemic state. Similar to HAPE, hyperbaric treatment may be necessary in HACE.

4. *List the signs and symptoms associated with reactions to various bites and stings, and describe the treatment for these conditions.*

Most bites and stings are unremarkable and uneventful, save for the local pain and possible swelling at the site. Keeping these wounds clean will help reduce the chance of infection and further injury. Anaphylaxis associated with insect stings is a serious emergency and should be treated accordingly. Bites associated with black widow or brown recluse spiders are unusual in presentation and should be evaluated by a physician for further treatment and follow-up. Snake bites are rare, and bites associated with envenomation are even more so. Treatment for these infrequent episodes is primarily aimed at reducing the spread of the venom through the body by minimizing movement of the affected area and transporting to an appropriate facility.

5. *Describe the injury patterns associated with lightning injuries and the concept of "reverse triage."*

Lightning is a form of electricity that is neither direct nor alternating current (DC or AC). For the briefest of moments the amount of energy and heat that is released during a lightning strike is nearly beyond comprehension. The injury patterns associated with lightning strikes are also unusual, ranging from "ferning" patterns on the skin associated with flashover phenomenon, to blast injuries after contact with superheated air, to asystolic cardiac arrest. You should be aware of scene safety issues if a lightning storm is still active.

If groups of people are affected by a strike, perform "reverse triage" and do perform CPR on those who present apneic and pulseless. Those victims who are alive after a strike will remain so. Those in cardiac arrest actually have a better than normal chance of resuscitation if basic life support is initiated soon after the strike.

Need to Do

The following skills are explained and illustrated in a step-by-step manner, via skill sheets and/or Step-by-Steps in this text and on the accompanying DVD:

Skill Name	Skill Sheet Number and Location	Step-by-Step Number and Location
Pulse Oximetry	12 – DVD	12 – DVD
Chest Auscultation	27 – Appendix A and DVD	27 – Chapter 11 and DVD

Connections

- The Diver's Alert Network (DAN) is a nonprofit organization affiliated with the Duke University Medical Center in Durham, NC. Its mission is to help protect the safety and health of divers. The emergency number to contact DAN for the location of a hyperbaric facility is +1-919-684-8111. You can also call collect at +1-919-684-4DAN. When the phone is answered, advise the operator that you are managing a diving emergency, and you will be connected directly to a DAN assistant or receive a return phone call. The DAN website is www.diversalertnetwork.org.

- The International Society for Mountain Medicine (ISMM) has a short tutorial on high-altitude illness at their website: www.ismmed.org/np_ altitude_tutorial.htm. The ISMM's mission is to "encourage research on all aspects of mountains, mountain peoples and mountaineers and to spread scientific and practical information about mountain medicine around the world."[1]

- You may want to review other causes of non-cardiac pulmonary edema in Chapter 29, Cardiology, and about intracranial pressure in Chapter 20, Head, Face, and Neck Trauma, in the textbook.

- Environmental conditions can often factor into complex cases. Problem-Based Learning Case 6, Come Out Swinging, will test your assessment and diagnostic abilities.

- Link to the companion DVD for a chapter-based quiz, audio glossary, animations, games and exercises, and, when appropriate, skill sheets and skill Step-by-Steps.

Street Secrets

- **Feel the Heat** On the patient, that is. Don't check for body surface temperature on the exposed areas of the skin—ambient temperature may cause you to feel inaccurately. Instead, check for temperatures close to the core, on the patient's chest or abdomen, or under the armpits. If these areas feel cool to the touch, you can be more confident that the patient may in fact be experiencing hypothermia. Don't forget to use the palmar side of your wrist to feel for skin temperature. Just be sure that your skin is intact in that region.

- **Be Safe** Many of the injuries and illnesses described in this chapter occur under risk-laden conditions—under water, at high altitudes, and at the extremes of heat and cold. You must be trained and prepared to handle yourself in these conditions, even as you help others. If you are working in an area where these types of events occur, take extra training to better protect yourself while working.

The Drug Box

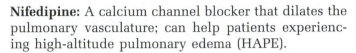

Nifedipine: A calcium channel blocker that dilates the pulmonary vasculature; can help patients experiencing high-altitude pulmonary edema (HAPE).

Diazepam: A sedative that can help reduce the extreme shivering brought on by rapid cooling measures utilized during heatstroke emergencies.

Diuretics: Furosemide may be helpful in helping to shift interstitial fluid out of the pulmonary tissue during HAPE, but it also increases the risk of dehydration.

Reference

1. International Society for Mountain Medicine website, "About ISMM." www.ismmed.org/ismm_info.htm (accessed November 18, 2006).

Answers

Are You Ready?

1. The irregular breathing pattern and level of unconsciousness are troubling. Because of the potential injury, you will need to manually stabilize the head and neck during the primary assessment. It is possible that you will need to ventilate the patient, rather than simply providing supplemental oxygen. He will need to be exposed quickly and checked for any possible injuries that may be hidden by his clothing. The circumstances may be a clue to Donald's medical condition. If Donald is a creature of habit, perhaps something happened to him that took him out of his normal routine. He might have been drinking more than usual, causing him to not be able to get back to his normal place of sleep. Or, he may have been assaulted or fallen and struck his head, causing confusion and altered mental status. If it was fairly cool the night before, hypothermia may have caused him to become confused and disoriented.

2. Patients like the one described can be frustrating to manage, but they still deserve your respect and care. See Chapter 3, Professional Ethics, for discussion on this topic.

Active Learning

2. a. decompression illness (type 1), ascent; b. oxygen toxicity, at depth; c. arterial gas embolism or pneumomediastinum, ascent; d. middle ear barotrauma, descent; e. nitrogen narcosis, at depth

3. a. false; b. true; c. true; d. false; e. false

You Are There: Reality-Based Cases

Case 1

1. There are several clues that key into the following conditions: new head trauma, Wernicke's disease, hypoglycemia, alcohol poisoning, and hypothermia. Given the patient's preexisting medical state, it may very well be a combination of several of these possible causes.

2. Airway protection with an oropharyngeal airway and bag-mask; supplemental oxygen and ventilation; cervical spine immobilization; IV fluid, with perhaps a fluid challenge; determine blood glucose level and CO_2 level; maintain body temperature and attempt passive rewarming efforts; transport to a trauma receiving facility for evaluation of head trauma.

Case 2

1. Although there are some signs of an infection, it is likely that Chris is experiencing high-altitude pulmonary edema (HAPE). The nausea, vomiting, and headache are alarming signs of high-altitude cerebral edema (HACE). Other differentials for the altered mental status include dehydration, hypothermia, hypoglycemia, hypoxia, and stroke.

2. Rapid descent to an altitude where excessive interstitial fluid in the lungs and brain can be reabsorbed by the body and administration of supplemental oxygen is the most effective way of managing this condition.

Test Yourself

1. d

Athletes and soldiers are at particular risk for heat illness given their degree of exertion in hot environments. Heat-related deaths are the third leading cause of death among American athletes, following head and spinal cord injuries and cardiac arrest.

2. c

The woman's symptoms (her complaints, her only slightly elevated temperature, and the diaphoresis) coupled with her history of significant water intake are indicative of heat exhaustion and hyponatremia. Hyponatremia occurs when oral intake does not keep up with sweat loss, resulting in abnormally low sodium levels.

3. Encourage the patient to rest in a cool area and drink a salt-containing sports drink or a 56–112 mEq salt solution (¼–½ teaspoon of table salt per liter of water). In severe cases of heat exhaustion, patients should be admitted for cautious correction of their volume and electrolyte imbalances.

4. Heat rash occurs when sweat gland pores are obstructed and staphylococcal infection results. To prevent heat rash in warm, tropical climates wear light, loose-fitting, clean clothing and avoid talcum powder.

5. False

Elderly and debilitated people are more likely to suffer from classic heatstroke. Young, active people generally suffer from exertional heatstroke.

6. c

Although the patient's body temperature is below 41°C, you should assume that it was higher before you were able to measure it. Suspect heatstroke. You should lower the patient's temperature, being careful to avoid "overshoot hypothermia," and administer fluid conservatively so as not to cause pulmonary edema.

7. 35, 95

8. b

Alcohol acts as a depressor and may lead to secondary hypothermia, also known as "urban" hypothermia because it is more prevalent in urban environments.

9. a

Patients who are moderately hypothermic have a core temperature between 32.2°C and 28°C. See Table 38-2 in the textbook for additional signs and symptoms.

10. Move the patient to a warm location, remove cold and wet clothing, and employ active, external rewarming techniques such as heat lamps, heating blankets, hot water bottles, and forced air warming systems.

11. a

Patients with core temperatures as low as 13.7°C have survived hypothermia. Defibrillation is usually unsuccessful until the core temperature is above 28°C, and in general, cardiac drugs are not recommended.

12. c

The extent of frostbite damage is classified based on depth, from superficial to deep.

13. d

Deep frostbite is characterized by hard, noncompressible tissue that will remain cool and gray or blue even after rewarming.

14. Chilblains

Erythema, edema, and pruritus are common manifestations of chilblains.

15. b

Frostbitten tissue is very fragile when thawed. Since the woman will be skiing back to the ambulance, it is best to wait until you return to begin rewarming. Rubbing or massaging frostbitten skin is contraindicated as it may cause more damage.

16. Boyle's law states that at a constant temperature, the absolute pressure and the volume of gas are inversely proportional. In other words, when the pressure within a given system increases, the volume of the gas will decrease; when the pressure decreases, the gas will expand. This law is particularly important to the understanding of dysbarism conditions.

17. CNS oxygen toxicity

   Oxygen toxicity may develop when people dive at pressures exceeding 1.6 atmospheres absolute for extended periods of time.

18. False

   Middle ear barotrauma (MEBT), the most common complaint among divers, is caused during descent. Approximately 30% of novice divers and 10% of experienced divers suffer MEBT.

19. Euphoria, a false feeling of well-being, confusion, loss of judgment or skill, disorientation, inappropriate laughter, diminished motor control, and tingling and vague numbness of the lips, gums, and legs. The symptoms of nitrogen narcosis usually resolve when the diver ascends to shallower water.

20. d

   Decompression illness (types 1 and 2), arterial gas embolism, and occasionally contaminated air (carbon monoxide poisoning) require recompression therapy. See Box 38-11 in the textbook for a list of diving disorders that do *not* require treatment in a hyperbaric chamber.

21. True

   Temperature regulation requires that thermosensors, the central integrative area of the CNS, and thermoregulatory effectors all work together to maintain homeostasis.

22. Mild

   During mild hypothermia, the body attempts to increase heat production by shivering. As fatigue and glycogen depletion develop, and the patient moves into the moderate and severe stages of hypothermia, shivering will lessen and cease.

23. b

   Patients with AGE should receive ground transport to a hyperbaric facility if possible. Air transport will further decrease the external atmospheric pressure, potentially worsening the illness. The patient should be placed in the supine position to maximize arterial-venous flow. The Trendelenburg position, once thought to reduce the degree of cerebral embolization, increases intracranial pressure and facilitates gas embolization to the coronary circulation.

24. c

   Arthropods include insects, scorpions, crustaceans, and spiders.

25. a

   You should remove the stinger as soon as possible, because a detached stinger may still continue to pulse and inject venom. Do not pluck or squeeze the stinger as this may cause more venom to be released.

26. False

   The black widow spider has a red hourglass shape on its ventral side. The brown recluse has a dark brown hourglass shape on its dorsal side.

27. Given the mechanism and the appearance of the injury on her hand, you should suspect that it resulted when the patient's fist struck the teeth of the other patient. Human bites are notorious for becoming infected and should be properly reported to the emergency room for exploration, irrigation, and antibiotic treatment.

28. c

   Animal bites from skunks, raccoons, bats, foxes, and woodchucks should be considered rabies risks.

29. d

   Although his symptoms exclude none of the possible diagnoses, you should initially suspect the most immediately life-threatening option: anaphylaxis.

30. c

   Jellyfish stings should be treated with an acidic solution. Vinegar is best, but acidic beverages such as fruit juices and certain soft drinks can also be effective. Contrary to popular opinion, urine has no effect and may actually make the injury worse.

31. a

   Shaving the area removes any undischarged nematocysts. Immersing the injury in warm water may also be effective.

32. Administer oxygen and remove him to a lower altitude.

   You should suspect high-altitude pulmonary edema (HAPE). Calcium channel blockers such as nifedipine may also be effective in treating HAPE.

33. Splash or side flash

   These types of injuries are more common than those caused by direct lightning strikes.

34. b

   Prompt rescue breathing is the most important treatment for submersion victims. If it can be safely accomplished while the patient is being extricated from the water, it should be.

chapter 39

Eyes, Ears, Nose, and Throat

Jimmy is a runaway who has been living on the street for the past several weeks. Police found him living in the park 2 days ago and brought him to the county shelter, where he has been living since then. The medical staff noted that he had a low-grade fever but no other flu-type symptoms yesterday. He began complaining of sharp chest pain this morning.

Your primary assessment reveals a young adult male who appears pale and warm to the touch. He is sitting nearly upright on the edge of his bed, with his feet on the ground. He is using his arms to sit upright, and his breathing is rapid. He has a rapid radial pulse.

Your partner reaches forward with a tongue depressor, wanting to get a better look at the patient's oral cavity.

1. What is your general impression of the patient?

   _____
   _____
   _____

2. What information should you look for next in order to manage Jimmy's condition?

   _____
   _____
   _____

3. Is it appropriate to use a tongue depressor in this case?

   _____
   _____
   _____

Are You Ready?

"Try to open your mouth," you say to Jimmy, as you look into his face. "I know it hurts, but try to open it a little." His eyes closed, Jimmy complies with your request, opening his mouth a little. A dribble of saliva trickles out. With your penlight you can easily see that his oral mucosa is reddened.

Active Learning

Anatomy Review

1. Identify the components of the eye in Figure 39-1, and describe the functions of those structures marked with an asterisk (*).

   a. _____

   b. _____

   c. _____

   d. _____

   e. _____

   f. _____

   g. _____

   h. _____

   i. _____

   j. _____

   k. _____

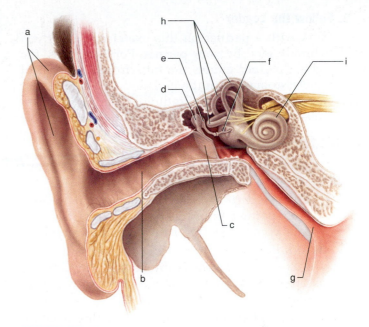

FIGURE 39-2

2. Identify the major parts of the ear in Figure 39-2, and give a brief description of their functions.

   a. _____

   b. _____

   c. _____

   d. _____

   e. _____

   f. _____

   g. _____

   h. _____

   i. _____

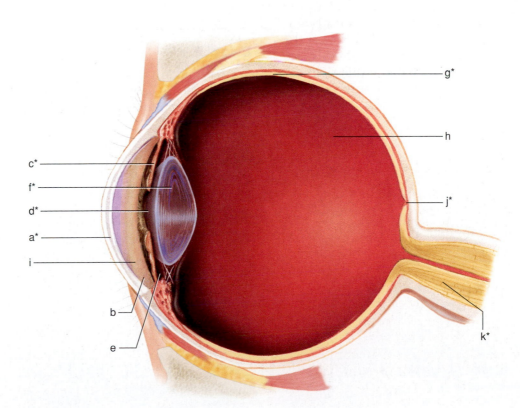

FIGURE 39-1

3. Follow the Leader

Work with a partner on this exercise. One of you is blindfolded by your partner. For 5 minutes, the sighted partner guides the blindfolded one out of the classroom, down the hallway, and into another classroom. Assist the blindfolded partner to sit in a chair or even lie down on a classroom table. Be careful to provide your directions very carefully and clearly, and please, no horseplay!

After the exercise is over, discuss your responses to the following questions:

- *Sighted partner:* How difficult was it to have your partner follow your directions? Did you find yourself stating your directions simply?
- *Blindfolded partner:* How difficult was it to follow your partner's directions? Did you feel nervous, even a little afraid of where you were going?
- *Both:* What did you learn from this exercise that you can apply to a patient who has both eyes covered because of an injury?

You Are There: Reality-Based Cases

Case 1 (*continued from chapter opener*)

Between breaths and spitting, Jimmy relates that he hasn't felt well for the past 2 weeks. It was difficult for him to eat because of pain in the right upper quadrant of his jaw. He has been drinking mostly fortified beer and soda in the past few days because the pain was so bad, and he felt like he couldn't close his mouth to chew. The pain radiated to his right ear about a week ago. The chest pain began this morning, and it feels like a "knife stabbing me in the heart."

The rest of your focused physical examination reveals the following:

- His right cheek appears to be puffy compared with the left cheek.
- His neck veins are flat. No tracheal tugging is noted. Stridor is noted upon auscultation of the neck.
- Breath sounds are clear and equal bilaterally.
- He is clasping his chest with both hands, saying that it "feels better" when he does so. Occasionally he coughs, which results in worsening of the pain. There is no sputum production.
- He has equal peripheral pulses.
- No edema is noted in his hands or ankles.
- His vital signs are: HR of 110, BP of 114/96, and shallow respirations with a RR of 20.

Jimmy's ECG is as shown in Figure 39-3.

1. What are the possible causes of Jimmy's presentation?

_____

_____

_____

2. Describe your treatment of Jimmy's condition.

_____

_____

_____

Case 2

You respond to a report of an "uncontrolled nosebleed" at the high-rise complex in your district. As you walk toward the apartment, the door opens. You see a male

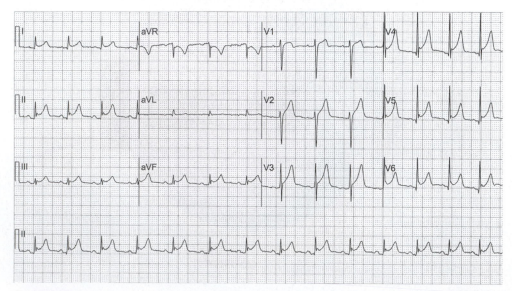

FIGURE 39-3

at the doorway, holding a towel to his face. Blood-stains are easily evident on the towel, as well as on the patient's hands and shirt. He appears quite anxious, motioning you with his hands to quickly come in.

1. What are your safety concerns at this point?

_____

_____

_____

It appears that the patient lives alone. Jake is a 67-year-old male who tells you he has never called for an ambulance. "My nose won't stop bleeding," he says, wiping it with the bloody towel as he paces back and forth. "It's been going on for an hour now. I've never had this happen to me before."

2. What can you instruct the patient to do right now?

_____

_____

_____

3. What should you do next?

_____

_____

_____

Jake's pulse rate is 104 and regular. His breathing rate appears adequate at 18 breaths per minute. His face is flushed, and his skin feels dry and warm. He also is complaining of tinnitus and a headache. He denies neck pain, chest pain, or shortness of breath. His pupils are equal and reactive to light. The rest of his physical examination is unremarkable.

Jake has a history of hypertension and hypercholesterolemia. He is prescribed hydrochlorothiazide. He has been trying to quit smoking cold turkey during the past 3 days. He denies any allergies to medications. He does not report any traumatic mechanism.

Using the intervention you described earlier, Jake's nosebleed slows and stops after 10 minutes. You evaluate his blood pressure and find that it's 220/112. His ECG shows a sinus tachycardia, and the pulse oximeter indicates a saturation rate of 97%.

4. What are possible underlying causes of Jake's condition?

_____

_____

_____

5. What will you do next?

_____

_____

_____

Test Yourself

1. The part of the eye that converts light images into neural transmissions is the _____.

2. Intubation is contraindicated for a patient with epiglottitis because
   a. the neck needs to be hyperextended.
   b. of the copious amount of secretions.
   c. it can stimulate spasms of the larynx.
   d. it may stimulate uncontrolled coughing.

3. Your patient is jutting his jaw and lifting his chin slightly in an attempt to align his airway into a better position for breathing. This is known as the _____.

4. When treating a patient with epistaxis, you should ask, "Was this event spontaneous?"
   True
   False

5. When irrigating a chemical from the eye, you should use the chemical antidote diluted with normal saline, if it is available.
   True
   False

6. Which of the following is a sign of anaphylaxis?
   a. Bradycardia
   b. Fever
   c. Vomiting
   d. Hypertension

7. Prehospital treatment of epistaxis includes
   a. tilting the head backward.
   b. digital pressure for 30 minutes.
   c. anterior nasopharynx packing.
   d. tilting the head forward.

8. The condition of the ear when inflammation narrows the eustachian tube, trapping viruses or bacteria, is called
   a. tinnitus.
   b. hemotypanum.
   c. otitis externa.
   d. otitis media.

9. The epiglottis is
   a. a bacterial infection at the opening of the oropharynx.
   b. a flap of soft tissue that seals the oropharynx during swallowing.
   c. a flap of soft tissue that seals the larynx during swallowing.
   d. a bacterial infection at the opening of the larynx.

10. The name of the space in the eye that is filled with aqueous humor is the _____.

11. Acute glaucoma results from a rapid decrease in ocular pressure.
    True
    False

12. The part of the ear that contains auditory sensory receptors that convert conducted vibrations into neural impulses is known as the
    a. auditory ossicles.
    b. auricle.
    c. vestibular labyrinth.
    d. cochlea.

13. Your patient is a 5-year-old with a foreign body up his right nostril. How should you treat this patient?

    _____

    _____

14. List three disease processes that can obstruct the airway.

    _____

    _____

15. A 20-year-old patient is bleeding from a knife wound to the anterior neck. You should
    a. apply cervical spine traction.
    b. stabilize the cervical spine.
    c. use a pressure point to control bleeding.
    d. cover the wound with a wet dressing.

Need to Know

The following represent the Key Objectives of Chapter 39:

1. *Recognize and care for patients with eye pain and/or sudden vision loss.*

   Eye injuries can be the result of either trauma or medical conditions. Regardless of the cause, the

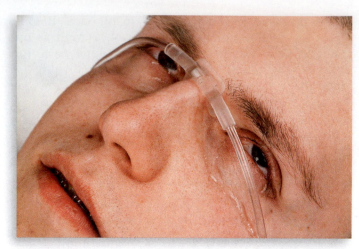

FIGURE 39-4 Use of a nasal cannula to irrigate both eyes simultaneously.

overriding goal is to minimize any further damage to the eye and loss of vision. Do not attempt to open an eye that is swollen closed. Cover both eyes by lightly bandaging them. Coach the patient not to squeeze his or her eyelids tightly and not to "look around." Consider providing an analgesic to help manage any pain or anxiety that might accompany the injury. Remember to remove contact lenses, either by irrigating them or, if necessary, manually removing them with a gloved finger. This is especially important for chemical contamination of the eye, in which the contact can cause the chemical to accumulate on the surface of the eye or cause the lens itself to adhere to the eye's surface.

Irrigate the eye with copious amounts of fluid (preferably 0.9% sodium chloride) if chemical contamination occurs. In cases in which both eyes have been contaminated by the chemical, a nasal cannula can be used to irrigate both eyes simultaneously (Figure 39-4).

Consider the force of the mechanism that caused the eye injury. Are there other associated injuries that you should look for? Will you need to immobilize the cervical spine if the forces involved were significant?

2. *Recognize and care for patients with ear pain, hearing loss, vertigo, etc.*

   Injuries to the external ear are generally not life threatening, although emotional trauma due to cosmetic damage can be significant. Tinnitus and vertigo may be signs of a more serious illness or injury and should be closely evaluated. Blood or clear fluid coming from the ear canal can be a sign of a serious injury to the internal ear apparatus and underlying skull.

Traumatic ear injuries are managed in the same way as other soft tissue injuries. Apply mild pressure to any external bleeding site. Do not pack the canal itself in an attempt to stop bleeding. In cases of avulsion, attempt to replace the loose piece back into its approximate location and wrap the area with gauze and dressing.

3. *Recognize and care for patients with throat pain.*

Throat pain can range from a very minor event such as soreness associated with the common cold, to a truly serious event such as epiglottitis. The paramedic should be most concerned about illnesses or injuries that can cause the upper airway to become obstructed.

Key signs of a compromised airway include a muffled or distorted voice or a complete loss of voice. The patient may speak in short, gasping sentences and may instinctively assume a sniffing position of the head and neck. Audible stridor may be heard. Young patients may drool or otherwise be unable to swallow in more severe cases of epiglottitis or other partial airway obstructions.

External injuries to the neck should be treated similarly to chest wounds, for which occlusive dressings are applied to help prevent any air leakage.

As with any other critical finding, manage loss of airway patency quickly. Relieve foreign body obstructions with BLS maneuvers or Magill forceps use. Assist with ventilations using a bag-mask if necessary; consider advanced airway approaches such as intubation or cricothyroidotomy if you are unable to maintain airway and ventilation with basic procedures. Apply spinal immobilization if the mechanism of injury to the neck may have affected the cervical spine. Swelling due to anaphylaxis can be managed through the administration of epinephrine and diphenhydramine.

4. *Describe the unique airway control issues associated with throat disorders.*

Swelling of the airway due to illness or trauma can be so significant that it causes a complete occlusion. An airway can close quickly and abruptly. You must stay alert for sudden changes in the patient's condition. Anticipate these changes and have both basic and advanced airway equipment immediately available to you in case you need it. Even if the patient appears to be stable, don't be lulled into a false sense of security.

5. *Recognize and care for a patient with a nosebleed.*

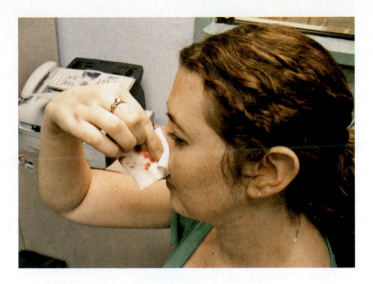

Because of the anatomy of the nasopharynx and nasal passages, nosebleeds are common and can appear quite dramatic. Control a nosebleed by firmly pinching the nostrils together and having the patient lean forward to avoid swallowing blood.

Consider the mechanism of injury to the nose and ascertain whether cervical spine precautions are needed.

A spontaneous nosebleed can be a sign of a more serious condition, such as acute hypertension. Assess the patient for underlying conditions that can result in a nosebleed.

Need to Do

The following skills are explained and illustrated in a step-by-step manner, via skill sheets and/or Step-by-Steps in this text and on the accompanying DVD:

Skill Name	Skill Sheet Number and Location	Step-by-Step Number and Location
Eye Drop Drug Administration	56 – DVD	N/A
Eye Irrigation	80 – DVD	N/A

Connections

- Chapter 29, Cardiology, in the textbook includes a more in-depth discussion of hypertension.
- Review Chapter 12, Airway Management, Ventilation, and Oxygenation, in the textbook for information on the use of Magill forceps.

- Chapter 32, Allergies and Anaphylaxis, in the textbook contains more detailed information and treatment approaches to life-threatening events such as anaphylaxis.
- Link to the companion DVD for a chapter-based quiz, audio glossary, animations, games and exercises, and, when appropriate, skill sheets and skill Step-by-Steps.

Street Secrets

- **Gauze for Grasping** Blood can be very slippery due to its viscous properties. To control a nose-bleed, use a small amount of gauze to better grasp the proximal end of the nose.
- **Reassurance** The sudden, unexpected loss of eyesight or hearing can be one of the most frightening events a person will experience. Your calm, reassuring, and professional demeanor will go a long way to support the patient.

The Drug Box

There are no specific drugs related to this chapter content.

Answers

Are You Ready?

1. Your primary assessment findings indicate that your patient is trying his best to compensate for an airway problem. He is sitting upright, using his arms to help keep his upper body as straight as possible. Both his respiratory rate and pulse are fast, which may be signs of respiratory compensation.

2. As you begin to treat the patient, you will need to determine the history of this condition quickly. This may be a challenge because the patient may not be able to answer your questions due to his level of distress. Closed-ended questions may be appropriate in this situation; asking the patient to shake or nod his head to your questions will help him conserve his energy so he can focus it on his breathing effort.

3. No. You have already noted that the oral mucosa has signs of infection, and the patient's inability to control his saliva is another indication that there may be significant edema in the back of the oropharynx that is preventing him from swallowing. The insertion of the tongue depressor could worsen this condition.

Active Learning

1. a. cornea—responsible for refracting light entering the eye; b. anterior chamber; c. iris—pigmented diaphragm surrounding the pupil that controls the amount of light entering the eye; d. pupil—the opening that allows light to enter the eye; e. posterior chamber; f. lens—focuses images and light onto the retina; g. retina—receives images from the lens; h. vitreous humor; i. aqueous humor; j. fovea centralis—the area of most acute vision; k. optic nerve—transmits impulses to the brain, where they are interpreted as images.

2. *External ear:* a. auricle—collects sounds from the environment and funnels them into the external acoustic meatus; b. ear canal (external acoustic meatus)—channels sound to the tympanic membrane; c. tympanic membrane—moves back and forth in response to sound waves and causes vibrations that are passed on to the auditory ossicles. *Middle ear:* d. malleus—attached to the tympanic membrane and in contact with the incus; when the tympanic membrane vibrates, the malleus transmits the vibration to the incus; e. incus—the middle auditory ossicle; assists in transmitting vibrations from the external ear to the inner ear; f. stapes—the innermost auditory ossicle which is bound to the oval window by ligaments; transmits the vibration from the auditory ossicles to the fluid of the inner ear; g. eustachian tube—helps maintain equal pressure on both sides of the tympanic membrane; *Inner ear:* h. semicircular canals—provide a sense of equilibrium; i. cochlea—function in hearing.

You Are There: Reality-Based Cases

Case 1

1. There are several possible causes for Jimmy's condition, including: abscess (tooth pain, reddened mucosa, drooling), adult epiglottitis (fever, drooling, ear pain), cardiac ischemia (chest pain, 12-lead ECG changes), pleuritis (sharp chest pain that worsens with cough); pericarditis (chest pain, 12-lead ECG changes, pain that worsens with coughing, some relief with positioning). Given the possibilities, a reasonable working assumption is a concomitant set of conditions: tooth or gum inflammation that caused the pericarditis.

2. Jimmy's airway is precarious; his body positioning and the oral secretions are indications of a serious problem. However, controlling the airway will be difficult, as any invasive management method could have serious consequences of closing the airway entirely. Since Jimmy is able to answer your questions, you could infer that he has enough oxygen going to his brain. That might lead you to think that continued positioning of the patient and keeping supplemental oxygen available may be your best approach right now. Humidified oxygen may be more comfortable. An intravenous line should be started, but transport should not be delayed because of the primary airway condition.

Case 2

1. It is not clear whether the nosebleed is from a traumatic or medical event. If trauma was involved, was there any violence involved? If you cannot ensure your physical safety, consider calling for the police to help secure the scene before you enter. Appropriate standard precautions are especially important when caring for patients with active external bleeding.

2. First, try to calm the patient. Because his nose is still actively bleeding, it will be necessary to try to contain the potential for contamination. Second, have the patient lean forward and firmly grasp the proximal end of his nose in order to clamp down on the capillary beds, which might be the source of bleeding. Using clean gauze may help provide a better grip on the area, since blood can be very slippery.

3. Next, conduct a primary assessment of the patient. Do not be distracted by the bleeding.

4. Although Jake has a medical history of hypertension, it would seem unlikely that his current blood pressure would be considered "normal." He may also be in a hyperanxiety state as he withdraws from nicotine use, resulting in an unusual rise in his blood pressure. A spontaneous nosebleed can result from a combination of these factors as the delicate capillary beds break down and bleed.

5. Conduct a secondary assessment consisting of a focused physical examination and history taking. Provide supplemental oxygen and transport the patient to an appropriate medical facility for further evaluation and possible control of the acute hypertensive event.

Test Yourself

1. Retina

   As light enters the pupil, changes in the shape of the lens focus light upon the retina. The retina then converts light images into neural transmissions, which are interpreted as sight by the brain.

2. c

   Epiglottitis is a bacterial infection of the epiglottis that is particularly hazardous. The epiglottis and the base of the throat are extremely sensitive to even the slightest irritation that can stimulate spasms of the musculature within the larynx, closing the airway.

3. Sniffing position

   The conscious patient with partial airway patency may attempt to assume a position that maintains maximal airway patency. This position is referred to as the sniffing position where the patient juts the jaw and lifts the chin slightly in an attempt to align the airway into a better position for breathing.

4. True

   In 90% of cases, bleeding from the nose originates from the rich vascular network of Kiesselbach's plexus. Because of its relatively exposed position along the anterior wall of the septum, irritation caused by dry air, frequent nose blowing, or the insertion of a finger can spark hemorrhage. Nosebleeds originating in this area are classified as anterior and are readily controlled with digital pressure applied for 10 minutes. Bleeding can also emanate from the larger, more posterior arteries supplying the nose. Blood loss in such instances can be profuse and flow down the posterior pharynx, threatening the airway and causing aspiration. Posterior epistaxis can occur without any inciting event, particularly among patients with bleeding disorders, poorly controlled hypertension, or those taking anticoagulant or antiplatelet medications such as Coumadin and aspirin. Successful management of posterior bleeding requires packing of both the anterior and posterior nasopharynx, which is not performed in the prehospital setting. Prompt transport of these patients is required. Ask all patients with epistaxis whether the event was spontaneous or precipitated by trauma, if any underlying medical condition exists that might predispose them to bleeding, and whether they take anticoagulant or antiplatelet medicines.

5. False

   Never use any chemical substance or "antidote" other than water or saline to flush the eye. Lactated Ringer's solution is preferred for irrigation, but plain normal saline may be used also.

6. c

   Signs of anaphylaxis include: respiratory distress, laryngeal edema, intense bronchospasm, vascular collapse, shock, pruritus, urticaria, and gastrointestinal manifestations including nausea, vomiting, diarrhea, and cramps.

7. d

   Nosebleeds are readily controlled with digital pressure applied for 10 minutes. Prehospital treatment of epistaxis entails sitting the patient upright with the head tilted forward to prevent blood from coursing down the posterior pharynx. Do not attempt to pack the nostrils in the field.

8. d

   Otitis media typically occurs when inflammation narrows the eustachian tube, trapping fluid and infectious organisms (typically viruses or bacteria) in the middle ear. Otitis externa connotes infection of the auricle or the external auditory canal. Tinnitus is the abnormal perception of sound when no external stimulus is present. Hemotympanum is bleeding within the middle ear.

9. c

   The oropharynx is also known as the throat. The superior opening of the larynx is protected by the epiglottis, a flap of soft tissue that folds over to seal the larynx during swallowing. Epiglottitis is a bacterial infection of the epiglottis that is at the opening of the larynx.

10. Anterior chamber

    The anterior chamber is the space between the cornea and the pupil of the eye. It is filled with circulating intraocular fluid called aqueous humor. Pressure within the globe is maintained by a careful balance in the volume of aqueous humor circulating within the anterior chamber and the more gelatinous fluid known as vitreous humor that fills the eyeball itself.

11. False

Acute glaucoma results from a rapid and abnormal increase in intraocular pressure due to a sudden imbalance between the production and drainage of aqueous humor in the anterior chamber.

12. d

The cochlea contains auditory sensory receptors that convert conducted vibrations into neural impulses perceived and interpreted by the brain and the vestibular labyrinth. The middle ear contains the auditory ossicles, a trio of delicate bones that conduct reverberating sound waves from the tympanic membrane (eardrum). The auricle, also called the pinna, is the funnel-shaped external portion of the ear.

13. Leave the object in place and transport the patient to the hospital.

Foreign bodies in the nose should be left in place and the patient transported to an appropriate receiving facility. Removal may require specialized equipment, and inappropriate attempts at extrication in the field may cause inadvertent aspiration of the object or damage to the nasal cavity.

14. Possible answers include: obstruction by a foreign body, swelling from allergic reactions, trauma, burns, or infection.

Any patient complaining of difficulty speaking, an inability to swallow, throat pain, or tightness demands immediate attention to airway patency. Patients should be monitored constantly for signs of airway closure. Early intervention is essential to prevent death due to hypoxia or suffocation.

15. b

Injury to the throat may involve the upper airway, jaw, and neck. Assume cervical spine compromise has occurred and stabilize accordingly. Cover all open wounds on the skin of the neck with occlusive dressings. Use direct pressure to control external bleeding.

chapter 40

Behavioral and Psychiatric Disorders

b. You and your partner pick her up, transfer her to your gurney, and begin transport.

c. Restrain the patient after planning the procedure with four to five people; then assess the patient as best as possible for causes of altered mental status.

d. Call the police to restrain the patient to a cot and then transport the patient.

_____

_____

_____

_____

Are You Ready?

You are evaluating an older female patient who lives in a long-term care facility and has been acting "inappropriately" during the past several days, according to the staff. She has become increasing agitated and verbally abusive to the staff, refusing to eat and throwing items at people who are trying to help her with the activities of daily living. You have tried to assess her vital signs and perform a physical exam, but she has not permitted you to do either. In fact, she has tried to slap and bite you as you try to assess her. The patient has a history of dementia, and the physician has ordered her to be taken to the hospital where she can be medicated and reevaluated.

1. Which of the following series of actions is most appropriate to follow in this situation? Why?

   a. Leave the patient at the facility and tell the staff to call you back when she is calmer.

Active Learning

1. Know Your State Law

Do you have the power to take a suicidal individual to the hospital against his or her will? In many states, paramedics and EMTs are not authorized to sign a transportation hold. What does your state law say? If you don't know, research your state law to learn this important information. Many times state laws are available on the Internet; you may wish to refer back to Chapter 4, Legal Issues, in this worktext, where you'll find an exercise pertaining to locating state laws. For example, Minnesota laws can be found at www. leg.state.mn.us/leg/statutes.asp.

2. Know Your System's Physical Restraint Policy

Many EMS systems' medical direction protocols or guidelines include a specific policy for the use of physical and/or chemical restraints. Are you familiar with yours? If there is a protocol, which of the concepts represented in Box 40-1 in the textbook does it address? If your system does not have a protocol, do you have the ability to ask your course medical director what his or her philosophy is on restraints? Some helpful documents include your textbook and the position paper from The National Association of EMS Physicians on the use of restraints, available online at www.naemsp.org/Position%20Papers/restraint.pdf.

3. Self-Defense

Despite your best intentions, you may find yourself facing an angry or hostile situation that you are unable to escape. Or you may find yourself managing a patient who has the potential to become violent while in your care. Investigate the availability of self-defense classes in your community. Check with your local police department. Verbal Judo is a method of active communication and de-escalation techniques that police officers and EMS responders can greatly benefit from. Is there a Verbal Judo class in your area? If not, contact your local crisis intervention volunteer hotline. Many times additional training for crisis volunteers can help you become more comfortable in assessing and managing patients who have altered behavior or mental illness.

4. Volunteer Opportunity: Behavioral Health

Volunteer to spend some time with an acute psychiatric facility or a mobile crisis intervention unit. Observing well-trained staff defuse a potentially violent patient will be of great benefit. Ask the staff about chemical restraints—what do they use? How do they administer the medication safely? How do they approach a patient who requires physical restraint? Gathering tips about these dangerous situations may be of great help to you when you are facing one for the first time.

5. Movie Time

Check out your local library or video rental store for *HBO: America Undercover: Suicide*, HBO Films, directed by Eames Yates (60 min, ISBN: 0-7831-2000-1, copyright 2001). This short documentary provides valuable and insightful information about suicide.

You Are There: Reality-Based Cases

Case 1

The police on the scene of a "domestic dispute" have called for EMS to evaluate one of the parties. You arrive on scene to find an officer outside the house talking with a very distraught female. The officer introduces the woman to you as the roommate of the patient, who is still inside the house with the other officers. When you interview the woman, she reports finding the roommate in her bedroom. He was threatening, glaring at her, and saying that he was going to kill her if she tried to take him to a "shrink." His pacing around the room made the woman nervous and caused her to flee the house.

1. What additional information should you determine before accessing the patient? Be specific.

_____

_____

_____

2. What equipment would you consider bringing with you into the scene?

_____

_____

_____

The woman tells you she did not know the patient very well, since he had only moved in about 2 months earlier. She had seen him take pills before, but he had not said what that medication was for.

The police officers inside the house report that they did not see any weapons on or near the patient. They had not yet restrained the patient, as they wanted you to evaluate him first.

You enter the house. The surroundings appear unremarkable, except for the bong sitting on the kitchen table. The smell of marijuana permeates the air. You make your way toward the back bedroom, where three police officers are waiting at the bedroom doorway and in the hallway. The patient is a male in his twenties, who is sitting on the edge of the bed. He is rocking back and forth and mumbling incoherently. His appearance is unkempt, and he smells as if he has not showered or bathed in several days.

3. Describe your initial steps to assess and manage this patient. Be as specific as possible. You are working with an EMT partner.

_____

_____

_____

One of the officers hands you the patient's identification card. Mike is 23 years old, according to the date of birth on the card. Your partner picks up a medication bottle with Mike's name on it. The prescription is for chlorpromazine. The bottle is empty.

4. Which of the following would be your most appropriate initial statement?
   a. "I want you to stop rocking and talk to me now."
   b. "Why is he not restrained?"
   c. "Mike, my name is _____, and I am a paramedic. Why are we here today?"
   d. "Can you stand up and walk over here, Mike?"

With your steady, reassuring words, the patient begins to talk with you. He says that over the past few days he's noticed his roommate looking at him strangely, as if trying to read his mind. He's tried to avoid her, but she has been "everywhere" he looks. He denies taking any street drugs or drinking any alcohol and says his medication "ran out" a few days ago. He knows who and where he is, but he is unable to tell you what day it is today.

5. What other information do you need to know about Mike?

_____

_____

_____

The physical exam appears unremarkable, with the smell of marijuana on the patient's clothing being the only major finding. He continues to rock back and forth but is much less agitated when he talks to you. Mike's pupils are slightly dilated but reactive. His vital signs are: HR of 124, RR of 20, and BP of 142/90. His skin signs are normal. He does not want you to put any electrodes on his chest and resists the placement of the stethoscope bell on his chest wall. As your exam continues, he leans over to you and whispers that he doesn't trust the police officers standing in the doorway. You observe his breathing rate increasing as he looks at the officers.

6. How can you reduce Mike's anxiety level?

_____

_____

_____

7. What might be causing Mike's presentation?

_____

_____

_____

Test Yourself

1. In what way does delirium differ from dementia?

_____

_____

2. When assessing a patient with a psychiatric illness, it is usually necessary to identify their specific condition.
   True
   False

3. What might you ask a patient when attempting to determine the patient's risk of suicide?

_____

_____

4. What groups have a higher proportional risk of suicide?

_____

_____

5. A schizophrenic patient insists she is "the only one who can warn the president about the invasion!" She is probably suffering from _____ schizophrenia.

6. Of the total number of patients who commit suicide, 90% of them have previously attempted it.
   True
   False

7. What is the main difference between psychosomatic and factitious disorders?

   _____

   _____

8. _____ disorders are characterized as being either unipolar or bipolar.

Scenario: You have been dispatched to a home where a man began acting strangely and intentionally locked himself in a room. His wife states the patient does not own any weapons.

9. You should
   a. assume that this patient must have a psychiatric disorder.
   b. quickly overwhelm the patient with force.
   c. approach the situation with extreme caution.
   d. tell the patient he will not have to be transported.

10. What term best describes a patient not acting within accepted societal norms?
    a. Schizophrenia
    b. Mood disorder
    c. Factitious disorder
    d. Behavioral emergency

Scenario: A 68-year-old Native American male patient has recently been diagnosed with a terminal illness and is now threatening to harm himself.

11. Your immediate treatment goal for this suicidal patient includes early identification of
    a. what he has already done to try to hurt himself.
    b. his number of risk factors and level of depression.
    c. whether or not he has a legal right to die.
    d. any other previous illnesses and the outcomes.

Scenario: You have been called to a dorm room where you encounter a 19-year-old female patient who seems to be hallucinating; she is babbling and rocking violently back and forth. Her roommate says the patient has been acting increasingly "bizarre" for the last few months. Upon physical examination, you find the patient's vital signs to be within normal range.

12. Which condition best describes the patient's state?
    a. Dementia
    b. Depression
    c. Delirium
    d. Psychosis

13. Likely causes of this patient's behavior could include
    a. drug withdrawal or mild anxiety.
    b. mania or schizophrenia.
    c. hypoglycemia or head injury.
    d. depression or hypoxia.

Scenario: The staff at a local homeless shelter states that a woman with a history of schizophrenia is experiencing muscle contractions in her face and neck. During your assessment you find a bottle of the drug Mellaril in her purse.

14. What do the involuntary muscle contractions in the face and neck of this patient most likely represent?
    a. A grand mal seizure
    b. A focal motor seizure
    c. A dystonic reaction
    d. An ischemic stroke

15. Treatment for this patient includes
    a. administration of Benadryl to reverse the reaction.
    b. oxygen and an additional bolus of Mellaril.
    c. subcutaneous epinephrine administration.
    d. scene safety, soft restraints, and rapid transport.

Scenario: A 27-year-old patient is sitting in his car in a parking lot complaining that his heart suddenly started racing and he became sweaty and could not catch his breath. His symptoms resolved prior to your arrival on the scene. He is alert and oriented and has experienced similar episodes in the past 4 months.

16. What is the most likely cause of the patient's symptoms?
    a. Hypotension
    b. Panic attack

c. Heart attack

d. Hypoglycemia

17. What body chemical is causing this patient's symptoms?

    a. Glucose

    b. Insulin

    c. Catecholamines

    d. Sodium bicarbonate

Scenario: A war veteran is experiencing a feeling of intense fear and paranoia. He is very agitated, claiming the enemy is all around him and is threatening to kill anyone who comes near. He also appears intoxicated and is bleeding from a small laceration on his right wrist.

18. How should a paramedic ensure this patient's safety?

    a. Remove any potential weapons from the area and reduce external stimuli.

    b. Leave the patient alone until he feels less threatened and willing to talk.

    c. Restrain the patient in the facedown position and secure all seat belts.

    d. Establish a rapport with the patient even if it requires lying to him.

19. What type of disorder is the likely cause of this behavior?

    a. Obsessive compulsive disorder

    b. Bipolar disorder

    c. Post-traumatic stress disorder

    d. Anxiety or panic disorder

Scenario: Over the past several months, you have noticed that your paramedic partner has become increasingly withdrawn, is unable to concentrate at work, and has not been interested in activities he once enjoyed.

20. The mood disorder your partner may be experiencing is _____.

21. Your partner tells you he has been feeling an unusual amount of stress for some time. Prolonged stress can lead to decreased levels of which three chemical substances in the brain?

_____

_____

Scenario: A 30-year-old highly agitated patient who seems to be hallucinating has been making verbal threats toward you and your partner. She does not want to go to the hospital and has repeatedly requested that you leave her alone.

22. While attempting to obtain the patient's history, the patient abruptly asks to use your pen so she can write down her medical history for you. Why should this concern you?

_____

_____

23. Several of the patient's friends who are on the scene seem to be making the patient more agitated. They are requesting that you allow them to take the patient to the hospital. How should you respond to the friends?

_____

_____

24. At what point should you consider physically restraining this patient?

_____

_____

Need to Know

The following represent the Key Objectives of Chapter 40:

1. *Assess and formulate a field impression and care for a patient with psychobehavioral symptoms.*

Patients who present in behavioral crisis can be some of the most frustrating and complex cases paramedics face in the field. Although EMS providers are well equipped to handle a variety of medical conditions, the only "tools" they have to manage the acute psychiatric or behavioral patient are a cool head, excellent communication skills, and the empathy necessary to manage the situation like any other.

There are three points to remember when approaching the psychiatric or behavioral patient.

    a. First, your safety and the safety of your crew are paramount. Be alert for signs of impending aggression that are exhibited by the patient, such as a confrontational stance, hiding of the hands, or a rising voice.

    b. Second, assume first that there may in fact be a medical condition involved in what otherwise appears to be bizarre behavior. Hypoglycemia, strokes, and seizures all can present as behavioral emergencies.

c. Finally, remember that any patient can present in crisis at any point during their medical emergency. The sense of being overwhelmed in the moment can cause a patient to present with far greater emotional involvement than the situation might indicate.

Providing treatment for these patients should follow these key points. Constantly remain alert as you engage and manage your patient, and look for signs of possible increased agitation and nervousness. Consider all possible medical conditions first as you treat, before settling upon a psychological cause of the behavioral emergency.

2. *Determine when a potentially violent situation involving a psychiatric or behavioral patient can be verbally de-escalated and when chemical or physical restraint may be necessary to control the situation.*

There will be times when a paramedic will confront a patient who is potentially violent or is intent on hurting himself or ones around him. At other times the patient may already be "acting out," that is, actually exhibiting violent or aggressive behavior. These are difficult situations for which there is no one absolutely correct management strategy. However, there are some basic principles to follow.

First, *keep calm.* The situation is already explosive, and there is no need to add to the stress, emotion, and confusion on the scene. A calm, steady voice and demeanor can go a long way in defusing the situation. Gather resources such as restraints and additional personnel as quickly as possible. Put together a plan of action quickly. For example: "Let's try to talk her down. In the meantime, why don't the two of you pre-

pare the restraints, while the other two move to the sides of the patient in case we have to restrain her. If that's necessary, I'll count to three and each one of us will restrain a specific, predesignated limb . . ."

Second, attempt to de-escalate the situation verbally. Sometimes a show of force and a steady, firm, and commanding presence will reduce the patient's aggressive behavior.

Third, restrain only when you have exhausted all nonphysical means of gaining control of the patient and you have confidence that you will succeed in the restraining process. You may need as many as five or more individuals to safely restrain a patient with the least risk of injury to rescuers or the patient.

Fourth, complete the restraining procedure completely. "Half restraining" patients can lead to a situation in which patients may hurt themselves or the rescuers around them.

Finally, remember to check your local system's policies and procedures regarding the restraint of patients.

Need to Do

The following skills are explained and illustrated in a step-by-step manner, via skill sheets and/or Step-by-Steps in this text and on the accompanying DVD:

Skill Name	Skill Sheet Number and Location	Step-by-Step Number and Location
Verbal Communications	63 – DVD	N/A
Physical Restraints	65 – DVD	65 – DVD

Connzections

- **Verbal Judo** Verbal Judo was developed by Dr. George J. Thompson as a way for police officers to defuse tense situations without resorting to physical methods. You can find more information about Verbal Judo at www.verbaljudo.com.

- Link to the companion DVD for a chapter-based quiz, audio glossary, animations, games and exercises, and, when appropriate, skill sheets and skill Step-by-Steps.

Street Secrets

- **Look Carefully**   In the hands of an angry or hostile person, nearly anything can become a dangerous weapon. As you size up the environment, make note of objects such as eating utensils, pens, tools, even dishes and glasses, and their proximity to the patient. If something is nearby the patient, and you are concerned about it being used as a weapon, divert the attention of the patient while you or a member of your crew moves it out of reach.

- **Be Handy**   Keep an eye on the patient's hands. When they are balled into fists or are constantly clenching, they might be giving you a nonverbal sign that the patient is anxious or angry. Be even more concerned when you cannot see the hands—they may be hiding a possible weapon.

- **Drugs and Behavior**   Many illicit drugs cause changes in behavior. Below are a few of the common drugs that are abused by patients, with their associated behavior patterns:

    - Amphetamines: Agitation, impaired judgment, hallucinations, delusions
    - Cocaine: Euphoria, impaired judgment, hallucinations (including tactile—such as formication—feeling like bugs are crawling on oneself), paranoid ideations
    - PCP: Belligerence, impulsiveness, delirium, psychotic symptoms
    - LSD: Visual hallucinations, delusions, flashbacks, severe anxiety, and/or depression
    - Marijuana: Euphoria, social withdrawal, hunger, anxiety, paranoid delusions, impaired judgment
    - Benzodiazepines: Somnolence
    - Alcohol: Disinhibition and emotional lability

The Drug Box

Benzodiazepines: Sedatives such as lorazepam, midazolam, and diazepam may be helpful in reducing the violent physical outbursts of the patient during restraint. Be vigilant for respiratory depression or arrest, since large amounts of the drug may be needed to subdue the patient.

Butyrophenones: Tranquilizers such as haloperidol can quickly control a hypermanic event. There are side effects as well, such as precipitating seizures, causing extrapyramidal reactions, hyperthermia, and

increased QT intervals that may lead to potentially fatal dysrhythmias.

Answers

Are You Ready?

1. c

   Having a plan and as sufficient resources as possible will help protect both the patient and rescuers from injury during the restraining process. This patient has demonstrated enough violent behavior to warrant restraint in the back of the ambulance.

You Are There: Reality-Based Cases

1. Determine whether any weapons were noted by the officers; the number of officers on the scene; whether there have been any similar prior events (and, if so, what were the outcomes); the patient's medical and psychiatric history, including medications and allergies; and whether any additional response resources (e.g., mobile crisis) are available or have been called.

2. In addition to the first-in equipment, it may be wise to have some type of restraining equipment available to you in case it is urgently needed.

3. Perform a scene size-up, checking for obvious weapons and weapons of opportunity. Position yourself between the patient and an exit route to allow you to retreat quickly if the patient becomes violent. Look for any clues to indicate a medical or psychiatric history, including medication bottles, pills, or tablets. Perform an initial assessment of the patient to confirm there are no life-threatening conditions to the airway, breathing, or circulation. Determine the patient's name and whether there were any interactions with the police prior to your arrival.

4. c

   This answer is best because it makes no assumptions and is not authoritative in nature, which may be perceived by the patient as a threat.

5. You should assume that Mike's complaint is due to a medical condition first. Therefore conducting a physical exam, obtaining a set of vital signs, and getting a complete SAMPLE history should be completed. Blood glucose levels should be evaluated on any patient presenting with an altered mental status.

6. If several of the officers are within view of the patient, asking all except one of them to step out of Mike's view may reduce his perceived threat level. Having one officer stay nearby will help maintain scene safety for you. Explain to Mike that the officers are on scene for his safety.

7. There could be several underlying reasons for Mike's altered mental status, such as hypoglycemia or drug ingestion. Mike's comments, demeanor, and prescribed medication suggest the possibility of paranoid schizophrenia.

Test Yourself

1. Delirium has a rapid onset and is usually temporary, while dementia progresses slowly. Delirium, like dementia, is also a disturbance in thought and reasoning but has a more rapid onset and is usually temporary.

2. False

   It may be difficult to distinguish between the various forms of psychiatric illness, but it is often not necessary to pinpoint the exact condition.

3. You should determine whether that patient has plans to kill herself or himself, and if so, ask the patient to describe the suicide plan. The more specific and realistic it is, and the more lethal the method, the higher the risk. For example, a vague statement like "I wish I was dead" is considerably different from a statement such as "I'm thinking of stepping in front of the 4 p.m. commuter train."

4. Groups that are at proportionately higher risk for suicide are adolescents ages 15–24, particularly teenage African American males, and adults over the age of 65. Native Americans have 1–1½ times the suicide rates of the national U.S. average. Men are more likely to commit suicide, but women make more attempts. Suicidal patients feel ambivalent about life and consider killing themselves as a viable alternative to continued suffering.

5. Paranoid

   The subtypes of schizophrenia include paranoid, disorganized, catatonic, and undifferentiated. Paranoid schizophrenics present with grandiose delusions, hallucinations, and feelings of persecution. Disorganized schizophrenia is characterized by disorganized speech and behavior. Catatonic schizophrenics exhibit physical symptoms of immobility or repetitive or excessive motor activity and bizarre postures. Undifferentiated schizophrenia cannot be categorized under the other three subtypes and usually presents with mixed symptoms.

6. True

   It is important to remember that 90% of patients who complete suicide have previously attempted it.

7. Patients with factitious disorders consciously try to deceive the caregiver, while patients with psychosomatic disorders believe what they say. In somatoform disorders, such as hypochondriasis or conversion disorder, patients consciously believe their physical symptoms are being caused by a medical problem. They seek the opinions of their health-care practitioners and are convinced that they need medical help. Patients with factitious disorders are consciously, actively working to deceive their medical practitioners.

8. Affective

   Mood or affective disorders are a grouping of illnesses that are characterized by longer-term sadness (unipolar) or a combination of sadness and mania (bipolar).

9. c

   Approach these situations with extreme caution and stay alert to potential threats throughout the encounter. Rule out life-threatening and reversible causes before deciding that the patient is suffering from a psychiatric disorder.

10. d

    Although some clinicians disagree over what constitutes normal versus abnormal behavior, it is clear that patients who are not acting within accepted societal norms, or who present a threat to themselves or others, must be carefully assessed. When altered behavior requires immediate attention to avert a serious outcome, it is considered an emergency.

11. a

    The treatment goal for suicidal patients is early identification of suicidal thoughts (ideation), potential risk (lethality) of a plan, and identification of anything they may have already done to try to hurt themselves.

12. d

    Psychosis is a state in which there is severe loss of contact with reality. Patients may have delusions, hallucinations, disorganized speech patterns, and bizarre or catatonic behaviors. The normal physical examination and vital signs, the young age of the patient, and the gradual onset of symptoms all suggest that this psychosis may be psychiatric in nature rather than medical.

13. b

    Psychosis may be seen in manic or schizophrenic patients but can manifest itself in other conditions such as drug intoxication, drug withdrawal, and dementia. This psychosis is probably not caused by a medical condition (such as hypoglycemia or head injury), since the patient's physical exam and vital signs are normal and the condition seems to have had a gradual onset. The memory aid MADFOCS can help you remember the factors that help differentiate between medical psychosis and psychiatric psychosis (see Table 40-1 in the textbook).

14. c

    Neuroleptic agents alter levels of dopamine in the brain and have a high frequency of adverse effects. Watch for signs of a dystonic reaction: tongue protrusion and involuntary contraction of muscles in the face and neck (torticollis). These reactions can look like a focal motor seizure.

15. a

    Giving diphenhydramine (Benadryl) will usually reverse dystonic symptoms and is the treatment of choice in the prehospital setting.

16. b

    A panic attack is a sudden onset of acute anxiety. This can include acute apprehension, fear, and feelings of impending doom. Patients experiencing a panic attack will present with physical symptoms of palpitations, tachycardia, shortness of breath, diaphoresis, chest tightness, and other catecholamine-related symptoms. Most patients who have a panic attack will recover without treatment and do not go on to develop chronic panic disorder.

17. c

The human body reacts to discomfort by engaging its fight-or-flight system, and the autonomic nervous system releases catecholamines to overcome the stressful challenge. Initially, anxiety can increase awareness and improve performance, but too much anxiety becomes overwhelming and dysfunctional.

18. a

Control the environment. If necessary, move to a safer location or reduce external stimuli (such as loud noise, televisions, or bystanders.) Work with law enforcement to properly search and disarm the patient. Ensure proper separation from objects that can be used as a nontraditional weapon, including your own scissors, pens, and multifunction tools clipped to your belt.

19. c

Post-traumatic stress disorder (PTSD) is a disorder in which a memory of a previous overwhelming or traumatic event is repeatedly reexperienced.

20. Depression

Depression is a progressive mood disorder that involves a persistent sadness, dysphoria, or loss of interest in usual activities.

21. Dopamine, norepinephrine, and serotonin

Prolonged stress, particularly when options appear hopeless, can lead to decreased levels of norepinephrine, dopamine, and serotonin in the brain. This leads to decreased levels of energy and interest and may be the reason why patients cannot improve their mood without using medications to alter their brain chemistry.

22. The patient may intend to use the pen as a weapon.

Look for objects that could be used as a weapon against you. Simple objects such as pens, scissors, kitchen utensils, or hand tools can appear harmless, but in the hands of an assailant they may be deadly.

23. Discreetly ask the police to dissipate the crowd.

When a crowd of people is forming around your scene, your interview and care may become more difficult. Discreetly enlist the help of other responders, such as law enforcement personnel, to dissipate the crowd. It is best to respectfully and professionally encourage onlookers to leave.

24. Physical restraint may be necessary if violence seems imminent or other efforts to de-escalate the scene have proven ineffective. Make sure that law enforcement officials are present to help secure the scene and enough personnel are on hand to restrain a patient should the patient become violent. If physical restraint is necessary, it should be performed as a last resort, and a minimum of five people should ideally be present. Sometimes a show of force alone is enough to deter a confrontation.

Problem-Based Learning Case 6
Come Out Swinging

Part I: The Case

Dispatch and Scene Size-Up

The call pager goes off, and your partner reads the text message. Groaning, she says, "Another call to the police substation to check on a prisoner. Didn't Medic 43 go out there earlier?"

You think about it for a second. "I'm not sure."

"Well, I hope the cops have a good reason to call us back."

A few minutes later you arrive at the substation. Entering through the galley, the station master greets you by buzzing the heavy steel door open. He motions back to the cell area. "He's in the back. I told the other medics that he needed to be taken to the hospital, but they said he was just drunk."

You can see the patient lying on the jail cot. Your partner wrinkles her nose. "Wow! That smell . . . is that *him*?" You have to agree; the odor is overwhelming. You notice that the patient's eyes are closed. From the odor and the stains on his pants, you determine that he is incontinent of urine, and maybe more.

You find out from the station master that the patient's name is Blaine Haven. Well known to the police, Blaine was arrested again for being drunk and disorderly in public. He has no known address and frequents the city's parks to sleep and get drunk. According to the arrest record, Blaine became unruly with some passersby and tried to assault one of them. The police were called, and, after a brief struggle, they subdued Blaine and took him to the station.

Blaine continued to be belligerent, banging against the police car cage with his body. Once he arrived at the station, however, he was more subdued. He was booked and placed into the holding cell, where he proceeded to doze off. When the station master went by the cell a couple of hours later, Blaine was difficult to awaken. Following policy, the station master placed a call to EMS. Medic 43 arrived and evaluated Blaine.

1. *Knowing that Medic 43 left the patient in the custody of the police after their evaluation, what would you assume about the patient's condition? What would you expect the previous crew to have performed during their evaluation?*

_____

_____

The Primary assessment (Initial Assessment) and Initial Differentials

You visually assess Blaine through the cell bars. He is curled up in a ball on the cell cot near the commode. His face is turned toward you, but his eyes are closed. His breathing is quiet, rapid, and shallow. You see evidence of fresh abrasions and small lacerations on his face and hands, covering the marks of previous injuries.

With another loud buzz, the door opens to let you and your partner into the cell. A police officer also steps in behind you. You kneel down near the patient, but at an arm's length away. Reaching over, you grasp the top of his shoulder firmly. This normally will get Blaine to rouse to an awakened state; today he simply moans and stiffens. His arms twitch slightly.

You carefully open his stained jacket. He has several layers of shirts on, all of them soiled. He has a few old, healed surgical scars on his chest as well as remnants of other less precise wounds. You do not observe intercostal muscle retraction or accessory muscle use. The smell of an unwashed body, coupled with stale beer and pungent urine, is nearly overwhelming. Your eyes begin to tear as you continue your primary assessment.

You note that Blaine's wrists are swollen and edematous. You are unable to detect a radial pulse. A check of a carotid artery reveals a thready, rapid pulse. Other than the abrasions and small cuts, there are no signs of severe bleeding.

2. *How does the patient presentation compare to your expectations? Based on this set of findings, would you consider Blaine to be sick, not sick, or not yet sick?*

_____

_____

History and Physical Exam (Secondary assessment and History)

You review the patient care report written by the previous crew.

47-year-old male, well known to PD and EMS, presents alert, belligerent, and resisting assistance. Strong odor of ETOH on breath. Refuses further physical examination and history by EMS, is verbally abusive when questioned. PD reports patient was detained after attempting assault. No fall or trauma associated with arrest.

The time of the patient care report was about 6 hours ago.

Blaine continues to breathe rapidly. The station master mutters, "I wish he would quit hyperventilating. Hey Blaine, quit faking. You'll still stay here tonight." Your partner nods her head in agreement.

You think for a moment. Why would Medic 43 leave this patient here? As you ponder this point, you sense that something is not quite right about this case. Blaine can present fairly intoxicated, but in your prior contacts, he has not been so intoxicated as to be this deeply unconscious. You reach down to recheck a radial pulse. As you do so, you smell something different: an odd, sweet smell that is vaguely familiar coming from his mouth.

You perform a secondary assessment; all the while your partner is chatting with the police officer. You find the following information:

His vital signs are HR of 110, RR of 28, and BP of 82/60. His ECG is as shown in Figure PBL 6-1.

His corneas are faintly yellow, and he has a disconjugate gaze.

A test of his blood glucose level shows a measurement of 200 mg/dL.

There is evidence of a green-tinged fluid spilled on his shirt and pants.

He has scattered wheezes that can be auscultated toward the base of both lung fields.

3. *List possible causes for Blaine's condition, based upon your current findings. Of your list, which ones are the most likely to be the cause of his presentation?*

_____

_____

Field Impression(s) and Formulation of Treatment Plan

You point out some of your findings to your partner. She is a bit more interested now. "Should we treat the wheezes?" she asks.

You look at Blaine's extremities again. They are swollen, and you can see bright green stains under his fingernails, similar in color to what's on his shirt. You check the pulse oximeter. In response to your partner's previous statement, you reply, "No, I don't think so. I think we should . . ."

4. *What were you planning to do next? What was the reading on the pulse oximeter?*

_____

_____

Transportation and Ongoing Care

En route to Community Hospital, you reassess Blaine's vital signs, breathing, and circulatory status. His blood pressure is now 88/70, and his heart rate is 100. The ECG is as shown in Figure PBL 6-2.

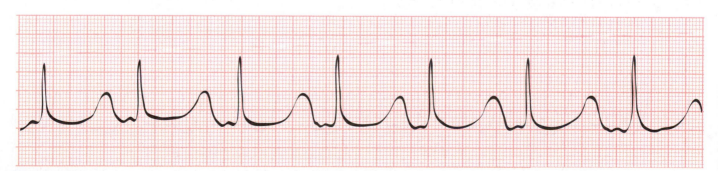

FIGURE PBL 6-1

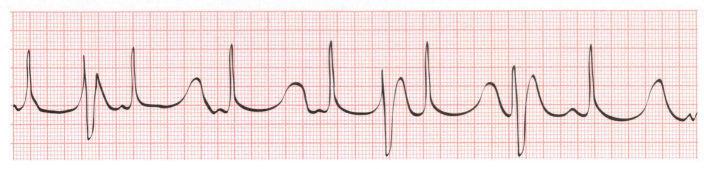

FIGURE PBL 6-2

The patient continues to be tachypneic. His extremities continue to spasm periodically. His level of consciousness has not changed.

After consultation with medical direction, you administer a medication intravenously. The ECG is now as shown in Figure PBL 6-3.

5. *What medication did you give to the patient, and why did you administer it? What positive benefit does this medication have?*

_____

_____

Transfer of Care, Follow-Up, and Outcome

You transfer Blaine to the hospital staff at Community Hospital. Blood samples are drawn for laboratory testing. Later on you review his chart. His lab values include:

Calcium: 6.1 mg/dL
Carbon dioxide: 25 mEq/L
Creatinine: 4 mg/dL
BUN: 70 mg/dL
Glucose: 180 mg/dL

Your prehospital treatment appears to have benefited the patient. His blood pressure has improved, and his respiratory rate has slowed to a more normal rate. His level of consciousness remains unchanged. The emergency department physician orders additional medication therapies and admits Blaine to the intensive care unit.

6. *What do the lab values tell you? What did the physician order?*

_____

_____

Long-Term Outlook

Blaine remains in the ICU for 72 hours. He is eventually discharged to an alcohol rehabilitation center and remains sober for 6 months. Unfortunately his addiction takes hold of his life and Blaine falls back into his familiar, destructive patterns. He reappears in the EMS system.

Part II: Debriefing

Responses to Part I questions:

1. There are several possible reasons why the patient was not taken to an emergency department for further evaluation. He may have refused further care, or his condition might have been of such a minor nature that further evaluation could be delayed until after his release. Or the patient may have been considered "stable" enough to be transported by another means. In any case, you would assume that the previous crew performed an appropriate primary and secondary assessment of the patient. You might also assume that the crew, documenting

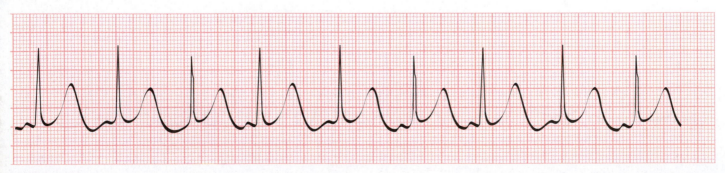

FIGURE PBL 6-3

their findings and the reasons for the nontransport, created a patient care report. What specific details would you expect to be documented?

2. Did the difference between his "normal" response to your painful stimulus and his current status catch your attention? Is it a clue that points to a potential, serious medical problem? Not immediately finding a peripheral pulse should have also provided a clue to your suspicion that intoxication is not the only reason for Blaine's altered level of consciousness.

3. Your primary and secondary assessment findings should give you real cause for concern. At the very least, you know that he is responsive to painful stimulus only, tachypneic, tachycardic, and hypotensive. In addition, his eyes are providing you several clues—a jaundiced cornea can indicate a hepatic or bile duct disorder, and the disconjugate gaze can point to a serious structural or metabolic problem. What smell did you detect? Would you expect ketones to be excreted with a blood glucose level of 200 mg/dL? What is unusual about the ECG tracing? How does the wheezing figure into your list of possible causes?

4. Your response to your partner's question appears to place the management of the wheezes at a lower priority than something else. Based on your findings so far, the unusual ECG tracing, coupled with the odd-colored substance found on the patient's fingers and clothing, seems to be contributing to his current condition. If this is an ingested substance, are there any other signs being presented that can help you better identify the toxin or poison? What treatment did you suggest? Clearly the need to control and manage the patient's airway is paramount; he is unconscious and at risk for aspiration. Obtaining an $ETCO_2$ reading might help differentiate why he is breathing so quickly. His hypotensive state is yet another concern. What are the specific management approaches for these conditions? What additional therapies might be useful in this specific case?

5. There could be several reasons for the patient's muscle spasms. How could the contractions be related to the ECG, blood pressure, and physical findings? Did you take Blaine's living conditions into consideration? What medical conditions are associated with being homeless as well as with being an alcoholic? Do any of these conditions relate to the patient's current presentation? At this point, you may have guessed that routine treatment for Blaine may not suffice. Did you figure out which medications to administer? Did your choice of medications address the ECG, neurological, and lab findings?

6. Did you look up the normal values for each of the tested items? You probably realized that one or more was abnormal. How do the lab values relate to the patient's condition and underlying suspected cause? How did your intervention improve the patient's condition? There were several follow-up actions that were probably ordered by the physician that built upon your initial interventions specific to the cause. Did you find out what they were?

Part III: Case Discussion

There are several facets of this case that are challenging. They include professional and legal concerns in addition to the clinical aspects.

Although the policies and procedures related to the care of a patient who is in the custody of a law enforcement agency will vary from one region to another, the legal and ethical obligations of the EMS provider to a patient do not. Your duty to act on behalf of this patient should not be clouded by previous perceptions of the patient, nor should the evaluation and nontransport decision made by the previous crew. Your partner was not happy about this situation initially, and she may be another source of pressure to minimize your assessment and management of this case. In these situations, you would be wise to weigh your options carefully and thoughtfully; using one of the ethical decision-making processes described in Chapter 3, Professional Ethics, in the textbook may help guide you to an appropriate decision.

The alcohol smell on the patient's breath that was reported by the previous crew brings up the issue about intoxication. Can a patient drink alcohol and still retain the right to refuse medical care? Because EMS typically does not have the ability to conduct blood alcohol testing or access test results at the time of evaluation, it is difficult to use the legal limits of intoxication as a basis of determination. Clearly describe the patient's behavior as your basis for making a medical decision to treat and/or transport—speech pattern, gait, coordination, and level of alertness can be documented clearly. It is as important to document the lack of findings as well as any pertinent ones.

Let's turn our attention to Blaine. Based on your primary assessment findings, it seems readily apparent that he is sick—quite ill, in fact. His altered level of consciousness is significant, even though he is frequently altered. Because of this fact, you must be able to protect and monitor his airway status throughout the remainder of the incident. Suction should be immediately available; if spinal injury is not suspected, placing the patient in the recovery position may be appropriate.

Focus on the breathing pattern—the station master was correct in the fact that Blaine is indeed hyperventilating, but not because he wants to. Something is happening that is causing the patient to sustain a very high breathing rate. Brain trauma, hypercarbia, metabolic or respiratory acidosis, or even simple hypoxia may be the culprit. The sweet smell that was detected—did you find it odd? The green substance that was on the fingers and clothing—did you guess that there was a possible ingestion? We will return to this possibility in a moment. Regardless of the actual cause, there is a need to determine whether the patient is adequately ventilating and oxygenating with the breathing pattern. You will need to assume for the moment that he is not and begin interventions such as providing high-flow oxygen, positioning the head and neck, and possibly even assisting ventilations with a bag-mask. Advanced airway equipment should be close by, in case basic airway management is insufficient. Remember that the best airway is the one that works, by the simplest means possible.

Turning your attention to circulation, there is no obvious major bleeding to control. His pulse rate and quality are poor; a subsequent blood pressure confirms your early suspicions. There are multiple conditions that can induce a hypoperfusing state; however, your first priority is to help the patient compensate or, at the very least, minimize any further loss of blood pressure. Preserving body temperature, keeping the patient flat, and initiating intravenous access are all part of that salvage process.

Now that your primary assessment is well under way, let's look at the findings you noted during the secondary assessment (focused history and physical exam). You will get very little information from Blaine at this point, given his mental status. His long-term history of alcoholism can give you some direction about his medical condition, such as liver and pancreatic dysfunction, chronic malnutrition, brain injury, and metabolic disorders. In addition, the need to ingest ethanol may be so great that an individual can be driven to drink alternative forms of the chemical, such as isopropyl alcohol, methanol, and ethylene glycol. The psychosocial aspects of alcoholism can also interfere with your assessment, especially with a chronic 9-1-1 system user. You must remain vigilant in making sure you evaluate these types of patients carefully each time.

Speaking of ingestion, did you surmise that there was a link between the green-colored stains you had noted early in your assessment and the patient's alcoholic state? Ethylene glycol is a component of antifreeze and has similar intoxicating properties as ethanol. However, ethylene glycol is quite toxic, causing a variety of problems. As the compound is metabolized in the body, glycolic acid is produced. The patient becomes highly acidic, which in turn causes a compensating hyperventilation syndrome to develop. The glycolic acid is transformed to highly toxic oxylate, which combines with available calcium in the bloodstream to form calcium oxylate. The patient can become hypocalcemic, causing involuntary contractions of the skeletal muscles, elongation of the QT interval of the ECG, and bronchospasm. The calcium oxylate deposits in the kidney, which can cause renal failure.

Treatment must be done rapidly to prevent possible death. You may have consulted with medical direction to administer sodium bicarbonate to help reverse the acidosis. Calcium chloride may also have been indicated. IV fluid therapy may help with a possible dehydration state. The emergency department physician may have followed up with pyridoxine and thiamine to speed up metabolism of ethylene glycol, as well as administering an antidote called fomepizole. As a temporizing measure, intravenous ethanol may be administered to compete with the ethylene glycol for its metabolism pathway.

Part IV: Further Learning Paths

- The open-source reference site Wikipedia has an extensive listing on the history and current state of homelessness. You can find this at http://en.wikipedia.org/wiki/Homelessness.

- The American Association of Poison Control Centers offers a listing of centers by state. You can find out more at www.aapcc.org/findyourcenter.htm.

- Are you familiar with the policies and that govern patients who are in police custody? Do these patients have the right to refuse or demand care at any time? You may want to look beyond your organization's protocols and review those of the local police agencies, as well as any state or national regulations or guidelines.

chapter 41

Obstetrics and Gynecology

Are You Ready?

Your partner, Gina, knocks on the front door of a suburban home. You were called to evaluate a woman who is experiencing abdominal pain. Shortly after knocking on the door, you see through a window that a woman is approaching slowly with a distinct shuffle to her gait. Nora, a 34-year-old female opens the door and asks you to come in. She appears to be in pain. She apologizes for calling, but in addition to experiencing pelvic pain and a fever over the past 4 days, she has started to feel a bit dizzy and didn't feel safe driving herself to the doctor's office. Your partner asks

Nora to sit down so that the two of you can talk to her and examine her.

1. Based on the information that you have thus far, what is your general impression of Nora's condition?

   _____

   _____

   _____

2. What is your initial approach in caring for Nora?

   _____

   _____

   _____

Nora noticed a purulent, foul-smelling vaginal discharge about a week ago. She states that she had douched twice a day in an attempt to get rid of the discharge, but it had only gotten worse. Four days ago she began to experience pelvic pain, pain on urination, and a low-grade fever. She has been alternating between taking acetaminophen and ibuprofen, but the pain and fever have persisted. She states that it is uncomfortable for her to walk. She takes birth control pills and is compliant with them. Nora tells Gina that she is sexually active and that she has had three sexual partners during the past several months. She started her period several days ago and is experiencing what she describes as a normal amount of bleeding. Nora has no other complaints, takes no other medications on a regular basis, and has no allergies to medications. Nora grimaces as Gina palpates the suprapubic region of her abdomen, and she feels warm-hot to the touch (her temperature is 99.6°F). Orthostatic vital signs reveal no orthostatic changes, but movement seems to exacerbate the pain.

525

3. What do you suspect is causing Nora's signs and symptoms?

_____

_____

_____

4. How will you proceed in your treatment of Nora?

_____

_____

_____

5. How would you describe Nora's acuity at this point in time?

_____

_____

_____

Active Learning

Anatomy Review

1. Label the structures of the female reproductive system shown in Figure 41-1.

   a. _____

   b. _____

   c. _____

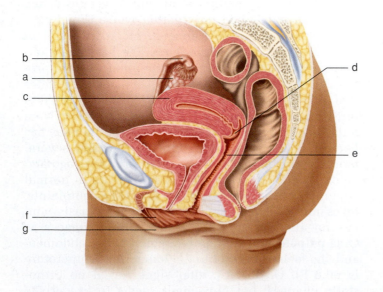

FIGURE 41-1

d. _____

e. _____

f. _____

g. _____

2. The space between the vagina and the anus is called the _____.

3. The female sex cell is called the _____.

4. Volunteer Opportunity: Obstetrics

There are a number of ways in which you can become more proficient and knowledgeable about obstetrics and gynecology. Childbirth skills are practiced during EMT and paramedic training, and during paramedic school many students have the opportunity to rotate through labor and delivery. Experience is by far one of the best teachers, and observational and hands-on experience with the guidance of an experienced practitioner is about as good as it gets. Consider volunteering some time in the following areas:

- Obstetric office where prenatal visits take place
- Antepartum unit of the hospital to observe patients with conditions such as preterm labor, premature rupture of membranes, and different causes of bleeding
- Postpartum unit of the hospital to observe the physiological changes that the mother goes through after childbirth

If you have the opportunity to follow patients with a midwife in the out-of-hospital setting, you can gain the experience of seeing differences in technique by a professional who focuses on natural childbirth. This is a beneficial experience to see how you may interact with this professional in the home should they request your assistance.

5. What's It Like?

Try this with a partner. Take a large, heavy-duty garbage bag and fill it with 3–4 gallons of water. Fold the top 2–3 inches of the bag over itself, and seal it with duct tape. Set it aside for the moment. Take a pant belt and loop it around your waist, above the navel but below the bottom of the rib cage. Fasten it so it does not slide down. Sit down. Now, carefully lift the bag filled with water and slide the taped side under the belt from left to right. Feed enough of the bag under the belt so that the water line comes up to the bottom of the belt. Fold the taped end of the bag over the front of the belt and use more tape to secure the bag to the belt.

Stand up carefully. The weight of the bag closely approximates the weight gain of a full-term pregnancy. You can try to move around slowly. Try keeping it on for 15–30 minutes. Do you feel the strain of the weight against your lower back? How does it affect your balance? If you were managing a pregnant patient, how might this exercise give you some ideas about how to accommodate the needs of this patient during extrication and transport?

You Are There: Reality-Based Cases

Case 1

Kisha Green is pregnant with her third child and has been doing everything that she can to be healthy and fit during her pregnancy. She has been taking a yoga class for pregnant women, eating healthy foods, taking her prenatal vitamins, and going to all her prenatal visits at her midwife's office. She has been working at staying healthy because during her last pregnancy she developed preeclampsia and ended up being bedridden during the last 2 months of her pregnancy.

Last week at her regular prenatal checkup, her midwife stated that Kisha had experienced a rapid weight gain, that there was protein in her urine, and her blood pressure was on the high side. Her midwife

told her that she needed to "take it easy for a while," disappointing Kisha.

Today you are called to Kisha's house by her husband because Kisha experienced a rapid onset of difficulty breathing. When you arrive on scene, Kisha is kneeling on the floor in severe ventilatory distress. Her husband Calvin is anxiously running around trying to get Kisha's clothes together so that she will be ready to go to the hospital. As you approach her, a firefighter is trying to place a non-rebreather mask on Kisha's face, but she keeps pulling the mask off. She is hyperpneic, using all of her accessory muscles with ventilation, and she has audible crackles that you can hear as you approach. Her skin signs are cool, pale, and diaphoretic with perioral cyanosis, and she is extremely anxious trying to breathe. You notice that she appears to be pregnant. In an attempt to prevent Kisha from having to speak, you turn to her husband and ask him if she is pregnant. He says, "Yes, 30 weeks."

1. How would you classify Kisha's condition?

_____

_____

_____

2. What is your initial priority in caring for Kisha?

_____

_____

_____

3. What other information do you need to know in order to develop a treatment plan?

_____

_____

_____

You track Kisha's ventilations with a bag-mask attached to high-flow oxygen at 15 liters per minute, and your partner assesses Kisha's lungs, places her on the ECG and pulse oximeter, starts an IV, and does a quick head-to-toe examination as the firefighters prepare to load her onto the gurney for transport to the hospital. Kisha continues to reach up and grab for the mask on her face despite your attempts at explaining what you are doing and the fact that she needs oxygen.

Her blood pressure is 220/130; her heart rate is 126, corresponding with a sinus tachycardia on the ECG monitor; and her respiratory rate is 40 with perioral cyanosis and continued severe ventilatory distress. She has an oxygen saturation of 90% being tracked with 100% oxygen via bag-mask. Her lungs have crackles in all fields, and she has generalized edema with jugular vein distention. Her husband states that Kisha had been complaining of a headache and some sort of visual disturbance.

4. What is a likely cause of Kisha's condition?

_____

_____

_____

5. What is your first priority at this point?

_____

_____

_____

6. How will you proceed with your treatment of Kisha?

_____

_____

_____

7. Where should you transport Kisha?

_____

_____

_____

Approximately 5 minutes out from the hospital, after the patient had been intubated and was showing improvement in her oxygenation and ventilatory status, Kisha began to have a full-body, tonic-clonic seizure. Her husband looked back from the front seat of the ambulance and said, "Oh no, is she having another seizure?"

8. What is the patient's condition called now?

_____

_____

_____

9. How will you manage the seizure?

_____

_____

_____

After the administration of magnesium sulfate, the seizures abate and Kisha presents postictal. She remains in a left lateral position with improving oxygenation and ventilatory status. Her blood pressure drops to 180/100 as the ambulance pulls into the hospital.

Test Yourself

1. How long does a term pregnancy last?
  a. 37–42 weeks
  b. 38–43 weeks
  c. 36–41 weeks
  d. 39–44 weeks

2. Your 16-year-old patient presents with severe abdominal pain. She also reports that she just had her period and that she "can't be pregnant." Her father states she was "feeling fine yesterday." The most serious condition to suspect is
  a. food poisoning.
  b. appendicitis.
  c. ectopic pregnancy.
  d. menstrual cramps.

3. Your patient complains of "cramps" and vaginal discharge over the past week. She also has a slight fever. She admits to being sexually active and is a smoker. You should suspect
  a. ovarian torsion.
  b. pelvic organ relaxation.
  c. pelvic inflammatory disease.
  d. a ruptured ovarian cyst.

4. On average, how much menstrual blood is lost during one cycle?
  a. 60–80 mL
  b. 100–120 mL
  c. 80–100 mL
  d. 120–140 mL

5. What causes an ovarian cyst?

_____

_____

6. Your 26-year-old patient states that she noticed an odorous vaginal discharge 2 days ago. She began to fear she had left in a tampon, and this morning she attempted to remove it. She presents with severe vaginal bleeding and the following vital signs: BP of 90/60, HR of 100, and RR of 36. You should
  a. sedate the patient and attempt to remove the tampon yourself.
  b. perform a thorough vaginal examination en route to the hospital.
  c. reassess ABCs and pack the vaginal area with gauze to control bleeding.
  d. apply a vaginal pad and treat for shock en route to the hospital.

7. Uterine prolapse can occur abruptly as a result of lifting a heavy object.
   True
   False

8. Your postmenopausal patient presents with acute abdominal pain, nausea and vomiting, dizziness, and low-grade fever. She states, "It felt just like an ovarian cyst, but then it got worse." What condition should you suspect, and how should it be treated?

   _____

   _____

9. Normal pregnancy lasts from the
   a. last day of the last normal menstrual period to the end of labor.
   b. last day of the last normal menstrual period to the start of labor.
   c. first day of the last normal menstrual period to the start of labor.
   d. first day of the last normal menstrual period to the end of labor.

10. The majority of all maternal deaths in America result from a combination of
    a. embolism, hemorrhage, and ectopic pregnancy.
    b. hemorrhage, ectopic pregnancy, and preeclampsia.
    c. preeclampsia, embolism, and hemorrhage.
    d. ectopic pregnancy, preeclampsia, and embolism.

11. While delivering a baby, you discover that it has a nuchal umbilical cord. If possible, you should
    a. clamp and cut the cord.
    b. relieve pressure on the cord.
    c. perform a cesarean section.
    d. pull the cord over the baby's head.

12. Which of the following is *not* appropriate when assisting a delivery?
    a. Lay the mother in a recumbent position.
    b. Encourage the mother to push only during contractions.
    c. Ask the mother to momentarily stop pushing when the head appears.
    d. Keep the baby's head level with the vagina

13. Dehydration and electrolyte imbalances during pregnancy are likely the result of
    a. abruptio placentae.
    b. hyperemesis gravidarum.

    c. ectopic pregnancy.
    d. placenta previa.

14. In which of the following situations are you *least* likely to transport a patient in labor?
    a. The mother's amniotic sac has just ruptured.
    b. The mother feels a strong pressure on her bottom and an urge to bear down.
    c. The woman has contractions 6 minutes apart, lasting for 30 seconds.
    d. The baby and placenta have already been delivered.

15. To break an intact amniotic sac, you should
    a. gently apply steady pressure with your index finger.
    b. quickly apply firm pressure with your index finger.
    c. gently apply steady pressure with your pinky finger.
    d. quickly apply firm pressure with your pinky finger.

16. An embryo that implants in the fallopian tubes is called a(n)
    a. ectopic pregnancy.
    b. eclampsia.
    c. abruptio placentae.
    d. placenta previa.

17. You arrive at the home of a 31-year-old female who is currently in labor. Her contractions are roughly 2 minutes apart, and you can see the top of the baby's head through the vaginal opening. At this stage you should
    a. transport the mother to the hospital at a normal speed.
    b. calm and reassure the mother.
    c. transport the mother emergently.
    d. assist in the birthing process.

18. Cord prolapse occurs when the umbilical cord
    a. becomes knotted or kinked.
    b. becomes twisted around the neck of the baby.
    c. tears during delivery.
    d. presents externally before the baby.

19. At what point during a pregnancy is a fetus most vulnerable to teratogens?
    a. 20 weeks
    b. 40 weeks
    c. 10 weeks
    d. 30 weeks

20. Multiple births increase the risk of all the following *except*

    a. abruptio placentae.

    b. premature labor.

    c. nuchal cord.

    d. breech delivery.

21. Of the three stages of labor, the _____ stage is generally the longest.

22. Labor is generally easier for mothers who have previously given birth.

True

False

23. Abruptio placentae is dangerous but typically painless.

True

False

24. A patient who is less than 14 days from her last menstrual period is more likely to have a pregnancy-related problem than a gynecological problem.

True

False

25. Under what circumstances would you want to transport a mother during the second stage of labor?

_____

_____

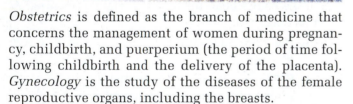

Need to Know

Obstetrics is defined as the branch of medicine that concerns the management of women during pregnancy, childbirth, and puerperium (the period of time following childbirth and the delivery of the placenta). *Gynecology* is the study of the diseases of the female reproductive organs, including the breasts.

The following represent the Key Objectives of Chapter 41:

1. *Outline the menstrual cycle.*

    Menarche is a female's first menstrual cycle. On average, menarche occurs between the ages of 12 and 13 years old. The duration of the menstrual cycle is typically 24–35 days and averages about 28 days. *Menstruation*, or the shedding of the thickened uterine wall if conception did not occur, lasts an average of four of those days. The average blood loss per menstrual cycle is approximately 60–80 mL. *Menopause* is the cessation of menses, which typically happens between 45 and 52 years of age.

2. *Describe common gynecological disorders.*

    a. *Infection-related.* Infectious agents can be broken down into two broad categories: non–sexually and sexually transmitted. Non–sexually transmitted diseases include candidiasis (yeast), bacterial vaginosis, and gardnerella. Sexually transmitted infections include syphilis, gonorrhea, chlamydia, herpes, condyloma, human papillomavirus (HPV), molluscum contagiosum, and trichomonas vaginalis. Common symptoms of gynecological infections include itching, pain, discharge, bleeding, and ulcerative lesions.[1]

    Pelvic inflammatory disease (PID) refers to infections that are located in the female upper reproductive tract. Complaints typically associated with PID are pain and fever. Risk factors include multiple sex partners, frequent douching, and recent intrauterine device (IUD) insertion. Because PID can be confused with several other serious conditions, such as ectopic pregnancy and appendicitis, the patient should be treated as if she is suffering from a life-threatening condition until proven otherwise.

    b. *Ovarian-related.* An ovarian cyst can be formed if follicular development is stopped during the normal ovulation cycle. These cysts can rupture abruptly. Signs and symptoms of a ruptured cyst include bleeding and severe, sharp pain that is classically localized to one side of the lower abdomen and pelvic area. Prehospital treatment for a ruptured ovarian cyst includes a primary and secondary assessment, assessing vital signs, and treating for possible shock.

    Torsion of the fallopian tube and ovary is frequently caused by rotation of the ovary due to cyst formation. Women who are taking drugs to increase ovulation are at increased risk for ovarian torsion. Signs and symptoms of ovarian torsion include unilateral pain, tenderness, or rigidity; nausea and vomiting; diarrhea or constipation; dizziness; and a possible low-grade fever.

    c. *Uterine conditions.* Dysfunctional bleeding is irregular uterine bleeding that is different from normal menstrual bleeding. This includes menorrhagia—greater than 80 mL or greater than 7 days of menstrual bleeding. Causes of dysfunctional bleeding include clotting disorders, fibroids, cervical cancer, hormones, and thyroid conditions.[2]

    d. *Vaginal conditions.* An object that has been inserted into the vagina is considered to be a foreign body (unretrieved tampons are most common). Signs and symptoms of an unretrieved foreign object include copious, foul-smelling vaginal discharge. Prehospital treatment of an unretrieved foreign body includes professionalism, maintaining the dignity of the patient, performing a primary and secondary assessment, and monitoring vital signs. Monitor the patient for signs of infection and shock.

Note: Table 41-1 in the textbook summarizes the causes of pelvic pain.

3. *Describe common complications associated with pregnancy.*

There are several conditions during pregnancy that require close monitoring of the patient. A fertilized egg that has implanted somewhere other than in the uterus, frequently in the fallopian tube, can result in an *ectopic pregnancy*. Ectopic pregnancies are usually diagnosed within the first 6 weeks of gestation, as the fallopian tube cannot accommodate the growing conceptus.[3] Signs and symptoms associated with ectopic pregnancy include vaginal spotting or bleeding and abdominal or pelvic pain. Because of the high criticality of a ruptured *ectopic pregnancy*, any woman of childbearing age (between 9 and 60 years of age) complaining of abdominal pain should be suspected of having an ectopic pregnancy until proven otherwise. Patients exhibiting any signs of shock should be treated with high-flow oxygen via non-rebreather mask and IV fluid resuscitation while en route to an appropriate receiving facility.

A *spontaneous abortion* (miscarriage) is the loss of pregnancy before 20 weeks gestation. Signs and symptoms include abdominal cramping; lower backache; and passage of blood clots, fetal or placental tissue, or other products of conception and vaginal bleeding. Care is mostly supportive. If possible, retain any products of conception that the patient has passed and transport such products with her to the hospital for evaluation.

Pregnancy-induced hypertension (PIH) is defined as a blood pressure greater than 140/90, diagnosed on two or more occasions at least 6 hours apart. Alternatively, PIH can also be determined based on deviation from the patient's baseline blood pressure after 20 weeks gestation. In this method, PIH is defined as a systolic blood pressure greater than 30 mm Hg over the baseline systolic blood pressure and a diastolic blood pressure greater than 15 mm Hg over the baseline diastolic blood pressure. This method takes into account patients who normally have a low blood pressure (e.g., 90/50).

A more serious form of PIH is preeclampsia (toxemia of pregnancy). Along with hypertension, patients with preeclampsia also exhibit generalized edema and have an increased production of proteins. Causes of this condition include placental dysfunction and systemic vasospasm. Signs and symptoms include hypertension, generalized edema, sudden weight gain, visual disturbances, and headache. Care is supportive, with close attention paid to signs of eclampsia.

Patients who have a history of preeclampsia and are actively seizing or in a coma are experiencing eclampsia. The cause of the seizure activity is likely to be hypertensive encephalopathy. Definitive care for the eclamptic patient is the delivery of the newborn in the hospital setting. Prehospital care for the patient having eclamptic seizures includes immediate transport of the patient to a facility capable of caring for a high-risk pregnancy patient, positioning the patient in a left lateral position (protects the airway of the mother and allows for optimal perfusion for the baby), administering high-flow oxygen, obtaining IV access, and treating seizure activity (e.g., benzodiazepines). If permitted, administer magnesium sulfate to treat the effects of toxemia.

Abruptio placentae is defined as the abnormal separation of the placenta from the uterine wall before the birth of the baby, usually during the third trimester. Signs and symptoms include sudden vaginal bleeding (not always present externally), firm uterus, and severe pain. Signs of shock may be present if bleeding is significant. Place the mother in a left lateral position with legs elevated, and begin transport immediately to an appropriate receiving facility. Administer high-flow oxygen and initiate IV access. Administer fluid if local protocol allows. Provide a vaginal pad for collection of blood and to help determine the amount of blood loss.

Placenta previa occurs when the placenta implants either partially or completely over the cervical os (Figure 41-2). If the placenta is stretched when the cervix begins to dilate, the placenta can tear and cause severe bleeding. Separation of the placenta from the uterine wall can lead to compromised fetal profusion and is considered a life-threatening condition for the mother and baby. Signs and symptoms of placenta previa include painless, bright red vaginal bleeding. Place the mother in a left lateral position, with legs elevated if possible. Transport to an appropriate receiving facility. Administer high-flow oxygen via non-rebreather mask, establish IVs, and provide fluid resuscitation. Provide a vaginal pad for collection of blood and to help determine the amount of blood loss.

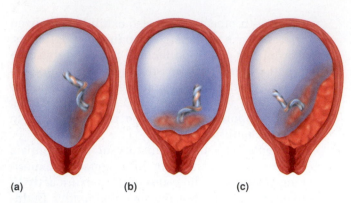

FIGURE 41-2 **Placenta Previa. (a)** Low-lying previa.
(b) Complete previa. **(c)** Marginal previa.

4. *Describe common complications of labor.*

Labor that occurs past 20 weeks after conception but before 37 weeks of pregnancy is called *preterm labor*.[4] Although successful deliveries have occurred, it is considered very risky for a newborn to be delivered so early. If you encounter preterm labor, provide a calm and supportive environment for the patient. Administer supplemental oxygen and establish IV access. Consider administration of tocolytics such as terbutaline sulfate (a beta$_2$-specific smooth muscle relaxant that relaxes the smooth muscle of the uterus and slows or stops contractions).

Fetal distress is very difficult to detect in the prehospital setting and requires advanced diagnostic equipment and training that paramedics do not routinely have. One of the key indicators for fetal distress in the prehospital setting is the presence of meconium. Meconium is the infant's first stool, thought to be released when the fetus is under stress. Prehospital management includes suctioning of the newborn's mouth and then nose with a bulb syringe as soon as the head emerges from the vagina. Continue to suction as the delivery completes. If meconium is suctioned from the mouth, consider direct laryngoscopy to see if meconium suctioning of the trachea with an endotracheal tube attached to a meconium aspirator is needed (Figure 41-3). Once the airway is clear, aggressively stimulate the newborn to breathe by drying and warming the body.

A *prolapsed umbilical cord* occurs when the cord presents through the cervix and vagina before the baby's head. The head subsequently compresses the cord, effectively cutting off its own oxygen supply. Prehospital management is aggressive. Position the mother in a knee-chest position.

Insert a gloved hand into the vagina, and lift the presenting part of the baby off of the cord. Once you have relieved the pressure of the presenting part of the baby from the umbilical cord, you are committed to maintain that position until the baby has been delivered. Administer high-flow oxygen via non-rebreather mask to the mother,[5] conserve body temperature, and transport emergently to a high-risk obstetrics receiving hospital (if possible). Obtain IV access en route to the hospital. Do not allow the mother to stand or lay on her back.

A *breech birth* occurs when the baby's initial presenting part through the birth canal is the buttocks, foot, or knees. For information on the prehospital birth of a baby, see Box 41-5 in the textbook.

When the umbilical cord is wrapped around the baby's neck, it is called a *nuchal cord*. If possible, loosen the cord and slip it over the baby's head. If the cord is too tight to loosen or slip over the baby's head, carefully clamp the cord in two places with hemostats and then cut the cord with round-tip scissors, making sure that you do not cut the baby's neck. Loosen the cord from around the baby's neck and continue with the delivery.

A *caul delivery* occurs when the baby is born inside an intact amniotic sac. If this occurs, identify the location of the baby's face. With your pinky finger, gently apply inward pressure toward the baby's mouth.[6] When the finger penetrates the sac, peel the sac back from the face and the rest of the baby's body. Continue with normal newborn assessment and care.

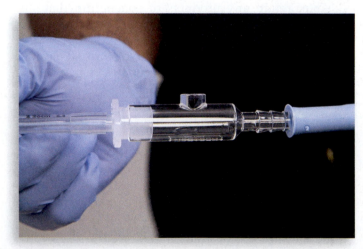

FIGURE 41-3 Endotracheal tube attached to a meconium aspirator to allow for meconium suctioning.

Need to Do

The following skills are explained and illustrated in a step-by-step manner, via skill sheets and/or Step-by-Steps in this text and on the accompanying DVD:

Skill Name	Skill Sheet Number and Location	Step-by-Step Number and Location
Meconium Suctioning	22 – DVD	22 – DVD
Abdominal Assessment	36 – DVD	N/A
Uncomplicated Childbirth	41 – DVD	N/A

Connections

- Chapter 13, Shock Overview, in the textbook provides more information on the different types of shock, including their signs, symptoms, and treatment.

- Chapter 30, Neurology, in the textbook contains more information on signs, symptoms, and treatment of various types of seizures.

- Chapter 33, Infectious and Communicable Diseases, in the textbook discusses gynecological infections in more detail.

- Chapter 34, Gastroenterology, in the textbook discusses and differentiates causes and treatment of abdominal pain, as well as assessment techniques for the patient with abdominal pain.

- A step-by-step guide to uncomplicated childbirth can be found in Chapter 41 of the textbook.

- An APGAR score sheet can be found in Box 41-4 in the textbook.

- Link to the companion DVD for a chapter-based quiz, audio glossary, animations, games and exercises, and, when appropriate, skill sheets and skill Step-by-Steps.

Street Secrets

- **High Index of Suspicion** Any woman of childbearing age with a complaint of pelvic or abdominal pain, whether the patient assures you that there is no possibility of pregnancy or not, should be suspected of having an ectopic pregnancy until

proven otherwise. The reason for the high index of suspicion is the potential life-threatening seriousness of this condition.

- **What's the Difference?** To differentiate placenta previa from placental abruption it is helpful to keep in mind that *p*revia is usually "*p*ainless," and *a*bruptio includes "*a*cute pain" 90% of the time.[7]

The Drug Box

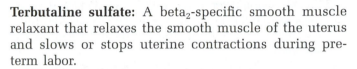

Terbutaline sulfate: A beta$_2$-specific smooth muscle relaxant that relaxes the smooth muscle of the uterus and slows or stops uterine contractions during preterm labor.

Oxytocin (Pitocin): Stimulates contractions of the uterus. Used in the prehospital setting to help manage postpartum hemorrhage.

Benzodiazepines (diazepam, lorazepam, midazolam): Can be used to treat eclamptic seizures.

Magnesium sulfate: Used to treat eclamptic seizures and signs and symptoms of toxemia.

References

1. I. K. Stone, "Sexually Transmitted Diseases," in G. I. Benrubi (ed.), *Obstetric and Gynecologic Emergencies.* Philadelphia: J. B. Lippincott Company, 1994, pp. 211–32.
2. S. J. Sondheimer, "Menorrhagia and Abnormal Vaginal Bleeding," in G. I. Benrubi (ed.), *Obstetric and Gynecological Emergencies.* Philadelphia: J.P. Lippincott Company, 1994, pp. 251–62.
3. L. V. Walsh, *Midwifery: Community Based Care During the Childbearing Year.* Philadelphia: W. B. Saunders Company, 2001, p. 424.
4. H. Varney, J. M. Kriebs, and C. L. Gegor, *Varney's Midwifery,* 4th ed. Sudbury, MA: Jones and Bartlett Publishers, 2004.
5. Ibid.
6. A. Frye, *Holistic Midwifery: A Comprehensive Textbook for Midwives in Homebirth Practice.* Vol. II, *Care of the Mother and Baby from Onset of Labor through the First Hours after Birth.* Portland, OR: Labrys Press, 2004, p. 465.
7. Ibid., p. 427.

Answers

Are You Ready?

1. Nora falls into the childbearing age range and is experiencing pelvic pain. A worst-case scenario would be that she is experiencing an ectopic pregnancy, which is

a potentially life-threatening condition. The duration of the pain, presence of fever, and pronounced shuffle may point to another condition, but think ectopic pregnancy until proven otherwise.

2. Start with an assessment of the ABCs. Perform a secondary assessment if no life threats are noted in the primary assessment and there is no indication to transport the patient emergently. A complete medical history focusing on the patient's current complaints, as well as PMH, medications, and allergies to medications, is also important.

3. Nora has many of the signs, symptoms, and risk factors associated with pelvic inflammatory disease (PID). Even though she appears to have PID, the signs and symptoms are similar to those experienced by people suffering from appendicitis, gastroenteritis, diverticulitis, and ectopic pregnancy.

4. Because it is better to assume and treat for the worst, treat the patient as if she is experiencing an ectopic pregnancy. Nora should be placed on supplemental oxygen, an IV should be established, and she should be transported to a facility capable of treating a patient with a possible surgical condition.

5. Nora appears stable, but it is safer to assume the possibility of deterioration in her condition rather than assuming that she has a benign condition that will remain stable.

Active Learning

1. a. ovary; b. uterine (fallopian) tube; c. uterus; d. cervix; e. vagina; f. labia minor; g. labia majora

2. Perineum

3. Ovum (oocyte)

You Are There: Reality-Based Cases

Case 1

1. Kisha has severe ventilatory distress, and she is 30 weeks pregnant. That makes her a critical patient.

2. Assess Kisha's airway, breathing, and circulation and intervene as necessary to support her ABCs. Provide high-flow supplemental oxygen as appropriate according to her presentation.

3. In reality, because Kisha has such a high-acuity condition, the priority is not so much to determine the exact cause of the problem but to support the ABCs at this point. Your prompt care during the primary assessment phase may very well determine the outcome of both mother and newborn.

4. With Kisha's history of preeclampsia, pre-pregnancy hypertension, the rapid onset of severe ventilatory distress with pulmonary edema, complaints of headache and visual disturbance, and a blood pressure of 220/130, you may be inclined to think preeclampsia or eclampsia. What about seizure activity or coma? Her husband is unable to answer any more questions, and you and your partner are doing all you can to oxygenate Kisha and assist her ventilations while trying to get her transported to the hospital.

5. Should you secure the patient's airway or begin transportation first? Because both need to be done and transport will occur no matter what, it may be prudent to begin transport and manage the airway and breathing en route to the hospital. This way, if you have any trouble with the airway or there are any unforeseen complications, you will be closer to definitive care. There are a number of ways in which this patient's airway and breathing can be managed, and no one way is better than any other as long as it accomplishes the goal of providing adequate oxygenation and ventilation. Because of the patient's inability to follow simple commands, the use of CPAP is contraindicated, although she might benefit from PEEP at this point. Other options for airway and breathing control include the use of a bag-mask with an NPA. Medication-assisted intubation is a possibility if it is approved for use in your EMS system. Nasal intubation is a possibility, but due to the fact that the patient is very hypertensive, any epistaxis incurred may be significant.

6. The treatment plan centers on control of the airway and breathing at this point, but the trouble with the breathing is likely directly related to the pregnancy and the fact that Kisha has a blood pressure of 220/130. Addressing the hypertension and the fluid on the lungs may directly impact the airway and the breathing. The treatment of pulmonary edema and hypertension during pregnancy varies between practitioners and between different EMS systems.

7. The patient needs to be transported emergently to the closest receiving hospital capable of caring for a critical obstetrics patient. Contact medical control for guidance.

8. The condition is called eclampsia because she is actively seizing.

9. Since you have already addressed the patient's ABCs and presenting signs and symptoms, controlling the seizure is the priority. Make sure that the patient is in a left lateral position and that you have a patent IV. Treatment for eclampsia is multifaceted and includes treatment for the seizure and the toxemia, which is likely contributing to the seizure. Management of this patient will vary based on local EMS protocols, but will likely include administration of a benzodiazepine and magnesium sulfate (not necessarily in that order). If you have not already done so, test the patient's blood sugar, as hypoglycemia is another possible cause of seizures.

Test Yourself

1. a

Pregnancy that ends with labor anytime between 37–42 weeks is normal and called a term pregnancy.

2. c

Because of the catastrophic nature and possibly preventable death from a ruptured ectopic pregnancy, any female patient of potentially childbearing age (ages 9 to 60) complaining of abdominal pain should be presumed to have an ectopic pregnancy until proven otherwise.

3. c

Pelvic inflammatory disease (PID) is caused by an infection that starts most often in the vaginal area but travels further up into the reproductive tract involving the fallopian tubes, ovaries, and uterus. The main pathogens are usually *Neisseria gonorrhea* or chlamydia, both sexually transmitted, and the infection is sometimes asymptomatic, which is why it goes untreated until the infection involves the reproductive organs and causes pain and fever. Specific risk factors for PID include late adolescence, multiple sex partners, frequent douching, recent IUD (intrauterine birth control device) insertion, prior history, and cigarette smoking.

4. a

Menstrual blood does not clot, and the total amount lost is from 60–80 mL per cycle. Menorrhagia is a term used to describe a large amount (> 80 mL) of menstrual bleeding and is considered "dysfunctional." The causes of dysfunctional bleeding include clotting disorders, fibroids, cervical cancer, hormones, and thyroid conditions among others.

5. During the normal ovulation cycle the follicle develops an egg, releases this egg (ovulation), and is converted into a corpus luteum. If follicular development is stopped for some reason, the follicle or corpus luteum can become filled with fluid and an ovarian cyst is formed.

If the cyst is formed early, within the first 2 weeks of the cycle (before ovulation), it is considered to be a follicular cyst (Graafian cyst). If the cyst is formed later in the cycle, it is called a luteal cyst. A ruptured ovarian cyst can lead to severe sharp pain and is localized to one side. Approximately 25% of menstruating women will experience this type of ruptured cyst. They are a relatively common finding and most are benign. A ruptured cyst can become complicated by bleeding, however, and may even become a life-threatening emergency.

6. d

If vaginal bleeding is severe and you suspect the bleeding is originating from an internal source, do not pack the vaginal area with gauze. Simply apply a trauma dressing to the external vaginal area or a vaginal pad to collect the blood, and focus on rapid transportation, as well as fluid resuscitation for patients who are hemodynamically compromised (blood pressure below 90 mm Hg). Scene removal of a foreign object is not recommended due to the increased risk of trauma and bleeding. As a general rule, paramedics do not perform vaginal exams.

7. True

Prolapse can be caused by overstretching or damage to the ligaments, muscles, and organs in the pelvis. Patients report some of the following symptoms: pelvic or vaginal pressure, heaviness in the lower abdomen, backache, and changes in urination or bowel habits. Less commonly, the prolapse happens abruptly after lifting heavy objects.

8. You should suspect ovarian torsion. Treatment includes carefully monitoring the patient for signs of hidden bleeding and shock while en route to the nearest hospital. Besides pain, patients may present with nausea and vomiting, unilateral abdominal tenderness or rigidity, diarrhea, constipation, dizziness, and low-grade fever.

9. c

Pregnancy normally lasts about 40 weeks from the last normal menstrual period (LNMP). Pregnancy duration is also approximately 38 weeks from the known conception date. Pregnancy that ends with labor anytime between 37–42 weeks is normal and called a term pregnancy.

10. b

Hemorrhage, ectopic pregnancy, and preeclampsia cause 59% of all maternal deaths in America. You should be highly suspicious of symptoms that resemble any of these three conditions.

11. d

A nuchal cord occurs when the umbilical cord is wrapped around the infant's head or neck. If some slack is available, it is easiest to flip the cord over the baby's head or push it down below the baby's shoulders while the head and body emerge. When a baby is born with the cord tightly wrapped around the neck, you must cut the umbilical cord.

12. a

You should not have the patient get into a recumbent position. It may be uncomfortable for her, and the pregnant uterus may press down on her vena cava, limiting oxygen for the baby. Semisitting or left side lying are more preferable positions.

13. b

Hyperemesis gravidarum is nausea and vomiting in pregnancy that lasts excessively long, throughout the entire pregnancy, or is severely pronounced and interferes with normal daily functioning. If the condition leads to dehydration and electrolyte imbalances with further chemical disturbances, medical treatment should be sought.

14. b

If the mother reports strong pressure in her bottom or an urge to bear down, it is probably time to deliver. Unless there are signs of a complicated birth, you should help deliver the baby on scene.

15. c

Gentle and steady pressure applied by the pinky finger is the most reliable way to break the amniotic sac. The smallest finger can most easily puncture the bag.

16. a

An ectopic pregnancy simply means that a fertilized egg has implanted somewhere outside its normal position in the uterus (usually the fallopian tubes). Implantations in locations other than the uterus rarely go to term and most often result in rupture of the structure unless diagnosed early enough. Ectopic pregnancy has a maternal death of about 10 percent.

17. d

If you can see the top of the baby's head (crowning), then birth is imminent. Unless there are signs of complications, you should assist in giving birth on the scene.

18. d

Cord prolapse occurs when the umbilical cord emerges through the cervix before the baby presents. A cord prolapse is a serious complication and usually requires an emergency cesarean birth to save the life of the infant. This is a life-threatening complication for the baby because as the baby moves down the birth canal it compresses the prolapsed cord and prevents oxygen from being delivered.

19. c

Teratogens are substances, medications, organisms, or physical agents capable of causing abnormal fetal development. The most important organs (such as the brain and heart) do most of their development early during the pregnancy, and it is at this time that they are most vulnerable. Though not as dangerous during later stages, women should do all they can to avoid teratogens during all stages of pregnancy.

20. c

Multiple births are at a high risk of premature birth, and in twin pregnancy, 40% have the additional consideration of one baby being breech. Another complication associated with multiple pregnancy is placental abruption after the birth of the first baby causing fetal distress or death for the second baby due to lack of oxygenation.

21. First

The first stage of labor, also called the dilation stage, generally lasts several hours. The second (expulsion) stage can last up to 2½ hours or can be over with a single push. The third (placental) stage rarely takes longer than half an hour.

22. True

Mothers who have previously had normal births generally go through labor more quickly and are at lower risk of complications. If a mother's previous birth had complications (such as the baby having been born preterm), she is at greater risk of similar complications.

23. False

Abruptio placentae is accompanied by severe pain. Other signs include vaginal bleeding and a firm uterus. Placenta previa is usually painless, however.

24. False

Ovulation typically occurs 14 days into a woman's menstrual cycle (if she has a 28-day cycle). If she has not yet ovulated, it is very difficult for a woman to be pregnant. However, timing is not enough to rule out pregnancy-related problems.

25. You may wish to transport a mother who is in the process of delivering if the birth is complicated or the pregnancy is high risk.

In an uncomplicated birth, if delivery is imminent, it is generally better to deliver the baby on the scene. In complicated circumstances (such as a prolapsed cord) or high-risk incidences (such as a premature labor), however, it may be better to deliver en route or at the hospital.

Special Populations

part

5

chapter 42

Neonatology

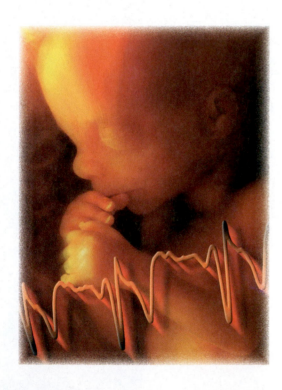

towel into the trash. What she found in the garbage can made her scream.

A newborn baby was in the trash, wrapped in bloody, wet paper towels. Diane came running into the bathroom to find Nancy trying to wrap the baby in her jacket. Nancy yelled for Diane to call 9-1-1.

1. Based on the information that you have obtained from this scenario, what will your initial action be?

_____

_____

_____

2. What factors are you concerned about, other than assessing and managing the patient's ABCs?

_____

_____

_____

Are You Ready?

Nancy and Diane were enjoying a stroll through the park one winter afternoon. Nancy asked Diane to watch her child so she could use the public restroom. As Nancy entered the restroom, a woman who appeared to be in her late teens ran out of the bathroom crying. Nancy went into the restroom and shivered as she entered the bathroom stall. A few minutes later, she finished washing her hands and went to toss the paper

3. How will the factors you identified in question 2 affect the patient?

_____

_____

_____

Active Learning

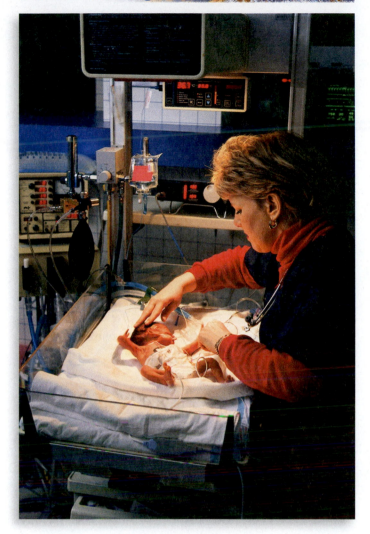

1. Volunteer Opportunity: Newborn

The experience of assessing and caring for neonates is one of the best ways to feel comfortable with this patient population, especially when there is something wrong with a neonate. Because this is something that paramedics do not have the opportunity to do on a regular basis, seek the opportunity to observe childbirth and newborn assessment in a local hospital.

2. Neonatal Resuscitation Course

The American Heart Association (AHA) and American Academy of Pediatrics (AAP) have developed a Neonatal Resuscitation Program (NRP) that teaches an evidence-based approach to the resuscitation of the newborn (including causes, prevention, and management of mild to severe neonatal asphyxia) in a manner that will optimize the provider's knowledge and skill in neonatal resuscitation. Take an NRP course in

your area to increase your confidence in caring for neonates.

3. APGAR Scoring

Read each of the following descriptions of a newborn infant. Score each presentation using the APGAR scale, or fill in the blank of the statement in order to fit the given APGAR score.

Newborn Description	APGAR Score
a. Crying, moves all extremities, pink throughout, heart rate of 150, breathing rate of 36	
b. Grimaces when stimulated, heart rate of 100, blue extremities, respirations of 12, arms flex	
c. Limp, heart rate of 100, skin color is _____ , no response to stimulus, breathing irregularly	3
d. Moves weakly, grunting, heart rate 110, blue all over, respirations of 40	
e. Unresponsive, blue all over, heart rate is _____ , breathing rate is 10.	2

You Are There: Reality-Based Cases

Case 1 (*continued from chapter opener*)

You arrive on scene shortly after the police and find Nancy and the baby in the back of the police car. When you open the door, a rush of hot air escapes from inside of the car. Nancy is holding the baby, who is still wrapped in wet towels and Nancy's jacket. You quickly step into the waiting ambulance and close the door. Nancy carefully hands you the baby.

1. The responding police officer had turned on his heater full blast. Was this good for the newborn? Why or why not?

_____

_____

_____

2. What complications can you anticipate based upon the scene findings thus far?

_____

_____

_____

3. Describe your management approach.

_____

_____

_____

Your partner attempts to obtain a history from Nancy as you assess the newborn. Your assessment reveals a neonate who appears to be fully developed and has an umbilical cord that is slowly oozing blood. You quickly clamp the cord and assess the baby's airway and breathing. You suction the mouth and nose of the baby with a bulb syringe, but you do not obtain any significant secretions. Breathing is agonal, and the patient has peripheral and central cyanosis.

4. At this point in the assessment, what should be done?

_____

_____

_____

5. How long will you perform each intervention before reassessing the patient?

_____

_____

_____

6. According to the AHA, what is the rate at which rescue breaths are delivered for a newborn patient?

_____

_____

_____

7. What is the next step in the assessment of the newborn?

_____

_____

_____

Despite your initial intervention, the patient remains cyanotic with agonal respirations and a brachial pulse of 60 bpm.

8. What is the appropriate intervention following these assessment findings?

_____

_____

_____

9. What is the compression-to-ventilation ratio for neonatal CPR?

_____

_____

_____

10. What is the target heart rate when performing chest compressions on a neonate?

_____

_____

_____

After 30–60 seconds of chest compressions and positive pressure ventilations, you reassess the patient and note that the patient continues to have agonal respirations and central and peripheral cyanosis with a heart rate of 60 bpm (palpated at the brachial artery).

11. What is the next appropriate intervention? Why?

_____

_____

_____

12. What is the most appropriate means of maintaining the patient's airway?

_____

_____

_____

After your interventions, your reassessment of the patient reveals decreasing cyanosis, a respiratory rate of 40 breaths per minute, a heart rate of 120 bpm, and a blood glucose level of 27 mg/dL. En route to a hospital that has a neonatal intensive care unit, you confirm ETT placement and continue to reassess the patient's ABCs and vital signs. You assist the newborn's ventilations and maintain the baby's warmth. You administer 10% dextrose via an umbilical IV.

13. After relinquishing the care of your patient to the physician in charge, do you have any further obligation as far as mandatory reporting surrounding the abandonment of the newborn?

_____

_____

_____

Test Yourself

1. Explain the difference between primary and secondary apnea.

_____

_____

2. What is the basic purpose of the APGAR score? At what point is it recorded?

_____

_____

3. Why do hypothermia and hyperthermia pose special challenges to infants?

_____

_____

4. Roughly how many out-of-hospital births require resuscitation?
   a. 1 out of 100
   b. 1 out of 1,000
   c. 1 out of 10
   d. 1 out of 10,000

5. A newly born patient has just been delivered and is not yet crying or breathing. Describe two ways you might stimulate the infant and what would be a healthy response.

_____

_____

6. An infant does not need intervention if the infant's APGAR score is 7 or greater.

   True

   False

7. Explain the proper equipment and procedure for administering positive pressure ventilation to a newly born infant.

_____

_____

8. Just after childbirth, most problems for newborn patients have
   a. cardiovascular-related causes.
   b. respiratory-related causes.
   c. hypothermia-related causes.
   d. hypoglycemia-related causes.

9. Which of these would be an antepartum factor for a neonate having a low birth weight?
   a. 19-year-old mother
   b. Premature labor
   c. Smoking
   d. Labor lasting 18 hours

10. In a newly born patient (immediately after birth), what pulse is typically easiest to use?
    a. Umbilical pulse, palpating where the umbilical cord attaches to the abdomen
    b. Dorsalis pedis, palpating the dorsalis pedis artery on the foot
    c. Apical pulse, auscultating the heart
    d. Brachial pulse, palpating the brachial artery in the upper arm

11. What is the most sensitive indicator for evaluating neonatal physiological distress?
    a. Respiration rate
    b. Reaction to stimuli
    c. Skin color
    d. Heart rate

12. You just helped deliver an infant who was born after 36 weeks of gestation. The patient displayed limited muscle activity, weak breathing, and a heart rate of 44. After administering positive pressure for 30 seconds, the heart rate increased to 53. What should be your next step?
    a. Perform endotracheal intubation.
    b. Administer chest compressions.
    c. Continue positive pressure ventilation only.
    d. Administer epinephrine.

13. What five questions should you ask to determine if a newborn infant needs resuscitation?

_____

_____

14. When treating a neonate with a respiratory complication, when would you use an invasive ventilation method without first trying a less invasive method?

_____

_____

15. When resuscitating a neonatal patient, you should reassess the patient every
    a. 1–2 minutes.
    b. 2–4 minutes.
    c. 30–60 seconds.
    d. 15–30 seconds.

16. Most infants born out of the hospital should be transported using an isolette.

    True

    False

17. A neonate is older than a newly born infant.

True

False

18. What is meconium, and what medical problems can it lead to?

_____

_____

Scenario: While delivering an infant, you discovered that he had a tight nuchal cord that you were forced to cut. The baby was initially pink, but during transport you notice that the patient's skin is pale. The infant is cool, has a weak brachial pulse and delayed capillary refill, and seems lethargic. You partner uses a glucometer to check the infant's blood sugar levels, and the glucose level is 60 mg/dL.

19. You should suspect

   a. narcotic withdrawal.

   b. secondary apnea.

   c. hypoglycemia.

   d. hypovolemia.

20. How should you treat this patient?

   a. Epinephrine, 0.01 mg/kg

   b. Naloxone, 0.1 mg/kg

   c. Isotonic fluid, 10 mL/kg

   d. 10% dextrose, 2–4 mL/kg

Need to Know

Neonatology is the study and treatment of neonates,[1] and neonate is defined as a baby from birth to 30 days.[2] The following represent the Key Objectives of Chapter 42:

1. *Explain the impact of the term of gestation on the health of the newborn.*

Premature birth is defined as birth before 37 weeks of gestation. Whether full-term or premature, newborns experiencing hypothermia or hypoxia are at risk for complications that will require prompt, aggressive resuscitation. Premature infants are at greater risk than full-term infants because of incomplete development of the body's systems.

2. *Describe the circulatory changes that take place during birth.*

Shortly after birth, a change from mother-placenta-dependent fetal circulation to independent, self-sustained neonatal circulation occurs (Figure 42-1).

The infant's chest passes through the birth canal, which squeezes out some of the amniotic fluid that has occupied the lungs until this point. As the chest comes out of the birth canal, it recoils and draws a small amount of air into the upper airway. Suctioning the mouth and nares of the baby when the head emerges from the birth canal and before the body has delivered allows for amniotic fluid to be removed and for less amniotic fluid to be drawn into the lungs during the first breath.

The first breath results from chemical and thermal changes. When the baby is delivered, the amount of assistance from the mother and placenta decreases dramatically. There is a sudden decrease of oxygen in the blood and an increase in the concentration of carbon dioxide. The pH falls, creating an acidotic state. All these changes stimulate the respiratory center in the medulla to initiate breathing. In addition to the chemical changes, when the newborn leaves the relatively warm maternal environment and enters the relatively cool external environment, the change in temperature stimulates the respiratory center to initiate breathing.

As the newborn begins to breathe, oxygen levels in the blood increase. This stimulates the closure of the fetal shunting system (foramen ovale, ductus arteriosus, ductus venosus) and allows for autonomous neonatal circulation.

There are several factors that can prevent the transition from maternal-fetal circulation to independent neonatal circulation. Persistent pulmonary hypertension in the newborn is caused by meconium aspiration and meconium-filled alveoli. This results in an increased pressure in the thoracic cavity which keeps blood from flowing to the lungs. Performing meconium aspiration and providing supplemental oxygen will reduce this condition (Figure 42-2).

Persistent fetal circulation results from hypothermia, which causes metabolic acidosis as brown fat is metabolized to generate energy and heat. This leads to an oxygen-poor, acidotic environment that causes a resumption of fetal circulation. A paramedic can manage this condition by drying and warming the neonate, supporting oxygenation and ventilation, and correcting hypoglycemia.

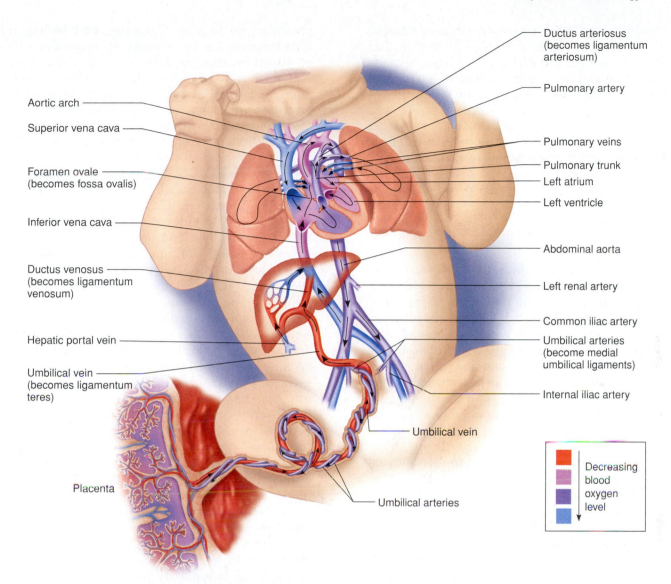

FIGURE 42-1 The general pattern of fetal circulation is shown anatomically.

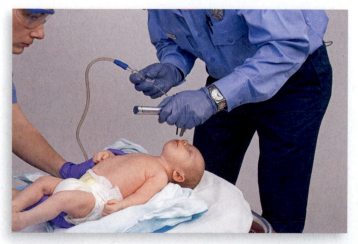

FIGURE 42-2 Performing meconium aspiration and providing supplemental oxygen will reduce the pressure in the thoracic cavity, which can prevent blood from flowing to the lungs.

3. *Differentiate between primary and secondary apnea, and describe the initial treatment approach for each.*

Because a ventilatory component is the primary cause of cardiopulmonary arrest in newborns, it is critical to identify and treat any respiratory compromise as early as possible. In primary apnea, the neonate attempts to compensate for fatigue. Primary apnea presents as an irregular breathing pattern that alternates between rapid breathing and apnea. Ensure that the neonate is dry, warm, and stimulated. If the problem is not corrected, consider blow-by oxygen or assisting ventilation with a bag-mask.

When primary apnea is not identified or corrected, the neonate can no longer compensate for fatigue and stops breathing, causing secondary apnea. Heart rate and blood pressure typically fall quickly. Treatment begins by assisting ventilations with a bag-mask device and high-flow oxygen. Ventilate a neonate experiencing secondary apnea at a rate of 40–60 breaths per minute for 30–60 seconds, and then reevaluate the patient. If the patient is pink and breathing at a rate of 40–60 breaths per minute, provide blow-by oxygen. If the patient has poor skin color and a respiratory rate less than 40 breaths per minute, resume bag-mask ventilations for another 30–60 seconds and then reassess again.

4. *Describe the assessment and treatment of a newborn.*

When the head emerges from the birth canal, suction the mouth and then the nose, unless there is an indication that the baby should not be suctioned (Figure 42-3). Once the baby has been delivered (note the time), dry, warm, and stimulate the baby. If the baby doesn't respond, stimulate the feet (flick with your finger or rub the bottoms of the feet) or the baby's back. If meconium is present, suction the meconium with a bulb syringe or a meconium aspirator via an endotracheal tube as appropriate. Clamp the umbilical cord when it stops pulsating or earlier if resuscitation is required.

If no indication for resuscitation or intervention of any kind exists, perform APGAR scoring at 1 minute and 5 minutes after birth (see Table 42-4 in the textbook for the APGAR assessment tool).

If the need for resuscitation exists, open the airway by placing padding under the shoulders, placing the airway into a neutral position. Assess

breathing by looking, listening, and feeling for air exchange for 10 seconds. A respiratory rate of 40–60 breaths per minute is considered normal for a newborn. If respiratory effort is sufficient, consider blow-by oxygen to help with a slower heart rate (see later in this section). If breathing is inadequate, begin assisting ventilations with a bag-mask. Intubation may be required if breathing does not improve with the ventilatory assistance.

Assess circulation by checking the brachial artery, umbilical cord, or apically for the pulse rate and quality (Figure 42-4). A normal heart rate is greater than 100 bpm. If the heart rate is between 60 and 100 bpm and there is abnormal skin color, provide blow-by oxygen to the side of the face or under the chin. If the heart rate is less than 60 bpm and there is spontaneous breathing, provide bag-mask ventilations with high-flow oxygen at 40–60 per minute for 30–60 seconds and reassess. If the heart rate remains less than 60 bpm, initiate CPR at a ratio of 3:1 (120 compressions and approximately 40 ventilations per minute). *Note:* Perform any needed intervention for 30–60 seconds and then reassess the patient. Provide further treatment based on the results of the reassessment for another 30–60 seconds, and reassess again. Continue this process until there are no further changes and then continue frequent reassessments.

If ventilation by bag-mask and CPR are not effective, obtain venous access while continuing with CPR. Although drug therapy is seldom necessary in the resuscitation of the neonate, epinephrine is typically the drug of choice.

FIGURE 42-3 When the baby's head emerges from the birth canal, suction the mouth and then the nose.

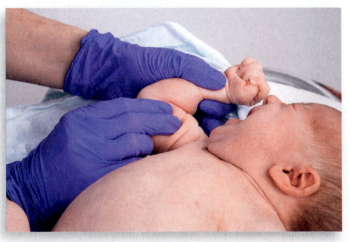

FIGURE 42-4 Assess circulation by checking the brachial artery, the umbilical cord, or apically for the pulse rate and quality.

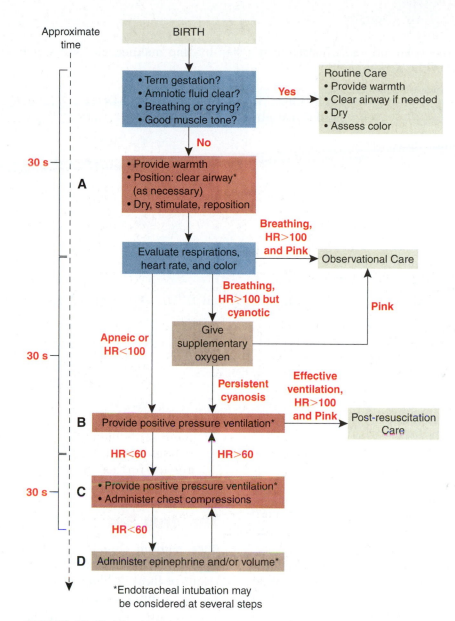

Approximate time

BIRTH

- Term gestation?
- Amniotic fluid clear?
- Breathing or crying?
- Good muscle tone?

Yes

Routine Care
- Provide warmth
- Clear airway if needed
- Dry
- Assess color

No

30 s

A

- Provide warmth
- Position: clear airway* (as necessary)
- Dry, stimulate, reposition

Evaluate respirations, heart rate, and color

Breathing, HR>100 and Pink

Observational Care

Breathing, HR>100 but cyanotic

Apneic or HR<100

30 s

Give supplementary oxygen

Pink

Persistent cyanosis

Effective ventilation, HR>100 and Pink

B

Provide positive pressure ventilation*

Post-resuscitation Care

HR<60   **HR>60**

30 s

C

- Provide positive pressure ventilation*
- Administer chest compressions

HR<60

D   Administer epinephrine and/or volume*

*Endotracheal intubation may be considered at several steps

FIGURE 42-5   The Neonatal Resuscitation Algorithm developed by the American Heart Association.

Consider fluid boluses when hypovolemia is suspected. Fluid resuscitation should be weight-based and should be limited to prevent fluid overload. The AHA Neonatal Resuscitation Algorithm is shown in Figure 42-5.

Connections

- Chapter 12, Airway Management, Ventilation, and Oxygenation, in the textbook contains additional information on airway management and ventilation.

- The American Heart Association's booklet–*Handbook of Emergency Cardiovascular Care* (2005 ECC Guidelines) contains the most current guidelines for the resuscitation of the newborn.
- Link to the companion DVD for a chapter-based quiz, audio glossary, animations, games and exercises, and, when appropriate, skill sheets and skill Step-by-Steps.

Street Secrets

- **Treat Aggressively**   When it comes to the assessment and treatment of neonates, assessments should be performed frequently. If there is any

Need to Do

The following skills are explained and illustrated in a step-by-step manner, via skill sheets and/or Step-by-Steps in this text and on the accompanying DVD:

Skill Name	Skill Sheet Number and Location	Step-by-Step Number and Location
Airway Positioning and Maneuvers	1 – DVD	1 – DVD
Oropharyngeal Airways	2 – DVD	2 – DVD
Endotracheal Intubation	7 – Appendix A and DVD	7 – Chapter 12 and DVD
Meconium Suctioning	22 – DVD	22 – DVD
Blood Glucose Assessment	26 – DVD	26 – DVD
Uncomplicated Childbirth	41 – DVD	N/A
Intraosseous Access and Drug Administration	45 – Appendix A and DVD	45 – Chapter 16 and DVD
Umbilical Vein Cannulation	46 – DVD	N/A
NREMT Pediatric Ventilatory Management	90 – DVD	N/A
NREMT Pediatric Intraosseous Infusion	91 – DVD	N/A

indication that the neonate is hypoxic or experiencing ventilatory distress, provide oxygen and assist ventilations with a bag-mask device.

- **Head Position** Make sure that the head of the neonate is not flexed or extended too far in either direction, as this can cause airway compromise or occlusion. Placing an object such as a towel or a pad under the baby's shoulders to keep the airway in a neutral position will help ensure that a patent airway is maintained.

- **Dry and Warm** Maintaining warmth in the prehospital setting is frequently a challenge. Neonates have very little ability to maintain body temperature, so make sure that newborns and neonates are dry and warm. If the neonate is not responding appropriately, suspect hypothermia as a possible cause. Skin-on-skin contact with the mother followed by covering the baby with warm, dry blankets is one of the best techniques for keeping a newborn warm. Heat loss through the head can cause hypothermia, so make sure that the baby's head is dry and that it is covered with a cap and that the body is covered with warm blankets.

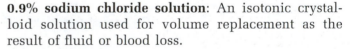

The Drug Box

0.9% sodium chloride solution: An isotonic crystalloid solution used for volume replacement as the result of fluid or blood loss.

Lactated Ringer's solution: An isotonic crystalloid solution used for volume replacement as the result of fluid or blood loss.

Epinephrine (Adrenalin, Sus-Phrine, EpiPen): A beta- and alpha-adrenergic agonist. The primary pharmacological drug used in neonatal resuscitation.

10% dextrose solution: Used for the treatment of hypoglycemia in a neonatal patient.

References

1. *Taber's Cyclopedic Medical Dictionary*, 20th ed., Philadelphia: F.A. Davis Co., 2005.
2. American Heart Association, "Recommended Guidelines for Uniform Reporting of Pediatric Advanced Life Support: The Pediatric Utstein Style." www.americanheart.org/presenter.jhtml?identifier=1211 (accessed December10, 2006).

Answers

Are You Ready?

1. Your first priority is to assess and treat any problems related to the baby's airway, breathing, and circulation.

2. Other factors that warrant concern include *hypothermia* and possibly *hypovolemia*. Hypothermia can lead to a number of other conditions, such as bradycardia, hypoxia, metabolic acidosis, and hypoglycemia.

3. When neonates get cold, they start to utilize glucose and brown fat in an attempt to maintain body temperature. The metabolism of brown fat can lead to metabolic acidosis because the end product is acid production. As the neonate burns available energy sources in an attempt to maintain body temperature, he or she will become hypoglycemic. Hypoglycemia for a neonate is a blood sugar less than 45 mg/dL. It is treated with dextrose 10%. Hypothermia that is not corrected can also lead to bradycardia and apnea. Blood or fluid loss in a neonate can lead to shock. It is important to remember that, since the neonate has a fixed stroke volume, cardiac output depends solely on the heart rate. As the body loses blood or fluid, it will attempt to compensate by increasing the heart rate. There is a limited supply of catecholamines in the neonate; once the catecholamines are exhausted, the compensatory mechanism will fail and the neonate will likely decompensate rapidly, deteriorating into cardiopulmonary arrest. For this reason, any signs of shock (e.g., tachycardia) need to be addressed early with supplementary oxygen and fluid resuscitation (per local EMS protocols).

Active Learning

3. a. 10; b. 6; c. blue all over; d. 6; e. less than 60

You Are There: Reality-Based Cases

Case 1

1. Yes, the officer was thinking clearly. Keeping the inside of the vehicle warm will help to reduce the possibility of hypothermia.

2. Beyond the primary concerns of the airway, breathing, and circulation, the delivery of a newborn outside of a health-care setting is cause for concern. Other concerns include: What is the likelihood of prenatal care? Is the newborn preterm? Will advanced airway management be necessary to support the airway?

3. Your management approach will likely follow the American Heart Association's Neonatal Resuscitation Algorithm, shown in Figure 42-5. Hypothermia is initially managed by ensuring that the newborn is dry and is being warmed (remove the wet towels; dry the neonate; and provide a warm, dry blanket and a warm, dry cap). Identification and treatment of hypoglycemia was discussed earlier in the case. Acidosis will likely be corrected during your management of the ABCs or via the newborn's own compensatory mechanisms. Be aware that one of the compensatory mechanisms that may be present is hyperpnea (using rapid respirations to blow off excess CO_2 in an attempt to correct the metabolic acidosis), a respiratory component that can lead to primary and/or secondary apnea. If the newborn appears to be tiring, assistance with ventilations can prevent deterioration into bradycardia and/or cardiopulmonary arrest. If the blood on the paper towels is from the newborn, the first action is to control the bleeding. If the baby presents with signs of shock, fluid boluses may be beneficial. The American Heart Association recommends an initial isotonic fluid bolus of 10 mL/kg that may be repeated once after reevaluation PRN. Administer fluid boluses to a neonate via an accepted means of vascular access (e.g., umbilical vein, peripheral vein, intraosseous route).

4. Ensure that the newborn is placed in a position that allows for an open airway by placing padding under the shoulders so that the airway stays in a neutral position. Provide positive pressure ventilations along with supplemental oxygen.

5. Each intervention should be performed for 30–60 seconds before reassessment occurs.

6. 40–60 breaths per minute when performed without compressions.

7. Reassess airway, breathing, and heart rate. If respirations do not increase and/or cyanosis persists, or if the heart rate is less than 100 bpm, continue ventilations and initiate chest compressions.

8. The baby remains cyanotic and displays agonal respirations and a heart rate of 60 bpm. The positive pressure ventilations have not improved the patient's vital signs, so chest compressions need to be added to the positive pressure ventilations.

9. The compression-to-ventilation ratio for neonates is 3:1.

10. The rate for compressions when performing CPR on a neonate is approximately 120 compressions per minute.

11. The next appropriate intervention will be to continue positive pressure ventilations, chest compressions, and obtain vascular access. Possible means of vascular access in a neonate include cannulation of the umbilical vein, IV access, and intraosseous access. Once vascular access has been obtained, the patient should be treated with fluid boluses or epinephrine. Vascular access will be needed for the administration of fluid boluses or epinephrine. The decision of whether to administer fluid or epinephrine is the dilemma. In this particular case, the newborn appears to be suffering from hypovolemic shock. If epinephrine is administered, the patient will receive the physiological effects of beta- and alpha-adrenergic stimulation resulting in increased heart rate, force of contraction, bronchodilation, and peripheral vasoconstriction. However, if the fluid volume in the vascular space is low, these effects may worsen the problem and increase the oxygen demands of the body tissues. Fluid bolus administration is likely the preferable treatment in this situation. Rapid transport to a facility capable of managing a

critical newborn is a top priority because the child may benefit from warming techniques that are not available in the prehospital setting and the administration of blood products if the baby has lost a significant amount.

12. Begin with a bag-mask and oral airway. If this is ineffective, if the patient needs to have the airway isolated due to secretions or blood in the airway, or if there is a problem such as swelling of the airway, a more advanced airway such as endotracheal intubation may be more appropriate.

13. Mandatory reporting of abuse and neglect varies from region to region. Whether you have mandatory reporting laws in your area or not, it is important that you cooperate with the local law enforcement agencies to make sure that the best interests of the baby are addressed. If you are not certain what your obligations are regarding this patient, contact your immediate supervisor and/or medical direction for assistance.

Test Yourself

1. Primary apnea is a newborn's futile attempt to breathe while fatigued. Secondary apnea occurs when the infant ceases to breathe completely.

   Primary apnea will manifest as a period of rapid respirations followed by a period of apnea. There will be no changes in heart rate or blood pressure during episodes of primary apnea. Secondary apnea corresponds to a considerable drop in both heart rate and blood pressure. Primary apnea is treated through stimulation activities such as tapping the feet, drying with warm towels, or gently rubbing the back. Simple stimulation will not correct secondary apnea episodes. The paramedic needs to assist ventilations. Use an appropriately sized bag-mask system connected to supplemental oxygen.

2. The APGAR score provides a preliminary assessment of a newborn's health using easily understood criteria. Current guidelines suggest obtaining APGAR scores at 1 and 5 minutes for all neonates.

   If the score is less than 7 points for the 1-minute or 5-minute assessment, an updated score should be recorded every 5 minutes until 20 minutes have passed or a score greater than 7 has been achieved. If a newborn requires resuscitative efforts, obtaining the APGAR score is not a priority. If desired, once the child is resuscitated successfully the APGAR score can be reconstructed for documentation purposes.

3. Newborns cannot regulate temperature very well. They have little body fat and can quickly deplete their energy trying to stay warm. Infants do not perspire like adults. They release heat by increasing respirations and heart rate.

   Infants also have a higher body surface area to volume ratio, and are unable to shiver, both of which increase the risk of hypothermia.

4. c

   Approximately 10% of all newly born infants require some assistance in breathing. The vast majority of these respond appropriately and fare well with just a few minutes of respiratory or ventilatory assistance.

5. The two common methods are rubbing the soles of the feet and rubbing the back. Rubbing the soles of the infant's feet should result in movement of the legs and flaring of the toes and should also stimulate the child to breathe and cry. Rubbing the infant's back should cause the back to slightly arch. The infant will dislike the gentle rubbing along the spine, which should trigger breathing and crying. It is never appropriate to dangle the child upside down or slap the child's bottom.

6. False

   While an APGAR score of 7 is generally considered normal, there are circumstances where an infant could score high but still need resuscitation, for example, if the infant was not breathing but received full points for the other scores.

7. Positive pressure ventilation is administered with a bag-mask device. Place only enough air into the lungs to cause the chest to begin to rise. If the chest is not rising adequately, reposition the head, suction the airway, check the mask seal, and try again. Always count aloud when providing positive pressure ventilations to maintain a rate of 40–60 breaths per minute.

   Be careful: The infant's lungs can easily be damaged if the paramedic is too excited or aggressive in supplying artificial respirations and the pressure valve (pop-off valve) is locked.

8. b

   Most problems arising during childbirth have respiratory causes, which are frequently corrected by suctioning the airway or with blow-by oxygen administration or bag-mask ventilation.

9. c

   Antepartum factors are variables that are present before labor begins. They include: smoking, no prenatal care, illicit drug use, mother's age (< 16 or > 35), medical conditions (such as hypertension, diabetes, and renal disease), multiple gestations, or trauma. A mother who is 19 years old generally does not present additional risks for low birth weight.

10. a

    The umbilical pulse is generally the easiest pulse to palpate in a newly born infant. Alternatives to the umbilical pulse are the apical and brachial sites. The apical pulse should only be used if the infant is pink or has other evidence of peripheral perfusion.

11. d

    The newborn heart rate is known to be the most sensitive indicator for evaluating physiological distress. Since the neonate has a fixed stroke volume, the cardiac output depends solely on the heart rate.

12. b

    According to the American Heart Association (AHA) Initial Resuscitation Algorithm for Newborns, if providing positive pressure ventilation fails to increase the heart rate above 60, you should move to the next step, which is administering chest compressions. Even though there was a slight improvement, it was not enough to rely on less invasive measures.

13. Was the baby at or near term (37–40 weeks)? Was the amniotic fluid clear of thick meconium, thin meconium, or any signs of discoloration that might indicate infection? Is the baby breathing and crying at least 30–60 times a minute? Is the heart rate at least 100 per minute? Does the baby have good muscle tone?

    If the answer to all these questions is "yes," the infant will most likely not need any additional resuscitation efforts.

14. If the infant has a heart rate of less than 60, you should skip blow-by oxygen and quickly begin performing positive pressure ventilation. In the rare case of congenital diaphragmatic hernia, you should intubate immediately, as bag-mask positive pressure ventilation can worsen the problem.

    Typically you would start by using blow-by oxygen. If that proved ineffective, you would switch to positive pressure ventilation. If the infant was still unresponsive, you may shift to endotracheal intubation.

15. c

    All treatments performed during neonatal resuscitation should be done for 30–60 seconds, and then the patient should be reassessed.

16. False

    A newly born infant and mother from an uncomplicated delivery situation can be transported by any paramedic crew in a standard ambulance containing standard supplies and equipment.

17. True

    According to the AHA, the term "neonate" is best used for any infant during the hospitalization phase immediately following birth. They use the term "newly born" to identify infants specifically at the time of birth.

18. Meconium is fetal fecal matter. It can be released if the fetus is stressed before delivery. As it floats around inside the amniotic sac, it can enter the fetus's mouth and nose. If the meconium is thick and tarlike or it contains chunks of any significant size, it may plug the bronchi if aspirated. To avoid respiratory compromise, you should suction out thick meconium with the meconium aspirator.

19. d

    Signs of hypovolemia due to blood volume loss include: pale color, cool skin, diminished peripheral pulses, delayed capillary refill time, lethargy, poor muscle tone, and later on, a lack of wet diapers. While dehydration is the primary cause of hypovolemia in older infants, hypovolemia in such recently born infants is more often caused by blood loss. An improperly clamped umbilical cord or a cord that was cut before it had stopped pulsating could be the cause of the hypovolemia. Some of the symptoms of hypovolemia are similar to hypoglycemia. When in doubt, a simple glucometer test can resolve the issue. (Hypoglycemia in neonates is defined as a blood sugar reading less than 40 mg/dL.)

20. c

    Hypovolemia is treated with isotonic fluid boluses of 10 mL/kg. After the bolus, reassess the infant and repeat a bolus of 5–10 mL/kg. Seek medical direction before infusing any more fluid into the newborn.

chapter 43

Pediatric Patients

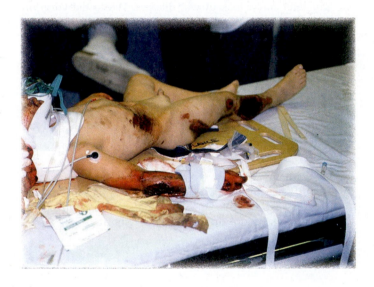

1. Based upon the mechanism of injury and the chapter-opening photograph, how would you rate the acuity of Jacob's condition?

_____

_____

_____

2. What is your first priority in caring for Jacob?

_____

_____

_____

3. Medical direction orders you to deliver fluid boluses per the American Heart Association standards. How much fluid will you deliver initially if Jacob weighs 44 pounds?

_____

_____

_____

_____

Are You Ready?

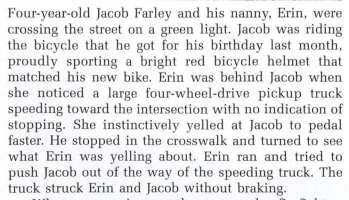

Four-year-old Jacob Farley and his nanny, Erin, were crossing the street on a green light. Jacob was riding the bicycle that he got for his birthday last month, proudly sporting a bright red bicycle helmet that matched his new bike. Erin was behind Jacob when she noticed a large four-wheel-drive pickup truck speeding toward the intersection with no indication of stopping. She instinctively yelled at Jacob to pedal faster. He stopped in the crosswalk and turned to see what Erin was yelling about. Erin ran and tried to push Jacob out of the way of the speeding truck. The truck struck Erin and Jacob without braking.

When you arrive on the scene, the firefighter-paramedic informs you that the woman is dead, and the child is alive and talking. The firefighters are attempting to extricate Jacob from under the truck.

Active Learning

1. Volunteer Opportunity: Pediatrics

Get involved in your community and learn about pediatric patients at the same time. First, pick an age group that you are least comfortable with or know the least about and go to the place where they are most likely to be (this exercise focuses on children from day care age through high school age).

If you choose preschool-aged children, for example, arrange to go to a preschool and offer to assist with some sort of education or prevention project. If you have knowledge regarding bicycle helmet sizing and use, arrange for the children to bring their bicycle helmets to school on the day that you will be there so that you can assist in helmet sizing and proper use. Attempt to find local businesses, public safety agencies, and bicycle helmet manufacturers that would be willing to donate helmets to children who cannot afford them. If you choose children of day care age, you might consider working with a representative of your local law enforcement agency to provide fingerprinting or identification cards for this age group.

There are a number of injury prevention topics that you can choose from, including motor vehicle safety, choking prevention, poisoning, bicycle and pedestrian safety, fire and burns, water safety, and firearms.

During the time spent with these children, you can experience firsthand how children of that age group function and behave. It is extremely helpful to have a teacher or a caregiver available to facilitate your interaction with the different age groups and assist you in learning about their normal behavior, growth, and development.

Once you have an idea of what is normal behavior, growth, and development, you will have a much better idea of what would be considered abnormal. After all, it is the abnormal presentations that you will be called to evaluate, treat, and transport.

When engaged with young children in these environments, you should always be accompanied by another adult to prevent any accusation of unethical behavior.

2. Assessment Practice

If you have the opportunity to spend time observing or volunteering in a pediatric clinic, a pediatrician's office, or the pediatric unit of a local hospital, you will be able to gain tremendous insight into the assessment and treatment of pediatric patients. Simply watching a practitioner who is well versed in the assessment of children is a wonderful way to develop your own assessment style, and if you have the opportunity to watch and then perform assessments with an experienced practitioner there to guide you, the experience will be even more valuable.

If you are unable to arrange such an experience, then practice assessing your children, children in your extended family, or children of friends or neighbors if they are willing to let you practice assessing their children.

3. Just How Safe?

Go to a store that sells infant-related furniture and devices. Find a changing table and measure the height of the changing surface to the floor. How does the height compare to the distance needed to meet trauma criteria? Repeat the measurement on a high chair and compare the heights. What did you find?

You Are There: Reality-Based Cases
Case 1

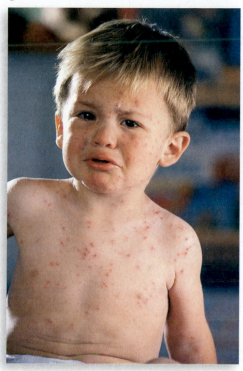

Ben is a 3-year-old who developed a rash over his entire body 3 days ago. He has stayed at home with his babysitter since the onset of the rash, and today he is complaining of abdominal pain and has a fever of 101°F.

The babysitter called 9-1-1 because she witnessed Ben having a full-body seizure.

When you arrive on the scene, you find Ben in a fetal position in bed. He is hot to the touch, responds to painful stimuli appropriately, has a very pronounced deep respiratory pattern, and his radial pulse is rapid and weak.

The sitter reports that Ben had been very tired and had vomited several times this morning.

1. How would you rate Ben's acuity based on the information that you have obtained so far?

_____

_____

_____

2. What is a possible cause for the rash seen in the photograph?

_____

_____

_____

3. What safety concerns might you have about the rash?

_____

_____

_____

4. What is your initial plan of action regarding this patient?

_____

_____

_____

5. What additional information do you need to obtain?

_____

_____

_____

6. List three possible causes for Ben's seizure.

_____

_____

_____

Your partner speaks to Ben's mother on the telephone. Ben has had a fever for the past several days, and the mother has been alternating between giving him acetaminophen and ibuprofen to address the fever per the pediatrician's instructions. The doctor informed Ben's parents that, from their description, Ben has chicken pox. Ben has been drinking an electrolyte replacement drink and water almost nonstop, and he has been urinating much more than usual. He has been trying to eat but is unable to keep anything down. Ben has received diphenhydramine and a topical lotion to help reduce the itching. The only medication that Ben takes on a regular basis is an over-the-counter multivitamin. He has had all his immunizations except the varicella vaccine. Ben's mother tells your partner where his immunization card is so that you can take it to the hospital with Ben. The immunization card shows that Ben has been immunized for polio, diphtheria, tetanus, pertussis (whooping cough), _Haemophilus influenzae_ type B, and hepatitis B. His mother states that he doesn't have any past medical history other than the "normal colds" that kids get. There is a history of diabetes and heart disease on the paternal side of the family.

The physical examination reveals the following: Ben maintains his purposeful response to painful stimuli, and he is hot to the touch. You remove his clothes down to his diaper. During the removal of his clothes, you are able to see that the rash appears to cover his entire body. You also note that his diaper is bulging with urine. His airway is clear and patent, and his breathing is rapid, deep, and slightly labored. His heart rate is rapid (164/bpm) and readily palpable centrally and peripherally. His blood pressure is 88/42. His ECG is a narrow complex tachycardia with no ectopy. His temperature is 101.2°F (axillary), his oxygen saturation is 96% on room air, and his blood sugar level is 592 mg/dL. Ben's lung sounds are clear and equal bilaterally, his reflexes are intact, and his secondary assessment is otherwise negative.

7. Has your initial impression of Ben's condition changed?

_____

_____

8. What other questions do you need to ask or what other tests should you perform to help support your general impression of Ben's condition and determine an appropriate treatment plan?

_____

_____

_____

9. Pathophysiologically, what do you think is causing Ben's current condition?

_____

_____

_____

10. Do you have any concerns regarding the previously discussed condition and pathophysiological process?

_____

_____

_____

11. Outline your treatment plan in order of priority.

_____

_____

_____

12. What considerations do you need to keep in mind while treating Ben?

_____

_____

_____

Case 2

The radio blares: "Good morning Metro dwellers, it's 6:25 in the morning, and you are listening to the Rock. Today is another 'spare the air' day, the fifth this week, and the weather bureau says that we can expect record heat and humidity for the next 3 days."

Eight-year-old Everett Price was already awake when the alarm went off. In fact, he had been up most of the night. An asthmatic since infancy, he had been up most of the night with his mother trying to manage a particularly bad attack. Everett's mother Alice had taken off 2 days this week from both her jobs to take care of Everett and his asthma.

Yesterday afternoon Everett overheard his mother talking with her boss, who told her that if she didn't come in tomorrow, she would have to start to look for a new job.

This morning when Everett went into the kitchen for breakfast, his mother asked him if he felt like he could go to school today. He felt horrible, but he told his mother that he felt fine and that he wanted to go to school. The short walk from the car to the library made Everett very short of breath, and as soon as he got there, he pulled his inhaler out of his backpack and took three hits. His shortness of breath worsened rapidly, and he felt like he couldn't breathe. Just then, Ms. Smart, his teacher, walked into the library and said hello to Everett. When he couldn't respond, Ms. Smart realized that Everett couldn't breathe and activated 9-1-1.

Shortly thereafter, the school nurse entered the library, put Everett on oxygen by mask and started to take his vital signs. The librarian said that an ambulance was on the way and the principal was contacting Everett's mother.

1. How would you rate the severity of Everett's condition?

   _____

   _____

   _____

2. What is the first priority after assessing scene safety and following standard precautions once you arrive on scene?

   _____

   _____

   _____

As you arrive in front of the school, the school nurse gives you a report regarding Everett's condition. She tells you that he has a history of asthma and has run out of his metered-dose inhaler medication. She reports that, when she first arrived in the library, she could hear audible wheezing and observed that he was very anxious. She placed him on oxygen, and now he is not wheezing and no longer seems anxious.

3. After hearing the nurse's report, can you slow down and relax, or should you hurry up and get to the patient as fast as you can? Explain your answer.

   _____

   _____

   _____

You arrive at the library. Everett is taking agonal breaths and is showing signs of perioral cyanosis. Assessment of his ABCs reveals that he has an open and patent airway and that there is almost no air movement on auscultation. His brachial pulses are very rapid and weak, and he has perioral and peripheral cyanosis, central mottling, and delayed capillary refill. His room air oxygen saturation is 76%.

4. What additional information do you need prior to initiating your treatment plan?

   _____

   _____

   _____

5. Describe your treatment plan in order of priority, giving a pathophysiological rationale for your decisions.

   _____

   _____

   _____

6. At what point will you transport, and where will you take the patient?

_____

_____

_____

Test Yourself

1. A child who creates a story about an "imaginary friend" is demonstrating the _____ defense mechanism.

2. What is a common secondary complication in febrile children?
   a. Hypoxia
   b. Hypothermia
   c. Hyperactivity
   d. Seizures

3. How do infants respond differently than other children to the effects of mild hypothermia?

   _____

   _____

4. The type of abdominal disorder that results from the slipping of a length of intestine into an adjacent portion, usually producing obstruction, is called _____.

5. You respond to a call for a sick 11-month-old child. Upon arrival, the patient's mother tells you that her son is normally alert and active but has become increasingly lethargic. You should
   a. use tools such as penlights, toys, or stickers to distract the child while you conduct a toe-to-head assessment.
   b. assure the mother that diminished activity is normal as a child transitions from the infant stage to the toddler stage.
   c. allow the child to participate in your assessment and use simple language that is age appropriate.
   d. ask the mother to leave the room while you conduct a toe-to-head assessment so the child will not be distracted by her presence.

6. You respond to a call for a 2-year-old with a seizure. The patient's mother tells you that her son has had two seizures in the last hour. The child has never had a seizure before, but the mother states he has been sick since last night so she dressed him in warm clothing and gave him an extra blanket. What is the most likely cause of the child's seizure?

   _____

   _____

7. Your pediatric patient was left in a hot, non-air-conditioned vehicle. He presents with lethargy and hot, dry skin. Which of the following conditions should you most suspect?
   a. Heat cramps
   b. Hypothermia
   c. Heat exhaustion
   d. Heatstroke

8. Use of which of the following is contraindicated in infants?
   a. Oropharyngeal airways
   b. Dual lumen airway devices
   c. Endotracheal intubation
   d. Nasopharyngeal airways

9. When treating a pediatric patient with a respiratory complaint, you should use a self-inflating resuscitation bag with a pop-off valve if available.
   True
   False

10. When administering dextrose to a pediatric patient, you should use the same concentration as you would for an adult patient.
    True
    False

11. Which age group suffers from "stranger anxiety" and should be engaged with an active assessment involving game playing?

    _____

    _____

12. A period of apnea in a pediatric patient resulting in skin color change and lack of muscle tone, followed by an apparent improvement, is termed _____.

13. Your 8-year-old patient has an obstructed airway. Which of the following methods for clearing the obstruction is contraindicated?
    a. Back blows and chest thrusts
    b. Abdominal thrusts
    c. Removal of the object with Magill forceps
    d. Blind finger sweep

14. In what ways do children respond differently to shock than adults?

_____

_____

15. You respond to the local elementary school playground for an asthma attack. Upon arrival you find a 9-year-old child who appears to be in distress holding her inhaler. She tells you that she has had asthma since she was 2 and uses two different inhalers. Discuss some things you could do to gain this patient's trust.

_____

_____

16. You are called to respond to an accidental injury where you find a small child with a head laceration. The child is conscious and answers all your questions appropriately. You estimate about a 200-mL blood loss. The child weighs about 20 kg. What other signs or symptoms would you expect to see in this patient?

_____

_____

17. You are caring for a 12-year-old cardiac patient with pulmonary edema. Medical control has ordered the administration of 1 mg/kg of furosemide. How much furosemide would you administer to this 65-pound patient?

_____

_____

18. When obtaining intravenous (IV) access in a pediatric patient, an EMS provider is *least* likely to use which of the following locations?
    a. Cephalic vein
    b. Subclavian vein
    c. Scalp vein
    d. Antecubital vein

19. What is the benefit of starting your examination at the toes and working up toward the head when conducting the physical examination of a pediatric patient?

_____

_____

20. You are called to the local high school for an unconscious patient. You are directed to the locker room where you find a female patient, whom you later learn is a senior celebrating the football team's victory. You notice a small flask next to the patient. She has suffered no apparent injuries or seizure activity, has snoring respirations, and has pupils

that are slow to react to light. What is likely the cause for her altered mental status?
    a. Sepsis
    b. Epilepsy
    c. Infection
    d. Alcohol

21. Which of the following characteristics is unique to the pediatric population?
    a. The liver and spleen are injured more often in adults than in pediatric patients.
    b. Blunt trauma to the abdomen of a child will likely not result in internal injuries.
    c. Skeletal trauma leads to secondary abdominal injuries more often in children.
    d. Children's ribs offer better protection to the liver and spleen, helping to prevent injury.

22. How do pediatric medication doses differ from adult doses?

_____

_____

23. A child has sustained blunt trauma to the chest. Which of the following complications should you *most* suspect?
    a. Internal hemorrhage
    b. Broken ribs
    c. Open chest wounds
    d. Superficial injuries

24. Fluid replacement for the pediatric patient should be administered at _____ mL/kg.

25. You are caring for a 1-month-old child who is sick and has been vomiting for 2 days. What is the highest systolic blood pressure that would indicate this patient is no longer compensating for his blood pressure?

_____

_____

26. _____ is a defect between the right and left atrial walls, which allows oxygenated blood returning from the lungs to mix with the nonoxygenated blood from the vena cava.

27. Which of the following should be your primary goal when treating a pediatric patient with a respiratory disorder?
    a. Finding and treating the cause of the respiratory disorder in all patients
    b. Preventing respiratory arrest that may lead to cardiac arrest
    c. Reducing the long-term effects of the airway disease
    d. Treating all respiratory patients aggressively with albuterol and oxygen

28. When using a colorimetric device to confirm placement of an endotracheal tube in a 4-year-old pediatric patient, which of the following will result in an appropriate color change?
    a. An improperly placed ET tube in a cardiac arrest patient
    b. The use of a pediatric-sized device
    c. The use of an adult-sized ET tube
    d. A child retaining CO_2

29. Air trapping in the alveoli due to reactive airway disease in a pediatric patient may result in
    a. impaired gas exchange.
    b. oxygen retention.
    c. decreased blood flow to the region.
    d. collapse of the bronchioles.

30. Children have a higher risk for head injuries.
    True
    False

Need to Know

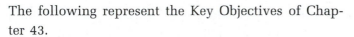

The following represent the Key Objectives of Chapter 43.

1. *Describe the epidemiology of the pediatric patient as related to trauma and illness.*

    Trauma remains the number one cause of death for children over the age of 1 year, and motor vehicle collisions are the leading cause of death among the traumatic causes of death in this age group.[1] When it comes to illness in the pediatric population, airway- and respiratory-related issues are the most common reason for EMS activation, followed by seizures and altered mental status.[2] Cardiac arrest in the pediatric population is rare and is typically the result of respiratory compromise or respiratory arrest.[3] When cardiopulmonary arrest takes place in the prehospital setting, it is almost always a terminal event.[4] This being the case, paramedics must maintain a constant state of awareness for conditions that can lead to cardiopulmonary arrest and address them early and aggressively.

2. *Describe the developmental characteristics of pediatric patients.*

    A basic knowledge of the expected developmental milestones for the pediatric population affords the paramedic the ability to identify atypical development and behavior. Atypical findings in these areas are an indicator that there may be an underlying medical condition that the paramedic needs to address. Review Table 43-1 in the textbook for a summary of expected behaviors for specific age groups.

3. *Describe the anatomical and physiological changes that occur during pediatric growth and development.*

    In the pediatric population, the head is proportionally larger than the body, especially in the occipital region. As a result children are at a higher risk for head injuries when they suffer traumatic injuries (falls, motor vehicle collisions, etc.) and positional airway obstruction when they are unconscious. The tongue is large relative to the size of the oral cavity and can obstruct the airway if the patient becomes unconscious. Until approximately age 5, the short, narrow trachea also increases the risk of airway obstruction, and the dependence on the diaphragm for breathing places children at a greater risk for metabolic acidosis due to inefficient CO_2 expiration when they suffer from conditions such as asthma or those that cause respiratory depression.

    The body surface area of infants is large relative to their weight, predisposing them to heat loss and hypothermia. Children also have very high metabolic rates that demand significant energy sources and oxygen supplies (pediatric patients' oxygen requirements are twice those of adults, and their oxygen reserves are smaller).

    Until their early teens, children have relatively fast respiratory rates, small lung volumes, and small alveoli. In addition, cardiac output is primarily rate dependent due to a relatively fixed stroke volume.

4. *Explain assessment techniques for the pediatric patient.*

    Three factors have proven to be very important in the assessment of pediatric patients. These are appearance, work of breathing, and circulation to the skin. The American Academy of Pediatrics uses these three factors in an assessment tool called the Pediatric Assessment Triangle (PAT) (Figure 43-1).

    The premise of the PAT is that each of the three components is equally important and interrelated. If there is a compromise to any of these components, the child's physiological baseline can be compromised. For example, if there is a compromise to the circulation of a child, then work of

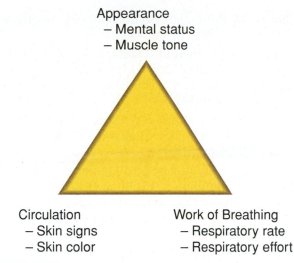

Appearance
– Mental status
– Muscle tone

Circulation
– Skin signs
– Skin color

Work of Breathing
– Respiratory rate
– Respiratory effort

FIGURE 43-1 The Pediatric Assessment Triangle (PAT).

breathing and appearance will soon follow. Therefore, if an abnormality is discovered during the assessment of a child using the PAT, it needs to be followed up with an immediate corrective action (treatment). If there is a compromise to any of the components of the PAT, the patient should be considered critical until proven otherwise.

Primary points to consider when performing the PAT assessment include:

Airway: Is the airway open? Is the airway patent?

Breathing: Is there adequate rise and fall of the chest? Does the child use accessory muscles with ventilation? Is there nasal flaring? Are there retractions? What are the breath sounds?

Circulation: What is the color and temperature of the skin? How is the skin turgor? What is the capillary refill time? Are peripheral and central pulses readily palpable? (If there is a noticeable difference between the central and the peripheral pulses, the child is likely in a state of hypoperfusion.)

Level of consciousness is another factor that plays an important role in the primary assessment of a pediatric patient. The AVPU scale can be applied universally to both children and adults. The Glasgow Coma Scale is modified in the verbal section to accommodate for age differences:

Best verbal response (V)
5. Infant coos or babbles (normal activity).
4. Infant is irritable and continually cries.
3. Infant cries to pain.
2. Infant moans to pain.
1. No verbal response.

Different approaches to patient assessment may need to be considered based on the patient's age and stage of development. Young children will typically be frightened by the presence of a stranger. If at all possible, ease into the assessment of children by performing a toe-to-head assessment as opposed to a head-to-toe assessment. This will get you down to their level and give the children confidence that you are not there to hurt them. This approach will ease you into your assessment of more personal areas including the head and the torso (see Chapter 43, Pediatric Patients, in the textbook for detailed information on specific assessment techniques for all the body systems).

5. *Describe the general treatment approach for pediatric patients in the prehospital setting.*

Assess the airway. If the airway is open and patent, and the patient requires ventilatory assistance and supplemental oxygen, ventilate with a bag-mask device attached to a high-concentration oxygen source, along with an airway adjunct such as an OPA to maintain the patent airway. If the patient can be managed with these basic interventions, no more invasive airway management techniques need be attempted. If the OPA and the bag-mask are not maintaining the airway, or if there is a need to isolate the airway, as in the setting of bleeding or vomiting into the airway, then more invasive techniques such as endotracheal (ET) intubation can be considered.

When it comes to determining the appropriate size equipment for ET intubation, there are a number of ways to approach this decision. For example, the choice of uncuffed ET tubes can be determined by a variety of methods, ranging from something as crude as comparing the diameter of the ET tube to the diameter of the patient's pinky finger, to more scientific approaches to determining the ET tube size such as the following formula:

4 + (Age in years/4)

= Size of ET tube in millimeters

The use of a length-based tape will give the paramedic not only the appropriate ET tube size, but also the appropriate size of the laryngoscope blade, etc. (Figure 43-2).

Intravenous (IV) access may be needed for a number of reasons. IO lines are typically reserved for patients who are *in extremis* due to the invasiveness of the procedure. When established, IO lines are as efficient as peripheral IVs in delivering fluid and medications to the central circulation.

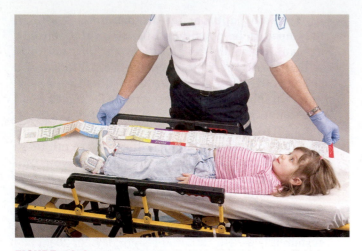

FIGURE 43-2 The use of a length-based tape will help the paramedic determine weight, equipment size, and medication dosages in children.

Medication administration is very rare in the prehospital setting because of the effectiveness of current oxygenation and fluid replacement capabilities. When medications are required, the paramedic should adhere to local protocols and/or adhere to national guidelines such as the American Heart Association's pediatric advanced life support (PALS) algorithms.

Connections

- The Centers for Disease Control and Prevention website (www.cdc.gov) provides information on childhood immunizations.

- Chapter 28, Pulmonary, in the textbook describes asthma in depth.
- Chapter 31, Endocrine, Electrolytes, and Acid/Base, in the textbook provides additional information on diabetes, diabetic ketoacidosis, and electrolyte disturbances.
- Chapter 33, Infectious and Communicable Diseases, in the textbook explains chicken pox and other childhood diseases.
- Kids represent a special and challenging part of the patient population. Problem-Based Learning Case 7, Bravery Comes in All Forms, will help you explore this group in greater detail.
- RSV and asthma. Respiratory syncytial virus can cause a variety of upper respiratory illnesses and bronchiolitis. There is a strong link between RSV and asthma that is not yet clearly understood. When assessing a pediatric patient with first-time wheezing, check for a past medical history of a stuffy nose, deep cough, low-grade fever, or ear infection.
- Link to the companion DVD for a chapter-based quiz, audio glossary, animations, games and exercises, and, when appropriate, skill sheets and skill Step-by-Steps.

Street Secrets

- **Pediatric Transport** Paramedics tend to be less proficient in the assessment and treatment of pediatric patients than they are with adults. Because of this, when on the scene of a critically ill or injured child, it may be prudent to begin transport as soon as possible ("scoop and run"), rather than performing a myriad of procedures ("stay and

Need to Do

The following skills are explained and illustrated in a step-by-step manner, via skill sheets and/or Step-by-Steps in this text and on the accompanying DVD:

Skill Name	Skill Sheet Number and Location	Step-by-Step Number and Location
Intraosseous Access and Drug Administration	45 – Appendix A and DVD	45 – Chapter 16 and DVD
Nebulized Drug Administration	52 – Appendix A and DVD	52 – Chapter 16 and DVD
Verbal Communications	63 – DVD	N/A
NREMT Pediatric Ventilatory Management	90 – DVD	N/A
NREMT Pediatric Intraosseous Infusion	91 – DVD	N/A

play"). Most interventions can be done while transporting the patient in the ambulance.

- **Just Do It** If, during the process of evaluating a pediatric patient, you find yourself debating whether or not to perform an intervention, a good rule of thumb is that the patient will probably benefit from the intervention. Because pediatric assessment and care is an infrequent part of the typical paramedic's day, paramedics tend to undertreat pediatric patients rather than overtreat them. For example, if you are considering the administration of oxygen to a patient who seems slightly dyspneic, but you don't want to upset the patient, you should administer the oxygen. If you believe that the patient is dehydrated, but you don't want to try to start an IV because "kids have small veins" and you are "not far from the hospital," try to start an IV en route to the hospital.

- **Temperature** Keep pediatric patients warm (especially trauma patients), but not too warm (especially children with high fevers). If a child has a high fever, remove the child's clothes down to the diaper or underwear to help cool the patient. *Do not* use rubbing alcohol to cool a child down, because it can be absorbed through the skin and its vapors can be inhaled, which can result in coma or seizures. If the ambient temperature is cold, a light blanket can be placed over the patient to prevent shivering (shivering is the body's natural heat-generating mechanism and should be avoided in children with fever).

The Drug Box

Albuterol (Proventil, Ventolin, Volmax): A beta-adrenergic sympathomimetic bronchodilator used to relax bronchial smooth muscle in patients who are suffering from asthma and other reactive airway diseases.

Metaproterenol (Alupent): A sympathomimetic bronchodilator used in the treatment of asthma and reversible bronchospasm.

Ipratropium (Atrovent): A synthetic anticholinergic similar to atropine used in the treatment of bronchospasm.

Epinephrine (Adrenalin): A beta-adrenergic agonist with some alpha effects. Used in asthmatics to treat bronchospasm through its beta$_2$ effects.

Terbutaline (Brethine, Bricanyl): A sympathomimetic used to treat reversible bronchospasm in asthmatics.

Magnesium sulfate: A magnesium supplement that is used to promote bronchodilation and improve airflow during asthmatic exacerbations.

Corticosteroids (prednisone, prednisolone, methylprednisolone, hydrocortisone, dexamethasone, betamethasone, etc.): Used to address the acute and chronic inflammation that results from asthma and other reactive airway disorders.

Combivent: A combination of albuterol and ipratropium.

References

1. Emergency Medical Services for Children, http://books.nap.edu/catalog/2137.html (accessed May 20, 2006).
2. Ibid.
3. A. G. Reis et al., "A Prospective Investigation into the Epidemiology of In-Hospital Pediatric Cardiopulmonary Resuscitation Using the International Utstein Reporting Style," *Pediatrics* 109, no. 2 (February 2002): 200–209.
4. Ibid.

Answers

Are You Ready?

1. Jacob is a critical trauma patient due to the mechanism of injury and apparent or potential injuries.
2. The first priority is to safely remove him from under the vehicle. Assess his ABCs while maintaining cervical spine alignment, and address any life threats discovered during the primary assessment.
3. If Jacob weighs 44 pounds (20 kg) and the initial fluid bolus for a pediatric patient is 20 mL/kg, then Jacob should receive 400 mL of an isotonic solution such as normal saline or lactated Ringer's solution IV.

You Are There: Reality-Based Cases

Case 1

1. Ben has a diminished level of consciousness following what may have been a seizure. He is febrile, and he has an obvious rash over a majority of his body. Ben is a critical patient.
2. The rash is classic for varicella, otherwise known as chicken pox.
3. Varicella is very contagious, especially since some of the blisters appear to be weeping. Isolate this patient from other people, and you should don a mask and eye shield in addition to gloves for your own protection.
4. The initial action for this patient is to assess his airway, breathing, and circulation and to correct any life threats that may be discovered during the primary assessment.
5. A secondary assessment should be performed. This should include a complete head-to-toe examination and a

complete set of vital signs (heart rate, blood pressure, respiratory rate, ECG, pulse oximetry, temperature) and a blood sugar level. The patient's babysitter should be questioned about the patient's prior medical history and any medications that he takes on a regular basis. If possible, obtain a complete SAMPLE history.

6. Children of Ben's age group are susceptible to seizures caused by a spike in temperature. Paramedics who encounter febrile pediatric patients frequently assume that the fever is the cause of the seizure. There are a number of other possible causes of seizures other than fever, including electrolyte imbalance secondary to emesis, epilepsy, hypoglycemia or hyperglycemia, poisoning, infection, trauma, psychosis (pseudo-seizures), hypoxia, arrhythmia, and hypovolemia.

7. If you assumed that the seizure was related to Ben's fever, your general impression has likely changed. Regardless, Ben remains in critical condition. Although fever is still a possible cause of the seizure, the results of the history and physical examination have brought up another strong possibility.

8. Additional assessment points include evaluation of the odor of Ben's breath and questioning about medications for the treatment of diabetes (insulin or an oral agent), how long the excessive thirst and urination have been present (did it start before the chicken pox became evident or after), how many diapers a day has Ben gone through since the onset of the excessive thirst and urination compared to his normal, and how much electrolyte replacement drink and water he has been drinking per day. Because the blood sugar was high, a repeat assessment of the blood sugar is warranted.

9. There is likely more than one disease process contributing to Ben's current condition. Chicken pox with a fever is likely one of the contributing factors, and hyperglycemia, with the possibility of diabetic ketoacidosis (DKA), is another possible contributing factor.

   Ben presented with the following signs: excessive thirst (polydipsia), excessive urination (polyuria), fatigue, nausea and vomiting, fever, tachycardia, atypical respiratory pattern (Kussmaul's respirations), and hyperglycemia. With a blood glucose level greater than 300 mg/dL, it is good practice to assume that the patient is experiencing DKA, even if he or she does not have a diagnosed history of diabetes. DKA results from a lack of insulin and involves a change in metabolism. In DKA normal glucose utilization does not occur; therefore alternative energy sources, including lipids and proteins, are metabolized.

   Diabetic ketoacidosis is frequently identified when marked hyperglycemia is discovered. (You learned about DKA in Chapter 31, Endocrine, Electrolytes, and Acid/Base, in the textbook; you may want to review that chapter in regards to ketone body production.) Early symptoms of DKA include increased thirst, excessive hunger, increased urination, and general malaise. Later signs include Kussmaul's respirations, coma, and hypotension due to dehydration.

10. The osmotic diuresis can lead to electrolyte imbalances such as hyponatremia and hyperkalemia or hypokalemia. *Hyperkalemia* (occurring when potassium is drawn out of the cells of the body secondary to the large concentration of sugar in the bloodstream) can cause weakness, peaked T waves, widened QRS complexes, and diarrhea. *Hypokalemia* (resulting from osmotic diuresis—elimination in the urine) can cause weakness and fatigue, flat T waves on the ECG, dysrhythmias, PVCs, decreased cardiac output, and respiratory arrest. *Hyponatremia* (resulting from osmotic diuresis) can cause weakness, altered mental status, seizures, abdominal cramping, nausea and emesis, and hypotension. DKA is frequently accompanied by a metabolic acidosis that can lead to an altered level of consciousness, weakness, hypotension, dysrhythmias and tachycardia, and a number of serious ECG changes depending on the associated electrolyte changes.

11. Since Ben's airway is patent and his breathing is deep and rapid, oxygen may be administered via nonrebreather mask with high-flow oxygen. Early transport to an appropriate facility is important because the definitive care for hyperglycemia is the administration of insulin, and insulin is seldom used in the prehospital setting. Because of Ben's tachycardia, it is prudent to assume that he is compensating for fluid loss (in the form of urine), and fluid replacement should be initiated. A peripheral IV should be established, and a 20-mL/kg fluid bolus should be delivered.

12. Do not administer more than one 20-mL/kg fluid bolus to these patients, as excessive fluid can lead to cerebral edema and many other problems. If the patient remains volume depleted after the administration of 20 mL/kg of isotonic IV fluid, contact medical direction for consultation. In addition, the potassium level needs to be evaluated and corrected prior to the administration of insulin or the patient may experience life-threatening arrhythmias as a result of the shifting of potassium back into the cells (hypokalemia) along with insulin and glucose.

Case 2

1. Everett is a critical respiratory distress patient who may be on the verge of respiratory failure.

2. After assessing scene safety and following standard precautions, the first step is to assess and treat any life threats to Everett's airway, breathing, and circulation.

3. There are two possibilities in this situation: one is that the patient has improved, and the other is that the patient has deteriorated. It is not likely that a patient who has been suffering from shortness of breath for several days with little relief from bronchodilator medications will improve with the administration of oxygen alone. The lack of audible wheezing may likely be an indication that his bronchospasm is so severe that he is no longer moving enough air to produce a wheeze. The fact that he no longer appears anxious may mean that he is exhausted and needs immediate intervention.

4. Ask the nurse for Everett's emergency contact card, which may contain up-to-date information about his medical history, medications that he is taking, and any allergies he has to medications. It will also have contact information for his mother, so you can have the nurse or your partner call and gather the information that you need.

5. The first priority of care for Everett is to provide 100% oxygen and supplement his agonal ventilations with a bag-mask. This should be done in conjunction with the administration of bronchodilating medications, which will cause relaxation of the bronchial smooth muscle and allow for air movement in the lungs and subsequent improvement in gas exchange.

   As you assist Everett's ventilations, keep in mind that individuals with asthma experience three primary problems: (1) First, the bronchioles spasm and constrict in response to a "trigger" or stimulus. (2) Copious amounts of mucus are excreted within the airway walls, which further restricts the airflow and begins to create obstructions at the alveolar level. (3) A fluid shift within the cells of the airway wall results in swelling and increases the potential for "air trapping." The air-trapping factor means that air can enter the airways but then becomes trapped and cannot be easily exhaled. When a paramedic provides positive pressure ventilations (whether it is via a bag-mask and a basic airway, via a bag-mask and an ETT, or via a continuous positive airway pressure device), there is an increased risk of exacerbating the air trapping even if you simultaneously begin to provide bronchodilator medications.

   There are a number of medications that can be administered to provide relief of severe symptoms of an asthma attack. They include epinephrine 1:1,000 delivered subcutaneously or intravenously, for both beta- and alpha-adrenergic effects. A beta agonist like albuterol may be helpful, but the loss of ventilation may render an updraft ineffective. Other possible medications include metaproterenol, Atrovent, terbutaline, magnesium sulfate, and corticosteroids.

6. It is best to transport early and provide a majority of the treatment while en route to a hospital. Focus on basic procedures to oxygenate and ventilate the patient while preparing for transport. You may need to establish vascular access prior to loading the patient, because vascular access will be easier to obtain while the patient is perfusing than if he deteriorates into cardiopulmonary arrest. It would also be important to have IV or intraosseous access in the event that fluid and/or medication administration is needed during the loading of the patient into the ambulance.

Test Yourself

1. Fantasy

   Creating a story or series of stories to buffer the impact of objectionable behavior through the use of imaginary characters is an example of the fantasy defense mechanism.

2. d

   If the rise in body temperature of a child is acute or rapid, the child may experience a febrile seizure.

3. Infants do not shiver.

   Like many mammalian newborns, human infants do not have the ability to shiver, most likely because they have poorly developed muscle tissue. In order to generate heat, infants burn a specific type of fat tissue called brown fat. Infants do not have a large reserve of brown fat and may lose body heat rapidly if hypothermic conditions are not corrected.

4. Intussusception

   Intussusception occurs most often in infants and toddlers, primarily in children under 2 years of age. Common symptoms include: urgent crying due to abdominal pain, vomiting, "currant jelly" stools, abdominal swelling or distention, lethargy, and shallow breathing. If left untreated, the child may develop fever and shock. Prehospital treatment includes symptomatic treatment (pain management) and transport. Definitive treatment usually requires a barium or air enema, or surgery.

5. a

   Pediatric patients between the ages of 1 and 12 months are in the infant stage of development. Healthy infants should be alert and attentive to activity around them and will track the paramedic with their eyes. Infants can straighten their extremities but may prefer flexed positioning. They can generally roll over starting at 3–6 months, can sit up by themselves at 6–8 months, and may start walking in the late stages of infancy. Infants may exhibit separation anxiety and be "clingy" to their parents. You should not separate an infant from his parents during your toe-to-head assessment, but you may want to distract him with a penlight, stickers, or toys. Infants are too young to take an active role in assessment, treatment, or care decisions.

6. Fever

   Febrile seizures are a normal reaction to a sudden or sharp rise in body temperature, most commonly seen in children less than 6 years of age. Based on the child's history of illness and apparent chills, it is likely that this child has a fever. The mother caused an additional increase in body temperature by dressing the patient in warm clothing and giving the child an extra blanket, which may have been enough to inhibit the body's ability to cool.

7. d

   Heatstroke is the most severe form of heat illness. It can occur even in people who are not exercising if the environment is hot enough. These patients have warm, flushed skin and usually do not sweat. Other symptoms of heatstroke include a body temperature above 103°F; a rapid, strong pulse; a throbbing headache; dizziness; nausea; confusion; and unconsciousness.

8. b

   Use of dual lumen airway devices (Combitubes and PTLs) are contraindicated in pediatric patients due to only being available in adult sizes and the potential damage they may cause to a child's airway.

9. False

A self-inflating resuscitation bag should be self-refilling and should not have a pop-off valve.

10. False

Dextrose must be diluted for use in pediatric patients. For newborns: 5–10 mL/kg of $D_{10}W$ bolus; for infants: 0.5–1.0 g/kg of $D_{25}W$ bolus; for children: 0.5–1.0 g/kg of $D_{50}W$ bolus; and for young adults: 0.5–1.0 g/kg of $D_{25}W$ bolus.

11. Toddlers (1–3 years old)

When assessing a toddler, paramedics should conduct a toe-to-head exam while making a game of the assessment process. It is also important to involve the parents because this age group suffers from separation or stranger anxiety.

12. An apparent life-threatening event (ALTE)

An apparent life-threatening event (ALTE) is a period of apnea accompanied by other respiratory complications (such as choking or gagging), skin color change, or change of muscle tone. Some have referred to ALTE as "near-miss SIDS," although an underlying organic origin is usually found.

13. d

A blind finger sweep is contraindicated in all pediatric patients 14 years of age and younger, as this may fully occlude the trachea by pushing the object farther down the airway.

14. Children typically present with signs and symptoms of mild shock at significantly lesser amounts of fluid loss. They remain in compensated shock longer than adults, but their vital signs deteriorate much more rapidly once they are in decompensated shock.

Children have proportionally less blood volume to body mass and typically present with signs and symptoms of shock at significantly lesser amounts of fluid loss. Most adults will not show significant signs of shock (BP below 90 mm Hg) until they have lost 25%–40% of their fluid volume, while children may become anxious or irritable and tachycardic with as little as 5% volume loss. Children have stronger, healthier cardiovascular systems, which have a remarkable ability to constrict. Their vascular system has the profound ability to shunt circulation from the extremities to the central circulation, allowing the patient to remain in compensated shock longer. Finally, the cardiac output capabilities of children are dictated by the rate of contractions. Infants and young children do not have the ability to increase their contractility or stroke volume and must therefore rely solely on increasing their cardiac rate.

15. The best way to gain this patient's trust is to communicate simply and directly with her, allow her to participate in assessment and treatments, and treat her with respect and professionalism.

School-aged children (aged 6–12 years) seem to have an innate ability to sense fear, joy, anger, shame, truth, dishonesty, and emotional projections by others. This places paramedics in a compromising situation if they attempt to be less than forthright with the child. Using toys and stories during your assessment may seem like condescension to this age group, and this patient won't want to be treated "like a baby."

16. Tachycardia and tachypnea (signs of compensated shock), followed by sudden deterioration of vital signs as the child enters a state of decompensated shock.

The total blood volume for a 20-kg patient would be 80 mL/kg × 20 kg = 1,600 mL. A loss of 200 mL would constitute a 12.5% blood loss (200 mL/1,600 mL = 12.5%). A blood loss of as little as 5% (80 mL/kg × 20 kg × 5% = 80 mL) may be enough to invoke shock in a pediatric patient. Because head injuries bleed a lot, you might expect to see tachycardia followed by hypotension because of the child's inability to effectively maintain stroke volume or cardiac output.

17. 30 mg

The dose of pediatric furosemide is 1 mg/kg; therefore, since 65 lb = 30 kg, you should administer 1 mg/kg × 30 kg = 30 mg.

18. b

IV access is generally achieved through venipuncture of the hand, radial, antecubital, medial cephalic, scalp, or external jugular vein just like for the adult. (*Note:* Local protocols may dictate the inclusion or exclusion of specific locations.) As technology and medical protocols continue to advance, the use of intraosseous (IO) access has also become an accepted practice.

19. Conducting a toe-to-head exam establishes trust and reduces the patient's fear of a stranger assessing the "personal zone."

The toe-to-head method forces you to get down to the patient's eye level. Starting your physical assessment from the toes also allows for the trust relationship to begin in earnest. There is less anxiety generated from a stranger touching the toes or feet than there would be touching the "personal zone"—the nose down to the symphysis pubis.

20. d

Based on these findings and the patient's age group (adolescent), it is likely her AMS is due to alcohol. Remember that members of this age group are susceptible to the influences of their peers, trusted adults, and their environment. The presentation of AMS may well be chemically induced (illicit drugs, prescription medications, over-the-counter medications, alcohol, or other consciousness-altering substances), whether intentional or unintentional. The U.S. Department of Health and Human Services, Substance Abuse and Mental Health Services Administration (SAMHSA) reports that 29% of young adults consume alcohol.

21. c

Abdominal trauma has several unique characteristics in the pediatric population. It is more common for a child to have an abdominal injury secondary to or associated with skeletal and head injuries. Because the rib cage does not fully protect their liver and spleen, these organs are injured at a higher frequency.

22. Medications are used less often with pediatric patients, and the dosage is more often weight-based in pediatric patients.

Medications are utilized with pediatric patients a small percentage of the time, especially when compared to adult patients. That being said, when necessary, *do not withhold* medications from patients simply because they are children. Medications administered to children are the same as those given to adults, with the exception of the dose.

23. a

A young child's ribs are soft and flexible and therefore less likely to break, even when the blunt force trauma is significant enough to cause internal organ damage and hemorrhage. You should always maintain a high level of suspicion for any condition that can lead to shock in a pediatric patient, since signs of compensated shock can be very subtle, and once a child is in decompensated shock his or her condition can deteriorate extremely rapidly. Internal hemorrhage is the most likely potential cause of shock in a child with blunt trauma to the chest, and you should therefore maintain a high index of suspicion.

24. 20

IV or IO access with infusion should occur at a rate of 20 mL/kg and may be repeated based on the patient's response and condition.

25. 60 mm Hg

Normal blood pressure in a 1-month-old ranges from 65–95 mm Hg systolic; therefore, a blood pressure of 60 mm Hg would be the highest pressure associated with decompensation.

26. Atrial septal defect

Atrial septal defect (ASD) is present in 4 out of every 100,000 people. If there are no other defects, the child may be asymptomatic. Children with ASD are susceptible to infective endocarditis, atrial fibrillation, and heart failure. Symptoms include palpitations, shortness of breath, and difficulty breathing.

27. b

Treatment for the respiratory disorder patient should be aimed at preventing the progression of respiratory arrest into cardiac arrest. This is accomplished by treating the disorder aggressively with oxygen. The treatments and medications vary based on symptomatology and cause, ranging from cold air exposure to the use of racemic epinephrine. The cause of respiratory disorders may not be apparent and is not always treatable in the prehospital setting.

28. b

A pediatric-sized device should be used in young pediatric patients. The dead air space in the adult-sized devices may cause false readings or facilitate retained CO_2 to be delivered back into the child resulting in an increasing hypercarbia and/or hypoxia. It is also worth noting that in cardiac arrest, the lack of color change may not be indicative of an improperly placed ET tube, because the presence of CO_2 in a cardiac arrest state diminishes over time. In this type of situation, do not remove an ET tube based solely on the change in color of a colorimetric device or lack thereof.

29. a

Reactive airway disease (RAD) is the result of the bronchioles spasming and constricting in response to a "trigger" or stimulus, causing a decrease in the diameter of the airways and an increase in airflow restriction. Massive amounts of mucus are excreted within the airway walls, which further restricts the airflow and begins to create blockages at the alveolar level. The final change is an increase in the fluids or a fluid shift within the cells of the airway wall, causing further restriction and increasing the potential for "air trapping." Once air becomes trapped in the alveoli, the potential for collapse is significant. The collapsed area continues to receive blood through the vascular system, but gases are not exchanged. As a critical mass of alveoli collapse, the significance of atelectasis and the degree of hypoxemia increase. As the unoxygenated blood continues to return to the heart and arterial system, the hemodynamic status of the child starts to deteriorate. It is easy to see why, once this vicious cycle begins, aggressive therapy is required.

30. True

A child's head is proportionally larger than the body, putting them at a higher risk for head injuries any time they defy the law of gravity.

Geriatric Patients

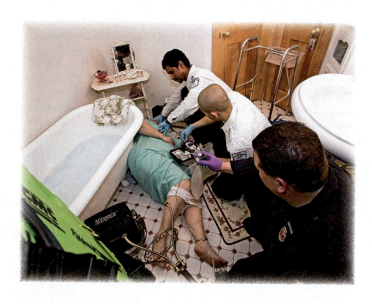

Are You Ready?

Sophie Peters was in pain. It kept her from getting up from the cool, tiled floor of her bathroom. How long had she been there? Sophie wasn't sure. With no windows in her small bathroom, it was hard to tell if it was night or day. She had come in to take her evening bath; everything seemed to be normal. She remembered suddenly getting very warm, and then nothing. She was disoriented; for a moment she thought she was getting out of the tub. But when she tried to sit up, a shattering, stabbing pain shot from her hip, up her spine, and down her legs. She cried out, but since she lived alone, no one heard her. Slowly she realized that she was lying on the floor, next to her tub. She could not sit up; any movement caused her pain to worsen dramatically.

As time went on, she contemplated her fate. Would she die here on the floor? She honestly couldn't answer her own question. She felt herself slowly become numb, except for the constant pain in her hip. Eventually she urinated on the floor; even in her agony she felt a bit embarrassed. Her phone rang a few times; she hoped it was her daughter calling to check on her.

Sophie dozed on and off through the pain. Slowly she became aware of something breaking in the front of the house—was that glass? She tried to call out, but she could not feel her lips move. In the sudden glare of the bathroom light an unfocused face appeared suddenly, as a paramedic knelt down to be close to Sophie. "Ma'am, are you okay? Can you hear me?" he called to her. "My name is Ahmid, I am a paramedic. We are going to take good care of you." Sophie again tried to respond but could not. Ahmid could see this. "Don't move ma'am. Let's get you out of here safely and then we'll talk, okay?"

1. If you were the paramedic, what steps would you take to manage this patient? What possible conditions concern you?

_____

_____

_____

Active Learning

1. Getting a Sense of the Situation

To get a better understanding of how the loss of senses can impact activities of daily living, try the follow activities:

a. *Sight.* Find a pair of glasses. If you do not have your own, use the safety glasses or goggles you have in the classroom. Cover one lens with opaque paper and put the glasses on. Have a friend or partner arrange a series of objects on a table, both close and far from you. Have a few additional objects placed on the floor. Now try to reach each article as if to pick it up. Were you able to do so on the first attempt, or did you have to adjust your "aim"? Why is that? Next, lightly smear a very thin coating of petroleum jelly over the lenses. Put them on and try to read this paragraph. You might try to read a newspaper article or the prescription information on a medication bottle.

b. *Sound.* Use a good pair of earplugs or earphones to greatly reduce your hearing ability. Have a friend or partner read something to you while sitting in front of you so you can see his or her face. Your partner should read the passage in a very quiet voice, like a whisper. Were you able to understand what was being said? Now, close your eyes and have your partner read another passage in the same low voice. Did you find it more difficult to understand what he or she said? Why is that? How does this exercise relate to your communications with a patient with a hearing impairment?

c. *Touch.* Don two pairs of examination gloves. If possible, use one size *smaller* than your regular size. Try to grasp objects of various sizes—for example, a baseball, a book, or a pill. How hard was it to grasp the smaller objects? Try a simple activity like tying your shoelaces. Was it a challenge? Do you think patients with arthritis have similar problems?

d. *Mobility.* Tie your shoes together in such a way that allows you to move your feet apart by no more than 12 inches. During the course of a few hours, try to move around as normally as possible (be careful about falling!). How difficult was it to move around, even when not walking? As a bonus, apply a couple of ladder splints to your knees in such a way as to keep them slightly bent. With your shoes still tied, try to move about. How can reduced mobility impact daily activities? Did you try walking up a stairway? What about picking something up off the floor?

2. Volunteer Opportunity: Geriatrics

Take a trip to a convalescent home or skilled nursing facility (SNF) after making arrangements with the administrator. Engage in any of the following activities:

- *Spend time with staff.* Ask about common conditions in their clients, including past medical history and medications. Ask how they manage clients with long-term mental status changes such as Alzheimer's disease or other forms of dementia. What techniques do they use to move clients comfortably and safely for both the patient and caregiver?

- *Interview a few clients.* Ask if you can perform a physical examination and elicit a medical history. Practice empathy and your communication skills—if possible engage with clients who are hard of hearing or visually impaired. Spend time simply talking with an older person. You may find the encounter to be quite illuminating. You might want to begin with a general question like, "Where were you born?" Let the conversation take its course. As trust is established, you might be able to delve into details of medical conditions that impact the client's life. Explore those relationships, and consider how you might be able to integrate your experience into future patient encounters.

The preceding exercise can also be easily done in the back of your ambulance. As an EMT you might be transporting geriatric patients to and from health-care facilities. Don't let the opportunity to practice your assessment and history-taking skills pass you by!

You Are There: Reality-Based Cases

Case 1 (continued from chapter opener)

Ahmid and his crew worked carefully and gently around the patient. Performing his primary assessment, Ahmid decided to immobilize Sophie's cervical spine and provide supplemental oxygen. He directed the crew to apply a cervical collar and remove the patient's soiled nightgown. They retrieved a few blankets from the closet and draped the patient to reduce any further heat loss and preserve modesty.

A physical examination and history was obtained. Findings included:

Age: 81.

Weight: 85 kg.

LOC: Confused to day, date, and time.

Vital signs: Irregular HR of 112, BP of 100/62, and shallow RR of 26; SpO$_2$ at 95% with high-flow oxygen.

HEENT: Bruise to left side of her head. Evidence of cut lip and tongue. (–) JVD. No accessory muscle usage noted. Medical pendant around neck indicating IDDM and HTN.

Chest: Equal rise and fall of the chest. Lung sounds were clear bilaterally, diminished at the bases. Pain upon palpation left lower aspects of rib cage. Bruising noted in same location. Chest wall cold to the touch.

Abdomen: Distended, soft, nontender to palpation. No obvious masses or bruising noted.

Pelvis: Incontinent of urine. Pain noted to left posterior and anterior hip. Externally rotated left leg that is shorter than the right. Large, reddened bruise noted in area of injury.

Extremities: Decreased pulses to lower extremities. Upper extremities have equal pulses, and decreased strength and sensation to left upper and lower extremities. Edema to both ankles.

Allergies to medications: Unknown.

Medications taken: Isophane insulin using an insulin pen device, Isoptin, HCTZ, Colace, multivitamin, calcium supplement.

Past medical history: Patient unable to provide medical history.

Last oral intake: Unknown

Events leading up to current condition: The patient's daughter contacted 9-1-1 after being unable to reach her mother by phone for a day. You estimate that your patient has been on the floor for approximately 24 hours.

1. What are possible underlying conditions that could explain Mrs. Peters' presentation? Which condition(s) are most likely?

_____

_____

_____

Test Yourself

1. A 74-year-old woman is complaining of upper-arm pain. She tells you that she tripped over a rug and fell to the floor landing on her right arm. The patient experienced no loss of consciousness and denies neck or back pain. She has a history of diabetes and high blood pressure. How should you care for her injury?

   a. Apply spinal immobilization and closely monitor her vital signs.

   b. Sedate the patient and realign the extremity.

   c. Transport the patient in a position of comfort.

   d. Splint the extremity and transport.

2. Which of the following is a normal physiological change in the cardiovascular system associated with aging?

   a. Loss of elastin and collagen

   b. Increase in the number of muscle cells

   c. Decrease in systolic blood pressure

   d. Decreased size of the myocardium

3. Which visual disturbance, commonly found in the elderly, presents with increased intraocular pressure and vision loss?

   _____

   _____

4. Which of the following groups of diseases is complicated by hypertension?

   a. Diabetes, renal failure, and seizure

   b. Stroke, blindness, and cataracts

   c. Diabetes, renal failure, and emphysema

   d. Diabetes, aneurysms, and myocardial infarctions

5. Which of the following statements about changes in lung physiology due to aging is *false*?

   a. Environmental stressors such as smoking can prematurely age lung tissue.

   b. Childhood infection may impact the health of lung tissue in geriatric patients.

c. Exercise tolerance is markedly decreased due to changes in recoil and elasticity.

d. Cardiorespiratory exercise may negatively impact an aging pulmonary system.

6. Preexisting diseases such as Parkinson's disease, Alzheimer's, dementia, and stroke can contribute to depression in the geriatric population.

True

False

7. What causes decreased respiratory function in geriatric patients?

_____

_____

8. Your geriatric patient is complaining of fatigue; headache; a weak, dry cough; and rhinitis. Your patient's symptoms are most likely caused by

a. respiratory syncytial virus.

b. *Escherichia coli.*

c. influenza.

d. *Mycobacterium tuberculosis.*

9. What is the difference between dementia and delirium?

_____

_____

10. Discuss some of the gastrointestinal changes associated with aging.

_____

_____

11. Ventricular hypertrophy may be caused by which of the following physiological effects of aging?

a. Decreased arterial collagen and elastin

b. Decreased heart rate

c. Inability of baroreceptors to compensate for changes in position

d. Degeneration of the sinoatrial node

12. You are a paramedic student completing your clinical rotations. You are asked to perform an assessment of a 79-year-old woman suffering from sepsis. Your patient appears sick but does not have an elevated body temperature. She is pale, cool, and clammy with an elevated heart rate. Her BP is 92/68. Why is the patient afebrile?

_____

_____

13. Discuss some history-taking techniques that may be helpful when obtaining a medical history from a geriatric patient.

_____

_____

14. _____ ulcers are a type of pressure ulcer that develop during periods of long-term bed rest.

15. You have repeatedly been dispatched to the home of an elderly man who complains of recurrent respiratory infections. Currently, he is complaining of a weak cough and chest wall pain. What should you suspect?

a. The patient is lonely and wants attention.

b. The patient's decreasing muscular strength is impairing his cough reflex.

c. The patient is not compliant with his medications.

d. An increase in the cilia lining of the respiratory tract is trapping foreign particles, causing frequent infection.

16. Which of the following statements regarding temperature regulation in the geriatric patient is *true*?

a. Impaired circulation results in impaired thermoregulatory mechanisms.

b. Decreased muscle mass results in the increased ability to maintain body heat.

c. Skin changes result in increased sweating that may lead to hypothermia.

d. Medications such as anticholinergics, amphetamines, and diuretics increase the risk for hypothermia.

17. Signs and symptoms including hematemesis, coffee ground emesis, and melena are commonly associated with which condition?

_____

_____

18. Your elderly patient is complaining of abdominal pain and constipation. Your patient tells you that this is a common problem and that she takes laxatives daily. You should suspect that her symptoms are caused by

a. chronic use of laxatives.

b. poor diet.

c. a lack of gastric secretions.

d. excessive gastric secretions.

19. You are called to a private residence for a 69-year-old male complaining of abdominal pain, urinary urgency, and inability to void. The man tells you the last time this happened the nurses at the hospital

had to insert a special catheter to drain his bladder. How would you care for this patient?

   a. Offer supportive measures and transport.

   b. Insert a catheter and drain the bladder.

   c. Recommend that the patient make an appointment with his urologist in the morning.

   d. Administer Lasix, an analgesic, and transport.

Scenario: A woman called 9-1-1 when she noticed that her elderly neighbor was acting strangely. When you arrive, the patient is confused. The neighbor claims that he was acting normally the previous day.

20. You should suspect

   a. Alzheimer's disease.

   b. Parkinson's disease.

   c. depression.

   d. medication toxicity.

Need to Know

The following represent the Key Objectives of Chapter 44:

1. *Recognize alterations in human anatomy and physiology as they relate to aging.*

   Gerontology is the scientific study of the process and problems of aging. As humans, we reach our peak "operating efficiency" in our twenties. After age 30, most people begin to experience slow, generally unnoticeable degradation of body systems. Although tremendous advances in both medicine and prevention activities have slowed the effects of aging, they occur nevertheless. Table 44-1 summarizes age-related changes by body system.

2. *Explain how geriatric pathophysiology can impact acute medical and traumatic conditions found during assessment.*

   Assessing the geriatric patient presents challenges unique to the population. Based upon the summary of changes found in Table 44-1, incorporate the following concepts into your assessment approach:

   a. Because of the generally long periods of time it takes for the aging processes to occur, geriatric patients can sometimes confuse acute events as a continuation of those chronic changes. Carefully clarify any vagueness surrounding the patient's chief complaint and medical history.

   b. The cause of the patient's chief complaint is often not simple. There are a variety of processes that interact with one another to produce the complex presentation that you see. Keep an open mind, and resist the temptation to "tunnel" to a single diagnosis.

   c. Age simply worsens many conditions that plague the human body. For example, your older patient who experiences a fall from a moderate height may become a "trauma activation" simply because he or she does not have the reserves necessary to compensate for any potential shock condition and may be more prone to serious fractures because of the bones' brittleness.

   d. Because of the body's general loss of sensing ability as it ages, classic presentations are often not seen. Cardiac ischemia is more likely to present as "atypical" pain or as "anginal equivalents"—shortness of breath, sudden syncope, and unexplained diaphoresis. Your index of suspicion for serious conditions should rise as the patient's age increases.

   e. Elderly patients are more prone to severe infection, such as pneumonia or sepsis.

   f. Usually benign dysrhythmias can be more harmful in older patients, because of impaired cardiac output associated with aging. Carefully monitor the patient's ECG and vital signs throughout the encounter.

   g. Diseases associated with hypertension are prevalent in geriatric patients. Strokes, acquired brain injury, and diabetic situations need to be carefully identified, assessed, and managed.

TABLE 44-1 Age-Related Changes by Body System

Body System	Anatomical and Physiological Changes	Resulting Effects
Respiratory	Loss of rib cage recoil Decrease in respiratory muscle strength Decrease in pulmonary capillaries and alveolar surface area Decrease in ability to sense hypercapnia and hypoxia Decrease in cough strength and gag reflex	Decrease in PO_2 Loss of reserve inspiratory volume Decrease in efficient gas exchange Less effective compensatory mechanisms Decrease in immune abilities
Cardiovascular	Decrease in vessel elasticity Decrease in lumen diameter due to arteriosclerosis Increase in heart size (hypertrophy) Decrease in baroreceptor sensitivity Decrease in electrical conduction cells	Increase in blood pressure, with increased workload on the heart Positional blood pressure changes Increased chance of dysrhythmia
Gastrointestinal	Decrease in taste and smell abilities Increase in tooth decay Decrease in GI motility Decrease in gastric enzyme production Decrease in mucous lining GI tract Decrease in blood flow to liver	Loss of appetite, less caloric intake Decrease in mastication ability Increase in constipation Decrease in nutrient uptake Increased risk of ulcerative disease Decrease in the liver's detoxification ability
Renal	Decrease in number of nephrons Decrease in regulatory hormone production Decrease in maintaining acid/base balance Decrease in bladder tone Increase in prostate size	Decrease in ability to regulate water in the body Decrease in ability to clear metabolic by-products (urea, creatinine, and ammonia) and drugs from bloodstream Decrease in ability to maintain balance of minerals, glucose, and blood pressure Decrease in ability to compensate for acidosis or alkalosis Urinary incontinence Increase in urinary frequency and urgency
Neurological	Decrease in hearing and vision Slowing of reflexes Decrease in tactile sensing and proprioception Decrease in temperature regulation Decrease in sleep ability	Decrease in ability to communicate and respond to environmental cues Increased risk of fall injury Decrease in ability to compensate for heat loss or gain Inability to generate fever in response to infection Increase in fatigue
Musculoskeletal	Decrease in muscle tone Decrease in bone strength	Decrease in endurance and metabolic rate Increase in fractures
Immune	Decrease in skin thickness, blood flow, mucosal linings, lymphoidal tissue	Decrease in ability to prevent infection

h. The older patient's mental status can be altered in subtle ways. As a reminder, try to ascertain the patient's underlying or baseline mental status from family, bystanders, or medical records and document all your neurological findings accurately.

i. Cognitive impairment can present in the form of delirium, dementia, or depression. Delirium is the acute presentation of AMS and should be assumed as efforts are made to determine the patient's baseline mental status. Keep in mind that even patients with dementia can have bouts of delirium secondary to a new illness or disease.

j. Abdominal pain in the elderly population is presumed to be serious until proven otherwise. A possible decreased sensorium, combined with many possible serious conditions that can exist in the abdominal cavity, make these complaints difficult to identify.

k. Be extremely precise and methodical about your physical examination of the geriatric patient. Remember that older patients may be vague or confused about their discomfort. It may take time to elicit specific details about such complaints.

l. Older patients are more likely to be taking an array of medications. Some of these medications may adversely impact others or your prehospital medication. Consult a drug guide if you are unsure of possible drug interactions.

m. Because of the liver's decreasing ability as it ages to detoxify the blood, a drug that you deliver may have a longer half-life than anticipated. For example, lidocaine should be delivered in half of the usual dose to an older patient to reduce the possibility of lidocaine toxicity.

n. A loss of musculoskeletal mass and strength may result in unusual body stature and posture. Pad and support necks, backs, and hips to help reduce the amount of pain and discomfort during procedures such as spinal immobilization and hip stabilization.

3. *Describe how geriatric pathophysiology affects communications between the patient and caregiver.*

a. Older patients can have difficulty understanding you or communicating with you because of possible hearing and vision loss. Ask patients to wear their hearing aids and glasses if they are available. Use clear, simple terms when asking questions, and position yourself in front of patients so they can see your facial expressions, mouth movements, and body language clearly as you speak.

b. Allow adequate time for the patient to respond to your questions. If the patient appears to pause, silently count to 10 before *rephrasing your query*. Use active listening techniques to ensure that your patient's response provided you with accurate information ("Mrs. Smith, I just want to confirm that your abdominal pain began sometime last evening; is that correct?")

c. Be especially respectful with your geriatric patients. Use formal names ("Mr. Smith") unless the patient corrects you ("You can call me Bob"). Whenever possible, speak directly with the patient and respect the patient's wishes, even when family is in the room.

d. Advance directives to withhold "lifesaving" or "heroic" resuscitation efforts may be present. Be sure that you fully understand what the legal instructions are before deciding upon your course of action. Contact medical direction if there is any question about the directive.

Need to Do

The following skills are explained and illustrated in a step-by-step manner, via skill sheets and/or Step-by-Steps in this text and on the accompanying DVD:

Skill Name	Skill Sheet Number and Location	Step-by-Step Number and Location
Verbal Communications	63 – DVD	N/A

Connections

- The American Geriatric Society (AGS), in conjunction with the National Council of State Training Coordinators, developed the Geriatric Education for Emergency Medical Services course after recognizing the need for continuing education in this area. More information on this one-day class can be found at www.gemssite.com. The AGS website can be found at www.americangeriatrics.com. Its mission is to improve the health, independence, and quality of life of all older people.[1]

- The American Association of Retired Persons (AARP) is the country's leading advocacy group for older Americans. Its website contains valuable information and resources for the health and social welfare of older people. The main page can be found at www.aarp.org.

- The Eastern Association for the Surgery of Trauma (EAST) is a not-for-profit group organized to furnish leadership and foster advances in the care of injured patients.[2] EAST published a "best practices" document for the surgical management of the geriatric trauma patient, which can be found at the federal National Guidelines Clearinghouse website, www.guideline.gov/summary/summary.aspx?ss=15&doc_id=2959&nbr=2185.

- Link to the companion DVD for a chapter-based quiz, audio glossary, animations, games and exercises, and, when appropriate, skill sheets and skill Step-by-Steps.

Street Secrets

- **Treat the Patient** In many situations, family members may try to "drive" the patient's decision-making process in regards to his or her health care. When a durable power of attorney exists, this may be appropriate; in these situations, try your best to inform the patient of the care plan that has been already worked out previously. However, if the family does not have the legal authority to manage the patient's medical affairs, tread carefully. Assess patients' mental status carefully to fully determine if they have the ability to make rational decisions about their health care. Keep at least one family member involved with the process, even if only as an observer. These actions may help reduce any question or confusion about what transpired on scene that may arise later.

- **Medications** Older patients tend to be prescribed quite a few medications for a variety of conditions. The potential for dangerous drug interactions increases when multiple physicians are involved in the prescription writing. Keep a drug reference guide handy when working; you can quickly look up medication interactions and side effects to see if they might be related to the patient's presenting signs and symptoms.

- **Not Your Grandparent's Hearing Aid** Today's auditory assistive devices are smaller and less noticeable than previous models. Look carefully at the patient if you suspect a hearing aid may be in use.

- **Mix It Up** Patients with five medications or more have a higher risk of experiencing adverse drug interactions.

The Drug Box

There are no specific drugs related to this chapter content.

References

1. American Geriatric Society website, www. american geriatrics. org/about/agsmission.shtml (accessed November 23, 2006).

2. EAST website, www.east.org/info.asp (accessed November 26, 2006).

Answers

Are You Ready?

1. Based on the photograph and details provided in the opening narrative, there are several key pieces of information to remember: The patient's downtime is significant, and hypothermia is a serious concern. The patient's own urine may be worsening the drop in core temperature, as heat is lost through both conduction and evaporation. There may have already been the beginning of tissue breakdown in the areas of the body being pressed by its weight against the floor. Sophie's mental status is also of concern. You will need to determine if her confusion is new-onset AMS, chronic, or an exacerbation. One clue to factor in is that she does live alone. Although that doesn't necessarily indicate that she has complete mental capacity normally, it is less likely that she is confused to the point of being unable to live on her own. Your patient is not absolutely sure what happened to her. It sounds as though she fell, but there may have been a possible medical cause for the fall. Sophie also has pain in her hip area. This is potentially an ill omen, considering the mortality rate from hip fractures in the elderly. In addition, the hip pain could be distracting her from any spinal cord injury associated with her fall.

   As you size up the scene and digest this information, remember that your basic assumptions of managing the patient's airway, breathing, and circulatory status come first. Secure her airway as you manually control her cervical spine. Determine if she has any respiratory distress and provide supplemental oxygen. Determine the location, quality, and rate of the pulse and control for any life-threatening bleeding. Start thinking about extrication; the room appears tight, and you will want to move her as soon as possible in order to stop the heat loss and conduct a further, more complete examination.

You Are There: Reality-Based Cases

Case 1

1. Like many of the geriatric patients you will encounter, Sophie has a variety of medical conditions that can interplay with each other and could have caused her to fall. In considering the signs, symptoms, and physical findings, it is interesting to note that your patient is not taking any medications related to atrial fibrillation. Is the dysrhythmia new? You should ask Sophie about it, understanding that she is currently confused and may not give you an accurate answer. Also, you can infer that she has a history of hypertension—the calcium channel blocker (Isoptin) and mild diuretic (HCTZ) point to that condition. Yet her blood pressure is borderline hypotensive considering the patient's weight

and age. It is possible that she is dehydrated after being on the floor. It could also be that the atrial fibrillation may be causing cardiac output to drop, causing both a blood pressure fall and a change in mental status. Sophie is also a diabetic, controlled by self-injection of insulin. You will need to rule out hypoglycemia or hyperglycemia as a cause of her AMS. Finally, hypothermia may be worsening any or all of these conditions. She is cold to the touch but not shivering. What might that imply about her core body temperature?

Test Yourself

1. d

Elderly patients often suffer from isolated extremity fractures.

2. a

During aging, microvascular changes affect the elasticity of vessels, patency of the lumen, and muscle strength. Together, these changes decrease the resilience and ability of the heart, arteries, and veins to compensate.

3. Glaucoma

Glaucoma presents with increased intraocular pressure, optic disk changes, and visual field loss. The pressure leads to damage to the optic nerve. Without early intervention, the vision loss is permanent.

4. d

Diabetes, renal disease, stroke, blindness, AMIs, and aneurysms are examples of the multiple diseases that have increased complications from hypertension. Hypertension may affect every organ system.

5. d

Normal lung aging is a benign process and has little impact on exercise tolerance in the elderly. In fact, exercise will strengthen muscles of respiration and increase endurance. The factors that promote illness include environmental stressors such as smoking, concurrent illness, childhood infection, and lack of exercise.

6. True

Signs and symptoms of depression include weight loss, insomnia, loss of interest, inability to concentrate, fatigue, irritability, hopelessness, feelings of worthlessness, thoughts of suicide, and isolation.

7. Loss of elastic recoil, ossification of the ribs and joints, a decrease in respiratory muscle strength, decreases in the pulmonary capillary network, and enlargement of the alveoli.

Stiffening of the chest wall (from loss of elastic recoil, ossification, and decreased muscle strength) results in a decrease in compliance and the reduction of respiratory capacity. This leads to a decrease in vital capacity, since the residual volume increases, even though total lung capacity remains the same. Decreases in the pulmonary capillary network and enlargement of the alveoli reduce the surface area available for gas exchange. These structural and mechanical changes impair gas exchange, resulting in a decrease in PO_2 while pH and PCO_2 remain fairly constant.

8. c

The influenza virus is a common cause of recurrent upper-respiratory infections in the geriatric population.

9. Delirium is frequently reversible, whereas dementia is more likely to be permanent.

Delirium is characterized by changes in level of attention and cognitive functioning; it is an acute presentation often seen in hospitalized patients or as the presenting symptom of an underlying medical disease. Dementia is the most severe form of cognitive impairment, characterized by a progressive impairment spanning memory deficits and the inability to perform motor functions, aphasia, and an inability to identify objects or engage in higher-level thought processes. These deficits lead to loss of daily functional ability.

10. With age, motility in the GI tract begins to slow. Gastric and digestive secretions are reduced. The protective layer of mucus that lines the surface of the tract decreases.

Decreased motility in the GI tract often leads to slower gastric emptying and constipation. The reduction in gastric and digestive secretions adversely affects the absorption of nutrients, leading to deficits of important substances. The decrease in the mucus layer means that the gastrointestinal tract is less protected from acid.

11. a

As geriatric patients lose collagen and elastin, their arteries stiffen, causing an increased workload. The heart accommodates the increased workload by enlarging (hypertrophy).

12. Geriatric patients are often unable to produce a fever.

Geriatric patients' bodies are often unable to generate a fever. Fever is a beneficial mechanism that deters bacterial and viral growth, stimulates the immune response, and increases phagocytosis.

13. Identify obstacles to communication and remedy if possible (i.e., make sure hearing aids and eyeglasses are used, if needed). Position yourself so the person can see your face clearly and make eye contact. When possible, decrease the noise level at the scene. Use open-ended questions to allow the patient to expand upon his or her answers. Allow the patient time to respond. It is essential to obtain the necessary information regarding age, present and past medical history, medication information, and potential presence of advance directives.

Approach geriatric patients anticipating that they are neurologically intact, since the majority of elderly do not have dementia. Treat all patients with dignity, respect, and sensitivity, and remember that older patients may have a realistic fear that going to the hospital may result in not being able to return home.

14. Decubitus

Pressure ulcers develop in areas where there is a lack of blood flow, usually due to pressure preventing adequate circulation. These are often over bony prominences such as the sacrum, heels, or greater trochanter. Long-term bed rest can put chronic pressure on these sites, leading to the formation of decubitus ulcers. Beginning as a reddened area, if blood flow is not reestablished, progressive tissue breakdown happens. Epidermal damage followed by dermal damage will continue through the subcutaneous tissue and deeper without adequate intervention. Pressure ulcers, venous stasis ulcers, and diabetic ulcers have different etiologies but can all result in cellulitis, osteomyelitis, or gangrene. Interventions include relieving the pressure at the site, dressing the wound, and preventing or treating infection.

15. b

Elderly patients are more vulnerable to recurring respiratory infections because the protective ability of the lungs to prevent and fight infection is decreased by the loss of muscle strength in the cough and gag reflexes. Additionally, the number of cilia in the lungs is reduced in geriatric patients—cilia are responsible for trapping and removing foreign particles.

16. c

Temperature regulation is compromised in the elderly. With slowed blood circulation, skin changes, and functional deficits in thermal regulatory mechanisms, the elderly have lost many of the protective responses that enable the body to adjust body temperature.

17. Gastrointestinal hemorrhage

The most common causes of gastrointestinal hemorrhage are peptic ulcer disease, gastritis, esophagitis, and diverticulitis, all of which have a higher incidence in the geriatric population. The signs and symptoms associated with gastrointestinal hemorrhage include hematemesis (vomiting bright red blood), coffee ground emesis, or melena (black, tarry, bloody stools), with significant blood loss, syncope, confusion, or shock. Interventions are based upon patient presentation and degree of acuity. Life threats need rapid airway, breathing, and circulatory support with transport to the hospital.

18. c

Abdominal pain and constipation may occur in the elderly as saliva, GI motility, and gastric secretions all decrease.

19. a

The patient is likely suffering from an enlarged prostate. You should focus on maintaining the patient's ABCs. Lasix should not be administered, as it may complicate his condition. Field catheterization is considered controversial. The patient needs immediate medical attention and should not wait until morning to receive treatment.

20. d

Sudden changes in mental status are often associated with delirium. Causes of delirium include hypoxia, respiratory distress, myocardial infarctions, metabolic disorders, and medication toxicity.

chapter 45

The Abused and Neglected

Are You Ready?

Dispatch sends you on a call to assist the police with a hysterical teenager. When you arrive on the scene, the police inform you that the victim was physically and sexually abused by her stepfather. The stepfather is in custody. A female police officer is the only person that your patient has been willing to speak with up to this point.

1. What can you do in this situation that will help reassure the patient and help maintain her dignity, while allowing you to gather all the information that you need and ensure that the patient doesn't have any potentially critical injuries?

   _____

   _____

   _____

2. What is the focus of the physical examination for a patient who may have been sexually abused?

   _____

   _____

   _____

3. With patients who are potentially victims of sexual abuse, what can you do to help law enforcement with preservation of evidence?

   _____

   _____

   _____

Active Learning

1. Know Your Resources

Contact as many of the following organizations that are available in your EMS system as you can. Ask them about their expectations of you as a paramedic and if there are mandatory reporting laws in your area (what is it that is mandatory to report, within what time frame do you need to make the report, and in what form does the report need to be, etc.) related to abuse, neglect, or domestic violence:

- Child protective services (CPS)
- Adult protective services (APS)
- Local law enforcement

- Local regulatory agencies
- Local hospitals

Ask representatives from these agencies if they have any additional information that may help you in the identification and treatment of abused and neglected patients.

2. **Volunteer Opportunity: Abused Patients**

Make an arrangement to spend some time at a women's shelter or with child protective services. Observe how case workers and investigators engage with their clients. Ask the professionals how paramedics can best handle these difficult cases.

You Are There: Reality-Based Cases

Case 1

As you arrive on scene, you see EMTs ventilating 5-year-old Trina Wilkinson with a bag-mask device. As you approach, one of the EMTs tells you that when they arrived Trina was lying prone in bed next to a basin full of emesis. She was completely unresponsive and was not breathing. Because the address was familiar, you had looked up a history en route to the call. You are shocked to discover that EMS had responded to that address 15 times in the past year. Each time it was for Trina.

1. Based upon the initial report from the EMT crew, how would you describe Trina's acuity?

_____

_____

_____

2. What is your priority for treatment?

_____

_____

_____

3. What additional information do you need in order to develop a treatment plan?

_____

_____

_____

While you examine the patient, your partner finds the patient's mother and asks her about the patient's history of the present illness. The mother states that Trina has some sort of undiagnosed blood disorder; she has bleeding problems, and she has difficulty eating. She was complaining of stomach pain this morning, and about half an hour ago, she started to have difficulty breathing. She has had no fever, and other than her chronic conditions she has been doing fairly well. Trina takes a number of medications, and the mother points to a dresser drawer full of liquid medications and syringes and feeding tubes to administer them.

When you hear of this, you are surprised because you noticed pill fragments in the emesis. You ask one of the EMTs to put the emesis basin in a paper bag and bring it to the ambulance. You take the opportunity to ask Trina's mother about the possibility of Trina getting into any medications and ingesting them. Her mother informs you that it is impossible for Trina to get into the medicine cabinet because it has a safety lock on it. She claims that, even if she got into the cabinet, all the medications are in childproof bottles and Trina is too weak to open them.

4. Do you have any concerns in addition to the patient's condition at this point? If so, how will you address them?

_____

_____

_____

Trina remains unresponsive and apneic. She has a scant amount of emesis in her airway and what appear to be a few additional pill fragments. You suction the oropharynx, and she appears to have an open and now patent airway. The patient has a delayed capillary refill. A comparison of central and peripheral pulses yields no significant differences, and the patient shows a sinus bradycardia on the ECG. Trina's blood pressure was 90/40 and her oxygen saturation was initially 72% on room air. Now that the EMTs have been ventilating her, she has a saturation of 94% on 100% oxygen, and her heart rate is 70. Her temperature is 98 degrees, $ETCO_2$ is 36 mm Hg, and blood glucose level is 86 mg/dL. You auscultate faint rhonchi in her bilateral upper lung fields, but the rest of the secondary assessment is unremarkable.

5. What is a likely cause for the rhonchi that you discovered when you auscultated Trina's lungs?

_____

_____

_____

6. What is your plan of action at this point?

_____

_____

_____

You manage Trina's airway and transport to a pediatric critical care facility, where you inform the physician and a child protective services (CPS) representative about the inconsistencies in the mother's story. Shortly afterwards a detective arrives and questions you about the call and what you saw and heard. You tell the detective all that you know, and he takes the container from your suction machine and places it in an evidence bag.

7. In regard to your documentation of this case, how should you proceed?

_____

_____

_____

Three weeks later you are reading the paper before work and you see a story about Trina and her mother. Her mother is being charged with aggravated child abuse and organized fraud for purposefully exaggerating or inducing chronic illnesses in her daughter. When you show up at work that day, you are met by your supervisor who delivers a subpoena for you to give a deposition in Trina's case.

8. What is the clinical term for the type of abuse with which Trina's mother is being charged?

_____

_____

_____

Test Yourself

1. You are called to a local elementary school by the school nurse. In her office you find a small child who appears to be scared and is holding his left arm. The school nurse tells you that she has noticed several injuries to the patient, and he has a history of multiple broken bones. The nurse has been unable to contact the child's parents. When questioning the child, which of the following responses should most raise your suspicion of abuse?
   a. "My mom tells me I have brittle bones."
   b. "I have hemophilia."
   c. "I fall down a lot and hurt myself."
   d. "My parents are rich."

2. You are called to the scene of a domestic violence incident. What is the most important action you can take prior to your arrival on the scene?

_____

_____

3. What is the order of the phases in the cycle of domestic violence?

_____

_____

4. What are some physical signs that are consistent with child abuse?

_____

_____

5. What clues in a child's behavior may indicate an abusive situation?
   a. Aggressive behavior in children under 6 years of age
   b. Children avoiding physical contact with any adult
   c. Passive behavior in children over 6 years of age
   d. Children who look to parents for reassurance

6. Individuals who were abused as children have a high risk of entering abusive relationships as adults.

True

False

7. How should you handle a situation where an abused spouse refuses transport?

_____

_____

8. In addition to maintaining their physical health, what factors should be taken into account with sexual assault patients?

_____

_____

9. You respond to the local quick stop for a "victim of violence" where you find a 36-year-old female with torn clothing and multiple bruises. Your patient is obviously injured and appears scared. She is requesting transport to a hospital on the other side of town for treatment. In assessing this patient, which action would *not* be appropriate?

a. Nonjudgmental questioning

b. Reminding the victim that assault is a crime

c. Asking the victim why she didn't leave sooner

d. Supportive care

10. You respond to the local nursing home for an elderly patient. Upon evaluating your patient you learn that she is upset that someone is "stealing" her money. The nursing home staff believes that the patient is paranoid and is suffering from a psychiatric disorder. What is likely the source of this patient's paranoia?

a. Physical abuse

b. Financial exploitation

c. Sexual abuse

d. Emotional abuse

11. A pattern of behavior that impairs the victim's sense of self-worth is an example of _____ abuse.

12. Which of the following is a sign of neglect?

a. History of multiple broken bones

b. Untidy home

c. Bruises in various stages of healing

d. Inattention to a child's emotional needs

13. When treating the victim of an alleged sexual assault, how should potential evidence at the scene be handled?

_____

_____

14. You are called to the high school dance for a sick student. Upon arrival you are directed to a 16-year-old male who appears to be upset. A bystander tells you that he believes the 16-year-old was raped. You take him to your ambulance for privacy during your assessment and questioning. He states that "it hurts" and is requesting to use the bathroom prior to transport. How would you handle this situation?

a. Allow the patient to use the restroom.

b. Have the patient change into scrubs after using the restroom.

c. Accompany the patient to the restroom and encourage him not to remove clothing.

d. Do not allow the patient to use the restroom.

15. You are called to the local grocery store to assist the police. You are directed to the break room where you see an infant in a car seat. The infant does not appear to be injured but is inappropriately dressed for the weather. A store worker tells you that she found the baby left in a cart near the entrance to the store more than 2 hours ago. What is your suspicion?

a. The infant's mother is teaching the infant a lesson for misbehaving.

b. The infant has been abused and left for someone to find.

c. The infant's mother likely forgot about the infant.

d. The infant has been neglected and abandoned.

Need to Know

The following represent the Key Objectives of Chapter 45:

1. *Identify safety issues for paramedics to address while caring for victims of abuse or neglect.*

The safety of the paramedic always needs to be a primary focus of any call. In the case of a call for an abuse or neglect victim, paramedics should approach the scene as they would the scene of a violent crime (abuse cases frequently involve violent crime). When dispatched to a call for abuse or neglect, you should ensure that law enforcement personnel are responding and, if not, request that they respond. If there is any indication that the scene is not safe for whatever reason, wait for the police to determine that the situation is safe prior to entering.

2. *Define the major types of child maltreatment.*

   Neglect is the failure to provide for a child's basic needs. Neglect can be physical, emotional, or medical in nature. *Physical abuse* occurs when the child suffers a physical injury at the hands of his or her caregiver. *Emotional abuse* is a pattern of behavior that impairs a child's emotional development or sense of self-worth. *Sexual abuse* includes physical acts such as fondling, genital or oral stimulation, intercourse, or sodomy as well as non-physical acts such as indecent exposure or obscene phone calls. *Sexual exploitation* forces a child to engage in prostitution or pornography.

3. *Describe findings in the history and physical examination that can be suggestive of child abuse.*

   The most consistent finding of abuse is a history that does not match the clinical examination. Examples of histories that may indicate abuse include:

   - The details of the history change over time.
   - The mechanism doesn't match the injury.
   - The child is not developmentally capable of sustaining injuries resulting from the mechanism that the parents claim.

   Examples of indications of abuse on physical examination include:

   - Bruising with a characteristic pattern (belt buckle mark, hand mark, etc.)
   - A physical examination that doesn't match the history
   - Burns of the perineum
   - Significant injuries ascribed to minor trauma

4. *Describe the role of the paramedic in the evaluation and treatment of the abused child.*

   EMS providers are among the few people who see patients in the home setting. They must constantly be aware of their surroundings and maintain a high index of suspicion when the possibility of abuse exists.

   Responsibilities of the paramedic related to abuse and neglect are:

   - Observe the interactions between the parent and the child.
   - Determine if the child is living in an environment that is safe and capable of meeting his or her basic needs.
   - Examine whether the injuries that the child has sustained are consistent with the parents' story of the mechanism of injury.

   - Notify any agencies (police, child protective services, etc.) to whom you are required by law to report possible abuse or neglect.
   - Document *objectively* all your observations on your prehospital report and on any suspected abuse or neglect paperwork. Documentation should not include your personal feelings or thoughts.

5. *Describe the patterns associated with domestic violence.*

   Domestic violence (DV) (also known as intimate partner violence [IPV]) is a pattern of assaultive and coercive behaviors, including physical, sexual, and psychological attacks, as well as economic coercion, that adults or adolescents use against their intimate partners.[1] The concept of the "cycle of violence" states that domestic violence occurs in three phases (tension-building, crisis, honeymoon) that, if unbroken, will continue to repeat themselves and increase in frequency and severity.

   The single most prevalent factor influencing whether a person becomes a victim of abuse or an abuser is whether a person witnessed or was the victim of abuse or neglect as a child.

6. *Describe how to approach a domestic violence scene.*

   When interacting with patients and potential perpetrators, maintain a professional and nonjudgmental attitude, and keep your safety and the safety of your partner as the main priority.

7. *Define the different types of elder abuse.*

Neglect and physical, sexual, or emotional abuse of an elderly person involves issues similar to those involving children. *Financial and material exploitation* is defined as illegally or improperly using an elder's funds, property, or assets. *Abandonment* is desertion of an elderly person by an individual who has physical custody of the elder or who has assumed responsibility for providing care to the elder. *Self-neglect* describes behaviors of a competent elderly person that threaten his or her own health or safety.

8. *Identify characteristics of elders who are at risk for abuse or neglect.*

   Elders with multiple medical problems, cognitive impairment, or dementia or who are socially isolated or financially dependent on their caregivers are at risk for abuse or neglect.

9. *List factors that indicate the potential for elder abuse or neglect.*

   Several scene findings warrant suspicion of elder abuse or neglect. A history of the injury or illness that is inconsistent with injuries, delay in seeking care, recurrent calls for untreated medical conditions,[2] an unclean or unsafe living environment, or a caretaker who does not permit a patient to answer your questions are red flag warnings of possible abuse. Physical findings may include dehydration; malnutrition; unwashed, soiled, worn, or bloody clothing; evidence that the patient has been lying in urine or stool; and unusual injury patterns.

10. *Describe assessment and management techniques for the sexual assault victim.*

    When interacting with a victim of a sexual assault, the paramedic should maintain nonjudgmental, supportive, kind, compassionate, and professional behavior. If at all possible, the paramedic examining the patient should be the same sex as the victim. Do everything possible to maintain the assault victim's dignity. Identify and manage any trauma that needs to be treated.

    Attempt to preserve any evidence by not allowing the patient to drink, brush teeth, shower, defecate, or urinate. Do not allow the victim to change clothes. Any evidence that is removed from the victim needs to be transported to the hospital in a paper bag (*not* plastic bags—*plastic bags may destroy biological evidence*). Notify local law enforcement if mandatory reporting exists in your area or if the patient requests you to do so. Document your findings in an objective manner free of personal bias or opinion. Avoid the term "alleged sexual assault," which carries a negative connotation; "sexual assault by history" is preferred.

Need to Do

The following skills are explained and illustrated in a step-by-step manner, via skill sheets and/or Step-by-Steps in this text and on the accompanying DVD:

Skill Name	Skill Sheet Number and Location	Step-by-Step Number and Location
Secondary assessment	33 – Appendix A and DVD	33 – Chapter 14 and DVD
Verbal Communications	63 – DVD	N/A
Documentation	64 – DVD	N/A

Connections

- Chapter 9, Safety and Scene Size-Up, in the textbook includes information on paramedic safety when caring for the victim of assault or domestic violence.
- Chapter 10, Therapeutic Communications and History Taking, in the textbook describes how to interview victims of abuse and/or neglect.
- Chapter 17, Documentation and Communication, in the textbook describes appropriate documentation for victims of assault or abuse.
- Chapter 33, Infectious and Communicable Diseases, in the textbook includes information on potential sexually transmitted diseases (STDs) associated with sexual assault.
- Chapter 44, Geriatric Patients, in the textbook provides additional information on geriatric patients, elder abuse, and neglect.
- Chapter 52, Teamwork and Operational Interface, in the textbook outlines how to work in a crime scene and preserve evidence.
- Link to the companion DVD for a chapter-based quiz, audio glossary, animations, games and exercises, and, when appropriate, skill sheets and skill Step-by-Steps.

Street Secrets

- **Safety First** Maintain a heightened sense of awareness when working on scenes involving potential abuse, neglect, or domestic violence. People who perform these acts have the potential for displaying unpredictable and potentially very dangerous behavior. Your safety and the safety of the victim should be your primary focus. Always err on the side of caution, and request the assistance of law enforcement before you even get on scene if you believe that the scene may present any possibility for danger.

4 **Need for Empathy** Victims of abuse are frequently frightened and humiliated by what has happened to them. Always treat these people with respect, empathy, and professionalism. Treat the victim of abuse as you would treat someone that you love if they were abused.

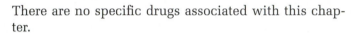

The Drug Box

There are no specific drugs associated with this chapter.

References

1. A. L. Ganley, "Understanding Domestic Violence," in D. Lee, N. A. Durborown, and P. R. Salber (eds.), *Improving the Health Care Response to Domestic Violence: A Resource Manual for Health Care Providers,* 2nd ed., The Family Violence Prevention Fund, 1998 (available at www.endabuse.org).
2. D. Anglin and H. R. Hutson, "Elder Abuse and Neglect," in J. A. Marx, *Rosen's Emergency Medicine: Concepts and Clinical Practice*, 5th ed. St. Louis, MO: Mosby 2002, pp. 875–82.

Answers

Are You Ready?

1. If the patient will interact with a female police officer, the officer should be allowed to remain with the patient. If your crew is all male, consider requesting that a female paramedic also respond, if there is no indication that the patient is suffering from any potentially serious injuries and the request would not take an excessive period of time. If there are no available female paramedics nearby, request that the female police officer assist you with gathering a history and stay with you while you perform your physical examination.

2. Your physical examination should focus on identifying any physical trauma outside the pelvic region that may require immediate intervention. In general, examination of the genitalia and perineum is not necessary in the field unless the patient complains of severe pain or significant bleeding.

3. Do not allow the patient to drink, brush teeth, shower, defecate, urinate, or change clothes (the clothing should be handled as little as possible). Any evidence collected on the scene (e.g., the victim's clothing, condoms, tampons, and towels) needs to be turned over to law enforcement or transported to the hospital in paper bags.

You Are There: Reality-Based Cases
Case 1

1. Trina is unconscious, unresponsive, and is not breathing, any one of which would distinguish her as a critical patient.

2. The use of the bag-mask at least indicates that the patient is in ventilatory failure. You must rapidly reassess the patient to confirm her unstable condition.

3. What is the history leading up to the patient's current presentation? What additional signs and symptoms does Trina present with? A complete SAMPLE history would be beneficial (the mnemonic AEIOU-TIPS may be helpful in determining the cause of the ALOC). Complete primary and secondary assessments including a full set of vital signs, oxygen saturation, ECG, end-tidal CO_2 reading, and temperature are needed. Because the patient has an altered level of consciousness, it is appropriate to evaluate the patient's blood sugar.

4. The inconsistency in the mother's story about the possibility of Trina getting into other medications than her own and possibly ingesting them, and the presence of what you believe are pill fragments in the emesis, are concerns. Coupled with an unexplained presentation of ALOC and apnea, these observations should raise a few red flags. Your priority is to manage the patient and to maintain objective and professional behavior. Avoid the assertion of any personal biases based on your feelings about the situation. Once you arrive at the hospital, you can relay your concerns to the physician in charge of the patient's care. Have the police officer accompany you to the hospital, and at the appropriate time, convey your concerns about the inconsistency to her as well.

5. The basin full of emesis, the emesis in her airway, the patient's unresponsiveness, and a history of difficulty swallowing all point to possible aspiration of emesis. There is always the possibility of a respiratory infection, but Trina lacks signs and symptoms that are typically associated with a respiratory infection, and the likelihood of aspiration is a much more plausible explanation.

6. Because of the patient's level of consciousness and the fact that she may have already aspirated, attempt to isolate the trachea with endotracheal intubation. An endotracheal tube will provide a direct means of suctioning any emesis that she may have already aspirated, as well as provide a patent airway. IV access in a peripheral vein is appropriate and will allow for fluid and medication administration. The patient needs to be transported emergently to a receiving facility capable of caring for a critical pediatric patient.

7. Documentation of any situation pertaining to patient care and observations that you make should be factual, objective, succinct, and nonjudgmental.

8. The clinical term for the type of abuse that Trina's mother is being charged with is *Münchausen syndrome by proxy* (MSBP). This term is applied when an adult, usually the mother, presents a false history to the physician regarding a child who is not suffering from any of the fabricated symptoms. This history causes the physician to perform unnecessary diagnostic procedures that do not result in any specific diagnosis. In 2002, a new terminology, *pediatric condition falsification* (PCF), was suggested by the American Professional Society on the Abuse of Children (APSAC).

Test Yourself

1. c

   In cases of child abuse, the child will commonly lie to cover up how the actual injuries occurred for fear of retribution. A history of broken bones and inconsistency in stories or injury patterns are also consistent with abuse. Children will generally not come out and accuse their abusers.

2. The most important action is to ensure that the police respond.

   Scene safety and personal safety are paramount in any call related to intentional injuries or violence. If it is known from dispatch information that the scene is one of domestic violence, law enforcement personnel should be summoned, and the EMS crew should not enter the scene until it has been secured.

3. The phases in order are tension-building phase, crisis phase, and honeymoon phase.

   Phase 1 is a tension-building phase. Arguing and an increase in verbal or minor physical abuse occur during this phase, along with a breakdown of communication. Often, the victim will feel the need to keep things calm. Phase 2, the crisis phase, involves the actual battering episode. Phase 3 is often described as the honeymoon phase, where denial and then apologies occur. The assailant may deny that the abuse took place or downplay the seriousness of the event; he or she may blame drugs or alcohol as the reason for the assault. The abuser may then become contrite, apologetic, and state that it will never happen again.

4. Strong indicators of physical abuse include: bruises in unusual locations, bruises in nonambulatory infants, bruises with a characteristic pattern (belt mark, hand mark, loop mark), cluster of bruises or bruises of varying age, burns in a stocking-glove pattern, burns of the perineum, femur fracture in a nonambulatory child, and significant injury ascribed to minor trauma.

   Identifying abuse and neglect can be difficult at times, but maintaining a high degree of suspicion for the presence of abuse can prevent a child from suffering further harm or even death. A careful history should be taken from the parent as well as from the child (if the child is able to give a history).

5. b

   Child abuse or neglect should be considered when a child exhibits any of the following behaviors: excessively passive behavior, especially in children under the age of 6; excessively aggressive behavior, especially in children over the age of 6; children who cry hopelessly during treatment, or children who cry very little, even with painful procedures; children who do not mind if their parents or caregivers leave the room; children who do not look to the parents or caregivers for reassurance; children who are wary of any physical contact; children who appear extremely apprehensive; and children who are constantly on the alert for danger.

6. True

   Adults who experienced childhood physical abuse are at risk of being involved in an abusive relationship during adulthood. Similarly, neglected children are at an increased risk of becoming violent as adults. Certain personality traits may be seen in either the abuser or the victim. These include low self-esteem; intense need for love or affection; uncontrolled temper, jealousy, and insecurity; and an unrealistic expectation of a relationship.

7. Because the victim is an adult, it is important to respect the victim's final decision to refuse transport. In addition many EMS systems provide information on safety planning, community resources, and shelter or hotline numbers to patients who elect not to be transported. This information should be relayed to the patient in private; any written information should be on a small, easily concealed card.

   Only the patient can assess the risks of leaving the abuser at the current time. The most dangerous time for a victim of intimate partner violence is the time frame after the victim has left the relationship. No police system or social service system can fully guarantee an individual's safety.

8. The paramedic should take an active role in emotional support.

   A nonjudgmental, supportive attitude is essential; tact, kindness, and a compassionate manner will help ease the victim's distress. Move the patient to a private area before obtaining a history or performing a physical exam, and provide a blanket or sheet to cover the victim if needed. A paramedic of the same sex as the victim should attend to the patient if possible.

9. c

   Being nonjudgmental and providing supportive care may be the best treatment that a paramedic can provide to an abused patient. Reminding the victim that assault is a crime may be a way to convince the victim that what she is experiencing is "not okay." Asking the victim why she did not leave sooner judges the patient and minimizes the situation.

10. b

    Financial and material exploitation is defined as illegally or improperly using an elder's funds, property, or assets. Examples include theft of Social Security checks, embezzlement, or the use of threats to enforce signing or changing legal documents.

11. Emotional

    Emotional abuse can be defined as any pattern of behaviors that impairs the victim's emotional development or sense of self-worth.

12. d

    Neglect is defined as failure to provide for a child's basic needs. Examples of neglect may include: physical neglect (failure to provide food, shelter, or appropriate supervision); emotional neglect (inattention to a child's emotional needs, failure to provide basic emotional support); medical neglect (failure to provide medical or mental health treatment); and educational neglect (failure to educate a child or attend to special education needs).

13. Disturb the crime scene as little as possible, especially prior to the arrival of law enforcement. Do not allow the patient to drink, brush teeth, shower, defecate, or urinate. The victim should not change clothes, and clothing should be handled as little as possible. If evidence needs to be transported to the hospital (e.g., the victim's original clothing, condoms, tampons, towels), paper bags, not plastic bags, should be used.

    Regardless of the patient's decision to file a police report or to pursue charges, and regardless of law enforcement's decision to request a forensic examination, hospital or clinic personnel should evaluate all sexual assault patients. Specially trained sexual assault nurse examiners may be used in certain areas of the country. All victims should be examined and treated for any traumatic injuries. It is important to transport these patients so that they may be treated prophylactically for sexually transmitted diseases and for pregnancy, if needed.

14. d

    Victims of sexual assault should not be allowed to remove clothing, change clothing, brush their teeth, shower, or use the restroom as evidence of the assault may be lost. If the victim wishes to remove clothing, it should be placed in a paper bag.

15. d

    The fact that the infant has been alone at the store for more than 2 hours rules out a forgetful parent. The fact that the infant is not appropriately dressed for the weather and was left abandoned in the parking lot indicates neglect. The infant is likely not "being taught a lesson for misbehaving" due to the infant's age.

Patients with Special Challenges

Are You Ready?

The police are on the scene of a "violent patient" and have requested your assistance in transporting the patient. You arrive at a hotel to find several officers confronting a young male who is standing in a corner at the end of a hallway. Hotel employees found the patient wandering around in the hallway, appearing agitated and upset. The manager and security guard tried to talk to the patient, but he screamed and ran down the hallway. The patient then tried to bite and scratch the guard when he attempted to take custody.

You size up the patient. He is standing, but not looking directly at the officers or you. He has his hands on his head, pulling on a cap and rocking slightly back and forth. He appears to be breathing fast and is pale.

1. Based upon the description of the events, will this patient require physical restraint immediately?

_____

_____

_____

2. What other actions should you consider before physically engaging the patient?

_____

_____

_____

As you discuss your options with the police officers, more security guards come down the hallway. A woman is with them; she is introduced to you as the patient's mother. She quickly tells you that the patient is autistic. The family is staying at the hotel, and somehow he left the room without being noticed. She called hotel security after searching the hotel for about 20 minutes, and they escorted her to the scene.

3. What will be your next steps in managing this situation?

_____

_____

_____

Active Learning

1. Life Spent Looking Up

This exercise will take a few hours to complete, so plan accordingly. If possible, borrow a wheelchair for a day. Adopt a mind-set in which you cannot use your legs for any reason. Try to navigate through an environment for at least 1 hour. You might try one or more of the following examples:

a. Try to move around your home or apartment. Perform the following tasks: Prepare lunch. Pretend to use the bathroom. Move from the chair to your bed and back again.

b. Go to a shopping mall. Get in and out of a car. Try on a shirt or blouse at a clothing store. Speak to a clerk at a checkout counter. Locate the elevator and use it to move from one floor to the next. Move through the mall. Order a meal at a restaurant or food court.

c. Try food shopping at a market. Try to reach items above and below your height. Retrieve one or more items from a freezer. Balance a shopping basket while moving through the store.

Afterward, reflect on these questions: Were you able to complete the tasks in the time it normally takes? Did it become more difficult to complete the tasks? Why? If you went out in public, how do you think you were perceived? How did you feel as you tried to complete the tasks?

If you performed this exercise correctly, you may have been very tired and sore at the end of the hour. What lessons did you learn that you could apply to your EMS practice when dealing with patients with physical disabilities?

Alternatively, you can perform this exercise even without a wheelchair. Simply adopt a sitting posture when attempting to perform each of the tasks. Do not use your legs if at all possible. What did you learn?

2. Volunteer Opportunity: Cancer Care

Arrange to observe patient care in an oncology unit at a hospital or in the home setting with a hospice nurse. If possible, participate in the care of the patient, including any medication administration and any type of patient moving.

You Are There: Reality-Based Cases

Case 1

You are on the scene of a young boy in acute respiratory distress. The mother reports that the 3-year-old began having trouble breathing earlier in the day. He has had bouts of respiratory distress during the past 3 months; the pediatrician prescribed albuterol as necessary for probable asthma. In the past 2 days the boy began complaining of fever, cough, and general fatigue.

As you begin your assessment, you note that the boy is supine in his bed, with pillows propping up his head and shoulders. He is pale and diaphoretic and takes shallow breaths. His radial pulse is weak and rapid. He appears listless and does not cry as you begin your assessment.

1. What are your next steps?

_____

_____

_____

2. What key pieces of information do you need to know right away?

_____

_____

_____

You have quickly completed your primary assessment and are now conducting a secondary assessment. The mother states that there is no other medical history and that there are no other medications other than the inhaler. She has given him four or five treatments since this morning, when the breathing trouble began. She also gave him one adult Tylenol tablet this morning, and another just before she called 9-1-1. She denies that the child has allergies to any medicine, and the last oral intake was this morning, when he had a few sips of soup broth. He has had very little to eat or drink since yesterday afternoon.

Your physical examination yields the following findings:

- He is very warm to the touch, with dry skin.
- There is no stridor or accessory muscle use.
- Breath sounds are clear and diminished in both lower fields.
- No unusual heart tones are evident.
- The ECG shows a sinus tachycardia, without ectopy.
- SpO_2 is 85% on high-flow oxygen via nonrebreather mask.
- $ETCO_2$ is 54 mm Hg.
- Neck veins are flat.
- The abdomen is soft and nontender.
- All four extremities are flaccid. He responds to your simple command of lifting an arm but only squeezes your fingers weakly.

3. Based on this information, what would you try to do next?

_____

_____

_____

4. List conditions that could be causing this patient's presenting signs and symptoms.

_____

_____

_____

Ventilating the patient improves both his oxygen saturation and carbon dioxide levels significantly. The patient appears to be more alert, blinking his eyes and trying to raise his hands to push the mask away. You are able to maintain a good mask seal, and with soothing, continuous encouragement, you continue to assist the patient's respirations en route to the hospital.

The patient is admitted to the pediatric ICU for 2 days before being moved to a med-surgery floor. A pediatric neurologist follows the case for a possible diagnosis of Duchenne's dystrophy.

5. Review Duchenne's dystrophy in chapter 46 in the textbook as well as doing a bit of research on the most common of all muscular dystrophies. Did the presenting signs and symptoms relate to this diagnosis? How closely are the signs related to other differential diagnoses that you suspected?

Test Yourself

1. Your blind patient has agreed to accept treatment and transportation. She is well enough to walk to the ambulance with aid. How should you guide her?

  a. Stay out of her way and announce obstacles as they appear.

  b. Stand behind her and gently guide her in the direction that she should travel.

  c. Place her hand in the crook of your arm and walk beside her.

  d. Grip her arm just above the elbow and slowly lead her to the ambulance.

2. When transporting a paralyzed patient with a tracheostomy, it is important to

  a. transport the patient in the supine position.

  b. have suction equipment readily available.

  c. realize that the patient is accustomed to medical procedures.

  d. transport the patient in Fowler's position.

3. You are called to the home of an elderly, deaf male. His granddaughter tells you that he does not know sign language and cannot read or write. How might you attempt to communicate with this patient?

_____

_____

4. Shortness of breath is common in obese patients and should be considered less concerning than dyspnea in patients who are physically fit.

True

False

5. You are treating an autistic child in respiratory distress. The child becomes extremely agitated when you try to touch her. Her father explains that she is hypersensitive and asks if you can take her to the hospital without touching her. You should

  a. suggest that the father transport the child in his own vehicle.

  b. refrain from touching the child and transport emergently.

  c. ask if there is a favorite toy or blanket that can be used to calm the child during your physical assessment.

  d. help the father understand the seriousness of the child's symptoms and the need for a physical evaluation, and then restrain the patient.

6. A man with Down syndrome was attempting to sit in a chair but slipped from the seat and fell to the ground. Immediately afterward, he began complaining of intense back and leg pain. You should suspect

  a. a fractured pelvis.

  b. a bruised coccyx.

  c. a spinal compression injury.

  d. a traumatic CNS injury.

7. Your patient has a severe stutter. He is becoming increasingly frustrated as he attempts to communicate his complaints to you. How might you help this patient?

  a. Whenever possible finish his sentences for him.

  b. Offer him the use of a pencil and paper.

  c. Tell him that communication is not necessary, and proceed with the physical exam.

  d. Ask questions that only require yes or no responses.

8. _____ patients are paralyzed from the waist down.

9. Very few patients with developmental or cognitive disabilities are able to understand you when you speak to them.

    True

    False

10. You arrive at the home of a patient who has not been taking his antipsychotic medication. His wife and children are present. When you attempt to approach him, he picks up a baseball bat and begins swinging it in the air. At this point, you should

    a. ask the patient whether he is having any suicidal or violent thoughts.

    b. leave the house with the wife and children and contact law enforcement.

    c. attempt to take the bat from the man and place him in restraints.

    d. calmly ask the patient to put down the bat and explain that you are here to help.

11. Urine, blood, vomit, and sputum from cancer patients may contain chemotherapy medications.

    True

    False

12. While performing a physical exam on a patient with a burned hand, you notice a discolored sore approximately 1 inch in diameter on the patient's forearm. When you ask him about it, he says that he noticed it a few months ago, but it has not yet healed. You should

    a. gently clean and bandage the sore, and recommend a topical application of vitamin E.

    b. suggest that the patient should ask his doctor for an oral antibiotic medication.

    c. treat the sore with antibiotic ointment and apply sterile bandaging.

    d. recommend that the patient should visit his doctor for an examination of the sore.

13. What are some of the causes of glaucoma?

    _____

    _____

14. Which of the following signs and symptoms are characteristic of cystic fibrosis?

    a. Wheezing, coughing with phlegm, and large appetite with poor weight gain

    b. Fever, headache, weakness, and muscle tenderness and spasms

c. Endocrine disturbances, cataracts, and prolonged muscle spasms in the fingers and facial muscles

d. Constipation, muscle weakness, slurred speech, and fatigue

15. You were called for a 4-year-old patient when his parents became increasingly concerned about his unusual behavior. The child is crying and occasionally tugs on his ears. He does not seem to mind being touched, but will not respond to your questions or to his parents. The parents assure you that he is ordinarily very verbal and outgoing. Other than irritability and a slightly elevated temperature, the child exhibits no signs of illness or injury. You should suspect that

    a. the child may be suffering from trauma-induced aphasia.

    b. the child may have a learning disability.

    c. the child may have a middle ear infection.

    d. the child may suffer from a congenital hearing defect.

Need to Know

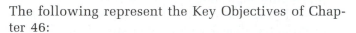

The following represent the Key Objectives of Chapter 46:

1. *Adjust your assessment and management approach for patients with physical impairments.*

(a)

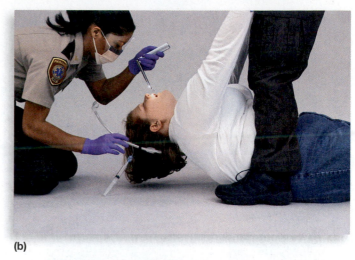
(b)

FIGURE 46-1   Airway Management Technique Modifications for Obese Patients. **(a)** Support the shoulders, neck, and head with a towel mound, or **(b)** have an assistant lift the arms and shoulders of the patient.

Review the information in Chapter 44, Geriatric Patients, in the textbook about hearing and visual impairment issues. Regardless of the patient's age, your ability to communicate with someone who has difficulty hearing or seeing you will be hampered. Remember the basics of communication: work with the impairment, not against it. Shouting at a hearing-impaired patient, for example, will likely not help. However, speaking in a slightly lower pitch and maintaining your body position in clear view of the patient's sight may make it easier for the patient to understand you. Similarly, for a poorly sighted patient try to locate the eyeglasses, and use your hands and body to guide the patient's movements when necessary.

Use active listening techniques for patients with speech impairments such as dysarthria or aphasia. Rephrasing their answers will allow you to confirm what you heard, as well as tell the patient that you understood what was said. If the situation permits, allow patients to use pen and paper to write out their responses. Try not to anticipate or complete a patient's sentences. Encourage the patient to use gestures (e.g., "Point to where it hurts"). Most importantly, give the patient time to formulate his or her thoughts and respond to your questions.

Obese patients pose significant challenges in assessment, treatment, and extrication. Remain professional and empathetic. Utilize additional personnel to minimize injury to yourself and other rescuers. Improvise your traditional equipment to secure the patient during extrication and transport. See the Connections section about ambulances specifically designed to handle very large patients.

Airway management in the obese patient is a challenge. Review the information provided in Chapter 12, Airway Management, Ventilation, and Oxygenation, in the textbook, and pay close attention to the technique modifications for supporting the patient's shoulders, neck, and head, such as a towel mound or having an assistant lift the arms and shoulders of the patient (Figure 46-1).

Patients with permanent forms of paralysis may have a variety of appliances and assistive devices to help them live longer and more comfortably. Whenever possible, integrate their regular method of movement during transfers. Be especially cautious about the patient's extremities—if paresthesia exists, the patient may not be able to tell whether an arm, leg, or finger is in an unusual position or if there is any pain.

2. *Manage patients with mental and emotional challenges appropriately.*

Review Chapter 40, Behavioral and Psychiatric Disorders, in the textbook for information about various mental illnesses and their presentations. Always consider whether a medical cause may be the source of apparent psychiatric behavior. As with all patients, your personal safety is your main priority. For patients who are suffering from acute episodes of their disorder, maintain a heightened sense of your surroundings and pay close attention to patients' verbal and body cues.

3. *Accommodate patients with developmental disabilities.*

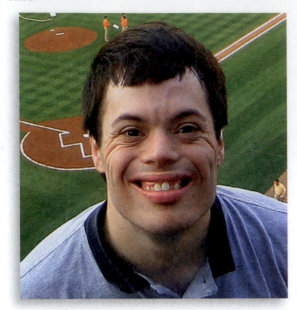

Although individuals with disabilities may have medical conditions that are more prevalent or unique, the greatest challenge may be the ability to communicate empathetically. As with physical impairments, allow patients with developmental disabilities the time to establish a dialogue with you. This may include a period during which you first need to establish trust before being "allowed" to perform a physical exam or apply equipment. An autistic child or a person with Down syndrome may very well understand what you are trying to say or do, but may be frightened or have difficulty controlling his or her impulses in response. Work with the disorder rather than against it. Integrate family, friends, and other trusted caretakers into your approach and management. There are several Web resources that are listed in the Connections section that provide further information about these disorders.

4. *Provide empathetic and professional care to patients with pathological challenges.*

There are several disease processes that can pose additional problems to the patient's chief complaint. Most can be accommodated with minimal effort, whereas others can require more resources and attention from you than is typical.

Arthritis is a common affliction. In many cases the pain or mobility issues are at most an inconvenience to the individual. However, some patients experience so much discomfort and reduction in their range of motion that procedures such as spinal immobilization or splinting can become quite difficult to perform without causing great pain. Pad as much as you can around joints, and work from the viewpoint of making the device fit to the patient, not the other way around. Take time to help the patient differentiate chronic pain from new-onset discomfort.

Cancer is another common condition seen in EMS patients. On occasion EMS may be called to an acute event that is the first sign of cancer; for example, a seizure may be caused by a brain tumor. However, most signs of cancer are more subtle and take time to develop. During chemotherapy a patient will become neutropenic or immunosuppressed and be much more susceptible to infection. Be precise on sterile technique and standard precautions. Avoid any unnecessary invasive procedures. In terminal cases, be sure that you fully understand any advance directives that may be in place. Cancer drugs are by their very nature very toxic. Do not handle them if you can avoid it.

Patients with *cerebral palsy* (CP) have difficulty controlling part or all of their body. It is easy to assume that all CP patients are also developmentally disabled; avoid making that assumption when communicating with such patients. Your primary accommodation will be to adjust your equipment toward unusual body positions; pad voids generously. Suction excessive secretions and maintain basic airways as needed.

Cystic fibrosis (CF) is a condition that afflicts the lungs and GI tract. The large amount of mucus that is produced hinders gas exchange in the lungs and digestive abilities. For patients experiencing respiratory distress, a beta agonist bronchodilator may be helpful in loosening secretion-plugged bronchioles, allowing for better air exchange.

Multiple sclerosis (MS) is a disease process that causes the myelin sheath surrounding the nerve fibers to degenerate over time, blocking nerve impulses at the site of destruction. This results in a variety of neurological impairments that can be debilitating or even fatal. Depending upon the location of the myelin sheath destruction, patients can experience vertigo, muscle weakness, slurred speech, visual disturbances, and numbness. Symptoms tend to become more frequent and longer lasting over time. Key illnesses to watch out for include urinary tract infections, respiratory infections, and muscle spasms.

Muscular dystrophy (MD) categorizes a group of related diseases that result in a progressive weakening and wasting of skeletal muscles. This condition results in loss of normal gait, muscle contractures, and even cardiac and endocrine disturbances. You will need to provide additional support for movement and padding for the unique positions the body might assume from later stages of MD for comfort during transport. Watch for cardiac dysrhythmias during your care.

Myasthenia gravis (MG) is an autoimmune disease that progressively weakens the voluntary muscles of the eyes, face, throat, and extremities. As the disease progresses, patients become noticeably weaker over the course of a day, especially after prolonged activity such as speaking or eating. Keeping the airway clear can become a challenge when the patient is in this weakened state. Be prepared to support the patient's airway and breathing effort.

Need to Do

The following skills are explained and illustrated in a step-by-step manner, via skill sheets and/or Step-by-Steps in this text and on the accompanying DVD:

Skill Name	Skill Sheet Number and Location	Step-by-Step Number and Location
Primary assessment	32 – Appendix A and DVD	32 – Chapter 14 and DVD
Secondary assessment	33 – Appendix A and DVD	33 – Chapter 14 and DVD
Verbal Communications	63 – DVD	N/A

Connections

There is a plethora of Internet resources for helping patients with disabilities. Following is a small sampling:

- The Master's Tech Home website, www.masterstech-home.com/ASLDict.html, provides both pictorial and animated demonstrations of American Sign Language (ASL) words, numbers, and letters.
- You can find information on bariatric (obese patients) ambulances at the Southwest Ambulance website at www.swambulance.com/site/images/images/bariatric_care_overview.pdf and at the American Medical Response website at www.amr.net/news/releases/2003/020303.asp.
- Learn more about autism at the Autism Society website: www.autism-society.org/site/PageServer?pagename=OnlineCourse. Autism care in the prehospital arena can be found at www.autismlink.com/info/ems.php.
- Locate information about Down syndrome at the National Down Syndrome Society website: www.ndss.org/index.php. The National Institutes of Health hosts a website at www.nlm.nih.gov/medlineplus/downsyndrome.html.
- One of the outcomes of myasthenia gravis is aphasia. You can find out more with this video Aphasia Hope Foundation: www.aphasiahope.org/media_resource.jsp?id=34.
- Chapter 46 in the textbook also references other chapters in the textbook. Review Chapter 4, Legal Issues, for handling patients with terminal illnesses. Chapter 20, Head, Face, and Neck Trauma, provides additional information on patients with head injuries.
- Link to the companion DVD for a chapter-based quiz, audio glossary, animations, games and exercises, and, when appropriate, skill sheets and skill Step-by-Steps.

Street Secrets

- **No RSI** Because of the effects that depolarizing drugs used during medication-assisted intubation have on the ACh receptor sites, this procedure is contraindicated in patients with myasthenia gravis.

The Drug Box

There are no specific drugs related to this chapter content.

Answers

Are You Ready?

1. It is possible that physical restraint will be required to protect the safety of rescuers and the patient. However,

as a health-care provider you need to assess the patient from "across the room" to see if you can determine if any potential life-threatening conditions exist.

2. If possible, establish a dialogue with the patient to try to "talk down" the patient. You and the other rescuers will also want to formulate a plan to safely bring the patient down to a controlled position. See Chapter 40, Behavioral and Psychiatric Disorders, in the textbook for more information.

3. The patient may be quite upset and anxious over being lost. It may take the assistance of the parent to help provide reassurance and instill a sense of trust. You will want to have the parent involved in your decision-making process; she may be able to tell, based on a lifetime of experience, whether he will be able to regain control of his fears and be calm. Understand that these cases may take time to manage and should not be rushed.

You Are There: Reality-Based Cases

Case 1

1. Your primary assessment reveals a child who is sick. Supplemental oxygen is needed at a minimum, but the level of arousal of the child is worrisome. Be prepared to manually ventilate the patient.

2. Prioritize your hunt for clues. You know that the patient is already doing poorly; his tachypnea and tachycardia are compensating for some underlying condition. It will be important to determine whether there is a primary cardiac dysrhythmia (even at this age), so ECG monitoring is critical. You also would want to know if the reported asthma condition could be the source of the problem, so auscultation of the lung sounds early is important, as is obtaining pulse oximeter and capnography readings. Can the parent provide any information about albuterol use by the patient? Are there any other medications or medical history in the child's background? Through subjective and objective findings, the intent is to quickly come up with a short laundry list of possible conditions that can be treated.

3. The higher-than-normal CO_2 and lower-than-normal O_2 readings should provide you clues that the patient is not ventilating adequately. Assisting his respirations with a bag-mask is needed. Increasing the minute volume could improve the patient's condition. It is a harder argument to make for the use of a beta agonist; lung sounds appear to be normal. However, because the patient is breathing so poorly, you may not be able to hear any wheezes that exist due to bronchoconstriction. More advanced airway management may be needed if manual bag-mask ventilations do not help.

4. There are several conditions to consider, including sepsis, dehydration, asthma, DKA, hypoglycemia, and neuromuscular disorders such as multiple sclerosis and muscular dystrophy. Additional testing by you and the

emergency department will be needed to determine the actual underlying cause.

5. Although unexpected, recognize that an "atypical" suspicion might become the underlying cause of the patient's presentation. If you thought of many other potential causes that are more "common," good for you! This case is a difficult one, but one of the main points is that, regardless of your suspicions, a reasoned approach to managing the signs and symptoms will be effective for the care of the patient.

Test Yourself

1. c

   Ambulatory blind patients should not be pushed or pulled. When leading this patient, walk beside her and allow the patient to hold onto your arm, rather than you holding onto hers.

2. b

   Airway obstruction from mucus is fairly common in tracheostomy patients, so suction equipment should be available.

3. You could try speaking into his ear in a clear, low-pitched voice. You could also try drawing pictures or symbols on paper, speaking so that your mouth is visible in case he is able to lip-read, using gestures, or enlisting the granddaughter's help in communicating with the patient.

4. False

   Although obese patients may become short of breath more easily than patients who are physically fit, you should never disregard any symptom that may indicate a serious medical condition. It is essential to adequately assess every symptom in order to identify and treat any life threats. When assessing any patient, you should determine if symptoms are new or part of a chronic condition, if any preexisting symptoms have been more severe than usual, and, if so, for how long.

5. c

   Many children with an autism spectrum disorder (ASD) have a favorite object (blanket, toy, etc.) or subject they like to discuss. Allow them to hold their object or discuss their interest. Restraint should only be used as a last resort. If a child is hypersensitive, restraint can be intensely painful and frightening.

6. c

   Compression injuries of the spine are associated with Down syndrome. Given the mechanism of injury, it should be your first suspicion. For other complications of Down syndrome see Box 46-9 in the textbook.

7. b

   When dealing with patients with speech impairments, patience is critical. It is important to allow them to express themselves fully and to offer aid, such as a paper and pencil, when possible.

8. Paraplegic

   Paraplegic patients are paralyzed from the waist down. Quadriplegic patients experience paralysis in the arms, legs, and trunk of the body and sometimes require artificial respiration to maintain life.

9. False

It is very important to establish a rapport with a patient who has a developmental disability before you initiate contact with that patient. Although they may not seem to comprehend you, patients with developmental handicaps are often capable of understanding your communication.

10. b

If there is any suspicion of violent behavior, leave the scene immediately and summon police assistance.

11. True

Chemotherapy drugs are harmful and can cause DNA mutation, birth defects in developing embryos, some types of cancer, and skin irritation. As body fluids from cancer patients may contain these drugs, you should exercise appropriate PPE precautions.

12. d

Sores that do not heal may be an indication of skin cancer. You should ask the patient to consult his doctor or an oncologist as soon as possible.

13. Glaucoma can occur as the result of an eye injury, inflammation, tumor, or in advanced cases of cataracts or diabetes. It can also be caused by certain drugs such as steroids. This form of glaucoma may be mild or severe. The type of treatment depends on whether it is open-angle or angle-closure glaucoma.

Glaucoma is a group of eye diseases that causes gradual visual impairment. Vision loss is caused by damage to the optic nerve.

14. a

Cystic fibrosis (CF) is characterized by very salty-tasting skin; persistent coughing, at times with phlegm; wheezing or shortness of breath; repeated lung infections; excessive appetite but poor weight gain; and greasy, bulky stools.

15. c

Otitis media (middle ear infection) is often characterized by irritability; fever; and temporary, mild hearing loss in children. Most children will experience otitis media at some point in their lives. Given his other signs and symptoms, coupled with the fact that he is normally verbal, the child's seeming unwillingness to communicate may be the result of this temporary hearing loss.

Problem-Based Learning Case 7
Bravery Comes in All Forms

Part I: The Case

Dispatch and Scene Size-Up

"Medic 3, Central."

You snap out of your slumber and reach for the microphone. "Go ahead, Central."

"Priority 1 response to 657 Mission Street, Apartment 302. Child having a seizure. Time out, 0312."

You rub your eyes and acknowledge the dispatch information. Your partner Dave grumbles something about the time of night. It's cold out; your unit has been posting at this location for the past hour, and it had been lightly snowing. With the vehicle heater running, it was hard not to doze off. Dave puts the transmission into drive, and you make your way into the night.

You arrive at the low-income apartment building at 0317. The fire department first responders have not yet arrived, although you can hear the siren coming from a distance. You load your stretcher with the first-in gear plus the pediatric bag and head for the elevator.

A distraught woman is looking for you as you head down the hallway. She is frantically waving her hands and asking you to hurry. As you enter the small apartment, you note how neat and tidy the room is. You also notice two children, about 3 or 4 years old, hiding behind the woman. She tells you that her name is Tonisha and that her oldest child Mosi just stopped seizing. She leads you to a small bedroom in the back of the apartment.

You turn on the overhead light and see several mattresses on the floor. On one of them is a boy who appears to be 6 years old. His eyes are closed, and you can hear wet, raspy sounds coming from his throat as he breathes rapidly. He appears almost ashen in color.

1. *Describe your first steps in your approach to this case.*

_____

_____

The Primary assessment (Primary assessment) and Initial Differentials

Your interventions clear the airway, but the soft, wet, audible sounds remain. Your patient has a radial pulse that is weak and rapid. There is a little blood coming from his mouth and lip. He also appears incontinent of urine.

You call Mosi's name, but he does not respond. He moans faintly when you apply a trapezius pinch, and you can feel him shrug his shoulder slightly.

Dave has been interviewing the mother while opening up the jump kits. He turns toward you and reports that the child has been sick for about 24 hours with a fever and cough. The mother described an episode of the child rolling his eyes upward and calling out, followed by classic clonic motions that lasted a "long time."

You auscultate lung sounds and confirm that Mosi has crackles in both lung fields.

2. *Should you intubate him to maintain his airway? Why or why not?*

_____

_____

3. *What safety precautions, if any, should you consider, given the short history provided by the parent?*

_____

_____

History and Physical Exam (Secondary assessment and History)

The mother reports that Mosi has a past medical history of sickle cell anemia. He has had a few episodes recently of abdominal and joint pain. They had gone to the pediatrician, who was going to refer them to a specialist, but she had not heard from the pediatrician yet. Mosi began feeling ill yesterday afternoon and missed school today. He had been complaining of having trouble breathing when the seizure occurred. He is not on medications and has no allergies to medications. Other than three doses of acetaminophen, a few sips of juice, and some soup broth, he has had nothing to eat since yesterday.

Your patient has a blood pressure of 76/50 and a heart rate of 136. His respiratory rate is 30, with an SpO_2 of 80% on supplemental oxygen. He feels warm to the touch. As you examine him, Mosi begins to blink and cry. He tries to speak, but his words are slurred and difficult to understand.

4. *List possible reasons for Mosi's signs and symptoms.*

   _____

   _____

Field Impression(s) and Treatment Plan

During your movement of the patient, you notice that he is able to move only his left arm and leg. The right extremities are flaccid.

His SpO_2 reading is now 86%. His breathing rate continues to be fast. You can palpate a blood pressure of 74 systolic. His heart rate is 130. The abdomen feels rigid when you try to palpate any of the quadrants, and he whimpers when you touch him. Bilateral distal pulses can be felt in his legs.

5. *Describe your treatment of this patient. Be specific and provide an organized approach.*

   _____

   _____

Transportation and Ongoing Care

Mosi is quiet as you transport him through the frigid night to University Medical Center. Although he doesn't speak, you can sense that he is in a lot of pain; tears continue to well up in his eyes, and he tries to grasp his right elbow with his left hand. His eyes track your movements and appear to focus on you. His lung sounds still sound "wet" but are unchanged from

before. You reauscultate his blood pressure at 82/64, with a heart rate of 124. His abdomen remains firm to the touch.

6. *Is your patient improving? Are there any other management techniques remaining to be done?*

   _____

   _____

Transfer of Care, Follow-Up, and Outcome

Dr. Gupta listens carefully to your report as the hospital staff goes to work transferring the patient from your care to theirs. Monitor leads are swapped and vital signs are reassessed. A nurse leans close to the patient's ear and reassures the frightened boy. In the bright lights of the resuscitation room, you can see that the patient is still very pale and breathing quickly. As you provide details of Mosi's condition, the physician's expression changes from puzzlement to apprehension. You ask, "Do you think he's in heart failure?"

She shakes her head. "I would have suspected something like that, given the fever and poor lung sounds, but with the history of sickle cell, I suspect it's something more." Picking up the room's wall phone, she asks the operator to page the hematologist.

7. *What do you think is the most likely explanation for Mosi's condition?*

   _____

   _____

Long-Term Outlook

Mosi stays in the pediatric intensive care unit (PICU) for 5 days. The hematologist and pediatric intensivist worked hard to resolve his chest condition. Unfortunately the hemiparalysis never completely resolves. Physical therapy helps Mosi regain the majority of function of his right side.

Part II: Debriefing

Responses to Part I questions:
1. Your primary assessment shows a sick child in need of immediate support. Do you need to suction, or assist his ventilations with a bag-mask? What other information could help you determine whether to support his ventilations or to provide supplemental oxygen?
2. Did you the weigh the pros and cons of placing an advanced airway in this patient? Remember the goal of airway management is to ensure oxygenation

and ventilation; the "best" airway is the one that does both as simply as possible. Did you consider other forms of airway control? If so, what did you consider? If you chose to intubate the patient, what were the factors that made you decide to perform the procedure?

3. Is there the possibility of an infectious cause for the patient's condition? Which disease would cause you great concern? What additional precautions would you take?

4. As always, think of body systems when evaluating the constellation of signs and symptoms. Based on the patient's vital signs, he could be in shock, perhaps sepsis with the history of fever. How would the presumed fluid overload in the lungs be involved with this situation? Does the sickle cell disease history play a factor? What can cause fluid buildup in the lungs?

5. Although your patient still continues to look "sick" he does show some improvement in his ability to carry oxygen in his body. What does that imply about the respiratory system? His other vital signs continue to show signs of shock. What treatment can you provide to support his blood pressure? How will the fluid overload in the lungs affect your treatment? Are you concerned about the extremity findings?

6. Your treatment appears to have improved his blood pressure, albeit marginally. Is there any other intervention you could consider to improve it further? With the change in his level of consciousness, you will need to reassess him. It would be a good time to determine if he can follow some simple commands. What would you ask him to do?

7. There are several potential causes for the signs and symptoms. Mosi appears to be pretty young for some of the findings, but does age rule out any of your suspicions? Did you determine that Mosi was experiencing acute chest syndrome? What about the strokelike symptoms? How are both of these conditions connected to sickle cell disease?

Part III: Case Discussion

As the case progressed, did you catch yourself wondering how a child this young has signs of pulmonary edema, as well as signs of a stroke? Your puzzlement should have led you on a search for disease processes specific to the pediatric population that can result in these findings. In particular, linking the sickle cell disease (SCD) history early could have led you to look into conditions related to that particular disease. We'll come back to this later.

There were several distracting findings that should have made you consider a variety of conditions. One

major cause would be infection; in particular, meningitis would be of major concern for your own health, as it is highly contagious. The fever history, altered mental status, and possible febrile seizure would be supportive of this theory. However, the hemiparalysis would be a very unusual finding in meningitis. Add the possible increased permeability of the capillary-alveolar membrane and hypotension, and you might consider sepsis as the culprit.

There are other noncardiogenic causes of pulmonary edema, including toxic inhalation, pulmonary infection, pancreatitis, aspiration, and multisystem trauma. Beyond a possible infection, it is unlikely that the remaining signs and symptoms support any of these causes.

Can a child have a stroke? It is rare, but absolutely yes—especially in children with SCD. Can you explain why? Certainly the misshapen form of the sickled cell has a direct influence on its ability to pass through the vascular system, especially in the capillary beds. A rapid clot buildup in the vasculature of the brain would produce ischemia just as surely as a lipid-based clot of an adult.

Did you link the chest findings and lung sounds to SCD? Did you find a particular syndrome in your research? SCD has far-ranging effects beyond the pain generated by the local ischemic events.

This is a very difficult patient to treat. You may have determined that IV fluid therapy can be helpful for SCD-related conditions and would have helped support the hypotensive state of the patient. However, the fluid you auscultated in the lungs may have prevented you from delivering any significant volume of normal saline or lactated Ringer's solution. A vasopressor such as dopamine could be helpful by increasing cardiac output, raising blood pressure, and helping to move fluid out of the lungs. Continuous positive airway pressure (CPAP) may have been helpful as well, although the patient may be too young for its use. Ultimately the patient will need to be admitted and given intravenous antibiotic therapy and even blood transfusions to correct the situation.

Part IV: Further Learning Paths

- eMedicine.com has several resources detailing sickle cell disease. You can search their website at www.emedicine.com.
- The American Sickle Cell Anemia Association is dedicated to providing resources for individuals and families at risk for sickle cell disease. Their website is www.ascaa.org/mission.asp.
- Another comprehensive website for SCD comes from the United Kingdom. The Sickle Cell Society website, www.sicklecellsociety.org/, has several areas for educational resources.

chapter 47

Patients with Chronic Illnesses

1. What are several causes of an obstructed tracheostomy tube?

_____

_____

_____

2. Is pulling the tracheostomy tube out the first thing that you should do?

_____

_____

_____

3. What are your options for managing the patient's airway?

_____

_____

_____

Are You Ready?

It is 0200 hours when you and your partner are dispatched for a resuscitation. You are approximately 5 minutes away from the scene when the first responder fire engine advises that CPR is in progress. When you arrive, you notice that there is a large crowd and the engine crew is performing CPR on a female lying on the sidewalk. Your partner goes to the patient, and you grab the equipment. As you approach the patient, you notice that she has a tracheostomy tube. Your partner is cutting the trach tube ties. He turns to you and says, "She's not moving any air through the tube. Should we pull it?"

Active Learning

1. **Volunteer Oppertunity: Living with Technology**

   An effective way to become familiar with the patients and devices that support patients in the home care setting is to work with patients in that setting. There are a number of ways that you can accomplish this goal:

   a. Arrange for an observational session with a home health-care provider. If you are interested in learning about preexisting vascular access devices (PVADs), schedule an observational session with an oncology home health nurse or infusion nurse.

b. If you want to learn about the access of arteriovenous shunts in dialysis patients, set up an observational session at a dialysis clinic where you can see a number of patients being treated at the same time.

c. If you are interested in learning more about ventilators, tracheostomies, and other airway devices, set up an observational session with a respiratory therapist in the home health-care setting or hospital. An observational session with a respiratory therapist is a valuable experience not only for gaining knowledge about ventilators and airway devices, but also for obtaining exposure to patients with a variety of respiratory conditions and presentations. You'll hear a variety of lung sounds and observe how different medications affect different patients.

You Are There: Reality-Based Cases

Case 1

You arrive on the scene of a motor vehicle collision to find the front seat passenger of one of the cars bleeding profusely from his groin. Once the area is exposed, you note a deep laceration to his right inguinal fossa caused by a glass vase on the patient's lap that broke during the collision. The patient is awake and alert, but slow to respond. He has cool, pale, and moist skin with a weak and rapid radial pulse of 118 and a respiratory rate of approximately 30. The bleeding from the patient's groin is difficult to control with direct pressure. The dressings that you have applied have already become saturated with blood, and the bleeding doesn't appear to be slowing. You and your partner apply additional dressings to the patient's groin and place him in c-spine precautions.

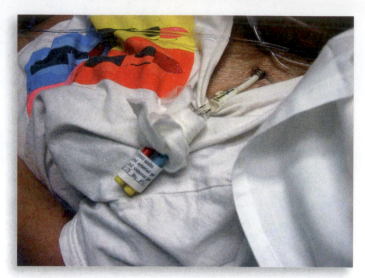

FIGURE 47-1 Vascular access device entering the left subclavian vein.

After you begin transport to the trauma center, you perform a rapid secondary assessment and discover that the patient has a vascular access device entering his skin inferior to the left clavicle (Figure 47-1). When questioned about the device, the patient's wife explains that the patient was on his way home from the hospital after having surgery for the removal of a brain tumor, at which time he developed renal failure. The device is being used for dialysis until he can be scheduled for surgery to create an arteriovenous (AV) shunt.

You notice that the patient is becoming less responsive, and when you reassess his ABCs, you discover that his ventilations are slower and shallower than when you first saw him. You are no longer able to palpate a radial pulse. The patient has weak and thready brachial pulses, and the bleeding from his groin continues.

1. Describe your top priority in caring for this patient.

_____

_____

_____

2. How will you address the patient's hypoperfusion?

_____

_____

_____

3. Is vascular access needed in this patient? If so, how will you obtain IV access?

_____

_____

_____

4. List three advantages and three disadvantages of central venous access devices.

_____

_____

_____

5. Describe the procedure for accessing a central line in the prehospital setting.

_____

_____

_____

Case 2

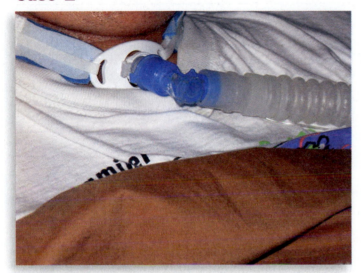

Charles Stanton is a prestigious neurosurgeon who has saved the lives of countless patients and developed a number of breakthrough techniques in neurosurgery. Three years ago, Dr. Stanton was diagnosed with amyotrophic lateral sclerosis (ALS), better known as Lou Gehrig's disease. Over the past 3 years, Dr. Stanton lost function in his arms and then his legs. Last year, his breathing became labored and he ultimately received a tracheostomy. Dr. Stanton has been at home for the past year with 24-hour-a-day nursing care. He is unable to feed himself, so he receives his nutrition through a gastric tube via a feeding pump (Figure 47-2).

Dr. Stanton has a specialized bed and wheelchair that are designed for optimal comfort and reduced chances of skin breakdown due to his immobility. His bladder is evacuated on a regular basis by a nurse who inserts a straight catheter into his urethra and bladder. Last month, Dr. Stanton had bright red blood in his stool. It was discovered that he had colorectal cancer. He met with an oncologist, who asked Dr. Stanton if he was willing to participate in a trial for a promising new chemotherapeutic agent. Dr. Stanton agreed and had a peripherally inserted central catheter (PICC) line inserted

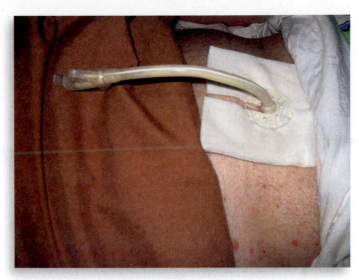

FIGURE 47-2 Gastric tube.

into his right antecubital fossa. He has received six doses of chemotherapy. On his last visit, it was discovered that his white blood cell count was extremely low. His doctor delayed the administration of subsequent doses of the trial chemotherapy medication until his white blood cell count returned to normal. Two days later the home health nurse called 9-1-1 because Dr. Stanton developed an altered mental status and a high fever (104°F). His blood pressure was recorded at 70/34, and his heart rate was 146.

1. What is the basic pathophysiology of ALS?

_____

_____

_____

2. What is your priority at this point?

_____

_____

_____

When you arrive on the scene, you are met by the patient's brother, who is his durable power of attorney for health care. He leads you into the patient's room, where the nurse is attempting to suction the patient's tracheostomy tube as the ventilator alarms (Figure 47-3). She states that Dr. Stanton's oxygen saturation is very low (76% on an FIO_2 of 30%).

3. What is your priority intervention at this point?

_____

_____

_____

FIGURE 47-3   Tracheostomy tube attached to a ventilator.

4. What pertinent questions should you ask about the tracheostomy tube?

_____

_____

_____

5. Describe the process of assessing and troubleshooting a tracheostomy tube.

_____

_____

_____

6. What is a simple way to improve the patient's oxygenation?

_____

_____

_____

7. What should you do if the ventilator continues to alarm despite your efforts?

_____

_____

_____

The patient's suction machine has been malfunctioning, so you remove the inner cannula of the patient's tracheostomy tube. The ventilator is reattached to the tracheostomy tube, and the FIO_2 is increased to 100%. The ventilator stops alarming, and the patient's oxygen saturation begins to slowly increase, but when your partner, Belinda, auscultates the patient's lungs, she hears rhonchi in all his lung fields.

8. What is the priority intervention or treatment at this point?

_____

_____

_____

9. What are two probable causes for Dr. Stanton's rhonchi?

_____

_____

_____

You suction the patient's tracheostomy tube while the nurse prepares a new inner cannula (Figure 47-4). You suction a large amount of formula-colored fluid from the patient's lungs.

10. What is your priority intervention at this time?

_____

_____

_____

In between suctioning and ventilating the patient, Belinda completes her assessment and updates the patient's vital signs. Dr. Stanton remains febrile, hypotensive, and tachycardic, but his oxygen saturation has increased to 94% on an FIO_2 of 100%. Belinda reports that the skin at the point of insertion for the PICC line is red, swollen, and warmer than the surrounding tissue. There are also red streaks running up the patient's arm from the point of insertion.

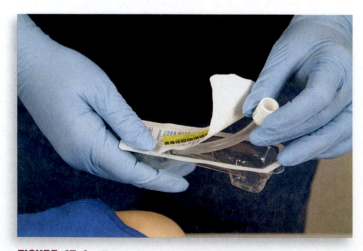

FIGURE 47-4   Example of an inner cannula.

11. What needs to be done prior to determining the best treatment for the patient's hypotension and tachycardia?

_____

_____

_____

12. Is the PICC line an option for use in treating the hypotension and shock? Why or why not?

_____

_____

_____

13. Beginning with the least invasive treatment, what are several possible treatments for hypotension and shock?

_____

_____

_____

Test Yourself

1. Patients undergoing hemodialysis are most likely to experience life-threatening emergencies caused by
   a. complications with the access device.
   b. malfunctions with the dialysis machine.
   c. infection at the access site.
   d. fluid or electrolyte imbalances.

2. A(n) _____ is a surgical opening that connects the end of the small intestines to the outside of the body.

3. An ostomy is
   a. a surgical opening created to release internal pressure.
   b. the surgical process used to insert a catheter.
   c. the surgical removal of some or all of an internal organ.
   d. a surgical opening created between the surface of the body and an internal organ.

4. Most calls involving home care devices are related to the patient's underlying medical condition rather than a problem with the device.
   True
   False

5. Which of the following questions is *not* one of the three that you need to ask patients with tracheostomy tubes?
   a. Is the tracheostomy tube temporary or permanent?
   b. How long has the patient had the tracheostomy?
   c. Is the upper airway patent or obstructed?
   d. Why did the patient receive a tracheostomy?

6. A 37-year-old male has a peripherally inserted central catheter to administer chemotherapy. His skin feels warm, and he is perspiring heavily. His vital signs are HR of 114, RR of 28, and BP of 82/57. The catheter insertion site is red, tender, and emits yellow pus. During the process of treating the patient, will you need to access the vascular system, and if so what will be your preferred manner of access?
   a. Yes, establish an intraosseous administration route.
   b. Yes, use the preexisting catheter site.
   c. No, you will not need to access the vascular system.
   d. Yes, establish another IV in a different site.

7. The major difference between oxygen delivery in the hospital setting versus the home care setting is the
   a. oxygen delivery method.
   b. ability to monitor the patient.
   c. mechanism used to warm and humidify the oxygen.
   d. source of oxygen.

8. How can home health-care providers be of use to an emergency responder?

_____

_____

_____

9. A central venous access device that has been implanted under the patient's skin should only be accessed using a specially designed needle.
   True
   False

10. Why might a patient prefer home health care to hospital care?

_____

_____

_____

11. A 67-year-old female has been placed on continuous formula feeding using a nasogastric feeding tube. She is now aspirating her formula. What should you do *first*?

   a. Visually confirm the placement of the tube.

   b. Remove the contents of the tube.

   c. Turn off the feeding pump.

   d. Remove the nasogastric tube.

12. Which of the following are you *least* likely to be called for regarding a chronically ill patient?

   a. Medical complications caused by home care equipment

   b. Hospice care assistance

   c. Medical complications caused by the chronic condition

   d. Malfunctioning equipment

13. What are some general differences between curative care and palliative care?

   _____

   _____

   _____

14. Which of these is *not* a factor contributing to the rise of home health care?

   a. A surplus of home health-care workers

   b. More patients choosing to stay at home

   c. Efforts to cut health-care costs

   d. Improvements in medical technology

15. What are some signs that a patient is experiencing urinary retention?

   _____

   _____

   _____

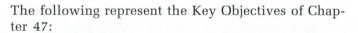

Need to Know

The following represent the Key Objectives of Chapter 47:

1. *Discuss the changes in medicine and managed care over the past 25 years, including their impact on the length of hospital admission.*

   The manner in which medicine is practiced has changed dramatically over the past 25 years. There have been considerable advances in practice, technology, and science. Hospital stays are shorter, and patients are being discharged into the out-of-hospital environment much sooner.

Changes in reimbursement for services has also changed dramatically. The insurance industry has had a dramatic impact on the practice of medicine, and as a result patients are being discharged more quickly and in more serious conditions than they would have been in the past.

2. *Describe how home health-care teams manage high-acuity and long-term-care patients without the services found in the in-hospital setting.*

   The advances in home health care are the result of advances in training, improvements in technology (biomedical equipment designed specifically for use in the out-of-hospital setting), and the availability of many of the same medical professionals that can be found in the hospital setting, such as nurse practitioners, physician assistants, respiratory therapists, and other allied health professionals. The out-of-hospital setting is becoming a "hospital" in a patient's home.

3. *Describe common home health-care equipment that paramedics may encounter in the home care setting, including their basic functions.*

   Oxygen equipment. Oxygen in the home can be delivered through liquid oxygen apparatuses and oxygen concentrators, as well as through compressed oxygen tanks. A variety of oxygen sources are designed to meet the varying needs of each individual home health-care patient.

   Ventilators. Ventilators can be reduced to a number of components: "a source of oxygen and air, warming and humidification system, valves controlling and monitoring gas flow, a user interface, a breathing circuit of plastic tubing and mechanisms for patient monitoring with alarm systems."[1] Mechanical ventilation in the home health-care setting is used for patients with chronic respiratory failure and patients with long-term neuromuscular disorders. Each individual patient requires personalized ventilator settings and parameters to meet his or her unique needs. An explanation for the use of each of these ventilator modes can be found in Table 47-2 in the textbook.

   Basic ventilator parameters include fraction of inspired oxygen (FIO_2), ventilator tidal volume, ventilatory rate, and inspiratory/expiratory ratio (I:E ratio). Table 47-3 in the textbook outlines basic ventilator parameters.

   Paramedics are typically called when the patient has taken a turn for the worse or there is a problem with the life support equipment. Troubleshooting problems with a ventilator is not a difficult task, especially in light of the fact that most problems that could exist with a ventilator are monitored by an alarm. When an alarm sounds, the control panel for the ventilator typically identifies where the problem exists, or at least the nature of the problem (a high-pressure or a low-pressure alarm, etc.). Table 47-4 in the textbook discusses the steps that the paramedic needs to take while troubleshooting a malfunctioning ventilator.

Tracheostomy tubes. A tracheostomy is a surgical opening in the neck that extends into the trachea. Tracheostomy tubes are the preferred airway for use in patients who require prolonged mechanical ventilation. Table 47-5 in the textbook offers an explanation of the different types of tracheostomy tubes and their uses.

Complications associated with tracheostomy tubes include mucous plug formation, decannulation or displacement of the tracheostomy tube, and bleeding at the incision (stoma) site. Treatment for these complications is discussed in detail in the textbook.

Nasogastric (NG) tubes. The most likely reason that an NG tube is used in the home health-care setting is to aid in the delivery of medication and formula to patients who are unable to receive their nutrition or medication by mouth.

Percutaneous endoscopic gastrostomy (PEG) tubes and gastric (G) tubes. PEG tubes and G-tubes are surgically implanted devices that extend from the surface of the abdomen into the stomach and are used for long-term nutritional support in individuals who are not able to receive their nutrition by mouth.

Foley catheters. The most likely reason for urinary catheterization in the home care setting is urinary retention.

Colostomy, ileostomy, and urostomy. These are artificial surgical openings that are designed to collect waste products from the body when the regular collection or excretion organs (the colon, the ileum, and the urinary bladder or urethra, respectively) are malfunctioning.

Preexisting vascular access devices (PVADs). Central venous catheters are designed to stay in place for extended periods of time for the treatment of chronic or long-term conditions. Long-term catheter placement prevents the patient from having vascular access started for each treatment and the negative side effects associated with frequent IV attempts.

Patient-controlled analgesia (PCA) pumps. PCA pumps are designed to allow patients to deliver their own IV pain medication according to their perceived level of discomfort with the touch of a button.

Connections

- Chapter 12, Airway Management, Ventilation, and Oxygenation, in the textbook includes additional information on the different airways and ventilators that may be encountered in the home health-care setting.

- Chapter 28, Pulmonary, in the textbook provides information on respiratory conditions that may be encountered in the home health-care setting.

- Chapter 34, Gastroenterology, in the textbook describes ostomies and how to care for patients who have these devices in the prehospital setting.

- Chapter 36, Urology, in the textbook outlines information on urinary catheters and urostomies, including how to care for the patient with these devices in the prehospital setting.

- Chapter 46, Patients with Special Challenges, in the textbook includes a discussion on patients with special challenges, the devices that they use, and how to manage these patients and their devices in the home health-care setting.

- Chapter 52, Teamwork and Operational Interface, in the textbook describes working with the home health-care professional in an attempt to provide the optimal care for the patient in the home health-care setting.

- Link to the companion DVD for a chapter-based quiz, audio glossary, animations, games and exercises, and, when appropriate, skill sheets and skill Step-by-Steps.

Street Secrets

- **Home Health Devices** Most of the devices that paramedics encounter in the home health-care environment, if approached with basic common sense, are straightforward to manage. If the patient's ventilator is experiencing a malfunction, turn it off, assess the patient's ABCs, and provide support for the patient's ventilations via a bag-mask device as needed while troubleshooting the problem with the ventilator. The same is true for care of patients with tracheostomies and those with a preexisting vascular access device such as a PICC line.

- **Patients with Tracheostomies** Patients with tracheostomies who are experiencing ventilatory distress should be treated in the same manner as patients without invasive airway devices. Assess the ABCs, and intervene whenever you discover a problem that compromises the integrity of the

Need to Do

The following skills are explained and illustrated in a step-by-step manner, via skill sheets and/or Step-by-Steps in this text and on the accompanying DVD:

Skill Name	Skill Sheet Number and Location	Step-by-Step Number and Location
Airway Positioning and Maneuvers	1 – DVD	1 – DVD
Bag-Mask Ventilation with 1 Rescuer	4 – DVD	4 – DVD
Bag-Mask Ventilation with 2 or More Rescuers	5 – DVD	5 – DVD
Foreign Body Airway Obstruction Removal—Advanced Techniques	6 – Appendix A and DVD	6 – Chapter 12 and DVD
End-Tidal Capnography	10 – DVD	N/A
Endotracheal Suctioning	11 – DVD	11 – DVD
Pulse Oximetry	12 – DVD	12 – DVD
Suctioning of Stoma	23 – DVD	23 – DVD
Evacuation of Gastric Contents	24 – DVD	24 – DVD
Intraosseous Access and Drug Administration	45 – Appendix A and DVD	45 – Chapter 16 and DVD
Central Line Access for Fluids and Drug Administration	47 – DVD	N/A

ABCs. You must be familiar with the basics of tracheostomy use, the different types of tracheostomy tubes, and how to troubleshoot problems with tracheostomy tubes once they occur.

- **Patients with Central Lines** Patients can have central lines for a number of reasons. Typically, they have a PVAD because they are undergoing a treatment that requires frequent and sometimes lengthy vascular access for medications, feedings (total parenteral nutrition [TPN]), or chemotherapy. PVADs are typically used by paramedics when the patient is significantly compromised (e.g., ALOC, severe respiratory distress, shock, cardiopulmonary arrest), but not for routine vascular access on a stable patient.

The Drug Box

There are no specific drugs related to this chapter content.

References

1. I. Greenwald and S. Rosonoke, "Mechanical Ventilation—Understanding Respiratory Physiology and the Basics of Ventilator Management," *Journal of Emergency Medical Services* (December 2003): 76; available online at www.jems.com (accessed April 1, 2005).
2. S. J. Seay et al., "Tracheostomy Emergencies—Correcting Accidental Decannulations or Displaced Tracheostomy Tube," *American Journal of Nursing* 102, no. 3 (2002): 59.

Answers

Are You Ready?

1. Any of the following answers is correct: foreign body obstruction, dislodged tracheostomy tube, damaged inner cannula, mucous plug, and airway swelling.

2. Pulling out the tracheostomy tube should not be your first action. Some of the risks of pulling the tube outweigh leaving it in place for a few seconds while you troubleshoot the problem. If you pull the tube without gathering some basic information about it,

you face the possibility of not being able to reestablish an airway.

3. The first thing is to remove the inner cannula. If that does not open the airway, insert a sterile French suction catheter into the tube to determine if you can clear the obstruction. Instill 3–5 mL of sterile normal saline into the tube and attempt to ventilate again to loosen up any thick mucus that may exist. Extubate the patient's tracheostomy only as a last resort.

You Are There: Reality-Based Cases

Case 1

1. Because the patient has a decreased level of consciousness and his respirations are ineffective, immediately assist the patient's ventilations with a bag-mask device along with high-flow supplemental oxygen. Insertion of a BLS airway (OPA or NPA) is warranted.

2. Position the patient in a manner that will promote blood flow to the vital organs. This can be accomplished in part by positioning the patient in a shock position. Stopping the bleeding is another top priority. One method that can free up the hands of you and your partner is to place military anti-shock trousers (MAST) over the dressings that you have applied and inflate them. The application of the MAST can tamponade the bleeding and shunt the blood in the lower extremities to the core of the body. Keep the patient warm, because cold can impact the patient's ability to stop bleeding. IV access and fluid replacement may be needed; remember that large amounts of crystalloids may not be effective in an uncontrolled bleeding situation.

3. Vascular access is important in a trauma patient and should be provided during transport to an appropriate receiving facility. In this case, the patient has a central line that is used for dialysis. Can you use it for your IV access? The answer is maybe. If you are trained in the use of preexisting vascular access devices, use the central line. If you are not trained or approved to use such a device, you will need to look for another type of access for this patient. Don't automatically conclude that if the patient has a central line, he or she does not have any other vascular access. Many times central lines are inserted not because the patient has poor vascular access, but because the patient routinely requires treatment that uses IV access.

4. Advantages of central venous access catheter use include they can remain in place for a long duration; they have the ability to deliver infusions that are not possible in peripheral IVs; when used with sterile technique, central catheters provide the greatest chance of preventing infections in immunosuppressed patients. Central venous catheters can be very cost effective for long-term venous access, can be used for blood sampling, and can reduce the number of times that a patient requiring long-term treatments must be stuck with a needle. Potential disadvantages of central catheter use include complications such as phlebitis, catheter occlusion, catheter-related thrombosis, catheter fracture or embolism, air embolism, catheter migration, and infection.

5. There are a few important points that must be observed when accessing a central catheter. The process for accessing the device is a sterile procedure. Carelessness in maintaining sterility can lead to serious infections and death. The patency of the catheter must be determined prior to use. If the procedure for determining patency is flushing the catheter, do not force the flush if resistance is met. Resistance may be the result of a thrombus that could be dislodged and create significant problems.

Case 2

1. ALS is a progressive neurodegenerative disease that affects nerve cells in the brain and the spinal cord. The progressive degeneration of the motor neurons in ALS eventually leads to the inability of the brain to initiate and control muscle movement. Despite the fact that an ALS patient may eventually become completely paralyzed, the mind remains alert.

2. The priority at this point is to assess and address any life threats discovered during the assessment of the patient's airway, breathing, and circulation.

3. The trach tube needs to be assessed for patency. Help in determining the problem with the patient's oxygenation and ventilation status can be found by checking for the source of the alarm.

4. Questions pertinent to the patient's tracheostomy tube include:
   a. Why did the patient receive a tracheostomy?
   b. Is the upper airway patent or obstructed?
   c. How long has the patient had the tracheostomy?[2]

5. If you suspect some form of obstruction, try the following steps:
   1. Attempt to suction the tracheostomy tube if sterile suction is available.
   2. If resistance is met while inserting the suction catheter, withdraw the catheter and remove the inner cannula.
   3. If suction is not available, remove the inner cannula and attempt to ventilate.

   Following these actions may resolve the problem, because it is typically the inner cannula that becomes obstructed with thick, dried mucus. After suctioning or removal of the inner cannula, reassess the ABCs and attempt to ventilate the patient to determine if the issue has been resolved. If the patient's signs and symptoms persist, continue your attempts to relieve the obstruction.

6. If the FIO_2 in the ventilator is set at 30%, ask the nurse to increase the FIO_2 to 100%. Or, if you are familiar with ventilator settings, increase the FIO_2 yourself, but be sure to inform the nurse that you have changed the FIO_2 setting.

7. Remove the patient from the ventilator and ventilate the patient with a bag-mask device.

8. Since the inner cannula of the tracheostomy tube has been removed, it would be good practice to replace it with a new sterile inner cannula. The next step should

be to address any issues with the patient's breathing. Since the patient has rhonchi in all his lung fields, it would be appropriate to suction the tube using a sterile French suction catheter and sterile technique.

9. Possible causes for the rhonchi include:

   a. Infection due to the low WBC count resulting from the chemotherapy

   b. An inability of the patient to clear his own secretions due to the ALS

   c. Aspiration of formula feedings into the airway

10. If you discover that the patient has formula-colored fluid in his airway, determine if formula is being administered via the gastric tube. If so, turn off and remove the formula tubing from the patient's gastric tube. Once the formula has been discontinued, continue the process of alternating between suctioning and then ventilating and oxygenating the patient until you no longer obtain formula with your suction attempts. If the patient remains in critical condition, this process can be accomplished en route to an appropriate receiving facility.

11. The patient should be assessed for a history of congestive heart failure and any other conditions that could be exacerbated by the treatments that you might administer. Since the patient has no history of CHF or any other condition that could be negatively affected by the administration of fluids, IV access should be established. Volume replacement may be provided to improve blood pressure.

12. The PICC line appears to have signs of infection; as such, it should be used only if the patient would die without its use and there is no other access available (e.g., peripheral IV or intraosseous access). If you have any doubt about using a PICC line (especially one that is infected), contact medical direction for consultation or use another means of vascular access.

13. The treatments for Dr. Stanton's hypotension and shock (beginning with the least invasive) are:

    a. Positioning—place the patient in a position that will optimize the flow of blood to his vital organs (e.g., shock position).

    b. Administer IV fluids while monitoring for the potential for fluid overload.

    c. If MAST or PASGs are used in your EMS system, consider their application.

    d. If the preceding interventions do not prove to be beneficial in improving the patient's hemodynamic status, consider the use of vasopressors.

Be aware of the possibility that positive pressure ventilation can influence the return of blood to the right side of the heart.

Test Yourself

1. d

   The true life-threatening emergencies that the dialysis patient will experience are typically conditions such as an excess or deficit of fluid and electrolytes, rather than complications with the access device or dialysis machine. Other underlying conditions often worsen these imbalances.

2. Ileostomy

   Complications for the ileostomy patient are relatively rare but include: intestinal obstruction, hemorrhage, hypoxia, and fluid and electrolyte imbalance. There is little that the paramedic can do for the patient with complications associated with ileostomies other than to provide supportive care and transport to a hospital for definitive care.

3. d

   Common ostomies include the colonostomy, ileostomy, and urostomy, all of which create an avenue for fecal or urinary wastes to be emptied. The tracheostomy (a surgical hole used for respiration) is another type of ostomy relevant to chronic care.

4. True

   When in a home care situation, keep it simple and return to the basics. Assess and manage the ABCs. Treat the patient, not the machine.

5. a

   The three questions may all directly impact your treatment of the patient. New tracheostomies are more likely to close up if the tube was removed, while older stoma may have shrunk. Patients with completely obstructed airways are at greater risk of asphyxiation than those with patent airways. Knowing why a patient received the tracheostomy is important as many problems stem from the need for a tracheostomy tube, rather than from a problem with the tube itself.

6. d

   The patient's catheter site is infected, and he shows signs of septic shock. You will need to administer fluids. You must establish a second IV to administer fluid treatment. You may only use the infected IV site if it is the only possible access and your medical director has approved you to do so. When intravenous routes are possible, they are generally preferable to intraosseous routes.

7. d

   While hospitals have oxygen plumbed into the walls and utilize portable oxygen tanks with regulators, oxygen for use in the home care setting typically comes in three forms: liquid oxygen, oxygen concentrators, and compressed oxygen stored in tanks. Other than this difference, oxygen delivery in a home care setting is remarkably similar to that in a hospital setting.

8. Home health-care providers have previous exposure to the patient, which gives them a baseline understanding of the patient's condition and the ability to anticipate complications. They are also familiar with the specific medical devices that the patient may depend on.

   For example, a home health-care worker may know what medications a patient is taking and if those medications might contribute to the current problem or affect the planned treatment.

9. True

   Central venous access ports that are surgically implanted under the skin (Mediports, Port-a-Caths, etc.) require special needles (Huber needles) to access them. Attempts to access these devices with anything other than a Huber needle may damage or destroy the device.

10. Home health care offers the comfort of a familiar environment and is less expensive than in-hospital care.

    Home health care is a popular choice for many patients, and given the aging population, the number of patients choosing home health care is likely to increase.

11. c

    The first task you must perform when caring for a patient who has aspirated formula from a continuous tube feeding is to turn off the feeding pump. Locate and turn off the power to the pump or unplug the pump. If this does not turn the pump off, remove the tubing from the pump and close the roller clamp. The other responses are steps that you will perform after turning off the feeding pump.

12. b

    Because palliative care (provided by hospice) and curative care (provided by the paramedic) have different goals and methods, there is little that a paramedic can do to care for the hospice patient other than provide supportive care such as pain management.

13. The goal of curative care is to cure patients, while the goal of palliative care is to reduce pain and discomfort. Curative care tends to be analytical, is based on diagnosis, provides scientific and biomedical care, focuses on the disease, views patients as parts, is based on "hard" science, has a hierarchical team, and views death as failure. Palliative care tends to be subjective, is based on symptoms, provides humanistic care, focuses on comfort, views patients as a whole, has an interdisciplinary team, and views death as normal.

    As a paramedic, you will generally provide curative care, but your patients may also be undergoing palliative care, so you should be aware of and value its principles.

14. a

    Efforts to cut health-care costs, such as the advent of diagnostic-related groups, mean that patients are being discharged from the hospital "sicker and quicker" than they had been previously. Advances in technology allow home-based treatments for conditions previously treatable only in hospitals. Furthermore, many patients prefer the comfort of home to the clinical hospital setting.

15. Signs of urinary retention include: an overwhelming need to urinate, restlessness, sweating, anxiety, bladder pain, and a feeling of bladder fullness.

    If untreated, urinary retention can lead to UTIs, stone formation, and potentially long-term structural damage to the bladder, ureters, or kidneys. If trained for the procedure, a paramedic may insert a urinary catheter in the patient either under standing orders or following the consultation of medical direction. If Foley catheter insertion is not an approved procedure, the patient should be transported to the hospital.

chapter 48

Patients from Diverse Cultures

1. What are your first actions?

_____

_____

_____

2. Should you ask the family to leave the room?

_____

_____

_____

Are You Ready?

It is 2:30 in the afternoon, and a Tongan family has called 9-1-1 to help with the 53-year-old mother of the household. She presents supine in bed with irregular snoring respirations. She barely moans when a painful stimulus is administered. Pulses are slow and palpable at the carotid arteries; her skin is warm, pale, and dry. You turn down the blankets covering the patient and see that she is still in her nightgown. She appears to weigh approximately 105 kg.

Her adult daughters are in one corner of the room; they are speaking in a language that you do not understand, but they appear to be praying. A Bible is lying open on the small night table where the daughters are kneeling. Despite the initial language difference, one of the women turns to you when you address them and responds in English.

Active Learning

1. Seeing Diversity

Diversity can take many forms. Think of diversity as pairs of eyeglasses, each with a slightly different prescription, color, and style. For example, your gender can color some of your opinions and likes and dislikes—a male may feel one way about sports, but his girlfriend may feel differently. How many kinds of "diversity eyeglasses" can you name?

_____

_____

_____

Next, try this with a partner who has also completed the diversity eyeglasses exercise. Compare your lists and match the ones you both have named, identifying those that were unique to your list or your partner's list. Were your lists alike or dissimilar? Why do you think that is?

2. Death Notification

Notifying the next of kin that a loved one has died can be a challenging experience for both the survivor and the notifier. Different cultures treat the concept of death differently. Religious beliefs, age, and other factors can also lead to diverse viewpoints about death. Regardless, a paramedic must approach the notification process with dignity and respect for others. Review the following online resources for additional information on this topic:

- The United States Department of Veterans Affairs' National Center for Posttraumatic Stress Disorder has a fact sheet online discussing the death notification procedure. It can be found at www.ncptsd.va.gov/ncmain/ncdocs/fact_shts/fs_death_notification.html.

- The Association of Death Education and Counseling publishes a journal called *Forum*. The July/August/September 2003 issue was dedicated to "those who defend and protect the public." You can find a PDF copy of this issue at www.adec.org/publications/forum/0307.pdf.

- Other resources exist online. Perform a search using terms like "death notification," "dying," and "grief counseling."

3. Who's in Your Neighborhood?

Your EMS system probably serves several different cultural populations within its jurisdiction. Do a little research on several of the major ones; there may be cultural centers where a representative is willing to speak to you about general viewpoints regarding health care, illness, and death. Better yet, arrange to have one of these representatives visit your class. Remember that what is said and portrayed are only general characteristics; you don't want to assume that every person from that culture feels the same way.

4. Complementary and Alternative Medicine (CAM)

CAM is often used as an adjunct to western medicine, and various CAM practices are common to other cultures. Explore the National Center for Complementary and Alternative Medicine at nccam.nih.gov.

You Are There: Reality-Based Cases

Case 1 *(continued from chapter opener)*

You learn that the patient was recently diagnosed as having panic disorder and was prescribed Xanax XR, 6 mg daily. She began this medication about 2 weeks ago. According to one of the daughters, the patient seemed to be "better" at controlling her "anxiety episodes" since being on the medication. The other daughter added that the patient had also been supplementing the prescribed medication with kava tea, a staple in the Tonga culture. The patient also has a history of type 2 diabetes, which has been diet-controlled for the past 10 years, and mild hypertension.

There was a family gathering at the patient's home last evening. A dispute occurred, which stressed the patient. One of the daughters helped her take one of her pills and poured a cup of kava tea, which seemed to help. Everyone left last night; the daughters came by today when the patient did not come to church in the morning.

The Xanax bottle is on the nightstand, along with an empty glass with some organic material at the bottom of it. After a few calculations, you determine that two of the tablets are missing.

The physical examination is unremarkable. Her pupils are dilated and very slow to react. Ventilating her with a bag-mask seems to improve her spontaneous respiratory rate; she is now breathing spontaneously at 6 times per minute. Her pulse rate is 110 and regular, and her blood pressure is 96/68.

1. How might you explain the patient's condition, given the circumstances of the situation and your findings?

_____

_____

_____

Test Yourself

1. Which racial or cultural group in the United States has the highest incidence of diabetes?

_____

_____

2. What is the difference between homeopathy and osteopathy?

_____

_____

3. Your patient is a lawyer residing in the affluent side of town. He is well known in your city, well educated, and often reported in the news. From his trim body it can be inferred that this patient regularly sees his doctor and maintains a healthy lifestyle.

True

False

4. You are called to a fight that occurred near the edge of an Ethiopian neighborhood. When you arrive, bystanders begin to scatter. The people who are too injured to run seem to fear you. You should

   a. smile to alleviate their fear, showing that you are just a "regular person" and similar to them.

   b. recognize that they are responding to your uniform, as they fear officials.

   c. use a stern and authoritative tone, ensuring immediate control of the situation.

   d. assume that their fear is the result of criminal guilt and call law enforcement for backup.

5. Groups such as the Bloods street gang and the Harley Owners Group (HOG) are, by definition, considered cultures.

True

False

6. Your elderly patient suffered a cardiac arrest. When you obtained his history, you discovered that your patient and his wife are immigrants from Italy. At the hospital, the patient is declared dead, and the doctor asks you to inform the family. On hearing the news, the wife falls to her knees, wailing loudly and crying "No!" She begins rocking back and forth, pulling at her clothes. Her daughter pats her shoulder and murmurs comforting words. You should

   a. call a nurse to help you place the woman in restraints and consider administering a sedative.

   b. ask the daughter to help you force her mother into a chair to get her to calm down.

   c. follow the daughter's lead and view this as an acceptable reaction to grief.

   d. ask the daughter if her mother has a history of psychiatric disorders or drug use.

7. Shamanism is a recognized form of traditional medicine.

True

False

Scenario: You are called to the scene of a domestic dispute where shots have been fired. Inside you find a Chinese man dead from a gunshot wound; a Chinese woman who speaks no English with gunshot wounds to her chest and leg; a 15-year-old girl who speaks broken English; and a 7-year-old boy crying hysterically who speaks very good English.

8. Communications about the background of the situation and treatment options will be challenging. You should consider all the following methods *except*

   a. calming the young boy so he can help you translate for his mother.

   b. waiting for a translator before starting treatment.

   c. patching a translator through from dispatch.

   d. using a pocket dictionary with familiar phrases.

9. How should you ask the children about their mother's medical history?

   a. "Please tell me about any health problems your mother has."

   b. "Does your mother have a history of health problems?"

   c. "Does your mother have any preexisting medical conditions?"

   d. "Please tell me about any preexisting medical conditions your mother has."

10. You begin treating the woman. The daughter brings you some herbs and insists that you use them to treat her mother. You should

   a. put the herbs on the wound as you continue to treat with other methods as well.

   b. keep shaking your head "no" as you push the herbs away.

   c. accept the herbs and tell her you will use them later.

   d. have her brother tell her that won't be necessary at this time.

Need to Know

The following represent the Key Objectives of Chapter 48:

1. *Explain how you, as an individual, bring bias into how you view your patients and into your interactions with them.*

Bias is simply the result of being raised as an individual. Think about it: Your upbringing is distinctly unique from that of virtually everyone on the planet. Your parents, your friends, your religious beliefs, your socioeconomic status, and countless other factors shaped your view of the world around you. The way you perceive ideas and concepts is like looking through a pair of eyeglasses, except the "lens" in this case is shaped not by your eye vision, but by your opinions and beliefs. To extend this metaphor, giving *your* pair of eyeglasses to another individual might result in an odd "view," one that is out of focus and unclear, even confusing. So it is when interacting with people who are different from you, whether the difference is based on age, sex, religion, or ethnic origin. Under normal conditions, the differences can be bridged through continual contact, dialogue, and interaction. In an emergency situation, it can be a challenge to try to understand a viewpoint that can be dramatically different from your own and incorporate those differences into the ongoing management of the patient's medical condition. It will be very helpful to adopt a tolerant, accepting mind-set about the actions of the patient, family, and friends during a very stressful time. Focus on the medical aspects of the case, and do not be distracted by what would seem to be unusual behavior.

2. *Describe how you can interact with a patient who is culturally different from you in a fair and professional manner.*

Your position as a paramedic is representative of authority; the warning lights on the unit, your uniform, and the radios all convey that sense to the patient and bystanders. It is imperative that you set aside your own biases and be professional, helpful, and empathetic. In one sense it is much like other challenges with communications: acknowledging what was said; using active listening techniques; and using other tools to make sure that you, the patient, and bystanders understand each other will provide a common platform to work from. Incorporating a better awareness of how other cultures and religions view illness, medicine, and health care will promote more trust and faith in your efforts to assist the patient.

Bias becomes dangerous when one ascribes a *value* to it—that is, when there is an inherent positive or negative judgment of the behavior being demonstrated. For example, a family may demonstrate great emotional distress after the death of a patient; they may cry loudly, throw things, and be nearly inconsolable. You, on the other hand, might personally be more of a stoic individual, believing that *not* showing great emotion is a *better* approach to showing grief. You might *disapprove* of the family's behavior, and although you may not say it out loud, your behavior or expression might indicate your distaste for the behavior. This is when your professionalism must prevail; cloak your value system so you can focus on helping the survivors through a traumatic time in their lives.

3. *Describe the basic steps to death notification that can help survivors begin the grieving process.*

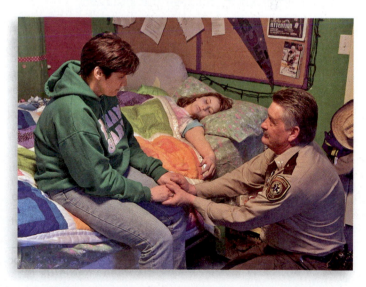

Review Box 48-2 in the textbook for some overarching themes regarding how different cultures view and accept death differently. Keep in mind that these concepts are highly generalized; many factors beyond race shape how individuals interpret and react to such devastating news. Acceptance and empathy will guide your actions in how you treat the survivors after a death occurs. Remember the following steps to death notification:

- Identify the individuals who must know about the death, and provide privacy and respect for their grief.
- Identify any specific belief sets that may need to be addressed. For example, a deeply religious individual may find comfort in the presence of clergy.
- Present yourself in a professional, caring, and empathetic manner. You will be setting the tone for what will follow. Identify resources that can be useful in these situations; for example, some EMS systems have access to critical incident teams that assist the community in situations such as death notification.
- When it is time to notify someone of a death, be straightforward and keep it simple. Sit down with the survivors to provide the news. Be prepared to answer any questions the survivors might have about your care during the patient's last minutes. If possible, guide the series of next steps. For example, you might ask the family if any preparations were made by or for the patient for a funeral. Offer to help make the initial contact to the funeral home for the removal of the body to that agency. Or explain how the agencies responsible for death scenes (medical examiner, police) will respond to and work with the next of kin to manage the situation.

Need to Do

The following skills are explained and illustrated in a step-by-step manner, via skill sheets and/or Step-by-Steps in this text and on the accompanying DVD:

Skill Name	Skill Sheet Number and Location	Step-by-Step Number and Location
Communication Challenges— Interpreter Services	62 – DVD	N/A
Verbal Communications	63 – DVD	N/A

Connections

- Review Chapter 10, Therapeutic Communications and History Taking, in the textbook for key

points regarding effective communication techniques that work across many cultures and belief systems.

- Culture in medicine is important. Beyond the civility of being a respectful person, there are benefits for understanding how culture shapes health care. See the Diversity Rx site www.diversityrx.org/HTML/ESLANG.htm for good information on this subject.
- Diversity Rx is a collaborative website that is cosponsored by the National Conference of State Legislatures (NCSL), Resources for Cross Cultural Health Care (RCCHC), and the Henry J. Kaiser Family Foundation of Menlo Park, CA. In addition to the link previously listed, check out a best practices document at www.diversityrx.org/BEST/index.html.
- Ready to wrap it up? Put on your thinking cap and work your way through Problem-Based Learning Case 8, Life Begins.
- Link to the companion DVD for a chapter-based quiz, audio glossary, animations, games and exercises, and, when appropriate, skill sheets and skill Step-by-Steps.

Street Secrets

- **Tincture of Time** Death notification and the events that happen afterward are dramatic. Be prepared to spend some time with grieving relatives and friends, especially if the death was unexpected. Be patient; try not to allow any feelings of impatience to show. Your behavior and actions will greatly help the family move into the grieving process.
- **Speak to Me** Using interpreters to overcome language barriers can be quite effective. Keep in mind that the interpreter has his or her own cultural lens that may shape not only how your questions are asked, but also how the patient's responses are translated. Try to direct the interpreter to simply ask the question and literally translate the response word for word.

The Drug Box

There are no specific drugs related to this chapter content.

Answers

Are You Ready?

1. The altered level of consciousness and snoring respirations detected on the primary assessment could indicate an impending loss of airway. Assuming no trauma is present, you should immediately lift the patient's chin to extend her jaw. A nasal or oral airway should be used to help secure a basic airway. It is probable that ventilatory assistance will be needed to ensure effective gas exchange. Since this patient will not be able to provide you with information, you will need to carefully examine the patient and surroundings to elicit the clues to the underlying cause(s).

2. This is a tricky situation, and the answer is a definite "maybe." Is there enough room for you to work? Are the daughters' voices too loud? What is the cultural value of praying in the presence of the patient? You will want to find out if removing the daughters from the room will result in a more anxious environment.

Active Learning

1. There are likely many more kinds of "diversity eyeglasses" than you imagined. Here are just a few: sex, age, race, sexual orientation, religion, height, weight, social class, economic status, marital status, parenthood, and veteran. Did you identify others?

You Are There: Reality-Based Cases

Case 1

1. Several aspects of the patient's medical history should focus your questioning and exam:
   - *Possible overdose.* The patient takes a potent benzodiazepine that she has only recently started using. Two pills are missing. In addition, kava has a sedating effect. Did you find out how this natural herb interacts with benzodiazepines?
   - *Diabetes.* Which procedure will you perform to determine whether the patient may be experiencing hyperglycemia or hypoglycemia? What other signs and symptoms would you look for?
   - *Hypertension.* Although described as "mild," hypertension is a risk factor for cardiac disease and stroke.
   - *Hypotension.* The patient, given her history and body weight, appears to be hypotensive, which may explain her decreased level of consciousness. Could it be from hypoxia or hypovolemia, or a combination of both? The improving heart rate may be an additional clue.

Test Yourself

1. Native Americans

   The National Center for Cultural Competence states that African Americans are 1.7 times more likely to have diabetes than Caucasians. Latinos are 2.0 times more likely and both Alaskan Natives and Native Americans are 2.8 times more likely to have diabetes than Caucasians.

2. Homeopathy is the practice of treating a person with small doses of drugs and substances in order to augment the body's natural defenses against disease. Osteopathy is the practice of enhancing the body's own healing power through the belief that the body contains all it needs to make itself well.

   Homeopathy is the study and use of substances designed to elicit and amplify the symptoms produced by the body's own immune response in order to help the body fight disease. Homeopathic practitioners believe that the body's response to an invader or disease is the same response needed to cure it. Osteopathy emphasizes the body's innate ability to heal itself, and osteopaths focus their efforts accordingly. Although doctors of osteopathy are fully licensed physicians who can prescribe medication and perform surgery, the fundamental philosophy of osteopathy is that the body contains its own best medicine.

3. False

   Without a physical exam and primary assessment you cannot assume anything.

4. b

   It is important to remember that in some cultures and foreign nations, people in uniforms are perceived as threatening and hurtful. Your presence may be frightening to some people. If you are respectful of the beliefs and values of your patients, and perform your job professionally in their time of crisis, your actions will speak volumes about both your capabilities as a paramedic and the entire medical and public health system you represent.

5. True

   The Merriam-Webster dictionary defines culture as "the customary beliefs, social forms, and material traits of a racial, religious, or social group." A culture does not necessarily imply a different country, skin tone, or foreign language. A variety of cultures and subcultures exist in both urban environments as well as rural areas. A gang, a church group, or a particular corporate office and its employees are examples of subcultures with various beliefs, behaviors, and traditions. Cultures may be defined by ethnicity, national origin, spoken language, race, religion, age, sexual orientation, physical challenges, or any combination of these or other unique characteristics.

6. c

   Cultural groups vary in their response to illness and injury. While some may favor stoicism and avoid showing or acknowledging pain, others consider an overt display of pain or grief appropriate and respectful. As long as grieving family members are not in danger of hurting themselves or others, they should be allowed to express their grief however they choose.

7. True

   Some of the most recognized forms of traditional healing include acupuncture, chiropractic, herbalism, holistic therapies, homeopathy, osteopathy, shamanism, and therapeutic massage. Clearly there are other methods used by certain cultures or ethnic groups—some of which are recognized as valid.

8. b

It is imperative to start treatment as soon as possible, and waiting for a translator through dispatch can waste valuable time. Look for other options that are closer.

9. a

When you are trying to communicate across a language barrier, consider the cultural value system of the person with whom you are communicating. Many Asian cultures, for example, believe it to be impolite to answer in the negative. Answers that should clearly be "no" will instead be given as "maybe" or "perhaps." It will be important to ask questions that do not require a "yes or no" answer to get accurate information. You should also speak as plainly and clearly as possible; in this situation the phrase "preexisting medical conditions" might be unclear.

10. d

Traditional healing methods, healing rituals, and herbal remedies continue to play an important role in many cultures throughout the world, and your patient's family obviously believes in their power. It is important to respect their values and their culture, yet you have a time-sensitive obligation to treat.

Problem-Based Learning Case 8
Life Begins

Part I: The Case

Dispatch and Scene Size-Up

"Engine 71; report of an imminent delivery. Fell Street off-ramp, on northbound 101. Highway Patrol on scene. Medic 27 en route from quarters, extended."

You and your crew roll out of the apparatus bay and head toward the freeway. It's late afternoon, and rush hour is in full swing. It will take you 8 minutes to reach the location, but it will take Medic 27 even longer. You mentally rehearse the steps for delivering a newborn, just in case.

Your fire engine slows down as you approach the scene. The driver judiciously uses the horn to clear traffic. You can see the highway patrol car at the bottom of the off-ramp, behind a minivan that is parked on the shoulder.

On arrival you pull your first-in bag and OB kit out of the side compartment and make your way toward the vehicle. You can see the patrol officer already has her OB kit out, and you hasten your step. Through the side window you see a woman lying on the middle row bench seat, her legs spread. The patrol officer is trying to coach the woman to slow her

breathing down. You can see blood and fluid spilling from the seat onto the floor of the minivan.

1. *Describe your initial actions as you approach the scene. What are your first concerns, based upon your observations?*

_____

_____

The Primary assessment (Primary Assessment) and Initial Differentials

Liza Munoz, age 22, appears to be full term. She is cyanotic, diaphoretic, and tachypneic. She nods at you with her eyes closed when you ask if she can hear you. A quick palpation of the right radial wrist detects a very faint, irregular, and fast pulse. The patrol officer has already started providing supplemental oxygen to the patient via non-rebreather mask.

The driver of the minivan identifies himself as the husband of the patient. He quickly tells you that they were heading toward University Medical Center but got caught in traffic. She went into labor about 90 minutes ago while at home.

2. *What are your concerns? What treatment will you begin immediately? What information do you need to elicit next?*

_____

_____

History and Physical Exam (Secondary assessment and History)

Liza's vital signs include a heart rate of 136 and respiratory rate of 30. Her blood pressure measures at 68/42. The pulse oximeter reads 78%, and capnography shows a carbon dioxide level of 20 mm Hg.

You quickly examine the patient's vaginal area. There is evidence of bulging, but no crowning is seen. The blood you see on the upholstery is fresh.

Responding to your questions, the husband reports that this is Liza's third pregnancy. The first two were uneventful, and she has received prenatal care during this pregnancy. She is about 10 days from term. She has no significant past medical history and is allergic to shellfish and certain antibiotics. She takes prenatal and calcium supplements. She was having difficulty catching her breath earlier in the day, something she had experienced earlier in her pregnancy. Her water broke while she was urinating, and the contractions started soon after that. Her first two pregnancies had ended in long labors, and the couple was advised to wait before coming to the hospital. Both of them went to pack their clothing for a short stay. Liza's respiratory distress worsened, and her husband became worried when she nearly fell a couple of times. He helped her out to the minivan and began the drive to the hospital. Halfway there she began to "pass out," and he panicked. He called 9-1-1 on his cell phone.

Liza begins to cry again, though it is weak. You can feel the abdominal wall become firm as a contraction begins. Her SpO_2 reading drops to 65%, and the ECG records a heart rate of 142. Liza's lips begin to turn blue.

3. *Is delivery imminent? If so, should you attempt to deliver or consider immediate transport when the ambulance arrives?*

_____

_____

Field Impression(s) and Treatment Plan

The contractions stop. Other than a small amount of blood-tinged fluid leaking from the birth canal, there is no other sign of imminent birth. Liza's respiratory rate is up to 36, and she only moans when you call her name. You are unable to find a radial pulse.

Auscultation of lung fields reveals faint, diminished breath sounds, with possible crackles posteriorly. You can palpate bilateral femoral pulses, although they are faint. Liza's eyes are half open, staring vacantly into space.

You ask for an ETA of the medic unit. Dispatch reports they are 2 minutes away.

4. *What might be causing Liza's condition? What should you do next?*

_____

_____

Transportation and Ongoing Care

The transfer to the ambulance is quick. Your update of the patient's emergent condition prepared the ambulance paramedic for the handoff. The ambulance pulls alongside the stopped minivan, with the highway patrol officer stopping traffic. Within 60 seconds you move Liza out of the minivan, onto the gurney, and into the ambulance. The unit begins to move toward the emergency department, the siren blazing a path through the stopped cars and onto the city streets.

You can feel another contraction begin. Liza moans but otherwise does not respond as before. The firefighter who is accompanying you to the hospital reports that the patient's jaw is stiff and he is having difficulty with her airway.

Her heart rate is still in the 130s. You are unable to palpate a blood pressure.

5. *What is the acuity of Liza's condition now? Has she improved or worsened since you first began treating her?*

_____

_____

Transfer of Care, Follow-Up, and Outcome

The delivery team from the obstetrical suite awaits your arrival at the emergency department, along with the surgical team. With no time to waste, the team moves the patient toward the elevator on your gurney, forgoing the transfer to the hospital bed in the emergency department.

Liza is in respiratory arrest. A slow, narrow rhythm moves across your monitor screen. One of the nurses climbs aboard the gurney and begins chest compressions. At the surgical suite entrance, you transfer the patient to the surgical bed. The medical staff pulls the patient inside, and the doors close behind them. After finishing your verbal report to one of the surgeons, you return to the emergency department. Liza's husband finds you there. Looking distressed, he asks how she is doing.

6. *Given what you know, what would you tell the husband?*

_____

_____

Long-Term Outlook

You find out later that a baby boy was delivered through emergency cesarean section and is doing well. Liza was resuscitated during surgery. No source of internal bleeding was found. She experienced disseminated intravascular coagulation (DIC) soon after being admitted to the ICU and remained on a ventilator for another week. She was eventually discharged home to be with her family.

7. *What are the most likely causes of Liza's condition?*

_____

_____

Part II: Debriefing

Responses to Part I questions:

1. Even though this appears to be a medical event, you are still operating very close to a major roadway. What steps should the engine company officer perform to ensure that the scene is as safe as possible? In regard to the actual incident, it certainly appears that there may be an imminent birth. Will you need to deliver in the vehicle or the ambulance, or will nature wait until you reach the hospital? And do you have concerns about the blood?

2. What does your primary assessment indicate? Did you decide what initial steps to perform? Were those steps related to the pregnancy? What information did you solicit from the husband? Certainly details such as the due date, any prenatal care, and previous pregnancies and deliveries are important—why?

3. You are in a difficult situation. Before you made your decision, did you take the mother's condition into consideration? She is clearly not doing well, especially when under the stress of contraction. The near-fainting episode is a serious sign of possible hypoperfusion, which does not bode well for the fetus. Why is that? It's not clear whether delivery is imminent. What other information do you need in order to make this determination?

4. There are several possible causes for Liza's presentation. If you could organize your responses according to the primary assessment, did you list any airway-related issues? What about concerns dealing with the breathing status? The crackles and diminished breath sounds are significant; her low SpO$_2$ reading is alarming. What could be causing these signs? Her circulation is also poor. You have already determined that, regardless of the cause, her lack of blood pressure is harming the newborn due to preferential shunting. Is bleeding a concern? Did you consider whether the hypoperfusion is due to a circulatory or respiratory cause? Are there any obstetrical conditions that could be contributing to her presentation? Based on your initial observations, what airway, breathing, and circulatory interventions did you provide?

5. Liza's condition is grim, having worsened since the beginning of the incident. With a decrease in her level of consciousness and a possible loss of her airway, it will take all your skill to frankly just keep her alive until you reach the hospital where more invasive procedures can be performed. Is intubation possible at this point?

6. Although the outlook for Liza and the newborn appears poor, at this point you cannot be absolutely sure what will happen next. How can you begin to prepare the distraught husband for the possible worst outcome of death without completely deferring to the hospital staff? After all, you did spend time with them during the initial workup, and he may continue to look to you for guidance and hope. Regardless of what you actually say, how you say it will be critical—you will want to be empathetic, supportive, and as respectful as possible.

7. Based upon the final findings, hypovolemia due to bleeding appears to have been ruled out. Given the sudden nature of the onset of Liza's illness, coupled with documented prenatal care, it would seem unlikely that the culprit would be a disease such as preeclampsia or diabetes. Based upon the primary respiratory findings, it appears like a pulmonary embolism, but how would the crackles that you auscultated figure into the cause?

Part III: Case Discussion

This near-tragic case serves as a reminder of how life can in fact "turn on a dime." Less than 2 hours earlier, Liza and her husband were getting ready for the birth of their next child. Now she lies unconscious while you struggle to keep her alive in the hopes of at least saving the child. Despite your efforts, she decompensates while in your care and in fact collapses in cardiac arrest at the receiving facility. You then have to console the husband about the possible loss of both his wife and baby. These types of EMS calls can be physically and emotionally exhausting to the paramedic. Remember to take time to be good to yourself; acknowledge any feelings you might have; and seek help from friends, family, and/or mental health professionals if needed.

By now you should have a solid understanding that, regardless of the underlying problem that is harming Liza, your initial focus is on the management of her airway, breathing ability, and circulatory status. Her advanced pregnancy and ongoing efforts to deliver a newborn complicate your resuscitation efforts. Remember that the body will preferentially shunt blood flow away from the fetus and back to the host (mother) when under stress. Your ability to impact the outcome of the newborn is therefore dependent upon your efforts to preserve the perfusion of the mother.

Liza appears to have a patent airway. No sounds of stridor can be heard, and breath sounds can be heard in both lung fields. She is tachypneic, although no accessory muscle use can be seen. This might indicate that there is no restriction to the lower airways; that is, asthma and COPD may be low on the suspicion index. Her oxygen saturation is disastrously low and improves only slightly with supplemental oxygen. This could very well be due to a hypoperfusion concern. Recall Fick's principle for a moment. It could be that blood flow is highly compromised; with fewer red blood cells (RBCs) circulating, less oxygen can be carried. There could be a pulmonary ventilation mismatch occurring, in which there is enough blood flowing, but not enough contact between the RBCs and the alveoli to transfer oxygen efficiently. Conditions that could cause the mismatch include pulmonary edema and pulmonary embolism. Finally, there may be a gas exchange problem at the cellular level in the tissues themselves. This is rare compared to the other two components of Fick's principle. We will come back to this in a moment.

Regardless of the problem, the low SpO_2 and $ETCO_2$ readings may direct your attention to inadequate ventilation. Is it possible that the downward movement of the diaphragm has been compromised by the presence of the fetus? Possibly, but the history provided by the husband doesn't appear to support that concern.

Assisting Liza's ventilation may be critical to her survival. Initiate bag-mask ventilations immediately to try to correct the blood gas levels. She may not be unconscious enough to facilitate a more advanced airway, and medication-assisted intubation may not be an option for you at this point. Basic positioning and airway control may be all that you can do at this early stage. Later on, the trismus may compromise even that procedure, so you will want to keep your airway toolbox open and available to you.

Liza has poor signs of circulation that worsen during your workup. With the possible precipitous labor, the observation of blood on the seat, and a firm abdomen, a ruptured uterus or a torn placenta (placenta abruptio) are possible conditions. However, the fact that no unusual bleeding was found during the surgical phase seems to minimize the possibility of catastrophic bleeding as a root cause of the hypoperfusing state. Did you consider other reasons, such as third spacing involved with anaphylaxis, or loss of distributive tone via sepsis? There is a history of allergic reactions, but it's unclear given the information whether she could be having anaphylaxis. There is no recent history of fever.

Return now to the pregnancy. There are a few conditions specifically related to a pregnancy. You know a fair amount about preeclampsia and eclampsia. Neither of these conditions would seem to be a likely culprit. What other obstetrical conditions exist that may cause a shocklike state and possible ventilation mismatch? One suspect is amniotic fluid embolism, which can create such a condition. A rare condition, its exact mechanism is unknown, but it is possible that an anaphylactoid-like state can be created if fetal proteins and tissue fragments like hair somehow enter the maternal bloodstream.

Certainly there are other conditions that can cause massive cardiopulmonary failure, such as a pulmonary embolism or even a myocardial infarction. As with the other Problem-Based Learning Cases you have worked on throughout this book, you should have a greater appreciation for the complexity of the human body, especially when someone becomes gravely ill or injured.

Part IV: Further Learning Paths

- The American College of Obstetricians and Gynecologists has a website that offers a variety of educational resources. The main page can be found at www.acog.org.
- A wide range of obstetrical and gynecological topics is covered at eMedicine, an online resource by WedMD. The website is www.emedicine.com/med/obstetricsgynecology.htm.
- Review the mechanism of anaphylaxis in Chapter 32, Allergies and Anaphylaxis, in the textbook.
- Review the mechanism of shock in Chapter 13, Shock Overview, in the textbook.

Operations

part 6

chapter 49

Ambulance Operations

Are You Ready?

Rick and Ann have been partners for 5 years. As usual, today they showed up to work a few minutes before their shift started. Rick headed directly to the shower to get ready for the shift, while Ann went to make a cup of coffee in the station kitchen and chat with the offgoing crew. Tom and Art were tired and eager to leave their shift. They had had a slew of runs, and Art was hurriedly entering the patient data into the station computer so it could be uploaded to the company's main server back at headquarters. Tom was already dressed in his civilian clothes and tossed the ambulance keys to Ann on his way out the door. When Ann called out to him, "Hey! How's the rig?" he responded, "No problem! We restocked everything we used." He jumped into his truck and drove off into the evening.

Art was hot on his heels, pushing himself away from the computer, picking up his gear bag, and waving to Ann as he headed out the door.

Ann finished making her coffee, silently commending herself for having seniority and being able to stay on swing shift, when the calls were fewer and better. She walked over to the garage door and noticed that one of the doors to the back of the ambulance was open. A mop bucket was sitting nearby. They must have cleaned out the rig, she thought to herself. Give it a few minutes to dry, and then I'll check out the rig.

The television was on in the dayroom. Ann sat down to sip her coffee, idly watching the evening news. Rick reappeared, dressed in uniform and with his hair still wet. They started chatting about their weekend off when the station bells sounded for a priority 1 response (light and siren), "Unconscious male at the city pool."

Ann turned off the television and went to the kitchen to drop off her coffee cup. Rick asked, "Did you check out the rig yet?" "Nope," she answered, "but Tom said that they restocked everything, and it looks like they mopped the floor."

"Should be okay then." Rick slammed the back door shut and climbed into the passenger seat. Ann settled into the driver's seat, fastened her seat belt, and started the diesel motor. Flipping on the lights, they eased out of the driveway and into the evening traffic. Rick reached over and turned up the CD player they had installed in the unit. "Check it out, I just bought this CD."

1. What are your concerns, if any, about this seemingly everyday shift change?

_____

_____

_____

Active Learning

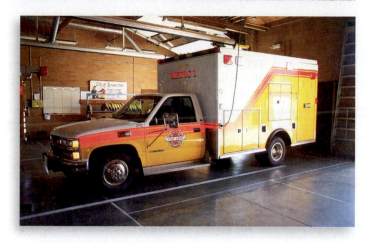

1. Defining "Ambulance"

What exactly defines an ambulance in your state? Are you familiar with your state or regional statutory regulations for the definition of an ambulance? Conduct an Internet search or go to your local or regional regulatory office to find statutes and ordinances that specify what an ambulance actually is. As a bonus, see if you can locate any regulation that specifies the minimum amount of equipment that needs to be stocked.

After your research, answer the following questions:

- Is there just one set of regulations that govern an ambulance or are there several sets of rules and laws?
- Is the language clear and unambiguous?
- Who enforces compliance with these regulations?
- Are there civil or criminal penalties for violation of ambulance regulations?

2. I *Am* an Ambulance Driver!

Research your state's Department of Motor Vehicles to learn who can be permitted to drive an ambulance. Then find any applicable laws that govern the operations of an emergency vehicle in your state. After finding the appropriate laws, answer the following questions:

- Can any person be certified to drive an ambulance? If there are restrictions, what are they?
- When driving with your lights and siren activated, what rules of the road are you permitted to supersede?
- Does the state's driving code define "due regard"? If so, what does it mean?

3. Penny Wise, Pound Foolish

For this activity, you will need some type of small toy with wheels, such as a lightweight plastic car or truck; a few pennies; a book or two; and a small board or piece of sturdy cardboard. Create a ramp, using the books as a base and the board or cardboard as the ramp. Carefully hold the wheeled toy at the top of the ramp. When ready, release the toy so it rolls down the ramp. Record how far it went. Now, if you were to weigh down the toy with a few pennies, what do you think the extra weight would do to the distance traveled? Will it be shorter or longer than without the pennies? Test your hypothesis by placing about 10 or more pennies on the toy and repeating the previous steps. Did the experiment results support your theory? How does this relate to driving an ambulance versus your private vehicle?

You Are There: Reality-Based Cases

Case 1 *(continuation of chapter opener)*

Dispatch reports that the fire department first responders are performing CPR on a teenage male as Ann and Rick arrive at the pool. After pulling the ambulance up in front of the main gate, Rick gets out and goes to open the side door of the ambulance. He picks up the jump kit to throw onto the . . . gurney? What gurney? Rick's eyes open wide just as Ann opens up the back doors. "Hmmm, Ann? What did you say about checking out the rig?"

1. What are your options at this point? How will you transport the patient to the hospital?

_____

_____

_____

Test Yourself

1. Which pieces of equipment should be carried on-scene to assist a patient with an altered level of consciousness?
   a. Cardiac monitor, splints, and oxygen/medical bag
   b. Oxygen/medical bag and suction equipment only
   c. Cardiac monitor, suction equipment, and patient carrying device
   d. Cardiac monitor, oxygen/medical bag, and suction equipment

2. You and your partner are discussing your careers in EMS. Your partner recalls the good old days when ambulances were nothing more than vans. What type of ambulance is your partner referring to?

   a. A "mod"

   b. A "vanbulance"

   c. A Type III

   d. A Type II

3. What is the difference between multiplex and duplex radio communications?

   _____

   _____

4. Why is it important to contact the receiving facility prior to arrival?

   _____

   _____

5. At what point should you brake when turning the ambulance?

   _____

   _____

6. Which phase of the EMS response includes making the unit ready for calls by ensuring the proper equipment is loaded and operable?

   a. Return to the station

   b. Preparation

   c. Dispatch

   d. Post-run

7. Why is it important to use a predesignated landing zone whenever possible?

   _____

   _____

8. Why is it important to tell dispatch you have arrived on the scene?

   _____

   _____

9. What are prearrival instructions?

   _____

   _____

10. A Type III ambulance consists of a van chassis with a modular- or box-type patient compartment.

    True

    False

11. Your partner is transporting you and your patient to the hospital. En route you give the following radio report: "Medic 1 en route to your facility with a 5–7 minute ETA. On board we have a 45-year-old male. Patient is receiving IV fluids KVO and oxygen at 4 liters per minute via nasal cannula. Administered three tablets of nitroglycerin, three baby aspirin, and 4 mg of morphine with no change in the patient's condition. Vital signs are BP of 102/68, HR of 122, and RR of 24." What, if anything, was omitted from this radio report that should have been included?

    a. Nothing was omitted

    b. The chief complaint

    c. The patient's ethnicity

    d. Request for orders

12. Exercising safe driving techniques when operating an emergency vehicle adheres to which law?

    a. Traffic laws

    b. Emergency vehicle operations

    c. Due regard

    d. Personal vehicle operations

13. You respond to a call for weakness and difficulty speaking. Your partner is driving, and you are navigating the route. What phase of the EMS response are you operating under?

    a. En route

    b. Transportation

    c. Preparation

    d. Arrival on scene

14. What type of radio equipment allows you to transmit over long distances from a fixed location?

    a. Mobile radio

    b. Relay station

    c. Handheld radio

    d. Base station

15. Prior to departing the receiving facility it is necessary to do which of the following?

    a. Provide a copy of your patient care report.

    b. Restock and refuel your ambulance.

    c. Request orders for medical administration.

    d. Deliver a complete patient report to the patient's primary physician.

16. What are some emotional factors that might impair your ability to operate an ambulance?

    _____

    _____

17. What piece(s) of equipment should always be brought to the patient's side?

    a. Oxygen-medical-trauma bag

    b. Splints and dressings

    c. Cardiac monitor

    d. Suction

18. If forced to park your ambulance in a manner that blocks part of the roadway, you should leave your visible and audible warnings on.

    True

    False

19. The _____ is responsible for the oversight of all communication equipment and interstate and international communications.

20. You and your partner have responded to a motor vehicle collision involving multiple vehicles on the interstate during rush hour traffic. Command has assigned you to a patient who has been ejected and presents with snoring respirations; a weak, thready pulse; and decreased lung sounds on the right. You are 15 minutes away from the nearest trauma center. How should you transport this patient?

    a. Nonemergency transport

    b. By helicopter

    c. Using lights and siren

    d. Call the medical examiner's office for transport; this is not a viable patient.

Need to Know

The following represent the Key Objectives of Chapter 49:

1. *Identify current local and state standards that influence ambulance design, equipment requirements, and staffing.*

   The federal specification standard for ambulances, KKK-A-1822, is revised every 5 years.[1] At the time of publication of this worktext, the current version of this Government Services Administration (GSA) specification is revision E, released in 2002. It describes a multitude of minimum requirements for ambulances, from size dimensions and weight-carrying minimums to motor, electrical, and sanitary safety standards. Many state and local agencies use this specification standard as a baseline for vehicle purchases.

   The American College of Emergency Physicians (ACEP) released a joint statement with the American College of Surgeons (ACS) in 2000 that specified a minimum set of equipment to be stocked on an ambulance.[2] Again, many governmental agencies use this guideline as the basis for their regulations for ambulance operators.

   Unlike ambulance design and equipment stock, national guidance for emergency personnel staffing is not so clear. The draft version of the National EMS Scope of Practice Document recommends that the minimum staffing of a transporting ambulance is the emergency medical technician (EMT), although it acknowledges that the emergency medical responder (EMR) may be part of a team staffing an ambulance in more rural areas of the country.[3] This document has not been released in its final form as of this writing. In the absence of national guidelines, most states have regulatory statutes that govern who should staff an ambulance, as well as their scope of practice.

2. *Explain the importance of completing an ambulance equipment and supply checklist at the beginning of each shift.*

   It is crucial to maintain an ambulance's operational readiness at all times. Basic items such as vehicle fuel, onboard oxygen, and a gurney are just as critical as advanced airway equipment and the drug box. The lack of any of these items could cause a delay in care or transport. Your local system may have protocols or procedures as to who has responsibility for this task; regardless it is your responsibility as a professional to ensure your operational readiness!

3. *Describe the proper way to drive an ambulance in emergent and nonemergent situations.*

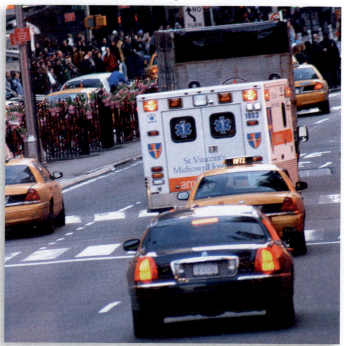

Ambulance crashes are a growing concern in the United States.[4] Most fatal crashes occur when the ambulance is proceeding straight through an intersection during an emergency run and collides with another vehicle. Most fatalities involve the driver of the nonambulance vehicle, although EMS providers have also been killed in these crashes. It is essential that you be trained to drive emergency vehicles proficiently and defensively. There are basic "rules of the road" to keep in mind while you are driving your response vehicle:

- Excessive speed has not been demonstrated to make a difference in patient outcome but does lessen your ability to control a top-heavy vehicle. Besides, ambulances are *trucks.* The only way to reduce their inherently choppy ride is to drive slower and more smoothly—no sudden stops or starts.

- Using safety belts while in the front and back of the vehicle will reduce your chances of injury or death. Secure children in appropriate safety seats, and always belt the patient onto the gurney.

- Securing items in the patient compartment will prevent them from becoming "flying missiles" in the case of impact or rollover.

- Looking further up the road and not directly in front of you will help you anticipate potential collisions rather than simply react to them. Intersections are especially dangerous. Have the rider in the passenger seat help you "clear" the intersection by looking for oncoming traffic approching the right side of the ambulance.

Obey all applicable driving laws and exercise due regard, especially during emergency runs. In most states, the use of the lights and siren does not allow you to violate traffic laws indiscriminately. It may be safer to have the mind-set that you are simply *requesting* the driving public to yield the right-of-way to you.

4. *List the factors in identifying the placement of ambulances in a community.*

Ambulance placement patterns are generally developed by one of two methods: static or dynamic. In static deployment, ambulances respond out of set stations for EMS calls and return to their stations when the calls are complete. In dynamic deployment, ambulances are constantly being moved from one geographical location to another ("posting" or "move-ups") in response to call volume in a particular area. By doing so, ambulances are continually being spread around so that most areas of the system can be reached within a specific time frame.

Whether dynamic or static deployment is used, several factors are considered in the placement of vehicles, including population density and fluctuations, traffic patterns, road conditions, and staffing. Global positioning systems can augment deployment strategies by providing exact locations of ambulances in real time.

5. *Describe the advantages and disadvantages of air medical transport.*

Air medical transport brings the advantage of speed to the transport of patients to hospitals. Air ambulances are often staffed with higher-trained EMS providers who can deliver certain procedures to the patient's side that are typically not within the ground paramedics' scope of practice. However, air transport is expensive, more dangerous than ground transport, and requires significant coordination between ground and air crews to minimize the risk of injury and delay of transport. Air transport can also be hampered by poor flying conditions and availability of a landing zone.

6. *Identify conditions in which air medical transport should be considered.*

If ground transport time is extended, generally beyond 20 minutes, then air transport by medical helicopter is a viable option. The condition of the patient, weather conditions, traffic patterns, road conditions, time of day, and number of patients are all factors to consider when deciding upon the use of a medical helicopter to transport your patient.

Need to Do

There are no psychomotor skills that directly support this chapter content.

💿 Connections

- The American Ambulance Association's mission is to promote health-care policies that ensure excellence in the ambulance services industry and provide research, education, and communications programs to enable its members to effectively address the needs of the communities they serve.[5] Their website is located at www.the-aaa.org.

- Are you curious about the GSA specification KKK-1822-E standards for ambulance construction? You can find them at http://apps.fss.gsa.gov/vehiclestandards/.

- The Association of Air Medical Services (AAMS) strives to ensure that every person has access to quality air medical and critical care transport.[6] Information about air medical transport services and becoming a member can be found at www.aams.org.

- Link to the companion DVD for a chapter-based quiz, audio glossary, animations, games and exercises, and, when appropriate, skill sheets and skill Step-by-Steps.

Street Secrets

- **Slow and Steady Wins the Race** The lights and siren on your emergency response unit do not give you permission to drive as fast as possible. In fact, there is little information to support the notion that rapid response will improve patient outcomes. Additionally, the time that is saved in a "code 3" or emergency response is often negligible compared with a routine response to the same location. Finally, your state laws about driving emergency vehicles probably have strict interpretations as to which rules an emergency vehicle operator can "violate" during an emergency run. Given these factors, take your time getting to an EMS event—the life you save may be your own or that of your crew or the general driving public.

The Drug Box

There are no specific drugs related to this chapter content.

References

1. KKK-A-1822 Specs Update. Emergency Medical Service. June 2005. www.emsresponder.com/publication/article.jsp?pubId=1&id=1791 (accessed March 28, 2007).
2. "Equipment for Ambulances: Joint Statement by the American College of Surgeons and the American College of Emergency Physicians," www.acep.org/NR/rdonlyres/AE62E47D-4700-4AD8-8A7B-3D168BDFFF29/0/ambulance_equip.pdf (accessed March 27, 2007).
3. National EMS Scope of Practice Model: Freedom within Limits. www.soundrock.com/sop/pdf/SoP_Draft_2.0.pdf.
4. Centers for Disease Control and Prevention. "Ambulance Crash-Related Injuries among Emergency Medical Services Workers—United States, 1991–2002," *JAMA* 289, no. 13, (April 2, 2003): pp 1628–29
5. American Ambulance Association, "Mission Statement of the AAA," www.the-aaa.org/about/mission.htm (accessed February 25, 2007).
6. Association of Air Medical Services, "AAMS Mission Statement," www.aams.org/AM/Template.cfm?Section=About_AAMS (accessed February 25, 2007).

Answers

Are You Ready?

1. There are a couple of key missteps that may dramatically impair Rick and Ann's ability to provide the community with high-quality service. First, without at least beginning to check out the unit, they do not know if they have the proper supplies and equipment to handle emergency calls. If the unit is low on fuel, they may not even be able to respond or transport the patient to the hospital. Second, the sound of the music may be distracting to Ann, who is driving the vehicle. At best, it may drown out any ambient sounds that might clue the crew in to the traffic patterns surrounding them as they head toward the incident. Can Ann be absolutely positive that the unit is ready to respond?

You Are There: Reality-Based Cases

1. Not having the ambulance gurney inside the ambulance is not only embarrassing, but it presents an operational challenge. Ann could return to the station to retrieve the stretcher, you could request a second ambulance for transport, or you could carry the patient out to the ambulance on a backboard and secure him somehow to the floor or bench seat of the ambulance. None of these options is satisfactory. The lesson learned here is to always check out the ambulance at the beginning of a shift.

Test Yourself

1. d

   For patients with complaints of altered mental status, the cardiac monitor, oxygen/medical bag, and suction equipment may be necessary in order to properly care for the patient. Each of these pieces of equipment should be brought to the scene to assist in your care of the patient. Remember, it is better to bring in the extra equipment and not need it than to look foolish when you need a piece of equipment left in the vehicle.

2. d

A Type II ambulance is the integral van body style with no modular box fixed on the chassis.

3. Duplex radio communications allow for the transmutation of two channels on a single frequency, while multiplex allows for a higher number of channels.

For example, duplex communication is typically used to both send and receive audio information (so that both people can talk at the same time). Multiplex communication could also allow the transmission of text data.

4. You should contact the receiving facility prior to arrival in order to allow the hospital the opportunity to make additional preparations prior to the patient's arrival.

It is important to contact the receiving facility prior to your arrival, even if you are less than a block away from the facility. This is a courtesy because there may be patients from other emergency units as well as walk-in patients requiring care. Lack of space at the receiving facility may result in diversion. In addition, advise online medical command about what treatments you initiated as per your standing order protocol and how the patient responded. If there are procedures that you wish to perform that require approval of online medical direction, this would also be the time to request approval. Contacting the receiving facility also gives the medical command physician the opportunity to order additional treatment or ask additional questions and to make preparations prior to the arrival of the patient. As an example, some hospitals have initiated stroke and heart attack centers. In many institutions, after a certain time in the evening, staff may be on call. Contacting the hospital will give them adequate time to call back the needed resources.

5. Before

While negotiating curves and turns, you will have to drive slower coming into those turns. Centrifugal force makes heavier objects track to the outside edge of a curve, making emergency vehicles prone to skidding. Avoid braking when going into a turn. Brake before heading into the turn and ease off the gas while making a turn.

6. b

The preparation phase generally occurs at the beginning of the shift and requires a complete check of the vehicle and its equipment.

7. Predesignated landing zones will be well known to the pilot, will be free of most obstacles, and are easier to find.

Predesignated landing zones have been picked because they are generally free of most obstacles that would be dangerous. They will also be easy to find, as most flight programs will have the predesignated landing zone pre-programmed into flight computers, with the appropriate global positioning system settings.

8. You should tell dispatch you have arrived on the scene so they know your current location.

Notify dispatch when you arrive at the scene. If you are directed somewhere different than where you were initially dispatched, update the communications center as soon as possible and be specific. If the situation rapidly deteriorates and you need help with the patient or your life is in danger, the dispatcher will send help to your last reported location.

9. Prearrival instructions are given by the emergency medical dispatcher (EMD) to assist the caller in caring for the patient.

Depending on the chief complaint, the EMD may give prearrival instructions to the caller. By following the EMD's instructions, the caller essentially becomes a first responder. This part of the EMD's job can be crucial. Appropriate prearrival care could mean the difference between a patient who has no chance of survival, regardless of scene and transport times, and one who has a chance of survival.

10. True

Type III ambulances are also referred to as "mod van" or "box" ambulances.

11. b

For medical notifications, the chief complaint and onset, current vital signs, relevant past medical history, and treatment should be communicated. This would include any medical conditions and medications that the patient is currently taking to treat them for diseases related to their chief complaint. Advise online medical command what treatments you initiated as per your standing order protocol and how the patient responded.

12. c

Anyone operating an EMS vehicle is subject to the law of due regard. Regardless of the emergent nature of medical crises, the driver must perform driving tasks safely and with consideration (due regard) for the people both in the emergency vehicle and in surrounding traffic. Driving blindly through intersections, lights and sirens blazing; failing to yield the right of way; speeding; and following too closely are all examples of failure to follow the law of due regard. The operator of an emergency vehicle is not exempt from traffic laws and may be criminally or civilly liable if death, injury, or property damage result from a crash.

13. a

During the response and prior to arriving at the scene, you are operating in the en route phase of the EMS response.

14. d

Base stations are generally in a fixed location. Some base stations are small enough to fit on a desktop; some are so large they require banks of consoles to contain them. They have larger antennas than portable or mobile radios and more power. This enables them to transmit over greater distances.

15. a

    Prior to leaving the hospital, complete your written patient care report. When you are done, make sure that you provide a copy of your written report to the emergency department staff. This becomes part of the patient's medical record and is important to the care of the patient. It is important to understand that this report is a legal document, and the terminology used should be appropriate and the content complete to reflect the patient's experience under your care. Data that is used to determine the future of paramedic practice is also pulled from these reports.

16. Examples include: if you are upset, just got into an argument, learned some upsetting news, or are too excited to focus on immediate tasks.

    Both positive and negative emotions can be distracting. Emotions play a key role in operating an emergency vehicle. If you are upset, just got into an argument, or have just received bad news, for example, refrain from driving.

17. a

    The oxygen-medical-trauma bag, containing the necessary patient care equipment, will always be removed from the ambulance when exiting to provide patient care.

18. False

    You should leave your visible warning (lights) on, but you should not leave your audible warning (sirens) on.

19. Federal Communications Commission

    The Federal Communications Commission (FCC) is an independent United States government agency charged with oversight of interstate and international communications by radio, television, wire, satellite, and cable. The FCC has jurisdiction over the 50 states, the District of Columbia, and all U.S. possessions. They assign radio frequencies for use by emergency service organizations, as well as designate the rules and regulations for speaking on the radio.

20. c

    If transport time by ground to the trauma center is less than 20 minutes, transport the patient via ambulance. Setting up a landing zone and dispatching the helicopter both take time to accomplish. If the patient is loaded and you are ready, go to the trauma center. Additionally, this patient has life-threatening injuries and should be transported emergently.

chapter 50

Medical Incident Command

Are You Ready?

You and your partner are sitting in the front seat of the ambulance. Your hat is covering your face as you try to fit in a short nap when all of a sudden you are violently shaken. The shaking continues, and you hear an earth-shattering crash outside. The first thing that comes to your mind is, "Earthquake!" You quickly lift your hat off your face just in time to see the houses on the opposite side of the street collapse onto a car that a man just got out of. The man runs into the street in an attempt to dodge the falling building. After what feels like a very long time, the shaking stops, and the man runs over to you. He points to the house that just collapsed on his car and yells that there are 13 people in his house. You look up and down the block and realize that the first floors of all the houses on the

block have collapsed, and the upper floors have fallen to the ground.

1. What is your first priority?

_____

_____

_____

2. What are some possible hazards that you need to be aware of on this scene?

_____

_____

_____

3. Is there anything that you can do while you wait for help to arrive?

_____

_____

_____

4. Describe the scene size-up that you would give specific to this scene based on the information that you have up to this point and on the chapter-opening photograph.

_____

_____

_____

Active Learning

1. START and SMART Triage

Using the following scenario and Table 50-1, triage the victims listed in Table 50-1 using START (as discussed in the textbook), and the alternative method called Smart Incident Command System (SMART) described on pages 636–638 by circling the appropriate color designation for each victim.

Scenario: The Jones brothers are known for their parties. Tonight is the first party that they have thrown in the new year. A majority of their guests are on the deck of the third-floor apartment. Everyone is having a great time until there is a loud cracking noise and the deck collapses. As the deck falls, it flips upside down and lands on top of the Jones brothers and eight of their guests.

You Are There: Reality-Based Cases

Case 1

It is 0030 hours. You are sound asleep when the automatic lights click on and the tones start to sound. As you sit up in bed, the dispatcher calls: "Engine 9, Engine 42, Truck 9, Rescue Squad 3, Medic 9, Medic 7, Medic 32, Battalion 10, EMS 3, respond for a multiple-car major MVC with people trapped. Westbound Interstate 42 at mile marker 54. Troopers on scene report numerous critical patients and two fatalities." When you hear "numerous critical patients and two fatalities," you go from being asleep to wide awake in a fraction of a second.

As you slide down the pole that leads to the apparatus floor and your ambulance, you gather your thoughts. The first thought is that you are one exit away from the scene, so you will likely be the first EMS unit to arrive. Your next thought is about ICS and what your responsibilities will be. Just as you suspected, you are the first unit on scene. A trooper runs up to you and informs you that there are three cars involved, with four patients in each car. He points to one of the cars and tells you that the passenger in the front seat is obviously dead and the driver is trapped. Then he points to the roadway and tells you that the patient who was ejected from another car is dead as well. Another trooper informs you that they have shut down the interstate at Broadway, and they will not reopen the road until you clear the scene and their investigation is complete.

1. Based on the preceding photograph and the information that you have received from the trooper, provide a scene size-up for this incident.

   _____

   _____

   _____

2. If you need additional or fewer resources, identify any additional resources that you need or extra resources that you can cancel.

   _____

   _____

   _____

3. If you are functioning as the incident commander (IC) and medical group supervisor (MGS), what role should your partner assume?

   _____

   _____

   _____

TABLE 50-1

Victim Presentation	START Triage				SMART Triage				
	Green	Red	Yellow	Black	Green	Red	Yellow	Blue	Black
Patient A: A 24-year-old male sitting on the sidewalk on the ground floor with a badly crushed arm that appears to have been crushed by the deck. He stands up and walks to the treatment area, cradling his arm, when you direct anyone who can walk to carefully walk to the green tarp area (treatment area) on the street.									
Patient B: A 27-year-old female who is gurgling blood from her mouth when she breathes at 12 breaths/min. Her capillary refill is 4 seconds, and she withdraws to pain.									
Patient C: A 23-year-old female who has a significant depression to the occipital region of her skull. She is initially apneic but begins to breathe when you open her airway. She has palpable radial pulses and is unresponsive.									
Patient D: A 26-year-old female who has a severely depressed open skull fracture with part of her brain lying on the ground next to her. She has infrequent respirations (4–6 breaths/min) and no peripheral pulses. She is unresponsive, and her husband is yelling at you to help her.									
Patient E: A 28-year-old male who has a piece of the deck impaled in his right anterior chest. He is breathing at 24 breaths/min. He has a radial pulse (capillary refill < 2 s) and is following your commands.									
Patient F: A 21-year-old female crushed by the deck on her chest. She is not breathing, she has no pulse, and she is unresponsive.									
Patient G: A 25-year-old male whose chest is torn wide open. You can see a majority of his liver. He has agonal respirations and delayed capillary refill, and is unresponsive. The firefighters tell you that it will take them 30 min to free him from the deck.									
Patient H: A 20-year-old female who has been decapitated. No breathing, no pulse, unresponsive.									
Patient I: A 30-year-old male who has both of his legs crushed under the deck. He is awake and breathing at 28 breaths/min. He has a capillary refill time of < 2 s, and he is following your commands.									
Patient J: A 19-year-old female who is unconscious and unresponsive with a large scalp laceration and blood dripping out of her right ear. She has rapid, deep respirations at 34 breaths/min and a capillary refill time of < 2 s.									

4. In a mass casualty incident (MCI), what roles do the personnel in the second-in ambulance typically play?

_____

_____

_____

5. What should happen with the "dead bodies" that the trooper pointed out to you?

_____

_____

_____

Your partner begins to triage the patients.

Of the four patients in the first car who are triaged, the following is discovered:

Patient A: A restrained 45-year-old driver is alert and oriented, but complaining of severe shortness of breath and chest pain. The patient's respiratory rate is 42 and shallow, and there is a weak, thready radial pulse at 136. Crepitus and subcutaneous air are noted upon palpation of the anterior chest wall.

Patient B: An unrestrained 38-year-old female passenger in the front seat who is alert and oriented, complaining of pain with obvious deformity to her bilateral femurs, glass lacerations to her forehead, and pain to her pelvis. Her skin is cool, pale, and moist. She has weak and rapid brachial pulses and an unlabored respiratory rate of 24.

Patient C: A restrained 10-year-old male located in the back seat behind the driver, complaining of head, neck, and back pain. He is conscious and alert with a strong radial pulse and a respiratory rate of 32.

Patient D: An unrestrained 5-year-old female in the back seat behind the front seat passenger who appears to be unconscious with agonal snoring ventilations and no palpable radial pulses. She appears to have a large hematoma to the right side of her head and a blown right pupil. In addition she has marked abdominal distention.

The second car that your partner triaged was turned sideways on the interstate and had significant damage to both the passenger's and driver's sides of the car.

Patient E: A restrained 27-year-old male in the driver's seat is trapped and shows signs of significant head and facial injuries. He is unconscious and has infrequent gasping ventilations. He has no radial or brachial pulses, but he has a weak and rapid carotid pulse. His chest has an asymmetrical expansion when he takes a breath, and his lower extremities appear to be badly broken.

Patient F: A restrained 23-year-old female is located in the front passenger seat. She has the A post (where the roof meets the hood of the car, framing the front windshield) of the car impaled in her face. She is unresponsive, does not appear to be breathing, and has no pulse.

Patient G: A restrained 20-year-old female is in the seat behind the driver. She is moaning and appears to have a depression to the left parietal region of her head. Her respiratory rate is 24, and she has bounding radial pulses. She appears to have a deformed left arm.

Patient H: A 2-year-old male is located behind the front seat passenger in his car seat. He is crying hysterically and following you with his eyes, but has no movement of any of his extremities. He has a respiratory rate of 52 and a heart rate of 100 beats per minute. He has obvious deformity of his cervical spine.

The third car in the accident has an empty driver's seat and three passengers.

Patient I: An unrestrained 7-year-old female in the front passenger's seat (with the air bag deployed) lies motionless in the seat. She has no ventilatory effort, and there remains no ventilatory effort after several attempts at opening her airway. She has no peripheral or carotid pulses.

Patient J: An unrestrained 27-year-old female passenger is in the seat behind the front passenger's seat. She is slumped over the top of the other back seat passenger. She is unresponsive, with rapid shallow respirations (36 breaths per minute) and a weak and rapid radial pulse. She has bleeding from her right ear and epistaxis from her bilateral nares.

Patient K: A restrained 9-year-old male is found under his mother in the back seat. He states that he thinks that he is fine, but he is afraid to move because he doesn't want to hurt his mother. He has a respiratory rate of 28 and a strong regular radial pulse. He has no complaints of pain or discomfort. He is able to move all his extremities, and when his mother is moved off of him, he is able to get out of the car and walk, but he refuses to leave his mother.

The trooper points out that the driver of the car was ejected and is lying in the roadway behind the car.

Patient L: An apparently unrestrained 28-year-old male lies prone on the ground with his face pointing up to the sky. He has considerable deformity of his neck and spine and has no ventilatory effort and no pulses.

TABLE 50-2

Patient	START Triage				JumpSTART Triage			
A	Green	Red	Yellow	Black	Green	Red	Yellow	Black
B	Green	Red	Yellow	Black	Green	Red	Yellow	Black
C	Green	Red	Yellow	Black	Green	Red	Yellow	Black
D	Green	Red	Yellow	Black	Green	Red	Yellow	Black
E	Green	Red	Yellow	Black	Green	Red	Yellow	Black
F	Green	Red	Yellow	Black	Green	Red	Yellow	Black
G	Green	Red	Yellow	Black	Green	Red	Yellow	Black
H	Green	Red	Yellow	Black	Green	Red	Yellow	Black
I	Green	Red	Yellow	Black	Green	Red	Yellow	Black
J	Green	Red	Yellow	Black	Green	Red	Yellow	Black
K	Green	Red	Yellow	Black	Green	Red	Yellow	Black
L	Green	Red	Yellow	Black	Green	Red	Yellow	Black

6. Using the START or jumpSTART triage criteria and Table 50-2, triage the patients by circling the appropriate category in Table 50-2.

As additional resources arrive on the scene, you transfer the role of IC to the battalion chief, and she directs you to take over the role of MGS. When the second-in ambulance arrives and checks in with you over the radio, you assign one of the crew members the task of setting up a treatment area and the other crew member the task of transport officer. You request that the transport officer begin to contact the trauma center and the local area hospitals to determine how many patients they can take.

During the extrication process patient E, the unconscious male driver who was trapped in his car with initial signs of significant head and facial injuries and infrequent gasping ventilations, has stopped breathing and no longer has a pulse. The officer of the rescue squad tells you that it will take another 10 minutes to extricate the patient. While en route to the scene, the EMS supervisor contacted dispatch and requested any available EMS aircraft. The dispatcher informs you that there are two medical helicopters available with a 7–10 minute ETA. Both have the capacity to carry one patient each.

The closest trauma center (a Level II trauma center) is approximately 20 minutes away by ground and 7–10 minutes by air, and there is a Level I trauma center that is over an hour away by ground and approximately 25 minutes by helicopter. There are two local community hospitals that are 15 and 20 minutes away, respectively.

The transport supervisor informs you that the Level II trauma center can handle two immediate patients and three minor or delayed patients. The local hospitals state that they can handle three minor or delayed patients each, and the Level I trauma center states that it can accept three critical trauma patients and three minor or delayed patients.

Two additional medic units have checked in and are waiting for instructions in the staging area in front of the crash scene.

Your partner (the triage supervisor) informs you that there are seven immediate (red) patients, one minor (green) patient, one delayed (yellow) patient, and three deceased (black) patients.

7. What should happen with patient E?

_____

_____

_____

8. What tasks do you need to coordinate with the incident commander?

_____

_____

_____

9. What should the incoming units do while they are waiting for assignments?

_____

_____

_____

10. What should you direct the triage supervisor to do now that the triage process is complete?

_____

_____

_____

Patient E has been retriaged as deceased (black). This makes the triage count of the patients as follows:
- Six immediate (red) patients
- One minor (green) patient
- One delayed (yellow) patient
- Four deceased (black) patients

11. Where should the patients be transported?

_____

_____

_____

12. How should the patients be transported (by ground, by air, etc.)?

_____

_____

_____

13. Critical (immediate) trauma patients should be transported to a trauma center. There are six critical trauma patients, and the two trauma centers together can accept five trauma patients. What are your options for managing this situation?

_____

_____

_____

Test Yourself

1. What elements does a scene size-up generally include?

_____

_____

2. What is the function of an incident action plan (IAP)?

_____

_____

3. When communicating with other agencies on the radio during a mass casualty incident, why is it important to use clear text?

_____

_____

4. Command posts are temporary locations where personnel and equipment are kept until they are needed on scene.

True

False

5. During a large-scale MCI, the incident commander is considering creating another division for a total of six divisions. What additional step should she take?

_____

_____

6. Once a staging area has been established, it becomes a functional unit under which section?

_____

_____

7. Why should paramedics use the ICS even for small events?

_____

_____

8. _____ is responsible for tracking hours of work and compensation during a large mass casualty incident.

Scenario: A building under construction has collapsed, trapping 30 workers. You have arrived on the scene, requested additional resources, and set up a command post. You are the incident commander.

9. You realize that there are two separate areas where extrication and treatment are needed. You should
  a. establish another command post to divide up the work.
  b. write an incident action plan because it is required.
  c. avoid dividing your resources in order to remain safe.
  d. assign resources and establish two division supervisors.

10. You begin treating patients after your supervisor arrives and takes over as the IC. This is called
  a. transfer of duties.
  b. transfer of command.
  c. transfer of control.
  d. transfer of scene.

Scenario: A passenger train has derailed and multiple people are injured. Many have self-extricated. Injured passengers can be found on both sides of the train.

11. Applying the incident command system, what is the best method for the initial management of this scene?
    a. Establish divisions on both sides of the train.
    b. Set up a command post on both sides of the train.
    c. Move all injured passengers to one side of the track.
    d. Plan for a single triage and staging area.

12. The railroad company has sent a representative to assist with the rescue effort. The title given to this advisor is
    a. technical specialist.
    b. administrative advisor.
    c. nonessential person.
    d. EOC advisor.

Scenario: A gas line explosion has destroyed several buildings and injured more than 50 people in a city with only one Level II trauma center. At approximately the same time, about a mile away from the scene, two cars collide head-on, seriously injuring three people.

13. Had the car crash *not* occurred at the same time as the explosion, it most likely would have been classified as
    a. a routine incident.
    b. a mass casualty incident.
    c. a multiple-casualty incident.
    d. a multiple-injury disaster.

14. How should you manage these incidents?
    a. Treat the car crash victims first because the scene can be cleared more quickly.
    b. Focus resources on patients who require advanced airways.
    c. Allocate resources to patients with the best chance of survival.
    d. Ensure that all patients who arrive at the hospital become priority patients.

Scenario: You are on the scene of a three-vehicle crash. Eight people are injured, and your squad has implemented START triage.

15. A patient with a small laceration on her cheek has exited her car and asks you if she can help with the injured. You should
    a. perform a quick assessment to determine primary triage designation.
    b. ask the woman if she has any medical training and allow her to assist you.
    c. ask the woman to go back to her car to await assessment by you or your partner.
    d. send the woman to the green "third priority" treatment area to await treatment.

16. Within the START triage method, all nongreen patients will be initially evaluated using what parameters?
    a. Respirations, pulse, and mental status
    b. Airway, breath sounds, and pulse
    c. Probability of survival and airway patency
    d. Resources and life-threatening conditions

Scenario: Three people were injured in a car crash. Patient 1 has an obvious, open skull fracture and is not breathing; patient 2 is an alert elderly man with a labored respiratory rate of 36; patient 3 is a child who does not respond to pain and is breathing 10 times per minute.

17. Using the START triage method, patient 1 would be classified as
    a. red.
    b. green.
    c. black.
    d. yellow.

18. Using the JumpSTART triage method, patient 3 should be classified as
    a. immediate.
    b. minor.
    c. delayed.
    d. nonurgent.

Scenario: You are the first ambulance on the scene of an apartment fire with an unknown number of people reportedly still inside the complex. Three police officers and two fire units have also arrived.

19. What is the first thing you should do?

_____

_____

20. If three separate "incident commanders" representing different agencies are required for this scene, the command structure is said to be unified.

True

False

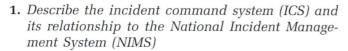

Need to Know

1. *Describe the incident command system (ICS) and its relationship to the National Incident Management System (NIMS)*

The incident command system (ICS), otherwise known as the incident management system, was developed in the early 1970s in response to a need for efficient management of rapidly moving wild land fires in the state of California.[1] The four pillars of the ICS system are that

a. It is an organizationally flexible system.

b. It is functional on a day-to-day basis as well as in incidents of grand scale.

c. It is standardized so that personnel from different agencies, large or small, can function in any role.

d. Its operations are cost effective.[2]

In order for these objectives to be carried out, the federal government, under a presidential directive to the Department of Homeland Security, created the National Incident Management System (NIMS).[3] State, local, and tribal agencies must adopt NIMS as a condition for receiving federal monies for training, equipment, and reimbursement for costs associated with assisting in the mitigation of large-scale incidents.[4]

As a result of the development of the ICS, the nation now has a system for managing incidents that allows for:

- Appropriate span of control ratios
- A standardized emergency response organizational structure
- Reliable incident information available to all agencies and personnel at an incident
- The ability for all the agencies responding to an incident to communicate effectively with one another
- A clearly defined chain of command
- Mutually understood terminology
- Clear incident objectives that allow for a coordinated response[5]

2. *Define key terms related to medical incident command.*

a. *National Incident Management System (NIMS).* A system responsible for developing a process that creates a clear chain of command and a consistent approach for federal, state, local, and tribal governments to work together.

b. *Incident command system (ICS).* A consistent incident management system that utilizes common and consistent terminology (the ICS is an integral component of NIMS).

c. *Incident commander (IC).* The only position that is staffed at every incident. The IC has the overall responsibility for managing the incident.

d. *Unity of command.* Each individual worker on a scene is accountable to only one supervisor.

e. *Unified command.* Allows for the sharing of the incident command function by two or more agencies or jurisdictions.

f. *Incident command post (ICP).* The place where the incident commander oversees incident operations. The ICP should be located outside of the incident.

g. *Staging areas.* Temporary locations where personnel and equipment are kept until they are needed on the scene.

h. *Buses.* Locations where primary logistical and administrative functions are coordinated and administered (the base may be located at the same place as the ICP).

i. *Camps.* Locations where resources are kept to support the incident operations (they provide food, shelter, water, sleeping areas, and sanitation to the workers at the incident).

j. *Helibases.* Locations for helicopter operations.

k. *Helispots.* Temporary locations that are used as landing zones.

l. *Incident action plan (IAP).* An oral or written plan containing the objectives and strategies for managing the incident (a hazmat incident is the only type of incident that requires a written IAP). The IAP should contain (1) what needs to be done, including incident objectives, strategies, evaluation of the progress that is being made in an attempt to mitigate the situation, and revision of the plan to meet changing conditions; (2) who is responsible for doing it, including personnel and resources; (3) how communications are accomplished; and (4) what is the procedure if someone is injured.

m. *Operational period.* A part of the IAP that describes the goals and objectives for a particular period of time (typically 12 hours, but can be more or less time).

n. *Span of control.* The number of people that a supervisor can effectively manage (between three and seven people, but the recommended number is less than five).

o. *Command staff*

1. *Public information officer (PIO).* Serves as a conduit for information to internal and external stakeholders, including the media.

2. *Safety officer.* Responsible for monitoring the safety conditions and developing measures to ensure the safety of workers on the scene.

3. *Liaison officer.* Serves as the primary contact for supporting agencies assisting with the incident.

p. *General staff.* The individuals in charge of each section.

1. *Operations section chief.* Responsible for the management of tactical operations (one of the operational areas will be EMS).

2. *Staging.* A functional unit under the operations section where arriving units can stand by until they receive an assignment.

3. *Planning.* Consists of four units and a number of technical specialists. This section is responsible for developing and documenting the IAP (including operational objectives and strategies established by the IC).

- *Technical specialists.* Individuals who are specially trained in their field or profession and are only activated when needed. They can be assigned anywhere in the organization, including the command staff.

4. *Logistics.* Responsible for the acquisition and coordination of required support resources.

5. *Finance and administration.* Typically established in incidents that last for several days or longer. Responsible for cost analysis, compensation, procurement, and tracking personnel and hours of work.

q. *Modular resource components*

1. *Branches.* Up to five branches per section. Branches are typically formed when the number of divisions or groups exceeds the recommended 1:5 ratio span of control. Branches often develop after divisions or groups. Branches are controlled by branch directors.

2. *Divisions and groups.* Up to five divisions or groups per branch. *Divisions* are used to divide an incident across geographical boundaries. *Groups* are established to control assignments that are related to a specific function.

3. *Units.* Up to five resource units per division or group (a resource unit is a company or a crew of an ambulance, a fire engine, a rescue squad, etc.).

4. *Strike teams.* Consist of a set number of the same type of resources.

5. *Task forces.* Any combination of resources put together to accomplish a specific mission.

- Both strike teams and task forces operate under a designated leader and have a common form of communication that they use during their assignment.

r. *Chain of command.* An orderly line of authority.

s. *Area command.* Provides oversight to the management of various incidents that are happening simultaneously around a single city.

t. *Transfer of command.* Typically takes place when an incident expands and later-arriving personnel take over command from the initial arriving personnel. The transfer is best accomplished face-to-face and needs to be communicated to all other workers at the incident.

3. *Define scene size-up and describe the components that need to be conveyed to the other responding units.*

A scene size-up is a brief report that summarizes the observation of first-arriving units. This report includes the following:

a. The designation of the first company arriving on the scene

b. A brief description of the type of incident and an estimate of the number of patients

c. Any obvious conditions or safety concerns

d. A declaration of the strategy to be used along with additional resources

e. The assumption of command (along with the designation of the name of the incident, for example, "Medic 47 will be Interstate 10 Command.")

f. The designated location of the command post[6]

Subsequent information, especially when the situation involves the care and transport of numerous patients, includes:

a. The best access for units to get to the scene

b. A location for a staging area

c. The best egress for units to take when transporting patients from the scene

d. Locations for treatment areas, helicopter landing zones (LZs), a morgue, medical supply, and so forth

e. The identity of the workers who take on the roles of triage, treatment, and transport groups

f. Periodic updates on the condition of the scene and progress in the transporting of patients

4. *Compare and contrast a multi-casualty incident with a mass casualty incident.*

A multi-casualty incident is an incident that produces more patients than a jurisdiction is routinely capable of handling.[7] It does not, however, exceed the capacity of the local hospitals, EMS providers, and other resources to manage.

A mass casualty incident involves a number of patients with severity of injuries that exceed the capabilities of the area EMS providers, hospitals, and facilities. In this type of situation, resources are allocated and utilized in a manner that allows for the patients with the best chances for survival and who require the least expenditure of time, resources, and personnel to be cared for first.[8]

5. *Describe the methods and processes for classifying patients during triage.*

Triage is the process of evaluating and classifying patients into categories based on predetermined triage criteria. Many systems use a color-coded method of identifying patients according to their acuity. Three commonly used triage systems are START, JumpSTART, and SMART.

a. START triage is a method of triaging patients that begins by removing all minor (green) patients from the equation and placing them in the treatment area.[9] The remaining patients are then evaluated using the mnemonic RPM:

R = respiration

P = pulse

M = mental status

Figure 50-1 shows the START triage algorithm.

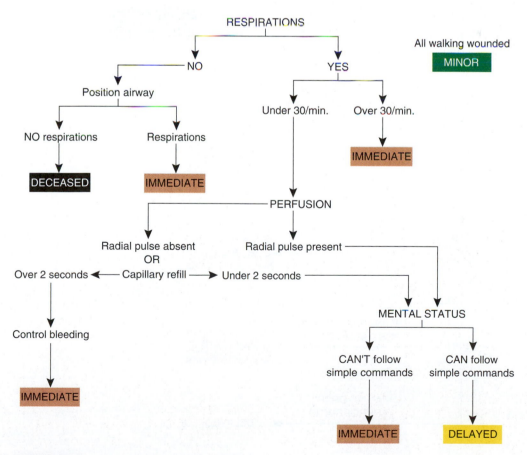

FIGURE 50-1 The START triage algorithm.

b. JumpSTART triage is a pediatric adaptation of the START method; it is shown in Figure 50-2.[10]

c. The SMART triage system is represented by the algorithm in Figure 50-3.

In this system patients are classified in the following manner:

- *First priority.* Patients who will likely survive, but have immediate life threats; usually coded by the color *red* and called "immedi-ate" in regard to the need for transportation off of the scene.

- *Second priority.* Patients who have injuries that may become life-threatening, but can tolerate a short delay in receiving care; usually coded by the color *yellow* or described as "delayed."

- *Third priority.* Patients who have nonurgent and localized injuries without systemic implications; usually coded by the color *green.*

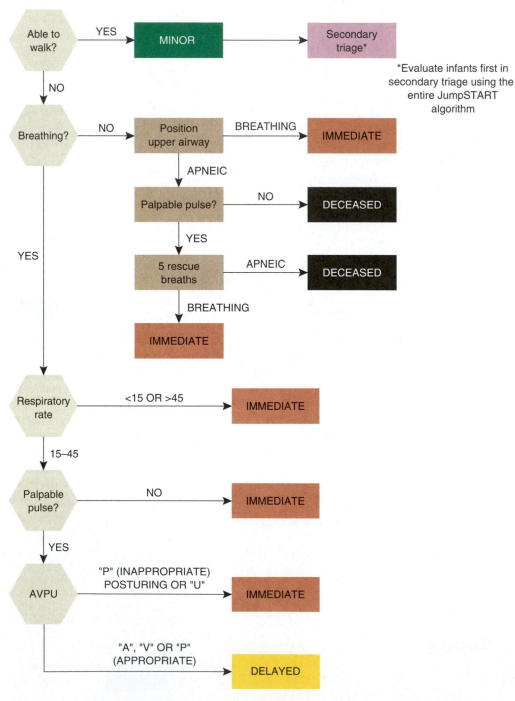

FIGURE 50-2   The JumpSTART MCI triage algorithm for pediatric patients.

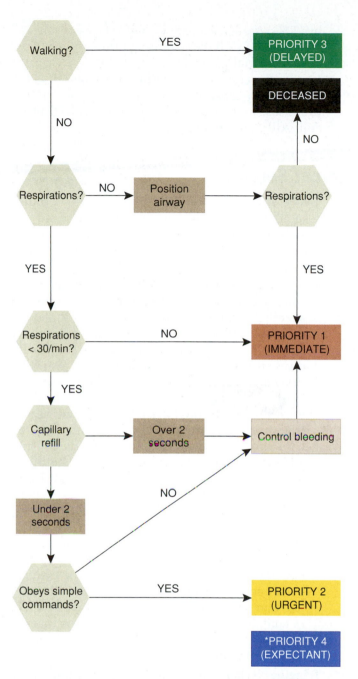

FIGURE 50-3 The Smart Incident Command System (SMART) triage system.

* Note that Priority 4 pertains to those patients who are not yet deceased, but have such catastrophic injuries that they cannot possibly survive and for whom treatment would be futile.

The group is often referred to as the "walking wounded" or the "hold" group.

• *Last category.* The last category is for patients who are dead or catastrophically injured and extremely unlikely to survive. This category is usually represented by the color *black* or classified as "expectant" or "deceased."

Patients are either initially triaged with colored (red, yellow, green, or black) plastic tape that is tied around an extremity or with commercially available triage tags. This process is typically performed using specific physiological criteria such as respirations, pulse, and mentation. The patient will receive the initial color-coded triage rating based on the results of the rescuer's interpretation of the triage criteria. Secondary triaging is completed as soon as the patient enters the treatment area (typically with triage tags). See Chapter 50, Medical Incident Command, in the textbook for additional information on triage criteria.

6. *Describe the function of the following multi-casualty incident ICS groups: medical group supervisor, triage group, treatment group, and transportation group.*

 a. *Medical group supervisor (MGS).* The primary focus of the MGS is to implement all medical group and branch functions necessary to triage, treat, and transport all patients according to the incident medical objectives. The MGS establishes command and control of the activities within a medical group, establishes the medical group with assigned personnel, and requests additional personnel and resources sufficient to respond to the magnitude of the incident. The MGS reports to the medical branch director or directly to the incident commander and supervises the triage unit leader, treatment unit leader, transport unit leader, and medical supply coordinator.

 b. *Triage group.* The triage group is responsible for overseeing personnel who locate and rapidly assess all the patients involved with the incident.

 c. *Treatment group.* The treatment group is responsible for designating an appropriate treatment area if the IC has not already established one. Patients are retriaged once they enter the treatment area, and their injuries are managed, generally under austere conditions.

 d. *Transportation group.* The transportation group assigns workers under their command to supervise communication with receiving facilities (determining how many patients a facility can take and the type of patients they are capable of treating) and track patients who are transported from the scene. This group works in conjunction with the MGS and the treatment supervisor to ensure that there are sufficient transportation resources and personnel to move the patients from the treatment area to the appropriate transportation vehicles. The group advises the treatment supervisor when resources are available for transporting patients, requests units from the staging area, and ensures that ongoing monitoring of patients takes place as they are readied and loaded into transport resources.

Need to Do

The following skills are explained and illustrated in a step-by-step manner, via skill sheets and/or Step-by-Steps in this text and on the accompanying DVD:

Skill Name	Skill Sheet Number and Location	Step-by-Step Number and Location
Airway Positioning and Maneuvers	1 – DVD	1 – DVD
Primary Survey	32 – Appendix A and DVD	32 – Chapter 14 and DVD
Verbal Communications	63 – DVD	N/A

Connections

- Chapter 5, Clinical Decision-Making, in the textbook describes clinical decision-making in the setting of multiple patients.
- Chapter 9, Safety and Scene Size-Up, in the textbook offers additional information on scene safety and scene size-up while responding to multi-casualty and mass casualty incidents.
- See Chapter 17, Documentation and Communication, in the textbook for additional information on communication and patient tracking while managing an MCI.
- Chapter 27, Trauma Patients and Trauma Systems, in the textbook explains the management of multiple trauma patients by prehospital personnel and medical facilities.
- Chapter 51, Rescue Awareness, in the textbook presents information on how to work with rescue personnel on the scene of an MCI.
- Chapter 52, Teamwork and Operational Interface, in the textbook discusses techniques for working with other agencies in small- and large-scale incidents.
- Chapter 53, Hazardous Materials Incidents, in the textbook outlines the responsibilities of EMS when managing patients who have been exposed to hazardous materials, including how to prevent the contamination of additional people and emergency personnel.
- For information and instruction on the Smart Incident Command System (SMART), created by TSG Associates, go to www.tsgassociates.co.uk/English/Civilian/training.htm and use the online tutorial.
- Link to the companion DVD for a chapter-based quiz, audio glossary, animations, games and exercises, and, when appropriate, skill sheets and skill Step-by-Steps.

Street Secrets

- **Two Critical Factors** When faced with a multi-casualty or a mass casualty incident, there are two factors that are critically important to the overall success of the operation: scene size-up and clear communication.
  - For a smooth-running MCI, first-arriving medical personnel need to perform an accurate and succinct *scene size-up*, which includes an estimate of the number of victims, request for additional resources, and a location for the additional resources to stage (this will also help prevent freelancing, as incoming units will need to check in once they are in the staging area). Regarding additional resources, a good rule of thumb is to divide the number of patients by 2 (to allow for two patients per ambulance) and add two ambulances to that number (to allow for enough personnel to handle the MCI and ICS positions). If there is no IC, the most experienced person from the first-in unit will become the IC and may also function as the MGS until transfer of the IC function can take place.
  - The other factor crucial to the success of an MCI operation is *clear communication*. All medical personnel need to be able to communicate with one another. It is the responsibility of the MGS in conjunction with the IC to make sure that everybody on the scene has the ability to communicate with one another.
- **Triaging** When you are faced with the task of triaging, triage by the criteria that are set forth by the system your region uses. You must maintain complete objectivity and keep emotions out of the process. It can be difficult to maintain objectivity, for example, when faced with injured children, but remember that the purpose of triage is to do the most good for the most people.

The Drug Box

There are no specific drugs related to this chapter content.

References

1. "History of ICS," Incident Command System National Training Curriculum, October 1994, p. 1.
2. Ibid, p. 2.
3. The White House of the United States of America, *Homeland Security Presidential Directive HSPD-5: Management of Domestic Incidents,* February 28, 2003, www.NIMSonline.com/docs/hspd-5.pdf (accessed June 30, 2005).
4. The White House of the United States of America, *Homeland Security Presidential Directive HSPD-8: National Preparedness,* December 17, 2003, www.NIMSonline.com/docs/hspd-8.pdf (accessed June 30, 2005).
5. "History of ICS," p. 2.
6. National Fire Service Incident Management System Consortium Model Procedures Committee, *Model Procedures Guide for Emergency Medical Incidents,* 2nd ed. Stillwater, OK: Fire Protection Publications, Oklahoma State University, 2002.
7. American College of Surgeons, *Advanced Trauma Life Support Instructor Manual,* 6th ed. Chicago, IL, 1977.
8. G. Super et al., *START: Simple Triage and Rapid Treatment Plan,* Newport Beach, CA: Hoag Memorial Presbyterian Hospital, 1994.
9. L. E. Romig, "JumpSTART Pediatric Triage Tool," www.jumpstarttriage.com/TheJumpSTARTAlgorithm.html (accessed June 30, 2005).
10. E. K. Noji and G. D. Kelen, "Disaster Medical Services," in J. E. Tintinalli, G. D. Kelen, and J. S. Stapczynski (eds.), *Emergency Medicine: A Comprehensive Study Guide.* New York: McGraw-Hill, 2004, pp. 27–35.

Answers

Are You Ready?

1. The first priority is your own safety. Don all your personal protective equipment. Call for help, then attempt to gather as much information as you can relevant to the location of the people in the house (what floor were they on, were they in the front or the back of the house, etc.) and other points of access (back entrance, roof, etc.), so that you can pass the information on to rescue personnel when they arrive.

2. Hazards at this scene include potential aftershocks, natural gas leaks, further building collapse, downed electrical lines, the potential for fire, and broken glass.

3. Things that you can do while you wait for help to arrive include the following:

   a. Isolate and deny entry to the collapsed building.

   b. Shut off the gas for the buildings if doing so does not pose a threat to your personal safety.

   c. Use the public address (PA) system in your ambulance to request people to call out if they can hear you. This can give you an idea of where people are and if people are able to respond to you. You can also offer some comfort by telling the people that help is on the way.

4. The scene size-up should include the following:

   a. The designation of the first company arriving on the scene—"Medic 82."

   b. A brief description of the type of incident and an estimate of the number of patients—"We have a building collapse that involves an entire city block on First Street between A and B Streets. We have reports of at least 13 people trapped."

   c. Any obvious conditions or safety concerns—"The upper floors of the buildings have collapsed on the ground floors, and there are downed electrical wires in the area."

   d. A declaration of the strategy to be used along with additional resources—"Requesting heavy rescue squad, additional fire suppression units for man power, and eight additional ambulances." Eight additional ambulances would allow for two patients per ambulance and an additional ambulance to cover the MCI supervisory positions, including your ambulance (triage, treatment, transport, and medical group supervisor [MGS]).

   e. The assumption of command (along with the designation of the name of the incident)—"Medic 82 will be First Street Command." When the person in charge of search and rescue shows up, you can transfer command to that individual and take over the role of MGS or take on any of the other roles that have not been filled.

   f. The designated location of the command post—"The command post will be at the corner of First Street and A Street." You can offer routes of access to the scene if you know how it will be best for units to arrive, and you can offer a location for ambulance staging so that the scene doesn't become a traffic jam of emergency vehicles.

Active Learning

1.

Patient	START	SMART
A	Minor	Priority 3
B	Immediate	Priority 1
C	Immediate	Priority 1
D	Immediate	Priority 4
E	Delayed	Priority 2
F	Dead	Dead
G	Immediate	Priority 4
H	Dead	Dead
I	Delayed	Priority 2
J	Immediate	Priority 1

You Are There: Reality-Based Cases
Case 1

1. "Medic 7 is on scene. The correct location of the incident is westbound Interstate 42 at mile marker 54. We have three vehicles involved. There are 10 patients and two fatalities. Troopers have shut down westbound 42 and are diverting traffic off the interstate at Broadway. The best access is to get on West 42 at Broadway. Have all responding ambulances park in front of the scene and report in to EMS command on the EMS channel for an assignment. Medic 7 is placing Interstate 42 command in service. Interstate 42 Command Post will be located at Medic 7 at the west end of the incident."

2. There are people trapped, so you will likely need a rescue squad and the engine companies for extrication, suppression if needed, and additional personnel. The truck can assist with extrication and labor, the battalion chief can take over as the incident commander, and the EMS supervisor can take over or share the medical group supervisor (MGS) position. If you are not comfortable canceling units or not sure what will be needed, keep all the units responding; it is better to have too many resources than not enough. You can always release units if you don't need them. There are a total of three ambulances responding, and there are 10 patients. You can use the rule of the number of patients divided by 2 (10 ÷ 2 = 5) plus two additional ambulances to handle the ICS/MCI positions (MGS, triage, treatment, and transport). Therefore, you will need a total of four additional ambulances.

   Some systems will automatically dispatch a medical helicopter to the scene of a major motor vehicle collision (MVC), depending on the availability of ground resources and the proximity of the scene to a trauma center or another appropriate receiving facility. If EMS aircraft are not part of the initial response, and you determine that they are needed, request the EMS aircraft as soon as possible, because it may take some time for the aircraft to arrive on the scene (remember that when EMS aircraft are requested, someone, usually the fire department with the assistance of law enforcement, should establish an appropriate landing zone [LZ]).

3. If you are the senior partner on the first-in unit, you should be the incident commander. It is not advisable to take on more than one role, because this will typically cause you to exceed the recommended span of control. If, on the other hand, you know that the battalion chief is minutes away and will take on the role of IC when you transfer command, you can then take on the role of MGS, since you already have all the information that you will need to function in this role. Since you and your partner are the only EMS personnel on the scene, it doesn't make sense to have one of you assume the role of IC and the other take on the role of MGS—that would leave both of you with no one to supervise. This situation would also delay the triaging of the patients, which is the role your partner should undertake.

4. The roles of the personnel in the second-in ambulance during an MCI are treatment supervisor and transport supervisor.

5. Depending on the policies and protocols of your EMS system, the determination of death in the field may need to be made by EMS personnel and based on specific criteria. If law enforcement in your area has the training and the authority to determine death in the field, then the patients who have been declared dead do not require any more of your attention. What is the case in your EMS system? Because the crash scene will require an investigation to determine what happened and whether anyone is at fault, the dead bodies should remain where they are unless they need to be moved in order to conduct rescue operations.

6.

Patient	START	JumpSTART
A	Immediate	
B	Immediate	
C		Delayed
D		Immediate
E	Immediate	
F	Deceased	
G	Immediate	
H	Deceased	Immediate
I		Deceased
J	Immediate	
K		Minor
L	Deceased	

7. Patient E needs to be retriaged. He should be classified as deceased. Efforts are redirected to patients who stand the best chance of surviving.

8. Since there are two EMS aircraft that are 7–10 minutes away, the setup of an appropriate landing zone needs to be addressed, and this task can be coordinated by the IC. In addition, you will need an extrication team to extricate the patients and a litter bearer team to transfer the patients who are extricated to the treatment area. If there are scarce resources, the extrication teams and the ambulance crews who are arriving on the scene can transfer the patients to the treatment area once they are extricated from the cars. The downside to using crews in this manner is that crews frequently bypass the treatment area and transport the patients. This is called "freelancing," which can cause a great deal of confusion and interfere with the ability to track patients. In addition, equipment from the incoming ambulances (e.g., backboards, c-collars, and oxygen) must be made available for use by the previously mentioned teams. The IC, in conjunction with MGS, can assign crews to these tasks.

9. The incoming units should get all their backboards, c-spine equipment, oxygen, and so forth, together for use by the extrication and litter bearer teams. They can also make their gurneys available to the litter bearer teams for use in transferring patients to the transporting units. While they are awaiting patients or tasks to perform, they should ready their ambulances for transport.

10. There is no specific role that the triage supervisor should take on once he or she has completed the initial round of triage, but it may make sense for this individual to assist in the treatment area, either with retriaging or coordinating with the transport supervisor which patients should be transported where, because he or she may already have a good idea of the acuity of the patients and where they should be transported.

11. In a perfect world, all the patients with a mechanism of injury who have the potential for significant injury would be transported to a trauma center. Therefore, the six immediate trauma patients should be transported to the trauma centers. Because of the mechanism of injury, the minor and the delayed patients would benefit from evaluation at one of the trauma centers as well, in case they turn out to have more serious injuries than previously thought.

12. Based on the information provided by the treatment supervisor, the Level I trauma center can handle three immediate (red) patients and three minor or delayed patients. The Level I trauma center is the furthest away; as such, it would make sense to fly the two most critical (immediate) patients to the Level I trauma center and send one of the lesser acuity (immediate) trauma patients to the Level I trauma center by ground. Two immediate (red) patients can be transported by ground to the Level II trauma center, along with the minor and the delayed patients. This leaves us with the problem of where to take the remaining trauma patient (discussed in question 13). The deceased patients should be left where they were found unless they interfere with your extrication and treatment of the other patients, in which case they can be moved to a makeshift morgue. The medical examiner needs to be notified about the public-view deaths and the need to come out to the scene to perform an investigation and collect the bodies.

13. There is no single correct answer to this question. This is the type of situation in which you are required to do some critical thinking, problem solving, and improvising. Consider the following possibilities:
    - Once you determine that there are more immediate patients than there are beds for them at the trauma centers, check to see if there have been any improvements in patient status when the patients are retriaged in the treatment area. If there is just one patient who was initially triaged as immediate who is now delayed, that patient can be transported to either of the trauma centers (likely the Level II trauma center by ground because it is the closest hospital with the greatest capabilities).
    - If there is no change in patient acuity during the retriaging of the patients in the treatment area, have the transport supervisor contact both of the trauma centers, report your situation, and determine if

either of them can handle one more immediate trauma patient.
    - If all else fails, have the EMS supervisor deal with the problem or contact medical direction for online consultation.
    - If at all possible, wait to transport the least critical of the immediate patients until a resolution to the destination problem is obtained.

Test Yourself

1. A scene size-up generally includes a brief description of the incident, safety concerns, the strategy to be used, assumption of command, and the location of the command post.

   The scene size-up is a brief report that summarizes the observations of the first-arriving unit and is delivered by the IC to incoming units. It usually includes the designation of the company arriving on the scene, a brief description of the incident situation, any obvious conditions or safety concerns, a declaration of the strategy to be used, the assumption of command, and the designated location of the command post.

2. The IAP is an oral or written plan containing the general objectives that reflects the overall strategy of managing the incident.

   Every incident requires an IAP, but only hazmat incidents need a written IAP. The IAP should outline what needs to be done, who is responsible for doing it, how communications are accomplished, and what is the procedure if someone is injured. The IAP typically spans a time frame of 12 hours, but it could cover more or less time. The time frame covered by the IAP is called the operational period. The IAP should be reviewed and updated at the conclusion of each segment of the operational period.

3. Codes may cause confusion, as all agencies may not use the same codes. It is for this reason that a "clear text" approach is needed for the ICS to be effective.

   It helps to make radio communications two-way, where the receiving parties repeat information in order to confirm accuracy.

4. False

   Staging areas are temporary locations where personnel and equipment are kept until they are needed on the scene. The status of all personnel, equipment, and supplies in the staging area is "available." Unlike the incident command post (ICP) or the base, it is acceptable to have more than one staging area for an incident.

5. She should begin to establish branches.

   Branches are typically established when the number of groups or divisions exceeds the recommended span of control 1:5 ratio for the IC or section chief. The single biggest reason to establish branches during an incident is because the span of control is exceeding recommended ratios. For this reason branches often develop after divisions and groups.

6. Operations

   Staging areas are temporary locations where personnel, equipment, and supplies are kept in an "available" status until they are needed on the scene. Typically, unless a staging area is established by the IC or operations section chief, incoming units will stage in an uncommitted position until they receive an assignment. Once a staging area is established, staging becomes a functional unit under the operations section, and all incoming units must check in with the staging supervisor. Units are then called up from the staging area as needed for the incident.

7. Frequent use of the ICS helps maintain proficiency.

When agencies frequently use the ICS on small incidents, they become more familiar with it and are able to easily implement the ICS during a large incident.

8. Finance and administration

When an incident requires significant management resources, including finance and administrative support, it may require the establishment of a finance and administration section. This could occur if management of the incident spans several days. This section is responsible for cost analysis, compensation, procurement, and tracking personnel and hours of work.

9. d

The incident commander may need to divide resources in order to accomplish the desired objectives. Divisions should be created and named, and supervisors need to be identified for those divisions.

10. b

When the role of incident commander is transferred to another individual following a face-to-face meeting, it is called a transfer of command.

11. a

Under the incident command system, every incident should have a single incident command post where the incident commander oversees all incident operations. Divisions can then be established to control assignments within a designated geographical area (i.e., each side of a derailed train). In this situation, it would not be practical to have a single triage area or move all patients to one side of the train, so divisions on either side of the train would be optimal. Keep in mind that implementation of the incident command system may vary from location to location depending on resources and local protocols.

12. a

Technical specialists may be required for certain incidents. They are individuals who are specially certified and are only activated when needed. They can be assigned anywhere in the organization, including the command staff.

13. c

A multiple-casualty incident is defined as an emergency incident that produces more patients than a jurisdiction is routinely capable of handling. During a multiple-casualty incident, the number of patients and the severity of their injuries do *not* exceed the capacity of area medical systems, hospitals, and facilities to render care, however. Thus, the car collision in this scenario would ordinarily be classified as a multiple-casualty incident,

since it would require more resources than a routine incident, but would not exceed the capacity of the area medical system.

14. c

In a mass casualty incident, the number of patients and the severity of their injuries exceed the capacity of area medical systems and facilities. This situation forces an allocation of resources that allows the patients with the best chance of survival and who require the least expenditure of time, equipment, supplies, and personnel to be managed first.

15. a

Patients capable of walking will most likely be classified "green," but you should always do a quick assessment before asking ambulatory patients to proceed to a designated minor (green) treatment area. Consider that it should take about 60 seconds for a responder to triage each victim for his or her primary triage designation. The early designation of a treatment area for ambulatory patients is important. You should not send this patient back to her car, as she may leave the scene and become difficult to locate.

16. a

After the minor (green) patients have been moved to the treatment area, the remaining patients are then evaluated using the mnemonic "RPM." With the RPM system, the *R* stands for respiration, *P* for pulse, and *M* for mental status. Using the system's given parameters, any victim in whom respiration is absent or above 30, perfusion is compromised (absent radial pulses or capillary refill time over 2 seconds), or mental status is unconscious or unable to follow commands gets categorized to the immediate (red) treatment section.

17. c

Nonurgent patients are either dead or catastrophically injured and extremely unlikely to survive. This category is usually represented by the color black.

18. a

Using the system's given parameters, any pediatric victim in whom respiration is below 15 or above 45, perfusion is compromised (using just absent radial pulses), or mental status is unconscious or demonstrates an abnormal response to pain is categorized to the immediate (red) treatment section.

19. Establish a command post and an incident commander.

It is important for the first-arriving ambulance to establish and communicate the identity of the incident commander, where he or she will be located (command post), and complete the initial scene size-up to determine the required response.

20. True

When command is shared by two or more agencies or jurisdictions, each jurisdiction is allowed a single representative, and this individual is also designated as "incident commander." In this situation, the term that applies to this shared command structure is "unified command."

chapter 51

Rescue Awareness

despite the use of shoring supports, the walls of the trench collapsed, burying Kimberly.

You and your partner are the first rescuers to arrive on the scene. When you approach the trench, you see that the scientists and the students are partway down in the trench, trying to dig Kimberly out by hand.

1. When you arrive on the scene, what should your initial concern be? Explain your reasoning.

_____

_____

_____

2. If you are the first-arriving unit, and you are the senior person on your unit, what is your role and responsibility when you arrive?

_____

_____

_____

3. What can you do while you wait for rescue personnel to arrive?

_____

_____

_____

Are You Ready?

A group of seismologists and geology students from a local university were performing a seismic hazard evaluation by excavating a fault to study the offset of layers and recurrence intervals of earthquakes. Kimberly Goldman was in the bottom of the trench when,

Active Learning

1. **Extra Credit**

   If you are interested in learning more about rescue operations, consider taking any of the following courses:

   - High-angle or cliff rescue
   - Swift-water or surf rescue
   - Technical rope rescue

- Structural collapse rescue
- Confined space or trench rescue
- Disaster medical specialist
- Wilderness search and rescue
- Diver rescue
- Vehicle extrication
- Big rig rescue
- Structural fire rescue

You might find these courses at a local fire department, fire academy, or regional rescue training center. Try performing a Web search for a course; there are several organizations that provide specialized rescue training.

2. Practice Makes Perfect

One of the best ways to gain experience in rescue operations is through simulated practice. Volunteer to work with your school or your provider to coordinate realistic simulated rescues of varying types. This may take a considerable effort on your part, but the more disciplines that are involved, the more realistic the experience will be and the more beneficial the exercise.

You Are There: Reality-Based Cases
Case 1

Yvonne Parker was on her way to pick up her two sons from soccer practice. The sun was starting to set behind her, and she could see the drivers in the cars driving the other direction shading their eyes from the bright sun. Yvonne looked away from the road to tune her car stereo. There was a huge crash, and dust, metal, and glass flew in every direction. Yvonne's car spun around, and when it all stopped, she was unconscious and trapped in her car.

Your ambulance and another ambulance from your district are dispatched to a motor vehicle accident with people trapped. En route to the scene, you hear the rescue squad go on scene. The officer from the squad states: "There are two vehicles with major damage and people trapped. More information to follow."

1. What additional information do you expect to hear from the officer of the rescue squad?

_____

_____

_____

2. How can this scene be made safer for the rescue workers and the patient?

_____

_____

_____

3. What type of PPE is appropriate for automobile extrication and patient care in the rescue area during extrication?

_____

_____

_____

4. Based on the photograph to the left, what hazards exist on the scene?

_____

_____

_____

Less than 2 minutes later the officer from Rescue Squad 2 gets back on the air and gives his scene size-up, which includes information that there are two patients in one car and one patient in the other car. The single patient is trapped in her car, and extrication is under way. He reports that fuel is leaking from the vehicles and requests that the first-arriving engine stand by with a charged hose in the event that there is ignition of the fuel, and that absorbent be placed on the fuel. He states that his crew is disconnecting the batteries from both cars. He is taking command and requests that Highway 123 Command be placed in service.

Moments later you arrive on the scene and report in to the IC. He informs you that they are peeling the roof off the minivan so that they can access the patient. He tells you that the other car has patients who are awake and complaining of extremity pain and some lacerations. He requests that you and your partner evaluate the patients.

5. What is your first priority?

_____

_____

_____

You go to the car with the two patients, and your partner goes to the car with the patient who is being extricated. There is considerable front-end damage to both vehicles, and they both appear to be leaking fuel. The two patients in the car are awake and alert with complaints of extremity and neck pain. Neither patient has any obvious trauma to his head, chest, or abdomen, and they both have strong radial pulses and pink, warm, and dry skin. Your partner's patient, Yvonne, has severe chest trauma (a flail segment to her anterior chest wall) with associated respiratory distress. She has cool, pale, and moist skin and a weak, rapid brachial pulse. She is disoriented.

You and you partner know that the closest trauma center is more than 1 hour away by ground and 20 minutes away by air.

6. What information or recommendation should you and your partner convey to the IC?

_____

_____

_____

7. Are there any other factors you need to consider in regard to the extrication and transport of your patient?

_____

_____

_____

8. What is your next step in caring for these patients?

_____

_____

_____

Test Yourself

1. A woman is trapped in a partially submerged car. The rescue team advises you that the patient is displaying signs of shock, but they do not feel that it is safe for you to access the woman in the water. You should

  a. put on a personal flotation device and treat the patient while the rescue team works to extricate her.

  b. ask the safety officer to overrule the rescue team's decision.

  c. ask the rescue team to relay their assessment findings and patient status reports.

  d. leave the scene and ask to be notified as soon as your skills are needed.

2. How would you reassure a patient during a rescue operation?

_____

_____

3. You arrive at the scene of a motor vehicle crash. As you approach the car, the driver is struggling to open her door. You notice an electrical line lying over the hood. The line is still and you see no sparking. What should you do?

_____

_____

4. When attempting a rescue, your primary concern should be

  a. scene safety.

  b. patient care.

  c. rapid extrication.

  d. patient confidentiality.

5. If a hazard is beyond your ability to handle, your priority should be

  a. ensuring the safety of arriving responders and bystanders.

  b. instructing rescue technicians after the patient has been accessed.

  c. enforcing the perimeter and controlling the scene.

  d. interviewing bystanders to obtain important information.

6. Why is "stored energy" a concern when performing a motor vehicle extrication?

_____

_____

7. How are vehicle air bag systems usually deactivated?

_____

_____

8. You and your partner arrive first at the scene of a "man down" in a business complex. As soon as you enter the building, you detect a sharp, noxious odor and a yellowish haze in the air. You should immediately

   a. exit the building and call a hazardous materials team.

   b. locate the patient and remove him from the building.

   c. ask all persons to quickly evacuate the building.

   d. put on your particulate respiratory mask before proceeding.

9. You are called to support a rescue operation for an adolescent girl who became trapped in an automobile when it struck a power pole. There are sparking electric wires hanging directly over the car. Which of the following considerations is _most_ important?

   a. The electrical hazard

   b. The comfort of bystanders

   c. The patient's condition

   d. The patient's age

10. List at least three hazards that are likely to be encountered at the scene of a motor vehicle crash.

_____

_____

11. All commercial vehicles transporting chemicals must display placards.

True

False

12. Which of the following vehicle parts is usually made from plastic laminate?

   a. The bumper

   b. The firewall

   c. The windshield

   d. The dashboard

13. In a rescue operation, when can the EMS provider access the patient?

   a. When the rescue crew determines that the scene is safe

   b. After the patient has been moved into the safe zone

   c. When the EMS provider's skills are necessary

   d. After the patient has been extricated from any entanglements

14. You are extricating a trapped patient from a motor vehicle when you notice a clear liquid leaking onto the pavement from the front of the vehicle. What should you do?

   a. Attempt to identify the substance leaking from the front of the car.

   b. Inform the rescue team that they will need to work faster.

   c. Find and attempt to seal the source of the leak.

   d. Notify fire officials of the development.

15. You and many other people are stranded by flooding. You expect that it will be at least 24 hours before relief arrives. You do not have any medical supplies. A man brings you to his friend who has a dislocated shoulder and is in extreme pain. The patient asks you to help him. You should

   a. have the friend help you reduce the dislocation.

   b. bind the patient's arm to his torso.

   c. administer an over-the-counter pain reliever.

   d. make him as comfortable as possible and wait for rescue.

16. During a rescue, who has ultimate authority over the operation?

_____

_____

17. What unique safety hazard must be considered when extricating a patient from a hybrid gas-electric car?

_____

_____

18. A bicycle helmet with a chin strap would be a good method of head protection in a swift-water rescue situation.

True

False

19. A building collapsed, trapping several individuals. Your patient is trapped in a narrow hallway beneath a pile of debris. After your initial assessment, you step out of the way to make room for the rescue technicians. When they pause during their work, you hear the patient making gurgling noises when he breathes. You should ask the rescue technicians to

   a. work more quickly.

   b. assess the patient and provide a status report.

   c. turn the patient's head to the side before resuming their work.

   d. stop so that you can suction the patient's airway.

20. What is the purpose of a vehicle's Nader pin?

_____

_____

Need to Know

The following represent the Key Objectives of Chapter 51:

1. *Identify the most frequently used method of organizing rescue operations and how this method accomplishes its desired effects.*

   The incident command system (ICS) is one of the most frequently used methods of improving the safety and efficiency of rescue operations. ICS accomplishes this goal by providing command, control, and coordination.

2. *Describe several factors that can influence rescue operations and/or patient care.*

   The ability to treat a patient's injuries when extrication is an issue is influenced by several factors, including access to the patient, the condition of the patient, and environmental conditions. Efforts between the extrication crew and the patient care team must be coordinated to allow rapid access and optimal patient care.

3. *Describe several things that you can do to improve patient outcome during complex rescue operations.*

   Make sure that you have the right equipment and resources for the job. Plan ahead for the possibility of extended operations. Maintain flexibility to improvise when conditions or situations change.

4. *Describe the five phases of rescue operations.*

   Phase 1. The scene size-up identifies the type of situation, the number of patients, potential or actual hazards, request for additional resources, and so forth.

   Phase 2. This phase involves gaining access to the patient, for example, on the face of a cliff or trapped in a building collapse. Formulate and implement a plan for patient access.

   Phase 3. Extricate the patient from the situation that he or she needs to be rescued from, while constantly being aware of and communicating any safety concerns to the rescue team. The patient needs to be reassessed frequently during this process.

   Phase 4. Package and load the patient.

   Phase 5. Treat the patient and then transport to an appropriate receiving facility.

5. *Identify potential hazards encountered with vehicular rescue operations and safety factors that you can implement in order to reduce the hazards.*

   a. For traffic hazards:
   * Place your apparatus between the traffic and your work area.
   * Provide adequate hazard lighting to make other drivers aware that you are working without making yourself a distraction to their safe driving.
   * Use cones, flares, or directional flashers to direct traffic away from the rescue area.
   * Wear clothing that is visible to other motorists.

   b. For fuel leaks:
   * Notify firefighters of the hazard.
   * Attempt to move rescuers, patients, and bystanders away from the source of the fuel leak.

   c. When there are high-voltage electric wires in electric cars and hybrids:
   * Request that the fire department disconnect the wires from the electrical source.

   d. When air bags do not deploy during impact:
   * Notify the personnel performing the rescue that there are nondeployed air bags that need to be deactivated.
   * Realize that not all air bags are deactivated by disconnecting the battery.

6. *Describe elements of vehicle construction that can impact rescue operations.*

   a. Newer vehicles employ unibody construction, which unifies the body and frame to create a stiffer vehicle overall. This type of construction leads to a quieter, more stable ride that also affords greater protection. However, unibody construction can impact vehicle extrication. If the unibody is compromised by cutting or bending, there is an increased risk of the structure collapsing, causing injury to rescuers and patients alike. Cribbing, shoring, and other methods of stabilizing a vehicle need to be used to minimize these occurrences.

b. Access to victims trapped in a vehicle depends on the vehicle construction. The following are possible points of entry:

- Doors and windows are possible points of entry. Check to see if the door is unlocked before trying to pry it open, and consider the fact that breaking glass can compromise the integrity of the rest of the car, especially with cars that come to rest on their roof. Breaking the glass can cause the roof-support posts to buckle and can crush patients who remain in the vehicle.
- The roof of the vehicle can be removed by cutting the windshield and the support posts (e.g., A posts and B posts) and bending the roof back or removing the roof completely.
- Some vehicles offer access through the trunk.
- Dashboards and steering wheels can be pushed or pulled back in order to free trapped patients.

7. *Identify different types of water rescue.*

- *Surface water.* Any form of water that is not rapidly moving (pools, lakes, etc.). Most drownings take place in surface water.
- *Swift water.* Any body of water that is rapidly moving (rivers, storm drains, etc.). Hazards associated with swift water include:
  - *Strainers.* When water moves through an obstruction (called a strainer), such as a storm grate or tree branches, the current can easily trap a person in the obstruction.
  - *Hydraulics.* When water flows over an object and creates a circulating effect behind the object, it can trap the object (victim, rescuer, etc.) in its current.
  - *Dams and hydroelectric sites.* These can pose the same hazards as discussed for strainers and hydraulics.

8. *Explain factors that influence survivability from a water incident.*

Age of the victim, duration of submersion, and temperature of the water are important factors in determining survivability of victims. When victims are submerged in water that is colder than 70°F, the mammalian dive reflex is triggered and the victim experiences a parasympathetic response in which the heart rate slows, blood pressure drops, and blood is shunted to the heart and brain. Laryngospasm may occur, and the patient will likely rapidly lose consciousness. Victims of cold-water drownings can survive if they are rescued and resuscitation is initiated in less than 1 hour. The rule of thumb for victims of cold-water drownings is that they "are not dead until they are warm and dead."

9. *List several possible hazards that can be encountered during a confined-space rescue.*

- Oxygen deficiency.
- A toxic atmosphere—gases, vapors, or fumes that have the potential to be harmful to humans.
- Engulfment hazards—any situation in which the rescuer has a chance of being buried (silos, etc.)
- Electrical hazards—any electrical supply or electrical source that has the potential to harm a rescuer. The electrical source should be disconnected and tagged so that it is not inadvertently turned back on.
- Mechanical hazards—such as blades, gears, and belts—located within the space in which the rescuer is working. The lockout/tagout method described on the FEMA website (www.fema.gov) provides details on how to shut off the power to such machinery and tag the power source so that it is not accidentally turned back on during the rescue operation.

Note: Before any confined space is entered, it needs to be tested for a toxic atmosphere, the potential for explosion, and oxygen deficiency or irregularity.

10. *Describe hazards and safety precautions associated with trench operations and cave-ins.*

The primary hazard associated with trenches and tunnels are cave-ins. Shoring is the most commonly used precaution against cave-ins, but the protection that it offers is only as good as the shoring that is used. Practice this critical skill frequently, if it is within your scope of responsibility. Otherwise, train with your local rescue crew if possible. Learn the terminology and basic principles of shoring and trench extrication.

Need to Do

The following skills are explained and illustrated in a step-by-step manner, via skill sheets and/or Step-by-Steps in this text and on the accompanying DVD:

Skill Name	Skill Sheet Number and Location	Step-by-Step Number and Location
Trauma Scoring	31 – DVD	N/A
Verbal Communications	63 – DVD	N/A
Bleeding Control and Shock	66 – DVD	66 – DVD
Seated Spinal Immobilization	68 – DVD	68 – DVD
Supine Spinal Immobilization	70 – DVD	70 – DVD
Rapid Extrication	72 – DVD	N/A
Crush Injury Management	79 – DVD	N/A
NREMT Patient Assessment Trauma	83 – DVD	N/A
NREMT Spinal Immobilization (Seated Patient)	92 – DVD	N/A
NREMT Spinal Immobilization (Supine Patient)	93 – DVD	N/A
NREMT Bleeding Control/Shock Management	94 – DVD	N/A

Connections

- Chapter 15, Pharmacology, and Chapter 24, Skeletal Trauma, in the textbook include more detailed discussions of pain management.

- Chapter 50, Medical Incident Command, in the textbook provides additional information on the incident command system (ICS).

- Chapter 53, Hazardous Materials Incidents, in the textbook describes how to operate within a hazardous materials scene.

- The National Association for Search and Rescue (NASAR) is dedicated to those involved in search and rescue operations. The organization's website is www.nasar.org.

- Link to the companion DVD for a chapter-based quiz, audio glossary, animations, games and exercises, and, when appropriate, skill sheets and skill Step-by-Steps.

Street Secrets

- **Leave It to the Experts** Safety, communication, and organization are the keys to any successful rescue operation. If you are not specifically trained in rescue operations, then let those who are specifically trained perform the rescue. If the rescuers have determined that it is safe for paramedics to enter the rescue space while they perform the rescue, do so only if you have adequate PPE. If you are not equipped with adequate PPE, ask the rescuers to bring the patient to you. Know your role in a rescue, and function in that capacity.

- **Stay in Touch** Again, communication is key—ensure that all personnel are on appropriate radio channels and that the operation is managed though the incident command system.

The Drug Box

There are no drugs specific to this chapter.

I SPY

Scenario:

An automobile has crashed, and patients are trapped inside. Extrication is under way by the fire department rescue crew, and a paramedic is directing patient care.

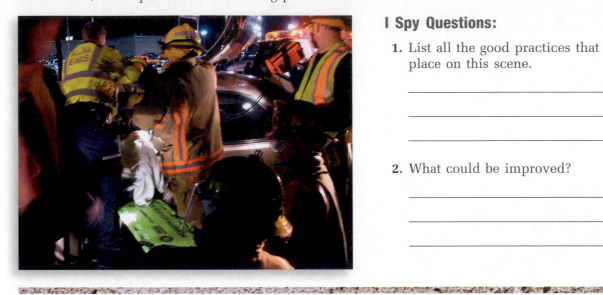

I Spy Questions:

1. List all the good practices that you can see taking place on this scene.

_____

_____

_____

2. What could be improved?

_____

_____

_____

Reference

1. National Fire Service Incident Management System Consortium Model Procedures Committee, *Model Procedures Guide for Emergency Medical Incidents,* 2nd ed. Stillwater, OK: Fire Protection Publications, Oklahoma State University, 2002.

Answers

Are You Ready?

1. Get the scientists and students out of the trench, as a secondary cave-in is a distinct possibility and could create additional victims. Isolate and deny entry to the area for the same reason, and request appropriate rescue personnel and equipment.

2. The senior person on the first-in unit assumes the role of incident commander (IC) and is responsible for establishing command, providing a scene size-up (exact location, type of incident, hazards, number of victims, additional resources, etc.), and maintaining scene safety.

3. While you wait for help to arrive, consider the following:
- Determine if there is only the one victim (have the supervisor of the group perform a personnel accountability survey).
- Determine the last place where the victim was located and approximately how deep the trench is at the spot where she was last seen.

- Determine how long the patient has been buried.
- Make sure that nobody is standing next to the edge of the trench, since weight and movement next to the edge could cause more dirt to fall on top of the victim.
- Prepare your equipment to treat the patient once she has been removed from the trench.
- Convey any pertinent information that you discover to incoming units.

You Are There: Reality-Based Cases
Case 1

1. The officer of the rescue squad will likely give a report based on his scene size-up and in accordance with the incident command system (ICS). The scene size-up should include:
- The designation of the first company arriving on the scene ("Rescue Squad 2")
- A brief description of the type of incident and an estimate of the number of patients
- Any obvious conditions or safety concerns
- A declaration of the strategy to be used, along with a request for additional resources
- The assumption of command along with the designation of the name of the incident
- The designated location of the command post[1]

2. Scene safety will be improved with placement of the apparatus that protects the scene from other cars. Cones and flares should be patterned to divert traffic away from the vehicles where rescue operations are taking place.

3. Personal protective equipment should include: helmet, eye protection, hearing protection (when the generator for the "jaws of life" is being used), protective clothing (turnouts or equivalent), gloves (firefighting for the rescuers, and protective or latex examination gloves for the paramedics), and protective footwear (to protect the feet from sharp objects that could penetrate the boots).

4. The hazards associated with this scene include broken glass, sharp metal, the possibility of nondeployed air bags, fluids leaking from the vehicles (radiator fluid, oil, gas, etc.), and other vehicular traffic.

5. Determine scene safety and don any personal protective equipment that you may need to work in this setting.

6. Because of the fact that the trauma center is more than 1 hour away by ground and only 20 minutes by air, recommend that the IC request a medical helicopter.

7. Other factors include the availability and the estimated time of arrival of a medical helicopter, and the time that will be necessary to extricate the patient from the automobile.

8. Repeat the primary and secondary survey on all the patients and address any life threats. Package the patients and prepare them for transport. Any care other than treatment of life threats and immobilization of the cervical spine should take place en route to the hospital, unless the patient who requires extrication will be trapped in the car for an extended period of time. If the extrication is prolonged, treatment of Yvonne should be initiated so that she is ready to be transported once the helicopter arrives.

Test Yourself

1. c

   If it is not safe to enter a scene, or the scene is unstable or dangerous, the initial assessment will likely be performed by the rescue crew and a report of patient status will be relayed to the paramedic. The EMS crew will then be directed to wait in a designated area to receive the patient once the extrication phase is finished and the patient is removed from the dangerous environment.

2. If the scene is safe, remain with the patient for the duration of the rescue; remain calm and provide encouragement; provide reassuring physical contact such as holding a hand when appropriate; and perhaps most importantly, talk to the patient and explain each step of the operation as it proceeds.

3. You should stay away from the vehicle until the power company arrives to assess the situation.

   You should never attempt to approach a vehicle when there are downed lines of any sort. Always assume that they are live until the power company arrives and assesses the situation. Even when they are not moving or sparking, the downed lines can still have an electric current.

4. a

   Safety is the first concern during rescue operations. This includes scene safety as well as crew safety, bystander safety, and patient safety.

5. a

   When hazards are identified that are beyond your ability to handle, the most important thing to do is to ensure the safety of the arriving responders and bystanders in the area. You may accomplish this by establishing a safe zone or perimeter outside of the hazard zone. "Enforcing" the perimeter and controlling bystanders, however, should be left to the police. Emotions can run high during this time, and it may take the presence of law enforcement to ensure people respect the boundaries that have been established.

6. When stored energy is released, it can injure anyone who happens to be in the way.

   Energy is stored when a motor vehicle crash occurs and metal and other components on a vehicle are altered. The release of this stored energy occurs during the extrication process when components of the vehicle, such as a door, are opened or removed. When the tension is released from a door, it can cause a sudden movement. As the crumpled metal springs back toward its original shape, it quickly releases the stored energy.

7. Vehicle air-bag systems are usually deactivated by disconnecting the battery.

   Air bag systems must be deactivated prior to the disentanglement phase of the extrication process. If the air bags have not deployed, they can cause severe injury or even death to a rescuer or patient who is directly in the path of one that unexpectedly deploys.

8. a

   If you encounter fumes indicating a hazardous material, it would be prudent to back away, begin to isolate the incident site, and call for a hazardous materials team. Additional hazards such as gas leaks, explosive devices, downed electric lines, and radioactive materials will require specialized resources beyond your capabilities.

9. a

   Often, scene conditions will greatly impact the ability of the rescue personnel to operate safely and effectively. Although bystander safety is important, their "comfort" is not your concern. Assessing the patient's condition is also very important, but it is secondary to assessing for hazards that may affect scene safety or impact patient care.

10. Options include: bystander hazard, electrical hazard, gas main hazard, and traffic hazard.

    Gas mains and electrical sources pose a risk of explosion and electrocution, respectively. Bystander hazards include bystanders walking into traffic or becoming hostile. Traffic poses a significant threat to scene safety, and efforts should be made to lead traffic away from the scene of the crash.

11. False

    Most chemicals can be legally transported without placards or warnings if they are under a specified weight, so always use caution when you see any sort of cargo in a vehicle crash.

12. c

    The front windshield is made of a three-layer system of glass, called plastic laminate, and is designed to remain intact in the event of a crash. This glass has to be cut out by utilizing commercial "glass master" tools or reciprocating saws.

13. a

    Once the patient is accessed, the rescue team will determine if it is safe for an EMS provider to enter the scene. If it is, and the EMS provider is wearing the appropriate protective clothing, the EMS provider will be given access to the patient.

14. d

    Be very careful when operating around a vehicle when a fuel leak is suspected. Notify fire officials immediately so that fire suppression measures can be taken in the event of a fire.

15. a

    During a rescue operation, long-term care requiring improvisation might include: repositioning or reducing dislocations; cleansing and care of wounds, including suturing; removing impaled objects; rewarming the patient; treating crush injuries; and terminating resuscitative efforts.

16. The safety officer

    If safety concerns arise, the safety officer may call a halt to the operation, even in the middle of performing a step. This individual has absolute authority to stop a task in progress, so all crew members should be alert to his or her commands.

17. The increased risk of electrical hazards

    Batteries (which are frequently located under the back seats) and high-voltage cables found running along the outer edges of the floorboards of hybrid cars can cause significant discharge of electricity if breached. Cables can run inside the car frame along the doorposts as well, so special care must be taken when cutting apart a hybrid car.

18. True

    The bicycle helmet has a four-point harness system (unlike, for example, a construction helmet) and is not particularly cumbersome. Fire helmets are not recommended in specialized environments requiring rope work, confined-space work, or swift-water rescue.

19. d

    Sometimes rescue operations will be halted so that you can properly care for your patient, such as when you need to perform suction to clear the patient's airway. Effective and coordinated communications among all personnel involved in this process are a must.

20. The Nader pin is a solid, steel pin that attaches the door to the frame so that it stays closed in the event of a crash.

    If the door hardware is mangled and the frame is bent, the door may not open. You may be able to pry it open with a pry bar, but often a hydraulic spreader will be required because of the strength of the Nader pin.

I Spy

1. All the firefighters are wearing protective clothing, helmets, and eye protection. There appears to be adequate light (one of the firefighters is providing light via a flashlight). There are emergency lights on the ambulance identifying the scene as an emergency scene. There is reflective material on the firefighters' turnouts (one of the firefighters is wearing a safety vest) and on the paramedics' bright green jackets so they can easily be seen at night.

2. When working in a rescue situation, all workers need to have appropriate personal protective equipment (the paramedics need to have personal protective equipment similar to that used by the firefighters).

Teamwork and Operational Interface

2. What limitations do you have as a paramedic operating out of your state?

_____

_____

_____

3. Where will you take the patient once you have assessed her and determined her medical needs?

_____

_____

_____

_____

Are You Ready?

You and your partner, along with the rest of your ambulance strike team (AST) from Texas, have just arrived in New Orleans to assist in the aftermath of a devastating hurricane. The strike team leader receives your assignment, and you head to a part of town that is primarily under water where there are reports of people trapped in their homes. En route to the assigned part of town, the strike team leader assigns you and one of the other units to rendezvous with a U.S. Coast Guard helicopter on a freeway overpass ½ mile to the east. They are lifting a pregnant woman from her home, and she may be in labor.

1. How will you communicate with the Coast Guard helicopter?

_____

_____

_____

Active Learning

1. Knowledge Is Power

In order for you to learn how to properly interact with the various agencies that you will encounter in your day-to-day career as a paramedic, you need to know what is expected of you—and what you can expect from other agencies. A good place to start is with the local EMS policies and protocols, as well as the standard operating procedures for your EMS provider. If you are left with any questions, contact your immediate supervisor and work your way up the hierarchy of your organization until you find the answers to your questions.

Next, contact representatives of the various agencies that you may interact with and ask them to explain what they expect from you in particular situations, and what you can expect from them. Examples of agencies that paramedics interact with include:

- Fire department
- Law enforcement
- Hospital personnel
- Military personnel
- Public health personnel
- Child protective services (CPS)
- Adult protective services (APS)
- Public works personnel
- Federal agencies such as the Federal Emergency Management Agency (FEMA); Department of Homeland Security; Federal Bureau of Investigation; Bureau of Alcohol, Tobacco, Firearms, and Explosives (ATF); Immigration and Naturalization Service (INS); and Centers for Disease Control and Prevention (CDC)

2. A Stick-ler for Details

To demonstrate the power of communication, try this exercise with 8–12 other students or friends. Find a lightweight stick that is about 8–10 feet long, such as a small wooden dowel. Split the group in half, with each group facing the other in two equal rows. Have everyone extend their index fingers out, palms down, and extend their arms. Line up everyone's fingers so that the stick can be laid over the top of every finger and not roll off. The stick should be balanced and be still when you begin the exercise.

The goal is to lower the stick to the ground, without having it roll off everyone's fingers. *The only constraint is that each index finger must be touching the stick at all times.*

What did you find out? Was it as easy as it sounds? At first, did the stick lower or rise? How did you finally complete the exercise successfully? How clear did your group's communication need to be?

You Are There: Reality-Based Cases

Case 1

The paramedic supervisor pops her head out of her office and asks the oncoming crews if anyone is interested in doing a standby to assist the police and the Drug Enforcement Administration (DEA) in a drug bust at a known methamphetamine lab. You and your partner look at each other with excitement in your eyes and at the same time yell, "We are!" You are both new paramedics. You went to paramedic school together, you studied together, you hang out together, and now you are partners. Your combined experience is just over 1 year, and you are eager to see it all.

Your supervisor sends you to the corner of Apollo Road and Athens Court and instructs you to check in with the incident commander. You do so, and he advises you that the SWAT team is just about ready to make entry, so you should stand by. Out of earshot, your partner eagerly suggests that you go around the neighbor's yard so that you can watch the SWAT team make their entry into the house. You are reluctant, but you really want to see all the action, so you agree. You get to the neighbor's front yard just as the entry team is breaking into the building. You hear shouting, loud banging, and struggling toward the side of the house. Your partner says, "Come on, let's check it out!" You both hunch down and start to sneak around to the side of the house. When you round the corner you see this:

You and your partner stop dead in your tracks, as does the man who almost ran right into you. He reacts by screaming, "Get down!" Your heart sinks, and you think, "This is it, our families will be told that their sons were killed because they were stupid." The man sees that you are paramedics and lowers his weapon. He yells several expletives at you, and he says, "I almost killed you both; get outside of the perimeter *now*." As he runs past, you see a badge on his belt. Your fear changes from the possibility of being killed by a drug dealer to being killed by your supervisor when she finds out what you did.

1. List several mistakes that were made by the EMS crew on this scene.

   _____

   _____

   _____

2. What should the EMS crew have done once they were on scene?

   _____

   _____

   _____

As soon as you and your partner get back to the command post, the IC starts yelling at the two of you. He tells you to get off of his scene and requests another ambulance to come and evaluate a suspect that the officers have detained in the house.

The second crew arrives minutes later with the fire department and checks in at the command post. The IC tells them to go with the officer at the front door and evaluate a patient. He advises that the suspect is combative and appears to be under the influence of methamphetamine.

3. Describe the considerations and precautions that should be taken as the crew enters the crime scene.

   _____

   _____

   _____

4. Describe considerations that the paramedics should keep in mind when working with a suspect who is in police custody.

   _____

   _____

   _____

Test Yourself

1. In a tactical situation, how does the "perimeter" established by law enforcement relate to areas of high risk?

   _____

   _____

2. What does Locard's principle mean for paramedics?

   _____

   _____

3. Whether formally or not, in most emergency situations the _____ is instituted and utilized to coordinate and direct the responders and resources in the most efficient manner.
   a. incident command system
   b. military structure
   c. mobile radio system
   d. funnel system

4. Whether working as the EMS commander or as a responding paramedic, prior knowledge of _____ and _____ is required for an operation to proceed smoothly.
   a. matrix, duplex
   b. funnel, unified command
   c. mobile radio, centralized dispatch
   d. incident command, unified command

5. What are some dangers posed by a methamphetamine lab?

   _____

   _____

6. The threat of bioterrorism is relatively rare in the 21st century and is not a component of planning and training of EMS personnel.
   True
   False

7. During a tactical operation, what should you do when asked to "stand by"?

   _____

   _____

8. What factors have contributed to the increase in diversions of ambulances away from hospital emergency departments?

   _____

9. Why might a law enforcement officer request that you place paper bags over a patient's hands?

_____

_____

10. Prisoners should not be handcuffed to the ambulance cot unless a _____ is immediately available.

11. EMS may have close interactions with law enforcement in which arena?
    a. Training
    b. Classroom
    c. Fire
    d. Tactical

12. EMS personnel are at substantial risk for encountering violence while on duty.
    True
    False

13. If called to a jail or prison to treat a prisoner, _____ should continually remain with the EMS crew while the patient is evaluated and treatment is initiated.
    a. the lead paramedic
    b. the EMS supervisor
    c. a community liaison
    d. police personnel

14. What is the lead federal agency responsible for emergency management activities after natural and terrorist disasters?

_____

_____

15. What are the two most prevalent models of EMS delivery in the United States?
    a. The private EMS model and the hospital-based EMS model
    b. The law enforcement EMS model and the community-based EMS model
    c. The public EMS model and the hospital-based EMS model
    d. The third service EMS model and the fire department–based EMS model

16. _____ on the part of the paramedic is necessary to avoid injury or scene contamination.
    a. Frequent radio communications
    b. Protocol familiarity
    c. Rapid patient assessment
    d. Heightened awareness

17. EMS crews should always strive for _____ when working with other agencies.
    a. collaboration
    b. separation
    c. competition
    d. maximum exposure

18. What other emergency service is the birthplace of the incident command system (ICS)?

_____

_____

19. In cases of complicated incidents involving multiple risks, what system allows all agencies with geographical or functional responsibilities to determine objectives and strategies for managing the incident?
    a. A unified command system
    b. A centralized dispatch system
    c. A simplex communication system
    d. A mobile radio system

Scenario: A convicted inmate requires transport from the county jail to the regional medical center after complaining of chest pain. The patient has a history of violence.

20. During transportation, you should place the patient in restraints,
    a. lock the unit's doors, and request a law enforcement escort.
    b. lock the unit's doors, but do not request a law enforcement escort.
    c. leave the unit's doors unlocked, and request a law enforcement escort.
    d. leave the unit's doors unlocked, but do not request a law enforcement escort.

21. During the 30-minute transport the patient experiences increased chest pain. He also reports difficulty breathing. You should
    a. remove the restraints, monitor cardiac function, and continue with BLS care.
    b. continue with oxygen, monitor cardiac function, and consider additional treatment with the patient restrained.
    c. continue oxygen and monitor cardiac function with the patient restrained, but wait for additional treatment.
    d. remove the restraints, continue with oxygen, consider morphine and nitroglycerin.

Need to Know

The following represent the Key Objectives of Chapter 52:

1. *List the basic functions of the federal government in coordinating large-scale events such as natural disasters and terrorist incidents.*

   The Federal Emergency Management Agency (FEMA) assists state and local agencies to prepare for, respond to, mitigate, and recover from large-scale emergencies by providing funding for such events.[1] Located within the Department of Homeland Security, FEMA has created the National Response Plan (NRP)—a best practices plan that is used to enhance the ability of the United States to respond to and manage large-scale domestic incidents by integrating public safety agencies into a unified structure.[2]

2. *Describe the role of the paramedic when interacting with law enforcement officials.*

   There are a number of situations in which paramedics will interact with law enforcement. Especially important are the following points:

   a. Understand what types of calls law enforcement officials should respond to with you. If they do not respond, request that they do.

   b. With dispatches for violent crimes, make sure that law enforcement is on scene and that the scene is safe and secure prior to entering.

   c. When assisting law enforcement with tactical situations, stage at the designated staging area, check in with the IC, and wait for instructions. Typically any patients will be brought to you or you will be escorted to a particular location by law enforcement personnel. Only specially trained personnel should be operating within the perimeter.

3. *Describe the functions of a tactical paramedic.*

   The role of the tactical paramedic can vary from team to team, but it typically includes:

   - Providing medical support within the perimeter of tactical operations.
   - Ensuring team health through adequate hydration and nutrition of members during training and on extended operations.
   - Tracking personnel rotations to avoid heat- and cold-related medical conditions.
   - Maintaining records of the team's health and fitness.
   - Instructing the team on basic first aid and self-treatment for injuries sustained when they cannot be accessed by the team paramedic.

Note that more than one-half of the care that the tactical paramedic provides for his or her team takes place during training exercises.

4. *List considerations for paramedic operations at crime scenes.*

   Locard's principle states, "Every contact leaves a trace and there is something left to be found."[3] If you come across something that you believe represents evidence of a crime, such as a weapon, bullet casings, a knife, or blood, advise law enforcement officials and then document your findings and actions clearly and concisely on the prehospital care report. Walk directly to the patient, or in a path designated by law enforcement; touch only what you need to in order to provide patient care; and exit along the same path that you took on your way into the crime scene. Be constantly aware of your surroundings, and let everyone know if you become aware of a safety hazard. If in doubt about anything related to the crime scene, ask law enforcement for guidance.

5. *Describe the paramedic's role in interacting with prisoners.*

   Prisoners are people who have a medical or traumatic complaint. It is the role of law enforcement to provide scene safety by disarming, securing, and restraining patients, but it is the paramedic's responsibility to ensure the following when interacting with prisoners:

   - Law enforcement officers must search a prisoner for any weapons or objects that could be used as weapons before paramedics care for the prisoner.
   - Never allow yourself to be left alone with the prisoner. Always have a law enforcement officer present when interacting with a prisoner.

- If the prisoner requires transport, make sure that law enforcement personnel with the ability to unlock handcuffs accompany you to the hospital so that the handcuffs can be removed if medically necessary.

Need to Do

The following skills are explained and illustrated in a step-by-step manner, via skill sheets and/or Step-by-Steps in this text and on the accompanying DVD:

Skill Name	Skill Sheet Number and Location	Step-by-Step Number and Location
Verbal Communications	63 – DVD	N/A
Documentation	64 – DVD	N/A

Connections

- Chapter 4, Legal Issues, in the textbook describes the legal responsibilities of paramedics when they interface with different agencies.
- Chapter 9, Safety and Scene Size-Up, in the textbook provides additional information about how to safely operate on scenes with multiple different agencies.
- Chapter 17, Documentation and Communication, in the textbook explains how to effectively and efficiently communicate with different agencies at the scene of medical emergencies.
- Chapter 40, Behavioral and Psychiatric Disorders, in the textbook outlines how to properly restrain patients.
- Chapter 50, Medical Incident Command, in the textbook includes a complete discussion on the organization and structure of the National Incident Management System (NIMS), incident command system (ICS), and unified command system (UCS).
- Chapter 51, Rescue Awareness, in the textbook explains how paramedics interact with other agencies during rescue operations.
- The website for the Federal Emergency Management Agency is www.fema.gov. More specific information for emergency personnel is given at www.fema.gov/emergency/index.shtm.

- Link to the companion DVD for a chapter-based quiz, audio glossary, animations, games and exercises, and, when appropriate, skill sheets and skill Step-by-Steps.

Street Secrets

- **The Golden Rule for Paramedics** First impressions can last a lifetime. It is always a good idea to put your best foot forward when interacting with different agencies, because there will be a time when you may need their help. If you conduct yourself in a personable and professional manner, you will likely develop strong ties and great working relationships with those agencies. On the other hand, if you are not a team player, and you are not willing to go the extra mile for the different agencies when they need your help, you are likely to get the same response from them when you need their help.
- **Safety, Safety, Safety** When working as a paramedic, there are countless ways in which injuries can be sustained. It is the responsibility of emergency workers to not only protect themselves from harm, but also to look out for the safety of all. The successful management of any type of emergency is not simply the mitigation of the problem. The true measure of success can be gauged by the operation's safety practices and the fact that nobody was injured or killed in the commission of their duties.

The Drug Box

There are no specific drugs related to this chapter content.

References

1. C. H. Schultz, "Disaster Preparedness, in" *Rosen's Emergency Medicine: Concepts and Clinical Practice,* 6th ed. St. Louis: Mosby, 2006, p. 2638.
2. *Homeland Security.* Department of Homeland Security. (February 18, 2005) www.dhs.gov/dhspublic/interapp/editorial/editorial_0566.xml. "National Response Plan." Department of Homeland Security (last updated May 25, 2006). www.dhs.gov/xprepresp/committees/editoral_0566.htm (accessed March 28, 2007).
3. N. C. Chamelin, C. R. Swanson, and L. Territo, "The Evolution of Criminal Investigation and Criminalistics."

Chap. 1 in *Criminal Investigation*, 8th ed., New York: McGraw-Hill, 2003, pp. 19–20.

4. "Public Health Consequences among First Responders to Emergency Events Associated with Illicit Methamphetamine Laboratories—Selected States, 1996–1999." *Morbidity and Mortality Weekly Reports* 49(45) (November 17, 2000): 1021-4 http://www.cdc.gov/mmwr/preview/mmwrhtml/mm4945al.htm (accessed March 28, 2007).

Answers

Are You Ready?

1. Communication capabilities, such as radio frequencies, are typically dictated when you are given an assignment. If you do not have a common radio frequency to communicate with the helicopter, communication will need to take place face-to-face with the crew once the helicopter lands. It is your responsibility to obtain this information when you are given the assignment; check with the strike team leader for assistance.

2. Leaving your local EMS jurisdiction to assist in a large-scale event such as this does not necessarily change your scope of practice. Mutual aid assignments are conducted under the same scope of practice that you use on a day-to-day basis.

3. As with communication capabilities, you should have been briefed on the means of travel (e.g., roads that are open) and available hospitals and medical aid stations that are capable of dealing with particular conditions. If you do not have this information, use your AST leader as a sounding board and a resource.

You Are There: Reality-Based Cases

Case 1

1. The EMS crew did not follow the incident commander's instructions and threatened the entire operation, while placing their own lives in jeopardy. They didn't stand by where they were told. They didn't have their equipment prepared in the event that an officer or a suspect was injured. They placed the entire operation in jeopardy because they wanted to see the action.

2. The EMS crew should have checked in with the IC, gone to their designated staging location, and readied their equipment in case a police officer, citizen, or suspect was injured. They might even have given the trauma center a heads-up that there was the possibility of injuries from the raid of a methamphetamine lab.

3. Considerations and precautions that paramedics should keep in mind when entering a crime scene include the following:
   - Scene safety is your foremost concern.
   - It is important that you protect and preserve evidence, but your main concern is to provide safe and effective patient care.
   - For every scene entered and every patient cared for, paramedics will leave their mark. Try to leave the smallest mark that you can on the crime scene without compromising patient care.
   - If you come across something that you believe represents evidence, advise law enforcement and document your findings and actions on the prehospital care report.
   - Be constantly aware of your surroundings, and let everyone know if you become aware of a safety hazard.
   - If in doubt about anything related to the crime scene, ask law enforcement for guidance.

4. Prisoners are individuals who have a medical or traumatic complaint and should be treated with respect. Suspects should be searched for actual or potential weapons before initiating care. Always have a law enforcement officer present when interacting with a prisoner. If the prisoner requires transport, make sure that law enforcement personnel with the ability to unlock handcuffs accompany you to the hospital.

Test Yourself

1. In any tactical situation, a "perimeter" is established by law enforcement. Inside this perimeter is the area of interest, which also corresponds to the area of highest risk.

   Depending on the situation, this perimeter may be quite small (e.g., a search warrant for a home may have a perimeter that is only as large as the home) or it may be huge (e.g., pursuing an active shooter in a wooded area may have a perimeter that is several miles in diameter).

2. Locard's principle states, "Every contact leaves a trace and there is something left to be found." In the EMS realm, this means that for every scene entered and for every patient cared for paramedics will leave their mark.

   Although it is important to attempt to preserve evidence for the purposes of criminal investigation, your first and foremost responsibility is to ensure adequate and safe patient care. However, with a little forethought and planning, both concepts can often be accommodated.

3. a

   Whether formally or not, in most cases an incident command system is instituted and utilized to coordinate and direct the responders and resources in the most efficient manner to manage the situation.

4. d

   Frequently, the first paramedic on the scene assumes the role of lead EMS officer at the command post. A supervisor or other designated paramedic may be assigned to relieve the first-arriving paramedic at the command post, depending on the type of situation or the duration of the incident. Whether working as the EMS commander or as a responding paramedic, prior knowledge of incident command and unified command systems is required for an operation to proceed smoothly.

5. Common chemicals found at a methamphetamine lab include acetone, sodium hydroxide, hydrochloric acid, and anhydrous ammonia. All of these are toxic. Burners and flames also create a risk of explosion or burn injuries.

   A study of injuries related to methamphetamine labs from 1996 to 1999[4] showed that first responders, law enforcement officers, or EMTs and paramedics suffered 51% of reported injuries. There has been an exponential growth in the number of methamphetamine labs since 1999, especially in rural America, and paramedics must be vigilant to avoid injury to themselves or others. If faced with a collection of burners, glassware, chemicals, or suspicious containers, paramedics should immediately remove themselves and any patients from the area without touching anything. Not only does this reduce the risk of contaminating evidence, but it may also reduce injury or death due to burns, respiratory problems, or explosions.

6. False

   Emergency medical services are very often among the first agencies to respond to incidents that ultimately prove to broadly threaten the public health. Frequently, the exact nature of the threat is not immediately apparent, resulting in exposure of paramedics to health risks and dangers that may only become evident over time. The threat of bioterrorism is a fact of life in the 21st century and must be addressed in planning and training of EMS personnel.

7. The expected response would be for the EMS unit to proceed to a safe staging area to await further orders from the incident commander (IC).

   This staging area is usually at the command post. Once there, EMS should check in with the IC and be ready to receive patients. Typically during tactical operations, an EMS unit will be asked to "stand by."

8. Ever-decreasing hospital bed capacities and emergency department overcrowding in America contribute to the increase in diversions.

   These diversions affect both day-to-day operations and surges caused by large-scale public health emergencies.

9. Law enforcement personnel may request that paramedics secure paper bags over the hands of suspects or victims of suspected gunshot or explosive injuries in order to minimize the contamination or loss of trace evidence of gunpowder or powder burns.

   You may comply with this request unless exposing the hands or wrists is necessary for the treatment of the patient.

10. Key

    The decision to restrain or not rests with officers of the jurisdiction in consultation with the lead paramedic. The accompanying officer should have keys available to open every restraint device on the patient in case the prisoner's medical condition necessitates immediate removal of the restraints. If for any reason an officer does not accompany the paramedic in the patient compartment of the ambulance, the paramedic should be given the keys.

11. d

    An area of EMS interaction with law enforcement is in the tactical arena. Law enforcement tactical operations occur during higher-risk situations such as hostage rescue, sniper situations, high-risk search warrants, and active shooter scenarios.

12. True

    On certain calls, it is a necessity to have law enforcement personnel present. The literature supports the conclusion that EMS personnel are at substantial risk for encountering violence directed at them while on duty. It is never a good idea to be first on the scene of an assault, only to find yourself confronting the assailant who is still on the premises.

13. d

    While the medical evaluation and treatment of a patient are the same whether the patient is a civilian or a prisoner, there are special considerations to keep in mind when responding to a request for service for prisoners. Scene safety is the responsibility of law enforcement officers, as is the appropriate disarming, securing, and restraining of the patient. Paramedics should never allow themselves to be alone with prisoners. Insist that law enforcement remain with you as you treat the patient and accompany you if you transport.

14. The Federal Emergency Management Agency (FEMA)

    FEMA is the lead federal agency responsible for emergency management activities after natural and terrorist disasters. FEMA assists state and local organizations to mitigate, prepare for, respond to, and recover from emergencies. The agency also provides funding for many disaster responses.

15. d

    The term "third service" represents an EMS service that is separate from either police or fire and may be operated by a private or public entity.

16. d

    Constant scene awareness on the part of the paramedic is necessary to avoid injury or scene contamination. Paramedics should avoid unnecessary walking about, moving items at the scene, and even touching the surroundings.

17. a

    Whatever the nature of the incident or the makeup of the responding agencies, cooperation between paramedics responsible for administering care and transport to ill or injured persons and other emergency response agencies is crucial. With the increasing likelihood of terrorist attacks, mass casualty incidents, or natural disasters, now more than ever before paramedics must be aware of these other agencies and their responsibilities and capabilities.

18. The fire service

The incident command system (ICS) is a scalable management system that can be used on emergency incidents of any magnitude. The fire service tends to follow this style of management at most incidents, including EMS calls. This system allows for a single incident commander (IC) with personnel or other managers reporting to the IC for orders.

19. a

In these instances, the incident command system may be expanded to a unified command system, which allows all agencies with geographical or functional responsibilities to determine objectives and strategies for managing the incident. Unified command also pro-

vides a forum for these agencies to make and relate consensus decisions.

20. c

Providers should consider transporting the patient with restraints in place while ensuring that the appropriate level of care is provided. Restraints may include handcuffs that are applied with the patient's hands in front versus behind the back. Treatment should follow local protocols.

21. b

Providers should be sure to thoroughly assess and treat all patients. Providers should always ensure their own safety first.

chapter 53

Hazardous Materials Incidents

Are You Ready?

You are dispatched to City Hall to evaluate a person who is experiencing symptoms after possibly being exposed to a mixture of cleaning solutions. You advise your dispatcher when you are on the scene, grab your equipment, and enter the building. You immediately see three people lying on the ground in front of the mayor's office. They appear to be seizing. Through the glass of the office door, you see several more people lying on the floor and slumped over their desks.

1. What is your initial priority?

_____

_____

_____

2. Is exposure to cleaning fluids the likely cause of the victims' conditions?

_____

_____

_____

3. What actions can you take immediately?

_____

_____

_____

4. What is your initial role as the first emergency worker on the scene?

_____

_____

_____

Active Learning

1. "Who Ya Gonna Call?"

Do you know who to contact if a hazardous materials event occurs? Locate the telephone numbers for organizations such as the local poison control center, the Chemical Transportation Emergency Center (CHEMTREC), Computer-AidedManagement of Emergency Operations (CAMEO), and the Agency for Toxic Substances and Disease Registry (ATSDR).

Laminate a card with these numbers on it so that you can carry it with you at all times.

2. Hazardous Materials ID

Pull out your Emergency Response Guide and drive around the industrial part of your town to practice identifying hazards displayed on different placards. With practice you will become familiar with how to use this guide and, in the event of an actual hazardous materials incident, you will be able to efficiently and effectively identify hazards and act appropriately.

3. Hazmat Courses

Prepare yourself for a hazardous materials incident by taking hazardous materials courses. The following courses are specifically designed for EMS professionals (but don't limit yourself to only these):

- Awareness and recognition
- EMS Level I Responder
- EMS Level II Responder

You Are There: Reality-Based Cases

Case 1

Parker and Addison are 5-year-old twins with more energy than any two children should ever have. Their parents jumped at the chance for the family to visit Uncle John on his farm because they thought it would be a place where the boys could burn up a lot of energy in a constructive manner.

The family drove overnight to the farm, and the boys slept the whole way. Uncle John drove up in his tractor as the car pulled into the driveway. He told the boys' parents to get some rest—he would keep the boys busy. The parents gladly went into the house to take a nap.

The boys went to explore the farm. When they arrived at the barn, they discovered Uncle John's World War II jeep. The jeep was just too much to resist. Parker jumped into the driver's seat, and Addison took the passenger seat. They pretended that they were in the war and jumped around in the jeep as if they were driving down a bumpy road. While jumping about, one of them bumped the emergency brake and the jeep began to roll forward. In seconds the jeep was rolling out the door of the barn and down toward a few storage tanks. Parker jumped out of the jeep and rolled on the ground, but Addison was too frightened. The jeep continued down the hill and crashed into one of the storage tanks. The tank ruptured, spilling liquid onto Addison and the jeep.

Parker ran toward the jeep and tried to pull Addison out. He too became drenched with the same fluid. Both collapsed to the ground. Their parents awoke to screaming and ran outside to see what was happening. They saw Uncle John running toward the boys, and they did so as well. Uncle John was able to pull both boys away from the site before he, too, was overcome by the effects of the liquid.

Aunt Betty heard the screaming and the boys' father yelling to call 9-1-1, and she ran for the phone. She told the operator that there had been a farming accident, dropped the phone, and ran outside. There, she saw all the family members sprawled out on the ground, the jeep crashed into the tank, and the liquid in the tank pouring out into the jeep. She ran back to the phone and told the dispatcher that they were all unconscious on the ground.

You are dispatched to this situation. You are 3 miles from the farm and are the only ambulance for another 30 miles.

1. What should your initial action be?

_____

_____

_____

2. What is your next priority?

_____

_____

_____

3. What should you do as soon as you arrive at the scene?

_____

_____

_____

4. How will you protect yourselves from the chemical spill?

_____

_____

_____

5. How will you identify the chemical that is involved in this incident?

_____

_____

_____

You stage approximately one-quarter of a mile away from the scene on a small hill upwind from the incident. Through your binoculars, you are able to see a placard on the tank and a UN identification number. The bottom of the placard reads UN2783. You convey this information to the dispatcher and the other responding units.

6. Use your *Emergency Response Guidebook* (ERG) (or go to the Pipeline and Hazardous Materials Safety Administration website at http://hazmat.dot.gov/pubs/erg/gydebook.htm) to provide the following information about the chemical Terbufos (*see below*):

   a. What are the potential health hazards?

   _____

   _____

   _____

   b. What are the potential fire and explosion hazards?

   _____

   _____

   _____

   c. What protective clothing should be worn?

   _____

   _____

   _____

   d. What initial care should be provided?

   _____

   _____

   _____

When the hazardous materials team arrives, they don their level A suits and approach the patients. While they place the twins on stretchers, the other team members set up collection pools for emergency decontamination, and you and your partner don Tyvek suits and air purifying respirators (APRs) so that you will be protected from the hazardous materials when the patients are ready for treatment. As this process is taking place, a farmer from up the road approaches the battalion chief who has taken over incident command. He states that he and Uncle John went in on the purchase of the chemicals because John crop dusts for both of their farms. He gives the IC a sheet that has the information listed in Table 53-1.

The IC announces over the radio the information that the other farmer has brought to his attention. The twins are brought to the decontamination area, and emergency decontamination is performed. When the twins have had all their clothing removed and they have been adequately irrigated and cleaned, they are transferred to you and your partner.

The boys present unconscious with hypoventilation, bradycardia, and excessive salivation. Tears are pouring down their faces, and they are incontinent of feces and urine. One of the twins is vomiting, and the other is seizing.

7. Describe the pathophysiology of organophosphate poisoning.

   _____

   _____

   _____

8. Describe your treatment for the twins in order of priority.

   _____

   _____

   _____

9. Will the adult treatment vary from the pediatric treatment?

   _____

   _____

   _____

TABLE 53-1

Trade Name	Common Name	Reportable Quantity	Shipping Name	Hazard Class	ID #	Placarding Required
Terbufos	Counter, lockin' load	Yes, in quantities > 100 lb/container	Organophosphate solid, toxic, n.o.s. (terbufos)	Poison B	UN2783	Poison

The rest of the victims are decontaminated and treated for organophosphate poisoning. The two additional ambulances have arrived on the scene and are ready to assist in transport of the patients.

10. Describe the most frequently used methods for reducing contamination of the ambulances and their equipment during the transport of the patients to the hospital.

_____

_____

_____

11. Should helicopter transport of these patients be considered?

_____

_____

_____

Test Yourself

1. Your patient is experiencing excessive salivation, lacrimation, and vomiting after being exposed to pesticides. Which treatment would be most appropriate?
   a. Epinephrine
   b. Atropine
   c. Sodium thiosulfate
   d. Amyl nitrate

2. Which of the following is a written source of information to aid in the identification of a placard?
   a. ERG
   b. CAMEO
   c. ChemTel
   d. CHEMTREC

3. Which level of PPE provides lightweight protection with a low fire rating and uses an air purifying respirator?
   a. Level C suit
   b. Level A suit
   c. Level D suit
   d. Level B suit

4. Which National Fire Protection Association (NFPA) standard makes recommendations for EMS personnel and hazardous materials training?
   a. NFPA 1561
   b. NFPA 473
   c. NFPA 472
   d. NFPA 704

5. Which of the following is an indicator of stress for a hazardous materials responder working within the incident?
   a. Increased heart rate
   b. 5% weight loss
   c. Increased respirations
   d. Decreased temperature

6. You respond to a multiple-vehicle collision involving a package delivery truck. You note liquids of different colors leaking from the back of the truck and giving off clouds of gas as they mix. Why is this a particularly dangerous hazardous materials scene?
   a. The driver may be seriously injured and unable to tell you what materials were on board.
   b. The materials may be unknown because delivery trucks are not required to be placarded.
   c. The MSDSs are kept in the cargo area and may have been damaged.
   d. It is not dangerous because delivery trucks do not carry hazardous substances.

7. You are on a hazardous materials scene performing a rehab function. Your patient is a hazmat responder complaining of chest pain and shortness of breath. Which of the following treatments would be appropriate?
   a. Administer the antidote to the chemical that is leaking.
   b. Perform a 12-lead ECG.
   c. Perform a preincident exam.
   d. Perform a rehab exit evaluation.

Scenario: You have responded to a hazmat incident. Your patient has been decontaminated and brought to you in the cold zone for transport. Upon examining the patient you note a white powdery substance on his skin. He says that the substance is causing a burning sensation.

8. What type of decontamination did your patient likely undergo?
   a. Secondary decontamination
   b. Gross decontamination
   c. Formal decontamination
   d. Total decontamination

9. Which parts of your patient are the most difficult areas to decontaminate?
   a. Legs and feet
   b. Back and neck
   c. Arms and hands
   d. Axillae and groin

10. If you became contaminated from this patient, how would you decontaminate yourself?

    a. Use baking soda and copious amounts of water.

    b. Use a high-pressure hose to remove contaminants.

    c. Blot the chemical with towels and flush with water.

    d. Inform the IC and report to the decontamination station.

11. Your personal safety is your primary concern during a hazardous materials incident.

    True

    False

12. How would you treat a patient with chlorine exposure?

    _____

    _____

13. What is your first priority when treating a patient exposed to a hazardous material?

    _____

    _____

14. Responders with no formal hazardous materials training should operate in the _____ zone.

15. You respond to a hazardous materials incident and are directed to enter the scene in order to provide care for an exposed patient. Your patient requires rapid intubation. In which zone should this procedure occur?

    _____

    _____

16. According to the fire diamond (NFPA 704) placard system, the color red indicates a reactivity hazard.

    True

    False

17. You respond to an industrial lab for an explosion. Upon arrival, you are told that your patient was exposed to hydrogen fluoride gas. Your patient presents with severe respiratory distress with pulmonary edema. What medication should you administer?

    _____

    _____

18. You respond to the local nuclear power plant for a radioactive leak. Hazmat responders bring you a 46-year-old male who has been exposed to, but not contaminated by, beta radiation during a radiation test. This patient poses little to no risk of contaminating you and your partner.

    True

    False

19. You are called to the university chemistry lab for a burn from a chemical spill. Upon entering the building you notice a diamond-shaped placard with the following information: a red square with the number 1, a blue square with the number 3, a yellow square with the number 1, and a "W" with a line through it in the white square. What is the most important consideration when entering this building?

    _____

    _____

20. The agency responsible for determining the level of exposure that is considered safe is the _____.

Need to Know

The following represent the Key Objectives of Chapter 53:

1. *Define "hazardous material."*

    A hazardous material is any solid, liquid, or gas that when released is capable of harming people, the environment, or property.

2. *Describe the three zones that should be established at a hazardous materials incident.*

    The zones are illustrated in Figure 53-1. The *hot* or *exclusion zone* surrounds the site of the hazardous materials release and should encompass all known or suspected hazards. Only trained and protected responders should be allowed access into this area. The *warm* or *contamination reduction zone* is the perimeter area around the hot zone and is determined by the length of the decontamination corridor. It contains the "decon" stations and functions as a safety buffer between the hot zone and the cold zone. The *cold* or *support zone* should be "clean" and free of hazmat contamination, including discarded protective clothing and respiratory equipment.[1]

3. *Describe the organization of a hazardous materials incident.*

    Safety and communication are key to a successful response to a hazardous materials incident. If you are the first unit on the scene, perform a scene

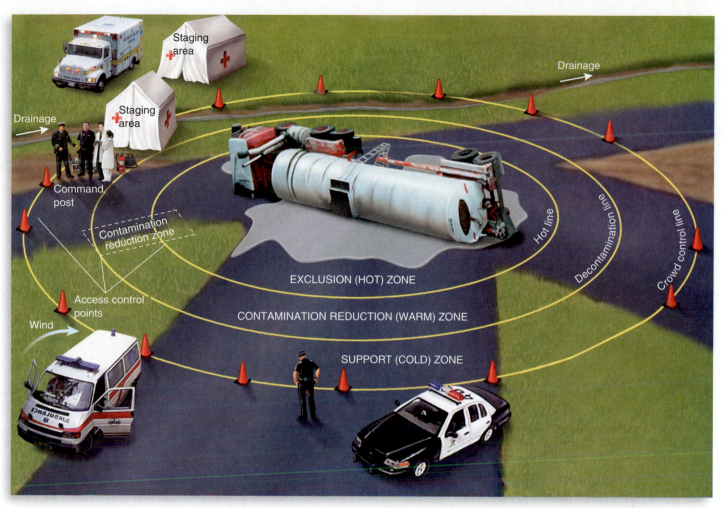

FIGURE 53-1   The work zones that should be established at hazardous materials incidents.

size-up; advise responding units of the exact location of the incident, hazards, access, egress, staging area, safety factors, and approximate number of victims; and request additional resources. Take command as IC until transfer of command can take place, and ensure that all responding emergency personnel have a means of communicating with one another. Determine a safe location, and establish the command post (Figure 53-2).

Isolate the area, and deny entry to anybody other than emergency personnel specifically trained in the mitigation of hazardous materials incidents. The initial isolation distance is the distance that all occupants should be evacuated in all directions from the site of the spill or leak.[2] Establish safety zones (hot, warm, and cold zones), and set up a decontamination area (Figure 53-3).

4. *Describe the methods used to identify a hazard.*

At least three resources need to be examined before decisions about health and safety can be made. They include:

a. Material safety data sheets (MSDS) or shipping papers—these are typically located in the cab of a truck, in the first engine of a freight train,

FIGURE 53-2   The command post should be established at a safe location.

FIGURE 53-3 Example of a decontamination facility.

on the bridge of a ship, and in marked tubes on the deck of a barge carrying hazardous materials.

b. Placard—this diamond-shaped sign on containers, buildings, and facilities (NFPA 704) is used to rapidly and easily identify hazardous risks. The placard is divided into four areas, each representing a specific hazard (Figure 53-4).

c. Department of Transportation (DOT) hazardous materials classification—the DOT *Emergency Response Guidebook* allows emergency personnel to utilize the placards to readily identify

FIGURE 53-4 Placards are used to rapidly and easily identify hazardous risks.

specific or generic hazards associated with the materials in question.

5. *Identify factors that influence how a hazardous material affects an individual.*

The concentration of the hazardous substance, the route of exposure, and the duration of exposure play a role in determining the dose received and, in turn, the response that a person will have to the exposure. Exposure to a hazardous material can occur through inhalation, absorption through the skin or mucous membranes, ingestion, and/or injection.

6. *Describe the types of personal protective equipment (PPE) that can be used by EMS personnel at a hazardous materials incident.*

EMS personnel should use PPE for which they have been adequately trained. Types of PPE include, but are not limited to:

a. Respiratory protection
   - N-95 mask
   - Air purifying respirator (APR)
   - Supplied air respirator (SAR)
   - Self-contained breathing apparatus (SCBA)

b. Skin protection
   - Level A protection is the highest level of respiratory, skin, eye, and mucous membrane protection (Figure 53-5a). It consists of a fully encapsulating chemical-resistant suit and SCBA.
   - Level B protection uses the highest level of respiratory protection but offers less skin and eye protection (Figure 53-5b). In conjunction with the SCBA it provides splash protection by way of chemical-resistant clothing.
   - Level C protection is for known airborne substances with continuously monitored concentrations (Figure 53-5c). Criteria for air purifying respirators must be met, and skin and eye exposures must be unlikely. It provides the same level of skin protection as level B, but a lower level of respiratory protection.
   - Level D is a work uniform (Figure 53-5d). It provides no respiratory protection and minimal skin protection. This is the appropriate level for awareness trained individuals.

7. *Explain the basic principles of decontaminating victims and emergency personnel at a hazardous materials incident.*

Early decontamination can prevent secondary contamination and can mean the difference between a minor injury and death. The most important and most effective decontamination is done immediately

(a) **(b)** **(c)** **(d)**

FIGURE 53-5 **Levels of Protection. (a)** Level A is the highest level of protection. **(b)** Level B uses the highest level of respiratory protection but offers less skin and eye protection. **(c)** Level C protection is for known airborne substances with continuously monitored concentrations. **(d)** Level D is a work uniform, which provides no respiratory protection and minimal skin protection.

after exposure. Ambulatory victims should be told to leave the hot zone and decontaminate themselves under the direction of the decontamination team.

Gross decontamination removes or chemically alters the majority of the hazard, but some residual contamination can remain. Secondary decontamination efforts further reduce or alter contamination. Effective decontamination means making the patient as clean as possible. Remove what you can and contain what you can't. Two methods can be used to determine if contamination reduction is effective:

- *Qualitative method.* A subjective decision usually involving a visual inspection.
- *Quantitative method.* Uses meters with objective environmental sampling techniques that can detect liquid and gases in small, numeric amounts to determine reduction effectiveness.[3]

The aggressiveness of contamination reduction should be based on the contaminant, the patient's condition, environmental conditions, and available resources.

8. *Describe the challenges of triaging patients who have been exposed to hazardous materials.*

Because patients directly affected by hazardous materials need to be isolated, triage may need to be performed by non-EMS personnel who are specially trained in hazardous materials response. There are several challenges associated with triage of patients exposed to hazardous materials. Patients identified as "immediate" should go through emergency decontamination before they can be definitively treated by EMS personnel. Basic first aid can take place during the decontamination process, but advanced procedures are typically rendered once decontamination is completed.

Some hazardous materials exposures do not result in immediately identifiable signs and symptoms. The onset of findings may be considerably delayed depending upon the hazardous material involved. It is important that paramedics are aware of the typical time frame for the onset of signs and symptoms for specific hazardous materials and manage these victims accordingly.

Children are generally more susceptible to toxic exposure and are more likely to receive a higher dose relative to body weight than an adult patient. This should be kept in mind when triaging patients exposed to a hazardous material. As a result, consider triaging and treating pediatric patients first.

9. *Describe the appropriate transportation of patients who have been exposed to hazardous materials.*

It is critical to decontaminate all patients as best as possible before transporting them to a hospital. Patients who have not been adequately decontaminated have a greater chance of causing secondary contamination of hospital personnel. To prevent secondary contamination of the ambulance, consider the following options:

- Cocooning—wrapping the patient in heavy plastic after gross decontamination has taken place, while ensuring that the face is uncovered (Figure 53-6).
- Enveloping the patient compartment—placing a plastic barrier on the inside of the patient compartment of the ambulance so that the equipment and cabinets are protected from secondary contamination (Figure 53-7).

Before leaving the scene, document all available and pertinent information, including hazards, known toxicology, degree of patient exposure, decontamination and treatments, as well as specific patient information (e.g., name, date of birth, vital signs, and SAMPLE history).

10. *Explain why and how rehabilitation should take place with rescue workers at a hazardous materials incident.*

Rehabilitation should be used for any incident in which the environmental dangers of heat, cold, humidity, physical exertion, psychological stress, impaired vision, limited mobility, and communication difficulties put the health and safety of

FIGURE 53-7   Enveloping involves placing a plastic barrier on the inside of the patient compartment of the ambulance so that the equipment and cabinets are protected from secondary contamination.

responders at risk. A rehabilitation officer should be part of every hazardous materials incident and should oversee emergency personnel before, during, and after the incident. Any emergency worker who is part of a hazardous materials team needs to be medically evaluated on a regular basis and must meet the medical standards established by his or her provider agency in order to be a part of the team. Because of the conditions that hazardous materials team members are exposed to when functioning at incidents, the following vital signs are typically assessed before, during, and after a team member works at a hazardous materials incident: heart rate, body temperature, respiratory rate and quality, blood pressure and capillary refill time, and body weight.

A 12-lead ECG should be obtained on any rescuer who complains of chest pain during a hazardous materials incident. Emergency workers who present with elevated body temperature and rapid heart rate should be removed from their protective clothing and cooled using fans (blowing ambient temperature air) and misting systems. Hydration with a mixture of 50% water and 50% electrolyte replacement drink is optimal at room temperature. Nutritious foods rather than fatty and salty foods should be encouraged. Rest periods of 10–20 minutes, or until body temperature, heart rate, and other vital signs return to normal should be planned into the operation so that cooling can take place and hydration and nutrition can be maintained.

FIGURE 53-6   Cocooning involves wrapping the patient in heavy plastic after gross decontamination has taken place.

Need to Do

The following skills are explained and illustrated in a step-by-step manner, via skill sheets and/or Step-by-Steps in this text and on the accompanying DVD:

Skill Name	Skill Sheet Number and Location	Step-by-Step Number and Location
Primary Survey	32 – Appendix A and DVD	32 – Chapter 14 and DVD
Autoinjector Drug Administration Device	59 – DVD	N/A
Putting On and Removing Gloves	60 – DVD	N/A
Handwashing	61 – DVD	61 – DVD
Verbal Communications	63 – DVD	N/A
Eye Irrigation	80 – DVD	N/A

Connections

- Chapter 9, Safety and Scene Size-Up, in the textbook describes scene safety and scene size-up during the management of a hazardous materials incident.
- Chapter 33, Infectious and Communicable Diseases, in the textbook describes biological agents that are considered hazardous materials.
- Chapter 50, Medical Incident Command, in the textbook provides information useful in managing hazardous materials incidents.
- Chapter 52, Teamwork and Operational Interface, in the textbook describes the role the paramedic plays in hazardous materials teams.
- Chapter 55, Responding to WMD Events, in the textbook discusses the hazardous materials component of WMD incidents.
- Link to the companion DVD for a chapter-based quiz, audio glossary, animations, games and exercises, and, when appropriate, skill sheets and skill Step-by-Steps.

Street Secrets

- **Slow and Steady** Responses to hazardous materials incidents need to be taken very slowly, with attention paid to the details. The operation needs to have a central focus on safety and prevention of exposing additional people to the hazardous materials. When these incidents are hurried, mistakes can be made and people can be unnecessarily exposed to harmful materials.
- **Hazmat versus WMD** An important thought to keep in mind when responding to and managing a hazardous materials incident is that the only difference between a hazardous materials incident and a weapons of mass destruction (WMD) incident is intention. Whenever you respond to a hazardous materials incident, constantly be aware of your surroundings and the possibility of secondary devices whether it appears to be a WMD incident or not.
- **Don't Keep It to Yourself** Communicate any hazards that you discover to all the other members of the hazardous materials team. Even if you think that everyone already knows about the hazard, make sure that you communicate your findings. The only "stupid" comment regarding safety at a hazardous materials incident is the comment that wasn't made.

The Drug Box

Atropine sulfate: An antimuscarinic agent that blocks acetylcholine at parasympathetic sites. Used to combat the effects of cholinergic agents and administered when signs of salivation, lacrimation, urination, defecation, gastric motility, and emesis (SLUDGE) are present. This is available in standard 1-mg pre-load syringes, multidose vials, and as the first autoinjector to be administered in a Mark I kit.

Pralidoxime chloride (2-PAM chloride): Reactivates cholinesterase inactivated by organophosphate pesticides allowing for degradation of accumulated acetylcholine. It is administered to patients who have been exposed to nerve agents or organophosphates as the second autoinjector found in a Mark I kit.

References

1. R. Stilp and A. Bevelacqua, *Emergency Medical Response to Hazardous Materials Incidents.* Albany, NY: Delmar Publishers, 1997, p. 18.
2. U.S. Department of Transportation, *Emergency Response Guidebook 2000.* La Grange, TX: Carlton, 2000, p. 4.
3. D. F. Peterson, "How Clean Is Clean? Assuring Decontamination Efforts Are Adequate," Firehouse.com, June 12, 2005, http:/cms.firehouse.com/content/article/printer.jsp?id=36029 (accessed March 28, 2007).
4. U.S. Department of Transportation, *Emergency Response Guidebook 2004.* http://hazmat.dot.gov/pubs/erg/gydebook.htm, pp. 252–3 (accessed February 12, 2007).

Answers

Are You Ready?

1. Your initial priority should be your own safety and the safety of your partner. The best initial plan of action should be to retreat and request that the police, fire department, and hazardous materials team respond.

2. Exposure to cleaning fluids is unlikely to cause such devastating effects in such a short period of time to such a large number of people.

3. The actions that you can take immediately include:
   a. Isolate the area and deny entry into the potentially hazardous environment.
   b. Perform a scene size-up and convey your findings to any responding units. Advise responding units of the exact location of the incident, any obvious hazards, the best access to and egress from the scene, an appropriate staging area (uphill, upwind, upstream, etc.), advice on any safety factors pertinent to the situation (anything that you could see, hear, or smell that could relate to the situation at hand, appropriate PPE for use by responding units, etc.), the approximate number of victims, and the need for additional resources.

4. Your role as the first emergency worker on the scene is incident commander (IC). In addition to providing a report concerning your scene size-up, you will need to take command ("City Hall Command"), identify the location of the command post, and ensure that all responding units are able to communicate with one another.

You Are There: Reality-Based Cases

Case 1

1. Attempt to gather more information on the nature of the call. It is unusual for multiple people to be involved in a farming accident. Request that the dispatcher clarify the nature of the incident and the number of patients, if possible. If there are more patients than you and your partner can easily manage, request additional resources (ambulances) as early as possible because they will take some time to get there.

2. The dispatcher has given you the number of victims and the fact that they were likely exposed to some sort of chemical. With this information, you should request additional ambulances for the transport of these victims, the fire department in case the chemical is flammable, a hazardous materials response team to manage the chemical spill and help decontaminate the victims (if necessary), and law enforcement to help control the scene.

3. As you approach the scene, you should be thinking safety. Until you know what the chemical is, you will need to keep a safe distance and provide as much information about the scene and the victims as possible without becoming victims yourselves. Attempt to determine the direction of the wind. Stage upwind, uphill, and upstream from the spill. When you are safely staged, use your binoculars to assess the situation and size up the scene.

4. Until the chemical can be identified, the best way to remain safe is to stay upwind, uphill, upstream, and a safe distance from the spill.

5. If you are the first on scene, look for any placards on the storage tank. If possible, use the information on the placard to identify the hazard. If you do not have copy of the *Emergency Response Guidebook,* relay the information from the placard to incoming units and the dispatcher so that the hazard can be identified. Ask the dispatcher to determine if the caller knows if there is a material safety data sheet (MSDS) for the chemical in the tank and, if so, where it is located.

6. a. Potential health hazards
      • The substance is highly toxic and may be fatal if inhaled, swallowed, or absorbed through the skin (avoid any skin contact).
      • The effects of contact or inhalation may be delayed.
      • Runoff of the substance may pollute waterways.
   b. Potential fire and explosion hazards
      • The substance is combustible; it may burn but does not ignite readily.
   c. Protective clothing
      • Wear a positive pressure self-contained breathing apparatus (SCBA).
      • Wear chemical protective clothing that is specifically recommended by the manufacturer.
      • Structural firefighters' protective clothing provides limited protection in fire situations *only*; it is not effective in spill situations where direct contact with the substance is possible.
   d. Initial care and first aid
      • Move the victim to fresh air.
      • Give artificial respirations if the victim is not breathing.
      • Administer oxygen if the victim is having difficulty breathing.
      • Remove and isolate contaminated clothing and shoes.

- In case of contact with the substance, immediately flush the skin or eyes of the victim with running water for at least 20 minutes.
- If there is minor skin contact with the substance, avoid spreading it on unaffected skin.
- Keep the victim warm and quiet.
- Ensure that medical personnel are aware of the material(s) involved and take precautions to protect themselves.[4]

7. Organophosphates bind to cholinesterase, causing the deactivation of acetylcholinesterase. The subsequent accumulation of acetylcholine at the neural synapse causes an initial overstimulation, followed by disruption of neural transmission in the central and peripheral nervous systems.

8. The priority of treatment is support of airway, breathing, and circulation. The unconscious patient with excessive salivation needs to have the airway suctioned and protected. Intubation is a likely solution to this problem. The patients should receive supplemental oxygen, and they should be monitored by ECG, pulse oximetry, and electronic capnography ($ETCO_2$ measurement). If Mark I autoinjectors have not yet been administered during the decontamination process, they should be administered now. If there is no access to Mark I kits, atropine sulfate and/or pralidoxime (2-PAM) should be administered per local protocols. Management of seizures should follow local protocols.

9. The only difference between adult and pediatric treatment for organophosphate poisoning is the dose of medications administered.

10. Possibilities for reducing contamination of the ambulance and equipment include *cocooning* (wrapping the patient in heavy plastic after gross decontamination has taken place) and *enveloping* the patient compartment (placing a plastic barrier on the inside of the patient compartment of the ambulance).

11. Helicopter transport of patients as shown in Figure 53-1 who have been exposed to poisoning is not frequently attempted due to the catastrophic results that would occur if the pilot was overcome by the poison during flight.

Test Yourself

1. b

   Patients exposed to organophosphate pesticides or carbamate pesticides should be treated with atropine to combat the parasympathetic effects.

2. a

   The *Emergency Response Guidebook* (ERG) is a written source of information that may be used to look up hazardous materials by placard ID number or by individual substance. CHEMTREC and ChemTel are hotline numbers, and CAMEO is an Internet resource.

3. a

   Level C suits are lightweight with a low fire rating and are the only suits to use an air purifying respirator.

4. b

   NFPA 473 identifies the levels of competence required of EMS personnel who respond to hazardous materials incidents and makes specific requirements for reducing accidents, exposure, and injuries.

5. a

   Key indicators of stress are an elevated heart rate and elevated body temperature.

6. b

   The U.S. Department of Transportation (DOT) requires placarding on loads of over 1001 pounds of most materials. Because delivery trucks often carry mixed loads and do not carry large enough amounts to be placarded or shipping papers, identification may be difficult or impossible.

7. b

   Responders should be encouraged to report to the rehab sector if feeling weakness, dizziness, chest pain, muscle cramps, nausea, altered mental status, or difficulty breathing. Even if symptom-free, responders should report to the rehab sector after extremely strenuous activity, using two SCBA bottles, 30 minutes in a hazardous environment, or failure of their PPE. A 12-lead ECG tracing should be obtained if the patient reports chest pain or has an irregular heart rate.

8. b

   Gross decontamination removes or chemically alters the majority of the hazard, but some residual contamination may remain. Secondary decontamination efforts further reduce or alter contamination. Formal decontamination is an enormous task. The process requires large numbers of responders and a lot of time and resources. Total decontamination is an unrealistic expectation for a decontamination corridor with a large number of casualties.

9. d

   Particular attention must be given to difficult-to-clean areas such as the scalp and hair, ears and nostrils, axillae, any folds of skin, under the fingernails, navel, groin, buttocks, breasts, genitalia, behind the knees, between the toes, and under the toenails. The axillae and groin are particularly difficult to decontaminate because of the thin skin and moisture of these regions.

10. d

   If prehospital providers become exposed, they should report to the decontamination station or inform command. For additional resources for specific decontamination procedures, see Box 53-5 in the textbook.

11. True

   During your scene size-up you should assess for possible scene hazards because your safety and your partner's safety are paramount. No treatment or assessment should occur until the scene can be deemed safe.

12. Simply treat the patient's signs and symptoms.

    Patients with any type of hazardous material exposure should be decontaminated before treatment is rendered. Once decontamination has been accomplished, assess and maintain the patient's airway, breathing, and circulation, and treat the patient's signs and symptoms.

13. Patient decontamination

    All contaminated patients should be decontaminated prior to receiving medical treatment. For example, gross decontamination will occur prior to spinal immobilization and other BLS procedures. Additional decontamination can occur simultaneously with BLS procedures by individuals wearing the appropriate PPE.

14. Cold

15. The cold zone

    Intubation should only occur in the cold zone after the patient has been decontaminated, since invasive procedures may act as a direct route for introduction of the hazardous material into the patient.

16. False

    Blue indicates a health hazard, yellow indicates reactivity, red indicates a fire hazard, and white indicates a specific hazard.

17. Calcium gluconate

    Exposure to hydrogen fluoride gas results in either an immediate or delayed onset of respiratory distress and pulmonary edema; these patients should be treated with the antidote—calcium gluconate.

18. True

    Beta particles are very high-energy particles that can penetrate a few centimeters of tissue. A person who has been exposed but has not been contaminated is *not* radioactive, presents no danger to responders, and does not need decontamination.

19. High health risk

    The NFPA 704 system uses placards on fixed facilities to indicate hazard risk. The hazards are numbered 0–4, with 4 being the highest risk. Blue indicates health, red indicates fire, yellow indicates reactivity, and white provides special information. Based on this information the blue square contains the highest number, and it can be determined that the chemicals inside pose more of a health hazard than any other type of hazard.

20. American Conference of Government Industrial Hygienists

    The American Conference of Government Industrial Hygienists is responsible for identifying what exposure levels are safe and do *not* cause permanent damage.

chapter 54

Special Events and Mass Gatherings

Are You Ready?

The sun shone hot over the sweltering, writhing mass of dancers and moshers; a steady, throbbing beat of synthesized drums and house music pushed the crowd into a frenzy. It was the third day of the annual Burning Man festival held in the Black Rock Desert in Nevada. In the middle of virtually nowhere, a city of more than 30,000 participants from all over the world materializes for 8 days, with art, music, and other creative activities taking center stage. People often stay up for days, using a variety of stimulants, both legal and illegal, to do so.

A volunteer EMS and field hospital is established, with 10 teams of EMTs and paramedics rotating on and off through the event, responding to a variety of incidents. Julian and Megan were just beginning their tour when their walkie-talkies crackled. A spotter near the dance floor has reported a "man down." After packing their gear into backpacks, the two medics hop onto their bikes and make their way to the "pit." Julian is quite excited; it is his first time here at Burning Man, and the energy in the air is palpable.

1. What medical conditions and traumatic injuries are likely to happen at an event such as this?

   _____

   _____

   _____

2. What are safety concerns unique to this special event?

   _____

   _____

   _____

Active Learning

1. Research

Conduct an Internet search for "EMS" and "mass gathering" for additional information on how systems manage these unique events. You may be surprised at how varied the response is from one region to the next. Identify the common attributes that you find, and think about how your local system implements the same principles. If your jurisdiction does not have a plan to handle mass gatherings, work on a plan for doing so. What resources would need to be developed? Where would those resources come from?

You Are There: Reality-Based Cases

Case 1 (continued from chapter opener)

The medics are directed by radio and volunteers to a man sprawled out on the desert floor. Julian begins his survey. The patient appears to be in his thirties, an African American who weighs approximately 80 kg. He is diaphoretic, with a grayish tint to his skin. A painful stimulus does not elicit a response. He is breathing rapidly, and Julian feels a faint radial pulse. There is no smell of alcohol on the man's breath, and there are no obvious signs of injury. A rapid examination of his torso does not reveal any tenderness or wounds. Breath sounds are difficult to hear because of the noise.

Bystanders have little information. He was seen in the pit throughout the night before, but it is unclear whether he left and came back. Although alcohol was not served by the event, alcohol and recreational drugs were being used by many of the participants. Someone noticed the patient lying on the ground just off to the side of the pit; he was there for several hours before someone recognized that there was a medical emergency.

1. Name the possible conditions that could be causing this patient's presentation.

_____

_____

_____

You actively cool the patient with fans and cooling towels and administer oxygen at 12 liters per minute via non-rebreather mask. An oral airway is placed without difficulty. You have also determined the following findings:

Vital signs: RR of 24, HR of 126, BP of 100/76.

SpO$_2$: 99%.

Blood glucose level: 8 mg/dL.

ECG: Sinus tachycardia with wide QRS complexes.

Physical findings: Core temperature is 41°C measured rectally; pupils are constricted and nonreactive; no lingual trauma; no smell of alcohol on breath; neck veins are flat; no stridor or accessory muscle use noted; equal and clear breath sounds; abdomen is flat, nontender to palpation; palpable femoral, distal pulses to both legs; no evidence of needle tracks along arms and legs.

2. Based on these additional findings, what treatment(s) will you perform on the patient?

_____

_____

_____

3. Should this patient remain at the on-site medical facility?

_____

_____

_____

Test Yourself

1. One of the activities associated with the _____ phase of a mass gathering event is scanning the crowd constantly for evidence of danger or foul play.

2. One common advantage of holding a mass gathering in a large, multilevel sports stadium is
   a. a low risk of terrorist threat.
   b. ease of access and egress.
   c. preexisting locations for first aid centers and emergency response vehicles.
   d. shelter from environmental hazards.

3. Transportation routes within and around the site of a mass gathering event
   a. will likely be labeled clearly on maps provided by the venue, in which case they require no further investigation.
   b. can be busy and dangerous and are therefore unsuitable for use by bicycles or golf carts.

c. require pre-event planning to ensure swift location of patients and determination of evacuation routes.

d. are designed to ease and maximize the flow of participants and are thus well-suited for the use of emergency vehicles.

4. Mass gatherings have a particularly high incidence of environmental emergencies.

True

False

5. The nature of mass gatherings often causes important deviations from everyday policies and protocols. Give an example of a deviation from protocol that would be acceptable when treating patients at a mass gathering.

_____

_____

6. What are the four phases of disaster management planning for mass gatherings?

_____

_____

7. Mass gatherings are defined in medical literature as any event with more than _____ persons.

8. When creating the medical operations plan for a mass gathering, members of the event planning team should

a. plan for a single central care area to streamline communication and dispatch.

b. strictly adhere to the policies and protocols of the local EMS agency.

c. only take into account the conditions most likely to be encountered, such as headache and minor trauma.

d. take into account factors such as the time of year and the demographic of the crowd.

9. List some of the ways you could practice public health hazard mitigation at a mass gathering.

_____

_____

10. When supporting mass gathering events, it is critical for the paramedic to be able to use which type(s) of communications equipment?

a. Pagers and landlines

b. The venue's equipment

c. A local 800-MHz trunking system

d. Walkie-talkies and cellular phones

11. A political convention would most likely be classified as a National Special Security Event (NSSE) in the National Incident Management System.

True

False

12. Which condition is *most* likely to occur at a mass gathering?

a. Anaphylaxis

b. WMD event

c. Dehydration

d. Cardiac arrest

13. Who should be included in the medical planning team for every mass gathering event?

_____

_____

14. While providing medical support at a 24-hour music festival at a large outdoor arena, you observe a cluster of patients with complaints of fever, nausea, and joint pain. You should first suspect

a. biochemical attack.

b. food poisoning.

c. severe dehydration.

d. hypothermia.

15. When planning for a mass gathering at a venue that has preexisting facilities for providing aid, you should

a. consider using the preexisting locations as stations from which to respond and in which to provide aid.

b. cut costs by relying solely on these preexisting locations as long as they are well stocked.

c. make sure all your personnel are stationed at these locations because that is where people will come for help.

d. not use the preexisting locations due to potential contract and liability conflicts.

Need to Know

The following represent the Key Objectives of Chapter 54:

1. *List factors that affect EMS response to special events and mass gatherings.*

Mass gatherings are generally defined as events with 1,000 participants or more. They vary tremendously from one event to the next; factors include geography, topography, ambient temperature, access and egress routes, age of participants, presence of intoxicants, and duration, to mention just a few. These factors must be considered when planning for an operation that covers the emergency medical needs of the event.

2. *Identify resources that can be deployed at special events and mass gatherings.*

Unique circumstances sometimes call for unique responses and management. It is not uncommon to engage a wide variety of response vehicles during a mass gathering event. Bicycles, electric carts, motorized all-terrain vehicles (ATVs), and motorcycles have all been deployed. This is especially true if the distance from the patient who needs to be carried to a medical facility or transport unit is quite far.

In addition to vehicles, the staffing may also be unique. Some large-scale events are covered by paid medical services, while volunteers may staff other events. Sometimes these events create logistical nightmares, especially if the medical staff is from outside the local regulatory jurisdiction. Temporary credentialing or licensing may be needed to fulfill statutory requirements to practice medicine at the event.

Equipment will also vary depending upon the event. For example, additional IV and oral fluids may be needed for hydration purposes. Antivenom for various poisonous animals may be required for events occurring in wilderness areas.

3. *Explain how paramedics work with teams that are unique in configuration, as well as under direct on-site medical direction, at mass gathering events.*

You can expect to work in teams that may comprise a wide range of practitioners, including physicians, nurses, and/or allied health professionals in addition to other levels of EMS providers. Having a good understanding of the protocols and local scope of practice, and a discussion with other team members prior to the start of the event, will help to define your role in the medical care continuum provided during the incident. If there is online medical direction being provided on-site, you should identify that physician and introduce yourself. Briefly discuss your expectations for medical oversight, as well as the physician's. By doing so, you can reduce the chances of any misunderstanding or confusion about team members' roles during the event.

Need to Do

There are no psychomotor skills that directly support this chapter content.

Connections

- Many regulatory agencies have policies and procedures in place for the oversight of EMS during a mass gathering event. An example of such policies is the EMS Plan for Mass Gatherings by the San Francisco EMS Agency, which can be found at www.sanfranciscoems. org/index.php?cat=no&name=massGathering& exten=html.
- eMedicine by WebMD provides an article containing additional information about planning for an EMS response to large-scale events at www.emedicine.com/emerg/topic812.htm.
- Several articles have been published in various trade magazines such as the *Journal of Emergency Medical Services (JEMS)* and *Emergency*

Medical Services Magazine. If your organization has a library of these, you might want to check the annual index issue to see if you can locate specific articles, such as the following:

- M. Nordberg, "EMS and Mass Gatherings," *Emergency Medical Services* 19, no. 5 (May 1990): 46–51, 54–6, 91.
- W. C. Butler and D. E. Gesner, "Crowded Venues. Avoid an EMS Quagmire by Preparing for Mass Gatherings." *Journal of Emergency Medical Services* 24, no. 11 (November 1999): 62–65, 67, 73 passim.
- W. C. Butler and D. E. Gesner, "Developing a Mass Gathering EMS Plan." *Journal of Emergency Medical Services* 24, no. 11 (November 1999): 66.
- R. B. Leonard and K. M. Moreland, "EMS for the Masses. Preplanning Your EMS Response to a Major Event." *Emergency Medical Services* 30, no. 1 (January 2001): 53–60.

■ Link to the companion DVD for a chapter-based quiz, audio glossary, animations, games and exercises, and, when appropriate, skill sheets and skill Step-by-Steps.

Street Secrets

■ **Take Care of Yourself** It's easy to get caught up in all the excitement related to the event. It is also easy to become fatigued and dehydrated yourself. Remember that your safety relates directly to your health; eat well, drink fluids, and get rest when you are supposed to. You may want to bring a distraction with you to a long-duration event, such as a book or music player. Refreshing the mind can be as important as refreshing the body.

The Drug Box

There are no specific drugs related to this chapter content.

Answers

Are You Ready?

1. Common problems that might be expected include minor injuries, such as dust in the eyes, lacerations to the legs and arms, and sprains and strains. Medical conditions are likely to include dehydration and heat exhaustion. If the event has a flow of alcohol and recreational drugs, overdoses are likely. Depending upon the age and health of the participants, you might want to remember that a myriad of medical conditions such as AMI, stroke, and diabetes might also appear.

2. The heat and dust of the desert can be aggravating factors to any preexisting medical conditions. Large masses of people, along with the use of alcohol and drugs, can also incite violent behavior, resulting in assaults to participants and rescue staff. The remoteness of the location also contributes to the planning of this event; a receiving facility may be very far away, requiring that most care be provided on-site.

You Are There: Reality-Based Cases

Case 1

1. Your answer should have included the following likely conditions: heatstroke, hypovolemic shock, hypoglycemia, alcohol or drug overdose, hypoxia, electrolyte imbalance, and stroke. Based upon the environmental findings, which ones were at the top of your list? Less likely answers may include: generalized seizure, sepsis, uremia, trauma, and psychosis.

2. Despite the apparent lack of gag reflex, the patient's oxygen saturation levels are within normal limits, reducing the need for assisted ventilations. However, his blood pressure is low, and he does show signs of shock. Given the environment and the described activities prior to the incident, intravenous fluid therapy is indicated. His ECG appears to be a sinus tachycardia, perhaps a response to a dehydrated state. A critical finding is hypoglycemia, along with a hyperthermic state. Intravenous dextrose is needed, along with continued cooling measures.

   Did you consider administration of naloxone for a possible narcotic overdose, based on the constricted pupils? Although not necessarily harmful, the fact that there is no sign of respiratory depression minimizes the need to administer naloxone. If the narcotic is contributing to the altered mental status, inhibiting its depressive effect could cause the patient to regain consciousness too rapidly, especially if there is a concomitant use of a stimulant.

   Did you consider intubation for airway control? Again, look at the oxygen saturation levels. Considering that hypoglycemia is a distinct cause for the patient's unconsciousness, intubation prior to dextrose administration may be unnecessary. If, after the "easy fixes" are done, the patient remains unconscious, consider advanced airway control.

3. Whether or not the patient stays at the temporary facility depends on the level of staffing, the equipment, and the facility, as well as any changes the patient may experience as a result of your actions. If lab processing is unavailable, or the patient does not improve, there may be no choice but to transfer the patient to a fixed medical facility.

Test Yourself

1. Mitigation

   The mitigation phase occurs as the event is in progress. Paramedics attending mass gatherings should be on high alert during the event and scan the crowd constantly for evidence of danger or foul play.

2. c

Stadiums, concert halls, and convention centers are examples of facilities specifically designed to host mass gatherings. Many have permanent locations for first aid centers, emergency response vehicles, and on-site medical staffing. Each venue has unique difficulties with access (entrance to) and egress (movement away from). Large venues or heavily attended mass gatherings are targets for those who wish to impact the most people with the least amount of effort.

3. c

These routes require pre-event planning to ensure paramedics will be able to rapidly locate a patient and determine the best route for evacuation if needed.

4. True

Environmental emergencies are an important subset of the problems that mass gathering participants tend to report. Venues are varied, and events take place in any season. Emergencies range from heat exhaustion and heatstroke to hypothermia and frostbite, as well as envenomations by snakes, arthropods, and marine life. Paramedics preparing for mass gatherings, particularly those in outdoor or remotely located areas, need to be familiar with the types of emergencies that may be caused by the environment and location.

5. Treat-and-release protocols will allow the paramedic to provide specific types of care, like administering dextrose to diabetic patients, and then to release patients without transporting them to the hospital. Another possible deviation from protocol would be field triage to an atypical destination, such as a clinic or rehydration unit.

Paramedics should be aware that all responses still need a minimum level of documentation. All laws, rules, and regulations regarding the privacy of patient records still apply in mass gatherings. Further, the paramedic must remember that appropriate role modeling for the public, as well as personal safety, demands the use of appropriate safety equipment on all types of vehicles, whether this includes seat belts, life vests, or helmets.

6. Planning, response, mitigation, and recovery

EMS operations at mass gatherings involve the basic actions of disaster management planning, which include the four phases. This model provides a good framework for planning and executing large-scale events.

7. 1,000

Mass gatherings, generally defined in medical literature as any event with more than 1,000 persons, are common occurrences that present uncommon challenges to EMS systems.

8. d

Certainly it is wise to prepare for the expected demographic for an event. An event's timing also has an effect on the medical response. This is true both for time-of-

year effects because of weather and time-of-day effects because of traffic patterns and hospital utilization.

9. Possibilities for hazard mitigation include: staffing rehydration units, providing information on safe-ride and designated driver programs, and distributing blankets during outdoor winter events.

10. b

It is critical that the paramedic be able to easily use the available equipment to avoid delays in dispatch and treatment. Many venues are equipped to participate in local 800-MHz trunking systems. If so, the paramedic will need to determine appropriate dispatch and tactical workgroups and frequencies. Other venues may rely on walkie-talkies, cellular phones, landlines, or pagers for communication.

11. True

Events like the Olympics, presidential inaugurations, and political conventions are classified as National Special Security Events (NSSE) in the National Incident Management System. NSSEs fall under the jurisdiction of the United States Secret Service.

12. c

The medical operations plan must take into account the most likely conditions that will be encountered. This generally includes headache, gastrointestinal upset, mild dehydration, and minor trauma. The plan should also consider the management of life-threatening conditions. Even though situations like cardiac arrest, anaphylaxis, and major trauma have a low expectation of occurrence, they require an immediate response and should be planned for.

13. Every event planning team should include a medical director in addition to police, fire, and other public safety representatives.

In addition to EMS, fire, and police agencies with which paramedics are already familiar, planning for larger events may involve input from emergency managers, public health personnel, and government agencies at the local, state, and federal levels. In particular, political events or events with high-profile participants may have separate response plans to ensure the safety of the attendees.

14. a

Careful observation on the part of the paramedic may provide the necessary clues to uncover more subtle forms of attack (most notably bioweapons) presenting as clusters of patients with similar complaints.

15. a

Preexisting medical facilities can often serve as stations from which to respond and in which to provide aid. If a physician is part of the response team, this is often a logical place to base the physician. Paramedics often staff these locations, sometimes working under offline treatment protocols. However, although it is tempting to rely solely on these preexisting locations, it is important to consider the specifics of the event to determine if these facilities are sufficient and appropriate for the expected needs.

chapter 55

Responding to WMD Events

Are You Ready?

You and your partner respond to a call on the out-skirts of town for a possible drug overdose. You are the first to arrive on the scene. When you look around, you don't see any activity in the house. You loudly announce, "EMS," but do not get a response. The front door is opened just a crack, so you knock on the door and slowly push it open. As the door opens, you notice a strange smell. Before you enter the house, your partner grabs you and says, "We need to get out of here." She points to the ground, and you see this:

1. How should you proceed upon discovery of this device?

_____

_____

_____

2. What type of assistance will you need?

_____

_____

_____

3. What considerations should you keep in mind?

_____

_____

_____

Active Learning

1. Are We at Risk?

An event involving a weapon of mass destruc-tion (WMD) might seem unlikely in your area; in fact, there are probably at least a few targets in your jurisdiction that, if attacked, could cause serious injuries, illnesses, and chaos. On a sheet of paper, list the general categories of potential weapons—chemical, biological, radioactive or nuclear, and explosives. Under each category, identify the possible targets in your response area. Is the list short or long? Consider helping to create scenarios that your organization can use for training.

FIGURE 55-1   Mark I autoinjector kit.

2. Use of the Mark I Kit

In the case of exposure to a nerve agent that produces an excessive sympathetic response (see the Need to Know section), you may need to inject the contents of a Mark I kit (Figure 55-1) into a patient, another rescuer, or yourself. Review the procedure for using this device.

Mark I Procedure

a. With the Mark I kit in front of you, pull the smaller of the two injectors (atropine 2 mg) out of the plastic clip.

b. Hold the autoinjector as you would hold a pencil (with your thumb and two fingers) (Figure 55-2a). *Do not touch the green end of the* *injector; the needle will penetrate clothing (even turnout pants).*

c. Palpate the area that you plan to inject to make sure that you are not going to inadvertently inject another object (e.g., a wallet or keys).

d. Remove the safety cap. *Do not hold your thumb over either end; an autoinjector will go right through your thumb and out the other side.*

e.   Place the green end of the autoinjector against the anterolateral thigh, and push firmly until you feel the injector activate (Figure 55-2b).

f. Hold in place for 10 seconds to complete delivery of the medication.

g. Use a secondary site (e.g., the other thigh) if the primary site is not accessible or for additional doses as indicated by symptoms and protocol.

h. Pull the large injector (pralidoxime chloride [2-PAM] 600 mg) out of the clip, and administer in the same manner as the smaller atropine injector (Figure 55-2c).

i. Rub the injected area to distribute.

j. Dispose of the used injectors in an appropriate sharps container.

Note: Some EMS providers (e.g., the U.S. military) are taught to leave the autoinjector with the patient to show the dose that was delivered to the patient.

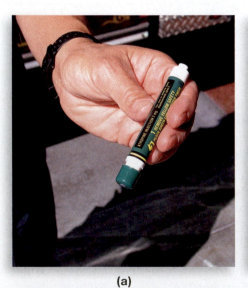

(a)

(b)

(c)

FIGURE 55-2   Use of Mark I Autoinjector. (a) Hold the autoinjector as you would hold a pencil (with your thumb and two fingers). **(b)** Place the green end of the autoinjector against the anterolateral thigh and push firmly until you feel the injector activate. **(c)** Pull the large injector (pralidoxime chloride [2-PAM] 600 mg) out of the clip and administer in the same manner as the smaller atropine injector.

You Are There: Reality-Based Cases

Case 1

Transit Authority Police have called for multiple ambulances and the hazardous materials unit from the fire department to assist them with a situation at the Main Street Station. Police officers have arrested two teenage boys who were seen running up the stairs at the station carrying handguns. As the officers were handcuffing the suspects, screams could be heard from the train platform, and people began to run past them to flee the station. A number of people were lying motionless on the platform and in one of the cars of the train. The suspects admitted to dispersing a mixture of sodium cyanide and hydrochloric acid on the train as it pulled away from the previous station.

As you arrive on the scene, you are told that the police have evacuated the station. Surveillance cameras show dozens of people lying motionless on the platform and in the train, and there are approximately 50 people in front of the station with complaints ranging from irritation of the eyes to severe ventilatory distress. The hazardous materials team from the fire department has already suited up and is heading down to the train platform to assess the situation.

1. What are your first actions to perform?

_____

_____

_____

2. What are the effects of combining sodium cyanide and hydrochloric acid, including the physical characteristics that result from the combination?

_____

_____

_____

3. What effect does this combination have on humans? Describe the pathophysiological effects of exposure to this combination.

_____

_____

_____

4. Is decontamination needed prior to treating victims exposed to this combination of substances?

_____

_____

_____

5. What is the prehospital treatment for a victim exposed to this combination of substances?

_____

_____

_____

A fire department battalion chief arrives on the scene and meets with you and the commanding officer from the transit police. The three of you discuss the situation and what you need to do to mitigate it.

6. What is the term used for the command style that utilizes figureheads from different agencies?

_____

_____

_____

7. In regard to the hazard on the scene and the treatment of the patients, what needs to be done at this point?

_____

_____

_____

The fire department's hazardous material unit sets up a decontamination area with pools and a shower tent. The hazmat team is appropriately clothed in PPE and ready to decontaminate the victims and rescuers.

Test Yourself

1. An unknown chemical gas has been detected in an office building. The first emergency personnel entering the building should wear which level of protection?

_____

_____

Scenario: Nearly two dozen people suddenly became sick at a shopping mall. Many of the patients, including your adult female patient, are exhibiting the following symptoms: tachycardia, dyspnea, cyanosis, and coughing that produces frothy, pink sputum. A police officer, one of the first on scene, reports having detected a greenish-yellow haze in the air and an unpleasant, sharp odor.

2. You should suspect
   a. cyanide poisoning.
   b. phosgene poisoning.
   c. anhydrous ammonia poisoning.
   d. chlorine poisoning.

3. After removing your patient from the area, you should
   a. remove her clothing, and decontaminate her skin and eyes with large amounts of water.
   b. keep her lying still and administer intravenous fluid.
   c. administer supplemental oxygen, and endotracheally intubate if necessary.
   d. administer amyl nitrate, sodium nitrate, and sodium thiosulfate.

4. In patients with viral hemorrhagic fever (VHF), the highest risk of secondary transmission occurs before symptoms appear.
   True
   False

5. Most cases of external radiation exposure do not constitute a medical emergency.
   True
   False

6. What are the three radiation guidelines for minimizing radiation exposure?

_____

_____

7. When an injured person is decontaminated as quickly as possible to enable medical staff to perform life-saving interventions, it is known as _____ decontamination.

8. An explosive device was detonated on a sidewalk in front of a tall brick building. You would suspect that the victims positioned _____ during the blast may have the greatest injuries.
   a. on the sidewalk, 100 feet from the detonation site
   b. on the sidewalk, 50 feet from the detonation site
   c. between the explosion and the building
   d. within the ground floor of the building

9. Which of the following is most likely to be classified as a WMD event?
   a. A reactor meltdown at a nuclear power plant
   b. An international flu epidemic
   c. Intentional food product contamination
   d. A hostage situation at a multinational corporation

10. The first known use of weapons of mass destruction occurred
    a. when Sir Jeffrey Amherst ordered the distribution of small pox–infected blankets to American Indians.
    b. when the United States Army Air Force dropped the atomic bomb known as "Little Boy" on the city of Hiroshima.
    c. when Japanese unit 731 dispersed plague-contaminated rice and fleas over Chinese cities.
    d. when the bodies of plague-infected Tartar soldiers were catapulted over the walls of a besieged city.

11. List one example of each of the following:
    a. Spraying device: _____
    b. Bursting or exploding device: _____
    c. Breaking device: _____

12. Why is the 1972 Biological Weapons Convention somewhat ineffective?

_____

_____

13. The symptoms caused by riot control agents should last no longer than _____ hours.

Scenario: Your patient is a 27-year-old woman presenting with blisters on her left arm and irritation of her nose and sinuses. She says she was on the subway when a stranger spilled a brown, oily liquid on her arm. The liquid "smelled like geraniums" and caused immediate irritation to the exposed skin. The patient has not had the opportunity to thoroughly cleanse her arm.

14. You should suspect

    a. phosgene.

    b. anhydrous ammonia.

    c. sulfur mustard.

    d. Lewisite.

15. Your initial treatment should be

    a. decontaminating the patient with whatever decontamination solution is available.

    b. supplemental oxygen administration and positive pressure ventilation.

    c. applying a sterile dressing to the blisters and intubating to protect the airway.

    d. supplemental oxygen administration and emergent transport to the nearest Level I trauma center.

Need to Know

The history of weapon of mass destruction (WMD) use traces back to the first recorded occurrence in 1346 when a biological attack was carried out in Kaffa. The dead bodies of Tartar soldiers who had been infected with plague were catapulted over the walls of the besieged city.[1] Over the past 20 years, the United States has experienced anthrax attacks, food product contamination, release of chemical weapons, and suicide attacks using explosive devices.[2]

The following represent the Key Objectives of Chapter 55:

1. *Describe the three classic methods of dispersion used to spread WMD agents.*

    a. *Spraying devices* are typically used to aerosolize liquid WMD agents.

       • Line source—poses a significant downwind hazard

       • Point source—smaller reach with moderate downwind hazard

    b. *Breaking devices* are used to encapsulate an agent and release it when the device is broken.

    c. *Bursting or exploding devices* incorporate an explosive device to break the agent container and disperse the agent.

2. *Define the terms* volatility, vapor, *and* persistence *as they relate to chemical warfare agents.*

Volatility is an agent's ability to evaporate to form an invisible vapor. *Vapor* is the gaseous form of a substance at a temperature lower than the boiling point of that substance at a given pressure. *Persistence* is the ability of an agent to remain a liquid hazard and to contaminate surfaces for 24 hours or longer.

3. *Describe the effects of nerve agents, their routes of absorption, their signs and symptoms, and general treatment for exposure.*

Nerve agents are the most toxic of all human-made chemical agents, yet are available in easily accessible forms such as organophosphates. They are easily absorbed through the skin, eyes, and lungs. Nerve agents inhibit acetylcholinesterase and cause the buildup of acetylcholine, which causes overstimulation of the sympathetic nervous system and results in the classic signs and symptoms represented by the acronym SLUDGE: salivation, lacrimation, urination, defecation, GI upset, and emesis. Nerve agents can cause sudden loss of consciousness, seizures, apnea, and death. Treatment includes decontamination, airway management and oxygenation, and Mark I autoinjector administration of atropine sulfate and pralidoxime (2-PAM).

Examples of nerve agents include sarin (GB), VX, tabun (GA), and soman (GD).

4. *Describe the effects of vesicants (blister agents), their routes of absorption, their signs and symptoms, and general treatment for exposure.*

Vesicants are chemical compounds that cause severe skin, eye, and mucosal pain and irritation. They are named for their ability to cause large, painful blisters on the bodies of those individuals who are exposed. Blister agents tend to be absorbed by inhalation or by liquid contact to the eyes, skin, and the airways. Signs and symptoms vary according to the agent used, duration of contact, and amount of agent. Signs and symptoms of exposure include: irritation to the eyes that ranges from mild conjunctivitis to ulceration or perforation; erythema of the skin that progresses to blister formation; and respiratory symptoms that begin with pharyngitis and can lead to dyspnea with a productive cough. Treatment for vesicant exposure includes: decontamination, supplemental oxygen, positive pressure ventilation as needed, bronchodilators for bronchospasm, and advanced airway procedures for upper airway swelling and compromise.

5. *Describe the effects of pulmonary agents, their routes of absorption, their signs and symptoms, and general treatment for exposure.*

The effects of pulmonary agents such as phosgene, chlorine, and anhydrous ammonia vary according to the specific agent, the dosage, and the duration of exposure. Pulmonary agents are typically absorbed via inhalation. Treatment for pulmonary agents varies depending on the agent, but all treatments include: decontamination, support for airway and breathing, supplemental oxygen, consideration of early intubation, treating volume depletion with isotonic fluid boluses, and avoiding the treatment of non-cardiac pulmonary edema with diuretics.

6. *Identify factors that should increase the paramedic's index of suspicion that a biological attack has occurred.*

There are several sentinel events that can provide clues to a biological outbreak. There may be an abnormally high number of patients complaining of respiratory symptoms who have an unprecedented mortality rate. Other EMS agencies within your geographical region may also be experiencing similar increases in patient volume and respiratory complaints. Livestock, pets, and other animals may become sick or die unexpectedly. There may be prior intelligence reports or claims by aggressors of a biological weapons attack.

7. *List the basic types of radiation, and discuss their effects on humans, their ability to be shielded, and the hazards that they pose.*

a. *Alpha radiation.* If alpha emitters are introduced into the body by inhalation, ingestion, or through a wound, localized damage can occur. Alpha particles are not able to penetrate through dead skin cells (epidermis). Alpha radiation is an internal hazard only.

b. *Beta radiation.* This type of radiation can penetrate into the germinal layer of the skin and, if left in contact with the skin, can cause damage. Beta radiation can also cause damage if deposited internally (it is both an internal and an external hazard).

c. *Gamma radiation.* This type of radiation readily penetrates most materials, including human tissue, at varying depths depending on the density of the tissue. It poses both an internal and external hazard to humans. Dense shielding is needed to prevent contamination of the skin.

d. *Neutrons.* Neutrons come to fruition through a process called *activation* (transmutation). Activation occurs when a neutron is captured by a stable nucleus, causing the nucleus to become radioactive. The radiation associated with neutrons is considered an external hazard.

8. *List three factors that paramedics must keep in mind when working around a radioactive source to minimize their exposure.*

a. Time—the shorter the time in a radiation field, the less the exposure.

b. Distance—the farther you are from the radioactive source, the lower the radiation dose.

c. Shielding—the use of shielding can reduce exposure to radiation.

9. *Describe the process of assessing a potentially radioactive scene.*

Rescuer safety comes first. Position yourself upwind, upstream, and uphill of a potential radioactive scene, don appropriate PPE, and wear your dosimeter. Perform a scene size-up. As soon as time and equipment availability permits, perform a radiological survey to assess for the degree of contamination. Establish a *hot line* to separate the clean from the contaminated areas of the scene. Identify an area for decontamination to take place, and set up the area for decontamination of patients and rescuers.

10. *List the phases of acute radiation syndrome (ARS).*

a. Prodromal phase—signs and symptoms appearing within 2 days of exposure.

b. Latent phase—the period of time after the prodromal phase and before signs of long-term illness begin.

c. Illness phase—radiation-related illnesses such as cancer occur.

d. Recovery or death phase—patients experiencing long-term illnesses survive or die.

11. *List the three different types of blast injuries that are associated with an explosion.*

    a. Primary blast injury—results from the direct effect of the blast wave on tissues and organs.

    b. Secondary blast injuries—caused by objects striking the victim (penetrating).

    c. Tertiary blast injuries—caused by the victim striking a stationary object (blunt).

12. *Describe safety practices that paramedics can employ to prevent their need for decontamination.*

    Staying "clean" and avoiding contamination is ultimately the best type of decontamination. Use disposable gloves, boots, aprons, and so forth that can simply be removed if contaminated. Only enter zones that you and your equipment are properly protected to enter.

13. *Differentiate between the different types of decontamination.*

    a. Emergency decontamination—designed to decontaminate injured crew members or people as rapidly as possible so that life-threatening procedures can be performed.

    b. Technical decontamination—the planned and systematic removal of contaminants from any-

thing or anybody that has come into contact with the hazardous agent.

14. *List the personal protective equipment that paramedics may be required to use when working at a WMD scene.*

    A self-contained breathing apparatus (SCBA) is the highest level of respiratory protection. An air purifying respirator (APR) or a cartridge mask is appropriate to wear in certain conditions, but has many more limitations than an SCBA.

    The National Fire Protection Association (NFPA) categorizes PPE according to its level of protection:

    • Level D—typical uniform that offers no respiratory protection and minimal skin protection.

    • Level C—protects against skin contact with a known substance and also affords the wearer some respiratory protection through an APR.

    • Level B—offers the user the maximum respiratory protection through the use of an SCBA and protection against chemical spills or splashes.

    • Level A—affords the rescuer the absolute highest level of skin and respiratory protection.

Need to Do

The following skills are explained and illustrated in a step-by-step manner, via skill sheets and/or Step-by-Steps in this text and on the accompanying DVD:

Skill Name	Skill Sheet Number and Location	Step-by-Step Number and Location
Autoinjector Drug Administration Device	59 – DVD	N/A
Putting On and Removing Gloves	60 – DVD	N/A
Handwashing	61 – DVD	61 – DVD
Verbal Communications	63 – DVD	N/A
Eye Irrigation	80 – DVD	N/A

Connections

- Chapter 9, Safety and Scene Size-Up, in the textbook includes detailed information on scene safety and scene size-up.
- Chapter 33, Infectious and Communicable Diseases, in the textbook describes biological agents used in WMD events.
- Chapter 50, Medical Incident Command, in the textbook explains how to manage WMD events.
- Chapter 51, Rescue Awareness, in the textbook explains the role of the paramedic during rescue operations resulting from a WMD incident.
- Chapter 52, Teamwork and Operational Interface, in the textbook describes the role the paramedic plays in the team that responds to a WMD incident.

- Chapter 53, Hazardous Materials Incidents, in the textbook covers the hazardous materials component of a WMD incident.

- The Center for Domestic Preparedness (CDP) is the branch of the U.S. Department of Homeland Security (DHS) that provides first responder training for CBRNE and WMD events. The website is http://cdp.dhs.gov/index.html.

- Link to the companion DVD for a chapter-based quiz, audio glossary, animations, games and exercises, and, when appropriate, skill sheets and skill Step-by-Steps.

Street Secrets

- **Safety First** Safety is the one consistent theme that runs through the response to a WMD event because, if it is not the first priority, the results can prove to be fatal. This is the type of operation in which teamwork, clear communication, and specialized training can truly make the difference between life and death for all parties involved. Paramedics must be alert and constantly aware of their surroundings, and any hazard that is discovered needs to be communicated to the team and addressed so that rescuer safety is not compromised.

The Drug Box

Atropine sulfate: An antimuscarinic agent that blocks acetylcholine at parasympathetic sites. It is used to combat the effects of cholinergic agents and is administered when signs of SLUDGE are present. This is available in standard 1-mg preloaded syringes, multidose vials, and as the first autoinjector to be administered in a Mark I kit.

Pralidoxime chloride (2-PAM chloride): Reactivates cholinesterase inactivated by organophosphate pesticides, allowing for degradation of accumulated acetylcholine. It is administered to patients who have been exposed to nerve agents or organophosphates as the second autoinjector in a Mark I kit.

References

1. R. Howard and R. Sawyer, *Terrorism and Counterterrorism: Understanding the New Security Environment.* New York: McGraw-Hill, 2003, p. 443.
2. E. Noji, "Introduction: Consequences of Terrorism." *Prehospital and Disaster Medicine* (July–September 2004): 163–4.

Answers

Are You Ready?

1. Remove yourself from harm's way. Backtrack as close as possible to the same way that you came in. Be aware of your surroundings, and look for any additional hazards as you head for safety. It is best that you do not use your radios to call for help, as the device could have a remote detonation capability that could be activated by radios.

2. Additional assistance for a possible explosive device would include local law enforcement (including a bomb squad), the fire department, and federal agencies such as the FBI and the Bureau of Alcohol, Tobacco, Firearms, and Explosives (ATF).

3. Bombs, especially those rigged as booby traps, are likely there to cause damage to a large number of people. They may be accompanied by secondary devices to specifically harm rescue workers. Always keep this in mind when responding to the scene of an explosive device or an explosion. Keep your eyes open, and report anything that you feel is out of the ordinary to the rest of the team and the IC.

You Are There: Reality-Based Cases

Case 1

1. The first priority is rescuer safety. Isolate the scene, and deny entry to anyone other than hazmat trained emergency personnel involved in the operation. Perform a scene size-up, and communicate your findings with other responding units. The scene size-up should include the exact location, type of incident, any hazards identified, number of patients, additional resources needed, a staging area for the incoming units, identification of the IC, and location of the command post.

2. The combination of sodium cyanide and hydrochloric acid or sulfuric acid produces a chemical weapon called hydrogen cyanide (HCN), also known as Zyklon B. HCN is a colorless gas or bluish-white liquid with a bitter almond odor.

3. Hydrogen cyanide can cause rapid death due to metabolic asphyxia. Acute exposure to cyanide can result in symptoms including weakness, headache, confusion, vertigo, fatigue, anxiety, dyspnea, and occasionally nausea and vomiting. Cyanide directly stimulates the chemoreceptors of the carotid and aortic bodies, causing hyperpnea. Cardiac irregularities are often noted.

4. Avoid dermal contact with cyanide-contaminated victims or with gastric contents of victims who may have ingested cyanide-containing materials. Emergency decontamination is necessary before the victims can be treated by EMS personnel.

5. Victims exposed to hydrogen cyanide require supportive care and rapid administration of specific antidotes (typically not available in the prehospital setting).

6. This is an example of a unified command.

7. Establish the hot, warm, and cold zones. With the resources that are available and the condition of the victims, triage needs to be performed to determine the priority for the decontamination and treatment of the different patients. Those patients needing emergency decontamination need to be addressed first, and those with minor signs and symptoms can wait for technical decontamination. If the antidote kit for treating these patients is not carried by EMS personnel, consider the possibility that the kits need to be brought to the scene to begin the treatment process.

Test Yourself

1. Level A

   Level A protection affords responders the absolute highest level of both skin and respiratory protection. The suit is fully encapsulating. This level of protection should be used anytime responders are working with unknown chemicals or substances. Once the type of chemical is distinguished, the wearer is recommended to downgrade to the appropriate level of protection.

2. d

   Chlorine is toxic to any body surface it contacts including the eyes, skin, respiratory tracts, and GI tract. After an exposure, patients may experience non-cardiogenic pulmonary edema. Although phosgene and anhydrous ammonia poisoning may both be characterized by respiratory distress, only chlorine gas is greenish-yellow in color with an acrid odor.

3. c

   Chlorine injures cells by reacting with water, producing hydrochloric acid (irritating) and free oxygen radicals. Affected patients should be given supplemental oxygen. Endotracheal intubation with assisted ventilation may be required. Although toxicity to the eyes and skin should be treated with copious flushing, in this scenario, your first concern should be to secure the patient's airway.

4. False

   The highest risk for secondary transmission of VHF is in the later stages of the disease when viral titers in the body are high and the patients may exhibit vomiting, bloody diarrhea, shock, and hemorrhage. Transferring patients may increase the potential for secondary transmission.

5. True

   Irradiation of the whole body or some specific body part in most cases does not constitute a medical emergency even if the amount of radiation received is high. The effects of irradiation usually are not evident for days to weeks, and while medical treatment is needed, it is not needed on an emergency basis.

6. Time, distance, and shielding

   EMS personnel must familiarize themselves with the radiation guidelines of time, distance, and shielding.

Time. The shorter the time in a radiation field, the less the radiation exposure. WMD personnel must work quickly and efficiently. A rotating team approach can be used to keep individual radiation exposures to a minimum.

Distance. The farther a person is from a source of radiation, the lower the radiation dose. Do not touch radioactive materials. Use shovels, brooms, and so forth, to move materials to avoid physical contact.

Shielding. Although not always practical in emergency situations, shielding offered by barriers can reduce radiation exposure.

7. Emergency

   Emergency decontamination procedures are designed to decontaminate an injured person or crew member as quickly as possible to enable medical staff to perform life-saving interventions. Individuals who qualify to receive emergency decontamination are those who cannot wait for technical decontamination to take place. Technical decontamination is the planned and systematic removal of contaminants from equipment, personnel, and anything else that has come into contact with the hazardous agent.

8. c

   If a solid structure such as a wall or building is present in the path of the explosion, the blast wave will rebound off this structure and generate a reflective force that is magnified almost nine times its original strength. As a result, victims caught between the blast and a building may suffer injuries two or three times greater than expected for the amount of explosive detonated and the distance from the explosion.

9. c

   Over the past two decades, acts of terrorism have ranged from the dissemination of aerosolized anthrax spores, intentional food product contamination, release of chemical weapons in major metropolitan subway systems, and suicide attacks using explosive devices. Epidemics can be naturally occurring; a meltdown could be an accident; and hostages can be taken with non-WMD (e.g., guns).

10. d

    The first known use of biological weaponry was in 1346 at Kaffa (now Feodosia, Ukraine), where the bodies of Tartar soldiers who had succumbed to plague were catapulted over the walls of the besieged city.

11. a. aerosol can; b. pipe bomb; c. glass bottle

    Spraying devices include: aerosol cans, garden sprayers, and crop dusters. Bursting or exploding devices pose both a chemical and explosion risk to bystanders, and include all types of bombs. Breaking devices include: balloons, lightbulbs, and vacuum bottles.

12. It only prohibits nations from conducting research or producing biological agents for offensive or hostile purposes, and it is difficult to differentiate between "offensive" research and "defensive" research.

    Although 140 nations signed and ratified the 1972 Biological Weapons Convention, problems related to verification and interpretation of "defensive" research have limited its effectiveness. The Center for Nonproliferation Studies at the Monterey Institute of International Studies has identified 31 nation states that have or had chemical or biological weapons programs and have cataloged at least 46 instances of their use.

13. 2

Most riot control symptoms should improve within 1 to 2 hours. Most skin exposures require little more than reassurance; however, with prolonged pain decontamination with soap and water may be helpful.

14. d

Lewisite is a vesicant that is rapidly absorbed by the eyes, skin, and lungs. The chemical agent produces blisters similar to sulfur mustard. However, Lewisite is highly irritating on initial exposure, producing visible lesions more quickly. Anhydrous ammonia has a pungent odor. Phosgene is a colorless gas that has a characteristic odor of freshly mown hay.

15. a

The most important factor for Lewisite treatment initially is decontaminating patients as soon as possible with whatever decontamination solution is available. Under emergency circumstances, dilute bleach, soap and water, or copious amounts of water are all acceptable decontaminants.

Appendix A: Skill Sheets

The skill sheets in this appendix correspond to the Step-by-Steps printed in this worktext. These and 70 additional skill sheets are available in PDF format on the accompanying Student DVD and the Student Online Learning Center at www.mhhe.com/chapleau1e. For a comprehensive listing of skill sheets and Step-by-Step skill demonstrations, see pages ix–xii in the front matter of this book.

You can use the skill sheets, along with the Step-by-Steps (when available), to practice your psychomotor skills. Remember that skill sheets are guidelines that present one medically acceptable manner in which the skills can be performed. As is true for many medical procedures, there are a number of correct ways to accomplish these skills, and the methods may vary from system to system. Your instructor will help to point out any important differences as appropriate. The following skill sheets are provided in this appendix:

Procedure/Skill Evaluation

Student: _____   Level: □ EMT-I □ EMT-P   Date: _____

Time

Evaluator: _____   Start: _____ End: _____   Total: _____ Pass/Fail: _____

Skill Sheet 6: Foreign Body Airway Obstruction Removal (unconscious patient)—Advanced Techniques

Conditions	The candidate should perform this skill on a simulated patient in the supine position under existing indoor, ambulance, or outdoor lighting, temperature, and weather conditions.
Indications	Any patient with a complete foreign body airway obstruction that is not relieved with BLS interventions.
Red Flags	Do not force object further down trachea. Incomplete airway obstructions usually do not require ALS intervention.

Use appropriate standard precautions.	
Assess Airway	
Position unconscious patient in supine position and open the airway.	
Verify complete obstruction.	
Attempt ventilation.	
If unable to ventilate, reposition airway.	
Reattempt ventilation.	
If still unable to ventilate, look inside mouth for visible obstructions.	
Perform BLS Maneuvers	
Perform abdominal thrusts, finger sweeps, etc. (as indicated).	
Visualize Hypopharynx	
Check equipment while assistants perform BLS maneuvers (suction, laryngoscope, Magill forceps).	
Slowly insert laryngoscope blade into mouth and anterior pharynx, and then pharynx and glottic opening, until object can be visualized.	
Do not rapidly advance blade deep into pharynx.	
Make all attempts to avoid pushing the object further down into airway.	
Remove Object	
Insert Magill forceps with right hand and remove object.	
After object has been removed, suction out any residual pieces until airway is clear.	
Unable to Remove Object	
If unable to remove object, have assistant continue abdominal thrusts.	
If object is below glottic opening and can't be removed with Magill forceps:	
Consider cutting the cuff off of an ET tube and attaching the ET tube to suction tubing (use a meconium aspirator or an improvised method depending on the suction tubing that is available).	
Create an airtight seal to grasp the foreign body.	
Remove object carefully past glottic opening and out of airway.	
If airway continues to be obstructed, consider cricothyroidotomy.	
Reassess Airway and Ventilate	
Consider placing ET tube while performing laryngoscopy.	
Alternatively, position airway, insert OPA or NPA, and attempt to ventilate.	
Verify chest rise and fall and adequate ventilation.	

Critical Criteria:
___ Use appropriate personal protective equipment.
___ Verify complete obstruction.
___ Perform BLS maneuvers.
___ Do not advance blade deep into pharynx (do not force object further into airway).

Procedure/Skill Evaluation

Student: _____   Level: □ EMT-I □ EMT-P   Date: _____

Time

Evaluator: _____   Start: _____ End: _____   Total: _____ Pass/Fail: _____

Skill Sheet 7: Endotracheal Intubation

Conditions	The candidate should perform this skill on a simulated patient in the supine position under existing indoor, ambulance, or outdoor lighting, temperature, and weather conditions.
Indications	Patients in respiratory failure or respiratory arrest, patients with an altered level of consciousness and an inability to protect their own airway, and patients in cardiopulmonary arrest.
Red Flags	Consider intubation as a tool for airway management, not as a goal. Esophageal placement can be fatal if unrecognized. Total time of ventilation interruption should not exceed 30 seconds.

Use appropriate standard precautions.	
Confirm BLS airway control is effective and ventilations are being provided correctly.	
If BLS is ineffective, adjust technique as necessary.	
Evaluate Anatomy for Intubation Approach	
Limited rotation and neck extension can limit access to airway.	
Receding chin can place glottic opening high and anterior to laryngoscopic view.	
Trismus or unusually narrow mouth opening can interfere with laryngoscope entry.	
Unusually short, squat neck places the glottic opening anteriorly.	
Abscess or other internal swelling can block passage of tube or view.	
Extend patient's tongue to view posterior oropharynx.	
A reduced or absent view of posterior oropharynx can indicate difficulty in visualizing the glottic opening.	
Decide If Any Modification to Intubation Approach May Be Necessary	
Can include one or more of the following:	
Continued bag-mask ventilation	
Alternative airway device (dual-lumen airway, laryngeal mask airway, retrograde guide wire, etc.)	
Modified laryngoscopy procedure (body position, ET tube introducer, etc.)	
Needle or surgical cricothyroidotomy	
Prepare Equipment	
Endotracheal tube	
Select proper endotracheal tube size.	
Adult: 7.0–7.5 mm for an average female, 8.0–8.5 mm for an average male.	
Pediatric: Use length-based tape to determine appropriate size, or one of the following formulas if length-based tape is not available:	
Peds uncuffed: [Age (in years)/3] + 4	
Peds cuffed: [Age (in years)/4] + 4	
For both adult and pediatric patients, have additional sizes immediately available.	
Open sterile package at proximal end of endotracheal tube.	
Attach 10–12 cc syringe to pilot balloon, and inflate cuff.	
Squeeze distal obturator cuff to determine if it holds air.	
Deflate cuff (completely); keep syringe attached.	
If needed, insert stylette into proximal end of ET tube.	
Confirm that distal tip of stylette does not extend past distal end of tube.	

continued

Skill Sheet 7: Endotracheal Intubation (*continued*)

Laryngoscope	
Select straight or curved blade.	
Adult: Generally a size 3 or 4 blade.	
Pediatric: Use length-based tape to determine blade size.	
Attach blade to handle and turn on light.	
Confirm that the bulb is "tight, white, and bright."	
Suction	
Have suction immediately available.	
Perform Procedure	
Place head, neck, and torso into proper position.	
Adult: Place head and neck into sniffing position, padding occiput and shoulders if needed.	
Pediatric: Elevate shoulders with padding, to move head into a neutral or slightly extended position.	
If cervical spine injury suspected, have assistant maintain manual stabilization.	
Discontinue ventilations and remove BLS airway adjunct.	
Open mouth with cross finger technique if needed.	
Suction if necessary.	
With laryngoscope handle in left hand, insert blade into right side of mouth until the tip of the blade is at the base of the tongue.	
Advance blade toward base of tongue and lift anteriorly to expose epiglottis.	
Tip of curved blade comes to rest in vallecula.	
Tip of straight blade lifts tip of epiglottis directly.	
Visualize and identify epiglottis, glottic opening, arytenoid cartilage, and vocal cords.	
Insert ET tube in right side of mouth and advance toward midline.	
Observe distal ET tube tip pass through glottic opening.	
Advance ET tube until tube marker is at vocal cords.	
Withdraw laryngoscope and close blade against handle, setting it aside.	
Secure tube against upper teeth with fingers of right hand.	
Inflate pilot balloon with syringe until firm, using left hand.	
Detach syringe from cuff.	
Note depth of tube at teeth.	
Remove stylette with left hand.	
Attach bag.	
If using esophageal detector device to confirm ET tube placement, utilize before attaching bag.	
Begin ventilating patient.	
Total time of ventilation interruption does not exceed 30 seconds.	
Confirm Endotracheal Tube Placement	
Use at least two methods of confirmation.	
If ET tube not correctly placed, deflate cuff, withdraw tube, and ventilate patient with bag-mask and OPA.	
Secure Endotracheal Tube	
Use commercial device according to manufacturer's directions.	
Reconfirm tube placement.	
Frequently reassess tube placement during patient encounter.	
Apply cervical collar to further restrict head movement during extrication.	

Critical Criteria:
__ Use appropriate personal protective equipment.
__ Use sterile technique.
__ Total time of ventilation interruption should not exceed 30 seconds.
__ Frequently reassess ET tube placement during patient encounter.

Procedure/Skill Evaluation

Student: _____ Level: ☐ EMT-I ☐ EMT-P Date: _____

Time

Evaluator: _____ Start: _____ End: _____ Total: _____ Pass/Fail: _____

Skill Sheet 13: Rapid Sequence Intubation

Conditions	The candidate should perform this skill on a simulated patient under existing indoor, ambulance, or outdoor lighting, temperature, and weather conditions.
Indications	Patients in respiratory failure or respiratory arrest, patients with an altered level of consciousness and inability to protect their own airway, and patients whose airways cannot be managed by conventional means (due to gag reflex, trismus, etc.)
Red Flags	Consider intubation as a tool for airway management, not as a goal. Esophageal placement can be fatal if unrecognized.

Use appropriate standard precautions	
Evaluate Anatomy for Intubation Approach	
LEMON law	
L — Look externally for masses, goiter, receding mandible, obesity	
E — Evaluate 3-3-2 rule: Adequate mouth opening, hyoid-chin distance, mouth-thyroid cartilage distance	
M — Mallampati scale: Class I through IV (I, II uncomplicated, III, IV difficult)	
O — Obstruction: abscesses, soft tissue swelling in upper airway	
N — Neck mobility: Limited range of motion of the neck	
Prepare Patient	
Inquire about allergies and previous medication reactions.	
Explain what medication you are giving and why.	
Assign specific duties to personnel on scene (ventilation, drawing up meds, etc.).	
Continue to oxygenate and assist ventilation with bag-mask.	
Monitor pulse oximetry and EGG.	
Prepare intubation and secondary airway equipment.	
Establish at least one IV for medication administration.	
Prepare Medications	
Check and recheck medication.	
Solution clarity and expiration date	
Ensure the 5 rights of medication administration.	
Consider Premedication	
Atropine	
Adults exhibiting or at risk of bradycardia	
All pediatric patients	
Lidocaine	
Patients with head injury to blunt an increase in intracranial pressure	
Sedate Patient	
Use medications and dosages per local protocols.	

continued

Skill Sheet 13: Rapid Sequence Intubation (*continued*)

Choose and administer sedative.	
Allow time for sedative to take effect.	
Paralyze Patient	
DO NOT administer paralytics without sedation.	
Use medications and dosages per local protocols.	
Choose and administer paralytic.	
Secure Airway	
Insert oral airway and continue bag-mask ventilations.	
Intubate patient using orotracheal method.	
If orotracheal intubation unsuccessful, attempt alternative airway.	
Dual-lumen airway	
Laryngeal mask airway (LMA)	
Bag-mask ventilations with OPA/NPA	
Cricothyroidotomy (last resort)	
Confirm tube placement.	
Use at least two methods.	
Secure tube with tape or commercial device.	
Place cervical collar to maintain ET position.	
Monitor Patient	
Closely monitor overall patient presentation, EGG, SpO_2, $ETCO_2$.	
Assess vital signs at least every 5 min.	
Closely monitor mental status.	
Additional doses of sedatives or paralytics may be required.	

Sedative Medications	**Paralytic Medications**	
Fentanyl (Sublimaze, narcotic agonist)	Succinylcholine (Anectine, neuromuscular agonist)	
Onset: 1–2 min.	Onset: < 45 sec.	
Duration: ~30 min.	Duration: 5–10 min.	
Midazolam (Versed, benzodiazepine)	Rocuronium (Zemuron, aminosteroid)	
Onset: 2–5 min.	Onset: 60–90 sec.	
Duration: 30–60 min.	Duration: 30 min.	
Etomidate (Amidate, non-barbiturate hypnotic)	Vecuronium (Norcuron, aminosteroid)	
Onset: < 1 min.	Onset: 1–3 min.	
Duration: 3–7 min.	Duration: 45–60 min.	
Propofol (Diprivan, alkylphenol non-barbiturate hypnotic)		
Onset: < 30 sec.		
Duration: < 30 sec. (infusion), 1–5 min. (bolus)		

Critical Criteria:
__   Use standard precautions.
__   Check for patient allergies and sensitivities to medications.
__   Check expiration date of medication.
__   Ensure that at a minimum 5 rights of medication administration have been followed.
__   Evaluate anatomy for intubation approach.
__   Administer sedative prior to administration of paralytic.
__   Ensure alternative airways are available if intubation is not successful.
__   Confirm tube placement (and reconfirm frequently).

Procedure/Skill Evaluation

Student: _____ Level: □ EMT-I □ EMT-P   Date: _____

                                     Time

Evaluator: _____ Start: _____ End: _____ Total: _____ Pass/Fail: _____

Skill Sheet 18: Continuous Positive Airway Pressure (CPAP)

Conditions	The candidate should perform this skill on a simulated patient in a sitting position under existing indoor, ambulance, or outdoor lighting, temperature, and weather conditions.
Indications	A patient experiencing respiratory insufficiency or failure, including pulmonary edema or bronchoconstrictive disease, who is able to follow commands and has oxygen saturations < 90%.
Red Flags	Contraindicated in patients with pneumothorax, apnea, unconsciousness, and full cardiopulmonary arrest. Relative contraindications include trauma with suspicion of elevated intracranial pressure, abdominal distention with risk for vomiting, and hypotension. Patients who have emphysema should be monitored closely when CPAP is applied, as they are at increased risk for barotrauma and pneumothorax.

Use appropriate standard precautions.	
Position the Patient	
Check for adequate blood pressure by the presence of radial pulses.	
Place patient in position that will optimize ease of ventilation (high Fowler, tripod, etc.).	
Prepare the Patient	
Assess patient prior to confirming use of CPAP:	
Primary and secondary survey, especially lung sounds	
ECG, oxygen saturation, $ETCO_2$ monitoring, vital signs	
Peak flow measurement, if available	
Explain procedure to patient.	
Prepare the Equipment	
Connect CPAP generator to a 50–psi oxygen source.	
Do not use oxygen regulator or a flow meter.	
Assemble mask and tubing according to manufacturer's instructions.	
Turn power and oxygen on.	
Set device parameters.	
Turn the rate (frequency) dial to 8–12 per minute.	
Turn the oxygen concentration dial to the lowest setting (28%–29% oxygen).	
Titrate oxygen concentration to an oxygen saturation > 92%.	
Set tidal volume to 10–12 mL/kg (based on local protocol).	
Set pressure relief valve at ± 40 cm H_2O.	
Occlude tubing to test for peak pressure required to activate pressure relief valve and adjust as necessary.	
Perform Procedure	
Have patient hold mask to his or her own face or apply head straps and ensure proper mask seal.	
Insert the CPAP valve into the mask (5, 7.5, or 10 cm H_2O pressure valve).	
Coach patient to breathe normally and adjust to air pressure.	
Frequently reassess patient for desired effects.	
Decrease in level of ventilatory distress	
Oxygen saturation > 92%	
Decreased adventitious lung sounds	
Absence of adverse reactions (barotrauma and pneumothorax)	

Critical Criteria:

___ Use standard precautions.

___ Ensure patient understands procedure.

___ Assess patient prior to and frequently after the application of the CPAP device.

___ Ensure proper parameters (pressure relief, tidal volume, oxygen concentration, rate, etc.).

___ Test pressure relief valve prior to application.

___ Reassess patient for desired or adverse effects.

Procedure/Skill Evaluation

Student: _____ Level: ☐ EMT-I ☐ EMT-P Date: _____

                                     <u>Time</u>

Evaluator: _____ Start: _____ End: _____ Total: _____ Pass/Fail: _____

Skill Sheet 19: Needle Cricothyroidotomy

Conditions	The candidate should perform this skill on a simulated patient under existing indoor, ambulance, or outdoor lighting, temperature, and weather conditions.
Indications	A patient whose airway cannot be managed by BLS or other ALS airway procedures.
Red Flags	This procedure cannot be used if the trachea is transected or if there is significant trauma to the cricoid cartilage or larynx. This technique is designed for short-term use only. It requires a high-pressure source of oxygen, which poses a great risk for spraying blood and body fluids on rescuers and can cause barotrauma in patients (pneumothorax, subcutaneous air, etc.). Does not isolate the airway; thus, aspiration of blood, emesis, etc., is a continued risk.

Don appropriate personal protective equipment.	
Prepare Equipment	
Attach three-way stopcock to oxygen source via tubing.	
Attach extension tubing to stopcock.	
Test to make sure flow is not obstructed.	
Attach a 10-mL syringe to a large-bore plastic catheter with needle.	
Prepare Patient	
Position patient supine if possible, hyperextending the head.	
Maintain neutral cervical alignment if cervical trauma is suspected.	
Locate cricothyroid membrane.	
Locate area inferior to thyroid cartilage.	
Locate area superior to cricoid cartilage.	
Palpate the "notch" between the two.	
Cleanse site thoroughly.	
Iodine or alcohol is preferred (iodine must be dry to be effective).	
Insert Needle into Cricothyroid Membrane	
Stabilize cricoid and thyroid cartilages with one hand.	
Insert needle/catheter, bevel up, through skin and lower half of cricothyroid membrane.	
Insert toward the feet at approximately a 45-degree angle.	
Gently aspirate with attached syringe while inserting.	
When syringe is able to aspirate air, stop advancing needle.	
Continue to advance catheter downward so that hub is flush with skin.	
Withdraw needle and immediately discard into approved sharps container.	
Attach oxygen source to catheter hub.	
Ventilate at approximately 6 breaths per minute with 100% oxygen.	
Allow an inspiratory/expiratory ratio of 1:3.	
Tape catheter to skin.	
Monitor Patient Closely	
Auscultate lung fields.	
Look for improvement in patient condition.	
Continuously monitor for complications and correct as needed.	
Control localized bleeding with direct pressure.	
Esophageal perforation, subcutaneous emphysema, or pneumothorax: Discontinue insufflation.	
Obstruction or kinking of catheter: Adjust position or recannulate.	

Critical Criteria:

__ Don appropriate personal protection equipment (gloves, mask, and eye protection recommended).
__ Insert needle/catheter at a 45-degree angle toward feet.
__ Aspirate syringe as needle is advanced.
__ Recognize incorrect placement.
__ Dispose of needle immediately into appropriate sharps container.
__ Monitor patient continuously for desired effects and complications associated with procedure.

Procedure/Skill Evaluation

Student: _____   Level: ☐ EMT-I ☐ EMT-P   Date: _____

Time

Evaluator: _____   Start: _____ End: _____   Total: _____ Pass/Fail: _____

Skill Sheet 21: Dual-Lumen Airway Device

Conditions	The candidate should perform this skill on a simulated patient in the supine position (stretcher, bed, or floor) under existing indoor, ambulance, or outdoor lighting, temperature, and weather conditions.
Indications	Patients in respiratory failure or arrest, without a gag reflex. Basic airway maneuvers do not maintain a patent airway.
Red Flags	Consider the dual-lumen airway as a tool for airway management use, not as a goal. Not designed for patients under 5 ft or over 7 ft tall. Other contraindications include recent ingestion of caustic substances, latex allergy, esophageal varices, trauma to the trachea, and bleeding below the pharynx. Total time of ventilation interruption should not exceed 30 seconds.

Use appropriate standard precautions.	
Evaluate Anatomy for Device Insertion	
Limited rotation and neck extension can limit access to airway.	
Trismus or unusually narrow mouth opening can interfere with device entry.	
Abscess or other internal swelling can block tube passage or view.	
Prepare Equipment	
Select proper size tube.	
37 cm for patients between 5 and 6 ft	
41 cm for patients over 6 ft	
Attach 100-mL syringe to blue port and test cuff.	
Attach 20-mL syringe to white port and test cuff.	
Lubricate distal tip with water-soluble jelly if possible.	
Have suction immediately available.	
Perform Procedure	
Place head, neck, and torso into "neutral" position.	
Insert left thumb into mouth to lift and control tongue.	
Insert airway in right side of mouth, advancing toward midline.	
Insert until teeth are between the black lines.	
Inflate oropharyngeal balloon to proper volume (80–100 mL).	
Inflate distal balloon to proper volume (5–15 mL).	
Total time of ventilation interruption should not exceed 30 seconds.	
Confirm Device Placement	
Ventilate through blue tube first.	
Assess chest rise.	
Assess for sound over stomach.	
Assess breath sounds.	
If unable to ventilate through first tube, ventilate through white tube next.	
Reassess chest rise.	
Reassess for sound over stomach.	
Reassess breath sounds.	
Secure tube.	
Continually reassess tube position during care and transport.	

Critical Criteria:
__ Use appropriate standard precautions.
__ Ventilation interruption should not exceed 30 seconds at any one time.
__ Continually confirm tube placement during patient encounter.

Procedure/Skill Evaluation

Student: _____   Level: □ EMT-I □ EMT-P   Date: _____

<u>Time</u>

Evaluator: _____   Start: _____ End: _____   Total: _____ Pass/Fail: _____

Skill Sheet 27: Chest Auscultation

Conditions	The candidate should perform this skill on a simulated patient under existing indoor, ambulance, or outdoor lighting, temperature, and weather conditions.
Indications	Any patient who is being evaluated by EMS.
Red Flags	Must be conducted over bare skin.

Use appropriate standard precautions.	
Prepare Equipment	
Clean diaphragm of stethoscope with alcohol prep or other disinfectant.	
Adjust auricles (earpieces) of stethoscope to fit properly.	
Auricles should be aimed slightly forward.	
Ensure proper placement in the ear canal.	
Prepare Patient	
Expose and inspect chest prior to listening to breath sounds.	
Position patient as to easily auscultate all lung fields.	
Perform Procedure	
Using light to moderate finger pressure, place bell on chest beginning at the fourth intercostal space, midclavicular line, on the closest side.	
Direct patient to inhale deeply and then exhale.	
Listen; then immediately listen to the same lung field on the opposite side.	
Repeat previous steps at the following sites:	
Midclavicular, fourth intercostal space	
Midclavicular, second intercostal space	
Midclavicular, above clavicles	
Midaxillary, fifth intercostal space	
Midaxillary, fourth intercostal space	
Posterior chest (each side):	
Area between top of scapula and spine	
Area between bottom of scapula and spine	

Critical Criteria:

__   Use appropriate standard precautions.
__   Listen bilaterally across lung fields.
__   Place bell over bare skin.

Procedure/Skill Evaluation

Student: _____   Level: □ EMT-I □ EMT-P   Date: _____

Time

Evaluator: _____   Start: _____ End: _____   Total: _____ Pass/Fail: _____

Skill Sheet 32: Primary Survey

Conditions	The candidate should perform this skill on a simulated patient under existing indoor, ambulance, or outdoor lighting, temperature, and weather conditions.
Indications	Every patient every time.
Red Flags	Life-threatening conditions must be identified and managed during the primary survey.

Use appropriate standard precautions.	
Scene Size-Up	
Consider scene safety concerns.	
Assess environment for clues to patient condition.	
Evaluate mechanism of injury or nature of illness.	
Determine number of patients.	
Evaluate need for additional resources.	
Primary Survey	
If mechanism suggests possible cervical spine injury, establish manual stabilization of the head and neck.	
Establish level of consciousness using AVPU.	
Evaluate and manage *airway* patency.	
Adjust patient position or perform basic airway maneuvers as needed.	
If BLS procedures fail to establish airway patency, institute ALS procedures.	
Evaluate and manage *breathing*.	
Assess breathing rate, tidal volume, and respiratory effort.	
Provide supplemental oxygen for patient with appropriate rate, volume, and effort.	
Assist ventilations with bag-mask if patient is in respiratory failure.	
If open wound is noted to neck or chest, apply immediate pressure with gloved hand to minimize air entry into thorax.	
If mechanism suggests tension pneumothorax, auscultate lung fields, percuss for hyperresonance, and check for JVD. Decompress if needed.	
Evaluate and manage *circulation*.	
Control major external bleeding.	
Assess presence, rate, and quality of peripheral pulse.	
Check carotid pulse if radial pulse weak or absent.	
Observe skin signs.	
Lay patient supine if pulses are weak or absent or if skin color is poor.	
Evaluate and manage *disability*.	
Reconsider level of consciousness.	
If patient has an altered mental status, be prepared for rapid airway control.	
If cervical spine injury is suspected, ask patient to move fingers and toes.	
Expose patient as needed to conduct physical examination.	
Inspect torso for major bleeding and life-threatening injury.	
Inspect pelvis and lower extremities for major bleeding or hip fracture.	
Decide if early transport is critical to patient care.	

Critical Criteria:
__ Use appropriate standard precautions.
__ Consider scene safety issues.
__ Establish need for cervical spine stabilization.
__ Manage airway threats immediately.
__ Manage breathing threats immediately.
__ Manage circulation threats immediately.

Procedure/Skill Evaluation

Student: _____   Level: ☐ EMT-I ☐ EMT-P   Date: _____

Time

Evaluator: _____   Start: _____ End: _____   Total: _____ Pass/Fail: _____

Skill Sheet 33: Secondary Survey

Conditions	The candidate should perform this skill on a simulated patient under existing indoor, ambulance, or outdoor lighting, temperature, and weather conditions.
Indications	Any patient who is being evaluated by EMS. The secondary survey focuses on the areas of the patient's past medical history and the body related to the presenting condition or chief complaint.
Red Flags	The patient's condition may prevent the paramedic from obtaining a medical history. Life threats found during the primary survey must be addressed before conducting a secondary survey. This checklist is not designed to be followed in the order presented nor is it implied that all steps must be done each time.

Taking a Medical History

Use appropriate standard precautions.	
Introduce self to patient if possible.	
Note Statistical Patient Information	
Age	
Sex	
Weight (kg)	
General cleanliness and grooming habits	
Identify Chief Complaint	
Use OPQRST mnemonic.	
Onset—events leading up to chief complaint.	
Provocation/palliation—actions taken by the patient that worsen or relieve the complaint.	
Quality—if complaint is of pain, an open-ended description of the pain.	
Radiation/related symptoms—if complaint is of pain, where is it being referred? Are there any other complaints of discomfort related to the chief complaint?	
Severity—rate discomfort on a 1–10 scale, or using a face scale.	
Time—when did the complaint begin? How long has it been going on? If intermittent, how many times?	
Elicit Pertinent Medical History	
Use AMPLE mnemonic.	
Allergies—to medications (prescribed, OTC, herbal/home remedies); environmental triggers	
Medications—prescribed, OTC, herbal/home remedies	
Past medical history—related to current complaint; other major disease processes, psychiatric, or trauma history	
Last oral intake—liquid or solid; amount ingested	
Events—recent changes in habit, diet, exercise, stress	
Note Current Health Status	
Tobacco, drug, and/or alcohol use	
Exercise	
Environmental conditions	
Patient's outlook	
Prior Health History	
General state of health	
Immunizations	
Family history	

Physical Examination

General Appearance (Inspect, Smell)	
Current state of health	
Growth and development	
Odors	
Examine the Head, Ears, Eyes, Nose, and Throat (Inspect, Palpate, Smell)	
Head: Hair and scalp	
Face: Symmetry, trauma, skin condition, scars	
Eyes: Sclera, conjunctiva	

continued

Skill Sheet 33: Secondary Survey (*continued*)

Lacrimal swelling or discharge	
Visual fields	
Visual acuity	
Pupils, both direct and consensual	
Extraocular movement	
Ears: (condition, shape, size)	
Bleeding or discharge	
Hearing acuity	
Nose: (condition, structure, shape)	
Bleeding, discharge, trauma	
Mouth, lips:	
Teeth	
Odors	
Masses or trauma in mouth or throat	
Examine the Neck (Inspect, Palpate, Auscultate)	
Symmetry	
Jugular vein distention	
Carotid pulses	
Carotid bruits, thrills	
Anatomical structures—thyroid gland, lymph nodes, stoma, masses	
Accessory muscle use, stridor	
Medical alert jewelry	
Cervical spine tenderness	
Examine the Chest (Inspect, Palpate, Auscultate)	
Overall shape and size	
Symmetrical rise and fall	
Anatomical structures: ribs, thoracic spine, musculature	
Intercostal, sternal notch retraction	
Anterior and posterior breath sounds	
PMI and heart tones	
Percussion	
Examine the Abdomen (Inspect, Palpate)	
Overall shape and size	
Discoloration patterns	
Tenderness	
Anatomical structures—liver, masses, flank, lumbar spine	
Examine the Pelvis/Genitalia (Inspect, Palpate)	
Lesions, discharge, swelling, priapism	
Anatomical structures: pelvic ring, pubic symphysis, genitalia	
Examine the Lower Extremities (Inspect, Palpate)	
Skin condition, scars, trauma, deformity	
Range of motion (ROM)	
Palpate pulses; assess color and temperature	
Symmetry between legs (strength, gait)	
Examine the Upper Extremities (Inspect, Palpate)	
Skin condition, scars, trauma, deformity	
Range of motion (ROM)	
Palpate pulses; assess color and temperature	
Symmetry between arms (strength, grip)	
Examine the Back (Inspect, Palpate, Auscultate)	
Skin condition, trauma, scars, deformity	
Tenderness	
If needed, auscultate posterior lung sounds	

Critical Criteria:
- __ Use appropriate standard precautions.
- __ Speak to the patient professionally and with respect.
- __ Use appropriate body language.
- __ Adjust interview technique for age or diversity factors.
- __ Use consistent, logical format to frame questions.
- __ Use a combination of open- and closed-ended questioning techniques.

Procedure/Skill Evaluation

Student: _____   Level: □ EMT-I □ EMT-P   Date: _____

Time

Evaluator: _____   Start: _____ End: _____   Total: _____ Pass/Fail: _____

Skill Sheet 37: ECG Acquisition

Conditions	The candidate should perform this skill on a simulated patient under existing indoor, ambulance, or outdoor lighting, temperature, and weather conditions.
Indications	Any patient exhibiting chest pain of possible cardiac origin or other symptoms of a possible myocardial infarction.
Red Flags	Avoid attaching electrodes to skin that is burned, injured, or otherwise not intact. Do not delay the management of life threats for acquisition of an ECG.

Use appropriate standard precautions.	
Prepare Equipment	
Select electrode placement sites.	
At least 10 cm from the heart for adults.	
Attach monitor cables to self-adhesive leads.	
Prepare Patient	
If possible, explain procedure to patient.	
Expose chest.	
Ensure skin is not broken or bleeding.	
Shave hair from site if particularly thick.	
Cleanse area with alcohol prep pad if dirty.	
Allow alcohol to dry before placing leads.	
Perform Procedure	
Turn monitor on.	

Limb Lead Monitoring		12-Lead Monitoring	
Attach limb leads to appropriate limbs (may be 3 or 4 leads).		Attach the 4 limb leads to appropriate leads.	
For MCL_1 attach LL lead to fourth intercostal space, just right of sternum.		Attach precordial (chest) leads. □ V_1—fourth intercostal space, right of the sternum □ V_2—fourth intercostal space, left of the sternum □ V_4—fifth intercostal space, midclavicular line	
Assess baseline rhythm.		□ V_3—on a line midway between V_2 and V_4	
Print ECG strip as necessary.		□ V_5—anterior axillary line on same horizontal level as V_4, between V_4 and V_5 □ V_6—midaxillary line at same level as V_4 and V_5	
		Connect cable for precordial leads to monitor, if necessary.	
		Ask patient to remain still and "breathe normally."	
		Acquire ECG reading.	

If artifact or "noisy data":	
View each individual lead on monitor to determine which one is "noisy."	
Reposition lead, replace if necessary.	

Critical Criteria:
__ Use appropriate standard precautions.
__ Accurately place leads on patient.
__ Ensure skin is clean and clear prior to lead placement.

Procedure/Skill Evaluation

Student: _____ Level: □ EMT-I □ EMT-P Date: _____

Time

Evaluator: _____ Start: _____ End: _____ Total: _____ Pass/Fail: _____

Skill Sheet 38: Synchronized Cardioversion and Defibrillation

Conditions	The candidate should perform this skill on a simulated patient under existing indoor, ambulance, or outdoor lighting, temperature, and weather conditions.
Indications	Defibrillation: ventricular fibrillation, pulseless ventricular tachycardia, when synchronization circuit is not working Synchronized cardioversion: unstable supraventricular tachycardia, unstable ventricular tachycardia; stable SVT or VT refractory to pharmacological interventions.
Red Flags	Do not delay CPR for any interval of time when defibrillating. Sedate alert patients if possible prior to cardioversion. *Electrical therapy is dangerous and can harm rescuers if they are in contact with the patient during delivery of electric charge.*

Use appropriate standard precautions.	
Prepare Equipment	
Manual paddles: connect to defibrillator and apply gel to paddle surface.	
Hands-off pads: check expiration date of pads and connect to defibrillator.	
Prepare Patient	
If possible, explain procedure to patient.	
Move patient to another location if on electrically conductive material (metal flooring, puddles of water, wet grass, etc.).	
Expose chest.	
Paddles—apex and sternum	
Pads—apex and sternum or anterior and posterior left chest	
Shave hair from site if particularly thick.	
Cleanse area with alcohol prep pad if visibly soiled.	
Allow alcohol to dry before placing pads or paddles.	
Dry patient if wet or diaphoretic.	
Perform Procedure	
If necessary, sedate patient.	
Attach electrodes to patient.	
Paddles: apply firm, even pressure against chest.	
Pads: remove adhesive backing and apply firmly to skin.	
Confirm rhythm on monitor.	
Set energy level, following manufacturer's recommendation.	
If performing a synchronized cardioversion, activate circuit by pressing button on monitor.	
Confirm synchronization by looking for arrows, dots, or other indicator above QRS.	
Charge defibrillator to appropriate energy setting.	
Clear the patient.	
Look around the patient and speak loudly, "One—I'm clear, two—everyone's clear, three, shocking."	
Deliver shock on "three."	
Paddles: press down firmly on patient and depress both shock buttons simultaneously.	
Pads: press shock button on defibrillator.	
Assess the Patient	
Confirm successful shock delivery by checking for rhythm conversion.	
If rhythm converted, check for corresponding pulse and blood pressure.	
If rhythm did not convert, prepare for additional electrical therapy as directed.	

Critical Criteria:
___ Use appropriate standard precautions.
___ Apply gel to paddles.
___ Ensure good contact between pad/paddles and patient.
___ Clear patient before delivering electric charge.
___ Assess patient and ECG rhythm before and after therapy.

Procedure/Skill Evaluation

Student: _____   Level: □ EMT-I □ EMT-P   Date: _____

Time

Evaluator: _____   Start: _____ End: _____   Total: _____ Pass/Fail: _____

Skill Sheet 39: Transcutaneous Cardiac Pacing

Conditions	The candidate should perform this skill on a simulated patient under existing indoor, ambulance, or outdoor lighting, temperature, and weather conditions.
Indications	Patient experiencing symptomatic bradycardia secondary to high-grade block; symptomatic bradycardia refractory to atropine.
Red Flags	Significant patient discomfort; consider sedation if IV access available. Ensure good contact between pads and patient to minimize energy levels needed for capture.

Use appropriate standard precautions.	
Prepare Equipment	
Ensure safety.	
Prepare pacing pads.	
Check expiration date of pads.	
Connect pads to pacing cable, then to monitor.	
Prepare Patient	
If possible, explain procedure to patient.	
Place ECG limb leads; ensure continuous ECG monitoring.	
Locate pad placement site.	
Expose chest.	
Locate apex and sternum or anterior and posterior left chest.	
Prepare Site	
Ensure skin is not broken or bleeding.	
Shave hair from site if particularly thick.	
Cleanse area with alcohol prep pad if visibly soiled.	
Allow alcohol to dry before placing pads.	
Dry patient if wet or diaphoretic.	
Perform Procedure	
Consider sedation.	
Attach electrode pads to patient.	
Remove adhesive backing and apply firmly and completely to skin.	
Confirm rhythm on monitor and patient symptomatology.	
Set desired rate.	
60–100 per minute, usually around 80 per minute.	
Set energy delivery level.	
Start at zero; slowly increase amperage until capture is seen.	
Electrical: look for QRS *and* T wave after each pacer spike.	
Mechanical: palpate for a carotid/femoral pulse with each QRS complex.	
Set amperage 10% above level of electrical capture.	
If no capture, consider other therapies.	
Continuously monitor rhythm and response to pacing.	

Critical Criteria:
___ Use appropriate standard precautions.
___ Place pads correctly.
___ Ensure good contact between pads and patient.
___ Check for electrical and mechanical capture.

Procedure/Skill Evaluation

Student: _____ Level: □ EMT-I □ EMT-P Date: _____

Time

Evaluator: _____ Start: _____ End: _____ Total: _____ Pass/Fail: _____

Skill Sheet 42: Intravenous Access

Conditions	The candidate should perform this skill on a simulated patient under existing indoor, ambulance, or outdoor lighting, temperature, and weather conditions.
Indications	Patients who require or may potentially require administration of fluids or intravenous medications.
Red Flags	Prep the site with as aseptic or medically clean technique as field conditions permit. Avoid starting an IV on the same arm as a dialysis shunt. IV infiltration, especially when medications are being administered, can cause serious and irreversible tissue damage. Avoid using areas of burned skin or heavy vein scarring. Establish a patent IV line within 6 minutes.

Use appropriate standard precautions.	
Prepare Equipment	
Prepare IV administration set.	
Select proper fluid.	
Check date, and clarity.	
Use warmed fluids if possible.	
Select proper administration set (macrodrip or microdrip).	
Close the roller clamp.	
Connect administration set to fluid.	
Hold fluid bag upside down and remove tab covering access port.	
Remove cap from sharp end of administration set; insert firmly into port on IV bag.	
Hang bag right-side up on IV hook or pole.	
Squeeze drip chamber gently until chamber is filled to line (approximately half full).	
Run fluid through tubing until free of air; then turn flow off.	
Prepare cannulation equipment.	
Select proper size angiocatheter.	
Consider intended use (e.g., fluid therapy, medication line).	
Consider size and fragility of vein.	
Gather tourniquet, gauze pad, alcohol prep, tape or commercial securing device.	
Prepare Cannulation Site	
Apply tourniquet or blood pressure cuff (inflated to just below diastolic BP):	
Proximal to wrist for hand veins	
Proximal to elbow for forearm veins	
Select site:	
Between knuckles, dorsal thumb, back of hands, ventral or dorsal forearms, ventral elbow (antecubital fossa).	
Palpate and look for veins that are straight and do not bifurcate proximally.	
Cleanse site.	
Wipe visible dirt from site with alcohol prep pad.	
Repeat with fresh alcohol prep pads until they are visibly clean after wiping.	

continued

Skill Sheet 42: Intravenous Access (*continued*)

Use fresh alcohol or iodine prep pad to wipe site outward, in a spiral motion.	
Do not palpate after wiping.	
Control site.	
Use nondominant hand to hold patient's hand or arm; pull skin taut.	
Ensure fingers are not in the potential path of needle.	
Perform Procedure	
Position angiocatheter correctly in hand.	
Bevel on needle facing upward	
Flashback chamber visible	
Index finger of dominant hand able to slide catheter over needle easily	
Insert needle into vein.	
Insert along path of vein at a < 45-degree angle to skin surface.	
Attempt to advance directly into vein with one smooth motion, without stopping.	
Monitor for and verbalize flashback.	
After flashback, advance angiocatheter an additional 1–2 mm into vein.	
Advance catheter with index finger while simultaneously pulling needle out.	
If angiocatheter is designed for needle-stick protection, advance until device engages.	
Remove tourniquet, unless blood sample required.	
Disconnect needle from catheter hub.	
Use nondominant hand to occlude vein proximal to end of catheter.	
Immediately place needle in approved sharps container.	
Connect IV administration set to catheter hub.	
Open IV fluid control fully to check IV patency.	
Ensure free flow through drip chamber.	
Inspect/palpate around cannulation site for infiltration (swelling/rigidity).	
If infiltrated, immediately discontinue IV and apply pressure with sterile dressing.	
Decrease flow to desired rate.	
Secure Site and Tubing	
Secure venipuncture site.	
Utilize transparent commercial device, if available (e.g., Tegaderm, Veniguard, Bio-occlusive).	
Wrap tape in chevron or "awareness ribbon" pattern around hub.	
Do not use nonsterile tape directly over site where catheter enters skin.	
Create a safety loop.	
Extend tubing a few inches distal to site.	
Curve tubing 180 degrees so that it runs proximally, creating a loop.	
Secure with tape.	
Tape at least once on tubing proximal to site.	

Critical Criteria:

__ Use appropriate standard precautions.
__ Maintain aseptic or medically clean technique throughout procedure.
__ Avoid catheter shear.
__ Observe for infiltration.
__ Establish a patent IV line within 6 minutes.
__ Dispose of sharps in an appropriate container.

Procedure/Skill Evaluation

Student: _____ Level: ☐ EMT-I ☐ EMT-P   Date: _____

Time

Evaluator: _____ Start: _____ End: _____ Total: _____ Pass/Fail: _____

Skill Sheet 45: Intraosseous Access and Drug Administration

Conditions	The candidate should perform this skill on a simulated patient under existing indoor, ambulance, or outdoor lighting, temperature, and weather conditions.
Indications	A patient who requires intravascular access for medication administration and/or volume resuscitation and for whom IV access is not readily available.
Red Flags	Long-bone deformity distal to access site on same bone; unable to locate landmarks.

Use appropriate standard precautions.	
Prepare Equipment	
Prepare IV administration set.	
Select proper fluid.	
Check date and clarity.	
Use warmed fluids if possible.	
Select proper administration set (macrodrip or microdrip set).	
Close the roller clamp.	
Connect administration set to fluid.	
Hold IV bag upside down and remove tab covering access port.	
Remove cap from sharp end of administration set and insert spike firmly into port on IV bag.	
Hang IV bag right-side up on IV hook or pole.	
Squeeze drip chamber gently until chamber is filled to line.	
Run fluid through tubing until free of air; then turn flow off.	
Select appropriate size needle.	
18 gauge for newborns	
15 gauge all others	
Prepare a 10-mL syringe with 5-mL saline.	
Prepare an additional syringe and a three-way stopcock.	
Prepare Patient	
If possible, explain procedure to patient and/or parent.	
Select appropriate site.	
Proximal tibia	
Distal femur	
Sternum/manubrium	
Superior iliac crest	
Clean site with alcohol and/or iodine.	
Stabilize site.	
Stabilize extremity from above.	
Pad underside of extremity so site is lying flat.	

continued

Skill Sheet 45: Intraosseous Access and Drug Administration (*continued*)

Perform Procedure	
Position needle correctly in hand.	
Needle shaft pointed 90 degrees perpendicular to bone.	
Fingers of stabilizing hand away from insertion point.	
Insert needle into bone.	
Manual needles: use a "boring" technique.	
Mechanical needles: follow manufacturer's directions.	
Feel a "pop" sensation as needle enters intraosseous space.	
Stabilize catheter and remove needle.	
Catheter will stand straight up if correctly inserted.	
Immediately place needle in approved sharps container.	
Confirm placement.	
Draw marrow sample using empty syringe.	
Flush needle with 5 ml saline using second syringe.	
If swelling noted, remove catheter.	
If flush difficult to administer, withdraw catheter slightly and reattempt saline flush.	
Secure catheter to site.	
Connect three-way stopcock to catheter hub.	
Connect IV administration set to stopcock.	
Open IV roller clamp and stopcock fully to check IV patency.	
Ensure free flow through drip chamber.	
Inspect/palpate around cannulation site for infiltration (swelling or rigidity).	
If infiltrated, immediately discontinue IV and apply pressure with sterile dressing.	
Decrease flow to desired rate.	
Administer Medication with Three-Way Stopcock	
Prepare medication.	
Confirm medication "rights."	
Turn stopcock valve off to all ports.	
Clean medication port.	
Insert medication syringe into open port on stopcock.	
Open stopcock valve to open medication port.	
Administer medication at appropriate rate and amount.	
Close stopcock valve to all ports and remove medication syringe.	
Open stopcock valve to flush remaining medication out of administration set, and return to desired drip rate.	
Assess for any changes to patient's condition.	

Critical Criteria:
___ Use appropriate standard precautions.
___ Use intraosseous needle in a safe manner.
___ Immediately dispose of sharps in appropriate container.
___ Observe for infiltration at site.
___ Ensure that 5 rights of medication administration are followed.

Procedure/Skill Evaluation

Student: _____   Level: □ EMT-I □ EMT-P   Date: _____

Time

Evaluator: _____   Start: _____ End: _____   Total: _____ Pass/Fail: _____

Skill Sheet 48: Intravenous Drug Bolus

Conditions	The candidate should perform this skill on a simulated patient under existing indoor, ambulance, or outdoor lighting, temperature, and weather conditions.
Indications	A patient who requires a medication bolus delivered intravenously.
Red Flags	Medications given through the IV route are rapid acting; deliver medications at appropriate rate and time intervals. Always observe for infiltration.

Use appropriate standard precautions.	
Inquire about allergies and previous medication reactions.	
When possible, explain what medication you are giving and why.	
Prepare Equipment	
Check patency of established IV.	
Check and recheck medication:	
Solution clarity and expiration date	
Right patient	
Right medication	
Right dose	
Right route	
Right time	
Assemble prefilled syringe or draw up medication into syringe.	
Expel air.	
Perform Procedure	
Clean injection site with antiseptic.	
Insert needle into medication port.	
Stop IV flow by pinching IV tubing near medication port or closing roller clamp, etc.	
Depress plunger on syringe and deliver medication at appropriate rate.	
Remove needle.	
Immediately place needle and syringe into appropriate sharps disposal container.	
Flush IV tubing.	
Readjust drip rate.	
Document dose and time of administration.	
Monitor Patient	
Continue to monitor injection site for signs of swelling or reaction.	
Obtain full set of vital signs.	
Monitor patient for adverse effects.	
Monitor patient for desired effects.	

Critical Criteria:
__ Use appropriate standard precautions.
__ Check for patient allergies and medication reactions.
__ Ensure at a minimum that 5 rights of medication administration have been followed.
__ Cleanse the IV port prior to injection.
__ Immediately dispose of sharps in an appropriate container.
__ Monitor patient for changes in condition.

Procedure/Skill Evaluation

Student: _____   Level: ☐ EMT-I ☐ EMT-P   Date: _____

Time

Evaluator: _____   Start: _____ End: _____   Total: _____ Pass/Fail: _____

Skill Sheet 49: Intravenous Drug Infusion

Conditions	The candidate should perform this skill on a simulated patient under existing indoor, ambulance, or outdoor lighting, temperature, and weather conditions.
Indications	A patient who requires medications continuously delivered intravenously.
Red Flags	Medications given through the IV route are rapid acting; pay close attention to the rate of administration. Always observe for infiltration of primary IV.

Use appropriate standard precautions.	
Inquire about allergies and previous medication reactions.	
Explain what medication you are giving and why.	
Prepare Equipment	
Check patency of established IV.	
Check and recheck medication:	
Solution clarity and expiration date	
Right patient	
Right medication	
Right dose	
Right route	
Right time	
Calculate drug dosage and drip rate.	
Assemble prefilled syringe or draw up medication into syringe.	
Expel air if needed.	
Select appropriate IV fluid.	
Check solution clarity and expiration date.	
Cleanse medication port of infusion bag with alcohol pad.	
Add medication to IV solution or spike premixed IV bag.	
Mark solution properly with medication label.	
Mark label with date, time, medication, concentration, preparer's initials.	
Select appropriate administration set (60 drops per milliliter set).	
Attach administration set to infusion bag.	
Connect bag to tubing.	
Fill drip chamber to line (approximately half full).	
Flush tubing.	
Maintain sterility of tubing end.	
Perform Proper Technique	
Clean medication port of main IV line with alcohol pad.	
Connect infusion IV set to main IV and stop flow of main IV.	
Set drip rate on infusion IV to deliver correct dose of medication.	
Secure infusion line to main IV line with tape or commercial device.	
Document dose and time of administration.	
Monitor Patient	
Continue to monitor injection site of main IV for signs of swelling or reaction.	
Obtain full set of vital signs.	
Monitor patient for adverse effects.	
Monitor patient for desired effects.	

Critical Criteria:
___ Use appropriate standard precautions.
___ Check for patient allergies and medication reactions.
___ Ensure at a mimimum that 5 rights of medication administration have been followed.
___ Cleanse medication port prior to insertion of needle.
___ Dispose of sharps immediately after use in appropriate container.
___ Ensure that infusion is set at proper rate.
___ Monitor patient for desired and adverse effects.

Procedure/Skill Evaluation

Student: _____   Level: □ EMT-I □ EMT-P   Date: _____

Time

Evaluator: _____   Start: _____ End: _____   Total: _____ Pass/Fail: _____

Skill Sheet 50: Intramuscular Drug Administration

Conditions	The candidate should perform this skill on a simulated patient under existing indoor, ambulance, or outdoor lighting, temperature, and weather conditions.
Indications	A patient whose condition requires the administration of a medication through the intramuscular route. A patient who does not have vascular access and for whom the required medication can be administered intramuscularly.
Red Flags	May not be effective in poorly perfused tissue.

Use appropriate standard precautions.	
Inquire about allergies and previous medication reactions.	
Explain what medication you are giving and why.	
Prepare Equipment	
Check and recheck medication:	
Solution clarity and expiration date	
Right patient	
Right medication	
Right dose	
Right route	
Right time	
Draw medication into syringe.	
Needle should be 20 gauge or smaller.	
Expel air from syringe.	
Prepare Patient	
Locate administration site.	
Deltoid muscle	
Vastus lateralis (lateral thigh) muscle	
Ventrogluteal or dorsogluteal muscles (buttocks)	
Administer Medication	
Cleanse site with alcohol prep pad.	
Pinch to lift skin slightly.	
Smoothly and quickly insert needle at a 90-degree angle to the skin.	
Advance into muscle layer.	
Attempt to aspirate by pulling back on plunger of syringe.	
If blood is aspirated, withdraw needle, control bleeding, and attempt injection at another site.	
Slowly depress plunger on syringe and administer medication.	
Remove needle.	
Immediately place needle and syringe into approved sharps disposal container.	
Apply sterile gauze and direct pressure to site.	
Document dose and time of administration.	
Monitor Patient	
Continue to monitor injection site for signs of swelling or reaction.	
Obtain full set of vital signs.	
Monitor patient for adverse effects.	
Monitor patient for desired effects.	

Critical Criteria:

__ Use appropriate standard precautions.
__ Check for patient allergies.
__ Ensure at a minimum that 5 rights of medication administration have been followed.
__ Insert needle at 90-degree angle.
__ Aspirate for blood prior to medication administration.
__ Immediately dispose of sharps in appropriate container.
__ Monitor patient for desired and adverse effects.

Procedure/Skill Evaluation

Student: _____   Level: □ EMT-I □ EMT-P   Date: _____

Time

Evaluator: _____   Start: _____ End: _____ Total: _____ Pass/Fail: _____

Skill Sheet 52: Nebulized Drug Administration

Conditions	The candidate should perform this skill on a simulated patient in a sitting or supine position (stretcher, chair, or bed) under existing indoor, ambulance, or outdoor lighting, temperature, and weather conditions.
Indications	A patient whose condition requires the administration of a medication through the nebulized route.
Red Flags	Equipment used to nebulize medications can vary significantly. Practice with your local system's equipment until you are comfortable with assembly and use.

Use appropriate standard precautions.	
Prepare Patient	
Assess patient to determine if in respiratory distress or failure.	
Inquire about allergies and previous medication reactions.	
Explain what medication you are giving and why.	
Prepare Equipment	
Check and recheck medication:	
Solution clarity and expiration date	
Right patient	
Right medication	
Right dose	
Right route	
Right time	
Assemble Device	
Equipment used to nebulize medications includes masks, handheld devices, and in-line nebulizers.	
Follow manufacturer's directions for proper assembly.	
Place medication into nebulizer chamber prior to sealing it tightly.	
Attach oxygen tubing to nebulizer chamber.	
When using an in-line nebulizer, attach a second oxygen source to the bag-mask if available.	
Administer Medication	
Adjust the flow of oxygen to the nebulizer to create a steady mist of medication (6–8 L/min).	
For conscious patient in ventilatory distress, instruct the patient to seal lips around mouthpiece, then breathe deeply.	
Keep handheld nebulizer mouthpiece securely in mouth, or	
Adjust mask so it fits snugly over patient's mouth and nose.	
For patient requiring assisted ventilations, use bag-mask to administer medication.	
Time bag squeeze to patient's inspiratory effort.	
Provide ventilations at a rate of 12–20 per minute.	
In-line nebulizers should be kept in an upright position.	
Carefully and correctly document dose and time of administration.	
Monitor Patient	
Obtain full set of vital signs.	
Monitor patient for adverse effects.	
Monitor patient for desired effects.	

Critical Criteria:
___ Use appropriate standard precautions.
___ Ensure at a minimum that 5 rights of medication administration are followed.
___ Assist ventilations as necessary.
___ Keep in-line nebulizer chamber upright.

Procedure/Skill Evaluation

Student: _____   Level: □ EMT-I □ EMT-P   Date: _____

Time

Evaluator: _____   Start: _____   End: _____   Total: _____   Pass/Fail: _____

Skill Sheet 53: Subcutaneous Drug Administration

Conditions	The candidate should perform this skill on a simulated patient under existing indoor, ambulance, or outdoor lighting, temperature, and weather conditions.
Indications	A patient whose condition requires the administration of a medication through the subcutaneous route.
Red Flags	May not be effective in poorly perfusing tissue.

Use appropriate standard precautions.	
Inquire about allergies and previous medication reactions.	
Explain what medication you are giving and why.	
Prepare Equipment	
Check and recheck medication:	
Solution clarity and expiration date	
Right patient	
Right medication	
Right dose	
Right route	
Right time	
Draw medication into syringe.	
Needle should be 22 gauge or smaller.	
No more than 1 mL of fluid should be delivered.	
Expel air from syringe.	
Prepare Patient	
Locate administration site (able to pinch about 1 in. of skin easily)	
Upper arms	
Abdomen	
Thighs	
Administer Medication	
Cleanse site with alcohol prep.	
Pinch to lift skin slightly.	
Smoothly insert needle at a 45-degree angle to the skin.	
Advance into subcutaneous layer.	
Attempt to aspirate by pulling on plunger of syringe.	
If blood is aspirated, withdraw needle and control bleeding.	
Slowly depress plunger on syringe and administer medication.	
Remove needle.	
Immediately place needle and syringe into appropriate sharps disposal container.	
Apply sterile gauze and direct pressure to site.	
Carefully and correctly document dose and time of administration.	
Monitor Patient	
Continue to monitor injection site for signs of swelling or reaction.	
Obtain full set of vital signs.	
Monitor patient for adverse effects.	
Monitor patient for desired effects.	

Critical Criteria:

__ Use appropriate standard precautions.
__ Check for patient allergies and medication reactions.
__ Check expiration date of medication.
__ Ensure at a minimum that 5 rights of medication administration have been followed.
__ Insert needle at 45-degree angle.
__ Immediately dispose of sharps in appropriate container.
__ Aspirate for blood prior to medication administration.
__ Monitor patient for desired and adverse effects.

Procedure/Skill Evaluation

Student: _____   Level: □ EMT-I □ EMT-P   Date: _____

Time

Evaluator: _____   Start: _____ End: _____   Total: _____ Pass/Fail: _____

Skill Sheet 58: Rectal Drug Administration

Conditions	The candidate should perform this skill on a simulated pediatric patient under existing indoor, ambulance, or outdoor lighting, temperature, and weather conditions.
Indications	A pediatric patient whose condition requires the administration of a medication via the rectal route.
Red Flags	Feeding tube or syringe (without needle) must be inserted deep enough into rectal space in order to deliver medication. Forceful insertion can perforate the bowel wall. Remove needle prior to insertion of syringe into rectum.

Use appropriate standard precautions.	
Inquire about allergies and previous medication reactions.	
Explain to parent what medication you are giving and why.	
Prepare Equipment	
Check and recheck medication:	
Solution clarity and expiration date	
Right patient	
Right medication	
Right dose	
Right route	
Right time	
Cut suppository for desired dose, if applicable.	
If medication is in liquid form, prepare delivery method.	
Draw up medication into syringe; remove and discard needle into sharps container.	

Choose administration option:
    a. Attach IV catheter or cut 3.0 ET tube.
    b. Attach short feeding tube.
    c. Use tuberculin syringe without needle.	

Thoroughly lubricate distal end of administration device or suppository and finger.	
Use water-soluble lubricants only.	
Administer Medication	
Gently insert tube, syringe, or suppository into anus.	
Continue until past both rectal sphincters.	
If suppository, push with gloved and lubricated finger.	
Slowly depress plunger to deliver medication into rectum.	
Hold buttocks closed to prevent medication from leaking out.	
Withdraw administration device.	
Hold buttocks closed for 5–10 minutes to allow medication to absorb, or tape buttocks together.	
Dispose of syringe and any other administration device into sharps container.	
Carefully and correctly document dose and time of administration.	
Monitor Patient	
Obtain full set of vital signs.	
Monitor patient for adverse effects.	
Monitor patient for desired effects.	

Critical Criteria:

___ Use appropriate standard precautions.
___ Check for patient allergies and medication reactions.
___ Ensure at a minimum that 5 rights of medication administration have been followed.
___ Lubricate administration device or suppository and finger before administration.
___ Pinch buttocks closed after administration.
___ Immediately dispose of sharps into an appropriate container.
___ Monitor patient for desired and adverse effects.

Procedure/Skill Evaluation

Student: _____   Level: □ EMT-I □ EMT-P   Date: _____

Time

Evaluator: _____   Start: _____ End: _____ Total: _____ Pass/Fail: _____

Skill Sheet 77: Management of Chest Trauma

Conditions	The candidate should perform this procedure on a simulated patient under existing indoor, ambulance, or outdoor lighting, temperature, and weather conditions.
Indications	Patient who has experienced a medical or trauma mechanism to the chest that results in loss of normal lung expansion, either due to negative pressure loss (pneumothorax) or excessive positive pressure (tension pneumothorax).
Red Flags	Increased possibility of infection. Application of an occlusive dressing can result in a tension pneumothorax forming; needle decompression is unlikely to reduce hemothorax and will create an open pneumothorax.

Use appropriate standard precautions.	
Apply supplemental oxygen and/or ventilate patient with bag-mask.	
Evaluate Patient for Chest Trauma	
Confirm trauma mechanism or medical condition that could cause an open pneumothorax or tension pneumothorax to form.	
Expose and *inspect* neck and anterior and posterior chest wall for signs of severe ventilatory compromise, including tachypnea, accessory muscle use, asymmetrical chest rise, and presence of open wound.	
If open wound is seen, apply direct pressure to site with gloved hand immediately.	
Palpate chest wall for cage integrity, presence of subcutaneous air, and asymmetrical chest rise.	
Auscultate for unequal lung sounds bilaterally along midaxillary lines.	
Percuss for presence of hyperresonance (air trapping) or hyporesonance (blood).	

Occlusive Dressing	Needle Decompression	
Select Occlusive Dressing	**Prepare Site and Equipment**	
Choose commercial occlusive dressing (Vaseline gauze, Asherman chest seal, etc.) or improvised occlusive dressing (plastic bag, plastic wrap, plastic bandage/gauze wrappers, etc.).	Locate site on affected side: Second intercostal space, midclavicular line, over the third rib / Fourth intercostal space, midaxillary line, over the fifth rib	
Wipe away excess blood.	Prep site with alcohol and/or iodine.	
Prepare site with alcohol and/or iodine.	Select large-bore IV catheter, at least 2 inches in length.	
Apply Occlusive Dressing	Prepare flutter valve as necessary.	
Immediately occlude wound with gloved hand.	**Insert Needle**	
Control bleeding with direct pressure, as needed.	Place tip of needle on top of the appropriate rib.	
Place occlusive dressing and tape securely to skin.	Drag needle tip over top of rib into the intercostal space.	
May tape on only three sides to leave a "flutter" valve to allow air to escape but not enter.	Insert needle with moderate force until air escape is heard or resistance decreases. If using syringe attached to needle, aspirate while advancing needle.	
If tension pneumothorax develops, tape fourth side and decompress the affected side with needle.	Advance catheter and remove needle.	
	Dispose of needle into appropriate container.	
	Secure catheter in place.	
	Attach flutter valve as necessary.	
Monitor patient for any changes.		
Continue transport.		

Critical Criteria:

__ Use appropriate standard precautions.
__ Identify tension pneumothorax quickly.
__ Insert needle over the top of the inferior rib.
__ Recognize developing tension pneumothorax after occlusive dressing application.

Credits

Photos

Chapter 1

Opener: Courtesy Greg Peterson; **2** (*top right*): Courtesy David Franzene; **1.1a:** National Library of Medicine; **1.1b:** Courtesy American Ambulance; **5** (*top right*): Courtesy Arthur Hsieh.

Chapter 2

Opener: © Digital Vision/Getty Images; **16** (*top right*): Royalty-Free/CORBIS.

Chapter 3

Opener: ©The McGraw-Hill Companies, Inc./ Rick Brady, photographer.

Chapter 4

Opener: ©The McGraw-Hill Companies, Inc./ Rick Brady, photographer; **30** (*top left*): Courtesy David Page; **31** (*top right*): Courtesy David Page.

PBL Case 1

Opener: © Photodisc Collection/Getty Images.

Chapter 5

Opener: Courtesy David Page; **38** (*top left*): © Dynamic Graphics/JupiterImages; **38** (*bottom left*): © Digital Vision; **40** (*bottom right*): © C Squared Studios/Getty Images.

Chapter 6

Opener: ©The McGraw-Hill Companies, Inc./ Rick Brady, photographer.

Chapter 7

Opener: ©The McGraw-Hill Companies, Inc/Joe DeGrandis, photographer; **56** (*top right*): Courtesy Peter T. Pons, M.D.; **7-1:** ©The McGraw-Hill Companies, Inc/Joe DeGrandis, photographer.

Chapter 8

Opener: © Imagingbody.com; **8-2:** © Photodisc/ Getty Images; **74** (*bottom left*): Courtesy David Page.

Chapter 9

Opener: Courtesy David Page; **84** (*left bottom*): Courtesy David Page; **85** (*top right*): Courtesy Kevin Boone; **87** (*top right*): Courtesy Arthur Hsieh; **88** (*top right*): ©The McGraw-Hill Companies, Inc./Rick Brady, photographer; **89** (**I Spy photo**): © Mark Downey/Getty Images.

Chapter 10

Opener: ©The McGraw-Hill Companies, Inc./Rick Brady, photographer; **10-1:** Courtesy of Kwikpoint of Alexandria, VA; **101** (**I Spy photos**): Courtesy David Page and Arthur Hsieh.

Chapter 11

Opener: Courtesy David Page; **106** (*bottom right*): © Steve Cole/Getty Images; **SBS 27-1** through **SBS 27-3:** ©The McGraw-Hill Companies, Inc./Rick Brady, photographer; **111** (*bottom left*): Courtesy Arthur Hsieh.

Chapter 12

Opener: ©The McGraw-Hill Companies, Inc./ Rick Brady, photographer; **120** (*top right*), **12.2** ©The McGraw-Hill Companies, Inc./Rick Brady, photographer; **SBS 6-1** through **SBS 6-3, SBS 7-1** through **SBS 7-7, SBS 13-1** through **SBS 13-3, SBS 13-5** through **SBS 13-8, SBS 18-1** through **SBS 18-4, SBS 19-1** through **SBS 19-5, SBS 21-1** through **SBS 21-5:** ©The McGraw-Hill Companies, Inc./Rick Brady, photographer; **SBS 13-4:** Courtesy Arthur Hsieh.

Chapter 13

Opener: ©The McGraw-Hill Companies, Inc./ Rick Brady, photographer; **147** (*top right*): ©The McGraw-Hill Companies, Inc./Rick Brady, photographer; **13-2:** ©The McGraw-Hill Companies, Inc./Rick Brady, photographer; **13-3:** ©The McGraw-Hill Companies, Inc./Rick Brady, photographer.

Chapter 14

Opener: Courtesy David Page; **154** (*top right*): Courtesy Arthur Hsieh; **155** (*top left* and *bottom left*): Courtesy David Page; **SBS 32-1** through **SBS 32-3, SBS 33-1** through **SBS 33-5:** ©The McGraw-Hill Companies, Inc./Rick Brady, photographer.

PBL Case 2

Opener: © Photodisc Collection/Getty Images.

Chapter 15

Opener: ©The McGraw-Hill Companies, Inc./ Rick Brady, photographer; **173** (*top right*): ©The McGraw-Hill Companies, Inc./Rick Brady, photographer; **175** (*top right*): ©The McGraw-Hill Companies, Inc./Rick Brady, photographer.

Chapter 16

Opener: ©The McGraw-Hill Companies, Inc./ Rick Brady, photographer; **187** (*all photos*): Courtesy Kevin Boone; **191** (*top left*), ©The McGraw-Hill Companies, Inc./Rick Brady, photographer; **SBS 42-1** through **SBS 42-6, SBS 45-1** through **SBS 45-5, SBS 48-1** through **SBS 48-4, SBS 49-1** through **SBS 49-2, SBS 49-4, SBS 50-1** through **SBS 50-4, SBS 52-1** through **SBS 52-6, SBS 53-1** through **SBS 53-4, SBS 58-1** through **SBS 58-4:** ©The McGraw-Hill Companies, Inc./Rick Brady, photographer; **16-2:** ©The McGraw-Hill Companies, Inc./Rick Brady, photographer; **SBS 49-3:** Courtesy Arthur Hsieh.

Chapter 17

Opener: ©The McGraw-Hill Companies, Inc./ Rick Brady, photographer; **212** (*top right*): ©The McGraw-Hill Companies, Inc./Rick Brady, photographer; **17-1:** © Photolink/Getty Images.

Chapter 18

Opener: © Royalty-Free/CORBIS; **218** (*bottom right*): © Digital Vision/Getty Images; **18-1:** © Photodisc Collection/Getty Images; **18-2:** C. Sherburne/Photo Link/Getty Images; **220:** Royalty-Free/CORBIS; **18-6:** Courtesy Kevin Boone.

Chapter 19

Opener: © Kim Steele/Getty Images; **229** (*bottom right*): Courtesy Greg Peterson; **234** (*bottom left*): Courtesy Bill Garcia; **234** (*bottom right*): Courtesy Arthur Hsieh.

Chapter 20

Opener: © Eddie Sperling; **240** (*bottom right*): Courtesy COL John P Gritz, USA-Ret. **247** (*top right*): ©The McGraw-Hill Companies, Inc./Rick Brady, photographer.

Chapter 21

Opener: Courtesy David Page; **253** (*top right*): Courtesy David Page; **SBS 77-1** through **SBS 77-6**: ©The McGraw-Hill Companies, Inc./Rick Brady, photographer.

Chapter 22

Opener: Courtesy David Page; **22-2**: Courtesy Kevin Boone; **22-3**: Courtesy Peter T. Pons, M.D.; **22-4**: Courtesy David Page.

Chapter 23

Opener: ©The McGraw-Hill Companies, Inc./ Rick Brady, photographer; **274** (*bottom left*): ©The McGraw-Hill Companies, Inc./Rick Brady, photographer; **274** (*top right*): © Kent Knudson/ Photo Link/Getty Images.

PBL Case 3

Opener: Royalty-Free/CORBIS.

Chapter 24

Opener: © Imagesource/PictureQuest; **Table 24-1 photos**: ©The McGraw-Hill Companies, Inc./Rick Brady, photographer.

Chapter 25

Opener: Courtesy Stephen Kotch, M.D.; **297** (*bottom right*): Courtesy University of Iowa Hospitals and Clinics; **299** (*top right*): Courtesy Peter T. Pons, M.D.; **301** (*top right*): ©The McGraw-Hill Companies, Inc./Rick Brady, photographer; **301** (*bottom right*): Courtesy Lee Ridge.

Chapter 26

Opener: Courtesy David Page; **26-2** through **26-5**: Courtesy Regions Hospital.**PBL Case 4**Opener: Courtesy David Page.

Chapter 27

Opener: Courtesy David Page; **321** (*top left*): Courtesy of Altoona Regional Health System Trauma Center, Altoona, PA; **323** (*bottom right*): Courtesy of Lee Memorial Health System, Fort Myers, FL; **324** (*bottom left*): Courtesy David Page; **28.4a, b**: (c)The McGraw-Hill Companies, Inc./ Dennis Strete, photographer.

Chapter 28

Opener: © Dynamic Graphics/JupiterImages; **332** (*left bottom*): ©The McGraw-Hill Companies, Inc./Rick Brady, photographer; **338** (*left bottom*): ©The McGraw-Hill Companies, Inc./Rick Brady, photographer.

Chapter 29, Section I

Opener: ©The McGraw-Hill Companies, Inc.; **29-10**: Courtesy Arthur Hsieh; **SBS 37-1** through **SBS 37-4**: ©The McGraw-Hill Companies, Inc./ Rick Brady, photographer.

Chapter 29, Section II

Opener: © Royalty-Free/CORBIS; **29-16**: © 2007 Arthur Hsieh; **371** (*top left*): © Dynamic Graphics/JupiterImages; **378** (*top left*): ©The McGraw-Hill Companies, Inc./Rick Brady, photographer; **29-25**: ©The McGraw-Hill Companies, Inc./Rick Brady, photographer; **SBS 38-1** through **SBS 38-3**, **SBS 39-1** through **SBS 39-3**: ©The McGraw-Hill Companies, Inc./Rick Brady, photographer; **29-24**: Courtesy David Page.

Chapter 30

Opener: Courtesy David Page; **30-2a**: © Corbis/ PictureQuest; **30-2b**: © Burke/Triolo/Brand X Pictures/JupiterImages; **30-2c**: ©Liquidlibrary/ JupiterImages; **30-2d**: Dynamicgraphics/ JupiterImages; **30-4(1)**: © TRBfoto/Getty Images; **30-4(2)**: © Cobris/PictureQuest; **30-4(3)**: © Photodisc Collection/Getty Images; **30-4(4)**: © Royalty-Free/CORBIS; **30-4(5)**: © Stockbyte/ PunchStock; **399** (*top right*): © Amos Morgan/ Getty Images.

Chapter 31

Opener: © J. Luke/PhotoLink/Getty Images; **411** (*top right*): ©The McGraw-Hill Companies, Inc./ Rick Brady, photographer; **412** (*bottom right*): ©The McGraw-Hill Companies, Inc./Rick Brady, photographer; **413** (*bottom left*): © PhotoLink/ Getty Images.

Chapter 32

Opener: © Ryan McVay/Getty Images; **429** (*top left*): ©The McGraw-Hill Companies, Inc./Rick Brady, photographer.

PBL Case 5

Opener: © Ingo Jezierski/Getty Images.

Chapter 33

Opener: ©Liquidlibrary/Dynamic Graphics/ JupiterImages; **438** © Dynamic Graphics/ JupiterImages; **442** (*top right*): © Brand X Pictures/PunchStock.

Chapter 34

Opener: © Dynamic Graphics/JupiterImages; **448** (*bottom left*): ©The McGraw-Hill Companies, Inc./Joe DeGrandis, photographer; **448** (*top right*): ©The McGraw-Hill Companies, Inc./ Rick Brady, photographer; **449** (*bottom right*): © Royalty-Free/CORBIS; **455** (*top left*): ©The McGraw-Hill Companies, Inc./Rick Brady, photographer.

Chapter 35

Opener: © PhotoLink/Getty Images; **461** (*bottom right*): © TRBfoto/Getty Images; **462** (*bottom left*): © Royalty-Free/CORBIS; **462** (*top right*): © BananaStock/PunchStock.

Chapter 36

Opener: © Keith Brofsky/Getty Images; **474** (*bottom right*): © Digital Vision/PunchStock.

Chapter 37

Opener: © Ryan McVay/Getty Images; **483** (*bottom left*): Courtesy Greg Peterson; **37-2**: © Meckes/Ottawa/Photo Researchers, Inc.

Chapter 38

Opener: ©The McGraw-Hill Companies, Inc./ Gary He, photographer; **492** (*top left*): Steve Mason/Getty Images; **492** (*top right*): © Alan and Sandy Carey/Getty Images; **493** (*bottom left*): Digital Vision/PunchStock; **496** (*bottom right*): ©The McGraw-Hill Companies, Inc./Rick Brady, photographer; **497** (*top left*): ©The McGraw-Hill Companies, Inc./Rick Brady, photographer.

Chapter 39

Opener: © BananaStock/PunchStock; **39-3**: Courtesy Minneapolis Heart Institute and Abbot Northwestern; **39-4**: ©The McGraw-Hill Companies, Inc./Rick Brady, photographer; **507** (*top right*): Courtesy Arthur Hsieh.

Chapter 40

Opener: © Keith Brofsky/Getty Images; **512** (*top right*): ©The McGraw-Hill Companies, Inc./Lars A. Niki, photographer; **516** (*bottom left*): ©The McGraw-Hill Companies, Inc./Rick Brady, photographer;

PBL Case 6

Opener: © S. Meltzer/PhotoLink/Getty Images.

Chapter 41

Opener: © Photodisc Collection/Getty Images; **527** (*top left*): © Adam Crowley/Getty Images; **41-3**: ©The McGraw-Hill Companies, Inc./Rick Brady, photographer.

Chapter 42

Opener: © Brand X Pictures/PunchStock; **539** (*top left*): © Royalty-Free/CORBIS; **42-2** through **42-4**: ©The McGraw-Hill Companies, Inc./Rick Brady, photographer; **Fig 42-5**: Adapted from 2005 *American Heart Association Guidelines for CPR and ECC.*

Chapter 43

Opener: Courtesy Peter T. Pons, M.D.; **551** (*top right*): © Brand X Pictures/PunchStock; **553** (*bottom left*): © TRBfoto/Getty Images; **43-2:** ©The McGraw-Hill Companies, Inc./Rick Brady, photographer.

Chapter 44

Opener: ©The McGraw-Hill Companies, Inc./Rick Brady, photographer; **565 (top left):** © Keith Thomas Productions/Brand X Pictures/PictureQuest; **568 (*bottom left*):** © Mel Curtis/Getty Images; **570 (*bottom left*):** ©The McGraw-Hill Companies, Inc./Rick Brady, photographer.

Chapter 45

Opener: © Emma Lee/Life File/Getty Images; **575 (bottom left):** ©The McGraw-Hill Companies, Inc./Rick Brady, photographer; **576 (*bottom left*):** ©The McGraw-Hill Companies, Inc./Rick Brady, photographer; **578 (*bottom right*):** © Royalty-Free/CORBIS.

Chapter 46

Opener: ©The McGraw-Hill Companies, Inc./Lars A. Niki, photographer; **586 (*bottom right*):** © TRBfoto/Getty Images; **46-1:** Courtesy David Page; **588 (*top left*):** Courtesy Charles Kauffman; **588 (*bottom left*):** © Geoff Manasse/Getty Images.

PBL Case 7

Opener: © BananaStock/PunchStock.

Chapter 47

Opener: © Getty Images; **596 (*bottom left*):** Courtesy Kevin Boone; **597 (*top left*):** Courtesy Kevin Boone; **47-1** through **47-3:** Courtesy Kevin Boone; **47-4:** ©The McGraw-Hill Companies, Inc./Rick Brady, photographer.

Chapter 48

Opener: Courtesy Arthur Hsieh; **606 (*bottom right*):** © Photodisc/Getty Images; **609 (*bottom left*):** ©The McGraw-Hill Companies, Inc./Rick Brady, photographer; **609 (*bottom right*):** Courtesy Arthur Hsieh.

PBL Case 8

Opener: © Geoff Manasse/Getty Images.

Chapter 49

Opener: © Ryan McVay/Getty Images; **619 (*top left*):** Courtesy Will Chapleau; **621 (*bottom right*):** ©The McGraw-Hill Companies, Inc./Luke David, photographer; **622 (*top right*):** © Royalty-Free/CORBIS.

Chapter 50

Opener: © J.K. Nakata, USGS Photo Library, Denver, Colorado; **627 (*top left*):** Courtesy David Page; **627 (*bottom left*):** Courtesy Greg Peterson.

Chapter 51

Opener: ©The McGraw-Hill Companies, Inc./John A. Karachewski, photographer; **644 (*top left*):** ©The McGraw-Hill Companies, Inc./Rick Brady, photographer; **644 (*bottom left*):** Courtesy Greg Peterson; **647 (*top left*):** ©The McGraw-Hill Companies, Inc./Rick Brady, photographer; **650 (I Spy photo):** Courtesy Greg Peterson.

Chapter 52

Opener: U.S. Coast Guard Photograph by Petty Officer 2nd Class NyxoLyno Cangemi; **654 (*bottom left*):** © Mikael Karlsson; **654 (*bottom right*):** Royalty-Free/CORBIS; **657 (*top right*):** Courtesy Mark Lindquist.

Chapter 53

Opener: © Donovan Reese/Getty Images; **663 (*bottom left*):** © Royalty-Free/CORBIS; **53-2** through **53-5:** ©The McGraw-Hill Companies, Inc./Rick Brady, photographer; **53-6:** Courtesy David Page; **53-7:** ©The McGraw-Hill Companies, Inc./Rick Brady, photographer.

Chapter 54

Opener: © Corbis Images/JupiterImages; **678 (*top left*):** ©The McGraw-Hill Companies, Inc./Jill Braaten, photographer; **678 (*top right*):** Courtesy London Ambulance Service Alistair Drummond Communications Department.

Chapter 55

Opener: ©The McGraw-Hill Companies, Inc./Rick Brady, photographer; **681 (*bottom left*):** ©The McGraw-Hill Companies, Inc./Rick Brady, photographer; **55-1** and **55-2:** Courtesy Kevin Boone; **683 (*top left*):** Steve Mason/Getty Images; **685 (*bottom left*):** © Getty Images.

Text and Illustrations

Chapter 1

1-1a: National Library of Medicine; **1-1b:** Courtesy American Ambulance.

Chapter 2

Table 2-1: Adapted from Clinical Guidelines on the Identification, Evaluation, and Treatment of Overweight and Obesity in Adults: The Evidence Report. National Heart Lung and Blood Institute, Department of Health and Human Services, National Institutes of Health; **2-1:** United States Department of Agriculture, Center for Nutrition Policy and Promotion; **Table 2-2:** Reprinted from Centers for Disease and Prevention, Department of Health and Human Services, July 2005.

Chapter 6

Tables 6-1 and **6-2:** Modified from: Patient Safety, "Do Not Use" List: Joint Commission on Accreditation of Healthcare Organizations, http://www.jcaho.org.

Chapter 42

42-5: Adapted from 2005 *American Heart Association Guidelines for CPR and ECC.*

Chapter 50

50-1: *G. Groths, R. Hook, et al. (1994). Start: Simple Triage and Rapid Treatment Plan. Newport Beach, CA: Hoap Memorial Presbyterian Hospital.* Reprinted with permission from the Critical Illnesses & Trauma Foundation; **50-2:** *JumpStart developed by Dr. Lou Roming, MD, FAAP, FACEP, Miami Children's Hospital, Miami, FL.* © Lou Romig, M.D., 2002.

A page number followed by 'i' indicates an illustration; 't' indicates a table.